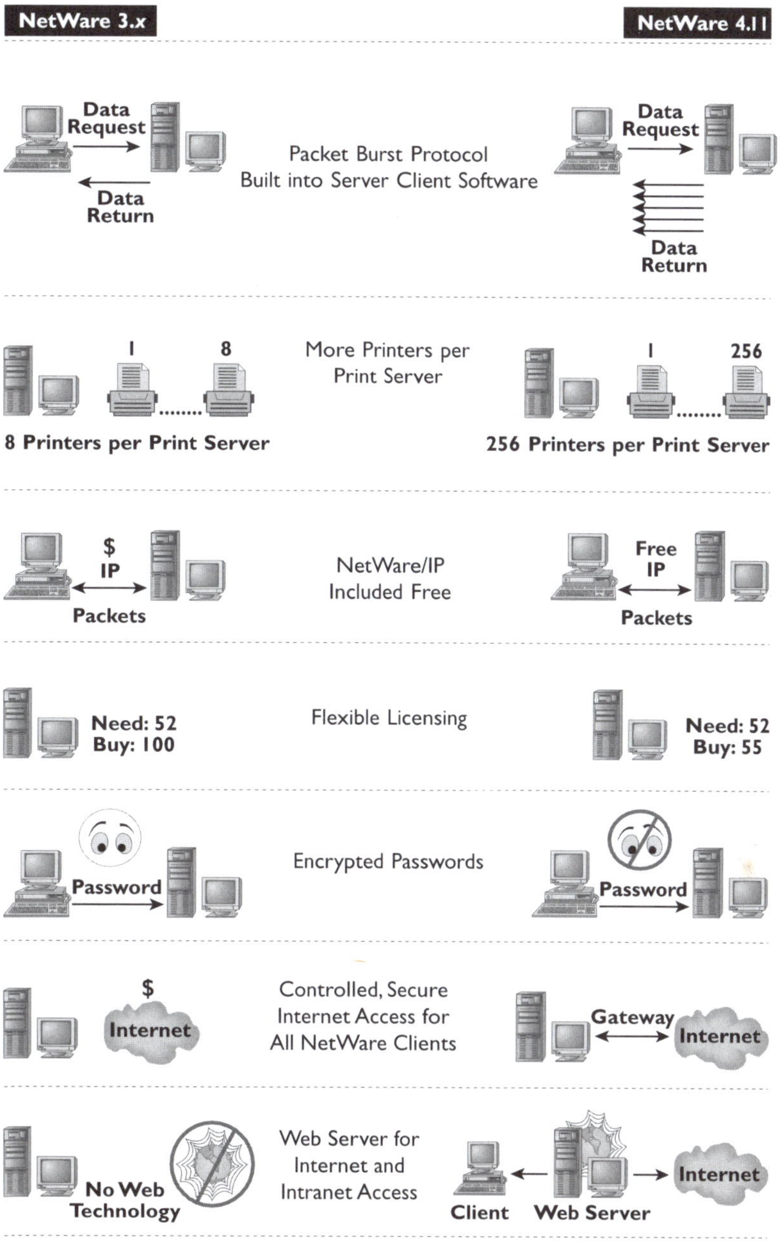

NetWare 3.x		NetWare 4.11
Data Request → ← Data Return	Packet Burst Protocol Built into Server Client Software	Data Request → ← ← ← ← Data Return
8 Printers per Print Server	More Printers per Print Server	256 Printers per Print Server
$ IP Packets	NetWare/IP Included Free	Free IP Packets
Need: 52 Buy: 100	Flexible Licensing	Need: 52 Buy: 55
Password	Encrypted Passwords	Password
$ Internet	Controlled, Secure Internet Access for All NetWare Clients	Gateway ↔ Internet
No Web Technology	Web Server for Internet and Intranet Access	Client ← Web Server → Internet

The Complete Guide to NetWare 4.11/ IntranetWare

GET THE BEST CONNECTIONS FROM NETWORK PRESS™

You CAN judge a book by its cover.

This Network Press™ title is part of a new, expanded series replacing Sybex's acclaimed Novell Press® book series. With Network Press, you'll find the same dedication to quality from a truly independent and unbiased point of view. Our unique perspective guarantees you full coverage of Novell, Microsoft, and the other network environments.

Building on 20 years of technical and publishing excellence, Network Press provides you the broadest range of networking books published today. Our well-known commitment to quality, content, and timeliness continues to guarantee your satisfaction.

Network Press books offer you:

- winning certification test preparation strategies
- respected authors in the field of networking
- all new titles in a wide variety of topics
- up-to-date, revised editions of familiar best-sellers

Look for the distinctive black-and-white Network Press cover as your guarantee of quality. A comprehensive selection of Network Press books is available now at your local bookstore.

For more information about Network Press, please contact:

Network Press
1151 Marina Village Parkway
Alameda, CA 94501
Tel: (510)523-8233 Toll Free: (800)277-2346
Fax: (510)523-2373 E-mail: info@sybex.com

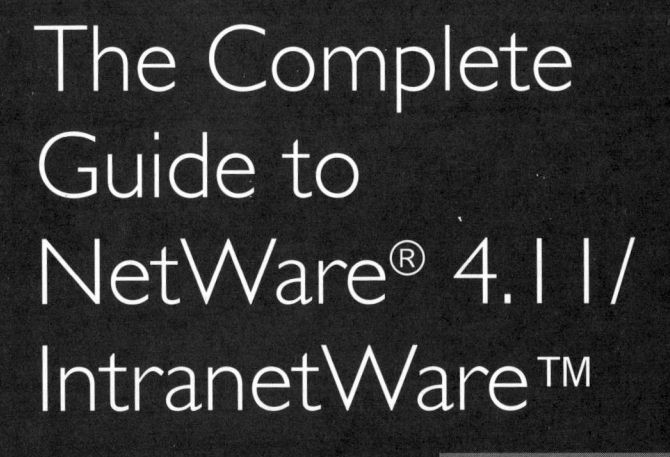

The Complete Guide to NetWare® 4.11/ IntranetWare™

Second Edition

James E. Gaskin

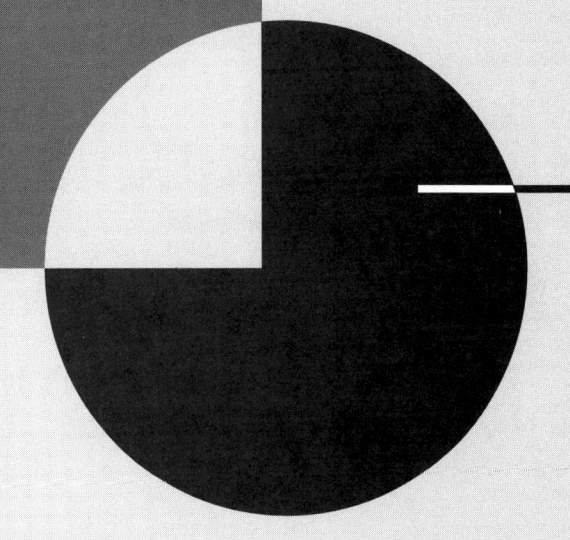

NETWORK PRESS®
SYBEX

San Franciso ■ Paris ■ Düsseldorf ■ Soest

Associate Publisher: Steve Sayre
Acquisitions Manager: Kristine Plachy
Acquisitions & Developmental Editor: Guy Hart-Davis
Editor: Marilyn Smith
Project Editor: Kim Wimpsett
Technical Editor: Kim Green
Book Designer: Seventeenth Street Studios
Graphic Illustrators: Patrick Dintino and Cuong Le
Desktop Publisher: Maureen Forys
Production Coordinator: Nathan Johanson
Indexer: Matthew Spence
Cover Designer: Archer Design

Screen reproductions produced with Collage Complete.

Collage Complete is a trademark of Inner Media Inc.

SYBEX is a registered trademark of SYBEX Inc.

Network Press and the Network Press logo are trademarks of SYBEX Inc.

TRADEMARKS: SYBEX has attempted throughout this book to distinguish proprietary trademarks from descriptive terms by following the capitalization style used by the manufacturer.

The author and publisher have made their best efforts to prepare this book, and the content is based upon final release software whenever possible. Portions of the manuscript may be based upon pre-release versions supplied by software manufacturer(s). The author and the publisher make no representation or warranties of any kind with regard to the completeness or accuracy of the contents herein and accept no liability of any kind including but not limited to performance, merchantability, fitness for any particular purpose, or any losses or damages of any kind caused or alleged to be caused directly or indirectly from this book.

First edition copyright ©1995 SYBEX Inc.

Copyright ©1997 SYBEX Inc., 1151 Marina Village Parkway, Alameda, CA 94501. World rights reserved. No part of this publication may be stored in a retrieval system, transmitted, or reproduced in any way, including but not limited to photocopy, photograph, magnetic or other record, without the prior agreement and written permission of the publisher.

Library of Congress Card Number: 96-70742
ISBN: 0-7821-1931-X

Manufactured in the United States of America

10 9 8 7 6 5 4 3 2

Acknowledgments

BOOKS ARE A trade-off; they save you time, but take plenty of mine. That time is often stolen from family, and I want to thank my family members for their patience. My lovely wife Wendy, handsome son Alex, and darling daughter Laura loaned me the time to make this book, and I appreciate that.

Third time is the charm for editor Marilyn Smith: this is our third book together; we added enough to the revision to count this as perhaps a fourth book. Her help has been above and beyond the call of duty. No doubt she also stole some time from her family.

The Sybex crew, once again, came through with flying colors. Kim Wimpsett managed the project from the editorial side, while Nathan Johanson and Maureen Forys handled the production details, politely working their way through the mountain of pages that make this book. Guy Hart-Davis did his usual excellent job keeping everyone and everything on track as much as he could while dragging me toward the finish. I'm sorry that Rudy Langer is no longer with us to enjoy this new book.

Novell folks still rate way up in the importance scale. Willie Donahoo, climbing ever higher at Novell, still has time for his old friends in the book business. The IntranetWare group was ably represented by Henry Sprafkin, who helped tie together all the new, Internet-inspired technologies that make NetWare into IntranetWare. Look for more and more features from Novell reaching toward the Internet and other systems, driven by Henry and the rest of that gang.

Kim Green provided technical editing for this version. He did an excellent job, checking each and every detail. With Kim backing me up, I'm more confident than ever that what you're about to read is correct, accurate, and helpful.

It's always nice to hear from readers, especially when clever readers like Daniel Foo Shih Chieh come up with solutions for network problems (Daniel's suggestion is in Appendix A). Other readers are welcome to follow Daniel's lead.

Since this book is a revision, I want to also acknowledge all the people who helped with the original version. There are many people at Novell that deserve special mention. First is the Novell Press group, headed by Rose Kearsley, who is ably assisted by Marcy Shanti. The technical support of Kelley J.P. Lindberg (herself the author of several excellent books) and Sandy Stevens (star of the NetWare 4 Days broadcasts) has been invaluable.

Many others at Novell deserve an acknowledgment. My friend Michael Bryant deserves special mention, as do the other Unix fans, Keith Brown, Brian Meek, and Mala Ranganathan. Jim Greene and Kevin Auger got me on track at the start, along with Blaine Homer, Milton Howard, and Dawn Drake.

Technical help was provided by many people, and I hope I cover them all. Dave Eckert provided valuable NDS information, along with Andy Marquez. Dan Montierth helped with troubleshooting, Howard Olson with general NetWare supervision, Allen Mark and Sandy Stevens again for Macintosh information, Craig Oler for printing, Jim Higgins for security, Troy Wilde for OS/2, Evan Porter for NDS setup, and Randy Stevens for OS/2 and SFT III. Bob Adams (not from Novell) helped with Chapter 17.

Outside Novell, Bob Timmons came through with his usual excellent support by providing an indestructible Acer Altos server, now starring in its second book in three years. Dan Garbarz loaned me an Apple 660av Macintosh. Michelle Gjerde and Wendell Watson of GATEWAY 2000 provided my other main server, a Gateway 2000 Pentium machine.

A project like this requires the help of many people. Many people helped me without knowing I was researching a book; they were just doing their job. Because of good people doing a good job, we have both this book and NetWare.

Contents at a Glance

Introduction	xxvi
SETTING UP THE NETWORK	**1**
Planning Your Network Before Installation	3
Installing NetWare 4.1x	55
Installing NetWare Directory Services and Optional Procedures	129
NetWare Directory Services: Overview, Planning, Expansion	199
Connecting PC Clients to Your Network	259
USING THE NETWORK	**347**
Creating and Managing Users (Now User Objects)	349
Handling More than One User at a Time	443
Arranging Network Printing	529
Securing Your NetWare 4.1x Network	663
NetWare 4.1x Administrator Duties and Tools	739
Providing Applications for Your Network Clients	931
Teaching Your Clients to Use the Network	989
INTEGRATING NETWARE WITH OTHER OPERATING SYSTEMS	**1085**
Using Macintoshes with NetWare 4.1x	1087
IntranetWare: NetWare, Intranets, and the Internet Combined	1123
Installing and Configuring OS/2 Clients	1197
Installing NetWare 4.1x Server for OS/2	1219
TAKING ADVANTAGE OF SPECIAL NETWORK FEATURES	**1241**
Installing and Using NetWare 4.1x SFT III for Complete Fault-Tolerance	1243
Using the NetWare 4.1x Enhancements	1257
Troubleshooting Your Network	1285
APPENDICES AND GLOSSARY	**1329**
Upgrading, Migrating, and Windows 95 Client Installation Support	1331
How NetWare 4.1x Differs from Earlier Versions	1345
NetWare 4.1x SET Commands	1365
Recommended Reading	1391
Glossary of Terms	1397
Index	1451

Table of Contents

Introduction ... xxvi

PART I   **SETTING UP THE NETWORK** ... 1

Chapter 1   **Planning Your Network Before Installation** ... 3

    Physical Network Types ... 4
        Ethernet Networks ... 5
        Token Ring Networks ... 7
        Token Ring and Ethernet: Practical Similarities ... 10
        Other Physical Network Options ... 12
    Planning for an Efficient File System ... 22
        Home Directory Sweet Home Directory ... 23
        NetWare System Directories ... 24
    Physical Space and Protection for Your Server ... 26
        Physical Security Considerations for Your Server ... 26
        Power Conditioning and Protection for Your Server ... 27
        Proper Tape Backup Precautions for Your Server ... 28
    Planning Cabling Installation ... 31
        Installing New Cabling ... 31
        Planning the Rest of Your Wiring Closets ... 33
    Network Protocols Used by NetWare 4.1x ... 34
        IPX/SPX and NCP ... 36
        TCP/IP ... 39
        AFP (AppleTalk Filing Protocol) ... 42
    A Note of Appreciation ... 43

Chapter 2   **Installing NetWare 4.1x** ... 55

    New, Improved NetWare Installation ... 57
    Requirements for NetWare Servers ... 58
        Choosing the Server's CPU ... 60

Figuring the Needed RAM (Buy More)	62
Choosing the Hard Disk (Buy a Bigger One)	63
Choosing the Server's NIC	66
Choosing the Server's CD-ROM Drive	68
Choosing the Server's Floppy Drive	69
Choosing the Server's Monitor	69
Setting Interrupts, DMA, I/O Ports, and ROM Addresses	70
Preparing for Installation	72
Creating the Server Installation Boot Disk	72
Preparing the Disk Drive for NetWare	76
Where Will Your Installation Files Come From?	81
Installing from a Server-Based CD-ROM	82
Installing from Floppies	83
Installing from a Remote Server's Network Installation Area	84
Running the INSTALL.NLM Program	88
The Simple Installation Method	89
The Custom Installation Method	91
Naming Your Server	92
Setting Your Internal IPX Network Number (Custom)	93
Copying Server Files to the DOS Partition (Custom)	93
Keyboard Mapping and File Name Format Choices (Custom)	94
Adding Extra SET Commands (Custom)	95
Starting Your Server Automatically (Custom)	95
Disk Driver Setup	96
LAN Driver Configuration	100
Adding Protocols to Your Network Driver (Custom)	102
Disk Configuration (Custom)	103
Managing NetWare Volumes (Custom)	106
Installing the NetWare License Software	115
Installing NetWare Directory Services—Almost Time	120
Intelligent Installations	121

Chapter 3	**Installing NetWare Directory Services and Optional Procedures**	**129**
	Details, Details, but Not Too Many	131
	Some Definitions	131
	What You Need to Know	132
	Configuring NDS during the First Server Installation	133
	Naming Your NDS Tree	133
	Notes on Network Time	135
	Setting the Server's Context	138
	Installing a New Server into an Existing 4.1x Network	141
	Installing the New Server into the Default NDS Tree	142
	Selecting a Different NDS Tree	144
	Continuing On and Setting Time Parameters	144
	Setting the Server's Context	147
	Finishing Installation and Your Next Steps	151
	Modifying the STARTUP.NCF File	151
	Modifying the AUTOEXEC.NCF File	153
	Copying Files to the New Server	154
	Other Installation Options	156
	Finished!	157
	Optional Installation Items, Procedures, and Products	158
	Creating a Registration Diskette	159
	Upgrading NetWare 3.1x Print Services	161
	Creating DOS, MS Windows, or OS/2 Client Install Diskettes	162
	Creating NetWare Upgrade/Migrate Diskettes	164
	Installing NetWare for Macintosh Software	165
	Installing NetWare MHS Services in NetWare 4.10	168
	Configuring Network Protocols	171
	Installing an Additional Server Language	175
	Changing the Server Language	176
	Installing Online Documentation and Viewers	178
	Installing Products Not Listed	182
	Removing NetWare Directory Services	184
	Warning, Warning	185
	Removing NDS from a One-Server Network	185

	Removing NDS from a Multiple-Server Network	187
	NetWare 4.11 New Products and Installations	188
	Installation Is Good, but It Will Get Better	190
Chapter 4	**NetWare Directory Services: Overview, Planning, Expansion**	**199**
	The Global Network View	200
	Advantages of NDS	201
	Objects Everywhere and Everything Is an Object	204
	Hierarchical Tree Structure and Schema	206
	[Root]: The Base, and Top, of Your NDS Tree	207
	Container Objects Make Up the [Root] Object	208
	Leaf Objects and the Bindery They Replace	214
	Planning Your NDS Tree	222
	Some Goals for Your NDS Tree Design	223
	Setting Up a Pilot System	224
	NDS Design Phases	225
	Design versus Implementation	227
	Developing Naming Standards	227
	NDS Example: Organizing by User Location (Bottom-Up)	230
	NDS Example: Organizing by User Function (Top-Down)	233
	NDS Example: Distributed Organization Chart with a WAN (Mixed)	236
	NDS Context Control and Management	238
	Why Context Is Important	239
	How to Use Contexts to Your Advantage	242
	Using Bindery Services to Provide Bindery Emulation	244
	How Bindery Services Works	244
	Why Bindery Emulation May Be Necessary	245
	Installing Bindery Services	246
	Using the Simple Installation Option with Bindery Services	247
	Maintaining Bindery Services	249
	Directory Designs and Discussions	250

Chapter 5	**Connecting PC Clients to Your Network**	**259**
	The NetWare DOS Requester: Moving beyond Shells	261
	Network Interface Card Installation and Setup	262
	Hardware Interrupts	264
	Base I/O Port Addresses	265
	Memory Addresses	265
	DMA Channels	266
	Client Files Required for Non-Client32 Clients	266
	ODI (Open Data-link Interface) Overview	267
	LSL.COM	268
	LAN Drivers (16 bit)	268
	IPXODI.COM	273
	NetWare DOS Requester (VLM.EXE)	274
	Installing Non-Client32 Clients	276
	Modifying the INSTALL.CFG File in NetWare 4.10	277
	Installing over the Network in NetWare 4.10	278
	Installing from the CD-ROM	279
	Installing from Floppies	280
	Running the INSTALL Program	282
	Attaching to the Network for the First Time	290
	NET.CFG Means Client Network Configuration for DOS and Windows 3.x Clients	291
	Standard NET.CFG Options for Typical Clients	292
	Complete NET.CFG Parameters and Options	294
	Installing and Configuring Client32	326
	Installing and Configuring Client32 for Windows 3.1x and DOS	327
	Installing and Configuring Client32 for Windows 95 Systems	334
	Too Many Client Options, Too Little Time	338
PART II	**USING THE NETWORK**	**347**
Chapter 6	**Creating and Managing Users (Now User Objects)**	**349**
	Users and NetWare 4.1x	350
	Creating User Objects with NetWare Administrator	352

	Loading Client Software and the NetWare Administrator Program	353
	Basic User Object Setup with NetWare Administrator	354
	Specifying Optional User Object Details with NetWare Administrator	358
	Configuring User Object Security with NetWare Administrator	376
	Creating User Objects with NETADMIN (DOS)	395
	Basic User Object Setup with NETADMIN	397
	Modifying User Object Details with NETADMIN	404
	User Object Security Configuration with NETADMIN	413
	The Users and You	437
Chapter 7	**Handling More Than One User at a Time**	**443**
	Who Manages the Users?	444
	NetWare 4.1x Tools for Managing Users and Resources	445
	Creating and Managing Groups (Now Group Objects)	446
	Creating and Modifying Group Objects with NetWare Administrator	447
	Creating and Modifying Group Objects with NETADMIN	466
	Saving Time with the User Template	479
	Creating a User Template with NetWare Administrator	480
	Creating a User Template with NETADMIN in NetWare 4.10	483
	Using Login Scripts	485
	Types of Login Scripts	487
	The Most Common Login Script Commands	491
	LOGIN.EXE Command Switches	495
	The Most Common Login Script Identifier Variables	496
	Creating and Managing Login Scripts	498
	A Sample Container Login Script	499
	A Sample Profile Login Script	502
	A Sample User Login Script	504
	Creating and Editing Login Scripts with NetWare Administrator	505

Table of Contents

Creating and Editing Login Scripts with NETADMIN	507
Creating and Managing Menus	511
The New Menu of NetWare 4.1x	511
Menu Script Commands	512
Converting Existing Menus	520
Swear Off Single Users	521

Chapter 8 Arranging Network Printing 529

NetWare Printing System Overview	531
The NetWare 4.1x Printing System Relationships	537
Using Quick Setup in PCONSOLE	538
Defining the Print Objects	538
Reviewing the Quick Setup Defaults	540
Saving the Setup	541
Setting Up and Managing Your Print System with NetWare Administrator	542
Using Quick Setup in NetWare Administrator	543
Creating the Print Queue Object with NetWare Administrator	545
Creating the Printer Object with NetWare Administrator	548
Creating the Print Server Object with NetWare Administrator	550
Specifying Print Queue Object Details with NetWare Administrator	552
Specifying Printer Object Details with NetWare Administrator	564
Specifying Print Server Object Details with NetWare Administrator	578
Viewing the Print Layout in NetWare Administrator	589
Viewing and Understanding Printer Status with NetWare Administrator	591
Creating and Modifying Printer Forms with NetWare Administrator	594
Creating and Modifying Print Devices with NetWare Administrator	596

	Setting Up Print Job Configurations with NetWare Administrator	602
	Using PCONSOLE for Print System Configuration and Management	605
	Creating the Print Queue Object in PCONSOLE	607
	Creating the Printer Object in PCONSOLE	608
	Creating the Print Server Object in PCONSOLE	609
	Configuring Print Server Object Details in PCONSOLE	610
	Configuring Print Queue Object Details in PCONSOLE	619
	Configuring Printer Object Details in PCONSOLE	629
	Using PRINTDEF for Print Device and Form Management	638
	Creating and Modifying Print Devices with PRINTDEF	639
	Editing Devices with PRINTDEF	639
	Importing Devices with PRINTDEF	641
	Exporting Devices with PRINTDEF	642
	Creating and Modifying Printer Forms with PRINTDEF	644
	Managing Print Job Configurations in PRINTCON	645
	Creating and Editing Print Job Configurations with PRINTCON	645
	Selecting the Default Print Job Configuration in PRINTCON	648
	Controlling the Print Server from the Server Console	649
	NPRINTER Updated: NPTWIN95	650
	Potshots on Printing	654
Chapter 9	**Securing Your NetWare 4.1x Network**	**663**
	Security: A Definition	664
	Where Is Your Security Plan?	665
	NetWare 4.1x Admin Compared with NetWare 3.x SUPERVISOR	669
	File System Security	670
	Directory Rights for Users and Groups	671
	File Rights for Users and Groups	674
	The IRF and File and Directory Rights	674
	Directory and File Security Guidelines	677
	Using File Attributes as a Security Enhancement	677
	File System: Directory Attributes	678
	File System: File Attributes	679

NDS Security		683
Object Rights versus Property Rights		684
The Access Control List (ACL)		686
How Rights Inheritance Works		687
The IRF and Object and Property Rights		687
NDS Security Guidelines		688
Security Management with NetWare Administrator		690
Revoking a Property Right		692
Setting or Modifying Directory and File Rights		693
Setting or Modifying Object and Property Rights		702
Security Management with DOS Utilities		709
Setting or Modifying Directory and File Trustees Using FILER		709
Setting or Modifying the Inherited Rights Filter with FILER		712
Setting or Modifying Object and Property Rights Using NETADMIN		713
Common-Sense Security Measures		715
Passwords and Login Restrictions		715
Virus Precautions		717
Using AUDITCON		719
Starting AUDITCON		720
Setting the New Auditor Password		722
Performing Audits		723
Viewing Audit Reports		725
NetWare 4.11 Security Improvements		726
When Security Stinks, Management Smells the Worst		728
Chapter 10	**NetWare 4.1x Administrator Duties and Tools**	**739**
	Managing Your Network with a Plan	741
	Managing Your Future Network	743
	Selling Your Network Plan to Your Boss	746
	Selling Your Network Plan to Your Users	749
	Supervisory Functions and the Necessary Rights	750
	Trustee Assignments	751
	Workgroup Managers to the Rescue	752

Installing NetWare Administrator	753
Creating a NetWare Administrator Icon on Windows *3.1x*	753
Configuring Windows 95 (Running Client32) for NetWare Administrator	755
Getting Familiar with NetWare Administrator	756
NDS Administration with NetWare Administrator	761
Creating Container Objects	762
Creating Leaf Objects	767
Moving Objects	770
Renaming Objects	772
Searching for Objects	773
Using NDS Manager to Manage Partitions and Replicas	776
Partition and Replica Management Guidelines	778
When You Mess Up NDS	779
Putting NDS Manager on the NetWare Administrator Tools Menu	780
Creating a New Partition	781
Merging Partitions	784
Viewing or Modifying Replicas	786
Viewing Server Partitions	789
Deleting a NetWare Server Object from NDS	790
Moving a Partition (and Its Container)	792
User Management	793
Using NetWare Accounting	793
Setting User Account Balances	799
Limiting User Disk Space	801
Using UIMPORT to Move Employee Database Records into NDS	803
Using NCUPDATE to Configure Non-Client32 Stations	805
Server Management	807
RCONSOLE for Remote Console Control	807
MONITOR Almost Everything	813
SET Command Overview	839
Using SERVMAN to Fine Tune Your File Server	844
DSTRACE Tracks NDS Synchronization Processes	851
DSREPAIR Means Directory Services Repair	853

	Using DSMERGE for NDS Tree Management	873
	Installing Additive Server Licenses	882
	Commonly Used Console Commands	883
	Managing Protocols and Remote Server Access with INETCFG	888
	Viewing Advanced IPX Statistics with IPXCON	896
	Using NetSync	897
NDS Administration with DOS Tools		906
	Starting and Moving Around in NETADMIN	907
	Creating Container Objects	908
	Creating Leaf Objects	911
	Managing Objects	911
	Using the Partition Manager in DOS: PARTMGR	916
	Starting Accounting with NETADMIN	919
Superb Supervision		920

Chapter 11 Providing Applications for Your Network Clients 931

Application Categories		933
Trends in Distribution, Metering, and Licensing		934
Application Server Guidelines		936
	Improving Disk-Write Performance	939
	Improving Disk-Read Performance	942
	Consolidating Application Licenses	943
Access Rights for Application Directories		945
	Managing Access Rights in Application and Data Directories	946
	Setting Rights to an Application Directory	946
Protecting Application Programs and Data Files		948
	File Attributes as a Safety Device	949
	Changing Directory and File Ownership	951
	Modifying File Rights with the Rights Command	953
Application Administration Tricks		957
	Drive Mapping Techniques	958
	Mapping a Fake Root	959
	Using Directory Maps	959
Some Application Guidelines		961

	Microsoft Windows	961
	GroupWise E-mail and Group Scheduling	966
	WordPerfect and PerfectOffice	968
	General Application Hints	970
	New with 4.11: NetWare Application Launcher	971
	Configuring Application Objects	972
	The Client Side of NAL	978
	Application Aggravation	980
Chapter 12	**Teaching Your Clients to Use the Network**	**989**
	Preparing the User Community	990
	Clients and the NDS Tree	992
	Using CX to Change Your Context	994
	NetWare User Tools:	
	One-Touch Convenience in NetWare 4.1	997
	Logging In from NetWare User Tools	998
	Using the Keyboard in NetWare User Tools	999
	Enabling the Hotkey for NetWare User Tools	1000
	Mapping Drives	1002
	Controlling Printing	1006
	NetWare Connections (Servers)	1014
	Sending Messages	1017
	Managing NetWare Settings	1019
	Customizing NetWare User Tools User-Defined Buttons	1022
	The Graphical Help Display	1023
	NETUSER for DOS Users	1025
	Configuring Printing	1026
	Sending and Receiving Messages	1028
	Mapping Drives and Checking Your Rights	1030
	Setting Attachments and User Details	1032
	Changing Your Context	1033
	Configuring Printing from the Command Line with CAPTURE or NPRINT	1035
	Using CAPTURE	1036
	Using NPRINT	1040

Setting Up Remote Printers	1042
Other Handy User Command-Line Utilities	1045
Checking Your Access with RIGHTS	1045
Checking File Attributes with FLAG	1046
Getting File, Directory, and Volume Information with NDIR	1047
Using FILER for File Management	1048
Managing Files and Directories	1049
Refining Search Parameters	1052
Selecting the Current Directory	1053
Viewing Volume Information	1053
Salvaging Deleted Files	1054
Purging Deleted Files	1056
Setting Default FILER Options	1056
Finding Help	1057
Getting Command-Line Help	1058
Using the DynaText Electronic Manuals	1059
DynaText and Windows 95	1064
Windows 95 Network User Support in NetWare 4.11	1067
WhoAmI and NetWare Information	1068
Sending Messages within Network Neighborhood	1070
Logging in from Network Neighborhood	1071
Mapping Drives from Windows 95	1072
Printing Doesn't Live Here Anymore	1074
Teach Your Users Well	1074
Setting Up Remote Printing	1077

PART III   INTEGRATING NETWARE WITH OTHER OPERATING SYSTEMS   1085

Chapter 13   Using Macintoshes with NetWare 4.1x   1087

Macintosh Networking Crash Course	1089
AppleTalk, EtherTalk, and TokenTalk and the Seven Layers of OSI	1090
Macintosh Network Addresses and Zones	1092

	Installing Macintosh Server Software	1094
	Preparing for Macintosh Server Installation	1095
	Loading the NLMs	1096
	Configuring the AppleTalk Stack	1100
	Configuring File Services	1106
	Configuring Print Services	1109
	Configuring CD-ROM Services	1113
	Installing Additional Language Support	1115
	Installing Macintosh Client Support	1116
	Adding the Macintosh Name Space	1117
	Installing Macintosh Clients	1118
	Navigating through NDS	1120
	Helping Macintosh and PC Users Work Together	1121
Chapter 14	**IntranetWare: NetWare, Intranets, and the Internet Combined**	**1123**
	Comparing NetWare and Unix	1124
	Unix (for NetWare People)	1129
	Everything in Unix Is a File	1130
	Daemons as NLMs	1130
	The NetWare and Unix Kernels	1131
	Networking, Print, File, and User Services Differences	1131
	Philosophical Differences	1132
	NetWare TCP/IP Support	1134
	TCP/IP Overview	1135
	Subnet Secrets	1142
	NetWare TCP/IP Components	1143
	Installing TCPIP.NLM	1146
	Using XCONSOLE	1151
	Using the IPTUNNEL Transport	1152
	Using NetWare/IP	1153
	How NetWare/IP Works on the Non-Client32 Client	1156
	Client32 and NetWare/IP Client Software	1159
	Installing and Using NetWare/IP	1160
	Running NetWare NFS Services	1164
	Managing NFS Services	1164

	Managing Name Services	1165
	Setting Up File Sharing	1166
	Setting Up Printing	1168
	File Transfer Services	1168
	One Product, Two Names: NIAS and/or NetWare IPX/IP Gateway	1170
	Installing the NetWare IPX/IP Gateway	1171
	Tracking Clients and Managing Your IPX/IP Gateway	1175
	Running the NetWare Web Server	1183
	Installing Web Server	1185
	Configuring and Managing the Web Server	1187
	Using the Multi-Protocol Router	1192
	Installing the MPR	1193
	Configuring the MPR	1193
	You, TCP/IP, the Internet, and the Web	1194
Chapter 15	**Installing and Configuring OS/2 Clients**	**1197**
	OS/2 Installation Options	1199
	Requirements for the OS/2 Station	1200
	Copying the OS/2 Client Diskettes for NetWare 4.10	1201
	Installing OS/2 Client Software from Diskettes	1202
	Installing OS/2 Client Software from the CD-ROM Disk	1205
	Configuring the OS/2 Client	1207
	Connecting to a Server	1208
	Finding OS/2 Utilities	1209
	Logging in from OS/2 Clients	1209
	The OS/2 Display	1209
	Using the NetWare User Tools Program in OS/2	1212
	Running NetWare Administrator from an OS/2 Workstation	1215
	OS/2 for NetWare Managers	1217
Chapter 16	**Installing NetWare 4.1x Server for OS/2**	**1219**
	Overview of NetWare Server for OS/2	1220
	Advantages of NetWare 4.1x Server for OS/2	1221
	Server Requirements	1222

	Installation Options	1224
	Installing from a CD-ROM	1224
	Installing from a Remote Network Installation	1225
	Choosing Your Installation Method	1226
	NetWare Installation Steps	1230
	Operation of NetWare Server for OS/2	1230
	Using the Performance Monitor Program	1233
	Managing Memory Allocation	1235
	Performance Tuning	1236
	Special NET.CFG Parameters	1237
	Surprisingly Stable	1239
PART IV	**TAKING ADVANTAGE OF SPECIAL NETWORK FEATURES**	**1241**
Chapter 17	**Installing and Using NetWare 4.1x SFT III for Complete Fault-Tolerance**	**1243**
	Overview of NetWare SFT III	1245
	Roles of the MSEngine and the IOEngine	1247
	Control and Startup Files for SFT III Servers	1248
	SFT III Server Log Files	1249
	Installing SFT III	1249
	Server Requirements	1250
	New Installations	1251
	Upgrading Existing NetWare SFT III Systems	1252
	Living with NetWare SFT III	1253
	Tolerant Thoughts	1255
Chapter 18	**Using the NetWare 4.1x Enhancements**	**1257**
	File Compression: Buy One Disk, Get Two Disks' Worth of Space	1259
	The File Compression Process	1259
	Checking File Compression Status	1261
	File Compression Management	1262
	Improved Performance of Peripheral Devices	1263
	Block Suballocation Saves Even More Space	1264
	MHS: Novell's Messaging Services for NetWare 4.10 Only	1265

	How MHS Works	1265
	FirstMail: Free E-mail Returns to NetWare 4.10 Only	1267
New Server Memory Management Techniques		1270
	Using the DOMAIN.NLM Utility to Load Suspect NLMs	1270
	Server Self-Tuning for Better Performance (and How to Improve It)	1271
SMS: Storage Management Services and SBACKUP		1271
	Components of SMS	1272
	Using SBACKUP	1273
	Backing Up NetWare 4.1x	1274
HSM: Hierarchical Storage Management for More Storage Space		1275
NLSP: Improved Routing for Your WAN		1276
SNMP: A Management Solution		1279
	SNMP for the NetWare 4.1x Server	1279
	SNMP Options in NET.CFG for NetWare Clients	1281
Exciting Enhancements		1283

Chapter 19 — Troubleshooting Your Network — 1285

General Troubleshooting Tips		1287
	Prevention Tips	1288
	Tips for Solving Problems	1291
Learning Your Network's Normal Operation		1293
	Tracking the Details	1293
	Tracking Normal Workstation Details	1302
	Tracking Normal Network Performance	1305
Component Failure Profiles		1308
Common Workstation Problems and Solutions		1310
	Workstation Can't Connect to the Server	1310
	Workstation Can't Use an Application	1312
	Workstation Shows "Not Enough Memory" Errors	1314
	MS Windows Doesn't Work Right	1315
	Printing Problems	1317
Common Server Problems and Solutions		1318
	Server Availability: A Management Decision	1319

	The Hardware Scale and the Costs		1320
	Operating System and RAM Problems		1322
	Freeing Server Memory Temporarily		1323
	Disk Errors		1324
Cabling Problems			1325
Tell Your Boss: Prior Planning Prevents Poor Performance			1327

PART V	**APPENDICES AND GLOSSARY**		**1329**
	Appendix A:	Upgrading, Migrating, and Windows 95 Client Installation Support	1331
	Appendix B:	How Netware 4.1x Differs from Earlier Versions	1345
	Appendix C:	Netware 4.1x Set Commands	1365
	Appendix D:	Recommended Reading	1391
	Glossary of Terms		1397
	Index		*1451*

Introduction

NETWARE 4.11 IS the latest version of the world's most popular network operating system, developed by the world's most successful networking company. Novell engineers took the file and print services that have defined networking for the past decade and added five new components of networking: directory services, messaging, routing, security, and management. Then, they took the best of the Internet (Web server, Web client, IPX-to-IP translation software, and software routing) and rolled it into the IntranetWare package. These services are what will define networking as we head toward the millennium.

Gee, this all sounds pretty fancy. What does it mean to you? If you're new to NetWare, it means NetWare 4.11 is the best network for companies small and large. If you're a current NetWare user, it means NetWare 4.11 builds upon the solid NetWare foundation you're familiar with and adds features necessary for the continued growth of your network.

Just as there are some new features in NetWare, there are some new features in this book. I've worked hard to present this huge wad of information in a friendly way.

Who Should Read This Book?

If you're a NetWare user already, this book builds on what you know from NetWare 3.x and adds the new features in steps. New management utilities are introduced by comparing and contrasting them with NetWare 3.x utilities, such as SYSCON and PCONSOLE. I've been working with NetWare for more than ten years, and I believe I have a good understanding of the "feel" of NetWare. I place these new features in perspective so you, experienced in NetWare but new to 4.1x, will understand where these features came from and how they fit into the current version of NetWare.

NetWare neophytes will find "ground-up" explanations for NetWare 4.1x features and utilities. As a PC networking consultant working with a variety of customer networks, I have learned to explain networking logically and clearly to people who don't have a background in NetWare. I regularly work with people new to networks and NetWare and can relay networking concepts to users familiar with their PCs.

Advanced users, especially those who are performing some network administration for their departments, will find quite a bit of interest here. I recommend recruiting subadministrators and point out the many areas where they are useful. If you fall into the power user or subadministrator category, you will like this book.

Those of you managing small networks will find clear directions on installing and configuring NetWare 4.1x for your company. Novell answered one criticism of earlier NetWare 4 versions by adding a new Simple Installation method. This streamlined installation and configuration process makes NetWare 4.1x easier to install and use than any previous version.

Those of you managing large networks will find many details about the advantages NetWare 4.1x offers administrators in your position. The book includes all you need to know about managing users by large groups, both when you're importing them into NetWare 4.1x and when you're controlling them afterward. Options for NetWare Directory Services suitable for large companies are provided with illustrations and recommendations.

The Politics of Networking

Something useful to both large and small companies is advice on dealing with your boss and your users. Networking is a political art form today. Network administrators must negotiate with competing groups demanding contradictory features in their network.

You know the seven protocol layers always explained in networking books? Well, here we spend time discussing the eighth layer: Politics. This layer is often the most important, yet it is left out of all computing manuals and reference books.

Politics and salesmanship are important requirements for the modern network manager. You must convince your management of your network's importance and continued need for enhancement. You must convince nervous users that the network will decrease, not increase, their daily workload. You must convince more users wanting more different things than ever before that your network is the best network design for them.

Perhaps we shouldn't call this "salesmanship," but refer to it as "user and boss expectation management." To help you with this management, each chapter ends with a few paragraphs of straight talk from me to you. These small sections are full of the advice and background I would give my best friend if she went into network management. In other words, the truth about more than technology—the truth about people on your network and how to handle them.

How This Book Is Organized

To help you find the information you need, this book is divided into four major sections:

- **Part I: Setting Up the Network, Chapters 1 through 5.** The chapters in this part cover what you need to know about installing your network. Two chapters are devoted to planning and installing NetWare Directory Services. This part takes you up through connecting workstations to the network.

- **Part II: Using the Network, Chapters 6 through 12.** The first two chapters in this part deal with those who are using the network: your users. The next chapter deals with a service those users take advantage of frequently (much too frequently in my opinion), which is network printing. Security, an important topic for many networks, is the subject of Chapter 9. The next chapter—the biggest one in the book—is a complete guide to network management and the NetWare 4.1x utilities that make those tasks easier than ever. The last two chapters in this part cover two basic user needs: applications and network training.

- **Part III: Integrating NetWare with Other Operating Systems, Chapters 13 through 16.** Does your network include Macintosh, Unix, or OS/2 systems? If it does, see the chapter that covers that system. Chapter 13 tells you what you need to know about MacNDS for the Macs on your network. For those networks that connect to Unix systems, Chapter 14 is the place to go. Chapter 14 also is where you should turn to learn how to take advantage of IntranetWare. Chapters 15 and 16 cover setting up OS/2 clients and installing NetWare 4.1x Server for OS/2.

> *I substantially revised Chapter 14, which was titled "Integrating NetWare 4.1 with Unix" in the previous edition, to cover IntranetWare and the changes this new direction brings to NetWare. Interestingly, people say in the same breath that they no longer care about Unix but are desperate to reach the Internet. What powers the Internet? Unix, of course. Always has, always will. For that reason, I left much of the Unix background information in the chapter. Besides, all the tools used to reach the Internet hosts work perfectly well when used to connect to local hosts.*

- **Part IV: Taking Advantage of Special Networking Features, Chapters 17 through 19.** In this part, you'll find coverage of Novell's SFT (System Fault Tolerance) III and NetWare 4.1x enhancements, which include the advancements in the NetWare 4.x versions other than NDS features. The final chapter is where you turn when you (I'm sorry to say, inevitably) have a problem with your network (or a network user or your boss).

Following Part IV are five appendices:

- Appendix A provides instructions for upgrading to NetWare 4.1x from earlier versions of NetWare.

- If you want to compare the features in NetWare 4.1x with earlier NetWare versions, and with other networks in general, see Appendix B for the details on what's new and what it does for you.

- Appendix C contains all the NetWare 4.1x server SET commands, for those of you who would prefer the command-line route to setting server parameters.

- If you're interested in my sources, and perhaps would like a look at a few of them yourself, you'll find the books I referred to for some of my information in Appendix D.

Finally, at the back of the book is a glossary of the terms used in this book. When you're not sure what I mean by a particular word, turn to the glossary for a quick definition.

I don't expect you to read this book straight through, cover to cover. (In fact, if you did, I might worry about you a little bit.) You are expected to skip around and dip in and out of the book regularly.

Many of the same network management functions may now be performed using a DOS utility (such as PCONSOLE or FILER) or a graphical utility called NetWare Administrator in Windows 95, Windows 3.1x, and sometimes in OS/2. Because I think that most of you will prefer one or the other, and read just the information about your preferred utility, management explanations and procedures are repeated: once for the NetWare Administrator graphical management utility, and once for the corresponding DOS utility. If you read both, you will get the same background information with minor variations, along with the precise procedure for the specific utility being discussed.

Special Features in This Book

Throughout the book, you will find several interesting features. Parts I and II include a special feature I call "case studies." These case studies, or progress reports, follow two mythical companies, MiniCo and MegaCorp, through the planning, installation, and configuration of their networks. The actions by both fictional companies are based on what I have seen in the real world, including published success stories and tales of network horror.

Oh yes, sometimes companies do things wrong. Both the right and wrong ways to approach some network management tasks are part of the case studies, just like in real life. You'll find the stories of MiniCo and MegaCorp at the ends of Chapters 1 through 12, with an extra look at how both companies handle IntranetWare at the end of Chapter 14.

The In a Hurry? instructions in this book supply the basic steps of a procedure without the embellishments. They appear throughout the chapters, just under the section heading and before the discussion of that task. These steps are here for quick-and-easy reference, for those times when you want to check yourself before a procedure.

If the In a Hurry? instructions give you everything you need, that's great. If you need more information about how or why to do the procedure (or maybe you're just interested), read the following text for the details. And, for extra convenience, all of the sets of In a Hurry? instructions (except chapters 15 and 16) are gathered in the easy-to-detach booklet that comes with this book.

Another bonus you get with this book is extra networking wisdom, in the form of "sidebars." Scattered throughout the book, you'll find special sections with advice about the politics of networking, some historical background on the topic at hand, and any other information I thought you might find interesting or helpful (or both).

And, as you may have grown used to if you read a lot of computer books, you'll see tips, warnings, and notes in the appropriate spots.

Hardware and Software Used for This Book

Many companies provided hardware or software to help me with this book. The generosity of these companies goes past just the equipment; many provided help and information above and beyond the call of duty. Without their help, this book would have been nearly impossible.

Hardware

Here's a list and some brief descriptions of the equipment I used:

- Two Gateway2000 P5-120s, each with the following:

    120 MHz Pentium processor
    32 MB RAM
    1.6 GB hard disk
    8x CD-ROM drive
    3Com 3C509 10BaseT Ethernet network adapter

- One Gateway 2000 P5-66, with the following:

    66 MHz Pentium processor
    16 MB RAM
    500 MB IDE hard disk
    CD-ROM double-speed drive
    3Com 3C509 10BaseT Ethernet network adapter

There have been three GATEWAY2000 systems used in the two versions of this book. They have all run various beta versions of all sorts of strange software products. None of the three systems have as much as hiccuped.

GATEWAY2000 was the primary server for most of the first version of this book. When it came time to test OS/2, this machine was reformatted and ran OS/2 Warp without a problem. The addition of NetWare Server for OS/2 still didn't strain the speed and performance of GATEWAY2000, even though we were technically exceeding the stated capabilities of the box. It just kept on running.

- Acer Altos 4500, with the following:

    EISA bus
    33 MHz 486 processor
    32 MB RAM
    500 MB SCSI hard disk
    Thomas Conrad TC5043-T 10BaseT Ethernet network adapter
    Adaptec 1542 SCSI controller
    MDI SCSI Express 600CDX2, dual CD-ROM drive attached

This machine, dubbed ALTOS486, is a repeat performer: it first appeared in my book *Integrating UNIX and NetWare Networks* (Novell Press, 1993) as both a Unix host and NetWare server (running Altos NetWare for SCO). It has performed for both books without a single blip or anomaly, no matter how much I abuse the poor thing.

- Home-built 386/33 (CLONE386), with the following:

    8 MB RAM
    340 MB hard disk
    3Com 3C509 10BaseT Ethernet network adapter

- BitWise Design, Inc. Portable System (312_NW), with the following:

    33 MHz 386 processor
    8 MB RAM
    200 MB hard disk
    Thomas Conrad TC5043-T 10BaseT Ethernet network adapter

- Macintosh Quadra 660AV, with the following:

    8 MB RAM
    300 MB hard disk
    CD-ROM
    Internal 10BaseT Ethernet network adapter

- Other hardware:

    LinkBuilder TP/8 wiring concentrator from 3Com Corporation
    Thomas Conrad TC5055 10BaseT wiring concentrator
    Uninterruptible power supply UPS from MinuteMan PM600, Para Systems, Inc.

Software

The software I used includes the following packages:

- NetWare 4.11, IntranetWare, and NetWare 3.12, from Novell, Inc.

- OS/2 Warp, from IBM, Inc.

- DS Standard, NDS Design and Modeling software from Preferred Systems, Inc.

- Collage Complete 1.1, screen capture, correct, and catalog software from Inner Media, Inc.

- Applause Image Utility for OS/2 (for all the OS/2 screenshots) from Solution Technology, Inc.

- John T. McCann's SofTrack, from ON Technology

- Windows 95 and Windows 3.1, from Microsoft. Word 7 (for writing the book)

How to Contact the Author

Use this address to reach me electronically:

- **Internet:** james@gaskin.com

Relax and have fun with NetWare and this book. This isn't a John Grisham story, so no lawyers or gangsters or gangs of lawyers are going to try and kill you. But like a John Grisham story, the hero (that's you) always wins in the end.

Setting Up the Network

PART 1

Planning Your Network Before Installation

CHAPTER

EVERY NEW NETWORK and installation must have a complete, detailed plan describing every particular. One customer told me, "We plan monthly and revise daily." Although he said it as a joke, a lot of networking truth is in that statement. Since a network is a collection of people, things will change because people change. That's a guarantee.

But even though things will change, you need a plan to provide a network framework. Once you have a plan, you can deviate from the plan. If you don't have a plan, you will wander about, getting more lost every day.

We'll get to what you need to plan for your network before you install NetWare, but first, let's set the scene. Let's begin with a look at the various types of networks, so you'll know how yours fits into the overall picture.

Physical Network Types

THE EARLY DAYS of NetWare were marked by a profusion of different types of network interface cards (NICs). Novell took an unusual approach to this proliferation: they supported every NIC they could find. While the early 3Com and Corvus networks ran only on their own NICs, NetWare ran on all these, as well as on Western Digital's and SMC's and Datapoint's and Proteon's, and on and on.

I once counted (in 1985) about 35 different versions of NetWare available for 35 different NICs. Now there are more than 200 NICs available, but they break down neatly into Ethernet, Token Ring, and Other. Other is getting a smaller piece of that pie graph every year.

If you are mostly Unix, you are also mostly Ethernet. Many people believe that "Open Systems" means Unix over Ethernet, but that's not exactly true. You will probably hear that from vendors of both Unix and Ethernet, however.

The majority of PC-only LANs are Ethernet as well. Ethernet was available before Token Ring, and the price of Ethernet cards has often been hundreds of dollars less than that of Token Ring cards. For these reasons, Ethernet got a big head start over Token Ring for NetWare networks. As more Token Ring vendors compete with IBM, the price difference between the two is lessening somewhat. But it's true that Token Ring still costs more than Ethernet.

If you are mostly IBM, you are also mostly Token Ring. IBM introduced Token Ring for the PC in 1984, and has had great success. By making it easy to connect Token Ring networks to 3270 cluster controllers, mainframes, AS/400s, and the like, IBM has made Token Ring the sales and technical equal to Ethernet.

IBM has now begun to support Ethernet in a major way, as the Unix vendors have started to support Token Ring. IBM's RS/6000 shipped from the factory with an Ethernet adapter, a first for Big Blue. Sun, DEC, HP, and other manufacturers now have Token Ring boards available for virtually their entire product lines.

That doesn't mean the two systems are interchangeable—not by any means. In fact, technically and philosophically, the two systems are as different as they could be.

Ethernet Networks

Developed by Xerox, Intel, and DEC in 1976, Ethernet was created where? You got it, PARC (Palo Alto Research Center). Credit for Ethernet belongs to Robert Metcalfe and David Boggs. Starting at 3 Mbps (megabits per second), Ethernet was soon bumped to 10 Mbps. At the beginning, its main purpose was to connect host systems to printers to provide quicker PostScript graphics printing, much faster than the speeds possible with serial lines. Metcalfe later founded 3Com, one of the earliest providers of Ethernet interface cards.

As defined in the IEEE 802.3 standard documents, Ethernet is a nondeterministic network access control method. This means that the network is available at all times for every node. When a node has information ready to transmit, it listens to be sure no one else is using the network, then sends a packet. Hence, the private car on the highway analogy. Leave when you want, and travel fast when the highway is empty.

The technical jargon for this access method used by Ethernet is CSMA/CD, for carrier sense multiple access/collision detect. This just means a node listens to the net (carrier sense), any node can get on at any time (multiple access), and when a collision occurs, it will be detected. Collisions are when two nodes send information at the same time and the two electrical signals get garbled. When a collision is detected, both stations wait a random number of microseconds before retransmitting. Users never know if a packet is being retransmitted; it happens randomly, and the retransmission scheme is so good that noticeable delays are avoided.

Ethernet nodes are strung together into an electrical bus, where each node connects to all other nodes. Visualize coax (coaxial cable), with the wire running from one node to the next, to the next, and so on. The new 10BaseT specification details how to run Ethernet over UTP (unshielded twisted-pair) cabling, like telephones use. This is still a bus topology electrically, even though every node must be connected to a central hub (as with Token Ring and its MSAUs). Inside the hub, the electrical signals still act as if they were on good old (okay, brittle, capricious, and prone-to-failure) coax. Figure 1.1 shows Ethernet on coax.

Ethernet packets carry anywhere between 46 and 1500 bytes of data. With routing and error-checking bits added, the smallest Ethernet packet is usually 64 bytes; the largest is 1518 bytes.

Every Ethernet interface card has a unique, 12-byte address assigned by the manufacturer. This address cannot be changed.

> **TIP**
>
> *After you install NetWare, you can see the Ethernet NIC address by typing* NLIST USER /A /B. *Under the NODE heading, you will see the 12-byte address for every active connection.*

FIGURE 1.1
Ethernet on coax

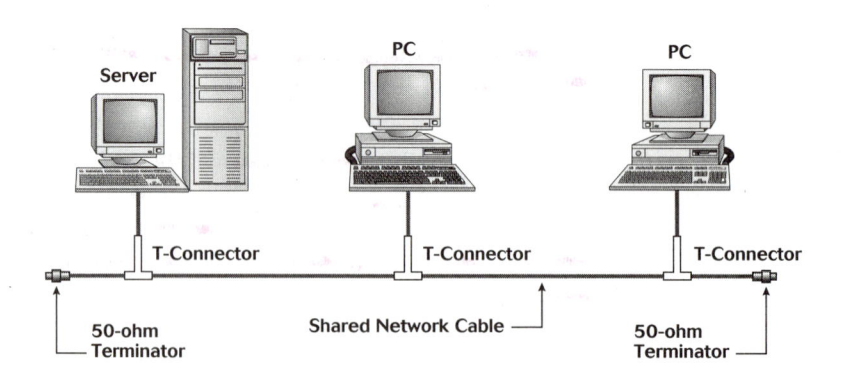

Switched Ethernet

Ethernet is a wonderful, high-performance technology until the network gets about 40 percent saturated with packets. With a high number of packets, more collisions occur, and more packets must be resent. The more you load standard Ethernet, the more problems you have.

Some people say that Ethernet doesn't really offer 10 Mbps throughput, since you can't reach 10 Mbps of data transfer by placing 20 systems, all spitting out 500 kbps, on the network. There are too many collisions and retransmissions, resulting in an actual throughput of 4 to 5 Mbps in this situation. This is technically true, but I feel the test is rigged to show the poorest side of Ethernet.

If you have only two systems on Ethernet, one sending and one receiving, you get close to a full 10 Mbps throughput. With send and receive packets from only two machines, few packet collisions will occur. Also, the shorter the physical network, the less chance of two packets corrupting each other. With a short network and two stations, I can get over 9 Mbps throughput from off-the-shelf Ethernet.

Some smart people decided that the problem with Ethernet was not the CSMA/CD access method, but the constant collisions. If they could figure out how to offer each computer on the network a dedicated Ethernet network—Eureka!

With an intelligent "matrix switch" bridge in the center of this picture, switched Ethernet can provide a dedicated network for high-performance systems such as servers. The earliest manufacturer of this equipment is Kalpana, so I copied that company's illustration (with permission), which is shown in Figure 1.2.

With switched Ethernet, shared network segments run at typical Ethernet speeds, but they are subject to overloading and multiple packet errors, just as with typical Ethernet. On the exclusive network segments used by the servers, there are virtually no collisions, so throughput approaches Ethernet's "theoretical maximum" of 10 Mbps.

Devices such as the Kalpana EtherSwitch and their now-numerous competitors may easily extend the life of Ethernet an extra decade. Prices on Ethernet switches are reasonable and prove to be an excellent value under the proper circumstances.

Token Ring Networks

For our purposes, Token Ring became a network option when IBM released the first 4 Mbps Token Ring cards in 1984, along with its PC Network software. Token-passing technologies had been examined and somewhat standardized by

FIGURE 1.2

Switched Ethernet

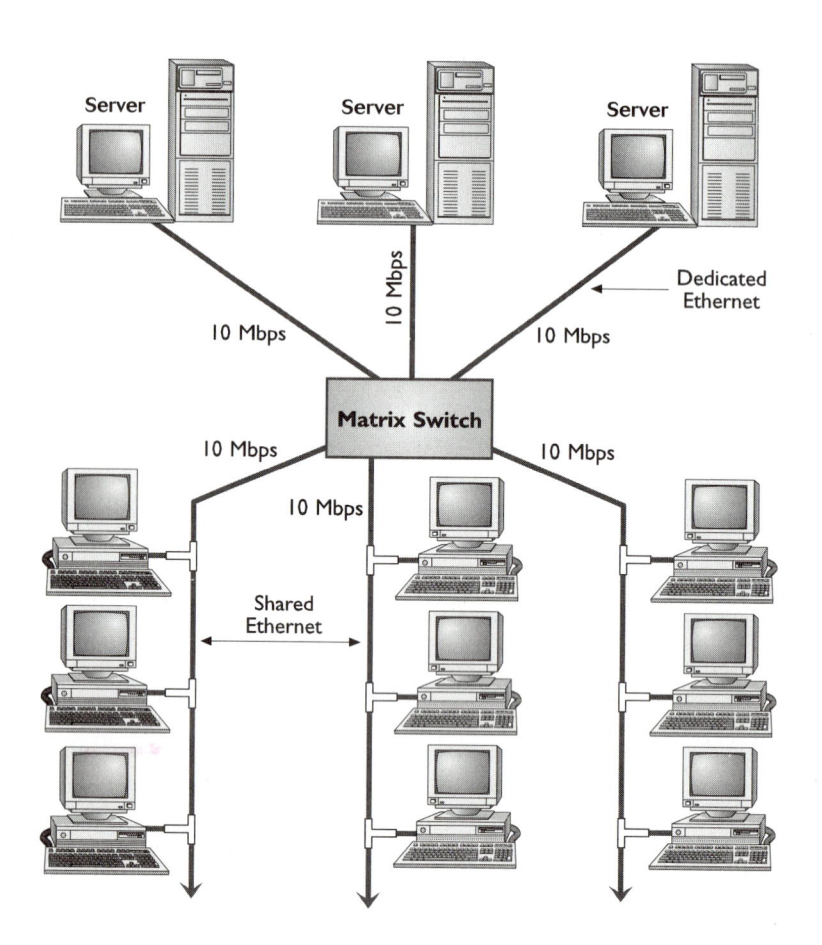

that time. Some IBM systems used a type of Token Ring before 1984, but the draft documents for IEEE 802.5 mark the beginning of Token Ring for this discussion.

Token Ring is a deterministic network access control method. This means that each node has a certain time slot when it can access the network to transmit a packet of information. An electrical signal goes from one station to the next, and if nothing is appended to that signal, the network is available. No matter when a node has information, it must wait for an empty token to come by. Hence, the bus and bus stop analogy. Whether the highway is busy or not, you must wait for the next bus before starting your travels. If the highway is busy, however, you have a special bus lane that avoids congestion problems.

Packets on 4 Mbps Token Ring can be as large as 4096 bytes. This requires consideration when connecting Token Ring and Ethernet because of the packet size difference. On 16 Mbps Token Ring, packets can be even larger, up to 16 kilobytes.

Token Ring sends signals from one node to the nearest active upstream neighbor (NAUN). Each node must be connected to a central hub called a multistation access unit (MSAU, often shortened to MAU). Each MSAU has an input and output port (Ring In and Ring Out) for connection to other MSAUs. The electrical wire path is circular, with the signal going to each active node in sequence before returning to our original station, hence Token Ring. Figure 1.3 shows the Ring In (RI) and Ring Out (RO) connections.

Like Ethernet, Token Ring interface cards are assigned a unique address when they are built. However, a feature called LAA (locally administered address) can override the built-in address with an address assigned when the

FIGURE 1.3

Token Ring network with Ring In and Ring Out connections

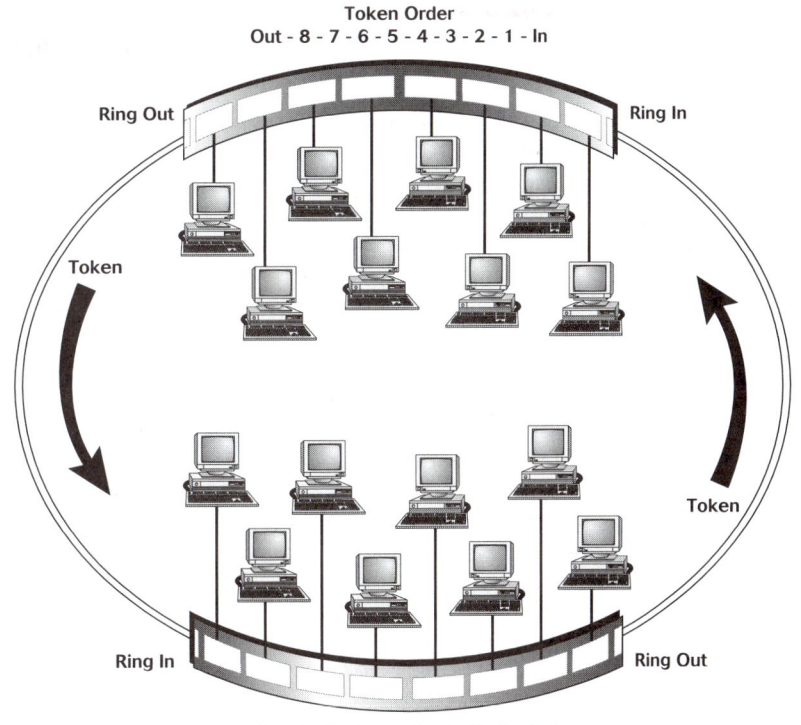

> *Ethernet fans feel they have democracy while the Token Ring group has dictatorship.*

NIC drivers are loaded. This is sometimes used to list a location code for each Token Ring card, but the network administrator must then track all assigned numbers and make sure no duplicates are created.

Token Ring advocates feel they represent civilization while Ethernet is chaos. Ethernet fans feel they have democracy while the Token Ring group has dictatorship. People get really bent out of shape if you criticize their particular choice of physical network connections.

Those of us in the integration business are above this, of course. We realize that both are good systems, and rarely is one considerably better than the other for any particular installation. While we may have our favorites (Ethernet), we know and appreciate both.

Token Ring and Ethernet: Practical Similarities

Although they have different speeds (10 Mbps for Ethernet; 4 or 16 Mbps for Token Ring), topology (bus for Ethernet; ring for Token Ring), and other technical differences, modern networks look amazingly similar. Both Token Ring and Ethernet installations have powered intelligent hubs with UTP wire pairs running from the hub directly to a workstation.

See Figure 1.4 and tell me which technology, Ethernet or Token Ring, is being illustrated. Can't, can you? The practical installation of Token Ring and Ethernet over UTP cable is almost exactly the same.

Does this somehow violate the "spirit" of the two networking protocols? Not at all. The situation merely acknowledges the influence of the market toward cleaner and neater solutions to common network problems.

Both Ethernet and Token Ring, in their traditional guise, have plenty of aggravations. But if you isolate each workstation on its own cable from the other workstations, limiting the effect a bad connection has on the network, you will have fewer headaches. Now when a cable or NIC goes bad, it doesn't take the entire network with it. If Joe kicks the wire lose under his desk, only Joe loses his network connection.

Management of the physical plant (fancy talk for wires and hubs) is easier with the scenario shown in Figure 1.4 as well. Each hub can be managed down to the individual port with the proper software. The ability to turn each hub port on or off from a remote location is old hat, as is the ability to monitor traffic levels by port.

FIGURE 1.4

A modern network—but Token Ring or Ethernet?

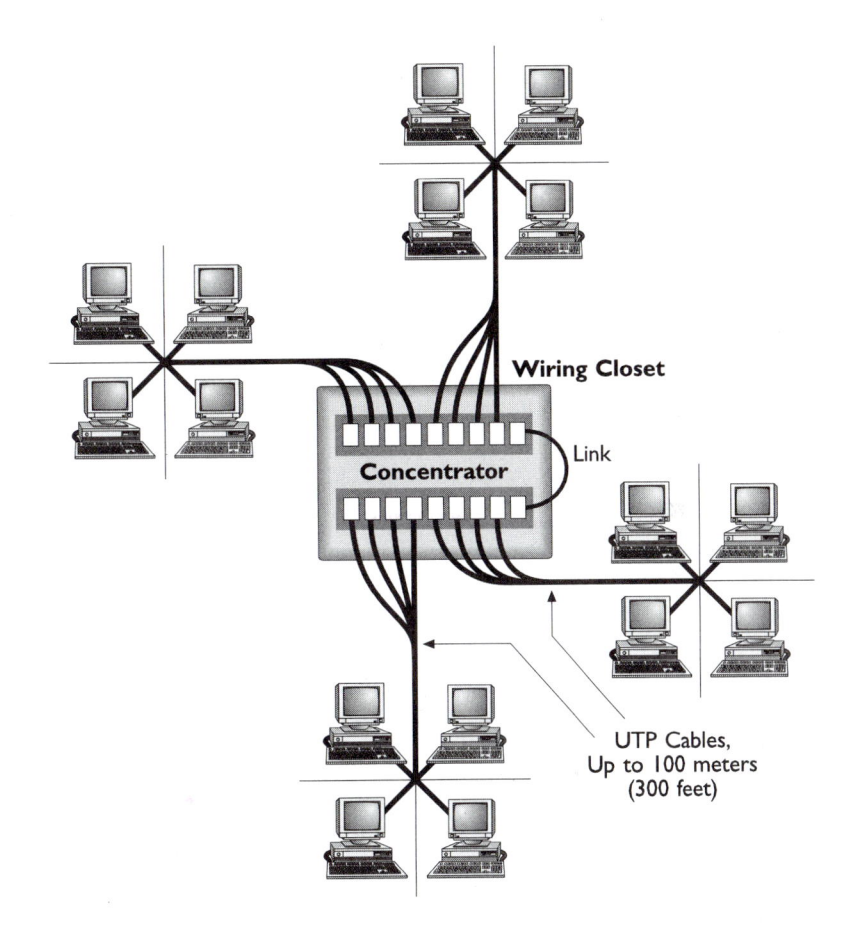

As a general rule for both UTP Ethernet and Token Ring, the distance between powered devices can only be about 330 feet (100 meters). Powered devices include hubs, PCs, bridges, routers, matrix switches, and the like. If you run cables north and south from a hub, you have a network diameter of more than 600 feet (180 meters). Since most buildings are much smaller than that, placing hubs in the middle of the area works well.

Hubs are connected with either UTP, coax, or fiber-optic cable. If fiber-optic cable is used, the distance between hubs can be more than a mile (as much as 2 kilometers). Your mileage may vary; check with the manufacturer of your premise's wiring equipment and use the manufacturer's guidelines.

Other Physical Network Options

You can never be too rich, too thin, or have too much network bandwidth. The eternal quest for speed means other faster networks are vying for the space now controlled by Ethernet and Token Ring.

Users strongly prefer UTP cabling for all network connections. Only if the speed is tremendously better will users consider using more expensive cable with shielding, more pairs inside the wire sheath, or the big price jump to fiber-optics.

The flip side of these users are the ones dying to find an application, such as video and audio, that requires fiber-optic cabling all the way to the desktop. Vendors pushing technology such as full-motion video want users to have enough fiber-optic cable installed so that the software runs well.

Fiber-optic cable is popular because it is immune to electrical noise and is almost impossible to tap without being detected. All the new fast technologies work on fiber-optic cabling first, then gradually learn how to suppress electrical noise well enough to run over coax, STP (shielded twisted-pair), or UTP cables. Another benefit of fiber-optic cable's electrical isolation is that it allows cable runs of more than a mile (as long as 2 kilometers) between hubs in a campus environment. The telephone companies run fiber-optic connections for dozens of miles between signal repeaters, but use single-mode fiber-optic cable rather than the dual-mode used in LAN connections.

One important consideration when discussing the "networks of the future" is that they no longer are data-only networks. Previously, voice and video traffic was analog, and this traffic needed a different transport mechanism than digital data. Today, everything is either digital already or will be soon. All the mess of the analog world (hundreds of shades of blue, increasing volume in a sound, and so on) has been replaced by the precision of digital transformation into ones and zeros. At least, everything is digital once it gets into the computer system.

The successful networks of the future will deliver high bandwidth on a reliable basis. High availability leans toward small, fast packets of data so transmissions can occur the instant they're needed. A delay of as little as 10 milliseconds introduces annoying echo into voice conversations, and is unacceptable. For video to become a part of the computer world, it must be clean and clear and deliver at least 24 complete new images per second, just like the television that so enthralls us.

Fast Ethernet (100BaseT)

In the infant years of Ethernet, the speed was bumped from the original 3 Mbps to 10 Mbps. Many vendors are trying to bump Ethernet once again, but this time by an order of magnitude to 100 Mbps.

In order to keep the name Ethernet, plans call for almost all the details but speed to remain the same as the Ethernet specifications for 10BaseT in use today. By building on distributed hubs with dedicated lines to each network device, control can be centered in the hubs. By ignoring the Ethernet standards for coax cable, the shorter network cable requirements imposed by the higher speed won't be a problem. Like 10BaseT, Fast Ethernet will be limited to about 330 feet (100 meters) between powered devices. A radius of about 660 feet (200 meters) from a hub in a wiring closet supports over 90 percent of desktops in corporate America today.

The most important consideration for those vendors proposing Fast Ethernet is the continued use of CSMA/CD for controlling network access. The MAC (Media Access Control) specifications of Ethernet describe everything in a speed-independent fashion. Only the interpacket gap is given in absolute time measurements; everything else is done on the basis of bits versus time. There is nothing in the CSMA/CD specifications that ties Ethernet to 10 Mbps.

Fast Ethernet is a local transport option only. Many people consider it unsuitable for real-time uses such as video, since collisions will still be a factor. Without a guarantee of regularly scheduled packets, video over Fast Ethernet may still jerk and waver on occasion. However, most computer applications used today will happily scream along at 100 Mbps. Of course, it only makes sense to put such speedy network connections on systems that can support it, such as high-speed buses inside servers and the like. All Fast Ethernet backbone products will include a bridge to standard Ethernet.

100BaseT will supposedly run over Category 3 UTP cable, but it will need four pair rather than the two pair used by 10BaseT. Don't believe the vendors when they say you will "probably" be able to use your existing cable. Plan on rewiring.

100BaseVG and AnyLAN

The competitors to Fast Ethernet wanted to fix what they considered the problem of Ethernet: the CSMA/CD network access method. Although both groups called themselves "Fast Ethernet" at one time or the other, cooler heads prevailed, and the CSMA/CD camp was declared Fast Ethernet. The other vendors, primarily IBM and HP, rechristened everything into AnyLAN, which now includes both Token Ring and 10BaseT Ethernet style networks.

You don't see how that works, right off? It's a stretch, but here goes: the hub acts as a traffic cop, and polls stations, somewhat like the token passing between stations in a Token Ring network. In addition, a demand priority scheme allows some nodes to gain access to the network before their turn. Those applications using demand priority will then be able to support real-time needs such as video to the desktop. The round-robin polling algorithm will service all other nodes before too long, so little or no delay will be seen by the other nodes.

Using the same hub-to-workstation design as 10BaseT, AnyLAN also allows up to four wiring concentrators (hubs) between communicating stations. AnyLAN supports STP and fiber-optic cable, with correspondingly larger distances supported.

The demand priority scheme has been available since 16 Mbps Token Ring cards appeared on the market, but no common applications use the demand priority functions (those used by audio and video data streams). This makes some people uncomfortable, and those people tend to prefer Fast Ethernet. Those people that need reliably delivered packets with no time fluctuation prefer AnyLAN.

This again is a local network system. Even with fiber-optic cable stretching up to more than a mile (2 kilometers), most installations will be for workgroups and servers rather than multiprotocol backbones. Again, don't believe vendors that "guarantee" your existing cable will support AnyLAN.

Wireless Networking

A fact of network troubleshooting: cables will kill you. They break, they get unplugged, they get cut, they cause problems. So let's dump'em!

Wireless networks have come a long way over the past year. They will go even farther to become a vital part of your network before the millennia. And, according to my friend Art, "wireless" as a name will go away, just as we no longer call cars "horseless carriages." He hasn't given me a better name yet. Too bad "Ether" net is already taken. Perhaps the IEEE 802.11 committee members will create a new name as they create standards for the emerging wireless market.

The fastest growth in the wireless (there's that name again) business is with laptops and PDA (Personal Digital Assistants, like Apple's Newton). PCMCIA (Personal Computer Memory Card International Association, or Personal Computer Makers Can't Invent Acronyms) slots have become popular as a

> And, according to my friend Art, "wireless" as a name will go away, just as we no longer call cars "horseless carriages."

connection point to your LAN across a wireless link. Other common uses for wireless connections include hard-to-wire locations, or in buildings protected by historical designations where it makes you nervous to drill holes in the floors and walls.

As Figure 1.5 shows, there are several ways to connect wireless stations into your existing LAN. Since wireless components are double or triple the cost of their wire-bound cousins, it's rare to see a completely wireless network.

The wireless grouping also includes infrared products that use light pulses rather than radio waves. Most people assume wireless means radio, but it only means "without wires."

FIGURE 1.5

A variety of wireless networking options

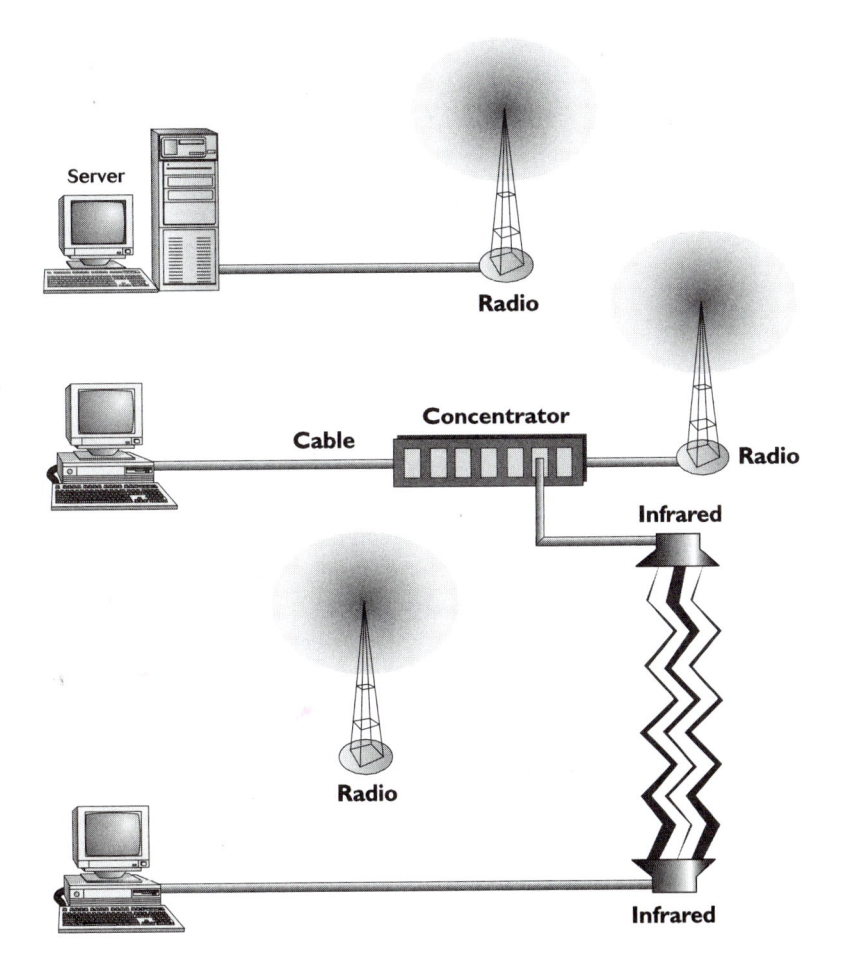

Some of the improvements with wireless products include support for standard protocols like TCP/IP and support for NetWare VLMs (Virtual Loadable Modules). Packet burst technology in NetWare 4 greatly improves performance. But be aware that transmission speed for wireless products is only around 2 Mbps. Plan your software distribution to put as much of the executable software as possible on the wireless client, to minimize user frustration.

Frequency hopping technology splits the send and receive frequency (either 900 MHz or 2.4 GHz) into up to 100 subchannels. Each transmission pair (the wireless network card and the access point to either the file server or LAN to wireless bridge) jumps around the subchannels in a predetermined pseudo-random pattern. This considerably lessens the chance of collisions and retransmissions.

FDDI

FDDI (Fiber Distributed Data Interface) is another method for reaching transmission speeds of 100 Mbps. Products are available and in general distribution, although the prices remain high because of low volumes and the complexity of FDDI.

Based on Token Ring ideas, FDDI uses a timed token-passing access method. The physical layout is a dual ring, with the token rotating around the ring in opposite directions. The dual counter-rotating rings provide redundancy if a cable is cut, and the protocol includes quite a bit of management support.

In spite of the *fiber* in the acronym, FDDI wasn't even a standard yet when companies started implementing FDDI over STP and UTP cabling. The specifications for UTP and STP support are now built into the protocol specification to enhance FDDI's use in workgroup situations.

Systems can be attached to the dual counter-rotating ring cabling directly, or connected by a single-attached cable to a concentrator. Again, this helps reduce the cost of connections and encourages smaller groups to participate. With a network length of 200 kilometers (yes, that's over 38 miles), FDDI can connect up to 500 stations on a single ring.

FDDI has lost the PR war against Fast Ethernet on the low end and ATM (Asynchronous Transfer Mode) on the high end, dooming it to niche applications. While it's possible to use FDDI to the desktop, the cost and complexity of the protocol limits most uses to backbones and specific high-throughput installations.

ATM

ATM is the newest high-bandwidth network option. Developed by the telephone companies as much as the data networking industry, ATM is a radical departure from Token Ring and Ethernet type networks.

Based on a matrix-switching technology similar to giant telephone exchanges and switched Ethernet, ATM uses 48-byte "cells" of data preceded by 5 bytes of routing information. These cells are fixed in length, and each cell's header contains all the information needed to route the cell to its destination. The higher-level applications are fooled by ATM into believing they have a dedicated connection between nodes.

ATM speeds are flexible, and technically they can range between 1 Mbps and 2.488 Gbps (gigabits per second). The most common speeds mentioned for ATM are 155 Mbps and 622 Mbps. The numbers are related to the SONET (Synchronous Optical NETwork) standard for North America and the corresponding SDH (Synchronous Digital Hierarchy) international standard. These higher speeds above 155 Mbps will likely be supported only in the long-haul network system.

Anything digital can be stuffed into the ATM cells. Advocates of ATM predict an end-to-end system of nothing but ATM cells whizzing about. Realistically, however, the cost and complexity of such high-speed interfaces will be applied to backbones, WANs, and special applications.

Fiber-optic cable is the transmission media of choice for ATM. True to form, however, work is underway to move ATM down to voice-grade UTP cable. So far, the signal only goes 10 feet before disintegrating. The minimum cable supported for ATM so far is Category 5 data-grade UTP. There is no market push to support lower-grade cable than Category 5, so make sure all your new cable is that level or above.

One consequence of the expense of ATM and its shared development by both data networking and telecommunications companies is the stranglehold large providers will probably have on the ATM product market. Unlike with Ethernet and Token Ring, small companies don't have the resources to play in the ATM league. The companies making and buying the ATM infrastructure are all big, big names: AT&T, IBM, WilTel, Hughes, MCI, DSC Corporation, BBN, Sprint, GTE, and Northern Telecom.

Routers will connect LANs to an ATM WAN framework, rather than having ATM come be the LAN. The overhead of ATM is high (1 byte of overhead for every 10 bytes of data in a cell), and only at high speeds does ATM make good sense.

ATM25

Of course, good sense is often ignored by the computer industry. IBM is busy promoting ATM25, or ATM directly to your PC. Rather than 155 Mbps, the ATM25 proposal offers 25 Mbps to the desktop.

Why 25 Mbps? Full-motion video with 24-bit color running at 30 frames a second means 720 Mbps. Compression ratios of 30:1, a fairly conservative estimate, give us 22 Mbps as the speed needed. A speed of 25 Mbps is slow enough to run over voice-grade UTP cables, being less than twice as fast as 16 Mbps Token Ring.

IBM believes the interface card cost of ATM25 can be kept low enough to be attractive as well. Adapters would need only one-third as many chips as required by 100+ Mbps ATM.

Running ATM on the desktop would ease the transition to ATM at the WAN level. Converting Ethernet or Token Ring down to 48-byte cells requires fast processing and large buffers, but connecting ATM25 to ATM would be considerably easier.

I immediately see two problems with this approach. First, 25 Mbps isn't enough of a speed increase over the 10 Mbps or 16 Mbps speeds of the currently available Ethernet and Token Ring products. Second, reworking all the existing LAN hardware or buying the pieces to integrate existing Token Ring and Ethernet systems with the ATM25 will cost a pretty penny.

Will ATM25 become popular? It will be helped by a strong move to offer videoconferencing to every desktop. ATM is a full-duplex technology, necessary for interactive video. But I wouldn't hold a fire sale on your existing network just yet. Give ATM25 another year or two before you jump into it big time.

ARCnet

An early (1977) network developed by Datapoint was named ARCnet (Attached Resource Computing network). It uses a token-passing scheme over a bus topology, somewhat like Token Ring. Slower (2.5 Mbps) and with smaller packets (512 bytes versus 4098 bytes) than IBM's 4 Mbps Token Ring, ARCnet typically runs over thin coax cable. The cable is, in fact, the same type as used by IBM for 3270 mainframe terminals, but adapters can convert the coax signaling scheme to work over UTP.

ARCnet interface cards were the first to get cheap; they regularly undercut Ethernet cards by $100 or more in the late 1980s. This accounted for their popularity, especially since AT class PCs couldn't overwhelm the slow 2.5 Mbps transfer rate. Low-cost passive and active hubs perform the same function as Token Ring's MSAU. See Figure 1.6 for some ARCnet cabling options.

The network addresses for each card were set, in octal, by a set of eight dip switches. Duplicate addresses mean trouble on a network, and only the most conscientious network administrator ever kept a good list of used addresses. Most installations involved arranging the dip switches into an attractive pattern and crossing your fingers. The octal address limits a single network to 255 addresses, with one address reserved for broadcast packets.

Unfortunately for ARCnet fans, Datapoint controlled ARCnet completely. Unlike Token Ring and Ethernet, there was never certification by the IEEE (Institute of Electrical and Electronics Engineers) Standards Committee for ARCnet as there was for Token Ring and Ethernet. The move to standardization is underway now, but it will likely be too little too late. The strength ARCnet had in the NetWare market has dwindled drastically the last few years as the higher performance Ethernet and Token Ring cards dropped in price, eliminating ARCnet's primary advantage.

ARCnet's PR has fallen so badly that a proposal several years ago for a 20 Mbps protocol called ARCnet Plus came and went, leaving nary a dent on the market. This was several years before full-duplex Ethernet could match the 20 Mbps throughput, and before Token Ring hubs supported matrix switching. In many ways, the system provided excellent technology at a fair price, but no one cared. The ARCnet reputation had fallen so far that outstanding performance couldn't pull ARCnet out of the hole it had dug for itself.

> *Most installations involved arranging the dip switches into an attractive pattern and crossing your fingers.*

FIGURE 1.6
ARCnet cabling examples

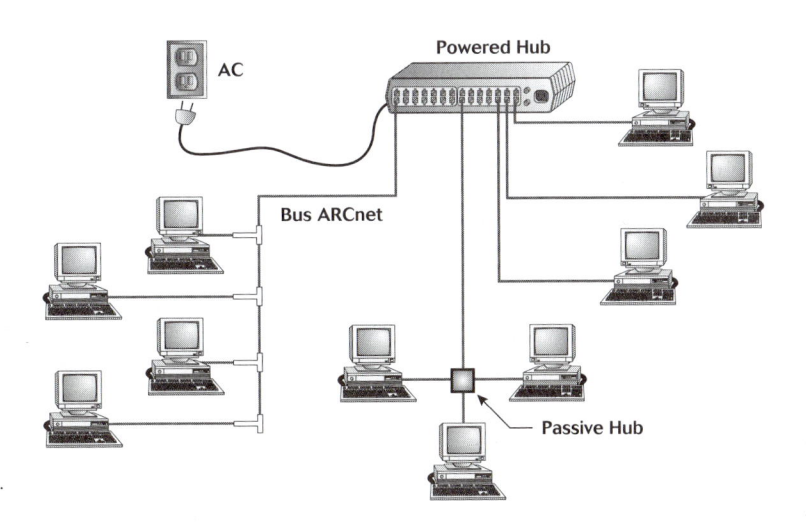

I see little reason for ARCnet to rebound in popularity, but it will be around for awhile. In the spring of 1994, I learned that the Nuclear Regulatory Commission allows only ARCnet cabling for network connections inside reactor containment buildings. Evidently, when the early tests were done, ARCnet was the most noise-immune cabling, and the standard has yet to be updated. Our tax dollars at work.

A Short History of NetWare

NetWare was developed by Novell Data Systems in the late 1970s, up in the hills of Utah. Using CP/M (Control Program for Microprocessors, the operating system of choice before the PC solidified DOS) and Unix as the guidelines, a multiuser microcomputer was being built. This was a typical time-sharing system, with dumb terminals attached by serial cables to a central box containing the CPU, disk, memory, and printer attachments.

This was not a particularly original idea, and the graveyards are full of similar companies started about the same time. The difference between the living and the dead was each company's approach to the Hot New Item: the IBM PC. Novell embraced it, believing a system that utilized the intelligence of the end node would always be better than one using dumb terminals. (At least this is the story told around campfires.)

Another stroke of genius was the search for a "file" server, not a disk server. In the early 1980s, Novell's competitors offered a way to split a large hard disk (maybe 50 whole megabytes!) into 5 or 10 MB partitions, one for each user and perhaps a common partition. Although this did help contain the capital budget for hardware, it did not allow any better communications between people, applications, or computers than the current rage, SneakerNet.

Once the folks at Novell moved to include the PC as a file server in all their future plans, they made another good decision. Rather than offering the NOS (network operating system) as a way to sell hardware, as did 3Com and Corvus, they concentrated on the NOS itself. They also made deals with every hardware vendor they could, helping to port NetWare to their hardware. This gave Novell a win-win situation whenever two different hardware vendors were bidding on the same business. No matter which of them won, Novell won as well.

(continued on next page)

Taking the early lead with NetWare/86 (for the Intel 8088/8086 processors), Novell also started the concept of a remote file system for PC networking. Not just a file repository any more, the file server actually began to control and secure files. Security became stronger, and the file-access controls allowed Unix software vendors to port their applications to NetWare. This allowed true multiuser programs to help push the sales of NetWare into typically Unix installations, particularly accounting systems and databases.

By 1986, network hardware independence was a given for NetWare, to the point that the file server could support multiple types of interface cards at the same time. Even more amazing, packets could be routed between network segments without the user being involved.

The push for more NetWare-aware applications was paying off as well. More than 2000 multiuser applications existed for the NOS.

With the advent of the PC AT, Novell focused most of its NOS development attention on the Intel family of processors. There had been an earlier PC file server, but the AT was such a hot machine that it outstripped the current workhorse, the Motorola 68000 powered S-Net server. With the gradual waning of the S-Net server, an S-100 bus system using 9-pin RS422 connectors (which look exactly like CGA or Token Ring connectors), the PC server era began. With the new support of the AT and Intel 80286 processor, NetWare officially became Advanced NetWare/286.

In 1988, NetWare for VMS made its appearance, along with Portable NetWare (now called NetWare for Unix) in early 1989. Macintoshes could now be supported by NetWare version 2.15 (late 1988), filling the Mac server hole left by Apple.

1989 saw the release of NetWare/386 version 3.0; currently shipping is version 3.12. The majority of current Novell users are connected to at least one NetWare 3.12 server. The rewriting done for NetWare 386 is what made NetWare for Unix and Processor Independent NetWare (PIN) possible. Modularity of the NOS was underway, continuing a trend Novell started back when the software engineers wrote support for more than one NIC in a server.

Released in early 1993, NetWare 4.0 continued the improvements to operating system modularity and introduced the object-oriented NDS (NetWare Directory Services). One network, one login, many servers.

(continued on next page)

> With NetWare 4.10, the tools network managers asked for, and more, were included. The network manager now has complete control over the NDS tree, able to prune, graft, split, and merge sections of the tree from the graphical NetWare Administrator program. With the Simplified and Custom Installation options, new networks are installed and running in about ten minutes of hands-on work. Novell set the pricing to match NetWare 3.12, meaning smaller companies that avoided NetWare 4 because they didn't feel they needed NDS at a premium are happy to try it on a "free" basis. Add the extra disk space provided by the file compression and other storage enhancements, and NetWare 4.10 actually costs less than a comparable NetWare 3.12 system.
>
> NetWare 4.11 does three important things: makes application support manageable with the Netware Application Launcher (finally fixed and working well), further improves all the graphical management tools, and infuses NetWare with TCP/IP and technology derived from the World Wide Web. Novell has gone so far as to coin a new name, IntranetWare, for the combination of NetWare 4.11, the Web Server, the new IPX/IP Gateway, and NetWare/IP. To emphasize the "Webization" of NetWare, Novell is selling the bundle of all the Intranet and Internet goodies for the same price as "basic" NetWare 4.11.

Planning for an Efficient File System

YOUR NETWORK USERS don't care about cabling, but they do care about their files. Let's look at some basic file system plans.

There are all sorts of "systems" recommended for handling the directory structure of hard disks. Unfortunately, no one system works for everyone.

There are two main philosophies on network file structure. One is user-centric, and revolves around user home directories and subdirectories for each application. The second is application-centric, and provides group directories where users can share files. Figure 1.7 illustrates the differences between the two philosophies.

Circumstances, not network administrator whims, will choose which system your network should follow. No matter which way you begin, you will wind up with a combination of both systems, because some software will force you into a new direction. Your only choice is which system comes first.

FIGURE 1.7

User-centric and application-centric file structures

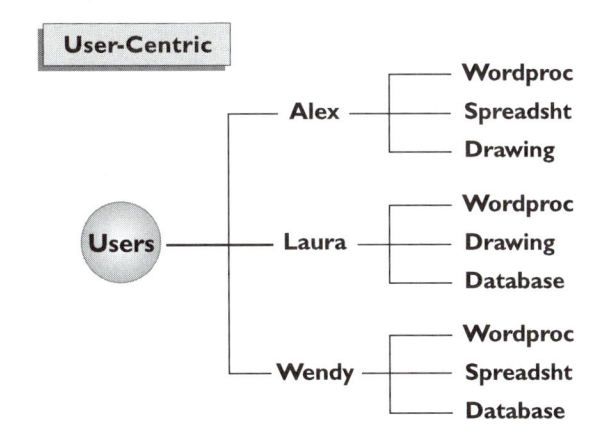

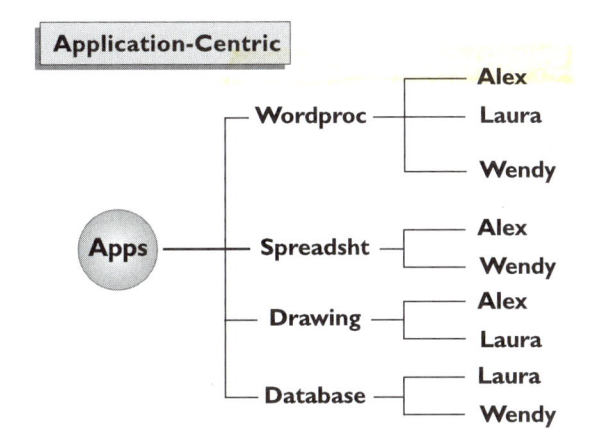

User-Centric

Users
- Alex
  - Wordproc
  - Spreadsht
  - Drawing
- Laura
  - Wordproc
  - Drawing
  - Database
- Wendy
  - Wordproc
  - Spreadsht
  - Database

Application-Centric

Apps
- Wordproc
  - Alex
  - Laura
  - Wendy
- Spreadsht
  - Alex
  - Wendy
- Drawing
  - Alex
  - Laura
- Database
  - Laura
  - Wendy

Home Directory Sweet Home Directory

One option that appears when you create a user is whether or not to create a "home" directory for that user. The home directory is a private subdirectory on the server for each user. This is the user's private area, and access to this directory is typically limited to the owner only.

Users like the home directory, because it's their own private space. They are free to create a goodly number of subdirectories underneath their home directory, just as on a personal hard drive. I encourage home directories, because it gives people a feeling of ownership on the network. If you can convince users to store their important information in their home directory, that information will be safely archived when you back up the server. With this backup, you can help them out when they accidentally type DEL *.* in the wrong place. You can't generally help them when they screw up their own hard drive.

No matter which file directory system you prefer, user-centric or app-centric, one piece of good advice comes directly from the Novell engineering group. Their strong recommendation is to keep applications and data in separate directories.

With modern applications, rarely do the executable files and data files wind up in the same directory. Many new applications are flexible when it comes to placing their data files somewhere besides directly beneath their primary directory, but some are not. We'll cover how to deal with uncooperative applications in Chapter 10.

NetWare System Directories

During installation, NetWare creates six (seven if you install the DynaText electronic documentation) special directories. These are referred to as the *system directories*, and you should take care to move the files in these directories only under the most extenuating circumstances. Never move system directories, even the DynaText files, on a whim. The documentation can be moved, but there's no reason to do so. The same advice goes for many of the system files and directories. It's less confusing in the future if you leave them in their default locations.

If you're familiar with earlier versions of NetWare, you know most of these directories already. The big four directories, there since the early days of NetWare, are SYSTEM, LOGIN, MAIL, and PUBLIC. The hidden DELETED.SAV directory showed up in NetWare 3.1, along with the ETC directory if you installed any of the Unix connection software. When the manuals went electronic, separate directories (DOC and DOCVIEW, if you install the electronic documentation) appeared to keep the information from being lost in a large PUBLIC directory.

Here's a summary of the directories created during installation:

- **SYS:DELETED.SAV:** A hidden, system directory that holds deleted files before they're purged.

- **SYS:ETC:** Contains sample files to help you configure the server, especially for TCP/IP support.

- **SYS:LOGIN:** Includes programs that are necessary for users to log in to the network, such as LOGIN.EXE. The two subdirectories are for OS/2 login programs and NLS (NetWare Language Support), containing subdirectories for login message files in the languages configured on the server.

- **SYS:MAIL:** May or may not contain subdirectories or files. Bindery servers include one subdirectory with a unique ID for each configured user.

- **SYS:SYSTEM:** Contains NetWare operating system files as well as NetWare utilities and programs for the supervisor. SYSTEM also has an NLS subdirectory, containing subdirectories for message files.

- **SYS:PUBLIC:** Has NetWare utilities and programs for all network users. SYS:PUBLIC has a special subdirectory for OS/2 utilities and a subdirectory called NLS, containing the message files for utilities.

- **SYS:DOC:** The directory with electronic versions of the NetWare manuals. It is created if you install DynaText.

NetWare takes precautions so the files in these directories aren't destroyed by accident. The SYSTEM, PUBLIC, LOGIN, DOCVIEW, and DOC directories are set to make it nearly impossible to delete or rename the files they contain (the files are set to Read-Only, Shareable, Delete Inhibit, and Rename Inhibit). If someone does manage to erase a few of these files, the installation process will copy them back out to the server for you (see the next chapter for details). Individual files can be extracted from the CD-ROM disk.

Companies with tape backup systems that can't quite cover the full disk contents often have an "operating system" tape with just the bare system files. Since the system files don't change except after updates, it's safe to not back them up every day.

Some companies also have an "application executables" tape that works the same way: just the application directories without any of the data. Since applications get upgraded all the time, and patches are applied to many programs on what seems to be a daily basis, this is advisable only if tape backup space is extremely tight.

Physical Space and Protection for Your Server

PERSONAL COMPUTERS TODAY are built to run in an office environment. No special air conditioning, raised floors, or expensive fire-dampening foam is needed. Even if you buy a superserver from Compaq, NetFRAME, or Tricord, an office environment is fine. So why should we make a big deal out of the physical space for your server?

Physical Security Considerations for Your Server

The biggest reason to lock up your server is security. The first part of any security program is to limit accessibility to what you are protecting. What people can't see, they don't try to steal or vandalize. Why do you think the police always tell you to lock packages in your car trunk, rather than leaving them in the back seat? Out of sight, out of their hands.

From a pure security angle, NetWare servers are more secure than any other network file server software. The NetWare files are kept in a separate disk partition from any DOS partition on the server. There is no quick and easy way to read the NetWare files from the file server, as there is with software that runs the network as an application under OS/2 or Windows NT. Those systems are workstations as well as servers, so the server portion of the file system is easily available from the server console. This is not so with NetWare.

This is not to say no mischief is possible from the file server. From a worst-case angle, a malcontent with access to your server can reformat the server hard disk without problem. The tools to format and partition the PC hard disk are included with the NetWare installation utilities, if the malcontent happened to forget his or her own DOS bootable diskette. The NetWare partition on the disk can be erased even more quickly, which does just as much damage to your network. Either way, you have a long day ahead of you, and your tape backup procedures will be severely tested.

Separate from actual harmful intent to your server, accidents happen more often to equipment out in the open. If your server is on a table, the table will get knocked over. Someone will "borrow" the monitor or the keyboard. Someone will spill coffee directly into the chassis air holes. If bad things can happen, let them happen to someone else's computer; keep your server safe.

> *If bad things can happen, let them happen to someone else's computer; keep your server safe.*

One customer had five servers clustered together, and they went down every evening. No diagnostics cleared up this mystery, until someone spent the night in the office. The cleaning crew unplugged one server for the vacuum cleaner (from the UPS), and the noise on the line sent the other servers into terminal weirdness.

Controlled environments are easier to make static-proof and generally safer for sensitive electronic equipment. Yes, this is contrary to the idea that the computers on every desk are safe, but they're really not. In the owner's manual of every computer is a warning about static electricity and how to avoid same. We all ignore that warning, with little consequence. However, since your file server may support dozens to hundreds of excitable people, crashing the server because of static buildup in the carpet will bring all those excitable people to a higher level of agitation. Better to keep the server in a locked room with a tile floor than risk that one-in-a-million, server-killing, static discharge from the carpet and your wool sweater.

The NetWare manuals go into detail about wearing static wrist-straps while working on the server. They give directions for ways to slowly bleed static away from your server (ground equipment through a one mega-ohm resistor). They also remind us to never open the chassis on a system with the power turned on.

You wouldn't do anything so stupid, would you? Well, I did, once, by accident. Take if from me, unplugging an Ethernet board from a powered PC will fry the motherboard.

Power Conditioning and Protection for Your Server

While you have the server in a locked room with tile floors, run dedicated power lines to that room. It's safest to run every network device from these dedicated lines, but that may not be possible. Use the idea of a dedicated line for every network printer, server, and wiring device to scare your boss into providing a dedicated circuit, at least for your server.

Ground the server (or all these dedicated circuits) to an earth ground if at all possible. Weird things happen with what's called a "floating ground," multiple grounds, and circuits that get cross-wired somehow. If your systems get flaky for no reason, an electrician may be a good person to call.

Always, always, always put the server on a UPS (uninterruptible power supply). There is no excuse for not doing so. UPS systems are cheap today, and many are smart enough to gently shut down your server.

The system works like this: a cable from the UPS connects to a server serial port. When a power blackout or brownout activates the UPS, the server software will communicate with the UPS over the connecting cable. When the UPS battery is in danger of being discharged completely, leaving the server without power, the monitoring software will down the server so all files are closed properly.

Few sites need to worry about power dropping out for more than a few seconds. Many sites do need to worry about power that has malformed signals and constant fluctuations. A good UPS will take care of these problems as well.

All powered network devices, such as wiring concentrators, modems, communication servers, bridges, routers, and tape backup systems, should be on a UPS. Remember to plug the server console monitor into the UPS as well, unless you have memorized all the proper shutdown keystrokes. Figure 1.8 shows the setup for a properly protected server.

Repeat: there is no excuse for having a server without a UPS. None.

FIGURE 1.8

The properly protected server

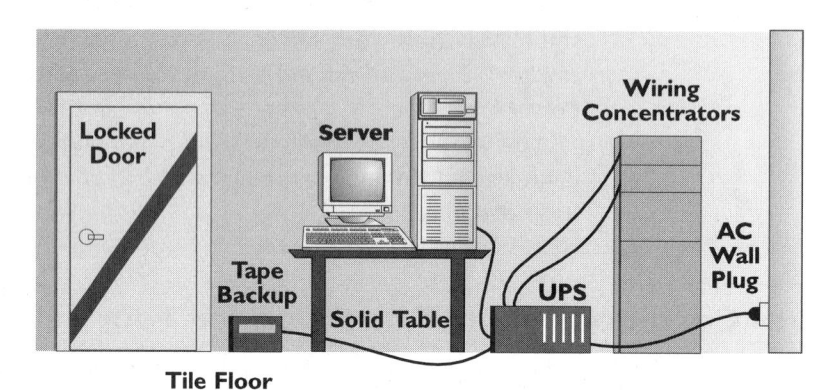

Proper Tape Backup Precautions for Your Server

Your file server must have a tape backup system. That's just as important as a UPS system, and maybe slightly more important. You will use the tape backup system more than you ever imagined.

Many people believe a tape is used to restore the entire file server disk contents after a catastrophic failure. That's not the most common use. You will constantly be replacing files for users, a single file or directory at a time. Users delete the wrong files for many reasons, but the result is the same: a needed file is gone.

Yes, NetWare tracks all deleted files, some for quite a long time, and you can sometimes reclaim them with a minimum of time and aggravation. Don't count on that. If it happens that way, count your blessings. Don't give up your tape backup system.

RAID (redundant array of independent disks) systems are great and work well, but they are no replacement for tape backup systems. How does RAID help when a person types DEL *.* on drive G: instead of drive C:? Get that tape backup system working today.

Some people use long, involved tape-backup schedules and tape-rotation schemes. Some software relies on complicated file tracking along with tape-rotation schedules to keep current files on as few tapes as possible. These are all too complicated and make me nervous. I'm sure the software accurately tracks every file and when it was last changed and backed up to tape, but I don't want to use five tapes to restore one directory.

The single best tape backup system is to back up your entire server disk every night. Period. Any day you need to reclaim a file that was deleted accidentally, you know exactly where that file is: on last night's tape. No logs are consulted to find where the deleted file went into the rotation, no "grandfather" rotations, nothing. Every night, every file.

Some file problems don't appear for quite awhile, such as a garbled or deleted accounting files. You don't need these files until the year-end reporting, so you need to keep some tapes for a long, long time. I recommend thirteen months of monthly tapes, six weeks of weekly tapes, and four weeks of daily tapes. See Figure 1.9 for a quick map of tapes moving through a daily, weekly, and monthly schedule.

The plan is simple: move a daily tape from daily use to weekly use every week (say Friday or Monday). Move a weekly tape to monthly use every week (last Friday or Monday of the month, for instance). After thirteen months, move a monthly tape back into the daily rotation. After a tape has been used 25 times, retire that tape to long-term storage. Don't press your luck and use tapes past their effective age.

Some newer tapes can now store up to 8 GB per tape, meaning you can often back up multiple servers on one tape. That's fine to do, and smarter tape backup software now backs up multiple servers all at one time, interspersing files from each server along the tape. If you have more servers than even that system can handle, get a second or third tape backup machine. You really are

FIGURE 1.9

Every night, every file backup and long-range safety system

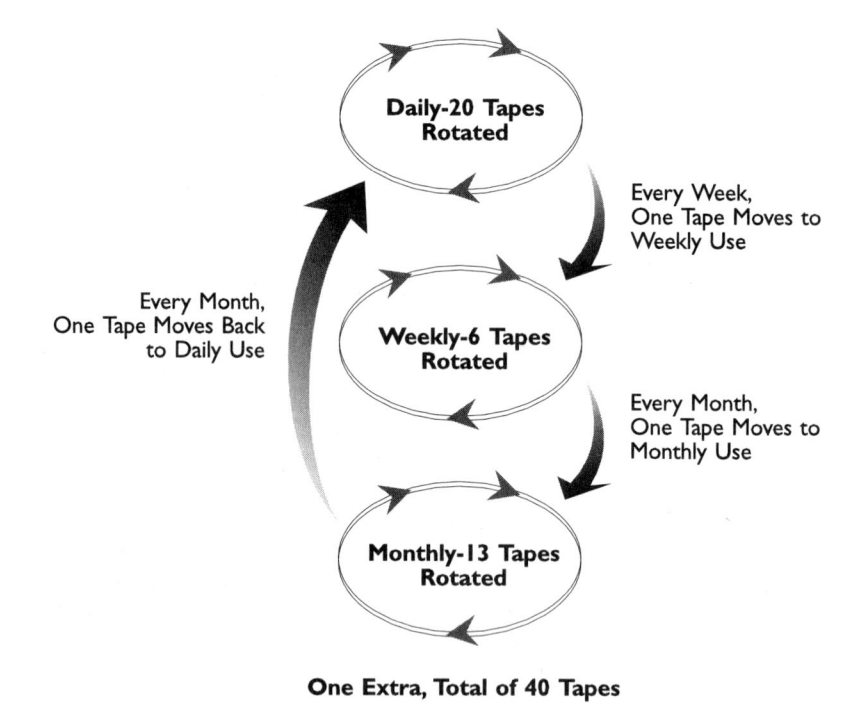

- Daily—20 Tapes Rotated
- Every Week, One Tape Moves to Weekly Use
- Weekly—6 Tapes Rotated
- Every Month, One Tape Moves to Monthly Use
- Monthly—13 Tapes Rotated
- Every Month, One Tape Moves Back to Daily Use

One Extra, Total of 40 Tapes

safer taping each file each night, and if you automate that procedure, people won't forget.

This system takes 40 tapes to start, and more as tapes get used 20 times and retired. Your boss may well complain about the cost of a large-capacity tape system and so many tapes. This is an excellent example of penny-wise and pound-foolish. Explain to your boss the true cost of re-creating files, and the downtime costs for all people waiting for the information being re-created. Explain to your boss how this is the single cheapest insurance your company has. Explain to your boss that the majority of small companies go out of business if all their data records are lost through a catastrophe. If all this fails, divert a PC purchase order into a tape backup system anyway. You absolutely must have one.

Some tapes must be kept off-site. Which tapes you ship away depends on how inconvenient the off-site storage is. Last week's tape may be too soon, but last month's tape may be too late. If your building has a bank in the lower floor, quickly get a safety deposit box. If not, pick a date you can live with for tape delay and send some tapes somewhere safe. I guarantee that if your server burns, the box of backup tapes next to it will burn as well.

If your information is sensitive, remember that each tape is a copy of your company's secrets. There are services that use armored cars to pick up and deliver backup tapes on a regular schedule. Check your Yellow Pages.

Planning Cabling Installation

YOUR NETWORK IS most likely already up and running to some degree. You probably have inherited the cabling with all its faults and quirks. If so, take this information and store it for when you add to your network.

Installing New Cabling

Stop right now. If you have a telecommunications department, go talk to those technicians before you do anything else. The people running the phones have been running cable since before you were born, and much of what they know through experience can help you. At best, you want to coordinate all cabling through one overseer; at worst, you should know when and where the phone people are running cable, and they should know the same about your plans.

Regardless of whether you are using Ethernet, Token Ring, or something else, you probably are using UTP wiring. This means you have wiring concentrators within about 330 feet (100 meters) of the computers they serve. This means you will become familiar with all the wiring closets in your building.

If you are not using UTP cabling with Ethernet or Token Ring, why not? Even though 16 Mbps Token Ring received UTP support later than all other cable types, it's on UTP today.

Those still using coax Ethernet, please see a doctor.

Those still using coax Ethernet, please see a doctor. If your application is important enough to justify spending thousands of dollars on networking hardware and software, it's important enough to justify a few hundred more dollars for UTP cable and equipment (eight-port 10BaseT hubs are under $500 now and still dropping). Bad or poorly installed cable is the source of the majority of network problems (90 percent at fault if you ask vendors of new cable). Use Category 4 UTP at a minimum, and preferably Category 5 for all new cabling. Pay the extra few cents for Category 5 connectors.

New installations give you an opportunity not to be missed: an up-to-date map of which wires go which way. Your existing cabling is already a mass of confusion, and more wires are lost or mislabeled every week. New cable will become another mass of confusion if you don't plan ahead and push your cabling contractor to do a good job of documentation.

Before you decide on a cabling contractor, get blueprints of your office. These don't need to be construction blueprints exact down to the inch, but that would be fine. These blueprints must at least have office walls to scale and proper labeling. Provide a set of these drawings to each prospective cable contractor.

As part of the installation price, require four items:

- Digital testing of each link
- Labels on each wall plate and wiring concentrator port
- A map with "as-installed" wiring routes and distances to each wall plate
- A warranty

The "as-installed" drawings need not be works of art, or exact engineering documents. You just need an idea of where wires are going and the length of each cable run. Placing the labels on the drawing helps check the work during installation and makes troubleshooting easier for you over the coming years. Figure 1.10 is an example of an adequate wiring plan document. The more notes you put on the drawing during installation, the better chance you'll have of tracking down problems later on.

You must participate in the partnership between cabling contractor and customer (you). Decide what you want before the bidding starts. Get your boss to sign off on the requirements, and stress that changing plans during installation will create more cost and future problems. Decide on the time for the wiring installation: during work hours is cheaper but more disruptive.

If there is any question whether a location will need a network connection in the future, put one there. The big cost in cabling is the hardware and labor, not a few extra pairs of wire. Labor costs less when running some extra cables during one visit than when scheduling a separate visit.

FIGURE 1.10

An acceptable wiring plan

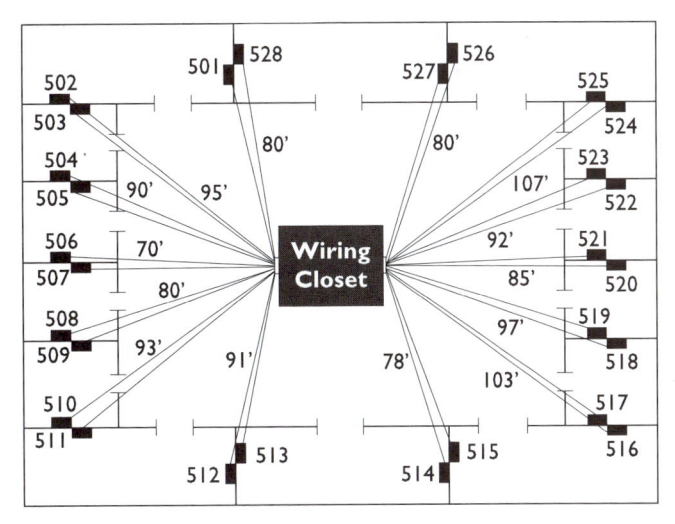

5th Floor
Two Connections in Every Office
Two Wire Exits from Wiring Closet
Four Pair Wires to Every Connector
Back-to-Back Wall Plate Wires
Pulled Together-Same Length
Distance-Tested with Digital
Ethernet Tester

Planning the Rest of Your Wiring Closets

Remember the discussion of dedicated power circuits? The wiring closets are good candidates for dedicated wiring because more and more networking hardware is going into the wiring closet.

If you can't get dedicated power, at least make sure there *is* power in the wiring closets. Telephone intermediate distribution frames (connections for bundles of phone wires to the floor and on to other floors) don't need power, so many wiring closets do not have AC wall outlets, especially the older ones. It's a bad feeling to hold a plug in one hand and suddenly realize there is no wall outlet.

At the least, you should add a small UPS to each wiring closet. Wiring concentrators take little power, but you should provide power backup for them in case the building's power supply drops or goes off. There's little advantage to having the server and your management workstation on standby power if the network cabling is dead.

Wiring closets have become good places to put servers, bridges, routers, communications gateways, and modems. The closets are usually locked, or locks can be added easily. Mechanical rooms like these closets are usually near the center of the building, making it easy to run cable to computers in all corners. Larger ones often have space for a rack to hold large amounts of equipment. Lacking that, the walls are lined in plywood to better attach telephone wiring connectors. That plywood is a good anchor for shelves to hold modems, bridges, routers, and even smaller PCs.

Respect any telephone equipment and cabling in the wiring closets. Once again, working with the telecommunications people will make your life easier. Networking is hard enough without asking for extra headaches. Eliminate one headache for yourself by being on good terms with the folks in the telecom department.

Network Protocols Used by NetWare 4.1x

A PROTOCOL IS A formal description of message formats and the rules two or more machines must follow to exchange those messages. We talk about protocols all the time, such as IPX/SPX (Internetwork Packet eXchange/Sequenced Packet eXchange), which is used by NetWare.

Protocols can be complex, but all we need now is enough information to get started building your network. If you run a NetWare-only network, IPX/SPX is the only protocol you will need. If your network involves Unix hosts, you will need to understand TCP/IP (Transmission Control Protocol/Internet Protocol). If your network supports Macintosh computers, you will need some understanding of AFP (AppleTalk Filing Protocol). Let's get started.

XNS: The Primordial Protocol

Once again, history takes us back to Xerox and PARC. The XNS (Xerox Network Services) protocol was developed along with Ethernet, which makes sense. What good is hardware without software?

Several assumptions were made when XNS was developed. First of all, every user in the network was expected to be using Ethernet. Since there was no other network transport media at PARC at the time, that was a safe bet. But multiple Ethernet networks were assumed to exist. That means there must be intelligent devices to link networks. This was the beginning of the router industry. The first information about XNS was published in 1980, well before the IBM PC appeared.

Routers are intelligent devices that send packets to the proper LAN segment based on protocol-dependent addresses within the packet. Routers must read the packet up through the network layer of the ISO/OSI network model to make the proper routing decision. A bridge is less intelligent, and merely reads the physical address of the packet's destination.

The basic unit of information transferred is the internet packet. Each packet must include additional addressing to ensure delivery to the proper network and host.

XNS had five layers, which correspond to the seven layers of TCP/IP:

- Level 0, the physical layer, handles transport media control (such as Ethernet, X.25, RS232c), and so on).

- Level 1, the network layer, includes IDP and internet addressing and routing.

- Level 2, the transport layer, includes RIP, SPP, PEP, error and echo protocols, sequencing, and flow control.

- Level 3, the datagram structure, includes RPC and Courier protocol, and provides structure for data; it assumes internetworking.

- Level 4, the application layer, contains the Clearinghouse protocol and directory services.

IDP (Internet Datagram Protocol) is an unreliable packet type. This means that the network protocol provides best-effort delivery, but if packets are lost, the higher-level software must recognize the loss and retransmit. IDP packets are used because they make good connections with minimal overhead. A guaranteed virtual circuit requires plenty of overhead and a reliable transport network, neither of which was available in the late 1970s.

(continued on next page)

> RIP (Routing Information Protocol), which rides on top of IDP, maintains a list of reachable networks and calculates the difficulty in reaching a specific requested network. RIP is still used quite a bit in IPX/SPX and TCP/IP, but people are trying to develop more functionality by using less overhead. RIP packets can generate lots of broadcast activity.
>
> RPC (Remote Procedure Protocol) provides a framework for client/server programming across a network. RPC provide a means for programs to execute locally, but query and control some parts of the application on a remote system. As you might tell from the development of RPC, XNS supposes there are multiple hosts on the network, and that some of those hosts are remote.
>
> SPP (Sequenced Packet Protocol) is the workhorse of the XNS transport layer. Unlike IDP, SPP provides a reliable means of data transmission. The protocol itself assigns sequential numbers to each datagram and assembles those datagrams in order at the receiving end. If a datagram is out of sequence, SPP will retransmit that packet without involving the higher-level applications.
>
> PEP (Packet Exchange Protocol) is a cross between IDP and SPP. It provides the reliability of SPP, but only for single packets. Any socket can be used as a source or destination address.
>
> Riding on top of all these was the Clearinghouse protocol. As you can see, XNS was a complete network system from the beginning. The designers of XNS made sure that support for X.25 packet networks, leased telephone lines, and dial-up lines was included in the specifications. At one time, Xerox had the largest worldwide corporate network, and XNS was the only protocol in the entire system.
>
> In biblical terms, XNS begat IPX/SPX. Simply put, Novell's IPX is identical to IDP (Internet Datagram Protocol).

IPX/SPX and NCP

IPX handles all the addressing, routing, and switching of packets to their destination. Each IPX datagram contains all the information needed for routing to its target. This avoids invoking virtual connections with the server, sapping server resources.

> *When packets contain all the information necessary for their delivery, they are often called* datagrams, *although some people use the terms* packet *and* datagram *interchangeably.*

SPX packets are guaranteed. The protocol sets up a direct connection between the two stations involved. Based on SPP, SPX guarantees a connection by having the destination node send an acknowledgment for received packets. If no acknowledgment comes within a certain time, the packet is resent. Too many missed packets, and SPX informs the user.

NCP (NetWare Core Protocol) is a higher-layer protocol proprietary to Novell. It is used for file access, print sharing, and application program support. For the casual user, NCP *is* NetWare. NCP runs over IPX or SPX, depending on the application. NCP provides the presentation and application layer interface for NetWare. NCP functions include:

- Create service connection
- Request (to server)
- Reply (from server)
- Destroy service connection
- Request being considered response (from server)

Some people, especially TCP/IP people, complain about IPX/SPX and its problems. While no one says IPX/SPX is the world's ultimate protocol, be sure to complain about the right things.

First, the constant (every minute from every server) broadcasts are not due to IPX/SPX but to RIP (Routing Information Protocol) and SAP (Service Advertising Protocol). RIP requires broadcasts to figure out routing, and SAP is required to allow NetWare clients to know what services are available on the network. TCP/IP handles this notification differently, which reduces broadcasts but increases setup and management complexity.

Second, the "ping-pong" packet trait is not due to IPX, but to NCP's DOS file service. Often called the "ack-ack" syndrome, NCP requests acknowledgment from receiving stations when packets are sent. This has roots in the fact that IPX is a non-guaranteed transport, meaning a higher-level protocol (such as NCP) must check that all packets are present and accounted for. In addition, performance over a LAN is fast, and the "ping-pong" packets are not noticeable. When used over slow WAN links, this asynchronous packet performance does become a problem. That's why we now have Packet Burst Mode.

IPX/SPX is the world's most popular protocol with application developers. More than 3000 applications are written to the DOS API (Application Program Interface) provided by IPX/SPX. The size is small (14 KB resident) and fast (800 Kbps and up with 16-bit Ethernet cards in my lab).

In Figure 1.11, there are a couple of new things. ODI (Open Data-Link Interface) was released in 1989 to separate the NIC device drivers from the software that connects the workstation to the network. By adding a layer of abstraction with ODI, one NIC can now support multiple protocols concurrently.

In the old days, each NIC needed a specific program generated for it for each configuration. This was called "genning a shell," as in generating a shell program. If you changed something on the NIC, such as the IRQ (Interrupt ReQuest), a new shell had to be generated. ODI did away with all this. More details will follow in Chapter 5, when we talk about connecting clients to your network. For now, here's a quick summary of how ODI fits together:

- **MLID (Multiple Layer Interface Driver):** Handles sending and receiving packets to and from the network.

FIGURE 1.11
How NetWare protocols stack up on a PC workstation

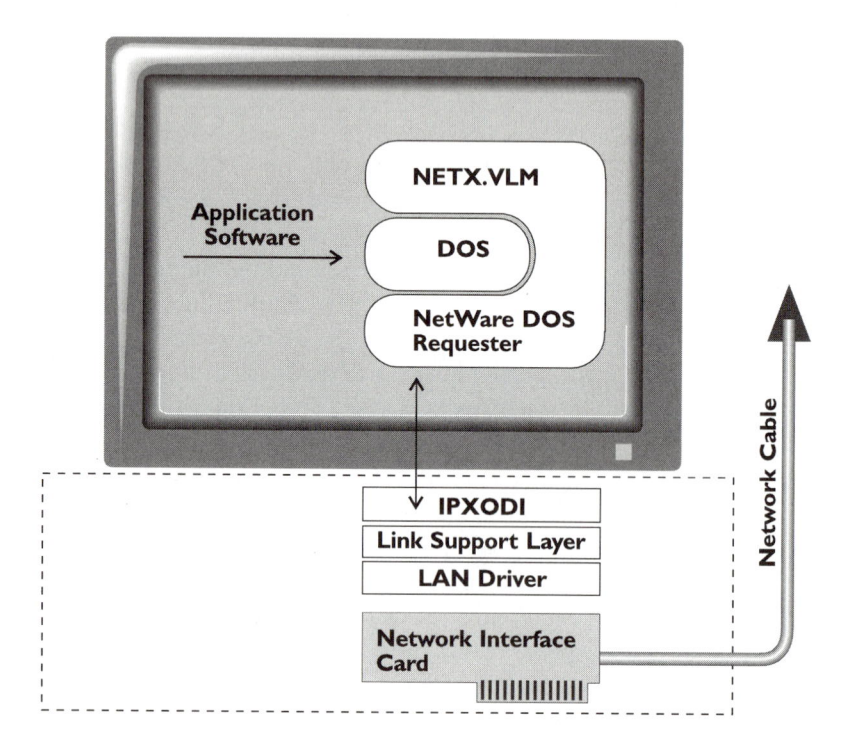

- **LSL (Link Support Layer):** Interface layer between the device driver and the protocol stack(s). Any ODI LAN driver can communicate with any ODI protocol stack through the LSL.

- **MSM (Media Support Module):** Interfaces ODI MLIDs to the LSL and to the operating system.

- **TSM (Topology Specific Module):** Controls operations specific to a particular network media such as Ethernet.

- **HSM (Hardware Specific Module):** Program normally provided by the network interface card vendor that contains details particular to that network card, such as initialization routines, reset, shutdown, packet reception, timeout detection, and multicast addressing. Will be named 3C509.COM or NE2000.COM or the like.

IPX, the standard protocol included with NetWare from the earliest versions, provides enormous benefits during installation and setup. NetWare handles all the client addressing and routing information, unlike other protocols that require tables of address information to be created during installation. With IPX, the unique serial number on each NIC, in conjunction with the network number assigned during server installation, is used for identification.

If your network is all NetWare, you will spend less than two minutes during installation dealing with protocol issues. That's the beauty of IPX: it doesn't have near the installation and management overhead of other protocols.

TCP/IP

Speaking of other protocols, TCP/IP has now received the U.S. Government's blessing as an "open protocol for open systems." Officially, as of mid-1994, TCP/IP has replaced OSI (Open Systems Interconnection) as an acceptable protocol (without special exemptions) on new government systems. How did TCP/IP get to this point?

First, it was developed to be a protocol for packet-switching WANs. In fact, it was developed to also support packet radio and packet satellite networks, two other mediums with shared communication channels and a penchant for lost packets.

Second, TCP/IP was under development at PARC. Robert Metcalfe and David Boggs were busy adding TCP/IP support to their newfangled Ethernet. David Farber at the University of California, Irvine was also working on TCP/IP, but on a ring concept network.

Third, the government was involved at the beginning. The original push for developing TCP/IP was from DARPA (U.S. Defense Advanced Research Projects Agency) in 1973. The ARPANET (Advanced Research Projects Agency NETwork) had been started earlier, and in October 1972 was publicly demonstrated.

This is all fine, but took place well over 20 years ago. What inside the development process gave TCP/IP its tremendous staying power in an industry known for having a short attention span?

Since the developers knew that packets would be lost across the early networks, TCP/IP was split into TCP (Transmission Control Protocol) and IP (Internet Protocol), and UDP (User Datagram Protocol) was added. IP became part of the network layer in the OSI reference model, responsible for internetwork considerations. A layer at a lower level takes care of the actual Ethernet, X.25, or other physical transport details. TCP provides sequenced, guaranteed transmission by relying on IP. UDP provides nonsequenced, transaction-like applications, such as packet voice.

> *The Internet made its appearance in 1973 in the guise of these early WAN experiments. The term* internet *will be used when speaking of any collection of networks that may or may not use official Internet standards. The* Internet *with a capital letter will refer to the official sanctioned network of networks that is the subject of so much hype lately. Information Superhighway, indeed.*

Figure 1.12 shows the TCP/IP protocol suite and how it fits into the OSI reference model. Table 1.1 lists the components of the TCP/IP protocol suite.

TCP/IP has the broadest support of any protocol today or tomorrow. If you say "open systems," many people hear "TCP/IP." Although TCP/IP comes with every Unix system delivered, there is nothing mandatory about Unix systems and TCP/IP. Some Unix hosts, such as ICL, use OSI for communications. UnixWare, Novell's Intel-based Unix software, uses IPX/SPX as the primary transport protocol. All that being true, the vast majority of computer users assume TCP/IP when you say Unix.

TABLE 1.1

Components of the TCP/IP Protocol Suite

COMPONENT	FUNCTION
IP (Internet Protocol)	Unreliable internetwork routing of datagrams.
ICMP (Internet Control Message Protocol)	Reports errors and responds to queries about remote conditions. This is an integral part of IP.
ARP (Address Resolution Protocol)	Maps Internet address to physical network address.
RARP (Reverse Address Resolution Protocol)	Maps physical network address to Internet address.
TCP (Transmission Control Protocol)	Provides reliable, connection-oriented delivery between clients; full-duplex connections.
UDP (User Datagram Protocol)	Provides unreliable, connectionless packet delivery service between clients over IP.
Telnet	Provides remote terminal connection services.
FTP (File Transfer Protocol)	File transfer protocol between hosts; carries ASCII, binary, and EBCDIC file formats.
SMTP (Simple Mail Transfer Protocol)	Rules for exchanging ASCII e-mail between different systems.
RIP (Routing Information Protocol)	Protocol that keeps a list of reachable networks for Internet packets.
DNS (Domain Name System)	Hierarchical naming scheme, with domain subnames separated by periods.

DOS and MS Windows versions of TCP/IP used to be memory-hungry and slow, but the situation today is greatly improved. Small and fast TCP/IP software packages for DOS and MS Windows are available from more than a dozen vendors.

Many companies have world-wide TCP/IP networks, including systems from mainframes down to tiny notebook computers. SNA (Systems Network Architecture) users by the boatload are busy moving to a combination TCP/IP and SNA network, or are replacing SNA completely. There is nothing in computing today that can't be accomplished across TCP/IP.

FIGURE 1.12

The TCP/IP protocol suite referenced with the OSI seven-layer model

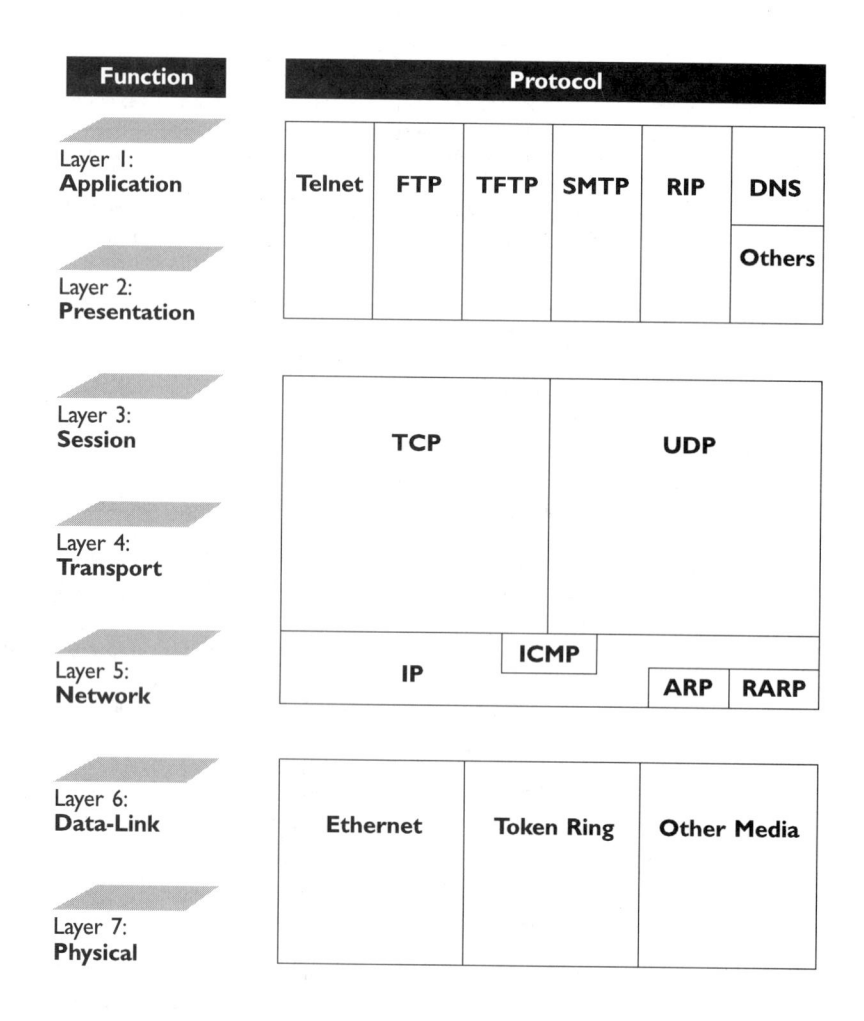

Function	Protocol
Layer 1: Application	Telnet, FTP, TFTP, SMTP, RIP, DNS, Others
Layer 2: Presentation	
Layer 3: Session	TCP, UDP
Layer 4: Transport	
Layer 5: Network	IP, ICMP, ARP, RARP
Layer 6: Data-Link	Ethernet, Token Ring, Other Media
Layer 7: Physical	

AFP (AppleTalk Filing Protocol)

AppleTalk is Apple Computer's suite of protocols that enables the hardware and software on an AppleTalk internetwork to interact and to exchange data. LocalTalk is the built-in network every Macintosh is born with, although non-Macintosh users often confuse LocalTalk the physical network and AppleTalk the networking software.

Most Macs today use either EtherTalk or TokenTalk, the Macintosh versions of Ethernet and Token Ring. New in NetWare 4.1x is the ability to make the Macintosh a full NDS (NetWare Directory Services) client, using IPX/SPX.

For those who don't want to use IPX/SPX yet, or need some background in network per Macintosh, Table 1.2 gives a quick rundown of AppleTalk protocols.

MacNDS requires System 7 software or later. Some Mac fanatics have mixed feelings about NetWare for Macintosh, and especially this new integration of the Macintosh and NetWare 4.1*x*. While better servers and enterprise support are great, true Mac fanatics really prefer the entire company to switch to Macintoshes and quit messing around with those Intel processors. That won't happen.

So the next best thing is to combine the best of Macintosh and the best of NetWare into something that will help the entire company. The more people that can share information with the Macintosh users, the higher profile the Macintosh gets.

This is another good example of the spirit of NetWare 4.1*x*: no matter who you are, come share with everyone else.

A Note of Appreciation

GREAT THINKERS AND developers stand on the shoulders of previous generations. The compression of technical development time is so intense today that great thinkers stand on the shoulders of other great thinkers in the next cubicle.

The advancements in computer networking are hard to see, because we're part of them. Think of the time from the first powered airplane flight (1906) to the first moon landing (1969). Many noted this enormous technological leap occurred in one lifetime. Technology has never moved so far so fast.

Following that reasoning, the development of computer networking has happened during the working life of people you and I can meet at conventions. Many of the people that drafted the plans to start the Internet are still working and pushing new technological boundaries today.

Imagine Wilbur and Orville Wright developing their first airplane from bicycle parts, and pushing technology the same way. Not only would Wilbur and Orville still be working, they would be part of the design team for the space station.

TABLE 1.2: AppleTalk Protocols

COMPONENT	FUNCTION
AARP (AppleTalk Address Resolution Protocol)	Maps AppleTalk addresses (network and node numbers) into LAN hardware addresses and helps each AppleTalk node acquire its unique AppleTalk address.
ADSP (AppleTalk Data Stream Protocol)	Allows two programs to communicate through a full-duplex data stream connection with reliable delivery.
AEP (AppleTalk Echo Protocol)	Support protocol that bounces a packet off another node.
AFP (AppleTalk Filing Protocol)	Application-level support protocol for file-sharing files. NetWare for Macintosh includes an AFP NLM to provide AFP support on a NetWare server.
ASP (AppleTalk Session Protocol)	Adds session functionality to ATP by guaranteeing delivery.
ATP (AppleTalk Transaction Protocol)	Provides reliable request and response transaction services through reliable packet exchange.
AURP (AppleTalk Update-based Routing Protocol)	Exchanges routing information only when a change occurs on the internetwork and IP tunneling.
DDP (Datagram Delivery Protocol)	Defines sockets and datagram delivery between sockets.
LAP (Link Access Protocol)	Data-link interface protocols for Ethernet (ELAP), LocalTalk (LLAP), and Token Ring (TLAP).
NBP (Name Binding Protocol)	Provides lists of service names to a user, and finds the network addresses of these names.
PAP (Printer Access Protocol)	Printer and print queue access on the AppleTalk network.
RTMP (Routing Table Maintenance Protocol)	Builds and maintains each router's routing table.
ZIP (Zone Information Protocol)	Associates zone names with network numbers and uses queries to maintain this mapping when new zones are added to an internetwork. AppleTalk uses zones to subdivide the internetwork logically so services are easier for users to find.

Does this mean networking (and flight) is as advanced as it can be? Of course not. We're on the brink of enormous leaps in technology, and the speed of new developments is increasing. Our children will pity us as technological cave people, as their children will pity them.

Take a moment to silently nod in appreciation for all the hard work that has gone before. Some of the smartest people in the world have pushed us this far, and they are still pushing. They deserve some appreciation.

How Their Networks Grew: Case Studies of Two Companies

Networks, like the people that use them, are not the same. Each network must be designed to meet the particular needs (and limitations) of its users. The case studies you'll find at the end of this and the following chapters will give you an idea of how two different companies went about building the best network for their situation.

We'll call the subject companies MiniCo and MegaCorp (and I hope that gives you some idea of the contrast that is being set up).

MINICO: COMPANY PROFILE

MiniCo is a book distributor and publisher of a few humorous gimmick books, including *How Gumby Got His Cadillac* and *Mammoths Galore*. It has three departments: Accounting, Sales, and Support.

Some key personnel include:

- Jack Mingo, President (uses a Macintosh)
- W.T. Quick (Bill), known as the Judge, Operations Manager (runs OS/2)
- Alexander von Thorn, Retail Book Distribution Manager
- Jim Lewczyk, Programmer
- Greg Oire, Marketing Manager
- Scott Elyard, Sales Manager

(continued on next page)

Its network setup includes:

- 3 servers
- 75 users
- 1 location
- 70 DOS and/or MS Windows clients
- 3 Macintosh clients
- 2 OS/2 clients

The Accounting department has 10 full-time users. Also, occasionally there are 5 extra users from the Sales and Support departments, who use the system for reporting purposes. The server is used for business accounting only and has just one volume. It is a 486/33, with 16 MB RAM and 500 MB disk. The one printer is a wide-carriage, dot-matrix, used for reports. The printer is connected to the server.

In the Sales department, there are 20 users. Additionally, 30 more users from the Support and Management departments use the system for reports, the database, and so on. The server is a 486/50, with 32 MB RAM, and 500 MB and 1 GB disks. It has two volumes, SYS (500 MB) and DEALS (1 GB). The Sales department has four laser printers, one with special letterhead paper loaded.

The Support department has 35 users in Support, plus 10 extra users from the Management and Sales departments. The server is a P66, with 64 MB RAM, and 500 MB and two 1 GB disks. It has Mac and OS/2 name spaces. Its two volumes are SYS (500 MB) and VOL1 (2 GB), spread across both disks. This department has six laser printers, including one color printer.

Several people need access to the Unix host to set up Web pages and copy files, but no serious integration is required. An Altos system runs SCO Unix and software for the Web Server. This system is controlled by the Retail Book Distribution Manager.

(continued on next page)

MEGACORP: COMPANY PROFILE

MegaCorp is an international conglomerate, specializing in financial services, private-label manufacturing for other companies, and a few high-tech consumer items (including MegaMouse, a 12-pound computer mouse for tennis, baseball, and golf enthusiasts who wish to exercise their forearms during their work day).

MegaCorp's headquarters are in Dallas, and it has branches in London, New York, San Jose, and Menlo Park, California. Many financial services products, both consumer and business, are controlled mostly in New York and London.

MegaCorp's CIO (Chief Information Officer) is Laura Kay, in Dallas, who dictates overall policy and controls the IS (Information Services) group's direction.

Its network setup includes:

- 50 servers
- 2500 users
- 5 locations

This company's servers are high-powered systems, optimized to support many users, even under heavy use. High-speed disks and controllers, along with plenty of RAM in each server, keep the number of servers low but the throughput high.

As much as possible, servers are controlled by the central IS department. Each physical location has central IS representatives along with some local support personnel. The exception is the five-user office in Menlo Park. All management for that site is done remotely by IS technicians in San Jose.

The headquarters office in Dallas has 1000 users and 20 servers. It holds the primary Unix installation for corporate use. The users rely on general office automation software, such as word processing, spreadsheets, and so on. There is also heavy use of e-mail and group scheduling with the GroupWise product. The majority of users require a Unix connection to run corporate software migrated from the mainframe. Some users still need access to the mainframe in New York.

(continued on next page)

> The London office handles financial services products, for both consumers and businesses, in Europe. It has 400 users and 8 servers. The small ICL Unix system runs OSI rather than TCP/IP. The users run general office software, and there is also lots of e-mail back to headquarters. A few users have Unix connections to the ICL system.
>
> In the New York office, which primarily handles financial services products, there are 700 users and 14 servers. It has 2 IBM mainframes, but no Unix systems. The users run general office automation applications and GroupWise. Almost everyone has mainframe access. There are no Unix connections to speak of.
>
> At the manufacturing site in San Jose, there are 400 users and 8 servers. It has the primary Unix installation for manufacturing support. Every user has Unix access. Also, workers use general office automation software and send lots of e-mail back to headquarters using GroupWise. The system has no IBM mainframe connections.
>
> The small office in Menlo Park, California, serves as a financial services customer's manufacturing and distribution site. It has just 1 server and 5 users. The server runs NetWare on OS/2 with an ISDN line back to the San Jose site. A standard dial connection is used for a backup link. The users run general office automation software and use GroupWise for e-mail. Most important data is accessed across the ISDN bridge to San Jose.

CASE STUDY

MiniCo: Planning Your Network Before Installation

MINICO HAS 3 servers, 75 users, and one location.

Physical Network Types

CONSIDERATIONS

The choices:

- Expand on the existing thin coax Ethernet.
- Install new 10BaseT Ethernet everywhere.
- Set up a new Token Ring network.

DECISION

Get new 10BaseT Ethernet for all systems, replacing the old thin coax.

EXPLANATION

MiniCo had a small existing Ethernet network, using thin coax cabling. This network served only the Accounting department's eight users. The cabling was replaced with new Ethernet 10BaseT cabling when the rest of the building was wired for the new network.

The slight performance advantage from moving to Token Ring was outweighed by the need to buy new network adapters for the existing machines. Staying with Ethernet was more cost-effective, because an inexpensive transceiver allowed the existing network adapters to work with the new 10BaseT cable and concentrators.

Planning for an Efficient File System

CONSIDERATIONS

The choices:

- Use one giant server for everyone.
- Have three servers to offer some fault-tolerance.

DECISION

Use three servers. Add two new servers, and upgrade the existing server.

EXPLANATION

The existing NetWare 3.x server was upgraded and kept for the Accounting department. The only application on that server is the accounting software. Two new servers were added to the network: one named SALES_1 and the other SUPPORT_1. Accounting software stays on ACCT, the Sales OU is on SALES_1, and the support and management staff uses SUPPORT_1. SUPPORT_1 supports the Macintosh name space.

MINICO CASE STUDY, CONTINUED

Physical Space and Protection for Your Server

CONSIDERATIONS

The choices:

- Keep the servers in the Accounting manager's office.
- Build a new room for the servers.
- Modify an existing office.

DECISION

Modify the office, adding a lock on the door and taking out the carpet.

EXPLANATION

The new network administrator moved the ACCT server out of the Accounting manager's office (where it had sat in the corner under a table). An office in the middle of the first floor was renovated, with shelving and a locked door. The heavy-duty, accounting report printer sits outside this room.

Planning Cabling Installation

CONSIDERATIONS

The choices:

- Have the PC and NetWare dealer install the cabling.
- Allow the building management to contract the cabling.
- Use the building management's telephone supplier.
- Use a small data-cabling specialist company.

DECISION

Hire the company that specializes in data cabling.

EXPLANATION

MiniCo already decided to install new 10BaseT Ethernet, which uses UTP (unshielded-twisted pair) cables. The network dealer for MiniCo wanted to do the network cabling, but cabling is only a sideline for that company; no employee is a full-time cable installer. The telephone company was price-competitive, but did not offer to test each cable with digital equipment. MiniCo felt more comfortable using a professional cable installation company that does cabling every day and has the proper digital test tools.

The site manager for the cabling company worked closely with MiniCo, arranging the layout and work situation. All the cable drops were tested, labeled, and marked on the floor blueprint. The building blueprint was used to diagram the sites for the Ethernet 10BaseT hubs. Arrangements were made to start the cabling at the end of the business day on Friday, and work on Saturday. This minimized the impact on MiniCo employees.

MiniCo: Planning Your Network Before Installation

MINICO CASE STUDY, CONTINUED

Network Protocols Used by NetWare 4.1x

CONSIDERATIONS

The choices:

- Work with the existing Macintosh and OS/2 computers.
- Replace those with more PCs.

DECISION

Keep the Macintosh and OS/2 systems and just enhance the network.

EXPLANATION

MiniCo did not have any legacy minicomputers to support, nor other existing computers to complicate the system. PCs are the majority of clients on the network, with standard software used. The few Macintosh systems use Ethernet network adapters, not LocalTalk. No system requires TCP/IP or SNA communications protocols.

CASE STUDY

MegaCorp: Planning Your Network Before Installation

MEGACORP HAS 50 servers, 2500 users, and 5 locations.

Physical Network Types

CONSIDERATIONS

The choices:

- Maximize use of existing cabling types, including three sites with a variety of Ethernet systems and two Token Ring sites.
- Choose one type and replace the other systems so they are all the same.

DECISION

Keep existing systems, but enhance them with switching technology whenever possible.

EXPLANATION

Although the CIO (Chief Information Officer) prefers a single network type, the cost-justification for replacing working systems has never been made. Switched Ethernet was already in use in two sites, with a pilot under way studying the performance differences between switched Token Ring, FDDI server backbones, and ATM25 to the desktop. Network switching systems, along with higher-speed bus adapters in the server machines, have improved the performance of the 10BaseT Ethernet above that of similar Token Ring systems in two locations.

The five sites are connected by a variety of WAN technologies:

- HQ and MFG have a T1 line between them.
- LON and NY have 256 Kbps leased lines back to HQ in Dallas and to MFG.
- The five-person Contract Control office in a customer's building connects over an ISDN dial-up bridge to the MFG plant in San Jose, CA.

Planning for an Efficient File System

CONSIDERATIONS

The choices:

- Set up centralized servers to be controlled by IS (Information Services).
- Install workgroup systems closer to the users.

DECISION

Both. Mission-critical systems run from centralized servers, while personal productivity and off-the-shelf software runs under the control of workgroup administrators.

MEGACORP CASE STUDY, CONTINUED

EXPLANATION

The eternal struggle between centralized versus decentralized systems never goes away. Internally developed software runs on IS-maintained servers for support and data-control reasons. All other software is under the control of a power user/workgroup administrator in each department, even though the servers are often in a centralized location.

Physical Space and Protection for Your Server

CONSIDERATIONS

The choices:

- Keep all servers under control of IS.
- Let workgroups control their own servers.

DECISION

Keep as many servers as possible under IS control.

EXPLANATION

Let local administrators control the noncritical servers, while servers with critical software are under control of IS. Most of the noncritical servers are in rooms controlled by IS but managed by the workgroup administrators.

This works out neater than it appears. IS handles the tape, battery backup, and physical security needs for each server under that department's control. Those noncritical servers under IS's control are managed (remotely) by workgroup administrators. These administrators do not have keys to the IS rooms; physical operations are done by IS. A few workgroups have physical control of their servers, but not many.

Planning Cabling Installation

CONSIDERATIONS

The cable-type choices:

- Connect UTP (unshielded twisted-pair) cable to each desktop.
- Connect fiber-optic cable to each desktop.
- Install fiber-optic for the server backbone networks.

The installation choices:

- Train and employ a MegaCorp cabling team.
- Hire outside contractors.

DECISION

Use UTP with extra wire pairs to each desktop. Use UTP or fiber-optic cable for computer room connections. Hire and train the cable installers internally.

EXPLANATION

UTP supports both Ethernet and Token Ring, allowing the same design to work in all buildings. The limitations of UTP for certain high-speed video applications have not proven a problem, but pilot programs are testing desktop videoconferencing within large buildings.

The in-house cabling team is handy. By combining the telephone and data wiring groups, one

MEGACORP CASE STUDY, CONTINUED

technician is able to handle all cabling problems for user connections. This cooperation between the Datacom and Telecom groups is unusual in the business world, but it is cost-effective.

Network Protocols Used by NetWare 4.1x

CONSIDERATIONS

The choices:

- Make the whole network all TCP/IP.
- Make the whole network all IPX.
- Use SNA gateways.
- Put dual protocol stacks on every PC.

DECISION

Use IPX within buildings, and use TCP/IP for remote connections and to host systems.

EXPLANATION

Most desktop systems use IPX to the servers. Remote routing is done with TCP/IP, either from the NetWare server or over NetWare/IP. SNA hosts now support TN3270 connections from PCs and Unix systems. The MFG building uses TCP/IP and NetWare/IP, because of its large Unix workstation installation. Macintosh systems use EtherTalk or TokenTalk, depending on their location.

Installing NetWare 4.1x

CHAPTER 2

NSTALLING NETWARE FOR the first time may give you pause. If you have never installed NetWare before, your anxiety about doing a new procedure is compounded by all your questions about NetWare particulars. If you have installed NetWare before, you may be concerned because NetWare 4.1x doesn't look exactly like NetWare 3.x, or any other earlier version.

Although it may give you little comfort now, NetWare 4.1x is the easiest version of NetWare to install in the history of the product. It's now shipped on a nice, shiny CD-ROM. The older versions of NetWare took a bushel basket of floppy disks and constant attention to feed those same disks in mind-numbing repetition. Mistype or forget something with earlier NetWare? Start all over, and feed those lousy floppies in one after another.

Even more exciting, NetWare 4.11 installation screens are almost exactly the same as those for the rest of the 4.x family. The differences are minor, and primarily concern support for the new features added to NetWare 4.11.

What will be different is the fact that you may not see some of the screens in 4.11 you saw in 4.10. The automated installation process has been improved, especially when you're using a server equipped with Plug-and-Play capabilities. Drivers for disks and network adapters are more often understood by the installation routines, meaning the installer (that's you) doesn't need to reenter driver information.

Do you have a dual-processor server? When Novell introduced SMP (Symmetrical Multi-Processor) support, the modified NetWare operating systems were licensed to the manufacturers. This allowed the vendors to make minor modifications to support their particular hardware. NetWare 4.11 has these improvements incorporated, so the software detects multiple processors during installation and adds the proper code.

You'll see the other improvements to NetWare 4.11 described in the appropriate places here and there throughout the book. In almost every case, however, what goes for version 4.10 also goes for version 4.11. A few of the 4.11 improvements are not backward compatible. Also, you wouldn't want to run a mixed network of 4.10 and 4.11 servers if you can help it. Otherwise, a good knowledge of 4.10 will cover 98 percent of 4.11, so you're in good shape.

New, Improved NetWare Installation

THE BIGGEST ADVANTAGES of NetWare 4.1*x* installation are:

- With the CD-ROM, you spend only ten minutes at the computer; the rest is done automatically by the installation program.
- All installation mistakes are easily corrected.
- Any changes you think of during or immediately after installation are easily made.

Let's take each item and squelch any remaining nervousness on your part. First, since there are no floppies to feed during installation, a new server can actually be installed with only ten minutes of your time spent at the keyboard. It will probably take you longer, at least the first time, because you will read all the help screens and peruse every word on each screen. If you are a typical NetWare administrator, you also won't fill out the worksheets completely, so you'll need to look up some information. That takes time, which pushes you past the ten minutes.

Later installations will take less time, because you will know the answers to the questions that appear during installation. Let me also offer hope for those of you installing from the floppies: the second NetWare 4.1*x* server in your network can easily be installed by copying information from the first server. If you must feed floppies, you will only feed them twice: once to install the first system, and the second time to load all the installation files onto the server hard disk for easy future installations.

Second, any time you make a mistake during installation, you can correct that mistake with little trouble. The installation program offers you several chances to stop and start all over. You have opportunities at every section to go back and redo any piece of that section.

Third, the installation program can be run anytime to fix any mistake or installation confusion. The new graphical NetWare administration tools make it easy to change common installation mistakes, like typos (there is no spelling checker in the installation program).

Of course, the "ten-minute install" works best when you take the approach of the cooking shows on TV. You should have all the necessary ingredients (information) at hand, so fill out those worksheets or at least gather all the specific details needed about your network. You should have a working oven (server) all preheated and ready to go, meaning properly configured with the correct disk drives and NICs. And, you should know the recipe, meaning you should read over the entire installation process once or twice to understand where you're heading with each step.

Okay, if you don't plan on filling out the worksheets, keep a pad and pencil beside the server during installation. Each time you must make a choice, or the installation program provides a randomly generated number for you, write it down. Save that paper, because you will forget the information. With luck, you won't need to refer to this information, or at least you won't lose the paper.

Requirements for NetWare Servers

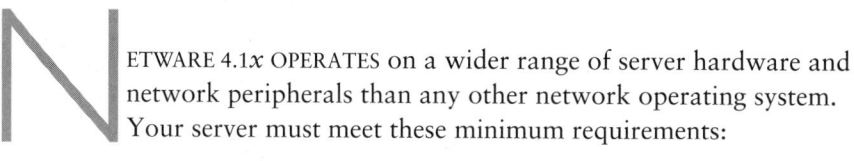

NETWARE 4.1x OPERATES on a wider range of server hardware and network peripherals than any other network operating system. Your server must meet these minimum requirements:

- A PC or PC compatible with a minimum 386 processor
- 8 MB of RAM
- 90 MB hard disk
- One NIC connected to a functioning network cabling system (NE2000, 3Com, Intel, SMC, and so on)
- A CD-ROM drive that can read ISO 9660 formatted CD-ROM disks (if you're installing from CD-ROM)

- 3.5-inch disk drive
- Monitor, video board, and keyboard

Technically, the list above will make a server. Practically, this server will be worthless to you. Your choice for server components should read like this:

OPTION	RECOMMENDATION
CPU	Intel 486DX or Pentium (or compatibles)
RAM	16 MB minimum, more is better
Hard Disk	500 MB minimum, more is better
NIC	EISA or PCI bus-mastering NIC
CD-ROM	2x speed CD-ROM drive minimum
Floppy	Basic 3.5-inch drive only (not 5.25)
Monitor	Low-end VGA card and cheap monitor

Each item on the list is necessary, but choosing some items demands more critical decision-making skills than others. The items requiring some soul-searching depend on your needs for this server. Our goal in this section is to discern which options best fit your situation for each particular server you will install.

If your company is like most companies, there is a constant struggle between what is wanted and what is affordable. Every network administrator would love to have nothing but superservers with more RAM and hard disk space than the company's mainframe. However, budget constraints exist in every situation. You may well talk your boss into a superserver, but you must justify that expenditure.

The only way to justify expenditures for most bosses is to give clear pictures of the options available, with the good and bad points of each option. Normally, the equation is simple: here are the good points, here are the bad points (usually price tag or required resources). Then you and your boss argue about the list of good/bad points for each portion of the server until some compromise is reached.

A question for you and your boss: What are the three most important functions for your planned server? The answers from you and your boss may be different. If so, problems will be your constant companion. Only when you and your boss are in agreement regarding the network will you both be happy with the choices you must make.

> **Living with Your Networking Decisions**
>
> The question "What are the three most important functions of *x?*" will reappear in various places throughout this book. If you are uncomfortable making decisions, I have one bit of advice: get over it. Business management, and especially networking, is nothing but decisions regarding the conflict between goals and constraints.
>
> Let me help take the fear out of decisions: every single one you make will be wrong next year. By this, I mean that technology will change, and better options will appear in the future. If you make the same decision next year as you made yesterday, you will be overlooking better options. Better equipment will be available, prices will be lower, or both, but things will change in the future.
>
> Don't beat yourself up over decisions made in the past that didn't work out as well as hoped. No one can blame you if you had the right priorities at the time you made that decision. The only action you can be blamed for is not revisiting poor decisions as time makes more options available.

Choosing the Server's CPU

As with all your server decisions, if money is no problem, pick the high-end option each time. If money is an issue, as it normally is, then you might be interested in a ranking of which server functions require the most CPU power. Here is a list of common server uses, ranging from supporting the clients with occasional file access to running large database applications (involving NLMs, or NetWare Loadable Modules) directly on the server:

Section 1: Low-End Requirements (1 point each)

- Standard client-support file service clients have local hard drives
- File service for clients without local hard drives
- File service for PC clients that run MS Windows locally but store applications on the server

Section 2: Mid-Level Requirements (2 points each)

- Shared database application files on the server with clients doing all the processing

- Communications gateway NLM applications on the server

- CD-ROM support on the server

- E-mail processing functions execute on the server

Section 3: High-End Requirements (4 points each)

- WAN connections are made from modems attached directly to the server

- Network and client management software NLMs

- Several NLM database application programs on the server

- One busy database application with heavy activity on the server

You can use this list to help you decide which type of CPU your server needs. Check each function that applies. Total the number of points for all the questions (combine all groups into one total).

- If your total is less than 5, the low-end server (a 486) will do fine.

- If your total is between 6 and 11, go with the midrange option (a low-end Pentium).

- If your total is more than 12, get the high-end system (a high-end Pentium).

- If you can afford one, get a Pentium Pro system. Then you won't need to worry about an upgrade for 18 months rather than just 12.

Actually, if your point total is close to the maximum in the first two categories, you should go with the higher-end server, because it's cheaper than upgrading.

When Pentium processors become comparable in price with 486s, buy Pentiums. If you're not comfortable with a lower-powered processor because of the server workload today or what may happen tomorrow, buy more horsepower. Your server demands will only increase, not decrease. Better to have too much horsepower than not enough.

Figuring the Needed RAM (Buy More)

Novell has a complicated method used to calculate necessary server RAM, and a "short-form" version of the same calculation. The short version is:

SERVER FUNCTION	RAM RECOMMENDED
Operating system, disk, and LAN drivers	8 MB
NetWare for Macintosh, NFS (Network File System), or other file system	2 MB
PSERVER, MONITOR, INSTALL, SERVMAN NLMs	2 MB each
Disk support	.008 times total disk capacity in MB
Cache buffers	1 to 4 MB

For a server with a 500 MB disk and the normal complement of NLMs, use this method:

8 MB + 2 MB + 4 MB (.008 x 500=4) + 1 to 4 MB (cache) = 15 to 18 MB

This is the official short form to figure RAM for your server. Personally, I say you should buy all you can afford. NetWare 4.1*x* can support up to 4 GB of RAM and 32 TB (terabytes) of hard disk space.

The important pieces of the formula above are the 8 MB of RAM for the operating system, 1 MB of RAM for each 100 MB of hard disk space, and as many more cache buffers as you can afford. Since cache buffers service users by keeping active files in RAM, the more the better.

Maybe we should develop some quick rule of thumb, such as 1 MB of cache buffer RAM for every 10 to 12 users. Assuming 40 users on the system described previously, use this calculation:

8 MB + 2 MB + 5 MB (1 MB for every 100 MB of disk space) + 4 MB (40 users) = 19 MB

No PC will support the odd configuration of 19 MB, so you'll either need to go up to 20 MB or 24 MB, depending on your server's memory configuration, or down to 16 MB. Some motherboard/BIOS combinations will take memory only in 4 MB chunks; some will take only 8 or 16 MB chunks.

Sorry this doesn't work out neatly. When possible, buy the higher RAM recommendation, not the lower number. In fact, NetWare 4.1x will happily use all the memory you can put in your server, so if money is not a constraint, pour in the RAM.

One of the systems I used to test NetWare 4.1x for this book was CLONE386 (386/33, 8 MB RAM, 300 MB hard disk, 5.25 floppy), an old server with many years of experience and trustworthy service. Unfortunately, unlike with network administrators, years of experience aren't an advantage for servers. Installation of NetWare 4.10 on CLONE386 turned out to be possible, but just barely. The 5.25-inch floppy was a pain because NetWare installation disks had to be copied to the old format from the 3.5-inch disks. The biggest pain was the 8 MB of RAM. Several times during various installation tests, RAM ran out and the installation stopped. The only installation that would work is the Simple Installation; adding the one extra NLM for some NDS authentication in the Custom Installation was one NLM too many.

The moral of this story is simple: buy more RAM. CLONE386 is an example of a bare-bones server that technically works, but would be irresponsible to foist on a customer. There may be a use for a server with only a 386 processor today, but not for a server with only 8 MB of RAM.

NetWare 4.11 makes this requirement even stronger. Although the base operating system hasn't grown too much, the extra goodies included (such as the NetWare Internet Access Server and Web Server) will tempt many into loading more than the basic system. When you try that, your realistic memory limit balloons past 12 MB to 16 MB, or more reasonably, 20 MB.

Choosing the Hard Disk (Buy a Bigger One)

No one complains about too much storage space, whether we speak of closets, car trunks, or server hard disks. My friend David Strom has this recommendation for beginning NetWare administrators: "Buy twice as much disk space as you think you'll need. Better yet, buy three times as much."

There are four types of disk interfaces available today on PCs:

- **ST506 (Seagate Technologies)**: Early PC interface; too slow for servers today.

- **ESDI (Enhanced Small Device Interface):** Popular with 386 machines, up to 15 Mbps transfer rates, two devices per controller; not a good server choice any more.

- **IDE (Integrated Drive Electronics):** Common, fast, low-cost controller that supports two drives per controller.

- **SCSI (Small Computer System Interface):** Parallel adapter interface running 4 Mbps or more, seven devices per SCSI adapter, data transfer path up to 32 bits wide. New variations include Fast and Wide SCSI and SCSI II. Popular for tape backup and CD-ROM drive support as well.

Novell pioneered an early version of asymmetrical coprocessing with the release of the DCB (Disk Coprocessor Board). A SCSI adapter, the DCB helped performance by doing some of the processing, keeping the CPU of the server free to service other system requirements. This did increase disk performance, but other systems now offer more speed without using the proprietary DCB.

Of the four drive types, only SCSI and IDE drives are commonly used in servers today. Let's talk about those two, along with RAID systems.

IDE Disk Controllers and Drives

If you buy a PC with an installed hard disk, chances are it will be an IDE system. IDE controllers are so inexpensive now that they are often bundled with the floppy controller and serial and parallel ports on a single, small interface card. Since the board needs only a few chips for the IDE portion, some manufacturers are building the IDE controller directly on the motherboard.

The chances of a PC with a small (500 MB or less) hard disk using IDE are great. Early versions of IDE controllers were limited to 525 MB, but now drives up to 1.2 GB are supported.

NetWare 4.1*x* support of IDE controllers is strong. The standard IDE.DSK driver included in the installation process works with all brands of IDE controllers. With the larger capacity available today, IDE drives are now good choices for servers. Local bus and PCI IDE controllers now support 32-bit access, making disk performance even better.

SCSI Disk Interfaces and Drives

Another technology "borrowed" from the world of Unix hardware, SCSI adapters and drives are the choice for serious servers and large server disks.

Technically, SCSI (pronounced "scuzzy") is an ANSI standard that details an I/O bus capable of supporting up to seven devices.

SCSI adapters use a short, 50-pin connecting cable when attaching to external disk drives. (IDE uses a 40-pin cable.) Since SCSI devices are "chained" together, a terminator must be used on the last device to anchor the chain.

SCSI is a popular adapter for CD-ROM drive connections. This popularity helps make SCSI devices more affordable, but some adapters are nonproprietary. These vendor-specific adapters use a 40-pin adapter cable, as does an IDE drive. These adapters will probably not run your file server disks.

High-performance needs of Unix workstations and servers are advancing the performance of SCSI devices every day. SCSI II, Fast SCSI, Wide SCSI, and Fast and Wide SCSI are improvements being advanced by various parties. The world of SCSI is also being pushed to support longer cable lengths to make disk clusters more convenient.

Adaptec SCSI adapters have the longest history in the PC hardware market. Years of experience making drivers for Intel-based Unix systems have been leveraged into a similar leading position in the NetWare server world. NetWare 4.1*x* includes support for many Adaptec, and other SCSI, adapters.

SCSI drives are excellent choices for servers. They were about your only choice for large (1 GB or more) drives and disk arrays until the EIDE (Enhanced IDE) drive controllers became popular. SCSI still works better for servers than EIDE, however, since SCSI drives have more flexibility, more throughput, and more field reliability.

RAID Disk Systems

Coming into popularity in the 1990s, RAID (redundant array of inexpensive disks, although some references now say independent rather than inexpensive) uses several disks to replace the storage capacity of a single disk. The advantage of RAID is fault tolerance; one disk can die, but the information is spread across all disks, so no data is lost.

How the data is spread determines the RAID level of a disk system. The levels range from 1 to 5, but RAID 4 and RAID 5 are generally used for servers, with RAID 5 the most popular. The best RAID systems allow bad disks to be replaced without downing the server, maintaining server uptime for the users in spite of what is ordinarily a catastrophic failure. Some vendors build cabinets with multiple power supplies and cooling fans to emphasize the fault-tolerant nature of RAID.

There are two warning notes attached to this rosy scenario, however. RAID systems do not, in any way, make a tape backup obsolete. Although a RAID disk system will continue if one drive goes bad, catastrophic failures can occur. More important, tape backup is most often used to replace files accidentally deleted. If you delete a file on a RAID disk system, the system will happily delete the file no matter how many disks hold part of that file.

The second warning is that reconstruction of a RAID system is not transparent. As the new disk in the system is populated to take the place of the failed drive, your server will be involved. The performance for clients will drop drastically.

Despite the warnings, RAID systems perform better in critical systems than any single drive available. No system is perfect, but RAID is a good step in the right direction. These systems will become more commonplace as prices settle and companies realize the value of the data on their server disks.

Choosing the Server's NIC

Whether your network runs Ethernet, Token Ring, or Other, the card in your server must carry the largest load. Each client talks to one system: the server. The NIC for the server is no place to save money.

Performance is best with an EISA or a MicroChannel Architecture (developed and used primarily by IBM) bus in the file server. EISA briefly took the lead in the server business, and then PCI and Local Bus started getting more popular. PCI came out to be the winner; go PCI if you have a chance.

The reason for the high-end bus for servers is the amount of data that can be transmitted at one time. EISA and MicroChannel both use 32-bit data paths, four times faster than the early 8-bit PC slots. In addition, both EISA and MicroChannel allow NICs to take control of the bus (bus-mastering) for high-speed transfer. Much like the early DCB adapters, bus-master cards take some load off the server CPU and increase network throughput.

All the above is true for PCI cards now; faster access and wider data paths are the selling point. Proprietary buses from a few of the major vendors still draw attention, but low-end PCs with PCI slots make fast yet inexpensive servers.

Early advice was to add several NICs in each server to handle higher network traffic loads. Now that switched Ethernet and Token Ring are available, my advice is to avoid multiple NICs. When you add the second network adapter in the server, the operating system turns on software necessary to route traffic between the two (or more) network segments. This means each and every packet coming to each network adapter must be examined and routed to either the server itself or to another network adapter. This overhead actually tends to slow server processing of packets in heavy network situations. If at all possible, do not use your server as a local router for your network segments. Figure 2.1 shows the possible and preferred setups.

FIGURE 2.1

Handling high network traffic levels

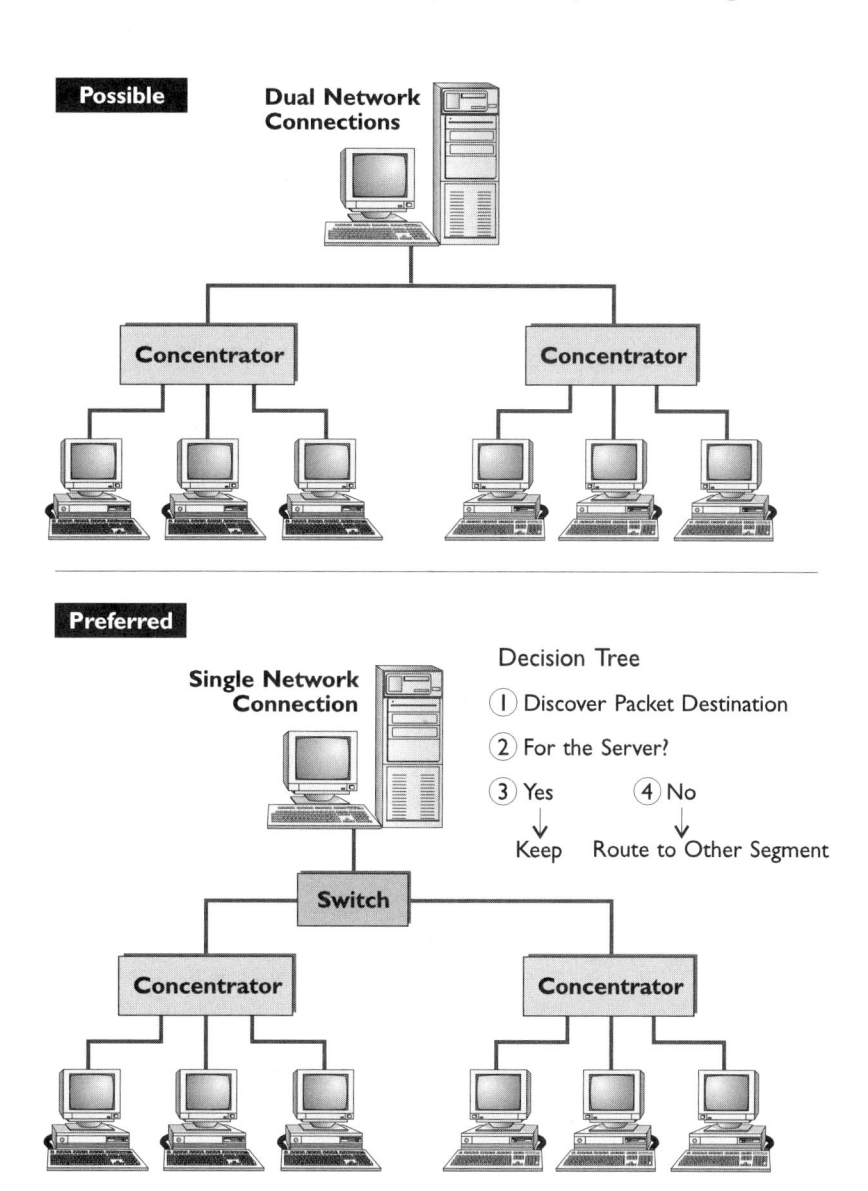

To paraphrase the old homily, put all your eggs in one basket, then really watch that basket. Put a stout network adapter in your server, and make sure it has been certified by Novell. Make doubly sure the card has the proper driver for not just NetWare, but for NetWare servers.

The NetWare operating system supports 65 LAN drivers right out of the box. Drivers for any other interface card can be added during installation by reading the vendor's configuration diskette.

One more suggestion: check your NIC vendor for new server drivers now and then. You can improve your server's performance by upgrading your drivers, and vendors supply new driver files on a regular basis.

Choosing the Server's CD-ROM Drive

The trick with the CD-ROM drives is not the drive itself, but the controller card that sits in the server. Since SCSI is an accepted standard, a NetWare-supported card in the server can easily run any new CD-ROM drive. So NetWare doesn't care about the drive, just the controller.

There are 15 drivers for various SCSI adapters included in the NetWare installation program. Just as with NICs, any vendors can supply their own Novell-certified drivers with their own SCSI card. Because NetWare servers are big business, most SCSI board manufacturers provide Novell drivers.

If you plan to use your CD-ROM drive as a NetWare volume after the server is installed, get at least a 6x drive. If you're not going to use the CD-ROM as a volume, it makes little difference; here's one place you can save some money. Just make sure the interface card for the CD-ROM drive doesn't interfere with the network adapter and disk controller.

IDE CD-ROMs are supported in NetWare 4.11, if that's important. The performance doesn't promise to be better than SCSI drives, however, so there's little reason to go out of your way to get an IDE drive and controller. Low-end servers with EIDE drives perform well, and these come standard in the less expensive servers if price is important.

> **WARNING**
>
> *There are cases of problems with some SCSI adapters when running both the hard disk and the CD-ROM drive from the same adapter. During installation, the adapter may become unstable and lock up the console keyboard. If that happens, take all the SCSI references out of your CONFIG.SYS file that boots your server under DOS before restarting the installation process. Then load the proper SCSI driver supplied by NetWare*

to load the CD-ROM as a NetWare volume, and use that volume as the installation files source. More details on resolving SCSI conflict problems during installation are in the section about disk driver setup, later in this chapter.

Choosing the Server's Floppy Drive

This is an easy selection, because any DOS floppy controller and drive will work under NetWare. You must have a floppy drive on the server to supply the license diskette during installation.

If you want to make your server slightly more secure, and plan on booting your server from the hard disk rather than a diskette in the floppy drive, you can remove the floppy drive after installation is finished. It may make the installation of some software slightly more difficult, but nothing serious.

There is nothing that forces you to remove the floppy drive. If you are using an IDE disk, your floppy controller is almost certainly located on the same controller as that for your hard drive. Removing the actual floppy drive saves you less than a hundred dollars.

Use a high-density, 3.5-inch floppy drive in your server. Most new software, including NetWare, comes on high-density, 3.5-inch diskettes. Low-density floppies or 5.25-inch drives are special items, and they will cause you some hassle one day, believe me.

Choosing the Server's Monitor

This is another easy choice—any cheap VGA video board and low-end monitor, even monochrome, will work fine on your server. If you order a server from a retail outlet and it comes with a nice monitor and VGA video board with more than 256 KB of memory, take them out and use them somewhere else. You will not use the monitor on a server enough to warrant spending ten dollars more than absolutely necessary.

The reason you want a low-end VGA video board is because of the memory a better video board would take. NetWare will use all the extended memory available in your server, but the video board memory carves a chunk out. The smaller that chunk, the better.

Once installation is complete, server console operations are done rarely. All normal console operations can be done across the network using the RCONSOLE.EXE program. Found in the SYS:SYSTEM directory, RCONSOLE allows any PC on the network to act as the server console, if the proper software is loaded on the server. A password specifically for the remote console function is part of the server configuration.

Setting Interrupts, DMA, I/O Ports, and ROM Addresses

Each of the interface cards discussed in this chapter so far requires some special configuration. The more of these cards in the server, the more difficult it may be to configure each one to work with the others.

Keep track of these settings for each server, and keep track of the paper with the final settings for each server. Having this paper will save you time when you add to or modify the equipment in your server. Some people keep the setting information in a notebook, some keep them by the server, some track the settings in a small database. Just remember to track them somewhere, and your life will be easier.

Interrupts

Interrupts are signals to the CPU in a system from a device under CPU control. Abbreviated IRQ for Interrupt ReQuest, the hardware lines that carry the signals to the CPU are required for every device in the system. The ISA bus has only eight IRQs, numbered 0 to 7, available. AT-class machines and above have sixteen IRQs (minus IRQ 2, which functions as an overlap point for the second interrupt controller chip that manages IRQs 8 through 15). Table 2.1 lists the IRQs and their devices.

TABLE 2.1 IRQs and Their Devices

IRQ	DEVICE
0	Timer
1	Keyboard
2	Second IRQ controller chip
3	COM2
4	COM1
5	Hard disk

TABLE 2.1 (cont.)
IRQs and Their Devices

IRQ	DEVICE
6	Floppy disk
7	LPT1
8	Clock
9	PC network
10–12	Available
13	Coprocessor
14	Hard disk
15	Available

DMA

DMA (direct memory access) is the quick method for transferring information from a mass-storage device of some kind into memory without using the CPU as a traffic cop. Because the processor does not need to be involved, performance is good. Network adapters rarely use DMA, but SCSI adapters often do. There are only five DMA channels, but these are plenty for NetWare servers.

I/O Ports

I/0 (Input/Output) describes the transfer of data between the computer and its peripheral devices. Disk drives, printers, tape storage systems and CD-ROM drives are considered I/O. A hexadecimal number describes a particular I/O port location for those peripherals in the server. Network adapters, SCSI adapters, and disk controllers require a particular I/O port number during installation. Examples are I/O port 300 for the 3Com 3C509 interface card and I/O port 330 for the Adaptec 1540 SCSI adapter.

ROM Addresses

ROM (read-only memory) addresses are necessary for those adapters that store their own operational code in hardware on the adapter. Expressed in large hexadecimal numbers, such as D000 or C800, these addresses are used most commonly in Token Ring interface cards. Any device may require a specific ROM address, but usually, you have only one or two of these devices in a file server. If you assemble the server yourself, make notes of the settings for each card you place in the server. Although the CONFIG command on the server console tells you the network adapter settings, it doesn't give the details for SCSI adapters, video boards, or anything else in the server. Even worse, if settings conflict, your server won't start.

Preparing for Installation

BEFORE STARTING THE ACTUAL NetWare installation process, you must verify that your server-to-be is properly configured. It must boot, have access to the hard disk and CD-ROM drive, and make connection to the network. In other words, before a PC can be a server, it must be a functioning workstation.

If your system came loaded with DOS and MS Windows and various applications, these will all be wiped out. If you want to keep the application software on the system, verify you have all the diskettes necessary to reload the applications elsewhere. Many preconfigured systems don't ship the floppies with the system, but have them stored on the hard disk. If that's the case with your system, get some floppies and copy those directories. Everything on the hard disk will be history.

I recommend that you put a DOS partition on the hard disk of your server machine, and boot from there. The rest of the hard disk will be one large NetWare partition. When you use FDISK to repartition your disk, everything will be wiped out. Even if you don't leave a DOS partition on the disk, all the programs that came with the system will be lost when you convert the bootable DOS partition into a NetWare partition.

Creating the Server Installation Boot Disk

A server installation boot disk is optional and not required by the NetWare installation when you boot the server from a DOS partition on the server hard disk. However, this working installation boot disk comes in handy. What we must create is a floppy containing all the necessary files to boot the machine and activate the CD-ROM.

Tables 2.2 and 2.3 show the CONFIG.SYS and AUTOEXEC.BAT files from a Gateway 2000 Pentium machine used in my lab for this book. As many retail systems do, this machine came with extensive software. What we are worried about now, however, is just enough software to make the CD-ROM usable for our forthcoming NetWare installation. These files were copied from the root directory of the Gateway 2000 PC and modified for use on the boot diskette. Modifications were made with an ASCII text editor before the server boot diskette was used to begin the installation process. Where a subdirectory is referenced to reach a file, the file is copied to the root directory of the boot diskette. The best example is the last line of the CONFIG.SYS file.

TABLE 2.2 CONFIG.SYS Modified for Server Installation

ORIGINAL LINE	REASON FOR CHANGE OR FUNCTION OF LINE
rem DEVICE=C:\DOS\HIMEM.SYS	NetWare will manage the PC's extended memory.
rem DEVICE=C:\DOS\EMM386.EXE NOEMS X=F000-F7FF	No DOS memory management can be used on NetWare servers.
rem DEVICEHIGH=C:\DOS\SETVER.EXE	NetWare ignores the DOS version.
rem DEVICEHIGH=C:\WINDOWS\IFSHLP.SYS	MS Windows is erased from the system.
DOS=HIGH,UMB	The address space for DOS is available during installation.
STACKS=9,256	Common command for environment space control.
FILES=50	This will have no impact after the server is installed.
BUFFERS=10	This will also have no impact.
rem LASTDRIVE=K	This setting was for the now-deleted MS Windows for Workgroups software.

TABLE 2.2 (cont.) CONFIG.SYS Modified for Server Installation

ORIGINAL LINE	REASON FOR CHANGE OR FUNCTION OF LINE
LASTDRIVE=Z:	This setting works for NetWare clients; necessary if you install across the network.
DEVICEHIGH=MTMCDAE.SYS /D:MSCD001/ P:340 /A:0 /M:30 /T:S /I:11	This is the important line; it's the driver for the CD-ROM drive.

The boot diskette was created by making a formatted, bootable floppy (from C:, type FORMAT A: /S). The entire root directory of the Gateway 2000 PC was then copied to the boot diskette (COPY *.* A:). The COPY command does not copy subdirectories, so there's no worry about copying a subdirectory to the floppy and filling it up before we get the files needed.

Every line in both files could have been cut except for the last line in CONFIG.SYS and the second line in AUTOEXEC.BAT, but that wouldn't illustrate the point as well. NetWare needs no memory management help from DOS, disk caching, mouse drivers, or anything else along that line. Only the lines necessary to start the CD-ROM to function as drive D: are needed on this boot diskette.

TABLE 2.3 AUTOEXEC.BAT Modified for Server Installation

ORIGINAL LINE	REASON FOR CHANGE OR FUNCTION OF LINE
rem @ECHO OFF	I prefer to see all messages to help with troubleshooting.
MSCDEX.EXE /D:MSCD001	Important file: MicroSoft CD-ROM EXtension program for CD-ROM control (placed in the root directory of the floppy).
rem C:\ANYKEY\ANYKEY30 T ANYKEY30	Gateway's keyboard enhancement program; unneeded on servers.
PROMPT PG	DOS prompt showing current working directory.
rem LH C:\DOS\SMARTDRV.EXE	NetWare provides its own server cache program.

TABLE 2.3 (cont.)
AUTOEXEC.BAT Modified for Server Installation

ORIGINAL LINE	REASON FOR CHANGE OR FUNCTION OF LINE
rem LH C:\WINDOWS\NET START	Unneeded command to start MS Windows for Workgroup networking software.
rem SET MOUSE=C:\MSMOUSE	Servers don't use a mouse.
rem C:\MSMOUSE\MOUSE	Servers still don't use a mouse.
rem PATH=C:\;C:\DOS;C:\WINDOWS;C:\MACHPCI;	DOS path is unnecessary during server installation, and these subdirectories are not on the boot floppy.
rem SET TEMP=C:\TEMP	No temp directory is needed.
rem WIN	Unneeded command to start MS Windows.

Two other files are necessary from the DOS directory: FDISK.EXE and FORMAT.COM, which are on the installation floppy. Both will be used to prepare the hard disk in the server machine.

The installation diskette with your NetWare package will perform some, but not all, of these functions. There is no reason for Novell to include drivers under DOS to cover the wide variety of CD-ROM adapters and drives on the market today. NetWare has a list of certified drivers for those CD-ROM drives that will be mounted as NetWare volumes. So if the CD-ROM on the server machine will be used for installation purposes, you will need to create your own installation boot diskette and copy the CD-ROM files to that diskette.

You can use the supplied Novell installation diskette and boot the soon-to-be server from its own hard disk that contains all the CD-ROM driver files. If the installation goes perfectly, you will not need this bootable installation diskette. However, if you stop somewhere in the installation and turn the machine off after you have modified the hard disk partitions, the bootable installation diskette will save you 30 minutes of frustration. All the files needed to start the PC and activate the CD-ROM will be in one place, rather than scattered who knows where.

Preparing the Disk Drive for NetWare

With a brand new server PC, there may be nothing on the hard disk. When formatting and partitioning the disk initially, you should decide if the server will boot from the hard disk or from the floppy disk. Novell and I strongly recommend that you create a DOS partition of 15 MB or so and boot the server from the hard disk.

If there are files on the hard disk (as is often the case with systems bought from retail outlets eager to add "value" by adding strange software of all types), all those files will be erased. You will erase them when you run FDISK and partition the disk.

If you do not have enough hard disk space for a NetWare installation, you'll see the message shown in Figure 2.2. If you forget to partition the disk, the installation program will remind you. Continuing with the installation will gain you nothing. With the new, friendlier installation process in NetWare 4.1*x*, pressing F1 will offer a suggestion on how to deal with the condition. The screen in Figure 2.3 shows the second page of the help screens.

FIGURE 2.2

What happens when the server doesn't have enough hard disk space

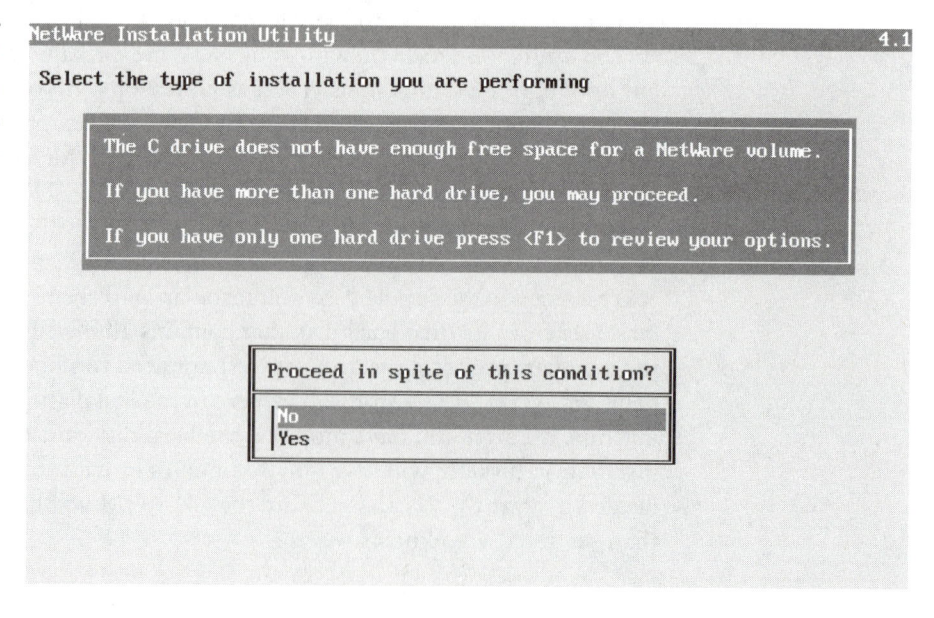

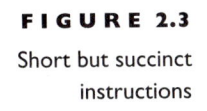

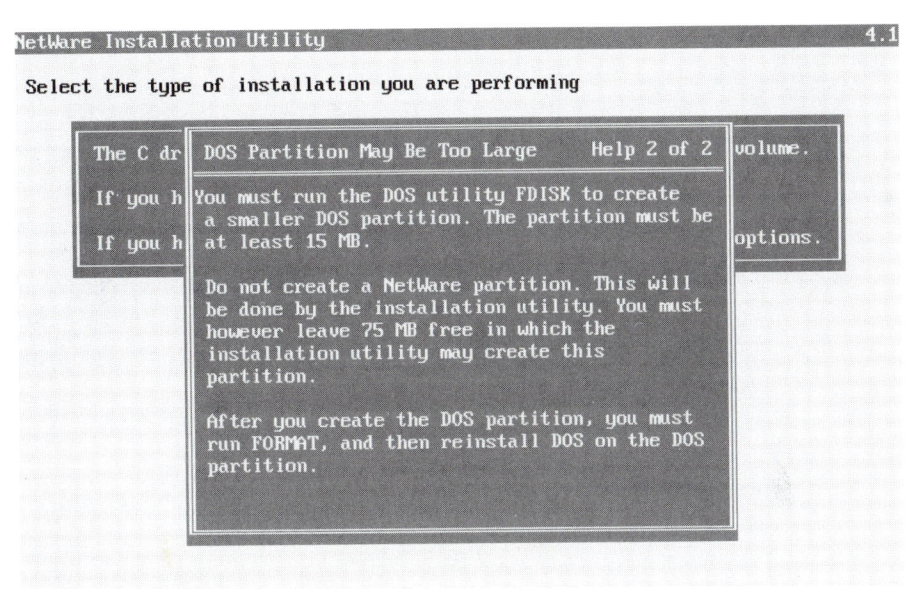

FIGURE 2.3

Short but succinct instructions

```
NetWare Installation Utility                                    4.1
Select the type of installation you are performing

    The C dr  DOS Partition May Be Too Large    Help 2 of 2   volume.
    If you h  You must run the DOS utility FDISK to create
              a smaller DOS partition. The partition must be
    If you h  at least 15 MB.                                 options.

              Do not create a NetWare partition. This will
              be done by the installation utility. You must
              however leave 75 MB free in which the
              installation utility may create this
              partition.

              After you create the DOS partition, you must
              run FORMAT, and then reinstall DOS on the DOS
              partition.
```

One more reminder: if you follow the directions in Figure 2.3 and rework your DOS partition, everything there will be deleted. Has a backup been done on this PC? If not, do a backup now if there is ever the smallest chance you or someone else will one day want some of the files.

Booting Your Future Server from the Hard Disk

To boot your server from the hard disk, there must be a DOS partition. Novell recommends 15 MB for the partition. This allows enough room for all DOS files, the NWSERVER directory for the NetWare files, and a little space for other server utilities. If you plan to boot the server from a floppy, this DOS partition is not necessary.

The 15 MB is a bit generous for the DOS partition, primarily because there's no reason to have a full DOS directory with all the assorted utilities. Many of the DOS utilities are MS Windows programs, and the server will never run MS Windows. If you want to cut the DOS partition down to 10 MB, copy only the DOS files from the first DOS diskette, and then delete any of those that are MS Windows-specific. However, with version 4.11, it's best to play it safe and use the recommended 15 MB, although you may waste some space. Depending on the hard disk and controller, choosing 15 MB in the installation program may become 16 MB when actually installed.

With a configured and working PC, you will need to use FDISK.EXE to make the adjustments to your disk partitions. It's painful to press the Y key to say, "Yes, completely wipe the disk contents, never to be seen again," even when you know there is nothing valuable on the disk. I suppose you need to accidentally erase a disk or two before you become paranoid about partioning a disk. If you haven't wiped away valuable files, you haven't been playing with computers long enough.

The steps for preparing the hard disk of your future server are:

1. Boot the system from the hard disk or your server installation floppy (better).
2. Run FDISK.EXE.
3. Delete the existing DOS partition.
4. Create a DOS partition using 15 MB of disk space.
5. Exit FDISK.EXE by pressing Escape.
6. Format the small DOS partition (type **FORMAT C: /S**) from the floppy.
7. Reboot the system and boot from the hard disk to verify previous steps.
8. Copy and verify that CD-ROM drivers initialize the drive (if the CD-ROM will be used for installation).
9. Copy and verify that NIC drivers connect to the network (if a network connection is needed for installation).
10. Begin NetWare installation.

Starting the file server is much faster with a DOS partition and booting from the hard disk. I prefer letting the installation program modify the AUTOEXEC.BAT program so that the NetWare server starts every time the system is booted. If something happens to make the server stop, such as a power failure, it's nice that the server can restart without someone typing a command or two.

Use the CD-ROM driver files you saved from the hard disk and placed on the installation boot floppy before you wiped the server hard disk. If a network connection is necessary for installation, copy the minimum client files needed from a working network client.

> *If you haven't wiped away valuable files, you haven't been playing with computers long enough.*

Booting Your Future Server from the Floppy Disk

There are at least two reasons some people recommend booting your server from the floppy disk rather than the server's hard disk. One reason is to leave the entire server disk for NetWare. The other is to prevent tampering with the server boot files, since the boot disk can be stored separately from the server.

Technically, booting from a floppy is possible and marginally attractive to some customers. But I don't buy it. Boot from the hard disk.

Let me answer the two supposed advantages of booting from the floppy. First, a large server hard disk (1 GB and up is typical for most larger company servers today) won't miss the 10–15 MB set aside for the DOS partition. The 10 MB is only one one-hundredth of a 1 GB drive!

Second, why would a company that allows access to the physical file server be scrupulous about keeping the server boot floppy safe? If a disgruntled employee or other miscreant wanted to cause damage, a boot floppy would be low on the mischief priority list.

Reasons to avoid a server boot floppy include the speed of booting and the limited space available on a floppy. Floppies take much longer to read than hard disks. Normally, the boot speed of a server doesn't matter, since the server is designed to keep running all the time. When a server is being rebooted more than one time, you are probably installing new hardware or software. Maintenance like this often requires you to boot the server many times in a short period of time. If this is the case, you will grow to hate the floppy as it slowly spins and spins and spins.

Another reason to avoid the server boot floppy is space. If the NetWare operating system gets larger, or the NetWare engineers change some of the startup details, more files may be needed than can fit on one floppy.

All this notwithstanding, a boot disk is possible. Make it bootable by formatting a blank diskette with the command FORMAT A: /S (assuming the floppy is in drive A:). If the installation files will be loaded from an attached CD-ROM drive, load the CD-ROM DOS drivers that activate your CD-ROM drive. If the installation files will be loaded from a remote server, you will also need NetWare client files that establish a link to your preferred remote server, but these files won't be needed after the installation is finished.

The combination of bootable diskette and other drivers must activate your CD-ROM drive for the installation disk, or connect you to the remote server holding the installation files. Once this is accomplished, skip to the section about running INSTALL.NLM and continue.

Keep the bootable diskette for the file server's boot diskette. You will need this after installation every time you restart the file server. The NetWare files that need to go on the boot floppy are listed in Table 2.4. These are the files I suggest you will need to get a server up and minimally working. The advantage of this method is the use of a single floppy diskette, meaning you can boot the server without changing diskettes.

If you're installing NetWare 4.10, replace all the locations listing NW411 in the table with NW410. Also, be prepared for Novell's installation design crew to change a few file locations as they prepare the actual shipping copies of the CD-ROM; think of these locations as guides rather than absolutes.

If you install the server using floppy diskettes, you will have an option to create the boot floppies. Two are needed, so the official method won't allow the server to boot unattended.

TABLE 2.4 NetWare Files to Put on Your Bootable Diskette

FILE	PURPOSE	LOCATION ON CD-ROM
SERVER.EXE	Main NetWare operating system file	\NW411\BOOT\NATIVE
Hard disk driver (varies; for example, IDE.DSK)	Activates hard disk controller	\NW411\DISKDRV
NIC driver (varies; for example, NE2000.LAN)	Activates NIC connection	\NW411\LANDRV
MSM.NLM and ETHERTSM.NLM (TOKENTSM.NLM for Token Ring)	Utility files for network communication	\NW411\LANDRV\CORE

The STARTUP.NCF and AUTOEXEC.NCF files will be created during the installation process. You dictate the locations of those two files in an installation screen, but the default is C:\ as a reminder to use a DOS partition. There is little extra room on the bootable diskette after these files are loaded.

> *Please keep in mind that some of this procedure may change, especially as later versions become available. By that time, one boot disk will probably be inadequate, meaning you will need to manually insert different floppies each time the server is rebooted. If this seems like an awful lot of extra trouble, you're right. Make that DOS partition. Don't make your life more complicated than it is already.*

Where Will Your Installation Files Come From?

IF YOU ARE INSTALLING your first NetWare server, you have no choice when deciding where your server installation files must be located. They must be loaded into a disk drive on your server. Most likely, the installation disk will be a CD-ROM. On rare occasions, new installations will be made by feeding floppy after floppy (after floppy) into a 3.5-inch floppy disk drive on the server.

If you are installing your second or seventeenth NetWare server, you have several options regarding the source of your installation files. The choices are listed in Table 2.5.

TABLE 2.5 Installation File Sources

SOURCE	SPEED OF INSTALLATION	HARDWARE REQUIREMENTS	EASE OF INSTALLATION
Remote server across network	Fastest option; no physical involvement during file copying	Existing network and server with space for installation files or the NetWare 4.1x CD mounted as a NetWare volume	Simple once target server connects to remote server as NetWare client
CD-ROM	Slower than across the network, but no physical involvement during file copying	CD-ROM available as DOS device on target server PC	Simple once CD-ROM is operational
Floppy diskettes	Slowest installation option, requires constant diskette changes	3.5-inch floppy disk drive	Simple but mind-numbing and tedious

There is little difference in the actual installation between loading your network operating system from a CD-ROM in the server or from another server three floors away. Most of the installation time is spent watching a seemingly endless list of file names zoom by. After answering a few questions at the beginning, you have little to do during the installation of NetWare 4.1*x* (unless you're installing from floppy disks).

Installing from a Server-Based CD-ROM

> **2.1 IN-A-HURRY**
>
> **Install NetWare from an Internal CD-ROM**
>
> 1. Mount and configure a CD-ROM drive on the target server.
>
> 2. Boot the server-to-be loading only DOS and the CD-ROM drivers.
>
> 3. Make the CD-ROM drive, with the NetWare 4.1*x* installation CD loaded, your current drive.
>
> 4. Type **INSTALL** in the root directory.
>
> 5. Skip to the section about running INSTALL.NLM.

On new NetWare servers, using the CD-ROM installation disk is the preferred method by far. An added bonus is the ability to leave the electronic documentation in the CD-ROM drive mounted as a volume. This method saves server hard disk space, while still allowing all clients access to the documentation just as they access any other NetWare files on the server.

The server-to-be machine must be functioning properly as a DOS system before it can be a server. Test the CD-ROM initialization files by rebooting the system loading only DOS and the CD-ROM startup drivers. If all is well, you can make drive D: your active directory and scan the CD just as you can your hard disk. These files are all you need for your server installation boot disk. Now you can start the NetWare 4.1*x* installation process with confidence.

Once your bootable installation diskette has started DOS and the CD-ROM drive, change to the drive letter designating the CD-ROM drive (normally drive D:). You will see the batch file INSTALL.BAT. You now can skip ahead to the "Running the INSTALL.NLM Program" section of this chapter.

Installing from Floppies

If you are installing NetWare 4.1x from floppies, your boss has done you no favors. The time spent messing with floppies during the initial installation and later maintenance sessions will far outweigh the cost of a low-end CD-ROM disk drive.

While floppy installation was the only option with earlier versions of NetWare, Novell is now trying to discourage the use of floppies as an installation media. Why? Formatted, labeled, and software-laden 3.5-inch floppies cost manufacturers about 80 cents each. Similarly prepared CD-ROM disks cost about $1.25. Add the cost of storage and extra shipping charges with all the floppy weight, and you can see which way the wind is blowing. It's blowing toward CD-ROM disks, friends.

Making Working Copies

The first headache is the official recommendation that you make working copies of all diskettes. Yes, all diskettes. If you can find a PC with two 3.5-inch floppy drives, here's how to make copies of each disk:

1. Boot a PC with DOS or OS/2.

2. Put your source diskette (NetWare disk) in drive A:.

3. Put your target diskette (blank disk) in drive B:.

4. Type **DISKCOPY A: B: /V** (the /V is for verify).

5. Repeat steps 1–4 for each NetWare disk.

DISKCOPY will erase everything on the target diskette and make a complete duplicate of the source diskette. Even the diskette label is copied. The diskette label is important in this instance, because the NetWare installation program needs some way to check that the correct disk is inserted during installation. That's why using DISKCOPY is strongly suggested—it's the only utility that copies the entire disk, including the diskette label, with one command.

If you don't have a PC with two identical floppy drives, don't feel bad. Many companies no longer have dual floppies on a PC, much less dual 3.5-inch floppy drives. If you have only a single 3.5-inch floppy drive, you must amend the previous DISKCOPY instructions slightly. Rather than typing DISKCOPY A: B: /V, you must reference the single 3.5-inch floppy both times. In other words, type:

```
DISKCOPY A: A: /V
```

And watch carefully when the utility requests the source and destination diskettes.

When all this is finished, extract the server installation boot disk from the mountain of diskettes that you have, insert it in the PC, and type:

```
INSTALL
```

The batch file will take off and begin the process. Now skip ahead to the section about running INSTALL.NLM.

Installing from a Remote Server's Network Installation Area

The fastest way to install NetWare is to use a remote NetWare server as your installation source. You can install from a NetWare volume or from a remote CD mounted as a NetWare volume. Even if this is the first NetWare 4.1*x* server you are installing, if you have another NetWare 3.*x* server available, it can be the source of all the installation files, saving you time and aggravation.

Installing from a NetWare Volume

This is probably the first NetWare 4.1*x* server you are installing into your network. I base that on your attention to the installation chapter. NetWare 4.1*x* is actually fairly simple to install, so as a good NetWare administrator, you probably won't need instructions more than the first time or two.

Since you're reading this section about running the installation process across the network, you already have a NetWare server or servers available. Most likely, these servers are NetWare 3.*x* of some level, with NetWare 3.11 being the most popular.

COPYING THE INSTALLATION FILES FROM THE CD-ROM DISK The easy way to copy the installation files from the CD-ROM disk to the NetWare

How Can a Network Be Faster than a CD-ROM?

If you're new to networking in general or NetWare in particular, you may wonder why transferring files from another PC over the network is faster than reading an internal CD-ROM drive. How can you send information through a bunch of network cabling, involve two different servers, and worry about other network traffic during your file transfer, yet still believe it's faster than an internal CD-ROM?

Two concepts: network throughput and file caching. The throughput from low-end CD-ROM drives is about 150 Kbps, not too much faster than any floppy drive. Double-speed CD-ROM drives get up toward 300 Kbps, and the newer triple- and quadruple-speed systems range from 400 Kbps to 500 Kbps. I know that those numbers don't multiply out exactly right, but there is a bit of fudging going on with performance numbers from some CD-ROM vendors right now. The double-speed numbers are reliable, but the higher-speed drives are not as high speed as the vendors would have you think. As the market settles down, vendor claims will settle down as well and become more reliable.

Network throughput for standard PC clients to a standard PC server (both using an ISA bus) ranges from 400 Kbps to 800 Kbps. Notice that this performance range is easily tested and has been verified by many independent sources. Even the fastest CD-ROM drive performs near the bottom of this scale.

Of course, the systems at both ends of the file copy and installation process at hand are both servers, and should have even higher throughput than standard ISA bus machines. If you are adding a server today for more than two dozen clients, it should support either EISA or PCI bus cards. This boosts the network throughput even more, well over 1 Mbps. These numbers are with standard 10 Mbps Ethernet; your mileage may vary, but it will probably vary upwards.

The final boost of performance comes with the file caching done by NetWare. Even when reading a slow CD-ROM drive, NetWare reads file blocks beyond the information needed to fill the current request. The file stays in the cache of the source NetWare server, so many of the file requests by the target server will be serviced by server RAM rather than server CD-ROM drive. If you have copied the installation CD onto the server hard drive, the performance boost by file caching is even more pronounced. Server hard drives are much faster than the fastest CD-ROM drive.

The moral of this story is simple: install from a remote server if possible. In fact, installation across the network is preferred.

server is by copying everything from a workstation with a CD-ROM drive. There are more than 5000 files or directories that collectively use about 125 MB of space, so make sure you have room on your target server before you start. The copying process will take a while, so start at lunch or at the end of the day.

The DynaText viewers and files are on a second CD-ROM. The total space if both CD-ROM disks are copied to a server hard disk is about 185 MB.

Here are the requirements for making a copy of the NetWare 4.10 CD-ROM on a different NetWare server:

- An existing NetWare server with 125 MB disk space available
- The target server configured as a NetWare workstation
- A workstation with a CD-ROM that can read ISO 9660 formatted CD-ROM disks
- A functioning network supporting all three machines

Follow these steps to make the copy:

1. Log in to the host server with proper rights to create a subdirectory.
2. Change to the root directory of NetWare volume (not SYS: unless you have plenty of disk space available afterwards).
3. Type **MD NETWARE** (or give it a more descriptive name, such as **NW411-CD**).
4. Type **CD NETWARE**.
5. Type **NCOPY D: /S /E /V** (assuming D: is the CD-ROM drive).

The switch options on the NCOPY command are /S for subdirectory, /E for empty directories, and /V to verify. Use NCOPY rather than XCOPY so that all the NetWare attributes on the files are copied properly.

COPYING THE INSTALLATION FLOPPY DISKS If you have the floppy diskette installation pack, all is not lost. You can copy the diskettes to a NetWare server and install other servers from this host server. Use the same procedure as outlined for copying the CD-ROM. Copy each and every diskette with the same command (use the DOS F3 key to repeat the last command).

Once the files from the CD-ROM are on your host server, you can begin installation. The target server must load the files necessary to log in to the host server. This requires loading the NetWare client shells or the NetWare DOS Redirector used by your other NetWare clients to connect to the server. Older NetWare shells using the NETX client files will work for installation, but they can't use NDS resources, so you will need to upgrade them. Create client diskettes on the server or use the CD-ROM on a workstation and run the INSTALL.EXE file from the CLIENT\DOSWIN directory to configure the server-to-be as a NetWare client.

Log in to the host server as Admin. Map a root to a drive from your workstation/server-to-be to the directory on the host server containing the NetWare 4.1x files. Next, type:

    INSTALL

INSTALL will prompt you to choose a language, with English as the default. You can now skip ahead to the "Running the INSTALL.NLM Program" section of this chapter.

Installing from a Remote CD-ROM Mounted as a NetWare Volume

For those of you with existing NetWare servers already containing CD-ROM drives, your job is simple. Place the NetWare 4.1x CD-ROM in the drive, mount the new volume, and then any NetWare client can reference that volume.

Once again, the server-to-be must be configured as a workstation. Log in from the target server as SUPERVISOR (for NetWare 3.x) or Admin (for NetWare 4.x) and make connection to the CD-ROM volume. Then follow these steps to mount the NetWare 4.10 installation CD-ROM on a remote server:

1. Dismount the current CD-ROM disk by typing **CD DISMOUNT** *volume-name* and remove the disk.

2. Place the NetWare 4.1x Installation CD-ROM disk in the drive.

3. Type **CD MOUNT NW411**.

4. From the workstation/server-to-be, log in to the host server as SUPERVISOR (for NetWare 3.x) or Admin (for NetWare 4.x) or equivalent.

5. Map a drive letter to the CD-ROM volume by typing **MAP N HOST_SERVER\NW410**.

6. Change directory to your language of choice (English in this example) by typing **CD NW410\INSTALL\ENGLISH**.

7. Type **INSTALL**.

This procedure brings you to the same point in the installation process as if the CD-ROM was inside the target server. You can now to continue to the next section.

Running the INSTALL.NLM Program

THE INSTALL.NLM PROGRAM does all the work for installation, and later for modification of many server and NDS parameters. You will use this program quite a bit as your network gets up and running.

Figure 2.4 shows the beginning screen that appears when you run the INSTALL batch file program. Notice that SFT III is included in the initial setup screen. We'll talk about SFT III later in the book (Chapter 16).

FIGURE 2.4
Beginning the installation process

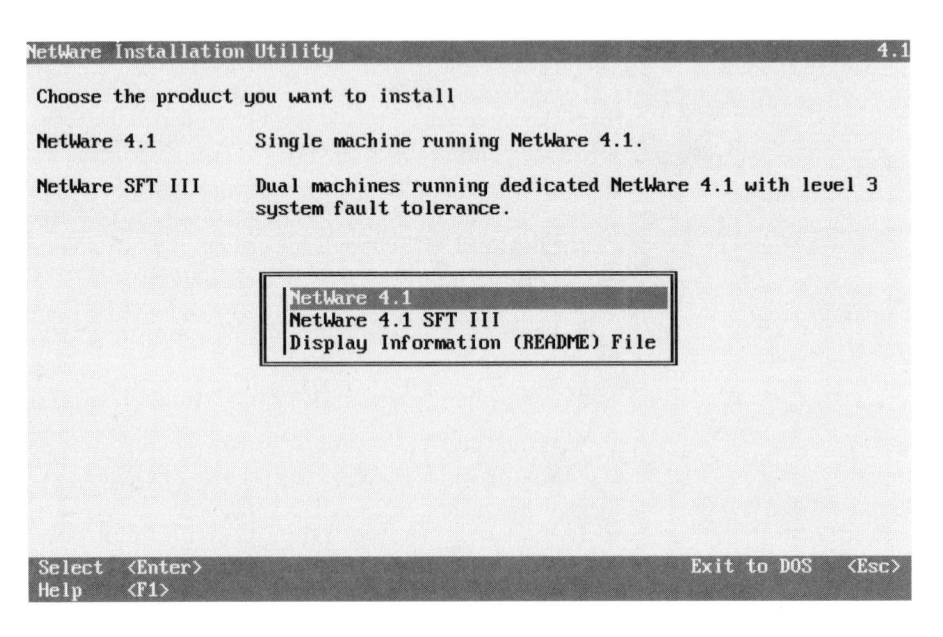

```
NetWare Installation Utility                                            4.1

Choose the product you want to install

NetWare 4.1           Single machine running NetWare 4.1.

NetWare SFT III       Dual machines running dedicated NetWare 4.1 with level 3
                      system fault tolerance.


                          ┌─────────────────────────────────┐
                          │ NetWare 4.1                     │
                          │ NetWare 4.1 SFT III             │
                          │ Display Information (README) File│
                          └─────────────────────────────────┘




Select   <Enter>                                        Exit to DOS   <Esc>
Help     <F1>
```

The steps you take with the server-to-be machine are:

- Boot DOS on the PC (without memory managers or other resident programs)
- Load CD-ROM drivers (if needed)
- Type INSTALL to start the batch file

It seems odd, but your PC technically becomes a server the minute the SERVER.EXE program is loaded. This program is the kernel of NetWare. Pick your choice of language for the server by highlighting the line you wish (most likely, the only line you can read) and keep going.

Of course, loading the SERVER.EXE program without any of the disk drivers and LAN connection software makes a useless server. As it sits now, the server can't communicate with anyone or anything else across the network. These details are configured during this section of the installation process. If you are loading the system from a remote server, the installation program will know which LAN drivers are being used. You will have the option to verify the drivers and accept them for the new server.

Many things in life force a choice: you can make it powerful or you can make it easy, but not both. NetWare changed the rules here with version 4: you now have an industrial-strength, enterprise operating system with an easy, quick setup option.

Customers using NetWare 4.1x as their first NetWare server, or those who have a typical LAN application, can now use the Simple Installation process to configure the server for their environment. The other choices are Custom Installation and Upgrade to NetWare 4.1x. The options are explained, albeit poorly, by the installation program, as shown in Figure 2.5.

The Simple Installation Method

If you choose the Simple Installation method, the installation program makes a variety of assumptions about your server and your network:

- There is an existing DOS partition on the server hard disk of 15 MB.
- DOS is installed on the hard disk.
- The server will boot from the DOS partition on the hard disk, not a floppy.

FIGURE 2.5

The first fork in the installation road

```
NetWare Installation Utility                                            4.1

Select the type of installation you are performing

Simple Installation      Install NetWare 4.1 on a new machine, allowing the
                         installation program to make most choices.
                         Note: Press <F1> to see the choices that will be made
                         for you.

Custom Installation      Install Netware 4.1 on a new machine, making choices
                         for such things as code page, network number,
                         installation directory, etc.

Upgrade to NetWare 4.1   Upgrade a machine that currently has either NetWare
                         3.1x or 4.x to NetWare 4.1


                     ┌─────────────────────────────────────┐
                     │ Simple installation of NetWare 4.1  │
                     │ Custom installation of NetWare 4.1  │
                     │ Upgrade NetWare 3.1x or 4.x         │
                     └─────────────────────────────────────┘


Select    <Enter>                                  Exit to DOS      <Alt-F10>
Help      <F1>                                     Previous screen  <Esc>
```

- All disk space not partitioned for DOS will be available to NetWare.
- Each server hard disk will contain a NetWare volume.
- NetWare will assign randomly generated IPX network numbers.
- STARTUP.NCF and AUTOEXEC.NCF will not be modified.
- The standard U.S. keyboard layout is used.
- IPX is the only network protocol used.
- NDS will be installed with a single Organization container for all objects.

These settings are used for the initial installation only; you are not bound to the choices forever. Most important, support for TCP/IP and AppleTalk protocols can be easily added later. NetWare 4.1*x* includes plenty of tools for modifying your NDS structure, so that structure can grow and change over time.

> *Speaking of NDS, the Simple Installation choice will be continued when you add a second server to the network. When the second server comes up to this installation point, it will ask if the Simple Installation model should be followed for the current server being installed. NetWare engineers, after much internal discussion, figured the limits for a "simple" installation as 20 servers and/or 1000 users. Since most NetWare networks are within that range, the basic setup will help many customers get started with NetWare 4.1x and grow into the enterprise-wide features as they are ready. No one is forcing NDS on you.*

If you choose the Simple Installation choice, you can skip the sections in the remainder of this chapter that have "Custom" in their headings.

Unix Connectivity Support

There are a variety of file "sets" (special upgrade files and the like) included with NetWare 4.1x to support Unix connectivity. The Simple Installation does not include all the available file sets, although you can install any of these sets later. The file sets that are copied to the server during installation are the System files and DOS, OS/2, and MS Windows utilities. Those that are not copied are the Unix utilities, client upgrade files, and upgrade and migration files.

The Custom Installation Method

If the Simple Installation parameters are a little too restrictive for your system, the Custom Installation choice is the right one. This installation isn't more difficult than the Simple method, just more flexible. If your NDS setup includes more than one container, the Custom Installation process gives you the flexibility to place your server in your choice of locations. You can set time zone parameters, rather than just reading the internal PC clock.

The Custom method allows you to set any or all of the default values for the following:

- Boot the server from a hard disk or floppy boot diskette.
- Have volumes that span multiple hard disks.
- Assign a specific IPX network number yourself.
- Partition hard disks with multiple partitions.

- Mirror hard disks for fault tolerance and performance.
- Specify volume names.
- Add support for multiple processors.
- Edit the STARTUP.NCF and AUTOEXEC.NCF files.
- Change the country code, code page, and keyboard mapping.
- Add support for nonrouting TCP/IP and AppleTalk as well as IPX protocols.
- Modify time zone parameters and container placement in NDS.

Usually, you will choose the Custom Installation option because you need to support a different hard disk arrangement or you have larger naming directory requirements. If any of the features in the previous list are appealing, choose the Custom Installation.

As with the Simple Installation, none of the choices you make during installation are binding and restrictive (except for three volume-specific settings). You may rework your server configuration files several ways after the network is up and running. You may also change your NDS setup by adding, modifying, or deleting objects.

Naming Your Server

As soon as you choose Simple or Custom installation, the program will ask for the name of your server. Some people warn you to choose a short, easily typed name. The default used to be FS1 in earlier versions of NetWare, translating to thousands of servers named FS1.

With NetWare 4.1x, there are few places a user will need to type the server name. In both DOS and MS Windows utilities, the names of all available servers are shown in a pick list. Choosing a server means either moving the highlight bar and pressing Enter in DOS, or clicking with the mouse in MS Windows. No typing involved.

Pick a name that means something to your users, say SALES1 or 4_FLOOR or EMAIL1 or (if you're a Unix naming convention fan) ZEUS, THOR, or DRAGON1. Most users do not interact with the file server, but with the volumes on that server; as in SALES1_SYS or DRAGON1_SYS. You can change the name of the server later, but that may create a bit of work if you have referenced the server SYS: volume in login scripts. Rather than go to that trouble, you can just provide an alias for the volume, or reference certain directories with a simple directory map name. We'll get to aliases, directory maps, and login scripts later; this is just to let you know that naming a server is less restrictive than it used to be.

> *It's tough to tell your CEO his main server is BOINGO.*

The official name instructions are 2 to 47 alphanumeric characters, including hyphen and underscore. No spaces are allowed; use the underscore or hyphen. And go with the urge to use meaningful names for your servers. It's tough to tell your CEO his main server is BOINGO.

Setting Your Internal IPX Network Number (Custom)

Each NetWare server needs a "virtual" network ID for the internal VIRTUAL_LAN frame type. This number has nothing to do with the server name, hard disk, or file system.

The internal IPX network number (called the internal network number in NetWare 3.*x*) provides a unique reference number for the server operating system. Since your server may have either two (or more) NICs or support more protocols than just IPX/SPX, the internal IPX network number helps the operating system know which packets go to which NIC using which frame type.

The number must be unique, and it must be between 1 and FFFFFFFE (hex). The installation program will supply a random number and ask you to accept that number. Unless you like to be cute (BABE is a popular address), take the recommendation. The number cannot match any other internal or external IPX network number, so don't be cute more than once.

There is a space on the worksheet in the Installation manual for this number. In rare cases, you may need this number, so write it down. You're supposed to have a pad and pencil beside the server during installation, remember?

Copying Server Files to the DOS Partition (Custom)

You may place your server boot files anywhere in the DOS partition you have on your server. The default is C:\NWSERVER, and this is where the Simple Installation method places them.

The files include the primary SERVER.EXE program, the disk drivers, and assorted NLM programs necessary to start the operating system talking to the hard disk and get the server started. Once these two systems start cooperating, the server comes up and the other files are read from the SYS:SYSTEM area. Figure 2.6 shows the progress bar across the top of the screen and the list of files scrolling by in the bottom portion.

FIGURE 2.6

File copy to your new server in progress

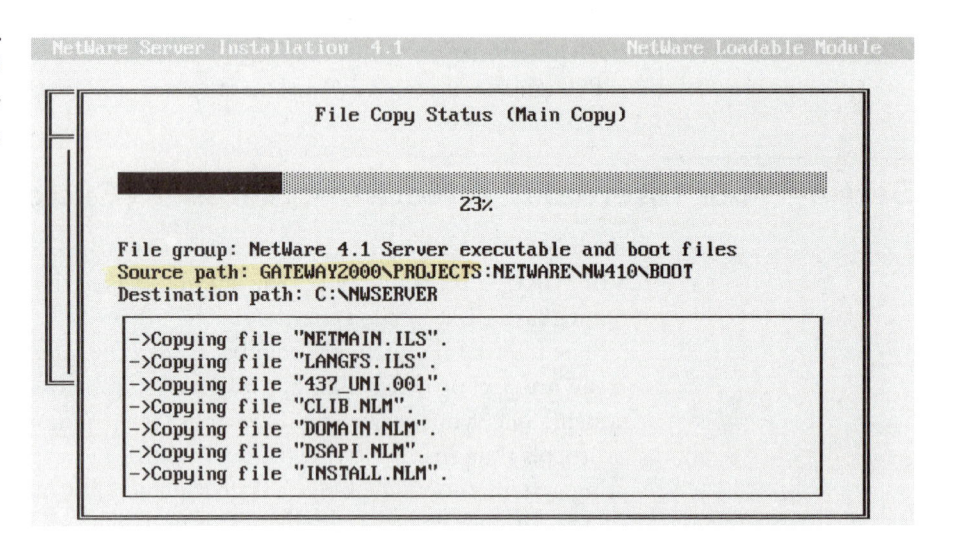

```
NetWare Server Installation 4.1                    NetWare Loadable Module

                    ┌──────────────────────────────────────────┐
                    │       File Copy Status (Main Copy)       │
                    │                                          │
                    │  ████████████▒▒▒▒▒▒▒▒▒▒▒▒▒▒▒▒▒▒▒▒▒▒▒▒▒▒  │
                    │                    23%                   │
                    │                                          │
                    │  File group: NetWare 4.1 Server executable and boot files
                    │  Source path: GATEWAY2000\PROJECTS:NETWARE\NW410\BOOT
                    │  Destination path: C:\NWSERVER
                    │                                          │
                    │  ┌────────────────────────────────────┐  │
                    │  │ ->Copying file "NETMAIN.ILS".      │  │
                    │  │ ->Copying file "LANGFS.ILS".       │  │
                    │  │ ->Copying file "437_UNI.001".      │  │
                    │  │ ->Copying file "CLIB.NLM".         │  │
                    │  │ ->Copying file "DOMAIN.NLM".       │  │
                    │  │ ->Copying file "DSAPI.NLM".        │  │
                    │  │ ->Copying file "INSTALL.NLM".      │  │
                    │  └────────────────────────────────────┘  │
                    └──────────────────────────────────────────┘
```

Notice the destination of the files being copied: C:\NWSERVER. You can't see here, but the files whiz by when copied from another server. Notice the source path is a server named GATEWAY2000 and a volume named PROJECTS.

Keyboard Mapping and File Name Format Choices (Custom)

With the Custom Installation option, you can choose different keyboard mapping and country codes. The Language Configuration screen offers choices for the Country Code, the Code Page, and Keyboard Mapping. The default choices are the safest by far in the United States. Each highlighted entry offers choices when you press the Enter key.

The next screen offers you a choice of DOS Filename Format or the NetWare Filename Format. Although you might expect the NetWare Filename

Format would be preferred, the installation program goes to the trouble to say RECOMMENDED for the DOS Filename Format to erase any confusion.

The NetWare format, which matches that used for NetWare 3.x, allows non-DOS characters in file names. This caused a few problems before, and causes more problems when considering multiple-language support. Workstations using NETX shells, rather than the recommended VLM files and the DOS Redirector, can place non-DOS characters in file names even on NetWare 4.10 servers. By selecting the DOS Filename Format here, that potential problem is avoided.

Adding Extra SET Commands (Custom)

SET commands are used in STARTUP.NCF and AUTOEXEC.NCF to configure operating system parameters. NetWare 4.1x's default parameters are designed to provide the best performance for most systems, but some equipment in the server demands particular parameters to work properly.

The one of interest has to do with ASPI (Adaptec SCSI Peripheral Interface) devices in EISA servers. Some EISA servers have trouble seeing memory above 16 MB and leaving buffer space under 16 MB for device drivers that don't work with the higher memory ranges. The suggestion from the installation program is to add:

```
SET RESERVED BUFFERS BELOW 16MB =200
```

to handle those drivers with memory difficulty.

Most SET commands are never changed, which is good because there are lots of them, mostly dealing with arcane details deep inside the NetWare operating system. The server utility SERVMAN allows a menu-driven interface to control most SET parameters, so you don't need to worry about your SET commands right now.

Starting Your Server Automatically (Custom)

While the Simple Installation makes the decision for you, the Custom Installation asks whether you want the server to start every time the PC is started. This is done by adding a few lines to the PC AUTOEXEC.BAT file. Nothing fancy—just moving to the NWSERVER directory and running SERVER.

The default AUTOEXEC.BAT listing does not start the server when the PC boots. If the NetWare operating system doesn't start automatically, someone must physically go to the server to start NetWare.

Disk Driver Setup

NetWare needs to know what type of disk and disk controller is in the server. There are quite a few controller definitions included with NetWare. You'll see a list of "Red Box CD-ROM Drivers" in the back of the Installation manual. New drivers certified by Novell will be available through technical support channels, such as NetWire and Novell's WWW (World Wide Web) server.

Vendors that add NetWare support for disk controllers can include the proper drivers on a diskette. The installation program allows you to add vendor drivers to your system, as shown in Figure 2.7. Here's a NetWare convention: press the Insert key to add something or open a pick list. In this case, pressing the Insert key will pop open a window asking the source drive of the new driver. Place the disk in the server's floppy drive, and the installation program will pick up the driver and save it on the server.

FIGURE 2.7
Installing disk drivers

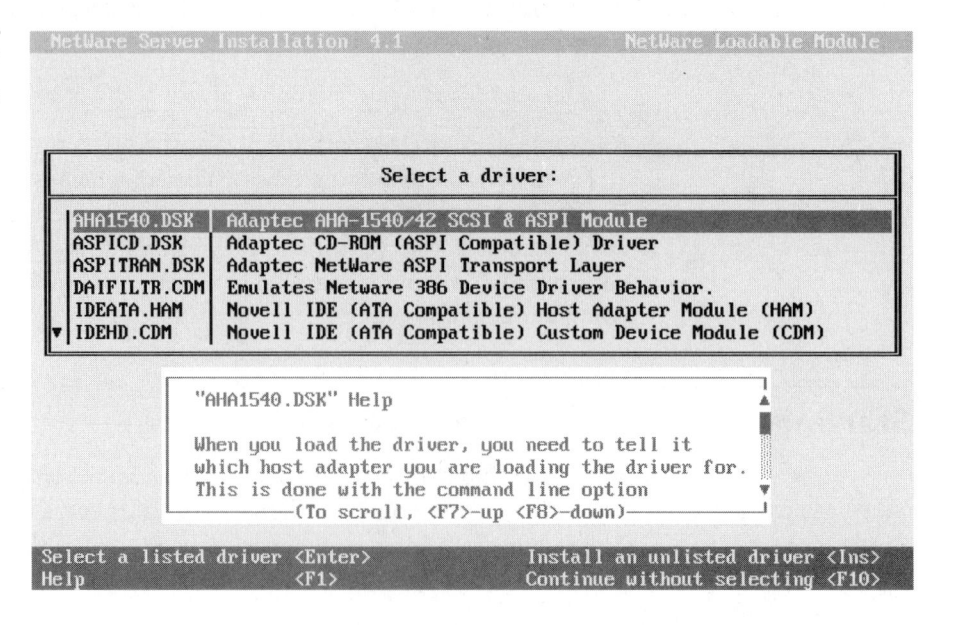

```
NetWare Server Installation  4.1                    NetWare Loadable Module

                          ┌─────────────────────────────────────────────┐
                          │              Select a driver:               │
                          ├─────────────────────────────────────────────┤
                          │ AHA1540.DSK  │ Adaptec AHA-1540/42 SCSI & ASPI Module        │
                          │ ASPICD.DSK   │ Adaptec CD-ROM (ASPI Compatible) Driver       │
                          │ ASPITRAN.DSK │ Adaptec NetWare ASPI Transport Layer          │
                          │ DAIFILTR.CDM │ Emulates Netware 386 Device Driver Behavior.  │
                          │ IDEATA.HAM   │ Novell IDE (ATA Compatible) Host Adapter Module (HAM) │
                          │▼IDEHD.CDM    │ Novell IDE (ATA Compatible) Custom Device Module (CDM) │
                          └─────────────────────────────────────────────┘
                              ┌──────────────────────────────────────┐
                              │ "AHA1540.DSK" Help                   │▲
                              │                                      │█
                              │ When you load the driver, you need to tell it │
                              │ which host adapter you are loading the driver for. │
                              │ This is done with the command line option │▼
                              └──────(To scroll, <F7>-up <F8>-down)──┘

Select a listed driver <Enter>         Install an unlisted driver <Ins>
Help                    <F1>           Continue without selecting <F10>
```

Running the INSTALL.NLM Program   97

The highlighted entry, an Adaptec 1540 SCSI adapter, controls both the hard drive and the dual Micro Design SCSI CD-ROM drives here in the ALTOS486 server in the lab.

Troubleshooting SCSI Conflict Problems during Installation

Unfortunately, too much going on through one controller during installation may cause problems. When installing NetWare from a CD-ROM to a hard disk, with both devices connected to the same adapter, some users have had their keyboards freeze. If this happens to you, it indicates the DOS drivers on the system are getting in the way of NetWare. You must eliminate all references to the CD-ROM drivers in your CONFIG.SYS and AUTOEXEC.BAT files, start the NetWare server, and let NetWare control both the hard disk drive and the CD-ROM drive.

Here is the procedure for dealing with SCSI conflict problems during installation:

1. Press Alt+Esc until you reach the console prompt (:).

2. Type **DOWN**.

3. Type **EXIT**.

4. Remove CD-ROM drivers from AUTOEXEC.BAT and CONFIG.SYS.

5. Save the files and reboot your system.

6. If NetWare doesn't start, type **CD\NWSERVER** (the location of your server boot files).

7. Type **SERVER**.

8. For Adaptec controllers, load the appropriate disk driver (such as AHA1540.DSK), then type **LOAD ASPICD** or **LOAD CDNASPI** from the console prompt.

9. From the console, type the following commands, pressing Enter after each one:

    ```
    LOAD C:NWPA.NLM.
    LOAD C:CDROM.NLM
    CD MOUNT NW411
    LOAD C:\NWSERVER\INSTALL
    ```

10. Pick up the Installation program where your left off and continue.

For the record, the ALTOS486 machine with the Adaptec 1540 driving both the hard disk and the dual Micro Design CD-ROM system had no problems during installation. You probably won't have problems either, but if you do, your problems are now over. Well, at least your keyboard lockup problem is over.

Monolithic Drivers versus the New NetWare Peripheral Architecture

Notice in Figure 2.7 the last two entries in the Select a Driver window:

```
Novell IDE (ATA Compatible) Host Adapter Module (HAM)
Novell IDE (ATA Compatible) Custom Device Module (CDM)
```

These are new in NetWare 4.1x. They are designed to replace the drivers with the DSK extension.

The DSK drivers are *monolithic* drivers, which means that a single driver controls the disk controller and all devices attached to that disk controller. The driver is the interface between the NetWare operating system and the adapter hardware and all the devices attached to the hardware adapter. The monolithic disk drivers are listed in Table 2.6.

TABLE 2.6 NetWare Monolithic Disk Drivers

SERVER ARCHITECTURE	CONTROLLER	DISK DRIVER TO LOAD
ISA	AT, IDE (ATA)	ISADISK, IDE
MicroChannel	ESDI, IBM SCSI	PS2ESDI, PS2SCSI
EISA	AT, IDE (ATA), EISA vendor proprietary	ISADISK, IDE, see vendor

There's nothing wrong with this approach. It's been working for years. When you add a new CD-ROM drive or tape backup unit to the SCSI adapter, everything will be fine, as long as the old driver supports the new hardware.

If the old driver doesn't support the new hardware, suddenly you must make a choice: scramble around to find a new driver that controls everything, or give up your new toy. Not a good choice.

This is exactly the scenario NPA (NetWare Peripheral Architecture) aims to eliminate. Rather than a single driver that controls all devices, NPA drivers are in two parts: HAMs and CDMs. HAM (Host Adapter Module) drivers control the interaction between the NetWare operating system and the physical host adapter plugged into the server bus. These drivers use the extension HAM. There will be one HAM driver for each adapter. CDM (Custom Device Module) drivers control the devices connected to the host adapters. There may be multiple CDM drivers for a single host adapter, since each device connected to the host adapter must have a specific driver. Table 2.7 shows the details.

TABLE 2.7 NPA Disk Drivers, HAMs, and CDMs

SERVER ARCHITECTURE	CONTROLLER	HAM TO LOAD	CDM TO LOAD
ISA	AT, IDE (ATA)	IDEHAM.HAM	HDIDE.CDM (for hard disk)
MicroChannel	IBM SCSI	PS2SCSI.HAM	HDSCSI.CDM (hard disk)
			CDSCSI.CDM (CD-ROM drive)
			MOSCSI.CDM (magneto-optical drive)
			SCSI2TP.CDM (tape device)
EISA	AT, IDE (ATA)	IDEHAM.HAM	HDIDE.CDM (hard disk)
EISA	EISA proprietary	See vendor	See vendor

The NWPA.NLM must be loaded before any of the HAM or CDM drivers.

If you never have more than one device connected to an adapter, this won't gain you anything. If you have ever told your boss the new tape drive he just spent thousands of dollars for won't work until you can find a new driver, you can appreciate the advantages of modular device drivers.

The NWPA.NLM driver must be loaded before the HAM and CDM drivers. The NWPA.NLM provides the interface between the NPA and the Media Manager. The Media Manager is the storage management layer of the NetWare 4.x operating system, providing a storage management interface between applications and storage device drivers.

New drivers will show up first with the devices they control. Remember to use the Insert key to redirect the installation program to look for new driver files in the floppy drive.

Once the disk driver is selected, you will have the chance to verify the parameters for that driver. Any changes to adapter settings should be made here. Once the parameters are set, you will have a chance to repeat the process for a second driver.

> **WARNING**
>
> Beware of problems upgrading old disk drivers. Sometimes the installation program will rename files, causing installation to fail. Make sure, if you have an IDE disk controller, that the IDE.DSK file hasn't been renamed to IDEATA.HAM or something similar. If it has, rename it back to IDE.DSK, and things will work better.

If you have two disks connected to a single host adapter, you need only one DSK driver. If you have two adapters, you need two drivers. If you have an adapter that uses the new HAM extension, you need one driver for the adapter, as well as a CDM driver for each device connected to that adapter.

LAN Driver Configuration

Like the disk controllers, the NIC needs a driver. Network adapter drivers have LAN as their file name extension. The next step in the installation process is choosing and configuring this LAN driver.

You must have at least one network adapter in the server for it to communicate with network clients and other servers. You may have as many as four LAN adapters in a server. They may all be the same type of NIC, such as Ethernet, or you may have four different topologies represented. It's possible to have Ethernet, Token Ring, Arcnet, and a WAN connector in one server. Possible, but not likely or practical.

Looking much like the corresponding screen for the disk drivers, the Choose the Server Drivers screen is shown in Figure 2.8. The help window in the bottom section of the screen provides some basic information about the LAN driver highlighted in the box above.

Once again, drivers not provided by the NetWare installation program can be loaded. Press the Insert key (instruction on the right of the bottom strip) and load the vendor-supplied disk into the floppy drive.

NetWare commands great respect among network adapter vendors because of the large market share. Many drivers are supplied by Novell as part of the installation process. Many vendors make compatible cards that work with these drivers, especially the NE2000 card.

FIGURE 2.8

Choosing your network adapter driver

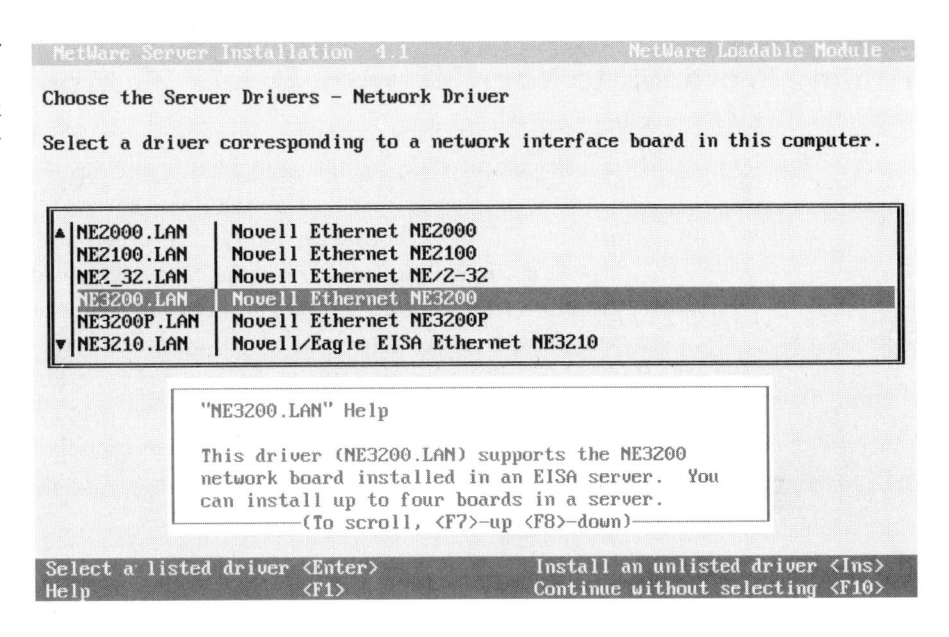

```
NetWare Server Installation 4.1                    NetWare Loadable Module

Choose the Server Drivers - Network Driver

Select a driver corresponding to a network interface board in this computer.

     ┌─────────────────────────────────────────────────────────────┐
   ▲ │ NE2000.LAN   │ Novell Ethernet NE2000                       │
     │ NE2100.LAN   │ Novell Ethernet NE2100                       │
     │ NE2_32.LAN   │ Novell Ethernet NE/2-32                      │
     │ NE3200.LAN   │ Novell Ethernet NE3200                       │
     │ NE3200P.LAN  │ Novell Ethernet NE3200P                      │
   ▼ │ NE3210.LAN   │ Novell/Eagle EISA Ethernet NE3210            │
     └─────────────────────────────────────────────────────────────┘

              ┌──────────────────────────────────────────────┐
              │ "NE3200.LAN" Help                            │
              │                                              │
              │ This driver (NE3200.LAN) supports the NE3200 │
              │ network board installed in an EISA server. You│
              │ can install up to four boards in a server.   │
              │          (To scroll, <F7>-up <F8>-down)      │
              └──────────────────────────────────────────────┘

Select a listed driver <Enter>        Install an unlisted driver <Ins>
Help                  <F1>            Continue without selecting <F10>
```

One interface card will have different drivers for use in a NetWare client or a NetWare server. Make sure you verify that a card vendor provides a driver for more than just "NetWare." If it goes into the server, the vendor must provide a server driver as well.

The installation program offers you a summary screen before continuing installation. If you forget to make a change and continue, you can come back after the server installation is finished.

There really is a reason for the "Continue without selecting <F10>" option in the bottom-right corner of Figure 2.8. For testing software separate from the network connections, such as NLMs that execute on the server, you may not want any packets leaving the server. Unix systems offer a "null" driver to start the networking software without a configured adapter; this is NetWare's equivalent.

The next screen or two adds the IPX protocol to the network adapters you chose. This is a process called *binding*, as in the command:

```
BIND IPX 3C509_1_E83 NET=1
```

This will be written into the server's AUTOEXEC.NCF file, starting the network adapter and binding IPX to the adapter so your server can talk to the rest of the NetWare world. Don't change anything on these screens, just press the Enter key.

Adding Protocols to Your Network Driver (Custom)

The Simple Installation process configures only IPX for your server. The Custom option allows you to add TCP/IP and AppleTalk protocols.

Figure 2.9 shows the cursor in the check square to add TCP/IP procotols to the 3Com 3C509 Ethernet card in the file server. The middle box in the screen shows the current parameters for the card, which are the default values.

If you choose to add TCP/IP, another box will pop open asking you to set the IP address and subnet mask for this node. If you are not sure what these are, your Unix administrator will provide those addresses for you. If your Unix friends are not available, do not make up an address and plug it in. If you do so, your Unix friends may not be so friendly because wrong addresses can play havoc with IP networks. You can add TCP/IP support later.

FIGURE 2.9

Your server adds another protocol

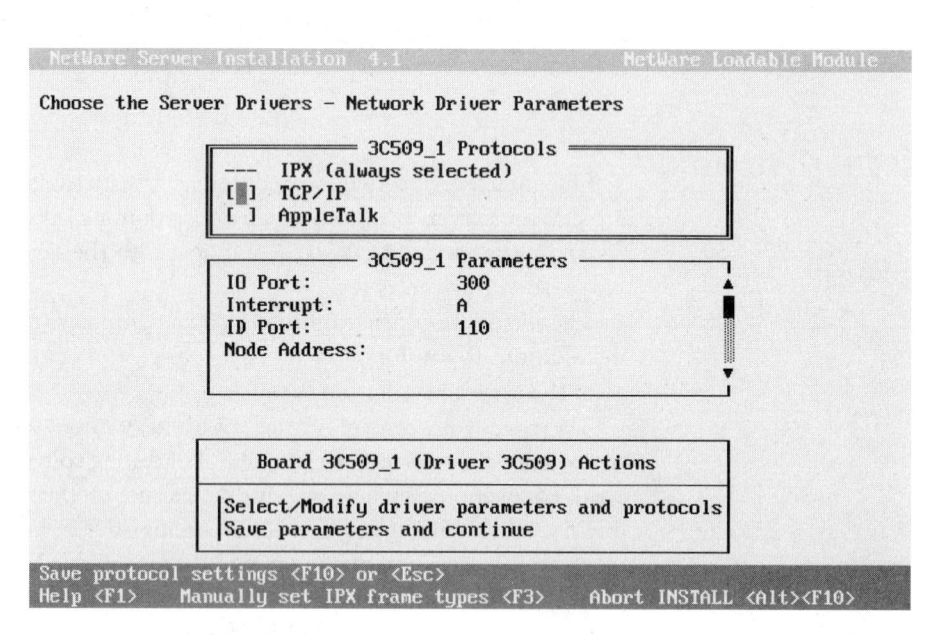

```
NetWare Server Installation  4.1                      NetWare Loadable Module

Choose the Server Drivers - Network Driver Parameters

                        ┌──────── 3C509_1 Protocols ────────┐
                        │ ───  IPX (always selected)        │
                        │ [■]  TCP/IP                       │
                        │ [ ]  AppleTalk                    │
                        └───────────────────────────────────┘

                        ┌──────── 3C509_1 Parameters ───────┐
                        │ IO Port:           300            │
                        │ Interrupt:         A              │
                        │ ID Port:           110            │
                        │ Node Address:                     │
                        └───────────────────────────────────┘

                        ┌───────────────────────────────────┐
                        │  Board 3C509_1 (Driver 3C509) Actions │
                        │                                   │
                        │ Select/Modify driver parameters and protocols │
                        │ Save parameters and continue      │
                        └───────────────────────────────────┘

Save protocol settings <F10> or <Esc>
Help <F1>    Manually set IPX frame types <F3>    Abort INSTALL <Alt><F10>
```

Notice the middle instruction on the bottom line of Figure 2.9 telling you how you can manually set the IPX frame type. This line appears only when you move the cursor to the one of the top two windows on the screen. There's no reason for that now; the binding screens coming up will do that for you as the network links become active.

Finishing this extra protocol screen dumps you back into the regular network driver process. You will have the choices of modifying the settings or continuing. You will then verify protocol binding for each installed card and selected protocol. Just press the Enter key.

Disk Configuration (Custom)

Now that the operating system can communicate with the disk, you get to configure the disk any way you want. The Simple Installation bypasses all this, using all the disk space except for the DOS partition for NetWare. If you have a large disk and wish to have more than one volume on it, you need to use the Custom Installation. The same goes if you wish to have one volume cover more than one disk.

Folks using the Simple Installation method will rejoin us at the "Installing the NetWare License Software" section. Those using Custom Installation can skip any of the following sections and move directly to the "Installing the NetWare License Software" as well. Just because you need to configure one detail doesn't obligate you to configure every single choice.

A Partition Isn't a Volume

Important: there is a difference between partitions and volumes. A *partition* of a hard disk is a portion that the operating system treats as a separate drive.

DOS supports multiple partitions on a drive, but only one can be the primary, bootable partition. DOS hard disks, like the ones in a NetWare server, can have multiple extended DOS and non-DOS partitions.

Only one NetWare partition can exist on a hard disk. Boot disks have a DOS partition along with a NetWare partition. Imagine the disk as a pizza, with one slice DOS and the rest NetWare. Non-boot disks in the server, whether internal or part of an external disk system, have one NetWare partition filling the entire disk.

Volumes, on the other hand, are logical portions of disk space created and controlled by the NetWare operating system. There can be multiple volumes per partition, or volumes may span several physical disks.

NetWare Disk Partitions (Custom)

The first disk configuration option has to do with partitions. Figure 2.10 shows the Create NetWare Disk Partitions screen, offering you a choice of manually configuring your disk partitions or letting NetWare do it for you.

FIGURE 2.10

Your partition creation choices

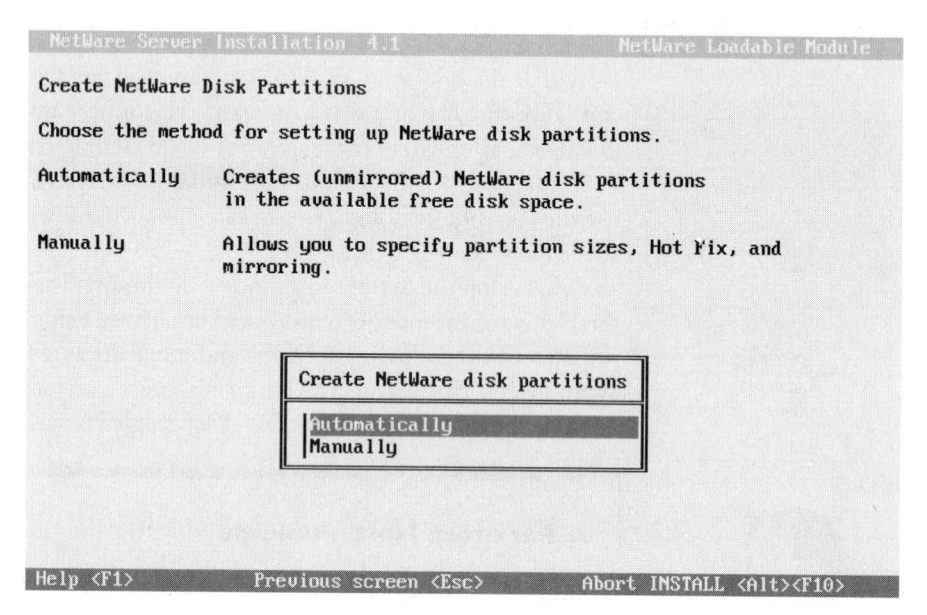

```
NetWare Server Installation 4.1                    NetWare Loadable Module

Create NetWare Disk Partitions

Choose the method for setting up NetWare disk partitions.

Automatically    Creates (unmirrored) NetWare disk partitions
                 in the available free disk space.

Manually         Allows you to specify partition sizes, Hot Fix, and
                 mirroring.


                      ┌─────────────────────────────┐
                      │ Create NetWare disk partitions │
                      ├─────────────────────────────┤
                      │ Automatically               │
                      │ Manually                    │
                      └─────────────────────────────┘



Help <F1>            Previous screen <Esc>         Abort INSTALL <Alt><F10>
```

If you choose Automatically, your next section is the Manage NetWare Volumes screen. If you choose Manual, you have (surprise) another few decisions to make before you get to your volume setup. If you plan on disk mirroring, the most common option of those listed, you must choose Manually.

Choosing the Manually option brings you to the Disk Partition Options screen. If there is a NetWare partition already on the disk for some reason (you're upgrading a system or reinstalling), the system will ask if you want to keep or delete the existing NetWare partition. Then you get to the screen shown in Figure 2.11.

FIGURE 2.11

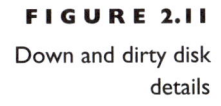

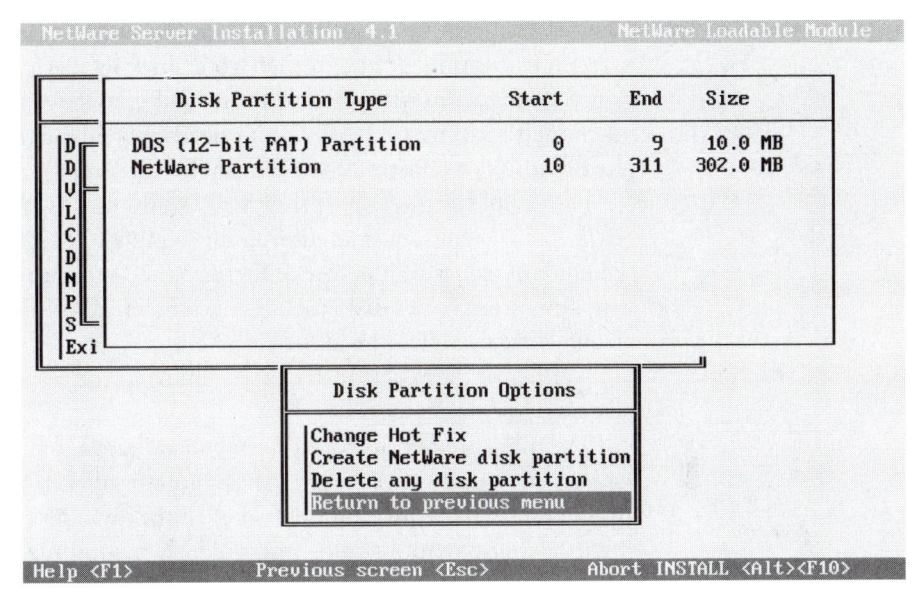

Down and dirty disk details

```
NetWare Server Installation 4.1                    NetWare Loadable Module

       ┌─────────────────────────────────────────────────────────┐
       │  Disk Partition Type        Start    End    Size        │
       │                                                         │
     D │  DOS (12-bit FAT) Partition    0      9    10.0 MB      │
     D │  NetWare Partition            10    311   302.0 MB      │
     U │                                                         │
     L │                                                         │
     C │                                                         │
     D │                                                         │
     N │                                                         │
     P │                                                         │
     S │                                                         │
    Exi│                                                         │
       └─────────────────────────────────────────────────────────┘
                    ┌──────────────────────────────┐
                    │    Disk Partition Options    │
                    ├──────────────────────────────┤
                    │ Change Hot Fix               │
                    │ Create NetWare disk partition│
                    │ Delete any disk partition    │
                    │ Return to previous menu      │
                    └──────────────────────────────┘

Help <F1>         Previous screen <Esc>        Abort INSTALL <Alt><F10>
```

Changing Hot Fix Settings (Custom)

Drilling down into the first choice, Change Hot Fix, allows you a chance to expand or decrease the number of disk blocks set aside. Hot Fix is a Novell utility that protects your information by marking bad spots on the hard disk as unusable. Any information already written to one of these bad spots is moved to a redirection area maintained by the Hot Fix utility. The default size of the redirection area is 2 percent of the disk space. The redirection area size can be changed, but there's little reason to go to the trouble. If you need to make the size bigger because your disk is developing more trouble areas, you need to replace your disk.

Disk Mirroring or Duplexing (Custom)

If there are two or more disks defined in your server, you are offered the chance to mirror or duplex your server drives. The Disk Mirroring Status screen shows each installed disk and its fault-tolerant status. They will be either Mirrored, Not Mirrored, or Out Of Sync.

Disk mirroring is common in NetWare servers. This is the technique of running two hard disks from one controller, and duplicating all disk writes to both disks. Disk mirroring is a fault-tolerant measure, which allows the system to continue if one of the two disks fails. Performance is improved, since information requested from the disk may be supplied by either disk. Although the mirrored disks don't need to be identical, you are obviously limited by the size constraints of the smaller disk.

Disk duplexing goes one step further and uses two disk controllers, one for each disk. This is considered even more fault-tolerant, since there are more redundant pieces of hardware. Performance is improved because disk reads are done from either disk, meaning your chances of the requested information being close to a drive head are doubled.

Neither of these options releases you from the responsibility of maintaining regular tape backups.

The disks are not mirrored during installation, of course. When visiting this screen later, an "Out Of Sync" message says mirroring has stopped and needs to be restarted by pressing the F3 key. For now, you can press the Insert key to choose your partitions to be mirrored, then continue with the installation.

> **WARNING**
>
> *You're offered a choice in the Disk Partition Options screen involving deleting a disk partition. However, the help screen says not to delete the DOS bootable partition. If you wish to change the details of an existing NetWare partition, you must first delete it, then re-create it with your new parameters.*

Managing NetWare Volumes (Custom)

The SYS: volume (and name) is mandatory. It must be on the boot disk if you have more than one disk, and it should be at least 100 MB in size. Novell recommends 75 MB as a minimum for NetWare (plus another 15 MB for the DOS partition), but if you add any of the extra files to support client installation files and the like, 75 MB is not enough. Print jobs that sit in the print queue get spooled to SYS: (unless you specify a different location), and bad things happen if a print job fills the volume.

Think about your network setup before you create volumes. You have three options for volume placement:

- **Several volumes per disk.** The advantages of this setup are that security is easy to control by volume and you have descriptive naming options, as well as better non-DOS name space support. The disadvantages are that artificial segmentation chops up available data space and it takes extra work to configure your backup system by volume.

- **One volume per disk.** This setup makes it easy to back up and restore the volume if the drive fails, but can still limit file space for large data sets.

- **One volume across two or more disks.** With this setup, there is an increase in performance since each segment will have its own disk. You'll also have unlimited file space as disks are added. However, one drive fault means restoring the entire multidisk volume.

Some companies structure the SYS: volume to hold application files. This is an easy choice, since the NetWare operating system files are already on the SYS: volume. Once configured, the SYS: volume won't need to be backed up often, since the information rarely changes.

Novell subtly encourages this idea. The next volume created has always been labeled VOL1: by default, intimating that SYS: is not really a volume, or it would be labeled number 1 in some manner.

My only concerns about this method are that applications are constantly upgraded, and each new upgrade takes more space than before. This means backup procedures should be done regularly. Since MS Windows applications often write files all over your local and server hard disk, you can't exclude the users of those applications from writing to the SYS: volume. If you write to the volume, sometimes you will need to delete from that volume. If you don't give users the ability to delete files on at least some parts of the SYS: volume, they will come to you with application problems caused by this security feature. If you do give users the ability to delete files on the SYS: volume, you need to back up that volume every single day.

The advantages of multiple volumes on a single disk include making separate volumes that support non-DOS name spaces. The long names from other operating systems (Windows 95, Macintosh, Unix, and OS/2) supported in the name spaces are controlled by extended attributes in the FAT (file allocation table). If you add, for instance, Macintosh name space support after a volume has been in use for awhile, the FAT will be fragmented as it marks the old file name locations and makes room for the new. This fragmentation will slow performance when files are read.

The backup and restore concerns come into play once again with the third option, where one volume spans two or more disks. Called *spanned* volumes (clearly enough), this method requires the entire volume to be replaced if one of

---

If you do give users the ability to delete files on the SYS: volume, you need to back up that volume every single day.

the disks crashes. For this reason, spanned volumes are excellent candidates for mirrored or duplexed drives. If one of the drives does crash, the fault-tolerance built into the system keeps the server up and working. When the drive is replaced, it merely needs to be synchronized with the remaining good drive of the pair to be ready for service once again. If the drive is big, this process may take a while, but not nearly as long as restoring files for the entire volume by tape.

If you're using the Custom Installation process, you have quite a few options for your new volumes. You can set volume block size, turn on file compression, turn on block suballocation, and migrate unused data in an orderly fashion.

First, you need to get the volume names set and the sizes configured. The first screen for this process is the Manage NetWare Volumes screen, shown in Figure 2.12. In this example, we have a small SYS: volume filling the single server disk.

FIGURE 2.12

Starting volume setup

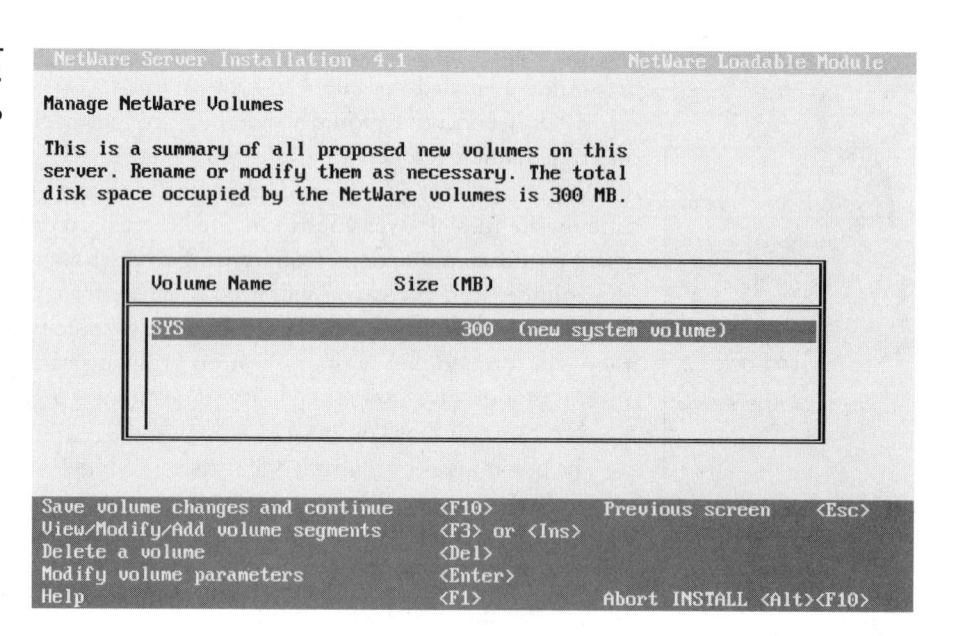

```
NetWare Server Installation 4.1                    NetWare Loadable Module
Manage NetWare Volumes

This is a summary of all proposed new volumes on this
server. Rename or modify them as necessary. The total
disk space occupied by the NetWare volumes is 300 MB.

        ┌─────────────────────────────────────────────┐
        │ Volume Name              Size (MB)          │
        ├─────────────────────────────────────────────┤
        │ SYS                      300  (new system volume) │
        │                                             │
        │                                             │
        │                                             │
        └─────────────────────────────────────────────┘

Save volume changes and continue   <F10>        Previous screen    <Esc>
View/Modify/Add volume segments    <F3> or <Ins>
Delete a volume                    <Del>
Modify volume parameters           <Enter>
Help                               <F1>         Abort INSTALL <Alt><F10>
```

Modifying Volume Segment Size (Custom)

Pressing F3 or the Insert key while highlighting the volume name on the Manage NetWare Volumes screen brings up the Volume Disk Segment List. This screen shows the volume segments on available disk devices. In our example, the only segment available is the 300 MB segment we've defined as the SYS: volume. Figure 2.13 shows the process of modifying the size of the SYS: volume. Notice that the second heading in the table is Segment No. (for Segment Number). Right now, there is only a single volume in the disk partition.

FIGURE 2.13

Making SYS: smaller

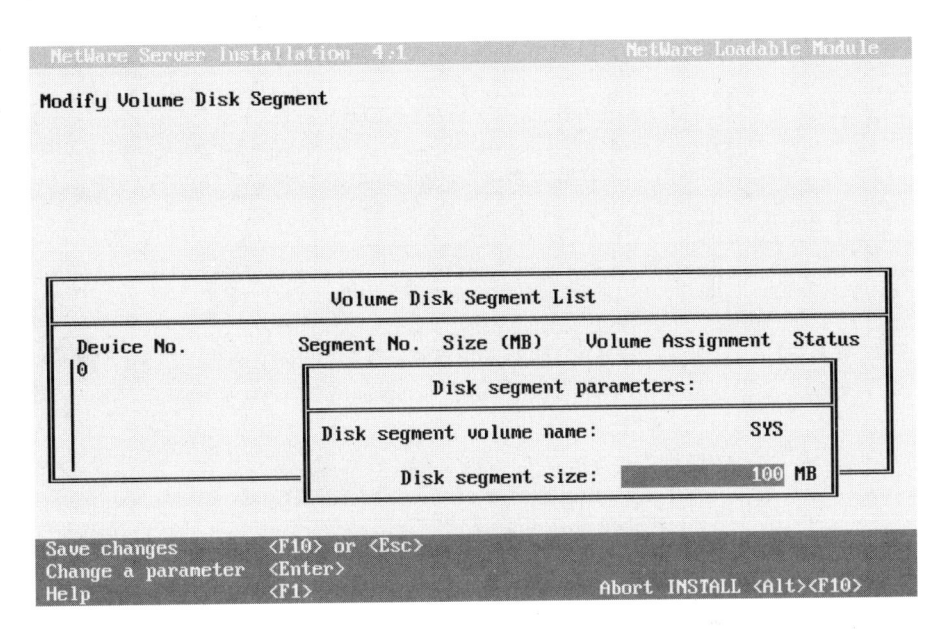

[Screen capture: NetWare Server Installation 4.1 — Modify Volume Disk Segment, showing Volume Disk Segment List with Device No. 0, and Disk segment parameters: Disk segment volume name: SYS, Disk segment size: 100 MB. Commands: Save changes <F10> or <Esc>, Change a parameter <Enter>, Help <F1>, Abort INSTALL <Alt><F10>]

Here we've made the SYS: volume 100 MB, down from the original 300 MB. Each volume can consist of up to 32 volume segments. Each volume segment can be on a separate disk. In fact, this is another way to improve performance. Multiple disks under the control of a single volume can all read in parallel, fetching information faster than any single disk can. If you could find a disk as big as 1 TB, NetWare could handle it. In fact, it could handle 32 of them, all configured as one volume.

Using the extra space we took from SYS:, we can create another volume. Figure 2.14 shows the same Volume Disk Segment List as in the previous figure, but with an addition: free space. The volume name and segment size are assigned after you press the Enter key with the highlight bar resting on the segment.

Pressing the Enter key while the free space segment is highlighted brings up another choice: should this space be used as a new volume, or make this a

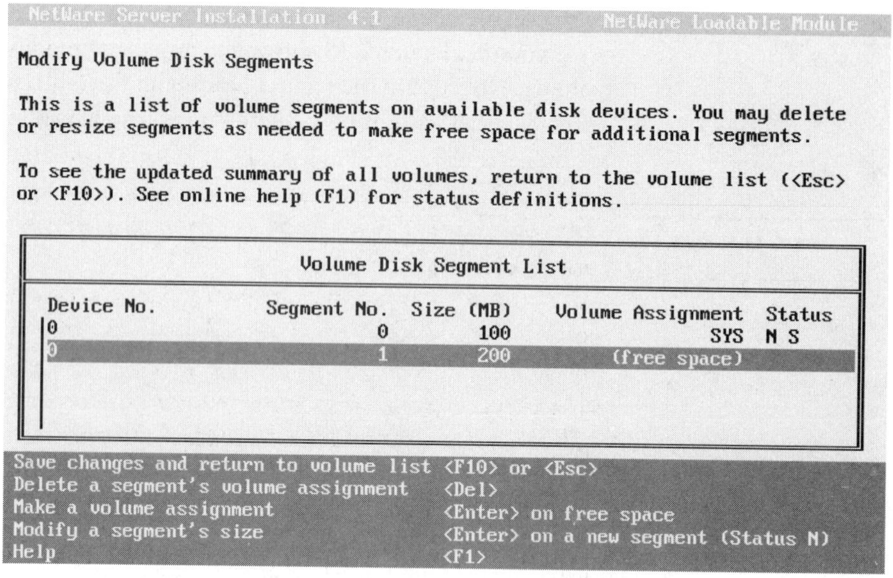

FIGURE 2.14

Preparing to turn free space into another volume

```
NetWare Server Installation 4.1                    NetWare Loadable Module

Modify Volume Disk Segments

This is a list of volume segments on available disk devices. You may delete
or resize segments as needed to make free space for additional segments.

To see the updated summary of all volumes, return to the volume list (<Esc>
or <F10>). See online help (F1) for status definitions.

    ┌─────────────────────────────────────────────────────────────────┐
    │                    Volume Disk Segment List                     │
    │ Device No.      Segment No.   Size (MB)   Volume Assignment  Status │
    │ 0                   0            100                   SYS    N S │
    │ 0                   1            200          (free space)        │
    │                                                                 │
    └─────────────────────────────────────────────────────────────────┘

Save changes and return to volume list  <F10> or <Esc>
Delete a segment's volume assignment     <Del>
Make a volume assignment                 <Enter> on free space
Modify a segment's size                  <Enter> on a new segment (Status N)
Help                                     <F1>
```

segment of another volume? This is where you make a segment on one physical disk part of a volume on another physical disk. If you make it a new volume, you again set the volume segment size, as shown back in Figure 2.13. If you decide to connect this segment to another volume, a pick list of available volumes appears. Press Enter on your choice.

Notice the Status label at the right end of the window? This indicates what kind of volume we're dealing with. The legend works as follows:

E	Existing volume
S	System volume (SYS:)
M	Mirrored volume segment
N	New volume still in memory; not yet saved to disk

Here you have another chance to think about your volumes and how they will be used. If you have four competing groups and a 1 GB disk, you may do the quick arithmetic and figure each group gets 250 MB and you're finished. After all, you don't want one group being able to snoop in the other group's volume, do you?

But that may not be the best long-term choice. With NetWare security, you can easily allow each group to have free reign in its own area, but no access to other disk areas. Plus, if you "hard-code" the four separate areas like that, it's tough to modify the arrangement. It's possible, but painful. If you have one big volume, as big as the disk, one group can get a bit larger than 250 MB without causing lots of trouble. If one of the other groups isn't using its entire space, the space is available to any other group with access privileges on the volume.

If a group moves, or gets its own separate server, having fixed volumes requires more work to reformat the volumes to fit your new arrangement. If you have one large volume, groups can come and groups can go without causing you or your other administrator buddies any grief.

In spite of the options across the bottom of the screen in Figure 2.14, you can't delete or change the name of the SYS: volume. However, we will explore setting all the parameters for the fun options you can see in Figure 2.15, which shows the Volume Information screen. Highlighting an entry, as the volume name is highlighted here, then pressing the Enter key allows you to change that entry.

FIGURE 2.15

Fun with volume details

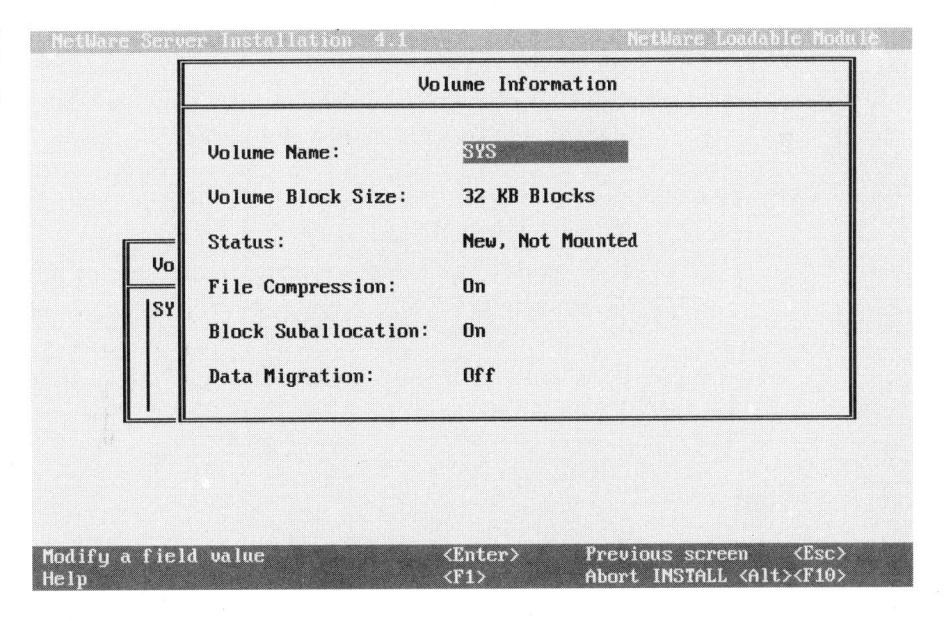

Naming Your Volumes (Custom)

If you didn't assign a name during the optional segment management, your first option is to name the volume. (As mentioned earlier, SYS: can't be changed.)

Volume names can be between 2 and 15 characters and can include all alphanumeric characters (all numbers and letters) as well as !@#$%&() but that's stretching your luck. Try something along the lines of MKTG or REPORTS for your non-SYS: volume names. The names must be unique per server, but it wouldn't hurt to keep track of them and make them unique on your whole network.

NDS will initially show all volume names as tied with their server names. In this case, the small disk drive belongs to an old 386/33 with 8 MB of RAM (yes, I know it's too little) named CLONE386. When NDS gets started, the default name for the volume shown in Figure 2.15 will be CLONE386_SYS:. You can display shorter volume names shorn of the server name if you wish; we'll get to these details later in the book (Chapter 8).

Many people caution you against long server and volume names. "Long names will frustrate your users, making them type," they say. I say hogwash. With NetWare 4.1x, users can avoid the command line completely if they wish. DOS and MS Windows user programs keep the command line well hidden from users. Choose names that do a good job describing the function of the volume, even if the name is a little long. It's just as easy to point and click on a long name as on a short name.

Volume Block Size Choices

The second changeable parameter in the Volume Information screen is the Volume Block Size. Volume blocks set the size of pieces of data stored in a volume. NetWare 4.1x sets the default block sizes based on the size of the volume. The NetWare default block sizes are as follows:

VOLUME SIZE	BLOCK SIZE
0 to 31 MB	4 KB
32 to 149 MB	16 KB
150 to 499 MB	32 KB
500+ MB	64 KB

Larger block sizes use less server RAM, since there are fewer to track. Unfortunately, the larger blocks will waste more disk space. A single file will be stored in each block, meaning an 87-byte batch file may "fill" an entire 64 KB disk block. To eliminate this waste, you can turn on block suballocation. We'll be there in just a second.

Unless you know your volume will hold large files, such as large database files, image files, or other consistently large data files, the defaults will work fine. If server memory is more limited than disk space, you may want to bump the block size up a bit, but it's better to buy more memory.

To change the volume block size, highlight that line in the Volume Information screen and press the Enter key. A pick list of your options will appear. Press Enter on your choice, and that block size will be filled into the screen. The highlight bar will move to the next option.

Another reason to go with the defaults and not guess about your block sizes is that these can't be changed after the volume is up and running. This shouldn't be a problem, but this item and the next three can't be changed on existing volumes. Changing the block size requires backing up the volume files and information (several times if you're the least bit paranoid), deleting the volume, and re-creating the volume.

File Compression Settings for Your Volumes (Custom)

The next field, File Compression, enables or disables file compression for the volume being configured. This setting cannot be changed on existing volumes. All is not lost, however. Using NetWare's administrator utilities, you can set individual files to be compressed or reject compression.

File compression is one of the big advantages of NetWare 4.*x*. Working intelligently in the background, file compression is applied to files that have not changed for a certain amount of time. The default setting is one week without being accessed, but that setting is configurable.

At a predetermined time of day (the default is midnight), all the files ready for compression will be crunched by the operating system when the server utilization level is low enough to indicate an empty network. The algorithm for compression tips the scales for fast decompression rather than being balanced; you don't care how long the file takes to shrink since it happens when you're not using the network. You do care that a previously compressed file, when accessed again, responds as quickly as any other file. The compression algorithm takes longer to compress than to decompress.

The details of compression times are set after the volume is up and running. Now we're just concerned about whether to support compression on this particular volume. The default is yes, as your answer should be. If you press the Enter key on this field, a short pick list of On and Off appears. Press Enter on your choice and continue.

One caveat to the normal On setting for file compression: your use of data migration. If you plan on using NetWare's High Capacity Storage System (HCSS) to place a large amount of files in near on-line storage, you must choose Off for file compression. The HCSS software needs to manage the file sizes and settings. This will be mentioned again when we choose data migration in just a bit.

Using Block Suballocation on Your Volumes (Custom)

Block suballocation, another feature of NetWare 4.*x*, is a fancy name for "let's pack in these files like a vacation suitcase." Rather than be limited to a large block size that wastes lots of space when a small file is stored there, block suballocation splits the remaining space of a partially used block into 512-byte segments. If an 87-byte batch file is placed into a new block, 63.5 KB will then become available for other file remainders. New files won't be placed here, just the ends of other files that are just a little larger than the configured block size. If the next file sent to the server is a 65 KB file, the first 64 KB of that file will fill a new block, and the remaining 1 KB will take two 512-byte suballocation blocks in the block with our 87-byte batch file.

You can see how this space savings will add up. Rather than wasting almost 128 KB in the examples just discussed, NetWare block suballocation works to keep these leftover corners of disk blocks full and under control.

Block suballocation and file compression work best together. Again, if you're planning HCSS, set block suballocation to Off, just as you must turn off file compression.

> *Block suballocation, another feature of NetWare 4.x, is a fancy name for "let's pack in these files like a vacation suitcase."*

Using Data Migration (Custom)

A common problem with large groups of data files is the need to keep them handy, but not necessarily immediately available. Hard disks, while coming down in price, still cost more per megabyte of storage than optical disk platters.

Imagine a newspaper's situation: lots of new stories every day that need instant file response. While reporters are writing and working on stories, those stories must be on the server hard disk and readily available. What about last month's stories? They must be kept, but the chances of needing any particular story are low. These would be excellent candidates for data migration.

To a user looking for an old story, up to 256 GB (yes, gigabytes) appear to be available on the volume. NetWare tracks which files have been migrated, and presents them to the user just like any current file. The retrieval time will be a few seconds slower, but the user doesn't need to do anything special when accessing these migrated files.

NetWare uses some hard disk space as a staging area for files going to or coming from (properly labeled *migration* and *demigration*) the near-online storage. An optical jukebox, an excellent example of near-online storage, will extend the capacity of a volume using data migration. Files are moved based on a configuration profile listing the age of the file and the storage capacity threshold of the hard disk space.

If you enable data migration, check again that both file compression and block suballocation are turned off for this volume. This is another setting that can't be changed for existing volumes, so think about any future plans for handling near-online storage requirements.

Saving Volume Changes

Press the F10 key to save your volume changes and continue. A verification screen will pop up to make sure you're ready to save the volume information, just press Enter once again. The volume setup time is much less than formatting the same size disk, so you won't wait long.

Installing the NetWare License Software

One of the diskettes included with your software is labeled as the license diskette. It will also have a user count, such as 5 User, 100 User, and so on. That's the disk asked for in Figure 2.16.

When the proper disk is inserted and verified, a window will say:

```
The Main Server License was successfully installed.
    Press <ENTER> to continue.
```

If a proper disk was not inserted, you will be offered a chance to try again. If you can't find your license disk, or this is a test setup of some kind, you can install the server license through the INSTALL.NLM program at a later time.

FIGURE 2.16

Verifying your NetWare license

```
NetWare Server Installation 4.1                          NetWare Loadable Module


       The license file will be installed from drive A:. Insert disk "MAIN
       SERVER LICENSE" (which contains the file "SERVER.MLS") into the drive.

       Warning:  Do not try to install this same license on any
       other server.
       Doing so will cause a copyright violation warning to be issued.

           Press <F3> to specify a different path;
           Press <Enter> to continue.



Continue                                          <Enter>
Specify a different source drive/directory <F3>
Continue without installing a license             <F9>    Delete last license <F8>
Help                                              <F1>    Abort INSTALL <Alt><F10>
```

However, you will not be able to log in more than one person at a time until the license is properly installed. The single-user limit allows lab setup and testing but not long-term abuse.

Novell has rejected some of the onerous copy-protection schemes other vendors use. This screen explains that each server has its own license disk with the SERVER.MLS file included. If a SERVER.MLS file from another operating system is used, error messages will appear on the servers and on workstations.

> **WARNING**
>
> *Software piracy is a multibillion dollar criminal market. Every piece of stolen software used takes money from the developer of the software that could be used to improve the product. Besides that, using software that you didn't purchase is no different than using an automobile that you didn't buy: it's theft.*

Establishing a Remote Server Link to the Source Files

If you are installing from a local CD-ROM drive (or floppies, you poor thing), you can skip right to the section title "Copying NetWare Files." If you are installing NetWare from a remote server, as I am for this demonstration, Figure 2.17 will be of interest.

FIGURE 2.17

Log in, once again

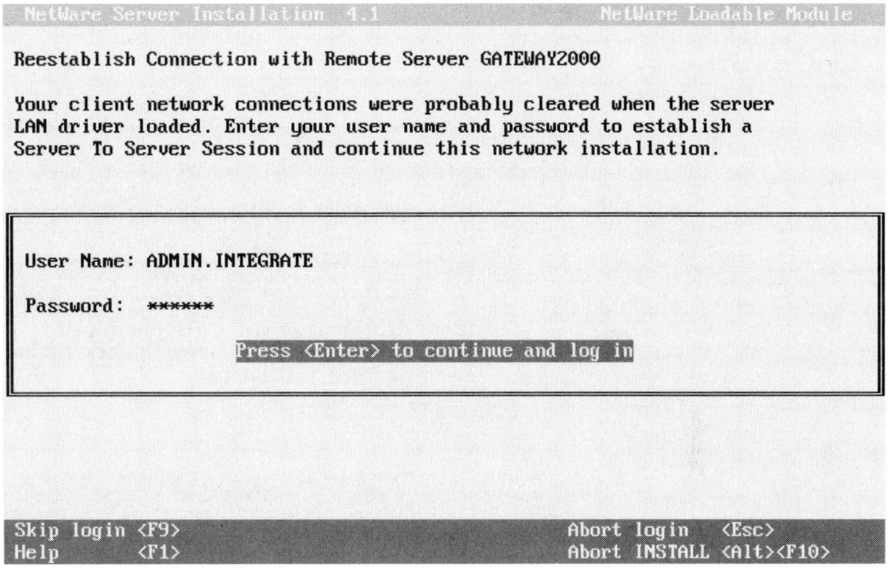

```
NetWare Server Installation 4.1                    NetWare Loadable Module

Reestablish Connection with Remote Server GATEWAY2000

Your client network connections were probably cleared when the server
LAN driver loaded. Enter your user name and password to establish a
Server To Server Session and continue this network installation.


┌─────────────────────────────────────────────────────────────────┐
│                                                                 │
│   User Name: ADMIN.INTEGRATE                                    │
│                                                                 │
│   Password: ******                                              │
│                                                                 │
│              Press <Enter> to continue and log in               │
│                                                                 │
└─────────────────────────────────────────────────────────────────┘




Skip login  <F9>                              Abort login   <Esc>
Help        <F1>                              Abort INSTALL <Alt><F10>
```

During the installation of your network drivers, the connection to the remote server was broken. Reestablishing the connection takes just your login name (on the host server, not the server you are installing) and the password.

This step is a necessary security precaution. Under no circumstances do you want someone to be able to connect to and take files from your system without going through some level of security.

Copying NetWare Files

Although the remote server connection was broken, the installation program remembers where files were coming from earlier. The path for the source files is presented to you for verification, as shown in Figure 2.18.

Notice the instructions in the main windows and across the bottom of the screen. If you are installing this from an internal CD-ROM drive, the source may be drive D: rather than the name of a remote server and volume.

In this case, the remote file source is a volume on server GATEWAY2000 named PROJECTS. The directory is NETWARE, as suggested by the earlier instructions for copying the CD-ROM disk contents to a server.

The installation batch file that begins the process is named INSTALL.BAT. The location of that file is exactly where Figure 2.18 says it is: in directory

FIGURE 2.18

The source of your new server's files

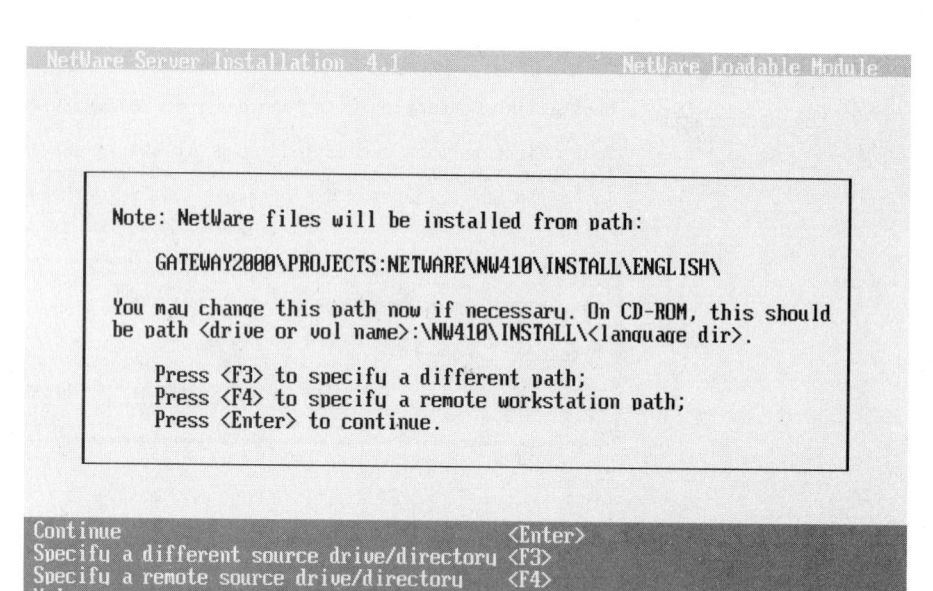

```
NetWare Server Installation 4.1                    NetWare Loadable Module


    ┌─────────────────────────────────────────────────────────────┐
    │  Note: NetWare files will be installed from path:           │
    │                                                             │
    │     GATEWAY2000\PROJECTS:NETWARE\NW410\INSTALL\ENGLISH\     │
    │                                                             │
    │  You may change this path now if necessary. On CD-ROM, this should │
    │  be path <drive or vol name>:\NW410\INSTALL\<language dir>. │
    │                                                             │
    │     Press <F3> to specify a different path;                 │
    │     Press <F4> to specify a remote workstation path;        │
    │     Press <Enter> to continue.                              │
    │                                                             │
    └─────────────────────────────────────────────────────────────┘


Continue                                           <Enter>
Specify a different source drive/directory         <F3>
Specify a remote source drive/directory            <F4>
Help                                               <F1>       Abort INSTALL <Alt><F10>
```

\NW410\INSTALL\ENGLISH. If you are installing support for French, Italian, German, or Spanish, reference that language as the last directory entry.

Selecting Optional NetWare File Groups to Install

Figure 2.19 is somewhat misnamed, since many people feel the files listed are not "optional." In the past, with the server-centric focus of NetWare, these files were required on each server. But with the single login to an entire network feature available with NetWare 4.x, there is little reason to have multiple copies of the same files.

The only set of files you can't see in the detail window in Figure 2.19 is Set up a Network Directory for Server Upgrade/Migration (16 MB). Each selection has an information screen that pops up, just like the bottom window explaining the NetWare DOS Utilities in Figure 2.19.

The default is for all files to be installed. Adding the file total, however, you see that 80 MB of disk space will be taken, besides the 20 MB of system files referred to in the opening message.

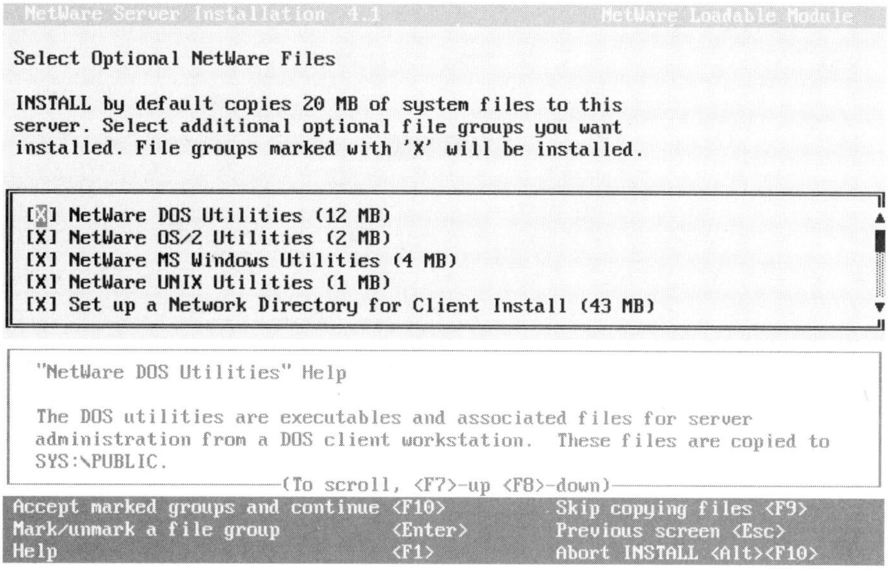

FIGURE 2.19

Selecting the NetWare files for your new server

```
NetWare Server Installation  4.1                    NetWare Loadable Module
Select Optional NetWare Files

INSTALL by default copies 20 MB of system files to this
server. Select additional optional file groups you want
installed. File groups marked with 'X' will be installed.

   ┌─────────────────────────────────────────────────────────────┐
   │ [X] NetWare DOS Utilities (12 MB)                           │
   │ [X] NetWare OS/2 Utilities (2 MB)                           │
   │ [X] NetWare MS Windows Utilities (4 MB)                     │
   │ [X] NetWare UNIX Utilities (1 MB)                           │
   │ [X] Set up a Network Directory for Client Install (43 MB)   │
   └─────────────────────────────────────────────────────────────┘

   ┌─────────────────────────────────────────────────────────────┐
   │ "NetWare DOS Utilities" Help                                │
   │                                                             │
   │ The DOS utilities are executables and associated files for server
   │ administration from a DOS client workstation. These files are copied to
   │ SYS:\PUBLIC.                                                │
   └─────────────────────────────────────────────────────────────┘
                    (To scroll, <F7>-up <F8>-down)
   Accept marked groups and continue  <F10>   Skip copying files  <F9>
   Mark/unmark a file group           <Enter> Previous screen     <Esc>
   Help                               <F1>    Abort INSTALL       <Alt><F10>
```

Disks are getting cheaper, but that's no excuse to waste disk space. In situations where there are more than two servers on your network, consider leaving some of these files off the hard disk.

If you have an active network, keep two copies of the file sets you need on servers. Servers after the first two need not have a full file complement. Such large file sets as those for client installation and upgrade/migration are particularly redundant.

Each of these files can be loaded any time through the INSTALL program. Each user who needs some of these files can be directed to any of the servers in that user's network context. In the case of CLONE386, only the SYS:\PUBLIC files are being loaded onto the hard disk.

Figure 2.20 is the File Copy Status screen, showing a progress bar inching from left to right. When copying files across the network, the progress is noticeable and continuous. The list of files scrolling in the bottom window goes way to fast to keep up with. The source and destination path will change as the files scroll by.

FIGURE 2.20

Smoothly copying files

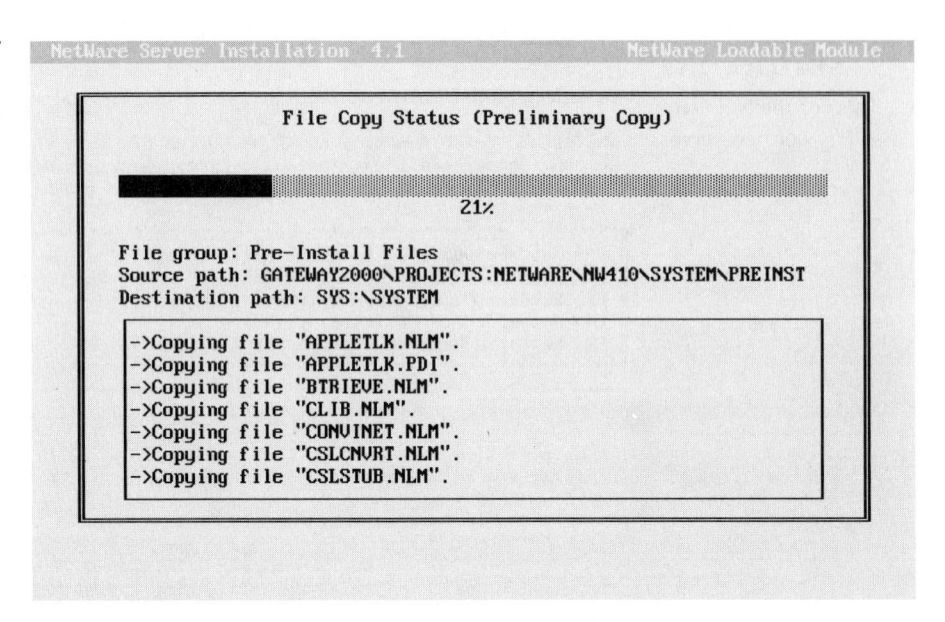

```
NetWare Server Installation 4.1                    NetWare Loadable Module

        ┌─────────────────────────────────────────────────────────┐
        │            File Copy Status (Preliminary Copy)          │
        │                                                         │
        │   ████████░░░░░░░░░░░░░░░░░░░░░░░░░░░░░░░░░░░░░░░░░░░  │
        │                         21%                             │
        │                                                         │
        │   File group: Pre-Install Files                         │
        │   Source path: GATEWAY2000\PROJECTS:NETWARE\NW410\SYSTEM\PREINST │
        │   Destination path: SYS:\SYSTEM                         │
        │   ┌─────────────────────────────────────────────────┐   │
        │   │ ->Copying file "APPLETLK.NLM".                  │   │
        │   │ ->Copying file "APPLETLK.PDI".                  │   │
        │   │ ->Copying file "BTRIEVE.NLM".                   │   │
        │   │ ->Copying file "CLIB.NLM".                      │   │
        │   │ ->Copying file "CONVINET.NLM".                  │   │
        │   │ ->Copying file "CSLCNVRT.NLM".                  │   │
        │   │ ->Copying file "CSLSTUB.NLM".                   │   │
        │   └─────────────────────────────────────────────────┘   │
        └─────────────────────────────────────────────────────────┘
```

Installing NetWare Directory Services—Almost Time

Next in the installation script is NetWare Directory Services. Although I dislike GOTO statements, I want to place one here. Read the next chapter titled "Installing NetWare Directory Services and Optional Procedures," and continue the installation without a break.

Any of these steps can be started from the INSTALL program at the server console. Looking at Figure 2.21, you will see all the major steps we have gone through laid out in order. In fact, the highlight bar is on Server Options (install/upgrade this server).

We will see this screen again as we talk about managing a NetWare 4.1x server. If you feel confused at all during this installation process, particularly the Custom Installation, take heart. The INSTALL program allows you to rework everything we've done to this point, and everything we will be doing with NDS.

FIGURE 2.21

The main installation screen for the INSTALL.NLM

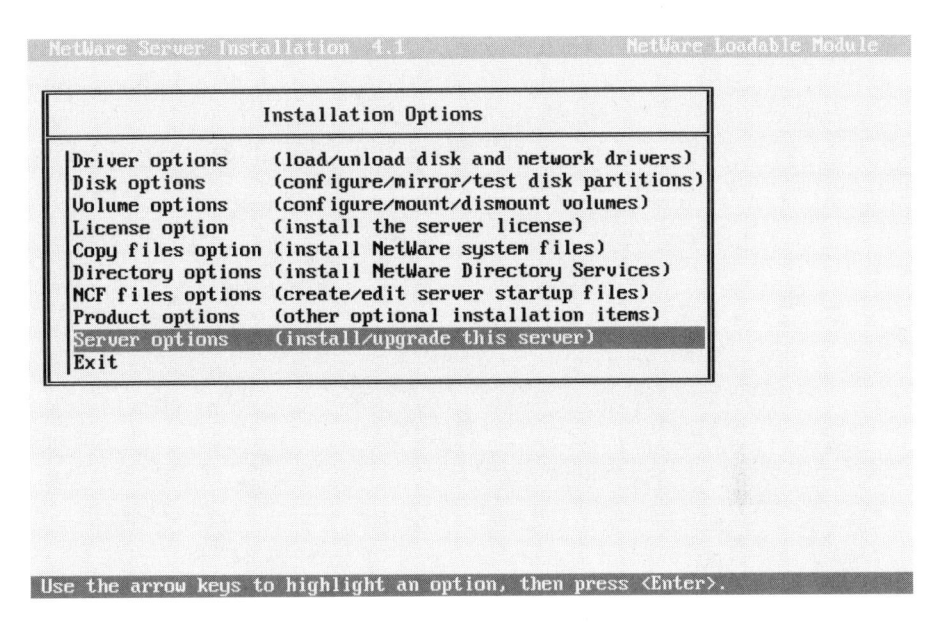

```
NetWare Server Installation 4.1                NetWare Loadable Module

              ┌─────────────── Installation Options ───────────────┐
              │ Driver options      (load/unload disk and network drivers) │
              │ Disk options        (configure/mirror/test disk partitions)│
              │ Volume options      (configure/mount/dismount volumes)     │
              │ License option      (install the server license)           │
              │ Copy files option   (install NetWare system files)         │
              │ Directory options   (install NetWare Directory Services)   │
              │ NCF files options   (create/edit server startup files)     │
              │ Product options     (other optional installation items)    │
              │ Server options      (install/upgrade this server)          │
              │ Exit                                                       │
              └────────────────────────────────────────────────────┘

Use the arrow keys to highlight an option, then press <Enter>.
```

Intelligent Installations

THE BEST INSTALLATION tool you have is time. Time to think about what you're doing, time to think about what your users need, and time to think and remember what that little nagging thought is at the back of your mind.

Time is not easy to get, especially for installations. People are waiting for the new software, and your management is eager to see some results from the money you spent. You are probably excited to see all the new things NetWare 4.1x has to offer, and in a hurry yourself.

But time spent thinking and playing with your new server during the initial installation will repay that time manyfold. Curious about the Simplified Installation process, even if it may not work for your system? Try it. Curious about the options available during the Custom Installation? Try a few. Will it hurt anyone? No.

Tell your boss the server arrived, but the software was back-ordered. Tell him it will take three to five working days to arrive.

Then play. You'll have the time, so you might as well use it. On the fifth day, tell your boss the software is here. Impress him with how quickly you zip through the installation process.

Time well spent. And it can't hurt at your perform review (and raise) time.

CASE STUDY

MiniCo: Installing NetWare 4.1x

MINICO HAS 3 servers, 75 users, and one location. For NetWare 4.1x installation, MiniCo had one existing server to upgrade and two new servers.

New, Improved NetWare Installation

CONSIDERATIONS

The choices:

- Get NetWare on diskettes, and avoid buying a CD-ROM drive for the servers.
- Get NetWare on CD-ROM, and buy CD-ROM drives for the servers.

DECISION

Order NetWare on CD-ROM, and buy a CD-ROM drive for one server.

EXPLANATION

Jack Mingo, President of MiniCo, didn't want to spend the extra money for a CD-ROM drive on the two new servers, and retrofit one to the existing ACCT server. After all, you only load the software once, right?

Alexander von Thorn (the Distribution Manager, who is handling the installation), faced with feeding scores of diskettes into the servers, threw a fit and convinced Jack to reconsider. What if we need to reinstall software, or to add modules later? These require more floppy feeding. Besides, being able to share a CD-ROM version of *Books In Print* may come in handy after the network is up and running.

The final agreement was to get a CD-ROM drive for one of the new servers. This server would install NetWare 4.1x, then mount the CD-ROM drive as a volume. The other servers would then install across the network, using the CD-ROM on the first server as the source of the installation files.

Requirements for NetWare Servers

CONSIDERATIONS

The choices:

- Buy one superserver.
- Buy three new servers.
- Upgrade the existing NetWare 3.12 server in the Accounting department to support NetWare 4.1x.

DECISION

Upgrade the existing server's software to NetWare 4.1x, but leave the hardware at the same level. This server is a 486/33, with 16 MB of RAM and a 500 MB IDE hard drive.

MINICO CASE STUDY, CONTINUED

Buy two new PC servers in tower cases from Gateway 2000. One of the new servers is a 486/50, with 32 MB RAM and 500 MB and 1 GB SCSI disk drives. The other is a Pentium P66, with 64 MB RAM and 500 MB and two 1 GB hard drives.

EXPLANATION

Leaving the accounting software on the ACCT server eliminated the need to upgrade the server hardware. The 500 MB IDE disk and drive controller wouldn't support a CD-ROM as a NetWare volume (but IDE CD-ROMs do work for installation).

The two new servers reflect the different needs of their respective departments. The 486 server is used in the Sales department, servicing customer databases and sales contact software. The Pentium server was placed in the Support department, which includes management. Shipment records, inventory, and business history files are kept in the Support department. Both the Macintosh and OS/2 name spaces are supported by this server.

Beginning the NetWare 4.1x Installation Process

CONSIDERATIONS

The choices:

- Make a bootable DOS diskette for each server.
- Copy all the boot files to floppy for each server.
- Copy and modify existing AUTOEXEC.BAT and CONFIG.SYS files for the server with the CD-ROM drive.

DECISION

Keep a bootable DOS boot diskette for the existing ACCT server and the new server with the CD-ROM drive.

EXPLANATION

Any boot diskette can be used with the new server without the CD-ROM drive. The configuration files for the existing server and the new server with the CD-ROM drive were kept. The AUTOEXEC.BAT and CONFIG.SYS files on the new server with the CD-ROM needed to be modified. The drivers for the CD-ROM drive were copied to the bootable floppy, and the configuration files changed to support the new file locations.

Both new servers came with MS DOS, MS Windows for Workgroups, and various other software. Since MiniCo's employees don't use most of the extra programs that were installed, the various program disks were stored in the server room, and all the installed software was erased.

Preparing the Disk Drive for NetWare

CONSIDERATIONS

The choices:

- Boot the server from the hard disk.
- Boot the server from a floppy disk.

MINICO CASE STUDY, CONTINUED

DECISION

Configure a DOS partition on each server and boot from there.

EXPLANATION

The space used by the DOS partition is a tiny fraction of the total disk space available. The advantages of a server automatically loading NetWare after rebooting far outweigh the lost disk space. Besides, booting from a floppy is more complicated to set up and use.

Where Will Your Installation Files Come From?

CONSIDERATIONS

The choices:

- Install from floppies.
- Install from the CD-ROM in the server.
- Install from another NetWare server on the network.

DECISION

Install the first new server from the internal CD-ROM drive, then copy the files to that new server for installation across the network.

EXPLANATION

Both upgrades and new server installations can be done across the network. In fact, across the network is the fastest possible option. Alexander von Thorn installed the first NetWare 4.1x system on the server with the CD-ROM drive, which was almost as quick as copying the files across the network. Then the appropriate files were copied to the server, so both the upgrade and the new server installation could take place across the network.

Running the INSTALL.NLM Program

CONSIDERATIONS

The choices:

- Use the Simple Installation method.
- Use the Custom Installation method.

DECISION

Take advantage of the Simple Installation method.

EXPLANATION

MiniCo has a single NDS tree, with no special protocol needs or disk configurations. The Simple Installation method works well for companies with this type of profile. Choices made during installation included:

- The 500 MB drive on each server was named SYS.
- The 1 GB drive on the SALES_1 server was configured as a single volume and called DEALS.
- The two 1 GB drives on the SUPPORT_1 server were configured as a single volume called VOL1 (the Support staff is fairly literal, and followed the example in the NetWare installation instructions).
- File compression and block suballocation were enabled on all volumes.

CASE STUDY

MegaCorp: Installing NetWare 4.1x

MEGACORP HAS 50 servers, 2500 users, and 5 locations. MegaCorp converted its existing servers from a network with a first-generation, rigid, and incomplete Directory Name Service. All existing servers were replaced with new, high-end servers.

New, Improved NetWare Installation

CONSIDERATIONS

The choices:

- Add a CD-ROM drive to each new server.
- Set up a specialized "installation" server in each location.

DECISION

A special installation server was created in the technical support area of each location.

EXPLANATION

Each building had a workbench set aside, with its own wiring concentrator (10BaseT or Token Ring, depending on the location). All new servers (*sans* CD-ROM drive) were configured, tested, and had NetWare installed at this bench.

The installation files came from the "installation" server. The installation network consisted of these two servers, so file copying went quickly across an empty network. Since the installation took place off the main network, the NDS information for each server was entered manually during installation. The MFG site (Manufacturing, in San Jose) handled the OS/2 client/NetWare server for the remote customer-site office (the one with one server running NetWare on OS/2, with an ISDN line back to MFG).

Requirements for NetWare Servers

CONSIDERATIONS

The choices:

- Reconfigure existing servers.
- Buy new PC servers (80 to 100).
- Buy new "servers on steroids," such as Acer, HP, ALR, IBM, or Compaq (50 to 60).
- Buy new superservers, such as NetFRAME or Tricord (10).

DECISION

Get new "servers on steroids," along with two superservers.

EXPLANATION

The important consideration for MegaCorp is network availability. All corporate information is delivered to the desktop by the LAN through

MEGACORP CASE STUDY, CONTINUED

the servers. Reliability and performance are critical, and each server can be upgraded to support multiple processors when that option becomes available for NetWare.

Since the employees at each location had their own favorite "server on steroids," several brands were chosen. The feeling was that having the strong, local support organizations for the respective server vendors was more important than pleasing the corporate people by using the vendor that they liked.

Servers chosen were Acer, HP Vectra, IBM, Compaq, and ALR models. Each server has 128 MB of RAM with dual SCSI-2 controllers supporting five 2.1 GB disk drives. This provides more than 10 GB of disk space, since each pair of drives was duplexed for fault-tolerance. Two NetFRAME superservers are in HQ (the headquarters office). Both have 256 MB of RAM and 20 GB of duplexed disk drives.

Beginning the NetWare 4.1x Installation Process

CONSIDERATIONS

The choices:

- Keep boot diskettes for each server.
- Keep reference boot diskettes for the server configurations used in each location.

DECISION

Keep two reference diskettes for each server type per location. None of the servers have CD-ROM drives installed, so it wasn't necessary to keep special CD-ROM configuration files.

EXPLANATION

The machines ordered by MegaCorp were built to be servers. No software or other "freebies" were included, so nothing needed to be erased from the disks.

Preparing the Disk Drive for NetWare

CONSIDERATIONS

The choices:

- Boot the server from the hard disk.
- Boot the server from a floppy disk.

DECISION

All MegaCorp servers use a DOS partition to boot the server.

EXPLANATION

A 15 MB DOS partition is placed on each server. Some NetWare utilities are placed in the partition to speed troubleshooting. The NetFRAME servers required a special disk partition on the installation PC that downloads the complete boot partition to the NetFRAME as part of the installation process.

Where Will Your Installation Files Come From?

CONSIDERATIONS

The choices:

- Install from floppies.
- Install from the CD-ROM in the server.
- Install from another NetWare server on the network.

MEGACORP CASE STUDY, CONTINUED

DECISION

Install from another NetWare server.

EXPLANATION

A specialized installation server was set up at each location, on a separate workbench. The server had a small (500 MB) hard drive, but 64 MB of RAM (to be reallocated later). A wiring concentrator was on the bench, giving a clear channel between the installation server and the new server being installed. All files were copied from the installation server across the two-station network.

Running the INSTALL.NLM Program

CONSIDERATIONS

The choices:

- Run the Simple Installation method.
- Use the Custom Installation method.

DECISION

Work through the Custom Installation method.

EXPLANATION

MegaCorp's network was far too complicated to use anything but the Custom Installation method. Each server was configured with the proper drive duplexing information. Other choices made during installation were:

- The SYS volume on each server was kept to 100 MB or less.
- Servers are named after locations and then functions, with the format HQ_XXX_S1 (HQ, Special Code, Server 1). For example, HQ_TAX_S1 is the name for the first server in the Tax department at HQ.
- Volumes are named sequentially, as in HQ_TAX_S1_V1 (HQ, Tax Department, Server 1, Volume 1). Applications are always on volume number 1 (not SYS).
- File compression and block suballocation were enabled on all volumes.
- Data migration was enabled on all volumes.
- TCP/IP and AppleTalk protocols were configured on all servers.

Installing NetWare Directory Services and Optional Procedures

CHAPTER 3

I'T'S TRUE THAT NetWare 4.1*x*'s object-oriented design is a considerable step forward from the server-centric NetWare 3.*x* design. That's why we took a break during this installation. But now we need to continue getting our first NetWare 4.1*x* server up and running.

The "first server" portion of the above paragraph is an important consideration. Although NDS (NetWare Directory Services) supports global networks, every NetWare 4.1*x* network starts with one server, installed into one NDS tree. That first server is the one we're concentrating on here.

This isn't the place to learn all about NDS and all the features and capabilities it includes. Chapter 4 goes into those NDS details. This chapter gives you enough information to get NDS started on your first NetWare 4.1*x* server. However, for more complex NDS installations, you should spend some time in the "Planning Your NDS Tree" section of Chapter 4 before proceeding with NDS installation. There you will see a variety of options for creating NDS trees for small and large company networks, both local and across long distances.

If one server is all you have, NDS will make life easier for you as an administrator and for your users. However, the real advantages come when multiple servers can be organized and managed as if they were all one set of resources available to the network users. To take advantage of these features, and the other NDS features that support thousands of users, check out the next chapter.

Details, Details, but Not Too Many

THERE ARE ONLY a few details you need here. You made harder decisions earlier in the installation process.

Some Definitions

Before you begin, skim over these quick definitions of the NetWare terms you'll be seeing:

- *Tree*: The hierarchical organization of the network. Like a directory structure for a hard disk, an NDS tree has a single root with multiple branches (directories) containing other directories and/or files (other branches and/or leaf nodes).

- *Container*: An object that can hold or contain other objects. The Tree (a special container), Country, Organization, and Organizational Unit objects are containers.

- *Organization*: A high-level container just below the Country level (if used) or the [Root] of the Tree and just above the Organizational Unit. There must be at least one Organization object in every NDS tree.

- *Organizational Unit*: The smallest container, below Organization. This container is not required, but it's often used for better management of workgroups, departments, or project teams.

- *Context*: A way to describe the position of an object within containers in an NDS tree. The context is a position reference point, similar to a user's home directory being a reference point in a file system tree.

- *Admin*: A User object created during NetWare 4.1x installation, similar to the SUPERVISOR in NetWare 3.x. Admin has the rights to create and manage all objects in the newly installed NDS tree.

- *Leaf objects*: Objects that don't contain any other objects. Leaf objects include users, printers, servers, server volumes, and the like. Leaf objects are effectively the bindery contents from NetWare 3.x.

What You Need to Know

To install NDS on a NetWare 4.10 server, you need to know:

- The name of your NDS tree
- Your time zone
- Your company (Organization) name
- Any company divisions (Organizational Units) (optional)
- The NDS location for the server (the default Organization or Organizational Unit)
- The password for your Admin user (or provide the password for new installations)

You'll need this information whether you are creating a brand new NetWare 4.1x network or plugging this server into an existing NDS tree. The process is remarkably similar in either case.

When you're installing your first NetWare 4.1x server, you must create an NDS tree and the context for the server being installed. For your subsequent servers, you must decide where in the existing NDS tree they should live.

When you're installing a new server in an existing NDS network, you can still create new NDS trees, Organizations, and Organizational Units during installation. The installation process will offer you the choice of installing the server into an existing context or creating a new context.

Although the best time to fix a mistake is immediately, if you make a mistake during server installation, it's not going to cause you any long-term trouble. If you later decide you don't like the name for a particular Organization or Organizational Unit, you can change it—no big deal.

Figure 3.1 shows four NDS tree arrangements. Each Organization or Organizational Unit is a context. The Simple Installation method follows the first illustration, with only a single Organization containing leaf objects. During NDS installation, you have the opportunity to create as many Organizations and Organizational Units as you desire.

FIGURE 3.1

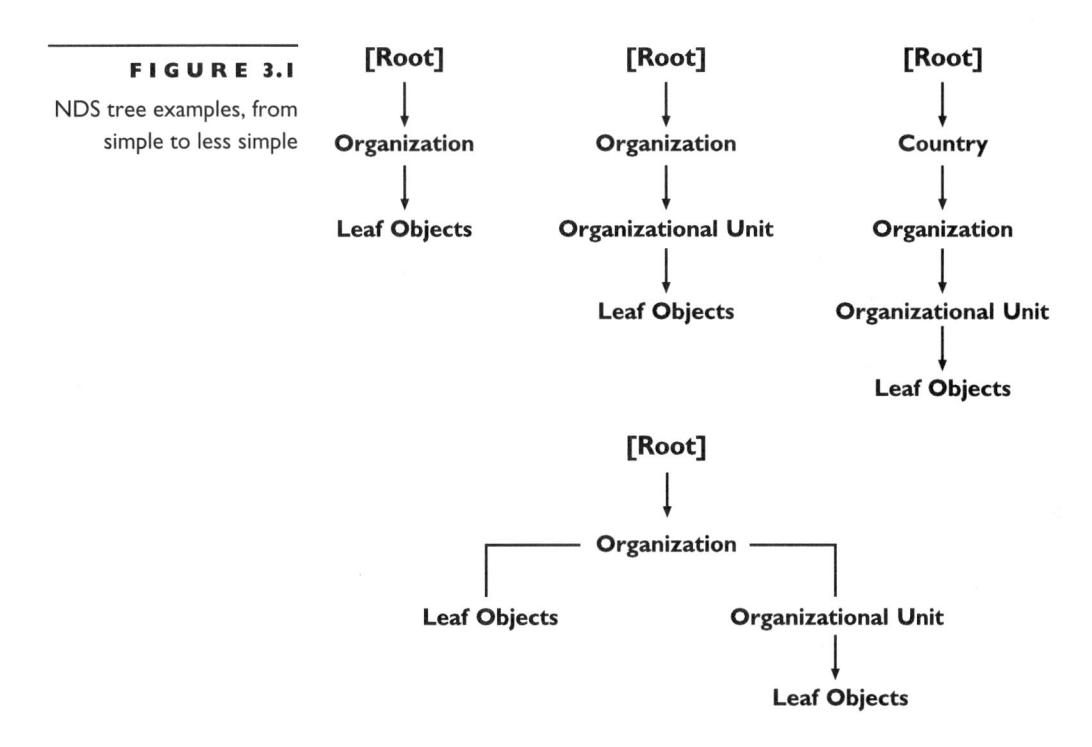

NDS tree examples, from simple to less simple

```
    [Root]              [Root]                 [Root]
      |                   |                      |
  Organization       Organization             Country
      |                   |                      |
  Leaf Objects     Organizational Unit      Organization
                          |                      |
                    Leaf Objects         Organizational Unit
                                                 |
                                           Leaf Objects


                        [Root]
                          |
            ——————— Organization ———————
            |                            |
       Leaf Objects            Organizational Unit
                                         |
                                   Leaf Objects
```

Configuring NDS during the First Server Installation

STARTING THE NDS installation process begins at the screen shown in Figure 3.2. If this is your first NetWare 4.1x server, the highlighted option will be the one you choose. Press the Enter key to confirm that this is the first NetWare 4.1x server on the network.

Naming Your NDS Tree

Since this is your first NetWare 4.1x server, you need to give your NDS tree a name and create it. The NDS tree naming details are:

- Must be unique across all connected networks
- May use letters A–Z

FIGURE 3.2

The beginning of NDS installation

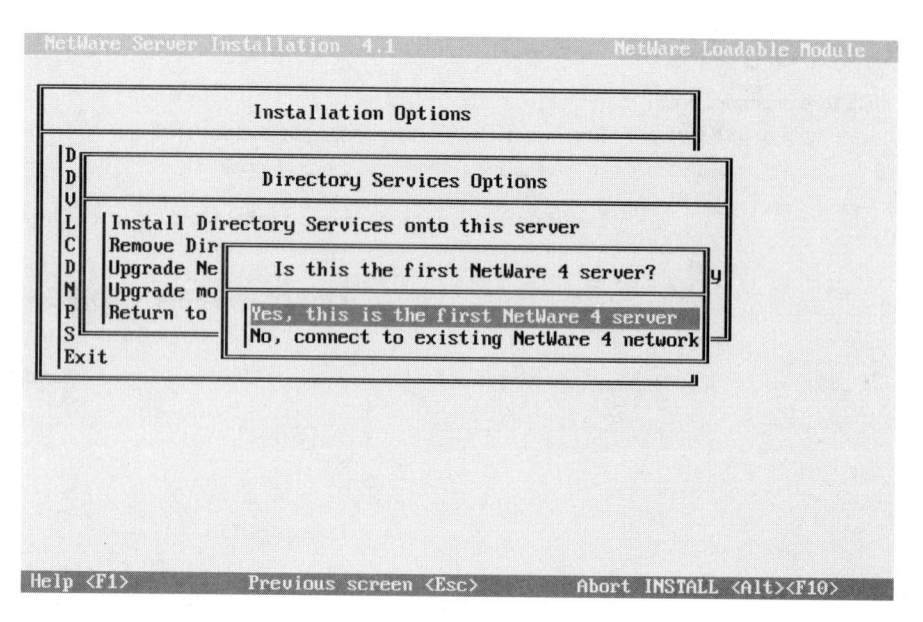

- May use numbers 0–9
- May use a hyphen (-)
- May use an underscore (_)
- May be any length, as long as the complete context name does not exceed 255 characters

There's no reason to give a long, descriptive name to the tree, because the Tree and [Root] objects are always implied (not shown) when listing contexts. This is not a problem, since Novell recommends only a single NDS tree per organization, and the client can see only one tree at a time.

NDS trees cannot be renamed or modified. Trees can be merged, but this is more advanced. Pick a unique name.

Since the demonstration network will be GCS, the NDS tree name I chose is GCS_TREE. Figure 3.3 shows the entry screen for the NDS tree name.

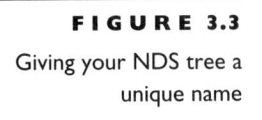

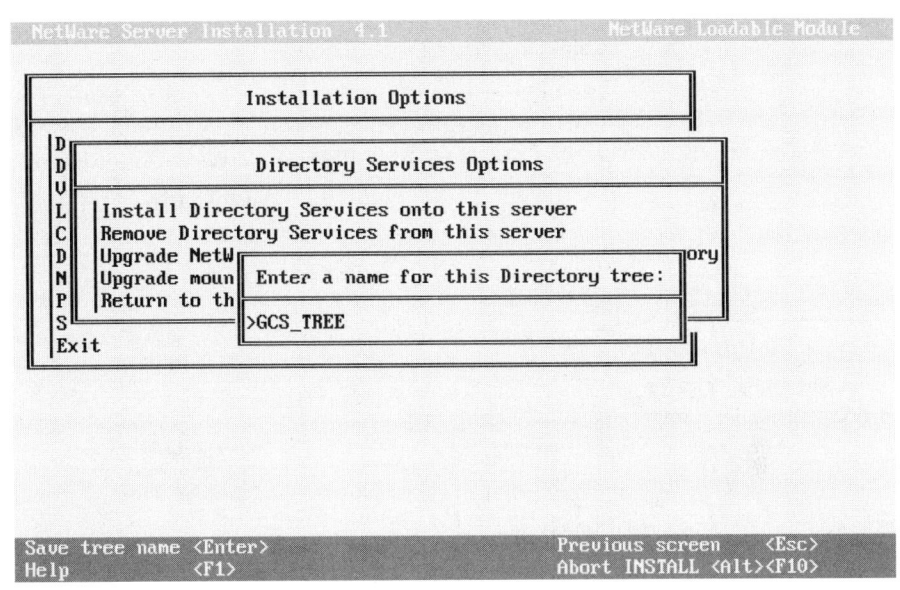

FIGURE 3.3

Giving your NDS tree a unique name

[Screenshot: NetWare Server Installation 4.1 — Directory Services Options dialog prompting "Enter a name for this Directory tree: >GCS_TREE"]

Notes on Network Time

Every PC includes a clock function, so every NetWare server has a clock built into the hardware. Servers have always used these clocks for certain operations, but the time of an event within a single server is not critical.

When you expand your network across multiple servers, time does become more of a concern. Some applications use time stamps on files or records, so a consistent time source is important to them. If there is only one server, you have a single time source. If you have two NetWare 3.x servers and you are attached to both, the time from one system may not match the time from the other one. If they don't match, time stamps on files and records across the two servers will not be reliable.

When you go a step further and spread your network Directory system across multiple servers, you have even more need for a single, reliable time source. Directory functions such as security changes and new user creation now require the participation of multiple individual servers. The most reliable means of tracking changes in a distributed network is by time stamps for each operation. Since multiple servers are involved, there must be a reliable time source for all servers to reference.

Selecting Your Time Zone

The next installation function is to choose a time zone for the server site. Thirty-seven different time zones are offered. Coverage ranges from Australia to New Zealand and all points in between (going west from Australia). Figure 3.4 shows the highlight bar on Central Standard Time in the U.S., where this book was written.

FIGURE 3.4

Choosing a time zone for a global Directory system

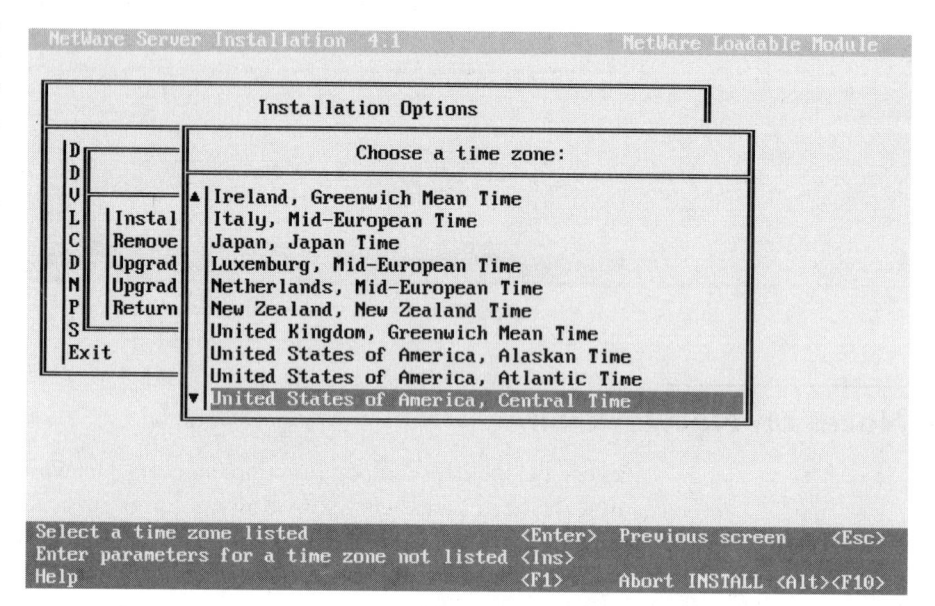

```
NetWare Server Installation 4.1                    NetWare Loadable Module

        ┌─────────────────────────────────────────────────┐
        │              Installation Options                │
        │  D┌──────────────────────────────────────────┐   │
        │  D│           Choose a time zone:            │   │
        │  U│                                          │   │
        │  L│ ▲ Ireland, Greenwich Mean Time           │   │
        │  C│   Italy, Mid-European Time               │   │
        │  D│   Japan, Japan Time                      │   │
        │  N│   Luxemburg, Mid-European Time           │   │
        │  P│   Netherlands, Mid-European Time         │   │
        │  S│   New Zealand, New Zealand Time          │   │
        │   │   United Kingdom, Greenwich Mean Time    │   │
        │Exit│  United States of America, Alaskan Time │   │
        │   │   United States of America, Atlantic Time│   │
        │   │ ▼ United States of America, Central Time │   │
        └─────────────────────────────────────────────────┘

Select a time zone listed                    <Enter>  Previous screen  <Esc>
Enter parameters for a time zone not listed <Ins>
Help                                         <F1>     Abort INSTALL <Alt><F10>
```

Press the Enter key to accept the highlighted time zone. If you choose the wrong time zone by accident, press the Escape key to move back one screen and choose the time zone again.

If your time zone is not listed in the pick list, you can add it yourself. Press the Insert key and describe your zone. Use the local time zone abbreviation if there is one, or make up your own if you must. This text string is used as a reference for your server; it's not some absolute value that must match other values. If you press Enter to add a time zone, you go to the screen discussed in the next section.

Configuring NDS during the First Server Installation

Verifying Your Server's Time Configuration

Since many time zones have modern "innovations" such as Daylight Saving Time (DST), time does not remain constant all year. One way to deal with this is to manually change the server time, just as you must change the clocks all over your house when the time changes. This is not considered fun by most people.

Realizing the lack of fun involved, NetWare engineers made a DST adjustment automatic in NetWare 4.1x. Figure 3.5 shows the default settings for a U.S. Central Standard Time server.

Notice the time server type is shown as Single Reference. Since there is only one server on this network, there can be only one server providing time for NDS operations and clients. The default for all first NetWare 4.1x servers on the network is Single Reference, and you should accept that default. We'll get to the various types of NetWare time servers shortly.

Just under the highlight bar in Figure 3.5 is the line:

```
Standard time offset from UTC    6:00:00 BEHIND
```

UTC (Universal Coordinated Time, or, better said, Universal Time Coordinated) is the new name for Greenwich Mean Time (GMT). GMT is the world time reference site in Greenwich, England. It's rare to need to change

FIGURE 3.5
Verifying server time settings

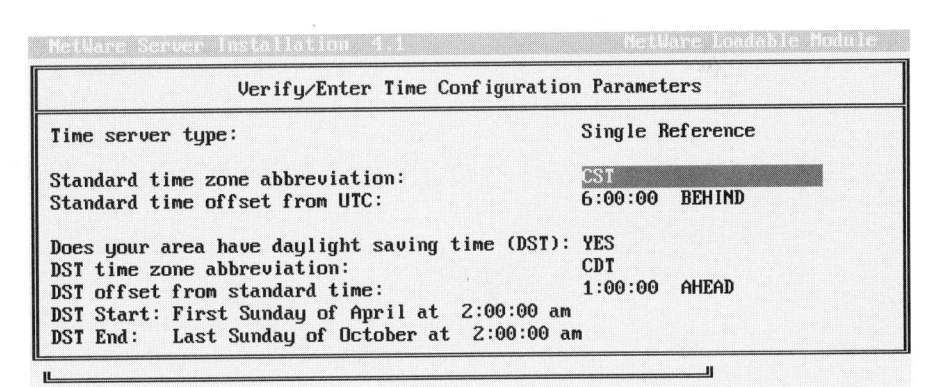

the deviation from UTC from that supplied by the installation program when you choose a particular time zone.

If you create your own time abbreviation and are east of UTC, use AHEAD with the number, since your time is ahead of UTC. For example, in Germany, you would type 1 and then press the Enter key to toggle to AHEAD. If your time zone is west of UTC, toggle to BEHIND, because your time is behind UTC.

Still rare in the U.S. are those sites that do not have DST. If you are in such a location, move the highlight bar over the YES entry and press the Enter key for a pick list of YES and NO. The pop-up window will verify that you do not have DST at some time during the year. When you choose NO, the rest of the information for DST will clear from the screen. If you have changed this by mistake and can't remember all the defaults, press the Escape key and rechoose your time zone. The defaults will reappear.

The offset from standard time to DST is set on the next line. You can vary the time (shown as 1:00:00 for one hour) and the clock offset method separately. U.S. locations use a standard hour and run ahead, which is the default.

Some locations pick odd times for starting and stopping standard time. If your location is one of those, the last two options allow you to modify the start and stop time for DST.

When you press Enter on the DST Start field, you are offered a choice for the start time of DST. Your choices for both DST Start and DST End are Weekday-of-Month (for example, the first Sunday in May) or Day-of-Month (for example, October 30).

When you are satisfied with the information in the screen shown in Figure 3.5, press the F10 key to continue. A small window may pop up while synchronizing the time with the network. On the first NetWare 4.*x* server in a network, the window will probably go by too fast to notice.

Setting the Server's Context

You must tell the server its location in the NDS tree. Every server is installed into a context, and the first server must define its own context. The server can change contexts later, but it's nice to get it right the first time.

In our demonstration so far, we've chosen only a name for our new NDS tree. The only default user for this new NDS tree is Admin, the manager of the entire newly created tree. Admin will be the SUPERVISOR equivalent for NetWare 3.*x* users.

Naming Your Organization and Organizational Units

To finish the installation, you need at least one Organization name. Organizational Unit names are optional, both during installation and when your network is up and running. Figure 3.6 displays the Context For This Server screen and the Organization name chosen for this NDS tree.

The Organization name can be the same as the name you gave the NDS tree itself, but that might be confusing to some users later. That's why the lab network tree has the name GCS_TREE and the Organization is named GCS. Clearly, it all belongs to the same company, but without any possible confusion with duplicate names for the Organization and the tree. The Organization name you type in and save will appear in the Server Context field, which shows O=GCS in Figure 3.6.

You can provide only one Organization per server, but you can have as many Organizational Units (OUs), shown as Sub-Organizational Units on this screen, as you wish. Only three OU fields appear, but you can add more by editing the Server Context field directly.

As you install your first server, keep in mind that this information doesn't pertain to this particular server only; you are creating a basic NDS framework. Maybe there is only one server involved right now, but your network may contain many more servers over time.

FIGURE 3.6

A simple context for server GCS

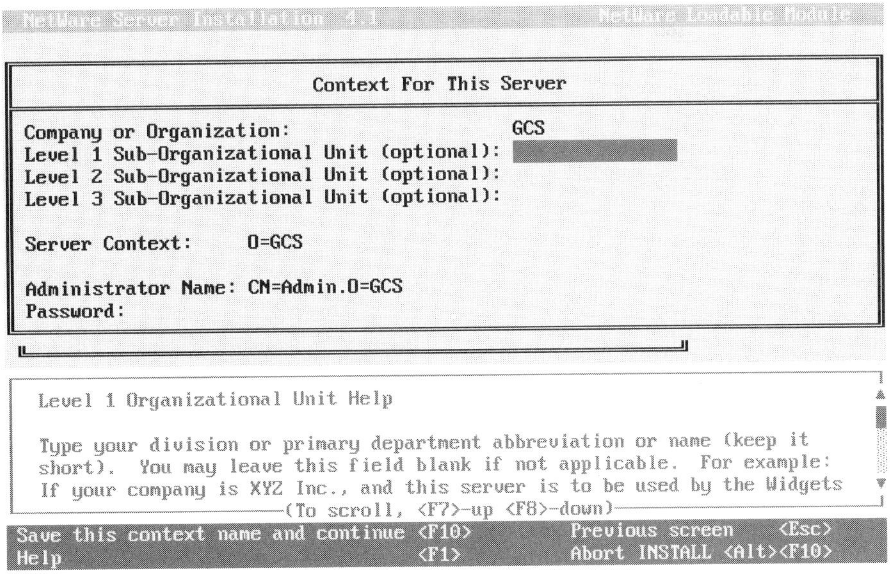

```
NetWare Server Installation 4.1                    NetWare Loadable Module

                         Context For This Server

    Company or Organization:                      GCS
    Level 1 Sub-Organizational Unit (optional):
    Level 2 Sub-Organizational Unit (optional):
    Level 3 Sub-Organizational Unit (optional):

    Server Context:        O=GCS

    Administrator Name: CN=Admin.O=GCS
    Password:


    Level 1 Organizational Unit Help

    Type your division or primary department abbreviation or name (keep it
    short).  You may leave this field blank if not applicable.  For example:
    If your company is XYZ Inc., and this server is to be used by the Widgets
                          (To scroll, <F7>-up <F8>-down)
    Save this context name and continue <F10>      Previous screen      <Esc>
    Help                                 <F1>      Abort INSTALL <Alt><F10>
```

Each field can contain up to 15 characters. Legal characters in this section are A–Z and a–z (uppercase and lowercase), along with 0–9 and the underscore (_) character. The limit for the total server context name is 255 characters.

Setting the Admin Name and Password

As you can see in Figure 3.6, the Administrator Name field is filled in automatically. The user name Admin is combined with the Organization name. In the example in Figure 3.6, the full Admin name is CN=Admin.O=GCS. CN is shorthand for container, as O is for Organization.

You can move the Admin down further in your tree, but it's better to leave Admin in the top Organization container.

Passwords are an art in themselves, and your company may have guidelines set already. If not, and you need to make up a password here, try to follow these guidelines:

- At least five characters long
- Include both letters and numbers
- Do not use the name of a loved one or your birthday
- Do not tape the password to your monitor

Move the highlight bar down to the Password field and type one in. You will be asked to retype the password for verification. Remember, someone logging in as Admin has full run of your network. Please use a decent password.

For Your Information: All the Details in One Screen

The tendency of network administrators to be distracted during installation and forget vital information is well known at Novell.

The tendency of network administrators to be distracted during installation and forget vital information is well known at Novell. For that reason, an FYI box will appear and tell you pertinent network information. Figure 3.7 shows an example.

Remember the pad and pencil you're supposed to have beside you during the installation process? Well, go find it, because you do need to write down the information shown in Figure 3.7. All the information in Figure 3.7 is easy to forget while NetWare 4.1*x* is still new. The only information you don't have on-screen that you will need is the password for Admin. Jot that down now while you're thinking of it (but please don't leave it next to the server).

FIGURE 3.7

Another chance to write down important information

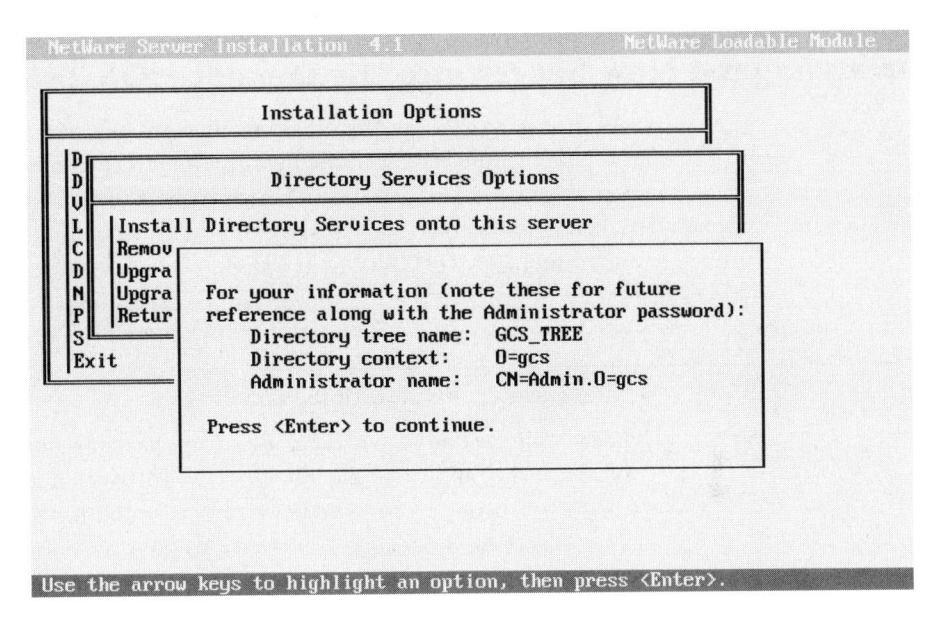

```
NetWare Server Installation 4.1                    NetWare Loadable Module

            ┌─────────────────────────────────────────────────────┐
            │              Installation Options                    │
     D      ├─────────────────────────────────────────────────────┤
     D   ┌──────────────────────────────────────────────┐
     U   │           Directory Services Options          │
     L   ├──────────────────────────────────────────────┤
     C   │ Install Directory Services onto this server   │
     D   │ Remov┌──────────────────────────────────────────────┐
     N   │ Upgra│ For your information (note these for future  │
     P   │ Upgra│ reference along with the Administrator password):│
     S   │ Retur│      Directory tree name:  GCS_TREE          │
         │      │      Directory context:    O=gcs             │
         │ Exit │      Administrator name:   CN=Admin.O=gcs    │
                │                                               │
                │ Press <Enter> to continue.                    │
                │                                               │
                └──────────────────────────────────────────────┘

 Use the arrow keys to highlight an option, then press <Enter>.
```

You can now skip ahead to the section concerning the AUTOEXEC.NCF and STARTUP.NCF files, titled "Finishing Installation and Your Next Steps." You're almost finished.

Installing a New Server into an Existing 4.1x Network

THERE ARE SOME differences between installing the first server and adding a second server into an existing NetWare 4.1x network. Some of the differences are obvious, but others are not. For example, when installing a second or third server, you may wish to add another container for that server by creating another Organizational Unit. These added pieces require a few more decisions during installation, but nothing serious.

Installing the New Server into the Default NDS Tree

As soon as you begin the NDS installation, you must decide whether to include the new server in the default NDS tree, create a new tree, or search for existing trees. The default NDS tree is the one first located by the new server when it connects to the network. If you are installing files from another server or from a CD-ROM drive mounted as a NetWare volume, the NDS tree used for connecting to the file source will be considered your default tree.

The Case against Multiple NDS Trees

Each NDS tree has its own database of objects that is not visible from another tree. NDS does not allow one client to cross over between trees. Clients in one NDS tree cannot see, browse, or use network objects in another tree. The only way to use those objects in the remote NDS tree is to leave the current tree and become a client of the remote tree (or connect as a bindery client, as described in Chapter 4).

If you're using the new Client32 software, however, multiple trees are not a problem. As you'll see in a bit, the Network Neighborhood desktop applet in Windows 95, after being enhanced by Client32, can see multiple trees. But this doesn't mean that your users won't get confused, so don't go tree crazy. One is best if at all possible.

Novell engineers are serious about this single NDS tree per company recommendation. If you persist in setting up multiple NDS trees, you will get a friendly warning. This is not to say you can't use multiple trees, just that you need to understand the implications of such a choice. Figure 3.8 displays the warning seen during installation.

The beginning NDS installation screen sets the NDS tree name. Figure 3.9 shows what happens when the installation program finds an existing tree, which is named GCS_TREE in this example. As you can see, despite the advice to keep a single tree, Novell does allow you the option of installing to another NDS tree.

The installation program recognized GCS_TREE as the single existing tree. As the screen shows, you can install the new server into the existing NDS tree (the most common option) or select another tree. The selection process also includes the opportunity to create a new tree.

If you choose to install your new server into the existing NDS tree, the installation program will continue with the time zone choices, and you can skip to that section. If you choose to select another tree, one must be found, as described in the next section.

Installing a New Server into an Existing 4.1x Network 143

FIGURE 3.8
Another single NDS tree sales pitch

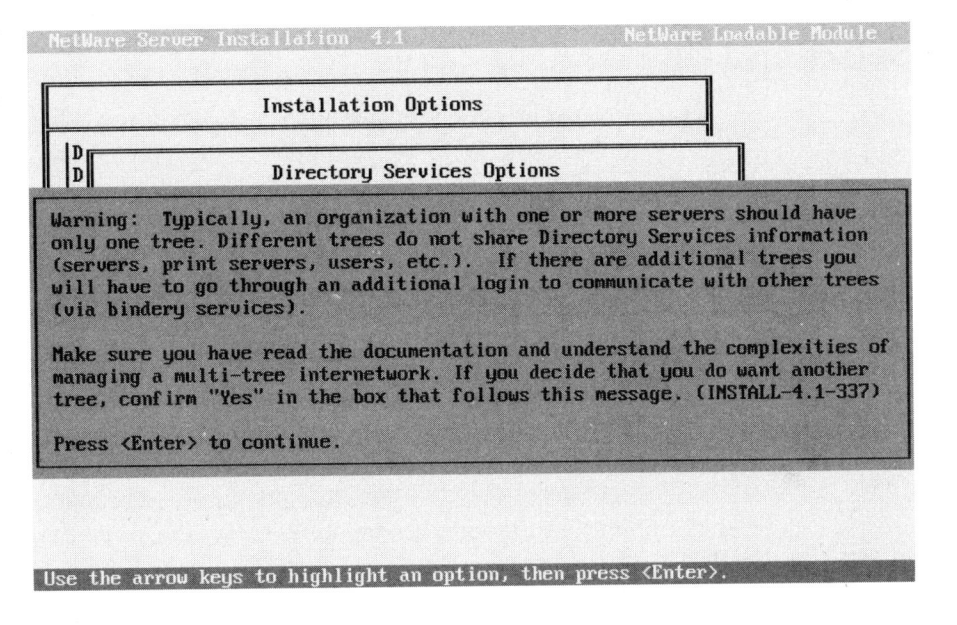

```
NetWare Server Installation  4.1                    NetWare Loadable Module

                    ┌─────────────────────────────────────────┐
                    │         Installation Options            │
                    ├─D┬──────────────────────────────────────┤
                    │ D│      Directory Services Options      │
┌───────────────────┴──┴──────────────────────────────────────┴─┐
│ Warning:  Typically, an organization with one or more servers should have │
│ only one tree.  Different trees do not share Directory Services information│
│ (servers, print servers, users, etc.).  If there are additional trees you │
│ will have to go through an additional login to communicate with other trees│
│ (via bindery services).                                                    │
│                                                                            │
│ Make sure you have read the documentation and understand the complexities of│
│ managing a multi-tree internetwork.  If you decide that you do want another│
│ tree, confirm "Yes" in the box that follows this message. (INSTALL-4.1-337)│
│                                                                            │
│ Press <Enter> to continue.                                                 │
└────────────────────────────────────────────────────────────────────────────┘

     Use the arrow keys to highlight an option, then press <Enter>.
```

FIGURE 3.9
Choosing your NDS tree

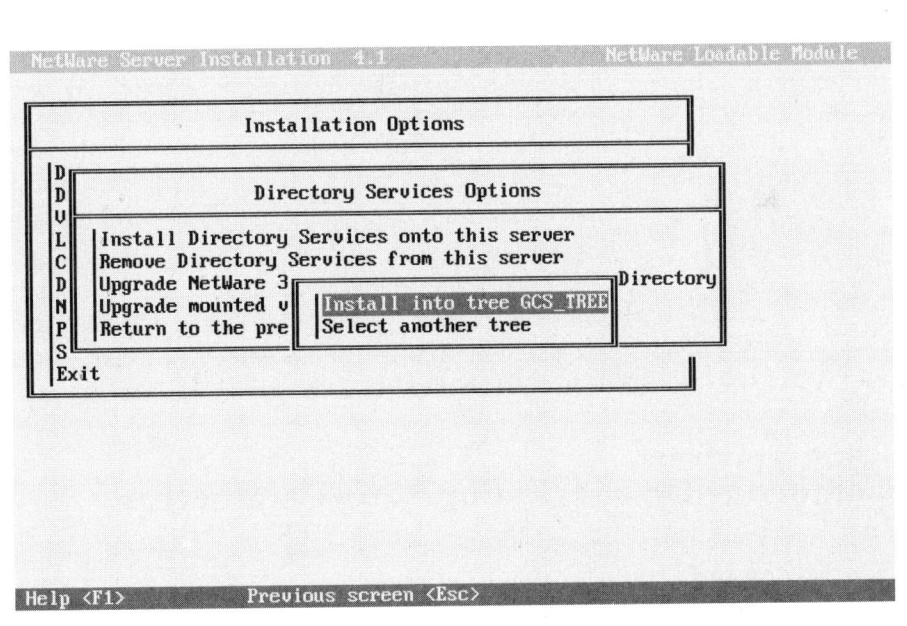

```
NetWare Server Installation  4.1                    NetWare Loadable Module

                    ┌─────────────────────────────────────────┐
                    │         Installation Options            │
                    ├─D┬──────────────────────────────────────┤
                    │ D│      Directory Services Options      │
                    │ U├──────────────────────────────────────┤
                    │ L│ Install Directory Services onto this server      │
                    │ C│ Remove Directory Services from this server       │
                    │ D│ Upgrade NetWare 3 ┌────────────────────────┐Directory│
                    │ N│ Upgrade mounted v │ Install into tree GCS_TREE │
                    │ P│ Return to the pre │ Select another tree        │
                    │ S└───────────────────┴────────────────────────┘
                    │ Exit
                    └────────────────────────────────────────────

 Help <F1>         Previous screen <Esc>
```

Selecting a Different NDS Tree

Picking Select a Tree checks the network for existing NDS trees. Since a second NDS tree may be connected through a router of some sort, there is the chance the connection is down or slow. If this is the case, a screen will appear asking if you want to recheck for a NetWare 4 network. Pressing the Enter key on that choice will once again broadcast a request from your server being installed to any other listening NetWare 4.1x servers.

When several trees exist in your network, all of them may respond to the request of your new server. If that's the case, simply highlight the tree you want from the pick list and press the Enter key. Continue on with the time zone configuration.

If your desired NDS tree is still not located, recheck that the network is configured correctly and the cabling system is intact. The new server must have a working LAN driver, including the proper frame type for the network. If the new server has been set up to use the Ethernet II frame type, it will not communicate with servers and clients using the Ethernet 802.2 frame type.

Once all the network details have been checked, and you're confident the servers should be seeing each other, there is one more process. Your network may have SAP (Service Advertising Protocol) filtering, to keep servers from broadcasting their location across the entire network. If that's the case, you must specify a specific address for a server in the tree you wish to reach.

Choose the Specify Address of Your NetWare 4 Server option. You will then be asked to supply the name of the NDS tree and the IPX address of that particular server.

With a specific name and network address available, the installation program will connect to the named server. The SAP filtering and any packet restriction settings on routers will allow packets that have a definite destination. You can then connect to your tree of desire and continue the installation.

Continuing On and Setting Time Parameters

After you've chosen the tree, your next step is to set the server's time zone and time synchronization parameters. The Choose a Time Zone screen (Figure 3.4) is the same no matter how many NDS trees your network supports. However, you'll see a difference on the Verify/Enter Time Configuration Parameters screen for your second and subsequent servers. Notice in Figure 3.10 that the field above the highlighted CST shows this to be a Secondary time server.

FIGURE 3.10

A secondary time server configuration

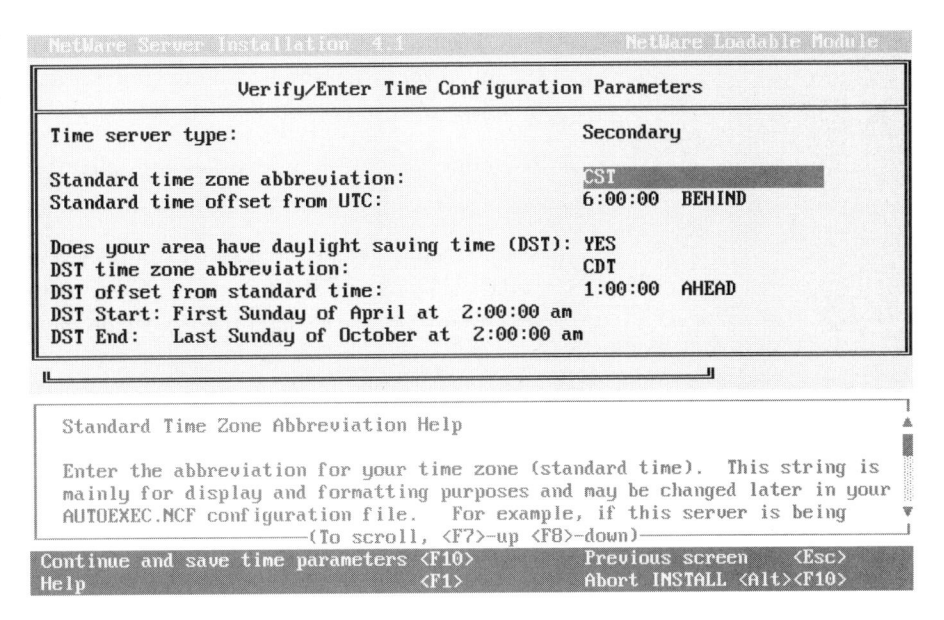

```
╔═ NetWare Server Installation 4.1 ═══════════════ NetWare Loadable Module ═╗
║              Verify/Enter Time Configuration Parameters                    ║
║                                                                            ║
║  Time server type:                         Secondary                       ║
║                                                                            ║
║  Standard time zone abbreviation:          CST                             ║
║  Standard time offset from UTC:            6:00:00  BEHIND                 ║
║                                                                            ║
║  Does your area have daylight saving time (DST): YES                       ║
║  DST time zone abbreviation:               CDT                             ║
║  DST offset from standard time:            1:00:00  AHEAD                  ║
║  DST Start: First Sunday of April at  2:00:00 am                           ║
║  DST End:   Last Sunday of October at 2:00:00 am                           ║
╚════════════════════════════════════════════════════════════════════════════╝
┌────────────────────────────────────────────────────────────────────────────┐
│  Standard Time Zone Abbreviation Help                                      │
│                                                                            │
│  Enter the abbreviation for your time zone (standard time).  This string is│
│  mainly for display and formatting purposes and may be changed later in your│
│  AUTOEXEC.NCF configuration file.  For example, if this server is being    │
└──────────────────────── (To scroll, <F7>-up <F8>-down) ────────────────────┘
 Continue and save time parameters <F10>       Previous screen        <Esc>
 Help                               <F1>       Abort INSTALL    <Alt><F10>
```

The existence of multiple servers on your network changes how the network tracks time.

When you set up your first NetWare 4.1x server, you chose the Single Reference time server type, since there was only a single server on the network. That same choice is still valid for one server on the network, but not for a second server (that's why it's called a *Single* Reference time server).

Time Servers and Their Uses

With multiple servers, we need to better understand what time servers do for the network. The types of time servers are:

- **Single Reference:** The only time provider on the network. This is the default for the first server on a network.

- **Primary:** Synchronizes its time with other Primary and Reference time servers and adjusts to the average of all other Primary time servers.

- **Reference:** Provides the time for all the network servers and clients to synchronize. Often the Reference time server is connected to an outside time source for accuracy.

- **Secondary:** Provides time to network clients, but does not collaborate work with other time servers to set the time.

All servers being installed into an existing NetWare 4.1*x* network will default to Secondary time servers. All time servers provide time to clients, but some time servers communicate with each other to decide the proper network time.

SINGLE REFERENCE TIME SERVERS A Single Reference time server provides time to all other servers and clients. Other servers must be configured as Secondary time servers, not Primary or Reference servers. The network administrator sets the time on a Single Reference server, although time can also be checked against an outside source, such as a radio clock. With a single-server network, time is rarely so critical as to require outside verification.

A Single Reference time server network has no time fault-tolerance. If all other servers rely on one server, and the server goes down, time will slip. Smaller networks with few servers are more likely to have a Single Reference time server. Other servers, if they exist, do not negotiate with a Single Reference time server to set the time; they just accept the time given.

REFERENCE TIME SERVERS More restrictive than the Single Reference time server, the Reference time server is often tied to an outside source for accurate time. While the Reference time server communicates with other servers to discuss the actual time, the other Reference and Primary time servers must accept the time from the Reference time server.

It is advisable to have multiple time servers if your network is geographically distributed. The delay in transmitting time information will skew your time settings across a WAN. The best plan is to have a Reference time server and an additional Primary server in each geographical location to provide time information for those clients and servers. The fewer time packets you have crossing your WAN, the better.

PRIMARY TIME SERVERS The Primary time server synchronizes time settings with at least one other Reference or Primary time server. Each server offers its time, then learns the time of the other servers, then an agreed-upon time is set for all Reference and Primary time servers.

Large networks use Primary time servers to offer alternative paths to other Secondary time servers. In WANs, a Primary time server will handle the long-distance connection to another time server source and pass that time along to local Secondary time servers.

SECONDARY TIME SERVERS Secondary time servers obtain time from a Single Reference, Reference, or Primary time server and pass that time to clients. The Secondary time server does not vote with other time providers to set the time.

Most servers will be Secondary time servers, especially in a large, distributed network. For best time keeping, make time server connections across the fastest network links possible.

Setting the Server's Context

Whether this server is the second or the seventieth, a context must be named and set for each server. Why? A server object is just one more item for a container to hold. Each object must be in a container. So, the server must be listed by context, which means we must identify which Organization or Organizational Unit holds the server object. You can simply place the new server into the same context as the previous one, or if your NDS design dictates, make this new server the start of a new context.

Setting the Admin Name and Password

No matter if the server is going into an existing context or creating a brand new one for itself, there is an existing NDS tree built and active. If there is an NDS tree, there is security, and you must log in to the tree.

Figure 3.11 shows the login screen for the NDS authentication process. There is only one NDS Admin user in this network, so the program displayed that name automatically. Notice the five asterisks indicating the password has been typed in the highlighted bar area.

If there are several Admin users or equivalents, you can press the Enter key while highlighting the Administrator Name field and type in the name of your choice. However, this is not the time to add a new Admin user to your NDS tree. If the name you provide does not exist and have Admin-level privileges, you will get an error message and be asked to try again.

FIGURE 3.11

Proving you belong to the NDS tree

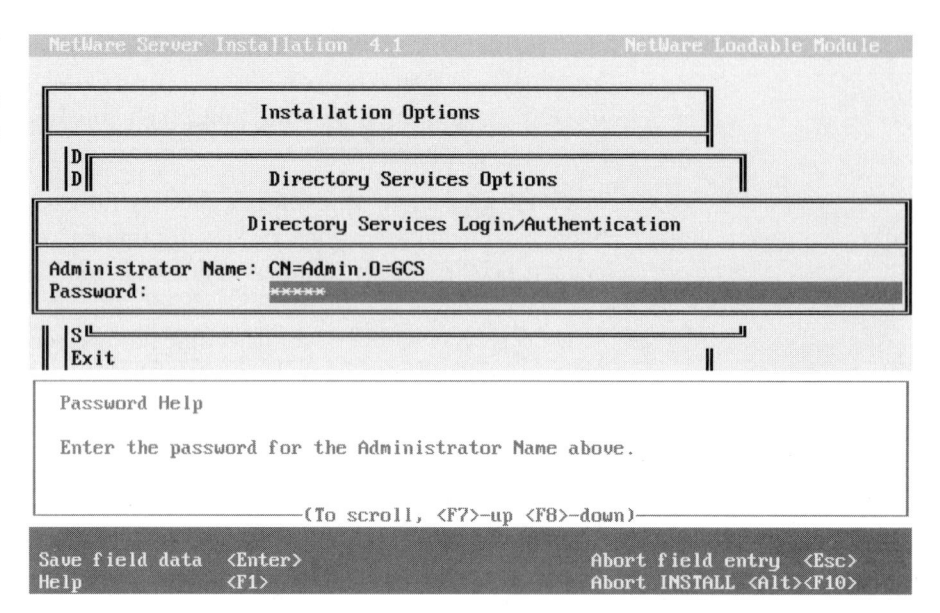

```
NetWare Server Installation 4.1                    NetWare Loadable Module
┌──────────────────────────────────────────────────────────────────────┐
│                        Installation Options                          │
├─D────────────────────────────────────────────────────────────────────┤
│ D                     Directory Services Options                     │
├──────────────────────────────────────────────────────────────────────┤
│                  Directory Services Login/Authentication             │
│ Administrator Name: CN=Admin.O=GCS                                   │
│ Password:           *****                                            │
├─S────────────────────────────────────────────────────────────────────┤
│ Exit                                                                 │
└──────────────────────────────────────────────────────────────────────┘
 Password Help

 Enter the password for the Administrator Name above.


 ─────────────────(To scroll, <F7>-up <F8>-down)─────────────────
 Save field data   <Enter>                    Abort field entry  <Esc>
 Help              <F1>                       Abort INSTALL  <Alt><F10>
```

Naming Your Organization

You can install this server into an existing Organization or set up a new Organizational Unit if you wish. Since an Organizational Unit is a container object, you can create a new one to hold the server you are installing.

When the highlight bar is on the Company or Organization field at the top of the Context For This Server screen, press the Enter key to accept the Organization name shown. If there are several Organization names defined in your NDS tree, a pick list will appear when you press the Enter key, offering a chance to highlight and choose the Organization you prefer.

If you want to create another Organization, type the Organization name in the field. The installation program will create the requested Organization, which will define the context for this server.

Naming Organizational Units

Once the Organization is chosen, you repeat the choose/create process for each level of Organizational Unit. Up to three levels will be installed by the prompts, but you can add more by directly editing the name in the Server Context field.

Figure 3.12 shows the new server being installed into an existing context described by the Organization name GCS and the Organizational Unit INTEGRATE. The small window in the middle of the screen labeled Choose a Name appeared when I pressed the Enter key with the highlight bar on the Level 1 Sub-Organizational Unit field.

FIGURE 3.12

Specifying a context in an existing NDS tree

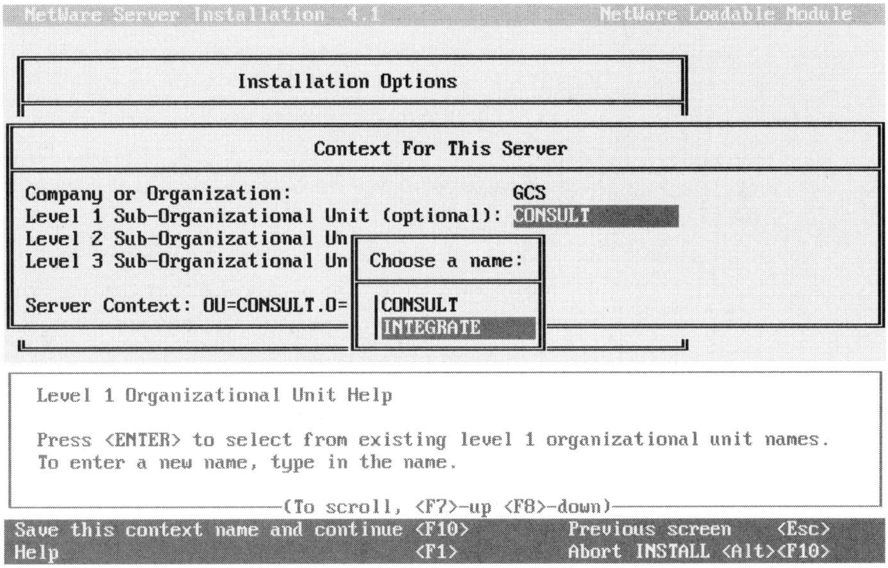

```
NetWare Server Installation  4.1                    NetWare Loadable Module
┌──────────────────────────────────────────────────────────┐
│                    Installation Options                  │
├──────────────────────────────────────────────────────────┤
│                  Context For This Server                 │
│                                                          │
│  Company or Organization:              GCS               │
│  Level 1 Sub-Organizational Unit (optional): CONSULT     │
│  Level 2 Sub-Organizational Un┌──────────────┐           │
│  Level 3 Sub-Organizational Un│ Choose a name:│          │
│                               │               │          │
│  Server Context: OU=CONSULT.O=│ CONSULT       │          │
│                               │ INTEGRATE     │          │
└───────────────────────────────┴───────────────┴──────────┘

  Level 1 Organizational Unit Help

  Press <ENTER> to select from existing level 1 organizational unit names.
  To enter a new name, type in the name.
  ─────────────(To scroll, <F7>-up <F8>-down)─────────────
  Save this context name and continue <F10>   Previous screen    <Esc>
  Help                                 <F1>   Abort INSTALL <Alt><F10>
```

The lab network NDS tree has a single Organization name, but two Organizational Units. Since CONSULT comes before INTEGRATE alphabetically, CONSULT appeared in the field.

Since CONSULT wasn't the Organizational Unit I wanted, I highlighted INTEGRATE and pressed the Enter key. That officially placed the server CLONE386 into a particular context. The full name of this server is now CLONE386.INTEGRATE.GCS.

Many servers can be placed into a single context. Each server must have a unique name because each server may broadcast available services across the network, and identical server names will be confusing to everyone.

The rule I suggest when designing your NDS is to keep the tree fairly flat. Some references may have you go overboard when segmenting your tree. Although you can have a server named SERVER1.DALLAS. SALES.WEST.US, the convenience may support the network designers more than the network users. Keep the hierarchical levels as shallow as possible. Some examples in the next chapter might help you design your NDS tree.

Once you press the F10 key to save this context name and continue, all the information you have entered for this server will be dispersed across the network. There is always a slight delay, especially if WAN links are involved. Figure 3.13 clues you into the situation.

Every change to NDS takes time to ripple out to all the connected servers. Remember to have some patience when making Directory changes. With NetWare 3.*x*, you can make a change and test it immediately; but you must wait a moment before testing changes in NetWare 4.1*x*. You don't need to wait long—just longer than with earlier NetWare.

Finally, insert the license diskette that contains the SERVER.MOF file into your floppy drive (or specify a different path) to complete the license procedure, and then press Enter.

FIGURE 3.13

The NDS installation program updating the network

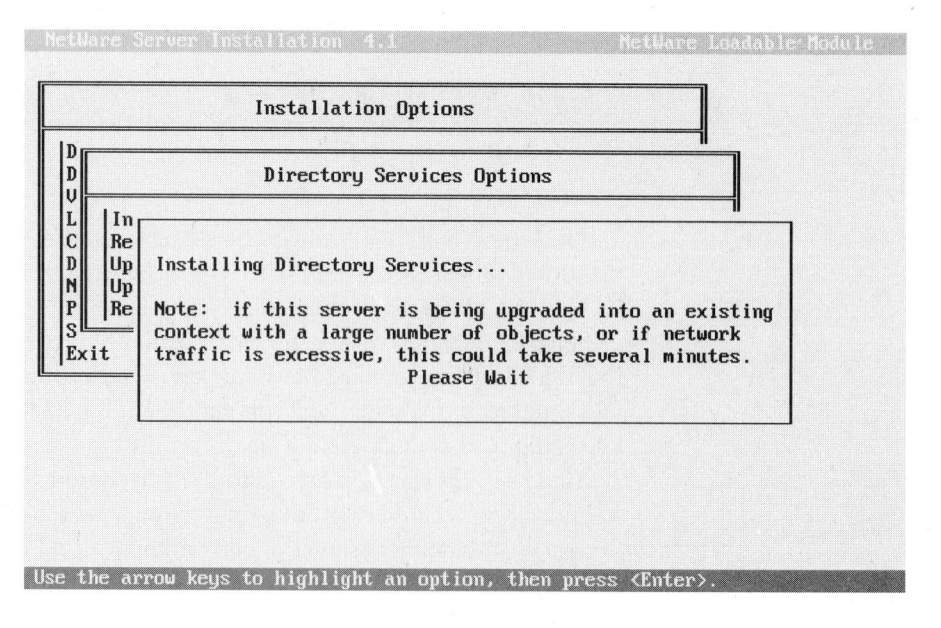

```
NetWare Server Installation 4.1                    NetWare Loadable Module

        ┌─────────────────────────────────────────────────────────┐
        │                  Installation Options                   │
        ┌─┬─────────────────────────────────────────────────────┐ │
        │D│            Directory Services Options               │ │
        │D├─┬─────────────────────────────────────────────────┐ │ │
        │U│ │                                                 │ │ │
        │L│I│                                                 │ │ │
        │C│R│                                                 │ │ │
        │D│U│  Installing Directory Services...               │ │ │
        │N│U│                                                 │ │ │
        │P│R│  Note: if this server is being upgraded into an existing
        │S├─┘  context with a large number of objects, or if network
        │Exit  traffic is excessive, this could take several minutes.
        │                         Please Wait
        └─────────────────────────────────────────────────────────┘

Use the arrow keys to highlight an option, then press <Enter>.
```

Finishing Installation and Your Next Steps

WE'RE ALMOST THERE—a complete, new server. One important job remains, and some optional jobs are available during the installation process.

Let's take care of the important job first. Your PC uses two files named CONFIG.SYS and AUTOEXEC.BAT to configure the machine upon startup. Your server needs the same job performed, but the files in this case are named STARTUP.NCF and AUTOEXEC.NCF.

Changes made in STARTUP.NCF and AUTOEXEC.NCF do not take effect until the server is rebooted. These files are read-only when the server starts.

Modifying the STARTUP.NCF File

The STARTUP.NCF file lives in the DOS partition on your server hard disk. It loads immediately after the SERVER.EXE program executes.

Disk drivers are the main concern of the STARTUP.NCF file. Different name spaces for Macintosh, OS/2, Unix, or FTAM files must be loaded before the actual disk driver gets going. The files referenced in the STARTUP.NCF file should be in the \NWSERVER directory of the DOS boot disk partition.

Some commands used in STARTUP.NCF to set up name space support are:

```
LOAD MAC.NAM
LOAD OS2.NAM
LOAD NFS.NAM
LOAD FTAM.NAM
```

Server parameter settings in STARTUP.NCF are made with SET commands, such as:

```
SET Maximum Physical Receive Packet Size
SET Auto Register Memory Above 16 Megabytes
SET Reserved Buffers Below 16 Meg
SET Maximum Subdirectory Tree Depth
SET Auto TTS Backout Flag
SET Minimum Packet Buffer
```

Another command you'll see in this file is:

```
PAUSE
```

The most commonly used of the above SET commands are:

```
SET Auto Register Memory Above 16 Megabytes ON
SET Reserved Buffers Below 16 Meg=200
```

These are used with EISA bus PCs, especially those with CD-ROM drives attached. Some EISA machines don't automatically register machine memory beyond 16 MB, which is the reason for the first command. Some CD-ROM drives don't handle extended memory for buffers well, which is why you may need the second command. These and other SET commands will be covered in depth in Chapter 10.

Figure 3.14 shows a fairly empty STARTUP.NCF file for the server CLONE386. When the Adaptec 1540 disk driver is loaded, the SYS: volume automatically mounts. Notice all the instructions across the bottom of the screen in Figure 3.14. If you guess from those hints that the editor for NetWare installation is capable of a decent level of text handling, you are correct.

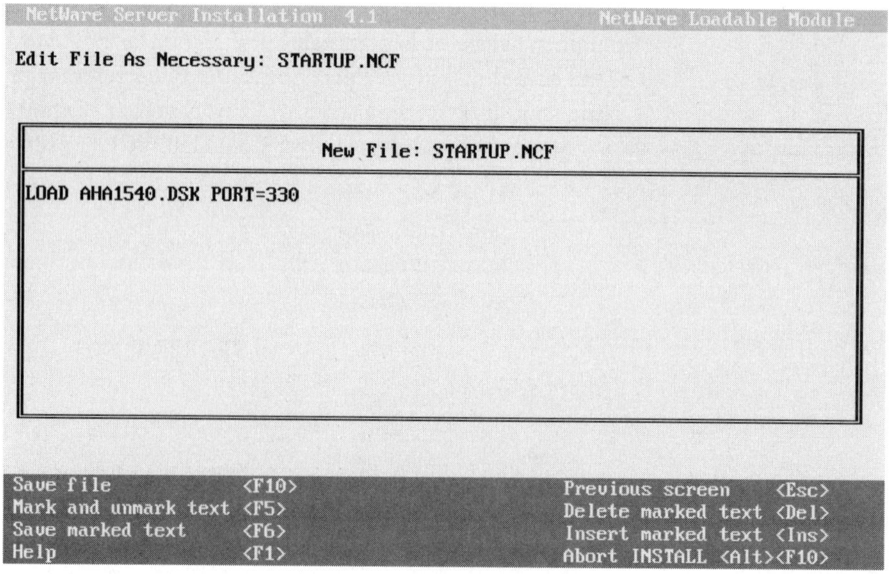

FIGURE 3.14

Your chance to modify STARTUP.NCF during installation

```
NetWare Server Installation 4.1                    NetWare Loadable Module
Edit File As Necessary: STARTUP.NCF

┌──────────────────────── New File: STARTUP.NCF ────────────────────────┐
│ LOAD AHA1540.DSK PORT=330                                              │
│                                                                        │
│                                                                        │
│                                                                        │
│                                                                        │
│                                                                        │
│                                                                        │
│                                                                        │
└────────────────────────────────────────────────────────────────────────┘

Save file          <F10>              Previous screen     <Esc>
Mark and unmark text <F5>             Delete marked text  <Del>
Save marked text   <F6>               Insert marked text  <Ins>
Help               <F1>               Abort INSTALL       <Alt><F10>
```

Editing STARTUP.NCF after Server Installation

There are two other ways to modify the STARTUP.NCF file through NetWare. Once the server is up and running, you can always type:

```
LOAD INSTALL
```

from the console prompt, then choose NCF Files Options (create/edit server startup files) from the menu. The screen that appears offers you a choice of creating or modifying both STARTUP.NCF and AUTOEXEC.NCF files. If you choose Edit STARTUP.NCF file from that menu, a window verifies that the file exists on the DOS partition of the server hard disk. Then the STARTUP.NCF file appears, looking exactly the way it does in Figure 3.14.

A second method for changing some of the STARTUP.NCF parameters is through the SERVMAN utility at the server console. The SERVMAN utility will be discussed in Chapter 10, which covers managing your network.

Modifying the AUTOEXEC.NCF File

The AUTOEXEC.NCF file executes after SERVER.EXE has started the operating system and STARTUP.NCF has loaded the disk drivers necessary to mount the SYS: volume. This is the first file read from the NetWare server portion of the file server hard disk. All other parameters configured during installation are set by the AUTOEXEC.NCF file.

AUTOEXEC.NCF sets the following server details:

- Time zone SET commands, including Daylight Saving Time details
- Bindery context (for emulating the bindery of NetWare 3.*x*)
- Time server type
- Server name
- IPX internal network number
- All LOAD and BIND commands for LAN drivers, protocols, and frame types
- Mount commands for server volumes
- NLMs loaded, such as REMOTE.NLM and PSERVER.NLM

154 Chapter 3 ▪ Installing NetWare Directory Services and Optional Procedures

Figure 3.15 shows the AUTOEXEC.NCF file for server GATEWAY2000, the lead server in the lab network. One clue that GATEWAY2000 is the lead server is the line near the middle of the screen that reads:

```
set Default Time Server Type = SINGLE
```

This shows it's a Single Reference time server. You want the main timekeeper of your network to be reliable and well-monitored.

FIGURE 3.15

A sample AUTOEXEC.NCF file

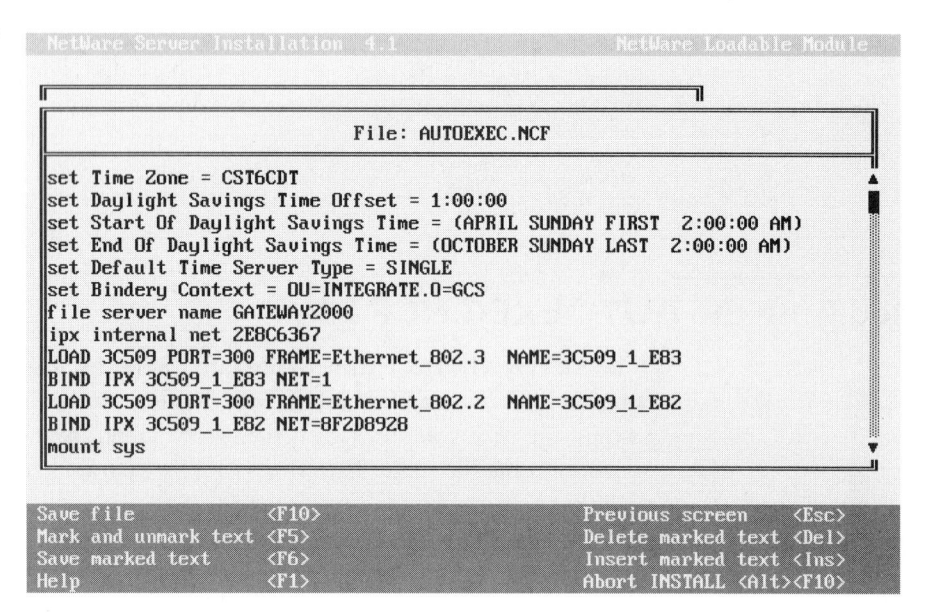

```
NetWare Server Installation  4.1              NetWare Loadable Module

                         File: AUTOEXEC.NCF

set Time Zone = CST6CDT
set Daylight Savings Time Offset = 1:00:00
set Start Of Daylight Savings Time = (APRIL SUNDAY FIRST  2:00:00 AM)
set End Of Daylight Savings Time = (OCTOBER SUNDAY LAST  2:00:00 AM)
set Default Time Server Type = SINGLE
set Bindery Context = OU=INTEGRATE.O=GCS
file server name GATEWAY2000
ipx internal net 2E8C6367
LOAD 3C509 PORT=300 FRAME=Ethernet_802.3  NAME=3C509_1_E83
BIND IPX 3C509_1_E83 NET=1
LOAD 3C509 PORT=300 FRAME=Ethernet_802.2  NAME=3C509_1_E82
BIND IPX 3C509_1_E82 NET=8F2D8928
mount sys

Save file            <F10>        Previous screen        <Esc>
Mark and unmark text <F5>         Delete marked text     <Del>
Save marked text     <F6>         Insert marked text     <Ins>
Help                 <F1>         Abort INSTALL    <Alt><F10>
```

Notice the same text-editing capabilities are available for the AUTOEXEC.NCF file as are available for STARTUP.NCF. Editing the AUTOEXEC.NCF file after the server is completely installed is done by following the same procedure described in the previous section for modifying STARTUP.NCF.

Copying Files to the New Server

Although a batch of files were copied to the server earlier in the process, those were only the "preliminary" files. Those files were necessary to support the rest of the installation process. All the LAN and disk drivers and minimum operating system files were transferred to the server.

Now that all the configuration options for the server have been made, the rest of the NetWare operating system files will be transferred. If you included the client support, client installation, upgrade and migration, OS/2, or Unix client support files from the Select Optional NetWare File Groups screen, all of these will be copied.

The source of the files is the location you described at the beginning of this installation process: internal CD-ROM, remote CD-ROM mounted as a volume, files copied to another server, or (shudder) floppies. Figure 3.16 shows this file copy in progress. The source is the NetWare files installed in the PROJECTS volume on the GATEWAY2000 server. The source for the files at the time of the screenshot is SYS:\SYSTEM on the CLONE386 server.

If you are copying these files across the network, as I am in Figure 3.16, the time will be short. Choosing all the optional file groups for installation will increase the time to completion. Installing from an internal CD-ROM will take longer than installing across the network, but will also be unattended. The difference between copying the files across the network and copying them from the internal CD-ROM drive is the difference between getting a fresh cup of coffee and getting a sandwich. Installing from floppies takes forever and requires constant attention. See why I suggested you splurge the few dollars necessary for a CD-ROM drive?

FIGURE 3.16

The main (and unattended) file copy process

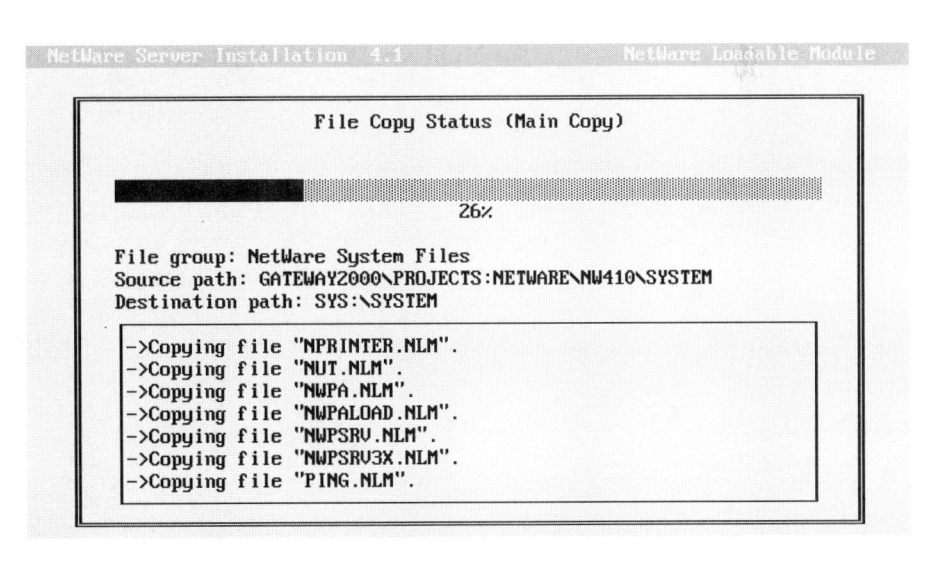

Other Installation Options

After the files are loaded onto your new server's hard disk, the Other Installation Options screen appears. Shown in Figure 3.17, the procedures listed are not absolutely necessary to your server functioning as a NetWare 4.1x server and full player in the NDS tree, but will be important to many people.

You know something is not showing because of the small down arrow in the bottom-left corner of the main window in Figure 3.17. The two procedures that can't be seen are Configure Network Protocols and Install Online Documentation Database and Viewers.

Notice your options in the bottom window:

```
Choose an item or product listed above
Install a product not listed
View/Configure/Remove installed products
Continue installation
```

The highlight bar automatically sits on the last option, Continue Installation, when this screen appears. As you add products to your network over time, you will return here and select some of these other installation actions. Now, however, the fact that the default location for the highlight bar is Continue Installation suggests that we should accept that recommendation and finish.

FIGURE 3.17

More procedures, if you decide to perform them

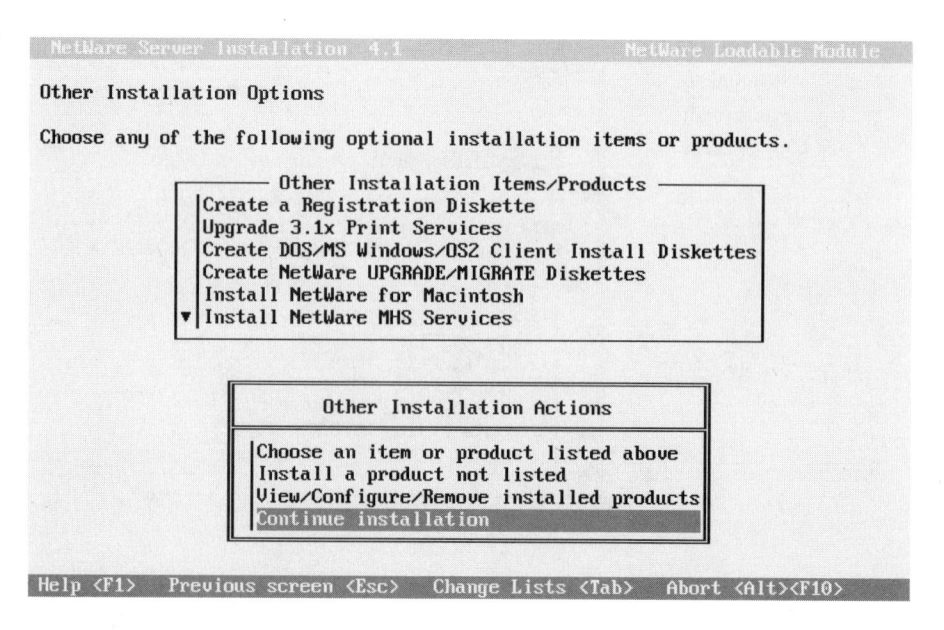

We'll come back to this screen again in the next major section, but I'm superstitious about installations. When I put a new card in a PC, I never put the screws in the case until I test things thoroughly. I put the case on, since I've had situations where the case grounded out wires and the like, but I never screw the cover to the case. That just seems to tempt fate.

Creating a registration diskette, the first option in Figure 3.17, seems to tempt fate in that same manner. And I don't want to install name services for Macintosh or MHS services or configure other protocols until I'm positive all is well with my server. My preference is to first finish up the installation.

Finished!

Whoa! Choosing Continue Installation does nothing except bring up the screen in Figure 3.18. Of course, the verbiage in the screen refers to plenty of other work to be done, such as gaining access to the online documentation and creating network users and the like. The server itself, however, is up and running in under ten minutes of actual hands-on time. Those of you who have been working with NetWare for several versions can now tell the youngsters in the area how hard it used to be with all the floppies and generating the operating system and walking uphill in the snow to work. But they won't listen; darn kids have no respect for the hard work we old-timers suffered through.

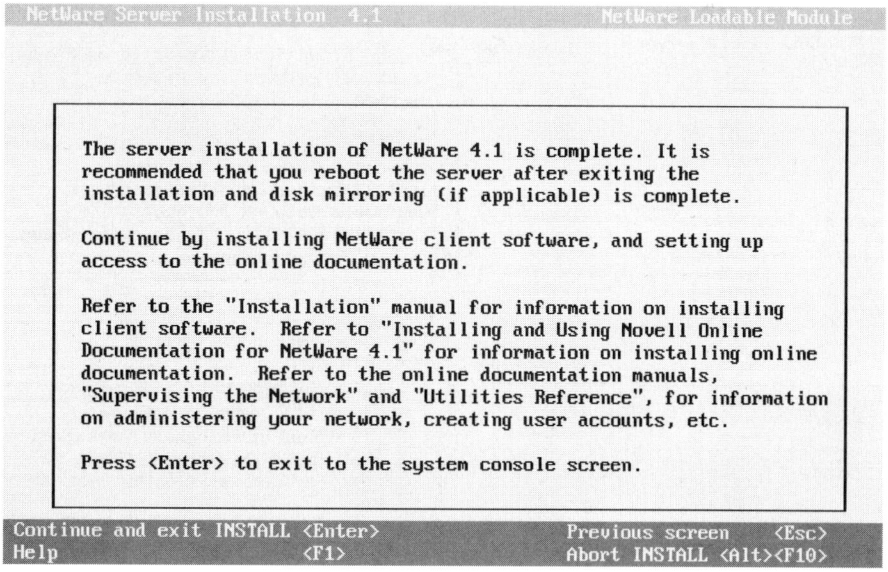

FIGURE 3.18
The last installation screen

```
NetWare Server Installation  4.1              NetWare Loadable Module

    ┌──────────────────────────────────────────────────────────────┐
    │ The server installation of NetWare 4.1 is complete. It is    │
    │ recommended that you reboot the server after exiting the     │
    │ installation and disk mirroring (if applicable) is complete. │
    │                                                              │
    │ Continue by installing NetWare client software, and setting up│
    │ access to the online documentation.                          │
    │                                                              │
    │ Refer to the "Installation" manual for information on installing│
    │ client software.  Refer to "Installing and Using Novell Online│
    │ Documentation for NetWare 4.1" for information on installing online│
    │ documentation.  Refer to the online documentation manuals,   │
    │ "Supervising the Network" and "Utilities Reference", for information│
    │ on administering your network, creating user accounts, etc.  │
    │                                                              │
    │ Press <Enter> to exit to the system console screen.          │
    └──────────────────────────────────────────────────────────────┘

Continue and exit INSTALL <Enter>          Previous screen      <Esc>
Help                    <F1>               Abort INSTALL <Alt><F10>
```

Optional Installation Items, Procedures, and Products

THERE ARE SEVERAL NetWare pieces that you may or may not want installed onto your server. Although I prefer not to add all the pieces until I'm sure the basic server operations are functioning, the process of installation is the same whether it's done during server installation or the next day.

NetWare 4.11 adds a few new wrinkles, as you might expect. The details for installing these are gathered at the end of this chapter. Don't feel cheated if some of the NetWare 4.10 menu options, such as creating a registration diskette, have gone away in NetWare 4.11; that's the way of all menu options.

Figure 3.19 shows the screen for Other Installation Items/Products that appears when you load the INSTALL.NLM program after the server is up and running. Notice it is slightly different than Figure 3.17, which appears during the server installation process.

The only option you can't see in Figure 3.19 is Install Online Documentation and Viewers, at the bottom of the top window. And this is the only one that isn't really "optional." If this is your first server, having access to the

FIGURE 3.19

Pumping up your server

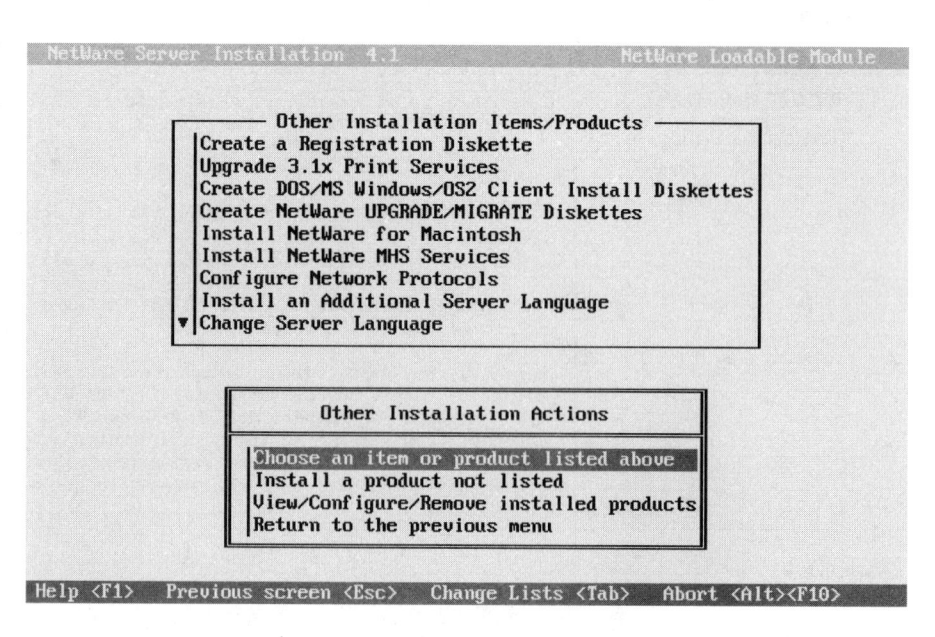

```
NetWare Server Installation 4.1                    NetWare Loadable Module

              ┌──────── Other Installation Items/Products ────────┐
              │ Create a Registration Diskette                    │
              │ Upgrade 3.1x Print Services                       │
              │ Create DOS/MS Windows/OS2 Client Install Diskettes│
              │ Create NetWare UPGRADE/MIGRATE Diskettes          │
              │ Install NetWare for Macintosh                     │
              │ Install NetWare MHS Services                      │
              │ Configure Network Protocols                       │
              │ Install an Additional Server Language             │
              ▼ Change Server Language                            │
              └───────────────────────────────────────────────────┘

                          ┌──────── Other Installation Actions ────────┐
                          │ Choose an item or product listed above     │
                          │ Install a product not listed               │
                          │ View/Configure/Remove installed products   │
                          │ Return to the previous menu                │
                          └────────────────────────────────────────────┘

  Help <F1>    Previous screen <Esc>     Change Lists <Tab>    Abort <Alt><F10>
```

Optional Installation Items, Procedures, and Products **159**

documentation is critical. We'll cover the options in their screen order, but you can skip to the last one and get your documentation taken care of first.

The procedure for adding any of the other installation items or products options shown in Figure 3.19 is to:

- Use the up arrow key to move the highlight bar from the bottom window.
- Highlight the desired item or product.
- Press the Enter key.
- Follow any subsequent instructions.

Most of the products listed in Figure 3.19 are located on one of the two NetWare CD-ROM disks. The first option, Create a Registration Diskette, also requires the use of the registration floppy included with NetWare.

Many of the product installations require additional NLMs to be loaded, so don't be alarmed if there is a slight delay. Some products may also require the Admin password.

Creating a Registration Diskette

3.1 IN-A-HURRY

Create Your Registration Disk

1. Get the registration disk and the addresses of your Novell reseller and the reseller's contact within your company.
2. Type **LOAD INSTALL** at the server console prompt.
3. Highlight Product Options and press Enter.
4. Highlight Create a Registration Diskette and press Enter.
5. Read the notice screen, and then press F10.
6. Provide the requested reseller information and press F10.
7. Provide your customer information and press F10.
8. Decide whether to include server-specific information (recommended).
9. Place the disk in the prepaid, preaddressed mailer and send it in.

In the old days, before NetWare 4.x, registration was accomplished by handwriting information on a tiny postcard and mailing same. That's why all your future upgrade and technical information for those products was addressed to "Snitih" instead of "Smith." Either your handwriting was terrible, or the clerk typing in registration forms messed up. Either way, creative names and other misinformation became embedded in the vendor's system, never to be put right.

With NetWare 4.x, Novell moved the blame for typos off its back and squarely onto yours. The included diskette will be loaded with information you provided (typed in yourself), then mailed back to Novell. There, the file will be dumped directly into the system without retyping. So if there's a mistake, look in the mirror.

From the server console type the command:

```
LOAD INSTALL
```

to bring up the Installation Options screen. Highlight Product Options by using the arrow keys or by typing **P**. Most NetWare screens will jump to the requested entry if you type the beginning letter or two.

Create a Registration Diskette is your first choice in the Other Installation Items/Products screen. To move the highlight bar to the top window, press the up arrow key four times. Highlighting Choose an Item or Product Listed Above in the bottom window and pressing Enter serves the same function.

You will see an information screen advising you to get your registration diskette and gather some address information. That screen is shown in Figure 3.20.

There are two screens to fill out, which appear after you press F10 from this information screen. The first is about your reseller, including its address and Reseller Access Number. This information is helpful, but not mandatory. The second screen gives information about your company and network. Some information, such as address, phone number, organization name, postal code, and country, is required before leaving this screen.

After pressing F10, you have the choice to copy specific server and site information to the registration diskette. Your server name, software version number, amount of server memory, cache buffers, server serial number, LAN interface card information, hard disk, and volume details are included. The information will be used by Novell tech support personnel if you call in for help. There's no downside to this, and it takes no work on your part, so you might as well agree, just in case it does help someday.

Included in your box of NetWare is a postage-paid return disk mailer, just for this registration diskette. Go ahead; you'll feel like a better person after you've registered.

Optional Installation Items, Procedures, and Products | 161

FIGURE 3.20
Information needed for your registration diskette

```
╔══ NetWare Software Registration  4.1 ═══════════ NetWare Loadable Module ══╗

  ┌─────────────────────────────────────────────────────────────────────┐
  │ This utility will aid you in the process of registering your        │
  │ software. In order to complete the registration process, you will   │
  │ need:                                                               │
  │                                                                     │
  │  1) The registration diskette included with the software            │
  │  2) The phone number and address of the person within your company  │
  │     who is the contact with your Novell Reseller.                   │
  │  3) The name and address of your Novell Reseller.                   │
  │                                                                     │
  │ Accuracy of the address information is critical to future           │
  │ communications between Novell and you.                              │
  │                                                                     │
  │                     <Press F10 to continue>                         │
  └─────────────────────────────────────────────────────────────────────┘

  <F10> Next screen                                          <ALT-F10> Exit
```

If this diskette and mailer are missing, check with your reseller. Some dealers that install the server software also submit the registration information. Before you panic, ask your dealer.

Upgrading NetWare 3.1x Print Services

3.2 IN-A-HURRY

Upgrade Your Print Services

1. Type **LOAD INSTALL** at the server console prompt.

2. Highlight Product Options and press Enter.

3. Highlight Upgrade 3.1x Print Services and press Enter.

4. Provide your login name and password.

5. Accept print system information to upgrade.

6. Test all newly defined printers, print queues, and print servers.

If your first NetWare 4.1*x* server used to be a NetWare 3.1*x* server, the NetWare 4.1*x* installation process will leave the older print system components alone during the upgrade. However, NetWare 4.1*x* graciously offers you a chance to upgrade the print system rather than going to the trouble of recreating it all under NetWare 4.1*x*.

Run the INSTALL program from the server console, choose Product Options, select Upgrade 3.1x Print Services, and press Enter. This begins the connection to the now-orphaned NetWare 3.1*x* printer system.

A valid Admin-level login name and password must be provided. Either type the name in where requested, or press Enter to search the NDS database. When you find the name you want, in the context you want, press Enter to accept and provide the proper password.

The upgrade process converts the Print Queue Operator to an Operator property of the Print Queue object. The NetWare 3.1*x* print queue becomes a Print Queue object. These are upgraded to full NetWare 4.1*x* print queues. All printers become Printer objects when the PUPGRADE.NLM program is run. This will take place during the Upgrade 3.1x Print Services operation.

Once you've upgraded the print system, check each printer, print queue, and print server. Printers are common sources of complaints, so head off as many of your problem-printout-possessed users as possible.

Creating DOS, MS Windows, or OS/2 Client Install Diskettes

3.3 IN-A-HURRY

Create Client Installation Disks

1. Type **LOAD INSTALL** at the server console prompt.

2. Highlight Product Options and press Enter.

3. Highlight Create DOS/MS Windows/OS2 Client Install Diskettes and press Enter.

4. Choose which client installation disk set you want to create, and then press F10.

5. Insert a formatted, high-density disk in the server's floppy drive and press Enter.

6. Insert each blank disk when requested (either 5 or 7 are necessary).

7. Label the disks as suggested by the installation program.

Optional Installation Items, Procedures, and Products   163

First bit of advice: don't create your client installation disks on the file server. The server is usually locked away in an inconvenient room, so feeding blank, formatted diskettes to it won't be handy. Writing to the floppy takes more server resources than it should, much like when you try to format a floppy in a background DOS box while running MS Windows. The disk copy procedure takes what seems like forever when using the server's floppy disk drive.

After starting the INSTALL.NLM program at the server console, open the Product Options window by highlighting that choice and pressing Enter. The third choice in the top window is to create the client installation diskettes. As you might expect, there is a screen that lets you choose what type of installation diskettes you want. Figure 3.21 illustrates your choices.

Notice that there is still an option (in NetWare 4.10, but not NetWare 4.11) to create 5.25-inch floppy disks, but only for the DOS and MS Windows file groups. The OS/2 disks will copy only to 3.5-inch floppies, since OS/2 appeared first with the PS/2 IBM computers that came standard with the 3.5-inch floppy disk drive. Take this as a hint to buy all your future systems with 3.5-inch floppy drives. Not a mandate; just a hint to those who watch trends.

Take your batch of five (for DOS and MS Windows) or seven (for OS/2) blank and preformatted disks, and copy the first one when asked. The program will stop (finally) and ask you for the second, third, and so on, disks.

FIGURE 3.21

Choosing your client installation program file groups

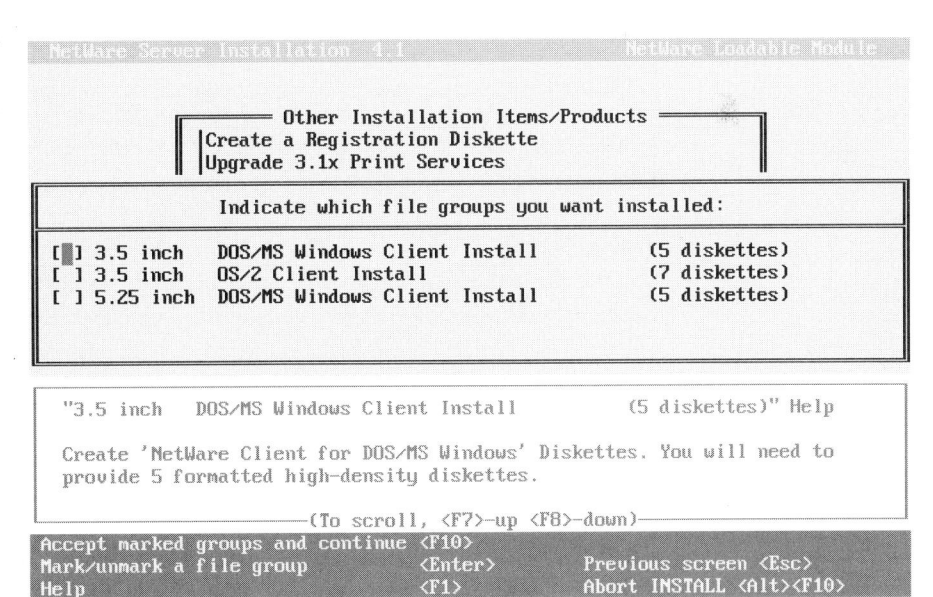

```
NetWare Server Installation  4.1                    NetWare Loadable Module
                ┌──────── Other Installation Items/Products ────────┐
                │ Create a Registration Diskette                     │
                │ Upgrade 3.1x Print Services                        │
                └────────────────────────────────────────────────────┘
      ┌────────────────────────────────────────────────────────────────┐
      │        Indicate which file groups you want installed:          │
      ├────────────────────────────────────────────────────────────────┤
      │  [■] 3.5 inch    DOS/MS Windows Client Install   (5 diskettes) │
      │  [ ] 3.5 inch    OS/2 Client Install             (7 diskettes) │
      │  [ ] 5.25 inch   DOS/MS Windows Client Install   (5 diskettes) │
      │                                                                │
      └────────────────────────────────────────────────────────────────┘

      ┌────────────────────────────────────────────────────────────────┐
      │  "3.5 inch    DOS/MS Windows Client Install   (5 diskettes)" Help │
      │                                                                │
      │  Create 'NetWare Client for DOS/MS Windows' Diskettes. You will need to │
      │  provide 5 formatted high-density diskettes.                   │
      │                                                                │
      └──────────────────(To scroll, <F7>-up <F8>-down)────────────────┘
 Accept marked groups and continue <F10>
 Mark/unmark a file group           <Enter>        Previous screen <Esc>
 Help                               <F1>           Abort INSTALL <Alt><F10>
```

The installation program will give you the proper labels to use on the outside of the disks. Proper disk volume labels will be written by the program on the disks. The last disk will include all the proper LAN drivers for assorted NICs.

The best way to create these client installation diskettes is by using the MAKEDISK.BAT program included in the \PUBLIC\CLIENT\ DOSWIN or \PUBLIC\CLIENT\OS2 directories. If you installed the client support files during the initial server installation, all these files are ready and waiting on your server disk. Change to the directory supporting your preferred client disks and run the batch file. The files will be copied to the floppy drive of your workstation much more quickly than to the floppy drive on the server.

Creating NetWare Upgrade/Migrate Diskettes

3.4 IN-A-HURRY

Create Upgrade/Migrate Disks

1. Type **LOAD INSTALL** at the server console prompt.
2. Highlight Product Options and press Enter.
3. Highlight Create UPGRADE/MIGRATE Diskettes and press Enter.
4. Choose which disk set you want to create, and then press F10.
5. Insert a formatted, high-density disk in the server's floppy drive and press Enter.
6. Insert each blank disk when requested (either 1 or 2 are necessary).

Just as you can create client diskettes, you can also create an Upgrade/Migrate set of diskettes. The floppy or floppies created will contain the important files necessary to begin a migration or upgrade for other NetWare 4.1x servers-to-be. Check Appendix A for the full details on upgrading or migrating to NetWare 4.1x.

Installing NetWare for Macintosh Software

> **3.5 IN-A-HURRY**
>
> **Install NetWare for Macintosh**
>
> 1. Type **LOAD INSTALL** at the server console prompt.
>
> 2. Highlight Product Options and press Enter.
>
> 3. Highlight Install NetWare for Macintosh and press Enter.
>
> 4. Verify the location of the source files.
>
> 5. Verify your intention to install NetWare for Macintosh.
>
> 6. Configure Final Installation Options.
>
> 7. Configure AppleTalk and Macintosh support files.

Novell was the first major LAN company to support the Macintosh computer. That heritage shows as Macintosh support has risen to a new level in NetWare 4.1x.

Load the INSTALL program from the server console, choose Product Options once again, and then choose Install NetWare for Macintosh. Several things will happen that will remind you of installing NetWare.

First, you must verify the location of the Macintosh support files to be loaded on the server. This location will be either the CD-ROM drive, if it's internal to the machine, or a remote server. If it is a remote server, it will most likely be the same source server that was used for the rest of the NetWare installation. Figure 3.22 shows this screen.

The source referenced on this screen is the external Micro Design dual CD-ROM drive mounted on server ALTOS486 as the NetWare volume NW41_940907. Not the typical volume label, but the CD-ROM disk in that drive was created on September 9, 1994, and the date was used as the label. The normal label is NW410.

If your file source is another directory, press F3 to specify that file path. To use a remote server, or directory on a remote server, press F4. If another server is referenced, you may be asked to provide a login name and password.

FIGURE 3.22

Installing Macintosh support files from a CD-ROM mounted as a NetWare volume

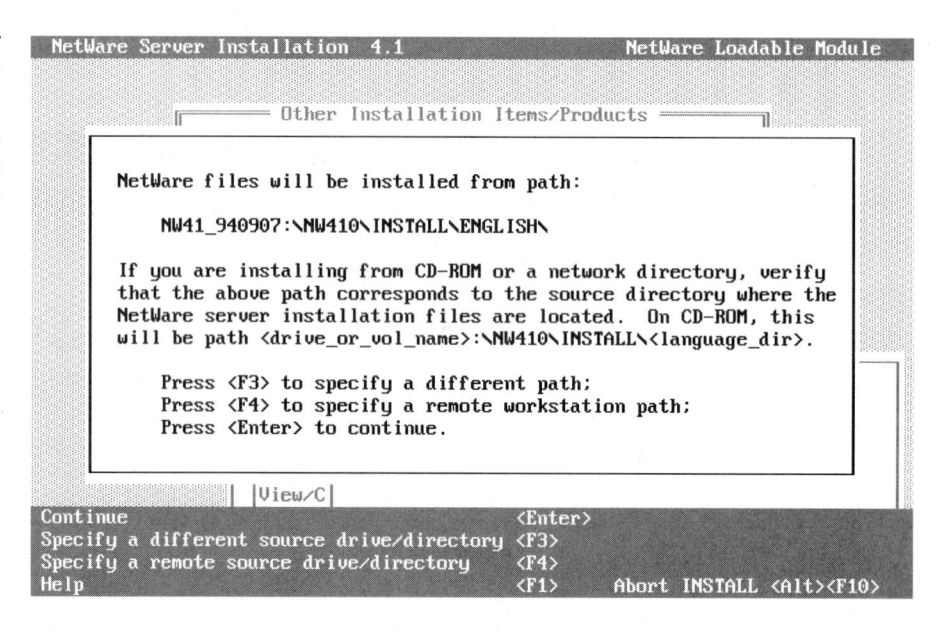

```
NetWare Server Installation  4.1                    NetWare Loadable Module

                ┌───── Other Installation Items/Products ─────┐
                │                                             │
                │ NetWare files will be installed from path:  │
                │                                             │
                │    NW41_940907:\NW410\INSTALL\ENGLISH\      │
                │                                             │
                │ If you are installing from CD-ROM or a network directory, verify
                │ that the above path corresponds to the source directory where the
                │ NetWare server installation files are located.  On CD-ROM, this
                │ will be path <drive_or_vol_name>:\NW410\INSTALL\<language_dir>.
                │                                             │
                │    Press <F3> to specify a different path;  │
                │    Press <F4> to specify a remote workstation path;
                │    Press <Enter> to continue.               │
                │                                             │
                └─────────────────────────────────────────────┘
                          |View/C|
Continue                                          <Enter>
Specify a different source drive/directory       <F3>
Specify a remote source drive/directory          <F4>
Help                                              <F1>     Abort INSTALL <Alt><F10>
```

If the source server is a NetWare 3.12 server, for instance, it may have no idea of the NDS context of the target server.

Another screen will appear, offering two choices: cancel or continue with the NetWare for Macintosh installation. Once you have verified that you do, in fact, wish to install NetWare for Macintosh, the screen in Figure 3.23 appears. These questions do the bulk of the installation work.

Pressing Enter pops up a pick list of all volumes on the server where the installation is taking place. The Macintosh name space, similar to the NFS name space, allows extended attributes that support the longer file names used by the Macintosh and its operating system. Support for data and resource forks is included. The name spaces are added per volume, not per server.

The second question offers to modify the AUTOEXEC.NCF file to automatically load Macintosh File Services. Normally this would be an automatic Yes, but some Macintosh applications may behave oddly if closed improperly. If Macintosh File Services are started immediately when the server reboots after a problem, an administrator may not get to the problem files to check them before other Macintosh users are connected.

FIGURE 3.23

Not really "final" but important NetWare for Macintosh questions

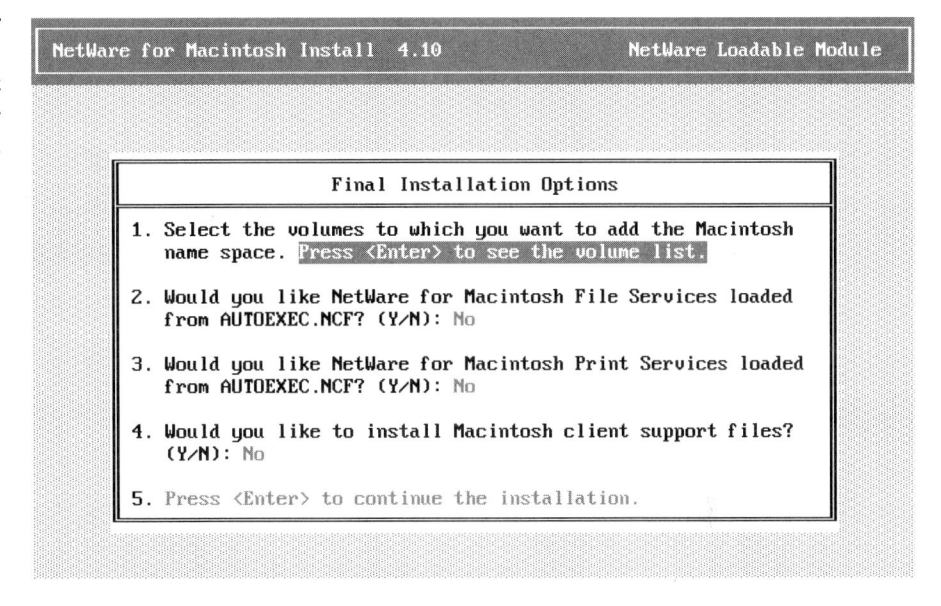

```
NetWare for Macintosh Install   4.10              NetWare Loadable Module


                        ┌─────────────────────────────────────────────┐
                        │           Final Installation Options        │
                        │                                             │
                        │  1. Select the volumes to which you want to add the Macintosh
                        │     name space. Press <Enter> to see the volume list.
                        │                                             │
                        │  2. Would you like NetWare for Macintosh File Services loaded
                        │     from AUTOEXEC.NCF? (Y/N): No
                        │                                             │
                        │  3. Would you like NetWare for Macintosh Print Services loaded
                        │     from AUTOEXEC.NCF? (Y/N): No
                        │                                             │
                        │  4. Would you like to install Macintosh client support files?
                        │     (Y/N): No
                        │                                             │
                        │  5. Press <Enter> to continue the installation.
                        └─────────────────────────────────────────────┘
```

The third question offers to make the same type of adjustment to begin Macintosh Print Services. It is possible to use Macintosh File Services separately from the Print Services, so it's valid to have this question stand apart from Question 2.

Question 4 offers to place Macintosh client support files on the server. These are then available to create client installation disk sets, just as you can create client disks for DOS, MS Windows, and OS/2. Say Yes to store a copy on the server.

Installing the Macintosh support software then leads to an entire section of configuration options shown in Figure 3.24. Skip ahead to Chapter 13, where NetWare for Macintosh is discussed in detail, for the answers to these questions.

Many of the listings in Figure 3.24 should remind you of the NetWare installation screens. Configuring protocols, languages, CD-ROM drivers, printing, and feeding your license diskette to the server should evoke fond memories of earlier NetWare installation procedures. Okay, evoke memories, fond or otherwise.

FIGURE 3.24

Beginning the NetWare for Macintosh configuration process

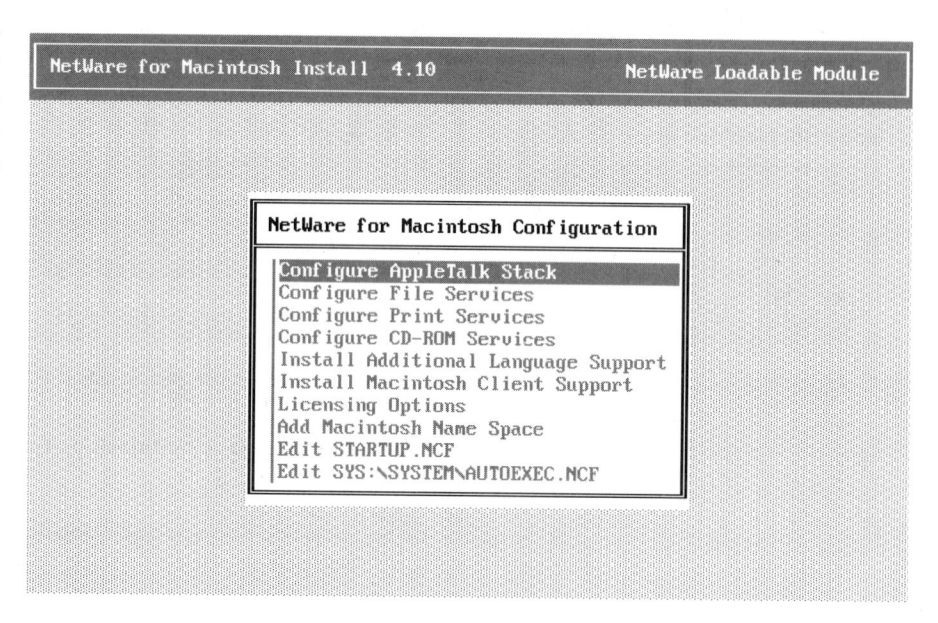

```
NetWare for Macintosh Install  4.10                    NetWare Loadable Module


                    ┌─────────────────────────────────────────┐
                    │   NetWare for Macintosh Configuration   │
                    ├─────────────────────────────────────────┤
                    │ Configure AppleTalk Stack               │
                    │ Configure File Services                 │
                    │ Configure Print Services                │
                    │ Configure CD-ROM Services               │
                    │ Install Additional Language Support     │
                    │ Install Macintosh Client Support        │
                    │ Licensing Options                       │
                    │ Add Macintosh Name Space                │
                    │ Edit STARTUP.NCF                        │
                    │ Edit SYS:\SYSTEM\AUTOEXEC.NCF           │
                    └─────────────────────────────────────────┘
```

Installing NetWare MHS Services in NetWare 4.10

3.6 IN-A-HURRY

Install MHS in NetWare 4.10

1. Type **LOAD INSTALL** at the server console prompt.

2. Highlight Product Options and press Enter.

3. Highlight Install NetWare MHS Services and press Enter.

4. Specify the source of your installation files.

5. Monitor file copy status and installation messages.

6. Provide a name a password for a Postmaster.

7. Specify whether or not this is the first MHS installed in the current NDS tree.

8. Choose a NetWare volume for the MHS files and mailboxes.

MHS (Message Handling Service) is Novell's popular protocol for communicating between different mail systems. This is a *store-and-forward* technology, meaning messages are passed from one mailbox to another and held until retrieved.

NetWare 4.10 (but not NetWare 4.11) includes basic MHS as an integral part of the operating system. The presence of MHS allows applications such as calendars, schedulers, and e-mail to work properly. Many third-party vendors use MHS as a foundation for applications such as workflow routing and EDI (Electronic Data Interchange). Novell, starting with NetWare 4.11, is pushing MHS off to gateway status within GroupWise.

Once again, load the INSTALL program at the server console, and choose Product Options. The choice for Install NetWare MHS Services is about in the middle of the upper window.

Since quite a few files are moved around for MHS installation, the location of the source files are important. Just as you did when installing the main NetWare software or the Macintosh services, specify the location for your source files.

Immediately, a progress bar will appear in a File Copy Status screen. Files will zip by, and the progress bar will march steadily from left to right. As soon as that finishes, a new screen, labeled Installation Status Messages, will appear. Details about files being moved and shuffled and created will scroll by, but neither of these screens requires the installer to do anything but watch.

Figure 3.25 does require some work, however. MHS functions as a postal service, albeit more reliably. Every postal service requires a Postmaster.

The default, and the name filled in by the installation program, is that of the NDS Admin. This makes sense, because the Postmaster needs wide-ranging authority and access. You can name another Admin-equivalent user if you prefer, if you are installing MHS after you have created some other users. Otherwise, if this is the first installation of your first NetWare 4.10 server, use Admin.

If you name the Admin user, you must correctly type the password. If you name another user, you must type his or her password. Do not try to create a user just to be Postmaster; it won't work here.

The installation program checks NDS before continuing. If there is no existing MHS system, you will be asked to verify that fact. Since we have a new network, we do not expect to have any other MHS systems in place.

The last bit of business is to place the MHS files and mailboxes on the server. If you have only one volume on your server, there is no question about location: everything goes into the SYS: volume. If you have more than one, however, the MHS installation program has some advice for you concerning the proper location for these system files. See Figure 3.26 for details.

170 Chapter 3 ▪ Installing NetWare Directory Services and Optional Procedures

FIGURE 3.25

Nominating your Postmaster General

FIGURE 3.26

Advice and a question of mailbox placement

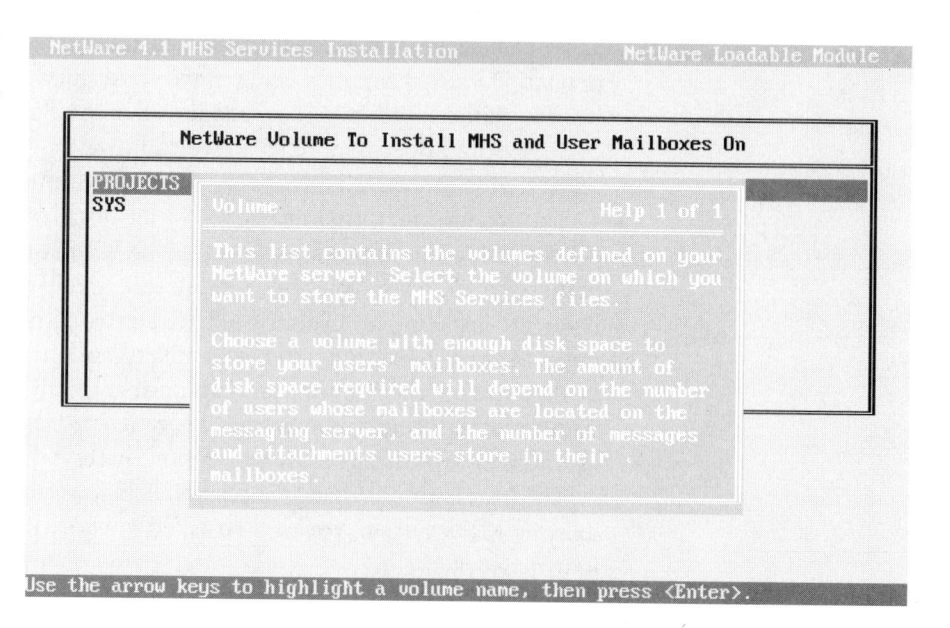

Since the server GATEWAY2000 has two volumes, SYS: and PROJECTS:, a choice was necessary. After reading the help screen in Figure 3.26, I chose to place the MHS files on the SYS: volume. I'm just a traditionalist at heart, and that can get me into trouble. Better to leave SYS: for only system files that do not change or grow and put MHS files elsewhere.

After you choose the file locations, you are returned to the Installation Status Messages screen. There it tells you everything is now complete.

Part of the installation process is to place all the shared FirstMail programs into the SYS:\PUBLIC directory. When a user types MAIL to load the DOS mail software, it will be executed from the SYS:\PUBLIC directory. The First-Mail system requires some configuration. Those details will be covered in the NetWare MHS section in Chapter 18.

Support for MHS and running FirstMail are connected, but MHS support does not mandate using FirstMail. Having FirstMail does not preclude using another e-mail application. Other e-mail applications will often rely on MHS support, however, especially if your network is using any kind of gateway between systems.

Configuring Network Protocols

3.7 IN-A-HURRY

Configure Your Network Protocols

1. Type **LOAD INSTALL** at the server console prompt.

2. Highlight Product Options and press Enter.

3. Highlight Configure Network Protocols and press Enter.

4. Agree to transfer LAN drivers and other controls to the INETCFG.NLM program.

5. Choose Protocols from the Internetworking Configuration menu.

6. Choose the protocol to be configured.

7. Follow the directions for each specific protocol.

8. Verify changes to AUTOEXEC.NCF.

This section is used only for enterprise networks, or those administrators with detailed knowledge of specific protocols. No casual choices are behind these menus.

Figure 3.27 brings the first clue that this section is not like other sections. All the work in developing the AUTOEXEC.NCF file is about to be modified, if you continue. As you see in Figure 3.27, a new program labeled INETCFG.NLM will now be used to manage all communication and protocol components on your server. Although the screen asks you to make a choice, your only choice is Yes if you need to modify any of the protocol settings.

If you load the INETCFG.NLM program directly on the console before authorizing the transfer of these details from AUTOEXEC.NCF, the system will ask you whether you wish to transfer the information now. You can say No and go into the menu shown in Figure 3.28, but you need to transfer the file information to successfully modify any protocol information.

The options in the menu deal with some items not standard in NetWare 4.1*x*, such as the WAN Call Directory. The choices in the menu address the following:

- **Boards:** Add a new network interface adapter or modify an existing one.

- **Network Interfaces:** Configure interfaces for WAN boards (LAN boards do not require this).

FIGURE 3.27
Cutting INETCFG.NLM into AUTOEXEC.NCF territory

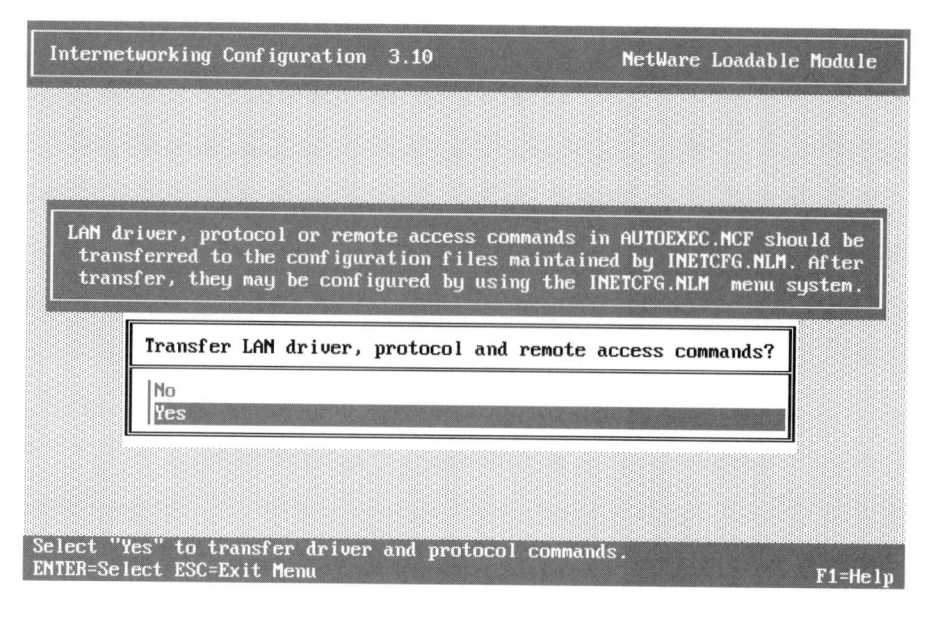

FIGURE 3.28

The Internetworking Configuration menu

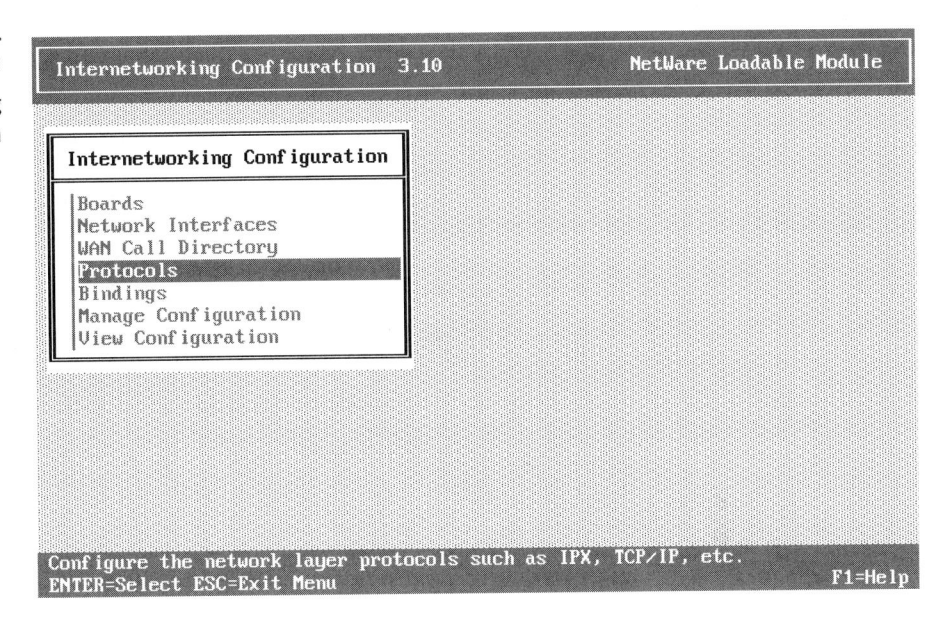

```
Internetworking Configuration 3.10                    NetWare Loadable Module

    ┌─ Internetworking Configuration ─┐
    │ Boards                          │
    │ Network Interfaces              │
    │ WAN Call Directory              │
    │ Protocols                       │
    │ Bindings                        │
    │ Manage Configuration            │
    │ View Configuration              │
    └─────────────────────────────────┘




Configure the network layer protocols such as IPX, TCP/IP, etc.
ENTER=Select  ESC=Exit Menu                                         F1=Help
```

- **WAN Call Directory:** Set up media-specific connection information for remote sites.

- **Protocols:** Enable and configure network protocols.

- **Bindings:** Associate a protocol with specific network interface adapters.

- **Manage Configuration:** Open a submenu to configure SNMP, remote access to this server, and edit the AUTOEXEC.NCF file.

- **View Configuration:** Display (but not modify) all INETCFG generated commands.

Many of the options from the menu in Figure 3.28 perform the same functions as the initial setup and configuration of network adapters and protocol bindings during installation. When you must modify existing server information, such as adding a new network interface adapter, the process will be the same as during installation. You just need to use a different road to reach your destination.

An example of what's behind some of these menus is shown in Figure 3.29. The menu path to this screen is reached by selecting Protocols then TCP/IP on the next menu.

FIGURE 3.29

TCP/IP modification within INETCFG

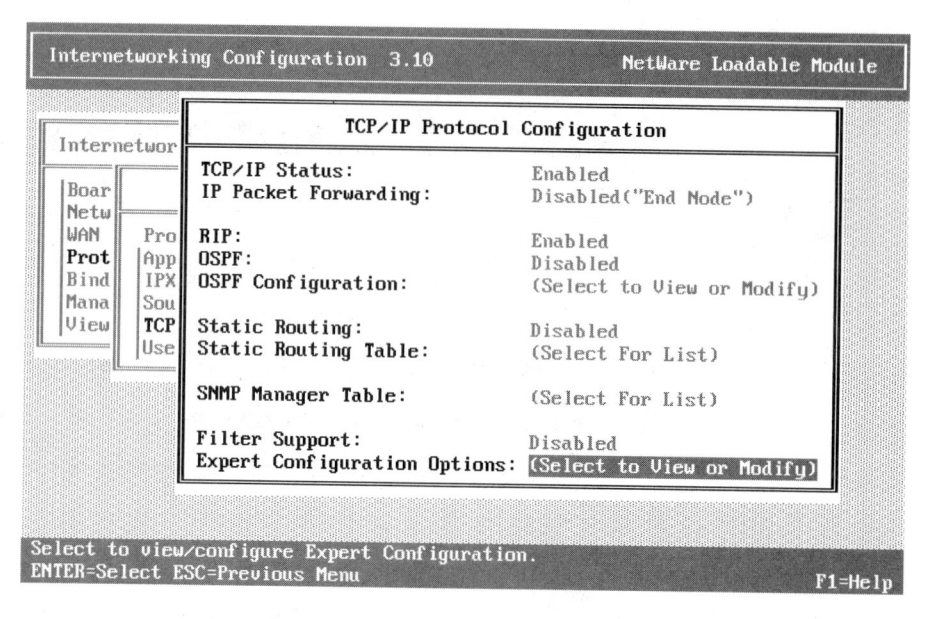

```
Internetworking Configuration   3.10            NetWare Loadable Module

                         ┌─────────TCP/IP Protocol Configuration─────────┐
   Internetwor           │                                               │
  ┌──────────┐           │  TCP/IP Status:            Enabled            │
  │Boar      │           │  IP Packet Forwarding:     Disabled("End Node")│
  │Netw      │           │                                               │
  │WAN    Pro│           │  RIP:                      Enabled            │
  │Prot   App│           │  OSPF:                     Disabled           │
  │Bind   IPX│           │  OSPF Configuration:       (Select to View or Modify)│
  │Mana   Sou│           │                                               │
  │View   TCP│           │  Static Routing:           Disabled           │
  │       Use│           │  Static Routing Table:     (Select For List)  │
  └──────────┘           │                                               │
                         │  SNMP Manager Table:       (Select For List)  │
                         │                                               │
                         │  Filter Support:           Disabled           │
                         │  Expert Configuration Options: (Select to View or Modify)│
                         └───────────────────────────────────────────────┘

Select to view/configure Expert Configuration.
ENTER=Select  ESC=Previous Menu                               F1=Help
```

The information in Figure 3.29 will not be needed unless your network has a sizable TCP/IP population. The defaults set by NetWare 4.1x may well be enough to allow your NetWare 4.1x server to function happily, even in a mixed Unix and NetWare network. But if more details are necessary on the TCP/IP protocol side, here is where to set them.

Notice the last option at the bottom of the screen in Figure 3.29, which says:

```
Expert Configuration Options: Select to View or Modify
```

Although you may believe that choices about RIP (Routing Information Protocol, the original protocol used for routing packs through the network) versus OSPF (Open Shortest Path First, a new means of WAN routing) belong in the expert category, the menu doesn't agree.

If you do work in a mixed NetWare and Unix environment, INETCFG will become important to you. There will be more information concerning these protocols and their setup and configuration when we discuss Unix and NetWare integration, in Chapter 14.

Installing an Additional Server Language

> **3.8 IN-A-HURRY**
>
> **Install Another Server Language**
>
> **1.** Type **LOAD INSTALL** at the server console prompt.
>
> **2.** Highlight Product Options and press Enter.
>
> **3.** Highlight Install an Additional Server Language and press Enter.
>
> **4.** Verify the source of the language files.
>
> **5.** Indicate which language-specific files you want to install.

NetWare 4.01 became multilingual. The NetWare operating system, used all over the world, now speaks to network users in five languages: English, French, Italian, German, and Spanish.

You can configure the following information:

- Date
- Time
- Currency
- Sorting tables
- Uppercase tables
- Legal file name characters

You can set the language for the server, message files, and console keyboard.

Multiple languages can be supported for clients. There are 19 languages available for the server to use on the console at this writing. Only the languages supported during the initial installation will be available.

The support files for an additional language besides the language chosen during installation are copied to the server using this menu option. As before, type LOAD INSTALL at the server console and choose Install an Additional Server Language in the Other Installation Items/Products window.

Verify the source of the new language files to be transferred to your server. The normal choices are an internal CD-ROM, remote CD-ROM mounted as a NetWare volume, or the NetWare installation files resident on a remote server.

Choose which language files you want transferred to your server by pressing Enter while highlighting your choice. This places an X in the checkbox beside the language of your choice. Accept your choice or choices by pressing F10.

Keep an eye out for additional NetWare languages. French, Italian, German and Spanish (known as FIGS internally at Novell) are the major languages supported, but more are added constantly. Also, remember that the language of the NetWare operating system has no effect on the language of your application. The German version of NetWare can't make your database display in German.

Changing the Server Language

> **3.9 IN-A-HURRY**
>
> **Change Your Server's Language**
>
> 1. Type **LOAD INSTALL** at the server console prompt.
>
> 2. Highlight Product Options and press Enter.
>
> 3. Highlight Change Server Language and press Enter.
>
> 4. Verify the source of the language files.
>
> 5. Select a default server language.
>
> 6. Clear all users and connections from the server.
>
> 7. Reboot the server.

After installing additional server languages, you may change the default server language. All the system messages will be displayed in the default language of your choice, unless client software specifically requests a different language.

At the server console, type LOAD INSTALL and choose Change Server Language from the Other Installation Items/Products menu. You must verify the source of the language files, since the installation program assumes they're coming from the location of the earlier installation files. Specify the full path of the source files, whether an internal CD-ROM, remote CD-ROM configured as a NetWare volume, or remote server file set. A window labeled Select Default Server Language will appear, offering the five supported languages, as shown in Figure 3.30.

There are quite a few files to be transferred and configuration files to be reset to support another default language. Many of these configuration files are not read except when the server starts. For this reason, restarting the server is necessary before the new language becomes available.

Remember that your network clients probably have the line:

```
SET NWLANGUAGE=ENGLISH
```

or the like in their AUTOEXEC.BAT files. The language referenced will be the default language at the time the client was installed. Each of those settings must change to reflect the new default server language. If they are not changed, that client will continue to display the language named in the SET parameter.

Do you manage servers that have a default language different than yours? If so, you may be happy to learn that you can change the console language without rebooting the server. Remote console operations can be done in the language of your preference, without disrupting the server's default language and the attached clients. For details, type LANGUAGE HELP on the server console.

FIGURE 3.30

Choosing the default language of your server

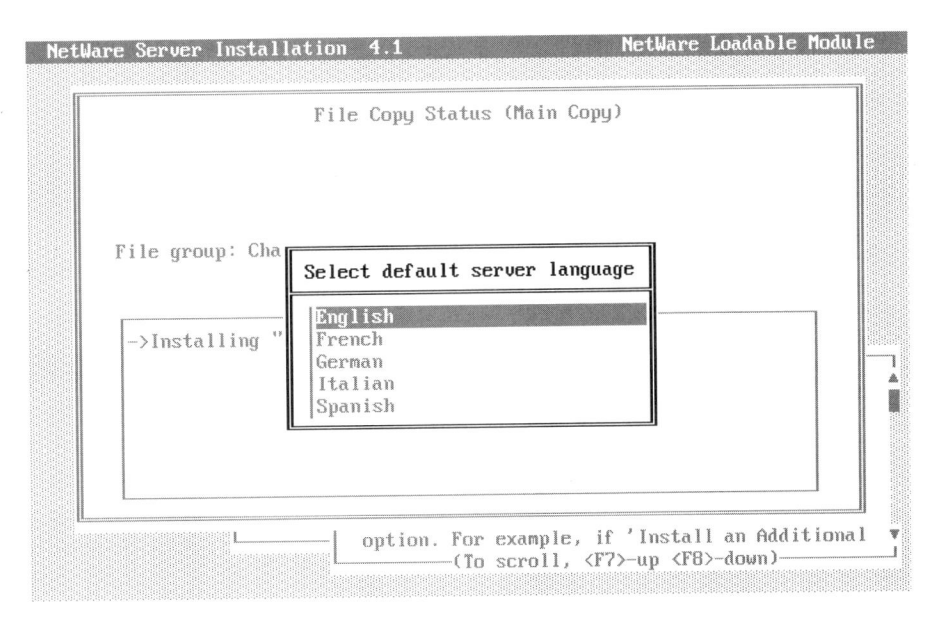

Installing Online Documentation and Viewers

> ### 3.10 IN-A-HURRY
>
> **Install the Online Documentation**
>
> 1. Type **LOAD INSTALL** at the server console prompt.
> 2. Highlight Product Options and press Enter.
> 3. Highlight Install Online Documentation and Viewers and press Enter.
> 4. Verify the source of the documentation files.
> 5. Choose the documentation file sets you want to install.
> 6. Verify the destination for the documentation files.

Of all these optional installation choices, this should be the one you choose first. Even if you have a CD-ROM drive on your server, placing the documentation files on the server hard disk will speed access times. It will also free your CD-ROM drive for a disk that contains too much information to load onto the server hard disk, such as clip-art or large reference works.

The documentation files only take about 60 MB (uncompressed) on the file server. Once the files are compressed, their effective size will be less than 30 MB. It's well worth the disk space to have all the documentation available to all users. Both DOS and Macintosh clients are supported by the new version of DynaText shipping with NetWare 4.1x.

From the server console, type LOAD INSTALL, then choose the Product Options menu selection once again. The information in Figure 3.31 appears. I highlighted the Install Online Documentation and Viewers line to pop open the help window in the bottom right of the screen.

I know the help screen says you should install all the other products first, and that looks somewhat contradictory to what I just said. However, the Novell engineers are speaking of "optional" products that I consider essential. If you need to support Macintosh clients, adding Macintosh support to your server is not optional; it's mandatory. Need e-mail? Then MHS is mandatory as well.

Optional Installation Items, Procedures, and Products **179**

FIGURE 3.31

Preparing to shelve your electronic manuals

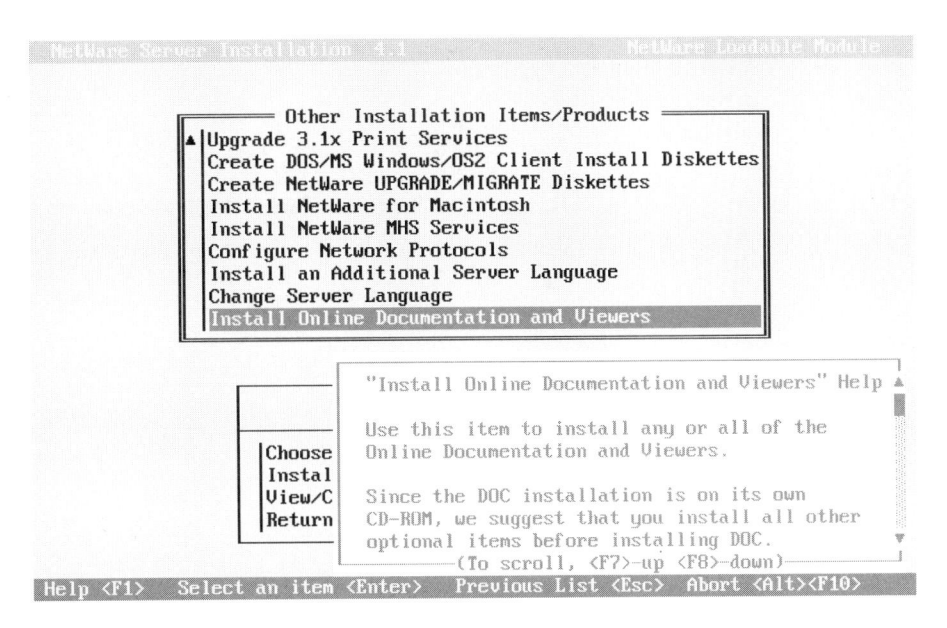

```
NetWare Server Installation  4.1                    NetWare Loadable Module

                ╒══════ Other Installation Items/Products ══════╕
                │▲ Upgrade 3.1x Print Services                   │
                │  Create DOS/MS Windows/OS2 Client Install Diskettes│
                │  Create NetWare UPGRADE/MIGRATE Diskettes      │
                │  Install NetWare for Macintosh                 │
                │  Install NetWare MHS Services                  │
                │  Configure Network Protocols                   │
                │  Install an Additional Server Language         │
                │  Change Server Language                        │
                │  Install Online Documentation and Viewers      │
                ╘════════════════════════════════════════════════╛

                          ┌─────────────────────────────────────────────────┐
                          │ "Install Online Documentation and Viewers" Help ▲│
                          │                                                 │
                          │ Use this item to install any or all of the     │
                  Choose  │ Online Documentation and Viewers.              │
                  Instal  │                                                 │
                  View/C  │ Since the DOC installation is on its own       │
                  Return  │ CD-ROM, we suggest that you install all other  │
                          │ optional items before installing DOC.          ▼│
                          │────────(To scroll, <F7>-up <F8>-down)──────────│
 Help <F1>      Select an item <Enter>     Previous List <Esc>   Abort <Alt><F10>
```

It's a good idea to get all the pieces up and cooperating on your server before adding the electronic documentation. Remember also that the documentation need only be on one server for all the local users.

If the source file location for the documentation installation is not correct, press F3 and give the correct location. If the source location is an internal CD-ROM in the server, give the DOS drive letter (D:). If the source is a remote server, give the full server and volume name to continue. The manuals don't change in size, so adding them to the SYS: volume is fine as long as you leave plenty of extra space available.

Figure 3.32 shows the pick list for installing the proper sets of electronic documentation. If there are no Macintosh clients on your server, you can save the space necessary for their viewer files.

Press Enter or the spacebar to place an X in the checkbox for the file sets you want to install. Once you have marked all your choices, press F10 to continue the installation.

Before the files start transferring to your server, you must verify the location for these files. Although NetWare usually lets you put files wherever you want to put them, some files need to be in a particular place that everyone knows about. Figure 3.33 shows the default destination and some dire warnings if you change the location.

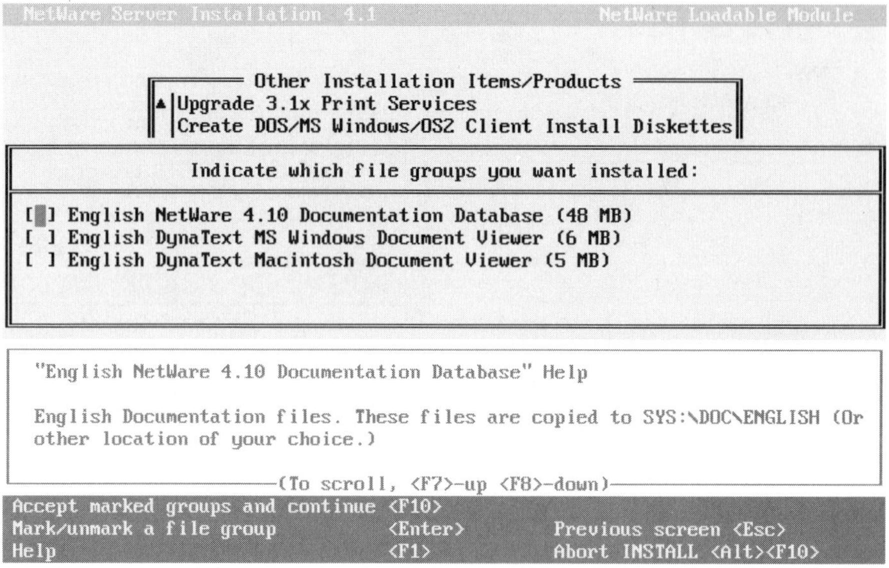

FIGURE 3.32

Selecting your documentation file sets

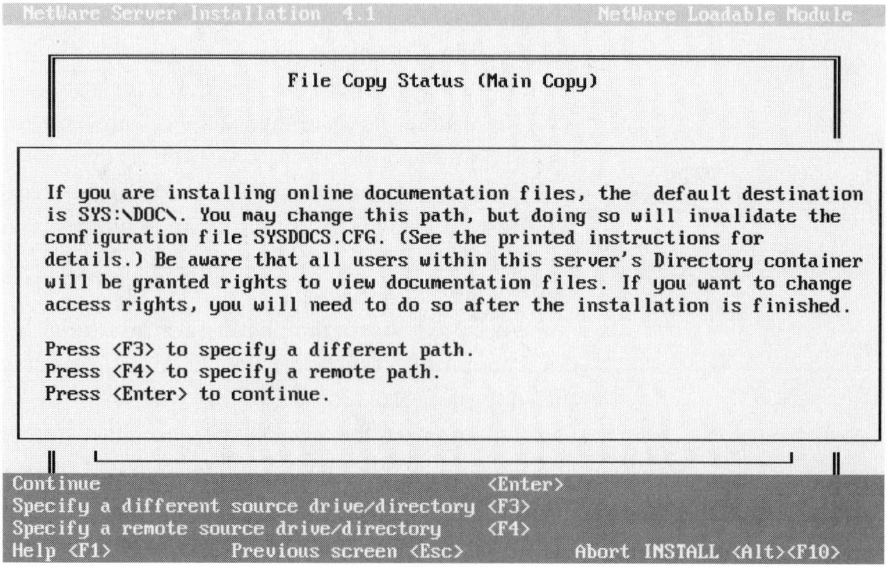

```
NetWare Server Installation  4.1                    NetWare Loadable Module
         ┌──────── Other Installation Items/Products ────────┐
         ▲│Upgrade 3.1x Print Services                       │
          │Create DOS/MS Windows/OS2 Client Install Diskettes│
┌─────────────────────────────────────────────────────────────────────────┐
│              Indicate which file groups you want installed:             │
├─────────────────────────────────────────────────────────────────────────┤
│  [■] English NetWare 4.10 Documentation Database (48 MB)                │
│  [ ] English DynaText MS Windows Document Viewer (6 MB)                 │
│  [ ] English DynaText Macintosh Document Viewer (5 MB)                  │
│                                                                         │
└─────────────────────────────────────────────────────────────────────────┘

┌─────────────────────────────────────────────────────────────────────────┐
│  "English NetWare 4.10 Documentation Database" Help                     │
│                                                                         │
│  English Documentation files. These files are copied to SYS:\DOC\ENGLISH (Or │
│  other location of your choice.)                                        │
│                                                                         │
│                    ──(To scroll, <F7>-up <F8>-down)──                   │
├─────────────────────────────────────────────────────────────────────────┤
│ Accept marked groups and continue <F10>                                 │
│ Mark/unmark a file group           <Enter>    Previous screen <Esc>     │
│ Help                               <F1>       Abort INSTALL <Alt><F10>  │
└─────────────────────────────────────────────────────────────────────────┘
```

FIGURE 3.33

Placing your electronic manuals on the proper shelf

```
NetWare Server Installation  4.1                    NetWare Loadable Module
┌─────────────────────────────────────────────────────────────────────────┐
│                      File Copy Status (Main Copy)                       │
│                                                                         │
├─────────────────────────────────────────────────────────────────────────┤
│                                                                         │
│   If you are installing online documentation files, the default         │
│   destination is SYS:\DOC\. You may change this path, but doing so will │
│   invalidate the configuration file SYSDOCS.CFG. (See the printed       │
│   instructions for details.) Be aware that all users within this        │
│   server's Directory container will be granted rights to view           │
│   documentation files. If you want to change access rights, you will    │
│   need to do so after the installation is finished.                     │
│                                                                         │
│   Press <F3> to specify a different path.                               │
│   Press <F4> to specify a remote path.                                  │
│   Press <Enter> to continue.                                            │
│                                                                         │
└─────────────────────────────────────────────────────────────────────────┘
 Continue                                       <Enter>
 Specify a different source drive/directory     <F3>
 Specify a remote source drive/directory        <F4>
 Help <F1>         Previous screen <Esc>        Abort INSTALL <Alt><F10>
```

Optional Installation Items, Procedures, and Products **181**

The previous screen describes the ability for all users to read the documentation files unless you change the access rights. If you want to restrict access, you must do so after installation. I can't imagine why you would want to prevent some users from seeing the DynaText files, but you can do so if you wish.

Since there are more than 50 MB of files, the transfer takes a few minutes. The installation program provides a progress bar so you will know the installation is still working. You can see in Figure 3.34 the source and destination locations for all the DynaText files. There are quite a few levels of files being loaded. Don't worry—you don't need to configure the locations of these files for your users. The document viewer application tracks all these files during execution.

Once the files are completely copied to your system, you will be returned to the INSTALL program.

It may never happen to you, but some network administrators get interrupted while they work. If you have ever had to stop a process to help solve some crisis (at least it was a crisis in the mind of the person that dragged you away from your installation), you will appreciate the screen shown in Figure 3.35.

FIGURE 3.34

Shelving your electronic manuals

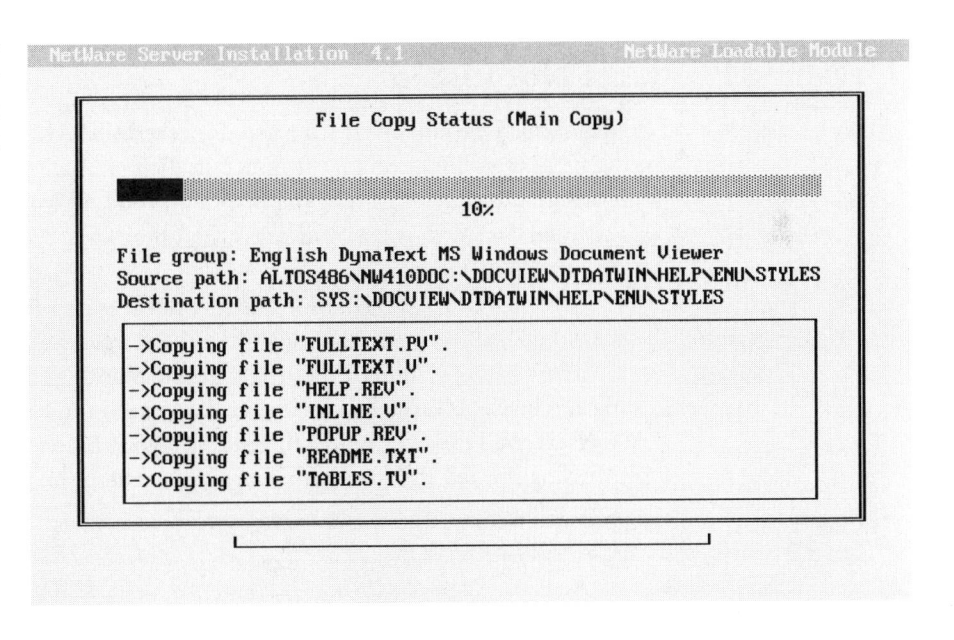

FIGURE 3.35

Restoring a stopped installation

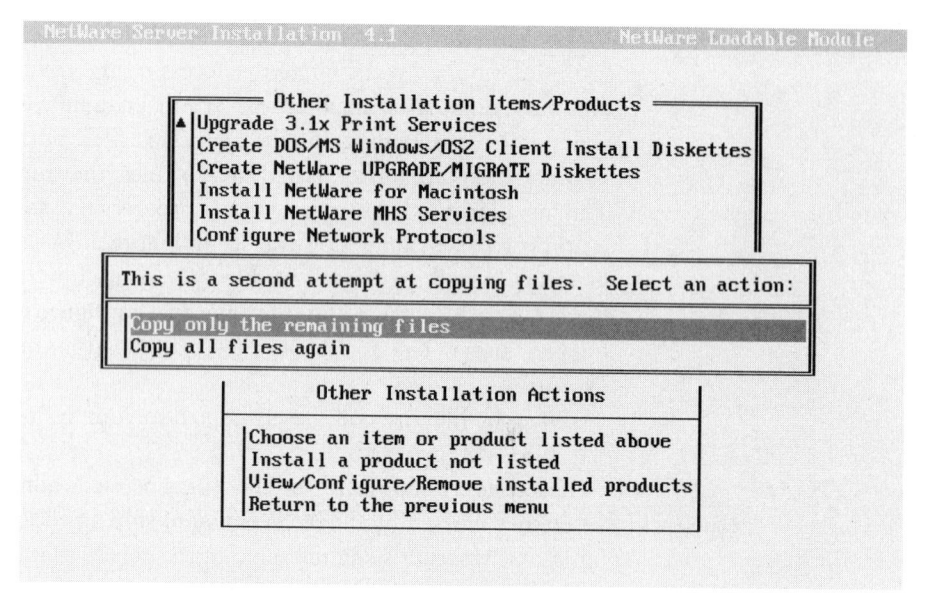

```
┌─ NetWare Server Installation 4.1 ──────────── NetWare Loadable Module ─┐
│                                                                         │
│         ┌──── Other Installation Items/Products ────┐                   │
│       ▲ │Upgrade 3.1x Print Services                 │                  │
│         │Create DOS/MS Windows/OS2 Client Install Diskettes│             │
│         │Create NetWare UPGRADE/MIGRATE Diskettes    │                  │
│         │Install NetWare for Macintosh              │                  │
│         │Install NetWare MHS Services               │                  │
│         │Configure Network Protocols                │                  │
│         └────────────────────────────────────────────┘                  │
│   ┌─ This is a second attempt at copying files.  Select an action: ─┐  │
│   │ Copy only the remaining files                                   │  │
│   │ Copy all files again                                            │  │
│   └──────────────────────────────────────────────────────────────────┘  │
│              ┌───── Other Installation Actions ─────┐                   │
│              │Choose an item or product listed above│                   │
│              │Install a product not listed          │                   │
│              │View/Configure/Remove installed products│                 │
│              │Return to the previous menu           │                   │
│              └───────────────────────────────────────┘                  │
└─────────────────────────────────────────────────────────────────────────┘
```

Installing Products Not Listed

Installing a product that isn't listed by the INSTALL program is basically the same as installing one that it does list. Type LOAD INSTALL at the server console prompt. Highlight the Install a Product Not Listed line in the Other Installation Actions list, and press the Enter key. You will then be greeted by the screen in Figure 3.36.

Any program can also be loaded from the server hard disk. This may sound backward, since we haven't installed the program yet, but it works.

The screen in Figure 3.36 offers you a chance to specify a different drive path when you press F3. So far, we have used the F3 key to reference remote file servers. However, you can reference your own server volume. After pressing F3, tell the installation program where the product to be installed is located:

```
SYS:\ directory_name
```

FIGURE 3.36

Third-party product installation

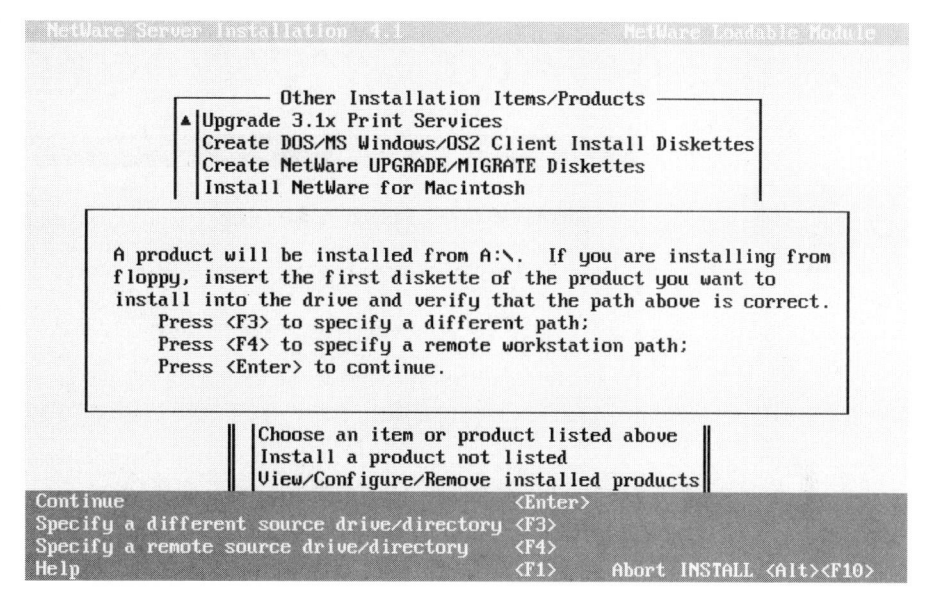

```
╔═══════════════════════════════════════════════════════════════════════════╗
║ NetWare Server Installation  4.1                    NetWare Loadable Module ║
╚═══════════════════════════════════════════════════════════════════════════╝
          ┌──────────── Other Installation Items/Products ────────────┐
         ▲│Upgrade 3.1x Print Services                                │
          │Create DOS/MS Windows/OS2 Client Install Diskettes         │
          │Create NetWare UPGRADE/MIGRATE Diskettes                   │
          │Install NetWare for Macintosh                              │
     ┌────┴───────────────────────────────────────────────────────────┴────┐
     │ A product will be installed from A:\.  If you are installing from   │
     │ floppy, insert the first diskette of the product you want to        │
     │ install into the drive and verify that the path above is correct.   │
     │    Press <F3> to specify a different path;                          │
     │    Press <F4> to specify a remote workstation path;                 │
     │    Press <Enter> to continue.                                       │
     └─────────────────────────────────────────────────────────────────────┘
                         ┌─────────────────────────────────────┐
                         │Choose an item or product listed above│
                         │Install a product not listed          │
                         │View/Configure/Remove installed products│
  Continue                                        <Enter>
  Specify a different source drive/directory      <F3>
  Specify a remote source drive/directory         <F4>
  Help                                            <F1>    Abort INSTALL <Alt><F10>
```

Before starting the installation, copy the product diskette to the file server volume of your choice. Make a directory for the server, as referenced above as *directory_name*. (Good example for clarity, but you realize the name is too long, don't you? Good.)

Copy the product diskettes by loading them into your workstation drive and copying them to the newly created server directory. Use NCOPY for safety:

    NCOPY A:*.* F: /S

This example guesses that A: is your local drive and drive F: is mapped to the newly created directory. Unlike the XCOPY command, NCOPY automatically verifies each file copy and also gets empty directories.

Removing NetWare Directory Services

> **3.11 IN-A-HURRY**
>
> **Remove NDS from a Server**
>
> 1. Type **LOAD INSTALL** at the server console prompt.
> 2. Highlight Directory Options and press Enter.
> 3. Highlight Remove Directory Services from this server and press Enter.
> 4. Read the NDS warnings.
> 5. Verify your intent to delete Directory Services.
> 6. Log in as Admin or equivalent.
> 7. Read the NDS warnings concerning the single NDS tree.
> 8. Verify your intention to delete the Directory.
> 9. Read the messages about further actions.

PARANOIA ABOUT PLANNING your NDS tree was rampant when NetWare 4 first hit the streets, because it was new. The tools to recover from mistakes were incomplete, and some customers felt it was easier to delete NDS than it was to fix it.

That's no longer true, even for the most paranoid of administrators. But if you do want to remove NDS, right at installation is a good time to do so. Installation is so quick with NetWare 4.1x that it actually may be quicker to reload NDS than rework a mangled tree.

Once again, we're back to the Installation Options screen. Type LOAD INSTALL at the server console prompt to reach this screen. Highlight Directory Options and press Enter to see the Directory Services Options menu. Highlight Remove Directory Services from this server and press Enter. Depending on the situation in your network, various warning messages will appear.

Warning, Warning

When you remove the Directory, you perform a lobotomy on your server.

NDS removal is a big deal, and should be done under the rarest of circumstances after the server has been put in use. However, during initial installation, you may want to play with different NDS arrangements. If one plan doesn't work well, it's little trouble to delete a basically empty NDS tree and reinstall. These instructions are given for those situations where NetWare 4.1x has been placed in a pilot network test mode, and no valuable information is contained on the server and no users are going to be stranded.

However, and this is serious, deleting a working NDS tree ERASES ALL USERS, OBJECTS, PRINTERS, PRINT QUEUES, AND GROUPS. Sorry for yelling, but this is an important point. When you remove the Directory, you perform a lobotomy on your server. This is the same as erasing the bindery files on a NetWare 3.x server.

No, it's actually worse than erasing bindery files. Bindery files concern only one server at a time. If you erase a bindery, only one server's worth of users are inconvenienced. With NetWare 4.1x, hundreds of users may suffer some aggravation.

Directories that are part of a large network may be referenced in scores or hundreds of different object descriptions. Some users may not discover the loss of the Directory information for that one server for weeks or months, but that just amplifies the hassle when they do realize it's gone.

Be careful about removing NDS. Try everything else before you dump the Directory.

Removing NDS from a One-Server Network

After you've run INSTALL and selected Remove Directory Services from the Directory Options menu, you'll reach the first warning. You must confirm again that you wish to delete Directory Services. Figure 3.37 shows one of the warning screens.

You cannot delete the Directory without proving you have the authority to do so. This would be a big security hole if just anyone could trash your server. Figure 3.38 shows the screen asking for the Admin password.

Once you are past the Admin login stage, you can delete Directory Services. Figure 3.39 warns you of the consequences for deleting the single replica of an NDS tree.

FIGURE 3.37

Warning! Warning!

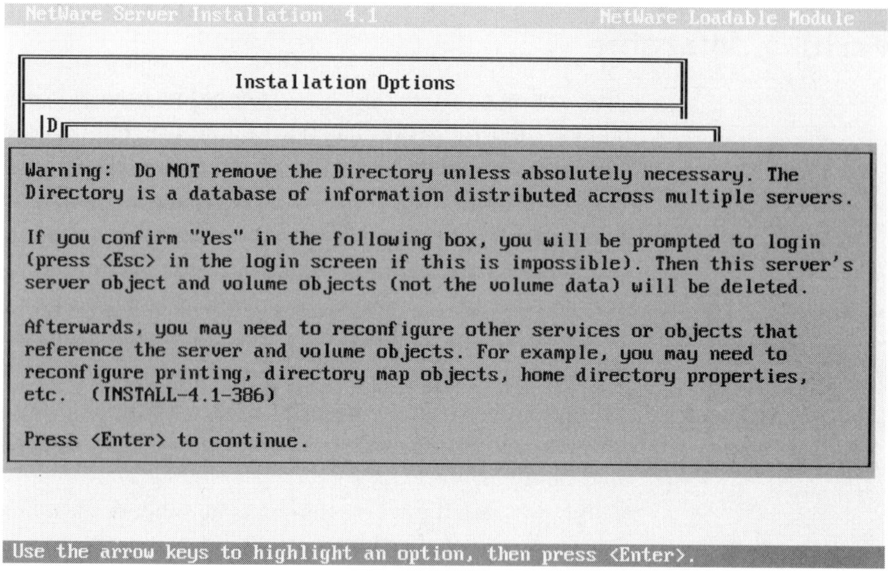

```
NetWare Server Installation 4.1                    NetWare Loadable Module
┌─────────────────────────────────────────────────────┐
│                  Installation Options               │
├─────────────────────────────────────────────────────┤
│ │D│                                                 │
│ ┌─────────────────────────────────────────────────┐ │
│ │ Warning:  Do NOT remove the Directory unless absolutely necessary. The │
│ │ Directory is a database of information distributed across multiple servers. │
│ │                                                 │ │
│ │ If you confirm "Yes" in the following box, you will be prompted to login │
│ │ (press <Esc> in the login screen if this is impossible). Then this server's │
│ │ server object and volume objects (not the volume data) will be deleted. │
│ │                                                 │ │
│ │ Afterwards, you may need to reconfigure other services or objects that │
│ │ reference the server and volume objects. For example, you may need to │
│ │ reconfigure printing, directory map objects, home directory properties, │
│ │ etc.  (INSTALL-4.1-386)                         │ │
│ │                                                 │ │
│ │ Press <Enter> to continue.                      │ │
│ └─────────────────────────────────────────────────┘ │
└─────────────────────────────────────────────────────┘
   Use the arrow keys to highlight an option, then press <Enter>.
```

FIGURE 3.38

Authenticating Admin before Directory deletion

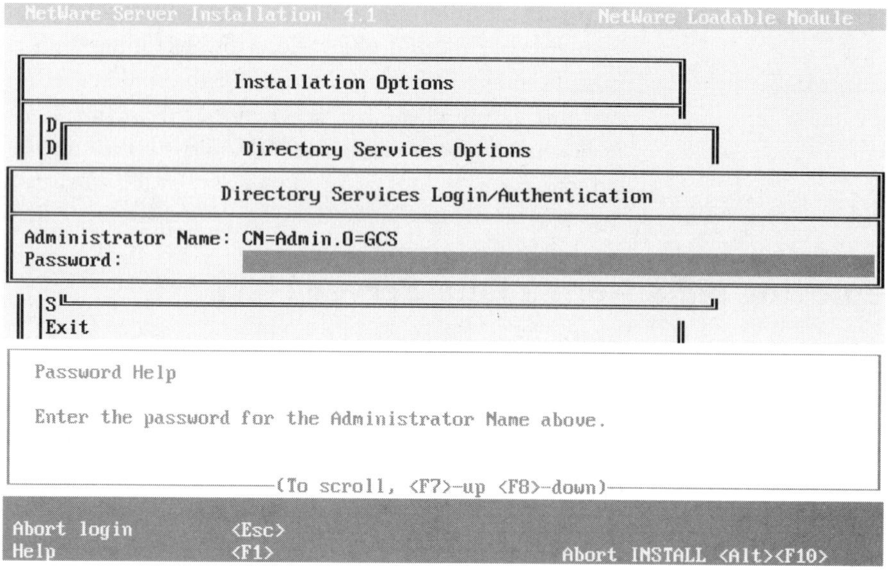

```
NetWare Server Installation 4.1                    NetWare Loadable Module
┌─────────────────────────────────────────────────────┐
│                  Installation Options               │
├─────────────────────────────────────────────────────┤
│ │D│                                                 │
│ │D│         Directory Services Options              │
│ ├─────────────────────────────────────────────────┤ │
│ │        Directory Services Login/Authentication   │ │
│ ├─────────────────────────────────────────────────┤ │
│ │ Administrator Name: CN=Admin.O=GCS              │ │
│ │ Password:    ▓▓▓▓▓▓▓▓▓▓▓▓▓▓▓▓▓▓▓▓▓▓▓▓▓▓▓▓▓▓▓▓▓ │ │
│ └─────────────────────────────────────────────────┘ │
│ │S│                                                 │
│ │Exit                                               │
├─────────────────────────────────────────────────────┤
│ Password Help                                       │
│                                                     │
│ Enter the password for the Administrator Name above.│
│                                                     │
│                                                     │
│              ─(To scroll, <F7>-up <F8>-down)─       │
├─────────────────────────────────────────────────────┤
│ Abort login          <Esc>                          │
│ Help                 <F1>               Abort INSTALL <Alt><F10>
```

FIGURE 3.39

One more warning

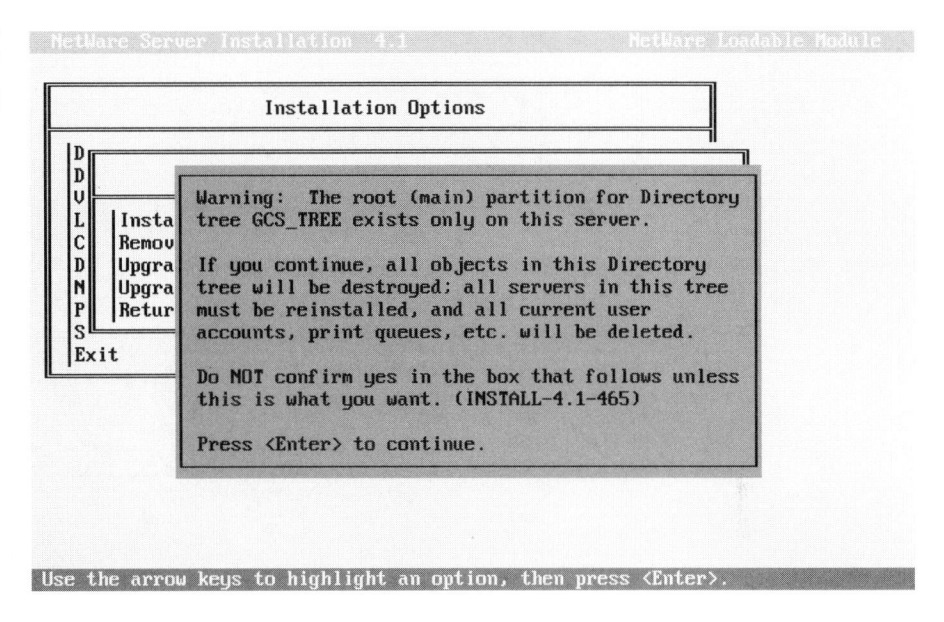

```
NetWare Server Installation 4.1                    NetWare Loadable Module

                    ┌─────── Installation Options ───────┐
                    │                                    │
         ┌──────────┴──────────────────────────────┐    │
         │ Warning:  The root (main) partition for Directory │
         │ tree GCS_TREE exists only on this server.         │
    Insta│                                                    │
    Remov│ If you continue, all objects in this Directory    │
    Upgra│ tree will be destroyed; all servers in this tree  │
    Upgra│ must be reinstalled, and all current user         │
    Retur│ accounts, print queues, etc. will be deleted.     │
         │                                                    │
   Exit  │ Do NOT confirm yes in the box that follows unless │
         │ this is what you want. (INSTALL-4.1-465)          │
         │                                                    │
         │ Press <Enter> to continue.                        │
         └────────────────────────────────────────────────────┘

Use the arrow keys to highlight an option, then press <Enter>.
```

This warning appeared on a single-server network. The default installation routines make the second server in an NDS tree a replica holder automatically. Although it would take some extra work, it might be possible for you to delete a single Directory installation and undo a network of several servers—possible, but unlikely. You might just take a deep breathe and think again before you continue, however.

Removing NDS from a Multiple-Server Network

Much of what happens during a Directory deletion on a single-server network happens with one of many servers. NDS is a serious service, and you shouldn't delete it cavalierly.

When there are multiple servers involved, time synchronization becomes another sticking point when deleting NDS. As Figure 3.40 shows, steps must be taken to guarantee time continues for the remaining servers and users in the tree.

Remember, there are better ways to fix an NDS tree than chopping it down. These options are described in Chapter 10, which covers network management. This is a last resort.

FIGURE 3.40

Time synchronization settings after NDS deletion

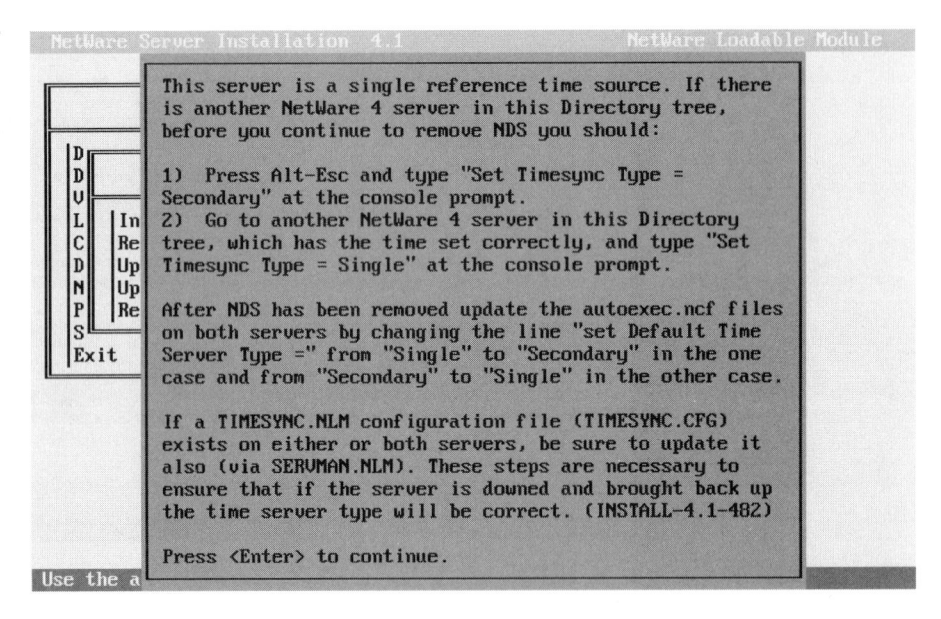

NetWare 4.11 New Products and Installations

GIVING USERS THEIR MONEY'S worth, Novell has added a few goodies to NetWare 4.11. Take a look at Figure 3.41 to see the new list of products you may choose to install.

The highlighted product, the NetWare Web Server, will be covered in a later chapter. In fact, the same chapter (Chapter 14) will also discuss NetWare IP and NetWare DHCP (Dynamic Host Configuration Protocol). If you care, look for the details in Chapter 14.

What's missing in the screen in Figure 3.41 is an easy way to install electronic documentation. Take your documentation CD-ROM, place it in your local CD drive or mount the CD-ROM on your NetWare server, and run the SETUPDOC.EXE program. You'll find this program in the root of the CD-ROM disk.

FIGURE 3.41

Choosing products to install with NetWare 4.11

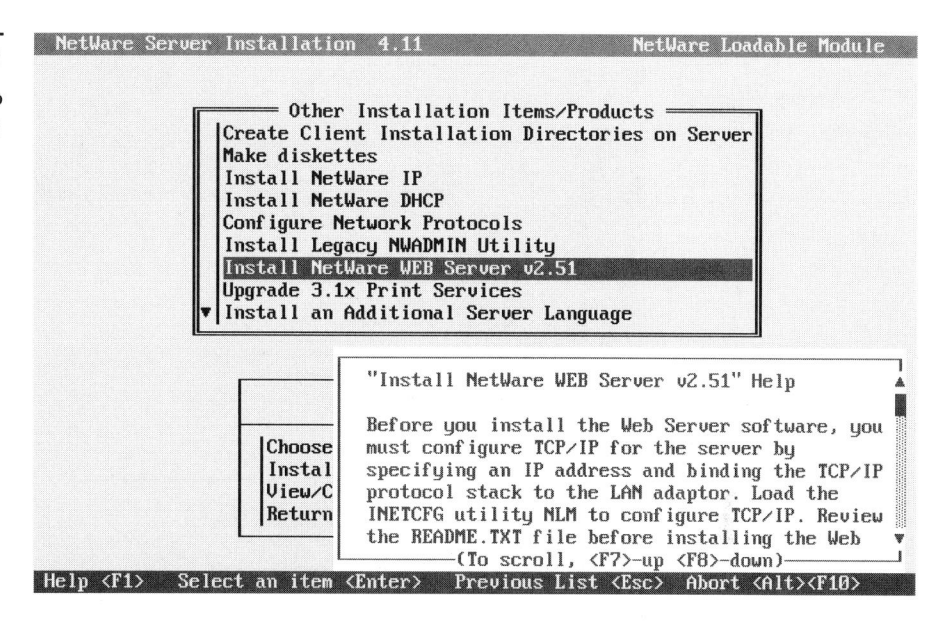

> Unlike the dull C-Worthy programs displayed in all the previous product installations, the SETUPDOC.EXE program starts a fancy Windows interface (I did tell you to run this under Windows—either 3.1*x* or 95—didn't I?). Take a look at the screen informing me of which "Document Collections" are about to be installed, in Figure 3.42.
>
> How do we get here? You are asked to install the collections and viewer separately. Click on the viewer installation, choose your locations for the source of your viewer and the destination, and let the system do the work. If you're lucky, your CD-ROM will include the CGMZV.DLL file missing from mine, and you'll be saved two hours of frustration tracking down that file. If they leave it off your disk as well, go straight to your NSE Pro disk or NetWire; the file isn't anywhere else close.
>
> After finishing the viewer installation, a viewer will be installed and an icon created. You can pick which group gets the icon, if it matters to you.
>
> The collections transfer is a bit easier, and you again choose the source (you could be copying the file from your local CD-ROM, a CD-ROM mounted on the server, or an installation server) and the destination. Let NetWare pick the default locations; no sense arguing with a computer program about where to put things. Software is squirrely enough without confusing it even more by moving the default locations.

FIGURE 3.42

A fancy Windows installation screen (finally)

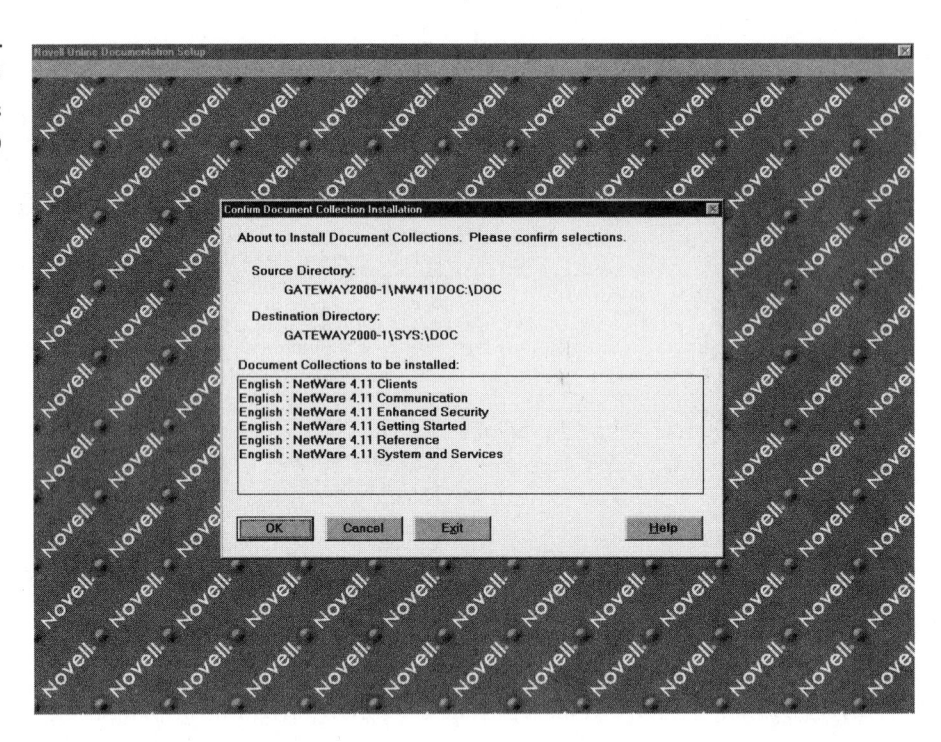

As mentioned, we'll get to see the new products included in NetWare 4.11 in Chapter 14. Since these products only involve the Internet and Unix interconnection, many of the NetWare networks being installed won't get into these details. If you fall into the growing ranks of Internet-connected companies, you'll enjoy Chapter 14 quite a bit.

Installation Is Good, but It Will Get Better

WHEN NOVELL INCLUDED the Simple Installation process for NetWare 4.10 (it actually got into 4.02), some network resellers were unhappy. How can you charge a customer for installation when the customer knows the installation process is a snap?

Customers, of course, are happy with this new installation feature. Installing NDS is simple, and any NDS tree mistakes can be easily corrected. What could be wrong?

What if this is too easy? What if customers figure, "no pain, no gain?" After all, NetWare is now almost as easy to install as DOS. It's easier to configure than MS Windows. How can this product be any good?

But only those with experience might take the "too-easy" view. Most people today *expect* things to be easier. You and I are in the computer business, and we know how much easier things are today than five years ago. People in the "real" world just see how computers are still more difficult to use than they should be.

Amazingly, the most difficult areas are those that home computer users most want. Have you installed a sound board and CD-ROM drive lately? Not simple. Modems are still killers, especially if they're cheap (and even worse if the cheap bundled software isn't configured for that particular modem).

The result of these problems is that people think computers are getting harder to understand, not easier. They may be right.

I'm waiting for the installation procedure that listens to the network and configures itself. The first disk that loads the SERVER.EXE program would start a network monitor, listen for the NDS information, and fill out several proposed configurations. You then choose your favorite, and get another cup of coffee.

That's the kind of installation routine I want. It would also make books like this shorter.

CASE STUDY

MiniCo: Installing NetWare Directory Services and Optional Procedures

MINICO HAS 3 servers, 75 users, and one location. MiniCo had one existing server to upgrade, and two new servers. All the servers needed to have NetWare 4.1x installed.

Details, Details, but Not Too Many

CONSIDERATIONS

The choices:

- Use the worksheets provided in the manuals and prepare for the installation.
- Don't use the worksheets and try to wing it.

DECISION

Try to wing it (couldn't find time to complete the worksheets).

EXPLANATION

Philosophically, "not to decide is to decide." If you don't prepare for a job, you won't do the job well. No one plans to do a bad job, they just do a bad job of planning. Unfortunately, the results are the same.

Configuring NDS during the First Server Installation

CONSIDERATIONS

The configuration requirements:

- Server name
- Server time zone
- Server context
- Admin name and password

DECISIONS

The server name was set as SUPPORT_1, planning for more servers in the future. The time zone was set for US Pacific, since MiniCo resides in Emdubville, California (in a building with a view of the ocean, the mountains, the forest, and the desert from the various windows). The server context was set as SUPPORT_1.SUPPORT.MINICO. The Admin name was given a password of canada.

EXPLANATION

Alexander Von Thorn (the Distribution Manager, who is handling NetWare 4.1x installation) followed the prompts the entire

MINICO CASE STUDY, CONTINUED

way through, accepting the recommendations of the installation program.

Installing a New Server into an Existing 4.1x Network

CONSIDERATIONS

The choices:

- Set up multiple NDS trees.
- Design a single NDS tree for the company.

DECISION

Use a single NDS tree.

EXPLANATION

MiniCo gained no advantage from separating the company into multiple trees. There was even discussion of keeping the network completely flat, as it would be under NetWare 3.*x*, but the separation offered by Organizational Units appealed to the Judge (a nickname for the Operations Manager). Keeping different functions within groups of like individuals seemed to appeal to his sense of order.

Finishing Installation and Your Next Steps

CONSIDERATIONS

The possible tasks:

- Load other name spaces (Macintosh, NFS, OS/2).
- Change any SET parameters.
- Add any other STARTUP.NCF or AUTOEXEC.NCF commands.

DECISION

Change the SET Auto Register Memory Above 16 Megabytes command to ON to allow the server to use all 64 MB of RAM.

EXPLANATION

Each server for MiniCo is different, and each required different SET parameters to make the memory acceptable to NetWare.

Optional Installation Items, Procedures, and Products

CONSIDERATIONS

The possible tasks:

- Create a registration diskette.
- Create client installation diskettes.
- Install NetWare for Macintosh support.
- Install NetWare MHS Services.
- Configure network protocols.
- Install Online Documentation and viewers.

DECISION

Alexander created the registration diskette and the client installation diskettes. He then loaded Macintosh support on SUPPORT_1, since Jack Mingo (MiniCo's President) and a few other people use a Macintosh. The online documentation package was also loaded on SUPPORT_1.

EXPLANATION

Unfortunately, Alexander didn't know how long it took for the server to create the client installation diskettes. Because he didn't read

MINICO CASE STUDY, CONTINUED

the manual before starting, he didn't know the diskettes could be created much more easily directly from the CD-ROM disk in any workstation.

Not knowing what to do about e-mail, Alexander didn't load NetWare MHS. The online documentation was installed on only one of the three servers, but Alexander had already installed it on his own PC as well.

Removing NetWare Directory Services

CONSIDERATIONS

The choices:

- Remove NDS from a single-server network.
- Remove NDS from a server in a multi-server network.

DECISION

No need to remove NDS.

EXPLANATION

In spite of a lack of prior planning, Alexander was able to make everything work on his servers and didn't need to remove NDS from any of the three.

Take a quick look at the map of MiniCo's network.

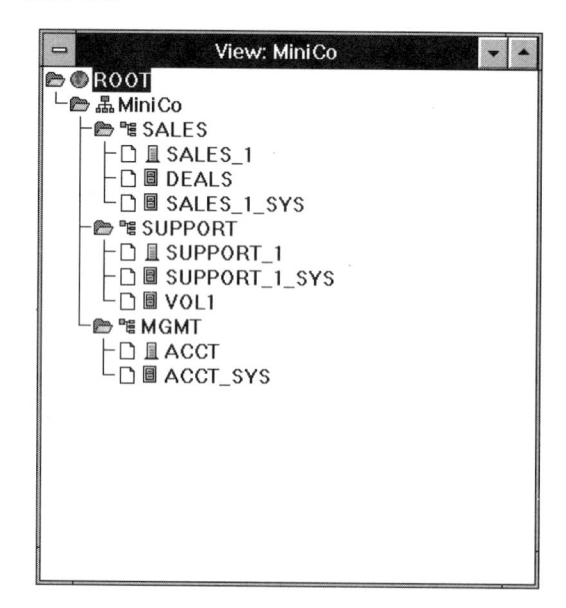

```
View: MiniCo
ROOT
└─ MiniCo
   ├─ SALES
   │  ├─ SALES_1
   │  ├─ DEALS
   │  └─ SALES_1_SYS
   ├─ SUPPORT
   │  ├─ SUPPORT_1
   │  ├─ SUPPORT_1_SYS
   │  └─ VOL1
   └─ MGMT
      ├─ ACCT
      └─ ACCT_SYS
```

CASE STUDY

MegaCorp: Installing NetWare Directory Services and Optional Procedures

Details, Details, but Not Too Many

CONSIDERATIONS

The choices:

- Use the worksheets provided in the manuals and prepare for the installation.
- Don't use the worksheets and try to wing it.

DECISION

Complete worksheets were created for each server well before installation.

EXPLANATION

A network planning committee, including members from each location, had met a total of five times during the planned transition to NetWare 4.1x. The last meeting concerned nothing but the details of NDS installation, confirming the role of each server in the network.

Configuring NDS during the First Server Installation

CONSIDERATIONS

The configuration requirements:

- Server name
- Server time zone
- Server context
- Admin name and password

DECISIONS

A rigid server name and context structure was developed before the NetWare 4.1x roll-out started.

EXPLANATION

All servers are grouped together in a SERVER Organizational Unit in each location. Directory Map and Alias objects are used to connect users to the proper volumes for applications and data. An example of a server name is HQ_TAX_S1, for the first server in the Tax department in the headquarters office (HQ) in Dallas.

Installing a New Server into an Existing 4.1x Network

CONSIDERATIONS

The choices:

- Set up multiple NDS trees.
- Design a single NDS tree for the company.

MEGACORP CASE STUDY, CONTINUED

DECISION

Design a single NDS tree for the whole company.

EXPLANATION

MegaCorp tried multiple NDS trees, but felt the inconvenience of jumping from tree to tree for management outweighed the advantages of separation. Using multiple Country and Organization containers provides all the necessary separation. A single tree, with redundant WAN connections, makes it easy for the central IS group to support the local technical team whenever necessary.

Finishing Installation and Your Next Steps

CONSIDERATIONS

The possible tasks:

- Load other name spaces (Macintosh, NFS, OS/2).
- Change any SET parameters.
- Add any other STARTUP.NCF or AUTOEXEC.NCF commands.

DECISION

Load Macintosh, NFS, and OS/2 name spaces during initial installation. Modify the SET Auto Register Memory Above 16 Megabytes command to reflect the 128 MB of RAM on the server. Add REMOTE.NLM and other management utilities to initial server script files.

EXPLANATION

All of MegaCorp's servers are configured to support all name spaces, since the company didn't want to limit the users of each server. Special memory configurations were set to support the large amount of RAM on each system. Every possible remote management utility was loaded on each server for easier support while in the field.

Optional Installation Items, Procedures, and Products

CONSIDERATIONS

The possible tasks:

- Create a registration diskette.
- Create client installation diskettes.
- Install NetWare for Macintosh support.
- Install NetWare MHS Services.
- Configure network protocols.
- Install online documentation and viewers.

DECISION

NetWare for Macintosh support was installed on all servers. Installation diskettes for various clients were set up to run from the server, with a boot diskette that installed NetWare to the workstation during the login procedure. NetWare MHS support installation was skipped, as was preparation of the registration diskette. A few select servers had the online documentation installed.

MEGACORP CASE STUDY, CONTINUED

EXPLANATION

Being a large corporate customer, MegaCorp bought NetWare through a Master License Agreement, and so the company didn't need a separate registration. MegaCorp uses Global MHS in a separate installation for e-mail transmissions. The first server per Organizational Unit always gets the online documentation installed, but no other servers are configured that way.

Removing NetWare Directory Services

CONSIDERATIONS

The choices:

- Remove NDS from a single-server network.
- Remove NDS from a server in a multi-server network.

DECISION

No need to remove NDS from any system.

EXPLANATION

Any server that showed the slightest deviation from the norm during installation was taken out of the loop and checked over thoroughly. If any disk error occurred, the disk was reformatted and tried again. If the disk showed a second error, no matter how small, it was returned to the manufacturer for a new one.

MegaCorp's procedures listed each step down the line. Any problems were dealt with by starting over. Too many times in the past, hours were wasted trying to fix some odd problem or another. Now, they simply wipe the disk and start over at the slightest hint of anything unusual.

Take a look at a high-level overview of MegaCorp's network:

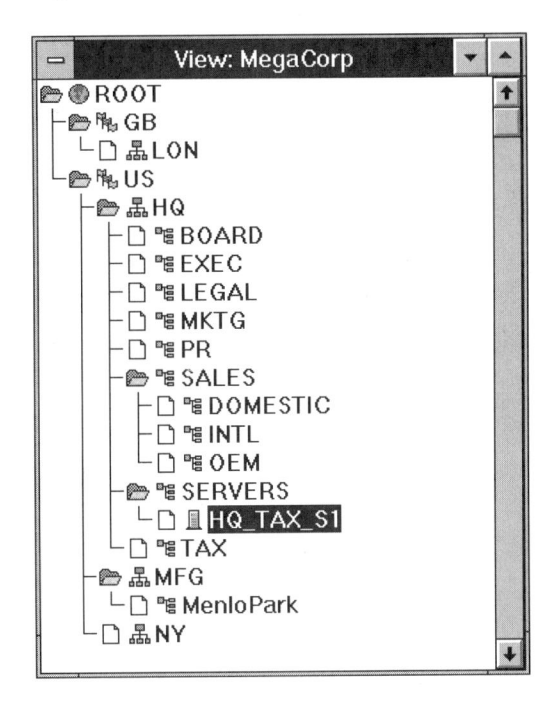

```
View: MegaCorp
ROOT
├── GB
│   └── LON
├── US
│   ├── HQ
│   │   ├── BOARD
│   │   ├── EXEC
│   │   ├── LEGAL
│   │   ├── MKTG
│   │   ├── PR
│   │   ├── SALES
│   │   │   ├── DOMESTIC
│   │   │   ├── INTL
│   │   │   └── OEM
│   │   ├── SERVERS
│   │   │   └── HQ_TAX_S1
│   │   └── TAX
│   ├── MFG
│   │   └── MenloPark
│   └── NY
```

NetWare Directory Services: Overview, Planning, Expansion

CHAPTER 4

MANY PEOPLE BELIEVE, mistakenly, that NDS (NetWare Directory Services) is the only improvement NetWare 4.x has over NetWare 3.x. Many people also believe, mistakenly, that NDS is some terribly complicated technology that bears no relationship to earlier NetWare software.

Put your fears to rest. NDS is the next step in network organization and administration, grouping servers the way NetWare 3.x groups users. NetWare 4.x is designed to provide user access and simplified management to an enterprise containing hundreds of servers as well as a single departmental NetWare server.

The Global Network View

OFFICIALLY, NDS IS a relational database distributed across your entire network. All servers in the network take part in supporting NDS, making all network resources available to NetWare clients. NDS provides global access to all network resources (users, groups, printers, volumes, and so on), regardless of where they are physically located. Users log in to a multiserver network and view the entire network as a single information system.

Fancy official words boil down to this: every client can see everything in the network from either a text-based or graphical program provided by NetWare 4.1x. More exciting for you as the administrator is the fact that this single network view works for management as well. You can view, change, add, or delete network resources anywhere in the network, without logging in to each server where the resource is located.

Imagine how the old phones worked: you picked up the handset, an operator asked the name of the person you wanted to connect to, and then the operator took care of the rest. NDS works exactly the same, except for one or two details. Instead of picking up the phone, a user executes the NWUSER (MS Windows-based NetWare User Tools), Network Neighborhood (Windows 95), or NETUSER (DOS-based) program. Instead of asking for a person by name, you highlight the resource name (with a mouse in NWUSER and Network Neighborhood or a cursor in NETUSER). Then you click (or press Enter), and you're connected. Except for those details, it's exactly the same.

Many users already think things are almost this easy, which is testimony to all your hard work managing your network. The reality is, of course, that previous NetWare versions focused on each server in the network. The NetWare 4.1x network focuses on the entire network. NDS is the database and associated programs that track all the pieces of the entire network.

Some procedural notes for our foray into NDS. References to Directory *assume the NDS Directory structure;* directory *assumes a file directory on a disk. The word* tree *refers to the NDS tree (I won't be talking about the oak, willow, or pecan type). And, while you might think* NetWare Directory Services *is plural and should be referred to in that manner, we've decided that it's a singular object and should be referred to in that manner. I will say, "NDS is" rather than, "NDS are." Although made of many pieces, NDS is a single item.*

Advantages of NDS

STRETCHING THE EARLIER telephone example a bit further, NDS looks like a giant network switchboard. Everything that happens in your network goes through the central authority of NDS.

Another analogy (in case you're collecting them) is that of a card catalog in a library. Each object in the library is listed on a card in the card catalog. If you want a library resource, such as a book, a map, a picture, a tape, a reference book, or a meeting room, the card catalog is the place to start. To make a stronger analogy for us, the card catalog should be used as the inventory tracking database as well. NDS tracks the location and disposition of all network resources.

NDS is a fundamental network service. A client (such as a user, application, or server) requests network information, services, or access. NDS finds the resource information and provides information, network services, or resource access based on the information contained in the Directory.

NDS provides the following:

- A global database providing access to, and management of, network information, resources, and services

- A standard method of managing, viewing, and accessing network information, resources, and services

- A logical organization of network resources that is independent of the physical characteristics or layout of the network

- Dynamic mapping between an object and the physical resource to which it refers

The "global" part of the database will help you, even if your network doesn't span continents. This ensures that NDS is available to every client and every server, and tracks every network resource.

Let's amplify two of the earlier points. The way that NDS handles network requests and activity is not much different than the way they were handled by the bindery, but some people insist in making things more difficult than they really are. The bindery has just as an important a role in earlier versions of NetWare as NDS does in NetWare 4.1x, but NDS has a larger scope. The necessity of a central network administration point has not changed.

NDS does have the ability to handle resources that are physically distant to the file server where you are connected. Since earlier NetWare versions have been completely server-centric, the idea of separating logical object location from the physical object location never came up. With NDS and NetWare 4.1x, the server-centric network has been replaced by NDS. Therefore, the physical location of a particular object in relation to a particular server is of less importance.

All these benefits come from a single login name/password sequence. This is the advantage of having all the servers work through NDS rather than individually. Before, you needed to connect to each server to use the resources controlled there. Now, you log in to the network, and all the NetWare 4.1x servers work together to provide services.

Quick Summary of NDS

All network requests go through NDS. Looking for a printer? Sending mail to another user? Looking for a file? Any client wanting information about or access to any (that means *any*) network resource must use NDS.

NDS contains logical resource information about network resources. The Directory contains information about each object connected to the network. The location of each object within the Directory tree may well be different than the physical location would indicate. NDS is a logical, not a physical, concept.

Here's how it works with the common network task of printing:

1. Client requests resource.	You need to print. You request a printer by its NDS object name.
2. A NetWare server responds.	A NetWare server, participating in NDS as they all do, looks for the printer object of that name in the Directory.
3. NDS locates object in Directory.	The particular printer object is located in the Directory database.
4. Resource location is identified.	Based on the property values found for the object, NDS discovers the physical location of the printer.
5. Client validity and authority are checked.	Your user name and rights are checked and referenced against the list of those eligible to use that particular printer.
6. Client is connected to resource.	You are connected to the requested printer.

Everything that happens in NetWare 4.*x* goes through NDS. Every network resource is tracked by NDS, and every network client uses NDS to find those resources.

Objects Everywhere and Everything Is an Object

OBJECTS HAVE BEEN mentioned many times. If you're wondering just what objects are and why they matter, you're not alone. The world of computing in general, and networking in specific, is gradually becoming objectified. (Okay, "object-oriented" is the proper term, although it lacks the playfulness of "objectified.")

An object is a distinct, separate entity, in programming or in networking. NetWare uses objects in the NDS structure to store information about a network resource, such as a user, group, printer, file server volume, and the like.

Directory objects are data structures that store information, not the entity they represent. Some of the entities are physical, such as users and printers, while other entities are logical, like groups and print queues. A Print Queue object stores information about the specific print queue and helps network clients find and use the queue, but the object is only information about the print queue.

Each object consists of properties. A *property* is a category of information that you can store about an object. Some properties are required to make an object unique; those will be mandatory when you create the object. The name of an object is a required property; for example, a User object name property might be "James."

Names can be up to 64 characters for every NDS object, but there is a limit of 256 characters for any complete NDS name. This should not be a problem, unless you give very long names or have way too many levels in your NDS tree.

Other properties will be available in the object, but not mandatory. For instance, the description property for James may say "author," or it may be blank.

The information within the property is called a *value*. In the example just given, the description property value for object James is author. Some properties may have multiple values. If the property is telephone number, for instance, both office and home numbers can be listed.

Objects, properties, and their values are stored in the Directory database. Some objects represent physical objects, such as User object James. Some objects represent logical, not physical, entities, such as groups and print queues. See Figure 4.1 for a graphical representation.

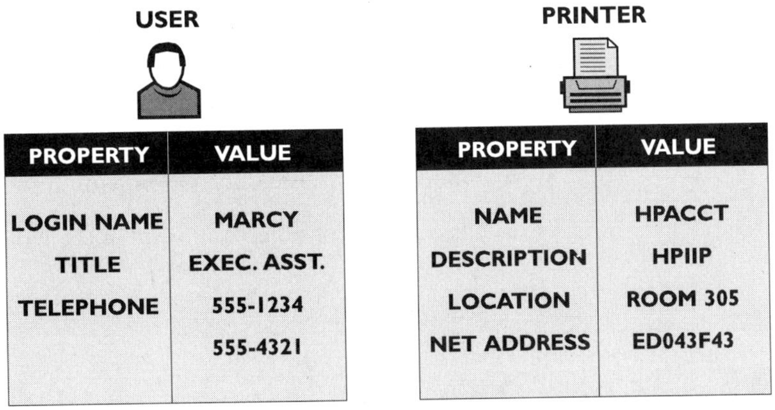

FIGURE 4.1

Examples of objects, properties, and values

USER

PROPERTY	VALUE
LOGIN NAME	MARCY
TITLE	EXEC. ASST.
TELEPHONE	555-1234
	555-4321

PRINTER

PROPERTY	VALUE
NAME	HPACCT
DESCRIPTION	HPIIP
LOCATION	ROOM 305
NET ADDRESS	ED043F43

Regardless whether the object represents a physical or logical entity, remember that the *object* we speak of is itself only a structure for storing information. There are no objects you can touch and manipulate physically in this definition.

The object for a device is not the device. That's easy to remember when speaking of printers, but can become confusing when speaking of logical items such as groups. The object describes the device, but it is not the device.

The *class* of an object is important. There are three types of classes, although one is slightly cheating. The *leaf* class of objects represents the actual network resources represented by the bindery in earlier NetWare. Examples are users, printers, servers, and volumes. Leaf objects cannot contain any other objects.

That job is performed by the *container* class of objects. Container objects hold, or contain, other objects. Container examples are the Organization and Organizational Unit objects. Container objects are called *parent* objects if there are actually objects inside the container. One container object is mandatory per tree.

Finally, there is the [Root] class, a "super" container class at the top of your NDS tree. This is created during installation, is mandatory, and slightly stretches the "class" metaphor. There can only be one [Root]. Each tree must have at least one Organization object. Remember naming your Organization during installation? That's when at least one mandatory Organization is created. You can create other Organizations during installation or later.

Here's a quick review of the NDS terms related to objects:

- **Object:** A unit of information about a resource
- **Property:** Information category stored about an object
- **Value:** The specific information within the property
- **Class:** Types of objects allowed in the Directory

Hierarchical Tree Structure and Schema

OFFICIAL STUFF HERE: NDS is consistent with the developing international standard, X.500. This specification, drawn by the IEEE (Institute of Electrical and Electronic Engineers), provides a global standard for organizing Directory information.

The X.500 specification describes a global "telephone book" to be used with the e-mail specifications detailed in X.400. Much of the "Information Superhighway" is being built according to X.500 guidelines. NDS follows those guidelines as well.

The Directory *schema* is the rules defining how the NDS tree is built. The schema defines specific types of information that dictate the way data is stored in the Directory database. The following information is defined:

- **Attribute information:** The type of additional information an object can or must have associated with it. Attribute types are defined within the schema by specific constraints and a specific syntax for their values.

- **Inheritance:** Determines which properties will flow down the tree to objects below the current object.

- **Naming:** Determines the structure of the NDS tree.

- **Subordination:** Determines the location of objects in the NDS tree.

These are all fancy terms for how the standard objects, such as servers, users, and print queues, are technically defined by NDS. The NDS schema can be modified to suit your network, which is exactly what we'll be doing soon.

[Root]: The Base, and Top, of Your NDS Tree

IT SOUNDS BACKWARDS to call the top of a hierarchical structure "root" but that's what we do. A statement such as "[Root] is automatically placed at the top of the NDS tree during installation" is true, but sounds weird. So what is this [Root], anyway?

Depending on your generation, [Root] is the Big Cheese, the Big Kahuna, or the Big Mamba Jamba. The [Root] object contains everything, which is why the icon for [Root] is a globe. The name of the tree, same name as the [Root] object, is entered during installation.

The [Root] object is the very first object in the Directory tree, and cannot be deleted or modified. All other objects, including Country and Organization objects, are contained within the [Root] object. Characteristics of [Root] include:

- Mandatory
- One per Directory
- Forms the top of the NDS tree
- Holds only Country, Organization, and Alias objects
- Created only during installation of the first NetWare 4.1*x* server on the network
- Cannot be moved, easily renamed, or deleted
- Does not have properties

> *Depending on your generation, [Root] is the Big Cheese, the Big Kahuna, or the Big Mamba Jamba.*

Analogies are fully stocked in our inventory room. In fact, that's a good analogy right there. The storeroom is [Root], the shelves are containers, and things on the shelves are leaf objects. You may have one wall for canned goods (an Organization) and two shelves named Peas and Lima Beans (Organizational Units, or OUs).

Or, your conglomerates' entire global network is [Root], with each individual subsidiary an Organization (container). Departments are Organizational Units (containers) made of file servers, file server volumes, users, printers, and all your other leaf objects.

NOTE

Do not confuse [Root] with the root directory of a file system. When you see [Root] with the brackets and the capital letter, it refers to the top level of your NDS tree. The root directory is the first directory of a volume or other hard disk, and has no relationship to the [Root] object.

For nature lovers, the tree trunk is [Root], branches are containers (with many containers from [Root]), and leaves are, well, leaf nodes. A single tree supports multiple branches, which support multiple leaf objects. Similarly, a single [Root] supports multiple Organizations and Organizational Units, which support multiple leaf objects.

Objects with rights to the [Root] object have those same rights all the way down the NDS tree. Unless blocked, a trustee of [Root] has authority over the entire network. The Admin user, created at the same time as [Root] during installation, has a trustee assignment including Supervisor rights to the [Root] object. This allows Admin all rights to all objects in the NDS tree. This equates to the SUPERVISOR user created during installation of earlier NetWare versions. Admin, as SUPERVISOR before, uses those rights to set up the network and create the framework for all users and other network resources.

WARNING

If you make any other user or group a trustee of [Root], that user or group will have the same rights as the Admin user. Leave Admin as the only individual trustee of [Root]. During NetWare 4.1x installation, the [Public] object is granted the Browse object right at the [Root] object of the NDS tree. This setting allows all users to see the entire NDS tree.

Container Objects Make Up the [Root] Object

Since [Root] contains everything, the next question is, "What is everything?" Everything, in terms of NDS, is containers, more containers, and leaf objects. Here's a summary:

- The [Root] object holds Country and Container objects.
- The Country object holds Organization objects.
- The Organization objects hold Organizational Units or leaf nodes.
- The Organizational Units hold other Organizational Units or leaf nodes.
- Leaf nodes are not containers.

[Root]: The Base, and Top, of Your NDS Tree

In Figure 4.2, you see a simple NDS design. Everything in the figure is a container except for the User and Printer objects.

Since no one can type anymore, or at least that's the impression I get, the "official" suggestion is to keep container names short. There are times when users must type a full listing of an NDS location. In Figure 4.2, the name for the user would be typed

```
USER.ORGANIZATIONAL UNIT.ORGANIZATION.COUNTRY
```

The [Root] name is always assumed to be included, since there can be only one [Root] per NDS tree.

Although the example for the user in Figure 4.2 looks like a lot of typing, it's rare for the user to type that much. There are programs for DOS (NETUSER), MS Windows 3.*x* (NWUSER), and Windows 95 (Network Neighborhood) that allow a user to move around the NDS tree without lifting a finger from the mouse or cursor keys.

For the few times a user must type a full Directory location, keep the names of the Organizations and Organizational Units fairly short. (You might also offer typing tutorial programs, but that's a diatribe for another time.) Don't, however, sacrifice clarity for a few keystrokes. Use the common abbreviations used elsewhere in your company; such as Eng for Engineering. Don't truncate Marketing to Mg; use Mktg.

FIGURE 4.2

Focusing on the top of a NDS tree

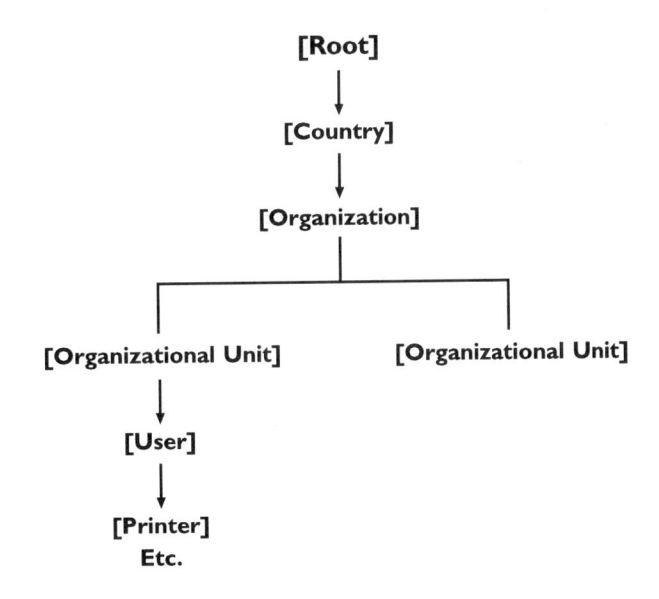

[Root]
↓
[Country]
↓
[Organization]
├── [Organizational Unit]
│   ↓
│   [User]
│   ↓
│   [Printer]
│   Etc.
└── [Organizational Unit]

The Country (C) Container

Characteristics of the Country container include:

- Optional for most networks
- Designates the country for your network
- Organizes all Directory objects within the country
- Must use valid two-character country abbreviation
- Holds Organization and Alias objects only
- Not part of the NetWare 4.1x installation program's defaults

NetWare 4.1x is a global network operating system, and the inclusion of a Country object makes that distinction clear. But the Country container is optional, even for those networks that do cross international lines.

If your network will connect to the Internet or a VAN (Value-Added Network) based on the emerging X.500 global directory specifications, the Country object is necessary. If your network will connect to a private network for remote communications, the Country object is optional. A network that's entirely local will have no need for the Country object. If you can avoid using the Country object, do so. Using it when you don't need to will only complicate things for your users and administrators.

If you do use a Country object, it can contain only Organization and Alias objects. No leaf objects are allowed.

There is a way to add the Country object during NetWare 4.1x installation, but you must know where and when. When you describe the context for the server being installed, you must type in the Country object description. Turn back to Chapter 3 and take a look at Figure 3.12. This is the screen where you may manually type the Country designation in the Server Context line (add .C=US to the start of the line). The screen doesn't tell you to do this, but it's the only shot you have during installation. You can add the Country designation later, using NWADMIN, if you prefer.

If you're in doubt about needing the Country object, you don't. Remember that even multinational networks don't require the Country object to function.

The Organization (O) Container

An Organization container has these characteristics:

- Mandatory (at least one per tree)

- Created under [Root] or Country only

- Typically represents a company, university, or department

- First level that can support leaf objects

- Placed in [Root] or Country objects

- Can contain Organizational Unit, leaf, and Alias objects

- Can contain a User Template (an object that can contain common information for groups of users)

- Named during installation, but subsequent Organizations can be created later

The next mandatory object after [Root] is the Organization container, indicated by the O abbreviation. There must be one Organization object per NDS tree, but one may be plenty. Smaller networks get along perfectly well with a single Organization object, using Organizational Units to separate workgroups or divisions. You may give the Organization the same name as your tree, but it's clearer during network use if you don't. In the lab network, the Organization is named GCS, while the tree is GCS_TREE. This pattern works easily and avoids confusion the few times you or a user may need to type the entire tree name and location.

The Organization object is the first container that can hold leaf objects. It can also hold Organizational Unit and Alias objects as well. You could create an NDS tree with a single Organization object, place all network resources in that single container, and have a flat network design modeled on NetWare 3.*x* layouts. The big advantage that this design has over a NetWare 3.*x* network is the ability to support multiple servers and their resources for all users with a single login.

Multiple Organization objects can exist in [Root], and each can contain as many Organizational Unit or leaf objects as you wish. Well, the upper limit of objects in a single container is 40,000. Practically, that's about 50 times more than enough. Users must be able to search the container without being overwhelmed.

Organization objects usually contain either Organizational Unit or leaf objects, with networks tending to lean toward one or the other. If your network is large, you may have several Organization objects, each containing multiple Organizational Units, each containing leaf objects. If your network is small, you may have many of your leaf objects in the Organization object, with few or no Organizational Units. Neither way is better than the other, and the choice is usually determined by company organization rather than philosophy.

The User Template is a convenient object for providing similar services for groups of users. This file holds information you can apply to new User objects as they are created. Common details for groups of users, such as file restrictions, language used, and the like, are put in the User Template object.

The first Organization must be named during the installation of the first NDS server in the tree. Later servers can be installed into the existing Organization or in a new one created for them. Organizations may also be created in the administrator utilities (NETADMIN for DOS or NWADMIN for MS Windows).

The Organizational Unit (OU) Container

Characteristics of the Organizational Unit container are:

- Optional

- Created in Organization or other Organizational Unit objects

- Typically represents a division, department, workgroup, or project team

- Contains Organizational Unit, leaf, or Alias objects

- Can contain a User Template

- Created during installation or later

The final container, the Organizational Unit (OU) object, is optional but helpful in grouping leaf objects. If you have a single Organization in your network, the Organizational Unit objects will be valuable in keeping straight which resources belong closest to which users. If you have multiple Organization objects, your company is large enough to subdivide each Organization into multiple Organizational Unit objects.

Organizational Unit objects are created within Organization objects, or within other Organizational Unit objects. Organizational Unit objects can hold other Organizational Unit objects, leaf objects, or Alias objects.

Organizational Unit objects can be created during installation, or later through normal administration utilities. These are useful as anchors for user login scripts.

Some early NetWare 4.0 administrators created an Organizational Unit object for each NetWare file server. They did this with the short-term goals of avoiding NDS and making the users feel more comfortable. Unfortunately, both goals backfired on most of the administrators. NDS offered more advantages than the learning-curve disadvantages, even with the first version, and it's even better and more flexible now. Second, users forced to change into an environment that closely re-created their previous NetWare 3.*x* network were forced to change for little personal benefit.

Container Rules

Each container has rules defining where it must reside and which objects it can contain. Table 4.1 summarizes these rules.

TABLE 4.1 Rules of Containment for NDS Objects

OBJECT	CAN EXIST IN	CAN CONTAIN	SAMPLE NAMES
Country	[Root]	Organization, Alias	US, FR
Organization	[Root], Country	Organizational Unit, Alias, leaf objects	GCS, UTDallas
Organizational Unit	Organization, Organizational Unit	Organizational Unit, Alias, leaf objects	Marketing, Integration

Figure 4.3 shows four examples of NDS trees that illustrate the rules of containment. The first example shows the simplest tree possible. All the other examples could have multiple Organization objects, spreading the network horizontally. There's no practical limit on the number of Organization objects that [Root] can hold, but there are reasons to keep the network from spreading too far. We'll cover many of those reasons when we speak of NDS replication and how to take advantage of the fault-tolerant nature of the NetWare 4.1*x* NDS tree (Chapter 10).

FIGURE 4.3

Some sample structures

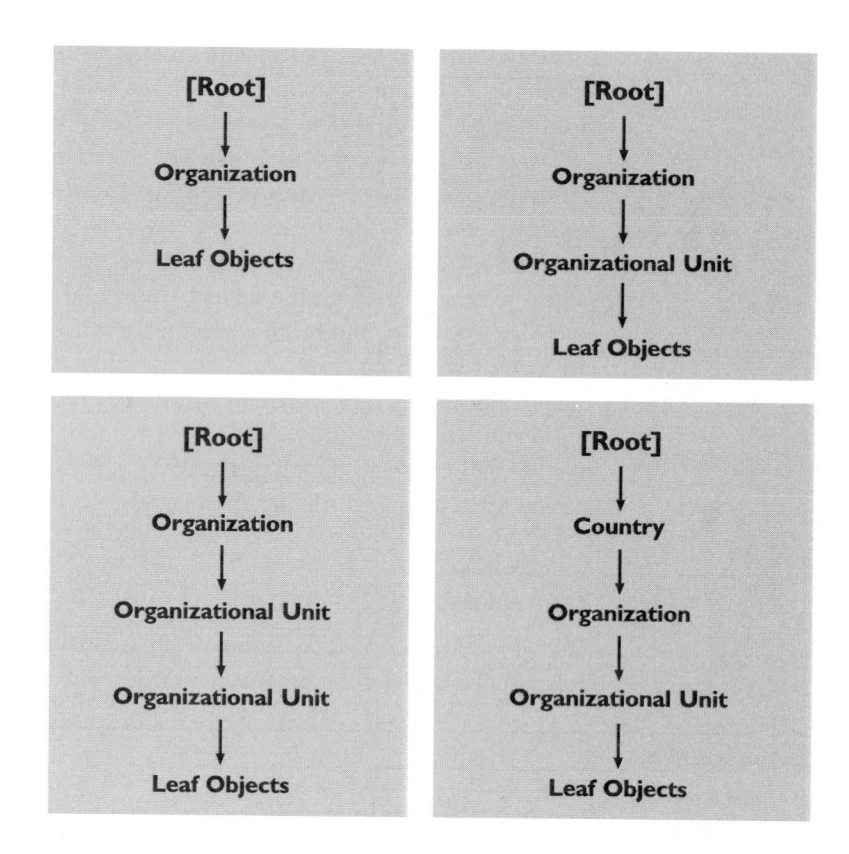

```
[Root]                    [Root]
  ↓                         ↓
Organization             Organization
  ↓                         ↓
Leaf Objects             Organizational Unit
                            ↓
                         Leaf Objects

[Root]                    [Root]
  ↓                         ↓
Organization              Country
  ↓                         ↓
Organizational Unit      Organization
  ↓                         ↓
Organizational Unit      Organizational Unit
  ↓                         ↓
Leaf Objects             Leaf Objects
```

Container objects hold (contain, get it?) other Directory objects. A container object that holds other objects, regardless of level, is officially called a *parent* object.

Leaf Objects and the Bindery They Replace

Now we've come to the point of all the new objects and containers and global NDS trees: leaf objects. These are the network resources that make networking worthwhile. Yes, these are all the bindery components you learned to love in earlier versions of NetWare.

Figure 4.4 is an image from early in the NDS development process of our lab network. The line divides the new NDS containers from the older bindery-type elements familiar to NetWare 3.*x* users.

FIGURE 4.4

Old and new demarcation point

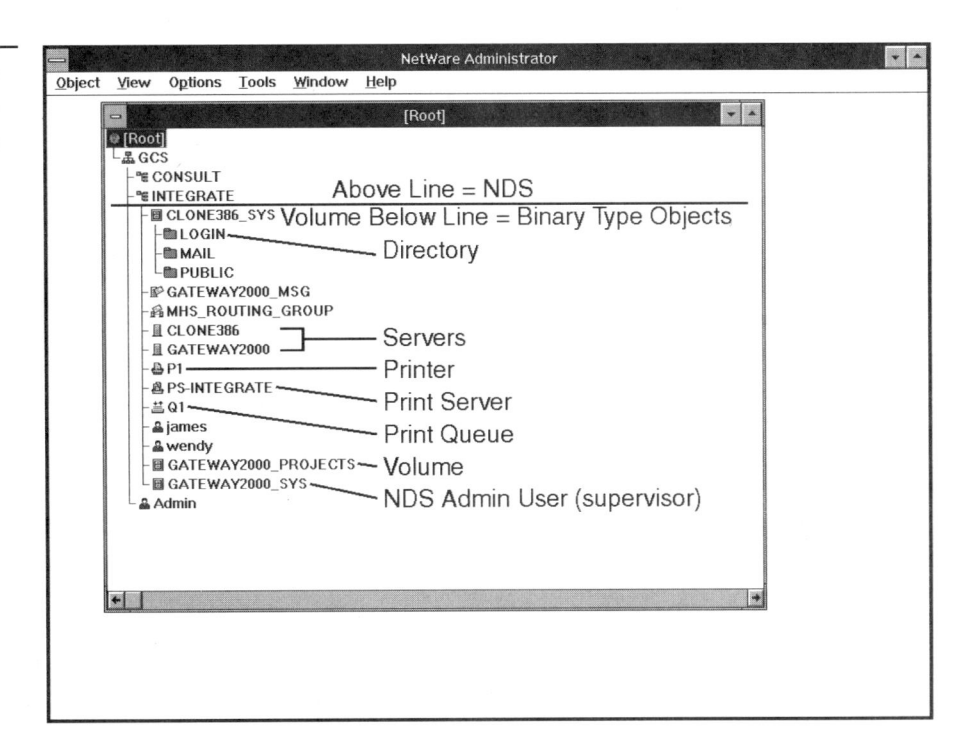

[NetWare Administrator screenshot showing NDS tree with [Root], GCS, CONSULT, INTEGRATE, CLONE386_SYS, LOGIN, MAIL, PUBLIC, GATEWAY2000_MSG, MHS_ROUTING_GROUP, CLONE386, GATEWAY2000, P1, PS-INTEGRATE, Q1, james, wendy, GATEWAY2000_PROJECTS, GATEWAY2000_SYS, Admin. Annotations: Above Line = NDS; Volume Below Line = Binary Type Objects; Directory; Servers; Printer; Print Server; Print Queue; Volume; NDS Admin User (supervisor).]

In Figure 4.4, you can see the [Root] object, with a globe icon, highlighted. Below [Root] is the Organization object named GCS. Two Organizational Unit objects are contained in GCS. The first, CONSULT, is not expanded. The second, INTEGRATE, is the main context for the lab network.

Labeled for you are a few of the leaf objects that directly correspond to earlier NetWare versions. You can see NetWare volumes, NetWare servers, users, standard NetWare system directories (such as LOGIN and PUBLIC), and even the troika of printer, print queue, and print server.

Later, you will see many pictures of the lab network as it grows and changes and transmogrifies to illustrate the flexibility of NetWare 4.1*x*. But now, let's see what new spin NetWare 4.1*x* has put on our old friends such as users and printers. We'll also look at some new items that never appeared until NetWare 4.*x* hit the market.

Leaf objects may have names as long as 64 characters, but be aware of your limits and your users. The total NDS name of an object cannot exceed 256 characters. Painfully long names for leaf objects will aggravate your users.

Remember that each item discussed here is represented by an icon for the object, not the device itself. That's the trick with object-oriented systems, you know. You always speak of the object representing some physical or logical item, not necessarily the item itself.

User

Here is the reason for the network: users. These icons of the User object represent the people who log in to the network and use the network resources.

The User object properties you can set are login restrictions, intruder detection limits, password and password restrictions, and security equivalences.

When you create a User object, you may create a home directory, just as in earlier NetWare versions. You can create User objects anywhere in the NDS tree, but your users must know that location in order to log in. It's best to create them in the context in which they will spend most of their time. This is only a matter of clicking on one context or another in the NWADMIN program.

Macintosh and OS/2 users must be created where the Bindery Services context is set for them to log in to. Bindery-based users don't use NDS contexts; they log in directly to a particular NetWare 4.1*x* server rather than to the NDS tree.

Group

Just as in earlier NetWare versions, a Group is a collection of users with common network requirements. Now, however, they are called members of the Group object.

The Group object is a list of User objects that can be located anywhere in the NDS tree. There is no requirement to limit Group object members to a particular context.

Group objects act as management shorthand. Rather than make many similar trustee assignments to individual User objects, applying these same trustee assignments to a Group object does the job for each User object listed in the Group object. Many of these same statements can be made for members of the same container, too. If you prefer groups, you can include members of different containers.

NetWare Server

Also called NCP (NetWare Core Protocol) Server objects, the NetWare Server object represents some machine running NetWare on your network. The Server object is created automatically when the server software is installed.

The NetWare Server object is used as a reference point for several other objects, such as NetWare volumes. The Server object's properties hold much information, such as that particular server's physical location, services provided, and the error log.

A bindery-based server (as in a NetWare 3.x server) must have an NDS Server object created for the server in order to access the server's volumes. The bindery server must be up and running when this happens, so the "Add New Object" routine in NWADMIN has a server to use for verification and reading during the installation process. Or, you can use DSMIGRATE and upgrade your 3.x servers, as Novell is pushing you to do.

NetWare Volume

The Volume object represents a physical NetWare volume on the network, automatically created during the NetWare 4.1x server installation. You may, however, need to create the Volume object inside NWADMIN to display the volume's icon. Clicking on the volume icon in NWADMIN displays the volume's file system.

The Volume object's properties include information such as the name of the host server, volume location, space limits for users, and available disk space.

Print Objects

The NetWare print objects include:

- **Printer:** Represents a physical network printing device. One Printer object is required for each printer in the network.

- **Print Server:** Represents a network print server, whether located on a NetWare server or separately. One Print Server object is required for every network print server.

- **Print Queue:** Represents a network print queue. A Print Queue object is required for every network print queue.

You must create the print objects by using the NWADMIN, NETADMIN, or PCONSOLE utility program. Some third-party print server devices may create the Printer object for you, but verify before trusting.

Directory Map

New in NetWare 4.*x*, the Directory Map object points to a particular directory on a volume. This works like the MAP command by representing what could be a long path name as an easily remembered label.

Directory Map objects help you manage your login scripts. In the login script, use a Directory Map object to refer to a particular directory. Then, if the path name changes, you won't need to update each and every login script that includes the directory.

A common example is a product upgrade. Say you use Visual Kumquat Designer version 2.4. As is their wont, the software makers release a new version, 2.401, which is not compatible with version 2.4. If you have a Directory Map object pointing to the directory holding Visual Kumquat Designer, you can place the new software in a newly created VKD_2401 directory. Then make a single change in the Directory Map object. That's all it takes to point all Directory Map requests from the old VKD_24 directory to the new VKD_2401 directory. You won't need to change a single login script; all users will automatically access the VKD_2401 directory.

Organizational Role

The Organizational Role object represents a position or role within the company organization. It is typically used for jobs that have well-defined requirements, but which are performed by a rotating group of individuals rather than a single person.

For instance, team leader may be a position that needs some access rights above and beyond those of the rest of the workgroup. Granting those rights to the Organizational Role rather than to individuals makes it easy to track which person has these extra rights at any one time. When the team leader changes, the next person can be assigned the Organizational Role. That user will immediately inherit all the team leader rights.

Profile

The Profile object contains a profile login script, a special login script used by individuals with common needs but little else in common. If the Profile object is listed as a User object's property, the Profile object's login script is executed when that User object logs in.

The Profile object provides a way for users that don't belong to the same context, such as accounting payroll clerks from multiple divisions, to share login script commands. For example, the profile login script may provide these users with access to particular directories or special printers. This process also works for a subset of users in the same container.

Computer

A Computer object represents any computer on the network that is not a server, such as a workstation, router, e-mail gateway, or the like.

Use the Computer object properties to store information about the system, such as network address, configuration, serial number, the person it's assigned to, and so on. The Computer object is informational only; it has no effect on network operations.

Alias

The Alias object points to another object in the NDS tree in a different location. When you use the Alias object, objects appear to be in places they really aren't. Using an Alias object is an easy way to allow users to access an object in another context.

This is fun: the Alias object is a representation of a representation of an entity. In other words, the Alias object takes the form of another object and makes it appear that the second object is in a place it's not really in.

When an object is moved or renamed, you have the option of leaving an Alias object in its place. This keeps resources in the (seemingly) same place for the users that rely on those resources, even after the resource has been moved. If you delete or rename an Alias object, the Alias itself is affected, not the object it's pointing to.

WARNING

Be careful when you're modifying an Alias object or an object that has an Alias. The Alias object takes the shape of the object it replaces or points to, so make sure you're modifying the object you actually want to change. Look for the small Halloween mask beside the Alias object.

If you wish to access the Alias object and the properties of the object it refers to, you need the Read right to the Alias name and the Read right to the properties of the object it refers to. These options may be set in NETADMIN in DOS or NWADMIN in MS Windows.

AFP Server

AFP (AppleTalk File Protocol) servers are those that support the Apple Macintosh computer protocols. The AFP Server object represents an AppleTalk server connected to your network. There is a good chance that the AFP server is acting as a router between the NetWare network and other Macintosh computers.

This object stores only information concerning the AFP server. The AFP Server object has no effect on network operations.

Messaging (MHS) Server

The Messaging Server object represents a messaging server (server-based application) that resides on a NetWare server.

The Messaging Server object is automatically created when Novell's MHS (Message Handling Service) software is installed on a NetWare file server.

Message Routing Group

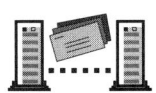

The Message Routing Group object represents a group of the aforementioned Messaging Server objects that can transfer messages between each other directly.

This is useful when several messaging servers are on the same network and need to exchange mail files and directory information.

Distribution List

The Distribution List object represents a group of e-mail addresses, such as a Quality Quorum that may not be in one regular Group together. When e-mail is sent to the Distribution List object, each member listed receives a copy. This is much quicker than sending e-mail to each user individually.

A Distribution List object differs from a Group object in these ways:

- Distribution List members do not have equal security to the Distribution List. Group members do have security equivalence with the Group.

- Distribution Lists work only for e-mail. Groups support login scripts and rights assignments.

- A Distribution List can include another Distribution List. Groups cannot include other Groups.

External Entity

The External Entity object represents a non-MHS address listing that has been imported into NDS and registered in NDS as a non-native NDS object. The NetWare MHS system uses this object to represent users from bindery-based directories to provide an integrated address book for sending messages.

If your network contains non-NDS and/or non-MHS servers, such as SMTP (Simple Mail Transfer Protocol, used widely by Unix systems) or X.400 systems, you can add those "foreign" addresses into the NDS database as External Entity objects.

E-mail users need only pick these External Entity objects from their address database. There is no need for the user to know or care about the actual e-mail system represented by the External Entity object.

Bindery and Bindery Queue Objects

The Bindery object represents an object placed in the NDS tree by an upgrade or migration utility.

The Bindery Queue object is exactly what you might expect: a print queue from a NetWare 3.*x* server placed in the NDS tree by an upgrade or migration.

Both of these objects are used by NDS to provide compatibility with bindery-based utilities. Many third-party print servers still require the bindery to function.

Unknown

The Unknown object is an NDS object that has been invalidated by losing a mandatory property. The NDS tree does not recognize the object. These Unknown objects appear when changes are made to NDS, such as when a NetWare server was deleted but the administrator forgot to delete the volumes for that server. The volumes will then appear as Unknown objects.

During large-scale changes to the NDS, some objects may briefly appear to be "unknown." This is caused by changes being made faster than NDS can synchronize. If you make changes and see Unknown objects, wait for awhile.

The best action is to delete Unknown objects that hang around. In the case of the orphaned volumes, re-create them if they belong to a server that has been re-created or modified.

Planning Your NDS Tree

NETWARE 4.1*x* USES building blocks in network design that were not available in earlier NetWare versions. These building blocks include the NDS tree, Organizations, and Organizational Units. Only when we speak of the leaf nodes, such as users, printers, servers, and volumes, do we overlap the pieces used by earlier NetWare.

Remember, the Country container object is available for use in those trees that span national borders, but unless you connect to an X.500 name service such as the North American Directory Forum, the Internet, or another X.500 service, avoid the Country container. If you learn after the fact that X.500 is necessary, you can add Country support later by modifying your tree.

While some administrators new to NetWare 4.1*x* fear these building blocks, many other administrators understand the advantages that the NDS tree offers to network architects. How many NetWare customers have a single server to handle every job? A few, but the normal sequence is to get one server, then have an application or two grow beyond that one server. Suddenly, the workgroup that started with one server has four servers.

With previous versions of NetWare, the management overhead quadrupled as the new servers arrived. With NetWare 4.1x, however, each server is just another object in the NDS tree. More importantly, each disk volume is just another object, and any one user can easily reference a dozen different volumes with a single network login.

Some Goals for Your NDS Tree Design

Plan your large NDS tree to perform the following functions:

- Fault-tolerance for the Directory database
- Decreased traffic on the network, especially over WAN links
- Easy look up of information and resources for users
- Simplified network administration and maintenance

> *Expect your network to change; expect to change NDS as a result.*

Keep these goals in mind, but let me say something: there is no one, perfect way to plan your NDS tree. The design that works for your network may not work for another network. The design for one division of your network may not work for another division. How your tree begins may not be how it ends. There are tools to modify the NDS structure, and those will be discussed in due course. Expect your network to change; expect to change NDS as a result.

Before we speak of specific planning and installation ideas, remember that adding NetWare 4.1x will be an adjustment for both you and your users. The users will need to feel comfortable with NetWare 4.1x; the more comfortable they feel, the easier the transition to the new network. Some hints for your rollout process:

- Run NetWare 4.1x in a lab environment.
- Demonstrate NetWare 4.1x to your power users before the upgrade.
- Train users before the upgrade (but not too long before).
- Draw NDS designs until everyone's priorities are covered.
- Coordinate with all other network administrators during the planning process.

Work with all other network administrators to develop a NDS tree that everyone can accept. No network design suits everyone perfectly, but you need to get the priorities covered. This will require input from all the other network administrators during the NDS design stage. The more closely everyone works together, the more successful your network will be.

When Novell implemented NDS on its global corporate network, managers met and talked (argued) about the design for months. Those wanting a purely geographical design disagreed with those wanting a design modeled strictly along job function lines. Finally, a hybrid network was designed and built. If the people at Novell themselves don't have a "magic" design that suits everyone, why should you?

When we speak of planning NDS design, we get into some gray areas, since each company and network is different. The process differs considerably depending on whether you will be doing all the setup and management, or you are one of many network administrators. If you do it all, your plans can be less detailed, because you will be the one making all the decisions as new questions arise. If you're working with a group of administrators, planning is the most important piece of the process. You and all other administrators must be in sync about NDS before starting.

The goal is supporting your users in the most efficient manner (for them) possible. Making resources easy to find for your users will speed their workday, but more selfishly, keep them from bothering you all the time. A good network design can save hours of network training.

Semantics can cause arguments in this section. Is a "bottom up" design the same as a "logical" design? Is "top-down" the same as "managed" or "preplanned"? Who cares? The important part is making the network fit your situation.

The focus here is on designing networks based on user function or user location. These roughly correspond to the top-down and bottom-up labels. As you might guess, a large network, or one that covers several geographic areas, will use a combination of both methods.

Setting Up a Pilot System

It will save you time and aggravation to have a pilot NetWare 4.1x server up and running before you begin the rollout. Even if the pilot server is running for only a week or two, the experience will be invaluable.

Build some sample users with different rights, and let people experiment. User 1 may have the run of the server, while Users 2 and 3 have specific areas only they use. Place instructions in the test area so users can log in and tour the network under each user name already created for them.

Be sure to make the pilot system available to the power users in your organization. You know the users I'm speaking of: those who read all the computer magazines, haunt the Internet or other electronic services, and informally help all the users in their area. They will be interested in the workgroup management facilities, since that kind of authority will verify what they've been doing unofficially for quite a while.

NDS Design Phases

Each network design, regardless of the architecture, has two phases: logical and physical.

Logical Phase

The logical phase focuses on the Directory structure and the process for implementing that structure. The steps in the logical design sequence are:

1. Determine the NDS tree structure.

2. Identify the naming conventions for your network.

3. Plan your implementation method.

Physical Phase

The physical phase focuses on how the Directory is accessed by the users during their workday. This phase also considers how information is stored on the servers and coordinated to provide accurate Directory and time information. The steps in the physical design sequence are:

1. Determine security considerations.

2. Set up Directory replication.

3. Synchronize Directory time.

The departmental design that served so well with the earlier versions of NetWare also works fine with NetWare 4.10. But NetWare 4.10 gives you many more options than the basic "one department, one server" design strategy.

Even better, you can take the departmental strategy and fold it into a bigger, more client-friendly framework.

> ### Designing for Users: Who Works with Whom, and for How Long?
>
> Don't get timid when designing your new company network. You must have the courage to ask questions. Some people you must question don't normally get involved in the network. You must, if no one else in your company ever has, make some sense of which people really work on which projects with which other people.
>
> This may sound easy, but if it is easy, you haven't dug down deep enough. You may have set up your existing network to mirror groups of people sitting close together in departments all in one building. That worked well with the limitations forced on large companies by departmental, server-centric networking. Although you can still set up your network in this manner, you are no longer limited to a departmental design.
>
> Are you familiar with the futurists (and network designers) and their new definitions of work? According to sources as varied as Alvin Toffler and developers of workgroup software like GroupWise and Lotus Notes, people shift and change their internal work partners on a regular basis. A project begins; a team is gathered. A project ends; the team members go in various directions.
>
> This is cleaner than what usually happens, of course. Theories, no matter how outlandish, pale beside the mess we people make of plans. If your life as a network administrator is typical, you are a member of ten ad hoc groups. You have meetings to choose new software, review current vendors, get authorization for a new server or two, and that doesn't count personnel, marketing support, remote computing, and network security. If you ever dream of pieces of yourself being pulled apart and flying in all directions, save the psychological counseling fees. You're just dreaming about your normal workday.
>
> E-mail and groupware help us deal with the mess we've worked ourselves into, but they can't do it all. Your network design for NetWare 4.1x will go a long way in helping improve the ease of user interaction. The easier it is for users to share information, the better the resulting project.

Design versus Implementation

Your network *design* is planning the NDS structure. Your network *implementation* is creating the NDS structure. You might think that the "design" component always comes before the "implementation" component. That's not true. The best designs always consider the problems of implementation and maintenance.

Are you upgrading from an earlier NetWare version? If so, some of the design choices will be made for you. The users, tied to a particular server throughout their NetWare experience, may wish to remain tied to that server. Create a comfortable environment for them by intelligent NDS design, and their transition will be smoother.

If you are upgrading, are you upgrading all servers at once? With a small network, it's possible to upgrade all servers in one pass, usually over a weekend. The user leaves an office with one network design and returns to the same office but with a different network design. If you aren't upgrading all the servers at once, you may wind up creating multiple NDS trees and merging those trees later.

Are you "seeding" the network with one NetWare 4.1x division and gradually expanding the NDS reach through the rest of the company? This offers more time for training users and coordinating departments, but it isn't magic. Bindery Services must be provided for those users caught between two departments that upgrade at different times.

If you create multiple NDS trees, a consistent naming convention must be agreed upon before the rollout begins. If a single NDS tree is created and expanded when each part of the company is connected, the naming consistency is just as important but a bit easier. The only advantage is that you will know about name conflicts as they arise during each department's installation, rather than all at once during the upgrade procedure. More work will be necessary to combine multiple trees into one tree than to create one tree and add to it.

Developing Naming Standards

With earlier NetWare versions, a "naming standard" generally meant using the last name and first initial for user login, or the first name and last initial. Large companies focused on the last name, while small companies and departments favored the first name.

With NetWare 4.1x and the global Directory database, a more complete naming standard must be developed. Names are needed for User, Printer, Print Queue, Server, Volume, Group, Organizational Role, Directory Map, and Distribution List objects. Lots of names will be needed before all is said and done.

Naming standards provide a framework for naming all network users and resources. These standards work best with consistency and a goal of making users comfortable while navigating a large network full of resources. The new search capabilities of NetWare 4.1x NDS work best when simple wildcard searching is possible. If all servers are named SRVsomething, a search with SRV* provides usable results. The same is true with printers: name all laser printers LJsomething, and searching for a printer becomes simple.

Name length for any object is the same: 64 characters. The caveat is that the total name length for the complete NDS name of an object cannot exceed 256 characters including periods, equal signs, and name type designators. Long names or deep NDS trees will cause users to work unnecessarily hard and may bump against your name length limit. Short but descriptive names have these characteristics:

- Make names easier to remember
- Simplify logins
- Use capitalization to increase readability
- Use hyphens rather than spaces
- Reduce NDS traffic across the network

If you are using Bindery Services, keep in mind the naming restrictions of NetWare 3.x. Keep names particularly short to fit all systems the user will be encountering.

Sample Naming Standards

If you are migrating some NetWare 3.x users, there will be some renaming necessary. If you have been planning to redo your naming standards, during the transition to NetWare 4.1x is a good time to make your move. Even if it's not technically true, everyone will believe you when you tell them they must change names because of the new network.

Table 4.2 shows some naming standards and the rationale behind them, along with some suggestions.

TABLE 4.2 Some Suggestions for Naming Standards

OBJECT	NAMING STANDARD	EXAMPLES
User	Limit names to 8 characters (8 character names make good home directories). Pick names that work with both the network and your e-mail package.	James E. Gaskin becomes JEGASKIN; Kelley J. Lindberg becomes KJLINDBE
Server	Server names must be unique on the network due to a SAP restriction, not NDS. Use a set of three- or four-letter codes for the location, division, and server. Airline city codes are good location designators (DFW for Dallas Ft. Worth; LAX for Los Angeles).	LAX-ACCT-001
Group	Base group names on the group function.	GP-ACCT for the accounting group
Printer	Use city codes as for servers, along with building location codes and printer type.	DFW-HP-LJ4SI
Print Queue and Print Server	Start with PQ or PS. Include the host server name and the numeric ID of each.	PS-GATEWAY2000-1
Organization and Organizational Unit	Use your company's internal abbreviations if possible. Reference a short version of the company name for the Organization object.	OU=SALES.OU=WEST.O=ACME

TABLE 4.2 (cont.)
Some Suggestions for Naming Standards

OBJECT	NAMING STANDARD	EXAMPLES
Organizational Role	Base the name on the job function. Always grant administrative rights to the Organizational Role rather than to particular users for ease of control when job descriptions change.	OR-ACCT_MGR
Profile	Base the name on the job function. Indicate if the Profile is mandatory with a Y or N as the last letter.	PR-PTRS-Y
Directory Map	Base the name on the application being mapped.	DM-WP, DM-EMAIL

Some may complain about the extra characters needed for the "type" designator at the beginning of each name, such as DM-EMAIL. This is not a requirement, of course, just a suggestion from Novell. If your company wants to rely on the icons under MS Windows to provides those clues, that's fine. But be consistent: don't have some groups labeled GP-EMAIL and other groups just labeled ACCT. Your users may be more aggravated by the confusion than they are about typing the extra characters.

NDS Example: Organizing by User Location (Bottom-Up)

This tree organization is often labeled the *departmental* or *workgroup* method, but the terms *bottom-up* or *user-location* method work just as well. The key point is that this is an independent group that will later be part of a larger group.

The Simple Installation track (see Chapter 3) works perfectly for this type of group. The guidelines for the Simple Installation used by Novell engineers are 10 servers or 500 users. Any less than that works well with the Simple Installation.

Some references assume this bottom-up plan can only be done by creating separate NDS trees for each department and joining them later. That method will work, and makes sense when the NDS trees that the department will later join are geographically dispersed. But instead, you can make the department a self-sufficient Organization inside an existing NDS tree. The important consideration in the user-location method is to set the department as a distinct entity from the rest of the corporate network, whether it be NetWare 3.*x* or NetWare 4.*x*. A group of users who share a location and a set of resources fits this profile, regardless of whether these users have their own tree or just their own Organization.

Departmental Design

Focusing on the department when designing your NDS tree makes sense under several circumstances. Especially with the new NDS utilities offered with NetWare 4.1*x*, there is no longer an administrative penalty to pay for developing a network design that must be changed later.

When the departments will stay isolated from each other, the bottom-up (figuring the department is the bottom of the organization chart) design works well. Another opportunity for this design is when there is no strong central administration group dictating standards. Even if there is a central group, it may not yet be prepared with a comprehensive plan that supports all departments. It won't be the first time the people doing all the work are inconvenienced by the HQ folks trying to figure out what they're doing, will it?

There are benefits of the departmental design, whether each group is a completely separate tree or just containers that don't interact. Each department can maintain the names used in earlier NetWare versions for ease of learning and minimal disruption. Although duplicate names are not allowed when the trees are merged, separate trees spread the learning curve out a bit. Forcing users to learn NetWare 4.1*x* at the same time as renaming all their network resources is a lot to handle all at once.

If the departmental design is used with separate trees for each group, there can be no sharing of information (except through Bindery Services, as explained later in the chapter) with NetWare 4.10. NetWare 4.11 users running Client32 software will be able to see multiple trees at one time. If each department is its own container, some sharing can be introduced gradually. This situation is perfect for Alias objects, which allow you to refer to other container resources. You don't need to teach the users all about contexts and the NDS hierarchy until they're ready to learn.

If you set up separate trees after a central plan is established, you'll need to use the DSMERGE utility (a server utility) to combine trees. Since leaf and

Alias objects can't exist at the root of the source tree, keep all objects down to at least the Organization level, no matter how small the tree. Remember that servers must have a unique name across the entire tree. Some minimal guidelines must be available for server names before you can integrate each department into the larger network.

Physical and Logical Views

Network diagrams are handy items, at least until they go out of date (which is constantly). With NetWare 4.1*x*, there are now two types of network diagrams to become obsolete: physical and logical views of your network.

The physical view of your NDS tree shows the branches clearly, with all network resources of that branch grouped together. Once the department tree is merged into the larger network, the current administrator may well continue to be the container administrator. The authority of the container administrator is similar to that of a full administrator, except that this authority is over only a specific container.

Figure 4.5 is a physical diagram of a departmental design network in its own tree. Both servers and volumes are represented, as are users, printers, and the like.

The physical diagrams are not what you are used to: the wire and all users, servers, and printers attached to that wire. You may have one diagram for each floor of your building, or just one large diagram for everything. Those are *wiring diagrams*, which prove useful when expanding and troubleshooting your physical network. What we mean by a *physical view* here is the icons strung together.

This is less important in small networks than in larger ones. However, if you have no naming designators (as is the case for the items in Figure 4.5), the icons help clarify which name refers to a Group, a Directory Map, or an Alias object.

Figure 4.6 shows the same information as Figure 4.5 but uses block diagrams and NDS abbreviations rather than icons. Admittedly, there is not a lot of difference when showing small networks.

Notice that the naming designators would help clarify some details in the logical view that didn't really need clarification in the physical view. Quick, without looking back at Figure 4.5, what is PAYROLL? Is it a group, a volume, or a directory map?

FIGURE 4.5

A departmental NDS tree, physical view

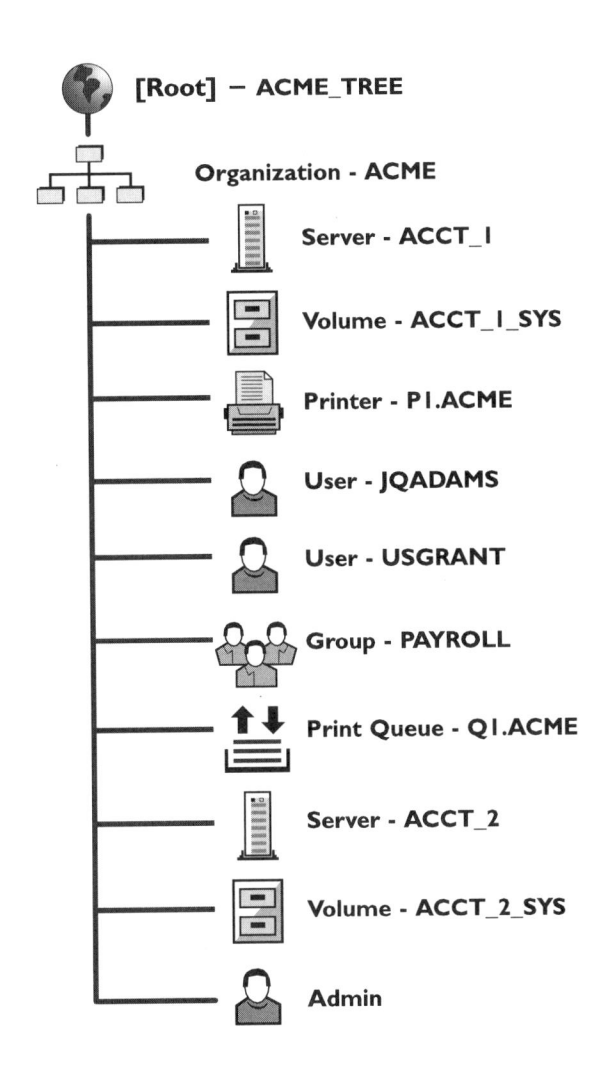

[Root] — ACME_TREE

Organization - ACME
- Server - ACCT_1
- Volume - ACCT_1_SYS
- Printer - P1.ACME
- User - JQADAMS
- User - USGRANT
- Group - PAYROLL
- Print Queue - Q1.ACME
- Server - ACCT_2
- Volume - ACCT_2_SYS
- Admin

NDS Example: Organizing by User Function (Top-Down)

The top-down design model works well when there is a central MIS (Management Information Services) or LAN control group in charge of the network. If your HQ folks know their business, this is the model you will likely use. If you are the MIS department, as often happens in smaller companies, this is a good option.

FIGURE 4.6

A departmental NDS tree, logical view

```
                    [Root]
                    O=ACME

                    ACCT_1
                    ACCT_2
                    ACCT_1_SYS
                    ACCT_2_SYS
                    P1.ACME
                    Q1.ACME
                    JQADAMS
                    USGRANT
                    PAYROLL
```

It's a delicate balancing act to design by user function. If the network is geographically wide, your WAN connections may be too slow to provide good service if half of your network traverses the WAN for normal business. If the network is physically in one place but contains too many servers to upgrade all at once, it may be difficult to use this model as well. However, this is a great design for networks that are mostly local and have clearly defined job descriptions that stretch across internal departments.

Organizational Design

There has been a trend for the past few years in business to place support functions (such as accounting, sales, design, engineering, human resources, and the like) directly in the departments they support. The model before was to always group like job functions, as in the bottom-up design method previously described. With the business pendulum swinging, however, your company may well decide to disperse these functions.

Figure 4.7 shows our mythical Acme Corporation built around a top-down model, grouping the various functions in separate Organizational Units. This design requires that you know and make sense of your company's organization.

This illustration makes good sense for the central planners, who don't need to worry which user sits in which cubicle. If you are responsible for maintaining the connection of user Guy H. Davis in cubicle 4-E-2, you may need an additional map.

FIGURE 4.7

An organizational view of Acme Corporation

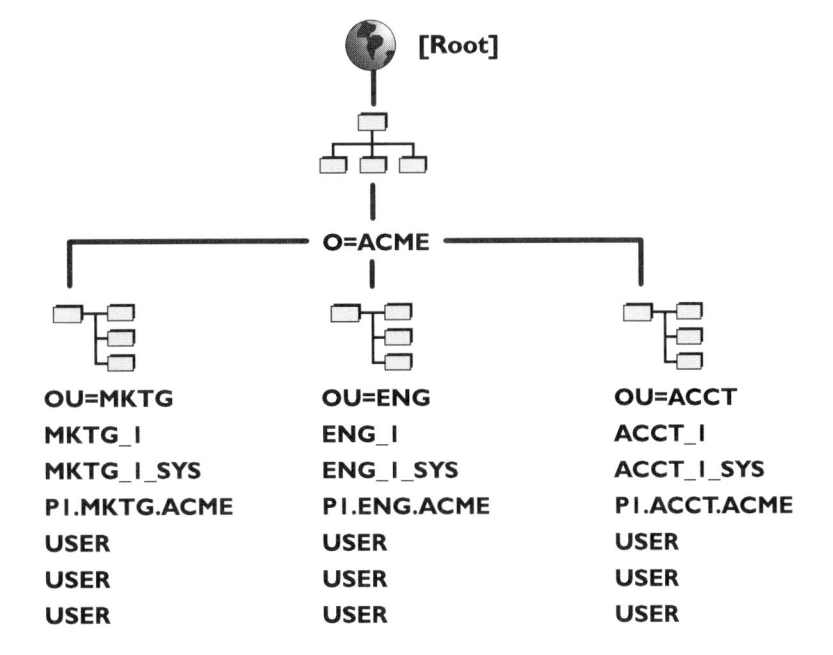

```
                    [Root]
                      |
                      |
                    O=ACME
      _____|_____
     |                |                |
  OU=MKTG          OU=ENG           OU=ACCT
  MKTG_I           ENG_I            ACCT_I
  MKTG_I_SYS       ENG_I_SYS        ACCT_I_SYS
  P1.MKTG.ACME     P1.ENG.ACME      P1.ACCT.ACME
  USER             USER             USER
  USER             USER             USER
  USER             USER             USER
```

The cable contractor that installed your network cabling was supposed to leave an "as-built" map showing each connection in each physical location. You probably can't find that now, so get the cubicle layout from the human resources space-planning department. On copies of the floor plan, label each user and his or her context in the NDS tree. This type of planning and forethought is rewarded during emergencies, but is difficult to maintain. Make an effort to start and maintain such a map for the feeling of self satisfaction if nothing else.

Notice that engineers are sitting next to marketing people, who are next to accounting people. This is slightly fictionalized, to enhance the contrast. If this were real life, translators would be needed between each cubicle.

The printers for two of the groups are in the west cubicle. Printers can be physically located anywhere on the network, either by connecting them to workstations or by using print servers that attach directly to the network cabling.

Even if your company begins the year by placing each group in the same physical location, normal business chaos will mangle that plan before long. People get promoted, people change jobs, the accounting department runs out

> *Even if your company begins the year by placing each group in the same physical location, normal business chaos will mangle that plan before long.*

FIGURE 4.8

A cubicle view of the organizational design

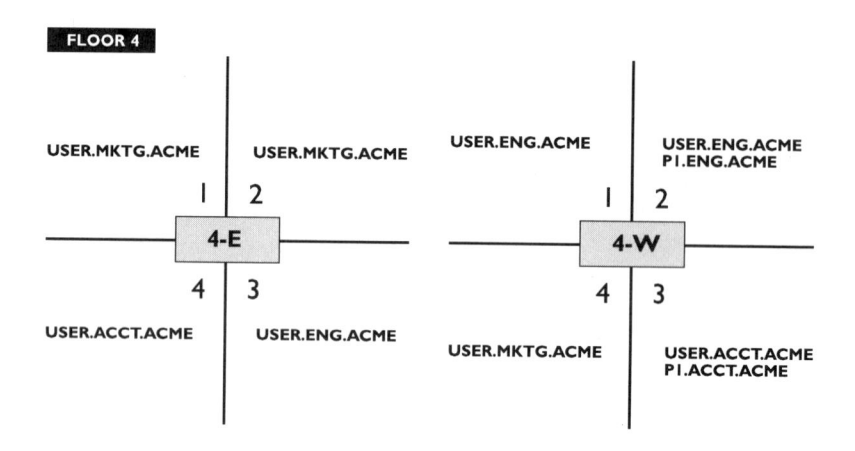

```
FLOOR 4

USER.MKTG.ACME   USER.MKTG.ACME        USER.ENG.ACME    USER.ENG.ACME
                                                        PI.ENG.ACME
       1  |  2                               1  |  2
        [4-E]                                 [4-W]
       4  |  3                               4  |  3

USER.ACCT.ACME   USER.ENG.ACME        USER.MKTG.ACME   USER.ACCT.ACME
                                                        PI.ACCT.ACME
```

of room so the managers place a few people in the marketing area, and so on—things just change. This type of map helps monitor that change. Can you track each cubicle user to their spot on the map in Figure 4.7? See, context names do help, don't they?

NDS Example: Distributed Organization Chart with a WAN (Mixed)

Let's say Acme Corporation has grown beyond its founders' wildest dreams. Hey, when marketing people and engineers learn to communicate, great things happen.

The new layout for Acme will probably be a mix of departmental and user-function designs. WAN considerations particularly push this mixed design, since small, remote offices often don't have enough personnel to keep job functions separate. But the slow WAN connections limit the practicality of using a top-down design.

Figure 4.9 shows the expanded Acme Corporation spreading across the country. The designers have chosen not to use the Country level, even though the company has grown into both Canada and Mexico. The design is clearly discernible without needing the extra layer of name contexts that the Country object introduces.

FIGURE 4.9

A global corporate/division/department/workgroup design

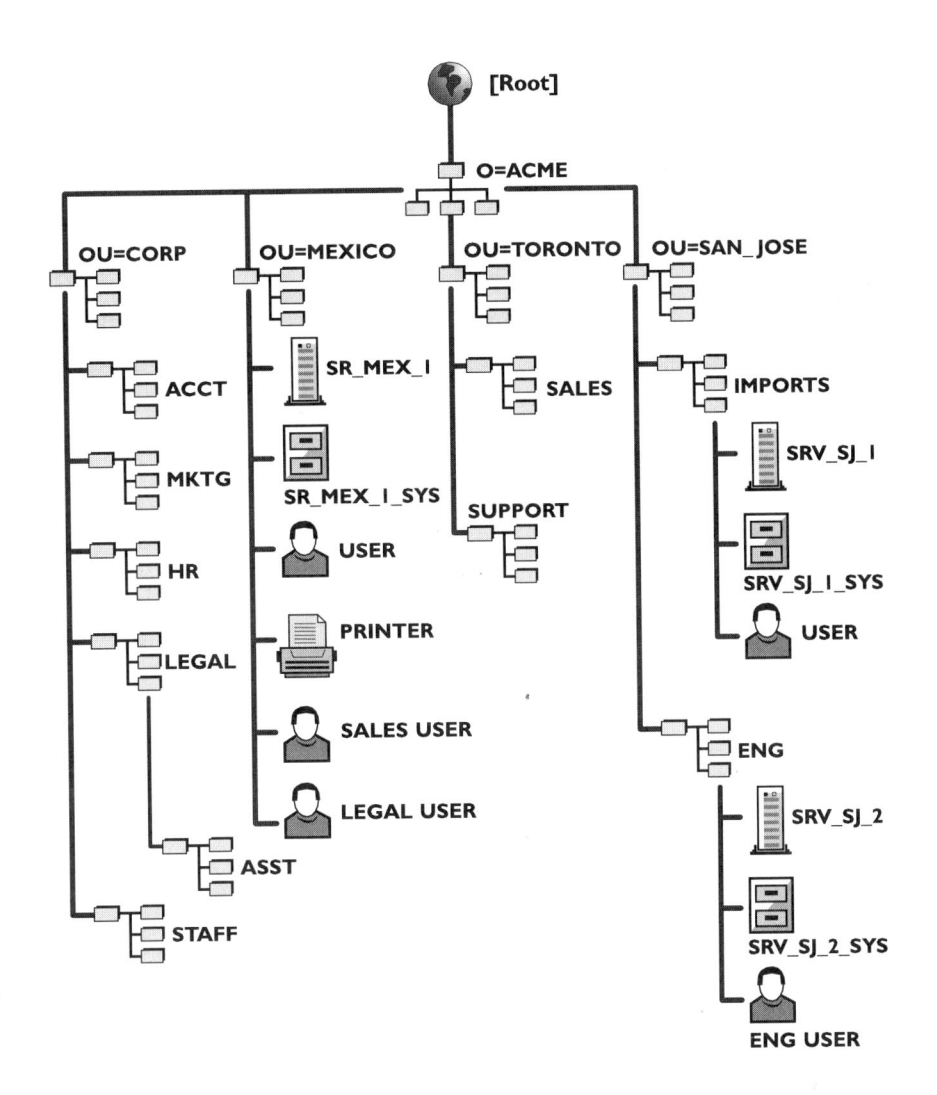

You should notice that OU=CORP is the largest and is not labeled by location. Each department has clearly defined groups, since more people in the corporate office tend to have specific job functions.

The other cities are labeled geographically, since that made the most sense during the design phase. In Mexico, the small office has no departmental subgroups or OUs within the Mexico OU. Toronto, a larger office, contains an

OU for both Sales and Support. San Jose includes two OUs, labeled Imports and Eng. Notice that although there are defined groups in San Jose, the file servers are named incrementally by the location.

Does this all make sense? Probably not, but it's a common situation. And the lesson to learn from this is twofold:

- NDS is flexible enough to cover your crazy company.
- No NDS design is inherently better than another.

NDS Context Control and Management

CONTEXT HAS COME UP several times, so let's nail it down completely. *Context* refers to the location of an object within the NDS tree. Not the physical location, but the logical position.

In the earlier example in Figure 4.9, the context of the first file server in San Jose is:

    SRV_SJ_1.IMPORTS.SAN_JOSE.ACME

The context here is given in *typeless* format. The rules are:

- **Typeful format:** Includes abbreviations for all containers
- **Typeless format:** No container abbreviations (also called *distinguished name*)

The translation of the above typeless name is "File server SRV_SJ_1 in the Organizational Unit Imports in the Organizational Unit San_Jose in the Organization Acme." In the typeful format, the name would be listed:

    CN=SRV_SJ_1.OU=IMPORTS.OU=SAN_JOSE.O=ACME

Personally, I prefer the typeless names and am glad they became available in NetWare 4.10. With typeless names, the trick to remember is that the Organization is to the far right, and the object (CN stands for Common Name of the object, remember?) is at the far left. Anything in the middle is an Organizational Unit.

See Table 4.1, earlier in this chapter, for the complete, official list of the rules of containment. For a shorthand and simplified list, remember that [Root] contains Organizations, and Organizations hold Organizations Units, which can hold other Organizational Units but not Organizations.

Why Context Is Important

> *Think of the context as the map with a red arrow saying, "You are here."*

Knowing where you are is important in every endeavor, especially when we're speaking of something like NDS, with the capacity for a global network. Think of the context as the map with a red arrow saying, "You are here."

Context, and knowing how to change your context, is just as important in the NDS tree as in a file system's directory tree. The biggest difference is that with NetWare 4.1*x*, you can have many drives mapped to different points in the file system tree, but only one active point in the NDS tree context.

Let's break this down into each component. First, the far left name is the common name, with the abbreviation of CN. The common name denotes a leaf object, such as a user, printer, server, or volume.

In Figure 4.10, PAT is the user name for both users. Although PAT by itself doesn't help us differentiate the two users, the rest of the name will always let us know which PAT is which. (Of course, using PAT_D or PJONES instead works without confusion.)

FIGURE 4.10

Find and describe Pat in as many ways as possible.

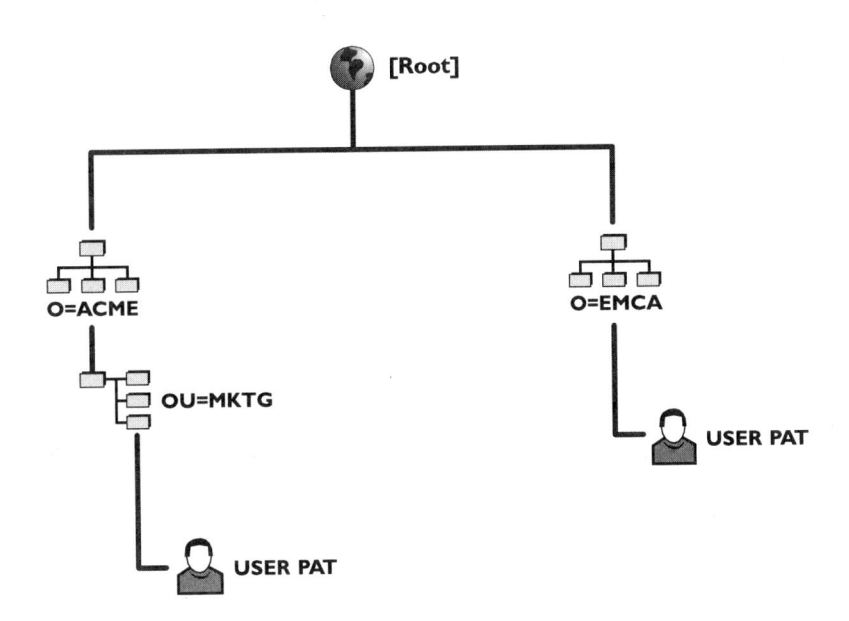

Since we don't know anything about PAT, or even if it's Ms. PAT or Mr. PAT, we need a better way to describe this PAT object.

Hence, we have *distinguished names*, another label for the typeless context of an object. The Novell manuals seem to favor context for names using the typeful descriptions with all the abbreviations, and referring to the typeless names as distinguished names. Works for me, although typeful and typeless seem a bit clearer. You can call it what you want on your own network.

The context works similarly to the directory context in a file system. The context acts as the CD command might work, by referencing where an object is located. People don't use this function of the CD command often, but just CD by itself will list your current directory. The Unix command pwd (for Print Working Directory) does the same thing. If you are in the same directory as the file you're looking for, just the file name is enough to reference the file. If you are in another directory, you must give a unique path name to the file.

The distinguished name for the PAT on the right is PAT.EMCA; the PAT on the left has the distinguished name PAT.MKTG.ACME. However, if you are also in the EMCA Organization with PAT, you can merely reference the name PAT without any of the extra identifiers.

What if PAT.EMCA wishes to send a message to the other PAT? How should that be addressed? The full distinguished name is PAT.MKTG.ACME. A subset of this is the *relative distinguished name*. Are you comfortable using the CD (Change Directory) DOS command to move up one directory level, then going down from there? If so, using the relative distinguished name should be comfortable for you as well.

When a network administrator with a context of O=ACME needs to refer to PAT.MKTG.ACME, there is a shortcut. Use either CN=PAT.O=MKTG or just PAT.MKTG, since both refer to the same object. If the administrator is already in the MKTG container, the reference would be either CN=PAT or just PAT.

A beginning period in a name tells the system the following name is complete and referenced from the [Root] of the current NDS tree. This works the same as a leading backslash in DOS path names for file designations.

The last trick is the trailing period in object naming. A name with a trailing period tells the system to start the partial naming one level up from the current context. This is rarely used. You are effectively removing one object name from the left side of the current context. For example, if your current context is:

```
OU=MKTG.O=ACME
```

and you enter the relative distinguished name:

```
CN=Admin.
```

NDS will remove the OU=MKTG object from the current context and append the relative distinguished name to the remainder:

```
.CN=Admin.O=ACME
```

Using CX to Change Your Context

Changing contexts is as easy as changing directories from the DOS command line. The CX command stands for Change conteXt just like CD stands for Change Directory.

Typing CX on the DOS command line will display your current context. In our example, if PAT on the right types CX, the result will be:

```
mktg.acme
```

Somewhat underwhelming, but often helpful.

The CX command line option is used more than the CD command line option, because there is no "Context" prompt like the DOS prompt that automatically shows your file system location.

The easiest way to use CX is to always type:

```
CX distinguished_name (.MKTG.ACME)
```

replacing *distinguished_name* with your desired context name, of course.

Both NETUSER and NWUSER make it easy to change your context as well. Although you point and click (or highlight and press Enter), the CX command is being used in the background. For ease of use when logging in to a server, the CX.EXE command is included in the LOGIN directory. If you connect to the NetWare server, you can then change your context before logging in to the system.

How to Use Contexts to Your Advantage

The context is most important when a user logs in to the system. As we just saw, there may well be several people with the same name. When PAT wants to log in, how will the system know which PAT this is?

Context helps here. NDS looks for objects in the following order:

1. The current context

2. The exact container specified by the typed object name

3. During login, the context of whatever server the user is currently attached to

There is no "search path" as in DOS and NetWare, sorry. The user doing the specification must provide the necessary context or the object will remain unfound. The exception is with the LOGIN program: If you start to log in from the wrong context, NDS will search the container of the server you are communicating with. If that context is not the right one for you, an error message appears, and you must try again.

This is not necessarily a disadvantage, however. One of the earlier examples of departmental groupings mentioned that the same setup works whether the department has its own tree or just an Organization. If the department has only an Organization, the users can treat that Organization in much the same way users currently treat NetWare 3.*x* networks.

Let's take that login problem PAT had just a moment ago. Some suggestions require you to type the full distinguished name every time a user logs in, looks for a printer, or references a network resource. But if everyone is in the same Organization, including all the various file servers for that department, full context names aren't necessary.

When PAT logs in, NDS searches the current context. *Voila!* The file server holding PAT's object is in that current context and login continues without a hitch.

The advantages of grouping similar users in Organizations or Organizational Units together with their file servers and other network resources makes NetWare 4.1*x* feel more comfortable. Users of earlier NetWare versions don't need to make a drastic leap of faith to take advantage of many of NetWare 4.1*x*'s strong points.

Setting a User's "Home" Context

Part of the reason some advisors make a big deal of using the shortest container names possible is to avoid having the users type many characters when typing their full context. Since NetWare allows a user to log in from any machine on the network (very handy for network administrators, this ability to gain your full rights from any desktop), worrywarts and concerned users will get confused if they need to type a long distinguished name.

Well, two things eliminate this problem for most networks. First of all, most users log in on their own computer the majority of the time. When networks started, it was more common for companies to have several users share a computer. Today, at least in the larger companies, almost every employee has full access to his or her own computer.

The advantage of this is the ability of placing user-specific commands in the NET.CFG file on the client PC workstation. In the NET.CFG file, the NetWare DOS Requester section will probably already exist. If so, use a text editor to add the name context line that applies to the particular user. In PAT's case, the following will show up in the NET.CFG file:

```
NetWare DOS Requester
    name context="PAT.MKTG.ACME"
    preferred tree=ACME_TREE
    first network drive=f
```

The preferred tree line is only necessary if your company has multiple NDS trees active on the network. That's rare.

When PAT begins to log in, the NET.CFG file will set the name context. NDS won't need to search for PAT's login script, since the system will know PAT belongs in MKTG.ACME before the LOGIN command appears.

If and when PAT does wander to another desk, there's still not much to remember to log in to the proper context. Have PAT type:

```
LOGIN PAT.MKTG.ACME
```

and then give the proper password when asked. PAT will be connected in the proper context without any problems.

If PAT uses Windows 95 and the Client32 software, you must use the Network Properties page to set a context. If PAT uses Windows 95 and the VLM client software, the previous instructions work, but you're not doing PAT any favors. Since Client32 will be mandatory in another revision or two, you might as well get all your clients up-to-date as soon as possible.

Using Bindery Services to Provide Bindery Emulation

NDS SUPPORTS BINDERY Services to allow users still using the NETX client shells to connect to NDS and to support third-party products, such as tape backup and print servers. Until all third-party products are current with the latest NetWare 4.1x release, Bindery Services will continue to be used.

If you have slipped into a comfortable mode with NDS over the last few chapters, give that up and remember what it used to be like. Bindery Services provides only some access to leaf objects on a server-centric basis within NDS. The global, distributed NDS database pretends to be a flat, limited structure for server resources and users. Only the leaf objects in specified containers can be seen under Bindery Services.

How Bindery Services Works

The *bindery context* refers to the container object where the Bindery Services feature is set. The bindery context is normally set during server installation, but only the first three servers installed on a partition automatically receive a replica of the NDS partition during installation. Without the replica, the server can't support NetWare 4's Bindery Services feature. When you upgrade a NetWare 3.x server to NetWare 4.1x, its bindery context is set.

You may add replicas to any NetWare 4.1x server you wish in order to support Bindery Services. Check Chapter 10 for details on using the Partition Manager program to add replicas.

Once the server in question is ready, up to 16 bindery contexts can be set for a single NetWare 4.1x server. This is done by using the SERVMAN utility at the server console or by directly modifying the AUTOEXEC.NCF file. The activation of Bindery Services is limited to the specific server modified.

Once active, Bindery Services responds to NETX requests (or NetWare 4.1*x* clients using VLM files with the /B switch at the end of their LOGIN command) from clients or applications. Leaf objects—and only leaf objects—are presented by Bindery Services as if they were a standard NetWare 3.*x* bindery. Containers are not presented under Bindery Services.

Information contained in NDS but not in the bindery is not visible under Bindery Services. The invisible items include:

- E-mail names
- Phone numbers
- Print job configurations
- Aliases
- Profiles
- NDS login scripts
- Directory maps

Why Bindery Emulation May Be Necessary

Even the most gung-ho NDS advocate may be forced to use Bindery Services sometimes.

Even the most gung-ho NDS advocate may be forced to use Bindery Services sometimes. During the transition to NetWare 4.1*x*, some NetWare 3.*x* servers may not be upgraded immediately. Some users may not wish to upgrade, or you may not have time to reach them all.

Print servers from most third-party vendors use Bindery Services to verify user access to the printers. While the companies are moving to support NDS, it takes time. And, marketing being the way it is, there are still a large number of NetWare 3.*x* server administrators out there buying the product. If the print server supports only NDS, it loses potential revenue. If it can use the bindery on NetWare 3.*x* systems and Bindery Services on NetWare 4.1*x*, the vendors don't see a strong reason to change quickly.

Make no mistake: There's no advantage for a NetWare 4.1*x* server to run Bindery Services except under these circumstances. NDS has far too many advantages to return to a server-centric system like the bindery.

Using Resources from Another Tree

There's one and only one valid reason to use Bindery Services in a pure NetWare 4.10 environment: cross-tree traffic. A NetWare 4.10 client can be connected to only one tree at a time. NetWare 4.11 and Client32 software running in Windows 95 changes this rule, although multiple trees are still not a good idea (if you ask me).

Multiple trees can exist on the same physical network under NetWare 4.10, as long as each tree name is unique. If someone, such as a network administrator, needs connections to multiple trees at once, Bindery Services is your only hope.

When you log in to the second tree, type:

```
LOGIN full.context.name /B
```

The /B forces NDS to handle this login with Bindery Services, even if the client is using the VLM client files for NetWare 4.1*x*.

Installing Bindery Services

If you are upgrading a NetWare 3.*x* server, and it's one of the first three NetWare 4.1*x* servers in the partition, Bindery Services will be installed automatically. The appropriate lines, such as:

```
SET BINDERY CONTEXT=MKTG.ACME
```

will be written into the AUTOEXEC.NCF file during installation.

You may later add Bindery Services by typing the SET command at the server console and listing the server's context in the command. To engage Bindery Services each time the server is restarted, you must add the SET command to the AUTOEXEC.NCF file manually. Remember that an NDS replica must be stored on this server to support Bindery Services.

The other option for adding Bindery Services is through the SERVMAN console utility. At the console, follow these steps:

1. Type **LOAD SERVMAN**.

2. Choose Server Parameter in the Available Options window.

3. Choose Directory Services in the Select a parameter category.

4. Press the Page Down key.

Using Bindery Services to Provide Bindery Emulation **247**

5. Press Enter to modify the bindery context setting.

6. Enter up to 16 valid bindery context listings, separated by semicolons.

7. Press Escape three times, then save the changes to your SYS:\SYSTEM\AUTOEXEC.NCF file.

8. Exit SERVMAN.

Figure 4.11 shows the screen to set the bindery context in the SERVMAN utility. Notice the help information in the bottom half of the window.

FIGURE 4.11

Setting the bindery context

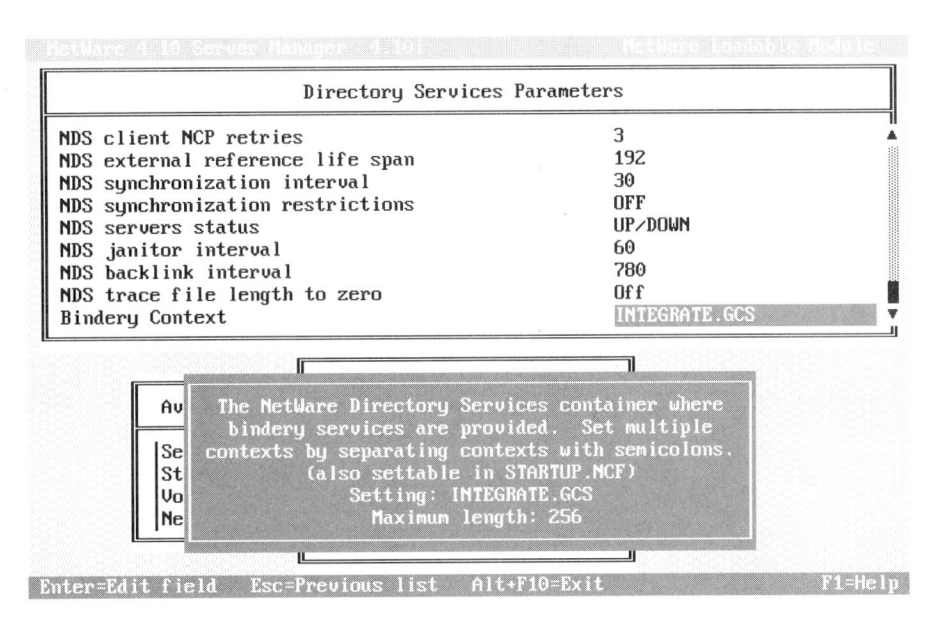

```
                    Directory Services Parameters
    NDS client NCP retries                    3
    NDS external reference life span          192
    NDS synchronization interval              30
    NDS synchronization restrictions          OFF
    NDS servers status                        UP/DOWN
    NDS janitor interval                      60
    NDS backlink interval                     780
    NDS trace file length to zero             Off
    Bindery Context                           INTEGRATE.GCS

         The NetWare Directory Services container where
         bindery services are provided.  Set multiple
         contexts by separating contexts with semicolons.
               (also settable in STARTUP.NCF)
                    Setting: INTEGRATE.GCS
                    Maximum length: 256

    Enter=Edit field   Esc=Previous list   Alt+F10=Exit        F1=Help
```

Using the Simple Installation Option with Bindery Services

A trick here: Any server in the container where the bindery context is set can support Bindery Services. With the Simple Installation process, which places all objects in a single container, a single bindery context setting will enable Bindery Services on all servers.

This makes sense after a little thought. In the most basic NDS plan, there is only one context. Setting the bindery context for the Acme Organization illustrated in Figure 4.12 allows bindery clients to connect to both servers.

FIGURE 4.12

A bindery context that overlaps the NDS tree

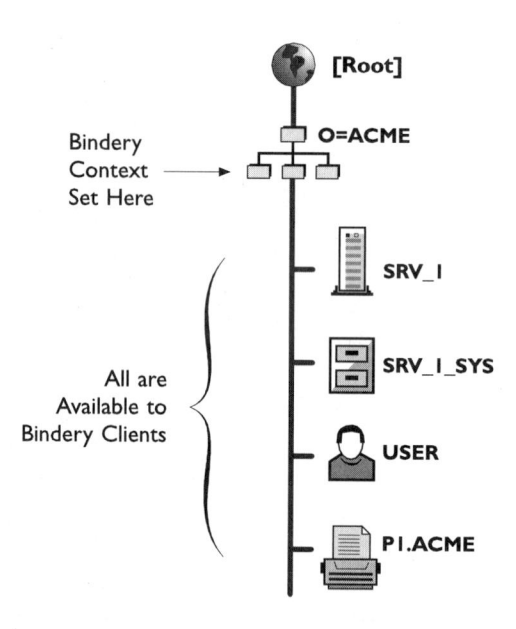

[Figure: NDS tree diagram with [Root] at top, O=ACME below (labeled "Bindery Context Set Here"), and leaf objects SRV_1, SRV_1_SYS, USER, and P1.ACME grouped as "All are Available to Bindery Clients"]

The single container NDS tree makes sense for the first NetWare 4.1x server in a network, especially as a way to roll out a pilot server. With this setup, clients can test the new NDS features while keeping the server resources available to all the bindery clients.

Notice that bindery clients can see only the NDS leaf objects that are covered by a bindery context. What if there are two Organizational Units in a company, and one of them is running Bindery Services? What can bindery clients see? Figure 4.13 illustrates this example.

As you might guess, leaf objects that do not exist in a container running Bindery Services are invisible to bindery clients. If Joe Bindery wants to connect to the Acme NDS tree, the only part he will see is the container OU=ACCT.O=ACME.

This can get more complicated, with NetWare 4.1x servers running Bindery Services to support a context they are not even in. The capabilities of Bindery Services are extensive.

Don't let your users push you into postponing the best parts of NDS while installing Bindery Services everywhere. Bindery Services is a short-term solution as all vendors get rolling with NDS-compliant products. The future is NDS, because the future of our networks is distributed. Bindery servers cannot keep up in the new world. Trying to avoid the short-term pain of

FIGURE 4.13

A bindery context that covers a portion of the NDS tree

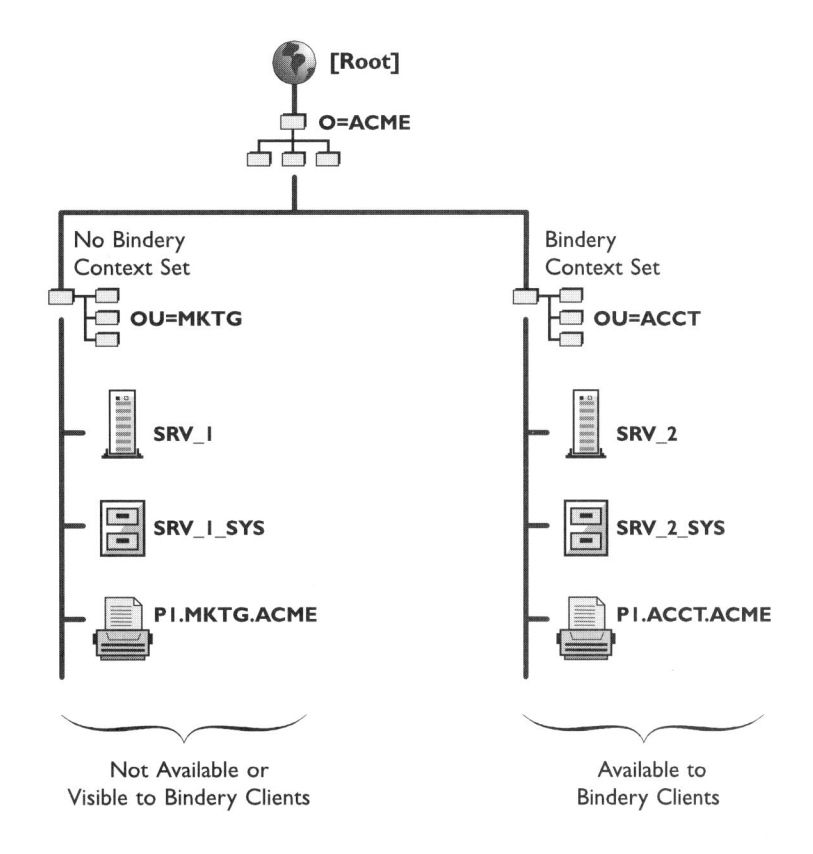

upgrading workstation clients will only lead to long-term agony when the change is forced on you under a strict deadline. Has any onerous job ever gotten better the longer it festers? No. If you (or your bosses) are still unconvinced about the value of NDS and the advantages of a global, distributed directory, just try it for a month. I guarantee that you won't go back.

Maintaining Bindery Services

The validity of each bindery context is verified each ten minutes, during NDS synchronization. If a bindery context isn't deemed valid, the Bindery Services will stop.

If a bindery client uses a login script from a NetWare 3.*x* server, any changes to that login script will not be replicated. Only the text file on the home server in the MAIL directory will be changed. The replication of user information changes is one of the big advantages of NDS and a major improvement over the server-centric bindery in earlier NetWare.

When the Bindery Services feature is in use, it cannot be disabled. Only by deleting a bindery context at the server console (BINARY ADD|DELETE [CONTEXT]) will you make Bindery Services unavailable while the server is up and running.

Directory Designs and Discussions

"ARE WE THERE yet?" If you have taken children on a car trip, you've heard those words too often.

In NetWare 4.1x, the Directory answers those questions. Are we there yet? Yes, we are. NetWare 4.0 wasn't there enough, but now we are there.

Where is there? That's the important question for every piece of your network. Where is there, and what's there? Where is anything? Where is everything?

It's all around the network, that's where. Everything now has a place, and there's a place for everything, just as your mother told you. The bindery of NetWare 3.x was always "there," on the file server, and only on one file server at a time. So why didn't Novell call NetWare Directory Services something like Bindery Plus?

My friend Art Wittman has a great analogy for this: We no longer refer to cars in terms of being carriages without horses (horseless carriages), we refer to them as cars. We no longer care about the previous technology of horses, we only care about our current technology of self-powered automobiles.

We will soon come to that point with NDS. NDS isn't an expanded bindery; it's a whole new network ballgame. Soon we'll speak of the "Directory" the same way we speak of the "Disk" and the server "Memory." In other words, it will be just another part of every good network.

> *Everything now has a place, and there's a place for everything, just as your mother told you.*

Will users like this? Sure, if the tools that make NDS simple for users are in place for them. Will all the users like this? No. All users never like all things. You will have as many users complaining because of the change as there will be cheering the new approach.

The trick is that complaining users will need to use the new network, whether they like it or not. Over time, they will all start complaining about something else, and will deny they complained about the network at all.

Change is constant, and so are complainers. Don't let a few ruin your work for the many. Go forth and set NDS loose upon your users. Realize the complainers will complain, but they are few and the Directory advancements are many.

CASE STUDY

MiniCo: NetWare Directory Service—Overview, Planning, Expansion

MINICO HAS 3 servers, 75 users, and one location.

The Global Network View and Advantages of NDS

CONSIDERATIONS

Benefits of NDS:

- Single login to all network resources.
- Easy-to-use, graphical tools for network navigation.

DECISION

NetWare 4.1x, with NDS, was an easy choice.

EXPLANATION

Being fairly new to networks, MiniCo had no real clue to what Directory Services were (the small NetWare 3.x network was used by only a few people). The big hooks that drew them to NetWare 4.1x were the tools used to save disk space. Paying for a single gigabyte, but storing 2 GB or more of files on that disk, has strong appeal to a company that watches its pennies.

Objects Everywhere, and Everything Is an Object

CONSIDERATIONS

The goals:

- Understand the Directory schema.
- Plan the network.

DECISION

Follow the installation routine and hope things work.

EXPLANATION

Using the Simple Installation method, MiniCo had little to worry about concerning objects, schema, and the interrelationships of network entities. The users needed to share applications, printers, and hard disks, not "objects" of some kind. The Simple Installation method takes care of the technical details for companies that have small, less complicated networks.

[Root]: The Base, and Top, of Your NDS Tree

CONSIDERATIONS

The choices:

- What to name the NDS tree.
- Whether to include a Country container.
- How many Organization and Organizational Unit containers to use.

MINICO CASE STUDY, CONTINUED

DECISION

Follow the Simple Installation guidelines.

EXPLANATION

No Country container is used unless requested during installation, and this container isn't necessary for smaller networks or those that will never connect their WAN to the outside world. Since MiniCo doesn't have a WAN, there was no reason to add the Country designation.

A single Organization with three Organizational Units made good sense during installation. Each server would control an Organizational Unit, and the users could easily share all the network objects.

Planning Your NDS Tree

CONSIDERATIONS

The goals:

- Fit everyone into the network easily.
- Make the network simple for the computer-phobics.

DECISION

Let the Simple Installation do the work. Planning was somewhat overlooked.

EXPLANATION

Jack Mingo, President of MiniCo, likes things simple. The one time Alexander von Thorn (the Distribution Manager, who is handling the installation) tried to discuss the network design with Jack, the boss taught Alexander how to spit nickels, instead. When Alexander asked the Judge (the Operations Manager) about the design, the Judge said he needed some time to consider. When installation time came around, the Judge was still considering, so Alexander went ahead.

NDS Context Control and Management

CONSIDERATIONS

The setup:

- Group the users in the proper Organizational Unit.
- Decide whether to have users log in to one server or all three.
- Use the name context setting in each user's NET.CFG file to help during the login process.

DECISION

Group the users by their functions, and log them in to each individual name context.

EXPLANATION

While much thought was given to having everyone log in to one server, the decision was made to separate people by department. People like to belong to a smaller group within the organization, and this feeling is encouraged at MiniCo. Once Alexander understood that NDS provided fault-tolerance between the three servers, the concern of limiting all users to one server was eliminated. If one server is down, those users can still be attached to the network and do some of their work.

MINICO CASE STUDY, CONTINUED

Using Bindery Services to Provide Bindery Emulation

CONSIDERATIONS

Reasons to use Bindery Services:

- Support network hardware that doesn't yet understand NDS.
- Support NETX client stations that haven't been upgraded.
- Access resources from another Directory tree.

DECISION

Bindery Services was automatically installed on the upgraded NetWare 3.x server. No other Bindery Services installation was needed.

EXPLANATION

A single-tree design eliminates one need for Bindery Services. Since there are only 75 users in MiniCo, all of their workstations were upgraded during the server installation. Therefore, there was no need for Bindery Services to support clients that had not yet upgraded to the client software provided with NetWare 4.1x.

CASE STUDY

MegaCorp: NetWare Directory Services— Overview, Planning, Expansion

MEGACORP HAS 50 servers, 2500 users, and 5 locations.

The Global Network View and Advantages of NDS

CONSIDERATIONS

Benefits of NDS:

- A single login to all network resources.
- A single point of network management.
- Easier network navigation than the previous system.
- Graphical administration tools, executable on MS Windows or OS/2 stations.
- Improved Macintosh support into NDS.
- Improved TCP/IP functionality and integration.
- Improved WAN efficiency using IPX/SPX protocols.
- Fault-tolerant NDS designs to help MegaCorp avoid a totally down network.

DECISION

NDS in NetWare 4.1x won over MegaCorp's current system, and those offered by other network operating system vendors.

EXPLANATION

Being a large company, MegaCorp had constant visits from companies hoping to convince the managers to move to a new network platform. Because of the advantages of NetWare 4.1x, the MegaCorp managers felt the time had come to rethink their decision of four years earlier, when NetWare 3.x had been replaced by another vendor's system. The local performance was worse with the replacement system, but the first-generation Directory Services provided a few advantages over the server-centric NetWare 3.x.

A central administration tool based on a GUI was important, since management personnel were now expected to support more systems per technician. NetWare 4.1x, with its combination of Packet Burst Protocol and Large Internet Packets built into the system, brought better performance across the WAN than that provided by the replaced system.

Interestingly, cost savings presented by disk savings had no strong impact on the decision.

Chapter 4 • NetWare Directory Services: Overview, Planning, Expansion

---

MEGACORP CASE STUDY, CONTINUED

Large companies always look for different advantages than small companies, and MegaCorp felt the ease-of-use across the network for the users and administrators outweighed all other considerations.

Objects Everywhere, and Everything Is an Object

CONSIDERATIONS

The goals:

- Understand the object orientation of NetWare 4.1*x*.
- Retrain all network support personnel on hierarchical tree structures with multiple levels.
- Have the programmer manager explain how objects are used in corporate program development.

DECISION

Go completely with NetWare 4.1*x* NDS, and avoid Bindery Services if possible.

EXPLANATION

Although MegaCorp's earlier network had a multiple-level directory structure, it was limited to three levels that didn't do a good job of representing the real network. The combination of the hierarchical tree structure, plus containers that can hold other containers, better solved some of the organizational problems at MegaCorp.

MegaCorp is particularly interested in taking advantage of the nature of the NDS database of properties to allow a single corporate database of personnel. Currently, every employee status change requires modifying seven different databases.

[Root]: The Base, and Top, of Your NDS Tree

CONSIDERATIONS

The choices:

- Whether to use a Country container.
- Whether to use one tree or more.
- How many Organization containers to use.
- How cluttered should the [Root] be.

DECISION

Use the Country designation, but keep one tree.

EXPLANATION

Since MegaCorp already had a presence on the Internet, it was felt that the corporate network would connect to either the Internet or a similar system within the next two years. The Country designation is important for X.500 compliance, so it was included.

The large Organization containers keep the [Root] from being cluttered. They also provide separation for management and keep users to their own Organizations unless central IS makes an exception. Most of the cross-Organization traffic comes through e-mail.

MEGACORP CASE STUDY, CONTINUED

Planning Your NDS Tree

CONSIDERATIONS

The goals:

- Select a tree name that reflects the company.
- Test the three favorite designs in the pilot lab.
- Design the tree based on company-wide criteria.
- Design the tree based on local considerations.
- Reflect the organization chart for departments in the tree.
- Keep the tree less than eight levels deep.
- Pick a network object naming convention.

DECISION

Use a single tree, named Mega_Tree, with geographical Organizations. Use functional Organizations beneath that level.

EXPLANATION

A single tree was deemed sufficient, especially with the large Organization containers separating the functional departments. The combination of large, rigid settings at the top of the tree, plus the flexibility for each location manager to reflect the organization of local departments, came to be seen as the best option during the pilot test.

Network names were codified for all network objects. Only central IS personnel have the option to make exceptions to these rules, and they do so rarely. With the users trained to use NetWare Tools, and the extensive use of Directory Map objects and Alias objects, users don't perceive the large network as difficult to navigate.

NDS Context Control and Management

CONSIDERATIONS

The setup:

- Guarantee users can log in properly no matter what their context.
- Use the name context setting for each user in their NET.CFG file.
- Keep users from needing to search too far up the NDS tree for services.

DECISION

Intelligent use of Organizational Units in each location to keep the tree from getting too deep. The login context is set by the NET.CFG file on each user's workstation.

EXPLANATION

Keeping the servers and their volumes together in the same Organizational Unit makes housekeeping simple. Using Container login scripts allows each user to gain access to the appropriate network resources at a high level. The NET.CFG file on each workstation maintains simple connections to the proper context. Each corporate user has his or her own station (sometimes two), so users rarely need to type their full name for login authentication.

MEGACORP CASE STUDY, CONTINUED

Using Bindery Services to Provide Bindery Emulation

CONSIDERATIONS

Reasons to use Bindery Services:

- Support cross-tree traffic.
- Support NETX clients.
- Support non-NDS network hardware.

DECISION

Use Bindery Services as little as possible.

EXPLANATION

All MegaCorp's NetWare clients were new, and all were loaded with the new client software. The older PCs were made into dedicated print servers, using the NPRINTER software included with NetWare 4.1x. The tape backup system (often a reason to remain with Bindery Services) was purchased new for the NetWare 4.1x installation.

Connecting PC Clients to Your Network

CHAPTER 5

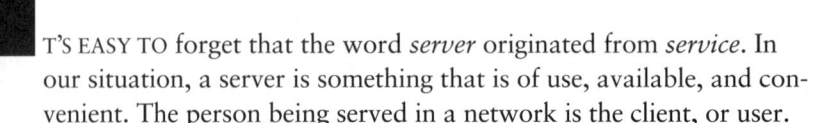

I'T'S EASY TO forget that the word *server* originated from *service*. In our situation, a server is something that is of use, available, and convenient. The person being served in a network is the client, or user.

NetWare provided a client/server system long before the term became a buzzword. In the early days, the only things a client needed were file and printer service. Today, much of a server's time is still spent providing controlled and shared access to files and printers.

But the client of today needs more than just access to files and printers. There are seven services that the modern client requires. In addition to file and print services, clients need directory, management, routing, messaging, and security services.

NetWare 4.1*x* supports DOS/MS Windows, Macintosh, Unix, OS/2, and Windows NT clients. The majority of NetWare clients are PCs with Intel microprocessors running some version of DOS. Often, the clients use a GUI (graphical user interface), usually Microsoft's Windows 3.1 or later. All these various clients can be connected to the same server at the same time and share all the server resources.

This chapter deals with PC clients. The other types of clients are covered in Part III. To be a NetWare client, a PC must:

- Be IBM PC-compatible

- Have one of these types of processors: Intel 8088, 80286, 80386 (SX or DX), 80486 (SX or DX), or Pentium

- Have a 1.2 MB (or larger) floppy disk drive (or a remote reset PROM on the network board)

- Have a network interface card and suitable network cabling

Using Client32 software for Windows 95 and other 32-bit client operating systems changes the rules quite a bit. Installation and use of Client32 software are covered separately from the DOS and Windows 3.1 client information. Skip to the end of this chapter if you're looking for Windows 95 and other Client32 information.

The NetWare DOS Requester: Moving beyond Shells

As the client PCs have become more complex and network services have expanded, the NetWare client programs have evolved to keep pace. Early DOS was completely unaware of the network, and the NetWare client software had to fool DOS into believing the file and print services of the network were really local. As DOS became more intelligent and network savvy, the NetWare client programs became more flexible and easier to control and modify.

When DOS was network-stupid, the NetWare client software "wrapped" around DOS, intercepting every software request for file or print services. This is where the *shell* label came from: NetWare client software literally became a shell around DOS. The network requests were handled, but every DOS request for local services was delayed because of the trip through the NetWare shell programs.

Novell has moved away from the shell technology, represented most recently by the client program NETX.COM. With NetWare 4, the shell was replaced by the NetWare DOS Requester. The advantages over the NETX.COM program are that the NetWare DOS Requester:

- Provides a modular architecture

- Takes advantage of memory-swapping technology and DOS redirection capability

- Includes the Packet Burst Protocol and Large Internet Packet (LIP)

- Uses a NETX module to communicate with the installed base of NetWare servers

- Can be fine-tuned for lower memory consumption

- Supports NetWare Directory Services, Bindery Services, and Personal NetWare

The client software included with NetWare 4.1*x* works with the DOS redirection functions. Rather than handling all the file requests in lieu of DOS, the

NetWare DOS Requester uses the DOS file-handling services. This close interaction between DOS and NetWare makes for a speedier and more robust client. The modularity of the new NetWare client programs allows better management and easier upgrading. Each small piece can be controlled or upgraded, so that you don't need to completely change all the client software to make a modification or to upgrade.

Network Interface Card Installation and Setup

BEFORE INSTALLING ANY of this nice new software, the PC must have a network interface card. The network interface cards have many names, depending on what you're reading:

- Network board
- NIC (network interface card)
- Board
- Adapter
- Drivers (the software that communicates between the computer and the interface card)

The network interface card connects your PC to the network cabling system. Every PC must have at least one interface card (or other means of communication) before the client software will load. Up to four adapters may be placed in a single PC running NetWare client software.

The adapter files provided with NetWare 4.1x or by the adapter manufacturer include all the default settings for each card. There are more than 50 driver files included with NetWare 4.1x, and the adapter vendor should also supply a driver file. In case the files are not the same, try the newest one first.

Adapter driver files are often upgraded. New driver files can make a tremendous improvement in workstation performance. Contact your vendor for details, or watch the Novell areas on CompuServe (NetWire), the Novell Web server (www.novell.com), or the Internet newsgroup (comp.sys.novell) for upgrade information.

Check the adapter's documentation for specific details on any jumper or switch settings for each adapter. Before opening a PC case to install any device, turn the computer off and unplug the system. The documentation with many adapters will warn you to work in a low-static environment (no carpet), and to work on a grounded pad with a wrist strap if you want to really be safe. That's great, but unrealistic for most situations. A clean desk and some care will be enough.

Adapters in your PC must work together with existing peripherals. There are four areas of connection between your adapter and your PC:

- Hardware interrupts

- Base I/O port addresses

- Memory addresses

- DMA channels

Each of these settings are required by the NetWare client installation program. If you don't know the following information for your network adapters, find the manuals for each adapter type you plan to use on your network. If you have an existing NetWare installation and client software, the NVER command will provide you with all the necessary information.

Here's a partial NVER listing, run from a client logged into a NetWare 4.1*x* server, showing the interrupt and port number:

```
DOS:V7.00
Link Support Layer: Version 2.11
LAN Drivers:
Board 1: 3Com EtherLink III Adapter
Version 1.30
Frame type: ETHERNET_802.3
Maximum frame size: 1514 bytes
Line speed: 10Mbps
Interrupt number: 10
Port number: 0300-030f
```

The same computer, running NVER from a client logged into a NetWare 3.12 server, shows this information (again, a partial listing):

```
NETWARE VERSION UTILITY, VERSION 3.75
IPX Version: 3.30
```

```
            SPX Version: 3.30
            LAN Driver: 3Com EtherLink III Adapter V.100
                        IRQ A, Port 0300
            DOS: NWDOS V7.00 on IBM_PC
```

As you can see, the newer NVER listing provides more information. But the important things to notice are the IRQ and port settings in both examples.

Later, when we cover the new Client32 for Windows 95 and other 32-bit client operating systems, we'll see a slightly different look to the NVER results. In fact, within the Windows 95 DOS box, the IRQ and port number both display as 0 (zero), since the client software is bound up inside the Windows 95 software. This may seem strange at first, but you'll get used to it.

Hardware Interrupts

Hardware interrupts (IRQs) are used by a device to request services from the PC's processor. These are normally shown as integers, but hardware IRQs are occasionally shown as hexadecimal numbers. Eight-bit interface cards have interrupts 2, 3, 4, 5, and 7 available. Sixteen-bit cards have additional interrupts 9, 10, 11, 12, 13, 14, and 15 (or 9, A, B, C, D, E and F). Interrupts support only one device. Standard PC interrupts and their assignments are listed earlier in the book, in Chapter 2 (Table 2.1).

With eight-bit interface cards, and PC and XT systems that have only eight bits available, interrupts are rare and valuable. Only interrupts 0 through 7 are available, and 0, 1, 2, 4, 5, 6, and 7 are already in use in most systems. The default for these eight-bit cards is often IRQ 3; a few still try to use IRQ 5 as a default. If you have a mouse on COM1 and a modem on COM2, there is no open interrupt for the network interface card. It's a good thing most of these old machines have been flushed out of the system.

Starting with the IBM AT with sixteen-bit slots, interrupts 8 through 15 become available, although IRQ 2 is lost as the step up to the higher interrupts. The hard disk in AT and newer machines tends to use IRQ 14, leaving IRQ 5 open.

However, the recent multimedia push requires more peripheral devices that need interrupts. CD-ROM drive controllers like IRQ 5, and sound boards often need an interrupt as well. Interrupts are becoming scarce again. Newer network interface cards often come with a default of IRQ 10, which is generally available.

Base I/O Port Addresses

Once the peripheral device has an interrupt assigned to request services from the CPU, it needs a specific address to send and receive messages from the CPU and other devices. Addresses are normally three-digit hexadecimal numbers (such as 280h or 340h), and are often expressed as a range bound by the low and high addresses. Most network interface cards, however, request a single address, such as 320h.

Each device must use a base I/O address. There are more addresses available than there are interrupts, so this setting is generally less trouble than the interrupt setting. The adapter documentation will specify the default I/O address and the options supported by the adapter card.

Memory Addresses

The memory address is the exact location in memory that stores a particular data item or program instruction. When installing network interface cards, only the first megabyte of RAM is available.

Not all adapter cards use a memory address. If your card will be started by a remote boot PROM (programmable read-only memory) chip, a memory address will be necessary. Token Ring and ARCnet adapters often use these memory addresses; Ethernet cards rarely do.

The memory address must be unique to the adapter. The addresses are expressed in hexadecimal with four digit-numbers, such as D000 or C400. Your adapter documentation will state whether a memory address is required and what the default address is.

If your PC uses a memory manager (which it probably does), you may need to exclude the adapter address range in your memory manager configuration. The Microsoft MEM-MAKER program will configure the address exclusion automatically if you run the program with the adapter drivers loaded. If you have a different memory manager, you will need to redo the setup to accommodate any memory set aside for the adapter's memory address needs. If you have Windows 95, you have a different set of memory control features.

DMA Channels

DMA (dynamic memory access) is a method of transferring information from a device such as a hard disk or network adapter directory into memory without passing through the CPU. Because the CPU is not involved in the information transfer, the process is faster than other types of memory transfers. The DMA channel must be unique for each device.

Ethernet adapters make more use of DMA channels than Token Ring adapters, but you must check the adapter documentation. Other devices that transfer large amounts of information, such as hard disks, CD-ROM drives, and sound boards, will compete for DMA channels with the network adapter. The DMA channels are labeled with decimal integers.

Client Files Required for Non-Client32 Clients

THERE ARE AT least four NetWare client programs to load on the client PC running DOS or MS Windows 3.*x*. Each program has multiple options, and the VLM.EXE program is actually a manager program that coordinates many small programs for the NetWare DOS Requester. Details are controlled in the NET.CFG text program, which we will see a bit later.

Each program is a TSR (terminate-and-stay-resident) program, meaning it must be loaded from DOS before starting any GUI applications. The files can load in upper memory (just like every other TSR fighting for space up there). The memory usage of the files when loaded is:

LSL.COM	5.3 KB
Network driver	4–8 KB
IPXODI.COM	16.5 KB
VLM.EXE	5–15 KB conventional; 35–45 KB upper memory

The LSL.COM, network driver, and IPXODI.COM programs can be loaded high with the LOADHIGH command, as in:

```
LOADHIGH LSL
```

Check your DOS manual. Different systems (such as Novell DOS 7, if any of you Novell die-hards are still using that product) use different commands. The VLM file will look for available upper memory automatically, so there's no need to specify the LOADHIGH command.

ODI (Open Data-link Interface) Overview

Released in 1989, ODI is the Novell specification that allows a single card to support multiple network interface card device drivers and protocols without conflicts. Using modular programming techniques, ODI defined the separation between protocol stacks and the device drivers needed for the physical interface card.

This makes life much easier in today's multiprotocol world. Before ODI, the only way for a PC to communicate with both a NetWare file server and a Unix host was to run two interface cards in the PC. Later, packet drivers were developed to support multiple protocols on a single network adapter, but each packet driver was specific to the hardware.

The diagram shown in Figure 5.1 may be helpful as you start stacking the client software programs on a PC. The bottom network boards are the physical network connections, and the diagram shows four, since four cards can be placed in one PC client.

FIGURE 5.1
Where the ODI client files fit in your PC

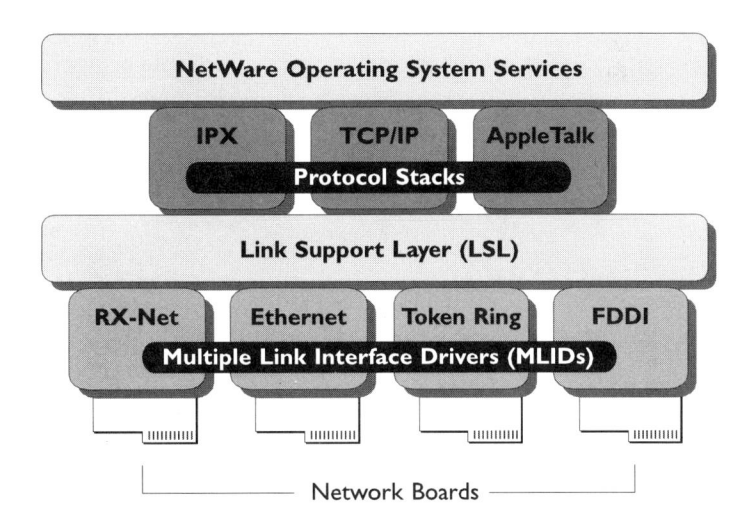

LSL.COM

The LSL (Link Support Layer) is an implementation of the ODI specification that serves as an intermediary between the NetWare server's LAN drivers and communication protocols, such as IPX, AFP, or TCP/IP. The LSL.COM program puts the packaged requests from IPXODI into the proper format for transmission on the particular client workstation's physical network. The LSL then takes replies from the network for the client workstation (via the LAN driver), removes the network-specific information it has added, and passes the reply to IPX.

The LSL.COM program is the first of the client programs loaded. To see the program options for LSL.COM, from the command line, type:

```
LSL /?
```

The program switches are:

LSL /?	Displays the help screen.
LSL	Installs the LSL software layer.
LSL /U	Removes LSL from memory.
LSL /C=[*path*]*filename*	Allows you to specify a configuration file to use instead of the default NET.CFG.

LSL.COM is supplied in the NetWare 4.1*x* client diskettes. Multiple network adapters supporting multiple protocols are handled by a single LSL.COM program. There is no need to load multiple versions of LSL.COM. Use the LOADHIGH command (again, check your DOS version) to push LSL into upper memory.

LAN Drivers (16 bit)

The LAN driver name depends on the interface card. One example is the driver for an NE2000 Ethernet interface card. Originally developed by Novell to help reduce the cost of network adapters, the NE family has become popular. Many other Ethernet card vendors make NE2000-compatible cards, allowing you to use the NE2000.COM program that comes with NetWare with their own brand of adapter.

Officially, the LAN driver is an MLID (Multiple Link Interface Driver). This device driver, written to the ODI specifications, handles sending and receiving of packets to and from a physical or logical LAN medium. For most users, MLID serves as a link between a workstation's operating system and the physical network parts. But MLID also understands logical LAN connections, such as those made through a serial port.

This bit of forward thinking will be important to you soon, if not now. The needs of remote users and the mobile business population guarantee more work will be done across POTSnet (Plain Old Telephone Service network). The craze for Internet connections is part of this trend. MLID is important for NetWare support over any network type.

The LSL program feeds requests to the LAN driver. The MLID then wraps the request into a network-specific packet and sends those requests to the network. Return packets are passed up to the LSL after being stripped of their network-specific header information.

Three smaller modules are included in the MLID:

- The MSM (Media Support Module) standardizes and manages primary details of interfacing ODI MLIDs to the LSL and operating system. It also handles generic initialization and run-time issues common to all drivers.

- The TSM (Topology Specific Module) manages operations unique to a specific media type, such as Ethernet or Token Ring. Multiple frame support is implemented in the TSM so that all frame types for a given media are supported.

- The HSM (Hardware Specific Module) is created for a specific network board. The HSM handles all hardware interactions. Its primary functions include adapter initialization, reset, shutdown, and removal.

The HSM performs packet reception and transmission tasks. Additional procedures may also provide support for timeout detection, multicast addressing, and promiscuous mode reception, depending on software configuration. For instance, LAN analyzers force the HSM into reading every packet on the network (promiscuous mode) rather than just those packets addressed to the workstation.

None of these modules are loaded from the command line; they are all internal. The options for the LAN driver program during loading are:

NE2000 /?   Displays the help screen.
NE2000   Installs the LAN driver.
NE2000 /U   Removes the LAN driver from memory.

Many LAN drivers are included with NetWare 4.1*x*. Their file names are the card name (for example, NE2000) with the COM extension. The supported network cards, and the drivers used to support them, are listed in Table 5.1.

> **NOTE**
>
> *The list of drivers that come with NetWare 4.10 is not exactly the same as the list of those included with NetWare 4.11. Table 5.1 shows the drivers included with 4.10, 4.11, or both versions. If you have an older card that is not supported by NetWare 4.11, ask the card vendor to provide a new driver (but if you have a NetWare 4.10 driver for the card, it will work with NetWare 4.11).*

TABLE 5.1 Drivers Included with NetWare 4.10 and/or 4.11

LAN DRIVER	CARDS SUPPORTED
3C501	3Com 3C1100 3Station Ethernet
3C501	3Com 3C501 EtherLink
3C503	3Com 3C503 EtherLink II, EtherLink II TP, EtherLink II/163C, EtherLink II/16 TP
3C505	3Com 3C505 EtherLink+
3C523	3Com EtherLink/MC, EtherLink/MC TP
3C5X9	3Com EtherLink III Parallel Tasking Family
CEODI	Xircom Credit Card Ethernet Adapter
E20ODI	Cabletron Systems Ethernet E20
E2HODI	Cabletron Systems Ethernet E2HUB
E30ODI	Cabletron Systems Ethernet E3010, Ethernet E3010-X, Ethernet E3020, Ethernet E3020-X, Ethernet E3030, Ethernet E3030-X, Ethernet E3040E, Ethernet E3040-X

Client Files Required for Non-Client32 Clients 271

TABLE 5.1 (cont.)
Drivers Included with NetWare 4.10 and/or 4.11

LAN DRIVER	CARDS SUPPORTED
E31ODI	Cabletron Systems Ethernet E31, Ethernet E31-X
ES3210	Racal-Datacom ES3210
EXOS	Novell/Excelan EXOS 205T Ethernet, EXOS 215 Ethernet
EXP16ODI	Intel EtherExpress ISA Family, MCA Family
HPMCAODI	Hewlett-Packard MC Adapter 16
IBMFDDIO	IBM FDDI
IBMODISH	IBM PS/2 Ethernet Adapter
ILANAT	Racal-Datacom InterLan AT/XT
INTEL593	Intel593-based adapter
INTEL595	Intel 82595-based adapter
INTEL596	Intel 596-based adapter
LANSUP	ODI module for IBM LAN Support program
MADGEODI	Madge Smart 16/4 PC Ringnode, AT Ringnode, MC Ringnode, MC32 Ringnode, EISA Ringnode, EISA Mk II Ringnode
NCRWL05	NCR WaveLAN
NE1000	Novell/Eagle NE1000
NE1500T	Novell Ethernet NE1500TN Ansel M1500
NE2	Novell/Eagle NE/2
NE2_32	Novell/Eagle NE2-32
NE2000	Novell/Eagle NE2000, Zenith Data Systems NE2000, National Semiconductor NE2000 InfoMover (many other cards use this and other NE drivers)
NE2100	Novell Ethernet NE2100, Ansel M2100, Wearnes 2110T, Wearnes 2107C, EXOS 105

TABLE 5.1 (cont.) Drivers Included with NetWare 4.10 and/or 4.11

LAN DRIVER	CARDS SUPPORTED
NE3200	Novell Ethernet NE3200, Intel EtherExpress32, EXOS 235T
NI5210	Racal-Datacom NI5210
NI6510	Racal-Datacom NI6510
NI9210	Racal-Datacom NI9210
NTR2000	Novell NTR2000 Token Ring Adapter
NULL	Not a working LAN driver. The NetWare client installation program copies this file to the client directory during installation for dedicated (Non-ODI) IPX drivers. You should contact the network board manufacturer for copies of the latest ODI drivers.
OSH391R	Proteon p1391 RapiDriver
OSH89XR	Proteon p189X RapiDriver
OSH990R	Proteon p1990 RapiDriver
PCMDMN	SC Ethernet PCMCIA Card
PCN2L	PCN II, PCN Baseband, PCN II/A, PCN Baseband/A
PE2ODI	Xircom Credit Card Ethernet Adapter
SLIP_PPP	Novell's LAN WorkPlace Asynchronous SLIP and PPP driver. This driver runs on workstations' serial hardware with either PPP or SLIP frame types, and it supports both direct-connection lines and indirect modem connections.
SMC8000	SMC EtherCard Plus Family Adapter
SMC8100	SMC Token Ring EliteFamily Adapter
SMCARCWS	SMC PC130/130E/270E, SMC PC500WS/550WS (short or long card), SMC PC600WS/650WS, SMC PS110//210/310 PS/2
T20ODI	Cabletron Systems Token Ring T20
T30ODI	Cabletron Systems Token Ring T30

TABLE 5.1 (cont.) Drivers Included with NetWare 4.10 and/or 4.11

LAN DRIVER	CARDS SUPPORTED
TCCARC	Thomas-Conrad TC6x42 ARCnet 8-bit Adapter, ARCnet 16-bit Adapter, ARCnet MC Adapter
TCE16ATW	Thomas-Conrad TC5045 Ethernet Adapter
TCE16MCW	Thomas-Conrad TC5046 Ethernet Adapter-16 bit
TCE32MCW	Thomas-Conrad TC5046 Ethernet Adapter-32 bit
TCNSW	Thomas-Conrad TC3042 TCNS 8-bit Adapter, TC3045 TCNS 16-bit Adapter, TC3046 TCNS MC Adapter, TC3047 TCNS EISA Adapter
TCTOKSH	Thomas-Conrad TC4035/TC4045 Adapter, TC4046 Adapter
TOKEN	IBM Token Ring Network Adapter II and 16/4 Adapter, 16/4 Credit Card Adapter, Network Adapter/A, Network 16/4 Adapter/A
TRXNET	Novell RX-Net, RX-Net II, RX-Net/2T
UBODI	Ungermann-Bass NIUpc/EOTP, NIUps, NIUpc, Personal NIU/ex, Personal NIU (look also under the new name for Ungermann-Bass: UB Networks)

IPXODI.COM

IPXODI (Internetwork Packet eXchange Open Data-Link Interface) is the software program that takes workstation requests the DOS Requester has determined are for the network, packages them with transmission information (such as their destination), and hands them to the LSL.

A header is attached by IPXODI to each data packet. The header specifies information that targets network delivery, announcing where the packet came from, where it's going, and what should happen after delivery.

Because IPXODI transmits data packets as datagrams (self-contained packages that move independently from source to destination), it can deliver the packets on only a best-effort basis. Delivery is assured by SPX.

The command-line options are:

IPXODI /?	Displays the help screen.
IPXODI /D	Eliminates Diagnostic Responder. Reduces size by 3 KB.
IPXODI /A	Eliminates Diagnostic Responder and SPX. Reduces size by 9 KB.
IPXODI /M	Uses Mobile IPX support. Diagnostic Responder and SPX will be loaded.
IPXODI /C= [*path*]*filename.ext*	Allows you to specify a configuration file to use rather than the default NET.CFG.
IPXODI /U	Unloads resident IPXODI from memory.
IPXODI /F	Forcibly unloads resident IPXODI from memory, regardless of programs loaded. Using this option can cause your machine to crash if applications are still using IPX/SPX.

NetWare DOS Requester (VLM.EXE)

The NetWare DOS Requester is DOS client software that provides the interface between DOS and the network. The VLM.EXE program is the modular executable program that calls a series of smaller programs with the VLM extension, called VLMs (Virtual Loadable Modules). These VLMs provide network features through APIs (Application Program Interfaces).

You don't need to decide which VLMs are required just to get the network up and running. The final command in the NetWare client software group, VLM.EXE, will manage the necessary modules. If you wish to fine-tune the client, you can make changes in the NET.CFG file. You have complete control over the VLMs loaded (although some VLMs are required).

The command-line options for the VLM.EXE program are:

VLM /?	Displays the help screen.
VLM /U	Unloads the VLM.EXE file from memory.
VLM /C= [*path*]*filename.ext*	Allows you to specify a configuration file to use rather than the default NET.CFG.
VLM /M*x*	The memory type the VLM.EXE file uses, where *x* is C (conventional memory), X (extended memory), or E (expanded memory).
VLM /D	Displays the VLM.EXE file diagnostics.
VLM /PS= <*server name*>	Preferred server name to attach to when loading.
VLM /PT= <*tree name*>	Preferred tree name to attach to when loading.
VLM /V*x*	The detail level of message display, where *x* is 0 (copyright and critical errors only), 1 (also warning messages), 2 (also VLM names), 3 (also configuration file parameters), 4 (also diagnostics messages).

WARNING *Do not use both the preferred server (/PS) and preferred tree (/PT) parameters. The second parameter will override the first.*

Child and Multiplexor VLMs

The two types of VLMs are *child* and *multiplexor.* A child VLM handles a particular implementation of a logical grouping of functionality. Different functions require different child VLM programs. For example, each of the NetWare server types has its own child VLM:

- BIND.VLM is for connections to NetWare 2 and 3 bindery servers.
- NDS.VLM is for connections to NetWare 4 NDS servers.
- PNW.VLM is for connections to Personal NetWare (NetWare desktop) servers.

Various implementations of transport protocols also have their individual child VLMs. For example, IPXNCP.VLM handles IPX protocol services. Other transport protocols may be defined in the future.

When memory space is critical, unneeded child VLM programs can be left out of the default client software. For instance, the client installation program will add only child VLMs for particular server types to your workstation if you agree that you need connection to those server types.

A *multiplexor* is a special VLM that routes calls to the correct child VLM. The NetWare DOS Requester multiplexors can be considered a parent VLM. Each multiplexor VLM ensures that requests to its child VLM reach the appropriate one. For example, NWP.VLM is the multiplexor that handles calls to and from the child VLM programs BIND.VLM, NDS.VLM, and PNW.VLM. Similarly, TRAN.VLM is the multiplexor that coordinates communication at the transport layer when its child VLM (IPXNCP.VLM and other transport protocols) are concurrently loaded.

Installing Non-Client32 Clients

PARADOXICALLY, THE BEST source for the client installation program is the file server itself. While this may sound like trying to install a new VCR with all the instructions on a VCR tape, it's not that bad. We actually will log in and use the network server as our installation source in a few moments.

If the workstation is running Windows 3.1*x*, you must exit and install from DOS. If your workstation is not yet running Windows but you plan to do so soon, install Windows before installing the NetWare client software. The NetWare support files for Windows will not install until Windows is resident on the workstation.

You need to set the language for the workstation. This is necessary for the installation program to know which language all the support and message files should use. Although you can skip this if the default language is English, it's better to get your workstation set for the language parameter now. It will be necessary later as well.

On the DOS command line, type:

```
SET NWLANGUAGE=ENGLISH
```

to set the default language of English. If you prefer another language, here are your choices:

SET NWLANGUAGE=FRENCH (or FRANCAIS)	French
SET NWLANGUAGE=GERMAN (or DEUTSCH)	German
SET NWLANGUAGE=ITALIAN (or ITALIANO)	Italian
SET NWLANGUAGE=SPANISH (or ESPANOL)	Spanish

All the required network hardware should be in place in the workstation before starting the installation. Token Ring systems must be connected to a live network for the software to accept the interface card. Ethernet cards can be separated from the network without problem, but it's really best to install the network client software onto a network-ready PC. That allows you to test the setup and software configuration immediately.

The installation program is DOS, and must run outside Windows. If you are running Windows, you must close and exit. The program makes changes to some of the Windows system files, so they must be closed during installation. All the Windows programs will be installed by the DOS program.

Modifying the INSTALL.CFG File in NetWare 4.10

The INSTALL.CFG file can help modify certain NET.CFG parameters if you plan on installing many workstations with the same configuration requirements. INSTALL.CFG is on the first floppy of the installation set, and in the \PUBLIC\CLIENT\DOSWIN directory in NetWare 4.10 (this doesn't apply to version 4.11).

In the [REQUESTER] section of INSTALL.CFG, the only default lines are:

```
FIRST NETWORK DRIVE=F
NETWARE PROTOCOL=NDS BIND
```

If you wish, you may add other NetWare DOS Requester options on the lines after the network drive designator. If you do this on the diskettes, keep track of which set of installation diskettes has which NET.CFG options. If you do this on the INSTALL.CFG file on the file server, be careful. Make copies of INSTALL.CFG for each different NET.CFG file, and rename the appropriate one to INSTALL.CFG immediately before you install to machines needing that configuration.

Be sure you don't forget and leave the INSTALL.CFG file renamed; if there is no INSTALL.CFG, the installation will blow up. All the files to be copied to the client, depending on your choices during installation, are listed in the INSTALL.CFG file.

Installing over the Network in NetWare 4.10

If you already have a NetWare 4.1x server on your network, the easiest way to install clients is to run the INSTALL program from that server. If your PC is already a workstation for a NetWare 3.x network, the NETX shell files you use will still connect to the NetWare 4.1x server. The connection will be under Bindery Services, meaning that you won't be able to take advantage of any of the NDS features and benefits. But that doesn't matter in this case, since you just want to gain access to the \PUBLIC\CLIENT\DOSWIN directory and run the INSTALL program directly from the server.

NetWare 4.11 changes the rules, even for Windows 3.1x and DOS clients. The directory with the client files is \PUBLIC\CLIENT\WIN31. The change from DOSWIN to WIN31 indicates the shift away from DOS is nearly complete, since DOS functions will only run under some version of Windows in the future. It's almost that bad already, but not quite. Your DOS stations are still supported under NetWare 4.11, but their days are numbered. If you have any DOS-only stations that you want to connect to a NetWare 4.11 server, you'll need to use the diskette installation routine. Yes, that means you'll need to make the seven diskettes and feed them one at a time.

If you haven't created any users on the NetWare 4.10 system, log in to the network as Admin. The basic drive mapping will cover all that is necessary. You will have a search drive mapped to the PUBLIC directory, which is mandatory. You will also have your first network drive pointing at the SYSTEM directory, which does you no good. Type:

```
CD \PUBLIC\CLIENT\DOSWIN
```

to move your current directory to the location of the INSTALL.EXE program. Once there, run the INSTALL program, as described shortly.

With a new network, there is still a way to save time and aggravation while installing client software on all the PCs that need it. After you have created a single workstation using the five-floppy-disk method, take a bootable diskette and put these files in the \NWCLIENT directory:

- LSL.COM
- The appropriate network adapter driver
- IPXODI.COM
- VLM.EXE
- All the VLM files from the C:\NWCLIENT directory
- The NET.CFG file configured for the stations to be installed

Add these to the root directory:

- A clean AUTOEXEC.BAT
- A clean CONFIG.SYS

The trick here is to make enough of a client diskette to get started and connected to the NetWare 4.10 server of your choice. All the necessary client utilities won't fit on a floppy disk, but you don't need those. All you need is enough to get connected and logged in.

You will need to edit the STARTNET.BAT file to change the references from drive C to drive A. The same goes for the AUTOEXEC.BAT and CONFIG.SYS files. The easiest way is to take the working files from the PC already set up and make your modifications.

Remember, you don't need any files except those NetWare files that connect you to the server. This is a diskette that boots, logs in, and starts the installation program.

Installing from the CD-ROM

If you want to install the client software to a workstation that has a CD-ROM drive, it works quickly and simply. It's similar to making the installation diskettes from the CD-ROM, as we talked about earlier.

Earlier versions of NetWare 4 required you to drill down into the directory structure to find the INSTALL.EXE program. With the addition of a small batch file in the root of the CD-ROM, life is much easier.

In NetWare 4.10, load the CD-ROM into your drive and move to that drive letter under DOS. This must be under DOS, not a DOS box inside MS Windows. Type:

```
CINSTALL
```

and the batch file of that name will start. This batch file changes your directory to the proper place on the disk and starts the INSTALL program for you.

This system does still work with the NetWare 4.11 CD-ROM. Of course, it's unlikely you'll have too many DOS-only stations with functioning CD-ROM drives, but if you do, you can avoid the floppy shuffle, at least for those stations. The sequence of batch file programs leading to the actual work is a bit different, of course. From the root of the CD-ROM, run the INSTALL.BAT file. Choose the appropriate language, press Enter to ignore all the legal restrictions the lawyers have included, choose Client Installation, and then pick NetWare DOS/Windows Client (VLM).

Installing from Floppies

Now that NetWare comes on a CD-ROM disk, if you're going to install from floppies, you will need to create workstation installation diskettes. This is not difficult, and you have two options for creating these diskettes. If you told the installation program to go ahead and load client files, your server has all the necessary programs. If not, they are on the CD-ROM, just waiting to be copied.

Creating Client Installation Diskettes in NetWare 4.10

No matter where the files come from, they will need to be copied to five blank, formatted diskettes. The installation program will put the appropriate disk label on the disks. You only need to label the disks for their functions, as specified by the MAKEDISK.BAT program.

The 2697-byte MAKEDISK.BAT program will lead you through all the steps in creating the five DOS and MS Windows client installation diskettes. The important considerations before starting are:

- Have five blank, formatted high density diskettes on hand.

- Make sure you have DOS utilities in your search path.

The program will ask you to specify which floppy drive on your workstation will be used, and suggest drive A: for you. After each diskette is full, you will be prompted for another. The minute you take the first diskette out is a good time to label it as suggested. Never carry around these diskettes without a label, or they will get lost. The labels for your diskettes are:

NetWare Client for DOS and MS Windows Disk 1 (WSDOS_1)

NetWare Client for DOS and MS Windows Disk 2 (WSDOS_2)

NetWare Client for DOS and MS Windows Disk 3 (WSDOS_3)

NetWare Client for DOS and MS Windows Disk 4 (WSDOS_4)

NetWare Client for DOS and MS Windows ODI LAN Drivers (WSDOS_5)

Be aware that this disk copy process takes some time to perform. The only thing that takes longer is to make these diskettes from the server. Although the INSTALL program from the console offers you a chance to make these diskettes on the server, avoid that at all costs. The time you save may be your own.

FROM THE NETWORK SERVER For PC clients, the important directory on the server is \PUBLIC\CLIENT\DOSWIN. This directory contains most of the necessary files in compressed format. If you look, you will see file names like SECURITY.VL_ everywhere. The NWUNPACK.EXE file in that directory will be used to expand the files during the copy process.

Once in the proper directory, start the MAKEDISK.BAT program. The proper syntax is:

```
MAKEDISK A: ENGLISH
```

but you will be prompted for the floppy drive letter if you forget. Although French, Italian, German, and Spanish are included, English is assumed if you forget to specify a language.

FROM THE CD-ROM If you have mounted the NetWare 4.1x distribution CD-ROM as a volume on a server, you can copy the files from there. If you haven't mounted the CD-ROM that way, don't worry about it. You can place the CD-ROM in any PC with a CD-ROM drive and copy the files under DOS.

The pertinent directory for this operation, whether the CD-ROM is on the server or in your PC, is \CLIENT\DOSWIN. The contents of this directory match the contents of the directory hiding under \PUBLIC on the server.

To start the MAKEDISK.BAT program, type:

```
MAKEDISK A: ENGLISH
```

(using the appropriate drive letter and language) from the command line to start the process. The same five blank, formatted high-density diskettes are needed, regardless of the source of the files.

The already slow process takes even longer when it's done directly from the CD-ROM, so don't start this if you need your computer anytime soon. The good news is that there are other options for installing the client software on various machines without these diskettes.

The first floppy of the installation set holds a program named INSTALL.EXE. You will be prompted for each diskette in the series.

Creating Client Installation Diskettes in NetWare 4.11

With NetWare 4.11, you'll need six blank, formatted diskettes to hold the client installation files. From the root of the CD-ROM, run the INSTALL.BAT file. Choose the appropriate language, press Enter to ignore all the legal restrictions the lawyers have included, choose Diskette Creation, and then pick NetWare DOS/Windows Client (VLM). The standard installation process will begin, after the lawyers have their say. See the next section for installation details, since the process is the same whether you're loading diskettes or using a server as the client file source location.

Running the program to download the Client32 software takes eight diskettes. Remember, no upgrade ever takes less RAM or disk space than the program it replaces.

Running the INSTALL Program

When you start the INSTALL.EXE program, it begins with the screen shown in Figure 5.2.

The highlighted entry asks if you want the destination directory to be C:\NWCLIENT. That's the default, and it's a good idea to keep the suggested directory. If you want to change the directory, simply press the Enter key, and you will be able to edit the destination directory name. When you see the cursor inside the highlight bar, backspace over the directory name and type in the name you prefer. The installation program will create the directory for you. \NWCLIENT is a new directory for the NetWare 16-bit client software.

FIGURE 5.2

The NetWare client installation utility

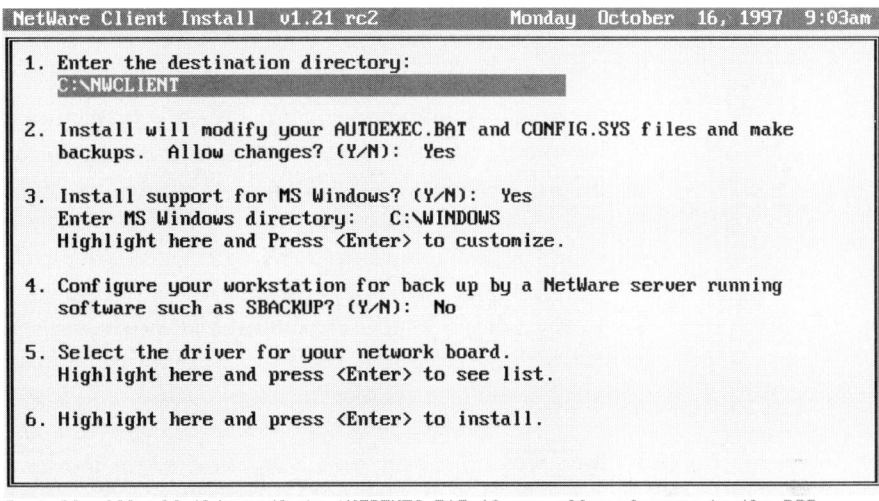

```
NetWare Client Install  v1.21 rc2              Monday  October 16, 1997  9:03am
 1. Enter the destination directory:
    C:\NWCLIENT

 2. Install will modify your AUTOEXEC.BAT and CONFIG.SYS files and make
    backups.  Allow changes? (Y/N):  Yes

 3. Install support for MS Windows? (Y/N):  Yes
    Enter MS Windows directory:    C:\WINDOWS
    Highlight here and Press <Enter> to customize.

 4. Configure your workstation for back up by a NetWare server running
    software such as SBACKUP? (Y/N):  No

 5. Select the driver for your network board.
    Highlight here and press <Enter> to see list.

 6. Highlight here and press <Enter> to install.


Install will add this path to AUTOEXEC.BAT if you allow changes to the DOS
configuration files.
Esc=Go Back    Enter=Edit/Select                              Alt-F10=Exit
```

If you have existing client software on this machine, this installation procedure will not disturb your current configuration.

The second step concerns whether you want the installation program to modify your AUTOEXEC.BAT and CONFIG.SYS files. As the screen says, there will be backups made. These backups have the extension BNW (Before NetWare). Changes to the AUTOEXEC.BAT and CONFIG.SYS files are minor (more minor than those made by many other inconsiderate software programs today).

In AUTOEXEC.BAT, your path statement is modified to add the NetWare client workstation directory, and a line is added to call the start-network batch file (STARTNET.BAT) from the same directory. For example, if your client workstation directory is NWCLIENT, the modifications appear as follows:

```
PATH=C:\NWCLIENT;
@CALL C:\NWCLIENT\STARTNET.BAT
```

The @CALL statement is added at the beginning of the AUTOEXEC.BAT file. You may want to move that statement farther down in the file, or even put it at the end. I have found that placing the network software load process at the end of everything else results in better memory utilization.

CONFIG.SYS is changed by the addition of one line:

```
LASTDRIVE = Z
```

In the past, NetWare wanted the client software to pick up at drive F:, but that was before the DOS Requester. Earlier versions picked up at the end of the local drives according to DOS, or drive E:. That left drive F: as the logical choice to begin the NetWare drive mappings. But now, remember, the NetWare DOS Requester works with DOS, so all 26 drives must be available to DOS. NetWare picks up its starting drive based on the line in the NET.CFG file.

Since these changes are minor, and the previous versions of both control files are saved for you, there is little danger in allowing the installation program to make these modifications.

If you have Windows 3.1x installed on your computer, the third step makes the installation choices to install the NetWare client support files for MS Windows.

As you can see in Figure 5.2, there are two questions to answer for Windows 3.1x installation and a submenu to "customize." Not to worry; the customization is simple. See the submenu in Figure 5.3.

The question of using more country codes should be an easy No for the vast majority of users. The second question about shared MS Windows files could be involved, but it's not. If you say Yes and press the Enter key, a new

FIGURE 5.3

Simple Windows 3.1x configuration questions

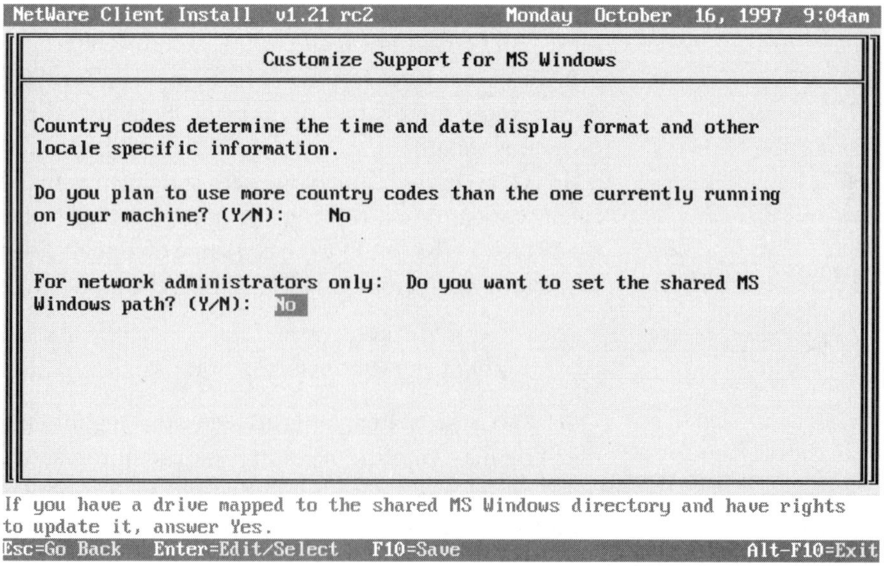

field pops up asking for the path to the shared directory. The information line across the bottom of the screen warns you that the path must be mapped and you must have the right to create files and directories.

Question 4 on the INSTALL screen opens an interesting can of worms, doesn't it? NetWare servers have traditionally been backed up by workstations, not the other way around. Chalk up one more advantage of NetWare 4.1x networking.

The submenu for Question 4 is shown in Figure 5.4. The SMS (Storage Management Services) server name is that of the server running software that coordinates backup between the host server and your workstation. TSA (Target Service Agent) is the software running on the client that works in tandem with the SMS server software.

If you have an SMS server, type the name in the first field. The next line asks for a unique name for your workstation. SMS requires more than just the hardware address normally used for Novell utilities. If you wish to specify a password, the third line is the place.

The buffers mentioned in the fourth field are 1 KB each. More buffers improve performance but take away from workstation RAM. To start, you should give the default of one buffer a test or two.

FIGURE 5.4

Hooking your TSA to your SMS

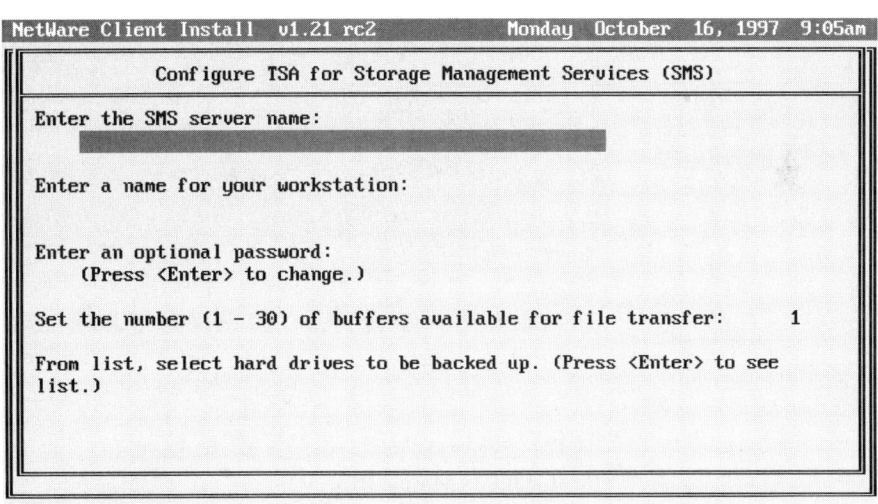

Chapter 5 • Connecting PC Clients to Your Network

Since the installation program has full control of your PC during installation, it's no trouble to read your local hard disk table. Pressing the Enter key pops open a small window labeled Backup Drives, which lists the local physical hard disks. Highlight your choice(s) and press Enter, then press F10 to save the information screen and return to the main installation screen.

Once there, Question 5 is the last, but it has several hidden screens. Once you "Highlight here and press <Enter> to see list" of network drivers, one of several things will happen.

With floppy diskettes, you must load the fifth installation disk, the one labeled for ODI LAN Drivers, when asked by the program. Figure 5.5 shows the screen asking for this diskette.

FIGURE 5.5

Locating LAN drivers

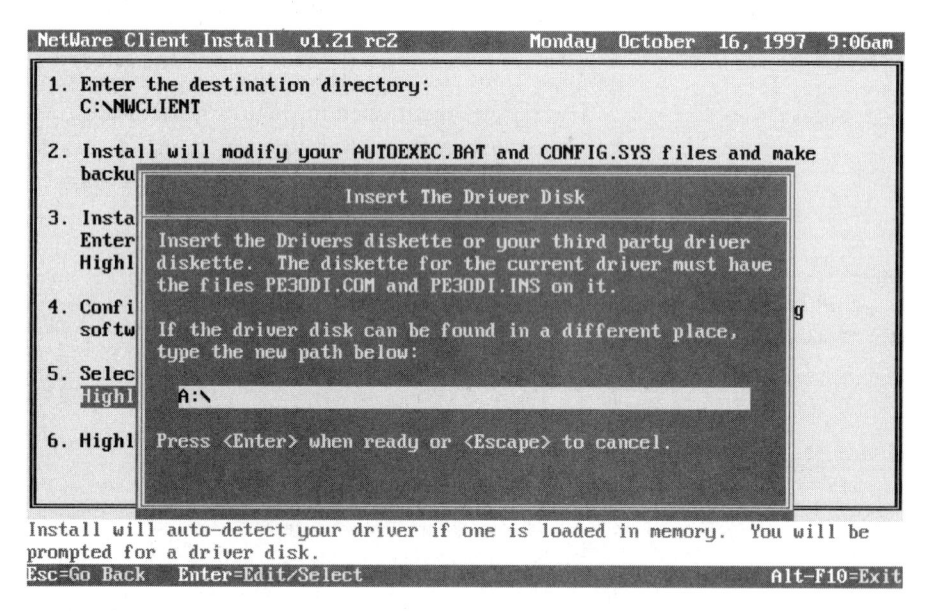

```
NetWare Client Install  v1.21 rc2           Monday  October  16, 1997  9:06am
1. Enter the destination directory:
   C:\NWCLIENT

2. Install will modify your AUTOEXEC.BAT and CONFIG.SYS files and make
   backu┌──────────────────────────────────────────────────────────────────┐
        │                     Insert The Driver Disk                       │
3. Insta│                                                                  │
   Enter│ Insert the Drivers diskette or your third party driver           │
   Highl│ diskette.  The diskette for the current driver must have         │
        │ the files PE3ODI.COM and PE3ODI.INS on it.                       │
4. Confi│                                                                  │g
   softw│ If the driver disk can be found in a different place,            │
        │ type the new path below:                                         │
5. Selec│                                                                  │
   Highl│ A:\                                                              │
        │                                                                  │
6. Highl│ Press <Enter> when ready or <Escape> to cancel.                  │
        └──────────────────────────────────────────────────────────────────┘
Install will auto-detect your driver if one is loaded in memory.  You will be
prompted for a driver disk.
Esc=Go Back    Enter=Edit/Select                                Alt-F10=Exit
```

The large box in the center of the screen is asking for the diskette with PE3ODI.COM and PE3ODI.INS on it. That may be one of the five installation diskettes, or it may be a diskette provided by the adapter manufacturer. In this case, the adapter is a Xircom Pocket Ethernet Adapter III, which is why the program is asking for the PE3ODI files. This screen is from the LAPTOP user we met briefly in a previous chapter.

If you are upgrading a workstation that already has an adapter card running NetWare client files, the installation program will know that. Figure 5.6 shows an information box from the installation program, at the same point as Figure 5.5. The difference here is that I loaded my NetWare client files before starting the installation.

FIGURE 5.6

Maintaining an existing network driver

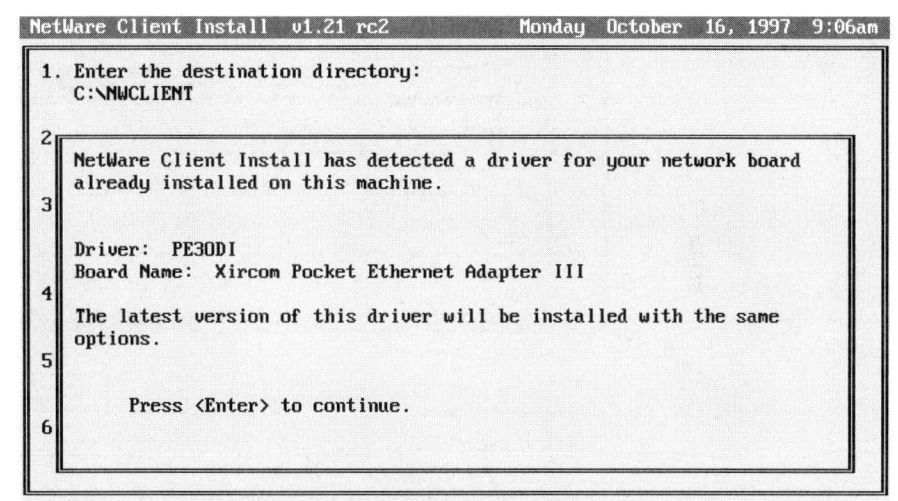

```
NetWare Client Install    v1.21 rc2         Monday   October  16, 1997   9:06am

 1. Enter the destination directory:
    C:\NWCLIENT

 2
   ┌──────────────────────────────────────────────────────────────────┐
   │ NetWare Client Install has detected a driver for your network board │
   │ already installed on this machine.                               │
 3 │                                                                  │
   │                                                                  │
   │ Driver:  PE3ODI                                                  │
   │ Board Name:  Xircom Pocket Ethernet Adapter III                  │
 4 │                                                                  │
   │ The latest version of this driver will be installed with the same │
   │ options.                                                         │
 5 │                                                                  │
   │        Press <Enter> to continue.                                │
 6 │                                                                  │
   └──────────────────────────────────────────────────────────────────┘

Install will auto-detect your driver if one is loaded in memory. You will be
prompted for a driver disk.
Enter=Continue                                                    Alt-F10=Exit
```

The system knows what adapter I'm using in this machine (the Xircom) and what the driver name for that adapter is (PE3ODI). It discovered this as part of the initialization routine for the installation. As the screen says, the installation program is more than happy to keep that driver and use it with the new client software and NetWare DOS Requester.

A third thing may happen here as well. It could be that you don't have a driver, or you need a new driver for a changed network interface card. For some reason, you need to choose and configure a driver from scratch.

Assume I'm changing the Xircom card for an NE2000 card (now in a docking station, for instance). When asked for a driver, I choose to look for the long list of available drivers that come with the NetWare installation program. The Network Board window shown in Figure 5.7 pops open, and I'm free to scroll through all the drivers and make my choice.

FIGURE 5.7

Choosing a network adapter driver

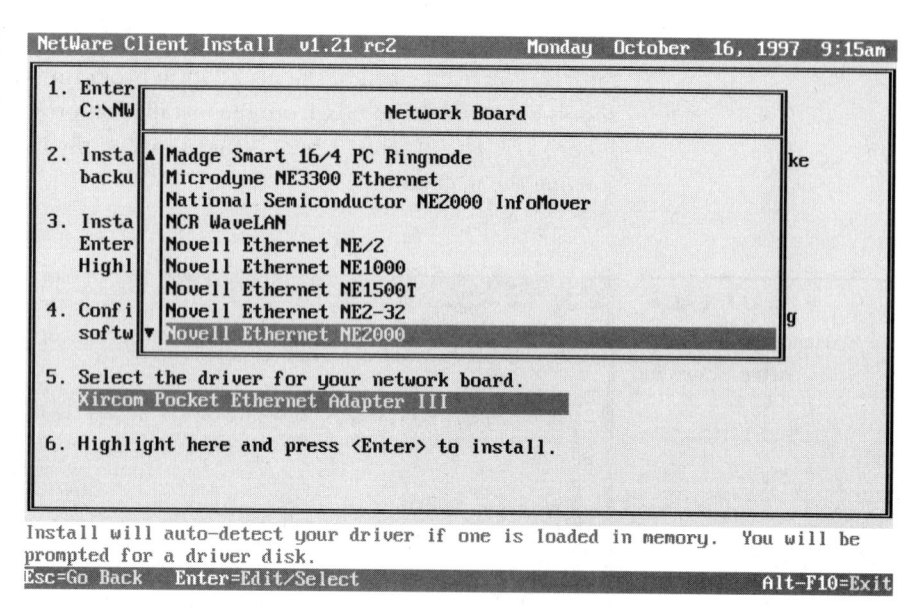

```
NetWare Client Install  v1.21 rc2           Monday  October  16, 1997  9:15am
1. Enter
   C:\NW ┌─────────────────────── Network Board ───────────────────────┐
2. Insta │▲ Madge Smart 16/4 PC Ringnode                              │ ke
   backu │  Microdyne NE3300 Ethernet                                  │
         │  National Semiconductor NE2000 InfoMover                    │
3. Insta │  NCR WaveLAN                                                │
   Enter │  Novell Ethernet NE/2                                       │
   Highl │  Novell Ethernet NE1000                                     │
         │  Novell Ethernet NE1500T                                    │
4. Confi │  Novell Ethernet NE2-32                                     │ g
   softw │▼ Novell Ethernet NE2000                                     │
         └─────────────────────────────────────────────────────────────┘
5. Select the driver for your network board.
   Xircom Pocket Ethernet Adapter III
6. Highlight here and press <Enter> to install.

Install will auto-detect your driver if one is loaded in memory.  You will be
prompted for a driver disk.
Esc=Go Back    Enter=Edit/Select                                Alt-F10=Exit
```

To find the driver you want, use one of these methods:

- Scroll with the up and down arrow keys.
- Use the Page Up and Page Down keys
- Type the first letter of the desired driver; the highlight bar will move to the first driver that begins with that letter.

As you saw in Table 5.1, there are plenty of drivers to choose from. If your network adapter doesn't have a driver listed with NetWare, you will be prompted to insert the disk from the manufacturer.

After choosing the specific board, you must configure that board. As we explained earlier this chapter, you may be asked to choose a base I/O port address, hardware interrupt, media frame type, and memory I/O address. See the box at the top of Figure 5.8 for the default settings for the NE2000 card chosen earlier.

Each field opens a double window that overlaps the current box. All the options for each setting are displayed, along with a small help message. Highlight your choice and press Enter, and the choice will be copied into the field in Figure 5.8.

FIGURE 5.8
Configuring the adapter

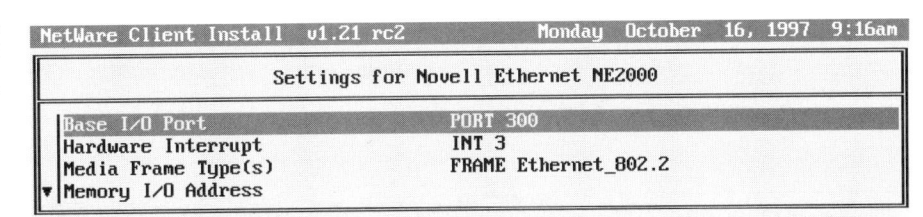

After you've chosen the adapter and configured the driver, all that's left is to copy the files to the workstation. You will be prompted to insert various diskettes at various times. A screen strongly reminiscent of the server installation program will chart your progress and give little hints and information. Figure 5.9 shows the beginning of the file-copy process.

FIGURE 5.9
Loading the client files to the workstation

As a courtesy, the installation program recaps much of the important information when the installation is complete. Figure 5.10 shows the final goodbye screen from the installation program.

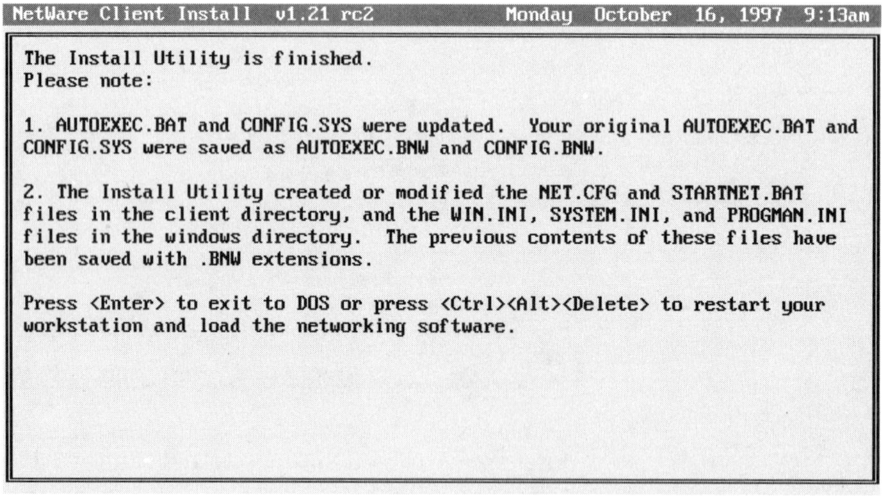

FIGURE 5.10

FYI about your client's installation

```
NetWare Client Install  v1.21 rc2           Monday  October  16, 1997  9:13am

The Install Utility is finished.
Please note:

1. AUTOEXEC.BAT and CONFIG.SYS were updated.  Your original AUTOEXEC.BAT and
CONFIG.SYS were saved as AUTOEXEC.BNW and CONFIG.BNW.

2. The Install Utility created or modified the NET.CFG and STARTNET.BAT
files in the client directory, and the WIN.INI, SYSTEM.INI, and PROGMAN.INI
files in the windows directory.  The previous contents of these files have
been saved with .BNW extensions.

Press <Enter> to exit to DOS or press <Ctrl><Alt><Delete> to restart your
workstation and load the networking software.
```

The final line doesn't say this strongly enough: You must reboot your computer before any of the new software is available to you. There were changes to AUTOEXEC.BAT and CONFIG.SYS, and those files are read only during the boot process. If there is nothing unusual about your configuration that requires modification of the NET.CFG file, you may now see what happens as you attach to the network for the first time.

Attaching to the Network for the First Time

Little in life feels as good as the first workstation connecting to the network. If things go well, Figure 5.11 shows what you should see when you reboot your newly configured PC.

The last line says which server has answered your login request. You are ready for business.

FIGURE 5.11

Rebooting a successfully installed client

```
[Novell DOS] c:\NWCLIENTSET NWLANGUAGE=ENGLISH
[Novell DOS] c:\NWCLIENTC:\NWCLENT\LSL.COM
NetWare Link Support Layer v2.11 (940817)
(c) Copyright 1990-1994 Novell, Inc. All Rights reserved

The configuration file used was "C:\NWCLIENT\NET.CFG."
Max Boards 4, Max Stacks 4

[Novell DOS} C:\NWCLIENTC:NWCLIENT\PE3ODI.COM
Xirom Pocket Ethernet Adapter III MLID V1.04 (930212)
(c) Copyright 1993 Xirom. All Rights reserved.

Pocket Ethernet Adapter III running inNon-Bidirectional mode

Int 7, Port 378, Node Address 80C72EED8F L
Max Frame 1514 bytes, Line Speed 10 Mbps
Board I, Frame ETHERNET_802.2, LSB Mode

[Novell DOS] C:\NWCLIENTC:\NWCLIENT\IPXODI.COM

NetWare IPX/SPX Protocol v3.00 (940901)
(C) Copyright 1990-1994 Novell, Inc. All Rights Reserved.

Bound to logical board I (PE3ODI): Protocol ID E0

[Novell DOS] C:\NWCLIENTC:\NWCLIENT\VLM.EXE
VLM.EXE-Netware virtual loadable module manager v1.20 (940831)
(C) Copyright 1994 Novell, Inc. All Rights Reserved.
Patent Pending

The VLM.EXE file is pre-initializing the VLMs.............
The VLM.EXE file is using extended memory (XMS).
You are attached to server GATEWAY20000
```

NET.CFG Means Client Network Configuration for DOS and Windows 3.x Clients

THE NET.CFG FILE is a small ASCII file, normally stored in the \NWCLIENT directory, in which you specify custom settings for the NetWare client software on that particular workstation. NET.CFG is workstation-centric; each PC workstation will have its own NET.CFG file, not a shared version somewhere on the network. This is somewhat similar to the AUTOEXEC.BAT file that configures each PC upon startup. NET.CFG configures the workstation-to-network interface.

You may not need to tinker with any NET.CFG file on your network. If you run only IPX/SPX on your network and use standard network interface cards, the installation program will set up everything a workstation needs. If your workstations fit this profile, feel free to skip on ahead (hey, it's your book).

If you do have a situation with multiple protocols on your network or multiple interface cards in a few workstations, or you need to keep workstation memory usage as low as possible, the NET.CFG program will become your friend.

Standard NET.CFG Options for Typical Clients

During DOS and Windows 3.1*x* client software installation, the installation program creates a default NET.CFG file and places it in either \NWCLIENT or the directory you specified to hold all client programs. The file looks similar to this:

```
Link Driver 3C5X9
    INT 10
    PORT 300
       FRAME Ethernet_802.3

NetWare DOS Requester
    FIRST NETWORK DRIVE = F
```

Let's take a quick look at the pieces. The Option lines (Link Driver and NetWare DOS Requester) are flush left, one per line. Each setting must be indented, and again, only one per line. Each line, including the last line, must have a hard return at the end. If you leave off the hard return on the last line, that setting or instruction will be ignored. I promise you will pull your hair trying to figure out what is wrong; I did.

There are many parameters with multiple settings inside NET.CFG, but most are not necessary under normal circumstances. Most parameters concern network interface card settings and NetWare DOS Requester options.

Rules for modifying NET.CFG are much like those for editing AUTOEXEC.BAT. You can add comments, beginning with a semicolon flush on the left margin. Imagine the NET.CFG listed previously after the switch from Ethernet 802.3 to Ethernet 802.2. It might look like this:

```
Link Driver 3C5X9
    INT 10
    PORT 300
```

```
          ;    FRAME Ethernet_802.3
               Frame Ethernet_802.2

     NetWare DOS Requester
     FIRST NETWORK DRIVE = F

     ; New frame type installed 10/16/95
     ; Kim W
```

This example shows a good form in client management: it leaves a record of what was changed, when it was changed, and who changed it. Obviously, not a real-world example.

Of the long list of NET.CFG parameters and settings, six are the most popular:

- EXCLUDE VLM=*path_vlm* specifies a .VLM file that VLM.EXE should not load. This parameter causes any VLM file listed in the VLM.EXE program default load table or in the VLM *vlm_path* parameter to not load when the VLM.EXE program runs. You must specify the complete file name, including the VLM extension. You must list this parameter after the NetWare Protocol section. For example, the following exclude printing support, security, and management diagnostics:

    ```
    EXCLUDE VLM=C:\NWCLIENT\PRINT.VLM
    EXCLUDE VLM=C:\NWCLIENT\SECURITY.VLM
    EXCLUDE VLM=C:\NWCLIENT\NMR.VLM
    ```

- FIRST NETWORK DRIVE=A–Z sets the first network drive to the letter of choice when the NetWare DOS Requester makes a connection to the NetWare server. This parameter accepts only the drive letter and not the colon. The default setting is the first available drive letter.

- NAME CONTEXT= "*name_context*" allows you to set your current position in the NDS tree structure. This parameter applies only to workstations connecting to a NetWare 4 network. The default is the root, which may cause confusion if duplicate user names exist. The quotation marks are required in this parameter setting. As example is:

    ```
    NAME CONTEXT="OU=INTEGRATE.O=GCS"
    ```

- PREFERRED SERVER=*any bindery server_name* sets the NetWare server you attach to first and helps guarantee your connection to the network. If the server specified has a connection available, the NetWare

DOS Requester attaches to that server. If this value and PREFERRED TREE are both used, the first protocol to make a solid attachment will be used. An example is:

```
PREFERRED SERVER=312_NW
```

- PREFERRED TREE=*any_tree_name* sets the tree you want to connect to first in a NetWare 4 network if you have multiple trees. If the tree specified has a server with a free connection, the NetWare DOS Requester attaches to that tree (obviously, this option is not necessary in a single-tree network). An example is:

```
PREFERRED TREE=MARKETING
```

- SHOW DOTS=[ON/OFF] sets whether or not the . and .. entries appear in directory listings. The NetWare server doesn't have directory entries for . and .. as DOS does. To see . and .. in directory listings, use SHOW DOTS ON. File manager utilities will be hindered if you can't move to a parent directory or subdirectory. The default setting is OFF. Setting SHOW DOTS=ON makes NetWare behave more like pure DOS for utilities and applications.

The "most popular" options vary per network, of course. If none of these look applicable, don't feel bad. If these don't cover your special circumstances, read the next section and see (almost) every option you have for the NET.CFG file.

Complete NET.CFG Parameters and Options

There are enough NET.CFG options and parameters to need their own manual. That's good when things are getting strange on you, because you have tools to use that can help. It's bad when you have to figure each area out before a good foundation has been built.

The following list shows the areas we're going to cover of the NET.CFG details. If there's something missing, check the table of contents. Desktop SNMP could be placed here, for instance, but I chose to put the information with other management topics (in Chapter 18). The areas we're looking at now are:

- NetWare DOS Requester option
- Link Driver option

- Link Support option
- Protocol IPX option
- NetBIOS parameters
- Named Pipes parameters
- Protocol ODINSUP option
- TBMI2 option

NetWare DOS Requester Option

The NetWare DOS Requester is the software modules that work together to control the DOS and MS Windows network connection. The bulk of the work falls on the VLM.EXE program, which manages all the VLMs.

The older NETX.EXE or NETX.COM programs have been replaced by the NetWare DOS Requester technology. The NETX.VLM module supplies the necessary NETX functions for software that expects the older NetWare shell.

This section of the NET.CFG program loads the VLM manager and related VLM files. The rest of the options under the NetWare DOS Requester heading in the NET.CFG file control communication between a workstation and the server and/or network.

Table 5.2 lists the current core modules in their default load order. Each of these modules is loaded by the VLM.EXE program. The table also includes descriptions and default values and indicates whether the module is required or optional for NetWare Directory Services (NDS), Bindery Services (BIND), or Personal NetWare (PNW) services.

TABLE 5.2 Core NetWare 4.1x VLMs

MODULE NAME	DESCRIPTION	NDS	BIND	PNW
BIND.VLM	NetWare protocol implementation using the bindery	Optional	Required	Optional
CONN.VLM	Connection table manager	Required	Required	Required
FIO.VLM	File Input/Output	Required	Required	Required
GENERAL.VLM	Miscellaneous functions for NETX.VLM and REDIR.VLM	Optional	Optional	Optional

TABLE 5.2 (cont.)
Core NetWare 4.1x VLMs

MODULE NAME	DESCRIPTION	NDS	BIND	PNW
IPXNCP.VLM	Transport protocol implementation using IPX	Required	Required	Required
NETX.VLM	NetWare shell compatibility	Optional	Optional	Optional
NDS.VLM	NetWare protocol implementation using Directory Services	Required	Optional	Optional
NWP.VLM	NetWare protocol multiplexor	Required	Required	Required
PNW.VLM	NetWare protocol implementation using Personal NetWare	Optional	Optional	Required
PRINT.VLM	Printer Redirector	Optional	Optional	Optional
REDIR.VLM	DOS Redirector	Required	Required	Required
SECURITY.VLM	NetWare enhanced security	Optional	Optional	Optional
TRAN.VLM	Transport protocol multiplexor	Required	Required	Required

Table 5.3 lists the current "non-core" VLMs. Non-core VLMs will not load automatically by default. These non-core VLMs are used by NDS, BIND, and PNW, but are not mandatory for any of the three. Use the VLM *path_vlm* parameter to load any non-core VLMs.

TABLE 5.3
Non-core NetWare 4.1x VLMs

MODULE NAME	DESCRIPTION
AUTO.VLM	Auto-reconnect/auto-retry
MIB2IF.VLM	MIB-II interface groups support
MIB2PROT.VLM	MIB-II support for the TCP/IP groups
NMR.VLM	NetWare management responder
RSA.VLM	RSA encryption for NDS authentication

TABLE 5.3 (cont.) Non-core NetWare 4.1x VLMs

MODULE NAME	DESCRIPTION
WSASN1.VLM	SNMP ASN.1 translation
WSREG.VLM	SNMP MIB registration
WSSNMP.VLM	Desktop SNMP module, which includes support for MIB-II System and SNMP groups
WSTRAP.VLM	SNMP trap

NetWare DOS Requester Parameters and Settings

Each of the parameters and settings in the NetWare DOS Requester section is optional. They are available to help fine-tune the performance and memory consumption of a particular workstation. They must all be indented under the NetWare DOS Requester heading in the NET.CFG file, as in:

```
NetWare DOS Requester
    BIND RECONNECT=ON
```

Many of these settings will not apply to your network. For instance, all the parameters that work with the PNW.VLM module pertain only to Personal NetWare. While this is an excellent product, if you are not using it, these settings will not be needed in your network. Table 5.4 lists the options.

TABLE 5.4 NetWare DOS Requester Parameters and Settings

OPTION	DESCRIPTION	VLMS APPLIES TO
AUTO LARGE TABLE	When set to ON, allocates a connection table of 178 bytes (instead of 34 bytes) per connection for bindery reconnects. Change the default setting of OFF to ON if the length of your user name and password is more than 16 characters.	AUTO.VLM, BIND.VLM
AUTO RECONNECT	When set to ON (the default), reconnects a workstation to a NetWare server and rebuilds the workstation's environment (excluding file-specific items) prior to connection loss. When this option is set to OFF, the AUTO.VLM load fails at preinitialization time.	AUTO.VLM, NDS.VLM, PNW.VLM

TABLE 5.4 (cont.)

NetWare DOS Requester Parameters and Settings

OPTION	DESCRIPTION	VLMS APPLIES TO
AUTO RETRY	Sets the number of seconds AUTO.VLM waits before attempting a retry after receiving a network critical error. The range is 0 to 3640; the default is 0.	AUTO.VLM, NDS.VLM, BIND.VLM, PNW.VLM
AVERAGE NAME LENGTH	Allows the NetWare DOS Requester to set aside space for a table of NetWare server names based on this setting and the value for CONNECTIONS. The range is 2 to 48; the default is 48. Save some memory by setting this number toward the low end if your servers have short names.	CONN.VLM
BIND RECONNECT	When set to ON, automatically rebuilds bindery connections and restores drive mappings and printer connections. The default is OFF.	AUTO.VLM, BIND.VLM
BROADCAST RETRIES	Sets the number of times the NetWare DOS Requester broadcasts a request. The range is 1 to 255; the default is 3.	PNW.VLM
BROADCAST SEND DELAY	Sets the number of ticks the NetWare DOS Requester delays between performing any function. The range is 0 to 255; the default is 0.	PNW.VLM
BROADCAST TIMEOUT	Sets the number of ticks the NetWare DOS Requester takes between broadcast retries. The range is 1 to 255; the default is 2.	PNW.VLM
CACHE BUFFERS	Sets the number of cache buffers the NetWare DOS Requester uses for local caching of nonshared, not transactionally tracked files. Each buffer allocated allows one file to be cached. Increasing the number of cache buffers speeds up the process of sequential reads/writes but also increases memory use. The range is 0 to 64; the default is 5.	FIO.VLM

TABLE 5.4 (cont.)
NetWare DOS Requester Parameters and Settings

OPTION	DESCRIPTION	VLMS APPLIES TO
CACHE BUFFER SIZE	Sets the buffer size (in bytes) for the cache buffers that the FIO module uses. Increasing the value of the parameter setting allows you to cache larger amounts of data, thereby increasing performance and also memory use. Do not set this higher than the maximum for your media type. The range is 64 to 4096 bytes; the default is the media maximum minus 64 bytes (e.g., Ethernet: 1500-64=1436). See the documentation for the cache buffer size for your media type.	FIO.VLM
CACHE WRITES	Sets the cache write requests to ON or OFF. Setting the value to OFF increases data integrity but decreases performance. Leaving the value set to ON (the default) can cause data loss if the NetWare server runs out of disk space between write requests.	FIO.VLM
CHECKSUM	Provides a higher level of data integrity by validating NCP packets. The settings are 0 (disabled), 1 (enabled but not preferred), 2 (enabled and preferred), and 3 (required). The default is 1. Setting the value to 2 or 3 increases data integrity but decreases performance. Note that Ethernet 802.3 frames do not support CHECKSUM.	IPXNCP.VLM, NWP.VLM
CONNECTIONS	Sets the maximum number of connections the NetWare DOS Requester supports. The range is from 2 to 50; the default is 8 (same as NetWare 3.x). Larger values than needed use memory to no advantage.	CONN.VLM, FIO.VLM
DOS NAME	Sets the name of the operating system used in the shell. The %OS variable in the login script uses this variable when mapping a search drive to the network DOS directory. The value for this parameter setting uses a maximum of five characters. The default is DOS NAME=MSDOS.	NETX.VLM, GENERAL.VLM

TABLE 5.4 (cont.)
NetWare DOS Requester Parameters and Settings

OPTION	DESCRIPTION	VLMS APPLIES TO
EOJ	When set to ON, tells the workstation not to send the server any end of job commands for closing files.	NETX.VLM, REDIR.VLM
EXCLUDE VLM	Specifies a .VLM file that VLM.EXE should not load. You must specify the complete file name, including the VLM extension. You must list this parameter after the NetWare Protocol section. See the section "Standard NET.CFG Options for Typical Clients" earlier in this chapter for examples.	VLM.EXE
FIRST NETWORK DRIVE	Sets the first network drive to the letter of choice (A to Z) when the NetWare DOS Requester makes a connection to the NetWare server. Use the drive letter without a colon. The default is the first available drive letter.	GENERAL.VLM
FORCE FIRST NETWORK DRIVE	When set to ON, specifies that the first network drive letter should be the same before and after you log out.	GENERAL.VLM
HANDLE NET ERRORS	Determines the default method for handling network errors. A network error is generated when the workstation doesn't receive a response from the NetWare server. The two values are ON (interrupt 24 handles network errors) or OFF (return NET_RECV_ERROR; for example, 8805h). The default is ON.	IPXNCP.VLM
LARGE INTERNET PACKETS	In the past, NetWare communicated across routers and bridges with a 576-byte maximum packet size to support the small 512-byte ARCnet packet size. However, Ethernet and Token Ring are capable of using larger packets. The settings are ON or OFF. When ON (the default), the maximum packet size negotiated between the NetWare server and the workstation is used, even across routers and bridges. Older routers and bridges may be hard-coded to the smaller size, however.	IPXNCP.VLM

TABLE 5.4 (cont.)
NetWare DOS Requester Parameters and Settings

OPTION	DESCRIPTION	VLMS APPLIES TO
LIP START SIZE	Specifies the packet size used by the NetWare DOS Requester when LIP negotiations are initiated. The default is 0 for off. The range is 576 to 655,535.	IPXNCP.VLM
LOAD CONN TABLE LOW	The initial release of NetWare 4.0 utilities required this parameter to be ON. This increased conventional memory requirements. If you are not using an initial release of the NetWare 4.0 utilities, the default setting (OFF) will give you better memory performance. The default setting loads the connection table in an upper memory block (UMB), if available.	CONN.VLM
LOAD LOW CONN	By default, this option is ON, and the connection manager, CONN.VLM, is loaded in conventional memory. If this parameter is set to OFF, CONN.VLM loads in upper memory, saving conventional memory but sacrificing performance.	CONN.VLM
LOAD LOW IPXNCP	By default, this option is ON, and the transport protocol implementation for IPX, IPXNCP.VLM, is loaded in conventional memory. If this parameter is set to OFF, IPXNCP.VLM loads in upper memory, saving conventional memory but sacrificing performance.	IPXNCP.VLM
LOCAL PRINTERS	Overrides the number of local printers on the workstation, which is normally determined by the BIOS and limited to 3. The range of this parameter is 0 to 9. The default is 3. By setting it to 0, you can prevent your workstation from hanging when you press Shift+Print Screen without any port capture or local printer connection.	PRINT.VLM
LOAD LOW REDIR	Specifies whether the Redirector is loaded into high memory. When set to ON, the Redirector is loaded into conventional (low) memory.	REDIR.VLM

TABLE 5.4 (cont.)

NetWare DOS Requester Parameters and Settings

OPTION	DESCRIPTION	VLMS APPLIES TO
LOCK DELAY	Determines the amount of time (in ticks) the NetWare DOS Requester software waits before trying to get a lock.	GENERAL.VLM
LOCK RETRIES	Specifies the number of times the NetWare DOS Requester attempts to get a lock on the network.	GENERAL.VLM
LONG MACHINE TYPE	Tells the NetWare DOS Requester software what type of machine is being used each time the %MACHINE variable is accessed. Use this parameter and setting to set the machine's search path to the correct version of DOS. You can set up to six characters. The default is IBM-PC.	NETX.VLM, GENERAL.VLM
MAX TASKS	Configures the maximum number of tasks that can be active at one time. Certain multitasking applications, such as MS Windows and DESQview, allow several programs to run concurrently. If you have problems running a new program, increase the value of this parameter. The range is 20 to 128; the default is 31.	CONN.VLM
MESSAGE LEVEL	Sets how you want to display load-time messages. Each message level implies the previous level's message (e.g., 1 implies 0). The values are 0 (always display copyright message and critical errors), 1 (display warning messages), 2 (display program load information for VLMs), 3 (display configuration information), and 4 (display diagnostic information). The default setting is 1.	NWP.VLM

	OPTION	DESCRIPTION	VLMS APPLIES TO
TABLE 5.4 (cont.) NetWare DOS Requester Parameters and Settings	MESSAGE TIMEOUT	Defines timeout in ticks (approximately on 1/8 second) before broadcast messages are cleared from the screen without user intervention. Handy if your workstation gets interrupted by messages and stops processing. However, there is no log of messages on the system, so you can't go back later and check for what you missed. The range is 0 to 10,000 (about 6 hours). The default is 0 (wait for user to clear message).	NWP.VLM
	MINIMUM TIME TO NET	Overrides the time-to-net value defined by the local router during connection time. The value is set in milliseconds (1000 = 1 second). This is used for bridged WAN/satellite links with time-to-net values set too low for workstations to make a connection under the following conditions: the server on the other side of the link is a NetWare 3.x or earlier not running Packet Burst or the transfer rate for the link is 2400 baud or less.	VLM.EXE
	NAME CONTEXT	Allows you to set your current position in the NDS tree structure. This applies only to workstations connecting to a NetWare 4 network. The default is the root, which may cause confusion if duplicate user names exist. You must use quotation marks around the context, as in "ou=integrate.o=gcs".	NDS.VLM
	NETWARE PROTOCOL	Allows you to list the order in which the NetWare protocols are used. The default is the order NDS, BIND, PNW. You can give priority to a specific protocol for login, load order, or other functions performed by the NetWare DOS Requester. Each protocol is separated by a comma or a space in the list, as in NETWARE PROTOCOL=PNW NDS BIND. If you use this, it must be the first parameter after the NetWare DOS Requester heading.	VLM.EXE

TABLE 5.4 (cont.)
NetWare DOS Requester Parameters and Settings

OPTION	DESCRIPTION	VLMS APPLIES TO
NETWORK PRINTERS	Sets the number of LPT ports the NetWare DOS Requester can capture, allowing you to capture and redirect LPT1 through LPT9. The range is 0 to 9; the default is 3. Increasing the number increases memory use. Setting the value for this parameter to 0 specifies that PRINT.VLM does not load.	PRINT.VLM
PB BUFFERS	Controls the use of the Packet Burst Protocol for file input/output. Packet Burst is automatically enabled in the NetWare DOS Requester. The values are from 0 to 10. A setting of 0 is off, and nonzero is on. The default is 3. Setting this to 0 decreases workstation memory use and, in some cases, decreases performance.	FIO.VLM
PBURST READ WINDOWS SIZE	Sets the read buffer size for MS Windows. The range is 2 to 64; the default is 10.	FIO.VLM
PBURST WRITE WINDOWS SIZE	Sets the write buffer size (in bytes) for MS Windows. The range is 2 to 64; the default is 16.	FIO.VLM
PREFERRED SERVER	Sets the NetWare server you attach to first and helps guarantee your connection to the network. If the server specified has a connection available, the NetWare DOS Requester attaches to that server. If this value and PREFERRED TREE are both used, the first protocol to make a solid attachment will be used. See the "Standard NET.CFG Options for Typical Clients" section, earlier in this chapter, for an example.	BIND.VLM
PREFERRED TREE	Sets the tree you want to connect to first in a NetWare 4 network if you have multiple trees. If the tree specified has a server with a free connection, the NetWare DOS Requester attaches to that tree. See the "Standard NET.CFG Options for Typical Clients" earlier in this chapter for an example.	NDS.VLM

TABLE 5.4 (cont.)
NetWare DOS Requester Parameters and Settings

OPTION	DESCRIPTION	VLMS APPLIES TO
PREFERRED WORKGROUP	Sets the Personal NetWare workgroup you attach to first and helps guarantee your connection to the network. If the workgroup specified has a connection available, the NetWare DOS Requester attaches to that workgroup. For example, you could specify PREFERRED WORKGROUP=MKT_9.	PNW.VLM
PRINT BUFFER SIZE	Determines the size (in bytes) for the print buffer. The print buffer acts as a cache for 1-byte print requests, which increases the size of some jobs. The range is 0 to 256; the default is 64.	PRINT.VLM
PRINT HEADER	Sets the size of the buffer (in bytes) that holds the information used to initialize a printer for each print job. If you send print jobs with many instructions in the header (such as initializing a printer for an emulated mode or changing defaults, font selections, page length, or orientation) and the printer is not delivering all the requested attributes, increase the size of the print header. The range is 0 to 1024; the default is 64.	PRINT.VLM
PRINT TAIL	Sets the size of the buffer that holds the information used to reset the printer after a print job. If your printer is not clearing out the buffer completely or resetting after each print job, increase the print tail size. The range is 0 to 1024; the default is 16 bytes.	PRINT.VLM

TABLE 5.4 (cont.)

NetWare DOS Requester Parameters and Settings

OPTION	DESCRIPTION	VLMS APPLIES TO
READ ONLY COMPATIBILITY	Determines whether a file marked read-only can be opened with a read/write access call. Certain applications require the value for this parameter to be set to ON, which is the default. Prior to NetWare 2.1, a program could open a read-only file with write access without getting an error, although any attempt to write to the file produced an error. To be compatible with DOS, NetWare 2.1 and later does not allow a read-only file to be opened for write access. Setting this ON causes the shell to revert to the old mode and allow the request to open the file to succeed.	REDIR.VLM
RESPONDER	Controls communication and response of the workstation. Helps in reducing the footprint of the NetWare DOS Requester on the workstation. The default setting is ON. The OFF setting will cause the workstation to ignore broadcasts and diagnostic communication.	PNW.VLM
SEARCH MODE	Alters the NetWare DOS Requester's method for finding a file if it is not in the current directory. The values for this parameter are 0 to 7; the default is 1. See the section "Using Search Mode with the DOS Requester" for details.	GENERAL.VLM
SET STATION TIME	Synchronizes the workstation date and time with that of the NetWare server that the workstation initially attaches to. The default setting is ON. Setting this option to OFF disables the synchronization feature.	VLM.EXE
SHOW DOTS	When set to ON (the default is OFF), shows . and .. in directory listings. See the "Standard NET.CFG Options for Typical Clients" section, earlier in this chapter, for details.	REDIR.VLM

TABLE 5.4 (cont.) NetWare DOS Requester Parameters and Settings	OPTION	DESCRIPTION	VLMS APPLIES TO
	SHORT MACHINE TYPE	Similar to LONG MACHINE TYPE, except that it is used specifically with overlay files. Use it when the %SMACHINE variable is accessed. Examples of files using this parameter include the IBM$RUN.OVL file for the windowing utilities and the CMPQ$RUN.OVL file that uses a default black-and-white color palette for NetWare menus. The maximum characters allowed in the name is four. The default is IBM.	NETX.VLM, GENERAL.VLM
	SIGNATURE LEVEL	Designates the level of enhanced security support. Enhanced security includes the use of a message digest algorithm and a per connection/ per request session state. The values are as follows: 0 (disabled; the SECURITY.VLM file will not load), 1 (enabled but not preferred), 2 (preferred), and 3 (required). The default is 1. Setting this option to 2 or 3 increases security but decreases performance.	NWP.VLM, SECURITY.VLM
	TRUE COMMIT	Selects whether the commit NCP is sent on DOS commit requests. The default is OFF, which opts for performance over integrity. Set this option to ON, which opts for integrity over performance, when processing critical data to guarantee data integrity. For example, use it with database applications.	FIO.VLM
	USE DEFAULTS	When set to OFF, overrides the default VLM files that the VLM.EXE program loads. The default is ON. See the section "Overriding the Default VLMs" for details.	VLM.EXE

TABLE 5.4 (cont.)
NetWare DOS Requester Parameters and Settings

OPTION	DESCRIPTION	VLMS APPLIES TO
VLM	Specifies a VLM file that VLM.EXE should load. This allows VLMs not listed in the default load table for the VLM.EXE program to be added to the table. You must specify the complete file name, including the .VLM extension. The maximum number of files you can add is 50. The following VLM files are not listed in the default load table: AUTO.VLM, NMR.VLM, and RSA.VLM. For example, to load AUTO.VLM, use VLM=C:\NWCLIENT\AUTO.VLM.	VLM.EXE
WORKGROUP NET	Provides a way for your workstation to find workgroup information outside your local network. If your workstation resides physically on a network segment other than the workgroup you want to connect to, this address setting (for example, WORKGROUP NET= 00123099:FFFFFFFFFFFF) will ensure that a connection is found. Note that this parameter should be modified only by the Personal NetWare utilities; it should not be edited manually.	PNW.VLM

USING SEARCH MODE WITH THE DOS REQUESTER By setting the SEARCH MODE parameter in the NET.CFG file, you can specify how the NetWare DOS Requester searches for a file that isn't in the current directory. In previous NetWare client software versions, search mode functioned only if the default drive was a network drive. The NetWare DOS Requester is global and affects all .EXE and .COM files, regardless of the current drive. Select the search mode that works correctly with most of your .EXE and .COM files.

Valid search mode values are as follows:

0   No search instructions. This is the default setting for executable files.

1   If a directory path is specified in the executable file, the executable file searches only that path. If a path is not specified, the executable file searches the default directory and network search drives.

2   The executable file searches only the default directory or the path specified.

3   If a directory path is specified in the executable file, the executable file searches only that path. If a path is not specified and the executable file opens data files flagged read-only, the executable file searches the default directory and search drives.

4   Reserved.

5   The executable file searches the default directory and NetWare search drives whether or not the path is specified in the executable file. If a search mode is set, the shell allows searches for any files with .xxx extension; otherwise, DOS searches only for .EXE, .COM, and .BAT files.

6   Reserved.

7   If the executable file opens data files flagged read-only, the executable file searches the default directory and search drives whether or not the path is specified in the executable file.

For example, the setting:

    SEARCH MODE=2

has the executable file search just the default directory or specified path.

OVERRIDING THE DEFAULT VLMS When set to ON, the USE DEFAULTS parameter in the NET.CFG file has the VLM.EXE attempt to load the following files:

- CONN.VLM
- IPXNCP.VLM
- TRAN.VLM
- SECURITY.VLM
- NDS.VLM
- BIND.VLM
- NWP.VLM
- FIO.VLM
- GENERAL.VLM
- REDIR.VLM

- PRINT.VLM
- NETX.VLM

When you set this parameter to OFF, it overrides the default VLM files that the VLM.EXE program loads. If you specify VLMs that are normally loaded by default in the NET.CFG file and don't set:

```
USE DEFAULTS=OFF
```

any default VLMs you specify will attempt to load twice, producing an error when the VLM files are loading.

With USE DEFAULT set to OFF, each VLM must be loaded specifically.

> **NOTE**
> *The EXCLUDE VLM parameter is a much better way to perform the function that was only available with the USE DEFAULTS parameter in NetWare 4.0.*

An example is:

```
USE DEFAULTS=OFF
CONN.VLM
IPXNCP.VLM
TRAN.VLM
SECURITY.VLM
NDS.VLM
;BIND.VLM
NWP.VLM
FIO.VLM
GENERAL.VLM
REDIR.VLM
PRINT.VLM
NETX.VLM
AUTO.VLM
```

Notice the semicolon before BIND.VLM, which makes that line a comment, so that the BIND.VLM module is not loaded.

Link Driver Options

The Link Driver section provides specific details to control the network interface card. Rarely do you need to get to this level of detail, but this shows that almost every aspect of the hardware interaction can be modified. Table 5.5 lists the Link Driver options.

TABLE 5.5 Link Driver Options

OPTION	PURPOSE	EXAMPLE*
ACCM [remote_host_address]	Specifies whether the PPP protocol should use the asynchronous control character map.	LINK DRIVER SLIP_PPP ACCM 000A0000
ACCOMP [YES/ NO]	Instructs the PPP protocol to compress the address and control field of the PPP header.	LINK DRIVER SLIP_PPP ACCOMP YES
ALTERNATE	Specifies an alternate board for the LANSUP.COM driver.	LINK DRIVER LANSUP ALTERNATE
AUTHEN PAP username password	Specifies whether the PPP protocol should use authentication. The PAP (Password Authentication Protocol) uses the user name and password to identify the local system to the remote peer host.	LINK DRIVER SLIP_PPP AUTHEN PAP MASMITH RMT1234
BAUD baud_rate	Sets the baud rate for PPP to use. Options are 300, 1200, 2400, 4800, 9600, 14400, 19200, and 38400.	LINK DRIVER SLIP_PPP BAUD 19200
COUNTER [protocol] timeout max_config max_term max_nak	Specifies a timeout value and three retry counters for the PPP protocol. All values are in decimal. The protocol can be LCP (Link Control Protocol), IPCP (Internet Protocol Control Protocol), or PAP. *Timeout* restarts timer timeout in seconds, *max_config* retries counter for configuration request, *max_term* retries counter for terminate-request, and *max_nak* retries counter for configuration-NAK.	LINK DRIVER SLIP_PPP COUNTER PAP 5 10 5 10

*The options must be on a single line, indented under the LINK DRIVER line. Ignore any word wrap shown in the table.

TABLE 5.5 (cont.) Link Driver Options

OPTION	PURPOSE	EXAMPLE*
DIAL *phone_number*	Specifies the phone number for the SLIP_PPP driver to dial when it's loaded. Use only when DIRECT is set to NO. The parameter accepts up to 30 modem modifier characters from the set of 0–9, *,#,A,B,C,D,-,(,),,,,P,T.	LINK DRIVER SLIP_PPP DIRECT NO DIAL (801) 555-1234
DIRECT [NO/YES]	Sets your SLIP or PPP as direct or not. Use NO if using DIAL or LISTEN.	LINK DRIVER SLIP_PPP DIRECT NO
DMA [#1/#2] *channel_number*	Allows the DMA channel to be configured for the workstation. Up to two DMA channels are supported.	LINK DRIVER NE2000 DMA=#1 3 DMA=#2 4
FRAME *frame_type*	Specifies the frame type used by the network adapter. You can support several frame types, or override the default frame type setting. Up to four frame types are supported for one Ethernet physical network (either four adapters with one frame type each or one adapter with four frame types). Token Ring networks support one or two frame types only.	LINK DRIVER NE2000 FRAME ETHERNET_802.2 FRAME ETHERNET_802.3
IRQ [#1/#2] *interrupt_request_number*	Specifies the IRQ for the adapter. If your network adapter supports more than one interrupt, you may enter two values, but this is rarely done.	LINK DRIVER NE2100 IRQ=#1 10
IPADDR [*remote_host_address*]	Specifies the IP addresses for PPP negotiation (in dotted-decimal notation).	LINK DRIVER SLIP_PPP IPADDR 199.1.11.2

*The options must be on a single line, indented under the LINK DRIVER line. Ignore any word wrap shown in the table.

TABLE 5.5 (cont.) Link Driver Options	OPTION	PURPOSE	EXAMPLE*
	LINK STATIONS *number*	Specifies the number of link stations needed for the LANSUP driver, to support the IBM LAN Support program.	LINK DRIVER NE2100 LINK STATIONS=5
	LISTEN	Signifies the passive end of a modem connection for the SLIP or PPP protocol. This parameter is used only when DIRECT is set to NO.	LINK DRIVER SLIP_PPP DIRECT NO LISTEN
	MAGIC *number*	Four-byte hexadecimal number that provides a way to catch data link anomalies.	LINK DRIVER SLIP_PPP MAGIC 1243FFFF
	MAX FRAME SIZE *number*	Sets the maximum number of bytes that can be put on the network by a LAN driver. If the line speed is 16 Mbps, the value for *number* must be between 632 and 17,960. If the line speed is 4 Mbps, the value must be between 632 and 4464. This parameter cannot be used with TASKID or TBMI2.COM.	LINK DRIVER NTR2000 MAX FRAME SIZE=2168
	MEM [#1/#2] *hex_starting_address* [*hex_length*]	Specifies a memory range to be used by the network board. Use the absolute address of the memory setting on the network adapter and the number of hexadecimal paragraphs taken by that board. *Hex_ length* defaults to 16 bytes and is rarely necessary.	LINK DRIVER EXOS MEM=D0000 400

*The options must be on a single line, indented under the LINK DRIVER line. Ignore any word wrap shown in the table.

TABLE 5.5 (cont.) Link Driver Options

OPTION	PURPOSE	EXAMPLE*
MRU *number* [M]	Specifies the maximum receive and transmit units (MRU) for the SLIP or PPP protocol. The optional parameter M instructs the SLIP_PPP driver to assume the worst-case scenario for character mapping, where every data byte in a packet is mapped into two bytes as required by the ACCM configuration.	LINK DRIVER SLIP_PPP MRU 960
NODE ADDRESS *hex_address*	Overrides any hard-coded node address in the network board, if the hardware allows it. Changing the node address on a board can create conflicts with other network boards. Don't do this unless absolutely necessary and you're prepared to track every network node ID to avoid duplications.	LINK DRIVER NE2100 NODE ADDRESS=12D34
OPEN *mode*	Specifies the active or passive open mode for the PPP protocols LCP or IPCP.	LINK DRIVER SLIP_PPP OPEN PASSIVE
PCOMP [YES/NO]	Instructs the PPP protocol to compress the protocol field of the PPP header.	LINK DRIVER SLIP_PPP PCOMP YES
PORT [#1/#2] *hex_starting_address* [*hex_number_of_ports*]	Specifies the starting port (*hex_starting_address*) and number of ports in the range (*hex_number_of_ports*). All values must be in hexadecimal.	LINK DRIVER NE2100 PORT #1 300 16
PROTOCOL *name* *hex_protocol_ID* *frame_type*	Allows existing LAN drivers to handle new network protocols. The example shows the option to use a new protocol XYZ with an NE2-32 network board.	LINK DRIVER NE2_32 FRAME=ETHERNET_SNAP PROTOCOL=XYZ 904A ETHERNET_SNAP

*The options must be on a single line, indented under the LINK DRIVER line. Ignore any word wrap shown in the table.

TABLE 5.5 (cont.) Link Driver Options	OPTION	PURPOSE	EXAMPLE*
	SAPS *number*	Specifies the number of Service Access Points (SAPs) needed for the LANSUP driver. Used with the IBM LAN Support Program.	LINK DRIVER NTR2000 SAPS=5
	SLOT *number*	Directs the driver to locate the board in the specified slot, instead of scanning for it. If you use more than one network adapter, you must specify each adapter after the LSL command in the batch file starting your client software, even if the boards are the same type (LSL NE2 NE2).	LINK DRIVER NE2 SLOT=1 LINK DRIVER NE2 SLOT=2
	TCPIPCOMP [VJ/NO] *slots comp_slot*	Enables Van Jacobson (VJ) header compression for the SLIP or PPP protocols.	LINK DRIVER SLIP_PPP TCPIPCOMP VJ 16 1

*The options must be on a single line, indented under the LINK DRIVER line. Ignore any word wrap shown in the table.

Link Support Options

The Link Support section of the NET.CFG file can be used to configure the number and size of the receive buffers, the size of the memory pool buffers, and the number of boards and stacks used by the LSL. You can also use this option to configure the LSL environment for managing Named Pipes and NetBIOS sessions.

The parameter:

```
BUFFERS number_of_buffers[buffer_size]
```

configures the number and size of receive buffers that the LSL will maintain. For example:

```
LINK SUPPORT
    BUFFERS=15 2800
```

sets fifteen, 2800-byte buffers.

The number of communication buffers must be large enough to hold all media headers and the maximum data size. If you make many connections, you should increase the number of buffers to improve performance. See the manufacturer's specifications for the settings available for third-party protocol stacks.

Buffer size is optional. The minimum size for IPX is 618 bytes. The buffer number multiplied by the buffer size (plus the header information) cannot be greater than 65,536 bytes. For example, 20 buffers multiplied by 1514 bytes equals 30,280 bytes.

The other Link Support option parameter is:

```
MEMPOOL number
```

Some protocols use this option to configure the size of the memory pool buffers that the LSL program will maintain. For example:

```
LINK SUPPORT
    MEMPOOL=1024
```

sets memory pool buffers at 1024 bytes.

Protocol IPX Options

Use the Protocol IPX options of the NET.CFG file to change the default value of the parameter settings for the IPX protocol. For example, usually a protocol binds to the first network board it finds. The BIND parameter forces the protocol to bind to the boards you specify. The parameter:

```
PROTOCOL IPX
    BIND=NE2000
```

binds to one NE2000 board.

The parameter:

```
PROTOCOL IPX
    BIND=NE2000 #2, #3
```

binds to boards 2 and 3. Board numbers are displayed when you load the network board drivers. Note that the equal sign is optional; you could enter the command as just BIND NE2000.

Table 5.6 lists the Protocol IPX parameters.

TABLE 5.6 Protocol IPX Parameters

OPTION	PURPOSE	EXAMPLE*
BIND *board_name* [*#number*]	Forces the protocol to bind to the boards you specify.	PROTOCOL IPX BIND=NE2000
INT64 [ON/OFF]	Allows applications to use interrupt 64h to access IPX services. IPX now uses interrupt 64h to maintain compatibility with earlier versions of NetWare. If an application's documentation requests interrupt 64h, or if you have an application that works on earlier versions of NetWare but hangs on NetWare 4.10, set the value for this parameter to OFF. The default is ON.	PROTOCOL IPX INT64=OFF
NT7A [ON/OFF]	Allows applications to use interrupt 7Ah to access IPX services. IPX now uses interrupt 7Ah to maintain compatibility with NetWare 2.0a. If an application's documentation requests interrupt 7Ah, or if an application works on earlier versions of NetWare but hangs on NetWare 4.10, set the value for this parameter to OFF. The default is ON.	PROTOCOL IPX INT7A=OFF
IPATCH *byte_offset, value*	Allows any address in the IPX.COM file to be patched with any specified byte_offset value. This is not a casual utility; use it only when absolutely sure of the requirements and your expected result.	PROTOCOL IPX IPATCH=XXX

*The options must be on a single line, indented under the PROTOCOL IPX line. Ignore any word wrap shown in the table.

TABLE 5.6 (cont.) Protocol IPX Parameters

OPTION	PURPOSE	EXAMPLE*
IPX PACKET SIZE LIMIT	Reduces the maximum packet size set by each network board driver. Even though a network board driver could send 16 KB packets on the wire, the wasted memory for most operations may be unacceptable. The optimum packet size for Token Ring drivers is 4160 bytes. For Ethernet, the optimum is 1500 bytes. Reduce the maximum packet size if you receive out-of-memory errors at the workstation. This is a new feature, and not all drivers support it. The range for the setting is 576 to 6500. The default is the lesser of either 4160 or the size specified by the LAN driver.	PROTOCOL IPX IPX PACKET SIZE LIMIT=1500
IPX RETRY COUNT *number*	Sets the number of times the workstation resends a packet. On networks that lose many packets, this retry count may need to be increased. IPX does not actually resend a packet. It uses this count to recommend the number of retries to the DOS shell and SPX. Increasing this number causes a longer delay for some network functions, such as establishing a NetBIOS session or registering a NetBIOS name. The default is 20.	PROTOCOL IPX IPX RETRY COUNT=30
IPX SOCKETS *number*	Specifies the maximum number of sockets that IPX can have open at the workstation. Some IPX-specific programs, such as management tools, may require more than the default number of sockets. The default is 20.	PROTOCOL IPX IPX SOCKETS =30

*The options must be on a single line, indented under the PROTOCOL IPX line. Ignore any word wrap shown in the table.

NetBIOS Parameters

NetBIOS is often mistakenly called a protocol. It is technically an application interface for network software. NetBIOS was popularized by IBM with its Token Ring cards introduced in 1984. It was supposed to take the network world by storm and swamp NetWare.

Unfortunately, NetBIOS is not routable, and this caused many problems early on. Since vendors created applications for NetBIOS at the urging of IBM and Microsoft, NetWare supported NetBIOS from the early releases.

That legacy support is still working here in NetWare 4.1*x*. Novell's NetBIOS program provides support for the new and existing NetBIOS applications through NET.CFG parameters. The NetBIOS parameters listed in Table 5.7 go under the Link Support heading in NET.CFG.

> **NOTE:** *The NetBIOS parameters should not be indented. They need to be flush with the left margin.*

TABLE 5.7 NetBIOS Parameters

OPTION	PURPOSE	EXAMPLE*
NETBIOS ABORT TIMEOUT *number*	Use this parameter to adjust the amount of time (in ticks) that NetBIOS waits without receiving any response from the other side of a session before it terminates the session. Increase this value if there are NetBIOS nodes across asynchronous lines or large internetworks. The default is 540 (approximately 30 seconds).	NETBIOS ABORT TIMEOUT=13500
NETBIOS BROADCAST COUNT *number*	Use this setting to specify how many times NetBIOS broadcasts a query or claim for the name being used by an application. Increase the value of this number if you have many LAN segments on the network with nodes that need NetBIOS support or cannot attach to a gateway. The range is 2 to 65,535. The default is 4 if NETBIOS INTERNET is set ON; 2 if it's set to OFF.	NETBIOS BROADCAST COUNT=8

*The NETBIOS parameters must be on a single line. Ignore any word wrap shown in the table.

TABLE 5.7 (cont.) NetBIOS Parameters

OPTION	PURPOSE	EXAMPLE*
NETBIOS BROADCAST DELAY *number*	Use this setting to specify how long NetBIOS waits between query or claim broadcasts. Increase this value if the packet loss rate is high or if the traffic is high. Reduce NETBIOS BROADCAST COUNT by a similar amount to maintain the same name resolution timeout value. The range is 18 to 65,535. The default is 36 if NETBIOS INTERNET is set ON; 18 if it's set to OFF.	NETBIOS BROADCAST DELAY=3000
NETBIOS COMMANDS *number*	Use this parameter and setting to specify how many NetBIOS commands can be buffered in the NetBIOS driver at any one time. The range is 4 to 250; the default is 12.	NETBIOS COMMANDS=64
NETBIOS INTERNET [ON/OFF]	Use this setting to transmit name-claim packets to and from all stations on the internetwork, or to and from stations on the local network only. The default is ON. See the section "The NetBIOS INTERNET Parameter" for details.	NETBIOS INTERNET=OFF
NETBIOS LISTEN TIMEOUT *number*	Use this parameter to adjust the amount of time (in ticks) that NetBIOS waits (when no packets are received from the other side of a session) before it requests a keep-alive packet from the other side to ensure the session is still valid. The range is 1 to 65,535; the default is 108 (approximately 6 seconds).	NETBIOS LISTEN TIMEOUT=2700
NETBIOS RECEIVE BUFFERS *number*	Use this parameter to configure the number of IPX receive buffers that NetBIOS uses. The range is 4 to 20; the default is 6.	NETBIOS RECEIVE BUFFERS=12

*The NETBIOS parameters must be on a single line. Ignore any word wrap shown in the table.

TABLE 5.7 (cont.) NetBIOS Parameters	OPTION	PURPOSE	EXAMPLE*
	NETBIOS SEND BUFFERS *number*	Use this parameter to configure the number of IPX send buffers that NetBIOS uses. The range is 4 to 250; the default is 6.	NETBIOS SEND BUFFERS=24
	NETBIOS RETRY COUNT *number*	Use this parameter to specify how many times NetBIOS transmits a request for connection or retransmits a failed communication. Adjust the parameter setting with the setting for NETBIOS RETRY DELAY to vary the timeout on establishing NetBIOS sessions. Increase the value of the setting if you have many LAN segments on the network with nodes that need NetBIOS support or cannot attach to a gateway. The setting range is 4 to 20. The default is 20 if NETBIOS INTERNET is set to ON; 10 if it is set OFF.	NETBIOS RETRY COUNT=50
	NETBIOS RETRY DELAY *number*	Use this setting to specify how long (in ticks) NetBIOS waits between transmissions while establishing a connection or resending a data packet. Adjust the parameter setting with the setting for NETBIOS RETRY COUNT to vary the timeout on establishing NetBIOS sessions. Increase the value of this number if you have many LAN segments on the network with nodes that need NetBIOS support or cannot attach to a gateway. The range is 10 to 65,535 ticks; the default is 10 (about .5 second).	NETBIOS RETRY DELAY=800
	NETBIOS SESSION *number*	Use this setting to specify how many simultaneous NetBIOS sessions can be supported by the NetBIOS driver. The range is 4 to 250; the default is 32.	NETBIOS SESSIONS=100

*The NETBIOS parameters must be on a single line. Ignore any word wrap shown in the table.

NETBIOS VERIFY TIMEOUT *number*	Use this parameter to adjust the frequency at which NetBIOS sends a keep-alive packet to the other side of a session to preserve the session. If no packets are being exchanged on the NetBIOS session by the software that established the session, NetBIOS sends packets at regular intervals to make sure that the session is still valid. The range is 4 to 65,535; the default is 54 (approximately 3 seconds).	NETBIOS VERIFY TIMEOUT=1350
NPATCH *byte_offset, value*	Use this parameter and setting to patch any location in the NETBIOS.EXE data segment with any value.	NPATCH=XX,YY

*The NETBIOS parameters must be on a single line. Ignore any word wrap shown in the table.

THE NETBIOS INTERNET PARAMETER When ON, the NETBIOS INTERNET setting is used to transmit name-claim packets to and from all stations on an internetwork, or to and from stations on the local network only. *Name-claim packets* are packets that attempt to establish the uniqueness of the name of the station that NetBIOS is running on.

If you are running NetBIOS applications on a single network with a dedicated NetWare server, set this parameter to OFF to speed up the delivery of name resolution and datagram packets.

If you are running on more than one network or LAN segment and will be communicating through bridges, or if you are running a nondedicated NetWare server, the value must remain at the default ON.

Named Pipes Parameters

Named Pipes are a communication API used by applications running across a network. Using Named Pipes, programmers can write client/server applications similar to writing file commands for a local application. Table 5.8 lists the Named Pipes parameters.

> **NOTE**
>
> *Like the NetBIOS parameters, the Named Pipes parameters should not be indented. They need to be flush with the left margin.*

TABLE 5.8 Named Pipes Parameters

OPTION	PURPOSE	EXAMPLE*
NP MAX COMM BUFFERS *number*	Specifies the number of communication buffers that the NP extender can use to transmit data to and receive data from the Named Pipes server. The range is 4 to 40; the default is 6.	NP MAX COMM BUFFERS=10
NP MAX MACHINE NAMES *number*	Controls the number of Named Pipes servers that the extender can communicate with. The range is 10 to 50; the default is 10.	NP MAX MACHINE NAMES=14
NP MAX OPEN NAMED PIPES *number*	Specifies the maximum number of Named Pipes the workstation can have open simultaneously. The range is 4 to 128; the default is 4.	NP MAX OPEN NAMED PIPES=6
NP MAX SESSIONS *number*	Specifies the number of Named Pipes servers the extender can communicate with in default mode. This parameter is not used in peer mode. The range is 4 to 50; the default is 10. The setting for MAXIMUM MACHINE NAMES overrides the setting used for MAXIMUM SESSIONS if both are used.	NP MAX SESSIONS=25

*The Named Pipes parameters must be on a single line. Ignore any word wrap shown in the table.

Protocol ODINSUP Option

ODINSUP (Open Data-link Interface/Network Driver Interface Specification Support) is a Novell interface that allows ODI and NDIS drivers to co-exist on the same workstation. This allows either a DOS or MS Windows workstation to connect to dissimilar networks and use them as if they were both a single, unified network.

The ODINSUP parameter is:

```
BIND odi_driver [number]
```

This binds the ODINSUP protocol to an ODI driver. When ODINSUP is bound to a driver, the network board for that driver is the board used for transmissions to and from the network. For example, this setting:

```
PROTOCOL ODINSUP
    BIND=NE2000
```

binds the ODINSUP protocol to the NE2000 driver.

TBMI2 Options

If you are still running Windows 3.*x* in standard mode, or using a DOS task-switching environment such as the DOS shell, TBMI2 (Task-Switched Buffer Management Interface) may be helpful.

In Windows, you should try these out if you plan to switch between DOS sessions, and your application bypasses the NetWare DOS Requester and accesses IPX or SPX directly. Not only is this unusual, but you must be running Windows in standard or real mode, another unusual event. You do not need task-switching files if you are running in enhanced mode or you will not switch between DOS sessions.

Table 5.9 lists the TBMI2 parameters.

TABLE 5.9 TBMI2 Option Parameters

OPTION	PURPOSE	EXAMPLE*
DATA ECB COUNT *number*	Specifies how many data event control blocks (ECBs) are allocated for use by DOS programs needing virtualization. These ECBs apply to most IPX and SPX send and receive packets. If a nondata ECB request is made when none is available, a data ECB is used. Each allocated data ECB requires 628 bytes of memory; the 60 ECB default requires 37,680 bytes. The maximum allocation also depends upon available memory; the total size of all ECBs must be under 64 KB, which normally limits the data ECB count to under 255. The range is 10 to 89.	TBMI2 DATA ECB COUNT=40

TABLE 5.9 (cont.) TBMI2 Option Parameters	OPTION	PURPOSE	EXAMPLE*
	ECB COUNT *number*	Specifies how many nondata event control blocks (ECBs) are allocated for use by DOS programs needing virtualization. These ECBs apply to most AES (asynchronous events services) events. If TBMI2 runs out of nondata ECBs, data ECBs can be allocated for use. Each allocated ECB requires 52 bytes of memory; the 20 ECB default requires 1,040 bytes. The maximum allocation also depends upon available memory; the total size of all ECBs must be under 64 KB, which normally limits the ECB count to under 255. The range is 10 to 255.	TBMI2 ECB COUNT=40
	INT64 [ON/OFF]	Allows applications to use interrupt 64h to access IPX and SPX services. IPX and SPX now use interrupt 64h to maintain compatibility with earlier versions of NetWare. If an application's documentation requests interrupt 64h, set the value of this parameter to OFF. The default is ON.	TBMI2 INT64=OFF
	INT7A [ON/OFF]	Allows applications to use interrupt 7Ah to access IPX and SPX services. IPX and SPX now use interrupt 7Ah to maintain compatibility with NetWare 2.0. If an application's documentation requests interrupt 7Ah, set the value for this parameter to OFF. The default is ON.	TBMI2 INT7A=OFF
	USE MAX PACKETS	Tells TBMI2 to use the maximum packet size as specified by the IPX MAX PACKET size.	TBMI2 USE MAX PACKETS
	USING WINDOWS 3.0	Tells TBMI2 to use TASKID. Setting a value of this parameter tells NetWare to identify tasks in each DOS BOX as separate tasks.	TBMI2 USING WINDOWS 3.0

*The options must be on a single line, indented under the TBMI2 line. Ignore any word wrap shown in the table.

Installing and Configuring Client32

FORGIVE AN OLD-TIMER'S musings, but I miss the days when a person actually knew what software did when it was installed, where the files were located, and how to fix a problem. Today, particularly with Windows 95, you start the process, hear the hard disk churn, and cross your fingers, hoping the process works properly. Because if it doesn't, you have no simple way to find the problem and fix the installation. Uninstall if possible, and reinstall until the operating system magic amulet you bought from the witch doctor at NetWorld+InterOp works its spell correctly.

> *Uninstall if possible, and reinstall until the operating system magic amulet you bought from the witch doctor at NetWorld+InterOp works its spell correctly.*

You can download software from the Novell Web site, if you would rather get started with Client32 before upgrading to NetWare 4.11. If you copy the files, just run the SETUP.EXE file from the local or network hard drive holding the Client32 files.

Client32 software that comes with NetWare 4.11 is stored in the \PUBLIC\CLIENT\WIN95 or \PUBLIC\CLIENT\WIN31 directories. Let's get started with the Windows 3.1 and DOS software.

Some Background on Novell's Windows 95 Client

Microsoft's move to real 32-bit client operating systems (Windows NT) and pseudo 32-bit (Windows 95) meant Novell had to make some major changes in the Windows 95 and NT client software. Of course, Microsoft developers made their own 32-bit NetWare clients, hoping to freeze Novell out of the loop. Microsoft's lack of a decent directory service caused the designers to ignore NDS in their Windows 95 client, implying that directory services aren't really all that important.

Well, NDS turned out to be important to NetWare users, and folks were upset. Aggravation was aimed in equal parts at Microsoft for making such an underpowered 32-bit client, and at Novell for being so slow in bringing out its own client for Windows 95.

Novell protested that Microsoft was making it impossible to bring out a good client, and Microsoft protested that wasn't true, and they went round and round until nobody cared. The fact that Novell took more than two years to deliver its first (nearly worthless) Windows NT client makes me suspect that Novell political

(continued on next page)

> infighting is just as much to blame for the late Windows 95 drivers as Microsoft's bad attitude. Either way, customers of both companies are being poorly served.
>
> NetWare 4.11 was released 13 months after Windows 95, so Novell has no excuses for the client shortcomings and installation hassles. Luckily for NetWare users, Novell has made a good Windows 95 client. If you don't believe me, check the various PC and network magazines; all agree Novell's client is better than Microsoft's. Of course, a NetWare client that's only "better than Microsoft's" doesn't mean it's a wonderful client. There are still installation hassles, so be wary.
>
> In the licensing terms for the new client, you'll notice that you may freely use these client files *only* when connected to a Novell operating system. If that seems strange, you must have missed Microsoft's File and Print Services for NetWare product running under Windows NT. To encourage the use of Windows NT servers as replacements for NetWare servers, Microsoft copied the basic NetWare 3.1 file and print servers, but running under Windows NT. The idea was that users could use their own NetWare client files to connect to the Windows NT server—the same files they use for connecting to the NetWare server.
>
> I have the dubious honor of being the person that pointed out (in a review in *Information Week*) that Microsoft, a stout defender of its own product licensing, was somewhat sleazy in encouraging the misuse of Novell client software. Turns out Novell's lawyers thought the same thing, and Microsoft was forced to release their own pseudo-NetWare client software for their own pseudo-NetWare server clone. Don't you love legal retribution?

Installing and Configuring Client32 for Windows 3.1x and DOS

Since the Client32 software must load in DOS before Windows 3.1*x* gets started, the installation of the DOS files are the most important part. The DOS installation looks almost exactly like that of the VLM file process we covered near the beginning of this chapter.

For some variety, we'll look at the Windows 3.1 installation screens. First, we're assuming the computer has a network connection, and so we'll load the Client32 files from a network server (assuming that these files were copied there when the server was installed). This is a good way to install clients, even for brand new machines. Keep a boot diskette that loads the proper drivers for your brand of network adapter card from the floppy diskette, and use that disk to get connected to the network. Then, using the Run option on the Windows 3.1 File menu, start the client download process by running the SETUP.EXE file from the \PUBLIC\CLIENT\WIN31 directory.

The first thing you'll see when loading Client32 software is a license agreement. This is new for Novell, and reflects the increasing legal climate chilling the computer business. Figure 5.12 shows the new artsy (you know, brooding and dark) background and the license agreement.

You'll notice you have no option concerning the licensing of Client32 software. You either accept the license, or you don't run the software. I'm not sure if this stand is completely legal, but that's not our problem in this book. Since you're using the client software to connect to a NetWare server, you have nothing to worry about, so click on Yes and continue.

The next dialog box sets the file target directory (\NOVELL\CLIENT32) and the location of your Windows 3.1*x* files (generally \WINDOWS). If you have moved either, you must direct the installation routine to the proper place. There's no good reason to move these directories, however.

Next comes the selection of your ODI files for your network interface card. Since I have network connection in place to reach the server, the software correctly assumes that I will continue using the same card in that machine. You

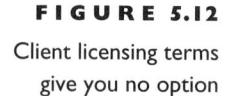

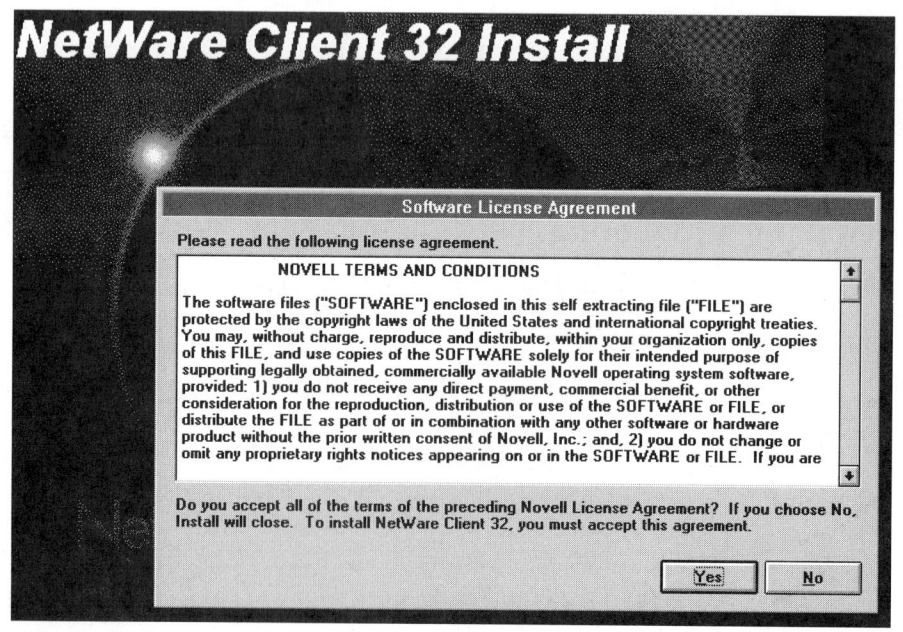

FIGURE 5.12

Client licensing terms give you no option

are given a chance to change the card settings if you wish, which is important if you're installing from floppies or the CD.

Figure 5.13 shows the next screen that pops up. This is new in our client installation universe, and includes two interesting items. First is the chance to load TCP/IP on the client machine. Your choice is between a full TCP/IP software stack, such as what is provided by LAN WorkPlace for DOS, and the NetWare/IP product.

The bottom checkbox is for the new IPX/IP Gateway that's available with the IntranetWare bundle. Using the gateway allows full Internet or intranet connection to TCP/IP-based services, such as Web servers, without running TCP/IP on your local machine. We'll talk more about this option in Chapter 14.

All we care about now on this screen is that the installation routine adds a line calling the STARTNET.BAT program from within the AUTOEXEC.BAT file. This means that the network support will load automatically. Most people need that connection available immediately, and this ensures that will happen.

The new file-copy status screen shows four diskettes, each covered with Novell balls. As the file contents are copied, each disk number is highlighted to indicate the progress. This is accompanied by a sales pitch for Client32 in the bottom-left corner of the screen. After the files are copied, you have a choice of rebooting (recommended), exiting to DOS, or exiting back to Windows. Unless you want to modify something, such as the STARTNET.BAT file loading commands, go ahead and exit.

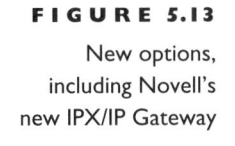

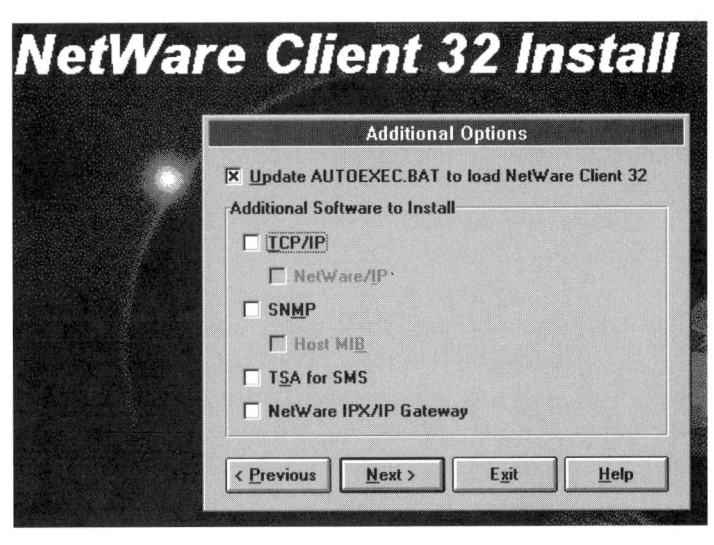

FIGURE 5.13

New options, including Novell's new IPX/IP Gateway

What's included in this STARTNET.BAT file? How is it different from the VLM configuration described earlier in the chapter? Let's see.

The following is the STARTNET.BAT from a DOS and Windows 3.1 station running Client32 software, in fact, the very one we installed just a bit ago. Read this over, and let me point out a few things.

```
SET NWLANGUAGE=ENGLISH
lh C:\NOVELL\CLIENT32\NIOS.EXE
lh C:\NOVELL\CLIENT32\LSL.COM
lh C:\NOVELL\CLIENT32\N16ODI.COM
lh C:\NOVELL\CLIENT32\NESL.COM
lh C:\NOVELL\CLIENT32\3C503.COM
LOAD C:\NOVELL\CLIENT32\LSLC32.NLM
LOAD C:\NOVELL\CLIENT32\PC32MLID.LAN
LOAD C:\NOVELL\CLIENT32\IPX.NLM
LOAD C:\NOVELL\CLIENT32\CLIENT32.NLM
```

The first line tells NetWare we're speaking English on this system. Nothing hard or unusual with this line.

I added the "lh" for "LOADHIGH" at the beginning of the following five commands. Novell doesn't do this, and it's necessary. This is one good reason to put off rebooting the system when the files are finished downloading.

The second line in the file:

```
lh C:\NOVELL\CLIENT32\NIOS.EXE
```

is new and different. What the heck is NIOS.EXE? NetWare Input Output System, or NIOS, takes its name from the BIOS (Basic Input Output System) in your PC. How new is this file, and the whole attitude that goes with it? The manual includes no information, except to refer you to the separate Help file under Program Manager or Windows 95 Help on the Start menu. Secrecy aside, the NIOS acts like the BIOS for the PC, only on the network. This is the traffic cop program that helps the right client program fit the right niche.

N16ODI.COM fills the role of the IPXODI.COM file under the VLM clients. Next is the NetWare Even Service Layer program, NESL.COM. This file appears only with the 16-bit ODI LAN driver files. Last in the first section is the 3C503.COM file, available from either 3Com or Novell. If your driver file is not included with NetWare, it should be on the driver diskette. If it's not there, you bought too cheap a network interface board, and you should return it and get a better one.

The last part of our STARTNET.BAT holds something never before seen on a client workstation: LOAD commands. Sure, you're used to seeing them on the server, but not the client. First comes the LSLC32.NLM, handling the Link Support Layer functions for the 32-bit client software.

The next two files, PC32MLID.LAN and IPX.NLM, perform the functions you would expect, and that we've spoken of several times before. They coordinate the client software to the driver for the network card and configure the IPX protocol details, respectively. Nothing too unusual here, although the LAN and NLM extensions do look odd, don't they?

Last is CLIENT32.NLM, which functions similarly to the VLM.EXE file on earlier clients. It handles final loading and configuration details. CLIENT32.NLM will take 25 percent of the available free memory for network file caching as a default. Check your Max Cache Size parameter and cut this down if the workstation is low on memory (aren't they all?). Giving this parameter a value of 0 (zero) will turn off caching, leaving the memory alone. Do this by saying:

```
MAX CACHE SIZE=0
```

on a line under the NetWare DOS Requester heading in the NET.CFG file.

Speaking of NET.CFG, Client32 for DOS and Windows 3.1*x* uses the same type of NET.CFG file as the VLM clients do. So you haven't wasted all your time trying to learn all the NET.CFG parameters after all.

Attaching to the Network for the First Time with Client32

What scrolls when you run the Client32 STARTNET.BAT program? If you look back at Figure 5.11, you can see the earlier STARTNET.BAT results from the VLM client files, and compare them to the following:

```
NetWare I/O Subsystem for DOS  v2.01 (960607)
(C) Copyright 1995, 1996 Novell, Inc.  All Rights
Reserved.

System configuration file at C:\NOVELL\CLIENT32\NET.CFG
Novell Link Support Layer for DOS ODI  v2.20 (960401)
(c) Copyright 1990 - 1996, by Novell, Inc. All rights
reserved.

The configuration file used was
"C:\NOVELL\CLIENT32\NET.CFG".
Max Boards 4, Max Stacks 4
```

```
Novell Nios to 16-Bit DOS ODI SHIM  v1.02 Alpha 01
(960423)
(c) Copyright 1996, by Novell, Inc. All rights reserved.

The Nios to 16-Bit DOS ODI Shim (N16ODI) has loaded
successfully.
Novell NetWare Event Service Layer for DOS ODI  v1.04
(960401)
(c) Copyright 1993 - 1996, by Novell, Inc. All rights
reserved.

3Com 3C503 EtherLink II MLID  v1.30 (931104)
(C) Copyright 1992 3Com Corporation.  All Rights
Reserved.
(C) Copyright 1991 Novell, Inc.  All Rights Reserved.

Connector is BNC/TP (Thin).  Programmed I/O Mode
Selected.
Int 3, Port 300, Port 700, Node Address 2608CACCB83 L
Max Frame 1514 bytes, Line Speed 10 Mbps
Board 1, Frame ETHERNET_802.2, LSB Mode
Board 2, Frame ETHERNET_802.3, LSB Mode

Novell Link Support Layer for Client 32  v1.02  (960529)
(c) Copyright 1996, by Novell, Inc. All rights reserved.

Novell 16-bit MPI to 32-Bit MLI SHIM for Client 32.
v1.02  (960501)
(c) Copyright 1996, by Novell, Inc. All rights reserved.

PC32MLID: Scanning for DOS ODI 16-Bit LSL
PC32MLID: DOS ODI 16-Bit LSL found at CAEE:1AF

PC32MLID: Shimming DOS ODI Board: 1, Name: 3C503, Frame:
ETHERNET_802.2.
PC32MLID: Shimming DOS ODI Board: 2, Name: 3C503, Frame:
ETHERNET_802.3.

PC32MLID registered as board 1, which Virtualizes DOS
ODI board 1.
```

Installing and Configuring Client32

```
    PC32MLID registered as board 2, which Virtualizes DOS
    ODI board 2.

    Novell IPX Protocol Stack for Client 32  v2.00  (960619)
    (c) Copyright 1989 - 1996, by Novell, Inc.  All Rights
    Reserved.

    IPX bound to 3C503 ETHERNET_802.2
        ODI Logical Board Number:  1
        Node Address:   02608CACCB83
        IPX Protocol ID:   0000000000E0
        Maximum Packet Size (Includes IPX Header):   1492
    bytes
        Transport Time:   1 milliseconds

    IPX bound to 3C503 ETHERNET_802.3
        ODI Logical Board Number:  2
        Node Address:   02608CACCB83
        IPX Protocol ID:   000000000000
        Maximum Packet Size (Includes IPX Header):   1496
    bytes
        Transport Time:   1 milliseconds

    Novell NetWare Requester CLIENT32 NLM  v2.01  (960620)
    (C) Copyright 1995,1996 Novell Inc.  All Rights
    Reserved.  Patents Pending.

    Attached to server GATEWAY2000-1
```

Well, there are some differences, aren't there? What strikes you first? The location of the STARTNET.BAT file, which is now in \NOVELL\CLIENT32 rather than in \NWCLIENT? That's a new location used by Client32. The NET.CFG file is in the same directory as the STARTNET.BAT file, as you would expect.

You may think that, since the STARTNET.BAT file has been put into a new subdirectory, you could easily switch back to the old VLM access method, merely by changing the reference to your old STARTNET.BAT file in the AUTOEXEC.BAT file. That's a good plan, and would work if Novell didn't erase the old files from your \NWCLIENT directory while installing the new version. Personally, I consider erasing files without asking, especially when upgrading a system, to be a serious breach of trust and possibly illegal.

Novell program designers obviously don't feel that way, or they would ask. Shame on them. Rename the \NWCLIENT directory before installing the software to give yourself a fall-back position. You may need to back up and start over, so save your \NWCLIENT directory, and don't delete it until all is well.

Here's the NVER listing from the DOS box from a system running Windows 95:

```
F:\>nver

DOS:      V7.00

LAN driver: ELNK3 Ethernet Adapter ETHERNET_802.2
Version 4.00 IRQ 0, Port 0

IPX API version:        3.32
SPX API version:        3.32

VLM: Version 32.00 Revision A  using Extended Memory

Attached file servers:

Server name:   486-33
Novell NetWare 4.11 (August 13, 1996)

Server name:   GWAY2K-2
Novell NetWare 4.11 (August 13, 1996)

Server name:   GATEWAY2000-1
Novell NetWare 4.11 (August 13, 1996)
```

This is not so different from what you see with a Windows 3.1*x* system. NVER still gives you important information, such as LAN driver, VLM 32 versions, and attached servers.

Installing and Configuring Client32 for Windows 95 Systems

There are no "messy" batch files and memory loading instructions with Windows 95. Although Microsoft pretends DOS doesn't exist, we know that DOS boots the hard disk and starts the Windows 95 shell, whether Microsoft wants to call it an operating system or not. However, the Windows 95 software is enough of an improvement over Windows 3.1*x* that we can live with the sleight of hand, going about our business in supposedly 32-bit software (although much of Windows 95 is still 16-bit).

How do you add Client32 to your Windows 95 system? It's not difficult, but you must do it from each workstation. There's no easy and reliable way to "preload" the network software, as you can do with DOS by copying a directory or two full of files and adding a batch file or two. Your frustration level will soar if you try to mass-upgrade Windows 95 clients.

Starting from the Control Panel, pick Network, then Client, then click on the Add command button. Microsoft graciously supplies a variety of clients from a variety of companies (although the cynical among us may think this is another attempt to dilute the importance of NetWare to Microsoft users). Double-click on Novell NetWare Client32.

If this icon doesn't exist, you must run the Novell installation routine. You can run the INSTALL.BAT file from the root of the CD-ROM disk, but it just tells you to try \PUBLIC\CLIENT\WIN95 and run the SETUP.EXE program. Don't try to check out these files if you're not ready to install them; once again, Novell installation engineers callously tell you they're erasing the old client, without allowing you to stop the process. To make matters worse, there's no easy renaming of the directory under Windows 95 as there is under DOS.

When you start the client installation, you will see screens much like those in Figures 5.12 and 5.13 (shown earlier), including the license statement. If there's a problem, you will be dumped into the Network Control Panel's Properties screen, where you may attempt to rectify what the installation program couldn't.

> **WARNING**
>
> *Prepare yourself for problems. Testing an early beta client, my Windows 95 Registry was completely trashed by the Novell client software. How trashed? Wipe the disk and reformat trashed. That has never happened to me before, in over a dozen years of Net-Ware involvement.*

Even the final client software is balky to install, especially when adding the IPX/IP Gateway protocol. In my experience, some files did not appear to be where they belonged; for example, sometimes the files requested weren't on the 4.11 CD-ROM or the NIAS (NetWare Internet Access Server, the official name for the IPX/IP Gateway) disk. Then, without explanation, a seventh attempt to install the client would prove lucky, and all the files would zip merrily to their assigned spots, the sun would shine, and all would be well with the world and my NetWare clients.

You may have a better experience than mine if you keep in mind that some files from Microsoft are required for this installation, but Microsoft wouldn't let Novell ship them with NetWare. Client32 installation prompts for CAB files or files on the Windows 95 CD. To simplify your Client32 installation, copy the Windows 95 CAB files to a directory that you can access, or have the Windows 95 CD in your CD-ROM drive.

One of the best ways to upgrade Windows 3.1x machines to Windows 95 and Novell's Client32 at the same time is to use the server-based Windows 95 installation routine (MSBATCH SETUP). See Appendix A for details.

Figure 5.14 shows the Network Control Panel for adding a client, which you use to update the client software on an existing Windows 95 system. Of course, the Windows software must know about the existence of Client32, so we're looking at a screen that won't show up during initial client installation, but only after you've tried and failed a time or two. Regardless, it's a screen you'll see many times as you try to control Windows 95 clients, so you may as well see it here first.

As you can see by the partially obscured command button that reads "File and Print S" in Figure 5.14, for File and Print Sharing, Windows 95 offers you a chance to emulate a NetWare 3.x server. DO NOT DO THIS! Sorry to shout, but enabling the ersatz NetWare server on a Windows 95 machine will

FIGURE 5.14

Novell client choices

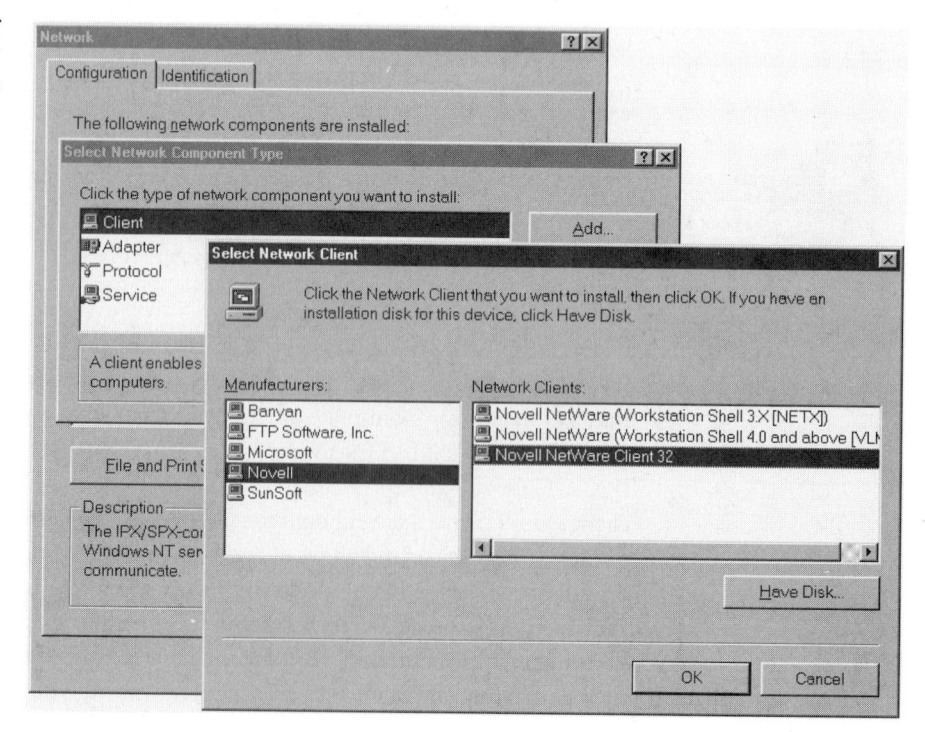

only cause you grief. If you want more grief in your life, hit yourself in the head with a hammer rather than enable the Windows 95 NetWare server option. The pain is about the same, but it's quicker than letting a dozen desktop servers turn your network security, backup, management, and user productivity to shreds. Make a rule today that no desktop servers are allowed, and your life will be better, I promise.

> *If you want more grief in your life, hit yourself in the head with a hammer rather than enable the Windows 95 NetWare server option.*

There's one more important point with the Windows 95 client that must be mentioned: Client32 software adds a network file cache, speeding access to and from network resources by utilizing part of your workstation RAM. Many reports have come from disgruntled users who have seen huge amounts of memory gobbled up by their Client32 software.

Avoid this RAM gobbling, especially on workstations without enough RAM (and who really has enough RAM?). The way to curtail RAM grabbing by Client32 software is one level deeper in the Network Control Panel. Figure 5.15 shows exactly where you can find this Properties setting, and the setting to use.

FIGURE 5.15

Stopping the RAM grab

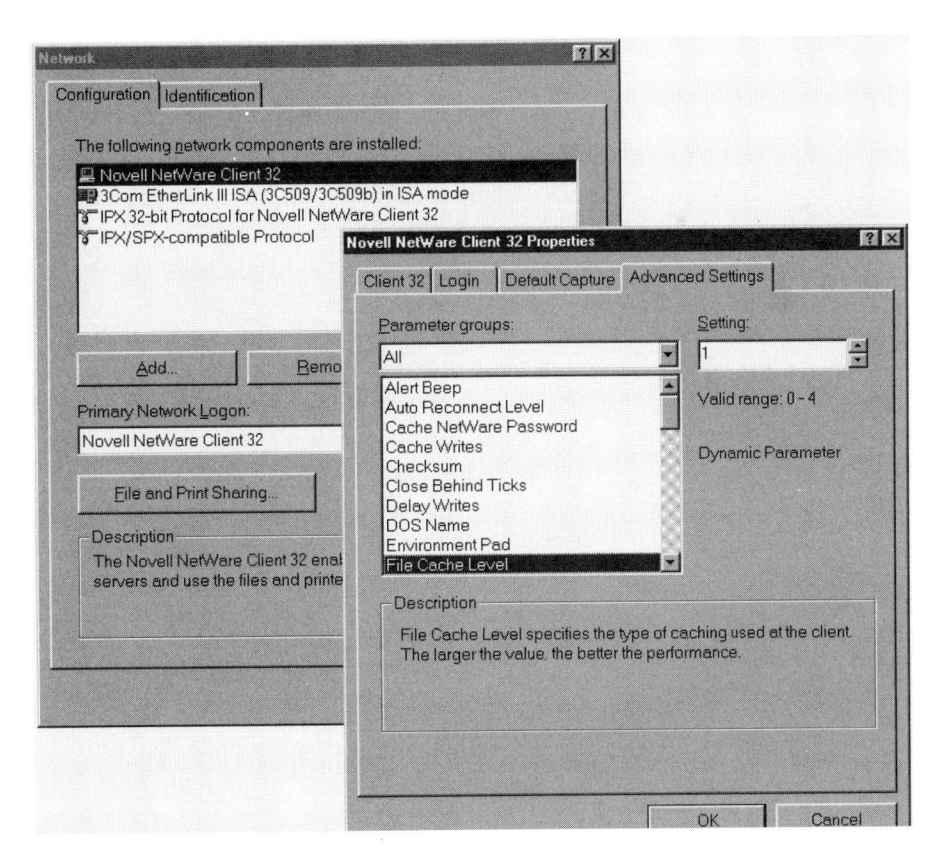

Never one to avoid a speed improvement if possible, I've set the lowest level of file cache. Setting the number to 0 (zero) eliminates the RAM file cache completely. Raising the number to 4 guarantees no application will have enough memory. Okay, that's a slight joke, but never underestimate an application's desire for RAM.

Window 95 isn't the ultimate desktop operating system, but it's what we have to work with today. It's harder to control in many ways than Windows 3.1, but it also works better most of the time. The extra pain of support may, or may not be, balanced by the new capabilities. Regardless, your company will migrate to Windows 95 or Windows NT before 1998, so get ready now.

Too Many Client Options, Too Little Time

WHEN I HAVE a problem with my car, I pull up the hood and look for a button that's labeled, "Push this and all will work again." Unfortunately, there isn't one of those, at least not on any of the cars I've owned.

When I have a problem with a computer or a network, I want to open the manual and see a heading that says, "James, here is the answer to your question." Unfortunately, there isn't one of those, either.

The only way for writers of technical manuals, and authors like your Humble Narrator, to answer every possible question is to present every possible option. This gives two disturbing impressions: that you should be using many of these options, and that the client configuration is difficult.

You will rarely need any of these parameters. The vast majority of networks will never require more than the standard configuration details for the standard network interface cards. NetWare works extremely well using the standard configurations for millions of users every day.

Of course, times change. The added client complexities of Windows 95 and Windows NT add a new layer of confusion and potential disaster. If you try to just "wing it" on client support, you may find yourself pulling more overtime than you, and your family, want.

However, if 100,000 people buy this book (please), a few will need to know how to set the strangest parameters for the strangest situations. Somewhere, some poor soul is trying to make NetBIOS work across an internetwork with a long delay while maintaining compatibility with NetWare 2.0a using ARCnet interface cards. I just hope this poor soul isn't you.

MiniCo: Connecting PC Clients to Your Network

MINICO HAS 3 servers, 75 users, and one location.

The NetWare DOS Requester: Moving Beyond Shells

CONSIDERATIONS

The choices:

- Use the newer Client32 client software.
- Use the older VLM NetWare 4.10 client software.
- Keep some of the original network stations on the older NETX client software.

DECISION

Move users to Client32 software.

EXPLANATION

There was no advantage to keeping the few NetWare 3.x clients on the older software when upgrading to NetWare 4.10. Using the VLM software that came as part of the standard installation diskettes was quick and easy. No software problems of any kind were reported.

Moving to Client32 for NetWare 4.11 became an easy choice, as well. Users upgraded their client software as they wanted, but there was no mandatory roll-out of the new software.

Network Interface Card Installation and Setup

CONSIDERATIONS

The choices:

- Choose between the two network interface cards offered by the dealer.
- Have the dealer install the network interface cards or have someone in-house install the cards.

DECISION

MiniCo chose the cheaper type of network interface card, and had an employee, not the dealer, install the cards.

EXPLANATION

MiniCo's dealer offered both SMC Elite (a new generation of Western Digital cards, one of the original Ethernet adapters, now owned by SMC) as the lower-priced card and 3Com 3c509 cards as the higher-end card. Jack Mingo (MiniCo's President) chose the cheaper cards, and decided Alexander von Thorn (the Distribution Manager, who handled the installation) could install them himself rather than pay the dealer to do so. Alexander thought that was a mistake, and it delayed the network by two weeks because of the extra time and trouble it took for one person to install all those cards.

MINICO CASE STUDY, CONTINUED

Some of the systems already had CD-ROM drives and speakers, making it harder for Alexander to find available memory and interrupt settings.

Client Files Required for Non-Client32 Clients

CONSIDERATIONS

The choices:

- Accept the standard files for client installation.
- Test and choose among the files that may not be required.

DECISION

Accept the standard client installation files.

EXPLANATION

Not having the resources or inclination to set up a pilot network and check every client file configuration option, MiniCo accepted the defaults and was happy with the results.

Installing Non-Client32 Clients

CONSIDERATIONS

The choices:

- Use the CD-ROM files for client installation.
- Develop an installation script.
- Run the SETUP.EXE program in the \PUBLIC\CLIENT\WIN31 directory.

DECISION

Use the network setup files, started by older NetWare client connection but upgraded during the immediate session.

EXPLANATION

Alexander created the DOS and MS Windows client installation disks during the initial NetWare 4.10 server installation, not knowing how long it would take. Although he meant to automate the procedure, Alexander never had the chance. Since the network wasn't a priority to anyone, installation happened after business hours or whenever anyone left his or her desk for an hour or so.

NetWare 4.11 installation time found a smarter Alexander, who used the VLM connections on the clients for initial connection to his first new 4.11 server. Once connected, each user ran the update themselves, or asked for support. In those cases, Alexander did the installation rather than take the time to write an installation script.

NET.CFG Means Client Network Configuration for DOS and Windows 3.1x Clients

CONSIDERATIONS

The choices:

- Accept the NET.CFG defaults.
- Test the multitude of NET.CFG options.

DECISION

Accept the default NET.CFG configuration.

EXPLANATION

Many of the configuration options available through NET.CFG apply to unusual network situations. Others may be of benefit to MiniCo, but Alexander didn't have the time or help necessary to check them out.

MINICO CASE STUDY, CONTINUED

Installing and Configuring Client32

CONSIDERATIONS

MiniCo could:

- Ignore Client32 except for the new systems.
- Add Client32 to all workstations, even DOS systems.

DECISION

Add Client32 to all systems.

EXPLANATION

Adding Client32 support for Windows 95 was forced onto Alexander when MiniCo agreed to rent space (both physical and network) to RoadTrip Productions, an even smaller publishing company. Each author/editor in RoadTrip Productions has a Windows 95 workstation, which requires Client32.

Terence Wright (Terry), an English import, heads the group. Most of his time is spent running production, but he is also the author of *The Staggering Man's Guide to English Pubs*. Terry's machine has a CD-ROM, so Alexander loaded the NetWare CD and installed the client software. Everything went without a hitch.

Loren MacGregor, author of *Victorian Programming Techniques* doubles as "Webmaster." In that capacity, he helped Alexander with the network needs of RoadTrip members. In fact, after Loren watched Alexander install Client32 on Terry's machine, he installed the rest of the RoadTrip systems without help.

Kimberly Borrowdale, author of *Names for Nether Regions* and editor for sex subject books, had a problem with her system: no CD-ROM drive. The same problem was found on Mike Barnard's portable, which he is using to write *Pedaling the Pacific* from his recombinant bicycle. Since Alexander had created an Organizational Unit for RoadTrip, along with user names and access rights for all the new folks, Loren used the meager Microsoft NetWare client provided in Windows 95 to make connections for Kimberly and Mike. This method took longer, since he had to configure and reboot the machine several times, but it did work.

Annabel Smyth, author of *Sermons with Snap* (and another English visitor) has an old DOS system that does not run Windows of any kind, much less Windows 95. Loren used the diskettes copied from the CD-ROM to install Client32 for DOS on Annabel's machine.

Linda Ryan writes the *Pommy: Mythic Battle Princess* books, and she is the educational liaison for RoadTrip and now helping MiniCo in the same area. Linda needed Client32 installed on her Windows 3.11 portable and on her desktop Windows 95 system. Loren used the diskettes once again on Linda's portable, and the CD-ROM on her desktop system.

The group's technical writer is Stan Shursky. At Stan's last on-site technical assignment, he used the older VLM clients with Windows 95. They worked, but he couldn't see any of the NDS structures. Running the Client32 upgrade from the server solved those problems.

MINICO CASE STUDY, CONTINUED

Jim Lewczyk, the programmer for MiniCo, was instrumental in getting RoadTrip into the MiniCo fold and attached to their network. RoadTrip published Jim's book, *I Fought the Lawn and the Lawn Won,* last year. His system was upgraded to Client32, even though he stayed with Windows 3.1.

MiniCo's hand was somewhat forced in regards to Client32, because of all the Windows 95 systems that arrived with the RoadTrip group. After seeing the ease of installation, performance, and auto-reconnect features, MiniCo put the Client32 software on all the systems.

MegaCorp: Connecting PC Clients to Your Network

CASE STUDY

MEGACORP HAS 50 servers, 2500 users, and 5 locations.

The NetWare DOS Requester: Moving Beyond Shells

CONSIDERATIONS

The goals:

- Examine the technology behind the new Client32.
- Use the pilot network to test the Client32 software for both Windows 3.1 and Windows 95 clients.

DECISION

Make adjustments necessary to upgrade the DOS Requester and VLM client software to the new Client32 version for all Windows 95 clients, and for those DOS and Windows 3.1 users who wish to upgrade.

EXPLANATION

Without DOS Requester and VLM client files, NDS will not function. MegaCorp was determined to find and fix any problems, large or small, with the client software before the roll-out. A few minor problems were found (and fixed) with some in-house software.

When it came time for NetWare 4.11, new Windows 95 clients were required to use the Novell network client, not the ones from Microsoft. Windows 3.1 clients who wished to upgrade were allowed to, as long as they got permission from their LAN department manager.

Network Interface Card Installation and Setup

CONSIDERATIONS

The criteria:

- Minimize installation time with new interface cards.
- Maximize performance of the network client.
- No jumpers to set on the interface card; must be software configurable.
- Bulk packaging is important to avoid cost and packaging waste.
- Excellent warranty for adapters through local resources and the vendor.
- Minimal chip count on the adapter to reduce possible failure points.
- Software diagnostics included with the adapter.
- Flexible installation options regarding interrupts, base I/O, and memory addresses.
- Single vendor for both Ethernet and Token Ring adapters.
- Support for all other protocols, such as TCP/IP/IP and SNA.

MEGACORP CASE STUDY, CONTINUED

DECISION

Use 3Com EtherLink III and TokenLink III cards for all clients.

EXPLANATION

3Com cards met all the criteria in the selection process. Although a few cards scored higher in either the Token Ring or Ethernet categories, it was decided the advantages of a single source for all client adapters outweighed other minor advantages.

The fact that 3Com commercialized Ethernet means every Ethernet software package supports the 3Com adapters. The TokenLink line is newer, but 3Com's reputation has pushed many vendors into providing strong support for this line.

All cards were installed by Central IS personnel. Configuration was made as automatic as possible, with the boot diskette loading enough information to connect to the network server and run a script to download the necessary files and configuration details. A log was kept of the settings for each client PC, and placed in that PC's See Also value in the NDS database.

No CD-ROM drives or speakers have been installed in standard client workstations, so this was not a concern for the vast majority of workstations. A few stations used in presentations did have extensive multimedia modifications, requiring the IS personnel to spend extra time to troubleshoot and verify the installation on those units.

Client Files Required for Non-Client32 Clients

CONSIDERATIONS

The choices:

- Accept the default client installation files.
- Test possible configurations to improve speed and lessen RAM impact.

DECISION

For the NetWare 4.10 installation, each VLM was tested for necessity in the MegaCorp network.

EXPLANATION

When NetWare 4.10 was installed, several VLMs were deemed unnecessary. Consequently, the NET.CFG files loaded each VLM individually.

Installing Non-Client32 Clients

CONSIDERATIONS

The choices:

- Use the client installation diskettes.
- Develop an installation script.

DECISION

Develop a custom installation routine.

EXPLANATION

Although the NetWare client installation routine is reliable and competent, it takes time. MegaCorp developed a boot diskette that automatically loaded the minimum network client

MEGACORP CASE STUDY, CONTINUED

files needed to connect to a server. From there, the custom login script exited to a batch file that copied the proper files to the proper location on the client. All configuration files were set during this download. The last step loaded a small text editor, so the installation technician could check the NET.CFG, AUTOEXEC.BAT, and CONFIG.SYS files.

Using the automated script, multiple workstations could be installed concurrently. Also, the file-copy process went much faster across the network than it could from the floppy drive. After the interface cards were installed and checked, the file download and configuration took less than four minutes per station.

NET.CFG Means Client Network Configuration for DOS and Windows 3.1x Clients

CONSIDERATIONS

The choices:

- Accept the default NET.CFG configuration.
- Test the multitude of NET.CFG options.

DECISION

Test and adapt the NET.CFG options for Client32 DOS and Windows 3.1 systems.

EXPLANATION

Since earlier VLM files were tweaked for NetWare 4.10, it should come as no surprise that the MegaCorp administrators decided Client32 software would be examined closely. NET.CFG files for Client32 software on Windows 3.1x clients were changed to reduce the amount of RAM used for local file cache (as were the File Cache Level settings under Windows 95).

Large and complex networks are the reason NET.CFG has so many options. Each network segment may need to modify timeout values for WAN connections, support Named Pipes, or configure NetBIOS for SNA gateway operations. Few of these options were included in the standard client installation. However, each configuration problem that was solved by a NET.CFG option was documented in the database for future support calls and workstation installations.

Installing and Configuring Client32

CONSIDERATIONS

- Stay with Windows 3.11
- Move to Windows 95
- Move to Windows NT
- Upgrade everyone at once, or upgrade in phases

DECISION

Accept only Windows 95 on new desktop and portable systems, and upgrade as required to support new applications. Make Client32 part of every upgrade, but don't retrofit Windows 3.1x systems.

EXPLANATION

Large companies move slowly, and MegaCorp is no exception. The details of upgrading to Windows 95 or Windows NT, rather than milking Windows 3.11 for another year, were debated furiously.

MEGACORP CASE STUDY, CONTINUED

Windows NT was deemed too expensive for the benefits. Plug and Play support for new hardware helped persuade MegaCorp to stick with Windows 95.

All new desktop systems were to be delivered with Windows 95. Selected users with Windows 3.1x were upgraded each month as their departments received new applications requiring Windows 95. No users were to be migrated to Client32 unless they received a new computer or application. No systems running DOS or Windows 3.1x were upgraded to Client32.

By using the existing NetWare client software included by Microsoft in Windows 95, MegaCorp technicians connected, under Bindery Services, to a particular server with the proper Windows 95 support files. The File Cache Level settings were made by hand. With planning, Windows 95 stations could be upgraded to a full, NDS-aware Client32 system in less than five minutes.

Using the Network

PART 2

Creating and Managing Users (Now User Objects)

CHAPTER 6

IN NETWORK SUPPORT departments, this is the first joke learned by rookies: *user* is a four-letter word. If your boss hears you, explain this joke mines the same humor vein as college professors that love teaching but hate students, salespeople that love selling but hate customers, and editors that love books but hate authors. The things we know best, we both love and hate, depending on the stress of the moment.

For those few moments when the stress overwhelms you and user does become a four-letter word, just remember that users require administration, which requires you. When users are a pain, it's often because they are undertrained and ill-equipped for their jobs as network clients.

The smart network user needn't like computers, but smart network administrators like both the business they're in and networking. Since users won't come to you until it's too late or something is broken, you must go to them. Learn their job function goals and provide them the proper tools to reach those goals, and your users will be happy and productive.

But first, before they can be a pain in the neck, users must be created on your new file server. With some management help, the users will pain you less. Except for that one user that drives everybody crazy; there's one on every network.

Users and NetWare 4.1x

THE USER OBJECT in NetWare 4.1*x* is the most fundamental object in NDS. Unlike the USER of earlier NetWare versions, this User object can contain information about the person it represents.

Just as with earlier NetWare, you can set or control every aspect of the User object's interface to the network. The only requirements for the User object are:

- A user name unique within the container

- A completed Last Name field (not empty)

That's it. Everything else for a User object is optional, but much is recommended. Each physical user on the network should have a unique User object, but that's not mandatory either.

If you are coming to NetWare 4.1*x* from an earlier version of NetWare, many of the User object properties will be familiar. User object details are as follows:

- **Group Membership:** When added to a group, the User object inherits the rights assigned to that group.

- **Home Directories:** Serves as personal disk space on the server. It's best if the directory is placed under an umbrella directory and uses the person's name for the directory name, as in SYS:\USERS\JAMES.

- **Security Equivalences:** Quick method of assigning the same rights to one User object as the rights held by another. This makes administration slightly more difficult, however, so verify the string of equivalent rights all the way through for each User object. If you assign JAMES the same rights as WENDY, JAMES suddenly has access to everything WENDY controls. Make sure that's what you want before granting this equivalence.

- **User Login Scripts:** Configurable network batch files that customize the User object's network environment by setting environment variables, mapping drives, attaching printers, and the like.

- **User Account Restrictions:** Security restrictions that limit a person's access to the network or limit the use of certain network resources. For example, limits can be placed on disk space used, connection times, and network computers from which to connect. Passwords can be made mandatory, with the user forced to change them at specified time intervals.

- **User Trustee Rights:** Allows the user to access directories and files. Must be granted by the Admin user or equivalent.

- **Print Job Configurations:** Specific print job details for each User object, or a container may have configurations for all the User objects within.

- **Account Manager:** The configuration of one User object with the Supervisor right to other objects. This allows the modification of the supervised object's rights. Without allowing full Supervisor rights, one object can be granted rights to other objects to fulfill certain functions, such as modifying phone numbers for each User object.

If you are the first user connecting to a NetWare 4.1*x* server, you will see only one configured user: Admin. The Admin User object is the NetWare 4.1*x* version of SUPERVISOR from earlier NetWare versions. Everyone else must be created using either the NetWare Administrator (NWADMIN) or NETADMIN program, for MS Windows and DOS respectively. SYSCON is no more. Some old NetWare hands will be saddened, others gladdened, but SYSCON is gone nonetheless.

For new installations, you must log in as the Admin User object to have the proper rights to create new users. Later, subadministrators can be allowed to create User objects in parts of your network. Workgroup administrators granted Admin equivalence can, of course, also create any NDS object.

Either of the two NetWare administration programs lets you handle both the creation and management of users. Any user information you enter during setup of the User object can later be modified in the same manner.

This is not a linear chapter: if you prefer MS Windows and NetWare Administrator, keep reading from here. If you prefer DOS and NETADMIN, skip ahead to the "Creating User Objects with NETADMIN (DOS)" section. The explanations are remarkably similar in both places.

Creating User Objects with NetWare Administrator

ONCE YOU ARE connected to the network and have the proper VLM client programs loaded for your MS Windows or OS/2 workstation, you can run the NetWare Administrator program,

NWADMIN. Novell manuals and technical support people reference this program simply as NetWare Administrator rather than as NWADMIN. The DOS program, NETADMIN, is also shorthand for NetWare Administrator.

The majority of NetWare 4.1x administrators will use an MS Windows system. So, when I reference NetWare Administrator, you know I'm speaking of the MS Windows (or OS/2) program.

NetWare 4.11 changes the rules slightly here, but not too much. Almost all administration should be done from a Windows 95 workstation, to take advantage of the Client32 software and pseudo 32-bit operating system. Of course, to run Client32 you must install Client32 on the workstation from the NetWare CD-ROM disk, a server connection made with an earlier version of the NetWare client software, or (heaven forbid) diskettes. No matter how you get there, the NetWare Administrator program looks more sculpted and three-dimensional under Windows 95, but the same information appears in NetWare 4.11 with Client32 software running as in the earlier NetWare 4.10.

Loading Client Software and the NetWare Administrator Program

Detailed instructions for client installation were in the previous chapter. If you've skipped ahead, and are in a hurry to log in to the NetWare 4.1x server and start administrating, do this (Windows 95/Client32 users should see the text after the steps):

1. Load the INSTALL.EXE program from the WSDOS_1 diskette and follow the instructions on the screen.

2. Exit the installation program and reboot your workstation.

3. From the network drive F:, log in to the network as Admin:

    LOGIN .Admin.ORGANIZATION_NAME

   and press Enter.

4. Map the next network drive to the PUBLIC directory of volume SYS:.

5. Change to the network drive that is mapped to the PUBLIC subdirectory.

6. Start MS Windows.

7. Select the NetWare program group or the program group that will hold the NetWare Administrator program.

8. From the Program Manager File menu, choose New and select Program Item.

9. Enter a description for the NetWare Administrator in the Description field.

10. In the Command Line field, type **NWADMIN.EXE** and press the Enter key.

11. Choose OK and save the changes before you exit.

For Windows 95 users, substitute the Start button and cascading menus starting at step 7 above. The program name is NWADMN3X.EXE for the Windows 95 version. (Don't ask me why the "3X" is there at the end of the name; I guess Novell engineers felt we all needed a bit more confusion in our lives.) Of course, if they had added 32, for the Client32 program, it would make sense. Perhaps the NWADMNS3X is a typo, and they meant NWADMN32. If you think of it that way, it will help you remember that NWADMN3X is the file you want.

Upon login, the Admin user has access to the root of the SYS: volume, to SYS:SYSTEM and SYS:PUBLIC, just as in earlier NetWare versions. The LOGIN command for Admin assumes the Admin object was placed in the main Organization container.

Basic User Object Setup with NetWare Administrator

6.1 IN-A-HURRY

Create a Basic User Object

1. Open NetWare Administrator, and move to the context for the new User object.

2. Press Insert to open the New Object pick box.

3. Choose the User object and press Enter.

4. Provide the Login Name and press Tab.

5. Provide the Last Name and press Enter.

When I say basic, I mean basic. The bare-bones User object created using the minimum configuration has no login script and no rights except those granted to the [Public] trustee object (similar to the EVERYONE group of earlier NetWare versions).

The first thing to do, as when performing any administration task while in MS Windows, is to load the NetWare Administration program. When the program opens, you will see the [Root] object with the globe icon. Each container you open displays the objects contained inside, both container and leaf objects. You can open a container by double-clicking on the container object or by choosing the Expand option from the View menu. (If you ask me, double-clicking is easier.) You may certainly use the key combinations of Alt+V then X for expand if you wish to avoid using the mouse.

Before we can create the User object, we must reach the context in which it will reside. Technically, you may create a User object in any context you wish, and the user will have access to the NDS tree. The trick is that the individual user must know his or her context when logging in, or the context must be placed in the LOGIN command. Practically, it's easiest to create each user in the same context as that user's primary server.

Non-NetWare 4.1*x* users (those using NetWare 3.*x* or earlier NETX shells on their workstations) must be created in the containers where Bindery Services is enabled. Their context is not important when they log in, because those users log in through Bindery Services. They log in directly to their target NetWare 4.1*x* server, bypassing NDS completely.

Once all the containers are open, or at least the container in which you plan to create a new User object, highlight the Organization or Organizational Unit name. To create a new object, you have three choices to start the process:

- Press the Insert key.

- Press the right mouse button on the container name, then click the left button on Create.

- Press Alt+O for Object on the main menu, then highlight Create and press Enter.

Old NetWare hands will no doubt press the Insert key, since that's the time-honored NetWare tradition. No matter which method you choose to start the Create process, you wind up with what's shown in Figure 6.1.

The NetWare Administrator program runs as a multiple-document interface (MDI) application. The main, full-screen NetWare Administrator window becomes the background for multiple secondary windows.

> **NOTE**
>
> *In Figure 6.1, I have moved the New Object subwindow to the right so it does not cover the NDS tree. For many of the illustrations in this book, the windows were moved about for clarity. So don't be alarmed when your screen doesn't look exactly like the one shown in the picture.*

In typical MS Windows fashion, you may left-click on the scroll bar to the right of the window until User comes into view, as it is in the screen in Figure 6.1. In typical NetWare fashion, you may also press the first letters of your choice until that choice appears under the highlight bar. In Figure 6.1, pressing U was all that was necessary to highlight User.

When the proper object is highlighted, press Enter or click on the OK button. You can cancel the process by clicking on the Cancel button or pressing the Escape key. Clicking on the Context button displays the context,

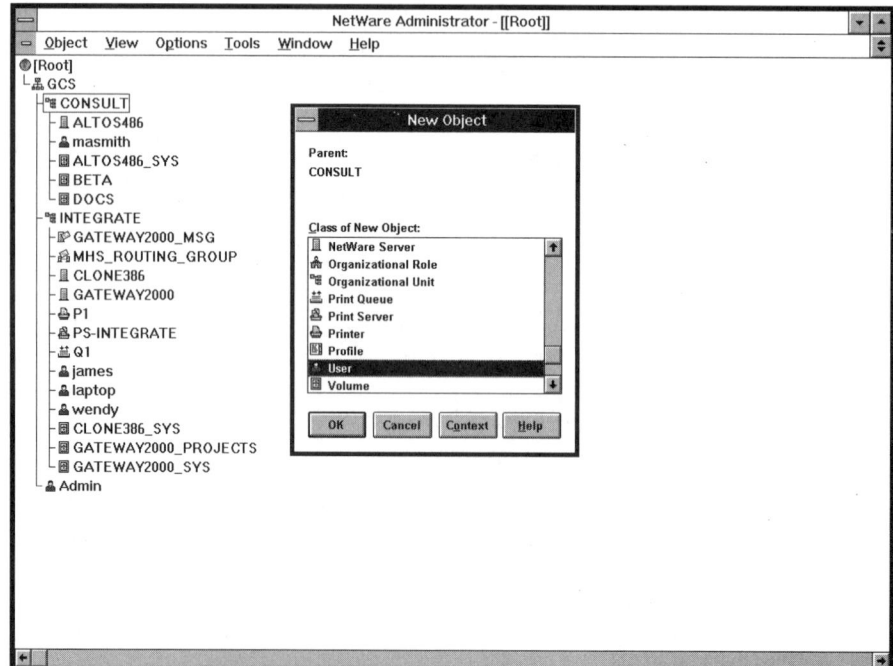

FIGURE 6.1

Beginning the process of User object creation

which echoes the listing under Parent at the top of the New Object window. Clicking on the Help button, or pressing the F1 key, pops open the standard MS Windows hypertext Help system, with information for your specific topic.

After choosing the User object and confirming your choice in the manner you feel most comfortable, the Create User window opens. This window has the two mandatory fields, Login Name and Last Name, along with four options. Figure 6.2 shows the Create User window.

The login name can contain spaces. Names are not case sensitive, but they will be displayed as typed in the Login Name field (MaSmith will display that way, but NDS regards it as identical to masmith and MASMITH).

The requirements for login names are:

- Must be less than 64 characters long

- Must be unique within the container

These restrictions aren't onerous, and are much more liberal than earlier NetWare versions. Which brings up an important point: if your NetWare 4.1x

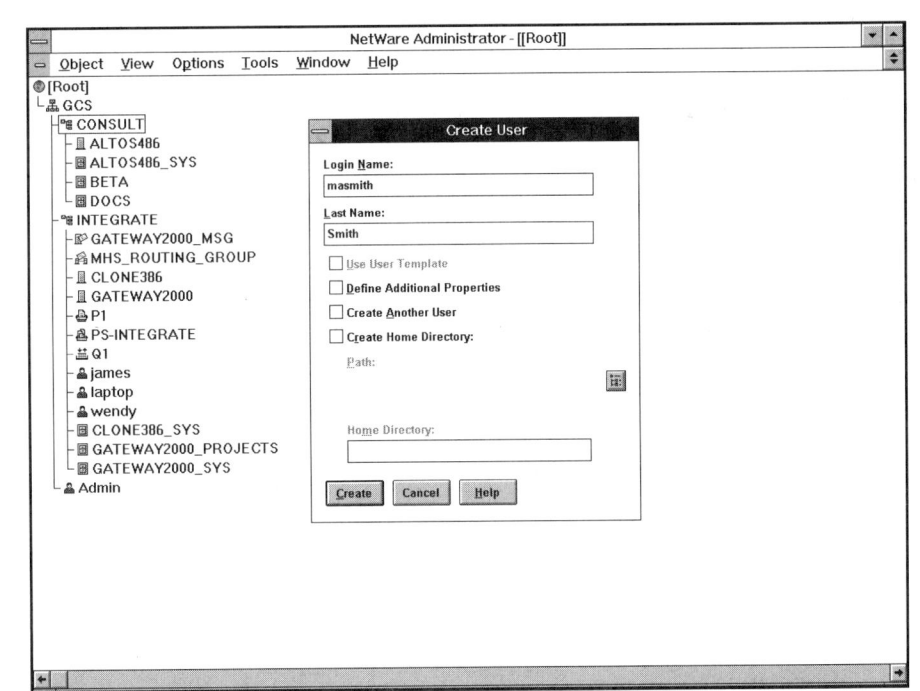

FIGURE 6.2

Creating MASMITH

server must support non-NDS clients, or work with earlier NetWare server versions, you must be mindful of the restrictions placed on login names by the bindery:

- Names longer than 47 characters are truncated.

- Spaces are shown as underscores.

- The following characters can't be seen by non-NDS clients: slash (/), backslash (\), colon (:), comma (,), asterisk (*), and question mark (?).

The special characters above are legal within NDS but not within bindery systems. These characters also have problems in DOS names. The path of least trouble is to develop a naming standard for users that allows only alpha and numeric characters. If e-mail is important to your company, verify names with that system before assigning them inside NDS. You want names that work across all applications and systems.

The Last Name field is mandatory, but has no restrictions except making the name fit into the field. You might wonder why this is here, looking so much like a database entry field. What about searching for users at a later date? This will be done, and last name is certainly an excellent search field. That's why this information is mandatory.

Specifying Optional User Object Details with NetWare Administrator

Notice in Figure 6.2 the four checkboxes below the Last Name field. Much more information is suggested for each user, even if it isn't mandatory.

- **Use User Template:** The user template is a file containing default information applied to new User objects, giving them predetermined property values within that container.

- **Define Additional Properties:** Opens a window with fields for more details about the User object.

- **Create Another User:** Saves this User object and lets you immediately create another.

- **Create Home Directory:** Make a personal directory for this user and grant that user all rights to that directory.

Of these four options, Define Additional Properties and Create Another User are mutually exclusive. If you choose one, the other option turns gray, indicating it's no longer valid.

Let's take a look at some of these. The first option, Use User Template is gray because we have yet to define a user template. We'll get to that soon.

Creating a Home Directory

> **6.2 IN-A-HURRY**
>
> **Create a Home Directory for a User**
>
> 1. Open NetWare Administrator and create a new User object.
>
> 2. Click on the Create Home Directory checkbox.
>
> 3. Click on the Browser button to see the available file systems.
>
> 4. Choose the proper location for the home directory, then click on OK.
>
> 5. Enter the name of the home directory in the Home Directory field, or accept the default (same as the User object name).
>
> 6. Click on Create, and the home directory will be created immediately.

I'm all in favor of the "Home Directory" concept that's been in use from the earliest days of NetWare. It encourages two important traits in your users:

- Placing personal working files on the server so they are easy to back up and restore

- Developing a sense of "ownership" of the server, since they have a personal stake

These may not be earthshaking, but they are important. Although backup systems are becoming more sophisticated, client backup is still difficult. The easiest backup system for you as the administrator is to back up only the server, knowing the user files will be taken care of at the same time.

The ownership feeling is a bit more ephemeral, but just as important. When NetWare networks were bought and supported by the department, the department "owned" the server and often felt protective toward it. The trend today is for servers to be centrally administered, making them more distant from the

Chapter 6 • Creating and Managing Users (Now User Objects)

If each person has a direct connection to a little piece of the network he or she "owns," that user has more positive feelings about the network.

departments. The department now has less control of the network composition, mission, and administration. Some of the aggravation formerly directed at the mainframe people is now being aimed at the central network authority. If each person has a direct connection to a little piece of the network he or she "owns," that user has more positive feelings about the network.

Creating the home directory is not at all difficult. Figure 6.3 shows the creation of a home directory for user MASMITH (in NetWare 4.10).

It's smart to group all the users under an "umbrella" directory (named USERS in the example in Figure 6.3). It makes for neater file systems, easier management, and smoother expansion. If all users are on the same volume, and the volume grows, another disk can be added and the volume spread across both disks without inconveniencing the users.

Notice in Figure 6.3 that we've created user MASMITH in the CONSULT Organizational Unit, but the home directories are all on the GATEWAY2000 server in the INTEGRATE Organizational Unit. This was not possible under earlier NetWare versions, and it illustrates another example of the value of NDS, even for small companies with only two or three servers.

FIGURE 6.3

Picking the home directory location

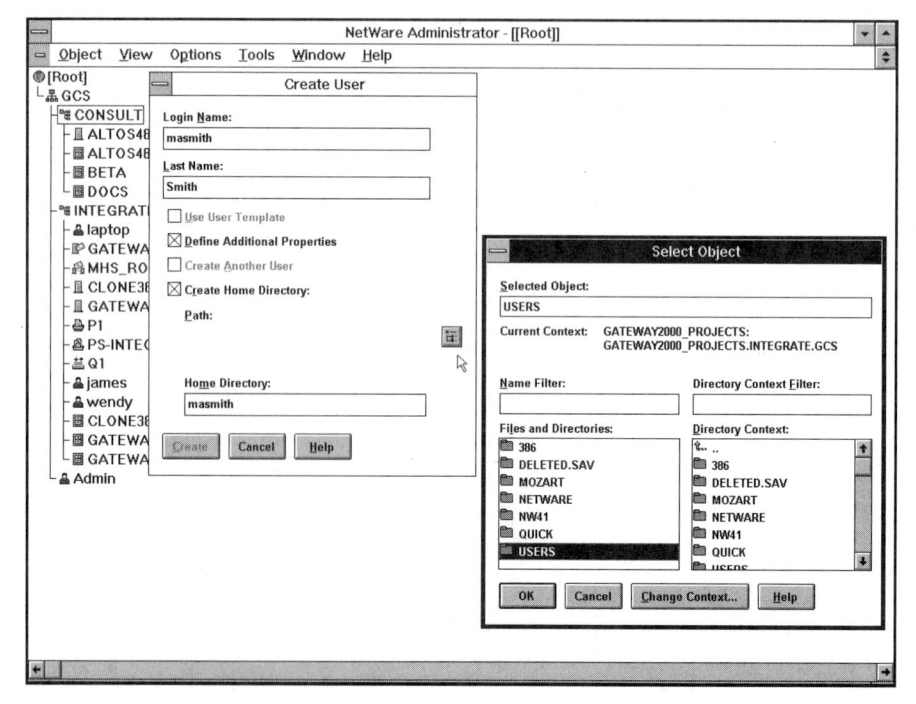

Users can use their home directory as if it were the root of their personal hard disk. They may create and delete files and subdirectories to their hearts' content. No user has, by default, the right to see or manipulate the contents of another user's home directory.

Don't put the user home directories on the SYS: volume if at all possible. That's been the tradition with NetWare administrators for years, but it's not a good idea. User-controlled space may grow quickly, filling the volume. If it's the SYS: volume that becomes full, your server gets weird and will likely shut down. If it's some other volume that gets full, a few users call and complain they can't save any more files. Of the two error conditions, the second is by far preferable.

When you click on the Browser button (the one that looks like a tiny map of the NDS tree) in the Create User dialog box, the Select Object dialog box, the active one in Figure 6.3, appears. Remember, directories and file systems are treated as objects now.

When the Select Object dialog box opens, the Directory Context box in the lower right shows the list of available servers and volumes in the context. To move around the NDS tree, double-click on objects in the Directory Context list box. In this example, double-clicking on the GATEWAY2000_PROJECTS volume shows the list of available directories. When the umbrella directory appears, you must click on the name in the Files and Directories pick list. Doing so will copy the directory name to the Selected Object field at the top of the dialog box, and the OK button will become active.

The Name Filter field in the Select Object dialog box allows you to restrict objects that appear in the left list box by using wildcards or object names. The Directory Context Filter above the right list box does the same for containers.

The Change Context button at the bottom of the dialog box allows you to see a different context. No Browser button is available; you must type the new context name. The Cancel button clears everything and returns you to the previous dialog box.

Clicking on OK closes the Select Object dialog box. Back in the original Create User dialog box, the home directory name, with its full context, is copied into the Path section. At the bottom of the dialog box, the Home Directory field contains the User object name. You may accept that name or type a different name into the field. Clicking on Create will immediately create the home directory and grant all rights to that directory to the user.

Adding User Identification Information

If you click on the Define Additional Properties checkbox in the Create User dialog box, you will find tons of things to fill out about this particular User object. Don't be overwhelmed; none of this information is mandatory. But many items are helpful, and you are probably already familiar with such things as the Login Script properties from earlier NetWare versions.

Figure 6.4 shows the main user Identification screen, identified in two ways. First, the screen name appears in the upper-left corner, just under the main title bar. Second, the Identification button on the right side is pressed and has black borders.

Let's take a quick look around this screen. In the title bar, the object class and name of the object are shown. Here, it's User:masmith (I told you the system remembers exactly how you typed the name). The page title shows just under the left side of the title bar. Page buttons line the right side, with the active one sporting a dark bar across the top and left side. The 3-D effect is used to make the active button look like it's pressed down.

FIGURE 6.4

Entering MASMITH identification information

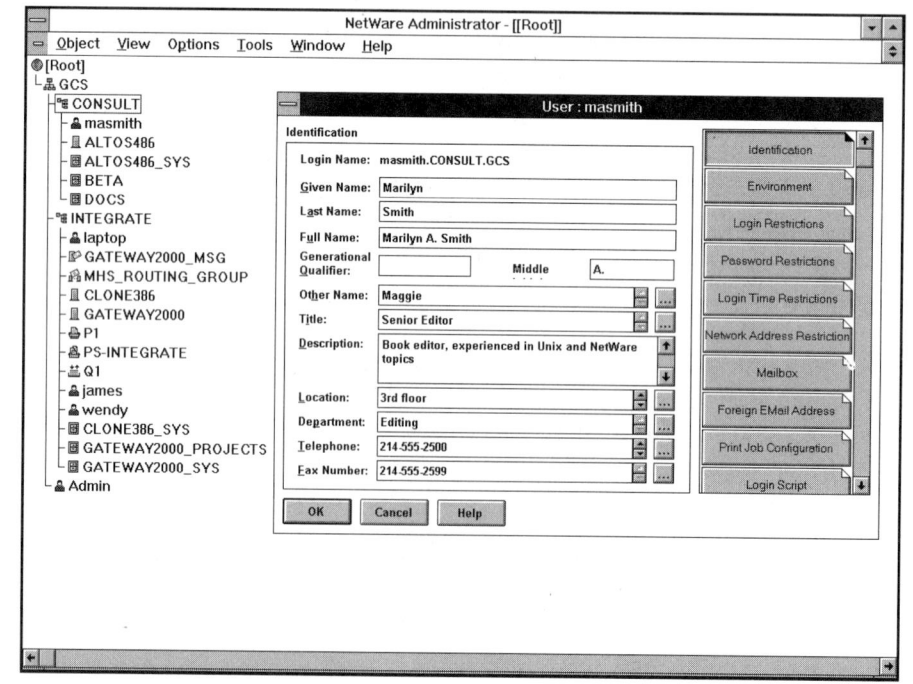

Creating User Objects with NetWare Administrator **363**

There are 17 pages represented by the buttons. Clicking on the scroll bar to the right of the buttons will pull the rest into view. When the turned-down corner of a page button is black, as the Identification button is in Figure 6.4, there have been changes made to that page, but those changes are not yet saved. Clicking on the OK button saves all the pages at once.

NetWare 4.11 adds the ability to choose which of those command buttons appear on the screen when you ask for the details about an object. There are new buttons for the NetWare Registry and the NAL (NetWare Application Launcher), which we'll talk about in Chapter 10. I don't recommend subtracting command buttons from the list that appears, more and more applications are starting to add their own buttons. If the list grows too much, paring it down may be worth the time and effort.

If your mouse arm is just too tired to reach all the way over to the command buttons, there is a shortcut if you're running Windows 95, believe it or not. Put your cursor anywhere on the foreground box, and click the right mouse button. The entire list of all command buttons will pop up in menu form.

> **WARNING**
>
> *The OK and Cancel buttons across the bottom of Figure 6.4 work on all of the pages represented by the buttons on the right. Each button represents at least one page of information. Do* not *click on the Cancel button unless you mean to cancel every change made on every field on every page during this session.*

Notice the More buttons to the right of the fields, starting with Other Name and running through the end. The three little dots on the button are really an ellipsis (Latin for "three little dots"). At the end of a sentence, the ellipsis indicates there is more not explicitly stated. The same is true here. Every field with a More button can hold multiple values, such as several phone numbers, titles, or the like.

When you start, the only information filled in is the Login Name (with full context) and Last Name fields. If you remember, these are the only two mandatory fields when creating a User object. However, the WHOAMI command-line utility presents the information in the Other Name, Title, and Description fields if they are not blank.

The fields in the Identification page contain plenty of information that can be useful when searching for particular people or locations on the network. The list of field names and uses are:

- **Given Name:** User's first name

- **Last Name:** User's last name (filled in automatically)

- **Full Name:** User's complete name
- **Generational Qualifier:** Jr., Sr., II, III, etc.
- **Middle:** User's initials
- **Other Name:** Nicknames, job function names, or other identification information (60 characters maximum per entry; duplicates are not allowed)
- **Title:** Position or function of user (60 characters maximum)
- **Description:** Function the user performs (30 lines of 37 characters each maximum)
- **Location:** Physical location, such as floor, wing, or mail stop
- **Department:** User's department, division, or workgroup
- **Telephone:** User's telephone numbers
- **Fax Number:** User's fax numbers or those available to the user

Why should you enter all these things? Seems like a lot of extra work, doesn't it? Well, what if your boss asks for all the network users on the third floor? How many network users are senior editors? How many network users will use the new fax modem when we replace the fax machine with the number 214-555-2599? These answers are easy to find if the database information is available.

> **NOTE**
>
> *Of course, if anyone had bothered to ask me, I would have replaced the fax number slot with an e-mail address, with room for multiple addresses. But then, I hate faxes, and much prefer e-mail. I'm surprised that Novell didn't add a spot for e-mail in NetWare 4.11, but perhaps they're expecting all NetWare customers to buy GroupWise. There is nothing stopping you from adding e-mail addresses in one of the fields that takes multiple entries, such as Location, but it would have been nice to have one that said "e-mail."*

Entering User Environment Information

The Environment page is strictly informative. None of the information you set here changes the User object's setup or configuration. Figure 6.5 shows this page. Notice the second button along the right side of the dialog box is pressed.

FIGURE 6.5

Environment information

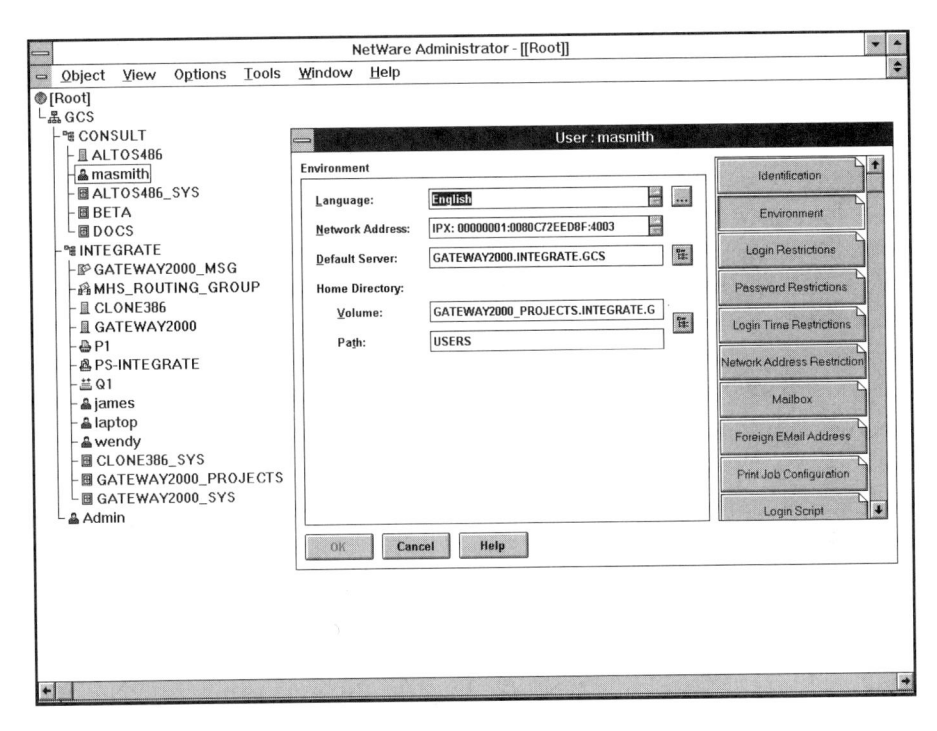

[Screenshot of NetWare Administrator showing User: masmith Environment page with fields for Language (English), Network Address (IPX: 00000001:0080C72EED8F:4003), Default Server (GATEWAY2000.INTEGRATE.GCS), Home Directory Volume (GATEWAY2000_PROJECTS.INTEGRATE.G) and Path (USERS).]

The fields on the Environment page are:

- **Language:** From the SET command, shows the language for system messages.

- **Network Address:** Address or addresses of the workstation this user is currently using to connect to the network. This will change when the user connects from a different station.

- **Default Server:** NetWare 4.1x server the user tries to connect to when logging in. This information is supplied by NDS.

- **Home Directory:** The volume and directory of the user's home directory. This is informational only; changes here don't add of modify anything in NetWare 4.10 (but you can add a new home directory through this field in NetWare 4.11).

The last line is important enough to repeat: the home directory is not set here, it is set during initial user setup. Do not try to create a home directory for a user from this page, or you will be disappointed, unless you're using NetWare 4.11. One of the little advancements that don't make the press release pages is the fact that now the home directory will be made for you from this screen.

Giving the User a Mailbox in NetWare 4.10

> ### 6.3 IN-A-HURRY
>
> **Set the E-mailbox Information**
>
> 1. In NetWare 4.10, open NetWare Administrator and locate the User object in the NDS tree.
>
> 2. Open the User dialog box by double-clicking on the User object name.
>
> 3. Click on the Mailbox button.
>
> 4. Click on the Browser button to open the Select Object dialog box.
>
> 5. Locate and click on the messaging server where the User object's mailbox is located.
>
> 6. Click on the OK button.

On the first User Information page, Identification, the physical address for the user is listed. Even more important today is the e-mailbox. You still get junk mail, but when you throw it away, it doesn't clog landfills.

Figure 6.6 shows the Mailbox Location field filled in on the Mailbox page. To set the mailbox location, start the NetWare Administrator program and locate the User object in the NDS tree. In our example, you can see that MASMITH is right where we left her, the only User object we've created in the CONSULT.GCS Organizational Unit.

When you locate the user, open the User dialog box by using one of these methods:

- Double-click on the name.

- Highlight the name and press the Enter key.

- Choose Details from the Object menu.

- Aim the cursor at the User object and press the right mouse button, then press the Enter key or click on Details.

FIGURE 6.6

Setting the e-mailbox location in NetWare 4.10

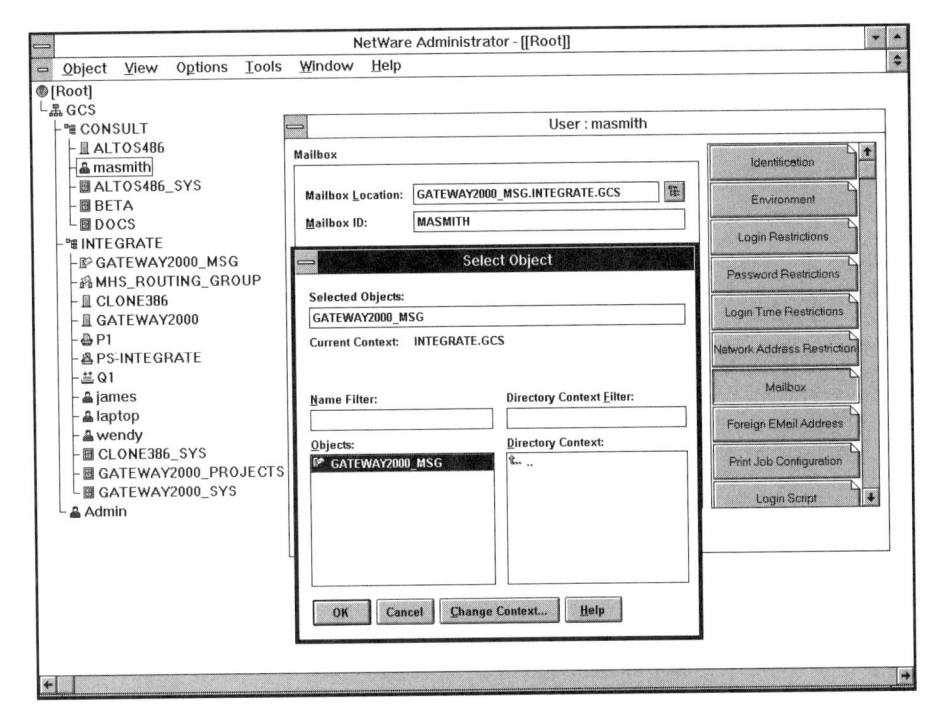

As you can see, NetWare Administrator makes it easy to get the details on your User object.

Open the Mailbox page by clicking on the appropriate button on the right side of the dialog box. If the Mailbox Location field is empty, click on the Browser button at the end of the field. You can tell this is a Browser button rather than the More button, because the diagram on the button is that of an NDS tree.

The Select Object dialog box opens, just as in Figure 6.3. Now, however, the Select Object dialog box is smart enough to know we don't care about volumes and directories, just messaging servers. When you move to a context holding a messaging server, as we have in Figure 6.6, the server name pops into the Objects pick list.

When the messaging server that supports the current user is chosen, the user name is automatically copied into the Mailbox ID field. Click on the OK button to save the information, but only if you're finished with all the pages of User object information. Both the OK and Cancel buttons apply to all pages, not just the one on display.

NetWare 4.11 is missing the e-mailbox. (Told you Novell wants you to buy GroupWise.)

Setting Foreign E-mail Address and Aliases in NetWare 4.10

> **6.4 IN-A-HURRY**
>
> **Set the Foreign E-mailbox Information**
>
> 1. In NetWare 4.10, open NetWare Administrator and locate the User object in the NDS tree.
> 2. Open the User dialog box by double-clicking on the User object name.
> 3. Click on the Foreign E-mail Address button.
> 4. Click on Set, under the Foreign EMail Address field.
> 5. Provide the user's foreign e-mail address and e-mail type in the Foreign EMail Address dialog box and click on OK.
> 6. Click on the Add button under Foreign EMail Aliases (if applicable).
> 7. Provide the user's foreign e-mail address and e-mail type in the Foreign EMail Address dialog box and click on OK.

There are two good reasons for having this information on foreign e-mail addresses: NDS supports NDS users getting their mail on remote mailboxes, and users outside your network may wish to address your users. If so, they will use their native system to address your users, and you may wish to keep track of those addresses.

Figure 6.7 shows the Foreign EMail Address page (with the smaller dialog box moved to the bottom of the screen so you can see the other fields). There are five e-mail types offered after you click on the down arrow button at the end of the Type field:

- **GMHS:** Global Message Handling Service from Novell.
- **PROFS:** PRofessional OFfice System, IBM's office automation and e-mail system for mainframes running the VM operating system.
- **SMTP:** Simple Mail Transport Protocol, the standard Unix e-mail exchange protocol.
- **SNADS:** SNA Distribution Services, another IBM product for file, document, and e-mail exchange.
- **X.400:** CCITT standard for exchanging e-mail between systems.

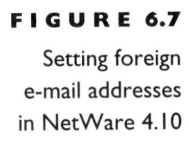

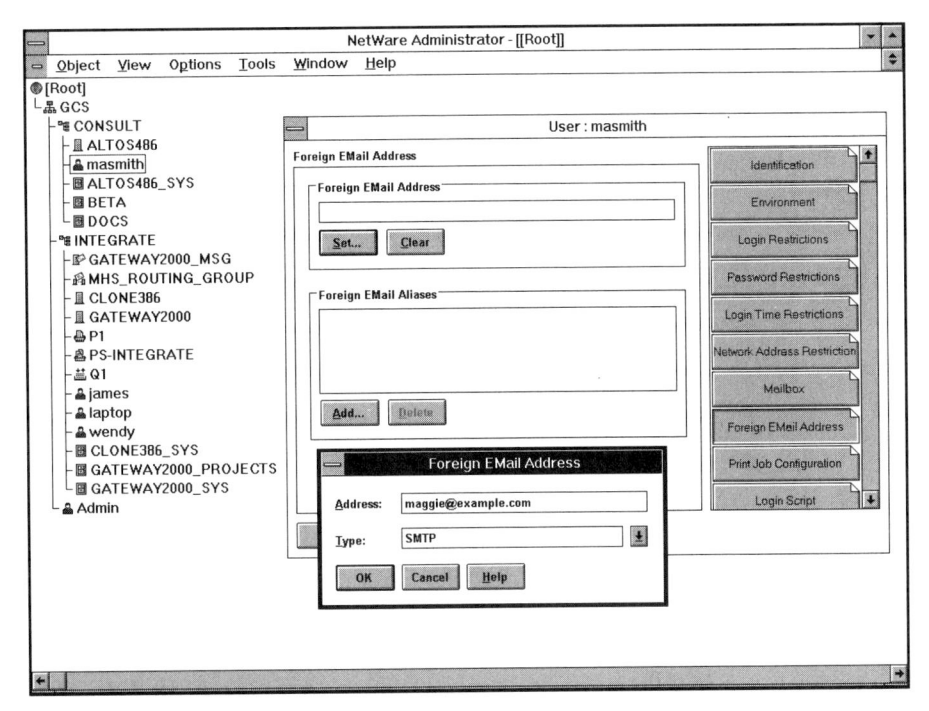

FIGURE 6.7

Setting foreign e-mail addresses in NetWare 4.10

This page is again for informational purposes, and doesn't effect any changes on your network. You may add only one foreign e-mail address, but multiple foreign aliases are allowed. The limit is one alias per e-mail type.

Having NDS clients with a foreign e-mail address isn't terribly unusual. The hassles of managing many of the LAN-based e-mail packages for remote clients and mobile users have heightened awareness of Unix-based e-mail. Several large companies are moving toward using a Unix e-mail package as the single e-mail system. By providing terminal access to local users and dial-up modem access to remote users, no LAN gateways are necessary.

As you might guess, NetWare 4.11 is also missing the Foreign E-mail Address command button. Of course, GroupWise handles these details for you, should you feel inclined to call your reseller and check out the most advanced e-mailing/scheduling/calendaring/task-watching groupware on the market.

Specifying Print Job Configurations

> **6.5 IN-A-HURRY**
>
> ### Create a Print Job Configuration
>
> 1. Open NetWare Administrator and locate the User object in the NDS tree.
> 2. Open the User dialog box by double-clicking on the User object name.
> 3. Click on the Print Job Configuration button.
> 4. Click on the New button.
> 5. Fill in the appropriate fields for this print job configuration, including a unique name for this user.
> 6. Click on OK in the Print Job Configuration dialog box, then again in the User dialog box.

Print jobs configurations are generally created at the container level, so that they are available to all users in the container. You can, however, create a personal print job configuration.

Any print job configuration is activated by using the Job option (J=) in the CAPTURE and NPRINT print utilities. You must specify which print job configuration you wish to engage by naming it as part of the CAPTURE or NPRINT command, as in:

```
CAPTURE J=PJ1
```

If you have a default print job configuration, those parameters will be in effect each time you invoke CAPTURE or NPRINT. You may override any of the defined parameters by using a command-line parameter with either print utility.

Figure 6.8 shows the Print Job Configuration page, with a new print job configuration being created. This screen is identical to the screen used to set up print job configurations for Organizations or Organizational Units.

Here we are adding a new print job configuration in addition to the one already listed in the background dialog box. The foreground dialog box opened when the New button was clicked. Beside the New button (but unseen because of the foreground dialog box) are buttons for Modify, Delete, and Default. The ms_print job in the background dialog box has been designated

Creating User Objects with NetWare Administrator 371

FIGURE 6.8

Creating a new personal print job configuration

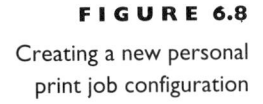

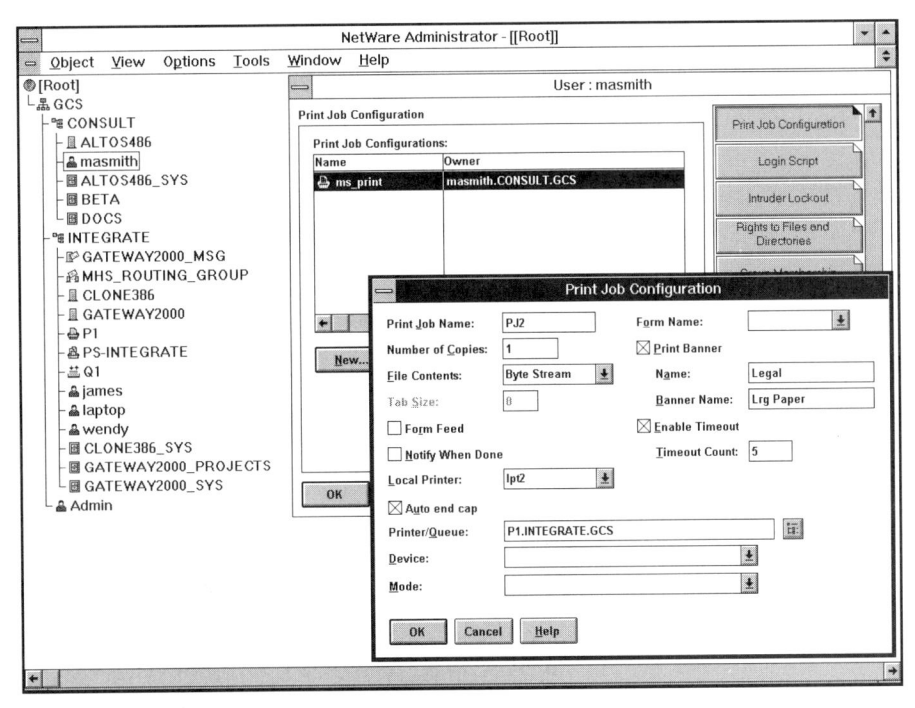

the default print job configuration, as shown by the small printer icon beside the print job configuration name.

The Print Job Configuration dialog box field names and acceptable values are:

- **Print Job Name:** Must be unique for this user. The name cannot be changed, although you can modify all other fields later.

- **Number of Copies:** The default is 1, but any number up to 65,000 may be entered.

- **File Contents:** Text or Byte Stream. Byte Stream is the default and also safest choice for general printing.

- **Tab Size:** Active only when the file contents are listed as Text. Refers to the width in characters each tab character should be when printed.

- **Form Feed:** When checked, the CAPTURE or NPRINT software sends a form feed to flush the job out of the printer.

- **Notify When Done:** When checked, the system will send the user a message when the print job is finished being spooled to the printer. It does not guarantee the printer has successfully printed the job itself.

- **Local Printer:** Chooses which parallel port your print job will be sent to. NetWare expands on DOS by allowing up to nine LPT designations. A modification to the user's NET.CFG file must be made to allow more than three LPT ports.

- **Auto End Cap:** When checked, tells the CAPTURE command to print the job when the application says it is finished.

- **Printer/Queue:** Designates the printer or print queue for this print job configuration. Clicking on the Browser button opens the Select Object dialog box, but the dialog box will show only printers and print queues.

- **Device:** Specifies a named print device for this print job configuration.

- **Mode:** Specifies a defined mode (such as Re-initialize) for the print device specified in the previous field.

- **Form Name:** Specifies a defined form for this print job configuration, chosen from a pick list that appears when the down arrow button is clicked.

- **Print Banner:** When checked, includes a banner page at the beginning of the print job.

- **Name:** Active only when Print Banner is checked. When this field is blank, the user name is inserted. The name listed in this field and the next can only be 11 characters long.

- **Banner Name:** Active only when Print Banner is checked. When this field is left blank, the printer port is inserted on the banner page. The name listed in this field and the previous can only be 11 characters long.

- **Enable Timeout:** When checked, forces CAPTURE to consider a print job finished if there is no activity for a defined number of seconds.

- **Timeout Count:** Active only when Enable Timeout is checked. Range is from 1 to 1000 seconds. For typical word processing print jobs, a short value (5–10) will be fine. For print jobs requiring lots of computer calculations, such as large reports or spreadsheets, the time should be longer. If a print job comes out in two or more pieces, this value is too low.

The ability to have print job configurations for particular users is good, but don't get carried away. It's much better to configure printing for groups of users at one time. That's why the print job configuration for a container is so much more useful than this one for individuals.

Specifying the User's Postal Address

> **6.6 IN-A-HURRY**
>
> **Set Postal Address Information**
>
> 1. Open NetWare Administrator and locate the User object in the NDS tree.
> 2. Open the User dialog box by double-clicking on the User object name.
> 3. Click on the Postal Address button on the right.
> 4. Fill in the fields in the top half of the window.
> 5. To copy the information to the Mailing Label Information, click on the Copy to Label button.
> 6. Click on OK to save the information.

The Postal Address page allows you to track either the home or business address for each user. The fields can be used for searching and to create a mailing label format. Figure 6.9 shows the Postal Address dialog box with information for user MASMITH.

After opening the NetWare Administrator program, find the user you want to give a physical address listing. Double-click on that name, or open the User dialog box in one of the other ways: select from the Object menu, right-click and press Enter, or just press Enter when the User object is highlighted. From the User dialog box, click on the Postal Address button on the right side. You will need to scroll down the buttons to find this particular button. After you click, the screen shown in Figure 6.9 appears.

No particular secrets here; no Browser buttons or pick lists. The only concern is if you plan to use this information for searching your NDS database later. Only the top half of the dialog box will be searched, not the bottom.

These fields accept all international postal codes. If you have international addresses, just supply the appropriate codes and countries in the Postal (Zip) Code field.

374 Chapter 6 ▪ Creating and Managing Users (Now User Objects)

FIGURE 6.9

Addresses the old-fashioned way

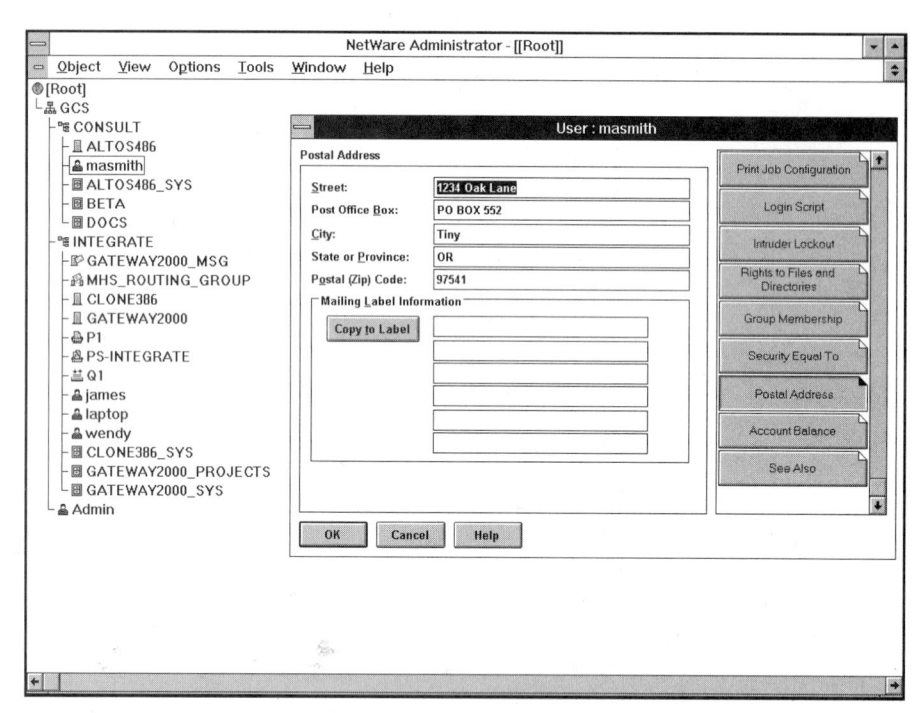

Setting the Account Balance

6.7 IN-A-HURRY

Set the Account Balance for a User

1. Open NetWare Administrator and locate the User object in the NDS tree.

2. Open the User dialog box by double-clicking on the User object name.

3. Click on the Account Balance button on the right.

4. Click to disable the Allow Unlimited Credit box to enable accounting.

5. Set the current Account Balance and the Low Balance Limit.

6. Click on OK to save your settings.

NetWare was the first network operating system to allow accounting. By tracking such details as connect time, disk space used, and service requests to a file server, NetWare accounting moved away from a PC LAN level toward mainframe-type control. Accounting is used by some network administrators to charge company departments, and by others to track when resources are being used more heavily than in the past.

If accounting is enabled on a server, the users of that server can be assigned a value for each server operation. The screen shown in Figure 6.10 tells you how simple it is to track the server resources consumed by a user.

The Account Balance field shows the remaining credits available for this user. The credits are set on the network resource itself, not here (see Chapter 10 for details). The Low Balance Limit field shows the credit level to warn the user before the account is disabled.

If you wish to track the accounting information for charge-back or overhead calculations, but don't wish to prevent users from reaching their network resources after they've used up their allotted credit, click on the Allow Unlimited Credit box. This will track the information needed for the accounting reports but never lock out users.

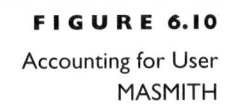

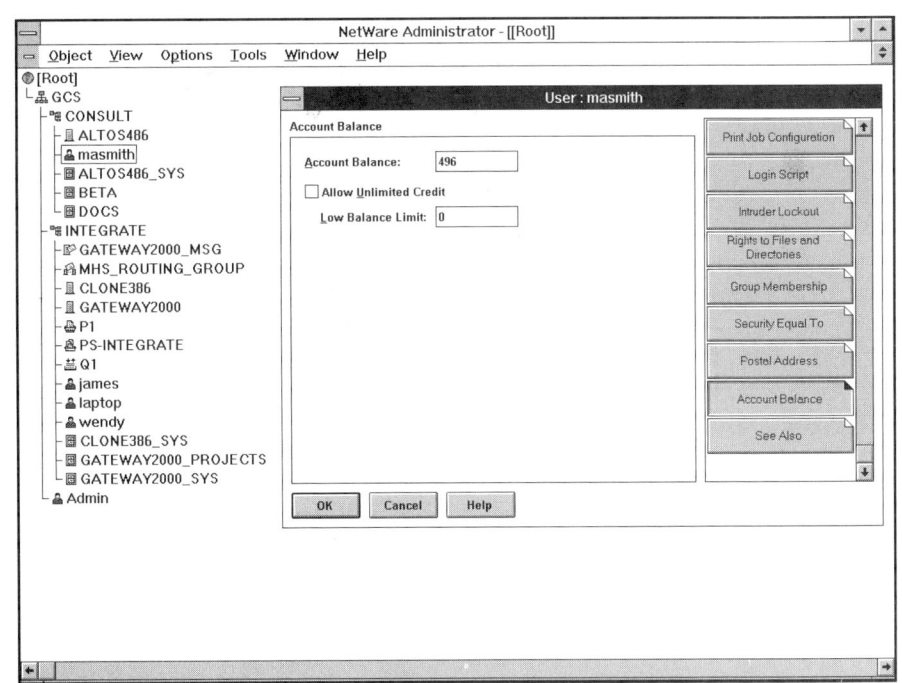

FIGURE 6.10

Accounting for User MASMITH

> **NOTE**
>
> *If a user's credits do drop to the level of the Low Balance Limit field and that user is locked out of the system, nothing happens to the user's information. The user will be back in business as soon as an administrator changes the Account Balance field.*

Adding Reference Information

6.8 IN-A-HURRY

Track Related Objects for a User

1. Open NetWare Administrator and locate the User object in the NDS tree.

2. Open the User dialog box by double-clicking on the User object name.

3. Click on the See Also button on the right.

4. Click on the Add button to list more objects related to the user.

5. Pick the related objects from the Select Object dialog box.

6. Click on OK to move the selected objects to the See Also page.

7. Click on OK to save the information.

The See Also page is strictly informational. It does not affect any network configurations. Figure 6.11 shows the process of adding new related objects to the user MASMITH (in NetWare 4.1). This page is a handy place to put items you may need for reference, such as the Computer object type used by MASMITH.

You cannot enter text in the See Also page. You can choose multiple objects in the Select Object dialog box. Just hold down the Ctrl key as you click the left mouse button on each object you want to select.

Configuring User Object Security with NetWare Administrator

So far, all the user configuration options we've covered have been informational. The last nine entry/information screens in the User section involve network security.

We'll get into more serious security discussions in later chapters. Now, however, we'll focus on the particular security information that is necessary to set up and manage individual User objects through the NetWare Administrator program.

Creating User Objects with NetWare Administrator **377**

FIGURE 6.11
Showing MASMITH is related to PS-INTEGRATE

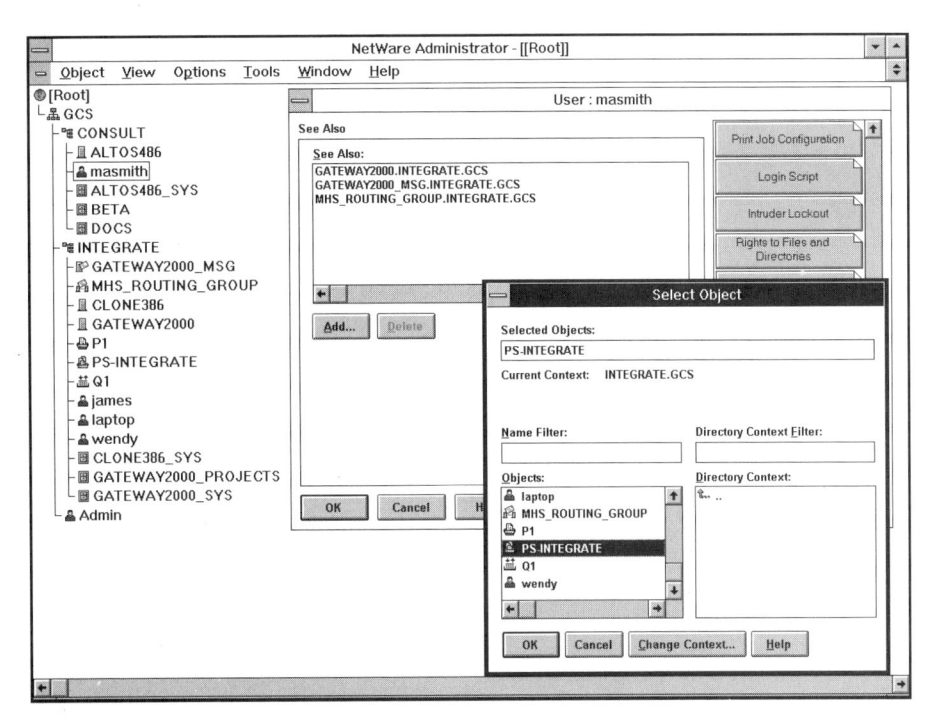

Adding a User Login Script

6.9 IN-A-HURRY

Create or Modify a User Object Login Script

1. Open NetWare Administrator and locate the User object in the NDS tree.

2. Open the User dialog box by double-clicking on the User object name.

3. Click on the Login Script button on the right.

4. Enter login script commands.

5. Click on OK to save the login script.

The login script was the single place to manage user configuration in the earliest NetWare versions. Later, more control was available in the system login script, but there could be only one system login script per server. That limited what could be done for any particular user or groups of users (or you ended up with a huge and unwieldy system script).

With NetWare 4.1x, there are four scripts that work together to control the network configuration of any one user. The user login script, once the most important, has now become somewhat less important.

The user login script executes last, and overrides all previous settings. This is the same relationship as with NetWare 3.x's system and user login scripts. But the extra scripts available in NetWare 4.1x make the user login script necessary only for unique needs for that particular user. We'll discuss the various types of login scripts in the next chapter, but if you do need individual user login scripts, the User dialog box's Login Script button is the one to click.

After starting NetWare Administrator and selecting the User object to examine, bring up the User dialog box by double-clicking on that User object. You'll notice that the Login Script button is toward the bottom of the screen shown in Figure 6.12. It may be completely hidden in your MS Windows display.

FIGURE 6.12

Adding a test login script for User MASMITH

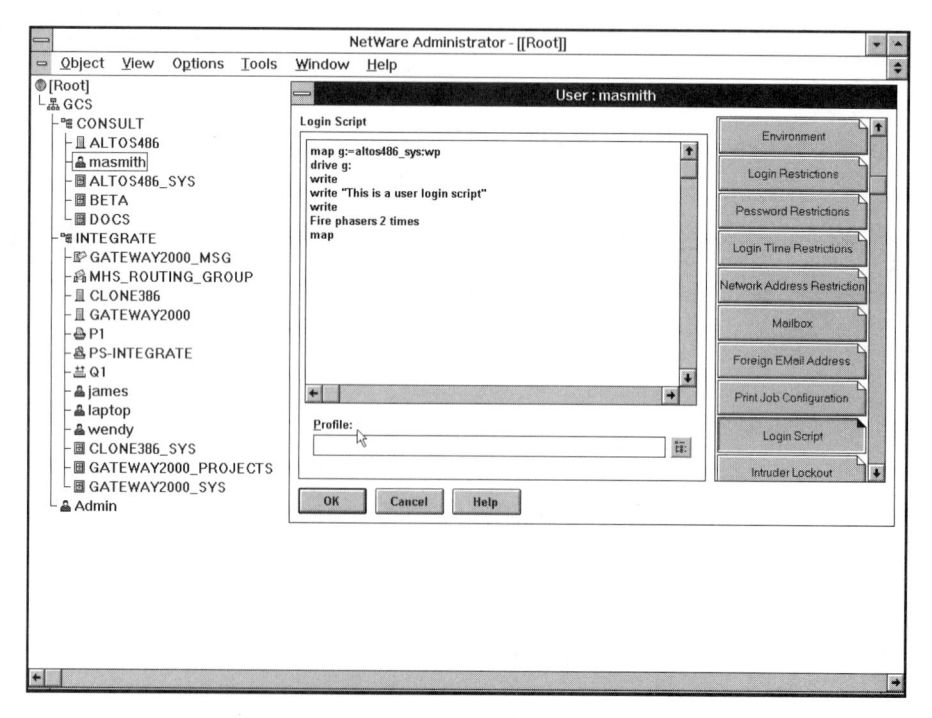

> *One important note: see the arrow pointing to the Profile field toward the bottom of the dialog box in Figure 6.12? That will become important soon. Since we haven't created a profile login script yet, we can't include it into the user login script here.*

In the Login Script page, enter the login script commands. See the next chapter for information about login script commands and syntax.

Setting Login Restrictions

6.10 IN-A-HURRY

Set Login Restrictions for a User

1. Open NetWare Administrator and locate the User object in the NDS tree.

2. Open the User dialog box by double-clicking on the User object name.

3. Click on the Login Restrictions button on the right.

4. Check the boxes to disable the account, set the account expiration date, or limit concurrent connections.

5. Read the last login time and date (if applicable).

6. Click on OK to save the restrictions.

Login restriction setup is one of the times that NetWare 4.1x focuses on the individual user. Normally, any configuration that can be done to a particular user can better be done working with a group. Restrictions on a particular user are useful at times, however, and this is where you set some of those restrictions.

Login restriction sounds like a way to stop someone from connecting to the network. That's only part of the value of the restrictions here. Maintaining tight network security often means limiting network access for users and tracking the resources used by each user.

After starting MS Windows and loading the NetWare Administrator program, choose the User object to be restricted and open the User dialog box. You will see a screen similar to the one shown in Figure 6.13. There are three action boxes and one piece of information in Figure 6.13.

Since users tend to share passwords and login names even when the manager yells at them not to, security heads south. One way to slow this trend down is by using login restrictions.

Chapter 6 • Creating and Managing Users (Now User Objects)

FIGURE 6.13

Restricting a user's access to the network

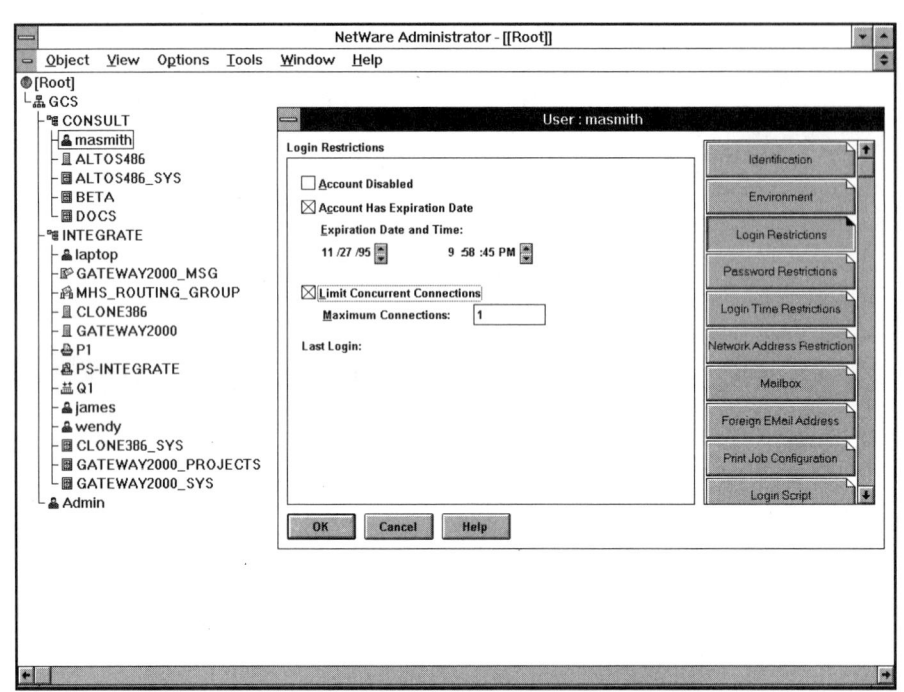

The Account Disabled checkbox is an excellent security tool when dealing with a shifting user base. This stops anyone from using this account, but does not erase the applicable login scripts, change passwords, or delete data.

When a user goes on vacation, check this box. It will stop coworkers from borrowing this user account while the user is gone. This also works well for temporary users. Let's say you bring in accounting help at the end of every month. Do you want to create and delete these users each month? No way. Create some generic accounting users, such as ACCT_1 and ACCT_2, and use the Account Disabled checkbox. When the temporary workers are gone, no one will be able to log in with the ACCT_1 or ACCT_2 names. When they come back, one click of the mouse sets everything back into place for them.

Account Has Expiration Date works similarly to Account Disabled. Once the expiration date is reached, the account disappears as far as any login attempts are concerned. The date can always be extended by changing it here. Have a group of visitors who need network access during their two-week stay? Set their user names with an expiration date, and you won't need to worry about other users getting access to their information after they're gone.

Limit Concurrent Connections controls one of the early advantages NetWare developed in the early days of NetWare: the ability to log in from two or more places on the network, but have the exact same rights and access for each login. Novell had this before any of its competitors.

If security is important in your network, however, this should always be set to only one concurrent connection per user. Limiting concurrent access is a good way to slow down the sharing of passwords among the users. If a second person tries to access the account of a person already connected, that user will get an error message.

There are other places to limit connections, and we'll cover them later in the book (in Chapter 9). If your default is to allow multiple connections, you can use the Login Restrictions page to limit particular users to a set number of connections.

The Last Login field displays the last time this user connected to the network. Only one historical connection is listed here.

Setting Password Restrictions

> **6.11 IN-A-HURRY**
>
> **Set Password Restrictions**
>
> 1. Open NetWare Administrator and locate the User object in the NDS tree.
> 2. Open the User dialog box by double-clicking on the User object name.
> 3. Click on the Password Restrictions button on the right.
> 4. Set the desired password restrictions.
> 5. Click on OK to save the restrictions.

The single most important user security tool is a good password system. If security is important to your company, password restrictions will be important as well.

Click on the Password Restrictions button on the right side of the User dialog box to see the screen shown in Figure 6.14.

Providing passwords for users usually isn't a good idea. Users like to feel their password is known to only them. Even though, as the administrator, you

FIGURE 6.14

Tightening password parameters

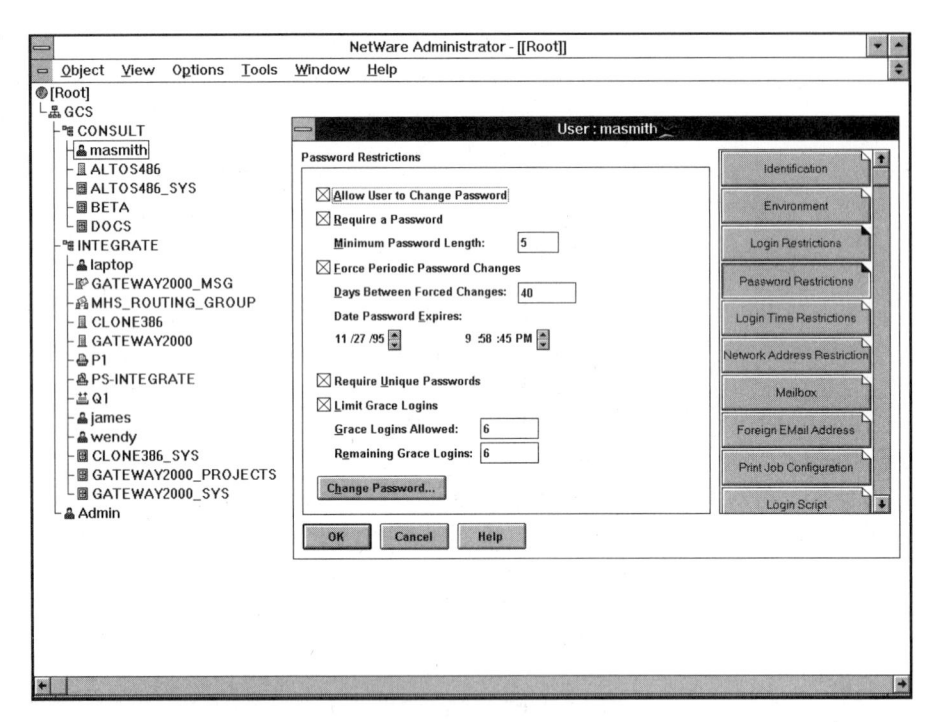

most likely have access to all their data files, users still feel more secure if they set their own passwords. A good compromise is to make a password-generating program available to the users; grace logins will be necessary for them to generate a new password before they can replace the old one.

Here, for the sake of our example, we have poor MASMITH restricted every which way. This looks like an enormous amount of extra work for the network administrator, and it may be. However, tight security takes time. Few networks use all these options. Most network administrators prefer to train users and teach them why security is important. Let's take a look at each option and see what choices we have.

- **Allow User to Change Password:** If your security is extremely tight, you may not allow the user to change his or her own password. This is both good and bad. It's good, because the passwords you choose will be better than the ones non-security minded users will choose. You will not pick his wife's name; users often choose a family name as the password. It's bad, however, because users will not easily remember the passwords you choose. This leads to passwords written down on calendars or desk blotters, which is not secure either. There's no good way to cover both these contingencies.

- **Require a Password:** If this box is unchecked, everything else in this dialog box turns gray to show it's unavailable. Checking this box allows you to set the minimum password length and choose whether to force periodic changes. The password minimum length can be between 1 and 999 characters, although setting this larger than 11 characters makes it impossible for Macintosh clients to log in. For security reasons, most experts recommend a password length of at least 5 characters. The longer the password, the harder it is to remember.

Although NetWare doesn't demand mixing alpha and numeric characters, some Unix systems do. Following the example of SCO Unix and requiring at least five characters including at least two numeric characters makes passwords much more difficult to guess. It also cuts down on using family names, unless someone on your network is related to 007.

- **Force Periodic Password Changes:** When this box is checked, the user will be forced to change his or her password at the interval you specify. The default for days between forced changes is 40 days (and 40 nights). The date the password will expire is listed on the screen for you. Changing that date does not change the Days Between Forced Changes field.

- **Require Unique Passwords:** When password changes are forced, the option to require unique passwords becomes available. If you choose not to have unique passwords, users can simply alternate between their son's name and their daughter's name for passwords. If you require passwords to be unique, NetWare tracks each user's last 20 passwords and does not allow duplication.

- **Limit Grace Logins:** If you force password changes, NetWare allows each user a few grace logins. In other words, even though the password is expired, NetWare will allow that password for a certain number of times. The default is six, and this dialog box displays how many grace logins are left. This is a friendly thing to do when forcing users to change passwords. If users must make up their own new passwords, they may not feel creative the morning their old password expires. The grace logins allow them to carefully consider their next password. If you or your department parcels out passwords, the user will need to contact you.

- **Change Password:** If you do want to change users' password for them, here's the place. Click on this button, and a smaller dialog box pops open with three fields. If you logged in as an Admin-equivalent user, you must type the old password, the new password, and retype the new password for verification. The Admin user doesn't need to enter the old password. You will see only asterisks for each letter you type. This feature also works when a user forgets a password; you can assign a new one here.

Setting Up Group Membership

> **6.12 IN-A-HURRY**
>
> **Add or Delete User Objects from a Group**
>
> 1. Open NetWare Administrator and locate the User object in the NDS tree.
>
> 2. Open the User dialog box by double-clicking on the User object name.
>
> 3. Click on the Group Membership button on the right.
>
> 4. To add a user, click on the Add button, choose a group or groups in the Select Object dialog box, and click on OK.
>
> 5. To delete a user, highlight the group name and click on Delete.
>
> 6. Click on OK to save your changes.

Groups are a marvelous tool when administering networks. Instead of dealing with each user, you can maintain a list of similar users and deal with the Group object. User objects inherit all the properties of their Group objects.

Be careful, a Group object is *not* a container. A Group object merely keeps a list of User objects. When some action is taken with that Group object, each User object listed as part of the group has that same action taken with it.

After opening the NetWare Administrator program and picking the User object to be added to a group, click on the Group Membership button on the right (you may need to scroll down past the other buttons). The Group Membership page will open, showing all the groups this particular user is a member of.

Creating User Objects with NetWare Administrator **385**

There is no practical limit to the number of groups one user can belong to, although making a group of two users may wind up being more trouble than it's worth.

If this particular user is not a member of any groups, click on the Add button. That calls the Select Object dialog box, as shown in Figure 6.15 (this figure shows the NetWare 4.10 version of the Select Object dialog box).

In the example, you can see that the context is currently CONSULT.GCS and the only group contained in this context is CONSULTANTS. In the Objects pick list, CONSULTANTS is highlighted. Clicking on OK will pop the group name into the Memberships listing in the Group Membership page.

The Delete button works as you would expect. After highlighting a group name, clicking on Delete erases the User object's name from the Memberships list. This screen is not where you delete the Group object itself; it just allows you to take this particular User object out of the Group object.

FIGURE 6.15

Adding MASMITH to the CONSULTANTS group

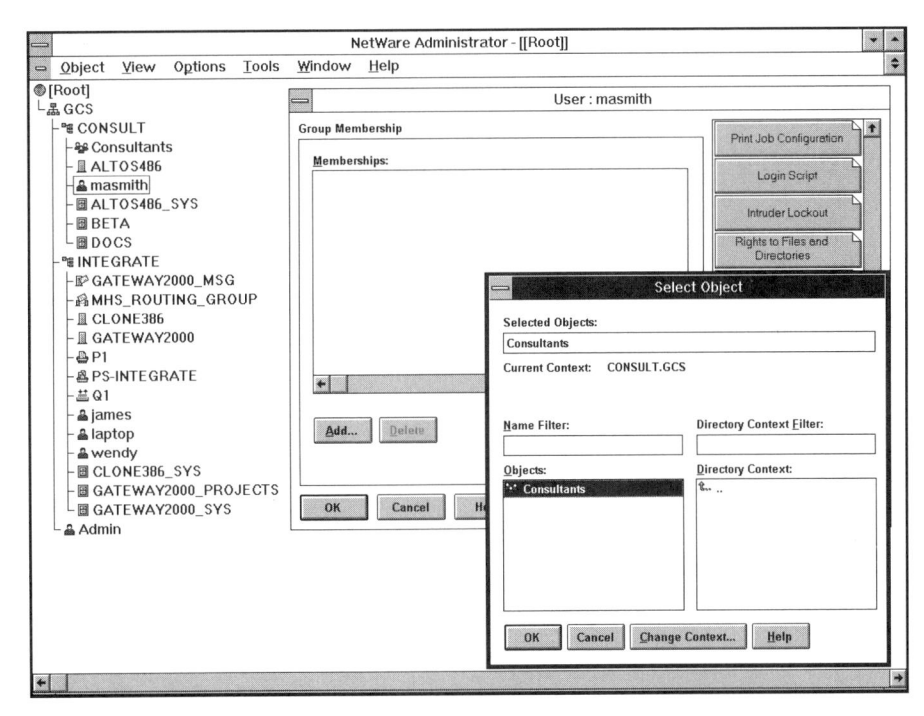

Setting Security Equal To

> **6.13 IN-A-HURRY**
>
> **Set Security Equivalence**
>
> 1. Open NetWare Administrator and locate the User object in the NDS tree.
> 2. Open the User dialog box by double-clicking on the User object name.
> 3. Click on the Security Equal To button on the right.
> 4. To add security equivalence, click on the Add button, choose objects in the Select Object dialog box, and click on OK.
> 5. To delete security equivalence, highlight the Security Equivalent object and click on Delete.
> 6. Click on OK to save your settings.

Security equivalence grants one User object the same rights as another object. This is the same idea as Group objects, where the members of the group all have the rights of the group itself. However, granting security equivalence of a User object to another User object is more dangerous than putting users in groups. We'll cover security equivalence and other security-related topics in Chapter 9.

Open the NetWare Administrator program and choose the User object to make equivalent to another object. In the User dialog box, click on the Security Equal To button, then on the Add button. The Select Object dialog box will appear, just as in Figure 6.16 (well, in NetWare 4.10; in 4.11, this dialog box looks a bit different). Notice that, in our example, MASMITH already has security equal to the group CONSULTANTS. That's the result of our last operation, when we added a User object to a Group object.

As an example, I have changed the context to INTEGRATE.GCS and am now able to make MASMITH equivalent to file servers or volumes as well as to other User objects. This inappropriate type of assignment would be dangerous, since MASMITH could suddenly have rights and access privileges of the server GATEWAY2000.

Deleting equivalence is simply a matter of highlighting the equivalent object in the Security Equal To box and clicking on Delete.

FIGURE 6.16

Modifying a User object's security equivalency

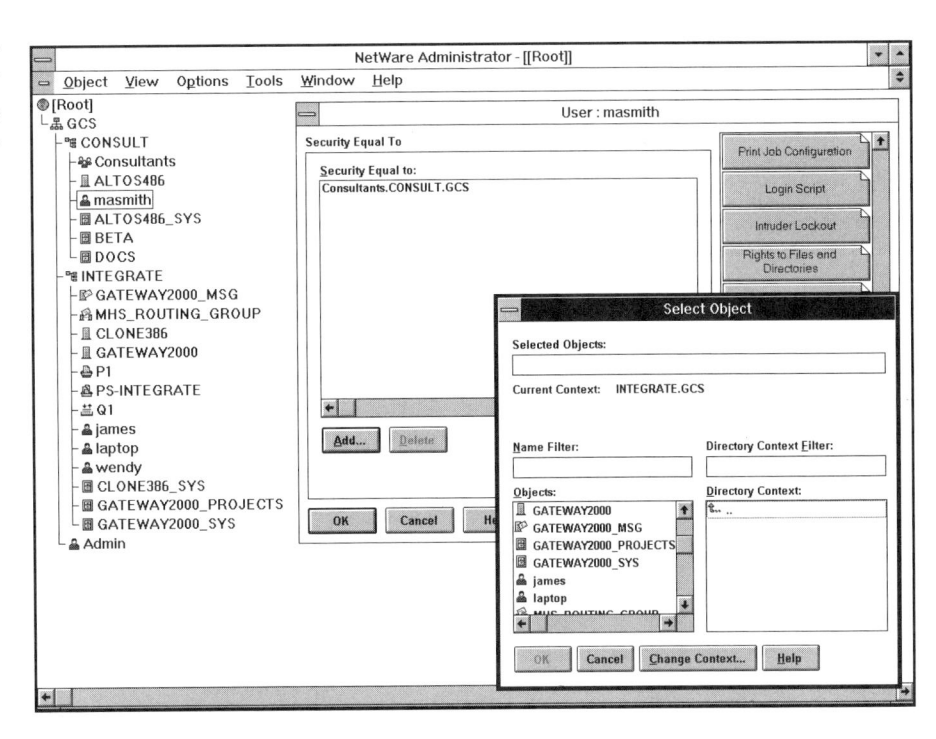

Setting Login Time Restrictions

6.14 IN-A-HURRY

Set Login Time Restrictions

1. Open NetWare Administrator and locate the User object in the NDS tree.

2. Open the User dialog box by double-clicking on the User object name.

3. Click on the Login Time Restrictions button on the right.

4. On the grid, indicate the times to lock out the User object.

5. Click on OK to save the restrictions.

There are several reasons to restrict access to your network. First, and most common, is to allow tape backup systems to work properly. Most backup systems skip open files. If users are logged in and still have applications open, the files in use will likely be skipped. Closing all connections before the backup starts eliminates that problem.

Security is another reason to restrict access. If no one in your company works the night shift, any user on your network at 1:13 A.M. is probably up to no good. Locking out all the users during the night and early morning limits your exposure to network tampering.

If you use login scripts to inform users of upcoming events with a MOTD (Message of the Day), you want them to log in to see it. If they stay connected overnight, the login script can't call the MOTD and display same. So set the Login Time Restrictions to force users to disconnect from the server during the night.

The name of this feature is slightly misleading. Along with restricting logins, this feature of NetWare 4.1*x* disconnects those users that are still connected at the beginning of the blocked time. Perhaps we should call this Connection Time Restrictions rather than Login Time Restrictions.

Open the NetWare Administrator program, choose the User object for your restriction operation, and click on the Login Time Restrictions button. This is one utility that really takes advantage of the graphical interface, as you can see in Figure 6.17.

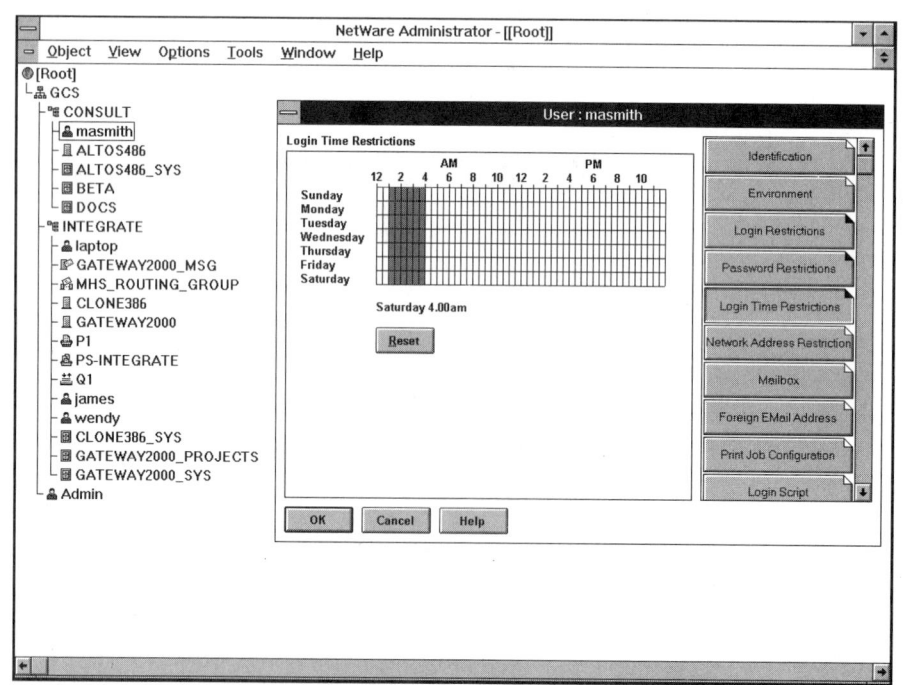

> *If no one in your company works the night shift, any user on your network at 1:13 A.M. is probably up to no good.*

FIGURE 6.17

Blocking out time

Each block on the time grid represents a half hour. White blocks allow connection; dark blocks restrict. Clicking on each block toggles its state: click on a white block and it turns dark, click on a dark block and it turns white.

Clicking on each half-hour block is cumbersome, so you can use a shortcut. Click on the first block of time to restrict, hold down the left mouse button, and drag the rectangle to the last time to restrict. When you release the mouse button, all the blocks within the rectangle will change state. You can also use your cursor keys: press the Shift key while you use the arrow keys to go across the grid.

Setting Network Address Restrictions

> **6.15 IN-A-HURRY**
>
> **Set Network Address Restrictions**
>
> 1. Open NetWare Administrator and locate the User object in the NDS tree.
> 2. Open the User dialog box by double-clicking on the User object name.
> 3. Click on the Network Address Restriction button on the right.
> 4. Choose the protocol the User object uses for connection to the network.
> 5. Provide the protocol address for the allowable workstation.
> 6. Click on OK to save your settings.

As you saw earlier (Figure 6.13), the Login Restrictions page for a user has a Limit Concurrent Connections checkbox. The second step in restricting the number of concurrent logins users can have is to restrict the workstations from which they can connect to the network. This is drastic and makes for more work for the network administrator, but it is possible.

There is one good way to use this to improve security without inconveniencing your users: make the restriction for your tape backup system. If your tape backup system runs from a network node, as most do, tie the backup User object to the address of the machine with the tape backup attached.

The User object for backup (usually called BACKUP or something equally creative and inviting to hackers and snoopers) has full rights over the network file systems, which could be a serious security breach if a person got hold of the backup user's user name and password. If that happens, but you have restricted the address for the backup User object, the thieving user must gain access to that physical workstation to cause problems.

After opening the NetWare Administrator program and choosing the User object to restrict, click on the Network Address Restriction button on the right. The Network Address Restriction page appears.

To add a restriction, click on the protocol for that user, then click on the Add button. A dialog box pops up asking for the specific address of that particular machine, as you see in Figure 6.18. Each protocol has different address requirements.

If you don't know the address for a particular user machine, from the DOS prompt, type:

```
NLIST USER /A
```

The active users for the network will be displayed along with their network and node numbers. Fill those numbers into the proper fields so the system knows exactly which workstation is allowable for this user.

Currently, you can restrict only AFP (AppleTalk Filing Protocol) and IPX/SPX.

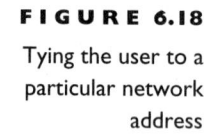

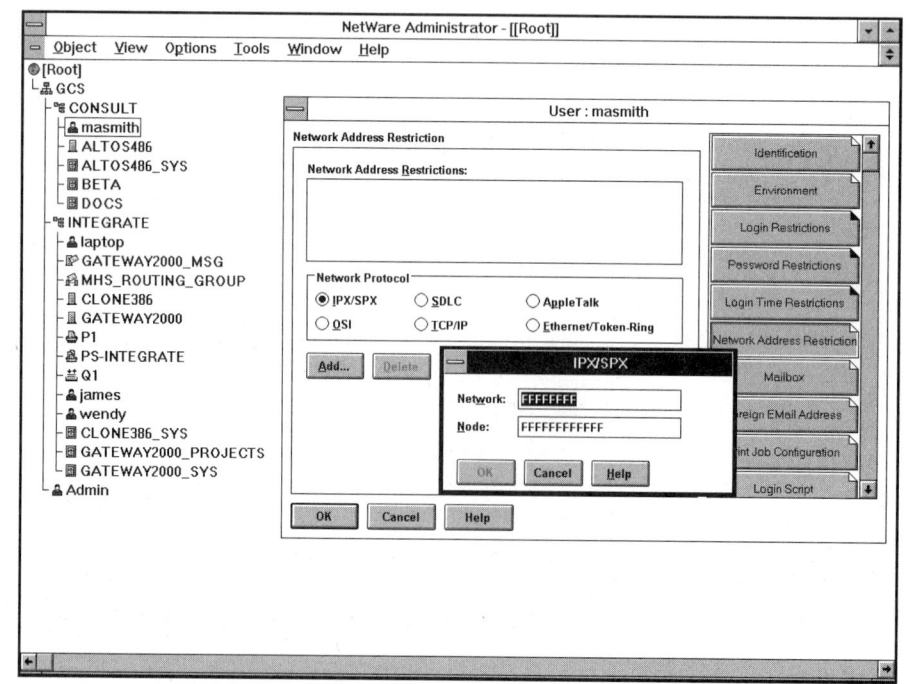

FIGURE 6.18

Tying the user to a particular network address

Resetting Intruder Lockout

> **6.16 IN-A-HURRY**
>
> ### Reset Intruder Lockout
>
> 1. Open NetWare Administrator and locate the User object in the NDS tree.
> 2. Open the User dialog box by double-clicking on the User object name.
> 3. Click on the Intruder Lockout button on the right.
> 4. Click on the Account Locked checkbox to reopen the account.
> 5. Click on OK to save the settings.

The intruder lockout function is a "gotcha" from NetWare, special delivery to hackers. If you have the intruder detection feature active, you will always know when someone connects to your network while guessing a password. Of course, you will also know when users forget their password, possibly even before they come crying for help.

Intruder detection must be set for the container (see Chapter 10) before this dialog box becomes active for the User object. You may have detection active on some containers but not on others.

Once again, start the NetWare Administrator program and open the dialog box for the user whose account has been locked. Click on the Intruder Lockout button on the right side. The page you'll see is shown in Figure 6.19.

There is nothing to do here except clear the workstation by clicking on the Account Locked checkbox. You can't lock the account by clicking on this checkbox. To lock an account, use the Account Disabled checkbox in the Login Restrictions dialog box (Figure 6.13), as explained earlier in the chapter.

Setting Rights to Files and Directories

After opening the NetWare Administrator program and choosing your User object, click on the Rights to Files and Directories in the stack of buttons on the right. The page you see in Figure 6.20 appears, without volume and directory listings.

6.17 IN-A-HURRY

Change Rights to Files and Directories

1. Open NetWare Administrator and locate the User object in the NDS tree.

2. Open the User dialog box by double-clicking on the User object name.

3. Click on the Rights to Files and Directories button on the right.

4. Click on Find beside the Volumes box to display file systems the user has rights to access.

5. To view assigned rights, click on the Find button, then highlight the volume or directory in the Volumes box and click on Add. Highlight the directory or volume in the Files and Directories box.

6. To grant access, click the Add button and choose the volume or directory to grant access.

7. To delete access, highlight the volume and click on the Delete button.

8. To grant or modify rights, highlight the object in the Files and Directories box and toggle the checkboxes in the Rights box.

9. Click on OK to save your settings.

This looks like the busiest page we've seen in all the User object information, but it's not too bad. However, rather than controlling access this way, when possible, assign rights to volumes and directories to groups, not individuals. When we get to Group object setup (in Chapter 7), you'll see that its screen looks just like this. You'll also get full definitions of all the trustee rights and other access controls in Chapter 9, which covers securing your network.

To find out which volumes and directories the user already has access to, click on the Find button. You will be asked where in the NDS tree you wish to search. The default is your current context, but you may request a search of the entire tree. If your NDS tree is large, you may be warned to expect a delay.

The Find button operates like a Browser button with a shortcut. When you click on Find, a small dialog box appears asking for the context you wish to search. If you know exactly where you want to look, it's easy to type in the name of the context. If you're not sure, or feel like doing less typing, there is a Browser button that opens the Select Object dialog box.

Creating User Objects with NetWare Administrator **393**

FIGURE 6.19

Intruder lockout activated by using the wrong password

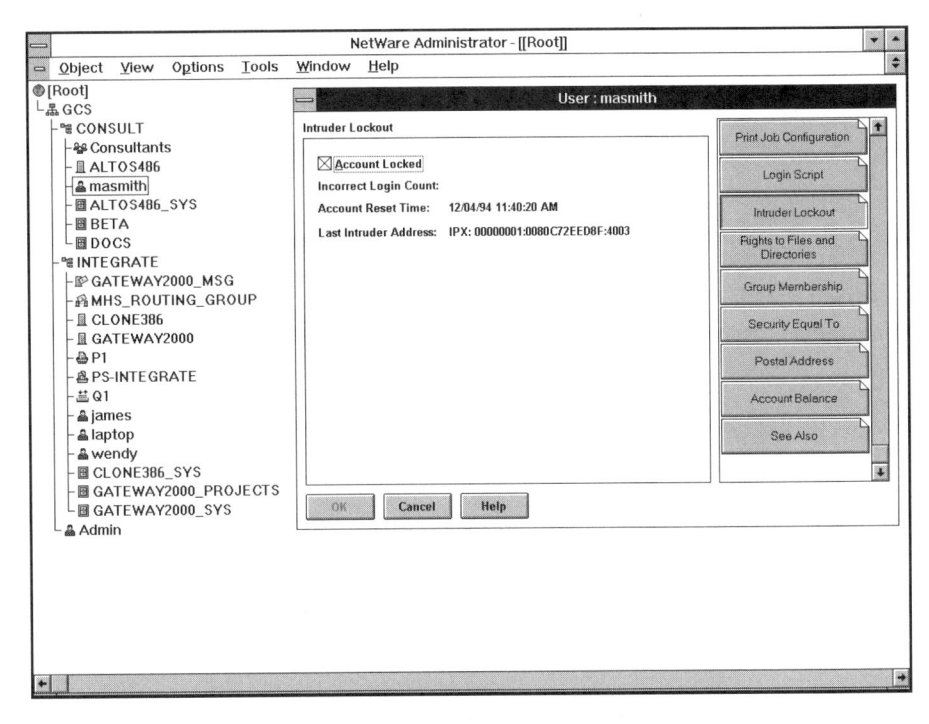

FIGURE 6.20

Directory and volume access control

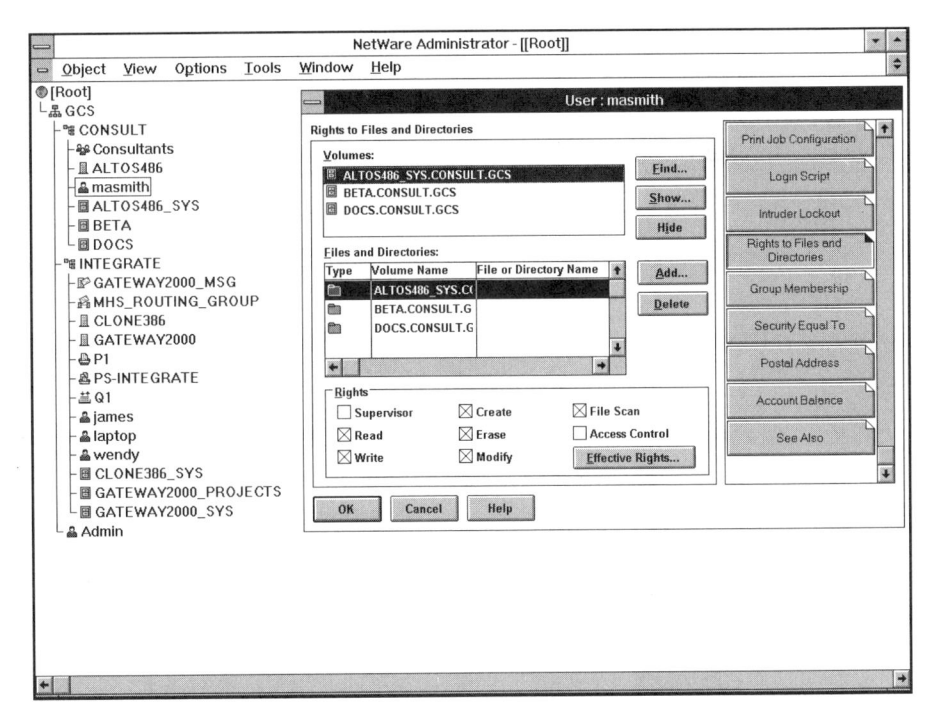

394 Chapter 6 ▪ Creating and Managing Users (Now User Objects)

When the list of volumes returns, the Volumes box will have an entry for each volume containing a directory of which the user is a trustee. When you highlight each directory, the Rights box just below the Files and Directories box will reflect the user's rights to that file or directory.

To delete trustee assignments, highlight the volume or directory and click on Delete. To modify rights to a particular directory or file, check the appropriate boxes in the Rights box. All the checkboxes are toggles, so if one is blank, checking it grants that right to that object.

The Effective Rights button displays the actual rights for the highlighted directory or volume object located in the Files and Directories box. When you click on this button, you'll see a small dialog box that includes the actual directory under examination, along with a Browser button to help you search more areas of the network. Figure 6.21 shows this Effective Rights dialog box.

Notice in this example that the Volumes box and the Files and Directories box are empty. To check rights, I clicked on Effective Rights and used the Browser button from there. From the Select Object dialog box, I moved to the other Organizational Unit, INTEGRATE, and looked down into the

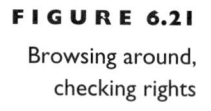

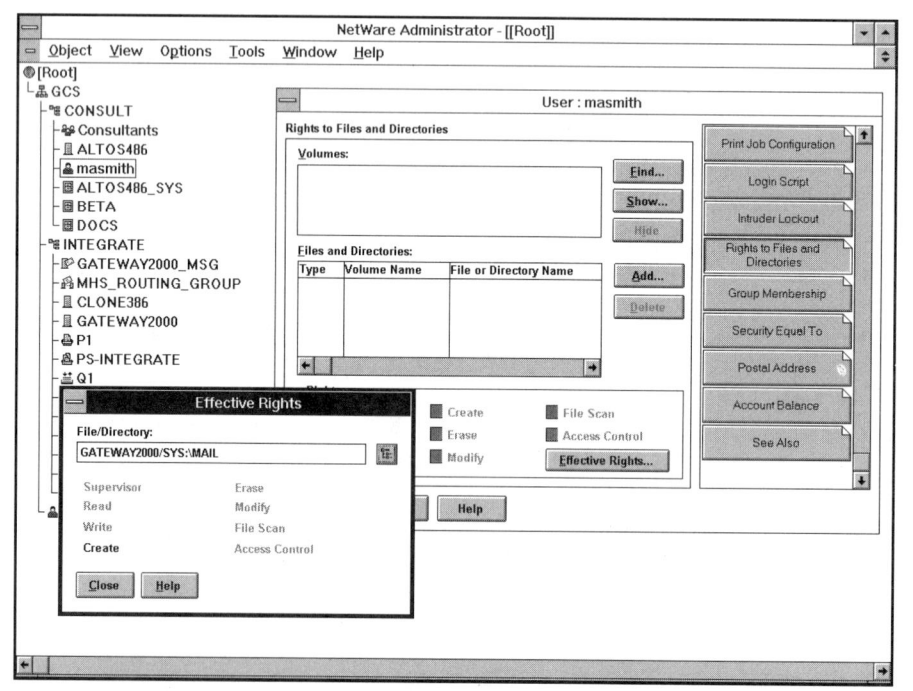

FIGURE 6.21

Browsing around, checking rights

GATEWAY2000\SYS: directory. Take another look at Figure 6.21, especially the Create right. Notice how it's in solid letters, rather than the faded gray? User MASMITH has only the Create right in the GATEWAY2000\SYS:\MAIL directory. In other words, she can send mail but can't check into other users' directories and see or manipulate their mail.

Creating User Objects with NETADMIN (DOS)

THOSE WHO HAVE worked with earlier versions of NetWare may be slightly discombobulated by the fancy NetWare Administrator program. Graphics, icons, and mouse commands are foreign territory to administrators of NetWare 3.x and before.

Figure 6.22 shows the opening screen of the NETADMIN program (listed as NetAdmin in documentation where they aren't trying to keep all the EXE programs in all capital letters). The opening screen, strongly influenced by SYSCON, hides all sorts of surprises for us under each of the menu options.

FIGURE 6.22
The opening of the NETADMIN program

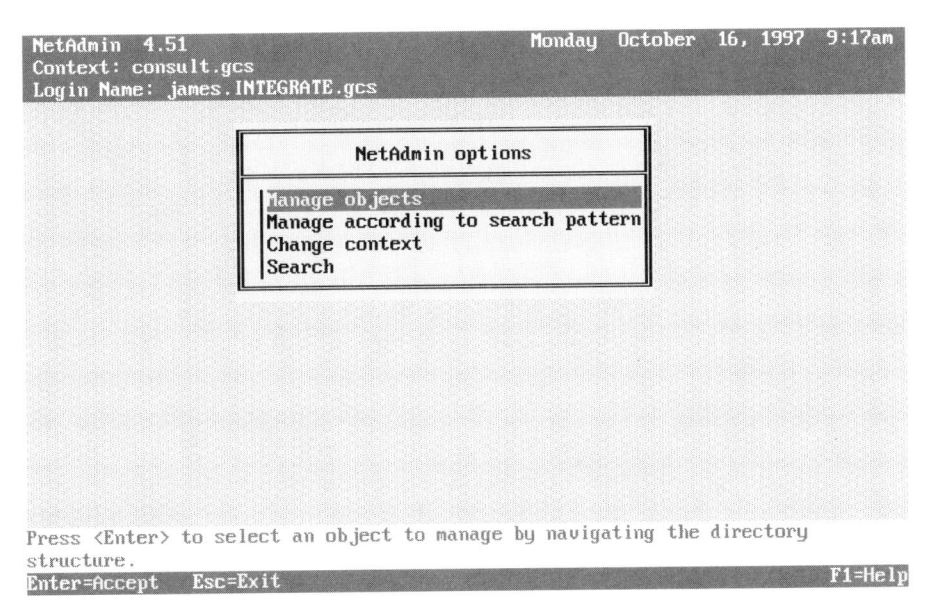

The look and feel of SYSCON is re-created faithfully, with a few advantages. The help screens, only an F1 key away, hold more information and provide better background than earlier NetWare versions. Most keyboard command combinations are listed in the status line at the bottom of the screen.

Some key combinations that aren't mentioned will be useful, and one major difference between NETADMIN and NetWare Administrator may catch you short. First, the Alt+F10 key combination will immediately call the Exit? choice, with Yes as the default. This is much quicker than pressing the Escape key ten times to back out of a deep menu structure. Another trick is to type the letters of your menu choice. NETADMIN will parse each letter and move to the first unique entry with those letters. Once there, just press Enter.

The catch may be when you do exit. In NetWare Administrator, choosing a Cancel button brings up the question:

```
Discard All Changes?  Yes  No
```

with the default set to Yes to discard your changes. Just pressing the Enter key will erase all the changes made. In NETADMIN, the default question when you press the Escape key to exit (to cancel what you're doing) is:

```
Save Change?  Yes  No
```

with the default set to Yes to save your changes.

When backing out of NetWare Administrator, you work to save your changes by changing the exit default. In NETADMIN, you work to cancel your changes, since saving is the default. This is a small point, but if you switch back and forth between DOS and MS Windows systems, remember to read the exit questions if you're using a program different than your regular utility.

Other keys that will help you are Insert, F5, and F10. The Insert key works much like the Browser button in NetWare Administrator. When in doubt about what to type into a field, press Insert, and a pick list may magically appear. The F5 key marks multiple items, just as clicking the left mouse button while holding down the Ctrl key does in MS Windows. Sometimes, the Escape key saves and exits, which is a holdover from early NetWare versions. (This Escape key function was built into the C-Worthy compiler used from the beginning by the first NetWare developers.) Most of the time, however, the F10 key saves screen information in NETADMIN, but you should read the bottom status line just in case.

Basic User Object Setup with NETADMIN

> **6.18 IN-A-HURRY**
>
> **Create a User Object with NETADMIN**
>
> 1. Start NETADMIN from the DOS command line and choose Manage Objects.
>
> 2. Choose the container where you want to create the user.
>
> 3. Press Insert, then choose User.
>
> 4. Fill in the Login Name and Last Name fields.
>
> 5. Press Enter to create the User object.

Basic user setup consists of two things: user name and user last name. For this section, I have deleted the user MASMITH created earlier so we can re-create that User object under NETADMIN. The goal will be to create the same User object using NETADMIN as we did using NetWare Administrator.

The first screen that appears when you choose the Manage Objects choice from the NETADMIN opening screen is the Object, Class screen, shown in Figure 6.23. Just as NetWare Administrator gives us constant clues about where we are in the NDS tree, so does NETADMIN.

Notice the upper portion of the screen. It tells you who you are (Login Name) and your context (CONSULT.GCS). It also provides the time and date, something missing from NetWare Administrator.

You can see in Figure 6.23 that there is currently no user created in this context. Unfortunately, there is less information displayed in the NETADMIN screens than in the corresponding NetWare Administrator screens. That's the advantage of high resolution for the NetWare Administrator program.

To modify an object on this screen, use the cursor keys to highlight that object and press the Enter key. As you can see on the bottom status line, pressing F10 performs the same function. If you press the Alt+F1 key combination, as referenced in the bottom-right corner of Figure 6.23, you'll see more information about other active key combinations.

Nothing too exciting is hidden from you, however. The other choices are Del=Delete, Esc=Exit, and F1=Help.

FIGURE 6.23

Beginning the User object creation process with NETADMIN

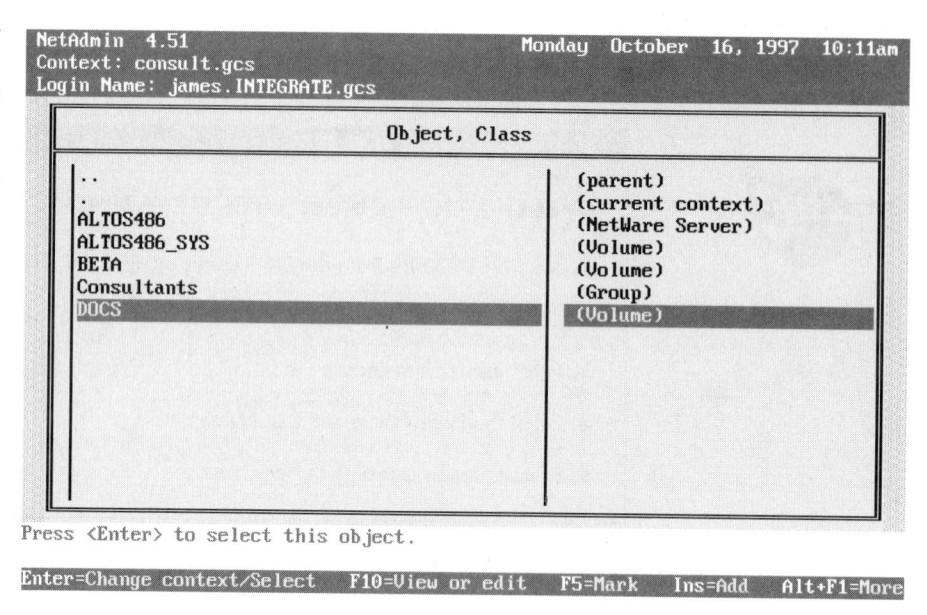

```
NetAdmin  4.51                              Monday  October  16, 1997  10:11am
Context: consult.gcs
Login Name: james.INTEGRATE.gcs
┌─────────────────────────────── Object, Class ───────────────────────────────┐
│  ..                                            (parent)                     │
│  .                                             (current context)            │
│  ALTOS486                                      (NetWare Server)             │
│  ALTOS486_SYS                                  (Volume)                     │
│  BETA                                          (Volume)                     │
│  Consultants                                   (Group)                      │
│  DOCS                                          (Volume)                     │
│                                                                             │
└─────────────────────────────────────────────────────────────────────────────┘
Press <Enter> to select this object.
Enter=Change context/Select    F10=View or edit    F5=Mark    Ins=Add    Alt+F1=More
```

Since we must re-create User object MASMITH, let's get going. While in the screen in Figure 6.23, press the Insert key to start the creation process once again. Figure 6.24 shows the pick list of objects we can create.

When the Select an Object Class window appears, you must either move the highlight bar with the cursor keys or type the first letters of your choice. When you have typed enough letters to specify a unique choice, you can then press the Enter key to create the object.

In our case, typing U is all that is necessary to move the highlight bar to User. After pressing Enter, the Create Object User screen appears, as shown in Figure 6.25. Notice just above the status line, where NETADMIN provides some helpful information.

> **NOTE**
>
> *Unfortunately, I'm unable to move the NETADMIN windows around the screen. While in NetWare Administrator, I regularly shifted the foreground window to uncover the background information, but I can't do that here.*

The login name must be less than 64 characters long and unique within the container. Names are not case-sensitive, but they will be displayed as they were typed in the Login Name field (MaSmith will display that way, but NDS regards it as identical to masmith and MASMITH). Spaces can be used and will be displayed as spaces within NDS.

Creating User Objects with NETADMIN (DOS) 399

FIGURE 6.24
Choosing the object to create

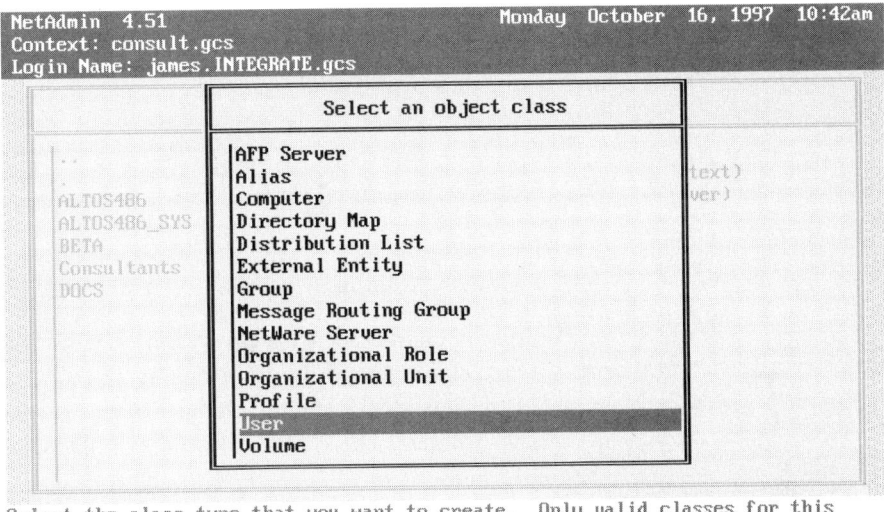

```
NetAdmin 4.51                              Monday  October 16, 1997  10:42am
Context: consult.gcs
Login Name: james.INTEGRATE.gcs

                         Select an object class
                    ┌──────────────────────────────┐
                    │ AFP Server                   │
                    │ Alias                        │        text)
         ALTOS486   │ Computer                     │        ver)
         ALTOS486_SYS│ Directory Map               │
         BETA       │ Distribution List            │
         Consultants│ External Entity              │
         DOCS       │ Group                        │
                    │ Message Routing Group        │
                    │ NetWare Server               │
                    │ Organizational Role          │
                    │ Organizational Unit          │
                    │ Profile                      │
                    │ User                         │
                    │ Volume                       │
                    └──────────────────────────────┘

Select the class type that you want to create.  Only valid classes for this
context are listed.
Enter=Accept   Esc=Exit                                              F1=Help
```

FIGURE 6.25
Creating User MASMITH

```
NetAdmin 4.51                              Monday  October 16, 1997  11:02am
Context: consult.gcs
Login Name: james.INTEGRATE.gcs

                            Object, Class

                         Create object User
   ┌─────────────────────────────────────────────────────────────────┐
   │ Login Name:                masmith                              │
   │ Last name:                 Smith                                │
   │ Mailbox location:                                               │
   │ Create a home directory?                          No            │
   │ Copy the User Template object?                    No            │
   │                                                                 │
   │ --- Home Directory Information ---                              │
   │ Volume object name:                                             │
   │ Path on volume:                                                 │
   │                                                                 │
   └─────────────────────────────────────────────────────────────────┘

Press <Enter> to edit the last name of the user. This is a required field.
Enter=Accept   F10=Save   Esc=Exit                                   F1=Help
```

If your NetWare 4.1x server must support non-NDS clients or work with earlier NetWare server versions, you must keep in mind the restrictions placed on login names by the bindery:

- Names longer than 47 characters are truncated.

- Spaces are shown as underscores.

- The following characters can't be seen by non-NDS clients: slash (/), backslash (\), colon (:), comma (,), asterisk (*), and question mark (?).

The special characters are legal within NDS but not within bindery systems. These characters also pose problems in DOS names. The path of least trouble is to develop a naming standard for users that allows only alpha and numeric characters. There's no advantage to placing unusual characters in the user name, and it can come back to haunt you.

If e-mail is important to your company, verify names with that system before assigning them inside NDS. You want to use names that work across all applications and systems.

The help information above the status line tells us that Last Name is a required field. In fact, it's the only required field. We can stop now, confident we have created a valid NetWare 4.1x User object. With the last name entered, there's an easy way to search for this user. Smith may be a popular last name, but it will certainly help narrow the field when we're sorting through a few hundred users later on.

Well, user MASMITH is legal, but not too functional. We best add some details to her.

Figure 6.25 shows several things the Novell engineers thought we should do for each user, or they wouldn't have put the options on the main page used to create a User object. The important things and some explanation are:

- **Mailbox Location:** E-mail is becoming the lifeblood of business today. Each user should have a mailbox, and NetWare 4.1x allows mailboxes to be on any server.

- **Create a Home Directory?:** Make a personal directory for this user and grant the user all rights to that directory.

- **Copy the User Template Object?:** This refers to the file containing default information applied to new User objects. The User Template object gives the user predetermined property values within that container.

> *There's no advantage to placing unusual characters in the user name, and it can come back to haunt you.*

Creating a Home Directory

> **6.19 IN-A-HURRY**
>
> **Create a Home Directory with NETADMIN**
>
> 1. Start NETADMIN from the DOS command line and create a new User object.
> 2. Toggle the Create a Home Directory? field to Yes.
> 3. Move the cursor down to highlight Volume Object Name and press Enter.
> 4. Type in the Volume object name or press Insert to browse for the object.
> 5. Highlight the desired volume and press Enter.
> 6. Accept the default home directory or type in the path.
> 7. Press F10 to accept and create the new user and the home directory.

The home directory is a section of the server volume that the user can treat exactly like his or her own hard disk. Users have a stronger feeling of owning the network if they have complete control over some portion of that network. This not only helps the users feel more friendly to the network, it also makes it much easier to back up their data files. If they keep those files in their home directory structure, they will be backed up with the rest of the server.

You can create the home directory now or later. It's best to automatically make the directory during initial user setup, so you might as well get into that habit now.

After listing the login name and last name for the new user, move the highlight bar down to the Create a Home Directory? field and press Y to toggle the field from No to Yes. Then cursor down once more to the Volume Object Name field just under the Home Directory Information label. The user name will be placed in the Path on Volume field automatically.

Press the Insert key to browse the NDS tree to find the volume that holds the home directories. It's best if you have a volume separate from the SYS: volume for this job. If the SYS: volume fills up because people put too much stuff in their home directories, your server will do strange things and stop.

The NETADMIN equivalent of the Select Object dialog box is shown in Figure 6.26. The highlight bar always starts at the top of the screen, ready to move up a level in the NDS tree with a single press of the Enter key.

FIGURE 6.26

Browsing with NETADMIN

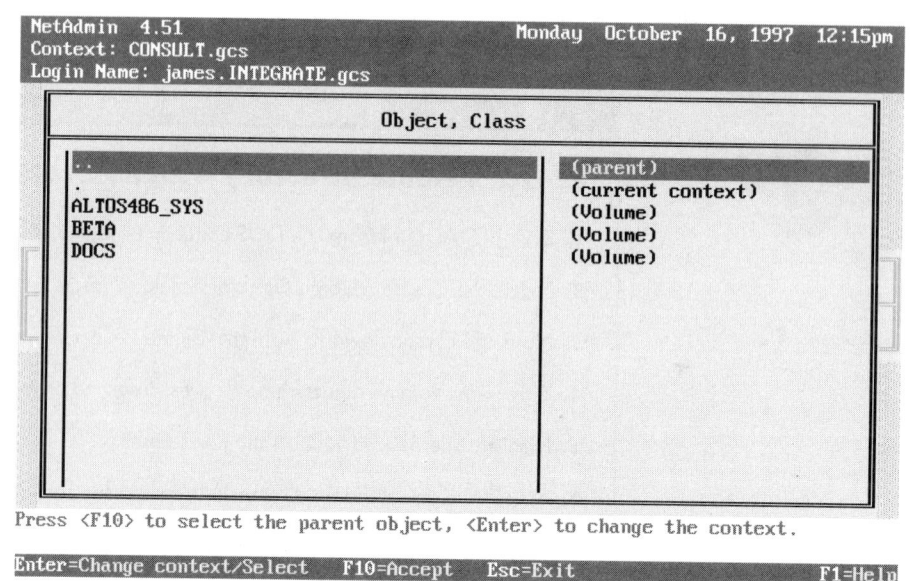

```
NetAdmin  4.51                              Monday  October  16, 1997  12:15pm
Context: CONSULT.gcs
Login Name: james.INTEGRATE.gcs
┌─────────────────────────── Object, Class ───────────────────────────┐
│ ..                                    │ (parent)                    │
│ .                                     │ (current context)           │
│ ALTOS486_SYS                          │ (Volume)                    │
│ BETA                                  │ (Volume)                    │
│ DOCS                                  │ (Volume)                    │
│                                       │                             │
└──────────────────────────────────────────────────────────────────────┘
Press <F10> to select the parent object, <Enter> to change the context.
Enter=Change context/Select    F10=Accept    Esc=Exit          F1=Help
```

Each screen showing the objects in a context, like Figure 6.26, corresponds to one level of the graphical NDS tree in the NetWare Administrator program. Pressing Enter on the two dots (..) that represent the parent container is no different than clicking on the container objects or using the CX command to change the context.

Since there is only a SYS: volume on the default server for this context, ALTOS486, all the user's home directories will be placed on the volume GATEWAY2000_PROJECTS. From the cursor location in Figure 6.26, there are three steps to locate and label the PROJECTS volume for user MASMITH:

1. Press Enter on the parent object, as shown in Figure 6.26 (this puts us in the O=GCS context).

2. Cursor down to the desired Organizational Unit (OU=INTEGRATE) and press Enter.

3. Highlight and press Enter on the GATEWAY2000_PROJECTS volume object.

As you can see (dimly) in Figure 6.27, the volume GATEWAY2000_PROJECTS.INTEGRATE. has been filled into the Volume Object Name field. The field's display length has truncated the full context name, but the system has not lost that information.

In Figure 6.27, the Path on Volume field has popped up to the top of the screen. If you wish to keep the user name as the directory name and leave it placed on the root of the volume, you are finished. If you wish, as I do here, to have some umbrella directory (named USERS in this example) under which all user's home directories reside, you must type in the full path name. As the status line says, press Enter to accept the configuration on the screen.

It may look a bit strange to separate the path to the home directory in this manner, but it's in keeping with NetWare 4.1*x*'s modular outlook. By separating the path from the volume, moving the home directories to another volume will be less work than if the entire path were listed as one value.

With the home directory taken care of, the user MASMITH will be created without a problem. The home directory will be set up, and the rights for MASMITH will be modified so she has complete access to her home directory. The system warns you that this may take as long as 60 seconds to create the User object and replicate that information around the NDS tree, but it won't take that long.

FIGURE 6.27

Last step in home directory creation

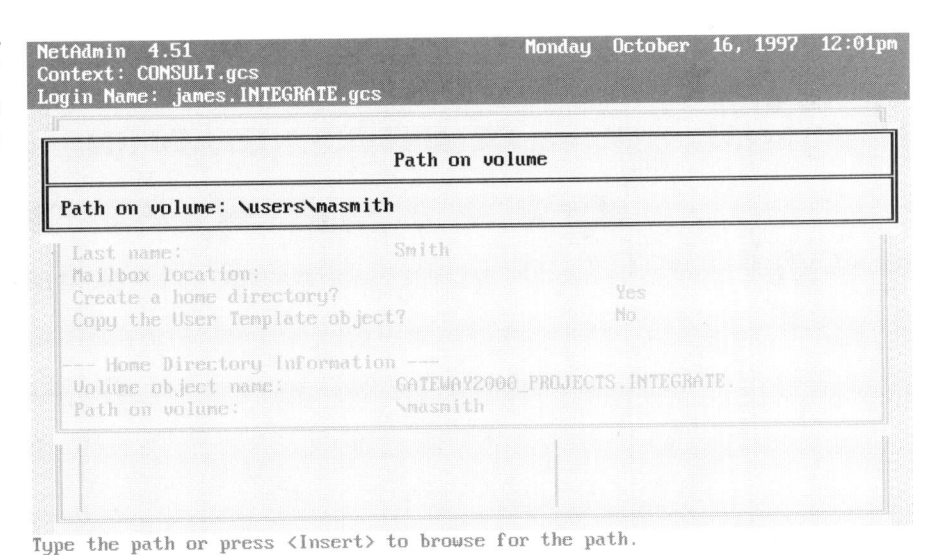

When everything is finished, the choice in Figure 6.28 appears. If you are creating more than one user, NETADMIN makes it easy for you to continue.

We are now officially finished creating user MASMITH. All the configuration to come appears to the system to be modifications.

FIGURE 6.28

Ready to repeat user creation

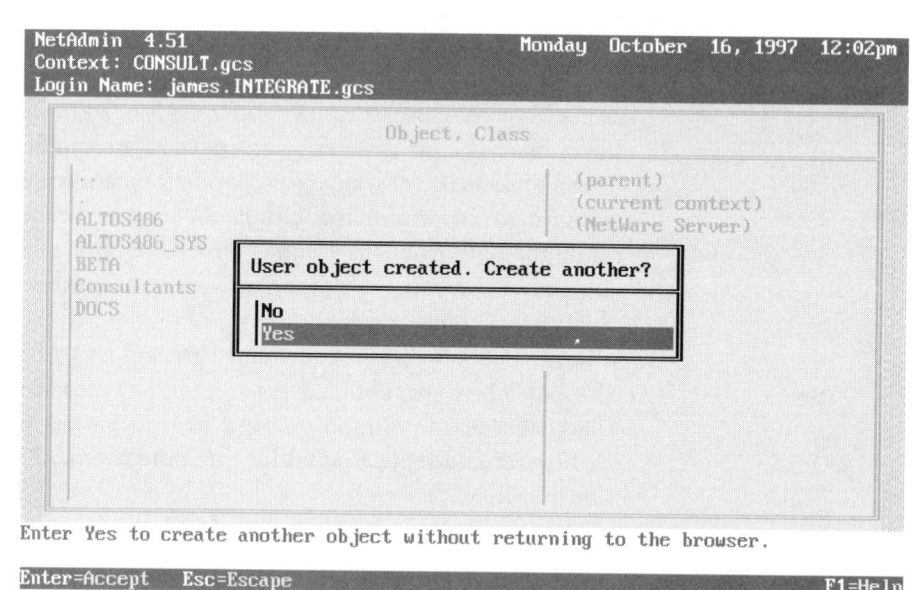

Modifying User Object Details with NETADMIN

6.20 IN-A-HURRY

Modify User Object Details in NETADMIN

1. Start the NETADMIN program from the DOS command line.

2. Highlight Manage Objects on the main menu and press Enter.

3. Highlight the User object to view or modify and press Enter.

4. Highlight View or Edit Properties of This Object and press Enter.

5. Choose which property of the User object to modify and press Enter.

We have an official user, named MASMITH, but no details about he, she, or it. To add information, run NETADMIN and choose the Manage Objects option. Then select the User object you created and choose the View or Edit Properties of This Object option. You'll arrive at the screen shown in Figure 6.29, ready to make the shell of the User object (MASMITH in this example) into a complete network user.

This menu takes the place of all the buttons running down the right side of the User dialog box in NetWare Administrator. If you have not used NetWare utilities before, you will be glad to hear they are consistently plain but functional.

Figure 6.30 shows the Identification information screen for our newly recreated user named MASMITH. The little arrows pointing down indicate that there can be more than one item in those particular fields. For instance, in the Other Name field, you may have both nicknames and job functions. The more of these you write down, the easier it will be to search databases for the information about your own users.

Each of these fields can be helpful later when you're searching for groups of people, such as those that use the fax machine with the number 555-2599. Why would you look for those people? Perhaps so you can tell them about the new fax server, or maybe you'll want to send them the cartoon that came from the marketing department.

The list of field names and uses are shown in Table 6.1.

FIGURE 6.29

The menu for User object setup and configuration

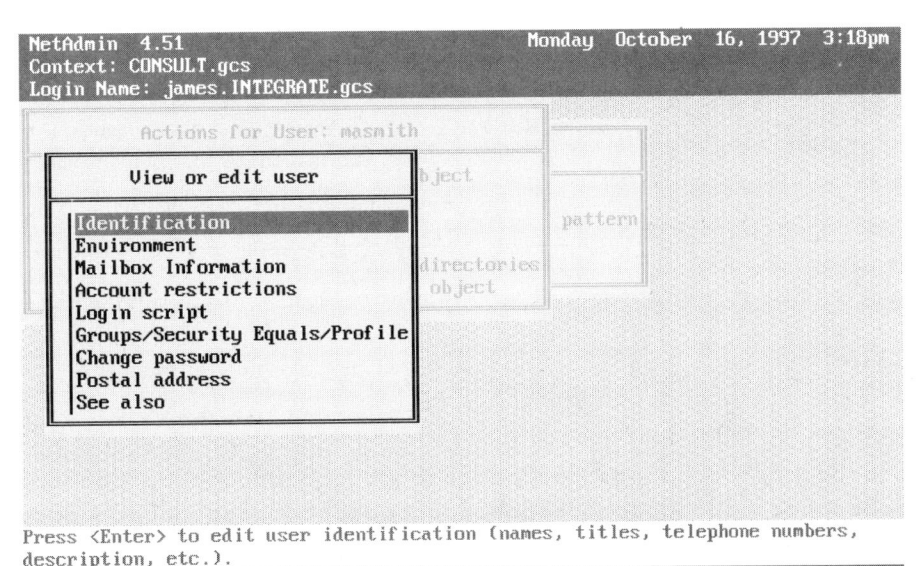

Chapter 6 • Creating and Managing Users (Now User Objects)

FIGURE 6.30
Providing personal information for MASMITH

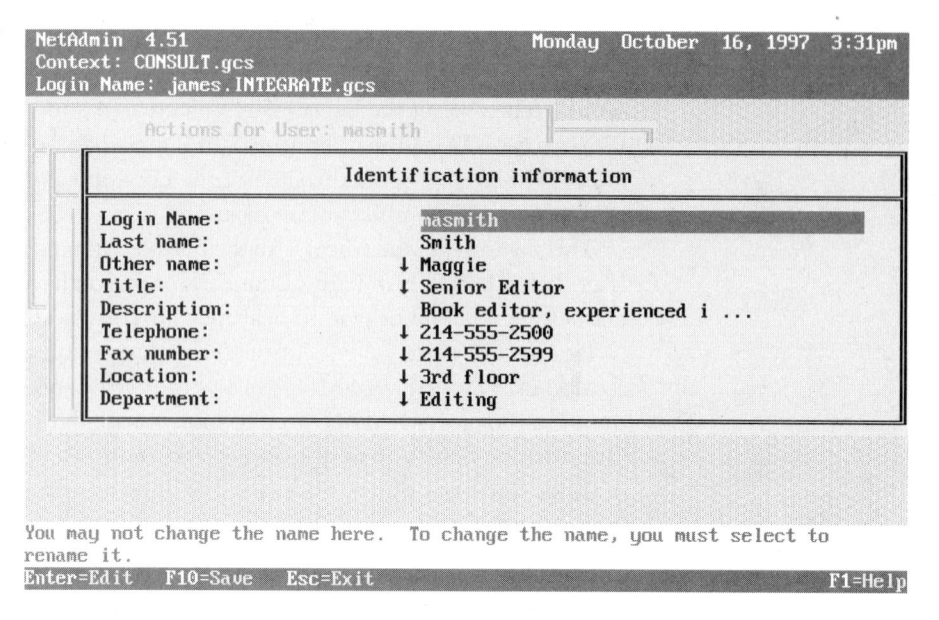

```
NetAdmin 4.51                                    Monday  October  16, 1997  3:31pm
Context: CONSULT.gcs
Login Name: james.INTEGRATE.gcs

                    Actions for User: masmith

                        Identification information

        Login Name:         masmith
        Last name:          Smith
        Other name:       ↓ Maggie
        Title:            ↓ Senior Editor
        Description:        Book editor, experienced i ...
        Telephone:        ↓ 214-555-2500
        Fax number:       ↓ 214-555-2599
        Location:         ↓ 3rd floor
        Department:       ↓ Editing


You may not change the name here.  To change the name, you must select to
rename it.
Enter=Edit   F10=Save   Esc=Exit                                         F1=Help
```

TABLE 6.1
NETADMIN Personal Information Fields

FIELD	DESCRIPTION
Login Name (not changeable here)	User's login name
Last Name	User's last name (filled in automatically)
Other Name	Nicknames, job function names, or other identification information (60 characters maximum per entry; duplicates are not allowed)
Title	Position or function of user (60 characters maximum)
Description	Function the user performs (30 lines of 37 characters each maximum)
Telephone	User's telephone numbers
Fax Number	User's fax numbers or those available to the user
Location	Physical location, such as floor, wing, or mail stop
Department	User's department, division, or workgroup

Specifying User Environment Information

Unlike the NetWare Administrator version of environment information, the NETADMIN version is not strictly for show. The fields you see when you select Environment from the View or Edit User menu, shown in Figure 6.31, are active and can be changed from this screen. The list of fields and their uses are shown in Table 6.2.

FIGURE 6.31
Your chance to change the home directory, among other things

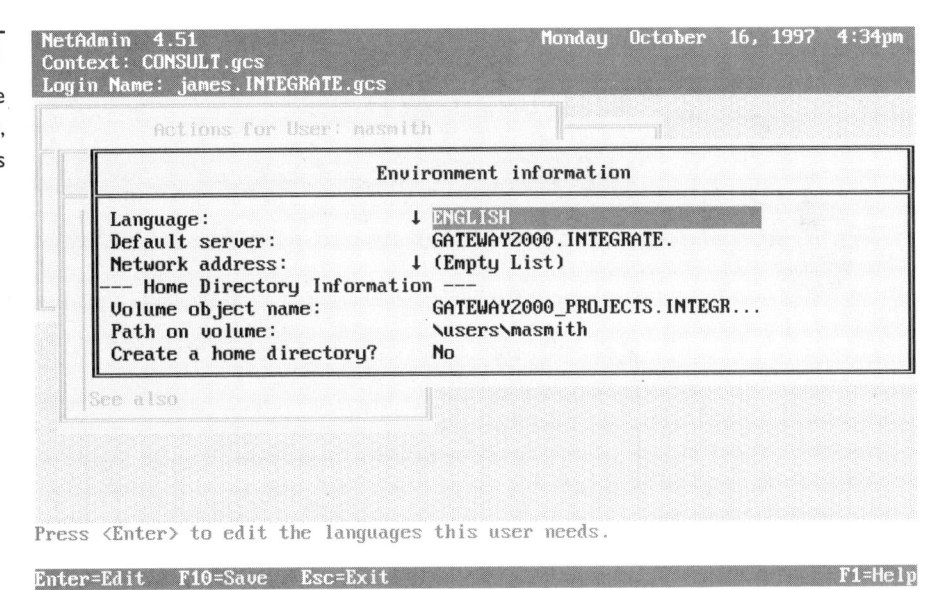

```
NetAdmin 4.51                                    Monday  October  16, 1997  4:34pm
Context: CONSULT.gcs
Login Name: james.INTEGRATE.gcs

                    Actions for User: masmith

                          Environment information
           Language:                     ↓ ENGLISH
           Default server:                 GATEWAY2000.INTEGRATE.
           Network address:              ↓ (Empty List)
           --- Home Directory Information ---
           Volume object name:             GATEWAY2000_PROJECTS.INTEGR...
           Path on volume:                 \users\masmith
           Create a home directory?        No

                       See also

Press <Enter> to edit the languages this user needs.
Enter=Edit    F10=Save    Esc=Exit                                    F1=Help
```

TABLE 6.2
NETADMIN Environment Information Fields

FIELD	DESCRIPTION
Language	From the SET command, shows the language for system messages.
Default Server	NetWare 4.1x server the user tries to connect to when logging in. This information is supplied by NDS.
Network Address	Address or addresses of the workstation this user is currently using to connect to the network. This will change when the user connects from a different workstation.
Home Directory	The volume and directory of the user's home directory. These are active fields, and changes can modify the home directory for this user (but not create one in NetWare 4.10).

Note that the home directory is not set here; it is set during initial user setup. Do not try to create a home directory for a user from this screen, or you will be disappointed if you're running NetWare 4.10; if you have NetWare 4.11, you'll be pleasantly surprised with its ability to create the new home directory for you. You can create a new home directory here with 4.11 by specifying the volume, path, and directory, and then choosing Yes.

If the user has a home directory, the information will be filled in the blanks by the system. If not, you must create the home directory manually. Again, filling in the home directory here will not make it happen.

Setting Up a User's Mailbox

> **6.21 IN-A-HURRY**
>
> **Set E-mailbox Information in NETADMIN**
>
> 1. Start the NETADMIN program from the DOS command line.
> 2. Highlight Manage Objects on the main menu and press Enter.
> 3. Highlight the User object to view or modify and press Enter.
> 4. Highlight View or Edit Properties of This Object and press Enter.
> 5. Highlight Mailbox Information and press Enter.
> 6. Press the Insert key twice to open the Object, Class window.
> 7. Locate the messaging server supporting this user and press Enter.
> 8. If the login name is acceptable as the e-mail name, leave this field blank.
> 9. Press F10 to save your settings.

As e-mail steadily infiltrates every company with more than one computer, e-mailboxes become mandatory for all LAN users. NetWare 4.10 includes MHS (Message Handling Services) for connections within the network and to the world outside your LAN; NetWare 4.11 does not include MHS.

From the NETADMIN program's View or Edit User menu, choose the Mailbox Information option to open the Mailbox screen, shown in Figure 6.32.

Open the Object, Class screen (which serves the same function as the Select Object dialog box in NetWare Administrator). Since we are only looking for

FIGURE 6.32

Setting the e-mail address

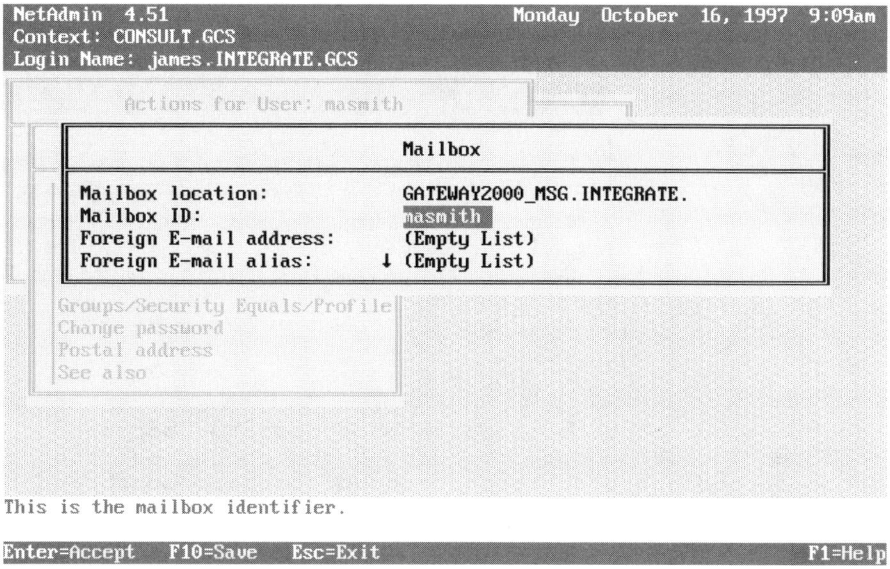

```
NetAdmin  4.51                                    Monday  October  16, 1997  9:09am
Context: CONSULT.GCS
Login Name: james.INTEGRATE.GCS

             Actions for User: masmith

                              Mailbox

          Mailbox location:    GATEWAY2000_MSG.INTEGRATE.
          Mailbox ID:          masmith
          Foreign E-mail address:   (Empty List)
          Foreign E-mail alias:   ↓ (Empty List)

          Groups/Security Equals/Profile
          Change password
          Postal address
          See also




This is the mailbox identifier.

Enter=Accept    F10=Save    Esc=Exit                            F1=Help
```

message servers, only message servers will appear in the window. Find the message server that will support the user and press the Enter key to select that server.

The Mailbox ID field will automatically use the login name, or at least the first eight characters of the login name. If any spaces or non-DOS characters are used in the name, NDS will force the name into DOS name compliance. If you leave this field blank and press the F10 key to save, the login name will be modified (if necessary) and plugged into this field.

Interestingly enough, the NETADMIN program included with NetWare 4.11 does include the e-mail and foreign e-mail address information. I suppose Novell engineers figured if you still want to use DOS administration tools with NETADMIN, you're probably still using MHS. That makes you a loyal Novell customer, although one with increasingly few people to communicate with over MHS.

Setting Foreign E-mail Address and Aliases

> **6.22 IN-A-HURRY**
>
> **Set the Foreign E-mail Address and Aliases in NETADMIN**
>
> 1. Start the NETADMIN program from the DOS command line.
> 2. Highlight Manage Objects on the main menu and press Enter.
> 3. Highlight the User object to view or modify and press Enter.
> 4. Highlight View or Edit Properties of This Object and press Enter.
> 5. Highlight Mailbox Information and press Enter.
> 6. Highlight Foreign E-mail addresses and press Enter.
> 7. Choose the e-mail type, provide the address, and press Enter.
> 8. Highlight Foreign E-mail alias and press Enter.
> 9. Choose the e-mail type, provide up to one address per e-mail type, and press Enter.
> 10. Press F10 to save your settings.

There are two good reasons for supplying information about foreign e-mail addresses: NDS supports NDS users getting their mail on remote mailboxes, and users outside your network may wish to address your users. If so, they will use their native system to address your users, and you may wish to track those addresses.

Figure 6.33 shows the foreign e-mail address information box. There are five e-mail types offered after you click on the down arrow button at the end of the Foreign E-mail Type field:

- **GMHS:** Global Message Handling Service from Novell
- **SMTP:** Simple Mail Transport Protocol, the standard Unix e-mail exchange protocol
- **SNADS:** SNA Distribution Services, another IBM product for file, document, and e-mail exchange

FIGURE 6.33

Setting foreign e-mail addresses

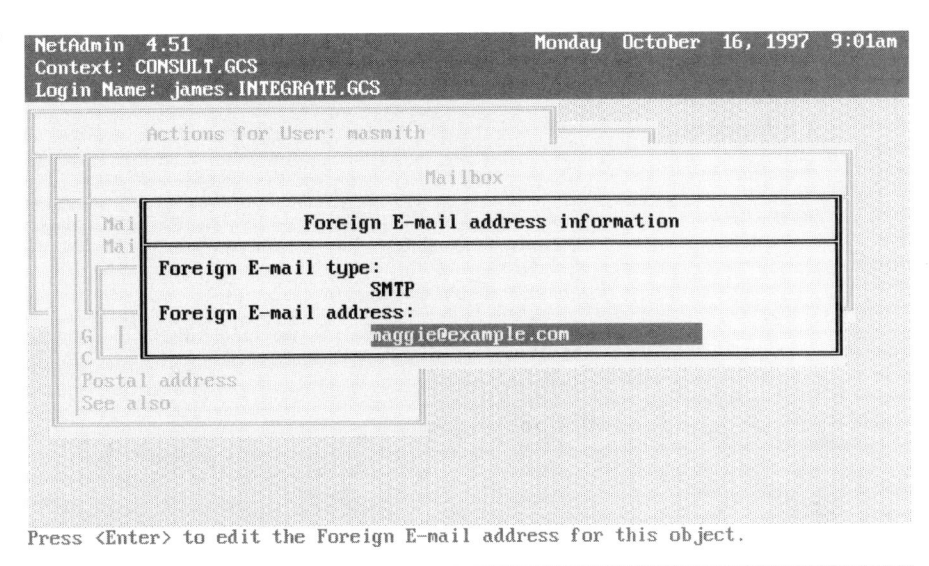

```
NetAdmin 4.51                              Monday October 16, 1997  9:01am
Context: CONSULT.GCS
Login Name: james.INTEGRATE.GCS

             Actions for User: masmith

                          Mailbox
             ┌─────────────────────────────────────────┐
             │   Foreign E-mail address information    │
             │                                         │
             │  Foreign E-mail type:                   │
             │           SMTP                          │
             │  Foreign E-mail address:                │
             │           maggie@example.com            │
             └─────────────────────────────────────────┘
             Postal address
             See also


Press <Enter> to edit the Foreign E-mail address for this object.

Enter=Edit   F10=Save   Esc=Exit                                    F1=Help
```

- **X.400:** The CCITT standard for exchanging e-mail between systems
- **PROFS:** PRofessional OFfice System, IBM's office automation and e-mail system for mainframes running the VM operating system
- **Other:** Another e-mail type

This screen is for informational purposes, and doesn't effect any changes on your network. You may add only one foreign e-mail address, but you can specify multiple foreign aliases. The limit is one alias per e-mail type. The procedure to set the foreign e-mail alias is exactly like that for setting the foreign e-mail address.

Recording the User's Postal Address

The Postal Address screen allows you to record either the home or business address for each user. The fields can be used for searching and to create a mailing label format. Figure 6.34 shows the Postal Address screen with information for user MASMITH.

FIGURE 6.34

Addresses the old-fashioned way

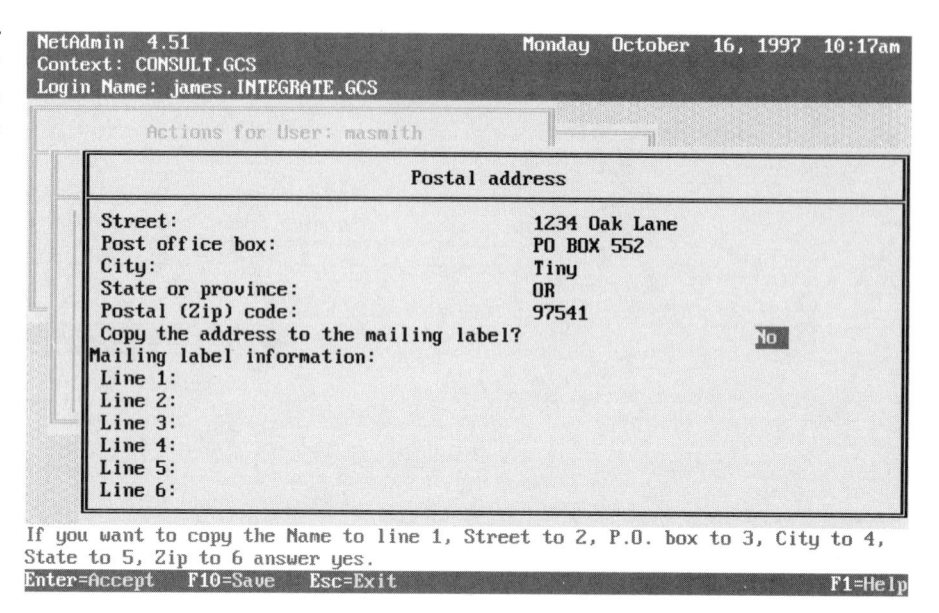

```
NetAdmin 4.51                              Monday October 16, 1997 10:17am
Context: CONSULT.GCS
Login Name: james.INTEGRATE.GCS

          Actions for User: masmith

┌──────────────────────────────────────────────────────────────────────┐
│                          Postal address                              │
│   Street:                           1234 Oak Lane                    │
│   Post office box:                  PO BOX 552                       │
│   City:                             Tiny                             │
│   State or province:                OR                               │
│   Postal (Zip) code:                97541                            │
│   Copy the address to the mailing label?              No             │
│   Mailing label information:                                         │
│   Line 1:                                                            │
│   Line 2:                                                            │
│   Line 3:                                                            │
│   Line 4:                                                            │
│   Line 5:                                                            │
│   Line 6:                                                            │
└──────────────────────────────────────────────────────────────────────┘
If you want to copy the Name to line 1, Street to 2, P.O. box to 3, City to 4,
State to 5, Zip to 6 answer yes.
Enter=Accept    F10=Save    Esc=Exit                             F1=Help
```

6.23 IN-A-HURRY

Set the Physical Postal Address in NETADMIN

1. Start the NETADMIN program from the DOS command line.

2. Highlight Manage Objects on the main menu and press Enter.

3. Highlight the User object to view or modify and press Enter.

4. Highlight View or Edit Properties of This Object and press Enter.

5. Highlight Postal address and press Enter.

6. Fill in the "snail mail" (physical) address for the user.

7. Toggle Yes or No to copy the address into a mailing label format.

8. Press F10 to save your settings.

Start the NETADMIN program and find MASMITH in the NDS tree. Type in the snail mail address information. It can be home or business; NetWare 4.1*x* doesn't care. The address in the top of the box will be the same as the one in the bottom, if you choose to have NETADMIN fill out the mailing label format for you. Press F10 to save and return to the View or Edit User menu.

Adding Reference Information

> **6.24 IN-A-HURRY**
>
> **Add User Reference Information in NETADMIN**
>
> 1. Start the NETADMIN program from the DOS command line.
> 2. Highlight Manage Objects on the main menu and press Enter.
> 3. Highlight the User object to view or modify and press Enter.
> 4. Highlight View or Edit Properties of This Object and press Enter.
> 5. Highlight See Also and press Enter.
> 6. Press Insert to add network objects that relate to this user.
> 7. Press F10 to save your settings.

The NETADMIN See Also screen is strictly informational. The information here has no effect on any network configuration. However, this screen is a handy place to reference information about the user, such as the Computer object type used by that user.

When you choose See Also from the User Object to View or Modify menu, you see the See Also screen. Figure 6.35 shows the process of adding related objects to MASMITH.

You cannot enter any text in this screen. Instead, you can press Insert and choose objects from the Class, Object screen. Press F5 for each highlighted entry you wish to mark.

User Object Security Configuration with NETADMIN

The arrangement of menu options in NETADMIN is a bit different than in the NetWare Administrator program. Where the MS Windows program uses a scrolling stack of buttons, the DOS ASCII graphics format of NETADMIN encourages the use of menus and submenus.

The submenu layout forces more artificial segmentation than the stacked buttons approach. That's the reason some of the security-oriented menu items in NETADMIN are put in one menu, and all the account restrictions are placed in a submenu. Compare Figure 6.36 here with the higher-level menu in Figure 6.29 at the beginning of the NETADMIN section.

414 Chapter 6 • Creating and Managing Users (Now User Objects)

FIGURE 6.35

Showing where MASMITH is related to the INTEGRATE Organizational Unit

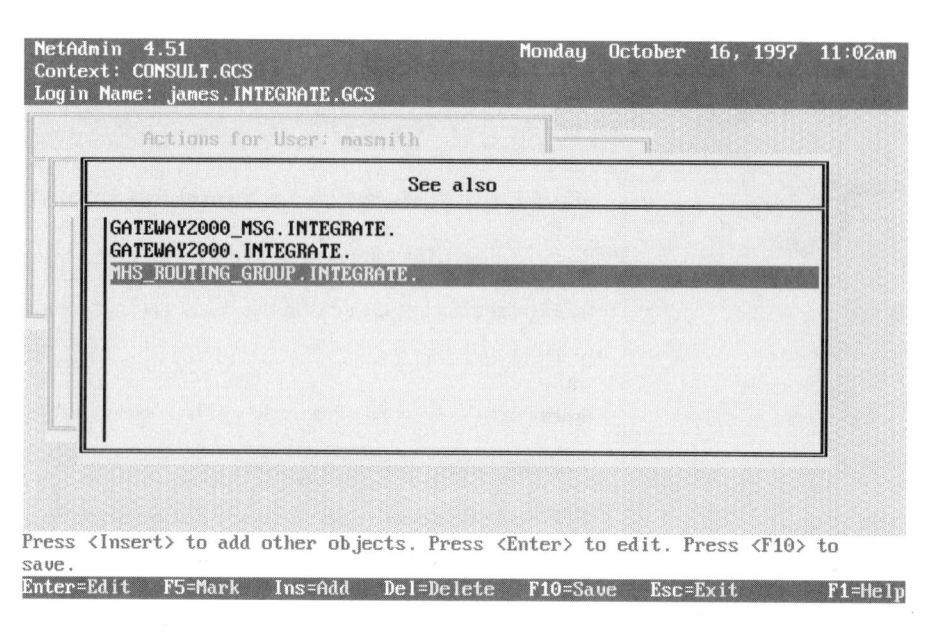

```
NetAdmin  4.51                              Monday  October  16, 1997  11:02am
Context: CONSULT.GCS
Login Name: james.INTEGRATE.GCS

         Actions for User: masmith
                          See also
    GATEWAY2000_MSG.INTEGRATE.
    GATEWAY2000.INTEGRATE.
    MHS_ROUTING_GROUP.INTEGRATE.




Press <Insert> to add other objects. Press <Enter> to edit. Press <F10> to
save.
Enter=Edit    F5=Mark    Ins=Add    Del=Delete    F10=Save    Esc=Exit    F1=Help
```

FIGURE 6.36

The NETADMIN Account restrictions submenu

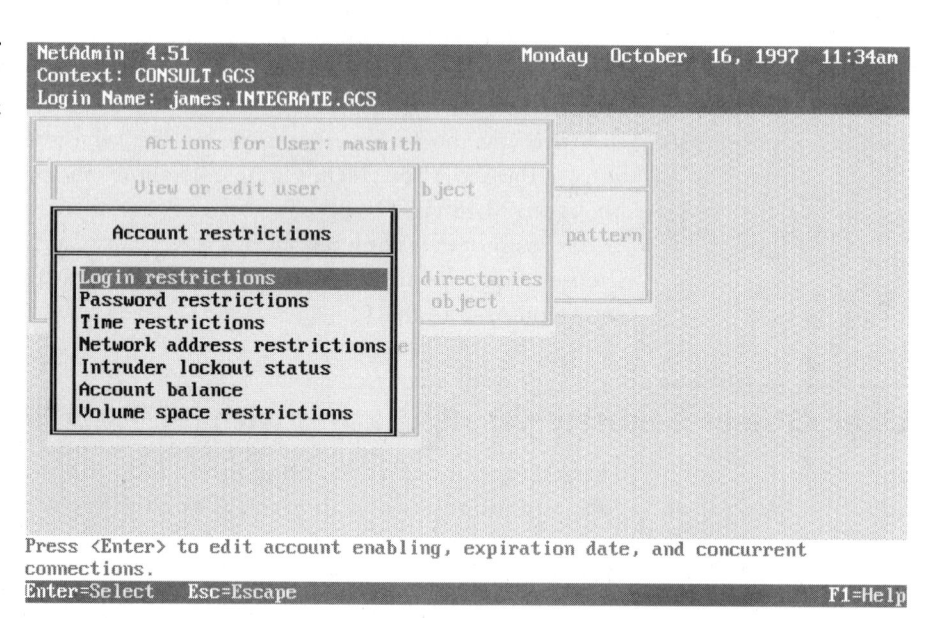

```
NetAdmin  4.51                              Monday  October  16, 1997  11:34am
Context: CONSULT.GCS
Login Name: james.INTEGRATE.GCS

         Actions for User: masmith
         View or edit user         bject
         Account restrictions              pattern
          Login restrictions
          Password restrictions    directories
          Time restrictions         object
          Network address restrictions
          Intruder lockout status
          Account balance
          Volume space restrictions




Press <Enter> to edit account enabling, expiration date, and concurrent
connections.
Enter=Select    Esc=Escape                                              F1=Help
```

We'll get to this submenu in just a bit. First we'll examine the security-related menu choices in the main View or Edit User menu, such as Login Script.

Creating a User Login Script

> **6.25 IN-A-HURRY**
>
> **Create or Modify a User Login Script in NETADMIN**
>
> **1.** Start the NETADMIN program from the DOS command line.
>
> **2.** Highlight Manage Objects on the main menu and press Enter.
>
> **3.** Highlight the User object to view or modify and press Enter.
>
> **4.** Highlight View or Edit Properties of This Object and press Enter.
>
> **5.** Highlight Login Script and press Enter.
>
> **6.** If no login script exists, decide whether to copy one from another user.
>
> **7.** Write or modify the login script for this particular user.
>
> **8.** Press F10 to save the script.

The login script was the single place to manage user configuration in the earliest NetWare versions. Later, more control was available in the system login script, but there could be only one system login script per server. That limited what could be done for any particular user or group of users, or else the system script became huge and unwieldy.

With NetWare 4.1x, there are four scripts that work together to control the network configuration of any one user. The user login script, once the most important, has now become somewhat less important.

The user login script executes last and overrides all previous settings. This is the same relationship as with NetWare 3.x's system and user login scripts. But the extra scripts available in NetWare 4.1x make the user login script necessary only for unique needs for that particular user.

After starting the NETADMIN program and working your way to the menu that lets you choose to edit the user's login script, you have a choice to make. In NetWare Administrator, the way to copy another login script is to use MS Windows block copy-and-paste functions. Long before MS Windows was available, NetWare provided an easy way to copy a login script from one user to the other. The choice you will be faced with is shown in Figure 6.37.

If you say Yes, a box pops up to ask for the object name of the login script owner. If you're not sure or don't want to type that much, press the Insert key, and the Object, Class screen will appear. This time, only similar objects will appear. No volumes or servers or printers or the like need apply.

Once you either copy a login script to modify or agree to write your own from scratch, the Login script box, which has basic text-editing capabilities, will appear. Some of the editing key commands are listed in Table 6.3. Login script commands and syntax are covered in the next chapter.

TABLE 6.3 NETADMIN Edit Key Commands for Creating or Modifying User Login Scripts

KEY	FUNCTION
F1	Help screens
F5	Mark text
F10	Accept (save)
Insert	Paste text saved to the buffer
Delete	Delete marked text
Ctrl+↑	Top of file
Ctrl+↓	Bottom of file
Ctrl+→	Next word
Ctrl+←	Previous word

Figure 6.38 shows a test login script for user MASMITH. This is strictly to test that the login script executes. The write lines will echo the text within the quotation marks to the screen during login script execution.

Creating User Objects with NETADMIN (DOS) **417**

FIGURE 6.37

To copy or not to copy

```
NetAdmin 4.51                          Monday October 16, 1997 11:35am
Context: CONSULT.GCS
Login Name: james.INTEGRATE.GCS

         ┌─────── Actions for User: masmith ───────┐
         │                                         │
         │     View or edit user        bject      │
         │                                         │
         │   Identification                pattern │
         │   Environm┌─────────────────────────────┴──┐
         │   Mailbox │ Script is empty. Copy script from another object? │
         │   Account ├────┐                                               │
         │   Login sc│ No │                                               │
         │   Groups/S│ Yes│                                               │
         │   Change p└────┘                                               │
         │   Postal address                                               │
         │   See also                                                     │

Enter Yes to copy a script from another object.
Enter=Accept   Esc=Escape                                        F1=Help
```

FIGURE 6.38

A test login script

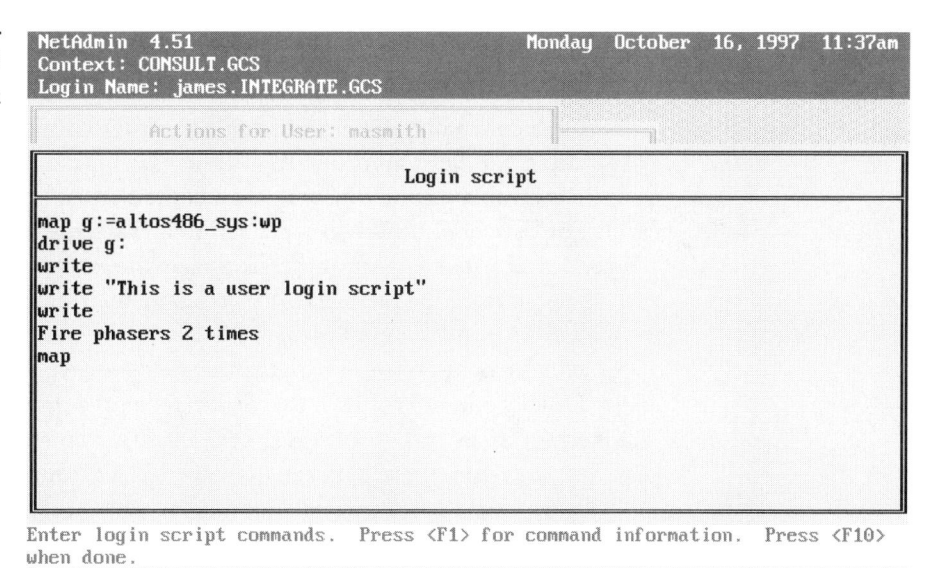

```
NetAdmin 4.51                          Monday October 16, 1997 11:37am
Context: CONSULT.GCS
Login Name: james.INTEGRATE.GCS

         ┌─────── Actions for User: masmith ───────┐
┌────────┴────────────────────────────────────────┴────────────────────┐
│                          Login script                                │
├──────────────────────────────────────────────────────────────────────┤
│ map g:=altos486_sys:wp                                               │
│ drive g:                                                             │
│ write                                                                │
│ write "This is a user login script"                                  │
│ write                                                                │
│ Fire phasers 2 times                                                 │
│ map                                                                  │
│                                                                      │
└──────────────────────────────────────────────────────────────────────┘
Enter login script commands.  Press <F1> for command information.  Press <F10>
when done.
F10=Accept   F5=Mark   Ins=Add   Del=Delete   PgUp=Page Up    Alt+F1=More
```

Setting Up Group Membership

> **6.26 IN-A-HURRY**
>
> **Add a User to a Group with NETADMIN**
>
> 1. Start the NETADMIN program from the DOS command line.
> 2. Highlight Manage Objects on the main menu and press Enter.
> 3. Highlight the User object to view or modify and press Enter.
> 4. Highlight View or Edit Properties of This Object and press Enter.
> 5. Highlight Groups/Security Equals/Profile and press Enter.
> 6. Press Enter on the Group field.
> 7. Press Insert to add a Group object to the Group Memberships box.
> 8. Type the Group name or press Insert to browse the NDS tree.
> 9. Press F10 twice to save your settings.

Groups are great when administering networks. Instead of dealing with each user, you can maintain a list of similar users and deal with their Group object. User objects inherit all properties of their Group objects.

Be careful, a Group object is *not* a container. A Group object merely keeps a list of User objects. When some action is taken with that Group object, each User object listed as part of the group has that same action taken with them.

After starting the NETADMIN program and finding the User object to add to a Group object, press Enter on the Groups/Security Equals/Profile menu choice. The next pop-up box has three fields for, you guessed it, Group, Security Equal To, and Profile. If the Group field says (Empty List), this user is not a member of any groups. Press Enter to rectify that situation, then press Insert to get to a point where you can actually add a Group object.

Figure 6.39 shows the text box used to add user MASMITH to the CONSULTANTS group. You can either type the Group object name in this field or press the Insert key to call up the Class, Object screen once again.

If a Group object is inside the Group Memberships box (in the background of Figure 6.39), you can modify or delete any of the Group objects. Deletion in this screen only takes the User object out of the group, it does not delete the Group object itself.

Creating User Objects with NETADMIN (DOS) **419**

FIGURE 6.39

Adding MASMITH to the CONSULTANTS group

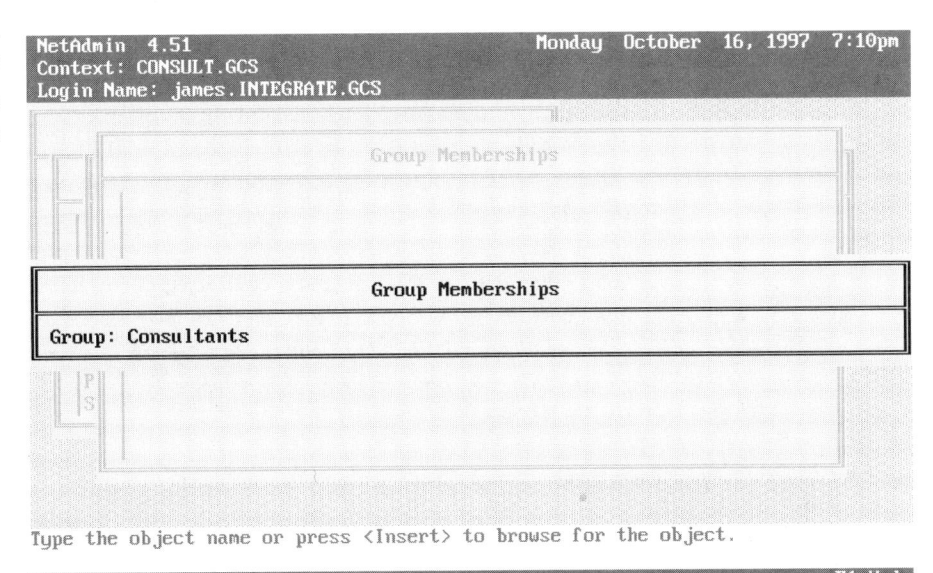

```
NetAdmin 4.51                                Monday October 16, 1997 7:10pm
Context: CONSULT.GCS
Login Name: james.INTEGRATE.GCS

                              Group Memberships




                              Group Memberships
          Group: Consultants




          Type the object name or press <Insert> to browse for the object.
          Ins=Add   Enter=Accept   Esc=Exit                          F1=Help
```

Setting Security Equal To

6.27 IN-A-HURRY

Set Security Equivalence in NETADMIN

1. Start the NETADMIN program from the DOS command line.

2. Highlight Manage Objects on the main menu and press Enter.

3. Highlight the User object to view or modify and press Enter.

4. Highlight View or Edit Properties of This Object and press Enter.

5. Highlight Groups/Security Equals/Profile and press Enter.

6. Press Enter on the Security Equal To field.

7. Press Insert to add a security equivalence to the User object.

8. Type in the object to be equivalent to, or press Insert to browse the NDS tree.

9. Press Enter to accept the new equivalence, then press F10 twice to save your settings.

Security equivalence grants one User object the same rights as another object. This is what happens with Group objects: the members of the group all have the rights of the group itself. Granting security equivalence of a User object to another User object is more dangerous than adding User objects to Group objects. See Chapter 9 for more on security equivalence and other security-related topics.

> **WARNING**
>
> *Using equivalence to give rights to a User object seems to save time in the short run, but may cause problems. Better to take an extra few seconds and grant rights to a Group object or to the individual User object. It's easy to forget that equivalent rights have been granted to a user, especially when something's wrong on the network and you're troubleshooting.*

After starting NETADMIN and working your way through the menus to the Security Equal To field, press Insert to add more equivalences. Notice in the background box in Figure 6.40 that the Group object CONSULTANTS is already listed as equal to MASMITH. That's because we added MASMITH to that group, and the rights of the group pass to the users in that group.

In Figure 6.40 we see that MASMITH is about to be equal (security-wise) to LAPTOP.INTEGRATE. The Organizational Unit name, INTEGRATE, is

FIGURE 6.40

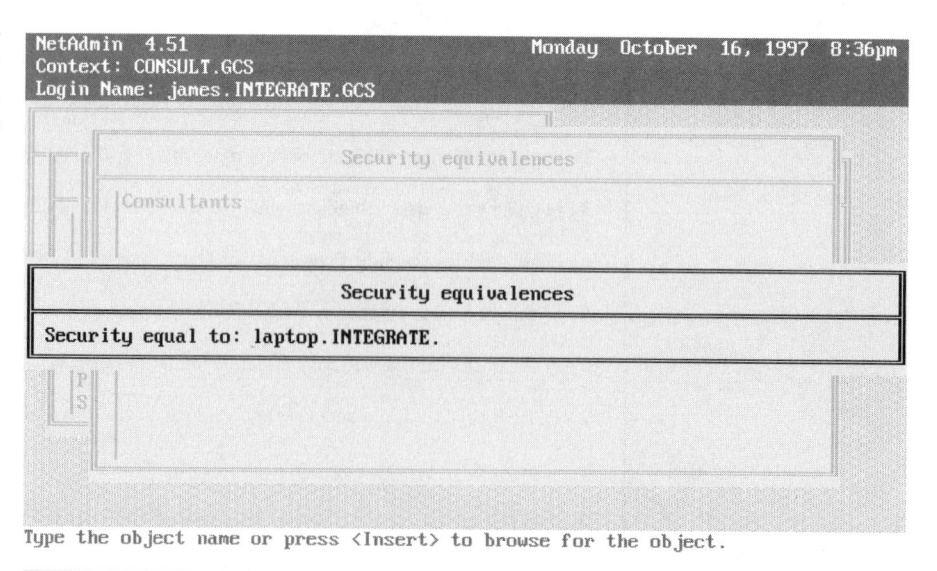

Granting security equivalence of user LAPTOP to user MASMITH

included so we'll know LAPTOP is from a different context. From the point where we are in Figure 6.40, we'll need to press F10 three times to save this information and get back to a menu.

Editing the Profile Script

Unlike NetWare Administrator, NETADMIN allows a bit more access to the profile login script. But we have a nice section on profile scripts coming up in just a bit (in Chapter 7), and I don't want to ruin the surprise. So, let's just exercise some patience and plan on doing the profile script explanation all in one place.

Setting Login Restrictions

> **6.28 IN-A-HURRY**
>
> **Set Login Restrictions with NETADMIN**
>
> 1. Start the NETADMIN program from the DOS command line.
> 2. Highlight Manage Objects on the main menu and press Enter.
> 3. Highlight the User object to view or modify and press Enter.
> 4. Highlight View or Edit Properties of This Object and press Enter.
> 5. Highlight Account Restrictions and press Enter.
> 6. Highlight Login Restrictions and press Enter.
> 7. Set the appropriate restrictions.
> 8. Press F10 to save your settings.

Login restriction setup is one of the times that NetWare 4.1x focuses on the individual user. Normally, any configuration that can be done to a particular user can better be done working with a group. Restrictions on a particular user are useful at times, however, and this is where you set some of those restrictions.

Login restrictions sounds like a way to stop someone from connecting to the network. That's only part of the value of these restrictions here. Maintaining tight network security often means limiting network access for users and tracking the resources used by each user.

Chapter 6 • Creating and Managing Users (Now User Objects)

When you choose Account Restrictions from the NETADMIN View or Edit User menu, you see the screen shown in Figure 6.41. The Login Restriction fields are described in Table 6.4.

TABLE 6.4
NETADMIN Login Restriction Fields

FIELD	DESCRIPTION
Account Disabled	Stops this account from being used. The default is No.
Account Has Expiration Date	Locks the account on the date listed. The default is No.
Date Account Expires	Lock out date for this account.
Limit Concurrent Connections	Determines whether the user can be connected from multiple clients. The default is No.
Maximum Connections	If connections are limited, how many are allowed. The default is 1.
Time Zone	Displays the time zone for this user.

FIGURE 6.41
Restricting MASMITH

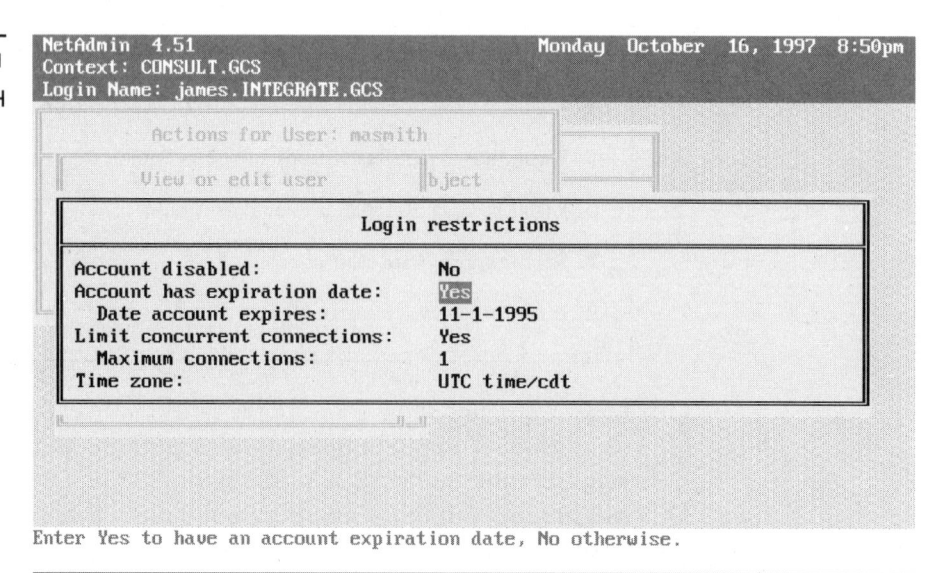

```
NetAdmin  4.51                              Monday  October  16, 1997  8:50pm
Context: CONSULT.GCS
Login Name: james.INTEGRATE.GCS

          ┌─────── Actions for User: masmith ───────┐
          │                                          │
          │   View or edit user          bject      │
          │  ┌──────────────────────────────────────┐
          │  │           Login restrictions         │
          │  │                                      │
          │  │ Account disabled:         No         │
          │  │ Account has expiration date: Yes     │
          │  │   Date account expires:   11-1-1995  │
          │  │ Limit concurrent connections: Yes    │
          │  │   Maximum connections:    1          │
          │  │ Time zone:                UTC time/cdt│
          │  └──────────────────────────────────────┘

Enter Yes to have an account expiration date, No otherwise.
F10=Save    Esc=Exit                                          F1=Help
```

Disabling accounts is handy when one person leaves temporarily and you want to be sure no other user has access to the absent user's information. While you as the network administrator know which files each user has access to, you don't know if one user shares their account and password with other users. You can put a crimp in this generosity by disabling accounts while people are on vacation. Limiting concurrent connections also cuts down on shared accounts and passwords.

Setting Password Restrictions

> **6.29 IN-A-HURRY**
>
> **Set Password Restrictions with NETADMIN**
>
> 1. Start the NETADMIN program from the DOS command line.
> 2. Highlight Manage Objects on the main menu and press Enter.
> 3. Highlight the User object to view or modify and press Enter.
> 4. Highlight View or Edit Properties of This Object and press Enter.
> 5. Highlight Account Restrictions and press Enter.
> 6. Highlight Password Restrictions and press Enter.
> 7. Set restrictions for this user.
> 8. Press F10 to save your settings.

Left to their own devices, most users pick terrible passwords. Family names are common, as are birthdays. If your going to have passwords, you might as well have good passwords. That's the idea behind password restrictions. Passwords you choose will be better than the ones non-security minded users will choose. You will not pick the name of the user's daughter. However, users will not easily remember the passwords you choose. This leads to passwords written down on calendars or desk blotters, which is not secure either. There's no good way to cover both these contingencies.

For security reasons, most experts recommend a password length of at least five characters. However, the longer the password, the harder it is to remember. Although NetWare doesn't demand mixing alpha and numeric characters, some

Unix systems do. Following the example of SCO Unix and requiring at least five characters including at least two numeric characters makes passwords much more difficult to guess.

Start the NETADMIN program and work your way down through the particular user settings to the Password Restrictions screen. The default password settings are to allow the user to change passwords, but not to require a password. As you can see in Figure 6.42, we have changed the defaults considerably. Table 6.5 describes the fields on this screen.

> *There's no place in NETADMIN to change a user's password. If you wish, you can use the SETPASS command-line utility.*

If you decide to force password changes, NetWare allows each user a few grace logins. In other words, even though the password is expired, NetWare will allow that password for a certain number of times. Allowing grace logins is a friendly thing to do when forcing passwords to change. If users make up their own new passwords, they may not feel creative the morning their old password expires. The grace logins allow them to carefully consider their next password. If you or your department parcels out passwords, the user will need to contact you.

FIGURE 6.42
Strict password restrictions

```
NetAdmin 4.51                              Monday October 16, 1997  9:08am
Context: CONSULT.GCS
Login Name: james.INTEGRATE.GCS

                          Password Restrictions

   Allow user to change password:        Yes
   Require a password:                   Yes
     Minimum password length:            5
   Force periodic password changes:      Yes
     Days between forced changes:        40
     Date password expires:              11-25-1995
     Limit grace logins:                 Yes
       Grace logins allowed:             6
       Remaining grace logins:           6
   Require unique passwords:             Yes
   Date and time of last login:          10-16-1995 1:50:41 am
   Time zone:                            Workstation time



Enter Yes to allow user to change password, No otherwise.

F10=Save   Esc=Exit                                              F1=Help
```

TABLE 6.5: NETADMIN Password Restrictions Fields

FIELD	DESCRIPTION
Allow User to Change Password	If your security is extremely tight, you may set this to No so that the user cannot change his or her own password.
Require a Password	If this is set to No, everything else in this box stays blank. Toggling this to Yes allows you to set the minimum password length and choose whether to force periodic changes.
Minimum Password Length	The password length can be between 1 and 999 characters, although setting this larger than 11 characters makes it impossible for Macintosh clients to log in.
Force Periodic Password Changes	When Yes, the user will be forced to change the password at the interval you specify.
Days Between Forced Changes	If you force password changes, the default for days between forced changes is 40 days.
Date Password Expires	The date the password will expire. Changing the Days Between Forced Changes field forces the Date Password Expires field to change, but not vice versa.
Limit Grace Logins	If you force password changes, NetWare allows each user a few grace logins.
Grace Logins Allowed	Number of grace logins. The default is six.
Remaining Grace Logins	This field displays how many grace logins are left for this user.
Require Unique Passwords	When password changes are forced, the option to require unique passwords becomes available. If you choose not to have unique passwords, users can simply alternate between their son's name and their daughter's name for passwords. If you require passwords to be unique, NetWare tracks each user's last 20 passwords and does not allow duplication.
Date and Time of Last Login	Shows the last successful login time and date for this user.
Time Zone	Displays the time zone for this user.

Setting Time Restrictions

> **6.30 IN-A-HURRY**
>
> **Set Login Time Restrictions in NETADMIN**
>
> 1. Start the NETADMIN program from the DOS command line.
> 2. Highlight Manage Objects on the main menu and press Enter.
> 3. Highlight the User object to view or modify and press Enter.
> 4. Highlight View or Edit Properties of This Object and press Enter.
> 5. Highlight Account Restrictions and press Enter.
> 6. Highlight Time Restrictions and press Enter.
> 7. Erase the asterisks to eliminate times the user can be connected to the network.
> 8. Press F10 to save the restrictions.

There are several reasons to restrict access to your network. First, and most common, is to allow tape backup systems to work properly. Most backup systems skip open files. If users are logged in and still have applications open, those files in use will likely be skipped. Closing all connections before the backup starts eliminates that problem.

Security is another reason to restrict access. If no one in your company works the night shift, the only users on your network at 1:13 A.M. are probably up to no good. Locking out all the users during the night and early morning limits your exposure to network tampering.

If you use login scripts to inform users of upcoming events with a MOTD (Message of the Day), you want them to log in to see it. If they stay connected overnight, the login script can't call the MOTD and display same. So set the Login Time Restrictions to force users to disconnect from the server during the night.

The name of this feature is slightly misleading. Along with restricting logins, this feature of NetWare 4.1x disconnects those users that are still connected at the beginning of the blocked time. Perhaps we should call this Connection Time Restrictions rather than Login Time Restrictions.

Run NETADMIN and plow through the menus to this user's Login Time Restrictions screen. The default is for all times to be available. The asterisk in a half-hour time block means login is allowed. Erase the asterisks for times to restrict access.

Block functions work: place the cursor on a starting time, press the F5 key, and move the cursor to the end time. If you press Insert, login will be allowed. Pressing Delete or the spacebar erases the asterisks.

Figure 6.43 shows the hours of 1:00 A.M. to 4:00 A.M. blocked out, allowing no network connections. Time is displayed in 24-hour format, making 2:00 P.M. display 14:00 o'clock. The Time Zone field in the bottom-left corner shows the current setting for this workstation, now displaying the UTC time set to cdt, or Central Daylight Time.

Setting Network Address Restrictions

The most restrictive control of users is to restrict the workstations from which they can connect to the network. This is drastic and makes for more work for the network administrator, but it is certainly possible.

There is one good way to use this to improve security without inconveniencing your users: make the restriction for your tape backup system. If your

FIGURE 6.43
Restricting network access during the early morning

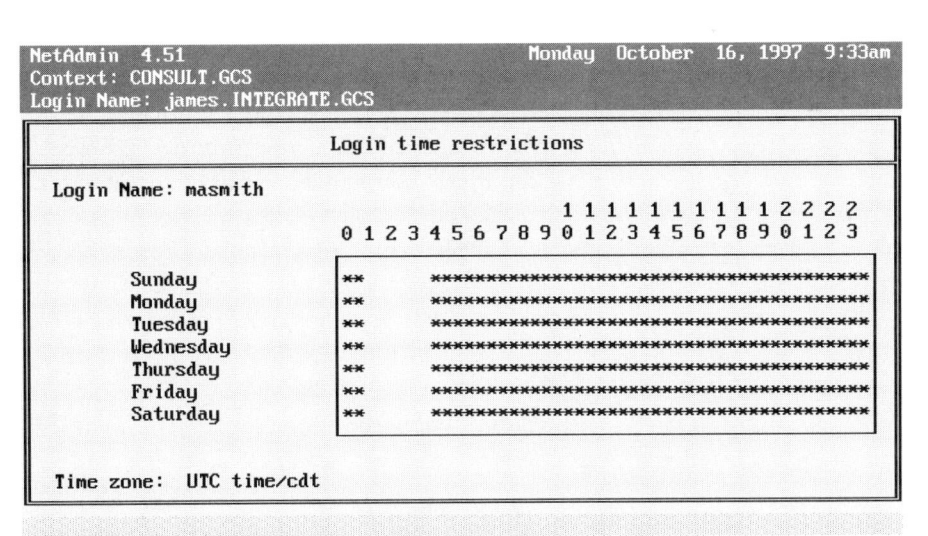

> **6.31 IN-A-HURRY**
>
> **Set Network Address Restrictions with NETADMIN**
>
> 1. Start the NETADMIN program from the DOS command line.
> 2. Highlight Manage Objects on the main menu and press Enter.
> 3. Highlight the User object to view or modify and press Enter.
> 4. Highlight View or Edit Properties of This Object and press Enter.
> 5. Highlight Account Restrictions and press Enter.
> 6. Highlight Network Address Restrictions and press Enter.
> 7. If the Network Address Restrictions box is empty, press the Insert key.
> 8. Choose the protocol for the allowed workstation and press Enter.
> 9. Provide the address details for the allowed workstation.
> 10. If desired, choose another protocol and repeat.
> 11. Press F10 to save your settings.

tape backup system runs from a network node, as most do, tie the backup User object to the address of the machine with the tape backup attached.

The User object for backup (usually called BACKUP or something equally creative and inviting to hackers and snoopers) has full rights over the network file systems, which could be a serious security breach if a person got hold of the backup user's user name and password. If that happens, but you have restricted the address for the backup User object, the thieving user must gain access to that physical workstation to cause problems. Figure 6.44 shows the screen used to restrict access for the IPX/SPX protocol used by NetWare.

The protocol options include AppleTalk, Ethernet/Token Ring, IPX/SPX, OSI, SDLC, and TCP/IP. Currently, you can restrict only AFP (AppleTalk Filing Protocol) and IPX/SPX.

If you don't know the address for a particular user machine, from a DOS prompt type:

```
NLIST USER /A
```

The active users for the network will be displayed along with their network and node numbers. Fill those numbers into the proper fields so the system knows exactly which workstation is allowable for this user.

FIGURE 6.44

Tying a user to a particular workstation

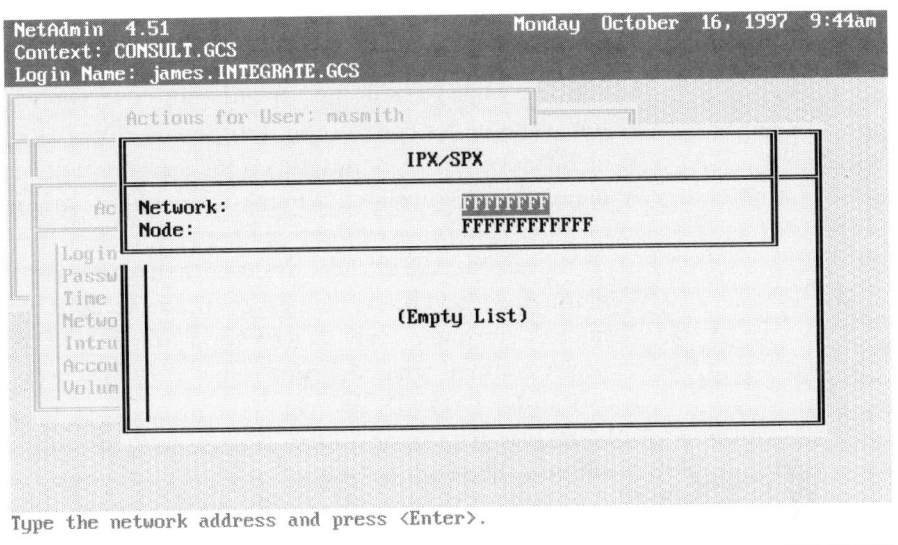

```
NetAdmin  4.51                          Monday  October  16, 1997  9:44am
Context: CONSULT.GCS
Login Name: james.INTEGRATE.GCS

            Actions for User: masmith

                           ┌─────────IPX/SPX─────────┐
         Ac                │ Network:    FFFFFFFF    │
                           │ Node:       FFFFFFFFFFFF│
         Login             │                         │
         Passw             │                         │
         Time              │                         │
         Netwo             │      (Empty List)       │
         Intru             │                         │
         Accou             │                         │
         Volum             │                         │
                           └─────────────────────────┘


Type the network address and press <Enter>.
Enter=Change   F10=Save   Esc=Exit                              F1=Help
```

Resetting Intruder Lockout Status

6.32 IN-A-HURRY

Check Intruder Lockout Status in NETADMIN

1. Start the NETADMIN program from the DOS command line.
2. Highlight Manage Objects on the main menu and press Enter.
3. Highlight the User object to view or modify and press Enter.
4. Highlight View or Edit Properties of This Object and press Enter.
5. Highlight Account Restrictions and press Enter.
6. Highlight Intruder Lockout Status and press Enter.
7. If locked, press Enter to clear.

NetWare's intruder lockout feature does exactly what it sounds like. If you have intruder detection active, you will always know when someone connects to your network while guessing a password. Of course, you will also know if someone forgets his or her password, possibly even before that user comes to you for help.

Intruder detection must be set for the container (see Chapter 10) before this dialog box becomes active for the User object. You may have detection active on some containers but not on others.

When you have intruder detection active on a container a user accesses, and that user forgets his or her password, the account will be locked. The assumption is that someone is up to no good while trying to hack your network. The reality is usually that someone forgot the password.

Run NETADMIN and climb the menu tree until you reach the Intruder lockout status for the affected user. If the account is really locked, the screen will look like Figure 6.45.

The help line at the bottom tells you everything you need to know:

```
When the account is locked, press <Enter> to unlock it.
```

Couldn't have said it better myself.

FIGURE 6.45

User MASMITH: busted

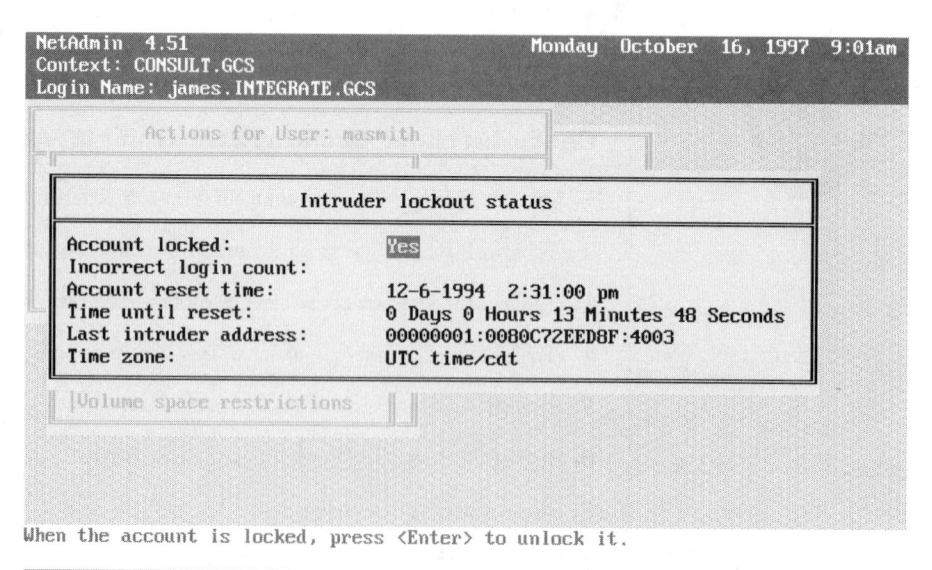

Setting a User's Account Balance

> **6.33 IN-A-HURRY**
>
> **Set the Account Balance with NETADMIN**
>
> 1. Start the NETADMIN program from the DOS command line.
> 2. Highlight Manage Objects on the main menu and press Enter.
> 3. Highlight the User object to view or modify and press Enter.
> 4. Highlight View or Edit Properties of This Object and press Enter.
> 5. Highlight Account Restrictions and press Enter.
> 6. Highlight Account Balance and press Enter.
> 7. Set the account balance, whether to allow unlimited credit, and the low balance limit.
> 8. Press F10 to save your settings.

NetWare was the first network operating system to allow accounting. By tracking such details as connect time, disk space used, and service requests to a file server, NetWare accounting moved away from a PC LAN level toward mainframe-type control. Accounting is used by some network administrators to charge company departments, and by others to track when resources are being used more heavily than in the past.

In NETADMIN, go through the menus to get to the Account Balance screen, shown in Figure 6.46.

The Account Balance field shows the remaining credits available for this user. The credits are set on the network resource itself, not here. The Low Balance Limit field shows the credit level to warn the user before the account is disabled.

If you wish to track the accounting information for charge-back or overhead calculations, but don't wish to prevent users from reaching their network resources, set the Allow Unlimited Credit field to Yes. This will track the information needed for the accounting reports but never lock out users.

If the user drops below the balance in the Low Balance Limit field, that user will be locked out of the system. However, nothing will happen to the user's information. The user will be back in business as soon as an administrator changes the Account Balance field.

FIGURE 6.46

Tracking network credits used

```
NetAdmin 4.51                          Monday  October  16, 1997  9:04am
Context: CONSULT.GCS
Login Name: james.INTEGRATE.GCS

         Actions for User: masmith
         View or edit user         bject
         Account restrictions            pattern

         ┌─────────────── Account balance ───────────────┐
         │ Account balance:        50000                 │
         │ Allow unlimited credit: No                    │
         │     Low balance limit:  100                   │
         └───────────────────────────────────────────────┘
         Volume space restrictions



Enter Yes to allow unlimited credit, No otherwise.

F10=Save   Esc=Exit                                             F1=Help
```

Setting Volume Space Restrictions

When disk space was expensive, the ability to limit each user's hard disk usage was popular. With fast hard disks selling for well under a dollar a megabyte now, this is less important. Better to buy more disks than to always adjust disk space allowances.

The idea that network disk space is valuable and to be used only for serious work clashes with the idea of making the network an attractive place for all users. Proponents of disk space limits say it forces users to clean out their closets and delete junk from the disk. That's certainly a good point.

It's possible to limit space on one volume while allowing unlimited space on other volumes. When used in this way, volume space restrictions can be valuable by pushing users to make use of volumes with plenty of open space.

After winding down through the menu system of NETADMIN, Volume Space Restrictions is the last choice for this user on the Account Restrictions menu. The default is not to limit space. Restrictions in place for user MASMITH are shown in Figure 6.47.

You set the limits in kilobytes, so the limit of 5000 KB translates to 5 MB. User MASMITH, when she checks her available disk space anywhere on the

> **6.34 IN-A-HURRY**
>
> **Set Volume Space Restrictions with NETADMIN**
>
> 1. Start the NETADMIN program from the DOS command line.
> 2. Highlight Manage Objects on the main menu and press Enter.
> 3. Highlight the User object to view or modify and press Enter.
> 4. Highlight View or Edit Properties of This Object and press Enter.
> 5. Highlight Account Restrictions and press Enter.
> 6. Highlight Volume Space Restrictions and press Enter.
> 7. Choose the volume on which to limit this user (press Insert or type the volume name), then press Enter.
> 8. Toggle the Limit Volume Space field (by pressing Y or N) to Yes to limit space.
> 9. Set the maximum disk space allowed on this volume for this user.
> 10. Repeat for other volumes if necessary.
> 11. Press F10 to save your settings.

ALTOS486_SYS volume, will see she has just over 3 MB available. If she tries to copy more files to a full disk, she will get an error message, just as if the disk were physically full.

Even when space is not restricted, this field is valuable. Volume space restriction will display the space used by any user on any volume. If you have a particular disk hog or two, this field will help you track their greed.

Do you have a boss that refuses to get more disk space, even though you really need some breathing room? When you set the volume space restrictions, set that boss's secretary a nice, tight limit. Too little disk space causes problems with lots of applications, especially those that use temporary files. When the secretary complains, the boss usually complies (Rule Number One in creative network management).

434 Chapter 6 • Creating and Managing Users (Now User Objects)

FIGURE 6.47

Limiting a user's disk space on volume ALTOS486_SYS

```
NetAdmin 4.51                              Monday  October  16, 1997  9:04am
Context: CONSULT.GCS
Login Name: james.INTEGRATE.GCS

        Actions for User: masmith
        View or edit user              bject
        Account restrictions                    pattern
        ┌─────────────────────────────────────────┐
        │              Account balance            │
        │ Account balance:       50000            │
        │ Allow unlimited credit: No              │
        │    Low balance limit:  100              │
        └─────────────────────────────────────────┘
        Volume space restrictions


Enter Yes to allow unlimited credit, No otherwise.
F10=Save   Esc=Exit                                                F1=Help
```

Setting Rights to Files and Directories

6.35 IN-A-HURRY

View Rights in NETADMIN

1. Start the NETADMIN program from the DOS command line.

2. Highlight Manage Objects on the main menu and press Enter.

3. Highlight User Object to View or Modify and press Enter.

4. Highlight View or Edit Rights to Files and Directories and press Enter.

5. Type the Volume Object Name: or press Insert twice to browse the NDS tree.

6. Choose the volume name and press Enter twice.

7. Press F10 to search for and then display the rights for the user.

8. Press Enter on the desired directory to view or edit trustee rights.

This section is one of the few places that NETADMIN falls short of the NetWare Administrator program. The problem in not NETADMIN per se, it's the low video resolution of DOS. The characters in the DOS program can't be made small enough to fit more information onto a screen. That's why NetWare Administrator does a better job than NETADMIN: more information is crammed on the screen at one time.

The biggest difference is that in NetWare Administrator, you see multiple volumes, and the directories on each that the user in question has rights to see and use. In NETADMIN, you can see only one volume's worth at a time.

Start through the NETADMIN menu tree, but stop before you go too far. Normally, you skip past the Actions for User menu to view or edit properties. This time, however, you must cursor down four times and press Enter on View or Edit Rights to Files and Directories.

Once you open the Rights to Files and/or Directories screen, there are four fields to fill, three of which are mandatory:

- **Volume Object Name:** Supply the volume name, or press Insert to browse.

- **Beginning Path:** Supply a directory on the volume to limit the search scope, or press Insert. If nothing is supplied, the search will start at the root of the volume.

- **Directories/Files:** Accept Directory or press Enter to open a pick list of Directory, File, or Directory and File. The more detailed the search, the longer it will take, and the more likely the search results will overload the program.

- **Trustee Search Depth:** Press Enter to open the pick list. Choose All subdirectories (default) or Current Directory only.

After giving a volume object name and modifying the other fields (if desired), press F10 to start the search and display the resulting list. Figure 6.48 shows the results of a rights search for user MASMITH on volume ALTOS486_SYS.

Currently, MASMITH has rights to only one directory on the ALTOS486_SYS volume. The rights (shown in abbreviation) are Read, Write, Create, Erase, Modify, and File Scan. To add more rights, press the Insert key. The box titled Trustee Rights Not Granted pops up in the bottom-right corner of the screen. This new box is shown in Figure 6.49.

Chapter 6 ▪ Creating and Managing Users (Now User Objects)

FIGURE 6.48

MASMITH's directory rights on ALTOS486_SYS

```
NetAdmin  4.51                                 Monday  October  16, 1997  5:21pm
Context: CONSULT.GCS
Login Name: james.INTEGRATE.GCS

           Actions for User: masmith

                    Rights to files and/or directories

    Volume object name:          ALTOS486_SYS
    Beginning Path:
    Directories/Files:           Directory
    Trustee Search Depth:        All subdirectories

                         Trustee directory, rights

           ETC/TEMP                                            [ RWCEMF ]




    Press <Enter> to view/edit; <F5> to mark multiple; <Insert> to add.
    Enter=Accept    F5=Mark   Ins=Add   Del=Delete   Esc=Exit         F1=Help
```

FIGURE 6.49

Adding more trustee rights for MASMITH

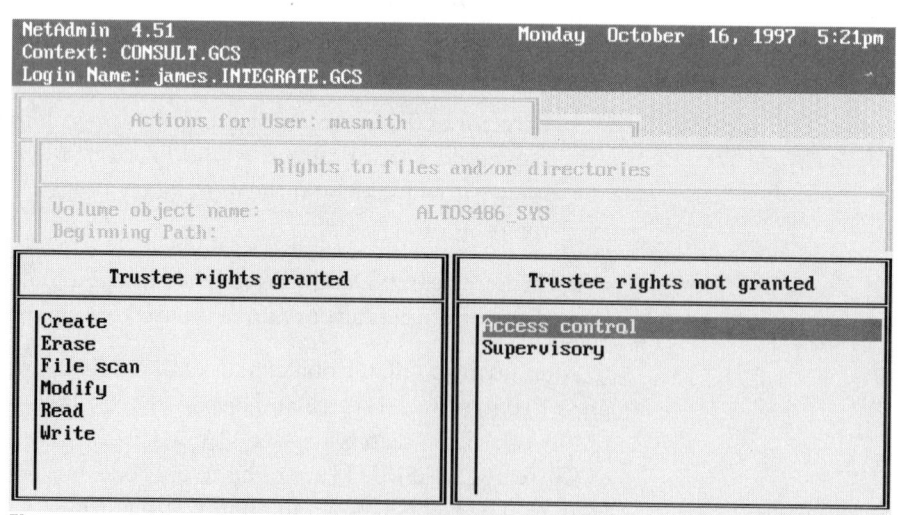

```
NetAdmin  4.51                                 Monday  October  16, 1997  5:21pm
Context: CONSULT.GCS
Login Name: james.INTEGRATE.GCS

           Actions for User: masmith

                    Rights to files and/or directories

    Volume object name:          ALTOS486_SYS
    Beginning Path:

          Trustee rights granted            Trustee rights not granted
         Create                            Access control
         Erase                             Supervisory
         File scan
         Modify
         Read
         Write



    These are rights not granted.  Press <Enter> or <Mark> then <Enter> to grant
    these rights.
    Enter=Accept    F5=Mark   F10=Save   Esc=Escape                    F1=Help
```

Although you can add these trustee rights shown in Figure 6.49 to the user, it's better to keep these rights away from individual users. In our example, user MASMITH's current rights are plenty to run any application from the directory on display.

The Users and You

None of this is flattering, is it?

AS STATED AT the beginning of the chapter, *user* is a four-letter word. So is *work*. The two are closely related.

Think of how the users on your network see you. If your company charges an internal budget for network hardware, software, and personnel, you're seen as an overpriced leech. If your company considers you overhead, you're seen as part of the group that sucks profits out of the profit-sharing plan, and hence out of the user's very own pocket. None of this is flattering, is it? Do you want to change this perception?

First, realize that you can't change everyone's mind. Some people won't like you or your job because they don't like computers. You'll never convert them, so be friendly but realistic.

Second, let users know that the internal prices for services are competitive or better than services purchased on the "outside." If they aren't competitive, figure out why not and fix the problem. If corporate management has set some outrageously high figure for labor or markup, you have a problem. It won't be easy to convince that same management to lower the internal rates; but if you don't, you'll never look good compared with the outside world.

Finally, let the users do some of your work for you. Believe it or not, they will love the opportunity.

This works especially well with vocal users and non-computer management. Most people believe their own job is rougher than anyone else's. If you offer them a chance to apply their business experience to your "deficiencies," they will quickly discover the problems you face every day. Let some of those bean-counters (excuse me, those esteemed accountants) debate the need between more server hard disk space, a new laser printer, a better tape backup system, or training for the new guy in the tech department. Maybe then they will appreciate your position a bit more. You might even offer to help them out a bit, or volunteer to handle your own payroll. Can't hurt to ask.

Seriously, the bottom line is this: the users are your job; the network is not. The network is a business tool for the users, supported by you. The activities of the users matter more than you and your network.

Is this terrible? Not if you adopt the proper viewpoint. Mechanics love cars, veterinarians love animals, and you love computers and networking. The first two groups need customers to support their favored occupation. So do you.

CASE STUDY

MiniCo: Creating and Managing Users (Now User Objects)

MINICO HAS 3 servers, 75 users, and one location.

Users and NetWare 4.1x

CONSIDERATIONS

The goals:

- Plan for new users on the network.
- Supply each user with a home directory.
- Plan groups for those functions reaching across containers.
- Plan login scripts for containers, Profile objects, and users.
- Decide on user account restrictions.

DECISION

Create users in batches as needed.

EXPLANATION

Since the Organizational Units cover all the employees in the company, Alexander von Thorn (the Distribution Manager who handled NetWare installation) didn't feel the need to spend a long time planning login scripts, groups, and account restrictions. Because the network was new to the majority of company employees, phasing in users in small groups as Alexander found time to add them didn't present a serious problem.

Creating User Objects with NetWare Administrator

CONSIDERATIONS

The choices:

- The level of information to provide.
- Whether to provide the information during user setup or later.

DECISION

Create a few users and see how it goes.

EXPLANATION

Not planning ahead, Alexander started creating users without creating print job configurations and preparing Profile objects. The first batch of users were all hand-configured for each security restriction and home directory placement. After the first group, Alexander stopped and read the manual. Then he better used the setup time for each user to provide more information immediately.

MINICO CASE STUDY, CONTINUED

Creating User Objects with NETADMIN

CONSIDERATIONS

The choices:

- Use the DOS utility NETADMIN.
- Use the MS Windows utility NetWare Administrator.

DECISION

Always use NetWare Administrator.

EXPLANATION

Although Alexander was used to NetWare 3.x non-GUI utilities, the advantages of the graphical interface convinced him to stay away from NETADMIN.

MegaCorp: Creating and Managing Users (Now User Objects)

CASE STUDY

MegaCorp: Creating and Managing Users (Now User Objects)

MEGACORP HAS 50 servers, 2500 users, and 5 locations.

Users and NetWare 4.1x

CONSIDERATIONS

The goals:

- Plan for user restrictions and generic profiles.
- Define a home directory policy.
- Organize users into functional job groups.
- Create login scripts for each container and user group.
- Decide which users must cross containers and need special group membership.
- Define information to be listed in the NDS database fields for users.

DECISION

Completely describe each user in the NDS database. User restrictions were set in place before the first user was created.

EXPLANATION

With large companies such as MegaCorp, the "personal" computer doesn't exist any more. Each computer is a corporate tool to be defined and controlled by the company, and each user's access to the network is part of that same control.

Thorough planning preceded the NetWare 4.1x installation, especially in the matter of handling users. Each user must fit into a predefined user type. Home directories are encouraged, but there is a limit on the amount of space each user is allowed in his or her home directory.

Creating User Objects with NetWare Administrator

CONSIDERATIONS

The setup:

- The user's home directory location.
- Print job configurations usable by newly created users.
- Security restrictions for users singly, in containers, and in groups.
- Default file access volumes for applications and data for each user.

MEGACORP CASE STUDY, CONTINUED

DECISION

Plan everything beforehand, and create a database using UIMPORT for much of the repetitive information.

EXPLANATION

Since the users were listed in the previous system's management reports, it was fairly easy to use some simple programs and create a feeder file for the UIMPORT program. The repetitive information was loaded into NDS without administrator intervention.

Each user in the database had his or her access rights listed, along with mailing address, location, telephone, and so on. MegaCorp plans to convert all employee information into the NDS database as a single repository of employee information over the next year.

Creating User Objects with NETADMIN

CONSIDERATIONS

The choices:

- Use the DOS utility NETADMIN.
- Use the MS Windows utility NetWare Administrator.

DECISION

Always use NetWare Administrator.

EXPLANATION

One of the advantages of moving to a new network platform was the availability of graphical administration tools. None of the Central IS technicians preferred NETADMIN over NetWare Administrator.

Handling More Than One User at a Time

CHAPTER 7

IN THE OLD days, it was easy to manage each user individually. Early NetWare systems often had a dozen or fewer attached workstations. The big network level started at about 25 workstations. PCs were new; only a few people in each company had access to a PC full time. No applications required more complexity than file and record sharing. The network stopped at the department; at the most, it went to the walls of the building.

Today, a large network starts at 500 users supported by 10 servers (according to the guidelines for the Simple Installation option). Most people connected to the network have full-time access to a computer, whether it's a PC running DOS or MS Windows, a PC running OS/2, a Macintosh, or a Unix system. Applications are mutating and replicating across the company, often with tools and technologies not yet fully developed. A logical workgroup may now include several continents.

You, the network manager, still have only 24 hours in your work day.

Luckily, improvements in technology make it possible for one lonely administrator to keep up with more users in more places than ever before. Early NetWare had a single group function to gather users; NetWare 4.1*x* has a variety of different ways to organize and manage network users and resources.

Who Manages the Users?

THE ASSUMPTION DURING this chapter is that the person managing network users is either the Admin or an Admin-equivalent user. In previous versions of NetWare, the assumption was that the person doing this work was either the SUPERVISOR or SUPERVISOR-equivalent. The name has changed, but the role is basically the same.

NetWare 4.1x allows more flexibility than previous NetWare versions. A User object may be granted rights to create objects, but not be able to access the information contained in the object. For that capability, either the Supervisor right must be given to that person or property rights must be granted along with the object rights. These new rights and how they relate to earlier NetWare versions and to each other will be explained in detail in Chapter 9. For now, do the work as the Admin user or equivalent, and there will be no surprises.

NetWare 4.1x Tools for Managing Users and Resources

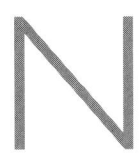

NETWARE 4.1x OFFERS six different ways to organize and manage network users and resources:

- **Organization object:** The largest grouping option. Your company may have one or several Organizations defined in an NDS tree. Trustee rights, login scripts, and user defaults may be assigned to all the User objects in the Organization object.

- **Organizational Unit object:** The second largest grouping option and the subunit for an Organization. A network will typically have many more Organizational Units than Organizations. Once again, trustee rights, login scripts, and user defaults may be assigned to all the User objects in the Organizational Unit object.

- **Group object:** Similar to the earlier NetWare ideas of groups, meaning a list of users sharing common items such as directory access rights. Objects in the same group may be from any part of the NDS tree. The Security Equal To property in the User object lists the Groups connected to the User object.

- **Profile object:** Depending on your NDS design, many users requiring similar work environments can be placed in different containers. The Profile object login script can be executed just before the User object login script. Each User object can have only one Profile login script.

- **Organizational Role object:** A leaf object that defines a specific operational role, such as operations manager or team leader. The expectation is that the person or persons inhabiting this role will change regularly, but the responsibilities and rights needed for the position will not change. The difference between a Group object and an Organizational Role object is that a Group object usually has many members and an Organizational Role object usually has only one or two.

- **User Template:** Technically a limited User object, the User Template functions as a list of properties that can be applied to newly created leaf objects. Common information, such as a fax number, login time restrictions, addresses, password restrictions, and language, can be placed in the User Template for easy replication. When a User Template is created, you can take information from the parent container's User Template (if one exists).

> *The NDS tree itself is not counted as a grouping resource for our examples. Resources can't be used across trees, and users can't be NDS clients in multiple trees at one time, unless you're running Client32 software.*

Before you can manage more than one user, you need to have a group of users. Although there are alternative options to the old NetWare implementation of a group, let's start with the Group object for old times' sake.

Creating and Managing Groups (Now Group Objects)

TECHNICALLY, THE GROUP object is a leaf object, like a User object or Printer object. The Group object, unlike Organization and Organizational Unit objects, is not a container.

Many of the group functions performed in earlier NetWare versions are more easily managed using rights and login scripts assigned to containers. The Group object is still, however, an efficient way to manage only one object (the Group object) instead of many individual User objects.

Practically, the Group object will do most of what is necessary in the area of granting file and printer rights to users listed as group members. After all, the group idea came from earlier versions of NetWare, where there were no object and NDS rights to worry about. The Group object in NetWare 4.1x carries the idea of a group of users into the new operating system by focusing on the file system and printer access rights accorded to Group object members.

Plenty of third-party products make extensive use of groups, especially the ability of groups to contain members from multiple containers. Services such as e-mail, fax-server, modem pool, and host-access gateways need groups. The applications generally build the groups themselves, but be prepared to help now and then.

Just as you can use either the NetWare Administrator program from MS Windows or the DOS-based NETADMIN program to create and manage User objects, you can use either of these administration utilities to work with Group objects. If you prefer to work with NetWare Administrator, continue with the next section. If you're a NETADMIN user, you can skip to the section titled "Creating and Modifying Group Objects with NETADMIN."

Creating and Modifying Group Objects with NetWare Administrator

7.1 IN-A-HURRY

Create a Group Object

1. Open NetWare Administrator, highlight the Organization or Organizational Unit container that will hold the new Group object, and press the Insert key.

2. Choose the Group object from the list, provide the Group object name, and press Enter.

3. Click on OK to create the new Group object.

Before you can place users in a Group object, you must create a Group object. This process is remarkably like that of creating a User object, as we did in the last chapter. The similarity is planned. In creating both groups and users, we are creating leaf objects, so the process should be almost identical. The differences appear as we configure the objects for their different roles.

> *Since the NetWare Administrator program does everything the administrator needs to do, the reference to offering the network on a silver platter is appropriate.*

First, we must open the NetWare Administrator program. While in Windows 3.1*x* running Client32 software, open the NetWare Tools group (or whatever group contains the NetWare Administrator icon) and double-click on the NetWare Administrator icon. If you look closely, you will see the icon is a hand offering an administrative program. Since the NetWare Administrator program does everything the administrator needs to do, the reference to offering the network on a silver platter is appropriate.

Windows 95 users will use the Start menu, move into the Programs menu, then pick up the Novell menu item. NetWare Administrator will be there in most cases; you can put the program shortcut anywhere you want, of course, including the desktop.

Once NetWare Administrator is started, I prefer to highlight and double-click on each container to open each of the Organizational Units. This allows me to see all the objects in each container, making it easier to avoid duplications. NetWare does not require you to open the container that will contain the new Group object before starting the process, but you may feel more comfortable if you can see everything in the container before you begin.

While the container name is highlighted, you can do one of three things to begin the creation of a new object:

- Press the Insert key.

- Click the right mouse button, then click on Create in the menu that appears.

- Open the Object menu, then choose Create.

NetWare vets will be comfortable with pressing the Insert key, a common function in earlier NetWare versions. If you are new to NetWare, pressing the Insert key whenever you're not sure of the next step can't hurt; in fact, it will often help.

Hard-core mousers will appreciate the increasing use of the right mouse button in NetWare 4.*x*. The NetWare Administrator program is even more mouse-friendly than it appears in the listing above. If you hold the left button while sliding the highlight bar down the menu items, releasing the button while highlighting Create launches the New Object dialog box.

Hard-core keyboard users will appreciate the Alt-key functions that speed menu operations. Most of the menu shortcuts available in earlier NetWare versions are still available in NetWare 4.1*x*. If you have some keystroke combinations memorized, try them. The keystrokes may well do the job you expect.

Creating and Managing Groups (Now Group Objects) 449

The result of any of the three options mentioned above is to open the New Object dialog box. From there, you can choose any of the new object classes listed. Since we want to create a Group object, highlight the Group entry using the cursor keys, the mouse, or by pressing the G key. The result is shown in Figure 7.1.

FIGURE 7.1

Preparing to create a new Group object

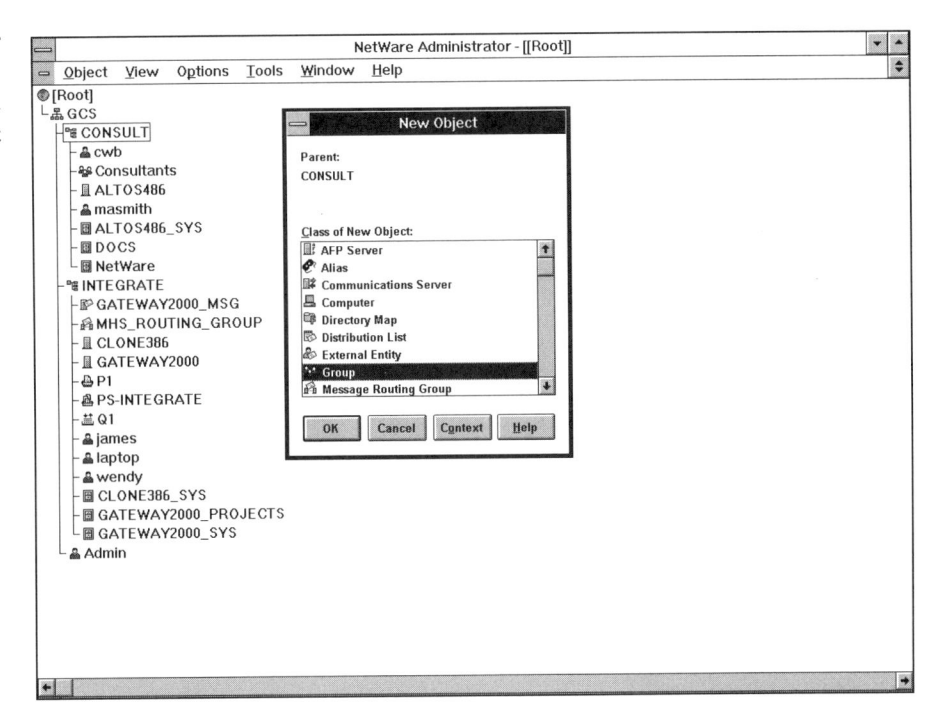

NetWare Administrator running under Windows 95 looks amazingly similar to what you see in Figure 7.1, so there should be no confusion. You're not thrown by the command buttons running down the right side of the New Object window rather than running along the bottom, are you? I didn't think so.

Once you begin to create your new Group object, a two-step process starts. The creation of the Group object takes little time and requires almost no detail. If you remember creating a User object, the process will be familiar.

When creating new User objects, the only information needed is the login name of the user and the last name of that user. Since Group objects don't have last names, the only information required before creating the Group object is the name of that Group object. Figure 7.2 shows the Create Group dialog box that appears after you choose Group from the New Object dialog box.

FIGURE 7.2

Choosing to configure this group before creating another

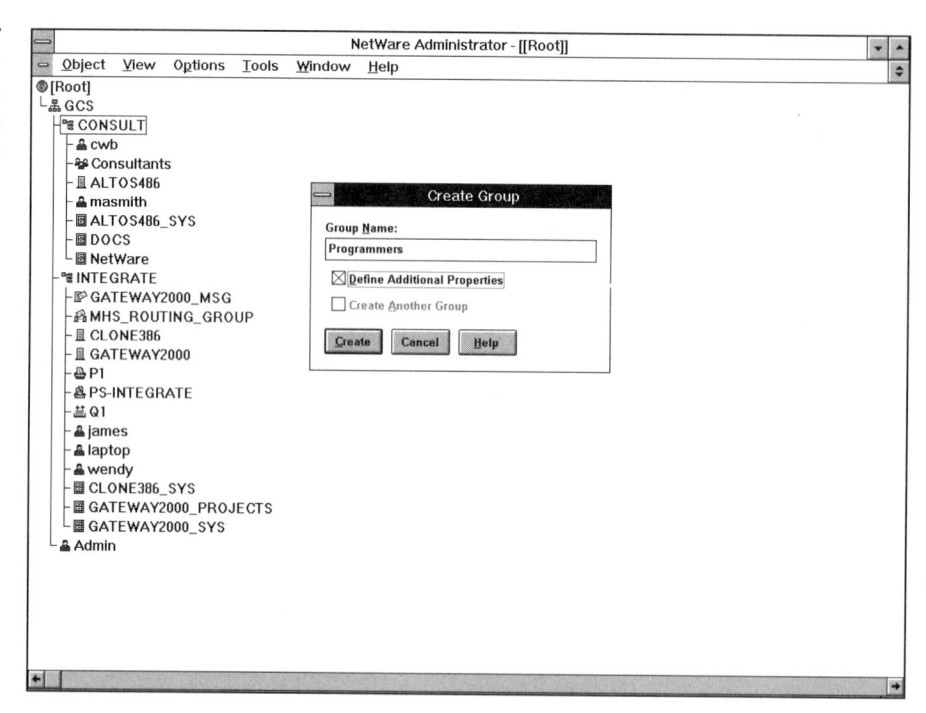

The naming rules for the Group object are the same as those for the User object (and all other leaf objects for that matter). Here is a short recap of naming rules:

- Names must be less than 64 characters long. Names longer than 47 characters are truncated for non-NDS clients.

- Names must be unique within the container.

- Names are not case-sensitive, but will be displayed as they were typed in the Group Name field (SalesSupport will display that way, but NDS regards it as identical to salessupport and SALESSUPPORT).

- Spaces can be used and will be displayed as spaces within NDS. Spaces are shown as underscores for non-NDS clients.

- The following characters can't be seen by non-NDS clients: slash (/), backslash (l), colon (:), comma (,), asterisk (*), and question mark (?).

Creating and Managing Groups (Now Group Objects) 451

You can check either of the two boxes below the name in Figure 7.2, but not both at the same time. If you choose Create Another Group, the Create Group dialog box will clear and be ready for the next name. If you choose Define Additional Properties, as we did in Figure 7.2, the new object is immediately created and placed into the NDS tree. The process for defining Group object properties is the same, whether done immediately after creating the object or by modifying an existing object.

Modifying the Identification of a Group Object

> **7.2 IN-A-HURRY**
>
> ### Identify a Group Object
>
> 1. Open the NetWare Administrator program, highlight the Group object to modify, and press Enter.
>
> 2. Fill in the optional information for the Other Name, Owner, Description, Location, Department, and Organization fields.
>
> 3. Click on OK to save the information and exit the Group dialog box.

Identification for a Group object is not required, but it is helpful when searching a large NDS system. All the fields in the Group dialog box can be searched.

If you're not currently running the NetWare Administrator program, start Windows 3.1x or Windows 95. Double-click on the NetWare Administrator program icon or menu choice, depending on your GUI interface. Once the program is running and the main browser screen is open, you must expand the container to see all the objects inside. Double-click on the container name, or press Alt+V then X to expand the list. Highlight the Group object to modify and press the Enter key, or double-click on the Group object to open the Group dialog box.

Figure 7.3 shows the Information page of the Group dialog box. The name is listed across the top, and the current page is shown in two ways: by the button depressed on the right and by the name in the top-left corner of the dialog box.

FIGURE 7.3

Providing searchable information for the PROGRAMMERS Group

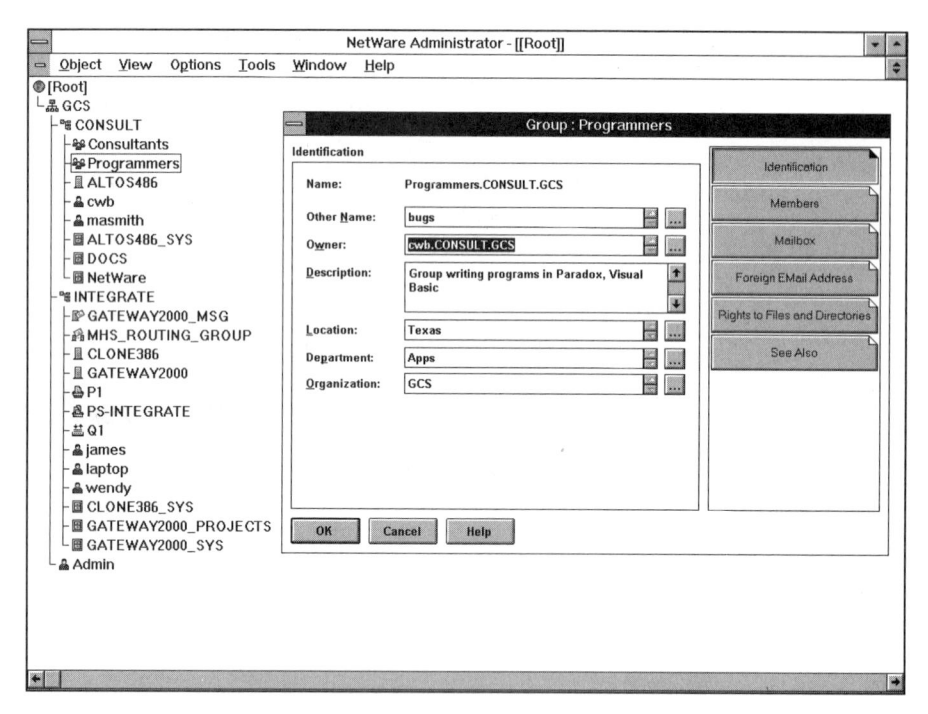

[NetWare Administrator screenshot showing the Group: Programmers Identification dialog with fields: Name: Programmers.CONSULT.GCS, Other Name: bugs, Owner: cwb.CONSULT.GCS, Description: Group writing programs in Paradox, Visual Basic, Location: Texas, Department: Apps, Organization: GCS]

Notice that all the fields on the Identification page for the Group object are a subset of the User object fields. The information here is optional, as is the corresponding information for User objects. You can fill in the fields as follows:

- **Other Name:** Allows more descriptive or alternative names for the Group object. Multiple entries are allowed, and they are viewed by clicking on the More button at the end of the field. Each entry in this field can be searched.

- **Owner:** Provides space to list owners or administrators for this group. NetWare 4.1x allows multiple subadministrators, a feature that will save you time once each subadministrator understands what they can and can't do. Multiple owners are allowed; to see them, click on the More button at the end of the field.

- **Description:** Holds free-form text, up to 30 lines of 37 characters of any text you find helpful concerning this Group object. Long description fields are scrollable. Unfortunately, the search program does not parse each word, so only a complete match of the Description field contents will result in a successful search. The scroll arrows are provided to help you if the text goes beyond the limits of the small field.

- **Location:** Provides space to indicate the physical location of this Group object. Multiple entries are allowed. This field allows any information up to 64 characters long and can be searched. With dispersed companies, this field is helpful when looking for all group members in a particular place, such as building, wing, or state.

- **Department:** Shows the company department to which this group reports. Multiple entries are allowed. Like Location, this field has a 64-character limit.

- **Organization:** Shows the organization to which this group reports. Multiple entries are allowed.

As in other dialog boxes, there are several buttons and screen areas that can speed things along. First of all, the page buttons take you to different pages of the same dialog box. The six page buttons shown in Figure 7.3 all pertain to information about the Group object named PROGRAMMERS. You can move up and down the page buttons using the Ctrl+Page-Up and Ctrl+Page-Down key combinations, or just place the pointer on the desired page button and click with your mouse.

The More buttons at the end of the fields allow multiple entries in those fields. Clicking once on the More button pops up a dialog box for the other field entries. The up and down scroll arrows included in the field make it easy to check other values in the field without using the More button.

As in all object dialog boxes, the OK and Cancel buttons at the bottom apply to all the pages of the dialog box. Don't click on OK when you finish modifying the first page if you plan on modifying more pages. There is no penalty if you do, but you will need to go through the steps necessary to return to the dialog box, wasting a bit of time and increasing your frustration level because you forgot, once again, that you shouldn't click on OK until you've finished all your work here.

When providing the owner name on the Group Identification page, you must supply the full name for the User object, even if the current context is set to the container for the Group object and User object to be labeled as Owner. Clicking on the More button opens the Owner dialog box. Click on the Add button, and then locate the User object you wish to make an owner of the group.

Modifying the Member List of a Group Object

> **7.3 IN-A-HURRY**
>
> **Add or Delete Group Members**
>
> 1. Open NetWare Administrator, and locate and choose the Group object to modify.
> 2. Click on the Members page button.
> 3. To add a user, click on the Add button. In the Select Object dialog box, choose one or more User objects to add to the group.
> 4. To delete a user, highlight the User object name in the Group dialog box, then click on Delete.
> 5. Click on OK in the Group dialog box to save your changes.

If you're not currently running the NetWare Administrator program, double-click on the NetWare Administrator program icon or menu listing. Once the program is running and the main browser screen is open, you must expand the container to see all the objects inside. Double-click on the container name, or press Alt+V then X to expand the list. Highlight the Group object to modify and press the Enter key, or double-click on the Group object to open the Group dialog box. Click on the second page button, Members, or press Ctrl+Page-Down.

To add a new User object to the list of group members, click on the Add button. The Select Object dialog box opens, with the current context listed. If the current context does not contain the User object you wish to add to this group, click on the up arrow in the Directory Context box. When you see the container holding the User object you want to add to the group, double-click on that name. The applicable objects for inclusion in a list of users will appear on the left side of the box.

> **NOTE**
>
> *These sections concerning group setup look amazingly like those for the user setup. If you read the user information, you will be able to perform the same procedures with groups as you do with users. If you did not read the user information first, excuse this note.*

Figure 7.4 shows the Group dialog box open, with PROGRAMMERS listed as the current Group object under examination. You can see the Members label in the upper-left corner of the dialog box and notice that the Members page button is depressed.

FIGURE 7.4

Browsing and selecting new PROGRAMMERS Group members

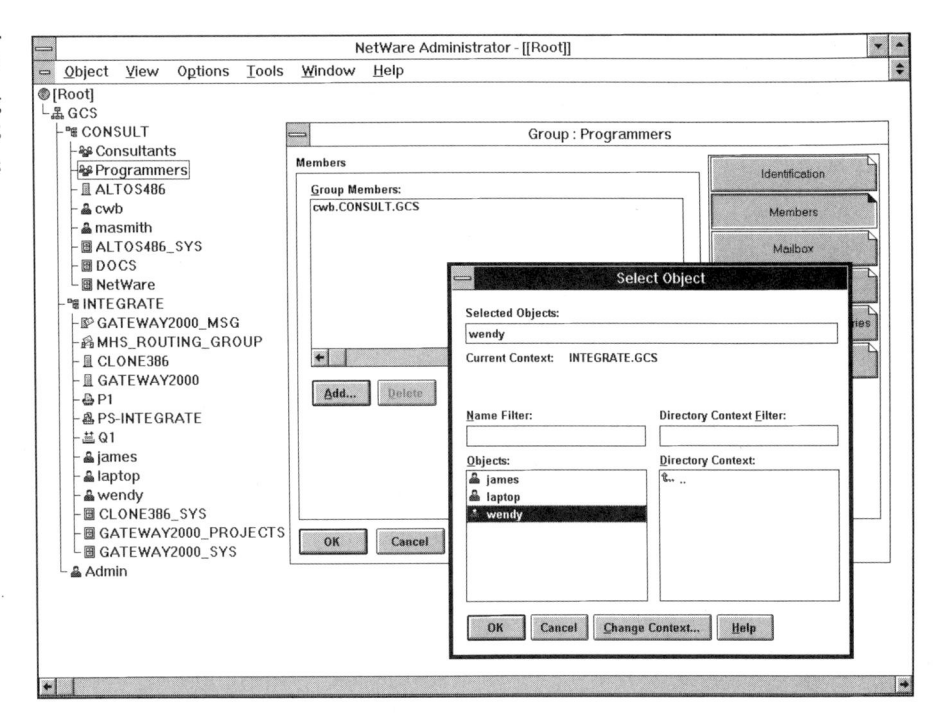

There are several things to notice about Figure 7.4. First, you see we have already added one user. CWB.CONSULT.GCS is in the Group Members list. The full name is listed.

In the Select Object dialog box, the User object representing user WENDY is highlighted. The Current Context is listed as INTEGRATE.GCS, meaning WENDY is in a different context than our previous user, CWB. No problem. This is one reason groups are still around, even though many of the group functions can be handled by login scripts in the Organization or Organizational Unit containers. Users from any container can be members of the same group.

Once the OK button is clicked, user WENDY will become part of the group PROGRAMMERS, joining CWB. By holding down the Ctrl key while clicking with the left mouse button, you can choose multiple objects at one time.

To delete a User object from the group listing, highlight the User object in the Group Members box. The Delete button will become active (no longer gray and faded). Click once on the Delete button, and the highlighted User object will be deleted from the list.

> **WARNING**
>
> *There is no undo feature when you delete a User object, so do this carefully. If you delete the wrong User object, click on the Cancel button rather than the OK button.*

Remember, this screen does not delete the User object itself, just the inclusion of that User object in the Group object membership list. See Chapter 10 for details on how to delete a User object entirely.

Something else you might notice in Figure 7.4 is the difference in the User object names. The three most popular user naming options are now on display in Figure 7.4. The new User object CWB is made of three initials. This method is handy, and works well with the User variables set in some network-aware programs, such as the WordPerfect word processor. The second option is that of User object MASMITH (this appears in the listing on the left side of the screen, next to the Group dialog box). This follows the suggestion of using the first two initials and first six letters of the last name. The last option is indicated by the User object WENDY. The first name, and first name only, makes the entire User object name. While this is friendly, first names tend to be duplicated quite a bit, forcing changes.

The three different styles are here to help you make a choice: which option do you like best? A friend once said, "I don't know what I want until it's right in front of me." If you're like my old friend, perhaps this will help you decide your naming style. Take a look, and see which option rubs you the wrong way and which rubs you the right way.

Job Description for Assistant Network Administrators

Adding members to, or subtracting them from, a group is a good job for assistant administrators. In fact, this is one area where the idea of workgroup administrator that first appeared in NetWare 3.x makes great sense. NetWare 4 takes this idea further, allowing added security constraints for the main Admin user to truly separate a container from the rest of the NDS tree.

(continued on next page)

Creating and Managing Groups (Now Group Objects) 457

> The assistant administrator, charged with responsibility for this group, can add and subtract members as necessary for the needs of the department. This can be done without bothering the main network administrator.
>
> Positive benefits happen two ways: the primary network administrator goes about his or her business, while the people in the department feel they have much more control over their own network destiny.
>
> This job is also one that doesn't take constant administration and worry time. People tend to stay in particular groups for a long time. When a user leaves, and you delete that user, the name is deleted from the User object list of members. When someone transfers, that user often keeps some of the old job's responsibilities, meaning the user will stay in the old group and become a member of an additional group as well.

Modifying the Mailbox for a Group Object in NetWare 4.10

7.4 IN-A-HURRY

Modify Group Object Mailbox Information in NetWare 4.10

1. In NetWare 4.10, open NetWare Administrator, and locate and choose the Group object to modify.
2. Click on the Mailbox page button.
3. Click on the Browser button at the end of the Mailbox Location field.
4. Select the messaging server that contains the Group object's mailbox.
5. Change the default Mailbox ID if necessary.
6. Click on OK to save the information.

Remember, NetWare 4.11 dropped the mailboxes. If you're working with NetWare 4.11 rather than an earlier version, don't go crazy trying to find the missing mailboxes.

If you have NetWare 4.10, and the group itself needs a mailbox, here's the place to set that mailbox. When mail is sent to a group, rather than to individual users, each member of the group automatically gets that message. A prerequisite for this ability is a functioning MHS system on at least one server in your network.

If you're not currently running the NetWare Administrator program, start it. Once the program is running and the main browser screen is open, you must expand the container to see all the objects inside. Double-click on the container name, or press Alt+V then X to expand the list. Highlight the Group object to modify and press the Enter key, or double-click on the Group object to open the Group dialog box. Click on the third page button, Mailbox, or press Ctrl+Page-Down twice.

Open the browser window by clicking on the Browser button at the end of the Mailbox Location field. This opens the Select Object dialog box we have seen before. Cruise through your NDS tree by navigating through the Directory Context box until the applicable message server appears in the left box labeled Objects. Figure 7.5 shows this discovery process.

When the message server is chosen, the Mailbox ID field will be filled in automatically. The ID is the first eight characters of the Group object's name.

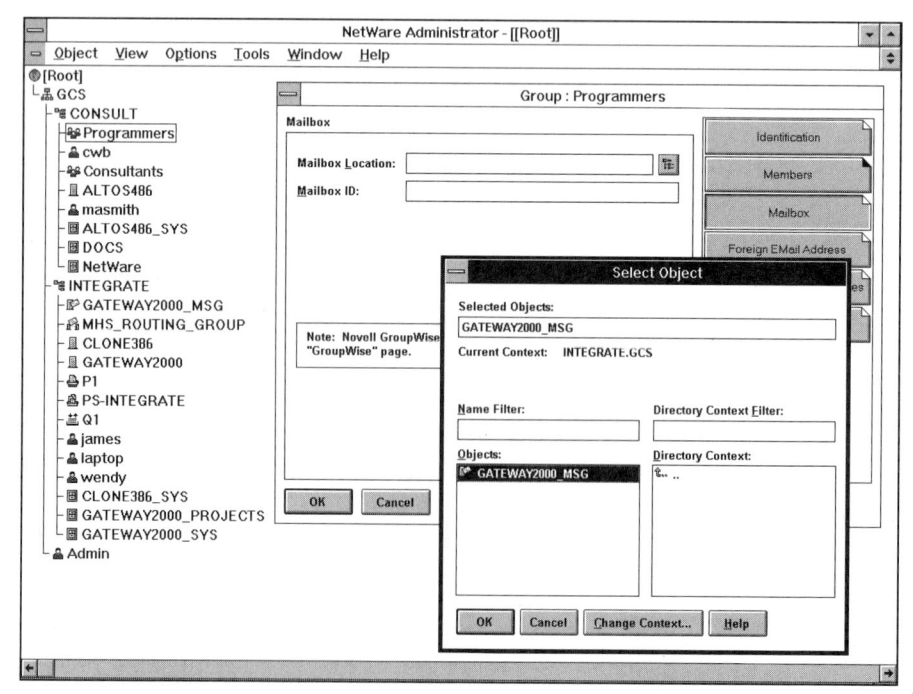

FIGURE 7.5

Identifying the message server for a Group object

Creating and Managing Groups (Now Group Objects) 459

If any of the first eight characters contain illegal DOS characters, such as spaces, those characters will be dropped. You can change the default, but there's little reason to do so unless your network contains other mailboxes that have the same beginning letters.

Click on the OK button to save the information and exit.

Modifying the Foreign E-mail Address for a Group Object in NetWare 4.10

> **7.5 IN-A-HURRY**
>
> **Modify the Group Object Foreign E-mail Address in NetWare 4.10**
>
> 1. In NetWare 4.10, open NetWare Administrator, and locate and choose the Group object to modify.
> 2. Click on the Foreign EMail Address page button.
> 3. Set the e-mail to be advertised to users outside your network.
> 4. Set the type of remote mail service.
> 5. Click on OK to save the information.

If your Group object expects to receive e-mail on an outside mail system, this is the place to set the remote mailbox name. The alias allows you to list addresses used by outside entities to address the group.

There are currently five remote e-mail types supported by NetWare 4.10 (but none in version 4.11):

- **GMHS:** Global Message Handling Service from Novell
- **PROFS:** PRofessional OFfice System, IBM's office automation and e-mail system for mainframes running the VM operating system
- **SMTP:** Simple Mail Transport Protocol, the standard Unix e-mail exchange protocol
- **SNADS:** SNA Distribution Services, another IBM product for file, document, and e-mail exchange
- **X.400:** CCITT standard for exchanging e-mail between systems

You can add only one foreign e-mail address, but you can have multiple foreign aliases. The limit is one alias per e-mail type.

In their wisdom, Novell executives deleted this function in NetWare 4.11. Another reason to buy GroupWise, at least in their minds.

Once the NetWare Administrator program is running and the main browser screen is open, you must expand the container to see all the objects inside. Double-click on the container name, or press Alt+V then X to expand the list. Highlight the Group object to modify and press the Enter key, or double-click on the Group object to open the Group dialog box. Click on the fourth page button, Foreign EMail Address.

You can type directly into the field if you remember the address exactly. If you don't know the full address, the Set button pops open another field, where you can put in part of the address and choose one of the five e-mail systems listed above. Click on OK to save the information.

Modifying the Rights to Files and Directories for a Group Object

7.6 IN-A-HURRY

Manage File and Directory Access for the Group Object

1. Open NetWare Administrator, and locate and choose the Group object to modify.

2. Click on the Rights to Files and Directories page button.

3. To view assigned rights, click on the Add button, then highlight each volume or directory you wish to view.

4. To add a volume, click on the Add button to open the Select Object dialog box and choose the new volume.

5. To delete access, highlight the volume and click on the Delete button.

6. To grant access, click on the Add button to open the Select Object dialog box and choose the volume or directory.

7. To grant rights, highlight the object in the Files and Directories box and toggle the checkboxes in the Rights box. To modify rights, toggle the checkboxes for each volume or directory.

8. Click on OK to save your settings.

This section is exactly like the corresponding section for the User object we worked with back in Chapter 6. There's a good reason for the similarity: here we are granting access to a single group, but the group includes many users. Although we modify only a single object, we affect anywhere from a few to hundreds of users all at once.

If you're not currently running the NetWare Administrator program, start. Double-click on the NetWare Administrator program icon. Once the program is running and the main browser screen is open, you must expand the container to see all the objects inside. Double-click on the container name, or press Alt+V then X to expand the list. Highlight the Group object to modify and press the Enter key, or double-click on the Group object to open the Group dialog box. Click on the Rights to Files and Directories page button.

First, you will want to check which rights the Group object has before granting any more rights. Find this information by clicking once on the Add button. Select the volume and click on OK. Highlight each directory, and the Rights box just below the Files and Directories box will reflect the group's rights to that file or directory.

To delete all trustee assignments from a particular volume, highlight the volume or directory and click on the Delete key. To modify rights to a particular directory or file, check the appropriate boxes in the Rights box. All the checkboxes are toggles, so if one is blank, checking it grants that right to that object.

The Effective Rights button displays the actual rights for the highlighted directory or volume object. When you click on this button, a small dialog box pops up, listing the actual directory under examination. It also has a Browser button to help you search more areas of the network.

Figure 7.6 shows the Select Object dialog box open in order to grant trustee rights to another directory. This dialog box appears after you click on the Add button.

By browsing up and down the NDS tree in the Directory Context box, the VB (for Microsoft's Visual Basic) directory is located. The VB directory is copied to the Selected Objects field at the top of the dialog box when the directory is double-clicked in the Files and Directories box below.

As before, you can select multiple directories by holding down the Ctrl key while clicking on the file or directory name with the left mouse button. If multiple items are chosen, each name will appear in the Selected Objects field, separated by a space from the previous name.

Once the files or directories are chosen, the rights must be granted. Figure 7.7 shows the changed checkboxes, allowing the group PROGRAMMERS near omnipotence over the VB directory.

Chapter 7 • Handling More than One User at a Time

FIGURE 7.6
Choosing the directory before granting rights

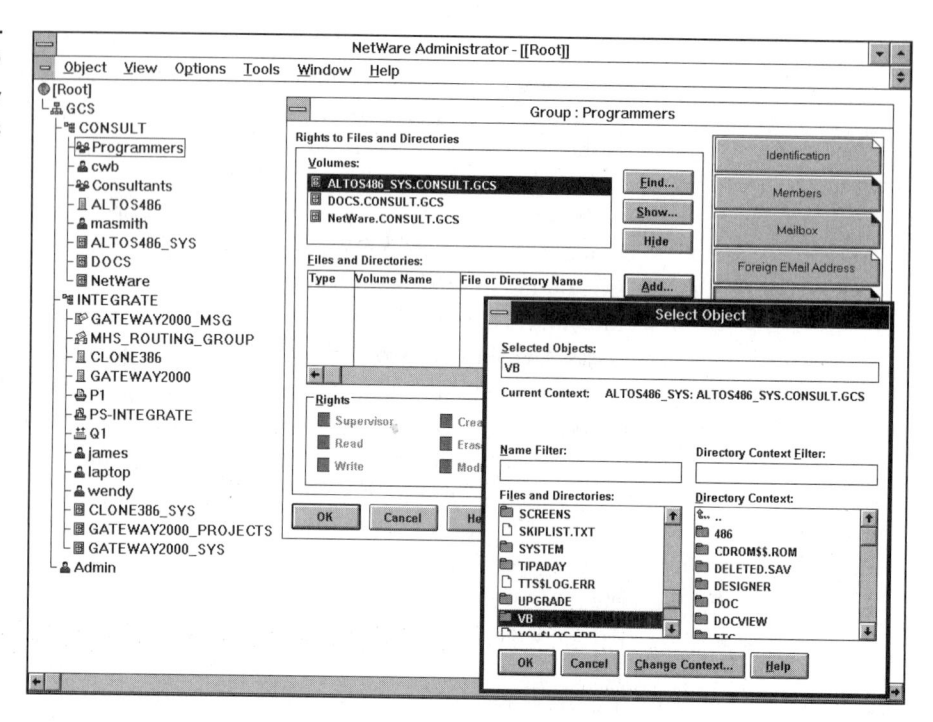

FIGURE 7.7
Granting PROGRAMMERS trustee rights to the VB directory

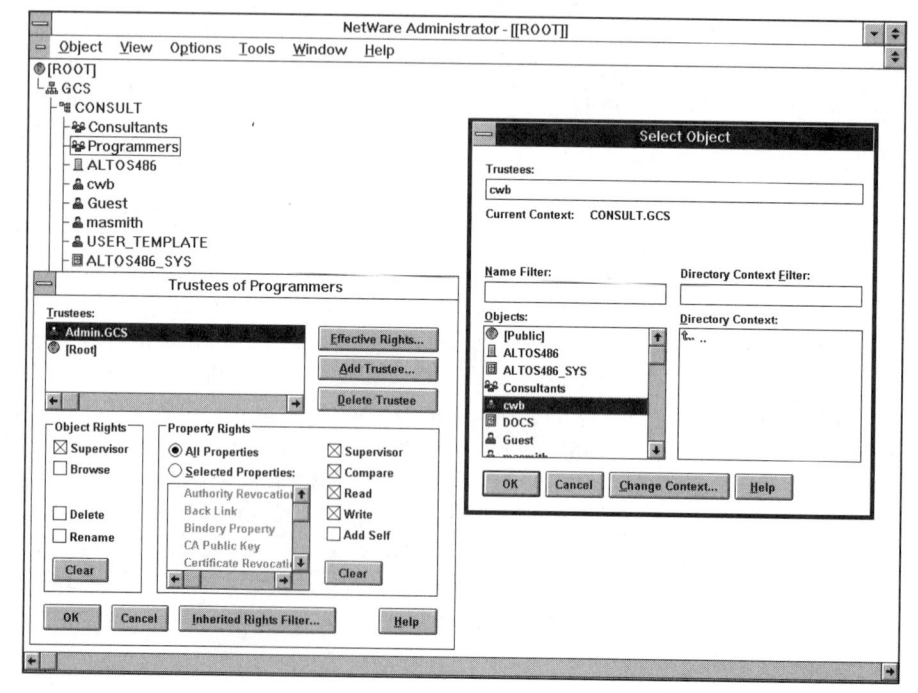

As far as file rights are concerned, each user in the PROGRAMMERS group now has complete control over the VB directory and all subdirectories. Read, Write, Create, Erase, Modify, and File Scan rights have been given to PROGRAMMERS. The only rights withheld are Supervisor and Access Control, neither of which affect the handling of files within the designated directories.

Subsequent members of the PROGRAMMERS group automatically receive these rights. Changes to these rights take place immediately, or at least as soon as the information gets spread around the NDS tree.

To remove a right, click on the checkboxes to toggle the setting. If the group has Modify rights, and you clear the checkbox, no member of the group will be able to modify an existing file.

When a group no longer needs access to a volume or directory, this same page handles that change as well. Highlight the directory or file name in the Files and Directories box, and the Delete button becomes active. Clicking on the Delete button removes the file or directory from the trustee list of the Group object. The users in the group no longer have access to those files or directories. This does not delete the files or directories themselves.

Modifying the NDS Trustees for a Group Object

7.7 IN-A-HURRY

Modify the NDS Trustees for the Group Object

1. Open the NetWare Administrator program and browse through the NDS tree to locate the Group object to modify.

2. Highlight the desired Group object and click the right mouse button.

3. Choose Trustees of This Object to open the Trustees Of dialog box.

4. To add a trustee, click on the Add button to choose the new trustee from the Select Object dialog box.

5. To delete a trustee, highlight the trustee and click on the Delete button.

6. To modify rights, highlight each trustee and toggle the appropriate checkboxes.

7. Click on OK to save the settings.

Chapter 7 • Handling More than One User at a Time

Groups have trustees, and PROGRAMMERS is no exception. Trustees are those network users or resources that have some control over the group. For more information about trustee rights and what they involve, see Chapter 9.

After opening NetWare Administrator, highlight the Group object whose trustee list you want to modify, and click the right mouse button. The same Trustees Of dialog box can be summoned by using the Object menu.

If you must add a trustee or two, you will once again use our friend the Select Object dialog box. Scroll through the dialog box to find the user (most likely) or other resource to make a trustee of the PROGRAMMERS group. Figure 7.8 shows user CWB gaining control over the group.

FIGURE 7.8

Gaining more control over PROGRAMMERS

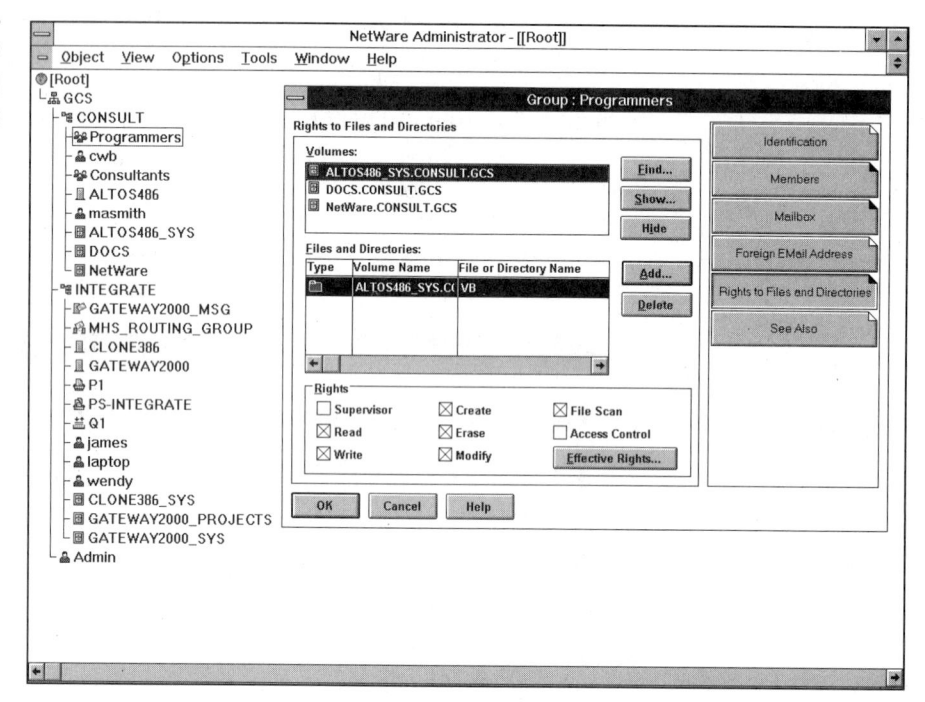

This screen should look familiar by now, since the process here is the same as adding trustees to volumes, servers, users, and so on.

> **WARNING**
>
> *Be careful in deleting trustees from a resource or group, because the users may have some procedures that require access to the resource they no longer have trustee rights for. This can cause some aggravation later, so think before granting or deleting individual trustee rights.*

Modifying the See Also Page for a Group Object

> **7.8 IN-A-HURRY**
>
> ### Add or Delete See Also Page Information
>
> **1.** Open NetWare Administrator, and locate and choose the Group object to modify.
>
> **2.** Click on the See Also page button.
>
> **3.** Click on the Add button, pick the related objects from the Select Object dialog box, and click on OK.
>
> **4.** Click on OK to save the information.

Purely informational, the See Also page is a place to make references for your group to other network resources. Which printer is the primary printer for the group? Place that printer name here. You can place any other related resource here, but not by typing in its name. Each object must be chosen through the Select Object dialog box, as shown in Figure 7.9.

FIGURE 7.9

Relating other objects to PROGRAMMERS

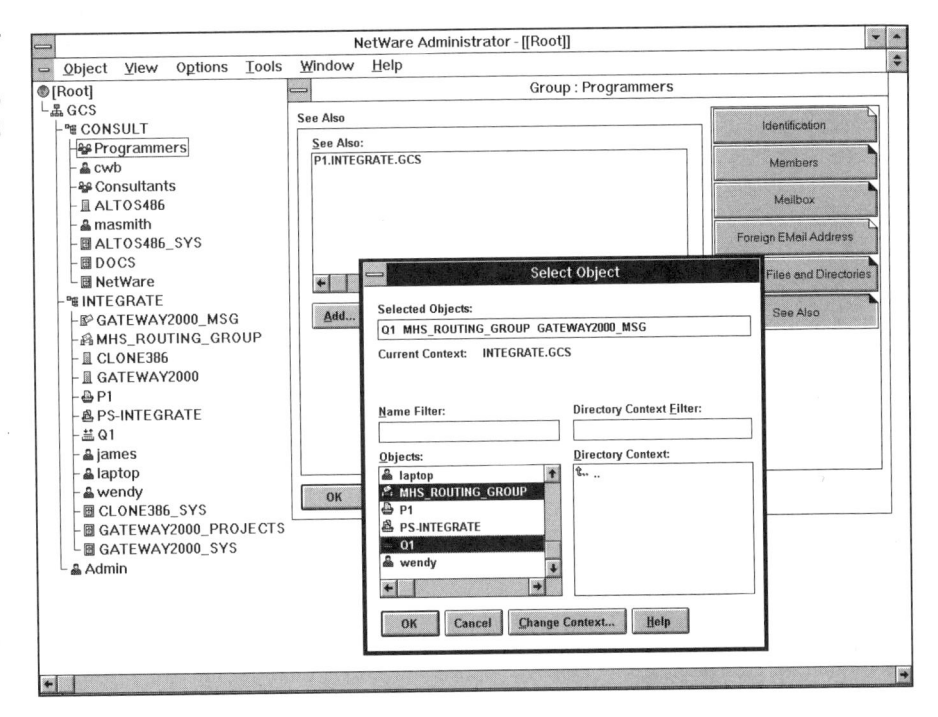

After opening NetWare Administrator, browsing, and choosing the Group object, click on the See Also page button. Click on the Add button to open the Select Object dialog box. To pick multiple items, hold down the Ctrl key while clicking with the left mouse button.

You can see in Figure 7.9 that both Q1 and the MHS_ROUTING_GROUP have been selected for inclusion in the Selected Objects box at the top of the screen. They will join the object already in the See Also list, which is a printer named P1.INTEGRATE.GCS, a good item to show here. In this example, the printer for the PROGRAMMERS group uses a printer from another Organizational Unit as their primary paper output device, and a note to that effect may come in handy one day.

Creating and Modifying Group Objects with NETADMIN

> **7.9 IN-A-HURRY**
>
> **Create a Group Object with NETADMIN**
>
> 1. Start the NETADMIN program from the DOS command line.
>
> 2. Choose Manage Objects from the main menu (highlight it and press Enter).
>
> 3. Move to the correct container for the new Group object and press the Insert key.
>
> 4. Choose Group from the Object Class list, type the name of the new Group object, and press Enter.
>
> 5. Press F10 to save the new object.
>
> 6. Respond Yes or No to the "Create another?" prompt.

The DOS administrator program, NETADMIN, owes quite a bit to the venerable SYSCON of earlier NetWare fame. It is not, however, a look-and-feel copy of the program. The screens are different, but all the same keystrokes work in NETADMIN as they worked in SYSCON. Table 7.1 lists these keyboard commands.

To create the Group object PROGRAMMERS, run the NETADMIN program from a DOS prompt. As stated at the beginning of the chapter, you must be either the Admin user or an Admin-equivalent user to perform most of the

TABLE 7.1
NETADMIN Keyboard Commands

KEY	FUNCTION
Enter	Accepts the information in the field.
Escape	Moves back to the previous screen or exits.
F1	Displays a context-sensitive help screen.
Delete	Erases the highlighted item.
F5	Marks an item.
F10	Saves and exits.
Alt+F10	Exits immediately (press Enter in the Exit? box).

functions discussed here. You must have the \PUBLIC directory in your path as well, or be in the \PUBLIC directory when starting the program.

You saw NETADMIN's opening screen in the last chapter, when we created a new User object. The first choice on the screen is Manage Objects, where the highlight bar sits. Most of the action happens in the submenus under this option. Press Enter to continue.

The Object, Class screen appears, showing the contents of the container from where you started the NETADMIN program. If this is not the proper context, press Enter on the parent option (top line, the .. representing the parent directory). The next Object, Class screen is the parent context, one level up from the first screen. If this is not high enough in your NDS tree, press Enter to move up the tree as many times as necessary to reach the context showing the container in which you plan to create the new Group object.

In our example, the container is .CONSULT.GCS, an Organizational Unit. After highlighting the container name and pressing Enter, the Object, Class screen appears, showing the contents of the CONSULT.GCS container. The action starts after pressing the Insert key to create a new object. Figure 7.10 shows the Select an Object Class pick list, with the Group object highlighted.

In the top-left corner, the current context and login name is displayed. The upper-right corner shows the current time and date (a feature missing from the NetWare Administrator program). The objects listed in the Select an Object Class list are the same as those seen in NetWare Administrator, of course. Highlight Group and press Enter.

FIGURE 7.10

Choosing to create a new Group object

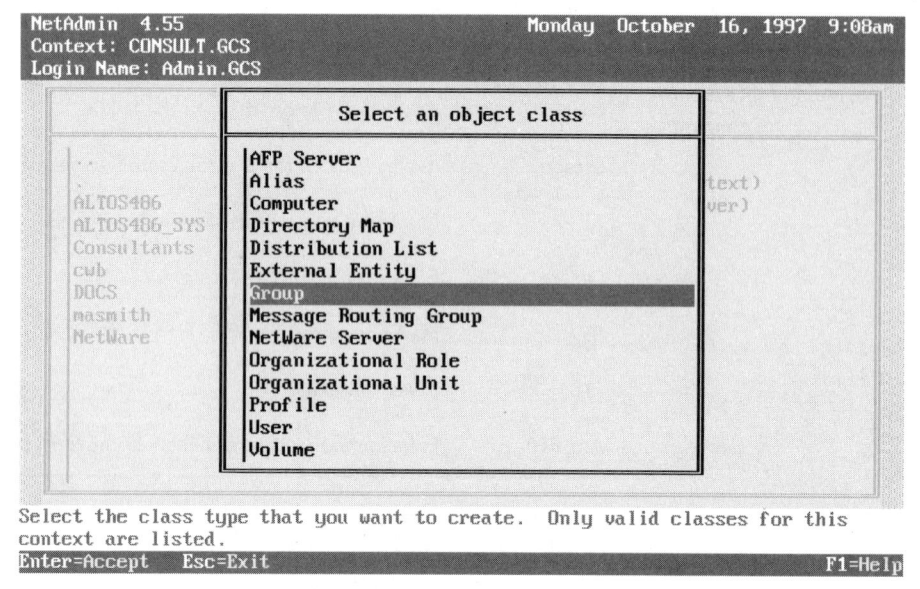

```
NetAdmin 4.55                           Monday  October 16, 1997  9:08am
Context: CONSULT.GCS
Login Name: Admin.GCS

                        ┌─────── Select an object class ───────┐
                        │ AFP Server                           │
                        │ Alias                                │
              ALTOS486  │ Computer                             │ text)
              ALTOS486_SYS │ Directory Map                     │ ver)
              Consultants  │ Distribution List                 │
              cwb          │ External Entity                   │
              DOCS         │ Group                             │
              masmith      │ Message Routing Group             │
              NetWare      │ NetWare Server                    │
                        │ Organizational Role                  │
                        │ Organizational Unit                  │
                        │ Profile                              │
                        │ User                                 │
                        │ Volume                               │
                        └──────────────────────────────────────┘

Select the class type that you want to create.  Only valid classes for this
context are listed.
Enter=Accept   Esc=Exit                                          F1=Help
```

The Create Object Group box opens, awaiting the name of the new Group object. Type the name here and press the Enter key. Either fill in the Mailbox location now or wait until the rest of the e-mail details are configured.

The naming rules for the Group object are the same as those for the User object (as well as all other leaf objects). Here's a short recap of the object naming rules:

- Names must be less than 64 characters long. Names longer than 47 characters are truncated for non-NDS clients.

- Names must be unique within the container.

- Names are not case-sensitive, but they will be displayed as they were typed in the Group Name field (SalesSupport will display that way, but NDS regards it as identical to salessupport and SALESSUPPORT).

- Spaces can be used and will be displayed as spaces within NDS. Spaces are shown as underscores for non-NDS clients.

- The following characters can't be seen by non-NDS clients: slash (/), backslash (\), colon (:), comma (,), asterisk (*), and question mark (?).

Creating and Managing Groups (Now Group Objects) 469

Press the F10 key to save the information. A box asking if you wish to create another Group object will appear. Say Yes or No, depending on your plans. The Group object is created and placed in the list, with the highlight bar remaining on it. This makes it handy to press Enter and continue setting up your new group.

Modifying the Identification Property of a Group Object

> **7.10 IN-A-HURRY**
>
> **Modify Group Object Identification with NETADMIN**
>
> 1. Start the NETADMIN program from the DOS command line.
> 2. Choose Manage Objects, move to the correct container for the Group object, and choose the Group object name.
> 3. Choose View or Edit Properties of This Object, then Identification.
> 4. Highlight the value to change and press Enter.
> 5. Add or edit the information.
> 6. Press F10 to save the information.

Figure 7.11 shows the Identification Information page for the PROGRAMMERS group all filled in. Notice the status line information across the bottom of the screen. Useful tips are displayed there regularly. This tip tells us that the name of the Group object cannot be changed here.

Notice the down arrows before the field entries. This indicates there is room for more than one value in each entry so marked. These fields are informational. They are used for searching purposes, not for any critical network design functions.

Open the NETADMIN program from any DOS prompt, and move through the menu structure to reach the container and Group object you wish to modify. Highlight that Group object and press Enter to open the Actions for Group box (which should reference our PROGRAMMERS group in our example).

FIGURE 7.11
A well-identified group

```
NetAdmin  4.55                          Monday  October  16, 1997  12:13pm
Context: CONSULT.GCS
Login Name: Admin.GCS

        Actions for Group: Programmers
      ┌─────────────────────────────────────────────────────────┐
      │              Identification information                 │
      │  Name:                    Programmers                   │
      │  Other name:            ↓ bugs                          │
      │  Owner:                 ↓ cwb                           │
      │  Description:             Group writing programs in ... │
      │  Location:              ↓ Texas                         │
      │  Department:            ↓ Apps                          │
      │  Organization:          ↓ GCS                           │
      └─────────────────────────────────────────────────────────┘




You may not change the name here.  To change the name, select rename on the
first menu.
 Enter=Accept    F10=Save    Esc=Exit                              F1=Help
```

Highlight Identification and press Enter. This brings up the screen in Figure 7.11. If there are no values in any of the fields, they will say (Empty List). Table 7.2 lists the fields and the information expected in those fields.

TABLE 7.2
Fields on the NETADMIN Group Identification Information Screen

FIELD	DESCRIPTION
Other Name	Any other identification labels used for this group. Multiple entries are allowed.
Owner	The person responsible for this group. Multiple entries are allowed.
Description	Free-form text window. Searches must match the entire contents of the Description field to succeed.
Location	Physical location of this Group object. Multiple entries are allowed.
Department	Shows the company department to which this group reports. Multiple entries are allowed.
Organization	Shows the organization to which this group reports. Multiple entries are allowed.

The primary use for this information is to provide good hooks for search operations later. Need to know how many PROGRAMMERS members are in Texas? The information in Figure 7.11 will make that search a matter of seconds rather than days.

Modifying the Member List of a Group Object

7.11 IN-A-HURRY

Modify the Member List of a Group Object with NETADMIN

1. Start the NETADMIN program from the DOS command line.

2. Choose Manage Objects, move to the correct container for the Group object, and choose the Group object name.

3. Choose View or Edit Properties of This Object, then Group members.

4. To add new User objects, press Insert.

5. To modify a User object, highlight it and press Enter.

6. Press F10 to save your changes.

Open the NETADMIN program from any DOS prompt, and move through the menu structure to reach the container and Group object you wish to modify. Highlight that Group object and press Enter to open the Actions for Group box. Press Enter to reach the View or Edit Group menu box, and press Enter on the Group Members option.

The background box in Figure 7.12 shows the Group Members box, with a single user listed. The foreground box, Group Members, is reached by pressing the Insert key from the background Group Members box.

Modifying Group objects with NETADMIN is just like modifying User objects with this utility (they're both leaf objects, after all). Pressing Insert opens the Object, Class screen, allowing you to browse through the entire Directory structure. In Figure 7.12, you can tell we went as far afield as another context, since user WENDY is from the INTEGRATE.GCS Organizational Unit. The trailing period in the name references the current Organization. Press Enter from the Group Members foreground box, and press F10 in the Group Members background box when it becomes active. This will save the information and take you to the View or Edit Group menu box once again.

FIGURE 7.12

Adding another PROGRAMMER

```
NetAdmin  4.55                              Monday  October  16, 1997  12:36pm
Context: CONSULT.GCS
Login Name: Admin.GCS

            ┌─ Actions for Group: Programmers ─┐
            │ View o                            │
            │        Group Members              │
            │ Ident   cwb                       │
            │ Group                             │
            ├──────────── Group Members ────────────┤
            │ Group Member: wendy.INTEGRATE.        │
            │                                       │
            │                                       │
            └───────────────────────────────────────┘

Type the object name or press <Insert> to browse for the object.
Ins=Add   Enter=Accept   Esc=Exit                              F1=Help
```

Modifying the Mailbox for a Group Object

7.12 IN-A-HURRY

Modify the Mailbox Information of a Group Object with NETADMIN

1. Start the NETADMIN program from the DOS command line.
2. Choose Manage Objects, move to the correct container for the Group object, and choose the Group object name.
3. Choose View or Edit Properties of This Object, then Mailbox Information.
4. Fill in the mailbox messaging server and mail address information.
5. Press F10 to save the settings.

Mail information for the Group object is set through the Mail Information page. When mail is sent to a group, rather than to individual users, each member of the group automatically gets that message. A prerequisite for this ability is a functioning MHS system on at least one server in your network.

Open the NETADMIN program from any DOS prompt, and move through the menu structure to reach the container and Group object you wish to modify. Highlight that Group object and press Enter to open the Actions for Group box. Press Enter to reach the View or Edit Group menu box, and then press Enter on the Mailbox Information option.

The primary information on these screens is detailing the messaging server supporting the group. You can either type this information into the Mailbox Location field or find it by using the Insert key to browse the NDS tree. You can change the Mailbox ID; the default is the first eight letters of the Group object name. Any non-DOS characters used, such as spaces, will be dropped from the Mailbox ID name.

The foreign e-mail address references the Group object's mailbox on a different (that is, not NetWare) mail system, such as Unix. If this is the case, place the name in the field. Five different foreign e-mail systems are listed in the pick list:

- **GMHS:** Global Message Handling Service from Novell

- **PROFS:** PRofessional OFfice System, IBM's office automation and e-mail system for mainframes running the VM operating system

- **SMTP:** Simple Mail Transport Protocol, the standard Unix e-mail exchange protocol

- **SNADS:** SNA Distribution Services, another IBM product for file, document, and e-mail exchange

- **X.400:** CCITT standard for exchanging e-mail between systems

- **Other:** Another e-mail type

Soon, access modules for the e-mail types listed above will be able to use NDS for delivery. The coming applications, available whenever Novell convinces the major e-mail vendors to support NDS, will require the foreign e-mail address to be entered on this screen.

Be aware that in NETADMIN, the e-mail type is listed first; in NetWare Administrator, the e-mail address comes first. Press F10 to save the address information.

Modifying the See Also Page for a Group Object

> **7.13 IN-A-HURRY**
>
> **Modify the See Also Page of a Group Object with NETADMIN**
>
> 1. Start the NETADMIN program from the DOS command line.
> 2. Choose Manage Objects, move to the correct container for the Group object, and choose the Group object name.
> 3. Choose View or Edit Properties of This Object, then See Also.
> 4. Press the Insert key to browse the NDS tree.
> 5. Pick items and network resources related to the Group object and press F10 to import them into the See Also box.
> 6. Press F10 to save the information.

Completely informational, the See Also listing is a good place to keep track of details about a Group object that may not be immediately apparent, and also to help in searches. Nothing listed in the See Also box affects the settings for the network or Group object itself.

Open the NETADMIN program from any DOS prompt, and move through the menu structure to reach the container and Group you wish to modify. Highlight that Group object and press Enter to open the Actions for Group box. Press Enter to reach the View or Edit Group menu box, and then press Enter on the See Also option.

You cannot enter text directly into the See Also box. If you have free-form text to enter, use the Description field on the Identification Information page. See Also is used to tag assorted network resources that relate to the Group object and keep an informational list.

Press the Insert key to open an input box, and press Insert a second time to start browsing the NDS tree. The highlight bar rests on the parent line for your current context, making it easy to move up the NDS tree with a single press of the Enter key.

To tag multiple network objects, use the F5 key. The marked items will change color. Once you have marked your choices, press F10 to accept the items, and they will be loaded into the See Also box.

Modifying the Rights to Files and Directories for a Group Object

> **7.14 IN-A-HURRY**
>
> **Manage File and Directory Access for the Group Object with NETADMIN**
>
> 1. Start the NETADMIN program from the DOS command line.
>
> 2. Choose Manage Objects, move to the correct container for the Group object, and choose the Group object name.
>
> 3. Choose View or Edit Rights to Files and Directories.
>
> 4. Press Enter and provide the name of a volume object, or press Insert to browse and choose one. Do the same for the Beginning Path field.
>
> 5. Choose whether to view directories, directories and files, or files while assigning trustee rights.
>
> 6. Choose whether to have the trustee rights apply to the current directory only or all subdirectories.

Open the NETADMIN program from any DOS prompt, and move through the menu structure to reach the container and Group object you wish to modify. Highlight that Group object and press Enter to open the Actions for Group box. Highlight and press Enter on the View or Edit Rights to Files and Directories option.

File and directory access management works better with NetWare Administrator than with NETADMIN, simply because of the amount of information that can be shown in the graphical screens. A disadvantage of the NETADMIN program is that you can't check the trustee rights for the group without pressing F10; this feature is built into the NetWare Administrator program.

The Rights to Files and/or Directories menu box opens. From here, you can set rights to one object at a time. Figure 7.13 shows the completed fields, after granting the group PROGRAMMERS the rights to use the VB directory on the ALTOS486_SYS: volume.

Press Enter in the Volume Object Name field to open a text-entry box. If you wish to type the volume name, you may do so. Otherwise, press the Insert

FIGURE 7.13

PROGRAMMERS with access to the VB directory

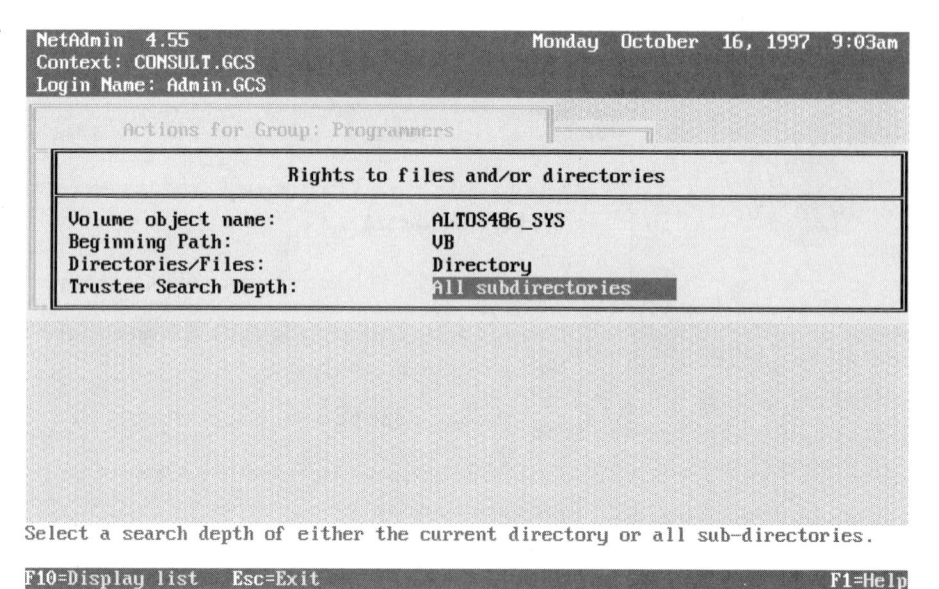

```
NetAdmin  4.55                           Monday  October  16, 1997  9:03am
Context: CONSULT.GCS
Login Name: Admin.GCS

         Actions for Group: Programmers
       ┌─────────────────────────────────────────────────────────┐
       │              Rights to files and/or directories         │
       │                                                         │
       │   Volume object name:        ALTOS486_SYS               │
       │   Beginning Path:            VB                         │
       │   Directories/Files:         Directory                  │
       │   Trustee Search Depth:      All subdirectories         │
       │                                                         │
       └─────────────────────────────────────────────────────────┘




Select a search depth of either the current directory or all sub-directories.
F10=Display list   Esc=Exit                                      F1=Help
```

key to browse the NDS tree. Once you've found the desired volume object, press Enter to fill the text box contents into the Volume Object Name field. The same process works for all other fields. The first press of the Enter key opens a text box, where you can type information or press the Insert key to browse.

Traditionally, rights are granted to directories, including all subdirectories and the files in all specified directories.

You can modify the other fields in the Right to Files and/or Directories screen as follows:

- **Beginning Path:** Supply a directory on the volume to limit the search scope, or press Insert. If nothing is supplied, the search will start at the root of the volume.

- **Directories/Files:** Accept Directory or press Enter to open a pick list of Directory, File, or Directory and File. The more detailed the search, the longer it will take.

- **Trustee Search Depth:** Press Enter to open the pick list. Choose All Subdirectories (default) or Current Directory Only.

After giving a volume object name and modifying the other fields (if desired), press F10 to start the search and display the trustee assignments. Press Enter to modify the trustee rights for the specified directory and subdirectories. Figure 7.14 shows the process of adding trustee rights for the PROGRAMMERS Group object on the ALTOS486_SYS:\VB directory.

FIGURE 7.14

Plenty of PROGRAMMER rights to the VB directory

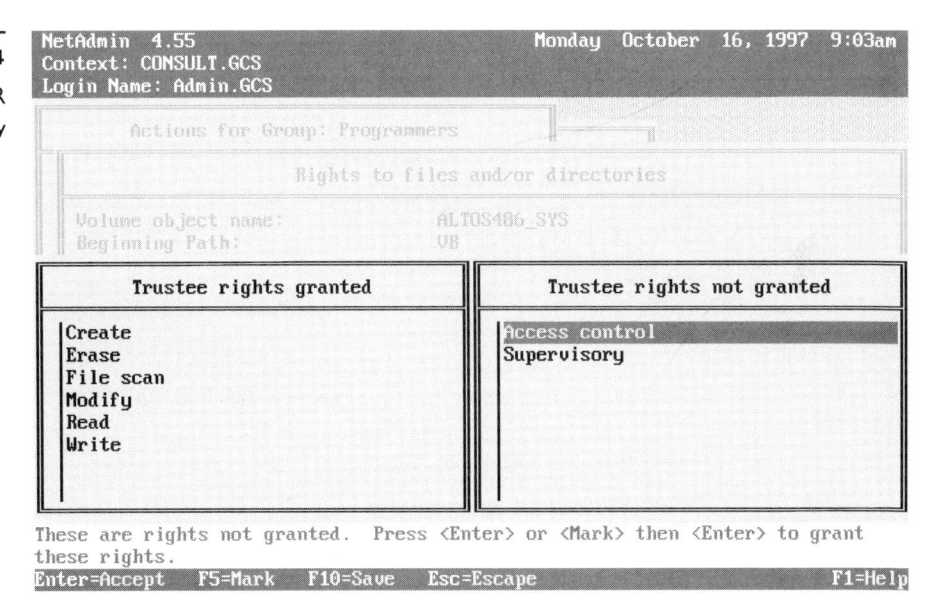

```
NetAdmin  4.55                              Monday  October  16, 1997  9:03am
Context: CONSULT.GCS
Login Name: Admin.GCS

              Actions for Group: Programmers
                   Rights to files and/or directories
        Volume object name:           ALTOS486_SYS
        Beginning Path:               VB

    Trustee rights granted           Trustee rights not granted
   Create                           Access control
   Erase                            Supervisory
   File scan
   Modify
   Read
   Write


These are rights not granted.  Press <Enter> or <Mark> then <Enter> to grant
these rights.
Enter=Accept    F5=Mark    F10=Save    Esc=Escape                    F1=Help
```

> **NOTE**
>
> *If you are the Admin or equivalent, many of these same changes to rights can be made with the FILER utility. See Chapters 9 and 12 for more information.*

Modifying the NDS Trustees for a Group Object

Trustees of this group PROGRAMMERS are those network users or resources that have some control over the group. For more detail about trustee rights and what they involve, see Chapter 9, which covers NetWare 4.1x security.

Open the NETADMIN program from any DOS prompt, and move through the menu structure to reach the container and Group object you wish to modify. Highlight that Group object and press Enter to open the Actions for Group box. Highlight and press enter on the View or Edit Trustees of This

478 Chapter 7 • Handling More than One User at a Time

> ### 7.15 IN-A-HURRY
>
> **Modify the NDS Trustee Rights of a Group Object with NETADMIN**
>
> 1. Start the NETADMIN program from the DOS command line.
> 2. Choose Manage Objects, move to the correct container for the Group object, and choose the Group object name.
> 3. Choose View or Edit the Trustees of This Object, then Trustees.
> 4. To add a new trustee, press Insert.
> 5. To view or edit an existing trustee, highlight an entry and press Enter.

Object option. Then press Enter on the Trustee menu option. You'll see a screen similar to Figure 7.15.

The existing trustees of this resource (in this case, the PROGRAMMERS Group object) are listed. Pressing Enter on any highlighted entry allows you to change the listed trustee rights (assuming you have the authority to make these changes). Pressing Insert will open a text box asking for a new trustee name. Pressing Insert a second time will open the Object, Class screen that we've seen so often.

FIGURE 7.15
Checking trustee rights for the PROGRAMMERS group

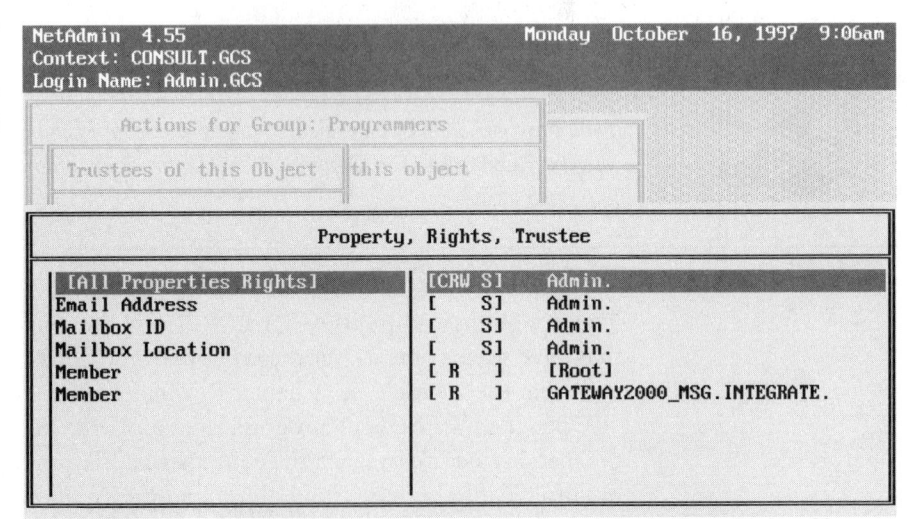

Saving Time with the User Template

NOW THAT YOU'VE gone through and created both User and Group objects by hand, so to speak, you're probably ready for some shortcuts. The first one to explore is the User Template. The name gives a clear indication of the purpose and function of this object: it provides a template of information for use when creating users.

Technically, the User Template is an NDS object holding default information common to many users. Here is some of the information you might include in a User Template:

- Login time restrictions
- Password restrictions
- Language
- Phone, location, and department information
- Print job configuration details
- Login scripts
- Group memberships
- Security equivalence settings
- Account balance information

A User Template may be created in any Organization or Organizational Unit objects. If a User Template exists in the container above, you may copy information from that User Template. In our example, if there were a template in GCS, the template created in INTEGRATE.GCS could include all the parent information as a starting point.

The User Template information is passed to a new User object if you check the Use User Template option when you create the User object. The information in the template may change later, but that change will not be reflected in the User object information. There is not a live link between the User Template and the User object; there is just a one-time copy process from template to user. Rights may not be granted via template.

No one may log in as the User Template, but it appears to be a normal User object during setup and modification. This is a helpful utility, not a security hole.

Creating a User Template with NetWare Administrator

> **7.16 IN-A-HURRY**
>
> **Create a User Template with NetWare Administrator**
>
> 1. Open NetWare Administrator and highlight the Organization or Organizational Unit container that will hold the Template.
>
> 2. Open the Object pull-down menu and choose Create or press Insert.
>
> 3. Provide information as you would for any other User object.
>
> 4. Click on OK to save the Template.

A Template is a leaf object that provides a basic set of properties and setup procedures to apply to new, but not existing, users. In NetWare 4.10, these are called User Templates. In NetWare 4.11, the name is shortened to Template.

In NetWare 4.10, open NetWare Administrator and click on the container for the new Template. Click on the Object pull-down menu item, or press Alt+O. Click on USER_TEMPLATE or type S to open the User Template. The template will be created immediately, even before you fill out a single field. In Figure 7.16, you can see that the User Template object is created underneath INTEGRATE.GCS even before the information is saved.

With NetWare 4.11 and Windows 95, the procedure is slightly different. As when you're creating a user, a small dialog box opens, asking for the name of the Template and whether you wish to create another Template or define additional properties. When you indicate (by checking the proper checkbox) that you wish to define additional properties, the dialog box opens, presenting the standard information for new objects.

Fill in the various pages of the dialog box exactly as you would for any other User object. In Figure 7.16, you can tell by the turned-down corners that information has been added to the Identification, Login Restrictions, Login Time Restrictions, Print Job Configuration, and Login Script pages. New in

FIGURE 7.16

User Template configuration

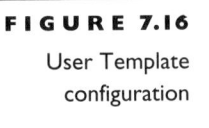

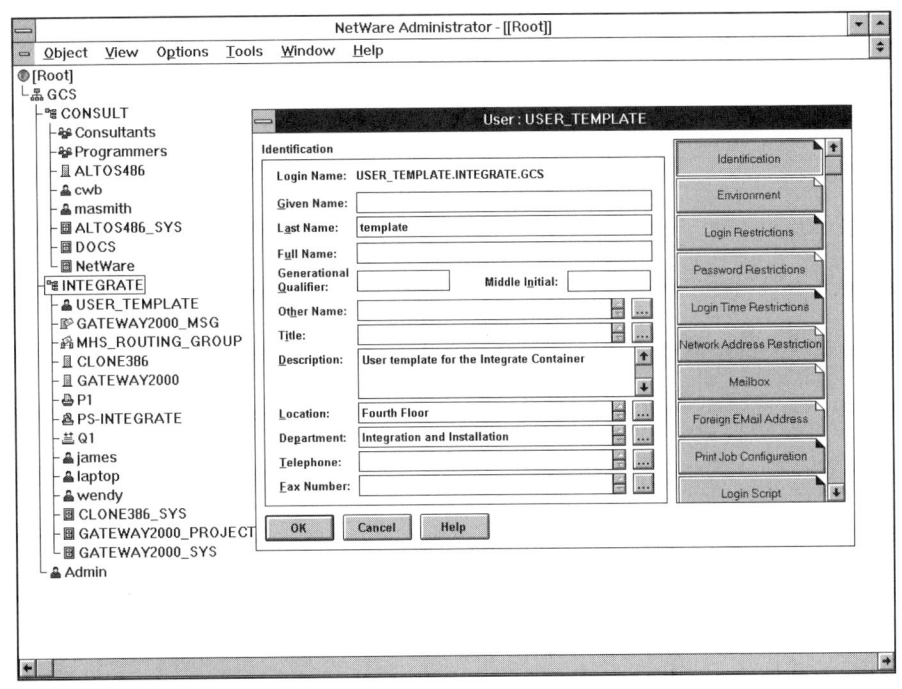

NetWare 4.11 are the turned-down corners for New Object's DS Rights, New Object's FS Rights, and Member of Template. Fill out the Template Members fields just as you would to add members to a Group object.

When the information is complete, click on OK to save it. When you create a new User object, the system will add these details into the proper properties. See Figure 7.17 for the first evidence of the existence of the User Template under NetWare 4.10; under 4.11 the object will be named Template.

When we created our first new User object back in Chapter 6, the Use User Template checkbox was gray and unavailable. Now, it's not only active, but the default is to use the template.

Does this work? See for yourself. Figure 7.18 shows a new User object in the process of being installed. The information from the User Template shown in Figure 7.17 has been copied into the fields for our new user DOUG. This is the result of providing the user's last name, accepting the default values, and making use of the template.

Chapter 7 • Handling More than One User at a Time

FIGURE 7.17

The Use User Template checkbox appears

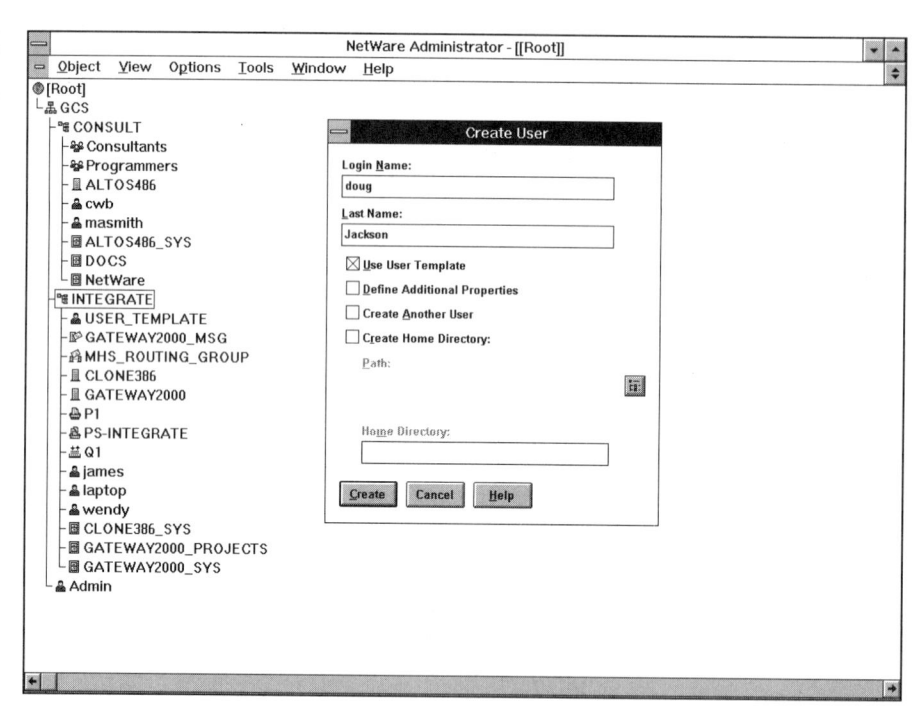

FIGURE 7.18

Applying the User Template to a new user

You might notice even the Description field came through exactly as it was in Figure 7.17. Learn from my mistake: don't put information about the User Template itself here; use it for information that applies to the subsequent users.

Creating a User Template with NETADMIN in NetWare 4.10

> **7.17 IN-A-HURRY**
>
> **Create a User Template with NETADMIN**
>
> **1.** In NetWare 4.10, start the NETADMIN program from the DOS command line.
>
> **2.** Choose Manage Objects from the main menu.
>
> **3.** Move to the correct container for the User Template, press Insert, and choose User.
>
> **4.** Name the user **USER_TEMPLATE**, with a last name of **template**.
>
> **5.** Modify the information for this special user as necessary.

There is no menu entry labeled Create User Template under NETADMIN running in NetWare 4.10. Since the template is just a specialized User object, however, we can create one ourselves.

Open the NETADMIN program from any DOS prompt, and move through the menu structure to reach the container you wish to hold the User Template. Press the Insert key, and choose User from the Select an Object Class list that appears. For the login name, type USER_TEMPLATE, in capital letters with an underscore. This will make our template look like the ones created by the NetWare Administrator program.

Give the last name as **template**, with lowercase letters, exactly as it is here. Then fill out special information that will apply to all, or at least most, of the new users created in this container.

When a new User object is created in NETADMIN, one of the toggle questions is "Copy the User Template object?" The default is Yes. Leaving the default will use the User Template object you created with the procedure outlined here.

NetWare 4.11 systems no longer support User Templates under NETADMIN. When you try to view a Template (no longer even called

USER_TEMPLATE) under NETADMIN, you get a stern "Objects of Unknown type are not maintained by this utility" message. Don't be surprised if you get the same message from NetWare Administrator as well.

Modifying the User Template with NETADMIN in NetWare 4.10

7.18 IN-A-HURRY

Modify a User Template with NETADMIN

1. In NetWare 4.10, start the NETADMIN program from the DOS command line.
2. Choose Manage Objects from the main menu.
3. Move to the container holding the User Template, highlight the current context entry (.), and press F10.
4. Choose View or Edit Properties of This Object, then select Edit the User Template.
5. Choose the item to modify from the View or Edit User list.

Open the NETADMIN program from any DOS prompt, and move through the menu structure to reach the container that holds the User Template object. You must make a special effort to force modifying the container itself rather than just seeing the objects inside the container. That's the reason you must highlight the current context listing (a single period, just as the current directory in DOS) and press F10.

Once you have done that, the Actions window that opens will offer actions to be taken against the Organization or Organizational Unit. In Figure 7.19, notice the menu box title in the background is Actions for Organizational Unit: CONSULT.

There are two menu items in the foreground window that deserve mention. First is the Edit the User Template choice, which is highlighted. Second is the Intruder Detection item, two lines above the highlight bar. These options clue you into the fact that this is not a typical User object View and Edit menu.

The editing of the User Template proceeds exactly like that of any other User object. Make the changes necessary and press F10 to save them and exit. Remember that changes made to the User Template have no effect on users already created.

FIGURE 7.19
Editing the User Template

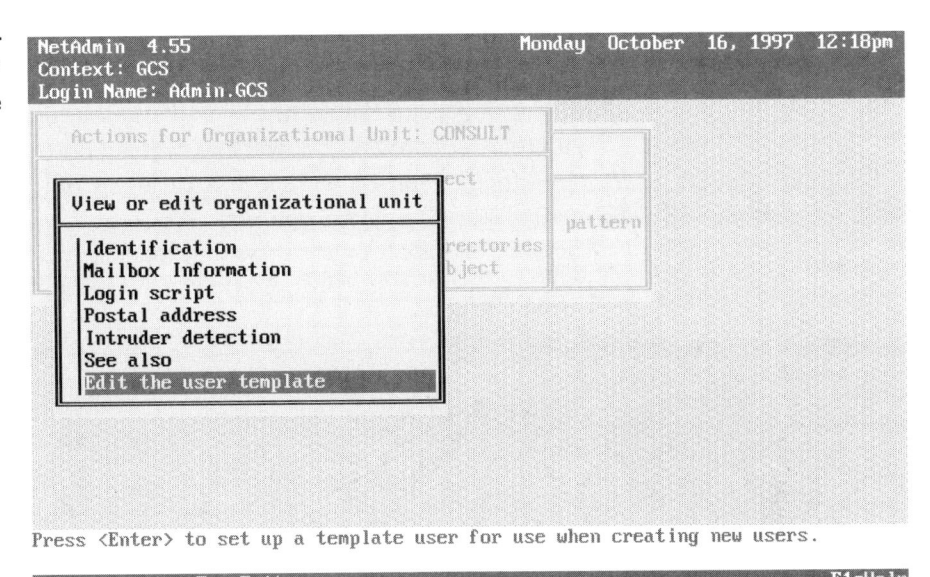

Using Login Scripts

LOGIN SCRIPTS ARE files containing instructions to configure the networking environment for users. These scripts are read and executed when a user logs in to the network. They are triggered by the LOGIN.EXE program. A login script is similar to an AUTOEXEC.BAT file for an IBM-compatible PC. Login scripts are properties of objects.

Login scripts are excellent ways to shield computer-phobic users from the network. With a well-designed login script, a user may never need to know any details concerning application locations and data file directories.

The most popular way to use login scripts is to MAP a drive to a particular directory. Using the MAP command dedicates a particular network drive letter, such as assigning drive H: to:

```
ALTOS486_SYS:\DOCVIEW\DTAPPWIN
```

The users merely change to drive H:, and they are automatically connected to the NetWare 4.1x DynaText file viewer on the server ALTOS486. The user does not need to type anything to get to this point.

There are four types of login scripts: Container, Profile, User, and Default. As with earlier NetWare versions, the last login script to execute has the last word, meaning it can change any and all information from previous scripts.

With four scripts available, you may wonder how to keep them all straight. It's not difficult, and you will see how each type of login script makes sense. Besides, all login scripts are optional.

The order of execution for these four login scripts is:

- Login begins
- Container object login script

    EXISTS = Execute and continue

    DOES NOT EXIST = Continue

- Profile object login script

    EXISTS = Execute and continue

    DOES NOT EXIST = Continue

- User object login script

    EXISTS = Execute and stop

    DOES NOT EXIST = Continue

- Default login script

    Executes if there is no User object login script

The User login script and the Default login script are an either/or situation. If you have a User login script, the Default script will not run. If you don't have a User login script, the Default login script will run. The exception is when a user has a NO_DEFAULT line in a Container or Profile login script, which prevents the Default login script from executing.

The primary use of the login script is to set different drive letters to provide users with an easy way to reach their applications. It is true that the entire network is open to users, and they can make use of any resource where they have been granted trustee rights. It is also true that the majority of users do not know how to navigate even a small network. Our job is to make network applications and other resources available to users with as little work on their part as possible. Login scripts go a long way in making the network easy for users to navigate.

> *It is also true that the majority of users do not know how to navigate even a small network.*

> **Users, Login Scripts, and You**
>
> The effectiveness of login scripts is evident when you speak to most users and ask them where any of their application directories are. Word processing is on drive G:, and the database is on drive M:. Does this answer tell you anything of value? No. It tells you that the user doesn't understand how NetWare handles drive redirection and has no clue about the network environment.
>
> You can take this two ways. You may regard the user as stupid and computerphobic, since he or she is unaware of fundamental network processes. This way guarantees you will burn out and become bitter toward the users before much longer. You may also regard this as a successful network setup on your part, since the user is able to function perfectly well without worrying about network technical details. This mental approach will make you much happier in your work.
>
> Perhaps the second method is the best way to approach network support in general and login scripts in particular. Your job is to provide a network foundation that supports the users' primary jobs without drawing attention to the underpinnings. Login scripts are your most direct tool to make the network an invisible connection between people and the resources they need.

Types of Login Scripts

Since the login scripts execute in the same order each time, there are some guidelines for each script's role. Container login scripts should focus on access to resources used by most network users, such as volumes and printers. Specific group needs can be answered by the Profile login script. Individual requirements belong in the User login script. The Default login script is not configurable.

If you're an old hand at NetWare, don't be surprised if it takes you a while to get used to the new login script arrangements in NetWare 4. It took me some time as well. For the first two months, I always tried to fix problems in individual User login scripts. With NetWare 4.1x, more control is managed more easily by using the Container and Profile login scripts than ever was possible with earlier NetWare user and SYSTEM login scripts.

The Container Login Script

The Container login script has the following characteristics:

- It is a property of an Organization or Organizational Unit.

- Each user can execute only one Container login script.

The Container login script is executed first. This replaces the SYSTEM login script from earlier NetWare versions. The SYSTEM login script was server-based; the Container login script is a property of the user's container. Whether the container is an Organization or Organizational Unit makes no difference. If the parent container for a User object does not have a login script, no other Container login script will be available for that user.

Use Container login scripts to:

- Establish network drive mappings to horizontal application directories.

- Establish a link to the user's home directory.

- Connect each user to the PUBLIC directory for NetWare utilities.

- Connect a default printer for the entire container.

- Activate menus or applications used by all members of the container.

- Send login messages to all container users.

You can use conditional IF statements based on login times, group membership, or other variables to make your Container login scripts more versatile.

The Profile Login Script

The Profile login script has the following characteristics:

- It is a property of a Profile object.

- A person can have only a single Profile login script.

- Many users may execute the same Profile login script.

The Profile login script works differently than an IF MEMBER OF... statement referencing a group in a login script. (Using the IF MEMBER OF... statement in login scripts is covered a little later in the chapter.) One important difference is that a User object may belong to many groups, but can have only one Profile login script. The Profile login script executes after the Container login script.

Use Profile login scripts to:

- Establish drive mappings to special data and/or application directories.
- Set specific search mappings for application directories.
- Connect to special-purpose printers (such as color or high-speed printers) unique to a group.
- Send login messages to a specific group.

The User Login Script

The User login script is a property of the User object. The User login script executes after both the Container and Profile login scripts. It is normally used for specific network details for one user only. There can be only one User login script per User object.

Use User login scripts to:

- Establish drive mappings to specific user directories.
- Send user-specific login messages.
- Activate menus or applications for each particular user.

The Default Login Script

The Default login script has the following characteristics:

- It is contained in the LOGIN.EXE program.
- It cannot be edited.
- It executes in the absence of the User login script.
- This type of login script provides minimal functionality.

The Default login script executes last, but only if there is no User login script. There is only one Default login script for the network.

The Default login script does not exist as text file to be edited. It is contained within the LOGIN.EXE program and cannot be changed. Since so little happens in this login script, few (if any) networks use only the Default login script.

The two ways to avoid the Default login script are:

- Have a User login script.

- Use the NO_DEFAULT command in a Container login script.

As an introduction to login scripts in general and some sample commands used, the following are the lines in the Default login script, along with a quick explanation for each one.

```
MAP DISPLAY OFF
```

MAP redirects a local drive letter to a network resource, either a regular drive or a search drive (similar to the DOS PATH command). MAP DISPLAY OFF prevents map commands from displaying on the screen, similar to the DOS command ECHO OFF.

```
MAP ERRORS OFF
```

Prevents mapping errors and the resulting messages from displaying on the screen.

```
MAP *1:=SYS:
```

Maps the first drive to volume SYS:. The *1 indicates a wildcard symbol for mapping the first non-local drive letter. This avoids possible problems in mapping particular drive letters (F: or G:) that may not be available for all clients.

```
MAP *1:=SYS:%LOGIN_NAME
```

Maps the first drive to the user's home directory, if LOGIN_NAME is the same as the user's home directory. If the user has no home directory, the first drive is still mapped to SYS:. The %LOGIN_NAME is an identifier variable, and will be interpreted differently for each person that logs in. The value given by the user as the login name will be captured by the login process and passed to this variable.

```
IF %1=Admin THEN MAP *1:=SYS:SYSTEM
```

If the login name is Admin, the first drive is mapped to SYS:SYSTEM instead of to the user's home directory. This is an example of the IF...THEN statement.

```
MAP P:=SYS:PUBLIC
```

For OS/2 workstation clients only. With OS/2, drive P: is mapped to SYS:PUBLIC. If the user is not using an OS/2 workstation, this drive mapping is ignored during the execution of the Default login script.

```
MAP INS S1:=SYS:PUBLIC; MAP INS
   S2:=SYS:PUBLIC\%MACHINE\%OS\ %OS_VERSION
```

The INS stands for insert, which places S1 (first search drive) into the DOS PATH statement in a way that does not overwrite any of the existing PATH commands.

If the user is using a DOS or MS Windows workstation, the first search drive is mapped to SYS:PUBLIC, where DOS-based NetWare utilities are stored. Then the second search drive is mapped to the directory where DOS is stored. The two MAP commands are joined by a semicolon. The default has always been a single command per line, and it's safer to write login scripts in that manner still. If the user logs in from an OS/2 workstation, these drive mappings are ignored during the execution of the Default login script.

```
MAP DISPLAY ON
```

This command allows MAP commands to display.

```
MAP
```

When the MAP command is used alone from the DOS command line or inside a login script, it displays a list of all drive mappings on the user's screen.

The Most Common Login Script Commands

You know the old story: 80 percent of the work is done by 20 percent of the blank. Fill in the blank with people, tools, circus elephants, or login script commands.

The complete list is located with the other commands in the online documentation. There are more login script commands than any one company will ever use. As you look over the list, you may think some commands seem strange. But remember that each command solves a problem for some customers. Every command has a use, no matter how specialized.

For our examples, the majority of all your login scripts will consist of the following few commands used over and over. These descriptions show the command, the explanation, and a usage example.

> **WARNING**
>
> *Always place a final carriage return at the end of each login script. The cursor should be on a line by itself, beyond the final login script command line, before saving the script. This will save you much troubleshooting; unless this is done properly, the last line may not execute.*

The ATTACH Command

The ATTACH command connects to bindery-based NetWare servers (NetWare 2.x or NetWare 3.x). This command can be used with NetWare 4.x servers to bypass NDS. This command no longer works from the command line; it only works from a login script.

An example is:

```
ATTACH 312_NW/JAMES
```

The # Command

The # command indicates an external program that will execute and return control to the login script. The example here is the most common, setting the print redirection from a local printer port to a network system printer using the CAPTURE command:

```
#CAPTURE Q=LASER_Q1 NB NFF TI=9
```

The COMSPEC Command

For COMmand SPECifier, the COMSPEC setting specifies the directory where the DOS command processor (COMMAND.COM) is loaded, especially when loaded from the network. OS/2 users shouldn't use this command. With the increased speed and size of local hard disks, more and more PCs are using paths to DOS and the local COMMAND.COM set when installing DOS, rather than pointing to a DOS version on the network.

An example is:

```
COMSPEC=S2:COMMAND.COM
```

The EXIT Command

EXIT stops execution of the LOGIN utility and executes an external program. This command doesn't apply to OS/2 workstations. An EXIT command placed in any login script stops any subsequent login scripts from running.

An example is:

```
EXIT "NMENU ACCOUNTING"
```

The FIRE PHASERS Command

The FIRE PHASERS command emits an electronic space gun sound that may fire up to nine times. Two is the tasteful limit, as in:

```
FIRE PHASERS 2 TIMES
```

This is helpful to signal login messages or the conclusion of a login process.

The IF...THEN Command

IF...THEN is a conditional statement used to perform an action only under certain conditions. Earlier NetWare versions with a single SYSTEM login script often used IF...THEN statements to check the user for group membership before mapping certain drive connections. Although it is still useful, some conditions requiring IF...THEN statements in the past can now be done with a combination of the Container and Profile login scripts.

The following example specifies that members of the group WIN31 will have the next available search drive (S16 tells the system to start with the highest possible search drive number, 16, and count down until it finds the next open search drive letter) mapped to the \APPS\WIN31 directory. The interior part is generally indented for clarity.

```
IF MEMBER OF "WIN31" THEN
  MAP INS S16:=SYS:\APPS\WIN31
END
```

The MAP Command

The MAP command maps drives and search drives to network directories and NDS objects. Examples are:

```
MAP G:=GATEWAY2000_PROJECTS:\REPORTS
MAP INS S16:=SYS:\APPS\WIN31
```

The PAUSE Command

PAUSE stops the execution of the login script until a key is pressed. It provides a handy way to force a user to look at the screen, since FIRE PHASERS tends to be ignored after the novelty wears off.

The SET Command

The SET command sets a DOS or OS/2 environment variable. For OS/2 workstations, SET commands affect the environment only while the login script is running. Values must be enclosed in quotation marks, as in:

```
SET PROMPT="$P$G"
```

$P sets the drive letter, and $G sets the symbol >.

The WRITE Command

WRITE displays messages on the workstation screen while the login script is running. It's best to put these commands at the end of the login script, so that they stay on the screen, or use them in conjunction with the PAUSE command.

All values, including special characters, must be in quotation marks. Special characters that help you control text strings are:

\r   Inserts a carriage return

\n   Starts a new line

\   Displays quotation mark

\7   Beeps the internal speaker

An example is:

```
WRITE "Welcome to the GCS Corporate Network \7"
```

LOGIN.EXE Command Switches

The LOGIN program allows you to gain access to the network. The normal syntax is:

```
LOGIN username
```

There are ways to modify the LOGIN program even before you get to a single login script. These command switches must be typed after LOGIN, followed by a single space, as in:

```
LOGIN /NS
```

If you wish to avoid the Novell NetWare splash screen and skip the "Enter your login name" prompt, type the command like this:

```
LOGIN /NB username
```

As with all NetWare commands, typing the command name followed by /? provides help, as in:

```
LOGIN /?
```

Table 7.3 lists the LOGIN command switches, along with a description of how they work.

TABLE 7.3 LOGIN Command Switches

SWITCH	FUNCTION
/CLS	CLear Screen. Clears the screen before starting the login process, wiping away the Novell NetWare login banner.
/NS	No Script. Prevents a login script from running. This prevents you from being logged out of any other servers you are connected to as well as eliminating the login script execution. This LOGIN command switch replaces the ATTACH utility from the DOS command line.
/NB	No Banner. Prevents the Novell NetWare red banner from being displayed during the login process.
/S path/objectname	Specify. Requests a specific login script file. Replace *path* with the path to the script. Replace *objectname* with the object whose script you want to run. This is handy for network administrators testing user setup.

TABLE 7.3 (cont.) LOGIN Command Switches	SWITCH	FUNCTION
	/B	Bindery. Specify a bindery login when connecting to a NetWare 4.x server. Bypasses NDS and uses Bindery Services for connection to that particular server.
	/PR=*profile objectname*	PRofile. Specify the Profile object script you wish to run.
	/NOSWAP	Prevents LOGIN from swapping to disk or extended or expanded memory.
	/SWAP=*path*	Tells LOGIN to swap to this path when external commands are executed. DOS only.
	/TREE	Specifies that you want to log in to a particular NDS tree. Overrides any settings in NET.CFG.

The Most Common Login Script Identifier Variables

Identifiers personalize login scripts. This works by using variables known to the NetWare client programs as information to fill in the blank of the identifier variable. For example, the user gives a login name as part of the login process. This name identifies that user to the system. After checking NDS for authentication, the system asks for that user's password. With the proper password, the user gains access to the network. By the time a user gets access to the network, the network knows everything about that user. Since this happens before the login script is started, the information about every user is available to personalize the login script using a common set of variables. The most familiar to many people is the greeting often used by network administrators. It's nice to see:

```
Good morning, JAMES
```

as you prepare for work in the morning. More important, it's easy for the administrator to make this happen. Table 7.4 describes the most commonly used login script identifier variables. When you use an identifier variable in a WRITE statement, it must be within the quotation marks, typed in all capital letters, and proceeded by a percent sign (%). In NetWare 3.x, the identifier variable didn't need to be within the WRITE statement's quotation marks, but this is a requirement in NetWare 4.

The requirement for identifier variables to be in uppercase letters suggests you should always use capital letters in all your login scripts. This looks a bit garish, especially to people with a Unix background. Using all capitals is, however, the easiest way to avoid potential problems with your login scripts.

TABLE 7.4 Common Login Script Identifier Variables

IDENTIFIER VARIABLE	FUNCTION	EXAMPLE
%GREETING_TIME	Uses the workstation clock to determine morning, afternoon, or evening time frame. Supplies the proper term for the time of the day upon login.	WRITE "Good %GREETING_TIME"
%LOGIN_NAME	The variable for the client's unique login name.	MAP F:=GATEWAY2000_SYS:USERS\%LOGIN_NAME
%MACHINE	Determines and displays the type of non-OS/2 computer used by the client.	WRITE "Your computer is: %MACHINE"
%OS	Determines and displays the operating system used by your system, such as MSDOS or DRDOS.	WRITE "Your %MACHINE is running %OS"
%OS_VERSION	Determines and displays the version of DOS, such as 3.3, 6.0, or 6.2.	WRITE "You are using version %OS_VERSION of %OS"
%STATION	Determines and displays your workstation connection number.	WRITE "You are connection number %STATION"

The %LOGIN_NAME identifier variable works well when first names are used for login names, less well if the naming system uses initials or name combinations. Being greeted by "Hello, CWB" is not particularly warm or friendly. However, this variable is great for mapping a drive to the user's home directory. Since the home directory name is the same as the login name, this variable will reliably map every user to that user's particular directory.

Creating and Managing Login Scripts

NOW THAT YOU know what login scripts are and the commands that are available, let's get scripting. First we'll use NetWare Administrator, then in the next section, we'll do everything with NETADMIN. Either way, you must have the trustee rights to create and modify the login scripts for each object. The easiest way to be sure of this capability is to be the Admin or equivalent.

The login script is an object property. Not all objects have login scripts, just users, Profiles, and containers. There are no mandatory login scripts, or even mandatory login script commands for containers, Profile, or User objects. The Profile script is stored in Organizations or Organizational Units as an NDS leaf object. Container scripts are stored in their respective containers. The User object login script is stored as a property of each User object. See Figure 7.20 for a graphical look at these storage locations.

FIGURE 7.20

Scattered scripts

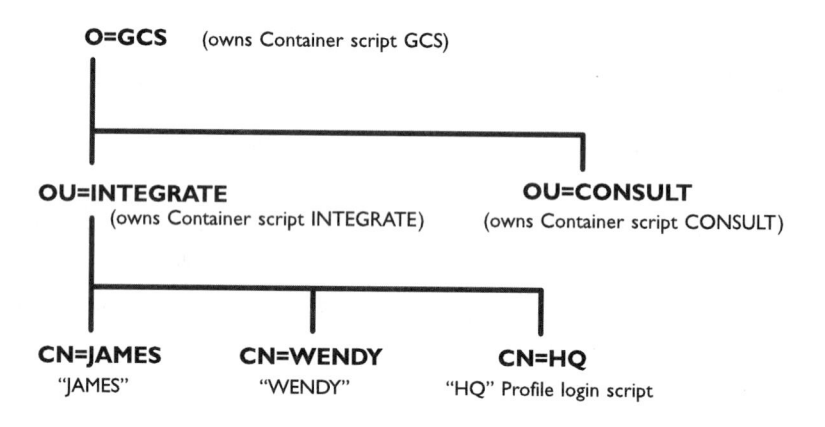

```
O=GCS    (owns Container script GCS)
   |
   +--------------------------------+
   |                                |
OU=INTEGRATE                    OU=CONSULT
   (owns Container script INTEGRATE)   (owns Container script CONSULT)
   |
   +----------+----------+
   |          |          |
CN=JAMES  CN=WENDY    CN=HQ
 "JAMES"   "WENDY"    "HQ" Profile login script
```

As Figure 7.20 illustrates, you must go to the particular object that owns the login script you wish to create or modify. There is no central database of login scripts. Before we get to the specifics of creating and editing login scripts with the NetWare Administrator or NETADMIN program, let's take a look at some examples of login scripts and see how they work.

A Sample Container Login Script

Let's look at our sample Container login script in Figure 7.21.

FIGURE 7.21

A sample Container login script in NetWare Administrator

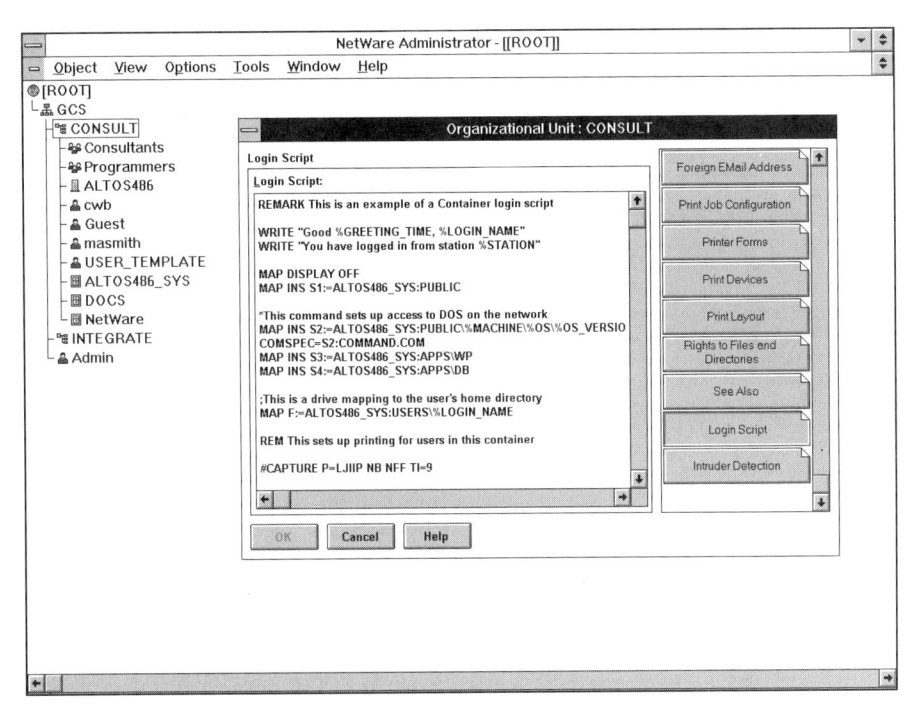

```
REMARK This is an example of a Container login script

WRITE "Good %GREETING_TIME, %LOGIN_NAME"
WRITE "You have logged in from station %STATION"

MAP DISPLAY OFF
MAP INS S1:=ALTOS486_SYS:PUBLIC

;This command sets up access to DOS on the network
MAP INS S2:=ALTOS486_SYS:PUBLIC\%MACHINE\%OS\%OS_VERSIO
COMSPEC=S2:COMMAND.COM
MAP INS S3:=ALTOS486_SYS:APPS\WP
MAP INS S4:=ALTOS486_SYS:APPS\DB

;This is a drive mapping to the user's home directory
MAP F:=ALTOS486_SYS:USERS\%LOGIN_NAME

REM This sets up printing for users in this container

#CAPTURE P=LJIIP NB NFF TI=9
```

Since the login script is longer than the text box (not unusual for Container login scripts), let me expand on it. Each line is followed by comments and clarifications.

    REMARK This is an example of a Container login script

REMARK allows you to add comments that are not executed. Four commands (REMARK, REM, ;, and *) perform this same function.

    WRITE "Good %GREETING_TIME, %LOGIN_NAME"

Displays the information inside the quotation marks. The resulting line will look something like:

    Good morning, James

Variables must be within quotation marks and in all uppercase letters.

```
WRITE "You have logged in from station %STATION"
```

Displays the connection number for this login.

```
MAP DISPLAY OFF
```

Turns off the information display to avoid multiple MAP statements clogging the screen. A later Profile or User login script will provide the MAP DISPLAY ON command.

```
MAP INS S1:=ALTOS486_SYS:PUBLIC
```

Inserts the first network search drive into the DOS path statement, allowing the NetWare utilities in the PUBLIC directory to be available to the user from anywhere on the system.

```
*This command sets up access to DOS on the network
```

Shows a different way to exclude lines from executing with the login script. Comments such as this are helpful to other administrators that work on the network. They are also helpful to you a year later when you have no idea what you were thinking when you set up this system.

```
MAP INS
    S2:=ALTOS486_SYS:PUBLIC\%MACHINE\%OS\%OS_VERSION
```

Inserts the second network search drive into the DOS path statement. This drive uses variables to point to the particular machine type and DOS version necessary for each user.

```
COMSPEC=S2:COMMAND.COM
```

Sets the DOS pointer to the correct COMMAND.COM file. This command must follow the network mapping to DOS in the login script, but it doesn't need to be the next command. It can also be set locally.

```
MAP INS S3:=ALTOS486_SYS:APPS\WP
```

Inserts the third network search drive into the DOS path, and gives access to the WP directory.

```
MAP INS S4:=ALTOS486_SYS:APPS\DB
```

Inserts the fourth network search drive, and points to the DB directory.

```
;This is a drive mapping to the user's home directory
```

Another comment line that doesn't execute.

```
MAP F:=ALTOS486_SYS:USERS\%LOGIN_NAME
```

Sets drive F: to the user's home directory. However, if another MAP command later uses drive F:, this entry will be overwritten. Since MS Windows setup demands constant drive letters, using a variable such as *1 for this mapping may not work.

```
REM This sets up printing for users in this container
```

The last, and most popular, line-exclusion command. REM works just as it does in a DOS AUTOEXEC.BAT file.

```
#CAPTURE P=LJIIP NB NFF TI=9
```

The crosshatch or number sign (#) starts execution of a COM or EXE file. Once the program is finished, control returns to the login script. Larger programs may not work, since the login script remains in memory during this procedure, taking about 70 KB of RAM.

```
#COMMAND /C CLS
```

Executes the external command to clear the screen, then returns to the login script.

```
;This command displays a DOS text file the administrator
;creates for daily messages
FDISPLAY ALTOS486_SYS:Admin\MESSAGE.TXT
```

Displays the file MESSAGE.TXT during the login process. FDISPLAY can handle word processing files. DISPLAY works only with text files.

```
PAUSE
```

Stops the login script until a key is pressed. It is identical to the DOS PAUSE command.

```
SET PROMPT="$P$G"
```

Same as the DOS SET statement, but the variable must be enclosed in quotation marks.

```
IF MEMBER OF
```

Adds conditional statements based on group memberships. For example:

```
IF MEMBER OF PROGRAMMERS THEN MAP
    P:=GATEWAY2000_PROJECTS:\APPS\SRC_CODE
```

You can see the ways in which this script is tailored to a large group of users: it sets the default printer, sends messages to the group, and maps drives to the user's home directory and the most generic applications.

A Sample Profile Login Script

Some coordination must happen between the Container and Profile login scripts. If you include User login scripts as well in your network, you must coordinate all three. Figure 7.22 shows a sample Profile login script.

Let's take a line-by-line look at this Profile login script.

FIGURE 7.22

Profile login script details in NetWare Administrator

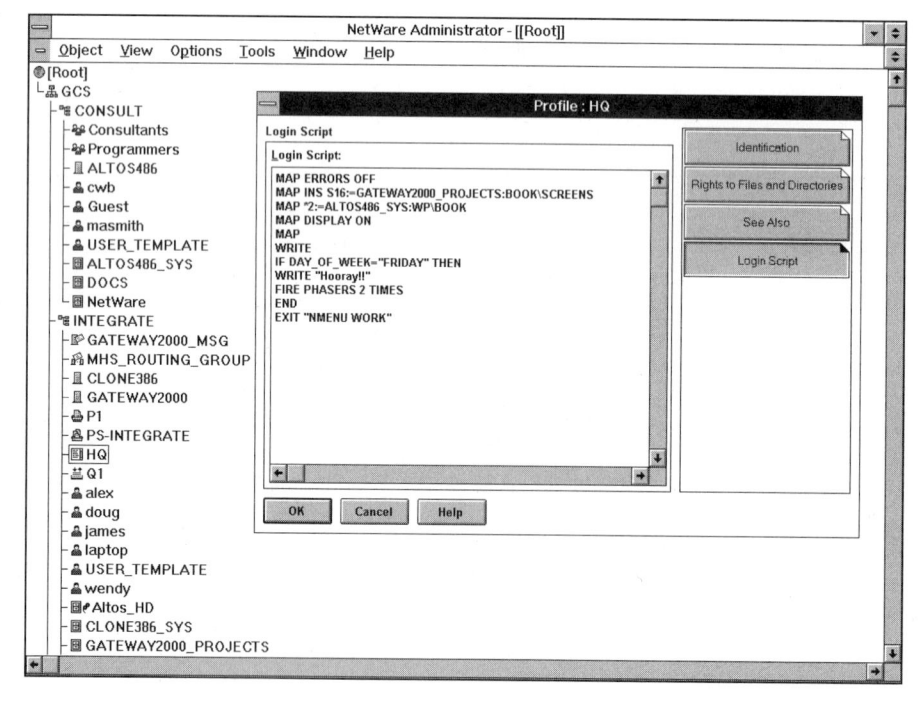

```
    MAP ERRORS OFF
```

If any drive mapping errors occur, they won't show on the screen. Even if MAP DISPLAY OFF is set, errors will still display unless you specifically exclude them with this command.

```
    MAP INS S16:=GATEWAY2000_PROJECTS:BOOK\SCREENS
```

Uses the highest search drive number, rather than relying on a specific drive letter designation.

```
    MAP *2:=ALTOS486_SYS:WP\BOOK
```

Also uses a wildcard to set the actual drive letter, although we are assuming there is only one other mapped so far.

```
    MAP DISPLAY ON
```

Remember in the Container login script we turned MAP DISPLAY OFF, but never turned it back on? Here it is.

```
    MAP
```

Executes the MAP command, listing all configured drives for this user.

```
    WRITE
```

With no text, the WRITE command inserts a blank line on the screen. This is generally used to separate information.

```
    IF DAY_OF_WEEK="FRIDAY" THEN
```

A simple example of the IF...THEN statement, using a date variable picked up by the NetWare client software from the workstation.

```
    WRITE "Hooray!!"
```

What's to explain?

```
    FIRE PHASERS 2 TIMES
```

Makes some noise for Friday, but only IF it is Friday, or THEN go to the END statement.

```
    END
```

End of the IF...THEN structure.

```
    EXIT "NMENU WORK"
```

Stops the login script execution and runs the specified program if there is one. This example goes from the login script straight to a menu.

A Sample User Login Script

Here we have a User login script that works well with the previous Container login script. Take a look at it in graphic format in Figure 7.23, then in text with some explanations.

FIGURE 7.23

A User login script with conditional commands in NetWare Administrator

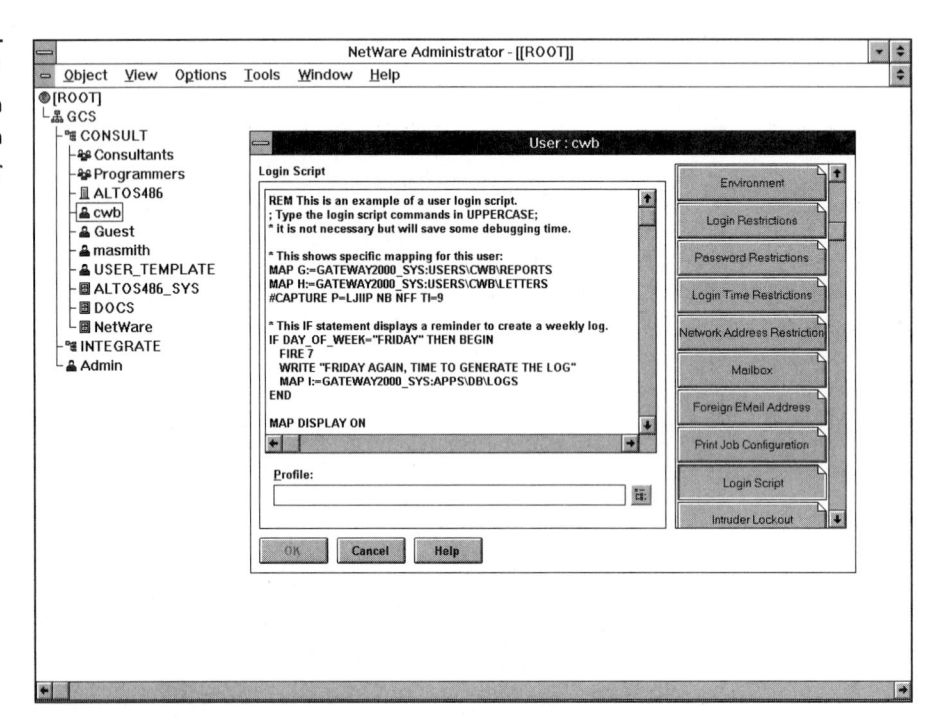

```
REM This is an example of a user login script.
; Type the login script commands in UPPERCASE;
*it is not necessary but will save some debugging time.
```

More comments, and the beginning of each line shows different ways to exclude comment lines from the login script. The line about using capital letters states a good idea. The commands themselves don't need to be in uppercase, but identifier variables must be. By getting in the habit of putting everything in uppercase except comments, you avoid a potential problem.

```
*This shows specific mapping for this user.
```

Comment line for a section of the login script.

```
MAP G:=GATEWAY2000_SYS:USERS\CWB\REPORTS
MAP H:=GATEWAY2000_SYS:USERS\CWB\LETTERS
```

Maps specific drive letters to specific directories.

```
#CAPTURE P=LJIIP NB NFF TI=9
```

Redirects all printing to the LJIIP printer.

```
*This IF statement displays a reminder to create a
  weekly log.
IF DAY_OF_WEEK="FRIDAY" THEN BEGIN
  FIRE 7
  WRITE "FRIDAY AGAIN, TIME TO GENERATE THE LOG"
  MAP I:=GATEWAY2000_SYS:APPS\DB\LOGS
END
```

This use of the IF...THEN structure is based on a variable, Friday. When DAY_OF_WEEK does equal Friday, too many phasers are fired (FIRE and FIRE PHASERS are the same command to the system) and a new drive mapping is set. On Friday, drive I: becomes available to the user in order to write the necessary log.

```
MAP DISPLAY ON
```

Turns on the map information display. If it is already on, there is no problem.

```
MAP
```

Executes the MAP command, listing all the drive mappings in place for this user.

Creating and Editing Login Scripts with NetWare Administrator

In the NetWare Administrator program, you can create or edit login scripts for containers and users. Browse down your NDS tree to find the object of your scripting endeavors. Once you've found it, open the Properties dialog box. For containers, you must press Enter or pull down the Object menu and click on Details. For profile and user login scripts, you can just double-click on the object to open the Properties dialog box.

> **7.19 IN-A-HURRY**
>
> **Create or Edit a Login Script in NetWare Administrator**
>
> 1. Open the NetWare Administrator program and click on the container, profile, or user to get the new login script or that has the login script to be modified.
> 2. Open the Properties dialog box by pressing Enter, or by double-clicking on a Profile or User object.
> 3. Click on the Login Script button.
> 4. Create or edit the login script.
> 5. Click on OK to save the script.

The Login Script button is with the other page buttons in the dialog box. If you do not find such a button, the object does not support the Login Script property. Printers and NetWare volumes, for instance, don't have login scripts.

When you click on the Login Script button, the dialog box is dominated by a text box. Type your login script, or edit the existing one, using the standard MS Windows text-editing commands and keystrokes. To copy a login script from one user to another, use MS Windows cut and paste commands.

Creating or Editing a Container Login Script

Once you have located the container needing a login script inside the NetWare Administrator program, open the Properties dialog box by pressing Enter while the container is highlighted or by pulling down the Object menu and clicking on Details. Then click on the Login Script page button to open the Login Script text box. From there, you can create a new Container login script or modify one that already exists.

Creating or Editing a Profile Login Script

The Profile login script executes after the Container login script but before the User login script. This type of script is still general, but more narrowly targeted to a smaller group of users within a larger container. Open NetWare Administrator and find the Profile object. Since this is not a container, double-clicking will open the Properties dialog box, as will pressing the Enter key. Then click on the Login Script button to open the Login Script text box. From there, you can create a new Profile login script or modify one that already exists.

If you haven't already assigned a user to the profile, continue with the following steps:

1. Select the User object, choose Details, then choose Login Script.

2. Type the name of the Profile object in the Profile field, located below the login script box.

3. Choose Profile object (use the Browse button to locate the Profile object), then Trustee of This Object, then Add Trustee.

4. Type the user's name and check the Browse and Read property rights.

5. Click on OK to save the settings.

Creating or Editing a User Login Script

Once the most used login script, the User login script has become less important in NetWare 4. It is still useful, however, and some situations can be handled only by a User login script. The main problem with individual login scripts is the time it takes to manage them in any kind of a dynamic network environment.

Open the NetWare Administrator program from either MS Windows or OS/2, and browse until you find the User object to get the login script. Open the Properties dialog box by double-clicking on the User object or by pressing Enter after the object is highlighted. You will probably need to scroll down the buttons to see the Login Script button. When you find it, click once to open the Login Script text box, then create or modify the User login script.

Creating and Editing Login Scripts with NETADMIN

Login scripts are the same, whether they are created and modified in NetWare Administrator or in NETADMIN. There are a couple of advantages to using NETADMIN, believe it or not. If you're an old NetWare hand, the login script sections of NETADMIN look and feel like the old SYSCON you grew up with.

7.20 IN-A-HURRY

Create or Modify a Login Script with NETADMIN

1. Start NETADMIN from the DOS command line.

2. Choose Manage Objects, then select the container, profile, or user to get the new login script or that has the login script to be modified. Press F10.

3. Choose View or Edit Properties of This Object, then Login Script.

4. If the login script is empty, choose whether to copy a script from an existing object. If you want to copy a script, specify the object to copy the script from (type the object name or press Insert to browse).

5. Edit the new or existing script.

6. Press F10 to save the login script.

Creating or Editing a Container Login Script

Start NETADMIN from any DOS prompt. Container login scripts are a property of the container object, meaning we must specify the container itself in NETADMIN, not the container contents. Highlight the container and press F10. Check that the Actions box has the name of the container. If so, press Enter while highlighting View or Edit Properties of This Object. Press Enter on Login Script.

If there is no login script for this container, you have the option to copy a script. If you know the object you wish to copy from, type it in. If not, press Insert to browse the NDS tree until you find a good source script. Unfortunately, there isn't a way to check the source login script during the browse process, so you'll need to know of a good script before you start. This feature doesn't exist in NetWare Administrator because the graphical interfaces support easy cut-and-paste between objects. In the DOS world of NETADMIN, that's not easy, so Novell has always had the ability to copy one script from another. But this right only exists when the login script is empty; you can't overwrite an existing script. You can, however, delete a login script and then import a new one.

Figure 7.24 shows the NETADMIN program in edit mode for a login script for the container Consult. Some of the script is out of sight. See the section titled "A Sample Container Login Script" for an explanation of each command in the example.

FIGURE 7.24

The sample Container login script in NETADMIN

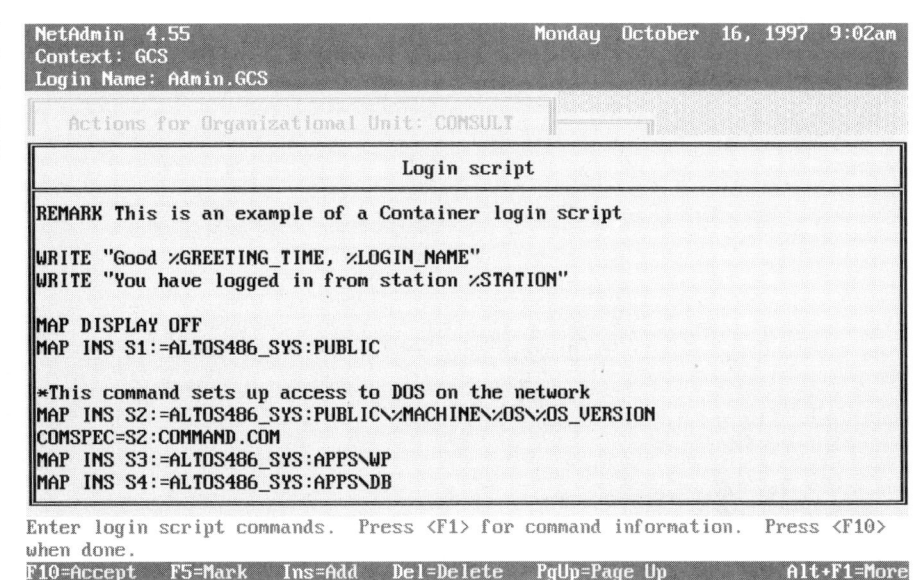

```
NetAdmin 4.55                              Monday October 16, 1997  9:02am
Context: GCS
Login Name: Admin.GCS

     Actions for Organizational Unit: CONSULT
    ┌─────────────────────────────────────────────────────────────┐
    │                       Login script                          │
    ├─────────────────────────────────────────────────────────────┤
    │REMARK This is an example of a Container login script        │
    │                                                             │
    │WRITE "Good %GREETING_TIME, %LOGIN_NAME"                     │
    │WRITE "You have logged in from station %STATION"             │
    │                                                             │
    │MAP DISPLAY OFF                                              │
    │MAP INS S1:=ALTOS486_SYS:PUBLIC                              │
    │                                                             │
    │*This command sets up access to DOS on the network           │
    │MAP INS S2:=ALTOS486_SYS:PUBLIC\%MACHINE\%OS\%OS_VERSION     │
    │COMSPEC=S2:COMMAND.COM                                       │
    │MAP INS S3:=ALTOS486_SYS:APPS\WP                             │
    │MAP INS S4:=ALTOS486_SYS:APPS\DB                             │

Enter login script commands. Press <F1> for command information. Press <F10>
when done.
F10=Accept    F5=Mark    Ins=Add    Del=Delete    PgUp=Page Up    Alt+F1=More
```

> **NOTE**
> *The examples of Container, Profile, and User login scripts in NETADMIN are the same as those in the sections that contain sample Container, Profile, and User login scripts, at the beginning of the discussion of creating and managing login scripts. The figures in those sections show the same examples in NetWare Administrator.*

Creating or Editing a Profile Login Script

The Profile login script executes after the Container login script but before the User login script. This type of script is still general, but it is more narrowly targeted to a smaller group of users within a larger container. Start NETADMIN and find the Profile that is in need of a login script or has a script that needs to be modified. Since a Profile object is a leaf object, you can browse and find it in the normal fashion without as much trouble as tagging a container object for modification. The Login Script menu choice is in the View or Edit Properties of This Object menu box. Figure 7.25 shows the sample Profile login script in NETADMIN.

Creating or Editing a User Login Script

Once the most used login script, the User login script has become less important in NetWare 4. It is still useful, however, and some situations can be handled only by a User login script. The main problem with individual login scripts is the time it takes to manage them in any kind of a dynamic network environment.

FIGURE 7.25

A sample Profile login script in NETADMIN

```
NetAdmin  4.55                          Monday  October  16, 1997  9:03am
Context: INTEGRATE.GCS
Login Name: Admin.gcs
                    Actions for Profile: HQ
┌──────────────────────────────── Login script ────────────────────────────────┐
│ MAP ERRORS OFF                                                               │
│ MAP INS S16:=GATEWAY2000_PROJECTS:BOOK\SCREENS                               │
│ MAP *2:=ALTOS486_SYS:WP\BOOK                                                 │
│ MAP DISPLAY ON                                                               │
│ MAP                                                                          │
│ WRITE                                                                        │
│ IF DAY_OF_WEEK="FRIDAY" THEN                                                 │
│ WRITE "Hooray!!"                                                             │
│ FIRE PHASERS 2 TIMES                                                         │
│ EXIT "NMENU WORK"                                                            │
│                                                                              │
└──────────────────────────────────────────────────────────────────────────────┘
Enter login script commands.  Press <F1> for command information.  Press <F10>
when done.
F10=Accept    F5=Mark   Ins=Add   Del=Delete   PgUp=Page Up       Alt+F1=More
```

Start NETADMIN and browse around until you find the User object in need of a login script or login script modifications. If there is no login script for this User object, you may copy one from another object. Figure 7.26 shows how our sample User login script looks in NETADMIN.

FIGURE 7.26

A User login script in NETADMIN

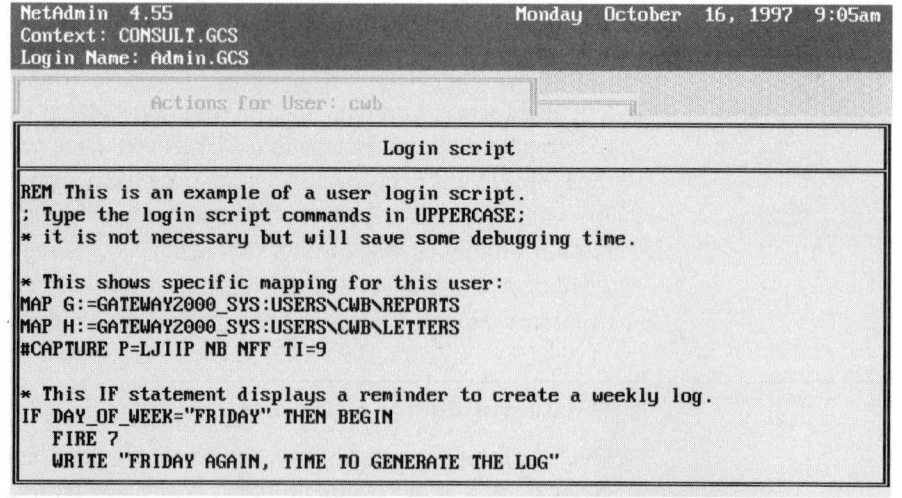

```
NetAdmin  4.55                          Monday  October  16, 1997  9:05am
Context: CONSULT.GCS
Login Name: Admin.GCS
                    Actions for User: cwb
┌──────────────────────────────── Login script ────────────────────────────────┐
│ REM This is an example of a user login script.                               │
│ ; Type the login script commands in UPPERCASE;                               │
│ * it is not necessary but will save some debugging time.                     │
│                                                                              │
│ * This shows specific mapping for this user:                                 │
│ MAP G:=GATEWAY2000_SYS:USERS\CWB\REPORTS                                     │
│ MAP H:=GATEWAY2000_SYS:USERS\CWB\LETTERS                                     │
│ #CAPTURE P=LJIIP NB NFF TI=9                                                 │
│                                                                              │
│ * This IF statement displays a reminder to create a weekly log.              │
│ IF DAY_OF_WEEK="FRIDAY" THEN BEGIN                                           │
│    FIRE 7                                                                    │
│    WRITE "FRIDAY AGAIN, TIME TO GENERATE THE LOG"                            │
└──────────────────────────────────────────────────────────────────────────────┘
Enter login script commands.  Press <F1> for command information.  Press <F10>
when done.
F10=Accept    F5=Mark   Ins=Add   Del=Delete   PgUp=Page Up       Alt+F1=More
```

Creating and Managing Menus

DOS MENUS HELP users who are not comfortable using the DOS command line. Information can be presented in layers, rather than overwhelming a user with every possible command on the screen at one time. The menu programs included with NetWare 4.1x allow you to build a menu structure that looks amazingly like FILER or NETADMIN. This can be done with any ASCII text editor and a few minutes of time.

> **NetWare and Menu Systems**
>
> NetWare has always contained a menu system as part of the package, and NetWare 4.1x is no exception. The menus in NetWare 4.1x are faster than those in previous versions and have no impact on workstation RAM. They are a subset of the Saber Menu System for DOS, one of the early add-on products for Novell NetWare that has grown and developed an entire suite of products.
>
> The use of menus has typically been limited to DOS in the past, although Saber does have a product that provides a menu structure for MS Windows users. Because DOS is waning, menus are waning as well. Icons with command structures hidden from view provide more flexibility than a straight ASCII menu system, no matter how powerful. Score another victory for the mousers.
>
> Some people (including your humble narrator) believe that a simple menu system such as NMENU could have changed the course of PC computing years ago. If IBM or Compaq had developed and standardized a simple DOS menu system, many DOS-haters would have been spared the agonizing frustration of facing a C:> prompt without the necessary training. But that's a story for another time and another book.

The New Menu of NetWare 4.1x

The operative program now is NMENU.BAT, rather than the previous version's MENU.EXE program. NMENU.BAT is located in the PUBLIC directory, so every user on the network has access. Each menu user must have

> With the proper menu settings, users can never escape and be forced to deal with the command-line interface.

Read and File Scan rights to PUBLIC, which the user will have as a matter of course. Menu users should also have a TEMP directory defined in their AUTOEXEC.BAT file or in their login script. If you like the new NMENU better than the old MENU.EXE, you're in luck. NMENU works with NetWare 2.*x*, 3.*x*, and 4.*x*. If you have a mixed operating system network, NMENU will work on all your systems.

One huge advantage of NMENU is the ability to keep users away from DOS. With the proper menu settings, users can never escape and be forced to deal with the command-line interface. Even better, if the only option to leave logs the user out of the network, there are no easy ways to violate network security. Special hot keys can be set to allow those users with experience and training to escape or exit to DOS. Without those hot keys set, the Escape key doesn't exit the menu; Ctrl+C does. The syntax to run a menu is simple:

```
NMENU filename
```

where *filename* is a written (and now compiled) menu batch file built with an ASCII text editor.

Remember the Profile login script earlier, with the line:

```
EXIT "NMENU WORK"
```

That login script moves a user directly from the login process to the menu system. This eliminates the confusion some computer users still feel when faced with a blank prompt and no hints as to where to get help.

Menu Script Commands

Menu files are made in ASCII and must be saved with an SRC extension (for SouRCe). Once the file is complete, you run the MENUMAKE program to compile the SRC file into a version of the file with the same name but new extension: DAT for DATa. The command works like this:

```
MENUMAKE WORK.SRC
```

Any subsequent changes to the original SRC file require the file to be compiled once again. There are two types of commands used in menu script files:

- Organizational commands govern the display of the menu.

- Control commands govern the actions of the menu.

Let's take a look at a sample menu. Figure 7.27 shows a menu to help the members of the PROGRAMMERS group. Notice the information on the top and bottom of the screen. These details are added automatically by the menu program. You don't need to remember to add them, but you can't modify them, either.

FIGURE 7.27

A basic DOS menu

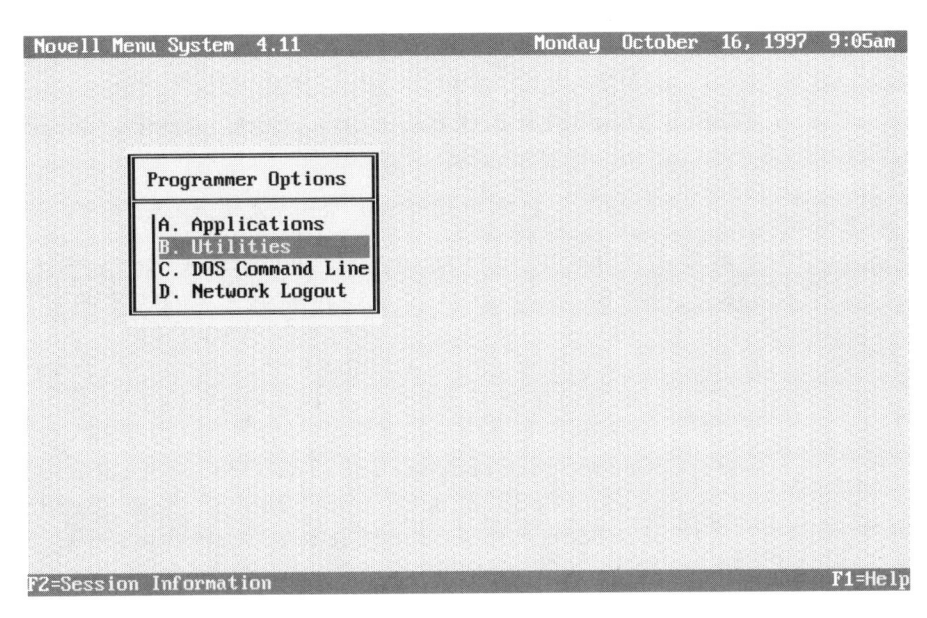

```
Novell Menu System   4.11                    Monday  October  16, 1997   9:05am


                  ┌─────────────────────────┐
                  │   Programmer Options    │
                  ├─────────────────────────┤
                  │ A. Applications         │
                  │ B. Utilities            │
                  │ C. DOS Command Line     │
                  │ D. Network Logout       │
                  └─────────────────────────┘




F2=Session Information                                                  F1=Help
```

You make your choices by highlighting a line and pressing Enter. A quicker method is to type the letter or number to the left of the line. Doing so will take you to that option immediately, without requiring a press of the Enter key. You can decide which letters or numbers are displayed, or allow NMENU to handle that detail for you.

Organizational Commands

There are only two Organizational commands, MENU and ITEM, but the ITEM command has four options.

THE MENU COMMAND The MENU command identifies the beginning of each menu screen within the menu file. Its syntax is:

```
MENU menunumber,menuname
```

You must supply a menu number and a name. The menu name becomes the title bar for the menu. There should be no spaces between the menu number and menu name, as in:

    MENU 1,MAIN MENU

Other menus can be called from within a menu, so each menu number must be unique. It's common to increase your numbering when you first write a menu by five or ten rather than using menu 1, menu 2, and so on. This leaves room to add the submenus you will create later.

THE ITEM COMMAND The ITEM command includes the text the user will see. Its syntax is:

    ITEM itemname {option option}

The menu program gives an indicator letter (A–Z) by default, but you can determine the character to precede it. Each option to be displayed in the window must be preceded by the word ITEM.

The menu items are listed in the order in which they are written. If you wish to force a character to be assigned to a menu item, type a caret (^) and the specific character before the option. Leave no spaces between the assigned character and the line item. If you specify one character, you should specify them all for that menu, since NMENU doesn't keep track of which letters are used and may duplicate a letter. An example is:

    ITEM ^Uutilities

which displays the Utilities option, with the letter U assigned to it.

The BATCH option for the ITEM command unloads the menu program from memory, freeing 32 KB of RAM. For example:

    ITEM WordPerfect 6.1 {BATCH}

Without this command, your applications will have less room to run. With this option, the CHDIR option is run automatically.

The CHDIR option returns you to your starting directory when you select an item. An example is:

    ITEM WordPerfect 6.1 {CHDIR}

The PAUSE option works like the DOS PAUSE command, stopping and displaying a "Press any key to continue" message. An example is:

    ITEM DOS Copy {PAUSE}

This does not work on multiple-screen text dumps until the last screen is displayed. To provide a page-by-page display for utilities such as DIR, use the /p option.

When a DOS command is executed with the SHOW option, the command name stays visible in the upper-left corner of the screen. An example is:

```
ITEM Copy Files {SHOW}
```

Control Commands

The Control commands perform the work of the menu system. The commands are EXEC, LOAD, SHOW, and GET*x*. The EXEC and GET*x* commands have several options.

THE EXEC COMMAND The EXEC command EXECutes command files. Application files with file names ending in EXE and COM are started in this manner. The EXEC command must be issued after the associated ITEM and any Control commands used by the ITEM. It should be indented on the line following the ITEM, as in:

```
ITEM WordPerfect 5.1 Plus for DOS
    EXEC wp
```

The EXEC command options are:

- EXEC CALL runs a batch file and returns to NMENU. For example:

    ```
    EXEC CALL UPDATE.BAT
    ```

- EXEC DOS provides temporary access to the DOS command line. Users must type EXIT at the DOS prompt to return to NMENU.

- EXEC EXIT leaves the NMENU system and puts the user at a DOS prompt.

- EXEC LOGOUT logs the user out of the network to a DOS prompt. The client files are still in memory, but the user is logged completely out of the Directory. This is important for two reasons: if you expect to reclaim your DOS memory, you must use the command names with the unload switch (LSL /u). If you have a remote printer attached, it needs the client software to remain resident so users can send their print jobs to the printer, but you don't need to be logged in for that to happen.

THE LOAD COMMAND The LOAD command starts a second NMENU program from within the first menu program. The second must be a compiled NMENU program file. The first menu goes into a hold state, with only the foreground menu active. There is no limit to the number of menus that can be loaded at one time.

THE SHOW COMMAND The SHOW *menu_number* command calls one of the submenus (up to 255 allowed) contained in a single script file. The called menu displays over the previous menu, slightly to the right. Replace *menu_number* with the number assigned to the submenu inside the main menu script file, as in:

```
SHOW 14
```

GETX The three GET*x* commands prompt for user input to be used by the menu program when you select an item. With a GET*x* command, the Enter key does not activate the command; use the F10 key as directed on the status line. Rules for GET*x* commands are as follows:

- The GET*x* command must be entered between the ITEM line and the EXEC line associated with the ITEM line.
- 100 GET commands maximum per ITEM.
- One prompt = one line.
- Up to ten prompts in each dialog box. Type a caret (^) at the beginning of each prompt that should be in its own dialog box.

The syntax is:

```
GETx instruction {prepend} length,prefill,{append}
```

where the parameters are:

instruction	Message to be displayed to user.
prepend	Data (inside braces) to be attached before the data the user types in.
length	Maximum number of characters the user is allowed to enter. The limit is 80.
prefill	A default response in the instruction field.
append	Information (in braces) appended to the end of the user input information.

The GET*x* commands are:

- GETO gets optional input from the user. For example:

  ```
  ITEM Directory Listing
     GETO Enter directory name: { } 40,, {}
     EXEC dir /p
  ```

- GETR gets required input from the user. The menu program will stop until a response is received or the user presses the Escape key to cancel the requested item. For example:

  ```
  ITEM Execute an Application {BATCH}
     GETR Enter path and application name: { } 80,, {}
     EXEC
  ```

- GETP stores input from the user as a variable for use by other menu commands. Variables are assigned %1, %2, and so on. For example:

  ```
  ITEM Copy Files {PAUSE]
     GETP Enter source: {} 80,, {}
     GETP Enter destination: {} 80,, {}
     EXEC NCOPY %1 %2
     EXEC DIR %2 /W
  ```

A Sample Menu with Explanations

How does all this look? As you saw earlier, the screen faithfully copies the look and feel of the other NetWare DOS utilities. Figure 7.27 showed the opening screen of our sample menu. Figure 7.28 shows the same menu, three layers deeper.

There are several interesting things to see here, and to relate to the menu code sample coming up. First, notice the menu placement. There is nothing you can do about that. Each menu overlaps the previous menu. Second, the colors are Novell's default DOS screen colors. They can be changed using the COLORPAL command, but it's a lot of trouble for little or no advantage. Study the COLORPAL command if you wish, but I recommend against changing the palate.

Third, on one of the submenus there are assigned characters, 1 and 2 rather than A and B. These characters are assigned for one box, but not the others. The details are in the third submenu labeled Utilities. There, specially assigned numerals are used rather than the system-assigned alpha characters.

FIGURE 7.28

Our sample menu expanded

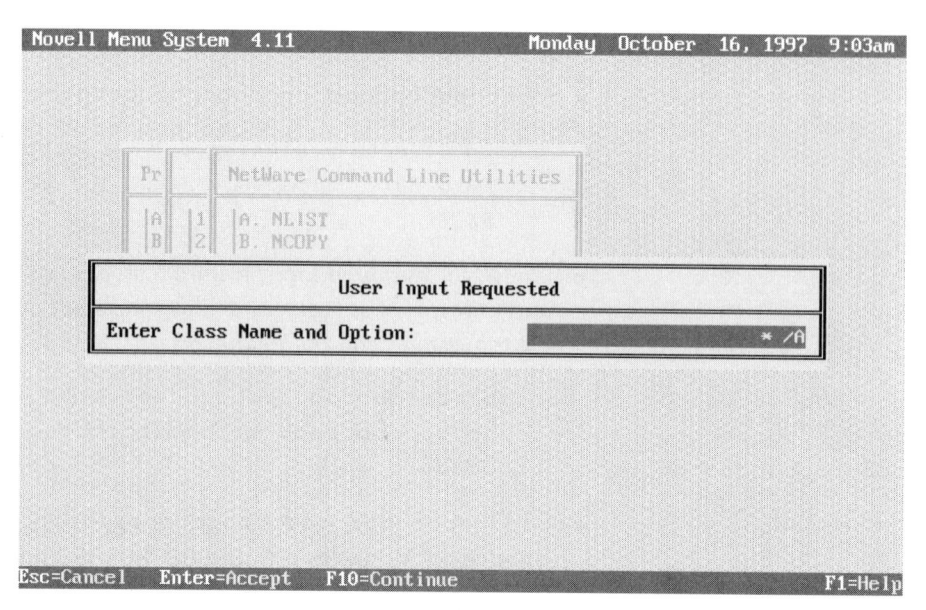

```
Novell Menu System   4.11                    Monday  October  16, 1997  9:03am

                Pr      NetWare Command Line Utilities
                |A|  |1|  |A. NLIST
                |B|  |2|  |B. NCOPY

                         User Input Requested
              Enter Class Name and Option:              * /A


Esc=Cancel    Enter=Accept    F10=Continue                          F1=Help
```

Fourth, the User Input Requested dialog box for the NLIST command is asking for user input. The default is showing in the highlighted text entry box, USER /A. If the user doesn't use the default, he or she can type the commands into the box to feed them to the NLIST command.

Here is the sample menu. Although the menu should be in one long ASCII file, I divided this into segments to provide explanations between each submenu:

```
MENU 01,Programmer Options
   ITEM Applications
      Show 05
   ITEM Utilities
      Show 10
   Item DOS Command Line
      EXEC DOS
   Item Network Logout
      EXEC LOGOUT
```

This is the main menu, the one in Figure 7.27. Look at the menu numbers: this is number 1, the next is number 5, the next 10. You have 255 total submenus available, but it's smart to group them by associated functions. If you leave some space in your numbering, your menu will read better and be easier to troubleshoot.

The last line, EXEC LOGOUT, makes this a fairly secure menu. If called from the login script, as is typical, the automatic LOGOUT command linked to the EXIT option on the menu makes sure there isn't easy access to the network from a DOS prompt.

```
MENU 05,Applications
   ITEM WordPerfect 51 Plus
      EXEC wp51
   ITEM Lotus123
      EXEC 123
   ITEM Q - Text Editor
      EXEC q
```

This is the first submenu listed in the primary menu. The execution is straightforward: EXEC wp51, EXEC 123, and so on. Replace the EXE file names of your applications (the EXE extension is not necessary, so you can say WP51 rather than WP51.EXE), and any DOS users will be able to start their applications without touching a command line.

```
MENU 10,Utilities
   ITEM ^1NetWare Menu Utilities
      SHOW 12
   ITEM ^2NetWare Command Line Utilities
      SHOW 14
```

This is the submenu with the assigned numbers for menu options rather than the system-assigned ascending characters. The SHOW commands are calling other submenus from later in the program.

```
MENU 12,NetWare Menu Utilities
   ITEM NETADMIN {BATCH}
      EXEC NETADMIN
   ITEM FILER {BATCH}
      EXEC FILER
   ITEM NETUSER {BATCH}
      EXEC NETUSER
```

The BATCH option is used to make as much memory as possible available for the NetWare utilities being called. No matter where the utilities are located on your system, when control returns to the menu, the BATCH option ensures that you will be back in your beginning directory.

```
MENU 14,NetWare Command Line Utilities
  ITEM NLIST {PAUSE}
    GETO Enter Class Name and Option: { } 25,* /A, {}
    EXEC NLIST
  ITEM NCOPY {PAUSE}
    GETR Enter Source { } 25,, {}
    GETR Enter Destination { } 25,, {}
    EXEC NCOPY %1 %2
    EXEC DIR %2 /w
  ITEM Display a MAP listing {SHOW CHDIR PAUSE}
    EXEC MAP
```

This submenu creates the dialog box requesting user input. You can get a feel for the GET*x* command function here. As you can see, it's not too difficult. As mentioned earlier, the GET*x* command must be between the ITEM and the EXEC for that ITEM.

Converting Existing Menus

This is all well and good, but what if you have invested a dozen hours in creating wonderful menus with the old MENU program? Do you need to throw them all out? Not at all.

Here's the syntax to convert old menus to new:

```
MENUCNVT old_menu_name
```

This couldn't be much easier. The MENUCNVT program converts the old MNU-extension file to a new file of the same name with the SRC extension. After conversion, the old menus must still be compiled with the MENUMAKE program.

Some network administrators may feel more comfortable with the older-style menu system. If you are one of those, feel free to develop the older MNU style of text file, and use the MENUCNVT to upgrade the menu to the NetWare 4.1*x* system. This doesn't cost you a nickel, and it lets you choose when to upgrade.

Swear Off Single Users

> *Let's get this title right: swear off, not swear at, single users.*

LET'S GET THIS title right: swear *off*, not swear *at*, single users. This slogan tells you to never, if at all possible, make changes to a single User object on your network. This has nothing to do with marriage status, but everything to do with maximum management. The work you do with a single User object will be repeated in the future. Why? If one user needs some part of his or her network access fixed, another user will need the same thing done. Maybe not today, maybe not this week, but sometime. You can bank on that.

So, if you bend this rule and make a change to user ALEX today, you will do something similar for user LAURA in the future. After a time, you'll discover you've done the same thing for users NICHOLAS, NATALIE, and BRADLEY.

One day, the fix you put in quickly "for one user" will blow up. A directory will be moved, an application will be upgraded, a printer will move to another print server, or something equally as innocent will happen. Then Alex, Laura, Nicholas, Natalie, and Bradley will all come to visit you in your office, loudly proclaiming "our network is broken."

So you'll scramble around for awhile looking for the problem. After a time, you'll remember you did something special to Alex's login script. Then you'll realize you did it to everyone's login script. Then you'll need to fix each individual login script. Then you'll swear not to do the same thing again.

Go ahead and swear that today, and avoid the trouble.

CASE STUDY

MiniCo: Handling More than One User at a Time

MINICO HAS 3 servers, 75 users, and one location.

Who Manages the Users?

CONSIDERATIONS

The questions:

- Who manages the network?
- Have full-time or part-time network management?

DECISION

Assign Alexander von Thorn (the Distribution Manager who handled setup) part-time as the lead manager, along with Jim Lewczyk (a programmer) and Scott Elyard (the Sales Manager) as part-time helpers.

EXPLANATION

MiniCo, in the person of the boss (Jack Mingo), doesn't believe its small network needs a full-time network manager. This is often a mental hurdle for smaller companies to get over. One day, the network will grow, or the company's reliance on the network will become so critical, that a part-time management crew will not be able to keep up. For the MiniCo decision-makers, it will come when they want to start using custom software to better organize their sales and distribution of books and related materials. Developing new programs means hiring new programmers, which means filling a full-time position to manage the computer part of the company. Even MiniCo has a chance to become a MediumCo, then a MegaCorp.

NetWare 4.1x Tools for Managing Users and Resources

CONSIDERATIONS

The goals:

- Design containers and groups to maximize user access to the network.
- Understand the Profile objects and the Template.

DECISION

Stick with the Simple Installation setup of containers, and look at the other options after the network is up and running.

EXPLANATION

Small companies often believe that the time spent investigating better management techniques is time wasted. Nothing could be further from the truth. In fact, undermanned

MINICO CASE STUDY, CONTINUED

companies such as MiniCo should spend the most time on training and research before a network is installed. Instead, they spend the least. That is why a small company's technician can't handle more than 50 to 100 users, while a large company regularly asks a network administrator to handle hundreds of users.

Creating and Managing Groups (Now Group Objects)

CONSIDERATIONS

The goals:

- Understand the Group object concept.
- Study the differences between the Group object and collecting users in containers.
- Designate users that will benefit more from groups than being grouped by container.
- Create appropriate Group objects and add members.

DECISION

Ignore groups and use containers and individual login scripts where containers don't work.

EXPLANATION

This is another example of short-term solutions to long-term problems. MiniCo didn't examine the value of the Group object before installation. Because the containers have been designed along the lines of the corporate divisions, some users didn't get all they needed from Container login scripts. Rather than creating a Group object to deal with those users, Alexander adjusted each user's login script individually. This will cost him some painful hours when the network expands.

Saving Time with a Template

CONSIDERATIONS

The goals:

- Examine and use the Template for users.
- Fill in the values in the Template and apply them to new users.

DECISION

Check into the Template when there is time.

EXPLANATION

Again, penny-wise but pound-foolish catches up with MiniCo. Checking out the Template takes time, and the two-week delay from installing all the interface cards himself (another one of management's "cost-saving" decisions) kept Alexander from researching other ways to catch up.

Using Login Scripts

CONSIDERATIONS

The goals:

- Examine the relationship between the four types of login scripts.
- Design login scripts for maximum coverage.
- Document the login script execution path for each container and each user within that container.

MINICO CASE STUDY, CONTINUED

DECISION

Hurry and get some users up and running with individual User login scripts.

EXPLANATION

Because of the sudden urgency to make up the time lost with the network interface cards, Alexander didn't quite understand the relationship between login scripts. The first users had individual login scripts, and then other users just copied those login scripts. Alexander thinks that soon he will have time to go back and rework the login scripts more efficiently (but since he is also the lead network manager, we know time is something he may never have again).

Creating and Managing Login Scripts

CONSIDERATIONS

The goals:

- Organize the relationships between login scripts.
- Test each login script separately and in sequence.
- Keep copies of each login script in a notebook for historical research.

DECISION

Create individual User login scripts, and plan on organizing, testing, and maintaining login scripts later.

EXPLANATION

Testing, analyzing, and organizing took too much time. Alexander thinks that later there will be some breathing room, and he will rethink and reorganize the login scripts (right!).

Creating and Managing Menus

CONSIDERATIONS

The choices:

- Use menus for the DOS users.
- Skip the DOS menu system.

DECISION

Skip the menus.

EXPLANATION

Few MiniCo users are still primarily DOS; only the accounting software hasn't been converted to MS Windows. Alexander set the login scripts for each of the Accounting department users to make the software accessible. Each user was also shown how to use the DOS NETUSER program to move around the network.

CASE STUDY

MegaCorp: Handling More than One User at a Time

MEGACORP HAS 50 servers, 2500 users, and 5 locations.

Who Manages the Users?

CONSIDERATIONS

The choices:

- Have Central IS personnel handle the network.
- Let a combination of Central IS and location IS (responsible to location management) people handle the network.
- Have Central IS personnel, including some at each location (responsible to Central IS), handle the network.

DECISION

Central IS handles the network, including some IS people stationed at each location.

EXPLANATION

MegaCorp realizes that computers run their company, second in importance only to the people themselves. A strong, centralized management staff makes the final decisions. Location managers don't always like the fact that the IS technicians on-site don't report to them, but the decision was made long ago.

In order to show appreciation for the location management and power users, Central IS holds a "Tech Fair" every six months. Location management chooses the power users from each site sent to HQ for a week of vendor demonstrations and training. When they return, these power users assist the IS technicians in implementation and strategic planning.

This combination of centralized planning but strong reliance on local resources has stopped any resentment from the locations towards HQ IS. Some companies aren't so lucky (or smart), and much time and money are wasted as managers of remote locations look for ways to thwart and embarrass IS personnel.

NetWare 4.1x Tools for Managing Users and Resources

CONSIDERATIONS

The goals:

- Understand and take advantage of Organizations, Organizational Units, and user groups.
- Investigate Profile objects and the Template for new objects.
- Design several network diagrams with different arrangements until one proves to be the best.

MEGACORP CASE STUDY, CONTINUED

DECISION

Design, study, research, and verify. Then install.

EXPLANATION

Large companies understand the cost of doing things right the first time. If you don't have the time or money to make something right at first, how are you going to find the time and money to redo it?

MegaCorp used its team of network administrators as guinea pigs in the pilot network, and called in power users from each location during the company's Tech Fair. The feedback from users at all levels prompted the Central IS group to reexamine the network design before installation strategy was decided.

Creating and Managing Groups (Now Group Objects)

CONSIDERATIONS

The goals:

- Understand the Group object concept.
- Study the differences between the Group object and collecting users in containers.
- Designate users that will benefit more from groups than being grouped by container.
- Create appropriate Group objects and add members.

DECISION

Create Group objects and group users as necessary when the Container login scripts don't provide all the connection needs.

EXPLANATION

Central IS set a hard rule: no individual User login scripts, period. This edict had a great impact on the handling of Group objects.

Many users were placed in various Group objects. Some groups are for applications use, some groups are for access to certain volumes, and some are based on specialized print needs. Use of Group objects allowed MegaCorp to control 2500 users without a single individual login script.

Saving Time with a Template

CONSIDERATIONS

The goals:

- Examine the Template for new objects.
- Plan the Template values for each container.
- Implement the Template for each new user.

DECISION

Take advantage of the time-savings offered by the Template.

EXPLANATION

Again, being faced with a lot of work forces one to find the quickest possible means to

MEGACORP CASE STUDY, CONTINUED

finish that work. For each user created, at least a few values were supplied by the Template.

Using Login Scripts

CONSIDERATIONS

The goals:

- Examine the relationship between the four types of login scripts.
- Design login scripts for maximum coverage.
- Document the login script execution path for each container and user within that container.

DECISION

Make every trustee assignment possible within the Container login scripts.

EXPLANATION

Following the Central IS rule of not using any individual login scripts at all required some convoluted Container login scripts at times, with multiple "IF MEMBER OF GROUP…" statements, but the philosophy at work was important.

No single user was to have special treatment, including the login script treatment. Whenever users seemed to require something special like this, IS management forced the technicians to create Group objects and rethink and rework Container login scripts.

Creating and Managing Login Scripts

CONSIDERATIONS

The goals:

- Organize the relationships between login scripts.
- Test each login script separately and in sequence.
- Keep copies of each login script in a notebook for historical research.

DECISION

Put everything possible in the highest Container login script possible, and track the history of each login script.

EXPLANATION

Details like printers and volume assignments are perfect for Organization Container login scripts. Each narrower requirement is answered in lower (Organizational Unit) Container login scripts.

Every login script iteration is kept in a log book. Historical login scripts are often helpful in tracking the growth of the network, or as troubleshooting tools when things go wrong over time. MegaCorp keeps copies of everything, and its WAN allows constant checking from Central IS to verify login scripts are working as they should.

MEGACORP CASE STUDY, CONTINUED

Creating and Managing Menus

CONSIDERATIONS

The choices:

- Use menus for the DOS users.
- Skip the DOS menu system.

DECISION

Not to use the DOS menu system.

EXPLANATION

The only DOS machines left on users' desks are those for special control and manufacturing functions. They have no need for a menu system, since they are dedicated to their function.

Arranging Network Printing

CHAPTER 8

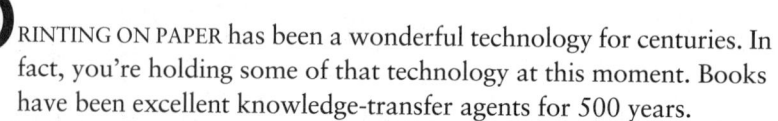

PRINTING ON PAPER has been a wonderful technology for centuries. In fact, you're holding some of that technology at this moment. Books have been excellent knowledge-transfer agents for 500 years.

Today, however, newer technologies highlight the disadvantages of printing on paper as the primary way to transmit information. Change is nearly impossible on paper; the contents of this book can be changed only with great difficulty, and no changes will be reflected in existing copies of the book. It's likely that some of the data in the report you received yesterday has already changed, but the printed copy of the report you have has remained the same. Business assumptions you make tomorrow based on that report may be mistaken. Even worse, when you check your paper files, you'll probably find several copies of the same report, all with slightly different information. Which copy is correct? Does this copy match the report your co-workers are using for their assumptions?

Even when you receive accurate printed information, the printed paper format makes it difficult to use the information. Most computer applications today allow you to share data between different files. Developing standards such as the OLE (Object Linking and Embedding) and OpenDOC technologies makes it possible to view a memo that contains graphs that change based on the current information. When you print that memo and graph, however, the information is locked and won't ever be accurate again.

Some people object more to paper printing because of the waste. Companies today discard tons of used paper every month. The idea of leveling a forest to turn trees into quickly discarded paper seems ridiculous.

Your users will complain more about printing than any other single network component. If you are new to the network administration game, you will soon hate paper because of the hassles printing causes you.

Whatever your personal reasons, limiting printing will save your company time and money. In the dynamic swirl of information, paper has been left behind. The less your company relies on paper to transfer knowledge, the stronger that knowledge will become.

However, since we're stuck with all this printing, we might as well do it right. NetWare 4.1x offers several advantages over earlier NetWare versions in the setup and control of the printing process. First, let's all agree on how the network printing process works in general, then we'll get to setting up and managing NetWare 4.1x printing in particular. This chapter covers the print objects and properties. The client side of printing is covered in Chapter 12.

NetWare Printing System Overview

EARLY PCS PRINTED to an attached printer containing little or no intelligence. The printer was often a small Epson dot-matrix unit, connected to the PC by a 10-foot cable. A diagram of this relationship is simple and uncluttered. Figure 8.1 re-creates the scene on many corporate desks in the early 1980s.

FIGURE 8.1
Printing the old way

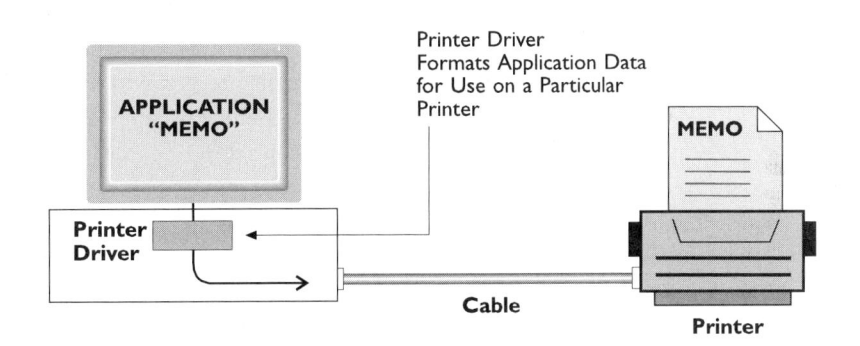

The components of this process are straightforward:

1. An application sends data (print stream) through the print driver to the designated printer.

2. The PC directs the print stream to the printer port.

3. A printer cable carries the print stream (now formatted by the driver) to the printer.

4. The printer puts characters on paper and responds to the PC indicating when the print stream may continue.

5. The printer cable carries the acknowledgment and request for more data to the PC.

6. The PC directs the request to the application.

7. Repeat the process.

This may look overly complicated for a single PC connected to a single printer, but even simple processes often require complicated underpinnings. Some details that may not be clear in the diagram and notes also impact the user sitting at this PC. For instance, notice there is a direct connection between the printer and the application. The application sends data through the printer driver and must wait for the printer to request more data. Printer cache buffers were tiny in the old days, so the application would patiently wait for each request for more data until all the print stream had been delivered to the printer. Unfortunately, the user was staring at a screen that flashed "Wait Wait Wait" or "Printing Printing Printing." Both meant the same thing.

Several things happened over the space of two or three years. First, people forgot how much time the PC saved them and grew impatient with the slow printing process. The printers were slow, the applications were slow, and the PC was useless until the print process was finished.

This was solved with stand-alone print spoolers, little devices that contained memory (sometimes as much as 256 KB!) that sat between the PC and the printer. The application would send the print stream, and the print buffer would accept it all quickly and tell the PC application everything was printed. Then the buffer would wait for the slow printer to finish printing. But the user could go back to work.

Print buffers helped, but each person still had his or her own printer, which was expensive. Worse, the printers were often dot-matrix printers, which produced crude characters and lots of noise. The loud BZZZZZZ of tiny pins hitting paper still send chills up my spine.

Laser printers appeared, and changed the world of printing forever. The quality was a thousand-fold better than the dot-matrix printers, but laser printers were expensive. Companies couldn't justify spending many thousands of dollars per PC to add laser printers for everyone.

The push to share laser printers probably has more to do with the growth of Novell than any other single factor. Thousands and thousands of networks were cost-justified by sharing one or two laser printers among the members of a workgroup.

> *The loud BZZZZZZ of tiny pins hitting paper still send chills up my spine.*

NetWare Printing System Overview

NetWare handles the printing today so that it can be routed through the network. Figure 8.2 shows our previous application's print stream reaching the printer through the network.

The components of this process are a bit more involved. First, at the workstation:

- The application generates print output "Memo" to print driver.

- The CAPTURE.EXE program checks destination: local or network printer?

- If local, CAPTURE ignores the print stream and it goes to the local printer.

FIGURE 8.2

Printing the NetWare way

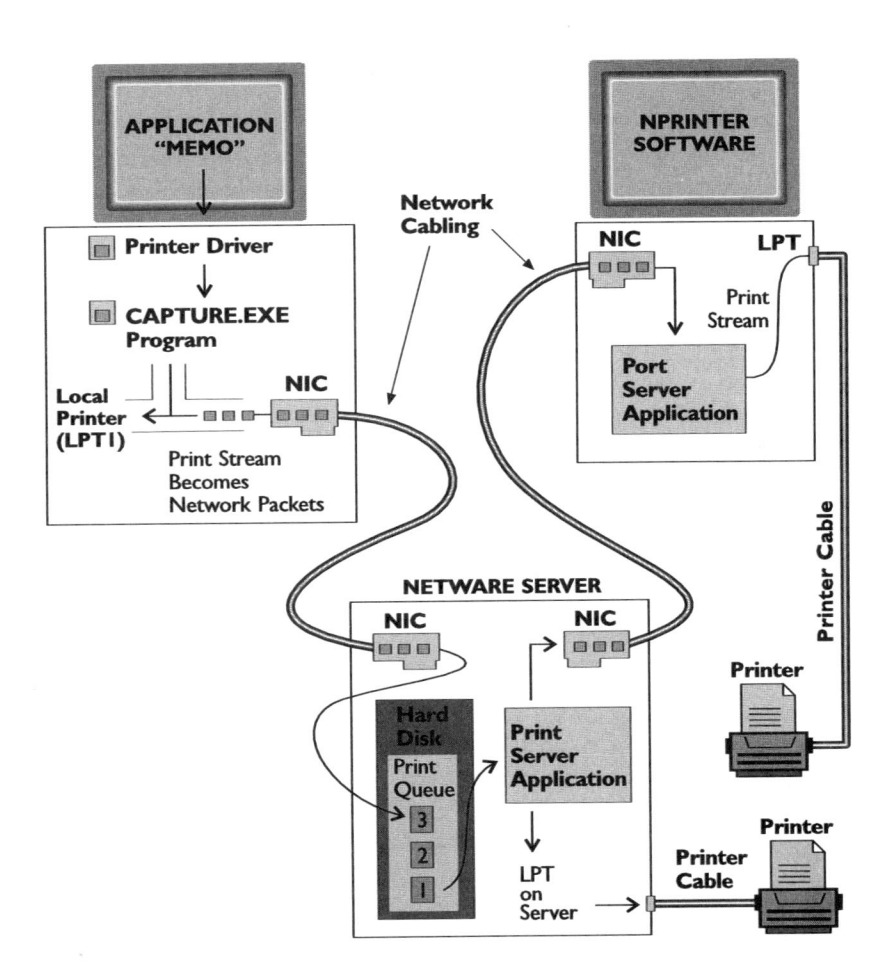

- If network, CAPTURE converts the print stream into packets the network understands.

- The network interface card addresses the packets and transfers them to the network cabling system.

- If an existing file is being printed with NPRINT, the CAPTURE program is bypassed and NPRINT feeds the print stream to the network card.

Some applications are network-savvy and print directly to the network client software. Most applications still have a default of printing to a locally attached printer. For these packages, the NetWare client software program CAPTURE redirects the print stream from the local printer port to the network. MS Windows clients can set the default printer to a network printer without using the CAPTURE program, but the effect is the same: The application doesn't know about the network printer; only the client does.

CAPTURE works by intercepting the print stream for particular printer ports and converting that print stream into packets that can travel over the network. These packets are sent to the network interface card, which addresses them to the server running the print server software. (We'll set up the client side of the print process in Chapter 12.)

If the printer port addressed by the application is still a local port, not controlled by CAPTURE, the NetWare software stays out of the way. It's possible to reference two printers in many applications and in MS Windows. Making one printer local and one printer available through the network is no problem.

The network cabling transports the print stream (now converted into data packets) across the wire to the file server running the print server software. The specific print server is referenced when the CAPTURE program is started, although the information may be changed by the user at any time. There is no practical limit on how many clients can feed print jobs to a print server. It's not limited to the number of concurrent licenses allowed by the file server software. Any NetWare client can send a print job to any NetWare print server.

The NPRINT.EXE DOS command-line program bypasses the decision process of whether the printer port is local or remote. In fact, NPRINT doesn't reference a printer port at all, just a network printer or print queue. If NPRINT is used, the process after it gets to the network card in the client workstation is the same as for the CAPTURE program.

Once the print stream (now split into data packets) leaves the workstation:

- The packets travel across the network cabling to the addressed file server hosting the print server software PSERVER.NLM.

- The server strips the addressing information from each packet and saves the print stream as a file on the server hard disk.

- When the last packet of the print stream is received, the application and the user running it are able to go back to work.

- The file is closed and the file name (assigned by NetWare) is fed into the queue with any other waiting print jobs.

- When the queue is empty (or sooner if the priority level for this print job is higher than the priority of the other waiting jobs) the file is transferred to the control of the print server.

- If the specified printer is locally attached to the file server, the print server software and the printer negotiate concerning forms and availability, and printing starts.

- If the specified printer is attached to a remote print server or to a workstation running the NPRINTER.EXE software, the print server passes the print job to the network card.

- The network card puts the print stream in packets, addresses them, and sends the packets on their way.

Once the print stream (once again split into data packets) reaches the remote workstation supporting the remote printer, these final steps happen:

- The network card strips the address information from the packets and passes them to the NPRINTER software.

- The port server software included in NPRINTER reassembles the print stream from the packets and initializes the printer port.

- NPRINTER negotiates with the locally attached printer. If it is printing in the background, time slicing is used to avoid disturbing the primary application.

This sounds much more convoluted than it seems to the users if everything is working properly. The users neither know nor care what happens underneath the surface. All they want is for their printouts to appear more quickly.

Being careful, the Novell manuals often include remote links and routers in their printing diagrams to emphasize NetWare's global reach. Nothing stops your printing setup from looking like that, of course. But no company today can get away with forcing users to traverse much distance when looking for their printouts. In the old days, mainframe users often went from one building to another in search of their paper. Huge printouts were stacked by the operations staff in cubbyholes waiting for the departmental wheelbarrow (okay, cart) to come and fetch paper by the dozens of pounds.

Today, an employee forced to walk more then five cubicles away for a printout might file a labor grievance. Users want fast printers close by. People will walk the length of the building for the fax machine without complaining, but they've been spoiled by personal printers. Most network users prefer a laser printer beside their desk, and will put up with a walk to the next cubicle for the color laser.

Many companies are working to make printing faster and easier. NetWare 4.1*x* includes a new version of NPRINTER that is considerably faster than previous versions. The client software for Windows 95 stations takes advantage of Microsoft's pseudo-multitasking for quicker printing. Third-party vendors make print server boxes that attach directly to the network cabling and eliminate the need for a PC running the NPRINTER software. These print servers cost less than a PC and speed up printing. Some print servers plug directly into the printer, and some need a printer cable to connect the printer and the network.

> *In NetWare 4.1x, print servers can control up to 255 printers, so there's less need for a print server on every server. Multiple print servers can exist in one container, but normally there aren't many print servers in a single container.*

Even though things are better than they were, printing will still be your largest network hassle. As you can tell from Figure 8.2, there are plenty of software and hardware pieces that must mesh together for printing to work properly. Any slip in any part of the journey may send your print job to the print job burial ground. Even though many print problems will have nothing to do with the network (how does the network know a person sent data to a printer without the right fonts?), you, as the network administrator, will be called upon to make things work again.

The NetWare 4.1x Printing System Relationships

AS WE SAW earlier with User objects, there are lots of properties we can set for each object in NetWare, but there are just a few critical properties that must be defined before the objects will work. For the print system, the following are mandatory:

- Print Queue object: Name and Volume properties
- Printer object: Print Queue(s), Port, Interrupt, Location, Printer Type, and Name properties
- Print Server object: Name and Printer properties

These few mandatory properties are easy to define, and it's easy to understand the need for each of them. The interdependencies of printing in NetWare 4.1x are a little different than in earlier versions of NetWare. This is because the Print object and Print Queue object are two separate entities in NetWare 4.1x. In earlier NetWare versions, the printer was just an extension of the print queue.

The three print system objects' mandatory values relate this way:

- Print Server object must know the name of the Printer object.
- Printer object must know the name of the Print Queue object.

All three pieces of the printing system must be created as objects inside NDS before any printing can happen. The Name property of a Print Queue object is added to a Printer object's Print Queue list to identify the print queue servicing the printer. The Name property of a Printer object is added to a Print Server object's Printer list to establish that the printer is servicing that print server.

Lost in all this "virtual" talk is the necessity of physically connecting the printer to the network in some manner. There are three ways to do this:

- A network-attached printer, plugged into the network cabling system directly
- A server-attached printer, connected by serial or parallel port to a file server
- A workstation-attached printer, connected by serial or parallel port to a workstation

There is nothing new in these physical methods of connecting printers. However, larger networks and smarter printers make the choice of a network-attached printer more practical for more networks today than ever before. Printers with their own network connection provide, by far, the best performance.

NetWare 4.1*x* can control NetWare 3.*x* printers and print queues through the NetSync utility. Information about NetSync is in Chapter 10, where we talk about administrator duties and tools.

Using Quick Setup in PCONSOLE

IF SETTING UP the printing system has been a problem for you in earlier versions of NetWare, you will love Quick Setup.

> **NOTE** *This feature is not available in NetWare Administrator for NetWare 4.10, although all the other PCONSOLE features are duplicated in that Windows 3.1x administration program. However, NetWare Administrator for NetWare 4.11 does include Quick Setup, as you'll see in the next section. The DOS-based NETADMIN program doesn't handle any printing operations.*

When you use PCONSOLE's Quick Setup feature, all objects are placed in the same context, and a new Print Server object is created in each context. The limitations of Quick Setup are that you can't use it to modify existing objects, and not all the properties of the new objects can be edited.

Figure 8.3 shows the PCONSOLE main screen, with the new Quick Setup option highlighted. Take a quick look before we start Quick Setup.

Defining the Print Objects

Four steps are involved in using PCONSOLE's Quick Setup option. Actually, there are only three steps if the defaults are fine, and they usually are (which is why they're the defaults).

As the Admin user or equivalent, start the PCONSOLE program from a DOS prompt. If you start the program while in the context in which you plan to create the printer, you can go directly to Quick Setup. If not, the Change

FIGURE 8.3

Preparing to zip through printer setup

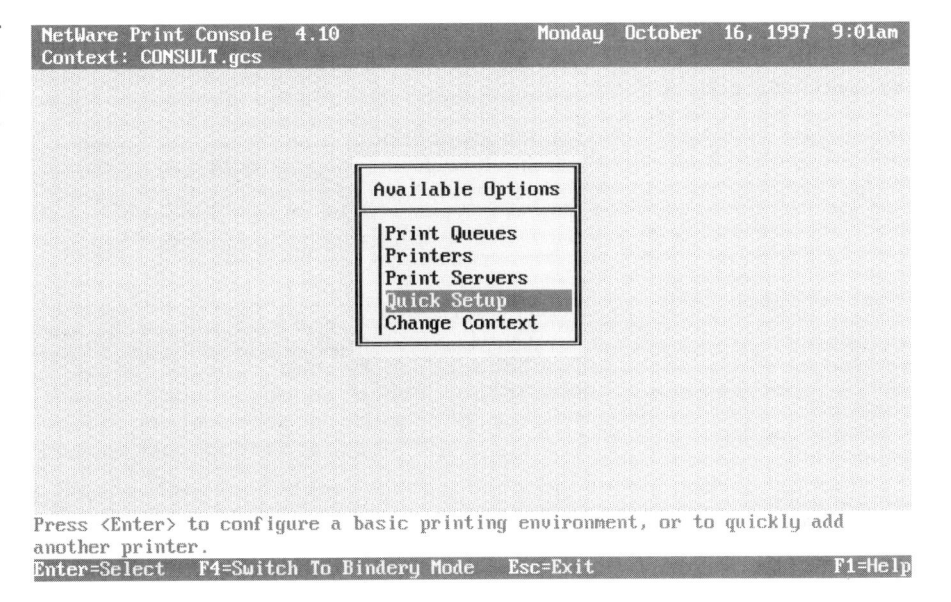

```
NetWare Print Console  4.10                Monday  October  16, 1997  9:01am
Context: CONSULT.gcs




                              ┌─────────────────────┐
                              │  Available Options  │
                              ├─────────────────────┤
                              │ Print Queues        │
                              │ Printers            │
                              │ Print Servers       │
                              │ Quick Setup         │
                              │ Change Context      │
                              └─────────────────────┘






Press <Enter> to configure a basic printing environment, or to quickly add
another printer.
Enter=Select   F4=Switch To Bindery Mode   Esc=Exit              F1=Help
```

8.1 IN-A-HURRY

Define New Print Objects with PCONSOLE's Quick Setup

1. Start PCONSOLE from the DOS prompt in the context you wish to create the print objects.

2. Choose Quick Setup (highlight it and press Enter).

3. Change any defaults.

4. Press F10 to save the settings.

Context option at the bottom of the PCONSOLE menu list opens an NDS browser (the same one as used in NETADMIN). Notice in Figure 8.3 that the upper-left corner of the screen tells us the program (NetWare Print Console 4.10) and the context (Context: CONSULT.gcs).

Highlight the Quick Setup choice and press Enter. If you type Q, the highlight bar will jump to Quick Setup. Otherwise, use the cursor keys. The screen shown in Figure 8.4 will appear.

540 Chapter 8 • Arranging Network Printing

FIGURE 8.4
Quick Setup defaults

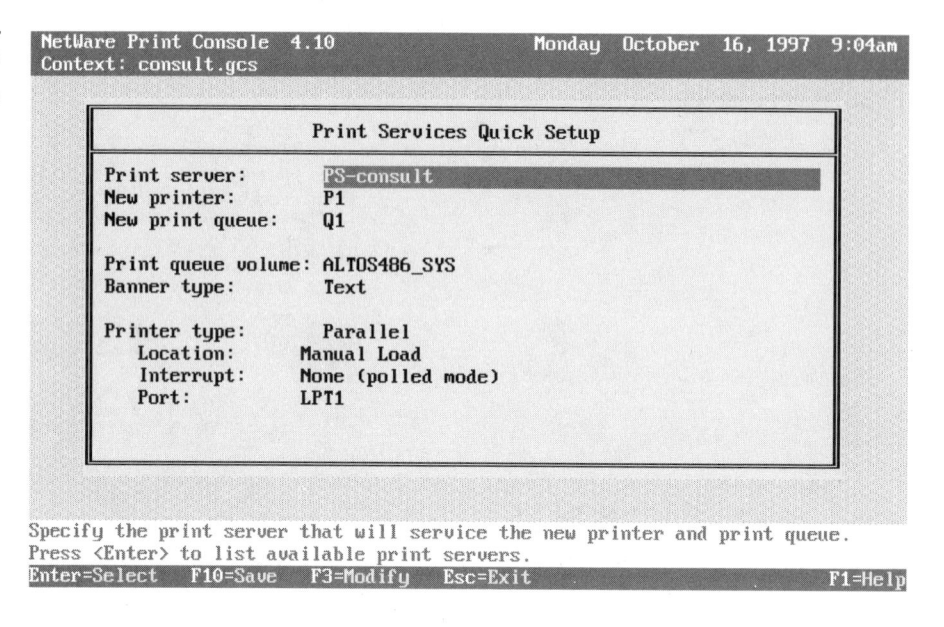

```
NetWare Print Console  4.10                   Monday  October  16, 1997  9:04am
Context: consult.gcs

                        ┌─────────────────────────────────────────────┐
                        │         Print Services Quick Setup          │
                        │                                             │
                        │   Print server:      PS-consult             │
                        │   New printer:       P1                     │
                        │   New print queue:   Q1                     │
                        │                                             │
                        │   Print queue volume: ALTOS486_SYS          │
                        │   Banner type:        Text                  │
                        │                                             │
                        │   Printer type:       Parallel              │
                        │      Location:        Manual Load           │
                        │      Interrupt:       None (polled mode)    │
                        │      Port:            LPT1                  │
                        │                                             │
                        └─────────────────────────────────────────────┘

Specify the print server that will service the new printer and print queue.
Press <Enter> to list available print servers.
Enter=Select    F10=Save    F3=Modify    Esc=Exit                       F1=Help
```

Generic printer setup at your service. If these values are acceptable, you can press F10 now and be finished. Be careful about pressing Escape to back out, because the default is to exit and save the changes, which is exactly opposite of what I would expect when using the Escape key. If these values need tweaking, you may do that now or later.

Reviewing the Quick Setup Defaults

The Print Server, New Printer, and New Print Queue fields are filled in automatically. The default names are based on whether these are the first print objects that have been created in this context. If you wish to change these names to something more descriptive, now is a good time to do so. Keep in mind the restrictions for naming objects, especially objects that may be referenced by NetWare 3.*x* clients or servers. Short names keep you out of trouble.

If there is an existing print server, that name will be placed in the appropriate field. If there are several, you may choose the one you wish by pressing the Enter key and picking the desired Print Server object from the pop-up list that appears.

There are two other values that may need specific attention at this point. The first field to think about is Print Queue Volume, which is set to ALTOS486_SYS in Figure 8.4.

This question never came up in earlier versions of NetWare. The print queues have always been on the SYS: volume, no matter how many volumes your server had. This led to problems at times, since print queues can overrun the space allotted to them. If that volume is SYS:, bad things may happen, such as your server shutting down. When there is no open disk space on the SYS: volume, the operating system loses its mind.

With NetWare 4.1*x*, you have a choice of placing the printer queues on any volume you wish. This will not stop print queues from clogging up now and then and overflowing (sounds like a sink, doesn't it?). But when they do overrun the available disk space, the volume that shuts down won't be SYS:. Your network will continue to operate, and you can fix the print queue problem without the added pressure of trying to restart the file server operating system with a full SYS: volume.

In our example, ALTOS486 has only one hard disk volume; two of the three volumes are CD-ROM drives. Since I've always put print queues on SYS:, I'm not as paranoid about this as about some things. If your network must be up every minute possible, however, the placement of the print queues is just one small detail to consider. Moving the print queues off of the SYS: volume can save you a network crash, and it's worth the move for that reason.

The second item you may want to change is the Location field under the Printer Type heading. By default, the printer is loaded manually. If this printer is attached directly to a file server, you can change to Auto Load, so the printer is loaded automatically when the server starts. This is handy, and is encouraged if you do have the printer hanging directly from the server, which is slightly discouraged.

We will discuss all the other fields that are configurable in the next section. The defaults will work for the majority of users. If you're not sure if they'll work, this is an easy way to set them and see if any modifications are necessary.

Saving the Setup

Once you have made your peace with the defaults or changed those that bother you, press F10 to save the setup. The screen in Figure 8.5 appears, displaying a message requesting patience. The creation process won't really take 60 seconds, unless your network is huge or you're setting up a Printer object for a remote context.

Once this is finished, all users in the context with the new Printer, Print Queue, and Print Server objects will have the rights to use them. Users outside the context of the Printer object must be granted the rights to use your new setup. This comes later.

FIGURE 8.5

Patience (just a little)

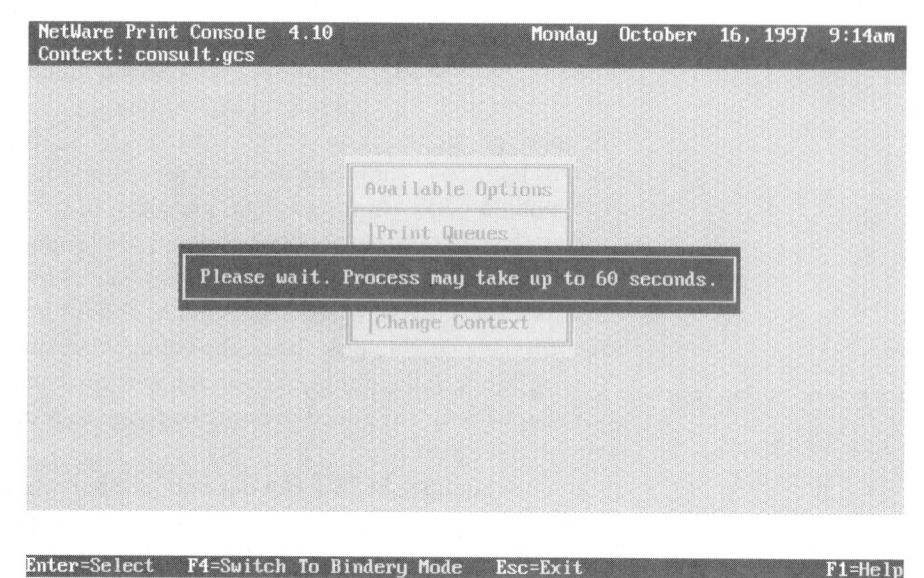

```
NetWare Print Console  4.10                    Monday  October  16, 1997  9:14am
Context: consult.gcs


                              Available Options
                              Print Queues
                    Please wait. Process may take up to 60 seconds.
                              Change Context



Enter=Select   F4=Switch To Bindery Mode   Esc=Exit              F1=Help
```

Next come the details of re-creating all the Quick Setup work through the NetWare Administrator program. These sections also explain many of the choices we accepted as defaults in Quick Setup.

Setting Up and Managing Your Print System with NetWare Administrator

NETWARE ADMINISTRATOR CONTROLS the printing system in exactly the same manner it controls all other system objects. Printer objects, Print Queue objects, and Print Server objects are all objects, and they are treated as such in NetWare Administrator. You can use NetWare Administrator to set up and manage each print system object.

> **NOTE:** *Speaking of NetWare Administrator, I would like to say something nice about the use of a GUI for administration. Although I'm a long-time DOS user and fan of SYSCON, the combination of functions and presentation in NetWare Administrator is far better than I imagined. Those of you who "grew up" on SYSCON and PCONSOLE may not believe it, but NetWare Administrator will convert you so well you won't ever go back to the traditional NetWare DOS utilities. At least I'm converted, and I'm betting you will be as well before this book is through.*

Using Quick Setup in NetWare Administrator

> **8.2 IN-A-HURRY**
>
> **Define New Print Objects with NetWare Administrator's Quick Setup**
>
> 1. Open NetWare Administrator and highlight the container for the new printer and print queue.
> 2. Click on the Tools menu, and then click on Print Services Quick Setup.
> 3. Change any defaults.
> 4. Click on OK to save the settings.

Here we are, staring at another improvement in NetWare 4.11 over NetWare 4.10. The inclusion of the Quick Setup option in NetWare Administrator is another example of DOS administration tools being moved to a graphical interface. Of course, the overhead of the graphical administration program takes longer to perform the same function as the DOS program, but we're not supposed to notice that.

There really aren't many differences between the graphical version of Quick Setup in NetWare Administrator and the DOS version in PCONSOLE. As you can see in Figure 8.6, the NetWare Administrator version includes more Print Queue details than the PCONSOLE version.

This time, I set the print queue up on a different volume. The network has mutated a bit over time, and now most of the systems and users have migrated over to the GASKIN tree. I picked the GATEWAY2000-1 system to hold the volume, although any volume would work.

FIGURE 8.6

New look, but same Quick Setup details

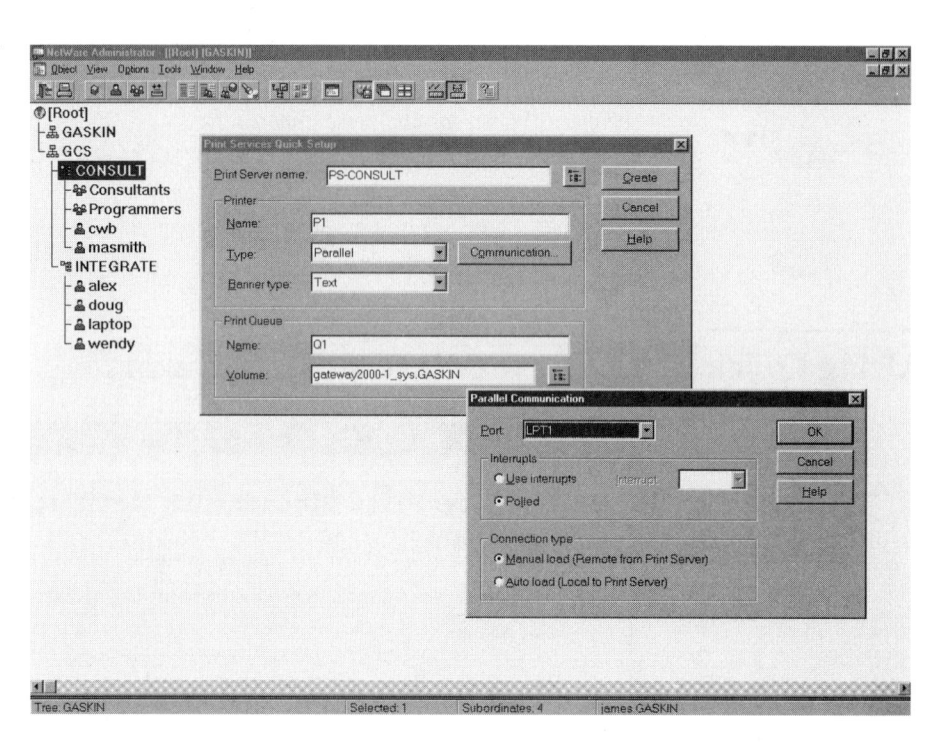

After making your selected container the active container, click on Tools in the NetWare Administrator menu bar. The last option on the Tools menu is Print Services Quick Setup, with the Q underlined for the mouse-impaired. Clicking on this final menu selection of the list opens the primary Print Services Quick Setup dialog box that you see in Figure 8.6.

The second dialog box open, titled Parallel Communication, was called by clicking on the Communication command button in the first dialog box. Novell programmers felt the need to put the queue information in the primary dialog box, leaving out the communication details provided by the PCONSOLE version of Quick Setup. By looking at the second dialog box, you can see that the defaults for the printers are the same in both versions of Quick Setup.

> **NOTE**
>
> *Figure 8.6 may be the first Windows 95 NetWare Administrator screen shown thus far in the book. We'll go into considerable detail in Chapter 10 about the minor differences in the new administration program that ships with NetWare 4.11. Here, however, you can tell that the program has evolved, but hasn't taken a giant leap forward.*

Creating the Print Queue Object with NetWare Administrator

> **8.3 IN-A-HURRY**
>
> **Create a Print Queue Object**
>
> 1. Open NetWare Administrator and highlight the container for the new Print Queue object.
> 2. Press Insert to open the New Object dialog box and choose Print Queue (highlight it and press Enter).
> 3. Keep the Print Queue object as a Directory Service Queue or click on Reference a Bindery Queue.
> 4. Provide a name for the Print Queue object.
> 5. Supply a name for Print Queue Volume (type it or click on the Browser button to select a volume).
> 6. Click on Create to exit the dialog box and create the Print Queue object.

As always, these administration chores should be performed by either the Admin user or equivalent. If you prefer (as I often do), a user with security equivalence to Admin (or with supervisory authority in the container) will work just as well for all NetWare administrative activities.

After logging in as an appropriate user, start NetWare Administrator. Open the NDS tree and highlight the container that will be the context for your new Print Queue object. Press the Insert key to open the New Object dialog box. Your screen should approximate the one shown in Figure 8.7, depending on your screen resolution, the size of your NDS tree, and whether you have the three-dimensional interface look that comes with Windows 95. The New Object dialog box shows your container in the upper-left corner. Currently highlighted is the Print Server option. Our goal now is Print Queue, the option above the highlight bar. Choosing this option opens the Create Print Queue dialog box, which is a typical dialog box for creating a new object.

Fill in all fields by clicking, typing, or browsing. The first two choices at the top of the dialog box offer a choice of making this Print Queue object a Directory Service Queue or a Bindery Queue, for NetWare 3.*x*. The default is Directory Service

FIGURE 8.7

Preparing to produce the printing system

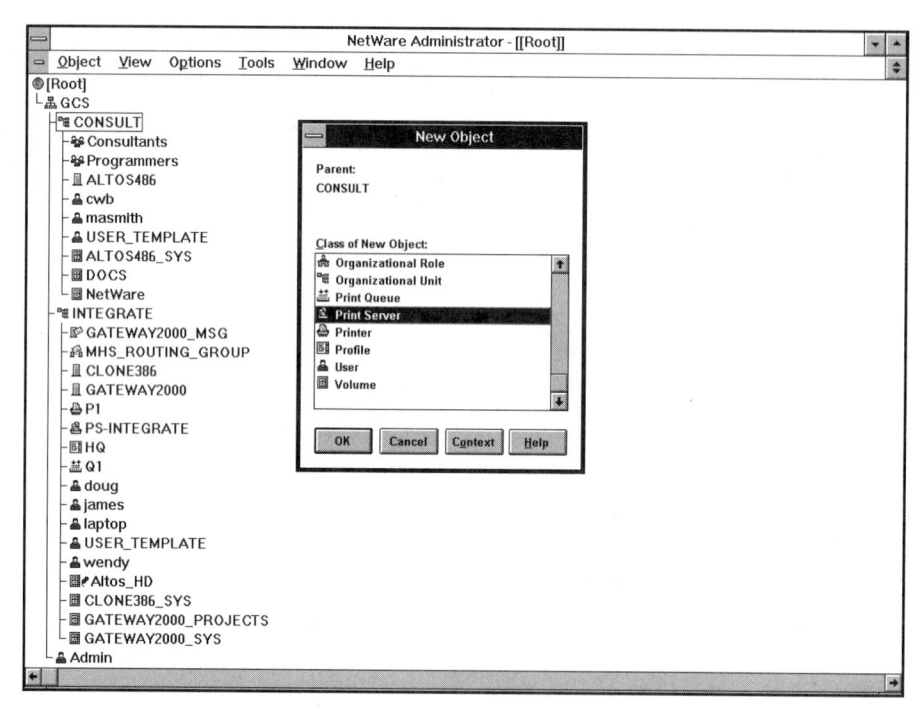

Queue, and the setting should stay that way for all new queues created inside NDS, unless you must support NetWare 3.*x* printing devices.

The Print Queue Name field is mandatory. In Quick Setup, the name created was Q1, so I used that same name (our previous Quick Setup information has been deleted). The name must be unique for the context. If the earlier Print Queue object still existed, another name would be necessary. Keep in mind the restrictions for naming objects, especially objects that may be referenced by NetWare 3.*x* clients or servers.

The Print Queue Volume field must be filled in as well. You can type the volume name, but it's easier to click on the Browser button (the button at the right end of the field), which pops open the Select Object dialog box. In Figure 8.8, the dialog box shows the applicable objects in our current context, CONSULT.GCS.

This shows an important point: The Print Queue object for CONSULT.GCS can exist on a volume in another context if necessary. The right side of the Select Object dialog box has a Directory Context window, showing the volumes in our current context. You can click on the up arrow and search for other volumes on the network. When the Volume object you want shows in the

FIGURE 8.8

Configuring our new Print Queue object

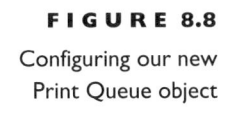

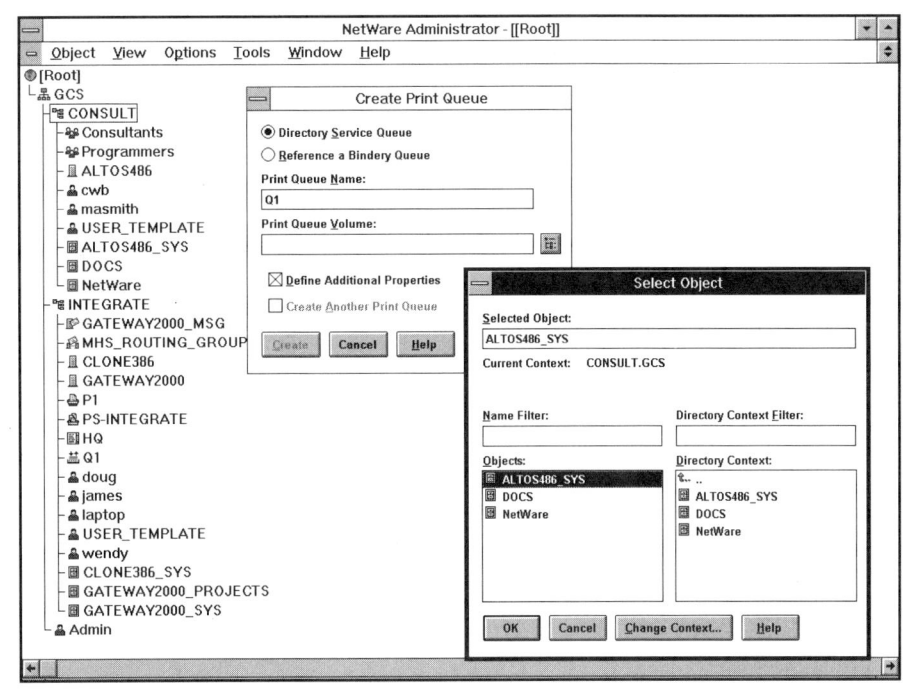

Objects box on the left side, highlight that volume and click on OK. As mentioned earlier, unlike previous NetWare versions in which print queues were always on the SYS: volume, NetWare 4.1x allows you to place printer queues on any volume you wish.

There are three volumes on ALTOS486, but only one is usable. Both the DOCS and NetWare volumes are Novell CD-ROMs that came with the product. Since they are CD-ROMs, they are read-only and can't be used as Print Queue object volumes.

The last two lines in the Create Print Queue dialog box are either/or choices. When you check Define Additional Properties, the default, the system takes you to the Properties dialog box after you click on OK here. If you are creating multiple print queues and plan on defining them later, you can check Create Another Print Queue. When you exit this dialog box, a new Create Print Queue dialog box will appear, awaiting the name of the next print queue to be created.

These two checkboxes are mutually exclusive, and they are both optional. I find it easier to configure an object immediately upon creation, but you may not. If you are creating multiple objects, you will certainly need to return later for configuration.

When you're finished with this dialog box, click on Create. If you checked the Define Additional Properties box, NetWare Administrator will immediately open the Print Queue:Q1 dialog box.

> **Taking Advantage of Power Users**
>
> Since a print queue is a workgroup-type item, decentralized management makes a great deal of sense. Anytime the users can control their part of the network, they feel more in control of their networking environment. Printing, since it's so localized and important to most groups, is a great area in which to grant some level of management authority to the workgroup. Besides that, it keeps you from being interrupted every time someone sends a PostScript file to a non-PostScript printer, causing it to go crazy. That kind of problem is best handled by an area workgroup manager.
>
> Power users, the ones that know more about computers and networking than anyone else in the department, are good candidates for providing administrative help. Whether you make these men and women official helpers or they do it on an unofficial basis, the service they provide will always be more timely than that from a central support group.
>
> Does that hurt your feelings? It shouldn't, if you understand how close-knit departments work. When a problem appears, everyone in the department turns to their expert, the power user, first. If he or she isn't available, they will call the official support people. If the power user can't solve the problem, he or she is expected to make contact with the support department.
>
> Graybeard alert: In the early days, there was no network career path and certification. The folks that became the network support group were all power users that found computers more fun than bookkeeping or inventory management or payroll or chemistry. Power users are a valuable resource for you; work with them rather than against them.

Creating the Printer Object with NetWare Administrator

As an appropriate user, start the NetWare Administrator program. Choose the container to hold the new Printer object and press the Insert key. The New Object dialog box will appear. Highlight Printer and press the Enter key.

> **8.4 IN-A-HURRY**
>
> **Create a Printer Object**
>
> 1. Open NetWare Administrator and highlight the container for the new Printer object.
>
> 2. Press Insert and choose Printer from the New Object dialog box.
>
> 3. Provide a name for the printer (the name must be unique in this context).
>
> 4. Click on Create to exit the dialog box and create the Printer object.

Figure 8.9 shows the sparse dialog box labeled Create Printer. Here you can see another advantage of NDS in general and better NetWare printing in particular. The name for a printer can be short and sweet, because it will be identified in its context (P1.CONSULT.GCS). In earlier NetWare versions, each printer defined on a server needed to be uniquely named. With the hierarchical naming conventions of NDS, P1 is a valid name a dozen times across the network, as long as each P1 is in a different context. All users in their home context can reference P1 and get to their default printer. That said, keep in mind the restrictions for naming objects, especially objects that may be referenced by NetWare 3.*x* clients or servers.

There are more items to configure for a Printer object before it can be used. You will need to check the Define Additional Properties box now and define these values immediately, or remember to come back and provide the values later. If you plan on setting up more printers now, check the Create Another Printer box.

Neither of these boxes must be checked to create the Printer object. But if you get interrupted during your workday, it's better to define the object as soon as you create it. Otherwise you may get dragged away from your desk and forget to configure a critical value.

There are mandatory values that must be defined for this printer before it will be operational. These include:

- Printer type (parallel or serial)

- Printer port (LPT or COM)

- Use interrupts or the new polling method

- Load the print server software manually or automatically

FIGURE 8.9

Naming your new printer

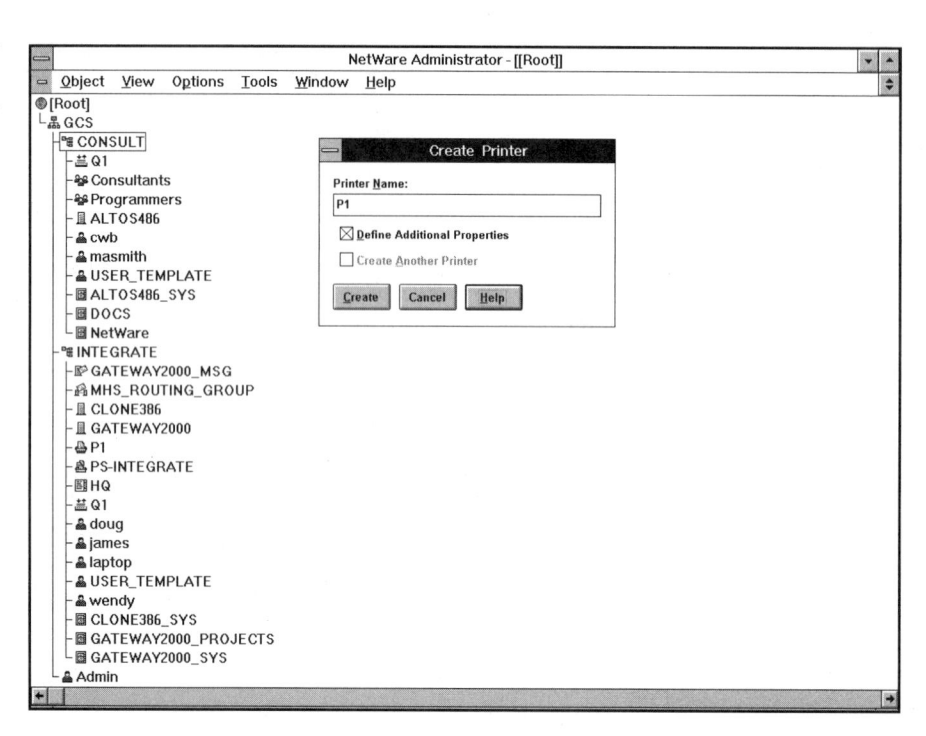

Creating the Print Server Object with NetWare Administrator

8.5 IN-A-HURRY

Create a Print Server Object

1. Open NetWare Administrator and highlight the container for the new Print Server object.

2. Press Insert and choose Print Server from the New Object dialog box.

3. Provide the Print Server object name.

4. Click on Create to exit the dialog box and create the Print Server object.

Once again, log in as an appropriate user to administer your network. Start the NetWare Administrator program. Highlight the container in which to place your Print Server object, and press the Insert key.

Setting Up and Managing Your Print System with NetWare Administrator **551**

The New Object dialog box will appear, listing the objects you have the authority to create in this context. Highlight Print Server and press the Enter key. Figure 8.10 shows the Create Print Server dialog box, with the name already filled in.

FIGURE 8.10

Re-creating the PS-CONSULT Print Server object

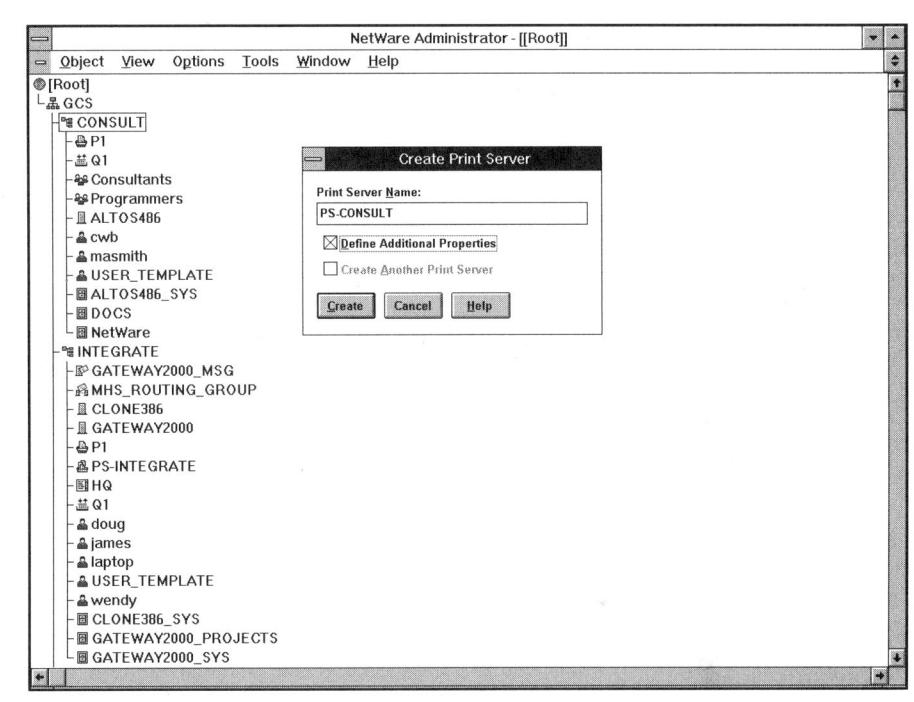

You must supply a proper object name for the print server. Remember the object-naming considerations for NDS, and the restrictions that apply to objects that may be accessed by NetWare Bindery Services clients.

The name for a Print Server object can be anything, but often starts with PS, as in PS-CONSULT. The icons for all the print devices are different, but the icons are also small. Labeling the Print Server object distinctively will help you find it in the NDS tree. The users never reference the Print Server object, so a longer name will not be an inconvenience.

The Define Additional Properties and Create Another Print Server checkboxes are optional items. There isn't much reason to have more than one or two print servers active in a context, so you'll probably move right on to Define Additional Properties.

When you click on the Create button, the dialog box closes. The new Print Server object will appear in your NDS tree immediately. There are still a few things to take care of before it's operational, however. See the section titled "Print Server Object Details," coming up.

Specifying Print Queue Object Details with NetWare Administrator

The Print Queue object has many of the same properties as other objects in NetWare 4.1x, plus a few extra. The queue was once the item most users identified with, since earlier NetWare versions forced users to direct print output to the queue and not to the printer. In NetWare 4.1x, the user is free to address either the printer or the print queue; the result is the same.

The next five sections go through all the areas of Print Queue object management. However, queues tend to get running and stay running. You shouldn't need to spend too much time managing your print queues.

Print Queue Object Identification and Operator Flags

> **8.6 IN-A-HURRY**
>
> **Identify the Print Queue Object and Set Operator Flags**
>
> 1. Open NetWare Administrator and double-click on the Print Queue object to configure.
>
> 2. On the Identification page, supply Other Name, Description, Locations, Department, and Organization values.
>
> 3. Change any of the Operator Flags options as necessary.
>
> 4. Click on OK to save and exit.

The Print Queue Identification page has the same properties that most other objects have. What is new on this page is the Operator Flags section, with a set of checkboxes.

While connected to the network as an appropriate user, start the NetWare Administrator program. Move through the NDS tree until the Print Queue object you want to manage is visible. Double-click on the Print Queue object or highlight the object and press the Enter key. Either way, the Print Queue object dialog box appears, with the Identification page showing.

The first two lines, Name and Volume, cannot be changed on this screen. These match the two mandatory fields entered during the creation of the Print Queue object. The other fields set the standard Identification values:

- **Other Name:** Any other identification labels used for this object. Multiple entries are allowed.

- **Description:** Free-form text window. Searches must match the entire contents of the Description field to succeed.

- **Location:** Physical location of this object. Multiple entries are allowed.

- **Department:** Shows the company department to which this object reports. Multiple entries are allowed.

- **Organization:** Shows the Organization to which this object reports. Multiple entries are allowed.

Figure 8.11 shows the Print Queue object dialog box for the queue we set up in the previous section. The values in the fields are strictly informational; they do not affect your network settings.

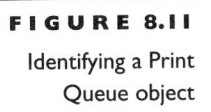

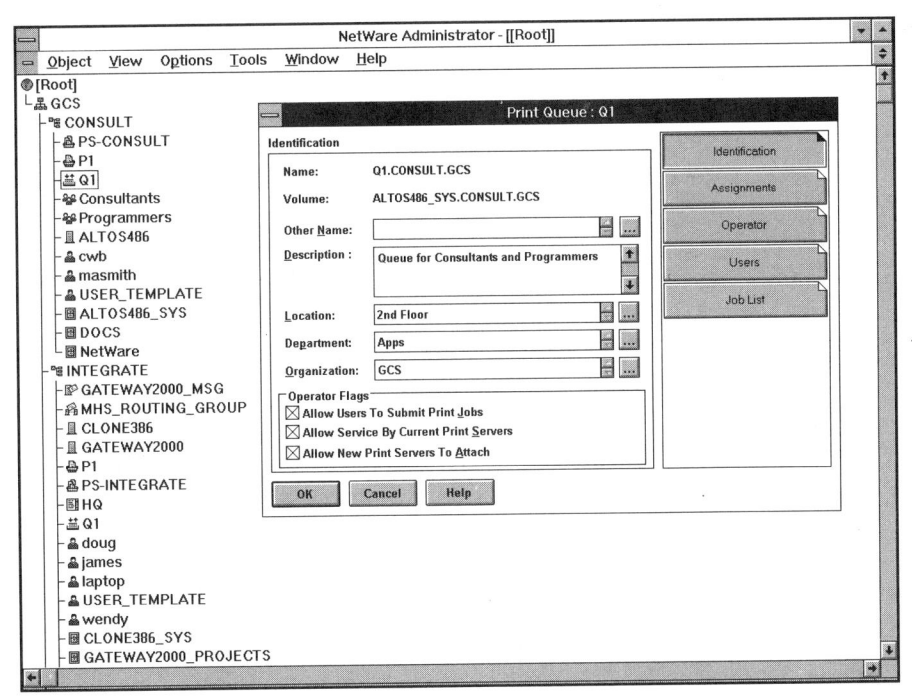

FIGURE 8.11

Identifying a Print Queue object

The Operator Flags choices in the bottom-left corner of the dialog box are new. The choices and definitions are:

- **Allow Users to Submit Print Jobs:** When Yes, queue users may submit print jobs to the queue.

- **Allow Service by Current Print Servers:** When Yes, assigned print servers may transfer jobs in the print queue to the proper printer.

- **Allow New Print Servers to Attach:** When Yes, allows print servers to attach to the queue.

You might remove the check for the first flag so that users can't send jobs to clog a full or problematic print queue. If a print server is being replaced or modified, these flags will unhook the connection between server and queue.

Viewing Print Queue Assignments

> **8.7 IN-A-HURRY**
>
> **View Print Queue Assignments**
>
> 1. Open NetWare Administrator and double-click on the Print Queue object to configure.
> 2. Click on the Assignments button.
> 3. View the information.
> 4. Click on Cancel to exit.

You can't make your print queue assignments from the Print Queue object, but you can see the assignments that have been made. The Assignments page is purely informational. Take a look at Figure 8.12 and see the blank screen. In a bit, we'll see how the information has been filled in for us on the Printer and Printer Server screens.

While connected to the network as an appropriate user, start the NetWare Administration program. Move through the NDS tree until the Print Queue object of interest is visible. Double-click on the Print Queue object or highlight the object and press the Enter key. Click once on the Assignments button on the right side of the dialog box.

FIGURE 8.12

An empty informational screen

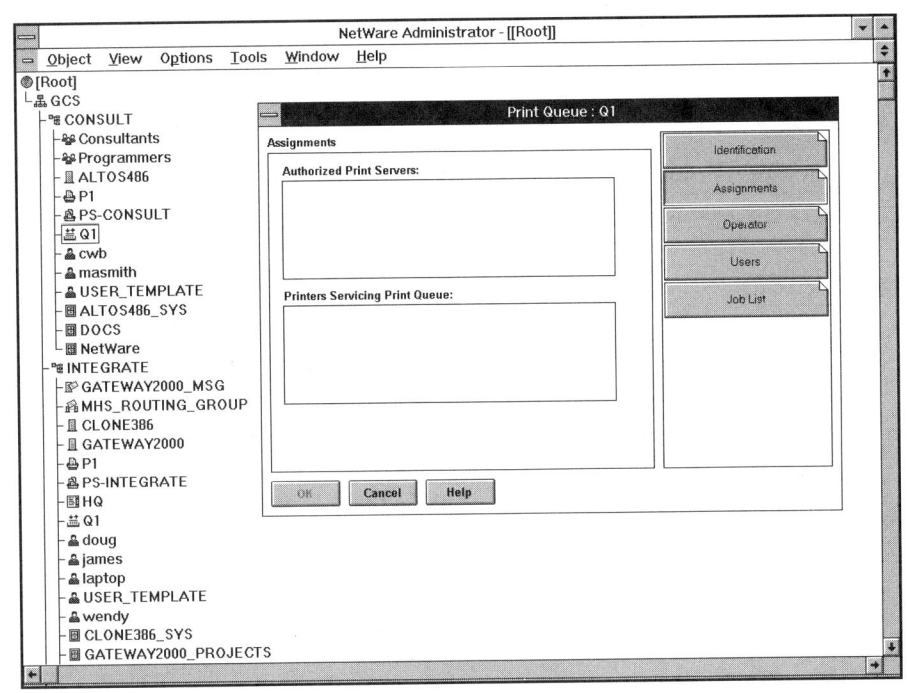

The top section of the dialog box, Authorized Print Servers, will be filled with print servers supporting this queue. Those assignments will be made in the Print Server dialog box.

The lower section of the dialog box, Printers Servicing Print Queue, will be filled with the printer (or rarely, printers) being fed by this print queue. That connection will be made in the Printer dialog box.

If you are doing this in order, don't feel like you've overlooked something when you see this screen. The OK button at the bottom-left corner never becomes active, because you can't ever do anything here. Again, this is strictly for your information, not for making changes.

Managing Print Queue Operators

A print queue operator can manage other users' print jobs, change the order of print jobs serviced, or delete those jobs from the print queue. A user listed as a print queue operator can also change the print queue status by modifying the

> ### 8.8 IN-A-HURRY
>
> **Add or Delete Print Queue Operators**
>
> 1. Open NetWare Administrator and double-click on the Print Queue object to configure.
>
> 2. Click on the Operator button.
>
> 3. To add an operator, click on the Add button. Choose the User object to add as an operator, and click on OK in the Select Object dialog box.
>
> 4. To delete an operator, highlight the User object name in the Operators list and click on Delete.
>
> 5. Click on OK to save your changes

three operator flags on the Identification page of the Print Queue dialog box. The Admin user, or equivalent, can assign users to be print queue operators.

As an appropriate user, such as the Admin user or equivalent, log in to the network and start the NetWare Administrator program. Browse the NDS tree listing until you find the Print Queue object to be modified. Double-click on the Print Queue object, or highlight the object and press Enter. You can also open the Object drop-down menu and choose Details. Once the Print Queue dialog box is open, click on the Operator button on the right side of the dialog box.

The list of current operators will appear in the Operators box that takes up the bulk of the dialog box. If the box is empty, or you wish to add another User object to the list of operators, click on the Add button.

The Select Object dialog box will open, with a view of the current context. The objects that can become Print Queue operators—User objects and Group objects—will appear in the Objects side of the dialog box. Even though they're listed, you cannot make Group objects into print queue operators. Notice that a user from another context can be designated as an operator. Highlight the desired user or users, and press Enter or click on the OK button. The selected User objects will be copied into the list of print queue operators. Figure 8.13 shows this process. In the example, I added Wendy to the list because she is one of the lead programmers.

If you wish to remove an existing print queue operator from the list, highlight that user name in the Operators box. When a name in the box is highlighted, the Delete button will become active. Click once on that Delete button,

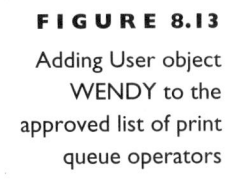

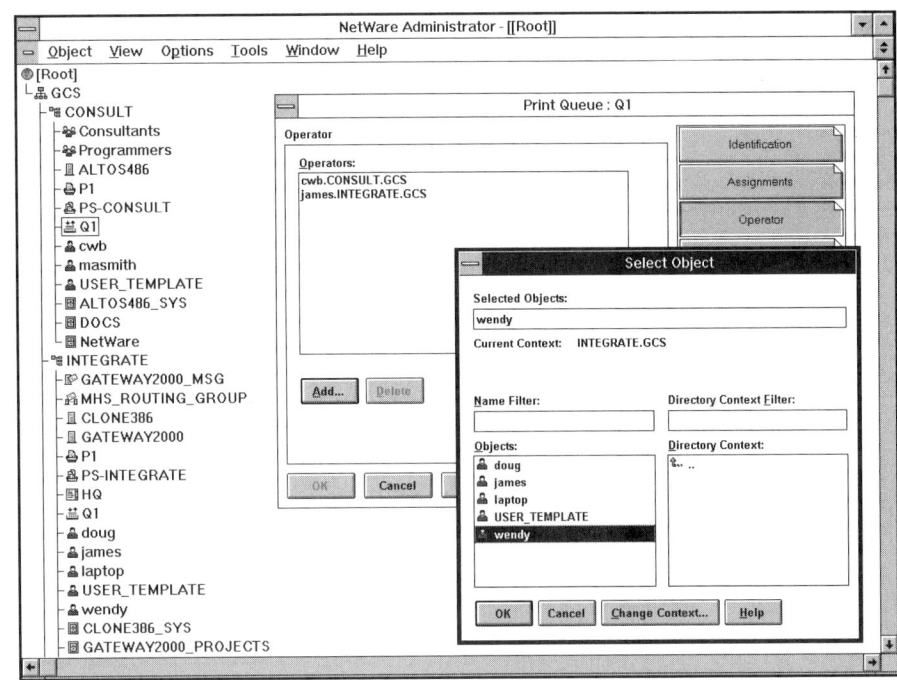

FIGURE 8.13

Adding User object WENDY to the approved list of print queue operators

and the user will no longer have the authority to operate the print queue. The user is not deleted; just that user's ability to affect the print queue is removed.

Did you notice someone missing in the list of operators? The print queue was set up not by Admin, but by an Admin-equivalent, JAMES.INTEGRATE.GCS. Unlike in earlier NetWare versions, the Admin user doesn't automatically control every piece of the network. Look at Figure 8.14, showing the trustee rights of the Admin user over Q1.CONSULT.GCS. Notice that Admin does not have the Supervisor rights checked, either for Object Rights or Property Rights. Since an Admin-equivalent user, JAMES.INTEGRATE.GCS, created Q1, that user has all those rights in place of Admin.

This never happened in NetWare 3.x systems. SUPERVISOR was always in control of each part of the network, no matter if a SUPERVISOR equivalent created the particular piece of the network under discussion. The new Admin user profile in NetWare 4.1x allows distributed networks to be administered by groups of managers, with more power going to the manager that creates objects than some (possibly) remote super-manager like SUPERVISOR.

FIGURE 8.14

Admin rights aren't absolute.

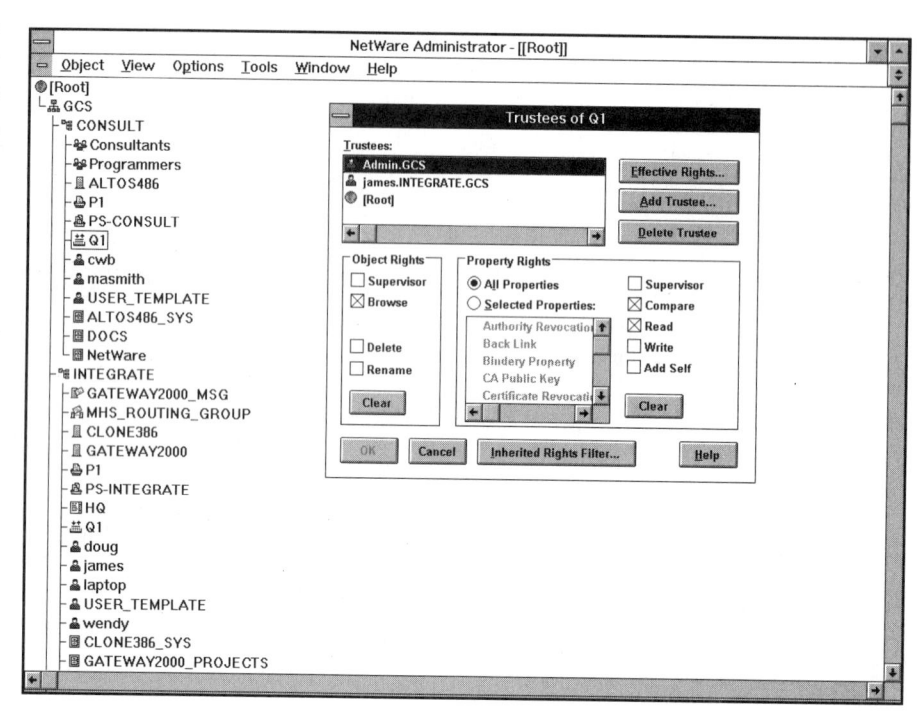

Managing Users in the Print Queue List

8.9 IN-A-HURRY

Add or Delete Print Queue Users

1. Open NetWare Administrator and double-click on the Print Queue object to configure.

2. Click on the Users button.

3. To add a user to the print queue's Users list, click on the Add button, choose the User object, and click on OK in the Select Object dialog box.

4. To delete a user, highlight the User object name in the Users list and click on Delete.

5. Click on OK to save your changes.

Setting Up and Managing Your Print System with NetWare Administrator 559

The list of approved users for a print queue automatically includes those users in the same context as the print queue. Others, both individual users and groups, may also use the print queue when listed on the Users page of the Print Queue dialog box.

While connected to the network as an appropriate user, start NetWare Administrator. Move through the NDS tree until the Print Queue object to be managed is visible. Double-click on the Print Queue object or highlight the object and press the Enter key. Click once on the Users button on the right side of the dialog box.

In Figure 8.15, two objects are already listed as users of the print queue Q1. CONSULT.GCS is the context where the print queue was created, so all members of that context have access automatically. JAMES.INTEGRATE.GCS is the Admin-equivalent user who created the print queue, so that user (me) has access. So why would anyone else need access?

The Group object PROGRAMMERS, highlighted in the Select Object dialog box in Figure 8.15, includes users from other contexts besides CONSULT.GCS. It's always easier to grant access to an object to a group rather than to each user individually.

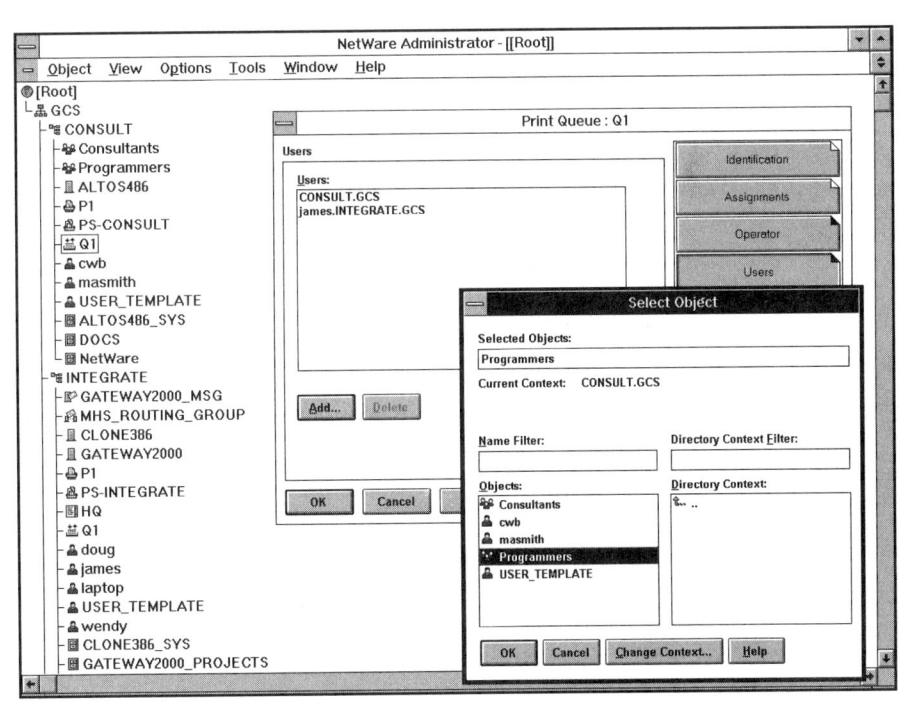

FIGURE 8.15

Adding a group to the list of approved Q1 users

WENDY, seen in Figure 8.14 (third from the bottom in the listing on the left side of the screen), is a member of PROGRAMMERS and so should have access to the print queue in CONSULT.GCS. The fact that she is not in the CONSULT.GCS context doesn't matter. She can still be added to the print queue access list. Who else is a member of the PROGRAMMERS group? Is DOUG? Doesn't matter, nor does it matter who joins the group in the future. If the group has access to a network resource, all the users in the group also have access.

Deleting User objects from the access list to the print queue works the same as deleting objects from any other dialog box: Highlight the user or users and click on the Delete button. The button will become active when one or more users is highlighted in the Users box area. The User objects are not deleted; this action just removes their ability to use the print queue.

Managing the Print Queue Job List and Job Details

> **8.10 IN-A-HURRY**
>
> **View or Modify the Print Queue Job List**
>
> 1. Open NetWare Administrator and double-click on the Print Queue object to configure.
> 2. Click on the Job List button.
> 3. To see details about a specific print job, highlight it and click on the Job Details button.
> 4. To hold, resume, or delete the highlighted print job, click on the appropriate button.
> 5. Click on OK to save and exit.

When there is a problem with a printer or print queue, the Job List page is the screen you will need to see. Print jobs stuck in limbo may be deleted, shuffled, postponed, or have their instructions modified. If you think that is a lot for one screen, you're right. The Job Details button opens another dialog box with lots of this information.

As an appropriate user, such as the Admin user or equivalent, log in to the network and start the NetWare Administrator program. Browse the NDS tree listing until you find the Print Queue object of interest. Double-click on the

Print Queue object, or highlight the object and press Enter. Once the Print Queue dialog box is open, click on the Job List button on the right side of the dialog box.

A screen similar to Figure 8.16 appears. The waiting jobs are listed in the Job List box, in the order they were received. When a print job is highlighted, the four buttons below the list box become active.

FIGURE 8.16

Print job control screen

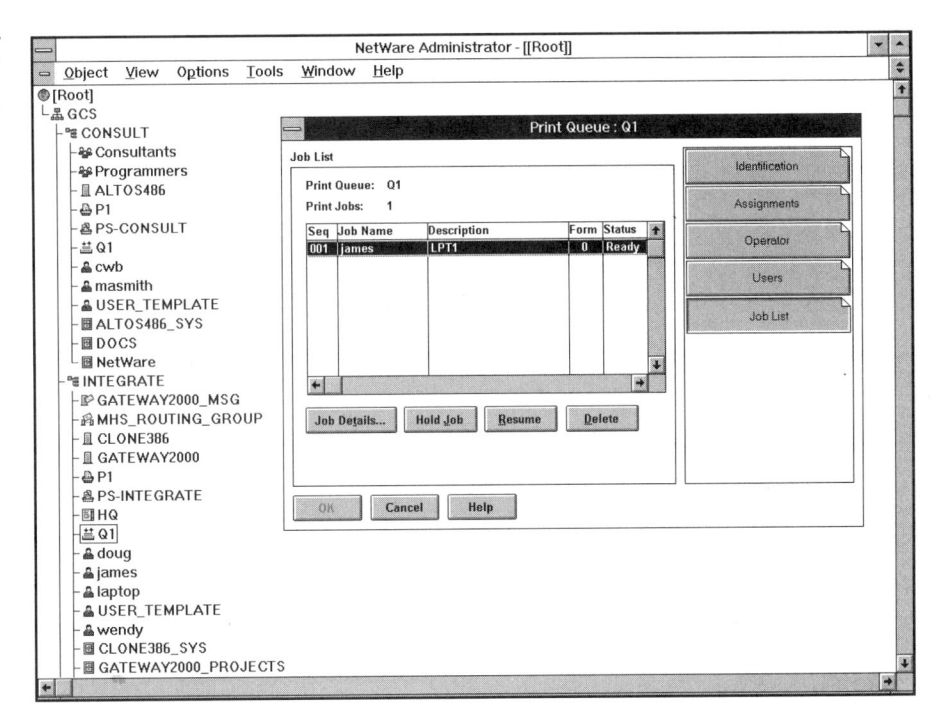

The buttons do the following:

- **Job Details:** Opens another dialog box with specific details for each print job.
- **Hold Job:** Holds a print job in the queue, postponing printing.
- **Resume:** Releases a held job, allowing it to print.
- **Delete:** Erases the highlighted print job or jobs.

Clicking on the Job Details button opens another world of print job information. Figure 8.17 shows the details for a print job. You can tell which print job; it's the one highlighted in the background dialog box.

In the upper-left corner of the Print Job Detail dialog box is the Print Job number, an eight-digit hexadecimal number. This is the random number assigned by NetWare to a print job to track the job through the system. The number is included on the Job List page, the dialog box in the background. The print job ID is the sixth column, after Status. You need to use the scroll bar to see the ID, but this number does you little good until you need to start troubleshooting.

Users can change the details of their own jobs only. If they highlight someone else's print job and look at the detail screen, the options will be gray and inactive. Administrators of the print queue have access to all options. The details for each print job are set by the user that submitted the job, or by the default print configuration information for the user. For instance, a print job that is particularly important to a user may have a request for the user to be notified when printing is complete, but the default is for no notification. Any default settings can be overridden by the CAPTURE command parameters (see Chapter 12 for details).

Table 8.1 shows the fields on the Print Job Detail screen.

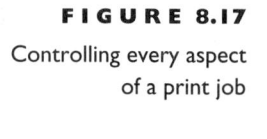

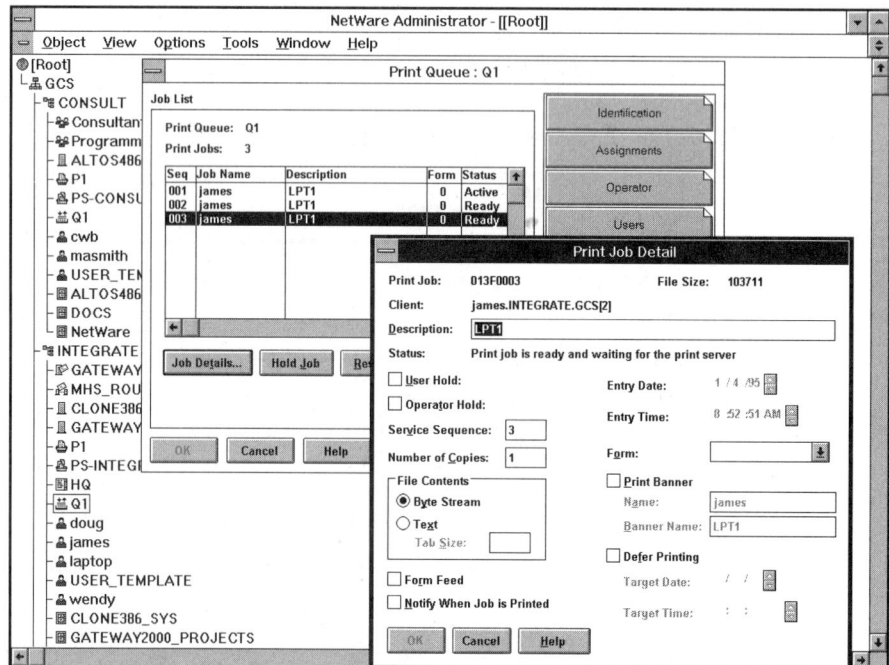

FIGURE 8.17

Controlling every aspect of a print job

TABLE 8.1 Fields on NetWare Administrator's Print Job Detail Screen

FIELD	DESCRIPTION
Print Job	Unique system-assigned ID number for this job.
File Size	Size in bytes of this print job.
Client	User who submitted this job.
Description	Descriptive information, which typically shows captured printer port.
Status	Descriptive line about the print job. Ready, Held, or Active in the Job List dialog box translates to more information on this screen.
User Hold	Job held by original submitter.
Operator Hold	Job held by the print queue operator or administrator.
Service Sequence	This job's position in the print queue.
Number of Copies	Instructions per print job for duplicates.
Byte Stream	Indicates the existence of non-ASCII data in the print file.
Text	Indicates the existence of only straight ASCII text in the print file.
Tab Size	Used only with text files, indicates the number of spaces used to represent the tab character inside the print stream.
Form Feed	Indicates whether or not a form-feed command is sent to the printer at the end of the print job.
Notify When Job Is Printed	Uses a system message to notify the user this print job is finished.
Entry Date	The date the print job was submitted.
Entry Time	The time the print job was submitted.
Form	Indicates whether a particular form will be used for this job. If a specific form was requested by the user when this job was submitted, that name will appear. In this screen, you can click on the down arrow and choose any defined forms.

Chapter 8 ▪ Arranging Network Printing

TABLE 8.1 (cont.)	FIELD	DESCRIPTION
Fields on NetWare Administrator's Print Job Detail Screen	Print Banner	Indicates whether the user wishes this print job to have an identification banner printed as the first page of this print job.
	Name	If the Print Banner is checked, the name of the user submitting the print job.
	Banner Name	If Print Banner is checked, the name of the print job. If not specified by the user, the printer port used by the CAPTURE program will be listed.
	Defer Printing	Delay printing until the specified Target Date and Target Time. This provides an easy way to postpone long or graphically complex print jobs to a less disruptive time.

> **NOTE**
>
> *The File Contents section of the Print Job Detail dialog box is not a security breach. This concerns only the type of file data: byte stream or text. Actual file information does not appear on this screen.*

Few print jobs require this level of control and intervention. These screens are valuable when dealing with a user who doesn't understand the printing process, or who sends huge jobs that get in the way of other users. These two screens are also handy in a heavy printing environment, since users can hold or delete print jobs if they realize there is a mistake or potential problem. In a normal network with a decent printing system, the print jobs are done before anyone can think to change any details. But if you need to change details, this is the place.

Specifying Printer Object Details with NetWare Administrator

There are more reasons to manage the Printer object than the Print Queue object. The mandatory settings are quick and simple:

- Print Queue(s)
- Port
- Interrupt
- Location
- Printer type
- Name

The optional fields cover similar areas of description we saw with the Print Queue objects. Using at least some of these optional fields will help you track and manage network resources. Older versions of NetWare didn't offer any search capabilities to the manager, but NetWare 4.1x offers quite powerful search features.

Printer Object Identification

> **8.11 IN-A-HURRY**
>
> **Identify the Printer Object**
>
> 1. Open NetWare Administrator and double-click on the Printer object to configure.
>
> 2. On the Identification page, supply values in the fields.
>
> 3. Click on OK to save the information and exit.

The only field that is mandatory on the Printer Identification page is the one that can't be changed: the printer name. Everything else is useful for management and tracking, but not required.

After logging in to the system as the Admin user or equivalent, start the NetWare Administrator program. Browse the NDS tree until the desired Printer object is located. Double-click on the Printer object name, or highlight the object and press Enter. The page that appears when the dialog box opens is the Identification page. Figure 8.18 shows some of the fields completed.

The fields on the Identification page are:

- **Other Name:** Any other identification labels used for this object. Multiple entries are allowed.

- **Description:** Free-form text window. Searches must match the entire contents of the Description field to succeed.

- **Network Address:** The 8-byte hexadecimal number of the file or print server hosting this printer.

- **Location:** Physical location of this object. Multiple entries are allowed.

FIGURE 8.18

Printer object identification information

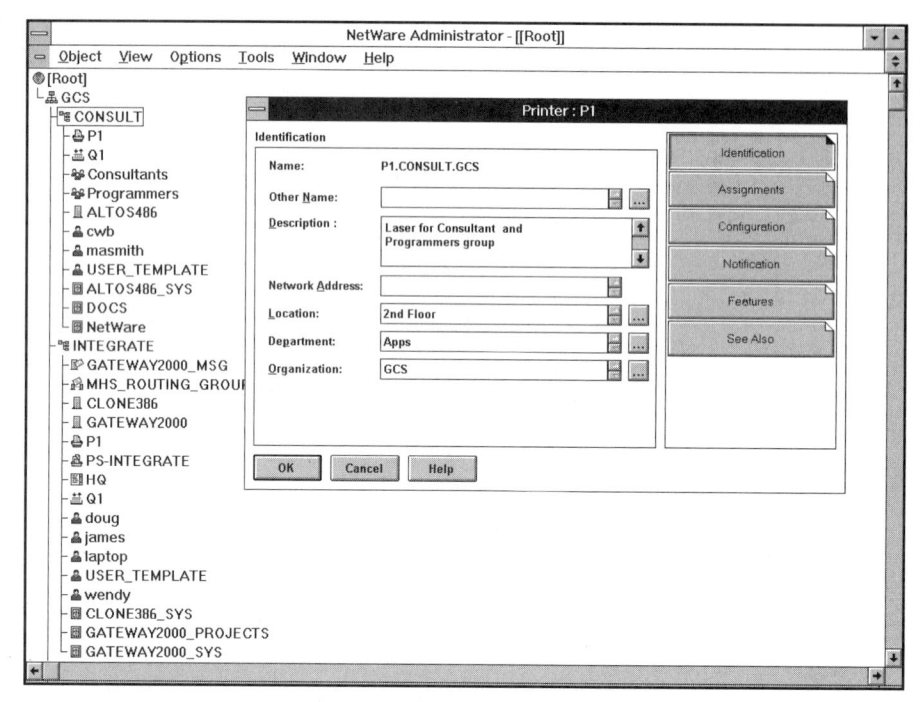

[Screenshot of NetWare Administrator showing Printer: P1 Identification dialog with fields: Name: P1.CONSULT.GCS, Other Name, Description: Laser for Consultant and Programmers group, Network Address, Location: 2nd Floor, Department: Apps, Organization: GCS]

- **Department:** The company department to which this object reports. Multiple entries are allowed.

- **Organization:** The organization to which this object reports. Multiple entries are allowed.

After you've filled in the Identification page information that you want to record, click on OK to save your settings and exit.

> *Remember that the OK and Cancel buttons apply to every page of the dialog box, not just the Identification page. If you have made changes on other pages and cancel this page, all changes will be lost if you proceed with the Cancel request. Fortunately, you will be warned by the system before this happens.*

Tying the Printer Object to a Print Queue

> **8.12 IN-A-HURRY**
>
> **Add or Delete a Print Queue Object from a Printer Object's List**
>
> 1. Open NetWare Administrator and double-click on the Printer object to modify.
> 2. Click on the Assignments button.
> 3. To add a Print Queue object to the Printer object, click on the Add button, highlight the desired Print Queue object, and click on OK in the Select Object dialog box.
> 4. To delete a Print Queue object from the Printer object, highlight the Print Queue object and click on Delete.
> 5. Click on OK to save and exit.

The Assignments page is the spot where you tie the Printer object to the Print Queue object. This step is necessary before anything will print. We'll take the final step in activating the printer when we connect the printer and the print server in the next section.

As Admin or equivalent, start the NetWare Administrator program. Browse your NDS tree until you find the Printer object to set up or modify. Highlight the object and press Enter, or double-click on it to open the Printer dialog box. Click on the Assignments button on the right side of the dialog box to open a dialog box similar to the one shown in Figure 8.19.

First, look at something that's not there: an entry for Print Server. We'll take care of that in the next section. Just below the empty Print Server field is the Print Queues box, also currently empty. This shows that the order in which you configure your print system doesn't really matter; some fields will stay empty for a time.

Many Print Queue objects may be defined in the Print Queues box, even queues from other containers. For now, we're adding the previously defined queue Q1 to our printer P1. Click on the Add button to open the Select Object dialog box, find your desired Print Queue object, and double-click to assign it to the printer.

Once there is a highlighted Print Queue object in the Printer dialog box, the Delete button becomes active. To delete (unhook) a print queue from this printer, just highlight the Print Queue object and click on Delete. This action does not delete the Print Queue object; it just disconnects this queue from this printer.

FIGURE 8.19

Tying a Printer object to a Print Queue object

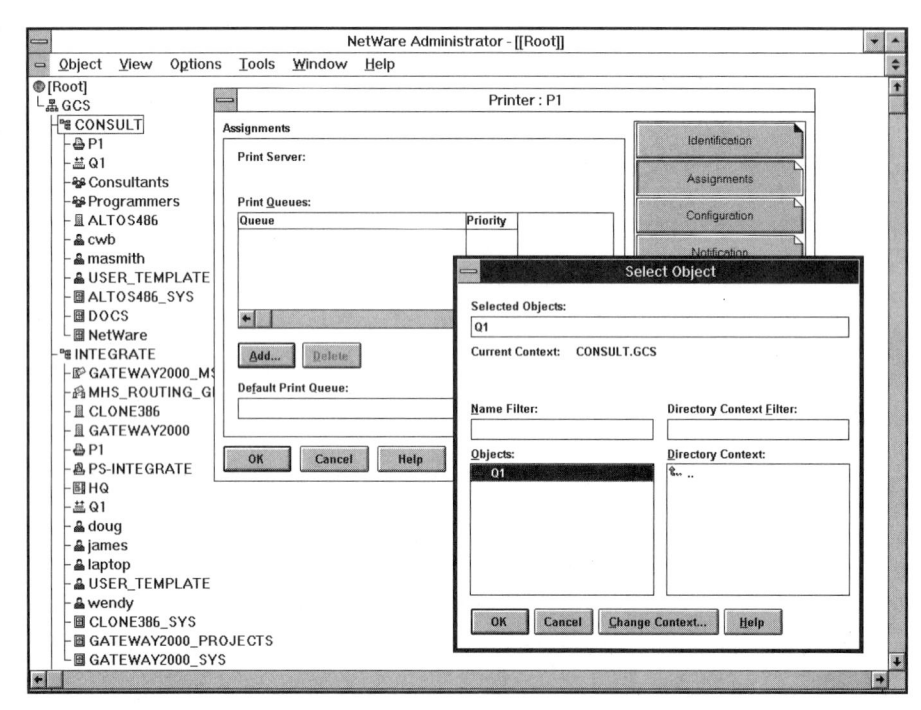

Modifying Printer Object Configuration

8.13 IN-A-HURRY

Modify a Printer Object

1. Open NetWare Administrator and double-click on the Printer object to modify.

2. Click on the Configuration button.

3. Supply the Printer Type, Banner Type, Services Interval, Buffer Size, Starting Form, and Service Mode for Forms values, or accept the defaults.

4. Click on the Communication button to configure the Printer Type values.

5. Click on OK to save and exit.

Setting Up and Managing Your Print System with NetWare Administrator 569

The Configuration page is the place to configure the physical details of how the printer communicates with the network. All manner of printers and communication details are controlled by this page of the Printer object dialog box.

Log in to the network as either Admin or equivalent. Start NetWare Administrator, and browse the NDS tree until you find the desired Printer object. Double-click on the Printer object, or open the Details dialog box from the Object drop-down menu. Figure 8.20 shows the Configuration page. The values shown here are the defaults for a printer physically connected to a NetWare file server.

FIGURE 8.20

The default printer configuration information

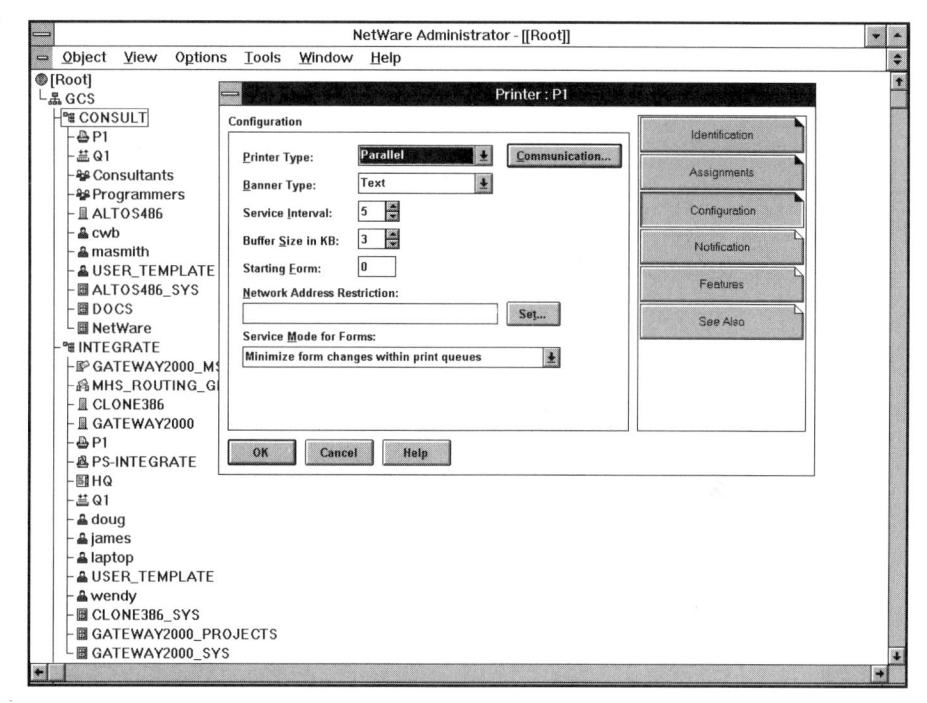

The server is not the best place to hang a printer in a busy network, but it used to be the only option NetWare gave you. Now, with workstation printers available to the entire network and third-party print servers doing so well, the server should be the last place to put a printer. Of course, a lightly loaded network, or an installation where every dollar counts, will happily use the traditional server-attached print devices.

The first option, Printer Type, has seven possible values:

- **Other/Unknown:** OS/2 printers or those configured by NPRINTER.

- **Parallel:** Standard Centronics parallel printer, the most common option.

- **Serial:** Asynchronous serial printers, attached to a server or workstation via a serial port.

- **XNP:** eXtended NetWare Printer protocol, a high-performance system for shared network printing.

- **AppleTalk:** Support for printers developed for the Macintosh network protocol.

- **Unix:** Designates printers attached to Unix systems.

- **AIO:** Asynchronous Input/Output. Designates printers attached to an asynchronous communications server or a multiple-port serial adapter.

The configuration details for each printer type will appear when you change the Printer Type field. They also appear when you click on the Communication button next to that field. All printer types, except Other/Unknown and XNP, require unique settings in the Communication dialog box. Other/Unknown and XNP printers are configured at the devices that connect them to the network cabling or remote system. XNP supports Macintosh and Unix printing; printer details are set on that end.

The second field, Banner Type, has two options. Text is the default. The other choice is PostScript. Use the default of Text, even if you do have a PostScript printer. Most PostScript printers sold over the last few years handle text in this manner, but problems persist. Keep the default until you can check your printer for problems, and then you can change the setting to PostScript if you need to.

The Service Interval field sets how many seconds go by before the print server checks the print queue for print jobs belonging to this printer. The default is 5 seconds; the range is 1 to 255 seconds.

The Buffer Size in KB field shows how large a piece of data can be for this printer. The default is 3 KB; the range goes to 20 KB.

If printer forms are used, the Starting Form field sets the form number to make active when the print server brings the printer on-line. Any form value between 0 and 255 is allowed.

If your security requirements demand that you restrict a printer to a particular address, set that address in the Network Address Restriction field. In extremely rare cases, print output can be copied to a recording device as well as printed. The two fields require you to list the network number and physical address of the print server or host. The Service Mode for Forms field dictates how often the print server will demand that you change printer forms (pre-defined page length and width setups) to accommodate print output to forms that are not mounted. When a print job calls for such a form, the print server holds that print job until the form can be mounted. The options in this pick list are:

- **Minimize Form Changes within Print Queues:** Requires you to change forms when print jobs demand a new form within this particular print queue, even if other print jobs in lower-priority queues for this printer are waiting to use the currently mounted form. This is the default setting.

- **Change Forms as Needed:** Forces the form changes for each print job as they appear. You will hate this setting, so don't use it if you can avoid it, unless you love servicing printers all day.

- **Minimize Form Changes Across Print Queues:** The printer will print all print jobs for the mounted form before stopping and requesting a form change. High-priority print jobs with a different form will be placed behind low-priority print jobs using the mounted form.

- **Service Only Currently Mounted Form:** The printer never requests a new form. All print jobs requiring a different form than the one mounted will be held indefinitely.

As you can see, multiple forms on one printer will always cause you grief. If there's any way to restrict your printing requirements so that no form changes are required on any printers, your life will go much more smoothly. Life is hard enough; don't make it worse by trying to print different forms on the same printer.

When you choose a Printer Type and click on the Communication button, you see settings for the port, interrupts, and connection type for the chosen type of printer. Figure 8.21 shows the Communication dialog box with the default settings for a parallel printer.

PARALLEL PRINTER COMMUNICATION SETTINGS For parallel printers, there are three choices for the Port field: LPT1, LPT2, and LPT3. The second area, Interrupts, offers a choice of the original LPT interrupt mode or the new polled printer communications.

FIGURE 8.21

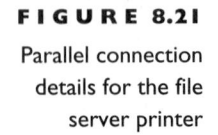

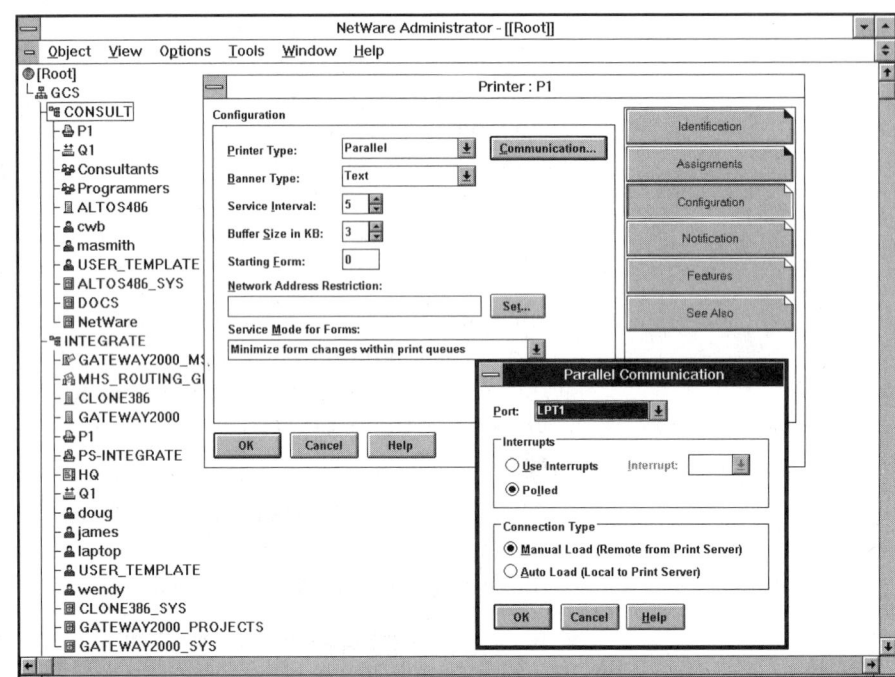

Parallel connection details for the file server printer

Polled communications let the operating system check on the status of the print queues without requiring a hard interrupt from the print server. In most cases, the performance is as good as the interrupt method, without the potential of conflicting interrupt settings. There are only so many interrupts to go around in a PC file server, as we saw during the installation chapters. While the IRQ for the first parallel port is generally available (IRQ 7), LPT2 and LPT3 use IRQ 5, a popular number. More than one printer hanging from the file server, demanding an IRQ, can squeeze your installation options. This squeeze doesn't happen with the Polled setting.

The Connection Type refers to port driver loading (NPRINTER.NLM and NPRINTER.EXE are port drivers). Printers connected to the file server may have PSERVER.NLM load automatically, which loads NPRINTER.NLM at the same time. These port drivers may also be loaded manually at the server console.

Printers connected to workstations must always use the Manual Load option. Printers attached to the network cabling via internal or external print servers load their own port drivers.

SERIAL PRINTER COMMUNICATION SETTINGS For a serial printer, the Communication dialog box has these settings:

- **Port:** COM1 through COM4
- **Interrupts:** Interrupts or Polled
- **Connection Type:** Manual or Auto Load
- **Line Control - Baud:** 300 to 38,400
- **Data Bits:** 5 to 8
- **Stop Bits:** 1, 1.5, or 2
- **Parity:** None, Even, or Odd
- **X-on, X-off:** Yes or No

APPLETALK PRINTER COMMUNICATION SETTINGS For an AppleTalk printer, the Communication settings are:

- **Names:** Seen by Macintosh clients
- **Type of Printer:** LaserWriter, ImageWriter, L.Q., DeskWriter, PaintWriter XL, or PaintJet XL300
- **Zone:** AppleTalk zone number
- **Hide Printer (from direct Macintosh access):** Yes or No

UNIX PRINTER COMMUNICATION SETTINGS You must have the optional LPR_GWY.NLM program to connect to Unix systems. The Communication dialog box settings for a Unix-type printer are:

- **Host Name:** Unix system host name
- **Printer Name:** Unix printer name as described on Unix host

AIO PRINTER COMMUNICATION SETTINGS For an AIO printer, the Communication settings are:

- **Port:** Supplied by manufacturer
- **Hardware Type:** Supplied by manufacturer
- **Board Number:** Supplied by manufacturer

- **Line Control - Baud:** 300 to 38,400
- **Data Bits:** 5 to 8
- **Stop Bits:** 1, 1.5, or 2
- **Parity:** None, Even, or Odd
- **X-on, X-off:** Yes or No

Notifying Users of Printer Problems

> **8.14 IN-A-HURRY**
>
> **Specify Users to Notify of Printer Problems**
>
> **1.** Open NetWare Administrator and double-click on the Printer object to modify.
>
> **2.** Click on the Notification button.
>
> **3.** To add a user to the Notification list, click on Add and select the user(s) to be notified about this printer's problems, then click on OK in the Select Object dialog box.
>
> **4.** To delete a user from the Notification list, highlight the user and click on Delete.
>
> **5.** Click on OK to save and exit.

When a printer has a problem, you have two choices: wait until someone calls and complains, or use the printer notification option. The normal printer problems are lack of paper, jamming, or going offline. The quicker someone knows about these problems, the quicker the simple remedies can be applied.

That someone can be anyone on the network, not just you. The owner of the print job, along with any other users you specify, can get a message. This is another opportunity for the workgroup administrator to help out.

After connecting to the network as either Admin or equivalent, start the NetWare Administrator program. Browse through the NDS tree until you find the particular printer you want to send notifications.

It's a good idea to decide your policy for printer notifications, and configure the notification details during initial printer setup.

Add users to the list by clicking on the Add button, which opens the Select Object dialog box, as usual. The eligible objects to be notified appear in the Objects portion of the dialog box. Highlight your choice or choices, and click on OK. Figure 8.22 shows an example of adding a user to the Notification list.

FIGURE 8.22

The print job owner is on the Notification list, and CWB is being added.

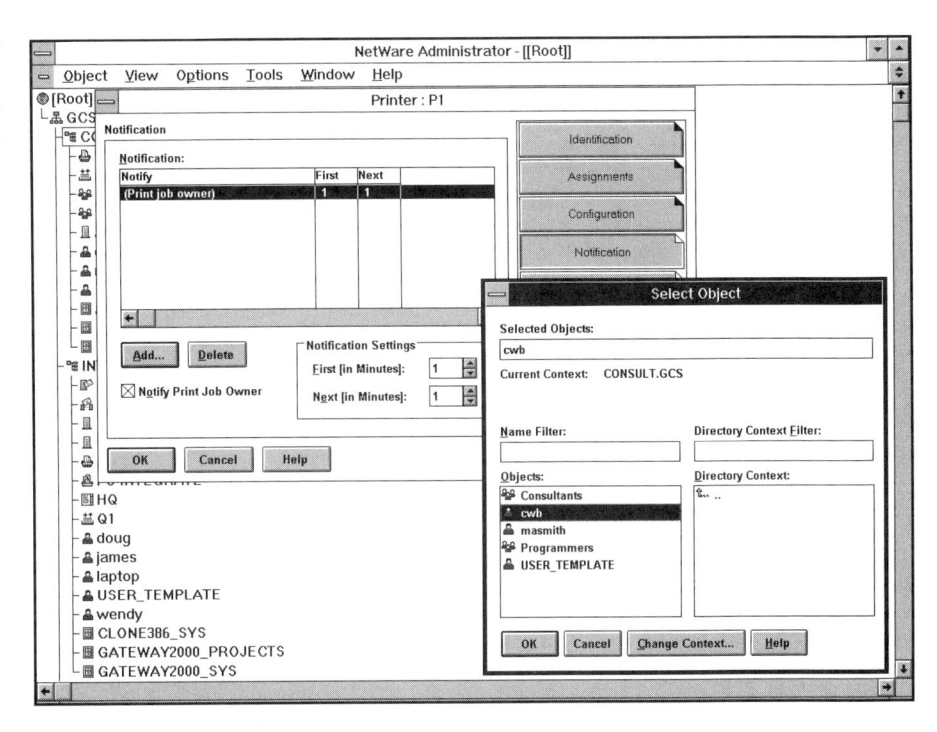

Delete users from the list the same way you delete any item from a list in NetWare Administrator. Highlight the object and click on Delete. The item is immediately deleted from the list, but not from the system.

The Notification Settings box sets the length of time before the first notification is issued, and the delay between each subsequent alert. In a nice bit of programming, the NetWare developers support different settings for each user on the list.

When user CWB is added to the Notification list, he will be given his first notice in one minute, and next notice in five, by default. The print job owner is assumed to be more interested in the print job than anyone else on the list, so that user's notifications are more frequent by default. The one-minute delay before the first notification allows almost enough time to change a font cartridge or add paper.

If someone turns off a printer that has you as one of its people to notify, you will be bombarded with messages about the printer being offline. Fortunately, these notification settings are easy to change.

Describing Printer Object Features

> **8.15 IN-A-HURRY**
>
> **Describe Printer Features**
>
> 1. Open NetWare Administrator and double-click on the Printer object to modify.
> 2. Click on the Features button.
> 3. Type the information in each applicable field; multiple values are allowed.
> 4. Click on OK to save and exit.

In support of creating manageable networks, each Printer object has several Features properties. Although these have nothing to do with running the network or the printers, they are handy for inventory and tracking purposes.

Log in to the network as either Admin or equivalent. Start the NetWare Administrator program. Browse the NDS tree until you find the desired Printer object. Double-click on the Printer object, or open the Details dialog box from the Object drop-down menu. Once the Printer dialog box is open, click on Features. A partially complete Features page is shown in Figure 8.23.

None of this information is read from the printer itself. You must enter all the information in the format that makes sense for later searching. For instance, if you care only about HPGL (Hewlett-Packard Graphics Language) and not the differences for HPGL4 or HPGL5, then type only HPGL in the Page Description Language field.

Each field with a More button (marked ...) to the far right supports multiple values. Click on the More button to open a small dialog box, allowing you to add more values.

Setting Up and Managing Your Print System with NetWare Administrator 577

FIGURE 8.23

Describing your printer

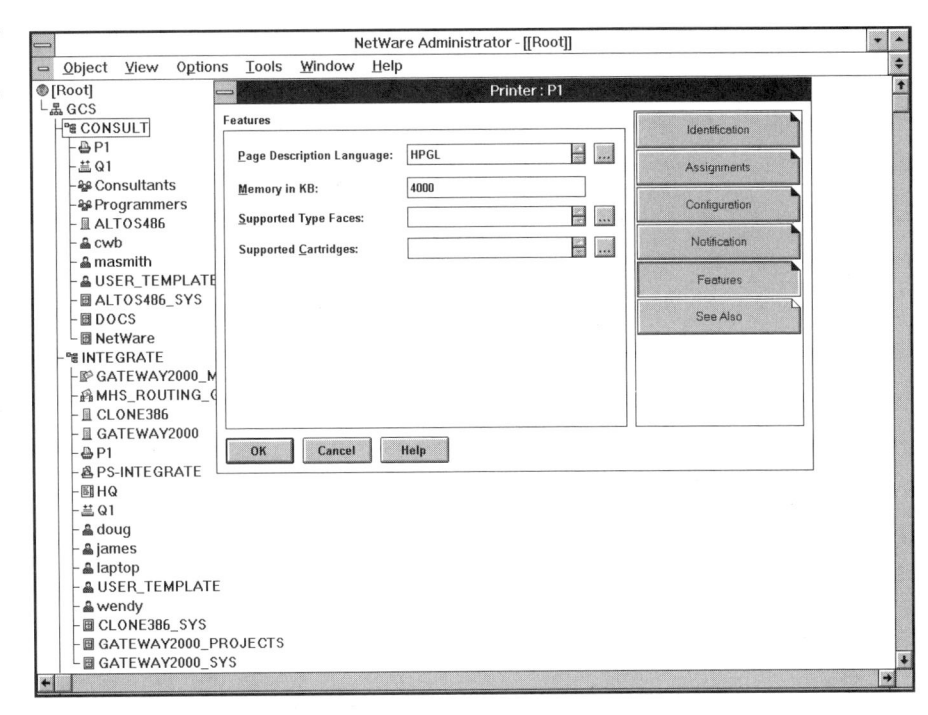

[Screenshot of NetWare Administrator showing the Printer: P1 Features dialog with fields for Page Description Language (HPGL), Memory in KB (4000), Supported Type Faces, and Supported Cartridges. The NDS tree on the left shows [Root]/GCS with CONSULT and INTEGRATE containers and their objects.]

Listing Objects Associated with the Printer Object

8.16 IN-A-HURRY

Add Printer Object See Also Details

1. Open NetWare Administrator and double-click on the Printer object to modify.

2. Click on the See Also button.

3. Click on Add, browse the NDS tree, and select objects for the See Also listing.

4. Click on OK in the Select Objects dialog box.

5. Click on OK to save and exit.

Like many other objects, the Printer object includes a See Also page to list associated objects. These objects have no impact on the workings of the printer or network. They are simply here to remind you of some connection between your current object and those listed.

Log in as an appropriate user, and start NetWare Administrator. Browse the NDS tree and select the Printer object you wish to modify, double-clicking to open the dialog box. Click on See Also to open the page shown in Figure 8.24.

To add objects, click on the Add button to open the Select Object dialog box. Browse and choose as many items as you wish to place on the page. To delete objects from the box, highlight them and click on Delete.

FIGURE 8.24

Associating WENDY with P1.CONSULT.GCS

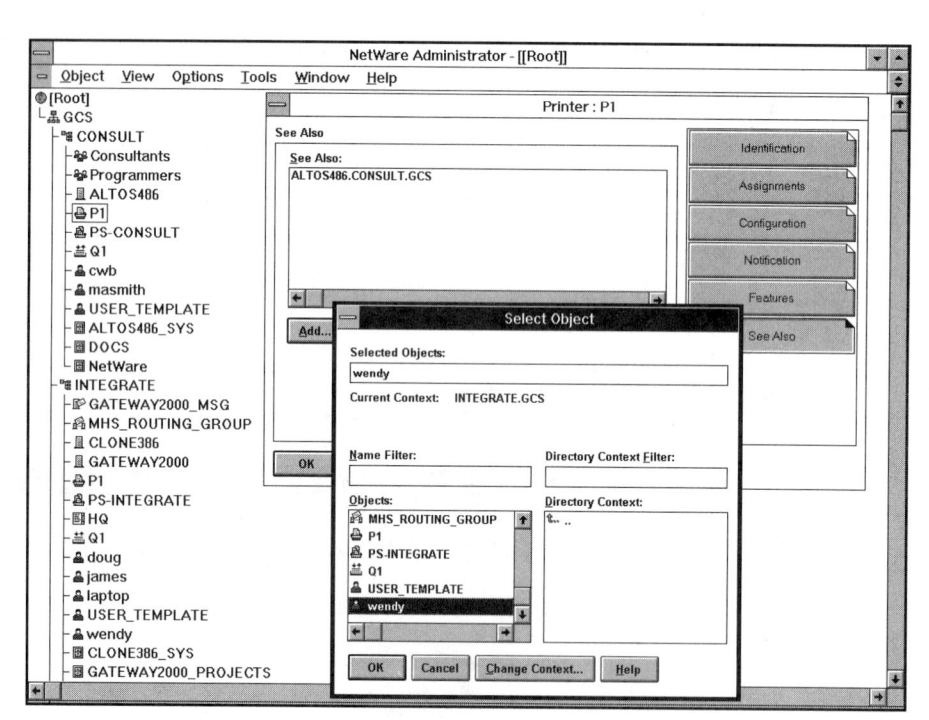

Specifying Print Server Object Details with NetWare Administrator

Now we're to the point of managing the Print Server object. Some of this can be done from the server console hosting the print server software, but more can be done from within NetWare Administrator than can be done at the server console.

Some of the items in this section should look familiar by now. That's one of the advantages of NetWare Administrator: Learn to manage one object, and you've learned to manage them all. Well, some details change, but the administration program makes those details easier to handle.

Print Server Object Identification

> **8.17 IN-A-HURRY**
>
> **Identify the Print Server Object**
>
> 1. Open NetWare Administrator and double-click on the Print Server object to modify.
>
> 2. Provide information in the descriptive fields of the Identification page.
>
> 3. Use the Unload button to stop a Print Server.
>
> 4. Click on Change Password to add or modify the Print Server password.
>
> 5. Click on OK to save and exit.

Most Identification pages have helpful, but not active, buttons and information. The page for the Print Server object offers a few extras.

Connect to the network as either the Admin user or equivalent. Start the NetWare Administrator program. Cruise your NDS tree until you locate the Print Server object to view. Double-click on the object, or highlight it and press Enter. You will see an Identification page, similar to the one in Figure 8.25.

There are some new things tucked into the standard object properties, aren't there?

- **Name:** Full NDS name for this print server.

- **Advertising Name:** The SAP (Service Advertising Protocol) name broadcast across the network every 60 seconds to tell the network this print server is available.

- **Other Name:** Any other identification labels used for this object. Multiple entries are allowed.

- **Network Address:** Protocol, internal address, and network address of the host server for this print server.

FIGURE 8.25

The Print Server Identification page

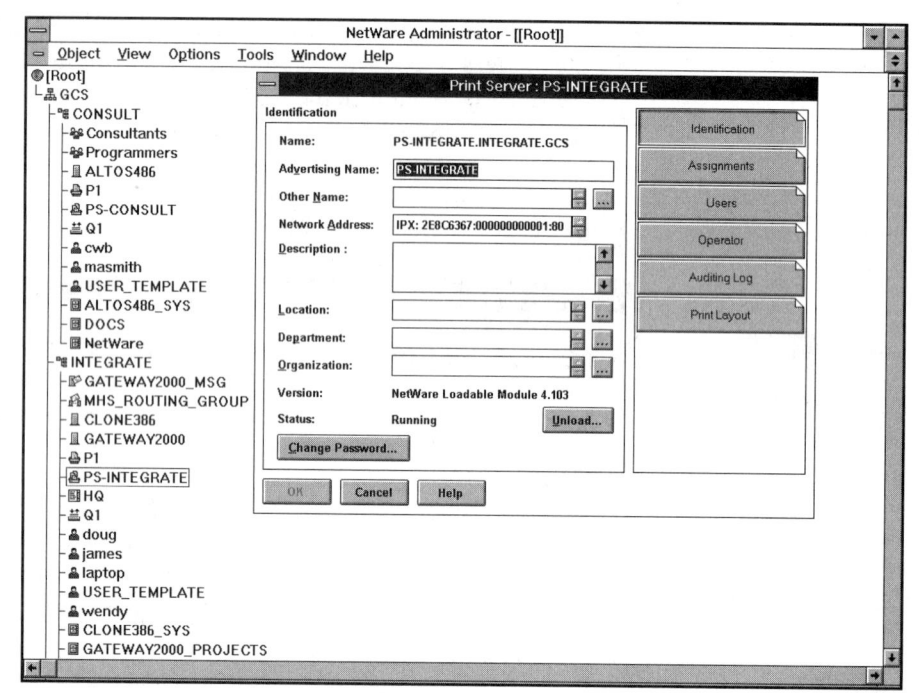

- **Description:** Free-form text window. Searches must match the entire contents of the Description field to succeed.

- **Location:** Physical location of this object. Multiple entries are allowed.

- **Department:** Shows the company department to which this object reports. Multiple entries are allowed.

- **Organization:** Shows the organization to which this object reports. Multiple entries are allowed.

- **Version:** The PSERVER.NLM version running this print server.

- **Status:** Shows the print server status: Running, Down, or Going Down.

The last two fields on this page, Version and Status, are not fill-in-the-blank items. The running version of PSERVER.NLM for this server is the NetWare Loadable Module (NLM) referred to as version 4.103. Novell makes regular updates of NLMs available through the company's FTP server (across the Internet), through NetWire (on CompuServe), and through NSE Pro (Network

Support Encyclopedia, Professional Version). This information saves you from looking up the actual file and comparing release date and file size to figure out if your NLM is in need of updating.

Status also refers to the PSERVER.NLM program. While the Running and Down states are clear, Going Down may seem strange. The reason for this odd state is that the print server can be told to finish the jobs in the queue, then shut down. The Going Down state may last for many minutes, depending on the queue backlog.

The Change Password and Unload buttons on this Identification page are two that we haven't seen in any other dialog boxes. Unload refers to stopping the PSERVER.NLM program on the file server. That's one way to change the state from Running to Down. Unfortunately, there isn't a Load button. Restarting the print server requires either going to the physical file server or using the RCONSOLE program (covered in Chapter 10).

The password will help limit access to the print server. Every time the print server is loaded, the password must be entered.

When clicked, the Change Password button opens a dialog box allowing you to type the old password (for verification of you), the new password, and retype the new password (for verification of your typing). If a password exists and you wish to erase it, type the old password, then press Enter on the New Password line. A message box will ask you to verify that you are serious about eliminating the password.

Changing Print Server Assignments

> **8.18 IN-A-HURRY**
>
> **Change Print Server Assignments**
>
> 1. Open NetWare Administrator and double-click on the Print Server object to modify.
> 2. Click on the Assignments button.
> 3. To add a printer, click on the Add button and double-click on the printer to add.
> 4. To delete a printer, highlight the printer in the Printers box, then click on Delete.
> 5. To change the printer number, highlight the printer in the Printers box, click on the Printer Number button, type the new printer number, and click on OK.
> 6. Click on OK to save and exit.

Here's the deal: Print Server objects work with Printer objects. Print Queue objects also work with Printer objects, even though Print Server objects take print jobs from Print Queue objects and feed them to Printer objects. Get all that? See why I recommend e-mail?

For our purposes, it's enough to remember that print servers serve printers, and print queues handle print job traffic. So let's work with a print server.

To get to a print server, log in to the network as either Admin or equivalent. Start the NetWare Administrator program, and browse through your NDS tree until you find the Print Server object to investigate. Either double-click on that object, or highlight it and press Enter. Then click on the Assignments button on the right. Something akin to Figure 8.26 will appear.

Notice we are now looking at the PS-INTEGRATE Print Server object, rather than the PS-CONSULT object we created earlier. This is to illustrate how easy it is to move and shift printers around, in case one printer (P1.CONSULT.GCS) breaks down.

To add a new printer, click on the Add button to summon the Select Object dialog box. As before, cruise around the NDS tree and double-click on the Printer object to add to the Print Server assignment list.

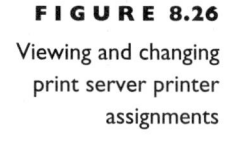

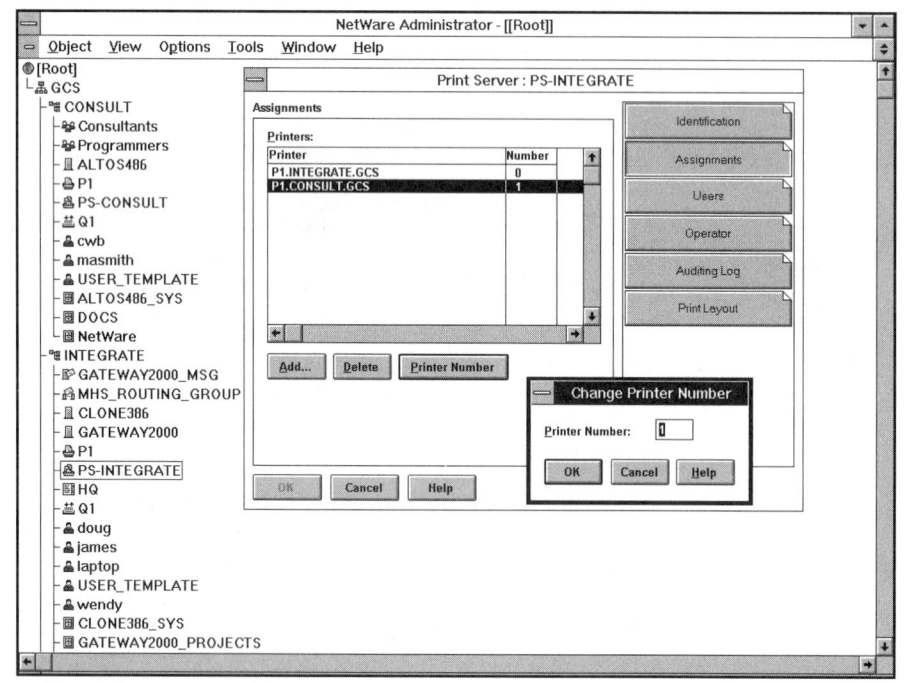

FIGURE 8.26

Viewing and changing print server printer assignments

Deleting a printer assignment requires you to highlight the printer in the Printers box and click on Delete. This eliminates the Printer object from this list, but doesn't delete the object itself.

As you can see in Figure 8.26, you can change a printer number within the Print Server object. Although most people don't know or care about this, the NPRINTER.NLM program requires, and NPRINTER.EXE allows, the loading of a port driver by specifying the print server name and logical printer number. This number may be referenced in batch files or applications requiring special printers. After the number is changed, the print server must be unloaded and reloaded for the changes to take effect.

Don't believe me? Check your server console, and after the line:

```
Loading Module PSERVER.NLM
```

you will see version and language details, then:

```
Network printer P1 (number 0) loaded
and attached to print server PS-INTEGRATE
```

This goes by quickly when the server is loading, and it's easy to miss. It makes sense, when you think about it, that NetWare will need some unique numeric way to identify printers supported by each print server. So if you want to change these, you now know how. When finished, click on OK to save the page and exit the Print Server dialog box.

Managing Print Server Users and Groups

> **8.19 IN-A-HURRY**
>
> **Add or Delete Print Server Object Users and Groups**
>
> 1. Open NetWare Administrator and double-click on the Print Server object to modify.
> 2. Click on the Users button.
> 3. To add a user or group, click on the Add button and mark the User and Group objects.
> 4. To delete a User or Group object, highlight the object in the Users box, then click on Delete.
> 5. Click on OK to save and exit.

Rights to use the Print Server object are not necessary to print. Only rights to the Print Queue object are necessary for printing; the rights to the Print Server object go along with that automatically.

The advantages to being a user of a particular Print Server object are these capabilities:

- Monitor the print server.

- See the print server status.

- Learn whether the print server needs some type of attention (rare, but possible).

As the Admin or equivalent user, start the NetWare Administrator program. Browse the NDS tree until the proper Print Server object is spotted, then highlight it and press Enter, or click on it with your right mouse button, highlight Details and press Enter. The Print Server object dialog box appears, listing the print server name at the top. Figure 8.27 shows this page for PS-INTEGRATE.

FIGURE 8.27

Adding a group to the PS-INTEGRATE access list

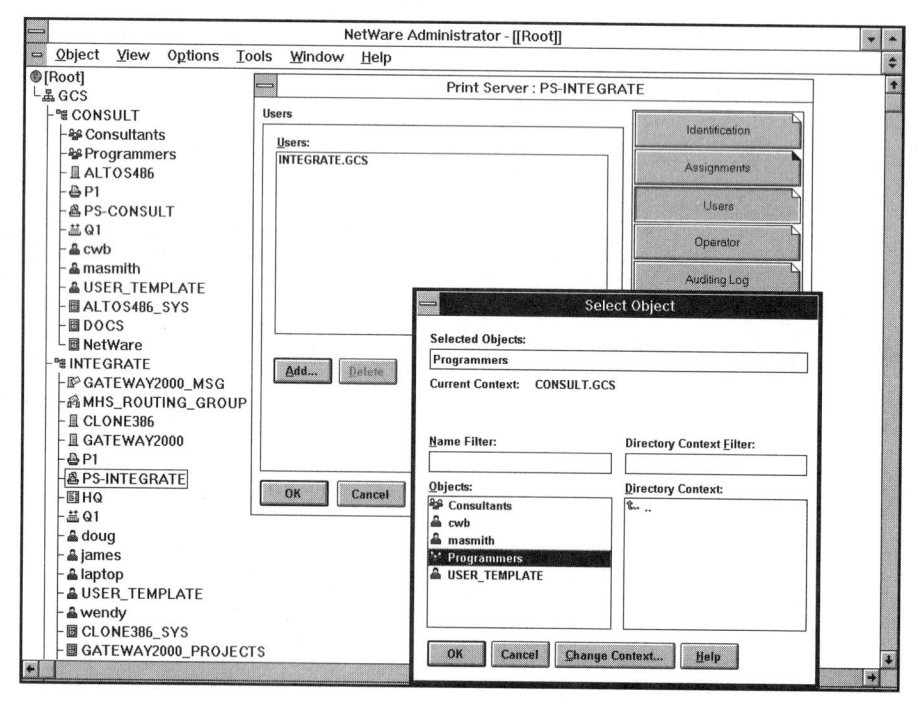

Why would we grant the PROGRAMMERS group rights to the print server? Programmers tend to test things, and those tests sometimes go awry. Since not all programmers are in the INTEGRATE container, adding them to the list of users for the print server allows any programmers who need access to have it.

Assigning and Modifying Print Server Operators

8.20 IN-A-HURRY

Add or Delete Print Server Operators

1. Open NetWare Administrator and double-click on the Print Server object to modify.

2. Click on the Operator button.

3. To add a user or group, click on the Add button, mark the User and Group objects to add, and click on OK in the Select Object dialog box.

4. To delete a User or Group object, highlight the object in the Users box, then click on Delete.

5. Click on OK to save and exit.

To add or delete a print server operator, log in to the network as Admin or equivalent, and start the NetWare Administrator program. Browse the NDS tree to find the print server of interest. Double-click on the Print Server object name. Click on the Operator button to see a screen similar to the one shown in Figure 8.28.

To add an operator, click on the Add button and cruise the Select Object dialog box. User and groups can be operators. Find the object(s) you wish to list as a Print Server object operator, and click on the OK button. This adds the chosen object(s) to the Operators box in the Print Server dialog box, as shown in Figure 8.28. Operators can see the print server status and down the print server. They also have authority to control the printers attached to the print server. Dead printer? An operator can reroute the printer output and the print jobs to a different print server until repair or replacement is finished.

Having a programmer be a print server operator makes good sense, especially if that programmer is writing programs that might do strange things to

FIGURE 8.28

Adding a print server helper

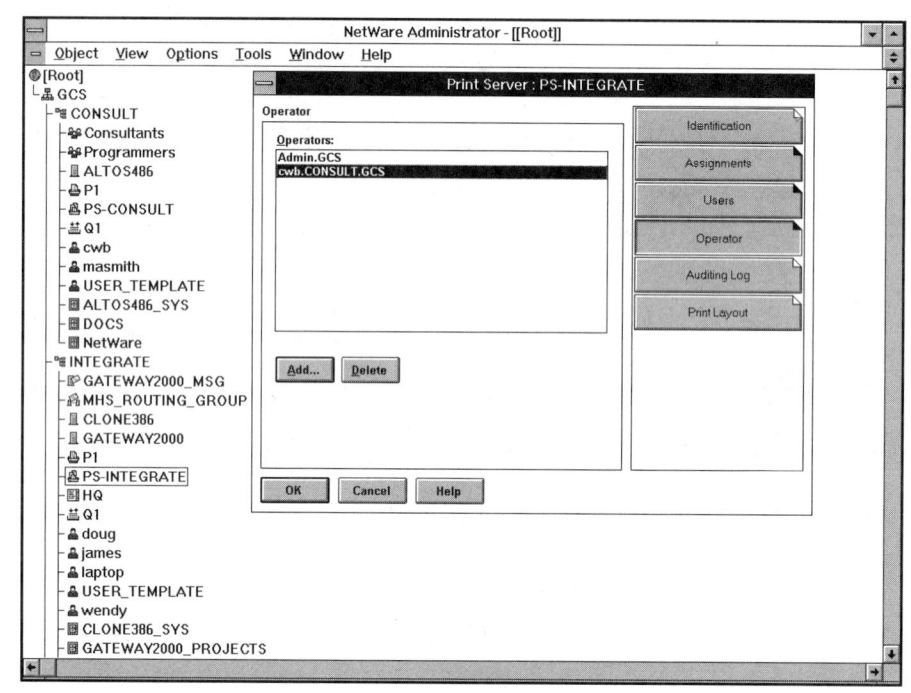

the printer when they're tested. But having help with the print system from anyone makes more sense than trying to do it yourself. Notice the only other operator listed so far is the Admin user. Do you want to answer every call for every paper jam and every form change?

Managing the Print Server Log

Log files, a listing of what happened where and when, are a staple of the mainframe and Unix worlds. They are late getting to the PC world, but items such as the log for the print server help rectify that oversight. The Print Server object log file tracks information such as:

- The internal ID number the operating system assigned to the print job
- The form used (if any)
- The print job name (if any)

8.21 IN-A-HURRY

Manage the Print Server Auditing Log

1. Open NetWare Administrator and double-click on the Print Server object to modify.

2. Click on the Auditing Log button.

3. View the Auditing Log for the print server, or click on View if the text box is empty.

4. To start logging, click on the Enable Auditing button.

5. To turn off logging, click on the Disable Auditing button.

6. To delete the log, click on Delete.

7. Limit the log size by checking the Limit Size box and setting the maximum size.

8. Click on OK to save and exit.

- The print queue name
- How many bytes a job took to print
- The user submitting the job
- When the job entered the print queue
- When the job actually printed
- Which printer serviced this job

Macintosh and Unix printers often supply this additional information:

- How long the print job took
- How many pages were printed

To see this information, connect to the network as either Admin or equivalent. Run the NetWare Administrator program and browse through the NDS tree until you find the print server whose log you wish to check. Double-click on the Print Server object, and click on the Auditing Log button. Figure 8.29 shows the Auditing Log page for Print Server object PS-INTEGRATE.

588 Chapter 8 • Arranging Network Printing

FIGURE 8.29

Tracking print jobs through better auditing

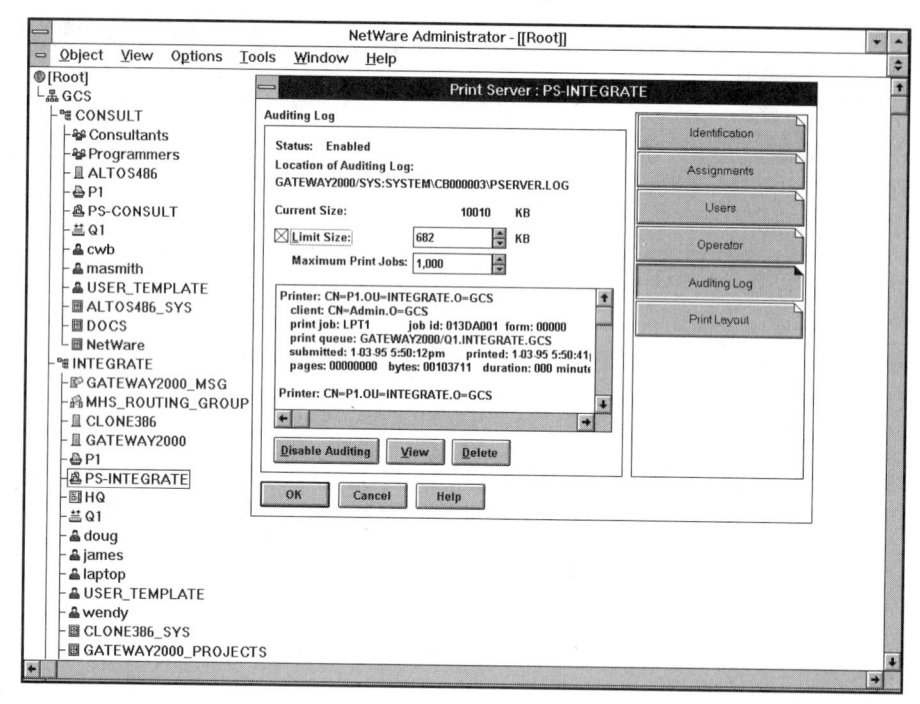

The top line, Status, tells whether Auditing is enabled or not. The status listed here will be the opposite of the button in the bottom-left corner of the interior dialog box. If Status is enabled, the button offers a choice to Disable.

The information in the Location of Auditing Log field is important, and not something you can change. It's important because Novell engineers realize that people that want this auditing information probably have a format they wish to use. Since it's impossible to guess what that format will be, the log is kept as a fixed-record-length ASCII file. The log may be read with any text editor, and managed by any database application that can import ASCII files.

There's a small problem with the Current Size information in NetWare 4.10. The size listed in Figure 8.29 is actually bytes, not KB. The display will show KB at some times, however, especially before you click on View to see the log file.

By checking the Limit Size box, you can keep the log from growing forever and taking over your hard disk. But keep in mind, if the maximum size is reached, the log stops recording instead of overwriting the earlier information. If limits are necessary, put this on your weekly checklist to keep the log from filling the space allotted and shutting down. You can change the size of the log by using the KB or Maximum Print Jobs text box scroll arrows. You can track nearly two million print jobs using 2 GB of disk space. Audit to your heart's content.

The actual audit log is read through the scrolling text window in the bottom portion of the dialog box. The entire log will scroll through the text box, but no changes can be made. If you view the log once, then come back to view it before another print job has gone through, the log may not appear in the window. Run a small print job through the print server to restart things.

Speaking of restarting things, you must unload and restart the print server software after the log is enabled (the default is disabled). Once the software is started, run a quick print job through to make sure the log picks up the information.

> **The Auditing Log and Your Quest for a New Printer**
>
> How could you use the numbers in the Print Server Auditing Log? Say you want another printer, and your boss doesn't want to pay for it.
>
> Track all the print jobs for the time going into the queue and the time coming out of the printer. If this is more than a minute or three, whip out your lost productivity argument. Paint visual images of high-priced employees waiting in line at the printer, cursing and complaining. Try to find a huge graphics file printout that backed up the queue for 20 minutes as your example. If your boss weakens, add a request for more file server memory. You always need file server memory, and more memory helps everything.
>
> If this doesn't work, ask your boss to list the workgroup personnel in order of printing importance. Lower-rated folks can be shunted to a print queue with a lower priority than the important printer people. Bosses hate to make this kind of decision, and will often authorize new hardware to avoid making this list. Remember to ask for more server memory while your boss is on the ropes.

Viewing the Print Layout in NetWare Administrator

The connections between printers, print queues, and print servers are somewhat abstract and hard to visualize. That's why Novell included a graphical representation of the print system interrelationships. This is another one of the new features of NetWare 4.1*x*.

8.22 IN-A-HURRY

View the Print Layout

1. Open NetWare Administrator and double-click on the Print Server object.

2. Click on the Print Layout button.

3. To update the diagram, click on Update.

4. To check the status of a listed object, highlight the object and click on Status.

5. Double-click on any object to collapse subordinate objects if the display is crowded.

To see this grand diagram, log in as either Admin or equivalent. Start the NetWare Administrator program, browse the NDS tree until the Print Server object you wish to check appears, and double-click on same. Click on the Print Layout button. A diagram similar to the one in Figure 8.30 will appear (the Status box appears after highlighting an object and clicking on Status).

FIGURE 8.30

The three legs supporting shared printing, and status information

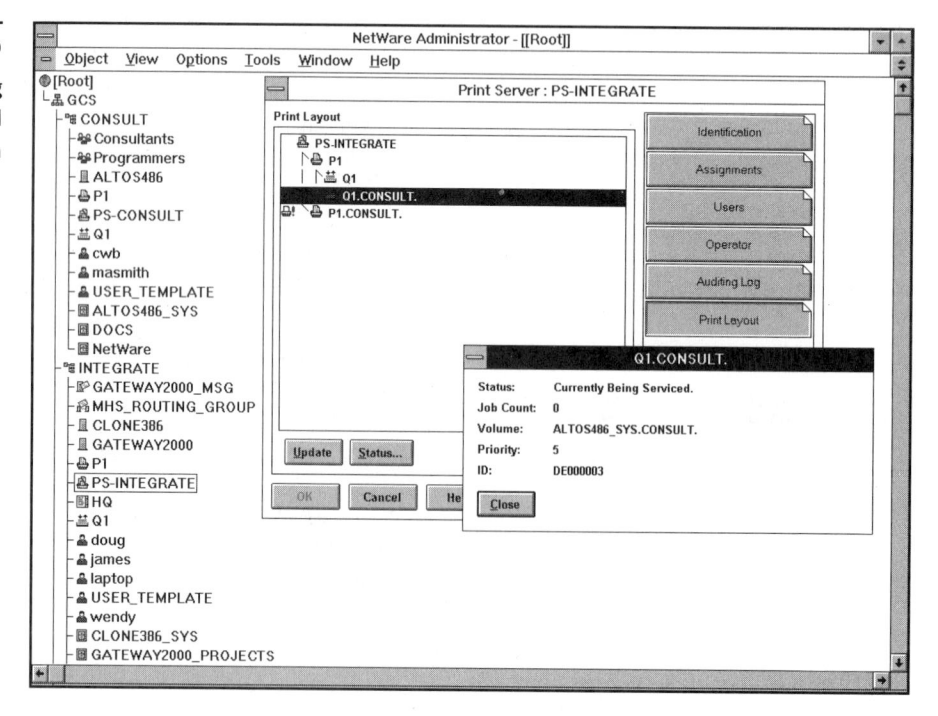

The Print Layout box shows standard icons for the Print Server object, the Printer Object, and the Print Queue object. The highlight bar is on Q1.CONSULT.GCS, a printer from another container redirected while P1.CONSULT.GCS is repaired or replaced.

P1.CONSULT.GCS has an exclamation point beside it, indicating trouble. Perhaps one of our programmers has sent some output there that locked it up, or perhaps it's just out of paper. The printer has been rerouted to the print server PS-INTEGRATE so users addressing that printer can still print. The Assignments page was used to make this happen. This movement is temporary, as shown by the dotted lines connecting printers and print queues.

To see the status of any print object, highlight the object and click on the Status button. If you prefer, you can click on the print object with the right button to open the Status box automatically. The box on display in Figure 8.30 is showing us some details for the print queue Q1.CONSULT.GCS.

Notice the trailing periods on P1.CONSULT. and Q1.CONSULT. in the diagram. Trailing periods represent the next level up, in our case GCS, which is shared by all devices in the diagram. Although the trailing periods aren't used by many network administrators, they do help keep the clutter down in this picture.

This same information can be seen through the Organization dialog box. Open the dialog box for an Organization object with printing defined, and click on the Print Layout button. The resulting page will look almost exactly like what is shown in Figure 8.30.

Viewing and Understanding Printer Status with NetWare Administrator

8.23 IN-A-HURRY

View and Change the Printer Status

1. Open NetWare Administrator and double-click on the Printer object to modify.
2. Click on the Printer Status button.
3. Use the command buttons to Pause, Start, Mount Form, Eject Page, or Abort Job, as necessary.
4. Click on OK to save and exit.

Now that we know about the three components that are part of every print job (the printer, the print queue, and the print server), we can better understand the Printer Status information. Although you won't spend lots of time checking this screen, it's handy when someone calls with a problem. If the problem is the wrong form or a huge job clogging the printer, you can tell immediately.

The NetWare Administrator program stays in communication with the servers after the program is started. This makes the Printer Status page real-time. When your printer goes from Waiting for Job to Printing as you watch, you'll understand the advantages of real-time management.

Start as an appropriate user on the network, and run NetWare Administrator. Browse the NDS tree until you find the printer to check, and double-click on the Printer object. Click on the Printer Status button. If you are not logged in as an administrator or user with authority to see printer information, the screen will look more like Figure 8.18 (the Printer Identification page) than Figure 8.31. Notice the buttons on the right side include Printer Status here, but not in the earlier figure.

Table 8.2 explains the fields listed on the Printer Status page.

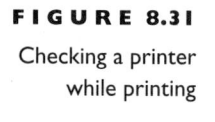

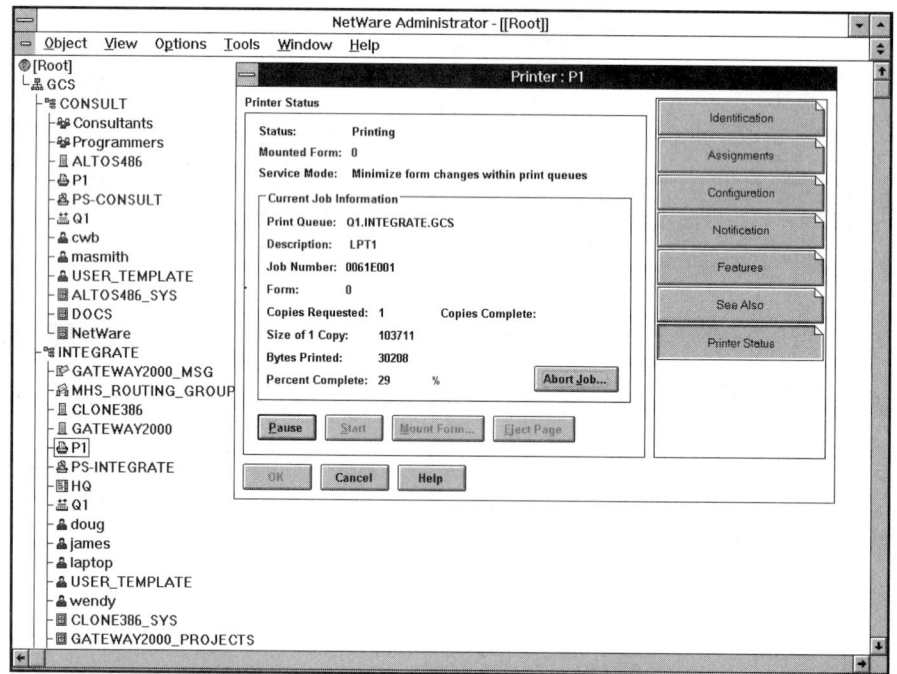

FIGURE 8.31

Checking a printer while printing

Setting Up and Managing Your Print System with NetWare Administrator 593

TABLE 8.2

Fields on NetWare Administrator's Printer Status Screen

FIELD	DESCRIPTION
Status	The printer status: Not Connected, Waiting for Form, Out of Paper, Printing, Paused, Stopped, Offline, Private, Waiting for Job, or Ready to Go Down.
Mounted Form	Defined form now loaded. If another form is needed, click on Mount Form for a dialog box listing all defined forms.
Service Mode	How jobs in the queue are processed according to forms usage.
Current Job Information	Listing of details about the current print job.
Print Queue	Queue submitting this print job.
Description	File name or port captured.
Job Number	Internal number assigned to this print job.
Form	Form used to print this job (if any).
Copies Requested	Requested copies per print job owner.
Copies Complete	If multiple copies are in process, which copy is currently printing.
Size of 1 Copy	Same as File Size field in the details portion for the Print Queue object.
Bytes Printed	Bytes processed by the printer for this print job.
Percent Complete	Ratio, listed per individual print job even for multiple-copy jobs.

The Printer Status page has four command buttons:

- **Pause:** Stops current job or changes printer from Waiting for Job to Stopped.

- **Start:** Moves from Paused to Printing, Stopped to Printing, or Stopped back to Waiting for Job.

- **Mount Form:** When clicked, opens a dialog box that lists the available forms and allows the form to be changed.

- **Eject Page:** Long-distance form-feed command to push a page from the printer.

> **NOTE:** You can see a screen with the same type of printer status information from the PSERVER.NLM console at the file server. However, opening the Printer Status page for the Printer object is easier than going to the server physically. It's also more friendly and usable than running the PSERVER screen with RCONSOLE.

Creating and Modifying Printer Forms with NetWare Administrator

8.24 IN-A-HURRY

Manage Printer Forms

1. Open NetWare Administrator, highlight the container to hold the Printer Form object, and press Enter.
2. Click on the Printer Forms button.
3. To create a Printer Form object, click on create and fill in the form name, number, paper length, and width.
4. To modify a Printer Form object, click on Modify and change the form name, number, paper length, or width.
5. To delete a Printer Form object, highlight the object and click on Delete.
6. Click on OK to save and exit.

All this talk about printer forms may lead you to believe they are some complex, amazing, outstanding feature of the printing world. Alas, they only set the paper boundaries. You can set length and width, but that's it.

Still, if you hate to print a regular letter on legal-size paper, or sometimes make the mistake of printing a legal-size document on letter-size paper, these forms can be useful. The NetWare Printer Forms feature can prevent these types of errors.

Different forms can certainly be the same length and width, of course. Just because the Request for Office Supplies form is the same size as the Request for Overtime form doesn't mean the two are interchangeable.

Setting Up and Managing Your Print System with NetWare Administrator 595

The form is created at the container level, and once created, it is available to all printers in the container. The file named PRINTDEF.DAT in SYS:PUBLIC holds the form definitions.

> **TIP** *Life is too short—don't use forms if you can avoid them. Printers are cheaper than management time for something as common as printing. If you have a need for both letter and legal printing, dedicate a printer to each. This may not make much sense in the capital budget, but it will certainly save management time and frustration.*

After connecting to the network as either Admin or equivalent, start NetWare. Since Printer Form objects are a container feature rather than a printer feature, highlight the container to hold the form. Once the container is highlighted, either press Enter or click the right mouse button to open the menu for the container, and then click on Details. Click on the Printer Forms button on the right side to open the dialog box shown in Figure 8.32.

The Name field can contain up to 12 alphanumeric characters. The first character must be a letter, and the name must be unique. If you use spaces, they appear as underscores.

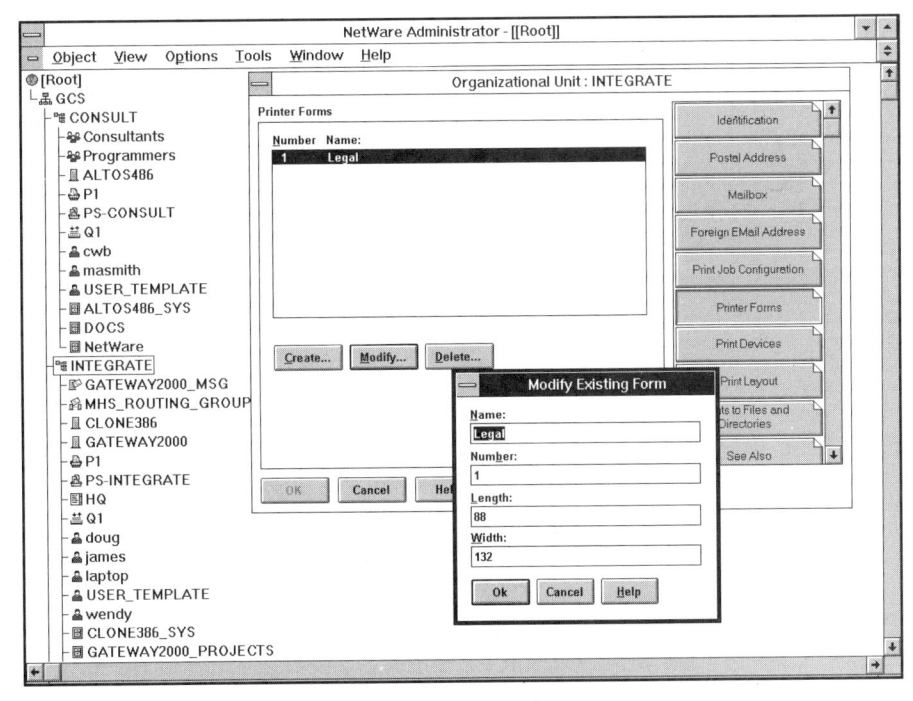

FIGURE 8.32

Modifying a printer form

The limits for the other page form fields are:

- **Number:** 0 to 254
- **Length:** 1 to 55
- **Width:** 1 to 999

These numbers are for your reference only. This information doesn't force any action or limitations on your printer; it only provides you a way to reference different paper sizes and hold printing until the right size paper is loaded.

Creating and Modifying Print Devices with NetWare Administrator

Here is another throwback feature, back to the time the laser printer was new and applications didn't know how to exploit all the features available. As a result, NetWare offered ways to set different print modes for printers with the few crude fonts and features available at the time.

Today this is less necessary, since the GUI has overwhelmed both the desktop and most applications. Printer drivers have become more complex for the vendors to support, while making life easier for users and network administrators.

Knowing life is not perfect, however, Novell provides 58 different printer definitions. Known as *print devices* inside NetWare, they can be modified to suit your situation. The included device files cover the popular printers, and they provide a good starting place if you must modify some printer functions. These functions are controlled by files with a PDF (Printer Definition File) extension, located in the PUBLIC directory.

Functions are actions, such as bold text or landscape orientation, that a printer can use. Modes are combinations of functions defined for specific printing needs. The string of functions are often sensitive to presentation order, so check your printer documentation for details.

Devices (printers) must be imported by the NetWare Administrator program or the DOS program PRINTDEF. During printing, the functions may be combined into print modes before being fed to the print device. The dance works this way:

- Print functions: Printer Reset, Landscape Orientation, and Typeface–Lineprinter

- Combined into mode: Report

- Print to printer device: HP LaserJet II/IID

Importing Devices

> **8.25 IN-A-HURRY**
>
> **Import or Delete a Print Device**
>
> 1. Open NetWare Administrator, highlight the container to hold the printer device, and press Enter.
>
> 2. Click on the Print Devices button.
>
> 3. Click on Import, choose a Printer Definition File (*.PDF) from the File Open dialog box, and click on OK.
>
> 4. To delete a print device, highlight it and click on Delete.
>
> 5. Click on OK to save the container Print Devices page settings and exit.

With five dozen predefined devices, you should be able to find the one for your printer, or a compatible printer, without too much trouble. If your printer is not represented, check with your NetWare dealer for new PDF file releases, or check with the printer manufacturer. If your applications have the printer drivers you need, the network files aren't necessary. It's better for your application to have the proper drivers than for you to set up the appropriate PDF file.

Open the NetWare Administrator program after logging in to the network as Admin or equivalent. Highlight the container that will hold the created print device and press Enter. Click on the Print Devices button on the far right of the dialog box. If Print Device objects exist, they may be modified or deleted by clicking on the appropriate buttons. To import a new print device, click on the Import button. The dialog box shown in Figure 8.33 will open.

The Files box in the dialog box will display only files with the PDF extension. As you can tell by the existence of the Directories box, you can easily search anywhere you have access to more PDF files.

There isn't any configuration that must be done at this time. If the printer works with your applications, no more configuration is necessary at all.

If you must create or modify print functions, a pop-up dialog box appears asking for the Function Name and Control Sequence. The unique name can be up to 32 alphanumeric characters, including spaces. The control sequences are the <Esc> <E> type codes sent to your printer to control various functions, such as printer reset, orientation, and font. The Help screen includes a complete listing of acceptable codes and good explanations.

FIGURE 8.33

Importing another print device into the INTEGRATE Organizational Unit

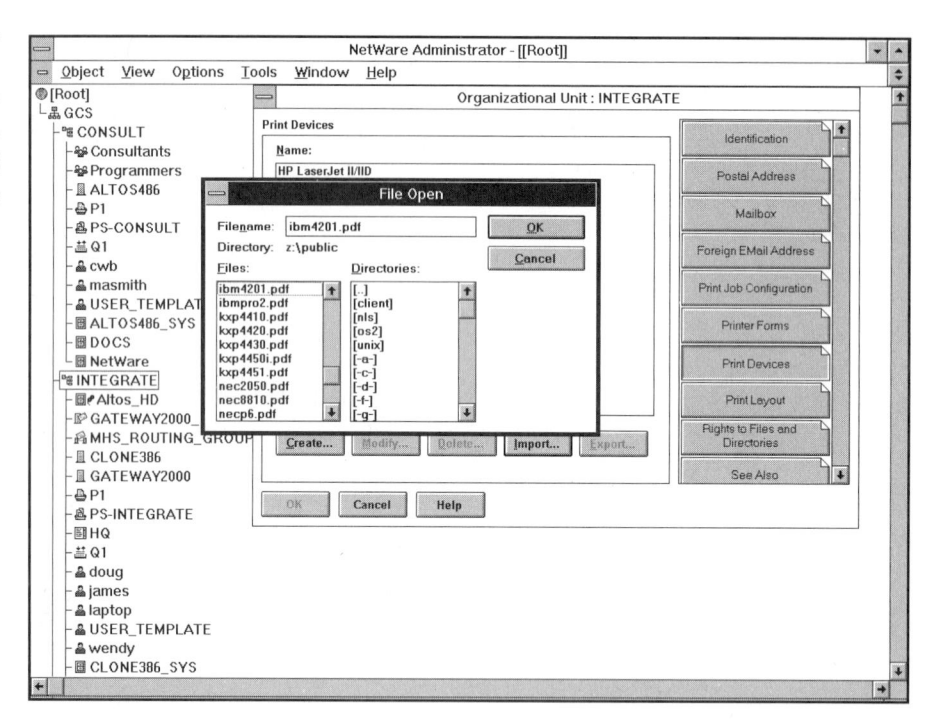

Exporting Devices

8.26 IN-A-HURRY

Export a Print Device

1. Open NetWare Administrator, highlight the container to hold the Printer Device, and press Enter.

2. Click on the Print Devices button.

3. Click on Export, choose a location to save the Printer Definition File (*.PDF), and click on OK in the File Save As dialog box.

4. Click on Cancel to exit the container Print Devices dialog box.

If one container has a definition for a print device, especially one that you have created or modified, you may want to share that device. The Export option on the Print Devices page will create the official Novell System PDF file for you. You may copy this file, including all modifications, anywhere you wish. This export feature makes it simple to import the copied file into other containers.

After connecting to the network as Admin or equivalent, run the NetWare Administrator program. Highlight the container where the print device export will take place (the source) and press Enter. Click on the Print Devices button on the right side of the dialog box, and then click on Export. The File Save As dialog box opens, as you can see in Figure 8.34.

FIGURE 8.34

Exporting a PDF file to another server

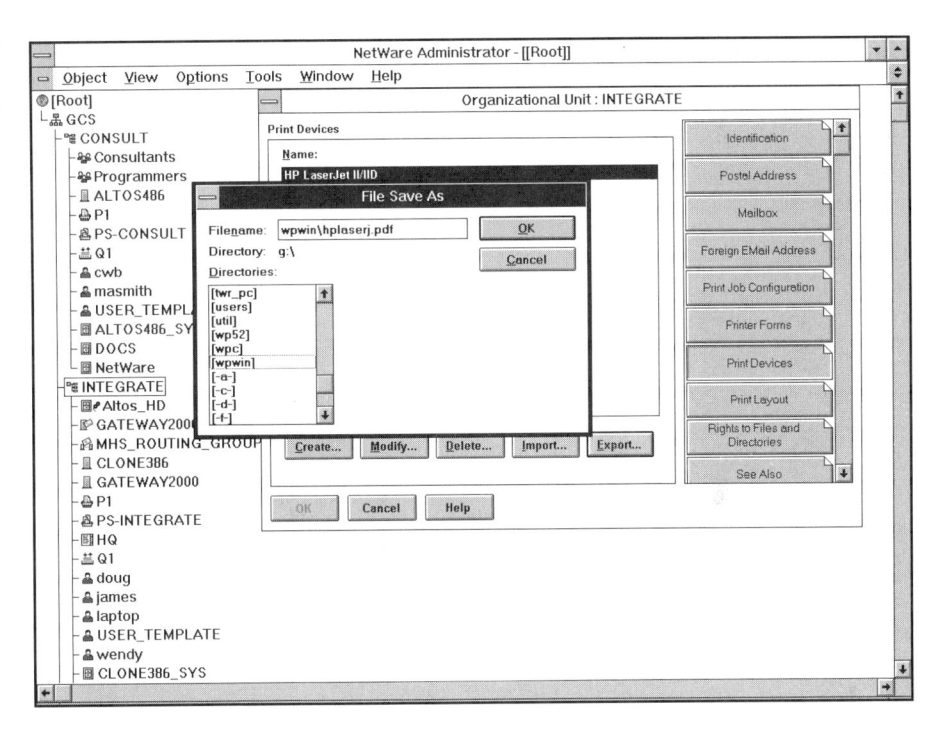

Once the PDF file is copied to another container, the Import utility can pick the file up and make use of it. Exporting is particularly valuable when a device has been customized. This allows you to copy, rather than re-create, all the work done setting up the print device.

Defining Print Modes

> **8.27 IN-A-HURRY**
>
> ### Define a New Print Mode
>
> 1. Open NetWare Administrator, highlight the container holding the printer device, and press Enter.
>
> 2. Click on the Print Devices button.
>
> 3. Click on Modify, and then click on Create Mode.
>
> 4. Type a unique name (eight alphanumeric characters or less, starting with a letter).
>
> 5. Highlight a function listed in the Device Functions list, and click on Add Above or Add Below.
>
> 6. Click on OK when the proper functions are listed in the Mode Functions list.
>
> 7. Click on Cancel to exit the container Print Devices dialog box.

Print modes define the font style, size, boldness, and page orientation. Although you can modify or delete modes for the existing printer list, these are dangerous actions and rarely needed. The safest, and most common, usage of print modes is to create new ones that set up the page to be printed in a special way.

Remember that specifying print modes means specifying new printer forms. This will require either separate printers for each form or extra printer management to load the proper forms.

WARNING

Print modes are not casual items to create and modify for fun. Check your printer's documentation carefully. The proper commands in the wrong order will lock up your printer just as tight as the wrong commands. These lockups require turning the printer off and back on to clear. Luckily, most users don't tend to play with these settings and cause trouble, even if they could find them buried in the NetWare Administrator program.

If you still need a printer form or two, log in to the network as Admin or an equivalent user. Start the NetWare Administrator program and highlight the container with the printer device that needs a new print mode and press Enter

Setting Up and Managing Your Print System with NetWare Administrator 601

(or click the right mouse button) and click on Details. Highlight a print device and click on Modify. In the Modify Existing Device dialog box, click on Create Mode to open the (surprise!) Create New Mode dialog box, shown in Figure 8.35.

FIGURE 8.35

Creating a new print mode

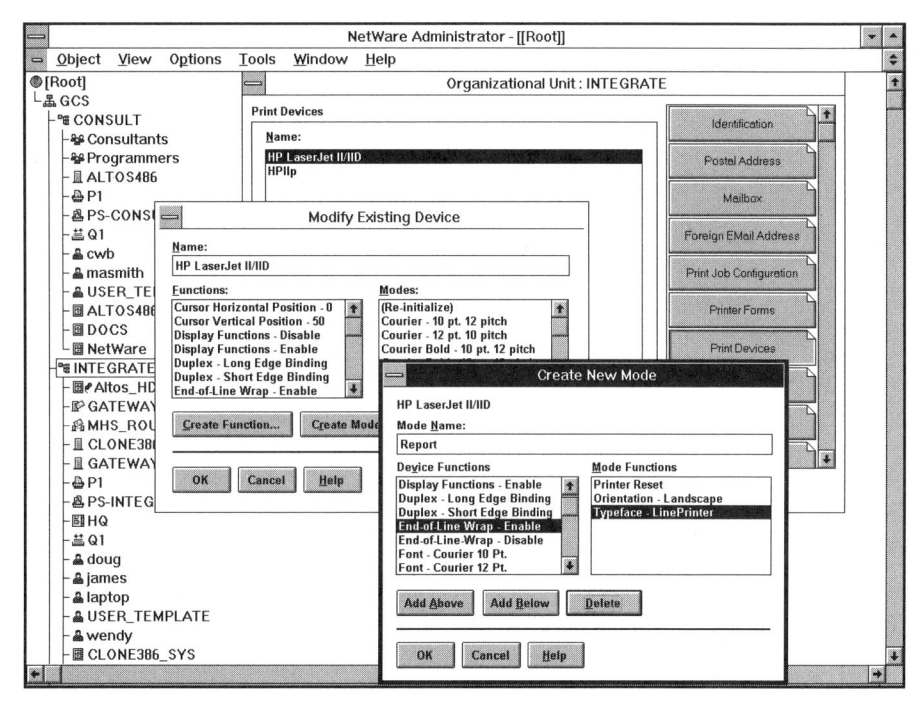

The list of printer function commands is in the left box, and the right box is empty until you choose the functions needed to make your new print mode. The name is first, so type a NetWare 3.*x* type name. This means eight letters or numbers, but beginning with a letter. This name must be unique. If you give an existing name (as in Report in the example shown in Figure 8.35), the error message will list several items that may be the error, and the system won't accept the duplicate name.

Pick each item from the Device Functions list, and click on Add Above or Add Below to move the function to the Mode Functions list. The entry will be placed above or below the highlighted mode function already in the box, if there is one.

Setting Up Print Job Configurations with NetWare Administrator

> **8.28 IN-A-HURRY**
>
> **Manage Print Job Configurations**
>
> 1. Open NetWare Administrator, highlight the container holding the print job configuration, and press Enter.
>
> 2. Click on the Print Job Configuration button.
>
> 3. To create a new configuration, click on New and enter the information.
>
> 4. To change an existing configuration, highlight the print job configuration name and click on Modify.
>
> 5. To set the default configuration, highlight that print job configuration name and click on Default.
>
> 6. Click on OK to save the settings.

Since users will wear out your beeper if the printing system has problems, these print job configurations are a wonderful network management tool.

Now that we've gone through lots of printing details, you may appreciate the labor-saving device known as a print job configuration more than you did previously. Although we haven't covered the user side of printing yet (that's in Chapter 12), almost every printing detail we've covered so far can be specified by the users. We can let them set their printing environment using command-line parameters every time they need to print, or we can create some print job configurations they can use. Since users will wear out your beeper if the printing system has problems, these print job configurations are a wonderful network management tool.

As with the other printing details, a good application will eliminate the need for most of this information. Applications today, routed to the proper printer, can quickly create beautiful or complex pages. Our job here is to make sure the minimum details are configured, and offer other print configurations for those applications that haven't gotten their printing support up to date.

Earlier versions of NetWare had only private print job configurations. Each of the configuration details could be the same, but the same configuration had to be copied to each user. In addition, there was a limit of 37 unique configurations that could be stored by the system.

NetWare 4.1x allows group configurations to be shared, while still allowing private ones for users if necessary. But you, as the administrator, need only create a default configuration, one time, for everyone. Users can create multiple configurations for different circumstances and easily reference them.

Each user in this container has access to the default Print Configuration object. If no instructions are issued to the contrary, the default Print Configuration object will provide the printing instructions for the user. Any of the defined print configurations can be declared the default configuration. In the upcoming figure, notice the Laser configuration has the little printer icon beside it. That says Laser is the default, and Default is not the default. See how flexible this is? To set the default, highlight one of the configurations and click on the Default button.

Figure 8.36 shows the Print Job Configuration page for the INTEGRATE.GCS container. The field names and acceptable values for the print job configurations are listed in Table 8.3.

FIGURE 8.36

The default print job configuration for a container

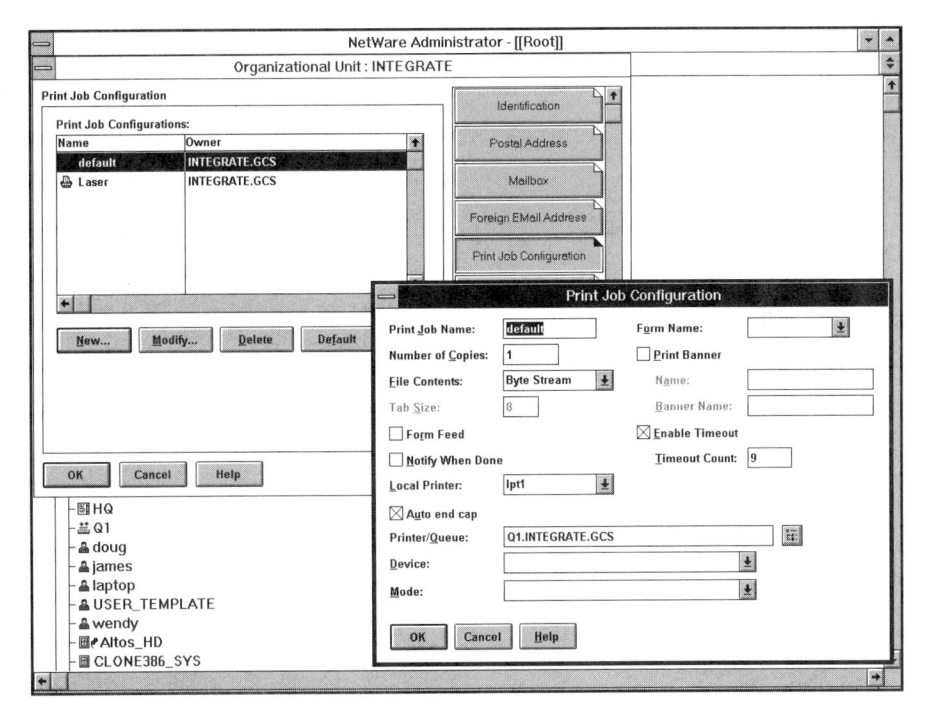

TABLE 8.3

Fields on NetWare Administrator's Print Job Configuration Screen

FIELD	DESCRIPTION
Print Job Name	Must be unique for this user. The name cannot be changed, although you can modify all other fields.
Number of Copies	The default is 1, but any number up to 65,000 may be entered.
File Contents	Text or Byte Stream, with Byte Stream the default and safest choice for general printing.
Tab Size	Active only when the File Contents is listed as Text. Refers to the width in characters each tab character should be when printed.
Form Feed	When checked, the CAPTURE or NPRINT software sends a form feed to flush the job out of the printer.
Notify When Done	When checked, the system will send the user a message when the print job is finished being spooled to the printer. It does not guarantee the printer has successfully printed the job itself.
Local Printer	Chooses which parallel port will be captured. NetWare expands on DOS by allowing up to nine LPT designations. A modification to the user's NET.CFG file must be made to allow more than three LPT ports.
Auto End Cap	When checked, tells the CAPTURE command to print the job when the application says it is finished.
Printer/Queue	Designates the printer or print queue for this print job configuration. Clicking on the Browser button opens the Select Object dialog box, which will show only printers and print queues.
Device	Specifies a named print device for this print job configuration.
Mode	Specifies a defined mode (such as Report) for the print device specified in the previous field.
Form Name	Specifies a defined form for this print job configuration, chosen from a pick list that appears when the down arrow button is clicked.
Print Banner	When checked, includes a banner page at the beginning of the print job.
Name	Active only when Print Banner is checked. When this field is blank, the user name is inserted. The name listed in this field and the next can be only 11 characters long.

TABLE 8.3 (cont.)	FIELD	DESCRIPTION
Fields on NetWare Administrator's Print Job Configuration Screen	Banner Name	Active only when Print Banner is checked. When this field is left blank, the printer port is inserted on the banner page. The name listed in this field and the previous one can be only 11 characters long.
	Enable Timeout	When checked, forces CAPTURE to consider a print job finished if there is no activity for a defined number of seconds.
	Timeout Count	Active only when Enable Timeout is checked. Range is from 1 to 1000 seconds. For typical word processing print jobs, a short value (5 to 10) will be fine. For print jobs requiring lots of computer calculations, such as large reports or spreadsheets, the time should be longer. If a print job comes out in two or more pieces, this value is too short.

Using PCONSOLE for Print System Configuration and Management

PCONSOLE IS THE time-honored, traditional method used by NetWare managers the world over to manage their printing systems. In NetWare 4.1x, it has been changed in two ways. First, it has been modified to reflect NetWare 4.1x features, such as contexts and containers and the like. Second, it has been superseded by the excellent print control software in NetWare Administrator.

As I've mentioned before, no one will admit to this officially, of course, but the DOS utilities such as PCONSOLE may go away someday. There are two trends that force this issue: DOS itself is going away, and managers overwhelmingly prefer GUI-based administration tools. However, the grim future doesn't detract from the usability of PCONSOLE today. The affection for PCONSOLE remains strong, even among those aware of the future. If not, why did the Quick Setup feature make it into PCONSOLE first (in NetWare 4.10), before it went into NetWare Administrator (in 4.11)? Oh, you think programming problems kept Quick Setup out of NetWare Administrator in NetWare 4.10? You're probably right.

There are three new features for PCONSOLE in NetWare 4.1*x*:

- **Quick Setup:** Allows you to create a complete print system setup in two minutes.
- **Integrated Setup:** PCONSOLE can now configure Unix and Macintosh printers.
- **Simplified Navigation:** The same functionality can be accessed from multiple menus.

The differences in PCONSOLE start on the opening screen. Where in the past there were three options at the beginning, there are now five. Check Figure 8.37 for the updated PCONSOLE screen.

FIGURE 8.37

PCONSOLE in the world of objects

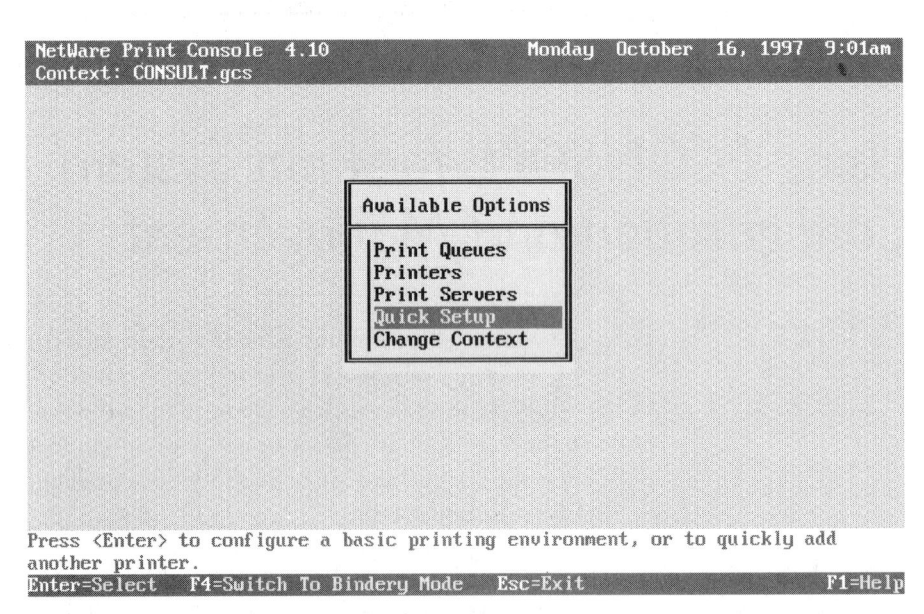

```
NetWare Print Console   4.10                          Monday  October 16, 1997  9:01am
Context: CONSULT.gcs

                              ┌─────Available Options─────┐
                              │ Print Queues              │
                              │ Printers                  │
                              │ Print Servers             │
                              │ Quick Setup               │
                              │ Change Context            │
                              └───────────────────────────┘

Press <Enter> to configure a basic printing environment, or to quickly add
another printer.
Enter=Select    F4=Switch To Bindery Mode    Esc=Exit                   F1=Help
```

In the past, you had a menu choice to Change Current File Server. NetWare 4.1*x* is no longer server-centric, so that choice has been replaced by Change Context. Since printers are separate from print queues in NetWare 4.1*x*, there is a menu item for Printers. The options to work with print queues and print servers are still there, just worded slightly differently. The Quick Setup option was described in the first part of this chapter.

Notice the status line, especially the second item:

```
F4=Switch To Bindery Mode
```

This is obviously new. It allows you to see Bindery Services objects on NetWare 4.1x servers, or to see NetWare 3.x print queues and print servers. When you're in Bindery mode, you can see only Bindery Services-type devices. When in Directory Services mode, you see only NDS print system objects, including printers. There are features in PCONSOLE that appear only in Directory Services mode.

Don't use PCONSOLE in Bindery mode unless you must support NetWare 3.x printing devices, such as third-party print servers, on a NetWare 4 server. Many hardware print servers that fit into printers are still not "NDS-smart," and must use Bindery mode as well. See the section on NetSync in Chapter 10 for more details.

Creating the Print Queue Object in PCONSOLE

> **8.29 IN-A-HURRY**
>
> ### Create a Print Queue Object in PCONSOLE
>
> 1. Start PCONSOLE, move to the context for the new print queue, and choose Print Queues.
>
> 2. Press Insert in the Print Queues menu to create a new Print Queue object.
>
> 3. Type the new print queue name.
>
> 4. Type the new print queue volume, or press Insert to browse for Volume objects.
>
> 5. Press Escape twice to exit, or press Enter to configure the new Print Queue object.

Log in as either Admin or equivalent. Having Supervisor rights to the container holding the new print queue will allow you to create and modify all the print system pieces.

After you connect to the network, start the PCONSOLE program. Either begin in the appropriate container, or use the Change Context menu option to move to the proper place for the new print queue. Highlight Print Queues on the menu and press Enter to open the Print Queues menu box. Press Insert to add a new print queue.

Filling in the New Print Queue Name field is mandatory. Keep in mind the restrictions for naming objects, especially objects that may be referenced by NetWare 3.*x* clients or servers. Short names keep you out of trouble. The official name limit is 64 characters, including spaces and underscores.

The Print Queue object's Volume field must be filled in as well. You can type the volume name, but it's easier to press Insert and choose one from the Object, Class screen. The Print Queue object for a container can exist on a volume in another context if necessary. Pick any volume in the Object, Class browser screen, even one from another context.

In earlier NetWare versions, print queues were always on the SYS: volume, no matter how many volumes your server had. This led to problems at times, since print queues can sometimes overrun the space allotted to them. If that volume is SYS, bad things may happen, such as your server shutting down.

With NetWare 4.1*x*, you have a choice of placing the printer queues on any volume you wish. This will not stop print queues from overflowing the available disk space on the volume, but if they do overrun the available disk space, the volume that shuts down won't be SYS:. Your network will continue to operate, and you can fix the Print Queue object problem without the added pressure of trying to restart the file server operating system with a full SYS volume.

After you've filled in the name and volume for the Print Queue object, you can skip to the section titled "Configuring Print Queue Object Details in PCONSOLE" to finish the setup. If you haven't created any Printer or Print Server objects, set up those first before configuring the Print Queue object.

Creating the Printer Object in PCONSOLE

8.30 IN-A-HURRY

Create a Printer Object in PCONSOLE

1. Start PCONSOLE and choose Printers.

2. Press Insert in the Printers menu to create a new Printer object.

3. Type the new printer name and press Enter.

4. Press Escape twice to exit, or press Enter to configure the new Printer object.

Printer object creation shows another advantage of NDS in general and better NetWare printing in particular. The name for a printer can be short and sweet, because it will be identified in its context (P1.CONSULT.GCS). In earlier NetWare versions, each printer defined on a server needed to be uniquely named. With the hierarchical naming conventions of NDS, P1 is a valid name a dozen times across the network, as long as each P1 is in a different context. All users in their home context can reference P1 and get to their default printer.

On the other hand, you may use up to 64 characters for the printer name. With the client programs available for users, they never need to type the full printer name. But keep in mind the restrictions for naming objects, especially objects that may be referenced by NetWare 3.*x* clients or servers.

As an appropriate user, start the PCONSOLE program. It's quicker to start from the proper context than to change using the PCONSOLE menu, but either way works.

Highlight Printers from the main PCONSOLE menu and press Enter. The Printers menu box will appear. It will be empty if this is your first printer. Press the Insert key and provide a name for the printer.

From here, you can skip to the section titled "Configuring Printer Object Details in PCONSOLE" to finish the setup. If you haven't created any Print Server objects, set up one of those first before configuring the Printer and Print Queue objects.

Creating the Print Server Object in PCONSOLE

8.31 IN-A-HURRY

Create a Print Server Object in PCONSOLE

1. Start PCONSOLE and choose Print Servers.

2. Press Insert in the Print Servers menu to create a new Print Server object.

3. Type the new print server name and press Enter.

4. Press Escape twice to exit, or press Enter to configure the new Print Server object.

Start PCONSOLE as either Admin or equivalent. From the main menu, highlight Print Servers and press Enter. Press Insert from the Print Servers menu to open the text box asking for the print server name. Using PS at the beginning of the name isn't required, but it is helpful. The users will never need to type the print server name, so the length isn't too important. If this object will be connecting to any NetWare 3.*x* servers, keep the name to less than 47 characters; 64 are allowed otherwise. But either maximum is much more than necessary.

After you type the name, press Enter. At this point, you will be warned the process may take up to 60 seconds, but it normally doesn't. Figure 8.38 shows the name for a new print server just entered.

Since all three of our print system pieces are now created, let's start configuring them.

FIGURE 8.38

Creating a Print Server object for laser printers

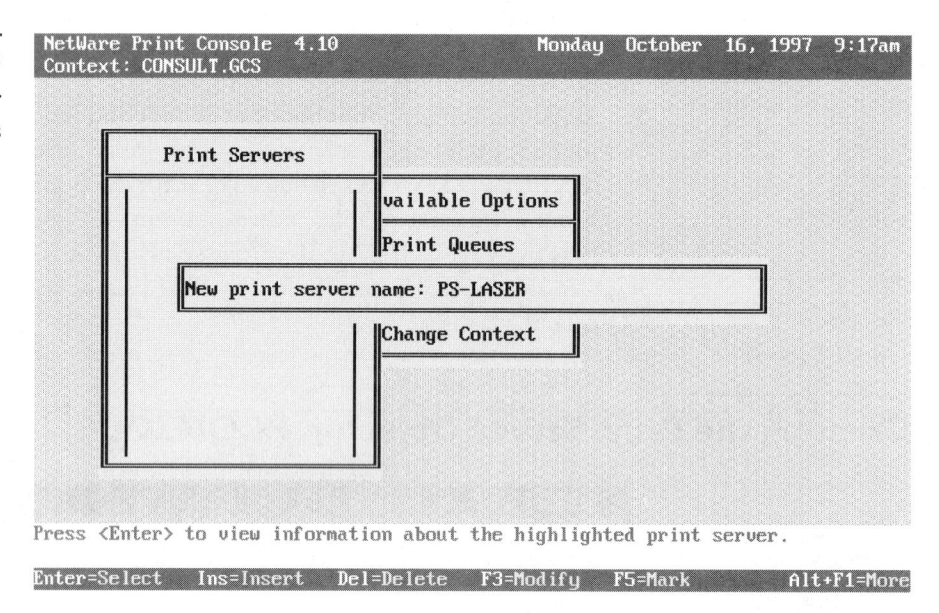

Configuring Print Server Object Details in PCONSOLE

The PCONSOLE version of the printing system leaves out many of the identification niceties provided by the NetWare Administrator program. PCONSOLE retains the uncluttered look of earlier versions, as you can see in Figure 8.39.

The Print Server Information menu changes depending on whether a regular user or the Admin user looks at it. In the figure, you can see the last two entries, Password and Audit. Neither of these are available to regular users.

FIGURE 8.39

Starting the Print Server object configuration

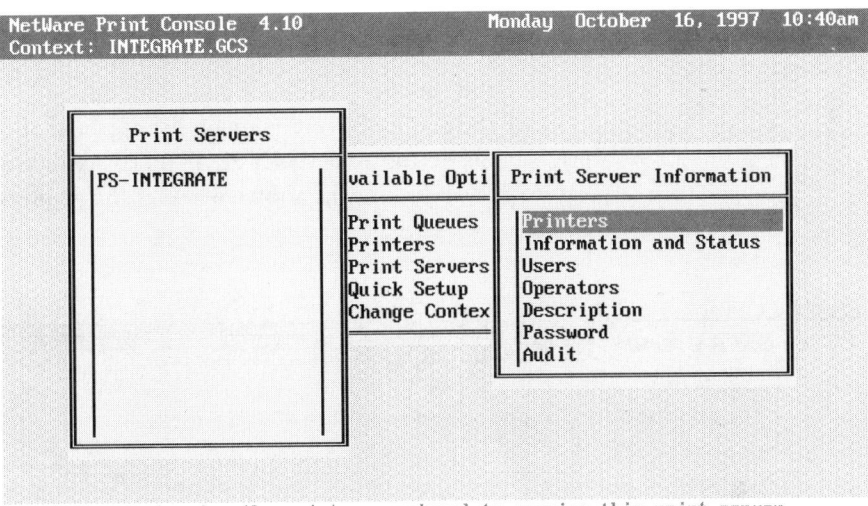

```
NetWare Print Console  4.10                    Monday  October  16, 1997  10:40am
Context: INTEGRATE.GCS

        ┌─────────────────────┐
        │    Print Servers    │
        ├─────────────────────┤
        │ PS-INTEGRATE        │ ailable Opti │ Print Server Information │
        │                     │              │ Printers                 │
        │                     │ Print Queues │ Information and Status   │
        │                     │ Printers     │ Users                    │
        │                     │ Print Servers│ Operators                │
        │                     │ Quick Setup  │ Description              │
        │                     │ Change Contex│ Password                 │
        │                     │              │ Audit                    │
        │                     │              │                          │
        └─────────────────────┘

Press <Enter> to view the printers assigned to service this print server.

Enter=Select    Esc=Exit                                              F1=Help
```

Managing Attached Printers

8.32 IN-A-HURRY

Add, Delete, or Rename Printer Objects in PCONSOLE

1. Start PCONSOLE and choose Print Servers.

2. Choose the Print Server object to configure, and then choose Printers.

3. To add a printer, press Insert and choose the printer from the Object, Class screen.

4. To delete a printer, highlight the printer name and press Delete.

5. To rename a printer, highlight the printer, press F3, type the new name for the printer, and press Enter.

6. Press Escape twice to exit the menu and save your changes.

This section is an excellent example of the simplified navigation feature of PCONSOLE: You can create a Printer object as part of configuring the Print

Server object. We won't do that now; we'll save the printer configuration for the printer section. But we will add and delete printers from the list supported by this print server.

Once the Serviced Printers menu list appears, all printers connected to the print server (in this case PS-INTEGRATE) are displayed. As the status line in Figure 8.40 says, this list shows whether the printers are active, configured, or both.

FIGURE 8.40

To delete or not to delete

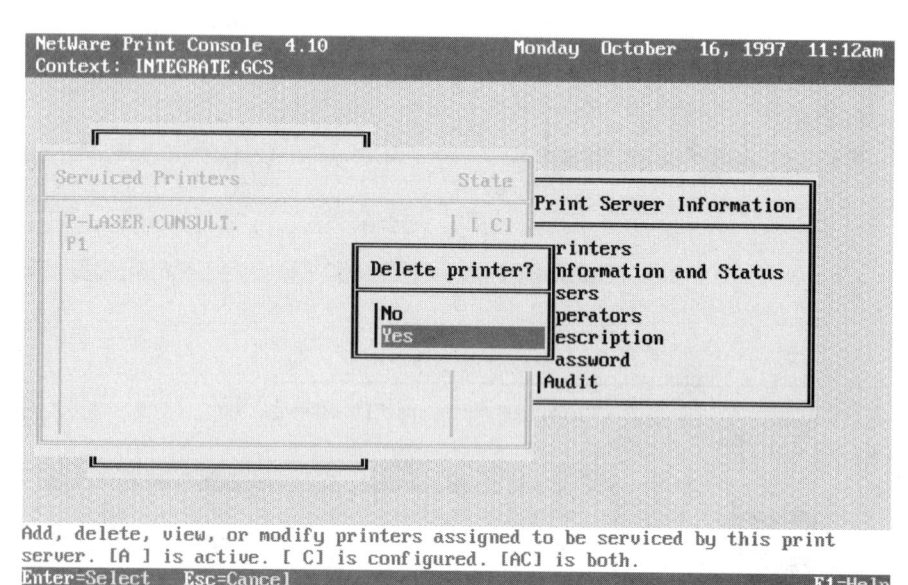

```
NetWare Print Console   4.10                Monday  October  16, 1997  11:12am
Context: INTEGRATE.GCS

┌─────────────────────────────────────┐
│ Serviced Printers           State   │┌──────────────────────────┐
│ P-LASER.CONSULT.            [ C ]   ││ Print Server Information │
│ P1                                  ││rinters                   │
│                    ┌──────────────┐ ││nformation and Status     │
│                    │Delete printer?│ ││sers                      │
│                    │              │ ││perators                  │
│                    │ No           │ ││escription                │
│                    │ Yes          │ ││assword                   │
│                    └──────────────┘ ││Audit                     │
│                                     │└──────────────────────────┘
│                                     │
└─────────────────────────────────────┘

Add, delete, view, or modify printers assigned to be serviced by this print
server. [A ] is active. [ C] is configured. [AC] is both.
Enter=Select    Esc=Cancel                                        F1=Help
```

Although you can't see the subtle difference in the printer names, I'm threatening to delete our new printer PS-LASER we created just a bit ago in the CONSULT container. How did that get here? I added it, by pressing Insert while in the Selected Printers menu list. The Object, Class browse screen opened, and I highlighted P-LASER and pressed the Enter key. That procedure is not particularly photogenic, because the Object, Class screen covers everything else.

You can rename a printer by highlighting the name in the list and pressing F3. A text box opens and asks you to Rename Printer To, leaving the current name in the box for you to edit. After renaming the printer, press Enter to save the name. The new name will be reflected immediately in the list.

Print Server Information and Status

> **8.33 IN-A-HURRY**
>
> **View or Change Print Server Status in PCONSOLE**
>
> 1. Start PCONSOLE and choose Print Servers.
> 2. Choose the Print Server object of interest, and then select Information and Status.
> 3. Choose the printer to check, then choose Current Server Status.
> 4. To change the broadcast name for the Print Server object, choose Advertising Name.
> 5. Press Escape to exit the menu and save your changes.

Since print server software runs on file servers, you might think you need to go to the physical file server to see how the print server is doing. Not so; just check the status through PCONSOLE. You can also stop the print server from this screen.

Figure 8.41 shows the Print Server Information and Status screen. There are only two items that can be changed from here: Current Server Status and Advertising Name.

FIGURE 8.41
Checking out the print server

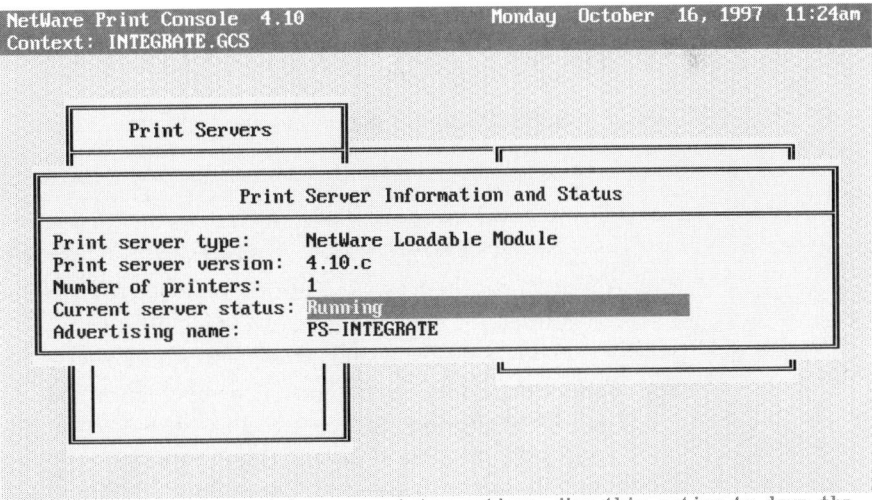

```
NetWare Print Console  4.10                Monday  October 16, 1997  11:24am
Context: INTEGRATE.GCS

        ┌─────────────────┐
        │  Print Servers  │
        └─────────────────┘
    ┌──────────────────────────────────────────────┐
    │      Print Server Information and Status     │
    ├──────────────────────────────────────────────┤
    │  Print server type:     NetWare Loadable Module
    │  Print server version:  4.10.c
    │  Number of printers:    1
    │  Current server status: Running
    │  Advertising name:      PS-INTEGRATE
    └──────────────────────────────────────────────┘

Press <Enter> to view print server status options. Use this option to down the
print server.
Enter=Select    Esc=Exit                                              F1=Help
```

There are three status levels:

- **Running:** The print server is active and functioning.

- **Going down after current print jobs:** The print server will reject new entries and stop after the current queue contents are finished.

- **Down:** The print server is not working.

The middle option is quite useful. It's similar to a checkout lane closing, but finishing with the people who are in the line already. You can set the print server to refuse any more print jobs. Once the last print job is finished, which may be quite a while depending on your print volume, the print server goes down.

Managing Print Server Users or Groups

> **8.34 IN-A-HURRY**
>
> **Add or Change Print Server Users or Groups in PCONSOLE**
>
> 1. Start PCONSOLE and choose Print Servers.
> 2. Choose the Print Server object of interest, and then select Users.
> 3. To add a user or group, press Insert and choose from the Object, Class screen.
> 4. To delete a user or group, highlight the name and press Delete, then verify the deletion.
> 5. Press Escape to exit the menu and save your changes.

Print server users are those individuals and groups who can see the Print Server object status. It is not necessary to list any users or groups in this screen in order for them to use a printer attached to the print server. That permission is granted for the print queue, not the print server.

Figure 8.42 shows the three people and/or groups currently allowed to check the print server status. The explanation line at the bottom of the screen is a bit misleading; everyone can use it, but these User objects can see the status. By default, all the users in the INTEGRATE container can see the print server status.

FIGURE 8.42

Doug and the Programmers have been added to the Print Server Users list

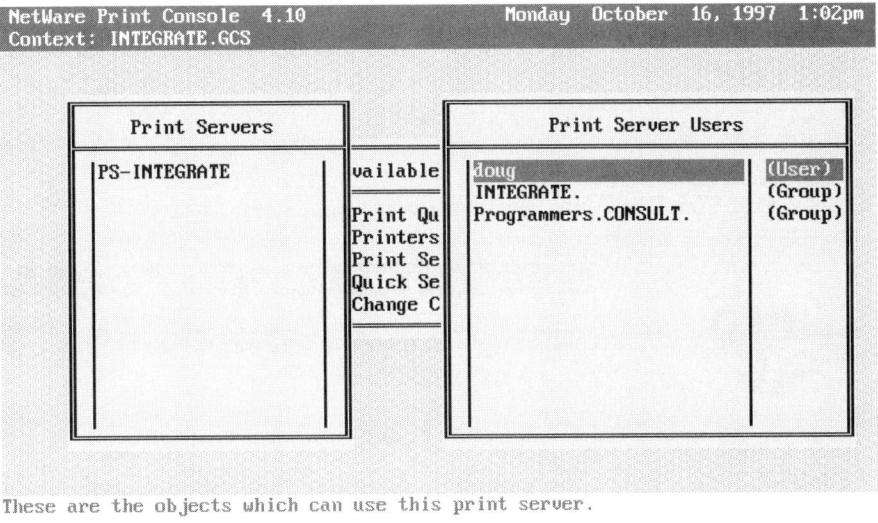

```
NetWare Print Console  4.10                    Monday  October  16, 1997  1:02pm
Context: INTEGRATE.GCS

         ┌─── Print Servers ───┐        ┌──── Print Server Users ────┐
         │ PS-INTEGRATE        │ailable │ doug                (User) │
         │                     ├────────┤ INTEGRATE.         (Group) │
         │                     │Print Qu│ Programmers.CONSULT.(Group)│
         │                     │Printers│                            │
         │                     │Print Se│                            │
         │                     │Quick Se│                            │
         │                     │Change C│                            │
         │                     │        │                            │
         └─────────────────────┘        └────────────────────────────┘

These are the objects which can use this print server.
Ins=Insert  Del=Delete   F5=Mark   Esc=Exit                           F1=Help
```

Managing Print Server Operators

8.35 IN-A-HURRY

Add or Change Print Server Operators in PCONSOLE

1. Start PCONSOLE and choose Print Servers.

2. Choose the Print Server object of interest, and then select Operators.

3. To add a user or group, press Insert and choose from the Object, Class screen.

4. To delete a user or group, highlight the name and press Delete, then verify the deletion.

5. Press Escape to exit the menu and save your changes.

Operators can see the print server status and down the print server. They also have authority to control the printers attached to the print server. For example, if a printer has problems, an operator can reroute the printer traffic to a different print server until repair or replacement is finished.

The procedure for adding print server operators is the same as that for adding users. Remember that any users on the network, including those who don't belong to the default container for the Print Server object, can become both print server users and operators.

Changing the Print Server Description

> **8.36 IN-A-HURRY**
>
> **Change the Print Server Object Description in PCONSOLE**
>
> 1. Start PCONSOLE and choose Print Servers.
>
> 2. Choose the Print Server object of interest, and then select Description.
>
> 3. Type a new description or edit the existing text.
>
> 4. Press Escape to exit the text box and save your changes.

A print server description can be viewed by anyone, but only an administrator of some level may add or change the description. Unlike the NetWare Administrator's Description field, this one is limited to 128 characters, with no extra lines and the like.

The description is useful for identifying print servers when there are so many you lose track, or when you set up a print server and someone else must administer it. Tricky details about the print server? Helpful hints for when things crash? Leave word here. Figure 8.43 shows an example.

The other option is to use the Description field for searches. However, for the search to be successful, you must match the information in the Description field exactly. If you plan to use this field for searches, print a list of acceptable description entries and use that list as the only options for this field. If you don't dictate the field's contents, searches will rarely work.

Setting or Changing the Print Server Password

Assigning a print server password will help limit access to the print server. Every time the print server is loaded, the password must be entered.

FIGURE 8.43

Print server description as warning

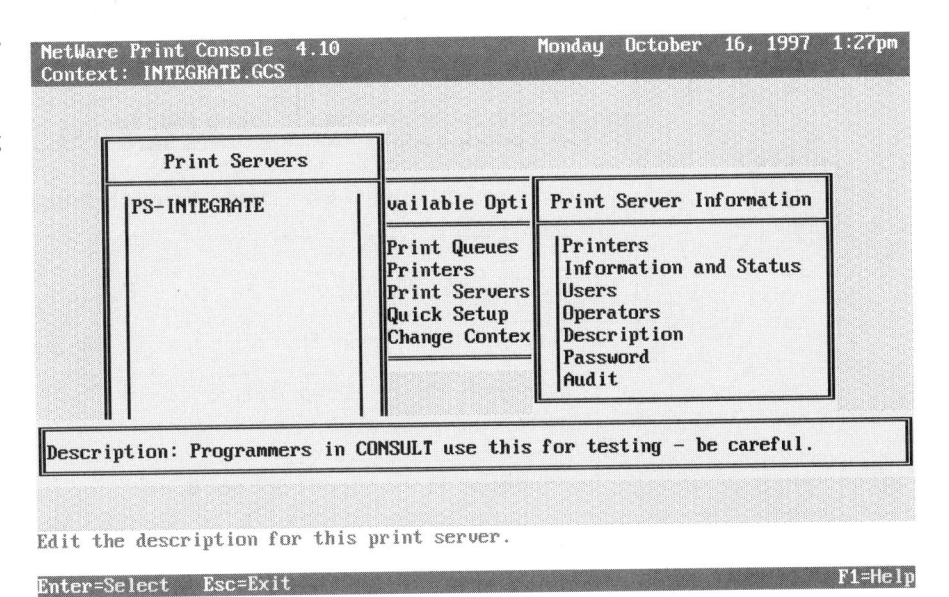

```
NetWare Print Console   4.10              Monday  October  16, 1997  1:27pm
Context: INTEGRATE.GCS

        ┌─────Print Servers─────┐
        │ PS-INTEGRATE          │ vailable Opti ┌─Print Server Information─┐
        │                       │ Print Queues  │ Printers                 │
        │                       │ Printers      │ Information and Status   │
        │                       │ Print Servers │ Users                    │
        │                       │ Quick Setup   │ Operators                │
        │                       │ Change Contex │ Description              │
        │                       │               │ Password                 │
        │                       │               │ Audit                    │
        └───────────────────────┘               └──────────────────────────┘

 Description: Programmers in CONSULT use this for testing - be careful.

Edit the description for this print server.

Enter=Select   Esc=Exit                                            F1=Help
```

8.37 IN-A-HURRY

Add or Change the Print Server Object Password in PCONSOLE

1. Start PCONSOLE and choose Print Servers.

2. Choose the Print Server object of interest, and then select Password.

3. Type a new password, and then retype it for verification.

4. Press Escape to exit the text box and save your changes.

As with all NetWare passwords, the new password must be typed, and then retyped for verification. If you're a sloppy typist, slow down for your passwords. If you're so sloppy you mistype the password twice in a row, I feel sorry for you. The only thing to do then is to delete the Print Server object and re-create it a minute later using the same name.

Viewing or Configuring the Print Server Audit Log

> **8.38 IN-A-HURRY**
>
> **View or Configure the Print Server Audit Log in PCONSOLE**
>
> 1. Start PCONSOLE and choose Print Servers.
> 2. Choose the Print Server object of interest, and then select Audit.
> 3. To configure the Audit Log, press Enter. Choose whether or not to enable auditing and limit the log file size.
> 4. Press Escape to exit and save your changes.

The Print Server object log file tracks information such as the print job's internal ID number (assigned by the operating system), the print queue name, the user submitting the job, when the job entered the print queue, when the job actually printed, which printer serviced this job, and other details. Macintosh and Unix printer logs often supply additional information, including how long the print job took and how many pages were printed.

As you can see in Figure 8.44, the setup for auditing a print server is simple. To enable the audit function (fancy for "start auditing"), highlight the Yes in the Enable Auditing field and press Enter. If you say No (the default), the rest of the fields will stay empty.

When you say Yes, you must then decide whether or not to limit the size of the audit log file. If you say Yes to the Limit Log File Size choice, you will keep the log from growing forever and taking over your hard disk. However, if the maximum size you set is reached, the log stops recording instead of overwriting the earlier information. If limits are necessary, put this on your weekly checklist to keep the log from filling the space allotted and shutting down. Change the size of the log by typing a number between 0 and 2,000,000. You can track nearly two million print jobs using 2 GB of disk space.

The Location of Auditing Log is important, and it's something you can't change. The log is kept as a fixed-record-length ASCII file. You can read the log with any text editor or database application that can import ASCII files.

You must unload and restart the print server software after the log is enabled. Once started, run a quick print job through to make sure the log picks up the information.

FIGURE 8.44

Auditing information in PCONSOLE

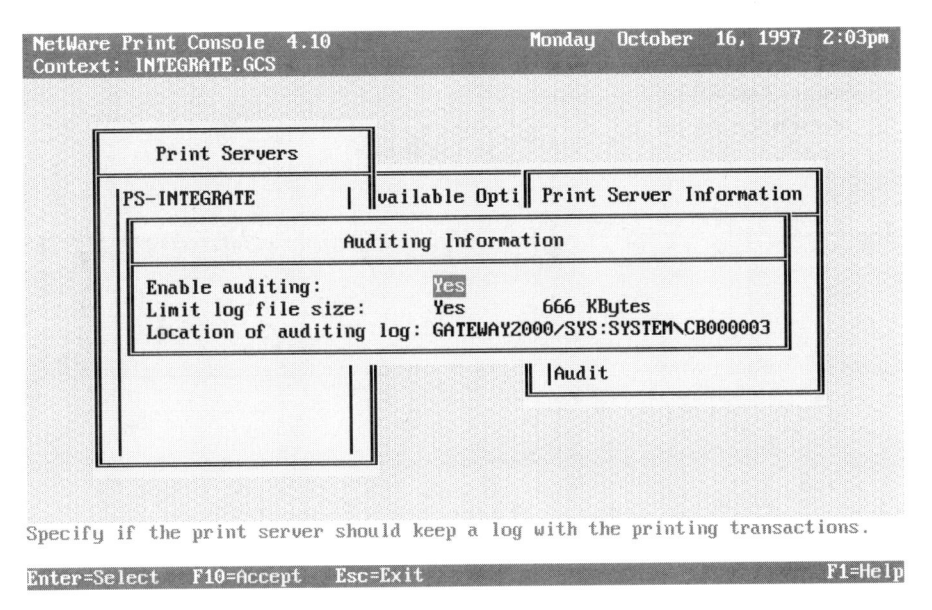

```
NetWare Print Console   4.10                    Monday  October  16, 1997  2:03pm
Context: INTEGRATE.GCS

         ┌─ Print Servers ──┐
         │ PS-INTEGRATE     │  vailable Opti │ Print Server Information │
         │                  ├─────────────────────────────────────────┐
         │          Auditing Information                              │
         │  Enable auditing:         Yes                              │
         │  Limit log file size:     Yes      666 KBytes              │
         │  Location of auditing log: GATEWAY2000/SYS:SYSTEM\CB000003 │
         │                                                            │
         │                                    │ Audit │               │
         │                                                            │
         └────────────────────────────────────────────────────────────┘

Specify if the print server should keep a log with the printing transactions.
Enter=Select    F10=Accept    Esc=Exit                            F1=Help
```

Configuring Print Queue Object Details in PCONSOLE

The Print Queue object has many of the same properties as other objects in NetWare 4.1x, plus a few extra. Figure 8.45 shows the Print Queue Information menu in PCONSOLE. Print queues are reliable. You'll probably manage print queues only because the printer has a problem. So, although you may use this menu often, it's almost never the fault of the print queue; the printer or bad printout from an application is usually to blame.

Viewing Current Print Jobs

When there is a problem with a printer or print queue, you will need to get to the screen that shows information about the current print jobs. You can delete, rearrange, postpone, or revise the instructions for print jobs from the print job summary screen.

You know this is the biggest part of print control when you consider the placement of the print job information in the menu system: press Enter three times and you're there. There, in this case, is the job summary screen, as shown in Figure 8.46.

FIGURE 8.45

Checking the Print Queue Information choices

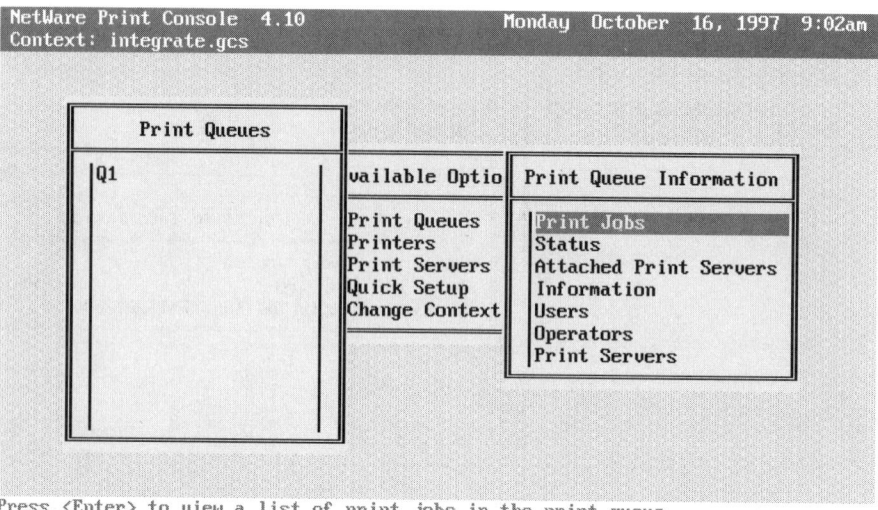

```
NetWare Print Console  4.10                  Monday  October  16, 1997  9:02am
Context: integrate.gcs

        Print Queues
    ┌──────────────────┐
    │Q1                │      vailable Optio   Print Queue Information
    │                  │      ┌──────────────┐ ┌──────────────────────┐
    │                  │      │Print Queues  │ │Print Jobs            │
    │                  │      │Printers      │ │Status                │
    │                  │      │Print Servers │ │Attached Print Servers│
    │                  │      │Quick Setup   │ │Information           │
    │                  │      │Change Context│ │Users                 │
    │                  │      └──────────────┘ │Operators             │
    │                  │                       │Print Servers         │
    │                  │                       └──────────────────────┘
    └──────────────────┘

Press <Enter> to view a list of print jobs in the print queue.
Enter=Select    Esc=Exit                                           F1=Help
```

8.39 IN-A-HURRY

View or Adjust Waiting Print Jobs in PCONSOLE

1. Start PCONSOLE and choose Print Queues.

2. Choose the Print Queue object of interest, and then select Print Jobs.

3. View the Sequence, Name (of user), Description, Status, Form Number, and Job ID of waiting print jobs.

4. To see the job details, highlight a print job and press Enter.

5. To add a print job, press Insert and give the file name, or press Insert again and browse for the job to print.

6. To delete a job, highlight the print job and press Delete.

7. Press Escape to exit the print jobs list.

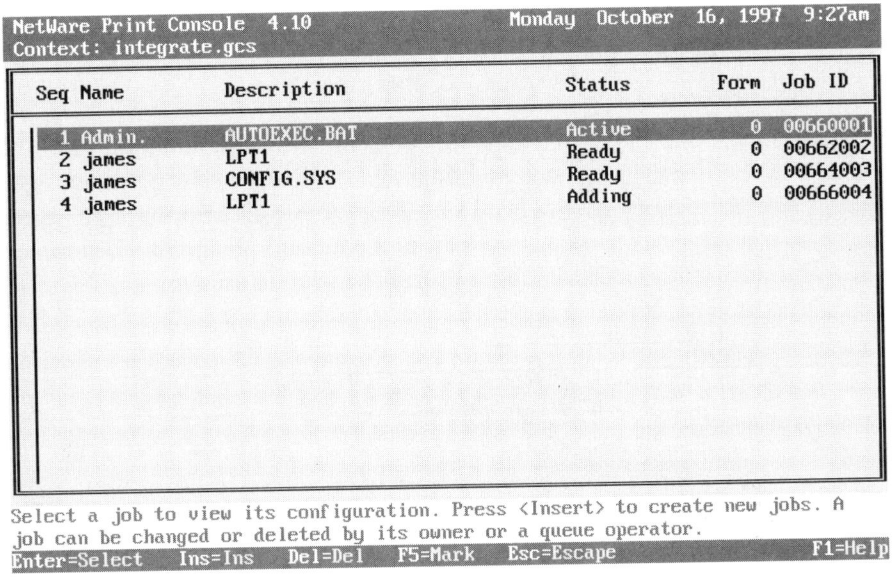

FIGURE 8.46

Print jobs in progress, ready, and being added to the print queue

```
NetWare Print Console  4.10                     Monday October 16, 1997  9:27am
Context: integrate.gcs

Seq Name         Description               Status          Form  Job ID
  1 Admin.       AUTOEXEC.BAT              Active            0   00660001
  2 james        LPT1                      Ready             0   00662002
  3 james        CONFIG.SYS                Ready             0   00664003
  4 james        LPT1                      Adding            0   00666004




















Select a job to view its configuration. Press <Insert> to create new jobs. A
job can be changed or deleted by its owner or a queue operator.
Enter=Select    Ins=Ins     Del=Del    F5=Mark    Esc=Escape         F1=Help
```

This screen holds the important information about your print jobs:

- **Seq (Sequence):** Sequence number of those waiting print jobs.

- **Name:** Name of the user who submitted the print job.

- **Description:** Name of the file submitted, or local printer port if redirected by the CAPTURE command.

- **Status:** The status of the print job: Active (being printed or processed), Ready (ready to be processed), Held (paused by the print job submitter), or Adding (file is currently being captured by the print queue).

- **Form:** Form number to be used, if any.

- **Job ID:** Unique system-assigned ID number for this job.

On this screen, the following keystrokes will help:

Enter	Shows detailed print job information.
Delete	Removes print job from the print queue.
Insert	Adds a new print job into the print queue.
F5	Marks multiple print jobs.

Chapter 8 ▪ Arranging Network Printing

    F7   Unmarks all previously marked print jobs.

    Escape   Exits this screen.

When you press Enter while highlighting one of the print jobs in the print queue, the Print Job Information screen provides great detail on the print job itself. The source of most of this information is a print configuration from either the client or a container. Figure 8.47 shows an example of this screen, and Table 8.4 describes the fields here.

FIGURE 8.47
Print job details and more details

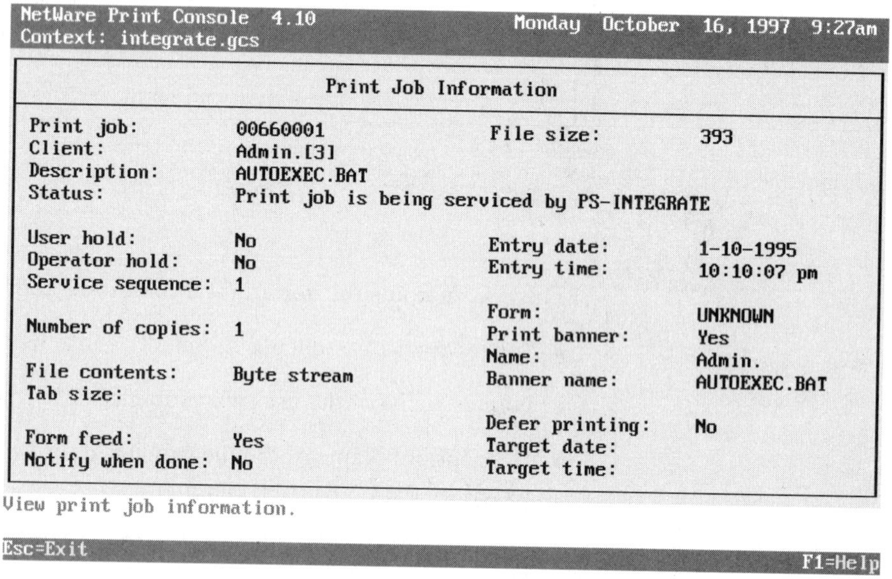

```
NetWare Print Console  4.10                    Monday  October  16, 1997  9:27am
Context: integrate.gcs

                        Print Job Information

Print job:       00660001                  File size:      393
Client:          Admin.[3]
Description:     AUTOEXEC.BAT
Status:          Print job is being serviced by PS-INTEGRATE

User hold:       No                        Entry date:     1-10-1995
Operator hold:   No                        Entry time:     10:10:07 pm
Service sequence: 1
                                           Form:           UNKNOWN
Number of copies: 1                        Print banner:   Yes
                                           Name:           Admin.
File contents:   Byte stream               Banner name:    AUTOEXEC.BAT
Tab size:
                                           Defer printing: No
Form feed:       Yes                       Target date:
Notify when done: No                       Target time:

View print job information.

Esc=Exit                                                              F1=Help
```

TABLE 8.4
Fields on PCONSOLE's Print Job Information Screen

FIELD	DESCRIPTION
Print Job	Unique system-assigned ID number for this job.
File Size	Size in bytes of this print job.
Client	User who submitted this job.
Description	Descriptive information, which typically shows captured printer port.
Status	Descriptive line about the print job. Ready, Held, or Active on the job list summary screen translates to more information on this screen.

TABLE 8.4 (cont.)
Fields on PCONSOLE's Print Job Information Screen

FIELD	DESCRIPTION
User Hold	Job held by original submitter.
Operator Hold	Job held by the print queue operator or administrator.
Service Sequence	This job's position in the print queue.
Number of Copies	Instructions per print job for duplicates.
File Contents	Not a security breach, this concerns only the type of file data. Actual file information is not available to this viewer. Byte Stream indicates the existence of non-ASCII data in the print file. Text indicates the existence of only straight ASCII text in the print file.
Tab Size	Used only with text files, indicates the number of spaces used to represent the tab character inside the print stream.
Form Feed	Indicates whether or not a form-feed command is sent to the printer at the end of the print job.
Notify When Done	Use a system message to notify the user this print job is finished.
Entry Date	The date the print job was submitted.
Entry Time	The time the print job was submitted.
Form	Whether a particular form will be used for this job. If a specific form was requested by the user when this job was submitted, that name will appear. In this screen, you can choose this field and select any defined forms.
Print Banner	Whether the user wishes this print job to have an identification banner printed as the first page of this print job.
Name	If Print Banner is checked, the name of the user submitting the print job.
Banner Name	If Print Banner is checked, the name of the print job. If not specified by the user, the printer port used by the CAPTURE program will be listed.
Defer Printing	Delay printing until the specified Target Date and Target Time. This provides an easy way to postpone long or graphically complex print jobs to a less disruptive time.

Viewing and Modifying the Print Queue Status

> **8.40 IN-A-HURRY**
>
> ### View and Modify Print Queue Status in PCONSOLE
>
> 1. Start PCONSOLE and choose Print Queues.
> 2. Choose the Print Queue object of interest, and then select Status.
> 3. View the current number of print jobs and number of active print servers.
> 4. Queue operators may set Operator flags affecting print queue services.
> 5. Press Escape to exit.

When you press Enter on the Status choice of the Print Queue Information menu, you see the screen shown in Figure 8.48. The top two lines in the screen give a quick view of how busy the print queue is (meaning how far behind the printer). These two lines are informational only and can't be changed from here.

FIGURE 8.48

Print Queue Status screen, showing a fully functional print queue

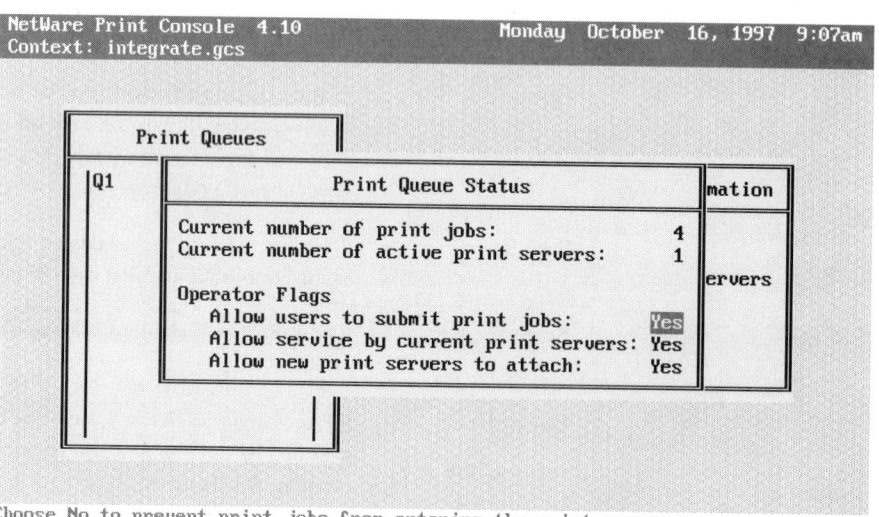

```
NetWare Print Console  4.10                    Monday  October  16, 1997  9:07am
Context: integrate.gcs

        ┌─ Print Queues ─┐
        │ Q1 │    ┌──────────── Print Queue Status ────────────┐ mation
        │    │    │                                            │
        │    │    │ Current number of print jobs:          4   │
        │    │    │ Current number of active print servers: 1  │ ervers
        │    │    │                                            │
        │    │    │ Operator Flags                             │
        │    │    │   Allow users to submit print jobs:   Yes  │
        │    │    │   Allow service by current print servers: Yes │
        │    │    │   Allow new print servers to attach:  Yes  │
        │    │    └────────────────────────────────────────────┘
        │    │
        └────┘

Choose No to prevent print jobs from entering the print queue.
Enter=Select    Esc=Exit                                          F1=Help
```

In cases where queues are clogged or print jobs need to be rerouted, the flags on the Print Queue Status screen can help. You can set the first flag to No so that users can't send jobs to a print queue. If a print server is being replaced or modified, you can set the flags to No to unhook the connection between server and queue.

The Operator Flags lines can be toggled Yes or No. Highlight the answer field for each line and press Y or N to toggle the setting for these flags:

- **Allow Users to Submit Print Jobs:** When Yes, queue users may submit print jobs to the queue.

- **Allow Service by Current Print Servers:** When Yes, assigned print servers may transfer jobs in the print queue to the proper printer.

- **Allow New Print Server to Attach:** When Yes, allows print servers to attach to the queue.

Viewing Attached Print Servers

8.41 IN-A-HURRY

View Print Servers Attached to the Print Queue in PCONSOLE

1. Start PCONSOLE and choose Print Queues.

2. Choose the Print Queue object of interest, and then select Attached Print Servers.

3. View the current number of print servers attached and the connection number to the NetWare server where the queue resides.

4. Press Escape to close the pop-up window.

This Attached Print Servers option is labeled well; highlight this entry on the Print Queue Information menu and press Enter, and you will see the list of attached print servers supporting this print queue. The text box opens underneath the Print Queue Information menu. If there is only one print server, the box is small.

There is no action available at this point except to press Escape and exit. You can't make any changes from this screen.

Viewing Print Queue System Information

> **8.42 IN-A-HURRY**
>
> **View Print Queue System Information**
>
> 1. Start PCONSOLE and choose Print Queues.
>
> 2. Choose the Print Queue object of interest, and then select Information.
>
> 3. View the Object ID number, supporting NetWare server, and supporting volume on that server.
>
> 4. Press Escape to close the pop-up window.

Another "look-but-don't-touch" screen, Print Queue System Information shows system assignments related to the Print Queue object. No changes can be made from this screen.

The object ID referred to is a unique number assigned by the system to this print queue when created. In earlier NetWare versions, a subdirectory with this number was created under the SYSTEM directory on the SYS: volume. In NetWare 4.1*x*, a subdirectory with this number (for example, CC000003) exists in the QUEUES directory on the volume listed.

Managing Print Queue Users

> **8.43 IN-A-HURRY**
>
> **Add or Delete Print Queue Users in PCONSOLE**
>
> 1. Start PCONSOLE and choose Print Queues.
>
> 2. Choose the Print Queue object of interest, and then select Users.
>
> 3. To add a user to the list of users allowed to send print jobs to this print queue, press Insert and choose a user or group from the Object, Class screen.
>
> 4. To delete a user, highlight the user or group, press Delete, and then verify the deletion.
>
> 5. Press Escape to close the pop-up window.

The list of approved users for a print queue automatically includes those users in the same context as the print queue. You can allow others, both individual users and groups, to use the print queue by adding them to the list of print queue users.

Figure 8.49 shows that everyone on this small network has access to this print queue; both containers are listed as group users, and the Admin user is listed because that is who created the print queue.

When you press the Insert key, the Object, Class browse screen opens, and you are free to cruise the network. The F5 key, as always, works to tag several objects, allowing you to mark multiple objects and have them all move into the list of approved users.

Highlight a user or group and press the Delete key to delete a user or group from the list of approved users. This affects only the ability of the user to send print jobs to this queue. It does not delete users or groups from the system.

Managing Print Queue Operators

A print queue operator can manage other users' print jobs, change the order of print jobs serviced, or delete those jobs from the print queue. A user listed as a print queue operator can also change the print queue status by modifying the three print queue operator flags we discussed earlier. The Admin user, or equivalent, can assign users to be print queue operators.

FIGURE 8.49
A print queue welcoming everyone

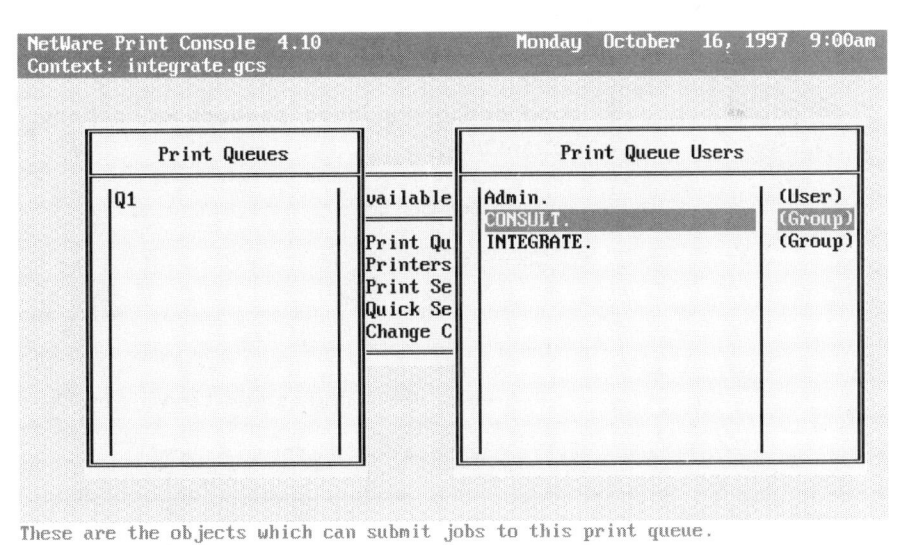

> **8.44 IN-A-HURRY**
>
> **Add or Delete Print Queue Operators in PCONSOLE**
>
> 1. Start PCONSOLE and choose Print Queues.
> 2. Choose the Print Queue object of interest, and then select Operators.
> 3. To add to the list of operators, press Insert and choose a user or group from the Object, Class screen.
> 4. To delete a user, highlight the user or group, press Delete, and verify the deletion.
> 5. Press Escape to close the pop-up window.

The Print Queue Operators screen looks and acts exactly like the Print Queue Users screen (Figure 8.49). Remember that a user from another context is free to not only use this print queue, but to be an operator. Any user from any context is free to do anything across the network, and this is just one example of that flexibility.

To delete a user or group from the list of operators, highlight the user or group and press the Delete key. This just removes the user or group as a print queue operator. It does not delete users or groups from the system.

Managing Print Servers for a Print Queue

> **8.45 IN-A-HURRY**
>
> **Add or Delete Print Servers for a Print Queue in PCONSOLE**
>
> 1. Start PCONSOLE and choose Print Queues.
> 2. Choose the Print Queue object of interest, and then select Print Servers.
> 3. To add a print server to the list, press Insert and choose a print server from the Object, Class screen.
> 4. To delete a server, highlight the print server, press Delete, and verify the deletion.
> 5. Press Escape to close the pop-up window.

Four sections earlier, we saw which print server is actively supporting this print queue. This option shows us which print servers have the rights to service this print queue.

The screen looks like the screens showing a list of users for the print queue (such as Figure 8.49). To add print servers to this list, press the Insert key to open the Object, Class screen. You will likely need to browse in another container to find another print server. Any print queue can be serviced by any print server, regardless of context.

To delete a print server from the list, highlight the print server name and press the Delete key. Press Enter again to verify you wish to delete the print server from this list. The Print Server object itself will not be deleted.

Configuring Printer Object Details in PCONSOLE

The PCONSOLE screens for the Printer objects work slightly differently than those for Print Queue and Print Server objects. In the Printer object screens, a large form, reminiscent of those in the NetWare Administrator program, has multiple forms hidden behind many of the entries. However, this arrangement is less intuitive than in the NetWare Administrator, since there's no easy way in text screens to show browser buttons and arrows indicating screen C is waiting behind screen B.

From the main PCONSOLE menu, highlighting Printers and pressing Enter opens a box that lists each of the printers assigned. Highlight the one of your choice and press Enter, and you will see a screen similar to that in Figure 8.50.

Setting the Printer Configuration and Printer Status

8.46 IN-A-HURRY

Configure Printer Object Details in PCONSOLE

1. Start PCONSOLE and choose Printers.

2. To add a printer, press the Insert key and type the unique name for the printer.

3. To delete a printer, highlight the printer name and press Delete.

4. To configure a printer, choose that Printer object, then highlight the printer configuration field to modify and press Enter.

5. Type the new information. If a submenu appears, fill out the appropriate fields and press Escape.

6. Press Escape to close the Printer Configuration screen.

FIGURE 8.50

The Printer object opening screen hiding many configuration screens

```
NetWare Print Console   4.10                    Monday  October  16, 1997  10:16am
Context: INTEGRATE.GCS

                        ┌─────────────────────────────────────────────────────┐
                        │              Printer P1 Configuration               │
                        ├─────────────────────────────────────────────────────┤
                        │ Print server:            PS-INTEGRATE                │
                        │ Printer number:          0                           │
                        │ Printer status:          (See form)                  │
                        │ Printer type:            Parallel                    │
                        │ Configuration:           (See form)                  │
                        │ Starting form:           0                           │
                        │ Buffer size in KB:       3                           │
                        │ Banner type:             Text                        │
                        │ Service mode for forms:  Minimize form changes within print queues │
                        │ Sampling interval:       5                           │
                        │ Print queues assigned:   (See list)                  │
                        │ Notification:            (See list)                  │
                        └─────────────────────────────────────────────────────┘

Specify the logical number (0-254, inclusive) assigned to this printer.
Enter=Select    F10=Save    F8=Port Driver Name    Esc=Exit            F1=Help
```

The first field of PCONSOLE's Printer Configuration screen, Print Server, cannot be changed from this screen. Everything else can be changed in a variety of ways.

The Printer Number field indicates which of the 255 printers that can be supported by this print server is assigned to our particular printer. If you have certain programs or batch files that are tied to a particular printer, this is where that number can be set.

PRINTER STATUS DETAILS The Printer Status field tells us that there is more beneath the surface: the field says "(See form)." When you highlight this field and press Enter, you'll see the form it's referencing. Figure 8.51 shows this printer in operation, printing away.

This acts the same as the Printer Status button under NetWare Administrator. Checking printer status leads to many possible answers. The Status field can show the printer as:

- Not Connected
- Waiting for Form
- Out of Paper

FIGURE 8.51

Status of a printer printing

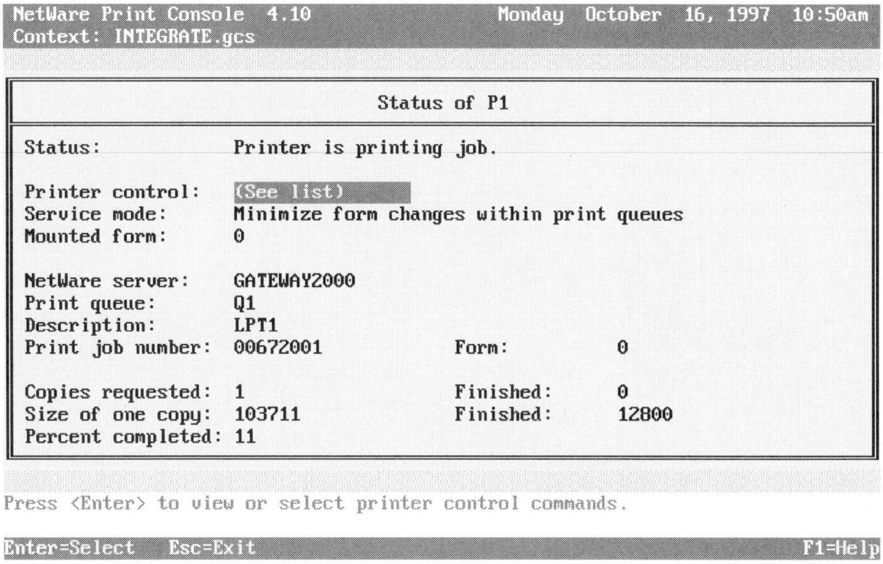

```
NetWare Print Console  4.10                    Monday  October  16, 1997  10:50am
Context: INTEGRATE.gcs

                              Status of P1
    Status:           Printer is printing job.

    Printer control:  (See list)
    Service mode:     Minimize form changes within print queues
    Mounted form:     0

    NetWare server:   GATEWAY2000
    Print queue:      Q1
    Description:      LPT1
    Print job number: 00672001          Form:          0

    Copies requested: 1                 Finished:      0
    Size of one copy: 103711            Finished:      12800
    Percent completed: 11

Press <Enter> to view or select printer control commands.

Enter=Select   Esc=Exit                                              F1=Help
```

- Printing
- Paused
- Stopped
- Offline
- Private
- Waiting for Job
- Ready to Go Down

Since the Status line gives the information in the list above, you can't change it. The next field, Printer Control, can be changed. The options that appear when you press Enter are:

- **Pause Printer:** The print queue operator command to stop current job. If nothing is printing at the time, this sets the printer to refuse more print jobs until a Start Printer command is issued.

- **Stop Printer:** Halts printing, sending any current job in process back to the print queue. The printer stays stopped until a Start Printer command is issued.

- **Start Printer:** Moves from Paused to Printing, Stopped to Printing, or Stopped back to Waiting for Job.

- **Form Feed:** Long-distance form-feed command to push a page from the printer.

- **Mark Top of Form:** Prints stars (****) across the page to help align paper in a printer.

- **Abort Print Job:** Stops printing and dumps the print job rather than returning it to the print queue.

- **Rewind Printer:** Pauses the printer, and prompts for parameters enabling you to print the job from a new position. It's easier if the printer is paused before being rewound.

The Service Mode field can be changed here, and we'll talk about that shortly.

The Mounted Form field can also be changed. This applies directly to a print job rather than forms for a series of print jobs. Highlight the number in the Mounted Form field, press Enter, and type in the new value for this print job. Wrong form loaded? Clogging up your printer? This is one way to deal with it.

The rest of the fields on the Status screen cannot be changed. You can see what is going by, but this screen doesn't let you modify any of the details. The Printer Control field is the place you want to be to hold, stop, or dump print jobs.

You can see a screen with the same type of printer status information from the PSERVER.NLM console at the file server. However, opening PCONSOLE's printer configuration screen for the Printer object is easier than actually going to the server. It's also more friendly and usable than running the PSERVER screen with RCONSOLE.

PRINTER TYPE DETAILS Back on the Printer Configuration screen, the Printer Type field sets the default at Parallel, referring to a printer physically attached to the file server. When you press Enter on this field, a pop-up list appears, with these options:

- **Parallel:** Standard Centronics parallel printer, the most common option.

- **Serial:** Asynchronous serial printers, attached to server or workstation via a serial port.

- **Unix Printer:** Designates printers attached to Unix systems.

- **AppleTalk Printer:** Support for printers developed for the Macintosh network protocol.

- **Other/Unknown:** OS/2 printers or those configured by NPRINTER.

- **XNP:** eXtended NetWare Printer protocol, a high-performance system for shared network printing.

- **AIO:** Asynchronous Input/Output. Designates printers attached to an asynchronous communications server or a multiport serial adapter.

When you highlight your choice and press Enter, you return to the Printer Configuration screen, with the highlight bar on the Configuration field. When you press Enter to get to the configuration details, you'll see something like the screen in Figure 8.52, which is for the parallel printer.

There are three choices in the Port field: LPT1, LPT2, and LPT3. The file server doesn't support more than three parallel ports.

The Location field refers to port driver loading (NPRINTER.NLM and NPRINTER.EXE are port drivers). Printers connected to the file server can have

FIGURE 8.52

Setting parallel printer details

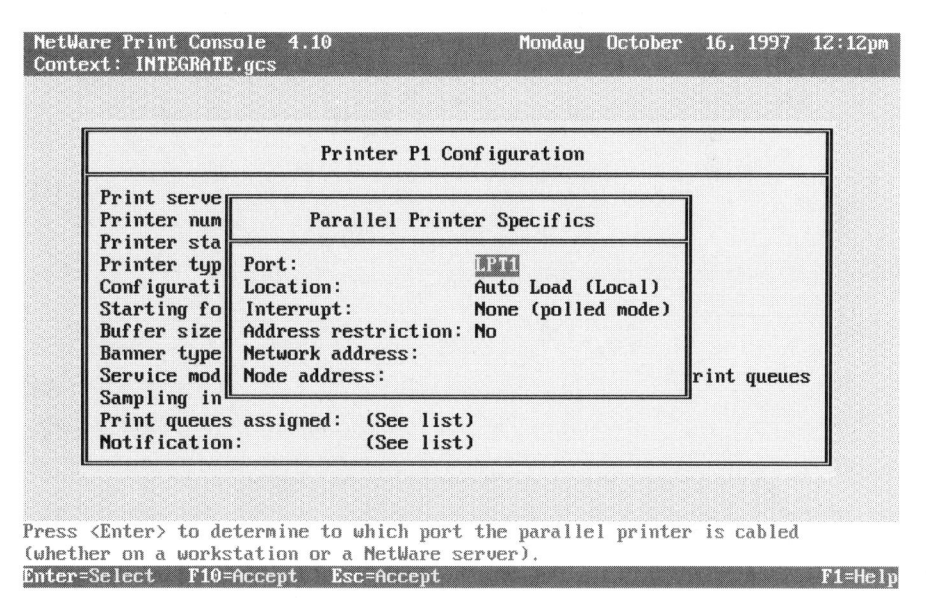

PSERVER.NLM load automatically, which loads NPRINTER.NLM at the same time. These port drivers can also be loaded manually at the server console.

Printers connected to workstations must always use the Manual Load option. Printers attached to the network cabling via internal or external print servers load their own port drivers.

The Interrupt option is a choice of the original LPT interrupt mode or the new polled printer communications. There are only so many interrupts to go around in a PC file server, as you saw during the installation chapters. Polled communications let the operating system check on the status of the print queues without requiring a hard interrupt from the print server. In most cases, the performance is as good as the interrupt method, without the potential of conflicting IRQ settings.

If you wish to restrict this printer to a particular physical address, the Network Address and Node Address fields allow you to do so. The Network Address field assumes a remote printer connection, and uses the current workstation number as a default. The Node Address field restricts the port driver from loading anywhere but that particular address.

For a serial printer, the printer type specifics are:

- **Port:** COM1 through COM4
- **Interrupts:** Interrupts or Polled
- **Connection Type:** Manual or Auto Load
- **Line Control - Baud:** 300 to 38,400
- **Data Bits:** 5 to 8
- **Stop Bits:** 1, 1.5, or 2
- **Parity:** None, Even, or Odd
- **X-on, X-off:** Yes or No

You must have the optional LPR_GWY.NLM program to connect to Unix systems. The printer type specifics for a Unix-type printer are:

- **Host Name:** Unix System host name
- **Printer Name:** Unix printer name as described on Unix host

For an AppleTalk printer, the printer type specifics are:

- **Names:** Seen by Macintosh clients
- **Type of Printer:** LaserWriter, ImageWriter, L.Q., DeskWriter, PaintWriter XL, or PaintJet XL300
- **Zone:** AppleTalk zone number
- **Hide Printer (from direct Macintosh access):** Yes or No

For an AIO printer, the printer type specifics are:

- **Port:** Supplied by manufacturer
- **Hardware Type:** Supplied by manufacturer
- **Board Number:** Supplied by manufacturer
- **Line Control - Baud:** 300 to 38,400
- **Data Bits:** 5 to 8
- **Stop Bits:** 1, 1.5, or 2
- **Parity:** None, Even, or Odd
- **X-on, X-off:** Yes or No

The Other/Unknown and XNP type printers are configured at the devices that connect them to the network cabling or remote system. XNP supports Macintosh and Unix printing; printer details are set on that end.

OTHER PRINTER CONFIGURATION DETAILS If printer forms are used, the Starting Form field on PCONSOLE's Printer Configuration screen sets the form number to make active when the print server brings the printer online. Any form value between 0 and 255 is allowed.

The Buffer Size in KB field shows how large a piece of data can be for this printer. The default is 3 KB; the range goes to 20 KB.

The next field, Banner Type, has two options. Text is the default, and the only other option is PostScript. Use the default of Text, even if you do have a PostScript printer. Most PostScript printers sold over the last few years handle text in this manner, but problems persist. Keep the default until you can check your printer for problems, and then you can change the setting to PostScript if you need to.

The Service Mode for Forms field dictates how often the print server will demand that you change printer forms (predefined page length and width setups) to accommodate print output to forms that are not mounted. When a print job calls for a form that is not mounted, the print server holds that print job until the form can be mounted. The options in this pick list are:

- **Minimize Form Changes within Print Queues:** Requires you to change forms when print jobs demand a new form within this particular print queue, even if other print jobs in lower-priority queues for this printer are waiting to use the currently mounted form. This is the default setting.

- **Change Forms as Needed:** Forces the form changes for each print job as they appear. You will hate this setting, so don't use it if you can avoid it, unless you love servicing printers all day.

- **Minimize Form Changes Across Print Queues:** The printer will print all print jobs for the mounted form before stopping and requesting a form change. High-priority print jobs with a different form will be placed behind low-priority print jobs using the mounted form.

- **Service Only Currently Mounted Form:** The printer never requests a new form. All print jobs requiring a different form than the one mounted will be held indefinitely.

The Sampling Interval field sets how many seconds go by before the print server checks the print queue for print jobs belonging to this printer. The default is 5 seconds; the range is 1 to 255 seconds.

In the Print Queues Assigned field, the "list" referred to shows active and configured print queues feeding this printer. As Figure 8.53 shows, queues can be changed in priority and they can be made the default queue.

You can see in the background, and in the helpful status lines across the bottom of the screen, that PCONSOLE does just as good a job of displaying information with text as NetWare Administrator does with pictures. Q1 is active, configured, and the default queue (not a leap of faith here, since it's currently the only print queue feeding this printer).

> **NOTE**
>
> As I mentioned before, the new version of PCONSOLE allows you to change some items from a variety of places. Although you may think the Print Queues Assigned option belongs strictly in the Print Queue menus, printer control demands some latitude in dealing with the print queues supplying print jobs. This screen allows that latitude.

FIGURE 8.53

Setting queue priorities from the Printer Configuration screen

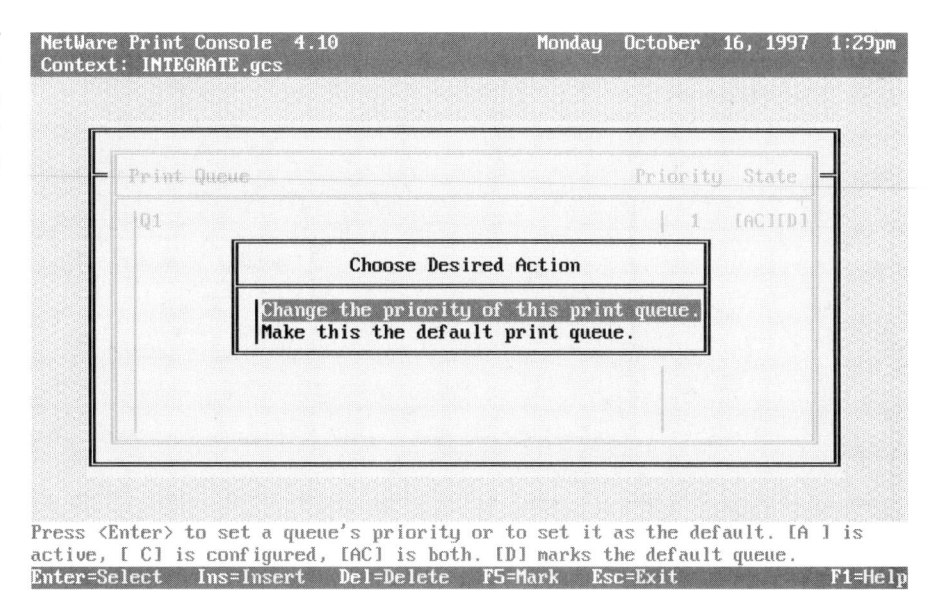

```
NetWare Print Console   4.10              Monday  October 16, 1997  1:29pm
Context: INTEGRATE.gcs
```

```
┌─ Print Queue ─────────────────────────────── Priority  State ─┐
│  Q1                                            │  1     [AC][D] │
│                                                                │
│              ┌──── Choose Desired Action ────┐                 │
│              │ Change the priority of this print queue. │     │
│              │ Make this the default print queue.       │     │
│              └──────────────────────────────┘                 │
└────────────────────────────────────────────────────────────────┘
```

```
Press <Enter> to set a queue's priority or to set it as the default. [A ] is
active, [ C] is configured, [AC] is both. [D] marks the default queue.
Enter=Select    Ins=Insert    Del=Delete    F5=Mark    Esc=Exit         F1=Help
```

The Notification field refers to a list of who will be notified about printer problems. The Object to be Notified list that appears when you press Enter on (See list) in the Notification field provides the expected information. The name of the user or group to be notified is listed. My favorite is (Print job owner). After all, if the person wants the printout, he or she will be strongly motivated to add paper or unjam the printer. Others can be listed, of course.

The Object Type tells us if the notified object is a user or group. For the owner of the print job, the first notification comes in one minute, and the next one comes in one more minute. You can have different settings for each user on the list. Figure 8.54 shows the box where these times are set.

The one-minute delay before the first notification allows almost enough time to change a font cartridge or add paper. If someone turns a printer off that notifies you in case of trouble, you will be bombarded with messages about the printer being off-line. Fortunately, these notification settings are easy to change.

FIGURE 8.54

Setting printer notification time and annoying follow-up reminders

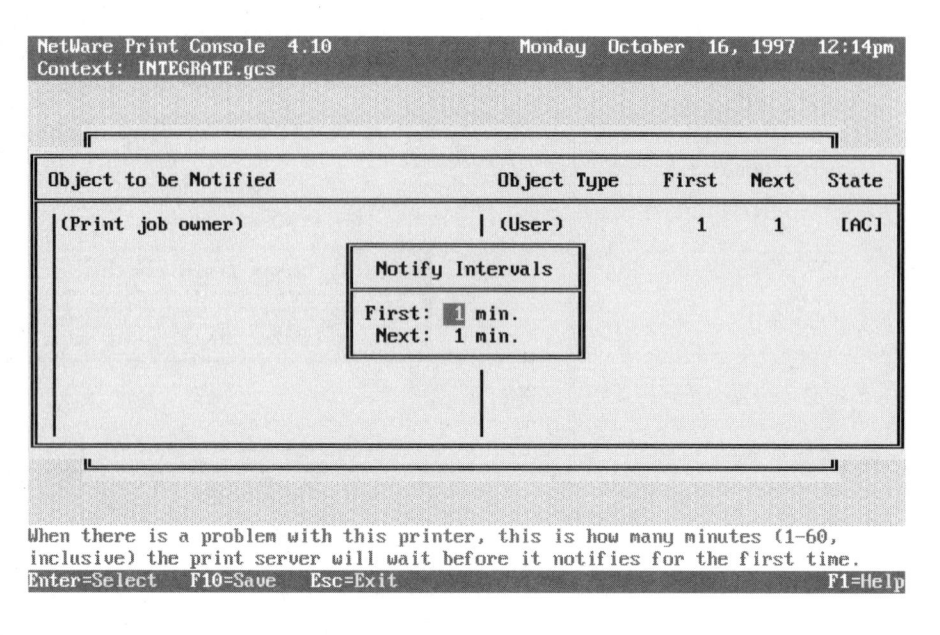

```
NetWare Print Console  4.10                    Monday October 16, 1997 12:14pm
Context: INTEGRATE.gcs

 Object to be Notified              Object Type       First   Next   State

 (Print job owner)                  (User)              1       1    [AC]
                          ┌─────────────────────┐
                          │   Notify Intervals  │
                          │                     │
                          │  First: 1 min.      │
                          │  Next:  1 min.      │
                          └─────────────────────┘

When there is a problem with this printer, this is how many minutes (1-60,
inclusive) the print server will wait before it notifies for the first time.
Enter=Select    F10=Save    Esc=Exit                                  F1=Help
```

Using PRINTDEF for Print Device and Form Management

IN NETWARE ADMINISTRATOR, Printer Forms and Print Devices are two different command buttons in the container properties. In NetWare 3.*x*, they have always been together in the same program called PRINTDEF (Printer Definitions).

There is a certain amount of logic to having these two features together. Each modifies the printer system in ways that benefit all users. Each limits the capabilities of non-supervisor level network clients to see and change the defined values. Both features are becoming less important as printers and applications get smarter.

Creating and Modifying Print Devices with PRINTDEF

You probably won't need to create *print devices,* Novell's name for printer definitions, because most of these functions are now handled by applications. However, if you must modify some printer definitions, NetWare comes with 59 different printer device files. These functions are controlled by files with a PDF (Printer Definition File) extension located in the PUBLIC directory.

Functions are actions, such as bold text or landscape orientation, that a printer can use. Modes are combinations of functions defined for specific printing needs. The string of functions are often sensitive to presentation order, so check your printer documentation for details.

Devices (printers) must be imported by the NetWare Administrator program, as explained earlier, or by the DOS program PRINTDEF, as explained in this section. During printing, the functions may be combined into print modes before being fed to the print device. The process works this way:

Print functions: Printer Reset, Landscape Orientation, and Typeface–Lineprinter

Combined into mode: Report

Print to printer device: HP LaserJet II/IID

Editing Devices with PRINTDEF

> **8.47 IN-A-HURRY**
>
> **Edit Print Devices in PRINTDEF**
>
> 1. Start PRINTDEF, choose Print Devices (highlight the menu choice and press Enter), and select Edit Print Devices.
>
> 2. To edit an entry in the Defined Print Devices list, choose the entry, then choose Device Functions.
>
> 3. To edit print device functions, highlight the entry and edit the name or control sequence.
>
> 4. To add print device functions, press Insert and provide the function name and control sequence.
>
> 5. To delete a print device function, highlight the function and press Enter.
>
> 6. Press Escape to close and exit.

If you must edit device functions, you can do it through PRINTDEF. As you can see in Figure 8.55, however, these functions are complex and prone to ruining your day in short order.

Nothing is gained by deleting functions you're not sure about. No memory is saved or performance enhanced that way. Adding functions is less dangerous, since the new function won't interfere with working systems. Changing functions is not for the faint of heart. The best way to use this information is with the help of both your printer manufacturer and applications developer. Almost anything else is guaranteed frustration.

FIGURE 8.55

Your chance to add, change, and delete illogical print functions

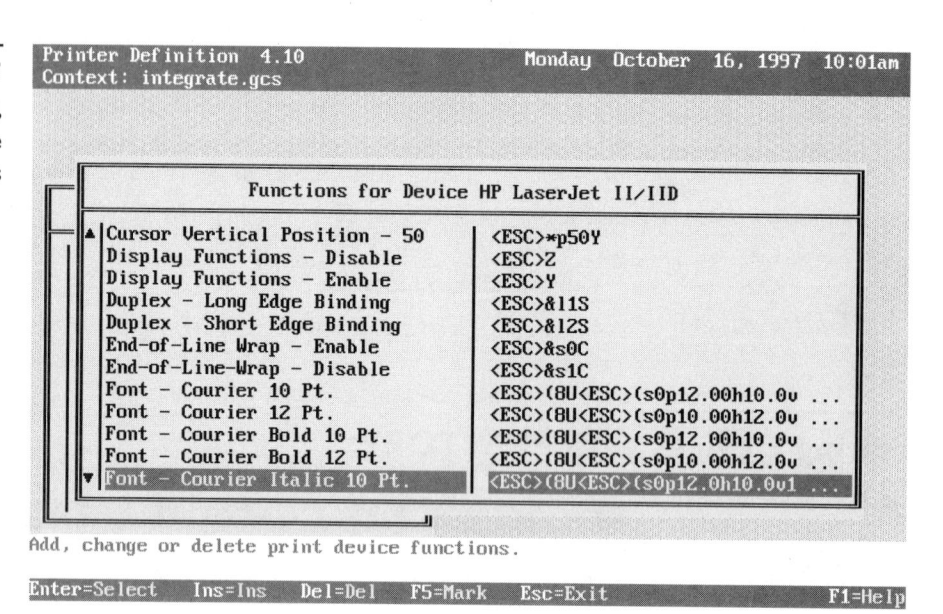

```
Printer Definition  4.10                    Monday  October  16, 1997  10:01am
Context: integrate.gcs

                    Functions for Device HP LaserJet II/IID
    ┌─────────────────────────────────────────────────────────────────┐
    ▲ │Cursor Vertical Position - 50       <ESC>*p50Y
      │Display Functions - Disable         <ESC>Z
      │Display Functions - Enable          <ESC>Y
      │Duplex - Long Edge Binding          <ESC>&l1S
      │Duplex - Short Edge Binding         <ESC>&l2S
      │End-of-Line Wrap - Enable           <ESC>&s0C
      │End-of-Line-Wrap - Disable          <ESC>&s1C
      │Font - Courier 10 Pt.               <ESC>(8U<ESC>(s0p12.00h10.0v ...
      │Font - Courier 12 Pt.               <ESC>(8U<ESC>(s0p10.00h12.0v ...
      │Font - Courier Bold 10 Pt.          <ESC>(8U<ESC>(s0p12.00h10.0v ...
      │Font - Courier Bold 12 Pt.          <ESC>(8U<ESC>(s0p10.00h12.0v ...
    ▼ │Font - Courier Italic 10 Pt.        <ESC>(8U<ESC>(s0p12.0h10.0v1 ...

Add, change or delete print device functions.

Enter=Select   Ins=Ins   Del=Del   F5=Mark   Esc=Exit              F1=Help
```

Device Modes

Print modes define the font style, size, boldness, and page orientation. Although you can modify or delete modes for the existing printer list, these are dangerous actions and rarely needed. The safest, and most common, usage of print modes is to create new ones that set up the page to be printed in a special way. Remember that specifying print modes means specifying new printer forms. This will either require separate printers for each form, or extra printer management to load the proper forms. Figure 8.56 shows the screen listing print modes for an HP LaserJet II/IID. Users can view these modes; those with Supervisor rights can make changes.

FIGURE 8.56

A small part of a Print Mode list

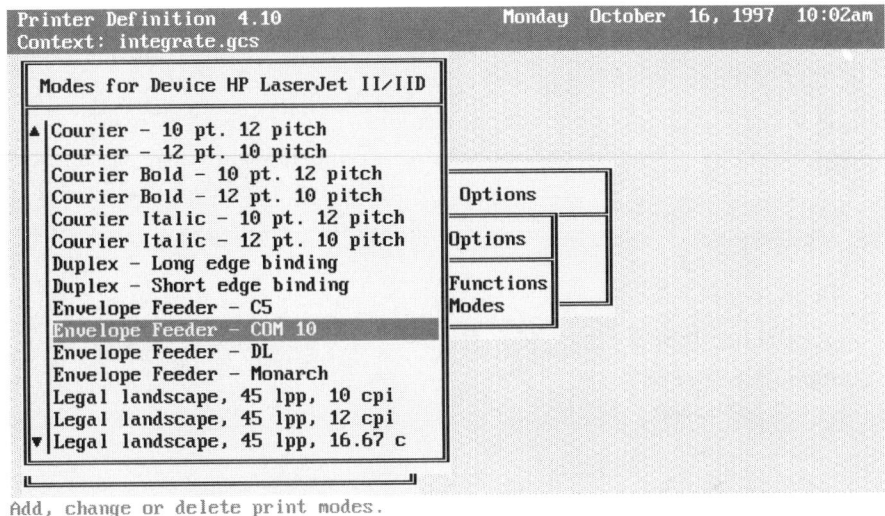

```
Printer Definition  4.10                Monday  October  16, 1997  10:02am
Context: integrate.gcs

 Modes for Device HP LaserJet II/IID
▲ Courier - 10 pt. 12 pitch
  Courier - 12 pt. 10 pitch
  Courier Bold - 10 pt. 12 pitch
  Courier Bold - 12 pt. 10 pitch          Options
  Courier Italic - 10 pt. 12 pitch
  Courier Italic - 12 pt. 10 pitch       Options
  Duplex - Long edge binding
  Duplex - Short edge binding            Functions
  Envelope Feeder - C5                   Modes
  Envelope Feeder - COM 10
  Envelope Feeder - DL
  Envelope Feeder - Monarch
  Legal landscape, 45 lpp, 10 cpi
  Legal landscape, 45 lpp, 12 cpi
▼ Legal landscape, 45 lpp, 16.67 c

Add, change or delete print modes.

Enter=Select   Ins=Ins   Del=Del   F3=Modify   F5=Mark   Esc=Exit        F1=Help
```

> **WARNING** *If you are stringing functions together to make a new print mode, make sure that you follow the correct order. The right function in the wrong place messes up just like using a wrong function. Bad functions or modes sent to the printer almost always require rebooting that printer.*

Importing Devices with PRINTDEF

> **8.48 IN-A-HURRY**
>
> **Import Print Devices in PRINTDEF**
>
> 1. Start PRINTDEF, choose Print Devices, and select Import from the Print Device Options menu.
>
> 2. To add a form, press Insert, then provide a name, form number, page length, and column width for the new form.
>
> 3. To delete a form, highlight the form name and press Delete.
>
> 4. Press Escape to close and exit.

The PDF files are placed in the PUBLIC directory of the SYS: volume during installation. As you can see in Figure 8.57, there is quite a list of PDF files available. If your printer is not listed, check with your NetWare dealer or the printer manufacturer.

Printer files can be imported from any existing server, your current server, or a manufacturer's diskette. The latest PDF is generally the best, but don't delete the older ones until you're sure the newer ones work.

FIGURE 8.57
Searching the Printer Definition Files

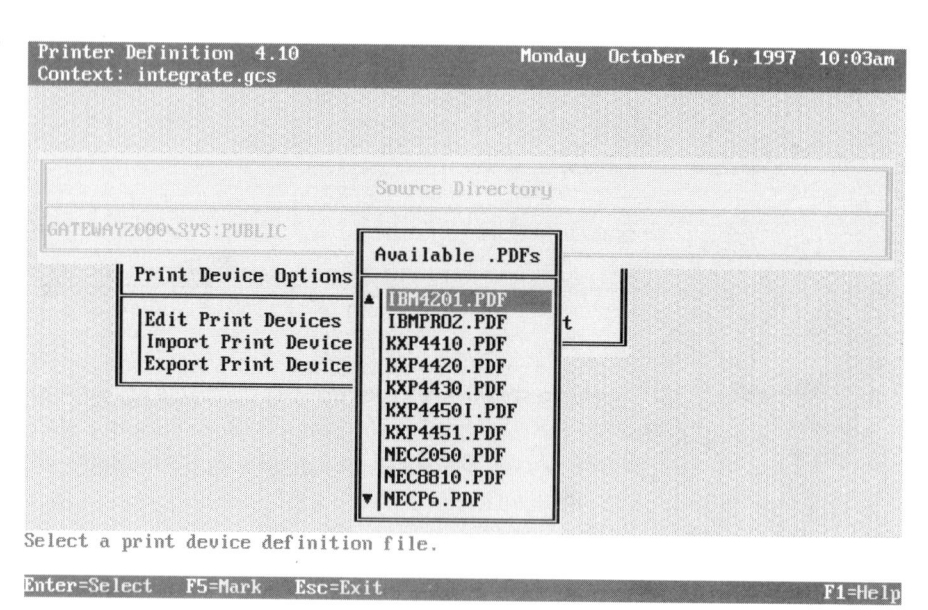

```
Printer Definition  4.10                    Monday  October  16, 1997  10:03am
Context: integrate.gcs


                              ┌──────────────────────────────────────────────┐
                              │              Source Directory                │
                              ├──────────────────────────────────────────────┤
                              │GATEWAY2000\SYS:PUBLIC                        │
                              │         ┌─────────────────────┐              │
                              │         │  Available .PDFs    │              │
                              │   ┌─────┼─────────────────────┼─────┐        │
                              │   │ Prin│▲ IBM4201.PDF        │     │        │
                              │   ├─────┤  IBMPRO2.PDF        ├─────┤        │
                              │   │Edit │  KXP4410.PDF        │  t  │        │
                              │   │Impor│  KXP4420.PDF        │     │        │
                              │   │Expor│  KXP4430.PDF        │     │        │
                              │   └─────┤  KXP4450I.PDF       ┘     │        │
                              │         │  KXP4451.PDF        │              │
                              │         │  NEC2050.PDF        │              │
                              │         │  NEC8810.PDF        │              │
                              │         │▼ NECP6.PDF          │              │
                              │         └─────────────────────┘              │
                              └──────────────────────────────────────────────┘
Select a print device definition file.

Enter=Select    F5=Mark    Esc=Exit                                    F1=Help
```

Exporting Devices with PRINTDEF

If one container has a definition for a print device, especially one that you have created or modified, you may want to share that device. The Export option for print devices will create a PDF file for you, and you can copy this file to wherever you wish. This Export option makes it simple to import the copied file into other containers. Figure 8.58 shows the Destination Directory browse screen.

FIGURE 8.58

Free to export to any volume or local drive

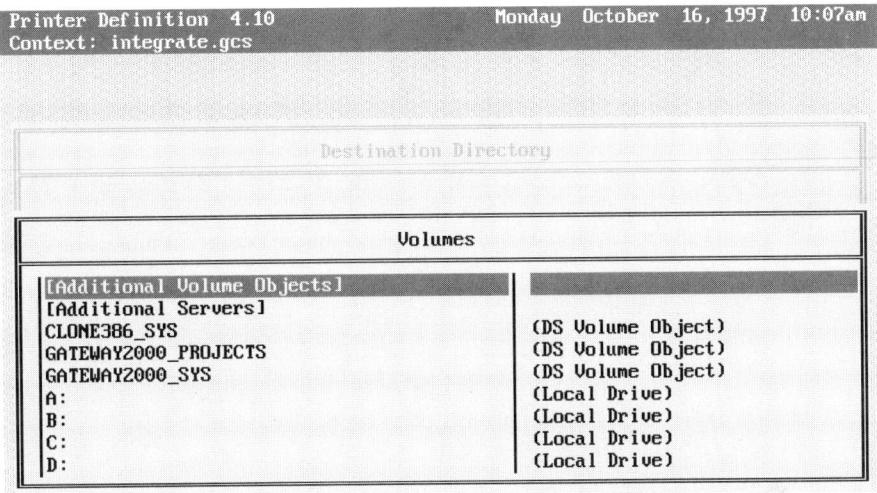

```
Printer Definition 4.10                    Monday October 16, 1997 10:07am
Context: integrate.gcs

                            Destination Directory


                                   Volumes
    ┌─────────────────────────────────┬─────────────────────────────┐
    │ [Additional Volume Objects]     │                             │
    │ [Additional Servers]            │                             │
    │ CLONE386_SYS                    │ (DS Volume Object)          │
    │ GATEWAY2000_PROJECTS            │ (DS Volume Object)          │
    │ GATEWAY2000_SYS                 │ (DS Volume Object)          │
    │ A:                              │ (Local Drive)               │
    │ B:                              │ (Local Drive)               │
    │ C:                              │ (Local Drive)               │
    │ D:                              │ (Local Drive)               │
    └─────────────────────────────────┴─────────────────────────────┘
    Press <Enter> to view the next level.  Press <Esc> to select the current path.

 Enter=Next Level   Esc=Select Current Path   Del=Log out        Alt+F1=More
```

8.49 IN-A-HURRY

Export Print Devices in PRINTDEF

1. Start PRINTDEF, choose Print Devices, and choose Export from the Print Device Options menu.

2. Choose the Print Device to export and press Enter.

3. Choose the destination directory for the device file. Press Insert to browse; backspace over the default directory listing to browse your entire network and local workstation.

4. Provide a unique file name and press Enter.

Once the PDF file is copied to another container, the Import utility can pick the file up and make use of it. Exporting is particularly valuable when a device has been customized. You can copy, rather than re-create, all the work you did to set up the print device.

Creating and Modifying Printer Forms with PRINTDEF

> **8.50 IN-A-HURRY**
>
> **Create or Modify Printer Forms in PRINTDEF**
>
> **1.** Start PRINTDEF and choose Printer Forms.
>
> **2.** To add a form, press Insert, then provide a name, form number, page length, and column width for the new form.
>
> **3.** To delete a form, highlight the form name and press Delete.
>
> **4.** Press Escape to close and exit.

With printer forms, you can set the page length and width. This may be useful if you need to avoid printing regular letters on legal-size paper, or worse, legal-size documents on letter-size paper. Figure 8.59 shows what you will see when you edit or create a new printer form.

FIGURE 8.59

Form creation or form editing—take your pick

The form is created at the container level, and it's available to all printers in the container. The file named PRINTDEF.DAT in SYS:PUBLIC holds the form definitions.

Managing Print Job Configurations in PRINTCON

THE ABILITY TO configure a print job, then reuse those parameters, is provided by the PRINTCON (PRINTer CONfiguration) program. Configurations can be associated by a name for a common set of print parameters. Destination, queue names, and printer names in NetWare 4.1x will trigger the predefined printing parameters.

As always, PRINTCON allows you to create, monitor, and modify print job configurations. You may also specify a default print job when one is not specifically listed with CAPTURE, NPRINT, or PCONSOLE. An additional item on the main menu allows you to change contexts, something the NetWare 3.x version had no need for.

There have been a few changes since NetWare 3.x, mainly in the location of the database and the ability to have a shareable print job configuration. The PRINTCON database is now an attribute of a container or User object. Because of this, you can modify a user's print job configuration through NetWare Administrator as well as through PRINTCON.

Creating and Editing Print Job Configurations with PRINTCON

As with the other printing details, a good application will eliminate the need for most of the information you would put in a print job configuration. Applications today, routed to the proper printer, can handle most printing tasks without user intervention.

In NetWare 4.1x, group configurations can be shared, or users can have private print job configurations. The administrator needs to create only a default configuration, one time, for everyone. Users can create multiple configurations for different circumstances and easily reference them.

646 Chapter 8 • Arranging Network Printing

> **8.51 IN-A-HURRY**
>
> ### Create or Modify a Print Job Configuration in PRINTCON
>
> **1.** Start PRINTCON and choose Edit Print Job Configurations.
>
> **2.** To add a configuration, press Insert, then provide print job details.
>
> **3.** To edit a configuration, press Enter on the configuration name and provide print job details.
>
> **4.** To delete a form, highlight the form name and press Delete.
>
> **5.** Press Escape to close and exit.

Each user in this container has access to the default Print Configuration object. If no instructions are issued to the contrary, the default Print Configuration object will provide the printing instructions for the user.

Figure 8.60 shows an example of the screen for editing a print job configuration named Laser. The fields on the Edit Print Job Configuration screen are described in Table 8.5.

FIGURE 8.60

Editing a print job configuration for the INTEGRATE container

```
Configure Print Jobs   4.10                   Monday  October  16, 1997  10:53am
Object: INTEGRATE.gcs

                      Edit Print Job Configuration "Laser"

    Number of copies:      1             Form name:        (None)
    File contents:         Byte Stream   Print banner:     Yes
    Tab size:                            Name:
    Form feed:             Yes           Banner name:
    Notify when done:      Yes

    Local printer:         1             Enable timeout:   Yes
    Auto endcap:           Yes           Timeout count:    10

    Printer/Queue:         P1.INTEGRATE.GCS
      (Printer)

    Device:                (None)
    Mode:                  (None)


 Choose Text or Byte Stream print job contents.

 Enter=Select   F3=Modify   F10=Save   Esc=Exit                         F1=Help
```

TABLE 8.5
Fields on PRINTCON's Edit Print Job Configuration Screen

FIELD	DESCRIPTION
Number of Copies	The default is 1, but any number up to 65,000 may be entered.
File Contents	Text or Byte Stream, with Byte Stream the default and safest choice for general printing.
Tab Size	Active only when File Contents is listed as Text. Refers to the width in characters each tab character should be when printed.
Form Feed	When checked, the CAPTURE or NPRINT software sends a form feed to flush the job out of the printer.
Notify When Done	When checked, the system will send the user a message when the print job is finished being spooled to the printer. It does not guarantee the printer has successfully printed the job itself.
Local Printer	Chooses which parallel port your print job will be sent to. NetWare expands on DOS by allowing up to nine LPT designations. A modification to the user's NET.CFG file must be made to allow more than three LPT ports.
Auto End Cap	When checked, tells the CAPTURE command to print the job when the application says it is finished.
Printer/Queue	Designates the printer or print queue for this print job configuration.
Device	Specifies a named print device for this print job configuration.
Mode	Specifies a defined mode (such as Report) for the print device specified in the previous field.
Form Name	Specifies a defined form for this print job configuration, chosen from a pick list that appears when the field is selected.
Print Banner	When Yes, includes a banner page at the beginning of the print job.
Name	Active only when Print Banner is set to Yes. When this field is blank, the user name is inserted. The name listed in this field and the next can be only 11 characters long.

TABLE 8.5 (cont.) Fields on PRINTCON's Edit Print Job Configuration Screen

FIELD	DESCRIPTION
Banner Name	Active only when Print Banner is enabled. When this field is left blank, the printer port is inserted on the banner page. The name listed in this field and the previous one can be only 11 characters long.
Enable Timeout	When checked, forces CAPTURE to consider a print job finished if there is no activity for a defined number of seconds.
Timeout Count	Active only when Enable Timeout is checked. Range is from 1 to 1000 seconds. For typical word processing print jobs, a short value (5 to 10) will be fine. For print jobs requiring lots of computer calculations, such as large reports or spreadsheets, the time should be longer. If a print job comes out in two or more pieces, this value is too short.

Selecting the Default Print Job Configuration in PRINTCON

8.52 IN-A-HURRY

Select the Default Print Job Configuration in PRINTCON

1. Start PRINTCON and choose Select Default Print Job Configurations (highlight it and press Enter).

2. Choose the configuration name you want to use as the default.

3. Press Escape to close and exit.

You can have several print job configurations, for any reason that appeals to you. The default parameters are used when the NPRINT or CAPTURE command is issued without specifying print job details on the command line.

The search order for NetWare 4.1x is to look for a private print job configuration. If one is not found for a user, the search continues in the NDS database.

Controlling the Print Server from the Server Console

MOST OF THE print information shown by RCONSOLE looks exactly like what we saw back in the Printer Configuration screens of PCONSOLE. Check Figure 8.50, then compare it with Figure 8.61 right here.

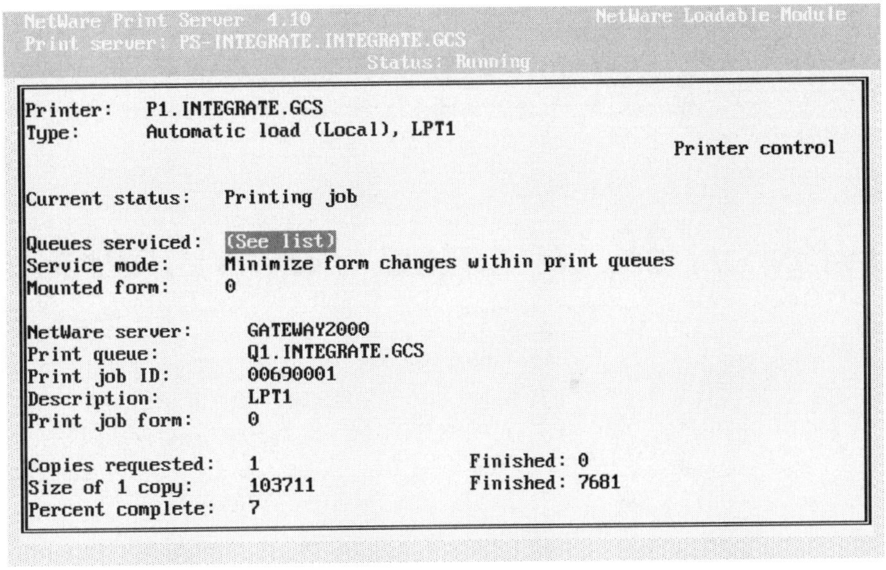

FIGURE 8.61

A print job from the print server point of view

```
NetWare Print Server  4.10                        NetWare Loadable Module
Print server: PS-INTEGRATE.INTEGRATE.GCS
                           Status: Running

Printer:       P1.INTEGRATE.GCS
Type:          Automatic load (Local), LPT1
                                                   Printer control

Current status:    Printing job

Queues serviced:   (See list)
Service mode:      Minimize form changes within print queues
Mounted form:      0

NetWare server:    GATEWAY2000
Print queue:       Q1.INTEGRATE.GCS
Print job ID:      00690001
Description:       LPT1
Print job form:    0

Copies requested:  1              Finished: 0
Size of 1 copy:    103711         Finished: 7681
Percent complete:  7
```

Every item, including the options for Printer Control, is the same as those described in the earlier sections. If you have only looked at the NetWare Administrator part of this chapter, you may want to refer to the sections that cover setting the printer configuration and printer status in PCONSOLE. That information will make the screen you see in Figure 8.61 much more understandable.

8.57 IN-A-HURRY

Check Printer Status at the Print Server Console with RCONSOLE

1. Go to the file server console, or use RCONSOLE to make a connection.

2. Change to the Print Server screen.

3. To check a print job, choose Printer Status, then choose the printer to check.

4. View the print job details, or choose Printer Control.

5. To check print server details, choose Print Server Information. To change the print state, press Enter on Current Status.

6. Press Escape to return to the printer list.

NPRINTER Updated: NPTWIN95

Time marches on, as any parent will tell you.

TIME MARCHES ON, as any parent will tell you. Time even applies to workstation-attached system printers, as NPRINTER gives way to NPTWIN95. Well, "gives way" may be an overstatement. After all, NPRINTER is still available, but now you have a good reason to never use it with a nondedicated system. Windows 95, on the other hand, no matter how Novell may curse it behind the scenes (heck, I curse it regularly, as you probably do as well) does function well enough to act as a decent nondedicated remote print server.

How hard is this to accomplish? Not too hard, actually.

First, find NPTWIN95.EXE. You may think that this file is in the set that was copied with your Windows 95 client files, but it isn't. You may want to copy the file to your local machine, but I advise against that. There are several DLL files that are necessary. None of these are tagged directly, and they are not in the path for standard clients. Check the \PUBLIC\WIN95 directory, and the NPTWIN95.EXE file will be there, begging to be run.

Second, copy the NPTWIN95.EXE program to each local Windows 95 workstation acting as a remote print station, or make a reference to the program on the server in your Startup folder. Either way will work.

Third, run the program on the aforementioned Windows 95 station and configure the application. Figure 8.62 shows the important details.

FIGURE 8.62

Configuring NPTWIN95

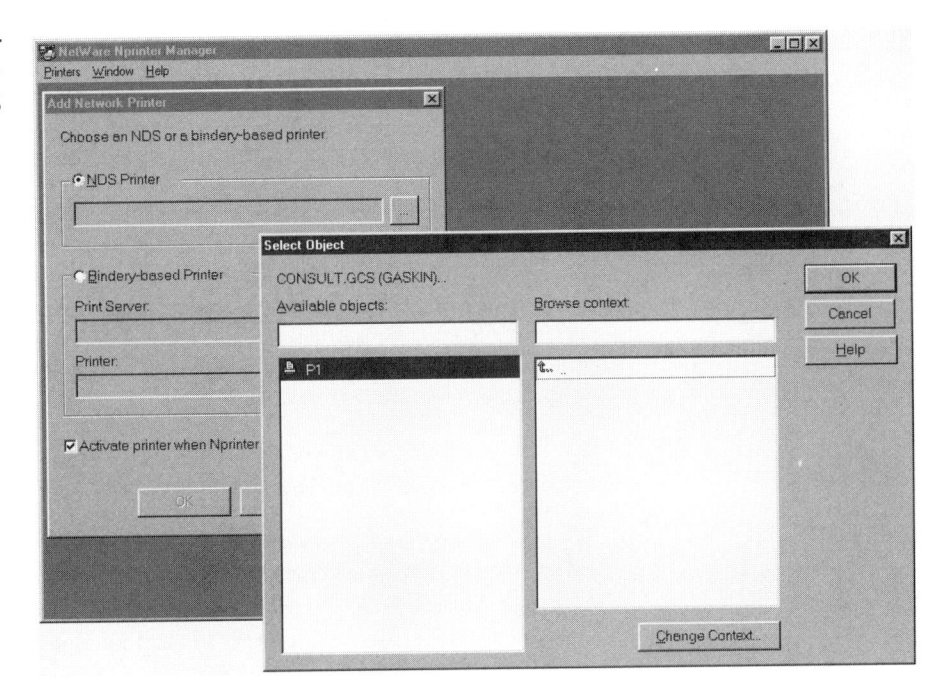

In Figure 8.62, I'm adding the printer we created using Quick Setup under NetWare Administrator earlier in the chapter. Nothing fancy here—just look around until you hit the right context, then pick your printer. Notice the NDS Printer button is active, as evidenced by the little black dot. Clicking next on the Browser button (the one at the end of that line with the three dots), brings up the Select Object dialog box. We've seen this many times, but this is the first time we've seen it in Windows 95. Are you impressed with the improvements? See, you were mistaken when you thought all you gained were 3D buttons.

Save the information, and verify the printer will be activated when the NPRINTER manager program starts. Although this checkbox is partially hidden in the figure, I believe you can get the idea from the words, "Activate printer when Nprinter..." that are visible.

The program will retreat to the Taskbar, staying out of the way on your Desktop. All of this is fine, and it works better than the old NPRINTER, but be careful. Users will turn off their systems, leaving your newly configured printer out of reach. Print servers are cheap (cheaper than upgrading PCs to handle Windows 95), and they don't turn themselves off. It's your choice, but at least you have a choice.

Coming Soon: NDPS (NetWare Distributed Print Services)

Novell engineers understand that network printing has been stuck in neutral for quite a while. How to fix that? NetWare Distributed Print Services, or NDPS, is the answer.

Not released with NetWare 4.11, NDPS will ship with the bug fixes (excuse me, "feature refresh") at the end of 1996, along with support for Java at the file server. At least, those are the plans as of fall 1996.

What's the big deal? Intelligent printers, more control over print output, easier printer selection, enterprise-wide printer management, and "virtual" printers are covered.

Let's take a look at each piece of the puzzle here. Intelligent printers will help by feeding detailed status and error messages back to the network. These messages will rely on the new NDPS Protocol, with network printers becoming just another intelligent agent on the network cable. An NLM will reside on the server to communicate with either the printer itself or with the print server that controls remote printers.

These advances are based on ISO 10175 DPA (Document Printing Application) specifications. I didn't know there was such a thing either, until researching NDPS. It seems a few groups of smart people have done more than just cuss printers; they've actually been trying to improve them.

Print jobs will be better able to find compatible printers. In fact, you may search for printers with the proper characteristics listed in their NDS entries. When you find one you like, the application and printer will negotiate through NDPS for the best performance.

(continued on next page)

Large companies with mainframes and/or Unix networks often invest in an enterprise-wide printer management system. NDPS attempts to offer many of the same features for NetWare users with large, complicated networks. Since the only printer management available for NetWare networks today works on single printers only, such as HP's JetAdmin, this improvement will be welcome.

Virtual printers are the heir-apparent to print queues. Rather than force the users to think print queue, NDPS focuses on printers. The fact that the network provides job spooling to specified volumes doesn't enter into the user–printer relationship. Of course, you may argue that your users have the same thing today, because you use intelligent names for your print queues. Nobody said virtual printers were new, just different.

Speaking of different, Novell has made special arrangements with HP and Xerox during the development of NDPS. This makes sense, because both companies are world leaders in printer technology. What is unusual is the exclusive license granted by Novell to both these companies. Other printer companies can't release products for approximately six months after Xerox and HP release their own NDPS systems.

As you might imagine, the other companies aren't happy about this. Of course, HP still holds the majority share of installed laser printers, but do you know who the second largest share belongs to? LexMark. What do you mean, who? LexMark is the company split off from IBM to focus on printing technology.

LexMark, and other laser printer manufacturers, are privy to the same ISO 10175 DPA specifications that Novell used to develop NDPS. So, although LexMark can't work on NDPS, those developers are busy developing their own management program, called MarkVision. How good is it? IBM included MarkVision with its OS/2 LAN offerings with the roll-out of LAN Server's new version.

Will NDPS raise the bar for network printer management, just as NDS has raised the standards for directory services? That's the idea. NDS has taken awhile to get rolling, and I bet NDPS will suffer the same slow start. Add in the fact that either new printers or print servers are needed to take advantage of NDPS, and you throw in another barrier to quick success.

Don't expect NDPS to revolutionize your network printing anytime in the near future. On the other hand, don't buy a network printer after the end of 1996 that doesn't support NDPS. Even one or two smart printers on your network will make a difference.

Potshots on Printing

THE PROGNOSTICATORS LIED to us all: the paperless office prediction is not only wrong, more paper is sold today than ever. You have as much chance of winning the lottery as your office does of going completely paperless in the next three years.

Should we say phooey and buy printers for everyone? No. In spite of what people want, the time for information primarily stored on paper is past. You make your children eat vegetables when they don't want to, and you must gently but firmly push your network into the 00's, when paper starts dying.

Don't be hard on your users when they complain, "My report doesn't look right. The graphic looked great on the screen but the printed version stinks! Why don't we have color lasers for everybody?"

Why not blow your top the seventeenth time you hear that type of remark in one day? Because to most people, what the computer does is not real. Paper is real. Until something in the computer is printed, they are not really sure if it exists.

Someday, when everyone is carrying their PDA that connects over a wireless network to the company Web server holding every document on magneto-optical disks rather than paper, the users will understand. But some of them will still print things when you're not looking.

CASE STUDY

MiniCo: Arranging Network Printing

MINICO HAS 3 servers, 75 users, and one location.

NetWare Printing System Overview

CONSIDERATIONS

The goals:

- Understand printing from more than just a "put marks on paper" standpoint.
- Diagram printing requirements per department.

DECISION

Plan to re-create individual printing convenience with shared printers.

EXPLANATION

Not having time to analyze the printing needs of MiniCo, Alexander von Thorn (the Distribution Manager who handled NetWare 4.1x setup) decided to let all the users who previously had their own laser printer to access that same printer on a shared basis. Users who didn't have a printer attached to their stations before also gained access to those printers.

The NetWare 4.1x Printing System Relationships

CONSIDERATIONS

The goals:

- Examine the relationship of the printer, print queue, and print server.
- Diagram printer locations throughout the company for maximum coverage with fewest printers.

DECISION

Keep printers where they were, and make them shared printers.

EXPLANATION

Each existing printer was changed from a personal printer to a network system printer. Some of the printers remained connected to workstations running the NPRINTER program. A couple of newer stations with Windows 95 run the NPTWIN95 program and support heavier-duty printers.

Using Quick Setup in PCONSOLE

CONSIDERATIONS

The choices:

- Use Quick Setup for most print system configuration.
- Use PCONSOLE for this configuration.
- Use NetWare Administrator for Quick Setup and continued maintenance.

MINICO CASE STUDY, CONTINUED

DECISION

Use Quick Setup exclusively.

EXPLANATION

The ability of the Quick Setup option to keep track of printer and print queue numbering made it easy for Alexander. Going down a hastily scribbled printer inventory, Alexander used Quick Setup to add each existing printer to the network. No forethought was required.

At first, Alexander used PCONSOLE, because he was familiar with the program from NetWare 3.1 and 4.10. After a bit, however, he started using NetWare Administrator to set up and manage printers.

Setting Up and Managing Your Print System with NetWare Administrator

CONSIDERATIONS

The goals:

- Set the naming convention for printers, print queues, and print servers.
- Define the print system operators (separate from the network administrators).
- Define and create print job configurations.
- Assign users the appropriate print job configuration.

DECISION

Let Quick Setup choose the names, and don't use any print job configurations. No one but the Admin user was listed as a print system operator.

EXPLANATION

Quick Setup uses sequential numbers to label print queues and printers. These designations work, but they don't provide any hints to the users about which printer is which, or what features each printer has.

If no print job configurations are defined, users must specify the printer control settings for banner pages, timeout values, and form feed each time a printer is captured. Alexander put these settings into the login scripts for each individual, because it was the quickest place to set up each user for the short-term. It also caused the most trouble in the long-term. When MiniCo decided to take more control of the printers, the time it took to go through each login script and take out the printer directions slowed down the improvement process considerably.

Using PCONSOLE for Print System Configuration and Management

CONSIDERATIONS

The choices:

- Use PCONSOLE for all printing management.
- Use NetWare Administrator for all printing management.

DECISION

Use NetWare Administrator.

EXPLANATION

Alexander got used to PCONSOLE when he managed the Accounting department's old network. PCONSOLE provides all the functionality in NetWare 4 that it did in NetWare 3, even if all

MINICO CASE STUDY, CONTINUED

the functions are available under NetWare Administrator. People tend to stick with what they know, and Alexander used the familiar PCONSOLE at first, but later he switched to NetWare Administrator.

Using PRINTDEF for Print Device and Form Management

CONSIDERATIONS

The choices:

- Use PRINTDEF for print device and print form management.
- Don't bother with print devices or print forms.

DECISION

Avoid PRINTDEF whenever possible.

EXPLANATION

All the applications in use at MiniCo have the proper drivers for the laser printers in use. There was no reason to import new print devices or modify features on the existing devices, so Alexander didn't deal with PRINTDEF during installation.

Managing Print Job Configurations in PRINTCON

CONSIDERATIONS

The choices:

- Use PRINTCON to manage print job configurations.
- Use NetWare Administrator to handle print job configurations.

DECISION

Use PRINTCON at first, but gradually start using NetWare Administrator

EXPLANATION

Again, because he had already managed the NetWare 3.x network, Alexander was familiar with PRINTCON. It was quicker for him to get the network up and running using utilities he was familiar with than learning how to use NetWare Administrator for those tasks. After Alexander started using NetWare Administrator for various other jobs, however, he started keeping the program open for all administration functions.

Controlling the Print Server from the Server Console

CONSIDERATIONS

The choices:

- Use the print server console to manage print servers.
- Use NetWare Administrator to manage print servers.

DECISION

Use the print server console, either physically or through RCONSOLE.

EXPLANATION

Because he was used to the DOS printing utilities provided by NetWare, Alexander stayed with the print server console when checking the print server or printer status. The fact that the server console loads so much quicker from the server than NetWare Administrator does from

MINICO CASE STUDY, CONTINUED

a workstation made this an easy choice, as well. This means that he needs to go to the file server running the print server or to use the RCONSOLE utility to make that connection, but he finds that few changes are necessary for working print servers.

NPRINTER Updated: NPTWIN95

CONSIDERATIONS

The goals:

- Add RoadTrip printers to MiniCo's system.
- Allow RoadTrip personnel to access MiniCo printers.
- Avoid buying print server hardware.

DECISION

Run NPTWIN95 on several RoadTrip Windows 95 workstations to convert personal printers into system printers, shared by MiniCo.

EXPLANATION

Adding the new group of folks from RoadTrip Productions forced MiniCo into the Windows 95 business. When it came to printing, this turned out to be a blessing rather than a problem. RoadTrip has a nice color printer that the company graciously allows MiniCo to access.

Using NPTWIN95 allows printers coming into the system from RoadTrip to be shared by MiniCo. Because Windows 95 workstations can handle moderate-volume system printers without severe performance impact, MiniCo and RoadTrip were able to avoid spending extra money on print server hardware.

CASE STUDY

MegaCorp: Arranging Network Printing

MEGACORP HAS 50 servers, 2500 users, and 5 locations.

NetWare Printing System Overview

CONSIDERATIONS

The goals:

- Understand printing from more than just a "put marks on paper" standpoint.
- Diagram printing requirements per department.

DECISION

Analyze each department's printing requirements before NetWare 4.1x implementation.

EXPLANATION

The number of printers used in each department was counted, as well as an approximate number of pages per day each produced. This resulted in some departments getting larger, faster printers. Other departments lost printers, or had faster printers replaced with slower printers. Corporate-wide, 50 printers were put in storage to be used as replacements when needed. The printer savings were the result of reallocation of resources made possible by NetWare 4.1x, as well as an increased internal reliance on e-mail and shared databases.

The NetWare 4.1x Printing System Relationships

CONSIDERATIONS

The goals:

- Examine the relationship of the printer, print queue, and print server.
- Diagram printer locations throughout the company for maximum coverage with fewest printers.
- Work with department managers to choose optimum printer placement.
- Discuss ways to print less with each department manager.

DECISION

Place fewer printers in more logical locations across the company.

EXPLANATION

Personal printers became a thing of the past when NetWare 4.1x was installed. There was nothing in NetWare that demanded this, of course, but Central IS took the network upgrade as an opportunity to strengthen the move toward less printing and more electronic sharing of information.

MEGACORP CASE STUDY, CONTINUED

Using Quick Setup in PCONSOLE

CONSIDERATIONS

The choices:

- Use Quick Setup for most print system configuration.
- Use PCONSOLE for this configuration.
- Use NetWare Administrator for print system setup.

DECISION

Use NetWare Administrator for all print system setup.

EXPLANATION

Although Quick Setup and PCONSOLE work perfectly well, MegaCorp planned the printing requirements of each department before the network was installed. Using NetWare Administrator, the Central IS network managers were able to graphically place printers (actually, printer Alias objects) in the proper departments with visual verification. In fact, it was easier to use their naming conventions when they bypassed Quick Setup.

Setting Up and Managing Your Print System with NetWare Administrator

CONSIDERATIONS

The goals:

- Set the naming convention for printers, print queues, and print servers.
- Define the print system operators (separate from the network administrators).
- Define and create print job configurations.
- Assign users the appropriate print job configuration.

DECISION

Printers follow a strict naming convention. Each container has an assigned print system administrator, and appropriate print job configurations are defined.

EXPLANATION

Printers are named by type (2 letters), building (3 letters), floor number, and direction. If more than one printer is located in the same direction, incremental numbers are assigned. For example, LJ-BLD-01-N2 describes a LaserJet, the three-letter building code, the first floor, and the second printer to the north.

Each department's print system administrator is responsible for the print job configuration maintenance (Central IS set up the configurations originally). New print job configurations and form changes are handled on the department level 95 percent of the time.

Using PCONSOLE for Print System Configuration and Management

CONSIDERATIONS

The choices:

- Use PCONSOLE for all printing management.
- Use NetWare Administrator for all printing management.

MEGACORP CASE STUDY, CONTINUED

DECISION

Use NetWare Administrator whenever possible.

EXPLANATION

Not having used PCONSOLE with earlier versions of NetWare (at least, not in the past four years), MegaCorp administrators had nothing to "unlearn" when moving to NetWare Administrator for printing management. Since the graphical management utilities were one of the reasons the company switched to NetWare, controlling the printing system through a Windows interface was planned from the beginning.

Using PRINTDEF for Print Device and Form Management

CONSIDERATIONS

The choices:

- Whether to define print devices and print forms.
- Use the printer FORMS feature in PRINTDEF or dedicate printers to particular forms.

DECISION

Use dedicated printers for necessary forms whenever possible.

EXPLANATION

The work process reevaluation that was performed prior to the network installation did away with many of the traditional but inefficient forms in use. Most of the forms were eliminated, but a few were deemed worthwhile. The few forms that are necessary are set up on preprinted paper in dedicated laser printers. Multiple copies are part of the print job configurations used with those printers.

This arrangement provides the forms that are necessary while rarely using the FORMS setting in print job configurations. Stopping printers to change forms slows down the department, and this is avoided whenever possible.

Managing Print Job Configurations in PRINTCON

CONSIDERATIONS

The choices:

- Use PRINTCON for print job configuration management.
- Use NetWare Administrator for managing print job configurations.

DECISION

Use NetWare Administrator.

EXPLANATION

NetWare Administrator saves time and keystrokes when managing the print system. MegaCorp managers had no previous strong loyalty to the DOS utilities, so encouraging the use of NetWare Administrator was successful.

MEGACORP CASE STUDY, CONTINUED

Controlling the Print Server from the Server Console

CONSIDERATIONS

The choices:

- Use the print server console to manage print servers.
- Use NetWare Administrator to manage print servers.

DECISION

Use NetWare Administrator for print server management.

EXPLANATION

NetWare Administrator covers all the same functions as the print server control screen on the server or through RCONSOLE. If the NetWare Administrator information doesn't seem right, the RCONSOLE option in the Tools menu in NetWare Administrator is always available for a quick check of the physical server console display.

NPRINTER Updated: NPTWIN95

CONSIDERATIONS

The choices:

- Attach system printers to Windows 95 workstations rather than print servers.
- Add more print servers for new areas.

DECISION

Use NPTWIN95 for some small workgroups with a central secretary, but use print servers for other groups.

EXPLANATION

Printer control is important for shared printers. By attaching a few system printers to workgroup secretaries' systems using Windows 95 workstations, MegaCorp is assured that these shared printers will be monitored closely. For the larger workgroups that need more printers than there are Windows 95 stations, print servers are used.

Securing Your NetWare 4.1x Network

CHAPTER 9

SECURITY: WHAT DOES it mean to you? Hackers sneaking in through your phone lines and deleting entire volumes? Illegal software on the system?

What does security mean to your boss? Inventory asset tags on all the computers, so you know the location of every piece of hardware? Competitors tapping into your system and stealing the plans for the roll-out of your new product line?

Security, like much of life, is a desirable abstract state sought through the use of material items. No two people think of the same thing when they hear security. Regardless of the situation, some people never feel secure. Other people may feel content and secure when actually their systems are vulnerable.

Security: A Definition

EACH COMPANY MUST come to an agreement of what security means, and the amount of effort that will be expended to reach a comfortable level of security. Securing your network, including all the physical and virtual items, will be expensive. This brings up another management decision point: how much security is enough?

How about a definition: Security is an aspect of networking administration concerned with ensuring that the data, circuits, and equipment on a network are used only by authorized users, and in authorized ways. This comes from the *Complete Encyclopedia of Networking* by Werner Feibel, published by Sybex (the folks that bring you this book).

Notice the order of items to be secured: data, circuits, equipment. Management often focuses security measures on physical items, such as computer hardware and telephone connections and modems. But if a computer is stolen, all that's necessary to replace that computer is money. Circuits must be protected from tampering and eavesdropping, and they must be available when needed.

If data is destroyed, years of work, effort, and thought are gone. Unfortunately, work, effort, and thought are not easily replaced.

Mr. Feibel suggests four threat areas to manage for your system security:

- **Threats to hardware:** These include theft, tampering, destruction, damage, unauthorized use, and ordinary equipment wear and tear.

- **Threats to software:** These include deletion, theft, corruption, and bugs.

- **Threats to information:** These include deletion, theft, loss, and corruption.

- **Threats to network operations:** These are interruption, interference, and overload.

Can you and your boss agree on these items? Do some of them seem outside the realm of security, such as ordinary equipment wear and tear? What about the threat of overload?

Some network managers think of security from a negative aspect only. Something is stolen or deleted. I don't believe that definition is wide enough to support the network needs of today.

Let's agree that system security means the system is available to authorized users doing their job. Anything that interferes with this is a security problem. If a file server is stolen, people can't do their work. What if the file server is overloaded or erratic? Isn't the result the same? People can't do their work. What if the file server is safe and running well, but someone deletes (either accidentally or on purpose) some of the system files? The result is the same once again: people can't do their work.

Where Is Your Security Plan?

IN 1988, THE INTERNET Worm ran amok, clogging thousands of computers and data circuits for days. The Worm was not destructive, but caused disruptions in computer services all across the Internet. Front-page stories were copied by paranoid managers and handed to network technicians with a question: Where is our security plan?

One of the responses of the Internet community to the Worm of 1988 was to establish CERT (Computer Emergency Response Team). This group responds to and helps resolve Internet security incidents. Part of the group's job is to help network administrators protect their systems against intruders before an attack is attempted.

The good news is that upgrading security takes surprisingly little work for most systems. Unfortunately, that's also the bad news. CERT estimates that 60 to 75 percent of network problems are caused by the following:

- Accounts with no passwords

- Poor passwords

- Unwatched guest accounts

- Poor user security management, especially giving users more rights than necessary

Are the listed problems familiar to you? Do you understand how easy these problems are to fix? We covered the user password details earlier; we'll talk about user rights in this chapter.

Before anything else, check the easy things. Many cars are stolen simply because the keys are left dangling from the ignition switch. Don't make things that easy in your network.

The Site Security Handbook

To help you devise your security plan, RFC 1244 was developed. Here is the opening:

```
Network Working Group              P. Holbrook
Request for Comments: 1244            CICNet
FYI: 8                            J. Reynolds
                                         ISI
                                     Editors
                                   July 1991
            Site Security Handbook
Status of this Memo
This handbook is the product of the Site Security Pol-
icy Handbook Working Group (SSPHWG), a combined effort
```

(continued on next page)

> of the Security Area and User Services Area of the
> Internet Engineering Task Force (IETF). This FYI RFC
> provides information for the Internet community. It
> does not specify an Internet standard. Distribution of
> this memo is unlimited.
>
> As is the norm, the information in this RFC may be freely copied and distributed. We'll quote two small sections, skipping most of the valuable information in this handbook.
>
> ```
> 1. 7 Basic Approach
> ```
> Setting security policies and procedures really means
> developing a plan for how to deal with computer secu-
> rity. One way to approach this task is suggested by
> Fites, et. al. [3, FITES]:
> - Look at what you are trying to protect.
> - Look at what you need to protect it from.
> - Determine how likely the threats are.
> - Implement measures which will protect your assets in
> a cost-effective manner.
> - Review the process continuously, and improve things
> every time a weakness is found.
> This handbook will concentrate mostly on the last two
> steps, but the first three are critically important to
> making effective decisions about security. One old tru-
> ism in security is that the cost of protecting yourself
> against a threat should be less than the cost of recov-
> ering if the threat were to strike you. Without
> reasonable knowledge of what you are protecting and
> what the likely threats are, following this rule could
> be difficult.
>
> The last two sentences apply to everyone in the computer business, but are difficult to quantify at times. You know what you have is valuable, but how valuable? How do you put a price on a database or spreadsheet templates or transaction history? Someone, preferably management, must assign some value to the information stored in your network. Quick estimate: how long will it take you to replace the database?
>
> *(continued on next page)*

Multiply that by twice as long, then figure a high rate per hour, and you're on your way to setting a value. You know what's coming from all this, don't you? Audit—inventory every server, workstation, network component, remote access device, wiring diagram, and each module of application and system software. Your manager will probably ask you to do this in your "spare" time. If you don't have a value assigned to what you're protecting, you don't know when the protection is more expensive than what's protected.

Another set of management decisions is described in this section:

```
2. 3 Policy Issues
There are a number of issues that must be addressed
when developing a security policy. These are:
1. Who is allowed to use the resources?
2. What is the proper use of the resources?
3. Who is authorized to grant access and approve usage?
4. Who may have system administration privileges?
5. What are the user's rights and responsibilities?
6. What are the rights and responsibilities of the sys-
   tem administrator vs. those of the user?
7. What do you do with sensitive information?
```

RFC 1244 may be retrieved from many different places on the Internet. The source for these quotes is the "Internet Info" CD-ROM, December 1993 release, available from Walnut Creek CD-ROM, Walnut Creek, California. They have since updated this CD to include 17,420 documents (including many more on security topics) for a price of $39.95. Check it out, along with their other products, at http://www.cdrom.com.

NetWare 4.1x Admin Compared with NetWare 3.x SUPERVISOR

THERE ARE TWO main security areas for NetWare 4.1*x*: file system and NDS security. If you are familiar with NetWare 3.*x*, you will be familiar with file system security. NetWare 4.1*x* added some attributes to support data compression and data migration features, and changed a bit of the terminology. But the majority of the details and the security goals are still the same. The main goal is to provide users access to and control of the proper files and directories.

NDS security is new with NetWare 4, as is NDS itself. Just as file system security controls which users may control which files, NDS security controls the same functions for the NDS objects. The two security systems are not in any way related. Let me repeat: having control over the NDS attributes of an object does not grant the rights to the files contained in that volume.

The Admin user is a supervisor's supervisor, able to control the network completely as the old SUPERVISOR did in earlier NetWare versions. The Supervisor right, however, may be granted to any user for particular NDS objects or containers. Being able to set up subadministrators for specific tasks, as we have spoken of before, can be a great help.

This flexibility of supervision is an important feature of NetWare 4.1*x*—one of the many features that place NetWare ahead of the competition. With global enterprise networking the norm for many companies today, the job of supervision is far beyond the abilities of any one person. NetWare 4.1*x* allows the supervision chores to be distributed in whatever method you prefer.

You can have different administrators for different parts of the tree, as well as different volumes, directories, or files. Admin may control the NDS design and overall setup but have no control over the files. File system supervisors in each container will handle those chores. Admin in Chicago may share duties with Admin in Cleveland, with each responsible primarily for his or her own city, but able to support the other network across the WAN if necessary.

> With global enterprise networking the norm for many companies today, the job of supervision is far beyond the abilities of any one person.

File System Security

NETWARE FILES ARE protected in two ways:

- Users must be granted the right to use files and directories.
- File and directory attributes provide hidden protection.

What is hidden protection? Suppose that Doug has the right to create and delete files in the \LETTERS directory. If he writes a letter named SLS_GOAL.OCT and decides he doesn't like that file, he can delete it. Files can be deleted from within applications or from the DOS prompt. He can even use the MS Windows File Manager.

What if Doug's mouse slips a fraction within File Manager, and he tries to delete the SLS_GOAL.PLN file, the template for all the sales goal letters? Is the file doomed?

Not necessarily. If the network administrator (probably you) has set the attribute to SLS_GOAL.PLN as Read Only or Delete Inhibit, Doug can't delete the file. However, if Doug also has the right to modify the file attributes (a bad idea, knowing Doug), he could change the Read Only or Delete Inhibit designation and delete the file anyway. But he would need to work at deleting the file; he couldn't do it by accident.

When Doug is granted the rights to use the \LETTERS directory, we call him a *trustee* of the directory, given to him by way of a *trustee assignment*. He has been trusted to use the directory and files properly. The trustee concept works with objects and NDS items, as we'll soon see.

Someone in authority must grant Doug, or a group or container Doug is a member of, the rights to use the file, directory, or object in question. The administrator is the person who places trust in Doug, making him a trustee of the rights of the object. This is referred to as making trustee assignments to a directory, file, or object. The trustee assignments are stored in the object's ACL (Access Control List) property.

The rights granted to users flow downhill. This means that the rights Doug has in one directory apply to all subdirectories. This idea works well, and the official name is *inheritance*. If your system is set up with \LETTERS as the main directory, and Doug has rights to use that directory, he will automatically have the same rights in the \LETTERS\SALES and \LETTERS\PROSPECT subdirectories. He will inherit the same rights in \LETTERS\SALES as he has in \LETTERS.

One way to stop Doug from having full access to a subdirectory is to use the IRF (Inherited Rights Filter). The IRF filters the rights a user may have in subdirectories, and will be covered later in this chapter. The other way is to explicitly make a new trustee assignment to this subdirectory. A new assignment always overrides the inherited settings.

[Public] is a special trustee, for use by all the users on the network, and can always be specified as a trustee of a file, directory, or object. Although that sounds similar to the group EVERYONE in earlier NetWare versions, containers act more like the EVERYONE group than [Public] does.

The rights to use directories and files are similar, so we'll take a look at the directory situation first. User's rights in dealing with files and directories are also similar, making explanations fairly simple and straightforward.

There are more reasons to grant rights to directories rather than files, not the least of which is the time savings. Even with wildcards available, I would rather set the rights of users to use a directory and all subdirectories than set their rights to the files in each directory.

Directory Rights for Users and Groups

What are these rights that users can have over a directory? And did that last sentence in the previous section mean subdirectories? Yes it did.

The rights available to users for a directory are summarized in Table 9.1.

TABLE 9.1 Directory Rights in NetWare 4.1x

RIGHT	DESCRIPTION
Supervisor (S)	Grants all rights to the directory, its files, and all subdirectories overriding any restrictions placed on subdirectories or files with an IRF. Users with this right in a directory can grant other users Supervisor rights to the same directory, its files, and its subdirectories.
Read (R)	Allows the user to open and read the directory. Earlier NetWare versions needed an Open right; Read now includes Open.
Write (W)	Allows the user to open and write files, but existing files are not displayed without Read authorization.

TABLE 9.1 (cont.)

Directory Rights in NetWare 4.1x

RIGHT	DESCRIPTION
Create (C)	Allows the user to create directories and files. With Create authorization, a user may create a file and write data into the file (authority for Write is included in the Create right). Read and File Scan authority are not part of the Create right.
Erase (E)	Allows the user to erase (delete) a directory, its files, and subdirectories.
Modify (M)	Allows the user to change directory and file attributes, including the right to rename the directory, its files, and its subdirectories. Modify does not refer to the file contents.
File Scan (F)	Allows the user to see file names in a directory listing. Without this right, the user will be told the directory is empty.
Access Control (A)	Allows the user to change directory trustee assignments and the IRFs for directories. This right should be granted to supervisory personnel only, because users with Access Control rights may grant all rights except Supervisor to another user, including rights the Access Control user doesn't have. The user may also modify file trustee assignments within the directory.

Let's see how these directory rights appear in NetWare Administrator. Figure 9.1 shows the group CONSULTANTS and the file and directory rights the members have.

The Effective Rights listing is in the separate dialog box in the bottom-right corner of Figure 9.1. This dialog box appears when you click on the Effective Rights command button in the Group: Consultants dialog box. Notice that on the right side of the dialog box, the Rights to Files and Directories button is pressed, which opened the main dialog box.

The Supervisor and Access Control checkboxes are clear in the Rights area. This means the group CONSULTANTS does not have those two rights. Giving a group of users the Supervisor right could be dangerous. Giving a person or group the Access Control right is equally dangerous. With the Access Control right, the user or group member can change his or her own rights and add more rights without your knowledge or consent.

These rights apply to the directory where they are granted, and to all subdirectories. Rights are inherited from the top directory levels through all the existing subdirectory levels.

FIGURE 9.1

An example of the rights a group can have

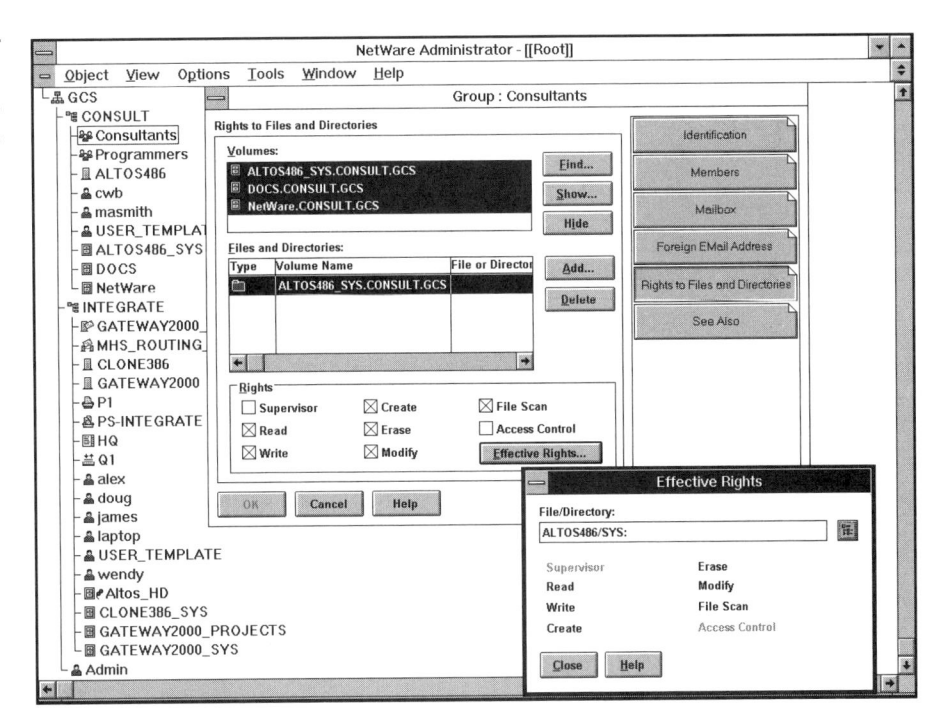

The rights are displayed (in DOS) as a string of the initials within brackets: [SRWCEMFA]. If some are missing, a space is put in their place. For instance, the most rights non-administrative users generally have are [_RWCEMF_]. As you can see, underscores were put in place of the S (Supervisor) and A (Access Control) rights. If the generic user listed previously didn't have the rights to Erase in a particular directory, the listing would look like [_RWC_MF_].

There are three minor diffences in how the rights are handled in NetWare 3.x and in NetWare 4.1x:

- The name Inherited Rights Filter (IRF) replaces the earlier name of Inherited Rights Mask (IRM); the actions are the same.

- New attributes have been added to files in NetWare 4.1x to accommodate compression and file migration.

- Users' home directories created during the initial user setup now include all rights, including Supervisor.

File Rights for Users and Groups

In contrast to directory rights, file rights address only specified files. Sometimes the files are specified individually, sometimes by a wildcard group (*.EXE, for example).

There are minor differences between how the rights are applied to a directory and to a file. Table 9.2 summarizes the file rights.

TABLE 9.2 File Rights in NetWare 4.1x

RIGHT	DESCRIPTION
Supervisor (S)	Grants all rights to the file, and users with this right may grant any file right to another user. This right also allows modification of all the rights in the file's IRF.
Read (R)	Allows the user to open and read the file.
Write (W)	Allows the user to open and write to the file.
Create (C)	Allows the user to create new files and salvage a file after it has been deleted. Perhaps this should be called the Re-create right.
Erase (E)	Allows the user to delete the file.
Modify (M)	Allows the user to modify the file attributes, including renaming the file. This does not apply to the contents of the file.
File Scan (F)	Allows the user to see the file when viewing the contents of the directory.
Access Control (A)	Allows the user to change the file's trustee assignments and IRF. Users with this right can grant any right (except Supervisor) for this file to any other user, including rights that they themselves have not been granted.

You might notice that the Create right is a bit different, and the Supervisor and Access Control rights apply to individual files. Why do we have the differences between directory and file rights?

The IRF and File and Directory Rights

Let's pretend your file system is set up so that all the accounting data is parceled into subdirectories under the main \DATA directory in the volume

ACCOUNTING. Many people on your network will need access to the information in these accounting files. Some will need to use the accounting programs, some will need to gather the information into reports, and others may need to write applications that use those data files.

Since directory rights flow downhill, this will be easy: give the group ACCOUNTING rights to use the \DATA directory, and the information in \DATA\AR, \DATA\AP, \DATA\GL, and \DATA\PAYROLL is available to everyone. But suddenly your boss realizes that giving everyone rights to see the information in \DATA\PAYROLL is not smart.

This is what the IRF was made for. The IRF controls the rights passed between a higher-level directory and a lower-level directory. In our example, that would be \DATA to \DATA\PAYROLL. The IRF does not grant rights; it strictly revokes them. The IRF default is to let all rights flow down unless otherwise instructed.

Figure 9.2 shows a simple look at our example. Everyone has access to all directories except for \DATA\PAYROLL. The IRF is blocking the rights for everyone in that directory.

There's a problem here: how does anyone see the \DATA\PAYROLL directory? The network administrator must specifically grant rights to the \DATA\PAYROLL directory for those users that belong there. The IRF filters between the parent directory and subdirectory. It does not dictate the rights assigned specifically to the subdirectory.

When you type RIGHTS from the DOS command line, you see your rights in the current directory listed with an explanation. If you have all rights in a directory, such as your home directory, the RIGHTS command will show something like the display for user ALEX in Figure 9.3.

FIGURE 9.2

Keeping prying eyes out of PAYROLL

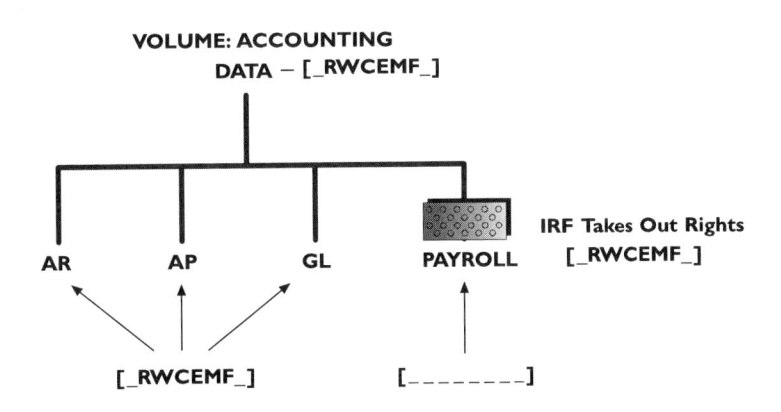

FIGURE 9.3

Results of the RIGHTS command

```
[Novell DOS] I:\HOME\ALEX>rights
GATEWAY2000\PROJECTS:\HOME\ALEX
Your rights for this directory:   [SRWCEMFA]
    Supervisor rights to directory.         (S)
    Read from a file in a directory.        (R)
    Write to a file in a directory.         (W)
    Create subdirectories and files.        (C)
    Erase directory and files.              (E)
    Modify directory and files.             (M)
    Scan for files and directories.         (F)
    Change access control.                  (A)

[Novell DOS] I:\HOME\ALEX>
```

If you have no rights in a directory, such as if our friend ALEX typed the RIGHTS command in the HOME directory above his own, the result would look something like this:

```
GATEWAY2000\PROJECTS:\HOME
Your rights for this directory: [    ]
```

There are two ways to approach the IRF: ignore it and set your file system up so that inheritance is never a problem, or take a minute to figure out how it works. The problem with the first option is that reality always rises up and bites you when you try to ignore problems, such as the previous example with the \DATA\PAYROLL directory. Since inheritance is always going to be with us, and the IRF makes good sense in certain situations, let's look at another view of the IRF.

First, let's add a complication: Group rights. Users may be assigned rights directly, or they may get them through group memberships. The individual and group rights are additive. If you have one right granted individually and another granted through Group membership, you effectively have both rights.

The IRF works against both the individual and group rights. The results of the individual plus group rights minus those taken away by the IRF are called the *effective rights*. Figure 9.4 stacks up the individual and group rights, subtracts the IRF, and shows the effective rights.

FIGURE 9.4

Stacking and subtracting rights

	Individual Rights	[_RWCE_F_]	[_RWCEMFA]	[_RW_E_F_]
	plus Group Rights +	[_____M_A]		[_R___MF_]
	minus IRF −		[_____M_A]	[__WE_M__]
	Effective Rights	[_RWCEMFA]	[_RWCE_F_]	[_R____F_]

Notice that the Supervisor (S) rights aren't mentioned anywhere. The IRF does not block the Supervisor right, whether granted to the individual or a group. This is true only of the directory and file rights IRF. Later, we'll see that the object rights are a different story.

Directory and File Security Guidelines

No two networks are alike and use the same security profile. However, some general guidelines are applicable:

- Design your network top-down: from tighter security at the higher directories to looser security in the lower directories.

- Fight the urge to grant trustee rights to individuals. Always look for groups first, second, and third before you work with the individual user.

- Plan for inheritance. Grant Read and File Scan rights high, and Create, Erase, and Modify rights lower in the NDS tree.

- Avoid granting any destructive rights high in the directory structure.

- Remember the Supervisor right for the file system cannot be blocked by the IRF. Grant that right carefully, if at all.

Using File Attributes as a Security Enhancement

FILE ATTRIBUTES IN NetWare, as in DOS and OS/2, detail the characteristics of a file or directory. NetWare administrators often call these attributes *flags*, from the NetWare DOS command-line utility (FLAG.EXE) that views and modifies those attributes.

Since we've decided that security includes making sure all network resources are available, the safety of files on the file server is important. Having files deleted or renamed by someone other than you is a security problem.

File and directory attributes are not a defense for cases of willful destruction and sabotage. They are a defense against mistakes and typos by innocent users. Haven't you ever had a user type DEL *.* in a directory on drive G: instead of drive C:? Having some of the files set as Read Only or Delete Inhibit may lessen the damage from a confused user.

Attributes control what can and can't be done with files and directories. They are also a limited form of virus protection. Since most viruses work by modifying executable files, keeping those executables RO (Read Only) will stop viruses from trying to rewrite files and save them back with the same name.

> **WARNING**
>
> *Of course, RO flags won't help with the new genre of Word macro viruses, or many of the other multitude of viruses out there. Flagging files RO is never enough virus protection; it just helps a little.*

File System: Directory Attributes

As is the case with much of NetWare, there are attributes for directories as well as files. Again, this makes sense. Unlike the rights to use an object, most directory rights don't directly affect the files in the directory. The attributes dealing with compression and data migration obviously do impact individual files. Since compression may be set by volume, the Immediate Compress attribute may be used more often than the Don't Compress attribute.

Table 9.3 lists the directory attributes with their abbreviations and descriptions.

TABLE 9.3 Directory Attributes in NetWare 4.1x

ATTRIBUTE	DESCRIPTION
All (All)	Sets all available directory attributes.
Don't Compress (Dc)	Stops compression on any files in the directory. This overrides the compression setting for the volume. New with NetWare 4.
Delete Inhibit (Di)	Stops users from erasing the directory, even if the user has the Erase trustee right. This attribute can be reset by a user with the Modify right.
Don't Migrate (Dm)	Stops files within the directory from being migrated to secondary storage. New with NetWare 4.

TABLE 9.3 (cont.) Directory Attributes in NetWare 4.1x	ATTRIBUTE	DESCRIPTION
	Hidden (H)	Hides directories from DOS DIR scans. NDIR will display these directories if the user has appropriate File Scan rights.
	Immediate Compress (Ic)	Forces the file system to compress files as soon as the operating system can handle the action. New with NetWare 4.
	Normal (N)	Flags a directory as Read/Write and nonshareable. It removes most other flags. This is the standard setting for user directories on the server handling DOS programs.
	Purge (P)	Forces NetWare to completely delete files as the user deletes them, rather than tracking the deletions for the SALVAGE command to use later.
	Rename Inhibit (Ri)	Stops users from renaming directories, even those users who have been granted the Modify trustee right. However, if the user has the Modify trustee right, that user can remove this attribute from the directory, and then rename the directory.
	System (Sy)	Hides directories from DOS DIR scans and prevents them from being deleted or copied. The NDIR program will display these directories if the user has appropriate File Scan rights.

Most of these directory attributes aren't used often to protect a directory from confused users. The options you will probably use the most are those that concern the operating system, such as Don't Compress and Immediate Compress. The Normal attribute will be used most often, if your network follows true to form.

File System: File Attributes

Most flagging happens at the file level, and doesn't get changed all that often. After all, once you set the files in a directory the way you wish (all the EXE and COM files Read Only and Shareable, for instance), there are not many occasions that require you to change them.

The time to worry about file attributes is during and immediately after installation of a new software product. Many product vendors today advertise, "Yes, it runs with NetWare," and they normally set the flags for you during installation. However, it's good practice to check newly installed applications, just in case the developers forgot to set a flag or three.

The available file attributes are listed in Table 9.4, with their abbreviation and meanings.

TABLE 9.4 File Attributes in NetWare 4.1x

ATTRIBUTE	DESCRIPTION
All (All)	Sets all available file attributes.
Archive Needed (A)	DOS's Archive bit that identifies files modified after the last backup. NetWare assigns this bit automatically.
Copy Inhibit (Ci)	Stops Macintosh clients from copying the file, even those clients with Read and File Scan trustee rights. This can be changed by users with the Modify right.
Don't Compress (Dc)	Stops the file from being compressed. This attribute overrides settings for automatic compression of files. New with NetWare 4.
Delete Inhibit (Di)	Stops clients from deleting the file, even those clients with the Erase trustee right. This can be changed by users with the Modify right.
Don't Migrate (Dm)	Stops files from being migrated from the server's hard disk to another storage medium. New in NetWare 4.
Hidden (H)	Hides files from the DOS DIR command. The NDIR program will display these files if the user has appropriate File Scan rights.
Index (I) (NetWare 4.0 and 4.1)	Forces the NetWare operating system to index this file's FAT entries in the server memory for faster file access. This happens automatically on any file with more than 64 FAT (file allocation table) entries.
Immediate Compress (Ic)	Forces files to be compressed as soon as the file is closed. New in NetWare 4.

Using File Attributes as a Security Enhancement 681

TABLE 9.4 (cont.)	ATTRIBUTE	DESCRIPTION
File Attributes in NetWare 4.1x	Normal (N)	Shorthand for Read/Write, since there is no N attribute bit for file attributes. This is the default setting for files.
	Purge (P)	Forces NetWare to automatically purge the file after it has been deleted.
	Rename Inhibit (Ri)	Stops the file name from being modified. Users with the Modify trustee right may change this attribute, and then rename the file.
	Read Only (Ro)	Stops a file from being modified. This attribute automatically sets Delete Inhibit and Rename Inhibit. It's extremely useful for keeping COM and EXE files from being deleted by users, and helps stop a virus from mutating the file.
	Read Write (Rw)	The default attribute for all files. Allows users to read and write to the file.
	Shareable (S)	Allows more than one user to access a file simultaneously. Normally used with the Read Only attribute so a file being used by multiple users cannot be modified. All the utility files in the \PUBLIC directory are flagged Sh (and Ro, Di, and Ri).
	System File (Sy)	Stops a file from being deleted or copied and hides it from the DOS DIR command. NetWare's NDIR program will display these directories as System if the user has appropriate File Scan rights.
	Transactional (T)	Forces the file to be tracked and protected by the Transaction Tracking System (TTS).
	Execute Only (X) (NetWare 4.0 and 4.1)	Stops a file from being copied, modified, or backed up. Used for EXE or COM program files, this attribute cannot be removed unless the file is deleted. Take care with this attribute. It can cause problems during updates (files can't be written over by a newer version), and some older backup software handles an Execute Only file by stopping.

File attributes are normally assigned to the files using a wildcard with the FLAG command, such as the command:

```
FLAG *.EXE RO S
```

This command says, "Change the file attributes of all files with the EXE extension to be readable, but not writable, and to share the file by allowing multiple clients to use the program file concurrently."

> **TIP** *When a user has a problem with a file, the first two things to check are the user's rights in that directory and the flags set on the problem files. One of these two settings, mismatched in some way, accounts for 80 percent or more of user file problems.*

Let's look at how to type an exploratory FLAG command and examine the results. Figure 9.5 shows the command and result.

In this example, we can see the file attributes for a few of the NetWare utility files. Most are Ro (Read Only), meaning they also have the NetWare attributes of Di (Delete Inhibit) and Ri (Rename Inhibit) set as well. Looking at the second set of attributes, you see this is true.

FIGURE 9.5

Checking FLAG settings in the \PUBLIC directory

```
[Novell DOS] Z:\PUBLIC>flag t*.*
Files         = The name of the files found
Directories   = The name of the directories found
DOS Attr      = The DOS attributes for the specified file
NetWare Attr  = The NetWare attributes for the specified file or directory
Status        = The current status of migration and compression for a file
                or directory
Owner         = The current owner of the file or directory
Mode          = The search mode set for the current file

Files                DOS Attr   NetWare Attr          Status  Owner           Mode
-----------------------------------------------------------------------------------
TEXTUTIL.IDX         [Ro----]   [---ShDi--Ri------]           .GATEWAY200...  N/A
TOSHP321.PDF         [Ro----]   [---ShDi--Ri------]           .GATEWAY200...  N/A
TYPEMSG.EXE          [Ro----]   [---ShDi--Ri------]   Co      .GATEWAY200...  0
TLIST.BAT            [Ro----]   [---ShDi--Ri------]           .GATEWAY200...  N/A
TCLASS31.DLL         [Ro----]   [---ShDi--Ri------]           .GATEWAY200...  N/A
TLI_SPX.DLL          [Ro----]   [---ShDi--Ri------]   Co      .GATEWAY200...  N/A
TLI_TCP.DLL          [Ro----]   [---ShDi--Ri------]   Co      .GATEWAY200...  N/A
TLI_WIN.DLL          [Ro----]   [---ShDi--Ri------]   Co      .GATEWAY200...  N/A
TESTING.BAK          [Rw---A]   [-----------------]   Co      .Admin.GCS      N/A
TESTING.DAT          [Rw---A]   [-----------------]   Cc      .Admin.GCS      N/A

[Novell DOS] Z:\PUBLIC>
```

The TESTING.DAT and TESTING.BAK files have been modified by the Admin user. You can tell because the flag is set to Rw (Read Write) and the Archive attributes are set, meaning they have changed since the last backup. The owner of these modified files is the Admin user. The rest of the files in the screenshot are owned by the server, GATEWAY2000. The ownership was set for these files during installation.

To check for all the various FLAG command line switches, from the DOS command line, type:

```
FLAG /? ALL
```

You'll see six screens' worth of information.

> *Don't think that FLAG is the only way to change file attributes. Both the FILER and Net-Ware Administrator utilities allow these same functions, just not as quickly and easily (in my opinion).*

NDS Security

SINCE NDS IS new to NetWare 4, the idea of NDS security is new to old NetWare hands. NDS security is concerned with the management and protection of the NDS database and its objects.

The SUPERVISOR user in NetWare 3.x was concerned about both file security (as we just discussed) and network resources security. The second part of the job included creating and managing users, setting network access privileges for all network users, and creating and managing network resources, such as printers and volumes.

The Admin user has, by default, all the rights and power of the SUPERVISOR. In NetWare 4, however, the management can easily be split between NDS security and file system security. It's entirely possible to have one administrator with no control over file and user trustee rights, and another administrator with no control over containers, Organizations, or Organizational Units. You can also set up subadministrators with complete control over their containers, having both file and property rights.

Let's be quite clear about this: file system and NDS security systems are (almost) completely separate from each other (the Supervisor right crosses the line). Having the rights to control a container gives you no authority over a file kept on a volume in that container, unless rights are granted to that volume.

The NDS database allows multiple management layers. You can create as many Organizations and Organizational Units as you wish, nesting the Organizational Units as many levels as you wish. As we'll see when we learn how the IRF works on object and property rights, it's possible to have the Admin of a network have full control over the Organization and the first Organizational Unit, but no control over the final Organizational Unit.

Object Rights versus Property Rights

There are two types of rights in NDS:

- **Object rights:** Determine what functions a trustee (user with the proper rights) can do to an object, such as creating, deleting, or renaming the object.

- **Property rights:** Determine whether a trustee can examine, use, or change the values of the various properties of an object.

Only in one case does an object right make any intrusion into the property rights arena: the Supervisor right. A trustee with Supervisor right to an object also has full rights to all properties of that object. But unlike with file and directory rights, the Supervisor right can be blocked on object and property rights by the IRF.

The opposite of the Supervisor right is the Browse right. This is the default right for users in the network. This allows users to see, but not modify, objects in the NDS tree.

Object rights concern the object as a whole in the Browser. Actions taken on an object in the Browser, such as moving a User object from one context to another, exemplify object rights.

Property rights concern the values of all the properties of an object. The User object that was moved in the last paragraph has 59 properties. The ability to change a property value, such as Minimum Account Balance or Telephone Number, requires property rights.

Objects have inheritance rights, meaning a trustee of one object has the same rights over a subsidiary object. If a trustee has rights over one container, that trustee has the same rights over any container objects inside the main container.

NDS Security

> When you turn your car over to a parking lot attendant, you give that attendant object rights: your car can be placed anywhere in the parking lot.

Let's play "Pick Your Analogy." Object rights are like moving boxes, and the box contents are properties. The movers have authority over the boxes (object rights), but not over the contents of the boxes (property rights). If one mover is a supervisor, that person has the rights to the boxes, and to the contents (property rights) of those boxes for management situations.

When you turn your car over to a parking lot attendant, you give that attendant object rights: your car can be placed anywhere in the parking lot. The attendant has full control over where your car is, and if it needs to be moved while you're gone. You probably exclude the Delete right from the attendant, however. The property rights to your car, such as the items in your trunk, glove compartment, and back seat, do not belong to the parking lot attendant. You have granted the attendant some object rights to your car, but no property rights. Do you think armored car drivers have object rights to the money bags, or property rights? Which would you prefer if you were a driver? Which if you owned the bag contents?

To keep things consistent, object rights and property rights overlap only on the Supervisor right. The trick is to remember that sometimes a C means Create, and sometimes it means Compare. Take a look at the official list of object rights in Table 9.5.

TABLE 9.5 Object Rights in NetWare 4.1x

RIGHT	DESCRIPTION
Supervisor (S)	Grants all access privileges, including unrestricted access to all properties. The Supervisor right can be blocked by an IRF, unlike with file and directory rights.
Browse (B)	Grants the right to see this object in the NDS tree. The name of the object is returned when a search is made, if the search criteria match the object.
Create (C)	Grants the right to create a new object, below this object, in the NDS tree. No rights are defined for the new object. This right applies only to container objects because only container objects can have subordinates.
Delete (D)	Grants the right to delete the object from the NDS tree. Objects that have subordinates can't be deleted unless subordinates are deleted first, just like a DOS directory can't be deleted if it still contains files or subdirectories.
Rename (R)	Grants the right to change the name of the object. This officially changes the Name property of the object, changing the object's complete name.

The object rights tend to be used by managers, not users. Create, Delete, and Rename rights are not the type of things normally given to users. The Browse object right is granted automatically to [Root], meaning everyone can browse the NDS tree. Remember, the Supervisor object right automatically allows full access to all property rights. The property rights are listed in Table 9.6.

TABLE 9.6
Property Rights in NetWare 4.1x

RIGHT	DESCRIPTION
Supervisor (S)	Grants all rights to the property. The Supervisor right can be blocked by an IRF, unlike with file and directory rights.
Compare (C)	Grants the right to compare any value to a value of the property for search purposes. With the Compare right, a search operation can return True or False, but you can't see the value of the property. The Read right includes the Compare right.
Read (R)	Grants the right to read all the values of the property. Compare is a subset of Read. If the Read right is given, Compare operations are also allowed.
Write (W)	Grants the right to add, change, or remove any values of the property. Write also includes the Add or Delete Self right.
Add or Delete Self (A)	Grants a trustee the right to add or remove itself as a value of the property, but no other values of the property may be changed. This right is only meaningful for properties that contain object names as values, such as group membership lists or mailing lists. The Write right includes Add or Delete Self.

The Access Control List (ACL)

The ACL (Access Control List) is the object property that stores the information about who may access the object. Just as Joe is a value of the Name property, the ACL contains trustee assignments for both object and property rights. The ACL also includes the IRF.

To change the ACL, you must have a property right that allows you to modify that ACL value for that object. Write will allow this, as will the Supervisor object right. Add or Delete Self is for users to add or remove themselves from a Members List property of a Group object.

Want to grant object or property rights to another object? You must have the Write, Add or Delete Self, or Supervisor right to the ACL property of the object in question.

Although it sounds as if the ACL is some list somewhere, it's really just one of many properties held by an object. Each object has an ACL. If a user is not listed in the ACL for an object, that user cannot change the properties of that object.

How Rights Inheritance Works

As we said before, rights flow downhill. Directory rights pass down to subdirectories, and container rights flow down to subcontainers. The only way to stop rights from flowing to a subcontainer is to use the IRF in the subcontainer. This forces users with rights to the parent container to also get the trustee rights to the subcontainer in a separate operation. That means the network supervisor (probably you) must go back and grant trustee rights to those users that need access to the subcontainer.

The system works well, with one exception: Selected Property rights are not inherited. If a user is granted trustee rights to an object for Selected Property rights only, those rights do not move down to the subcontainer or other objects. Figure 9.6 shows the process of granting user WENDY Selected Property rights to the SYS: volume of server ALTOS486.

Selected Property rights always take precedence over inherited rights. Even without an IRF, setting particular trustee rights in one container puts those rights in effect, no matter which rights are assigned to the container above.

The IRF and Object and Property Rights

The IRF works the same with object and property rights as it does with file and directory rights. The IRF doesn't give rights to anyone; it only takes rights away.

You, as network manager, set the level of rights users should have to an object. If a particular user has more rights than that, the IRF will filter that particular user to the level of access you set.

The big difference in the IRF when dealing with object and property rights is the ability to block the Supervisor object right. This gives some departments a warm fuzzy feeling, since no one except their administrator can control their part of the NDS tree. But care must be taken in organizing your system.

NetWare helps safeguard against accidentally eliminating all supervision for part of your tree by not allowing you to block the Supervisor object right

FIGURE 9.6

Granting limited rights that cannot be inherited

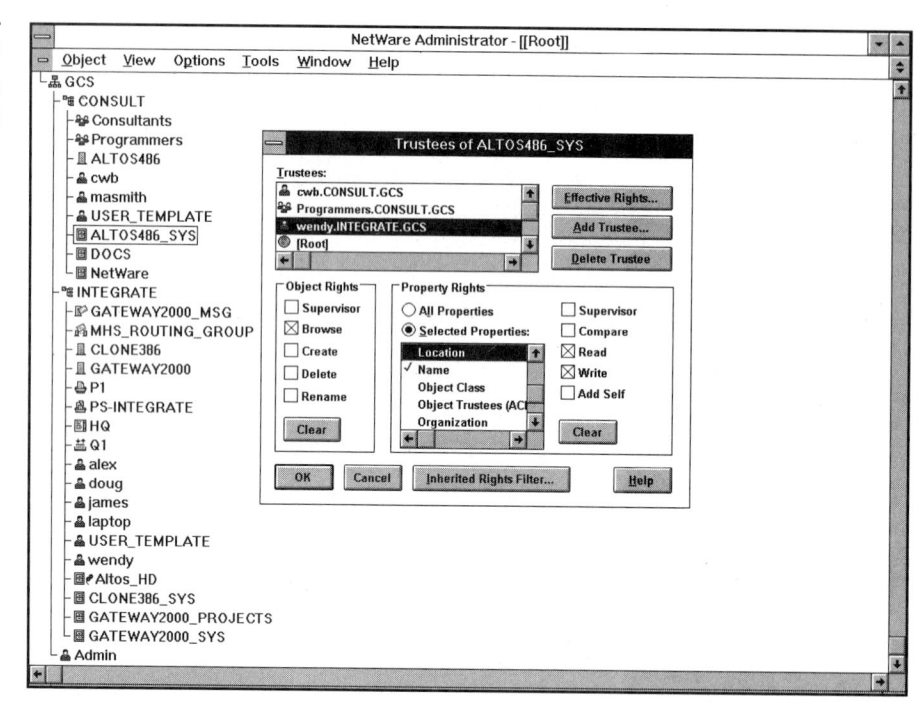

to an object unless at least one other object has already been granted the Supervisor right to that object. The problem comes if the other Supervisor object is deleted. Deleting the sole Supervisor for part of your NDS tree leaves part of the system without management, which is not a good thing.

This is a good reason to never delete the Admin user, even if you have one or two Admin-equivalent users. Over time, something will happen to both equivalent users, and suddenly your network will not have anyone able to perform supervisory functions over the entire tree.

So, when you grant someone the Supervisor trustee right to a section of the NDS tree, also grant them all other trustee rights. This precaution allows that person to maintain the ability to Create, Delete, Rename, and Modify objects, even if the Supervisor right is blocked by the IRF.

NDS Security Guidelines

Security management is not the most exciting stuff in the world 99 percent of the time. The goal of this section is to help you ensure that the 1 percent of security management that is exciting—a security breach—happens only in the mildest way possible.

Realize that few users need to create, delete, or modify objects during their normal workday. Those users who have occasion to need these trustee rights should be made an official or unofficial helper. The designation of "Power User for Marketing" will help that person feel better about spending extra time helping other users without getting paid for it. At least recognize those power users, since recognized helpers will help keep security strong, not tear it down. The big problems come when someone accidentally gets too many rights, not when the department's power user has defined a new printer.

A CNI (Certified NetWare Instructor) friend of mine offers these guidelines for granting rights:

- Start with the default assignments. Defaults are in place to give users access to the resources they need without giving them access to resources or information they do not need.

- Avoid assigning rights through the All Properties option. Avoiding All Properties will protect private information about users and other resources on the network.

- Use Selected Properties to assign property rights. This will allow you to assign more specific rights and avoid future security problems.

- Use caution when assigning the Write property right to the ACL property of any object. This right effectively gives the trustee the ability to grant anyone, including himself or herself, all rights, including the Supervisor right. This is another reason to use extreme care when making rights assignments with All Properties.

- Use caution when granting the Supervisor object right to a Server object. This gives Supervisor file system rights to all volumes linked to that server. This object rights assignment should be made only after considering the implication of a network administrator having access to all files on all volumes linked to a particular server. Furthermore, granting the Write property right to the ACL property of the Server object will also give Supervisor file system rights to all volumes linked to that particular server.

- Granting the Supervisor object right implies granting the Supervisor right to all properties. For some container administrators, you may want to grant all object rights except the Supervisor right, and then grant property rights through the Selected Properties option.

- Use caution when filtering Supervisor rights with an IRF. For example, a container administrator uses an IRF to filter the network administrator's rights to a particular branch of the NDS tree. If the network administrator (who has the Supervisor right to the container administrator's User object) deletes the User object of the container administrator, that particular branch of the NDS tree can no longer be managed.

Here's my security slogan: Grant to containers or groups; ignore the individuals. The more individual users you administer, the more time and trouble it will take. I've known some NetWare managers to make groups holding only one person. That sounds stupid, but consider the alternative: when a second person comes, and then a third person, you'll find yourself handling each one by hand. If there's a group in place, each new person that arrives takes only a few seconds to install and have all the necessary trustee rights and network resource mappings applied.

Whenever possible, handle security (access to network resources) through the container. If not a container, then a group. If not a group, look harder to make the need fit an existing group or develop a new group. The more adamant you are about securing your network by groups rather than individual users, the lighter your network management burden. The more you use the container to grant rights, the neater things are.

If you prefer NetWare Administrator for your management tasks, read the next section. If you prefer the DOS administration tools, skip to the "Security Management with DOS Utilities" section up ahead.

Security Management with NetWare Administrator

WHEN NDS IS first installed, there are two objects, Admin and [Public]. The default rights, and the reasons for the rights, are:

Admin	Supervisor object rights to [Root]	Allows Admin to create and administer all other network objects.
[Public]	Browse object rights to [Root]	Allows all users to see the NDS tree and all objects on the tree.

When you create User objects, each has a certain set of default rights. These rights include what the User object can do to manage itself, such as Read and Write the user's login script and print job configuration. To get around in the NDS tree, users are also granted limited rights to [Root] and [Public].

Here's a summary of the default User object trustee, default rights, and what these rights allow a user to do.

The User has these default property rights:

- [R]: Read right to All Property Rights, which allows the reading of properties stored in the User object.

- [RW}: Read and Write property rights to the user's own Login Script property, which allows users to execute and modify their own login scripts.

- [RW]: Read and Write property rights to the user's own Print Configuration property, which allows users to create print jobs and send them to the printer.

The [Root] object has this default property right:

- [R]: Read property right to Network Address and Group Membership, which identifies the network address and any group memberships.

And the [Public] object has this property right by default:

- [R]: Read property right to Default Server property, which determines the default server for the User object.

As you can see, the default NDS rights are fairly limited. A new user can see the network, change his or her own login script and printer configuration, and wait for help.

If that's too much—perhaps you don't want users to have the ability to change (and mess up) their own login scripts—change it. Merely revoke the User object's Login Script property right. Figure 9.7 shows the User object details, with the Write capability for the Login Script property revoked. The Read capability is necessary so the user can log in.

Revoking a Property Right

> **9.1 IN-A-HURRY**
>
> **Prevent a User from Modifying His or Her Own Login Script**
>
> 1. Open NetWare Administrator from some version of Windows.
>
> 2. Highlight the User object to modify and click the right mouse button.
>
> 3. Highlight Rights to Other Objects and click the left mouse button.
>
> 4. Click on OK in the Search Context dialog box that appears.
>
> 5. Highlight the User object by clicking the left mouse button.
>
> 6. Click on the Selected Properties radio button and highlight the Login Script in the Properties list.
>
> 7. Clear the Write checkbox while Login Script is highlighted.
>
> 8. Click on OK to save and exit.

Think of this as a prelude to the other security management tasks we're going to do in the following sections. First, you must start NetWare Administrator from MS Windows 3.1 or Windows 95 running Client32 software, and highlight the User object that you want to modify. But don't press Enter after you highlight the user, or you'll get the multipage dialog box about the User object (and that doesn't include the object or property rights information). You must either click the right mouse button and then choose Rights to Other Objects or use the Object pull-down menu.

When we get to the dialog box for the User object (as you can see in Figure 9.7 in the previous section for user LAPTOP), we want to change the Property Rights setting. Before the Property Rights section becomes active, the Assigned Objects list must have a highlighted entry. In our example, highlight User object laptop.INTEGRATE.GCS. Then click on the Selected Properties radio button, which makes the properties pick list active. Scroll through the list, find Login Script, and click on it.

The default is to have both Read and Write capabilities. By clicking on the Write checkbox, that right is cleared from our user. The change will become

FIGURE 9.7

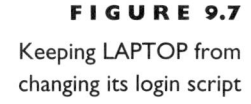

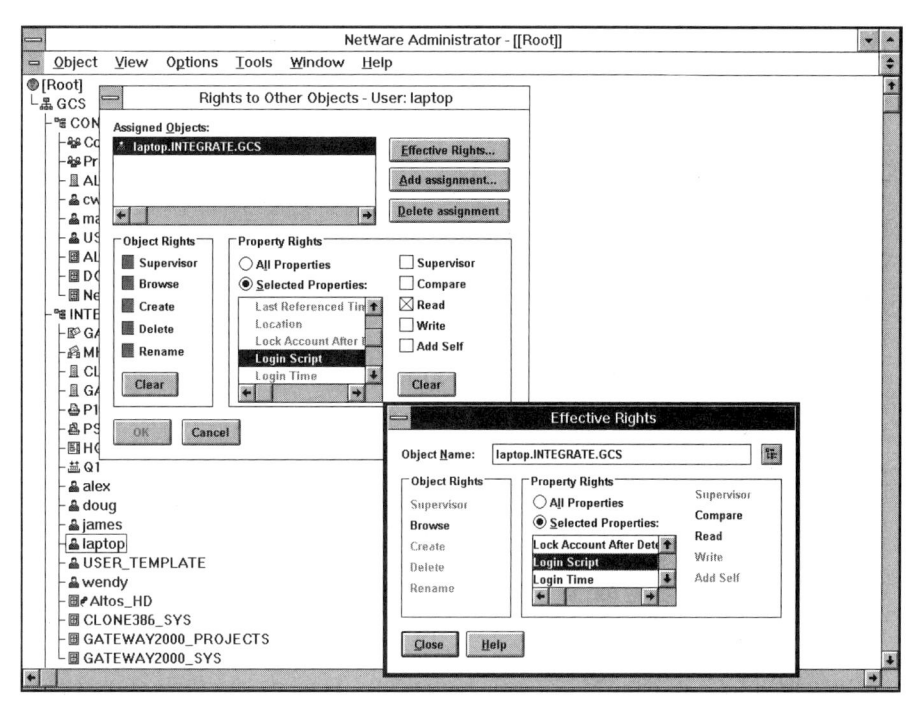

Keeping LAPTOP from changing its login script

active after the dialog box is saved with the new setting and the NDS database has a second to digest the change.

In Figure 9.7 (shown earlier), I also opened the Effective Rights dialog box by clicking on the Effective Rights button. When I highlighted Login Script, the rights for User LAPTOP to its own login script were shown: Compare and Read were bold, the rest were dim. So now we know user LAPTOP has the capability to read and therefore execute the login script, but not to change it.

The other way to stop users from playing with their login scripts is to bypass them entirely. Remember the sequence of login script execution? The User object's login script comes last. Just use the NO_DEFAULT command in the container login script, and the personal login script for everyone in the container will be bypassed. Then users can make all the changes they want in their login scripts, but it won't make a bit of difference.

Setting or Modifying Directory and File Rights

There are two ways to allow a user, or group of users, access to a directory. You can go through the user side, and use the rights-to-files-and-directories approach. Or you can go to the directory to be accessed and use the trustees-of-this-directory angle.

Which method you use depends on whether you're making one directory available to lots of users, or granting trustee rights to one set of users to lots of other network objects. We'll take a look at both angles.

First, let's take a different view of the network inside NetWare Administrator. Each time we've seen it before, there has been one big window with the network objects running down the left side. This view is the quickest and works well with a small network. But for some tasks and some networks, other views are handy. NetWare Administrator is very flexible in its presentation of your NDS tree.

Figure 9.8 shows the use of the Browser utility. With the Browse function, you can divide the network into as many different views as you wish. In fact, you can look at the same information in so many different ways that you might get confused if you're not careful.

This is the same network we've seen before with NetWare Administrator, but sliced a different way. The far-right window is the [Root] view, which has been the only view we've seen so far. The middle window is the INTEGRATE Organizational Unit, shown in its own window instead of underneath the CONSULT Organizational Unit. The far-left window is the GATEWAY2000_PROJECTS

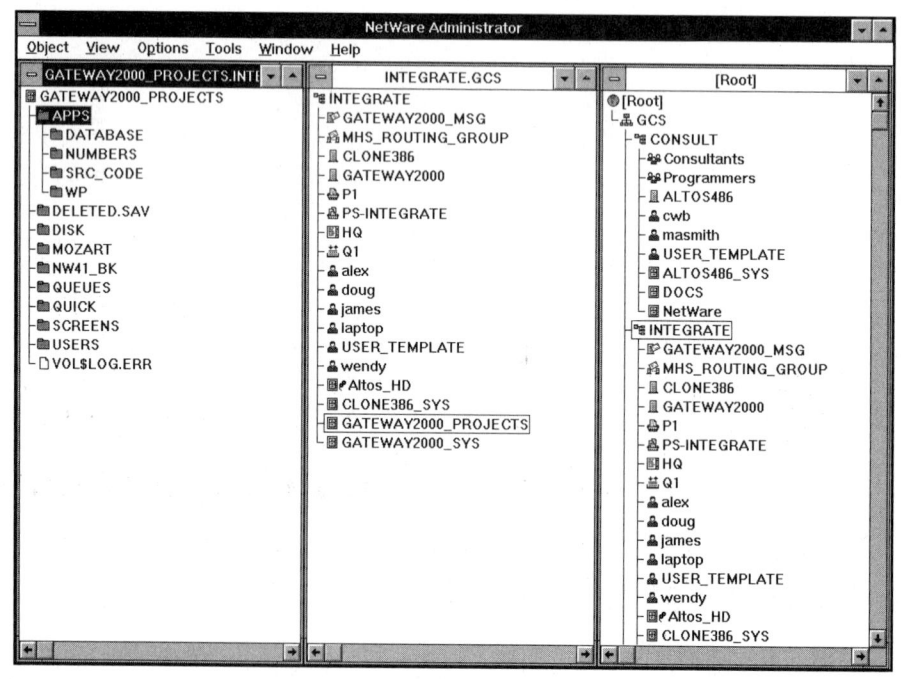

FIGURE 9.8

Browsing and exploding our network view

directory, expanded from the INTEGRATE window to show all the directories. The highlighted directory, APPS, is expanded to show the four subdirectories DATABASE, NUMBERS, SRC_CODE, and WP.

Opening a Browser Window

> **9.2 IN-A-HURRY**
>
> **Open a Browser Window in NetWare Administrator**
>
> 1. Open NetWare Administrator from MS Windows or OS/2.
> 2. Double-click on the Organizations and Organizational Units you wish to expand.
> 3. Highlight the object to place in a new Browser window.
> 4. Click the right mouse button to open a floating menu.
> 5. Click on Browse.

Officially, each display window in NetWare Administrator is a Browser window. But since the first window always opens in full-screen mode when you start NetWare Administrator, it's hard to think in terms of the display being just one of many windows.

After opening NetWare Administrator from Windows, double-click on all the container objects you wish to expand. (I have always expanded both Organizational Units, INTEGRATE and CONSULT, in the main window for each screen copy.) Then highlight the object you wish to place in its own Browser window. Click the right mouse button to open a "floating" menu. Click with the left mouse button on Browse to see the previously highlighted container in a new window. The container expands automatically and displays its contents in the new window.

You can also use a drop-down menu to start a Browser window. Highlight the object to set in its own window and click on the Tools menu. The drop-down menu contains the Browse option, which you can click on to open a new Browser window.

If the item highlighted cannot be browsed, as is the case with a User object, you cannot open a Browser window for it. The Browse choice in both the Tools menu at the top of the screen and the floating menu will be gray and unavailable.

From the Group or User's Point of View

> ### 9.3 IN-A-HURRY
>
> **Grant Trustee Rights to a Volume or Directory**
>
> 1. Open NetWare Administrator from Windows.
>
> 2. Double-click on the Group, container, or User Object to grant trustee rights.
>
> 3. Click on the Rights to Files and Directories command button.
>
> 4. Click on the Show button to open the Select Object dialog box.
>
> 5. Move through the NDS tree and choose the volume containing the directory or files to be accessed. (To select multiple items, hold down the Ctrl key while clicking on the volume name.) Then click on OK.
>
> 6. Highlight a volume name and click on the Add button to open the Select Object dialog box again.
>
> 7. Choose the directory, file, or volume to make accessible to this object.
>
> 8. Highlight a volume or directory in the Files and Directories window to display the rights available to that object. To modify the rights, check or uncheck the boxes in the Rights box at the bottom of the dialog box. Repeat as necessary for each volume, directory, or file.
>
> 9. Click on OK to save and exit.

You can easily grant trustee rights for a single object to multiple volumes, directories, or files. The object gaining the rights should be a group of some kind, such as an Organization, Organizational Unit, or Group object, but it works for single User objects as well.

Start NetWare Administrator after connecting to the network as a user with authority over both ends of this transaction: user side and network resource side. The Admin user is the safest, obviously, but users with Supervisor rights to the container objects involved can do the work as well.

Open the object that will be granted the trustee rights, then click on the Rights to Files and Directories command button on the right side of the dialog box. The Rights to Files and Directories page appears. The process is now two-fold: you must choose the volume containing the directories and files to make available, then choose the particular directory or file. Click on the Show button to open the Select Object dialog box.

Figure 9.9 shows an example of assigning rights this way. In the Select Object dialog box (bottom right), the SRC_CODE directory has been chosen, moving it into the Selected Objects text box at the top of the dialog box. You can tell that the DATABASE directory was chosen previously, since it shows up in the Files and Directories section of the main dialog box.

The chosen directories are in a different context than the PROGRAMMERS group. This is not a problem, but you will need to create an Alias object for the remote volume to enable the group to connect to these directories during login. We'll get to that in the management chapter coming right up (Chapter 10).

Multiple directories and files may be chosen at one time in the Select Object dialog box. Just as in any other MS Windows utility, hold down the Ctrl key while clicking the left mouse button. Consecutive items in a list may be chosen by clicking one item, moving to the end of the consecutive items you want to highlight, and holding the Shift key while clicking the left mouse button.

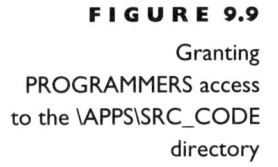

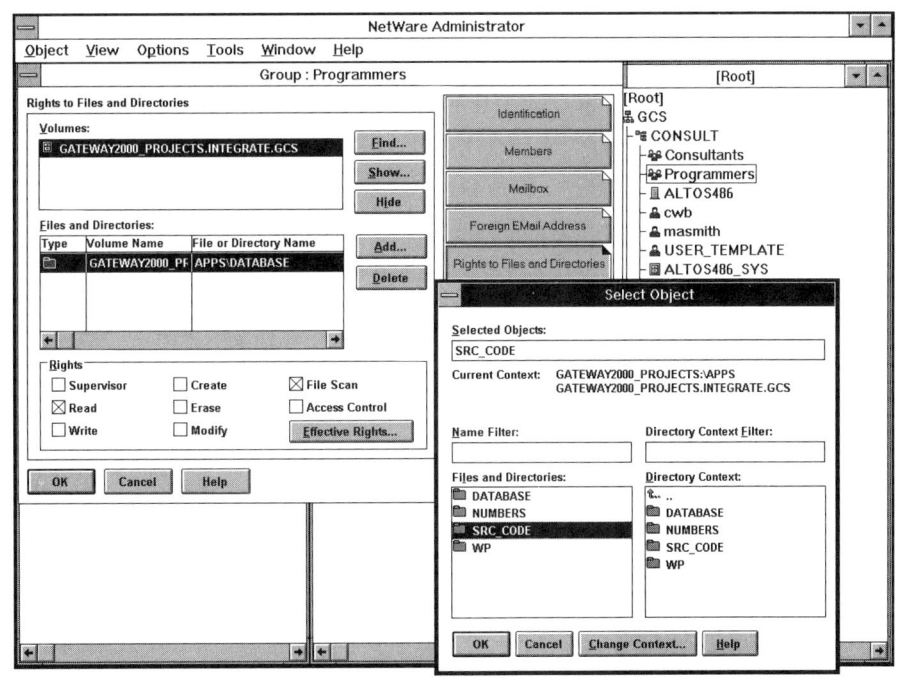

FIGURE 9.9

Granting PROGRAMMERS access to the \APPS\SRC_CODE directory

Figure 9.9 shows only the directory level in the Select Object dialog box. If you clicked another time on any of the entries in the Directory Context box on the right, the file system would be exposed. When the proper directory or file is shown in the Files and Directories list on the left of the Select Object dialog box, click on that name. Then click on OK to close the Select Object dialog box and refocus attention on the main dialog box, now displaying one or more file system objects.

The default rights to any new volume, directory, or file are Read and File Scan, as you can see in Figure 9.9. These rights are probably not enough for your purposes. To modify the rights for each chosen item, highlight that item in the Files and Directories list. Then click on the desired rights in the Rights section. For PROGRAMMERS, all rights except management functions (Supervisor and Access Control) are given. See Figure 9.10 for a display of the effective rights.

You can grant trustee rights to a Volume object rather than to a directory or file. If you do, the object with those rights has complete access to the root directory, meaning the entire volume. If you have enough volumes to parcel

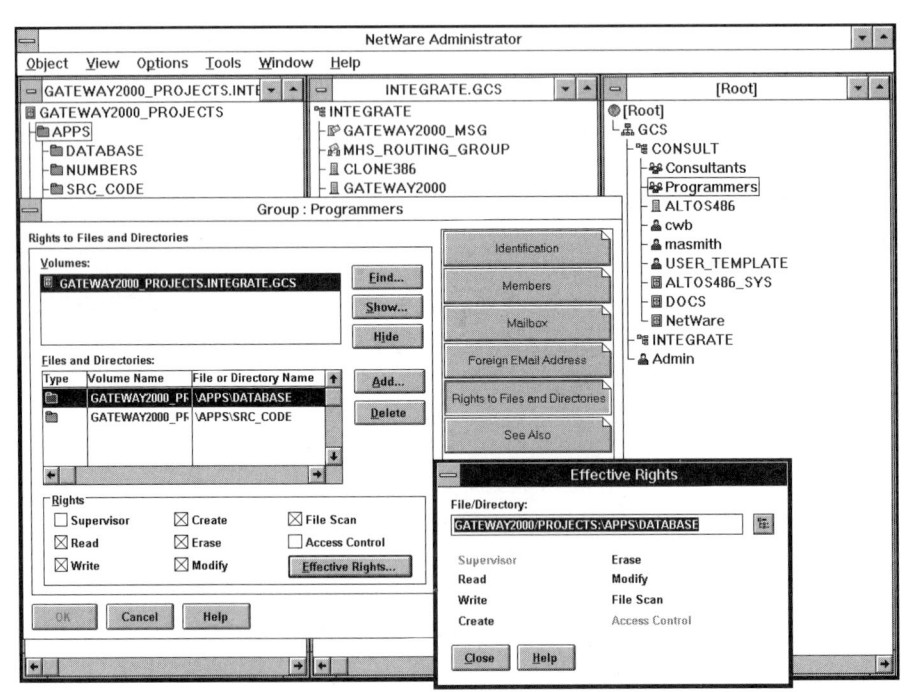

FIGURE 9.10

Granted rights are bold; excluded rights are gray

them out in that manner, that's great, but most networks grant rights to a directory. That allows plenty of accessibility for the users, since they can build a full directory structure, while still maintaining an easy method of control.

Granting rights to a directory in another container is not a problem, but one more step may be needed. If the users wish to map a drive to another container in their login script, they can't get there from here. You must create an Alias object for the remote volume, and then map the groups and users to the Alias.

From the Directory or File's Point of View

9.4 IN-A-HURRY

Grant Trustee Rights to a Group or User

1. Open NetWare Administrator.

2. Highlight the volume, directory, or file to make available to more users and press Enter.

3. Click on the Trustees of this Directory command button on the right side.

4. Click on the Add Trustees button to open the Select Object dialog box.

5. Move through the NDS tree and choose the groups or users to be allowed access. (To select multiple groups and users, hold down the Ctrl key while clicking on the names.) Then click on OK.

6. Highlight the groups and/or users in the Trustees window to display the rights available to that object.

7. To modify the rights, check to add or uncheck to delete rights in the Rights section at the bottom of the dialog box. Repeat as necessary for each group or user.

8. Click on OK to save and exit.

This is the best method to use when granting several users or groups trustee rights to the same volume, directory, or file. One screen allows you to choose multiple trustees at once, and yet assign different rights to each of them if you wish. Although this can work with volumes and files, let's use a common scenario: making a group of users trustees to a directory.

Start the NetWare Administrator program. Browse through the NDS tree as necessary to highlight the object to make available to the new user or users. In our example, the \APPS\NUMBERS directory is the one to be shared with the PROGRAMMERS and CONSULTANTS groups.

Once the file is highlighted, press Enter to open the dialog box. You can also click the right mouse button, or pull down the Object menu choice from the top of the screen, and choose Details from either. This opens the main dialog box, from whence you must click on the Trustees of this Directory command button.

In our example, there are currently no trustees of this directory, so the Trustees box is empty. Clicking on Add Trustee pops open the ubiquitous Select Object dialog box, listing only those items that can be a trustee to a directory. Figure 9.11 shows this dialog box in action, with the two groups that we want to make trustees highlighted and ready. Multiple trustees can be chosen by holding down the Ctrl key and clicking on each desired choice.

The Inheritance Filter list shows all rights are being passed through to all subdirectories, which is the default. I see no reason to change that situation for our example, so let's leave the IRF alone for now.

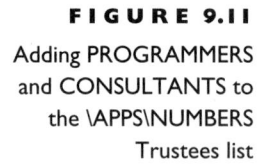

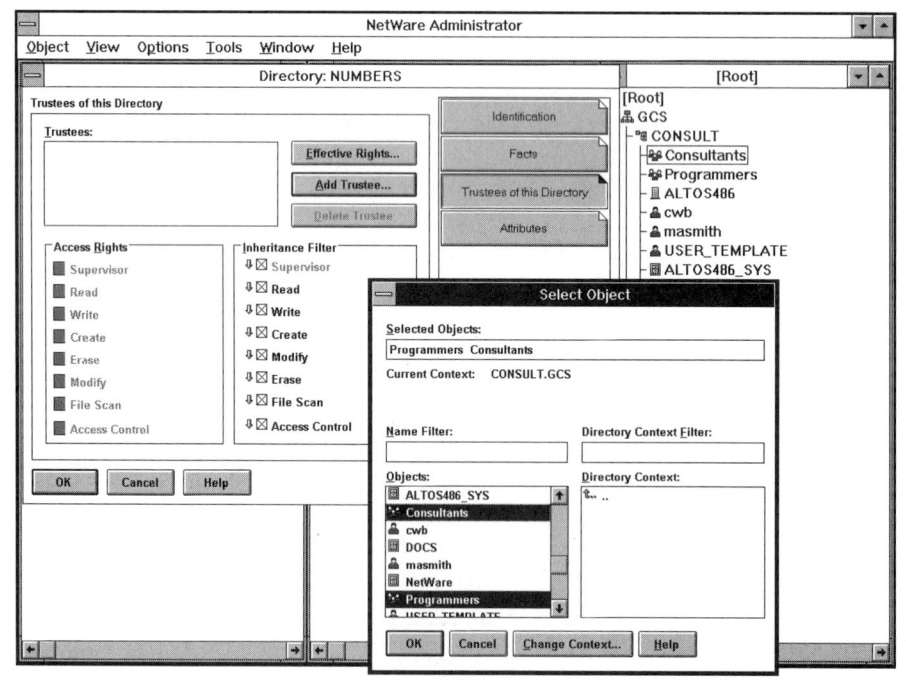

FIGURE 9.11

Adding PROGRAMMERS and CONSULTANTS to the \APPS\NUMBERS Trustees list

Security Management with NetWare Administrator

The Access Rights checkboxes are all unavailable. Why? There's nothing in the Trustees list to have any access rights. As soon as we click on OK on the Select Object dialog box, the two chosen groups will be listed as trustees, and the Access Rights boxes will become more important.

Once the new trustees are copied to the list, checking the Access Rights for each group will set the level of control the group has over the directory. Since few groups should ever have Supervisor rights, leave that and the Access Control box unchecked.

Here in Figure 9.12, we see that all normal access rights for a group to a directory have been granted. The Effective Rights dialog box shows in bold letters which trustee rights are granted, with Supervisor and Access Control still dim and gray. The reason the fold-down corner on the Trustees of this Directory button isn't black in Figure 9.12 is because the Access Rights display and the Effective Rights dialog box won't be updated until the new trustees rights have been saved to the NDS database. Click on OK to save and exit, then reenter to check that all the rights you planned to grant have in fact been granted. It's easy to slip a mouse-click here and there, so make it a habit to check yourself.

It's easy to slip a mouse-click here and there, so make it a habit to check yourself.

FIGURE 9.12

The effective rights to \APPS\NUMBERS for two groups

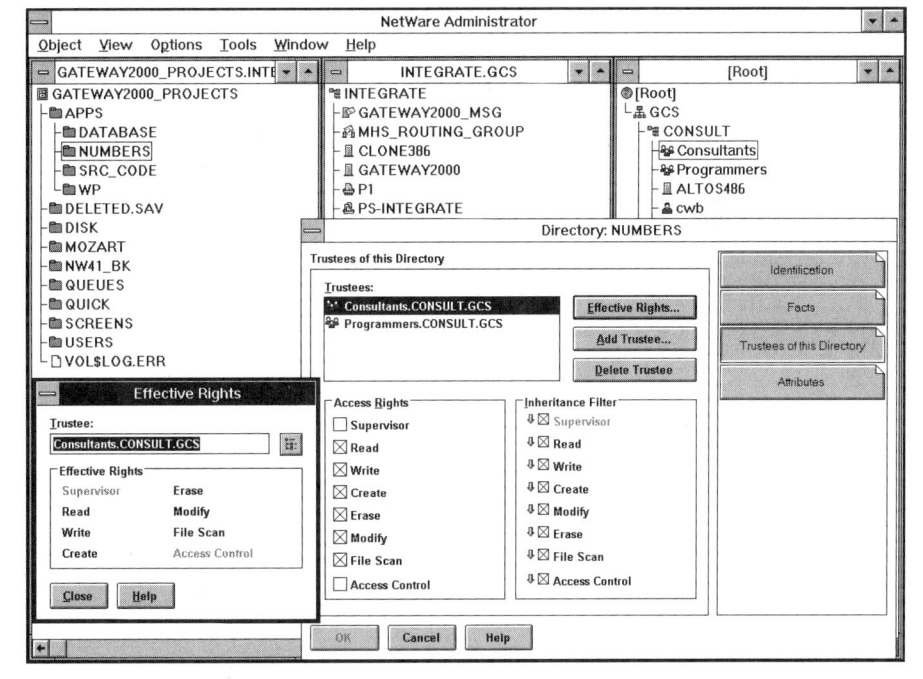

By moving these dialog boxes around, you can see the \APPS\NUMBERS directory marked in the left window, and the CONSULTANTS group marked in the right window. The middle window displays the INTEGRATE Organizational Unit, but the point of connection with the left window, the GATEWAY-2000_PROJECTS directory, is obscured behind the main dialog box.

Once again: granting rights to a directory in another container is not a problem, but one more step may be needed. If the users wish to map a drive to another container in their login script, they can't get there from here. You must create an Alias object for the remote volume, and map the groups and users to the Alias.

Setting or Modifying Object and Property Rights

NetWare Administrator offers drag-and-drop trustee assignments to some NDS objects. That means you can, for instance, drag a User icon over to a network object such as a Volume, and drop that User object there. Trustee rights are granted for the dropped to the droppee, although only the basic Read and File Scan rights are included. Granting any more rights requires going through the Trustees of this Object menu item.

FIGURE 9.13

Dragging WENDY into Trustee Rights to PS-INTEGRATE

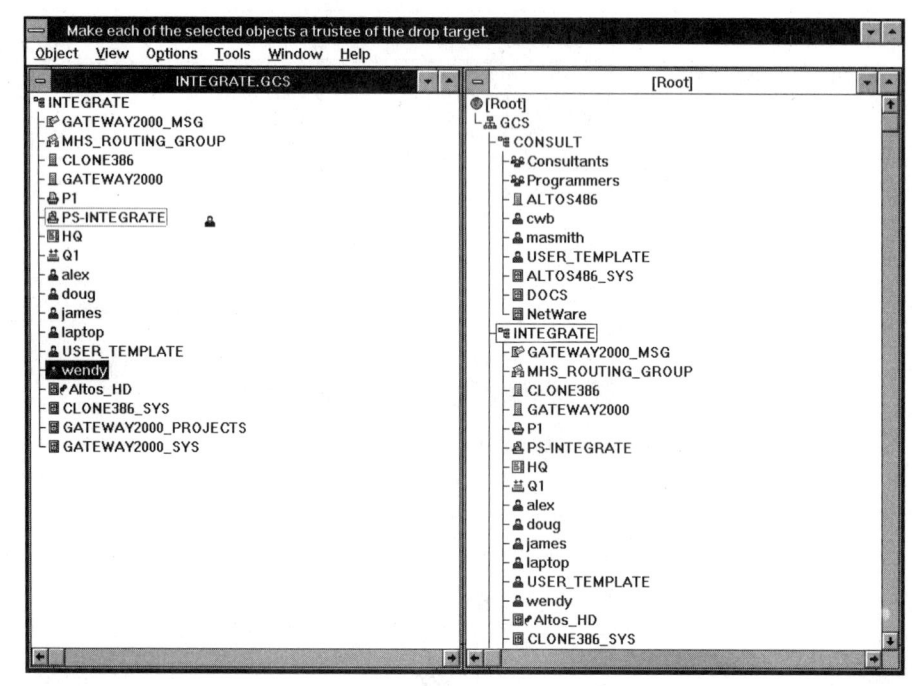

This drag-and-drop feature is far ahead of NetWare 4.1x's competition. Although the mouse can't manage your network by itself, easier administration means more time for you to stay a jump ahead of your users.

Let's take a look at drag-and-drop in action. Figure 9.13 shows the Browser window in two pieces, the right one with the [Root] display we've used almost exclusively, and the left window showing the INTEGRATE Organizational Unit display. Notice that User object WENDY is highlighted. This is the first part of the drag-and-drop activity. The tiny User object icon, a Lego-like head and shoulders drawing, is floating close to the print server PS-INTEGRATE.

While the WENDY User icon is floating up and down the NDS tree, several things happen. As the object moves, the dotted box that surrounds PS-INTEGRATE in the example moves along with the icon. If the dragged object has the ability to become a trustee of the object being indicated by the dotted box, the status line on the very top of the screen announces the ability to make each of the selected objects a trustee of the drop target. In other words, you can drop and gain some control over the target.

Once the target is reached and the icon released, the Trustees of This Object menu item is automatically checked, popping open the dialog box of the same name.

From the Target Object's Point of View

9.5 IN-A-HURRY

Drag-and-Drop Trustee Rights

1. Open NetWare Administrator.

2. Highlight the object to be given the trustee rights.

3. Click and hold down the left mouse button on the object.

4. Move the object icon over the NDS tree until the target object is indicated by the dotted line.

5. Release the left mouse button.

6. Modify any of the object or property rights using the checkboxes.

7. Click on OK to save and exit.

Dragging-and-dropping is a handy way to grant object and property rights from one object to another. Even if you have multiple objects that need rights to the target object, this is a fun way to open the Trustees Of dialog box.

After connecting to the network as an appropriate user, start NetWare Administrator. In this example, we have the two Organizational Units displayed in one window, and the INTEGRATE Organizational Unit opened separately in the left window.

Find the object to make a trustee of our target object and click and hold down the left mouse button on that object. As you move the mouse up and down the NDS tree, you'll see the icon for the object moves along with you (as in Figure 9.13, shown earlier). The dotted-line box will surround each object you pass over, indicating exactly which object is your target at that second.

When the dotted line surrounds your target, drop the object by releasing the left mouse button. The Trustees Of dialog box will open, with the trustee object added to the trustees list and highlighted. The Browse Object right and the Compare and Read property rights are granted automatically in this process. Take a look at Figure 9.14 for the status of this operation.

FIGURE 9.14

Click and save, or grant more rights for WENDY to PS-INTEGRATE

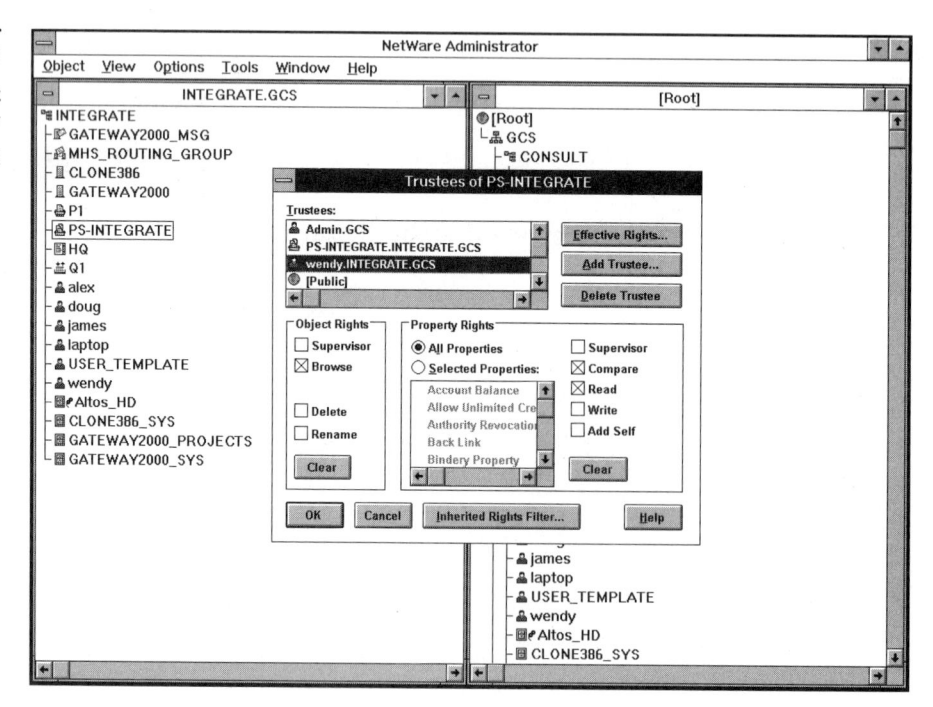

If you wish to change any of the trustee rights, this is the time to do so. Use the checkboxes to add or delete rights. Click on OK to save and exit.

More trustees can be added to this screen by clicking on the Add Trustee command button. This opens the Select Object dialog box once again, and all the objects that can be a trustee of the target object are displayed. Change context by using the Change Context button or the up arrow in the Directory Context box. The process is exactly like that of adding more directory and file trustees.

You may skip the drag-and-drop operation if you wish. To open the Trustees Of dialog box (as shown in Figure 9.14), highlight the target object and click the right mouse button. This opens the floating menu containing a Trustees of This Object choice. Click there, and the dialog box opens, without any assignments. All the trustees must be added through the Select Object dialog box. After choosing the trustees you need, highlight each and modify any of the object and/or property rights for each trustee. Finally, click on OK to save and exit.

From the Trustee Object's Point of View

9.6 IN-A-HURRY

Give an Object Trustee Rights to Other Objects

1. Open NetWare Administrator.

2. Highlight the object to be given trustee rights to another object.

3. Click the right mouse button and choose the Rights to Other Objects menu item.

4. Modify the Search Context text box to include your entire NDS tree, check the Search Entire Subtree box, and click on OK.

5. Click on the Add Assignment button, and then choose the object(s) to become a trustee to in the Select Object dialog box. (To choose multiple items, hold down the Ctrl key while clicking.) Click on OK to save your choices.

6. Modify any of the object or property rights necessary using the checkboxes.

7. Click on OK to save and exit.

Want to give an object trustee rights to more than one other object at a time? Here's the place. This procedure allows you to grant trustee rights to multiple objects from one screen.

As the Admin user or equivalent, start the NetWare Administrator program. Highlight the object, such as a user, group, or container, that you wish to make a trustee of one or more other objects. The floating menu opens, offering you Rights to Other Objects. Take that offer.

The first step is to discover what the object already has rights to. This requires our first real search operation. Figure 9.15 shows the Search Context dialog box open, with one important change already made and another pending.

When the dialog box opens, the current context is highlighted in the text box. You can press the Delete key and retype the context, or use the button to the right of the text box to open your friendly Select Object dialog box to set your context. We'll get to the Select Object dialog box soon enough, so just move the cursor to the beginning of the text with the Home key, and delete the Organizational Unit CONSULT from CONSULT.GCS. This makes the

FIGURE 9.15

Searching for the rights of PROGRAMMERS to other objects

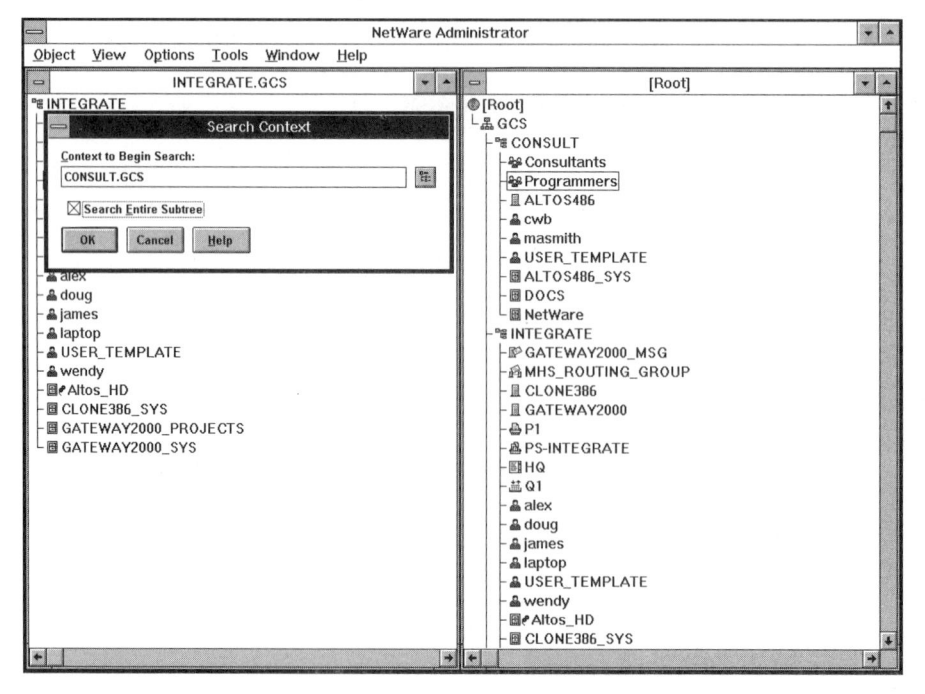

context to search GCS, our Organization level containing everything in this demonstration network. This step has not yet been taken in Figure 9.15.

The step that has already been taken is to check the Search Entire Subtree box. You might think that this indicates that checking the box will do the same as directing the search from the main NDS tree down, but it doesn't. You must take both of these steps to see everything this object has trustee rights over.

The dialog box that appears when you click on OK in the Search Context dialog box is labeled Rights to Other Objects and shows the class (Group) and specific name (PROGRAMMERS) of the current object. All the objects the named user, group, or container already has some property or object rights to are listed in the Assigned Objects list. The Rights checkboxes will be unavailable until you highlight one of the objects in the list.

Our goal is to Add Assignment, so we must click that command button. Now your friendly Select Object dialog box appears, as shown in Figure 9.16. Browse through the NDS tree using the list boxes or the Change Context button, and highlight the object or objects to gain trustee rights over. In our example, PROGRAMMERS are now taking over the CLONE386 server and CLONE386_SYS: volume.

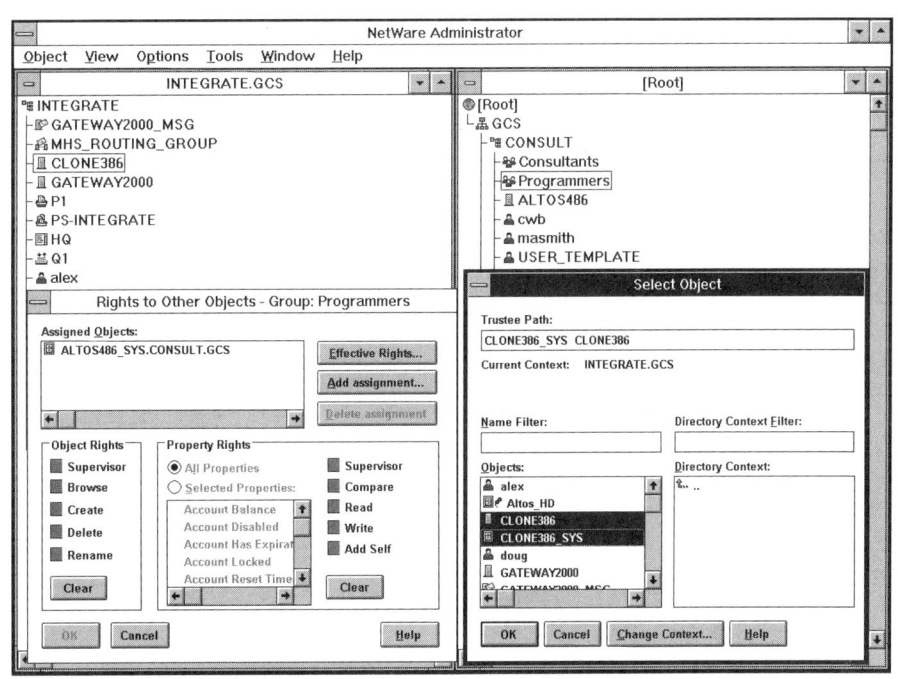

FIGURE 9.16
PROGRAMMERS are selecting another server to control

Notice that we may once again tag several objects in one screen by using either the Ctrl-key-and-multiple-click or the Shift-key-and-inclusive-click technique. We can see the current context of the items we're choosing, not the context of the objects gaining the trustee rights. Click on OK to save your choices and move them to the Rights to Other Objects dialog box for final configuration.

Figure 9.17 shows the final step in this process. Both of our chosen objects may be configured concurrently. As long as one or more items in the Assigned Objects list is highlighted, the checkboxes will apply to all. Check the rights you wish the object to have over the target object (in our example, the rights of PROGRAMMERS over CLONE386). When you're finished, click on OK to save and exit.

The same process works for modifying existing rights to objects. In that case, making sure you search the entire network for all objects is even more important. If you wish to delete the assignment, highlight Assigned Objects and click on the Delete Assignment command button. The rights assignment, not the object itself, will be deleted.

FIGURE 9.17

Granting object and property rights to more than one object at a time

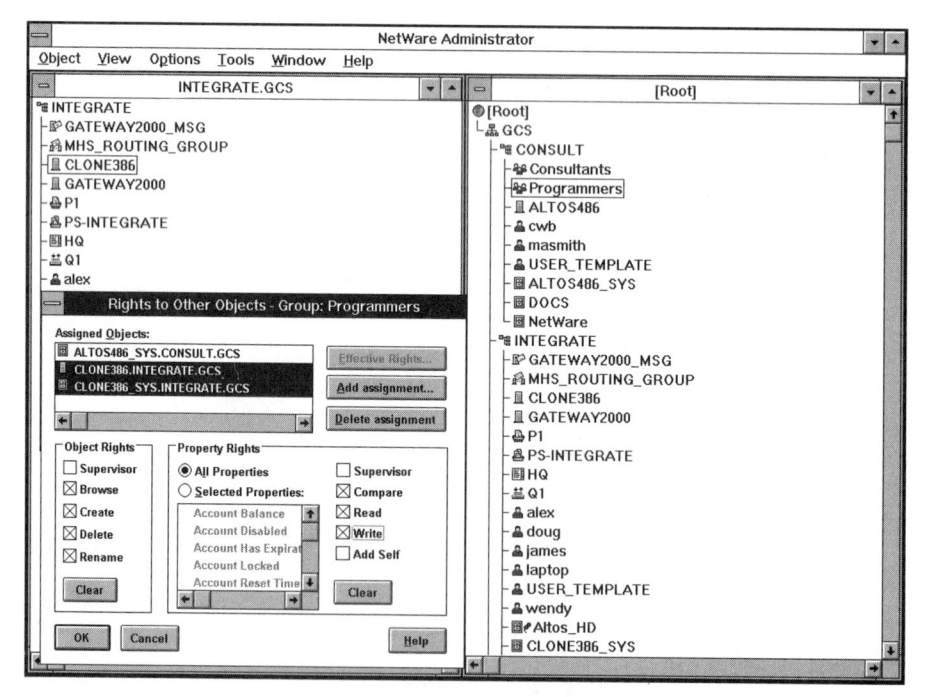

Security Management with DOS Utilities

UNTIL NETWARE 4, DOS utilities were the only tools the overworked NetWare manager had to help corral the network. If you're moving from NetWare 3 and are ready to get to work managing users and their access using SYSCON, let me break this to you gently: it's gone. Type:

    SYSCON

at a DOS prompt, and this is what you see:

    This utility is not supported with 4.x NetWare products.

    Use NetAdmin (DOS) or NWAdmin (WINDOWS and OS/2) for
    administrative tasks.

Sorry, but SYSCON is no more. The functions that were in SYSCON are spread between NETADMIN and FILER. Makes you mad enough to strangle the next mouse you see, doesn't it? Better make peace with your mouse soon, because administrative life is easier using NetWare Administrator in MS Windows than using NETADMIN in DOS.

Better make peace with your mouse soon, because administrative life is easier using NetWare Administrator in MS Windows than using NETADMIN in DOS.

Setting or Modifying Directory and File Trustees Using FILER

One of the functions now in FILER is granting trustee rights to particular directories. It's a bit more awkward than in the NetWare Administrator program, since it's more difficult to see and tag multiple directories. You can set the IRF for more than one directory at a time, but not trustee rights.

As a supervisor-level user such as Admin or workgroup administrator, type FILER from the DOS prompt. The program name is the same for users and administrators, but the options presented to those with Supervisor rights are more extensive.

When the first FILER screen opens to the Available Options menu, press Enter immediately for the Manage Files and Directories choice. This leads to a Directory Contents window, which lists the subdirectories, current directory, parent directory, and a backslash for the root directory.

If you highlight the subdirectory and press Enter, you'll get the subdirectory contents. This is not what we want, so press Enter again on the double

> ### 9.7 IN-A-HURRY
>
> **Manage Directory and File Trustees Using FILER**
>
> 1. While connected as Admin (or another supervisor-level user), type **FILER** from the DOS prompt.
>
> 2. Choose Manage Files and Directories.
>
> 3. In the Directory Contents window, locate and highlight the directory.
>
> 4. Press F10 to open the Subdirectory Options menu, then choose View/Set Directory Information.
>
> 5. Highlight the Trustees field and press Enter.
>
> 6. Add or delete trustees, or modify any entry in the Trustees list.
>
> 7. Press Escape to save and exit.

dots for the parent directory, and try it again. This time, highlight the directory that needs its trustee list adjusted, and press F10 instead.

The resulting screen, Information for Directory *x,* will look similar to Figure 9.18. The important field for us now is the Trustees field, currently highlighted in Figure 9.18.

To see what trustee rights the group has, press Enter on the Trustees field. The trustee information will be listed by trustee name, type of network object, and the rights. Figure 9.19 shows this screen, with a second trustee, user WENDY, added to the directory.

The help information across the bottom of the screen tells the story: press Insert to add users, Delete to remove users, and Enter to change the trustee rights of a user. Notice that WENDY and PROGRAMMERS are from two different contexts, and have different trustee rights to the DATABASE directory.

When you press the Enter key, the pop-up menu named Trustee Rights opens, listing the trustee rights held by the user. Rights can be added and deleted by pressing Insert and Delete as appropriate. You can add or remove multiple rights by using the F5 key to tag more than one right. The effects are the same as doing it one by one. The F1 key brings up context-sensitive help in all these screens.

Security Management with DOS Utilities **711**

FIGURE 9.18
Group PROGRAMMERS in the Trustees list for the DATABASE directory

```
FILER  4.21                                Monday  October  16, 1997  9:07am
Context: INTEGRATE.GCS
Volume object:
Current path: GATEWAY2000\PROJECTS:APPS
┌─────────────────── Information for directory DATABASE ───────────────────┐
│ Owner: james.INTEGRATE.GCS                                               │
│                                                                          │
│ Creation date: 1-21-1995                                                 │
│ Creation time: 10:50am                                                   │
│                                                                          │
│ Directory attributes: ↓ <empty>                                          │
│ Current effective rights: [SRWCEMFA]                                     │
│                                                                          │
│ Inherited rights filter:[SRWCEMFA]                                       │
│ Trustees: ↓ Programmers.CONSULT.GCS                                      │
│                                                                          │
│ Limit space: No                                                          │
│ Directory space limit:           Kilobytes                               │
└──────────────────────────────────────────────────────────────────────────┘
Press <Enter> to view, add or delete users, or their rights.

Enter=Select    Esc=Escape                                         F1=Help
```

FIGURE 9.19
Adding another trustee to the directory

```
FILER  4.21                                Monday  October  16, 1997  9:31am
Context: INTEGRATE.GCS
Volume object:
Current path: GATEWAY2000\PROJECTS:APPS
┌──────────────────────────┬──────────────┬──────────────────────────────┐
│ Trustee name             │ Type         │ Rights                       │
├──────────────────────────┼──────────────┼──────────────────────────────┤
│ Programmers.CONSULT.GCS  │ Group        │ [ RWCEMF ]                   │
│ wendy.INTEGRATE.GCS      │ User         │ [ R    F ]                   │
│                          │              │                              │
└──────────────────────────┴──────────────┴──────────────────────────────┘
Press <Insert> to add users. Press <Delete> to remove users. Press <Enter> to
change users' rights.
Esc=Escape   F5=Mark   Del=Delete   Ins=Insert   Enter=Select      F1=Help
```

Setting or Modifying the Inherited Rights Filter with FILER

> **9.8 IN-A-HURRY**
>
> **Manage a Directory's IRF with FILER**
>
> 1. While connected as Admin (or another supervisor-level user), type **FILER** from the DOS prompt.
>
> 2. Choose Manage Files and Directories.
>
> 3. In the Directory Contents window, locate and highlight the directory.
>
> 4. Press F10 to open the Subdirectory Options menu, then choose View/Set Directory Information.
>
> 5. Highlight the Inherited Rights Filter field and press Enter.
>
> 6. Add or delete items, or modify any entry in the Rights list.
>
> 7. Press Escape to save and exit.

The IRF sets which rights may be inherited from one directory to a subdirectory, or for a file. As the Admin user or equivalent, start the FILER program from a DOS prompt. Move through the menus until you have reached the directory or file you wish to set as the filter. The process is just the same as setting trustee rights, except that you now want to highlight the Inherited Rights Filter field and press Enter.

Remember that the Supervisor right can't be deleted from directory and file rights. If you try to limit the Supervisor right, a polite error message reminds you of that fact.

The background window in Figure 9.20 shows the list of Inherited Rights being passed down to subdirectories at the moment. Since Access Control is one of those active rights, I decided to delete that and the Erase right. (What doesn't appear in this list is what is getting filtered.) Sometimes you don't want files deleted if they become a problem; you just want to rename them and move them aside.

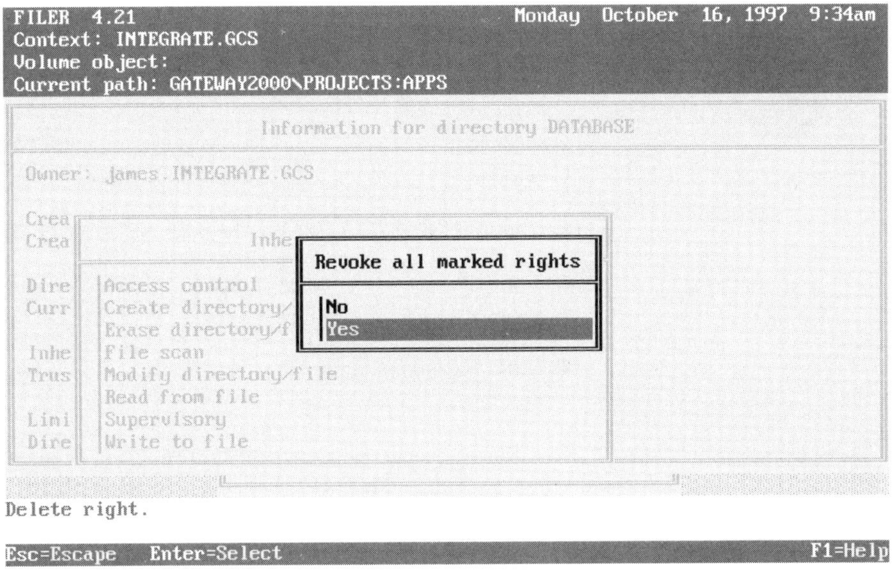

FIGURE 9.20

Revoking inherited rights in the DATABASE directory for the subdirectories

Since I wanted to revoke two rights, I used the F5 key. If only one right was being eliminated, the question box would say "Revoke Right," with the No or Yes choices.

When you are finished setting the IRF, press Escape. The changes will be saved, and you will return to the Subdirectory Options menu. If you wish to exit the FILER program quickly, use the Alt+F10 key combination. But note that any changes you made will not be saved unless you use the Escape key to move back at least one screen level before using the Alt+F10 key combination to exit.

Setting or Modifying Object and Property Rights Using NETADMIN

Prepare for lots of searching the Object, Class browser screen, or typing the full name of different users and objects, when you assign rights using NETADMIN. The process of searching for property and object rights information for a user other than the Admin or equivalent takes some extra keystrokes.

> **9.9 IN-A-HURRY**
>
> **Manage Property and Object Rights with NETADMIN**
>
> 1. While connected as a supervisor-level user, type **NETADMIN** from the DOS prompt.
>
> 2. Choose Manage Objects from the main NETADMIN menu.
>
> 3. In the Objects, Class screen, locate and highlight the object whose object or property rights you want to modify.
>
> 4. In the Actions menu for the selected object, choose View or Edit the Trustees of This Object.
>
> 5. To view available rights, choose Effective Rights. Then type the trustee name to check or press Insert to choose a trustee from the Objects, Class screen.
>
> 6. To change rights, choose Trustees from the Trustees of This Object screen. To add a trustee, press Insert. To delete a trustee, highlight it and press Delete.
>
> 7. To change property rights or object rights, highlight either [All Property Rights] or [Object Rights] and press Enter. To add a right, press Insert. To delete a right, highlight it and press Delete.
>
> 8. Press Escape to save and exit.

Once you've drilled down through all the menus, you will reach a screen similar to the one shown in Figure 9.21. This figure is comparable to Figure 9.16 (a NetWare Administrator screen) as far as the information involved is concerned. Whether you prefer NETADMIN or NetWare Administrator, you can see that the GUI shows more information on one screen. It's also easier to reach than the menu in NETADMIN, judging by keystrokes used and menus waded through.

FIGURE 9.21

The PROGRAMMERS still control volume CLONE386_SYS

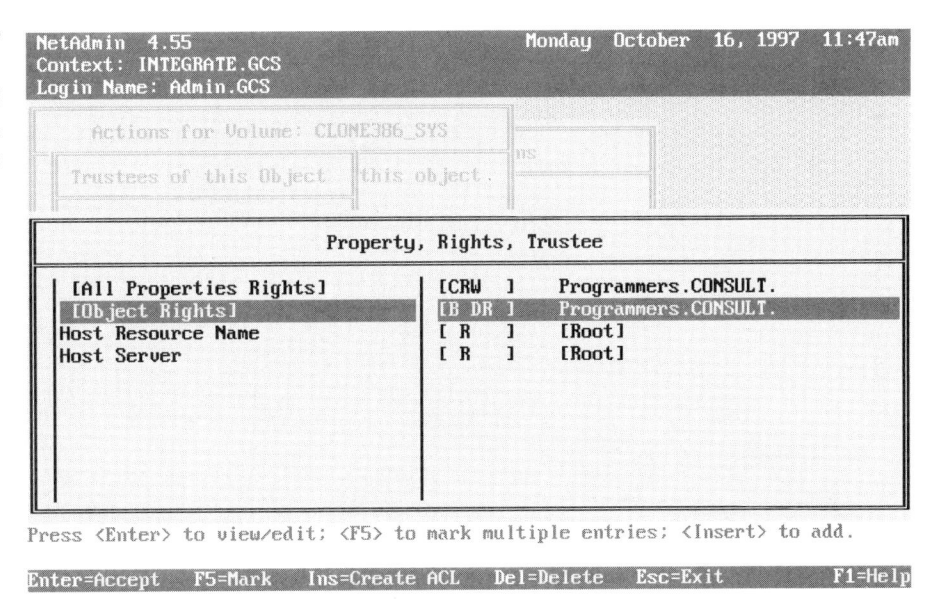

```
NetAdmin  4.55                               Monday  October  16, 1997  11:47am
Context: INTEGRATE.GCS
Login Name: Admin.GCS

         Actions for Volume: CLONE386_SYS
         Trustees of this Object   this object.

                           Property, Rights, Trustee

         [All Properties Rights]       [CRW  ]    Programmers.CONSULT.
         [Object Rights]               [B DR ]    Programmers.CONSULT.
         Host Resource Name            [ R   ]    [Root]
         Host Server                   [ R   ]    [Root]




         Press <Enter> to view/edit; <F5> to mark multiple entries; <Insert> to add.
         Enter=Accept   F5=Mark   Ins=Create ACL   Del=Delete   Esc=Exit        F1=Help
```

Common-Sense Security Measures

ALONG WITH FILE system and NDS security, security practices include passwords, login restrictions, virus precautions, and other common-sense measures.

Passwords and Login Restrictions

During user creation and setup, we spoke at length about the value of login and password security. Much of Chapter 6 concerns these very topics. Rather than repeat all that information here, I'll provide a quick synopsis. For more details, you can thumb back to Chapter 6, and review it with a new understanding of security.

- **Passwords:** Each user must have a password. Here are some tips for your passwords:

    The longer the password the better. Novell's default minimum is 5 characters; try for 6 or lucky 7.

    Encourage the use of alpha and numeric characters in the password.

    Set passwords to expire (the default is 40 days).

    Let the system keep track of passwords to force unique ones. The limit is 20.

    Limit the grace logins; two is enough.

- **Login restrictions:** Using login restrictions, you can limit users' network access and track the resources they use. Here are some tips for setting login restrictions:

    Limit concurrent connections for all users.

    Set an account expiration date for all temporary workers.

    Disable accounts for users away from the office.

There are a few more common-sense ideas to combat the problem of slipping security. When the network is new, or a security problem has occurred, everyone is conscientious. After a time, however, human nature takes over and everyone gets sloppy.

Your network changes constantly, and each change is a potential security disaster. Add a new user? Did you take care to match the new user with an existing group with well-defined security and access controls? How about new files created by the users themselves? Do you have a plan for watching the access level of those files? Do the users have the ability to allow other users' access into a home directory? If so, no private file will be safe. Don't allow sharing within each person's private directory. Send the file by e-mail or have a common directory for users to put files to share. Do *not* allow them more file rights to the \PUBLIC directory, even though some will ask for it.

Watch new applications. Many vendors have modified NetWare rights for files and directories for years, especially during installation. Are these loopholes closed in the new application directories you created just last week? Better check.

> *Your network changes constantly, and each change is a potential security disaster.*

Virus Precautions

Viruses are always a concern, even if they are statistically insignificant. People worrying about viruses waste more time than viruses waste. But knowing that virus attack is rare doesn't make you feel any better, or get your network back to normal any faster if it does happen.

There are some precautions you can take without adding optional software to your network or much time to your day. Mark all EXE and COM files as Read Only. Viruses generally function by modifying executable files. If all your executable files are read-only, viruses have a much harder time getting started.

Keep a tight watch on user's access rights to system areas—there shouldn't be any. Only managers, with a proper understanding of virus prevention, should have access to system files.

Do not allow users to bring disks from outside and load them to the network before being tested. Some companies go so far as to lock floppy drives, not so users can't steal from the company, but so the user can't load infected software. This is difficult to enforce, and not good enough to be your only prevention step. Better to offer a virus-free check station for users to test floppies than try to ban floppies altogether. If you ban them, people will just sneak them into the building.

The days when users regularly downloaded unknown files from bulletin boards and booted their systems with those disks are long gone. That's good. BBS sysops (SYStem OPeratorS) now pride themselves on running a clean board. That's good also. But the amount of files copied from unknown sources across the Internet is growing tremendously, and that's bad. Unix administrators often don't know which DOS and Windows files are on their systems, and they don't have the time or tools to test them for viruses. That's bad.

Feel free to restrict or eliminate FTP (File Transfer Protocol) programs from your Internet suite of applications, except for those trustworthy users who understand the need for virus protection. Although you can't always stop users from downloading files with a Web browser such as Netscape, keeping the FTP programs away from the general user population can't hurt.

Special virus-protection software is available for networks, often in conjunction with software metering or network user management. If your company is overly concerned with a virus attack, the software may give some peace of mind. However, virus software used inconsistently is worse than none at all. When you have none, people are more careful. When you have virus software used poorly, people develop a false sense of protection.

Some of the virus-protection features the optional programs provide are:

- Easy installation and configuration. NetWare versions are run as NLMs.
- Block unprotected clients from logging in to a protected server.
- Distribute protection to multiple servers and clients.
- Include an administration program for MS Windows as well as DOS.
- Send alerts to the specified users when a questionable event occurs.
- Schedule when and how security sweeps are made.
- Report on status and other statistics.

There are two major camps in the virus-developer community regarding the primary means of protection. One idea is to track the signature of all viruses. The *signature* is a piece of code inside the virus that identifies that virus, usually included by the virus criminal as an ego enhancer. As more viruses are discovered, the signature database must grow. Those systems that scan for known virus signatures should receive regular database updates.

The other option is to register a CRC (cyclical reduncy check) of every executable file on the server when the file is installed. The CRC is checked each time the file is read from the server. If the CRC value changes, this means that the file has been tampered with. The alert sounds, and the software shuts down the use of that file.

I lean toward the CRC method, for several reasons. First, a new virus obviously can cause you problems, and this is eliminated with the CRC method. Second, the overhead of checking a large virus database with every file-read request will only get heavier. As the demands on servers grow, this overhead will become burdensome. Finally, my friend John McCann was one of the first programmers to make quality add-on NetWare utilities, and he says the CRC method is better. Since he knows more about NetWare programming than anyone else I know, I'll take his word for it. (It's especially easy when I agree with his conclusion anyway.)

Some of the major NetWare-specific virus protection programs are:

- Central Point Anti-Virus for NetWare from Symantec Corporation
- Dr. Solomon's Anti-Virus Toolkit for NetWare 6.69 from S&S Software International Inc.

- InocuLAN from Cheyenne Software, Inc.
- LANdesk Virus Protect from Intel Corporation
- Norton AntiVirus for NetWare from Symantec Corporation
- NetShield from McAfee Associates, Inc.

If your manager is particularly scared of a virus attack, use that fear to your advantage. Clip an article about a virus attack and the resulting damage to the company. Nearly every single report includes a line about how the company had an inadequate backup procedure in place, meaning extra loss. If you've been angling for a bigger tape backup system or an upgrade, play the cards you're dealt and hit your manager with the tape backup request in one hand while waving the virus attack article in the other hand. Is this dishonest? Not at all. Some people need to be pushed into doing the right thing. You should take care to push your manager when he or she is already staggering. This way, you don't need to push noticeably hard, but you still get what your network needs.

Using AUDITCON

WHO WATCHES THE watchers? That question first appeared concerning the Roman army. How do you monitor a person that has all the power? In our case, the network administrator has full control of the network. You can limit that authority in some cases, but generally the administrator controls the network countryside as completely as the Roman soldiers controlled their territory.

We in the modern world know who watches the watchers: auditors. NetWare 4 is the first network operating system that allows true auditing of network events by a person with power only to watch, not to change. The network administrator has always been the network auditor, but that leaves a security hole. Would your bank trust the branch manager with all that money without checking the books regularly? Of course not. Now your network can be audited by an outside individual with full access to network events, but no control to change the network in any way.

Officially, auditing examines records to verify that transactions are accurate and the confidential information is handled securely. NetWare auditing

Would your bank trust the branch manager with all that money without checking the books regularly?

allows independent auditors, separate from the regular NetWare administrators or users, to audit network transactions. Changes to NDS; a volume's content, files, or directories; and server status are considered transactions for auditing purposes. Network events that can be audited include:

File or directory events	File and directory creation, modification, or deletion
	File and directory salvage, move, or rename operations
	Print queue creation, service, and deletion
Server events	Server going down
	Bindery object creation or deletion
	Volume mounting and dismounting
	Security rights changes
NDS events	Object create, move, rename, and delete operations
	Security equivalence changes
	User object logins and logouts

Because NetWare did not include auditing in earlier versions, some third-party products are available for this task. Ask your dealer for names of popular audit and management programs.

> **TIP**
> *An extra benefit is the large volume of DynaText, entitled "NetWare Enhanced Security." That chapter of DynaText provides excellent information in great detail about the security and network auditing features. If your management is serious about security and auditing, this chapter will be the first place to start. The details about using the AUDITCON program are in the "Supervising the Network" volume.*

Starting AUDITCON

Setting up auditing doesn't take much work on your part as the network administrator. The user account doesn't need to be named AUDITOR, and in fact will be more secure if it isn't. One important part of security is to keep valuable things hidden; the user name AUDITOR draws attention, while LKGASKIN doesn't get a second look.

As Admin or equivalent, create a new user to be the auditor, giving this user all rights to a home directory. This is necessary for the auditor to store reports from the audit process. Since the AUDITCON program and supporting files are in the SYS:PUBLIC directory, rights to Read and File Scan are necessary, but those trustee rights should be standard for the network.

9.10 IN-A-HURRY

Start the Volume-Audit Process

1. While connected as the Admin or equivalent user, create an auditor user and a home directory for that user.

2. Assign the auditor Browse rights in all containers to be monitored.

3. Verify the auditor has Read and File Scan trustee rights in SYS:PUBLIC to run the AUDITCON program and support files.

4. From the DOS command line, type **AUDITCON** to start the program.

5. Change the server or volume if desired. Current information is listed at the top of the screen.

6. Choose Enable Volume Auditing from the Available Audit Options menu and press Enter.

7. Enter a password for the volume, and then verify the password.

8. Notify the auditor of the password.

Start the AUDITCON from a DOS prompt. If you did not start the program from the server or volume you wish to audit, change that with the opening menu options. A pick list will appear offering you the available servers or volumes. Highlight one and press Enter. Once you've decided on the server and volume, choose Enable Volume Auditing from the main menu.

The "Enter volume password" prompt appears, as shown in Figure 9.22.

After verifying the password by retyping, your job is done. The auditor will take over from here and should change the password immediately. Once that password is changed, you (the network supervisor) have no way of knowing what it is. If the auditor forgets the password, you can't be of any help, except to create a new auditor and do this all over again.

The described process sets up auditing on a volume. To start auditing for a container, choose Audit Directory Services, rather than Enable Volume Auditing, from the Available Audit Options menu, and set a password for the container. Each container is audited separately; subcontainers aren't audited with their parent container.

FIGURE 9.22

Setting the password for the auditor

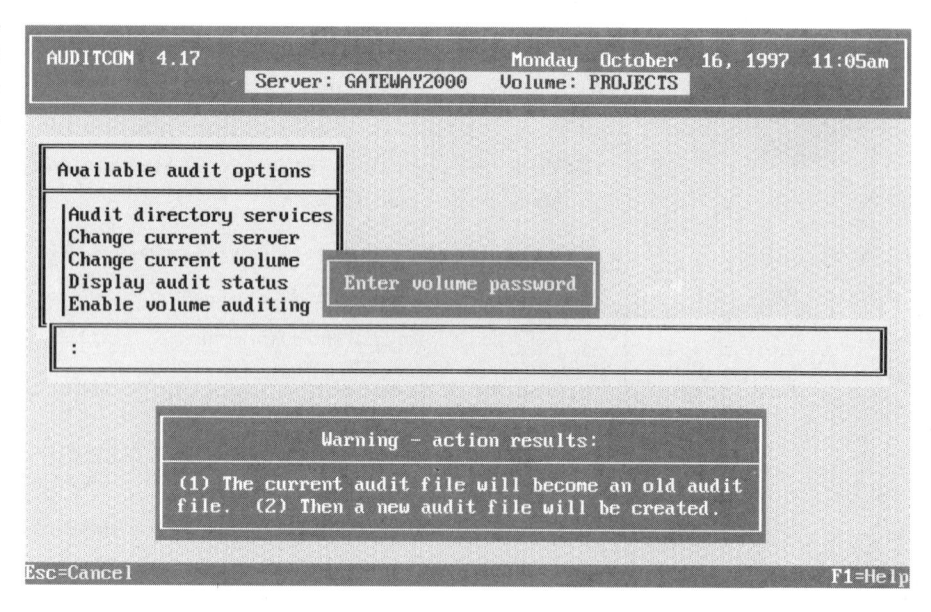

```
AUDITCON  4.17                              Monday  October  16, 1997  11:05am
                    Server: GATEWAY2000    Volume: PROJECTS

    ┌─────────────────────────┐
    │ Available audit options │
    ├─────────────────────────┤
    │ Audit directory services│
    │ Change current server   │
    │ Change current volume   │   ┌──────────────────────┐
    │ Display audit status    │   │ Enter volume password│
    │ Enable volume auditing  │   └──────────────────────┘
    └─────────────────────────┘
    ┌──────────────────────────────────────────────────────┐
    │ :                                                    │
    └──────────────────────────────────────────────────────┘

                ┌──────────────────────────────────────────────┐
                │          Warning - action results:           │
                ├──────────────────────────────────────────────┤
                │ (1) The current audit file will become an old audit │
                │ file.  (2) Then a new audit file will be created.   │
                └──────────────────────────────────────────────┘
Esc=Cancel                                                     F1=Help
```

Setting the New Auditor Password

> **9.11 IN-A-HURRY**
>
> **Securing the Auditor's Password**
>
> **1.** As the assigned auditor user, start AUDITCON from the DOS prompt.
>
> **2.** Choose Auditor Volume Login and type your password.
>
> **3.** Select Auditing Configuration from the Available Audit Options menu.
>
> **4.** Select Change Audit Password from the Auditing Configuration menu.
>
> **5.** Enter the current password, enter the new password, and then retype it to verify.

When the auditor changes his or her password, the NetWare administrator no longer knows the password for AUDITCON.

This must be the first act of the auditor. If this step is not taken, the audit results will not be regarded as accurate by most auditing procedures. Allowing one of the audited people to access the audit procedure does remind one of having foxes guarding henhouses, doesn't it? Don't take a chance on your auditing work being criticized for something so easy to fix. Have the auditor change passwords immediately.

Performing Audits

> **9.12 IN-A-HURRY**
>
> **Audit File System Events**
>
> 1. As the assigned auditor user, start AUDITCON from the DOS prompt.
> 2. Select the proper volume if necessary (you will start on the volume of the DOS prompt).
> 3. Select Auditor Volume Login and type the password.
> 4. Choose Auditing Configuration and set the audit by event, file/directory, or user.
> 5. Choose the details for events, files and directories, or users from the submenus.
> 6. Enable volume auditing if that has not been done.
> 7. Press Escape to save your changes and exit.

There are more options to monitor and audit than you want to know about. You will likely configure the system to audit almost everything the first time. After you wade through pages and pages of dull details, you will then focus your auditing quite a bit more.

Figure 9.23 shows just a few of the options to track on one volume of one server. If you activate each of these options, plus the other pages not shown in the figure, you will spend your life deciphering file activities.

Don't think you have fewer choices when auditing the NDS activities. Figure 9.24 shows the corresponding screen for the INTEGRATE.GCS container. Since each container is audited separately, tracking the parent container GCS wouldn't help with information here.

Most of the activity for the file system will be created by users during their normal user jobs. As you might guess by the listing, you can track file activity for all files, no matter who does what with the global option. The user or file option

724 Chapter 9 • Securing Your NetWare 4.1x Network

FIGURE 9.23

Just a few of your audit options for the file system

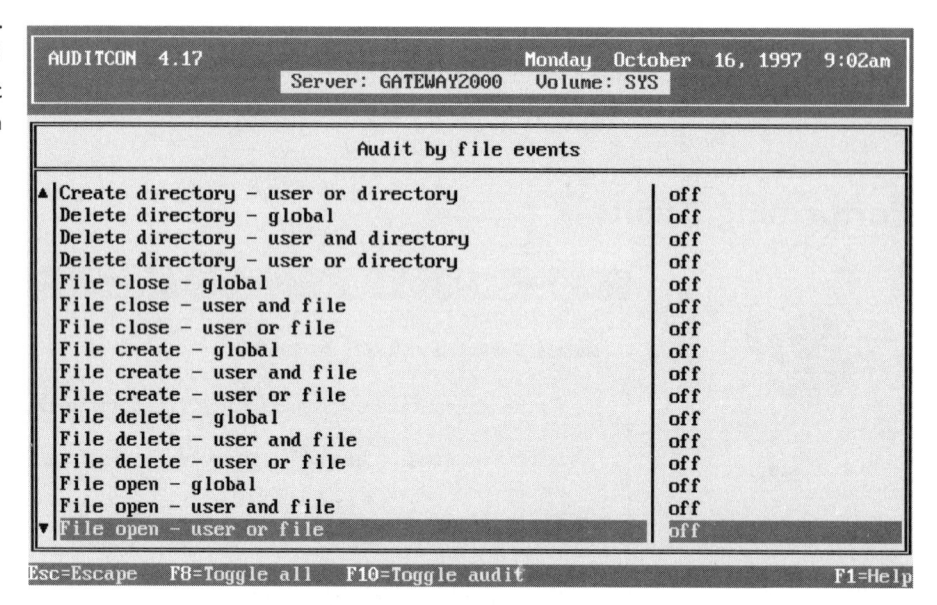

```
AUDITCON  4.17                              Monday  October  16, 1997  9:02am
                    Server: GATEWAY2000    Volume: SYS

                            Audit by file events
  ▲ Create directory - user or directory              off
    Delete directory - global                         off
    Delete directory - user and directory             off
    Delete directory - user or directory              off
    File close - global                               off
    File close - user and file                        off
    File close - user or file                         off
    File create - global                              off
    File create - user and file                       off
    File create - user or file                        off
    File delete - global                              off
    File delete - user and file                       off
    File delete - user or file                        off
    File open - global                                off
    File open - user and file                         off
  ▼ File open - user or file                          off

  Esc=Escape   F8=Toggle all   F10=Toggle audit                      F1=Help
```

FIGURE 9.24

Half your audit options for NDS events

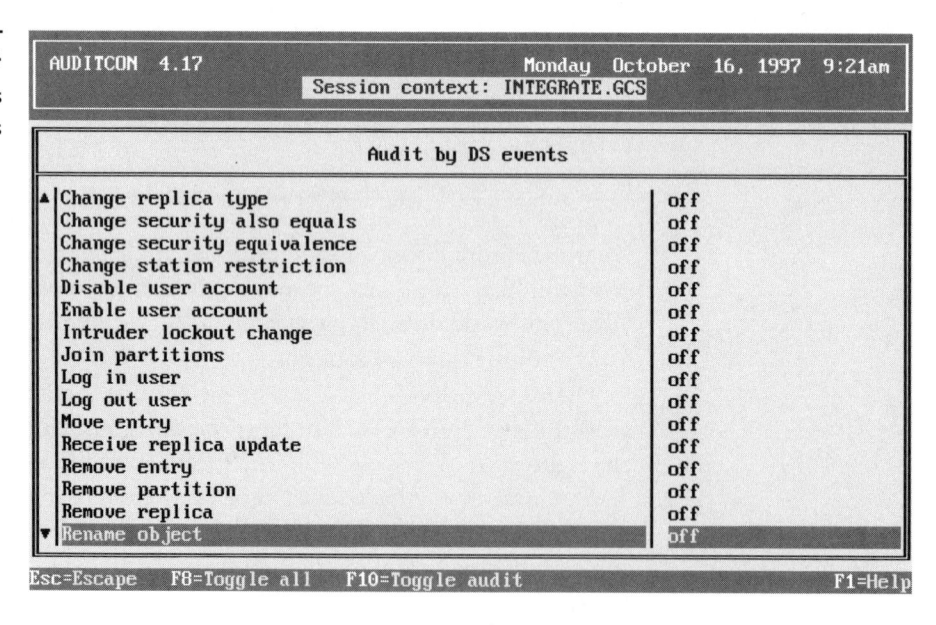

```
AUDITCON  4.17                              Monday  October  16, 1997  9:21am
                    Session context: INTEGRATE.GCS

                            Audit by DS events
  ▲ Change replica type                               off
    Change security also equals                       off
    Change security equivalence                       off
    Change station restriction                        off
    Disable user account                              off
    Enable user account                               off
    Intruder lockout change                           off
    Join partitions                                   off
    Log in user                                       off
    Log out user                                      off
    Move entry                                        off
    Receive replica update                            off
    Remove entry                                      off
    Remove partition                                  off
    Remove replica                                    off
  ▼ Rename object                                     off

  Esc=Escape   F8=Toggle all   F10=Toggle audit                      F1=Help
```

tells the system to track that particular user or file, no matter where it is in the volume or who instigates the action. You might watch all files in the \APPS\SRC_CODE directory, for instance, or track all files deleted by user CWB.

This section should be entitled "Watching the Watcher," since most events being tracked by this configuration screen can only be done by the NetWare administrator. Feeling just a bit paranoid?

The arrows at the top and bottom on the left side of the event listing indicate there is more in each direction.

Being audited may make you unhappy, but companies under strict guidelines must do this. Don't take it personally if a big audit of all computer systems is under way, and you, the network administrator, are in the spotlight as well. After all, if you weren't so honorable and noble as you are, you could really trash the network. Read the Internet newsgroup comp.sys.novell sometime, and you'll see plaintive requests for ways to undo damage done by departed, and angry, network managers.

Viewing Audit Reports

9.13 IN-A-HURRY

Configure and View Audit Reports

1. As the assigned auditor user, start AUDITCON from the DOS prompt.

2. Select the proper volume if necessary (you will start on the volume of the DOS prompt).

3. Select Auditor Volume Login and type the password.

4. Choose Auditing Reports, then View Audit File to see the current file. Other choices allow viewing old files and setting report filters.

The variety of trackable items is nearly matched by the variety of ways to view the resulting report. As you can see in Figure 9.25, AUDITCON gives you flexibility in viewing audit files and the reports from those files.

The amount of archived audit file history is configurable, as are the report formats. The submenu for Edit report filters offers:

- Report by date/time

- Report by event

- Report exclude paths/files

FIGURE 9.25

Reports ready to slice and dice your way

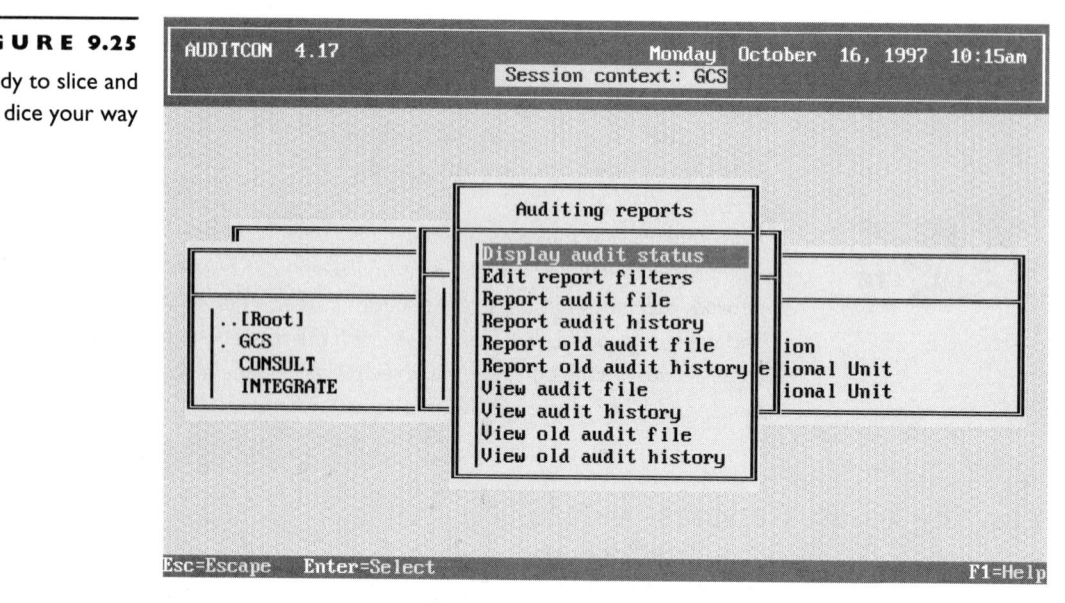

```
AUDITCON  4.17                         Monday  October  16, 1997  10:15am
                          Session context: GCS

                          ┌─────────────────────────┐
                          │    Auditing reports     │
            ┌─────────────┤ Display audit status    ├─────────────┐
            │             │ Edit report filters     │             │
            │             │ Report audit file       │             │
            │  ..[Root]   │ Report audit history    │             │
            │  . GCS      │ Report old audit file   │  ion        │
            │    CONSULT  │ Report old audit history│e ional Unit │
            │    INTEGRATE│ View audit file         │  ional Unit │
            │             │ View audit history      │             │
            │             │ View old audit file     │             │
            │             │ View old audit history  │             │
                          └─────────────────────────┘

Esc=Escape    Enter=Select                                         F1=Help
```

- Report exclude users
- Report include paths/files
- Report include users

Finding a way to view the audit trails won't be a problem, even if finding the time to do so is. If these options aren't enough for you, the reports are exported as TXT files. You can then bring them into another program and slice and dice them any way your heart desires. Have fun.

NetWare 4.11 Security Improvements

EVER-EVOLVING FEATURES required Novell to add some bang to the security section of NetWare 4.11. Novell could have done this by adding a few extra security screens everyone ignores, marked the security matrix as "improved," and gone on with their business.

Security became much more prominent than that. Novell hired one of the original developers of the U.S. Government's "Red Book" security project. That developer, and other work done by Novell deep inside the operating system, helped NetWare 4.11 be certified as a "C2 Red Book" network. This is a big deal.

First of all, it's a big deal because Microsoft made so much noise about Windows NT getting C2 security. The Novell folks can't stand for Microsoft to beat them in any purchase order check-off category, and that's what was happening. The fact that Windows NT was only C2 secure in stand-alone mode left the door open for Novell to top Microsoft, at least in the PR war.

Second, it's a big deal for customers who support and use such security systems already, such as the government, the armed forces, and paranoid corporations. It's true the government has a sizable NetWare installed base, and there are huge areas of some departments that can't run computer equipment rated lower than C2.

Does C2 security do much for you? Probably not. Realistically, C2 level security is a giant hassle and few companies go to that much trouble. If your company is one of the C2 adherents, you know of what I speak.

I will be amazed if your company increases your NetWare security profile up to the C2 level, unless you work for one of the aforementioned groups such as the military. For one thing, only C2-authorized software can run on a NetWare NTCB (Network Trusted Computing Base). All those NLMs you have? Gone, unless they've been certified.

Are you and the other administrators certified? Gone. Do you have NetWare 3.*x* networks still running on your corporate network? Gone. Only secure systems can run on a secure network. Do you have your server under lock and key? Gone until that's done. Have you limited access to remote console programs, such as RCONSOLE? Gone. See what I mean: it's more trouble than it's worth.

> *The fact that Windows NT was only C2 secure in stand-alone mode left the door open for Novell to top Microsoft, at least in the PR war.*

When Security Stinks, Management Smells the Worst

A "ROCK AND A HARD PLACE" describes security. The tougher the security, the more people will hate the network. Looser security makes for happier users, but more virus problems and file mishaps. Remember that your company routinely allows access to every room of your building to the lowest paid, and least monitored, employees: cleaning crews. The biggest risk is crews employed by the building management, especially those that use temporary helpers. Do you have any idea what these people are doing? Does your management? Probably not.

This is one of the areas where hard choices must be made, and your management must make them. If your bosses won't do their jobs, push a little. If they still refuse, document the security measures in place, the reasons for those measures, and apply them absolutely. When users complain to their bosses, and their bosses complain to your boss, let your boss modify the procedure. Then get you boss to sign any changes. Accountability is shared; blame is yours alone.

Don't let management overcompensate for lousy security elsewhere by tightening the screws on the network. That's like a bank with a huge vault full of cash, while the bearer bonds, cashier checks, and negotiable securities are laying out on the counter, ready to be picked up and carried away.

Force management to define a consistent security profile. It makes no sense to restrict network users to the bone while leaving the president's file cabinet unlocked. People looking to steal information, both from the inside and outside, will happily take paper or computer disks. While it isn't legal to steal a report off your computer system, it is legal to grab a printout of that same report out of the dumpster.

Inconsistent security control runs both ways. I once had a customer so worried about security he refused to have a fax server on the network. The owner was afraid of dial-in hackers going through the fax-modem into the computer system. We finally convinced the owner this was impossible.

The flip side was a major oil company in the mid-1980s that had the typical tight security on its mainframe. Terminal and user IDs were tracked, users were monitored, and passwords were everywhere—the whole bit. Then someone noticed it was possible to copy information from the mainframe to a

PC connected with an IRMA board (an adapter in the PC that connected via coax to an SNA cluster controller, effectively making the PC a 3270 terminal).

A management committee studied the matter, and verified that yes, anyone could copy any information from the mainframe to disks and paper. The information could then be dropped in the trash, carried home, or sold to a competitor. All these options obviously violated the company's security guidelines.

What did the managers do? They decided to ignore the problem, and placed no security on PCs with IRMA boards beyond what they had on the terminals the PCs replaced. It was noble to trust the employees, but inconsistent security. Those users with PCs deserved security training and a warning about the severity of potential security leaks. They got nothing because corporate management was too lazy to do its job. If a problem developed, who would be blamed? Yep, the computer managers who had no control over the decision.

CASE STUDY

MiniCo: Securing Your NetWare 4.1x Network

MINICO HAS 3 servers, 75 users, and one location.

Security: A Definition

CONSIDERATIONS

The goals:

- Define security.
- Develop a security profile for the company.

DECISION

To MiniCo, security means keeping things from being stolen. No time was dedicated to security issues during the planning and installation of the network.

EXPLANATION

MiniCo's executives have an old-fashioned idea about security: locks on the doors keep things secure. The company has never addressed security. Employees don't know what on the network is secure or why. Passwords are lackadaisical, and no auditing or virus protection is in use.

Where Is Your Security Plan?

CONSIDERATIONS

The goals:

- Examine the current security plan.
- Revise the security plan to accommodate the new network.

DECISION

Cross your fingers.

EXPLANATION

MiniCo didn't have a security plan to revise. Security has never been a concern. The company has a warm, family atmosphere, where everyone feels appreciated. This goes a long way toward eliminating employee mischief, but it doesn't protect the company against mistakes, outside snoops, or disasters.

NetWare 4.1x Admin Compared with NetWare 3.x SUPERVISOR

CONSIDERATIONS

The choices:

- Maintain Admin as the sole network supervisor.
- Separate containers and assign subadministrators to different network areas.

DECISION

Have a single supervisor: the Admin user.

MINICO CASE STUDY, CONTINUED

EXPLANATION

Coming from NetWare 3.x, Alexander von Thorn (the Distribution Manager who is also the lead network administrator) was used to a single user having full control over the entire network. With NetWare 4.1x, he has left the Admin user in the supervisor function. When he has supervisor functions to perform, Alexander logs in as Admin. Otherwise, he logs in as AVT.

File System Security

CONSIDERATIONS

The goals:

- Plan the file system rights from the top down.
- Map the file inheritance rights down through the file system directory tree.
- Grant destructive rights carefully.
- Avoid granting rights to individuals when possible.

DECISION

Grant rights for each container to the server volume in that container so all users can use the software they need.

EXPLANATION

Rather than taking the time to understand all the implications of granting file trustee rights, Alexander quickly granted every user in each container the rights to the user's own server volumes. This allowed everyone to have the rights to see, use, and delete everything. At least he managed a group of users at once, rather than modifying 75 login scripts.

This turned out to be a mistake. Files were deleted by accident, and people soon learned they could look at files they shouldn't have access to view. Alexander needed to stop his own projects, study file security, and rework the rights of all users in each container.

Using File Attributes as a Security Enhancement

CONSIDERATIONS

The goals:

- Understand file attributes.
- Organize files in ways to take advantage of file attribute protection.

DECISION

Place files on the servers and let the users have access.

EXPLANATION

Lack of preparation again cost MiniCo. Rather than understanding file attributes, Alexander just lumped many applications and data files in the same directories. This made it impossible for him to set file attributes at the directory level, since the data files couldn't be set to Read Only as the executable files required. Rather than change attributes file by file, Alexander just let everyone have full access. Later, he needed to reorganize the files.

MINICO CASE STUDY, CONTINUED

NDS Security

CONSIDERATIONS

The goals:

- Understand NDS security and how it differs from file security.
- Plan the granting of NDS rights, taking into consideration the downhill flow of NDS rights.
- Evaluate where to use object rights and where to use property rights.

DECISION

Quickly skim the object and property rights discussion in the hurry to get the network up and running.

EXPLANATION

Unfortunately for MiniCo, object and property rights are not the same as file system rights. Because he didn't understand the difference, Alexander allowed many users full access and control over the SUPPORT_1 file server. Luckily, Alexander caught his mistake before someone used this undeserved authority to rename the server or delete a few users.

Security Management with NetWare Administrator

CONSIDERATIONS

The choices:

- Use NetWare Administrator for security management.
- Use NETADMIN, FILER, or DOS command-line tools for security administration.

DECISION

Use FILER and the DOS command line first, then NETADMIN or NetWare Administrator.

EXPLANATION

Coming from a NetWare 3.x part-time management background, Alexander didn't know how much better the tools in NetWare Administrator were than those provided by Novell in the past. He spent way too much time looking up switches for the DOS command-line utilities, when he didn't need to use a command-line utility at all.

Security Management with DOS Utilities

CONSIDERATIONS

The choices:

- Use NETADMIN for the majority of security management.
- Use FILER and command-line utilities.
- Avoid using any DOS utilities.

DECISION

Stick with the DOS utilities.

EXPLANATION

Alexander was used to SYSCON, but that utility is no more. NETADMIN looks similar to SYSCON in some areas, so Alexander stayed with that. He was frustrated with all the extra keystrokes after a time, and started checking into NetWare Administrator.

MINICO CASE STUDY, CONTINUED

Common-Sense Security Measures

CONSIDERATIONS

The goals:

- Plan user security.
- Prepare user account restrictions for all user types.
- Establish password rules.
- Enforce regular password changes.
- Guard against virus attacks.

DECISION

Use the default user account restrictions, don't worry about passwords, and hope that virus attacks have been overhyped.

EXPLANATION

This is another example of MiniCo getting only halfway to the right network configuration. The defaults for user account restrictions are intentionally loose, since it's the job of each network administrator to set the limits for the network, not Novell. However, some tightening of the default network security levels are strongly encouraged. All we can do now is cross our fingers and hope for the best for MiniCo.

Using AUDITCON

CONSIDERATIONS

The choices:

- Use AUDITCON or a third-party package to monitor the network's security and activities.
- Don't bother monitoring these activities.

DECISION

Don't worry about it.

EXPLANATION

MiniCo is a small company, and everyone trusts Alexander to do a good job on the network. Management isn't interested in tracking who opens which file; they just want to make sure that people get their work finished somewhere near the deadline.

CASE STUDY

MEGACORP

MegaCorp: Securing Your NetWare 4.1x Network

MEGACORP HAS 50 servers, 2500 users, and 5 locations.

Security: a Definition

CONSIDERATIONS

The goals:

- Define security.
- Develop a security profile for the company.

DECISION

Develop and explain a full security plan to all employees.

EXPLANATION

Before the first network server was contemplated, security was an issue at MegaCorp. The network was installed after a security review, and protection procedures were in place before the first NetWare client was connected.

Where Is Your Security Plan?

CONSIDERATIONS

The goals:

- Evaluate all areas of the current security guidelines.
- Revise the guidelines where needed to accommodate the new network.
- Inform all employees of the security guidelines that have changed.
- Reiterate to all employees the importance of security in all activities.
- Locate and evaluate NetWare-aware security software and hardware.

DECISION

Perform all the above.

EXPLANATION

Security is important to MegaCorp, an international firm that develops and manufactures its own products, as well as providing financial services to customers. When there was only the mainframe, the Central IS group dictated security. As LANs became more important, security was evaluated in light of the "personal" computer on the desktop.

Data, equipment, and telecommunication links are all under the security umbrella. Any disruption of service is seen as a security breach, and dealt with quickly.

MEGACORP CASE STUDY, CONTINUED

NetWare 4.1x Admin Compared with NetWare 3.x SUPERVISOR

CONSIDERATIONS

The choices:

- Maintain Admin as the sole network supervisor.
- Separate containers and assign subadministrators to different network areas.
- Appoint subadministrators, but leave the Central IS group in charge as a super-supervisor.

DECISION

Maintain Central IS as Admin over the entire network, but allow subadministrators to do much of the day-to-day network management.

EXPLANATION

A large network like the one at MegaCorp requires multiple administrators. So the question becomes not "if" there will be multiple supervisors, but how to manage and control all those supervisors.

Proper training is given to all subadministrators, whether they are Central IS personnel on location or power users in a department. Each subadministrator knows the penalty for locking out the master Admin user: severe discipline or possible termination.

File System Security

CONSIDERATIONS

The goals:

- Plan the file system rights from the top down.
- Map the file inheritance rights down through the file system directory tree.
- Understand the Inherited Rights Filter.
- Grant destructive rights carefully.
- Avoid granting rights to individuals.

DECISION

Grant file and directory rights to many users at once, whether by container or user group.

EXPLANATION

The applications are organized to facilitate granting rights to entire volumes of program files and data files at once. There are many volumes available, making it simple for Central IS at MegaCorp to plan the placement of application programs on one volume, and data files and users' home directories on other volumes. This allows restricted file rights of Read Only and File Scan on the application programs with a single setting per container per volume.

Destructive rights (Erase and Modify) are granted only to users in their home directories. When necessary, users are granted these rights in data file directories as required by the applications.

MEGACORP CASE STUDY, CONTINUED

Using File Attributes as a Security Enhancement

CONSIDERATIONS

The goals:

- Understand file attributes.
- Organize files and directories in ways to take advantage of the protection provided by file attributes.
- Work on a large-scale basis by setting file attributes at the directory level for large groups of users.

DECISION

Control file attributes for file protection in every application volume.

EXPLANATION

MegaCorp regards files being accidentally erased just as seriously as files being infiltrated by a computer virus. After all, the result is the same: a needed file is unusable.

Application files are stored on different volumes than the data files and the users' home directories. File attributes are set at the directory level, and flow down the tree through all the directories. Users are granted access by the container or user Group object, never individually.

NDS Security

CONSIDERATIONS

The goals:

- Understand NDS security and how it differs from file security.
- Plan the granting of NDS rights, considering the downhill flow of NDS rights.
- Evaluate where to use object rights and where to use property rights.

DECISION

Strictly control users' access to object and property rights.

EXPLANATION

Knowing the mischief (real or accidental) that could be caused by someone with more power than training, MegaCorp was careful when assigning object and property rights. The difference between the rights was explained to users, and they were shown how to use them properly.

Security Management with NetWare Administrator

CONSIDERATIONS

The choices:

- Use NetWare Administrator for security management.
- Use NETADMIN, FILER, or DOS command-line tools for security administration.

DECISION

Use NetWare Administration whenever possible.

EXPLANATION

The advantages of graphical administration have been proven to MegaCorp. Since nearly all security management can be done from

MEGACORP CASE STUDY, CONTINUED

within NetWare Administrator, MegaCorp expects the network administrators to use this tool.

Security Management with DOS Utilities

CONSIDERATIONS

The choices:

- Use NETADMIN for the majority of security management.
- Use FILER and command-line utilities.
- Avoid using any DOS utilities.

DECISION

Use NetWare Administrator whenever possible.

EXPLANATION

The graphical interface of NetWare Administrator saves many keystrokes and much time over the DOS interface of NETADMIN and FILER. All types of management, including security management for files, directories, and objects, is possible through NetWare Administrator.

Common-Sense Security Measures

CONSIDERATIONS

The goals:

- Plan user security.
- Prepare user account restrictions for all user types.
- Establish password rules.
- Enforce regular password changes.
- Guard against virus attacks.

DECISION

Prepare user account restrictions and apply them to all users. Passwords are mandatory and must be changed every 30 days. Passwords must be seven characters long and include two numbers. Management uses an virus-protection software on every server.

EXPLANATION

MegaCorp is serious about security. Managers have fired employees who left sensitive information on their screens when they got up and left their station.

The security for each user type describes the particular user account restrictions in place for those users. Few users are allowed more than one concurrent login. None are allowed access to the system between midnight and 6:00 A.M. All users must have a password that follows the password rules. The system tracks the last 20 passwords, so users can't change back and forth between their children's names.

Symantec's Norton AntiVirus for NetWare 2.0, released just as MegaCorp was coming online, was the first virus-protection product to work with NDS. By using this product on every server, MegaCorp was able to have more confidence in the virus protection than was ever possible with the previous network software.

MEGACORP CASE STUDY, CONTINUED

Using AUDITCON

CONSIDERATIONS

The choices:

- Use AUDITCON or a third-party package to monitor the network's security and activities.
- Don't bother monitoring these activities.

DECISION

Use both AUDITCON and several third-party products.

EXPLANATION

Many vocal critics of Central IS fear that IS personnel are somehow "spying" for HQ. This isn't true, of course, even though network supervisors have full reign of the network. To quiet critics, Central IS allows individuals from nervous departments to run the AUDITCON utility and see the kind of activity that exists on their network. Once a department can see for itself how boring network management usually is, the criticism subsides for awhile.

Central IS itself tracks user activity at a file level on a random basis. Wary of the overhead of monitoring everyone doing everything, IS personnel randomly watch the activities on one volume or another for a few days. As long as the activity falls within historical norms, IS moves on to the next volume. If some activity looks suspicious, IS investigates further.

NetWare 4.1x Administrator Duties and Tools

CHAPTER 10

WHAT ARE ADMINISTRATOR duties? The short answer is anything you, as the administrator, do on the network is an administrator duty. When you're playing a network game such as Duke Nukem or Quake, you're not wasting time, you're testing the network's graphics performance under load.

The long answer to the question of administrator duties is to list everything that is expected of you. Take a look at the standard list of administrator duties:

- **Plan the network**

    Design the cabling

    Decide on server location and other equipment placement

    Devise the NDS structure

    Create the User list and appropriate access privileges

    Define application and data storage requirements

- **Install the network**

    Perform or oversee the physical cabling installation

    Configure server machines

    Install NetWare on the servers

    Install or upgrade workstation software

- **Support the network users**

    Make all network resources available to authorized users

    Provide protective, but not restrictive, security

    Train the users as necessary

Protect network files and data from mishaps

Maintain a high level of network performance

Leap tall buildings in a single bound

Plan for the future

Understand network growth

Foresee and avoid network bottlenecks

Watch new technologies and investigate ones appropriate for your network

If you're a perfectionist or can't live with chaos, get another job. Likewise, leave if you're sensitive to real or imagined criticism. Need constant praise to maintain your self-esteem? Good luck, and tell your therapist "Hello" for me.

NetWare administration is a thankless job about 90 percent of the time; 5 percent of the time, it's worse. The rest of the time, though, makes up for everything. When the network hums along and nothing can disrupt either the network or your good mood, no job in the world can beat the life of a network jockey. The light that goes on in people's eyes when they start to understand how the network can help them is wonderful to see.

Other, more specific administration topics are scattered about the book. Check the chapter about printing (Chapter 8) if you have questions about printing not covered here. You'll find plenty of information about setting up users and other objects in Chapter 6. If you don't find your topic here, check the index or the table of contents, and I bet you'll find what you're looking for.

Managing Your Network with a Plan

NOW THAT YOU'VE seen the list of what a "good" network manager should be doing, you may feel like taking up a career in something less challenging, like brain surgery or astrophysics or juggling chainsaws. No one can do everything on that list of standard administrator duties, can they?

No, of course not. All you can do is work hard and work smart. I can't help you with the work hard part, but perhaps we can make some progress in the working smarter department.

If the network is new to your company, everyone will be thrilled for a few weeks. No matter how poorly the network is running, it's still a thousand-fold better than no network.

If your company has just moved up to NetWare from some other network, such as a peer-to-peer workgroup solution that was outgrown much too quickly, people will still think this is amazing. Again, even a poor NetWare network is a hundred-fold better than the best peer-to-peer system whose capabilities have been surpassed. Most peer-to-peer networks reach the end of their rope at about eight users, but your management won't justify the cost of a server and separate operating system like NetWare until at least twenty users are screaming for improvements.

The supervision and plans for stand-alone workstations, or even a small underpowered workgroup network, are not sufficient for a NetWare network. If you are new to this, you must upgrade your thinking quite a bit.

Some books go into long, detailed plans on how to manage your network. I've even seen books with timesheets, planning every hour for you.

There used to be a trend where company management tried to make the network a "utility," such as what is provided by the electric or telephone companies. Flip a switch, there's the network. Of course, this was before the electrical service started fluctuating widely enough to reset everyone's VCR at home, and a few software problems downed large parts of the national long-distance network.

Management doesn't use the utility example as much anymore. But it's not a bad idea to emulate, with slight provisions.

Having electrical and telephone service available at every moment is a fact of modern life we have grown to love. But both these services spent decades as monopolies. There are advantages to monopolies, not the least of which is the ability to mandate the infrastructure and set rules for the users.

Translate the electrical grid throughout the city into a plan for supporting network connections in every corner of your company. When management complains about building the network for sections of your company that are not yet inhabited, point to the growth trends and economy of wiring as many connections as possible to maximize every labor hour by the cabling contractor. If you built a new building, would you expect to see the electrical company executives standing in the street, scratching their heads and wondering how to get power to you? Of course not. Don't let that be the case with your network.

> *If you built a new building, would you expect to see the electrical company executives standing in the street, scratching their heads and wondering how to get power to you?*

Managing Your Future Network

This may seem like an odd chapter heading. How do you manage a network you don't have yet? By making sure the network you want is the one you eventually build, of course.

If you're driving from Baltimore, Maryland to San Francisco, California, how do you get there? By driving west. You may drive north or south for a bit now and then, but most of the time, you keep driving west. When you come to an intersection, you want to go west if at all possible.

You get to your future network the same way. You must decide what your future network will look like, and move toward that vision with every network decision. There are choices to make every day when running a large network, and you want to choose the option that will get you closer to your future network.

Deciding what your network of the future will be must be done with your management. We can always say networks tomorrow must be larger, faster, have more disk storage, and be more fault-tolerant than the networks of today, but those guidelines are a little too vague to serve as directions.

What does larger mean for your future network? Does it mean more users? Does it mean more locations? Does it mean more types of clients to service? More types of data to carry across the network? If it means geographically larger, then a method of WAN connections and data distribution may be necessary. More clients, or different types of clients, need support in the physical cabling and network protocol area. Is your boss hot to run video across the LAN? Does she want to teleconference across a campus using desktop-mounted cameras and microphones? Then you must move toward a network transport layer that guarantees support for priority packet types and real-time data streams.

What type of storage will be needed? Do you want more hard disk space, stringing gigabytes together? Or does your network information better suit a plan using HSM (Hierarchical Storage Management)? Do you keep some data on server hard disks for immediate access, some other data on magneto-optical jukebox platters with a few seconds of delay, and other data on tape? Or does your company need to move more toward a large disk cluster, with every byte available instantly through any file server? Each option has a learning curve and a foundation that can be laid today.

Does "fault-tolerant" mean absolutely no service interruptions? Or does it mean you must recover from a hardware failure within a certain number of minutes? How about two hours? How much does it cost your company when the network is completely down? Can you work with your management to set that number? If you don't know how much it costs when your network is broken, how will you know how much you can spend to make sure it doesn't break? Should you plan for an extremely well-protected central server cluster, or maintain high network availability by distributing network access and replicating the data? These two options are directly opposed to each other, and will make a difference in every network plan and hardware purchase over the next few years.

Many of these questions can only be answered after you (and your management) develop a network philosophy. Once everyone agrees on the philosophy of your network and the types of service that will be provided to your network clients, you have a decision framework. Is your philosophy to move toward a single network protocol for every client, say TCP/IP? Then you want to start learning about NetWare/IP, MacTCP, and details about the upcoming TCP/IP protocol stack in Windows 95. Do you prefer to make the fewest changes possible on the clients, and force your servers to support multiple protocols? Then your learning curve is different, as are your choices in WAN equipment.

Perhaps this section could be called "Developing Your Network Philosophy" rather than "Managing Your Future Network." A well-developed network philosophy today helps you make decisions concerning all parts of your network for tomorrow.

A Sampler of Management Slogans

If you're currently running a network, you know that "interrupts" happen not only to computer CPUs but to your day. Every phone call may be a disaster on the other end. Your day is not your own.

Make a mental change, and make it simple: You run your network, not the other way around.

Sure, you say, that's easy for me to say, sitting back in Texas. Nobody's hollering for my head because the laser printer goes off-line every time the president sends it a spreadsheet.

Let's talk some network advice as stated by your grandmother. Sayings that are simple, short, and clear but echo longer and louder than you would expect. Perhaps we can get Granny to stitch these slogans onto some pillows for the office.

(continued on next page)

"Up Is Good, Down Is Bad"

Every network resource should be available at all times. That's a "good" thing. Unavailable network resources are "bad" things. This seems amazingly simple, but it needs to be said. But sometimes, the definition of "up" needs to be slightly reworked.

The users will complain that the network is terrible when the only problem is their favorite network printer is not working properly. Show them the other network printers, and they will rephrase their network complaint. Instead of "no printing" it becomes, "print over there." The printing system itself is working, even if their particular printer is not.

"Maximize Uptime by Scheduling Downtime"

Maintenance time should be scheduled for your network every day or every week. If your network is smaller, there is probably time every night or early morning for the network downtime.

Downtime need not be serious, with major overhauls of server and hard disk. You may want to reorganize print servers. You may need to add a new protocol to a network segment. You may need to readjust the physical wiring and add an extra concentrator or two.

This type of network maintenance isn't serious, but it is necessary. Even more necessary is to make sure your management understands that the network is always available, when people need the network. If no one is in the office at 5:00 A.M., who cares if the network is down? If you need to shut down a database running as an NLM on a server to get every system file on a backup tape, shut it down.

There will always be reasons to take the network off-line for maintenance. If you schedule regular downtimes, it never becomes a question or a concern to management. When your network has been running for 86 days and you say it must be taken off-line, people will think the reason for the downtime is more serious than it really is. Perhaps we should say this is another example of managing not the network, but your management's expectations.

"Promote Confidence through Paranoia"

To make your users confident in your network, you must be slightly paranoid. You must constantly have a nagging worry in the back of your mind, forcing you to examine every inch of your network for flaws and weaknesses.

(continued on next page)

> Like the old joke says, you're not really paranoid if they really are out to get you. If you run a network, fates are actively conspiring to make it break. So you're not paranoid, you're just doing your job.
>
> Spare parts are a good example of paranoia. Does your boss demand an HA (High Availability) system—not quite fault-tolerant and able to continue in the face of hardware failure, but able to resume operations fairly quickly? Then keep available spare parts for all the servers that must keep running. If your main server's main data lives on a Maxtor 1 GB drive, you better have another one on the shelf, or another server ready to take the backup files and start running immediately.
>
> Do you imagine a server's power supply is making some kind of strange noise, but you're not quite sure. Replace it. That's an example of paranoia that will enhance your network by minimizing downtime.
>
> "Every User Is an Honored Guest but a Potential Criminal"
>
> The chapter about security should make this warning clear, but it's worth restating. Your worst security problems are the people on the end of your network wires.
>
> Retail executives will tell you much more stolen property goes out the back door with the employees than out the front door with the shoplifters. While you would like to think your fellow employees will not knowingly harm your network or steal your data, the sad truth is that one or more of them will. The man in the elevator with you yesterday evening may have had an illegal copy of WordPerfect in his briefcase. The woman beside him may have had the marketing plan for the next quarter in her purse.
>
> You must provide network access to all users in order for them to perform their jobs. Any more access than necessary will only lead to trouble.

Selling Your Network Plan to Your Boss

One problem with network (or personal) philosophies is that everyone has his or her own. While this makes for a more interesting society at large, it makes it more difficult for you to plan and run your network unless some agreement is reached.

No matter how brilliant your network plan, or comprehensive your network philosophy, all is lost unless your boss agrees. I've met some wonderful network administrators who failed because they and their bosses never agreed on the network. I've also met some very "un-technical" network administrators who built amazing, complicated networks with the full support of their bosses in particular and their company in general.

The key here is for you and your boss to share the same network vision and philosophy. If you have been hired to support an existing network, the boss's philosophy is probably well set, and you must go with that. If you built the network from nothing, your philosophy has been the guide. The trick is to get your boss to agree with the work you've done and help you continue on the same path.

Just as you get pressure from higher in the management chain, so does your immediate manager. So you are now in a situation where you must sell not only to one layer of management, but another layer or two above that.

Yes, sell. Your boss must be sold on the facts that you know what you're doing technically, and that your ideas for network growth make sense. Don't assume your boss will understand the technical parts and agree because your choice of technology is superior to all other options. It's not, and your boss won't.

I prefer to lay out the network choices in such a way as to "lead" people to the conclusion I have already reached. This only works when the facts support my idea, so it helps me to verify I'm on the right track before I must present the case to anyone.

We can call this method the "Pros and Cons Weighing of Technical Alternatives," but in sales, it's really the "Ben Franklin Close." Evidently, old Ben used this trick on the other Founding Fathers to sell them life insurance during the Revolutionary War.

This method works by listing three columns: the decision to be made, the pros, and the cons. In sales, you actually sit with the customers and write down each element of the chart, letting them come up with some of the pros and cons. If you think this won't work with your boss, think again. It works every time, because your boss helps list the pros and cons for the decision with you. If your boss picks the "wrong" decision, you'll know why because you went over the reasons together. Either you didn't know your facts or your boss feels differently about the situation than you do. Better to find out during a discussion than from a rejected proposal.

Let's say that you feel the need for a software metering product, but your boss doesn't want to spend the money. Sit down together, and draw a line separating a page into two columns labeled Pro and Con. Write the decision to be made across the top of the page, such as Start Software Metering Y/N. Now ask your boss for the primary objection, and write that down. Ask for the next, and the next. You may have a list like this:

- Too expensive
- Too much management time
- Current software inventory system works okay
- Inconvenience the users

After your boss is finished, you can write down a list similar to the following:

- $5 per user
- Installation reads the NetWare user list and automatically builds access tables
- No one knows how many copies of each program have been purchased
- Users are now copying software illegally and trying to install it themselves
- Tracks application use
- Forces all applications onto the server, meaning consistent backup and easier upgrades
- Lists software that users may not know is available, especially between departments
- Demonstrates compliance with software-use laws to auditors

In case the pros and cons don't line up exactly, draw lines between each. If you're careful with the two lists, your columns will look like this when you're finished:

Too expensive	$5 per user
Too much management time	Installation reads the NetWare user list and automatically builds access tables
	Demonstrates compliance with software use laws to auditors
	Forces all applications onto the server, meaning consistent backup and easier upgrades

Current software inventory system works okay	No one knows how many copies of each program have been purchased Tracks application use
Inconvenience the users	Lists software that users may not know is available, especially between departments Users are now copying software illegally and trying to install it themselves

Every objection from your boss has at least one response. Several of your responses apply to more than one of the objections. For example, to the objection "Too expensive," you can say that the cost of the metering software is a new cost, but it reduces the cost of software purchases since everyone can better share. It also saves time (money) with better backup and upgrades, and tells which applications are really used. If you have 20 copies of presentation software that only six people are using, you'll save money when it's time to upgrade by upgrading only six copies.

Will Ben Franklin come to your rescue every time your boss gives you a hard time? No, but the idea of selling your boss rather than arguing will help. Everyone needs to be sold on ideas, and often resold several times. The sooner you understand that selling is a big part of network management, the better off you'll be.

Selling Your Network Plan to Your Users

You're not through with sales when you convince your boss of your positions. You must still convince the users that the way you run the network provides them the best support within the constraints dictated by management.

What constraints? Generally money. The network would run faster if you had a row of superservers, like those shiny NetFRAME cubes, stacked against the wall. Storage space wouldn't be a problem if you had an extra gigabyte of hard disk for every workgroup. User applications would run better if each desktop came equipped with a fast Pentium computer with 32 MB of RAM.

The users understand these types of constraints. Each of them wants more desk space in a bigger office, a company car, more vacation time, paid trips to conventions, and a bigger bonus. They're probably so worried about their constraints, they haven't given much thought to your problems.

This is where your network philosophy can help clarify exactly what the network can and can't do. If you (and your boss, of course) can condense your

Each of them wants more desk space in a bigger office, a company car, more vacation time, paid trips to conventions, and a bigger bonus.

network philosophy into a mission statement, your users will better understand what to expect from the network today and tomorrow. The shorter the mission statement, the better. Two paragraphs is too much.

How would your users like this: "Our network will be available a minimum of 20 hours every business day, providing secure access to applications, data, printers, and host access services." This tells the story quickly, but doesn't promise 24-hour satisfaction of every tiny network desire they may have.

Unless there is an immediate network problem, unhappy users are expressing a conflict between their expectations and your network reality. Align the users' expectations to the network you can provide, and everyone will be happier.

Supervisory Functions and the Necessary Rights

WHEN THE FIRST NetWare 4.1x server is installed in a new network, the Admin user is created. Granted the Supervisor right to the [Root] level of the network, Admin controls the entire new network through inheritance.

Let's take a quick look at what rights go where:

Directory rights	Apply only to the directory in the file system where they are assigned. Directory rights are part of the file system, not NDS. These rights are inherited by subdirectories and files unless blocked or redefined. A User object may be granted directory rights to any directory on a volume.
File rights	Apply only to the file to which they are assigned. Trustees inherit rights to a file from the directory rights above the file.
Object rights	Apply to NDS objects. Object rights are inherited from higher objects, or are assigned directly to a given object. Inherited object rights pass down with continued inheritance. Assigned object rights do not flow down the NDS tree.

Property rights — Apply to the properties of NDS objects. Rights can be assigned to specific properties of a given object. Rights to a specific property do not flow down the tree through inheritance.

All Property rights — Allow the trustee assignment to apply to all rights of the given object with one assignment. The All Property rights trustee assignment, unlike Property rights, does flow down the NDS tree through inheritance.

Trustee Assignments

A *trustee* is a user or group granted rights to a directory, file, or object. This user or group is then called a trustee of that directory, file, or object. Although this naming reminds me of bad prison movies, the root of the term trustee comes from trust. A trustee is trusted to properly use the objects placed in his or her trust.

Trustee assignments grant rights for one object to another object. The trustee rights assignments are kept as part of the object to which they grant access.

The trustee assignments are stored in a trustee list. The trustee list for an object is stored in the ACL (Access Control List) property. Every object in the network has an ACL property.

[Public] is a special trustee, and acts somewhat like the group EVERYONE in earlier NetWare versions. Rather than granting EVERYONE rights to a directory in NetWare 4.1x as you did in NetWare 3, you might instead specify the rights of [Public] in that directory. [Public] may also be a trustee of a file or other object, besides just a directory.

If a user has no specific trustee rights to an object, directory, or file, that user automatically has the same rights as the [Public] trustee. [Public] is assigned the Browse right to the [Root] of the NDS tree, and so has the ability to read all of the tree. This allows all users to see the available network resources.

More coverage of rights across the network can be found in Chapter 9, which is about security. If you've skipped to here and bypassed Chapter 9, skimming back through that information may eliminate any confusion.

Workgroup Managers to the Rescue

Although I'm wary of granting workgroup administrators complete control with no Admin supervision, I think they are a valuable tool in your network management toolkit. In fact, proper use of workgroup administrators will keep you closer to your end users than a crowded elevator.

To restate one last time: Please do not lock Admin out of parts of your NDS tree. Some departments will cry and moan how they need "security" from prying eyes in the "corporate" computer room. Don't fall for it, and be ready when they go over your head to your boss. Then be ready when they go over your boss's head.

Use the argument about training and maintaining a support staff as a starting point. You and your group (if you have one) are trained to know all parts of the network and are able to support each other. If a department has its own administrator and has locked you out, what do those employees do when this person is on vacation? How about sick days? What about when the employee quits or transfers? If you are able to help out by still maintaining access to that departmental branch of the NDS tree, none of these situations are a problem.

Say a directory gets deleted accidentally (hey, it happens all the time). Assuming the department has a good backup plan in place and follows that plan, replacing the directory's files are no problem. But what if the only administrator with access to the tape backup software is in the Cleveland airport? If Admin is not blocked, you can step in and save the day. If Admin is blocked, you can call the airlines and get the estimated arrival time for our wandering administrator. But you can't retrieve the files.

Now let's talk about the good side of workgroup administrators. They are closer to the department's problems, and hence quicker with easy solutions than you are. More than that, they serve as your cheerleader in the department. If you make them feel special by sharing information and responsibility, the workgroup administrators can help make the network better.

How? Let's take a look at some ways the workgroup administrators, and by extension the user community, can work with you:

- Involve them in pilot projects. Two great benefits come from their involvement. First, they know more about how your end users work than you do, and will make sure all the bases are covered. Second, they will spread the word about your new project and generate positive word-of-mouth among the groups that will most likely need to pay for the new service. This makes your job of selling the benefits much easier.

- Have them let you know how the users really feel. Your network clients won't tell you the truth. This is not really their fault, it just works that way. Formal questionnaires and focus groups help, but the little things won't get passed along. Your workgroup administrator will know what users are happy about and what they hate.

- Let them help you define training goals and courses. Generic application training is always helpful. Specific job-related training on those same applications is invaluable, but difficult to identify and develop. Your workgroup administrator will know where your training courses are falling short, and how to stretch them back out again.

- Ask them to explain the computer decisions made by you (or your department) to the users. No one likes hearing pronouncements handed down from above, and your network users are no exception. Having one of their own able to translate "HQ" talk into "people" talk will soften the resistance to network changes. Of course, if you're involving them in pilot projects, there won't be any surprises.

Are there more ways the workgroup administrator can help? Many more ways are available, but they depend on your situation. Remember, power users are your friends.

Installing NetWare Administrator

NOW IT'S TIME to get out your primary management tool and unleash it. Let's install NetWare Administrator, and then look at how the program itself works, with all the options.

Creating a NetWare Administrator Icon on Windows 3.1x

To say that we are "installing" NetWare Administrator is a bit strong, perhaps. The NWADMIN.EXE file and necessary DLL (Dynamic Link Libraries) files are copied to the \PUBLIC directory on each server (except those with the absolute minimum installation). Some of the support files for NetWare client

10.1 IN-A-HURRY

Install NetWare Administrator on Windows 3.1x

1. Connect the workstation to the network and log in as Admin.

2. Map a network drive to the \PUBLIC directory.

3. Start Windows 3.1x and highlight the Group to contain the NetWare Administration program.

4. From the Program Manager File menu, choose New.

5. Select Program Item, then OK.

6. Type **NWAdmin** or **NetWare Administrator** in the Description field and press the Tab key.

7. Choose Browse and select the drive in the drive list box that points to SYS:PUBLIC.

8. Select NWAdmin.EXE from the File Name list box and click on OK.

9. If the icon does not appear, click on the Change Icon Button, then select an icon, then click on OK.

10. Click on OK to keep the icon and save the new item in the Group window.

---

and administration functions are copied to each Windows PC as part of the normal workstation installation process. What we must do is create an icon for NetWare Administrator in a Windows group of your choice. As part of the deal, an NWADMIN.INI file is copied to your PC to track NetWare Administrator configuration details on your particular system.

These instructions assume you installed the support for the "legacy" (older) NetWare Administrator program during installation, or that you have a NetWare 4.10 network. If you have NetWare 4.11, and wish to use 16-bit administration programs, you must go to the INSTALL utility and add the older NetWare Administrator program to your system from the NetWare CD-ROM if it wasn't added during installation.

After you add the workstation files to your PC and connect to the network, log in as the Admin user. Start Windows 3.1x. If you want to put the NetWare Administrator program in the NetWare Tools group that was created during workstation configuration, click somewhere in that group to make it active. From the File menu, choose New. The New Program Object dialog box will appear, asking if the new object is a Program Item (default) or Program Group. Choose Program Item and click on OK.

The Program Item Properties dialog box now appears, asking for the description to place under the icon. Novell suggests NWADMIN, but that's too stark for my taste, so I entered NetWare Admin and let the title word-wrap. Click on the Browse button to open the dialog box to wander around your available files and directories. Use the Drives list box to point to the mapped drive pointing to the SYS:\PUBLIC directory. Make sure this drive mapping will be the same as used later, since Windows references the drive letter in the Command Line and Working Directory fields.

Windows will try to scare you away from referencing an application on a network drive, but tell the warning box that you do indeed wish to maintain that pointer. Then the working directory name will be placed in the appropriate field, the icon will appear in the NetWare Tools group, and you're ready to start administering.

Yes, NetWare Administrator will work under OS/2 as a Windows 3.1x application. Installation procedures work the same as just mentioned for "regular" Windows on your OS/2 machine. There is no native OS/2 version as of yet, and Novell hasn't decided whether to make one (at least, not by the time that this was written).

Configuring Windows 95 (Running Client32) for NetWare Administrator

Here's where all the work will happen, and where we'll spend most of our time in this chapter. You may run the older NetWare Administrator program on a Windows 3.1*x* system, but Novell loudly says that only 32-bit administration programs are the future. If you run 16-bit utilities, your days are numbered; the upgrade looms.

There's nothing difficult about running the NWADMN95.EXE program, once you discover where on the file server it resides. If you search \PUBLIC first, you will be disappointed. Check the \PUBLIC\WIN95 directory; NWADMN95.EXE and supporting files are hiding there.

Make a shortcut on your Windows 95 workstation to this directory and file name. I put this file in the NOVELL folder, but you may put it on the Desktop or in any folder you wish. You might even choose to put it on the Start menu.

Getting Familiar with NetWare Administrator

Using NetWare Administrator is quite a bit different from using the old SYSCON program in earlier NetWare versions. Although everyone familiar with the SYSCON will have a nostalgic twinge for the old days, I predict you will grow comfortable in NetWare Administrator within a short time.

Go ahead and play with the program. Click, drag, drop, expand, collapse, and search. The amount of information that can be packed into the NetWare Administrator screen makes it far more useful than the old SYSCON and more informative than the current NETADMIN DOS-based program.

Although the largest difference between NetWare Administrator that shipped with NetWare 4.10 for Windows 3.1x and the version shipping with NetWare 4.11 is the look and feel of the interface, there are some substantive changes as well. For example, the ability to add or remove items from the toolbar is the result of increased functionality in the improved Windows 95/NT interface. Better Help screens mean quicker productivity for network managers new to NetWare. Besides all that, the Windows 95/NT interface offers a more polished and three-dimensional look. Some companies feel it's better to look good than work good; fortunately, here you get both.

> *No one will say so officially, but my guess is that DOS utilities have a life span through NetWare 4.2 at most. Since DOS has disappeared from most new computer shipments, there will be little reason for Novell engineers to continue upgrading products for a non-existent operating system. My guess is that Windows 95 and NT will corner the market on management applications because of their 32-bit platform. Look for all vendors to move their control applications to a 32-bit platform; Windows 3.1x has room on your management station for a short time only.*

So far in this book, you've seen plenty of pictures of the NetWare Administrator program, but all from the earlier, 16-bit version. Take a look at Figure 10.1 to see a view in the 32-bit version that comes with NetWare 4.11.

In the far-left browser window, the [Root] view is collapsed to show the minimum information. Our two Organizational Units, CONSULT and INTEGRATE, are all that are listed, along with the Admin user. The middle browser window shows CONSULT.GCS. INTEGRATE.GCS is shown on the far right. You may have up to nine browser windows open at one time.

Many of the menu options depend on which object is highlighted in the browser window. When the program opens, what looks like the entire program is really just the first browser window, open to your current context.

Installing NetWare Administrator **757**

FIGURE 10.1

Three browser windows, three views, one network

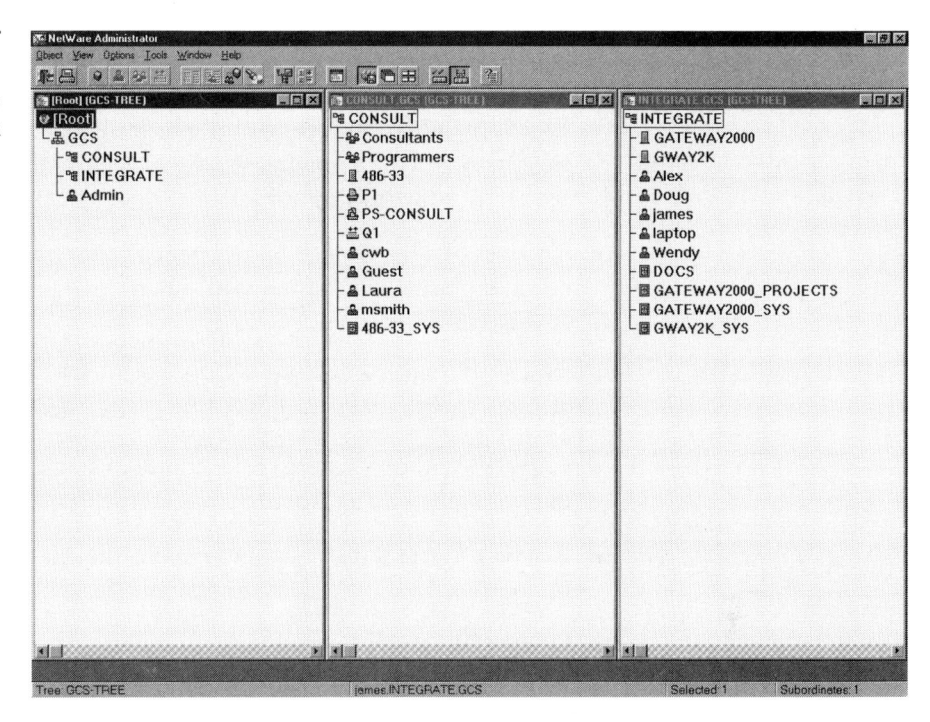

Most operations in NetWare Administrator require you to highlight an object in a browser window, then take some action using a menu choice.

The menu bar has six options. When you highlight a menu or a menu item, the description displays just above the menu bar. Menu choices that are grayed are not available for the highlighted object. Each menu option is described in the following sections.

The Object Menu

The Object menu has these commands:

- **Create (Ins):** Opens a dialog box to create a new object, or a directory if used on a Volume object. Insert is this option's shortcut key.

- **Details (Enter):** Opens an information dialog box about the object, file, or directory highlighted. The same dialog box opens when you double-click on a leaf object.

- **Details on Multiple Users:** With NetWare 4.11, you may now choose multiple objects and take some action on all highlighted objects at one time.

- **Rights to Other Objects:** Shows which rights the highlighted object has to other objects. You must specify which part of the NDS tree you wish to search to gather this information.

- **Trustees of This Object:** Shows which other objects have rights to the selected object. This option is also used to set the object's Inherited Rights Filter (IRF).

- **Move (F7):** Moves selected leaf objects or files to other locations; destinations are selected in a dialog box that appears.

- **Copy (F8):** Allows you to make copies of single or multiple files. A destination dialog box appears once the Copy option is chosen.

- **Rename:** Opens a dialog box to rename the selected object. You have the option to keep the old name to maintain existing references to the object.

- **Delete (DEL):** Deletes and purges the selected object. There is no recovery available. Containers must be empty before they can be deleted.

- **Browse:** Open a new browser window with the selected object at the top.

- **Search:** Opens a Search dialog box to help find objects in the NDS tree matching the specified pattern. Found objects are listed for further action.

- **Print (Ctrl+P):** Prints the objects in the browser window. NetWare Administrator can wrap long listings into two columns.

- **Print Setup:** Opens a standard Windows 95 Printer Setup dialog box.

- **Exit:** Closes the NetWare Administrator program.

The View Menu

The View menu has these choices:

- **Show Hints:** When checked, shows hints above the main menu bar.

- **Show Toolbar:** When checked, displays the toolbar under the menu bar.

- **Show Status Bar:** When checked, displays the status bar on the last line of the screen.

- **Show Quick Tips:** Pops open the little help line beside the cursor when you linger on an icon.

- **Configure Toolbar and Status Bar:** Opens a Preferences dialog box that allows you to pick the icons that appear on the toolbar and the information panels that are on the status bar.

- **Set Context:** Changes the context shown at the top of the browser window or panel.

- **Go Up a Level (Backspace):** Sets the root of the browser window up one level in the NDS hierarchy.

- **Sort and Include:** Includes or excludes certain object classes from the browser window and sets sort preferences.

- **Expand (+):** Displays objects in the selected container or volume. The + key or double-clicking works in the same way.

- **Collapse (-):** Hides all objects contained in the selected object. Double-clicking or the - key works in the same way.

The Options Menu

The Options menu choices are:

- **Save Settings on Exit:** When checked, opens to the same network view when the program is restarted.

- **Confirm on Delete:** Verifies that you do wish to delete the object. Deleted objects are not salvageable.

- **Get Alias Trustees:** When checked, this option allows you to manage the trustees of an Alias object, rather than the actual object the Alias is representing.

- **Get Aliased Object Trustees:** When checked, this option allows you to manage the trustees of the actual object, not the Alias referring to the object.

The Tools Menu

You'll find these tools listed on the Tools menu:

- **Internet Connections:** Starts your favorite Web browser and displays bookmarks for quick Internet connections (at least with the Novell-logo version of Netscape).

- **Salvage:** Allows you to recover previously deleted files, or permanently trash them.

- **Remote Console:** Opens a DOS box and starts the Remote Console utility program.

- **NDS Browser:** Starts a new browser window.

- **NDS Manager (optional):** Calls the NDS Manager (NDSMGR32.EXE) from within NetWare Administrator, if you have configured your Windows 95 Registry properly. We'll explain how to put this command on your Tools menu when we talk about the NDS Manager.

- **Install License:** Opens a submenu that allows you to install license files or metering configuration information.

- **File Migration:** Migrates files from bindery servers.

- **DS Migrate:** Starts the Novell-modified DS Migrate program from Preferred Systems, for NetWare 3.*x* system conversion.

- **Print Service Quick Setup:** Starts the Quick Setup routines for easy printer installation, which were formerly only inside the PCONSOLE command-line utility. See Chapter 8 for details.

The Window Menu

Here are the choices on the Window menu:

- **New Window:** Starts a new browser window, copying the same settings as in the existing browser window.

- **Cascade (Shift+F5):** Traditional Windows Cascade command to overlap all open windows with only the titles showing.

- **Tile (Shift+F4):** Traditional Windows Tile command to arrange all open windows to completely display without any overlap. Windows will be truncated to fit the size available.

- **Arrange Icons:** Traditional Windows Arrange Icons command to straighten the icons.

- **Close All:** Shuts all open browser windows. Open browser windows are listed by the name of their container.

The Help Menu

The Help menu lists these options:

- **Help Topics:** Presents a Windows 95/NT-style tabbed Help page listing help topics and index. Error messages for NetWare and NDS are included in the Help Topics.

- **Novell Support:** Calls your Web client software and connects to the Novell support Web site.

- **Show Welcome Screen on Startup:** Allows you to continue the "Did You Know?" tips each time you open NetWare Administrator or cancel them.

- **About NetWare Administrator:** Displays traditional Windows 95 version and copyright information, included the version of NetWare Administrator in use.

NDS Administration with NetWare Administrator

THE MOVE TO a graphical utility for management reinforces the object-oriented foundation of NetWare 4.1x. Perhaps it's just me, but the ability to open containers, and see their containers, which might hold even more containers, helps emphasize the idea of inheritance. Drilling down through your network from the highest [Root] context through an

Organization, and through one or more Organizational Units, and through a Volume object, and through a directory, down to an individual file displays the organization like a giant network x-ray.

A distributed database takes a while to "ripple out" the changes. Just as the waves in a pond take a moment to reach the bank from a pebble splash, so too does NDS take a bit of time to synchronize all servers. The control over user information is quick, just as it was with SYSCON. The control over NDS takes a bit longer. Try to wait for results twice as long as you think is possible, and you'll be about right.

Creating Container Objects

10.2 IN-A-HURRY

Create a Container

1. Log in to the network as the Admin user or equivalent and start NetWare Administrator.

2. To create an Organization, highlight the [Root] level. To create an Organizational Unit, highlight the Organization or Organizational Unit that will hold the new container.

3. Press the Insert key.

4. Choose to create an Organization or Organizational Unit.

5. Type the name of the new container. You can check either Define Additional Properties or Create Another Organizational Unit (or Create Another Organization) but not both. Check Define User Defaults if you want the container to inherit the parent container's Template.

6. Click on Create, then Yes or No for the Template if the Define User Defaults box was checked in the previous step.

An Organization can contain anything, except another Organization. Only [Root] can contain an Organization. All leaf objects may be contained in an Organization. Single-server NetWare 4 networks may easily be a single Organization holding all servers, users, and network resources, mimicking a flat, NetWare 3 network.

Used more often is the Organizational Unit. Any container, including another Organizational Unit, can contain an Organizational Unit. Typically, there are multiple Organizational Units per Organization.

The process of creating either container is exactly the same. The difference is only where you put the container. Figure 10.2 shows the creation process for a new Organizational Unit, TECH_CON, being added within INTEGRATE.GCS. The name for this Organizational Unit will be TECH_CON. INTEGRATE.GCS.

The Country container object is rarely used, and should be avoided if possible. The hierarchy is as follows:

- The Organization container can exist in a [Root] or Country container. It can contain Organizational Unit, Alias, and all leaf objects. Some examples of Organization names are GCS and UTDallas.

- The Organizational Unit container can exist in an Organization or another Organizational Unit container. It can contain Organizational Unit, Alias, and all leaf objects. Some examples of Organizational Unit names are INTEGRATE and TECH_CON.

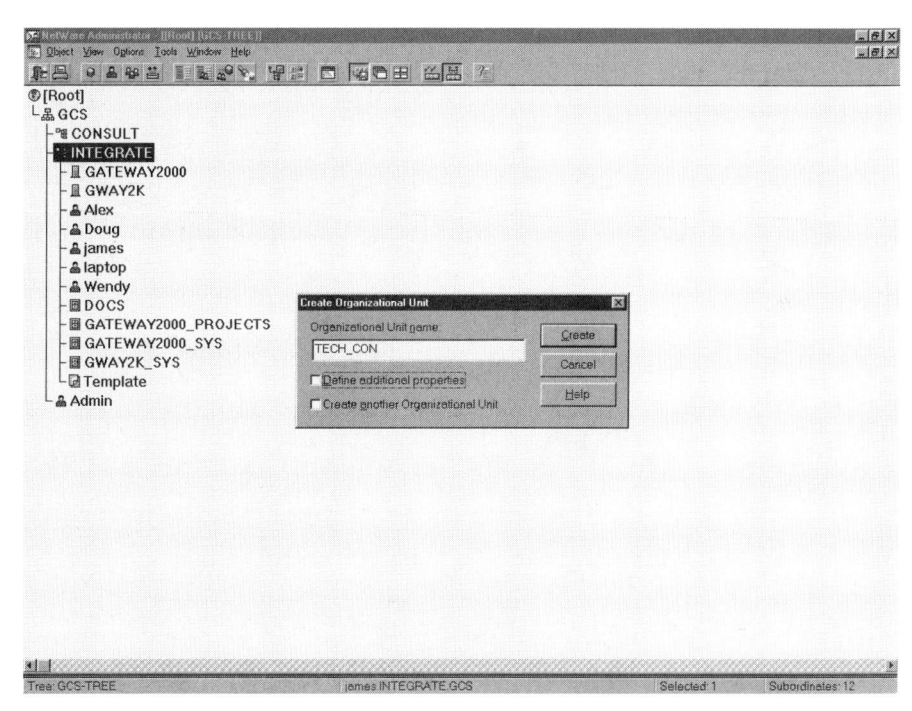

FIGURE 10.2

Creating a new Organizational Unit

Containers have as many details about themselves as do User and Group objects. In fact, the dialog box for the Organizational Unit INTEGRATE.GCS has as many pages as there are in the User and Group object dialog boxes. Check out Figure 10.3 to see what I mean. The screen in Figure 10.3 should be familiar, since it's the same as for a User object or Group object. The users in INTEGRATE.GCS have rights to files and directories, because their container has rights to those files and directories.

This is an advantage of NetWare 4.1x over earlier NetWare versions. Using container objects similar to how you used a group in NetWare 3 allows you to grant trustee rights to files and directories without modifying any of the User object's rights individually. NetWare 4.1x Group objects do have the advantage of being able to grant trustee rights to User objects from different containers, and so they are still useful.

The only improvement in this screen from the similar screen in NetWare 4.10 is that addition of the Path command button beside the Files and Directories list. When you click on this button, as I've done in Figure 10.3, a little information box appears to inform you of the full path name of the volume highlighted in the Files and Directories list.

FIGURE 10.3

Showing that a container has access to directories and files, just like a user

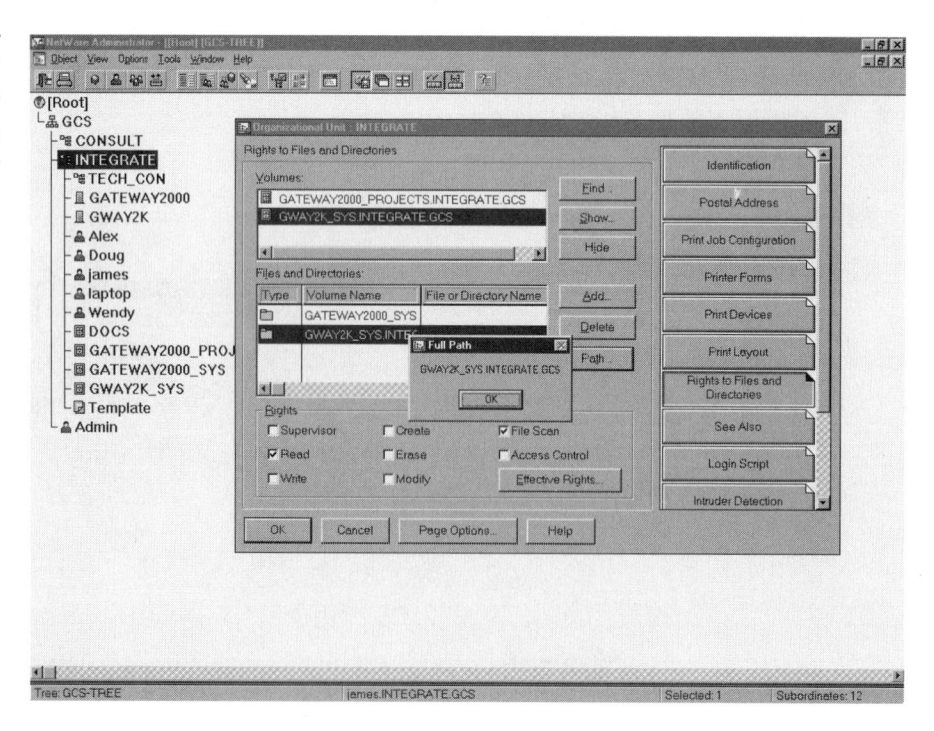

Let's take a second to reiterate the naming rules and guidelines for NDS objects:

- Must be less than 64 characters long. Names longer than 47 characters are truncated for non-NDS clients.

- Must be unique within the container.

- Names are not case-sensitive, but will be displayed as typed in the Name field (SalesSupport will display that way, but NDS regards it as identical to salessupport and SALESSUPPORT).

- Spaces can be used and will be displayed as spaces within NDS. Spaces are shown as underscores for non-NDS clients.

- The following characters can't be seen by non-NDS clients: slash (/), backslash (\), colon (:), comma (,), asterisk (*), and question mark (?).

Setting Intruder Detection

> **10.3 IN-A-HURRY**
>
> **Set Intruder Detection**
>
> 1. Log in to the network as the Admin user or equivalent and start NetWare Administrator.
>
> 2. Highlight the container to modify, or immediately modify a new container with the Define Additional Properties box checked during setup.
>
> 3. Click on the Intruder Detection command button on the right side (at the end of the list).
>
> 4. Check Detect Intruder and accept or modify the default settings.
>
> 5. Check Lock Account After Detection and accept or modify the default settings.
>
> 6. Click on OK to save and exit.

Every new container deserves some security from the first moment of creation. You should get in the habit of thinking of security every time you create an object.

If you are setting up a new container, you may wish to check the Define Additional Properties box (see Figure 10.2, shown a bit earlier in the chapter).

If you are creating several containers at one time, that's not an option. If you want to set intruder detection for an existing container, open that container object's dialog box, click on the Intruder Detection command button, and adjust the settings from there.

Intruder detection works on the idea that anyone trying the same user name with multiple password attempts is up to no good. We've talked about the simple passwords people choose if you let them choose their own, and other employees and crooks know to try the obvious choices first when trying to break into accounts. Figure 10.4 shows the setup screens for Intruder Detection, along with NetWare's much too lenient default settings.

As you can see, the default setting for Incorrect Login Attempts is set to 7. This is way too high. If an employee coming back after a liquid lunch can't type a password in three tries, send that person home in a cab. The reset interval is 30 minutes, meaning three bad password guesses in 29 minutes will be counted as a possible intrusion. Since someone trying to crack the password will probably try several at a time, 30 minutes is enough for employees. But it isn't enough for outside attackers, who know about these detection settings. Set the time longer, such as one or two days.

> *If an employee coming back after a liquid lunch can't type a password in three tries, send that person home in a cab.*

FIGURE 10.4

Stopping the password guessing game

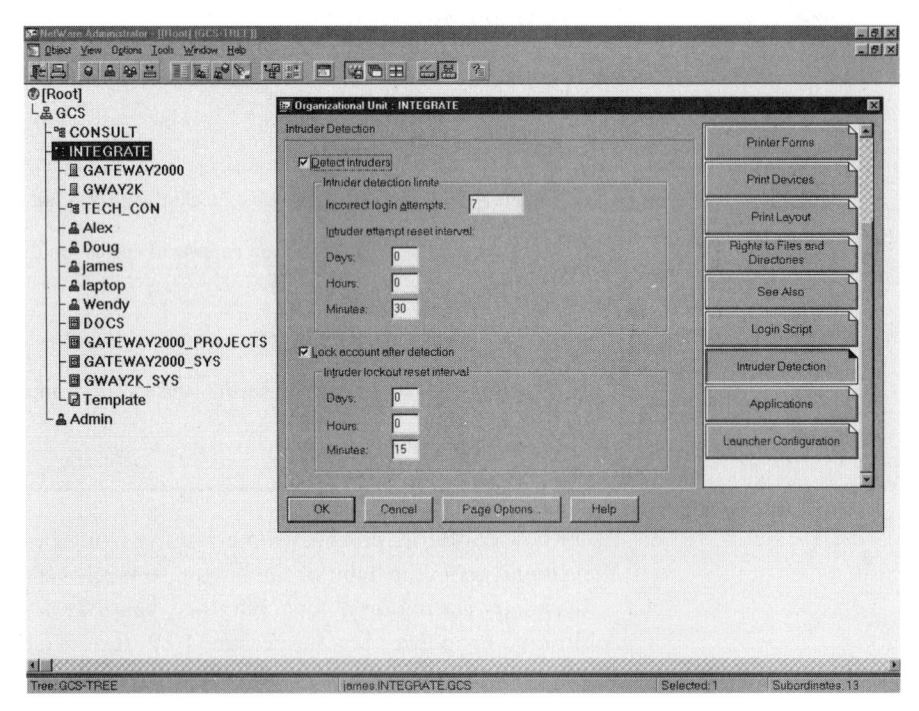

The second checkbox tells the system what to do after the maximum password retries is exceeded. The server console will beep, and the account should be locked, when the proper password isn't given in the set number of tries. Again, the default is far too short. Some recommend that the account be locked for a day or more. What if someone is trying to break the account on Friday evening? Locking it for only one day lets the perpetrator try again Saturday and Sunday evening without detection. Since you can reset the locked account easily by clicking the Intruder Lockout command button for the user, set the lock to last for three days and protect your system through the weekend.

Creating Leaf Objects

10.4 IN-A-HURRY

Create a Leaf Object

1. Log in to the network as the Admin user or equivalent and start NetWare Administrator.

2. Highlight the container for the new leaf object and press the Insert key.

3. Choose the leaf object to create from the New Object list.

4. Name the new leaf object. If necessary, provide file or location information.

5. Check a box to either Define Additional Properties or Create Another leaf object if you wish.

6. Click on Create to save the new object.

The process for creating a leaf object is basically the same, no matter what object you are creating. The differences are related to whether the new object depends on a directory or volume path, or on some other reference to the NDS tree that a User or Group object won't need.

As an example, let's create a Directory Map object, since we haven't done one of these before. A Directory Map represents a particular directory in the file system. It's helpful two ways in login scripts:

- It references a specific directory in the file system without requiring the entire path name.

- You can move the directory and change only the Directory Map description, not every login script that uses the Directory Map.

After highlighting the container for the object and pressing the Insert key, the New Object list box opens. Choose your object by double-clicking or by highlighting it and clicking on OK. Then the Create dialog box opens (the dialog box title always indicates which type of object you are creating). Figure 10.5 shows us creating a Directory Map object.

Since a Directory Map object works with the file system, the Create dialog box has more information than usual. Here, we need to detail the volume used and path within that volume. The Select Object dialog box is called by clicking on the Browser button on the right side of the Path field.

Now that we've taken a quick look at Directory Map object creation, let's switch over to the setup of another leaf object that needs some rights. Suppose that new user Laura is now part of the CONSULT Organizational Unit. Her job is to help out with the graphics work. To do this, she needs access to the \SCREENS directory and all subdirectories under that directory.

Open up the Laura object by double-clicking on the name. Scroll down the User dialog box until you can see the Rights to Files and Directories command button. Click on that button to display that page of information for user Laura.

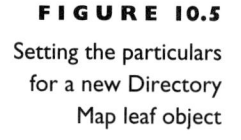

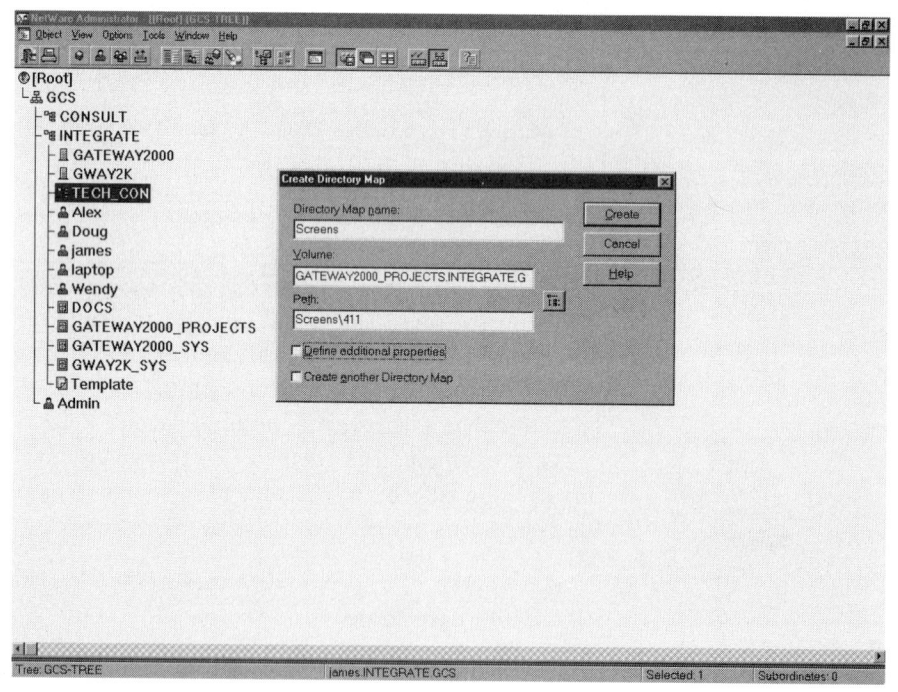

FIGURE 10.5

Setting the particulars for a new Directory Map leaf object

NDS Administration with NetWare Administrator 769

Figure 10.6 shows the process of granting Laura rights to the directory in question. Being a member of the CONSULT Organizational Unit, she is automatically granted access to the volumes you see listed in the upper-left part of the dialog box. I highlighted the 486-33_SYS: volume, then clicked on the Add button to open our old friend, the Select Object dialog box. By scrolling through the directory context list, I found and highlighted the \SCREENS directory.

Once you've closed the Select Object dialog box and accepted the specified directory path, click on the OK button. The last step is to grant the trustee rights for the directory. This is accomplished by clicking on the checkboxes in the Rights section of the main dialog box. To give all the necessary user rights to the directory (and all subdirectories through inheritance), check Read, Write, Create, Erase, Modify, and File Scan.

NetWare 4.10's NetWare Administrator program required you to highlight the volume(s) in question and click on OK in the Select Object dialog box. In the spirit of productivity, NetWare 4.11 only requires you to double-click on the directory name. Don't squander all your saved time at once.

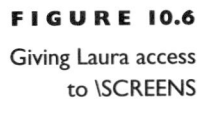

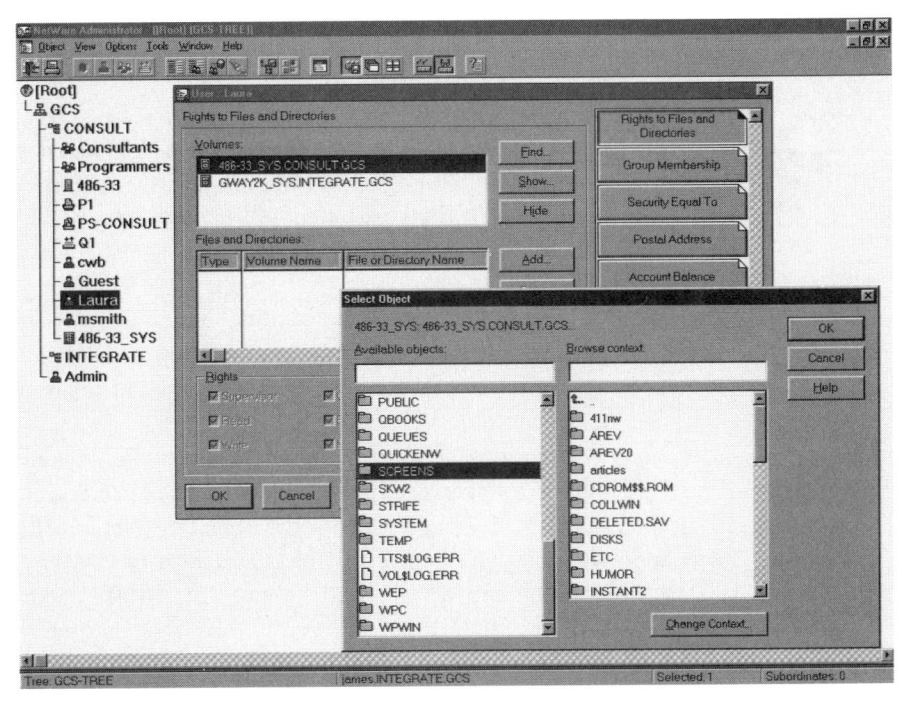

FIGURE 10.6

Giving Laura access to \SCREENS

Moving Objects

> **10.5 IN-A-HURRY**
>
> **Move an Object**
>
> 1. Log in to the network as the Admin user or equivalent and start NetWare Administrator.
> 2. Highlight the object to be moved and press the F7 key.
> 3. Type the new location or use the Browser button to open the Select Object dialog box.
> 4. Choose the new location and click on OK to exit the Select Object dialog box.
> 5. If available (NetWare 4.10), choose to check the Create Alias in Place of Moved Container box.
> 6. Click on Create to save the settings.

When you move a leaf object, all NDS references to the moved object are changed. The common name of the object will remain the same, but the full name showing the context will change.

Earlier versions of NetWare 4 allowed moving leaf objects only. Now, however, you may move any container object as well, but with some caveats. A container object can be moved only if it is the root of an NDS partition that has no subordinate partitions. Check NDS Manager information coming up soon for more details.

Let's correct a mistake of mine made just a bit ago. There's no reason to put the Directory Map object into a container three levels deep, especially since all network users may want access to the files referenced by the Directory Map object Screens.

After logging in to the network as Admin or equivalent, open the NDS display so you can see the Directory Map object Screens. Your first thought might be to drag-and-drop the object into its new location, but that won't work. If you do grab an object and start to move it, notice the help information that appears above the menu line: "Make each of the selected objects a trustee of the dropped target." Oops, this isn't what we want. Drag your object to the top or bottom of the screen before letting it go, or you will create a trustee assignment that you don't want.

Here's the tricky way to move this same object: hold down the Ctrl key while you're dragging-and-dropping. (This isn't in the manual, so don't tell anyone, okay?)

The "official" way to move an object is to highlight the object and either press F7 or choose Move from the Object menu. This opens the Move dialog box, showing the current location and a text box awaiting the destination. You can type the destination or use the Browser button. Figure 10.7 shows the Select Object dialog box being used to move Screens to a more reasonable location. SCREENS.TECH_CON.INTEGRATE.GCS will, once I click on OK in each dialog box, become SCREENS.GCS, a much more manageable handle. I have now corrected the mistake I made previously.

If you remember NetWare 4.10's NetWare Administrator program, you may recall that the Move dialog box included an option to create an Alias object in place of the moved object. That option no longer exists. Either Novell's research showed people didn't use that function or the designers forgot to upgrade those lines of code. Either way, once you move an object, the only way to leave an Alias in its place is to create one yourself.

FIGURE 10.7

Moving Screens up two NDS tree levels

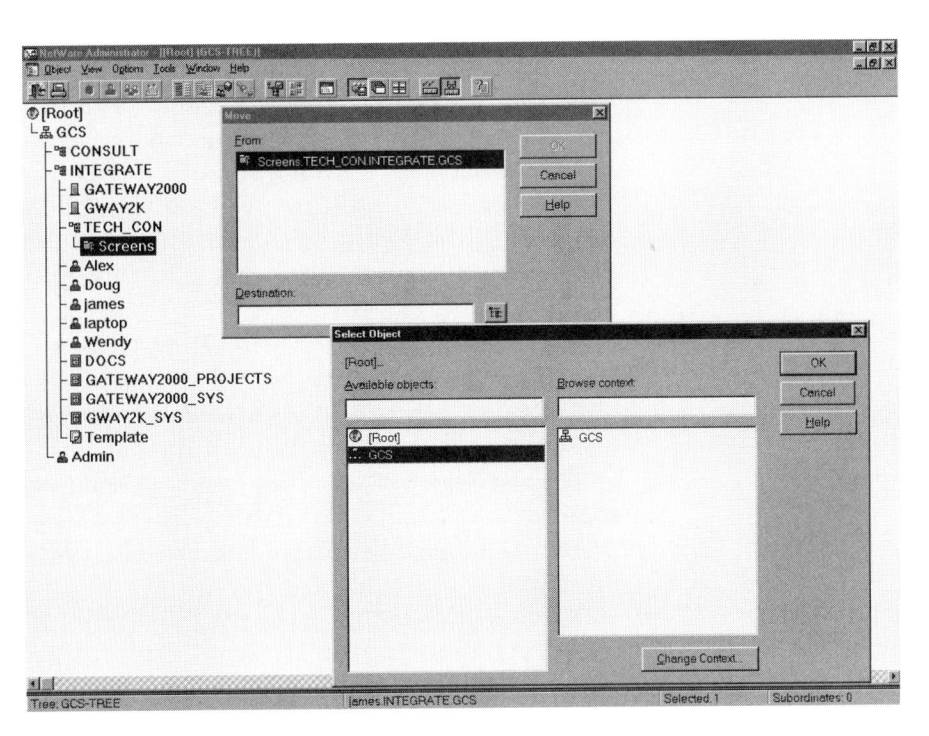

Renaming Objects

> **10.6 IN-A-HURRY**
>
> **Rename an Object**
>
> 1. Log in to the network as the Admin user or equivalent and start NetWare Administrator.
> 2. Highlight the new leaf object to be renamed.
> 3. Pull down the Object menu and choose Rename.
> 4. Type the new name.
> 5. Check whether to save the old name, and whether to create an Alias if renaming a container.
> 6. Click on Create to save.

This may come as a shock to you, but things in your network will change. Some brilliant VP will decide that SLS+MKTG must become MKTG+SLS, and every reference in the company, including the network Organizational Unit, needs to change. Luckily, this is easier and much cheaper than getting new business cards (quicker, too).

To change an object's name, you just highlight the object that needs the name change and pick Rename from the Object menu. A small dialog box appears, asking for the new name. Figure 10.8 shows the process of renaming TECH_CON to TECH_CON_1.

With this step, all references to TECH_CON will become TECH_CON_1, throughout the entire NDS tree. What about the users that will go looking for TECH_CON, only to be disappointed? As you can see in Figure 10.8, there are two ways to make sure the users can find the container.

The first checkbox asks if you wish to save the old name. This will keep the name as an Alias in the NDS database, so searches for the old name will work. The search results will tell the users (or other network administrators) what the new name for the object is.

The second checkbox creates an Alias object with the name of the original object. The Alias object points to the object with its new name. Users with references to the newly renamed object in their NET.CFG file or login script will

FIGURE 10.8

Renaming a container, and taking all the proper precautions

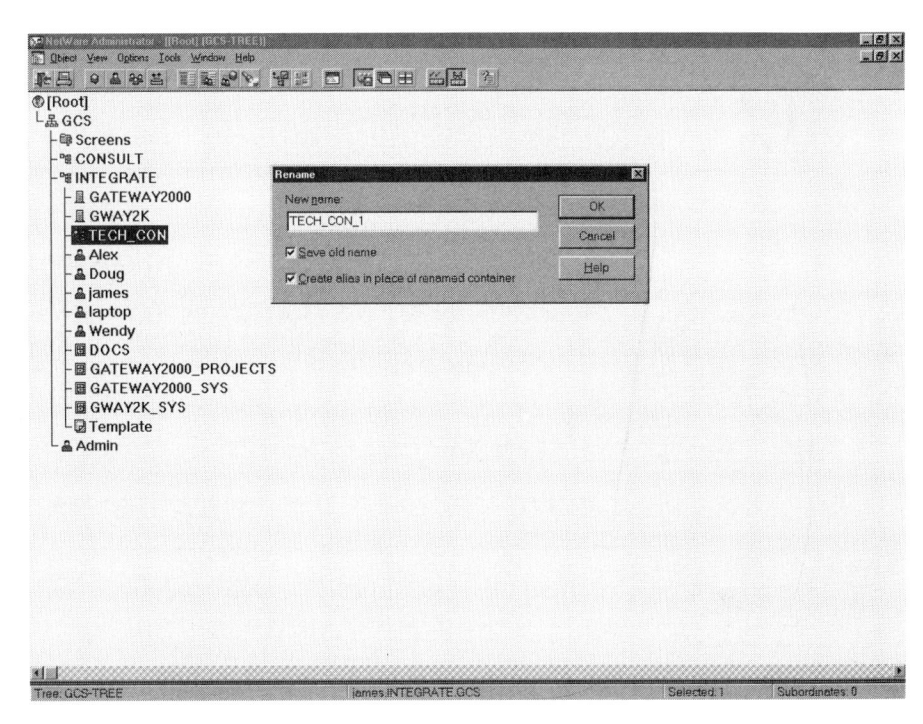

be connected properly. However, if there's no Alias object or modification made to login scripts, users that reference the container name in their NET.CFG may not be able to log in.

This problem of a now-antiquated NET.CFG file is addressed by the NCUPDATE utility. A command placed in the renamed container's login script will update the user's NET.CFG file. You'll find more on this utility in the "User Management" section, a bit later in this chapter.

Searching for Objects

As your network and NDS database both get larger, finding objects with specific properties will get tough. Your users will be okay, since they spend most of their time in specific containers using a small set of servers and volumes. You, however, must patrol the entire network.

The Search option on NetWare Administrator's Object menu (or clicking the flashlight icon on the toolbar) makes life much simpler. You can list search

> **10.7 IN-A-HURRY**
>
> **Search for Objects**
>
> 1. Log in to the network as the Admin user or equivalent and start NetWare Administrator.
> 2. Highlight the container from which to start the search (optional).
> 3. Pull down the Object menu and choose Search, or click on the flashlight icon.
> 4. Choose your search filters in the dialog box, or open a previously saved search filter.
> 5. Click on OK to start the search.
> 6. Use the search results in their own browser window.

requirements based on an enormous number of options, and save the search query for reuse. Once the search is finished, the results display in their own browser window, so they are easy to keep in one place and remain available for quick reference.

Make sure you run the search utility as a user with as many trustee rights as possible. The minimum rights required for a search are the Browse rights to objects so you can see the entire network, and the Read and Compare property rights, so you can match a particular value to the object of your search profile.

Figure 10.9 shows a search about to start. Since NetWare 4.1x no longer has the SECURITY.EXE file used in NetWare 3, this search operation will list all users that are equivalent to Admin. One of the most serious security breaches is when the wrong person has the ultimate network access privileges, and this type of search can tell you if this has happened.

Setting a Search Filter

There are several steps in setting up a search filter. Here are some suggestions for the Search dialog box fields:

- **Start From:** The context you have highlighted when calling the Search dialog box is placed in the Start From field. If you don't wish to start from that point, click on the Browser button at the end of the field and move through the NDS tree until you find your preferred context.

FIGURE 10.9

Searching for users who may be security risks

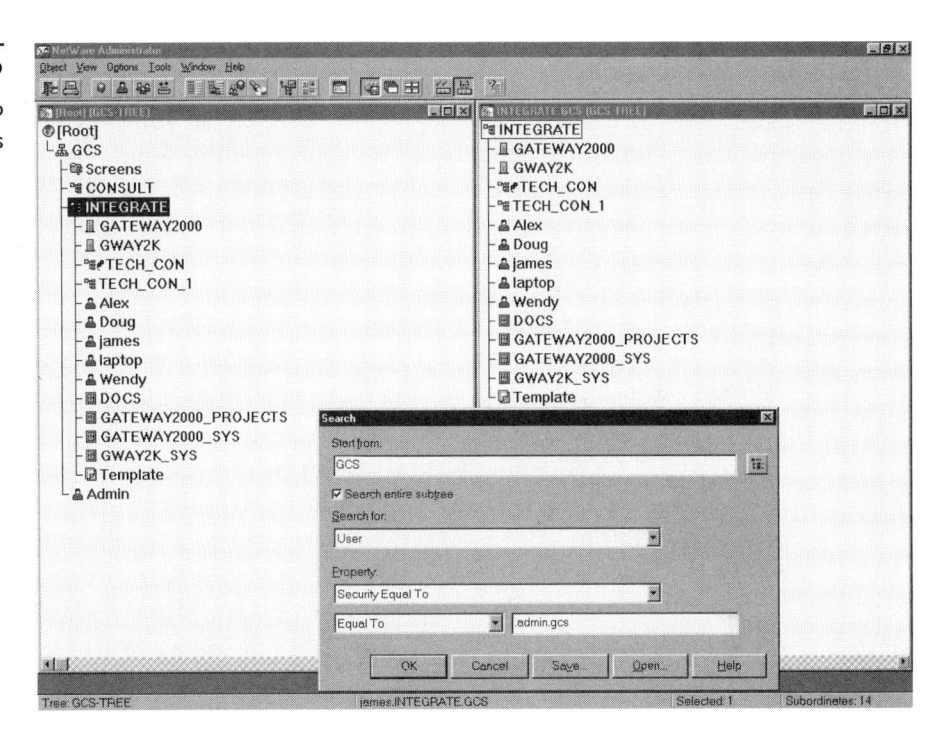

- **Search Entire Subtree:** Checking this option searches the current container and all subordinate containers. When it isn't selected, the search utility looks only in the current container.

- **Search For:** Every leaf object, plus additions such as volume, Organization, and Organizational Unit, may be searched for. The default is User, figuring that some network client will be causing the problem you are searching to resolve.

- **Property:** Specifies the property value to search, based on the item in the Search For field. None is the default, somehow meaning all.

The field directly below Property could be called the Boolean field, since the contents tend to be Equal To or Not Equal To, Present or Not Present, Greater Than or Less Than, and the like. If you use this field to indicate a number or text, such as Equal To or Greater Than, enter the value in the text box to the right. In our example in Figure 10.9, Equal To .Admin.GCS is specified for the search.

Search results appear in a separate browser window, waiting for you to take some action. You may minimize the window, keeping it available for use but out of your way while you go about your business within NetWare Administrator. Using the defaults of the Search window gathers all users in the container in one tidy spot. If your container is getting so large these search results are used regularly, you need to rethink your network design.

Saving Search Criteria

The search results always inhabit their own browser window entitled Search. There's no way to save the search results for reuse later, but you can save the search criteria.

Notice the command buttons across the bottom of Figure 10.9. OK, Cancel, and Help we expect, but Save and Open are a surprise in NetWare Administrator. Once you have the search questions set the way you want them, click on Save. A Save As dialog box appears, prompting you to put the saved procedure files in the \PUBLIC directory with an extension of SCH.

If you later click on Open, the File Open dialog box arrives, aimed at the \PUBLIC subdirectory. The File Name list box is set for the SCH extension, so you merely need to double-click on the name of the procedure you want to retrieve.

Once summoned, the Search dialog box waits for you, with all the previously configured information in the proper places. You may then click on OK and conduct the same search operation, or modify any of the field's contents before starting the search.

Using NDS Manager to Manage Partitions and Replicas

THE NDS DATABASE tracks all the network objects and their rights to use the network. The database is spread around the network for two main reasons: fault-tolerance and speed of execution. The closer the database is to a user requesting services, the sooner those services can be provided. Having more copies of the database running on the network prevents one server from locking everyone out of the network.

NetWare 4.1x divides the Directory into partitions. Each partition is a distinct unit of data in the NDS tree. A partition includes a container object, all objects contained therein, and the data about those objects. No file system information is included in a partition. An object can only be in one partition, but copies of the partition allow the object to be accessed from anywhere in the network. Subordinate partitions are labeled *child* partitions; the partition above that is called the *parent* partition.

A replica is a copy of one partition. Replicas provide fault-tolerance within each partition by copying the database to multiple file servers. A lost partition can be re-created by using a replica. There are four types of replicas:

- **Master replica:** The primary replica of a given partition. Used to create new Directory partitions or to read and update Directory information. The Master replica should be near the NetWare manager responsible for maintaining the partition. Only one Master replica of any partition can exist.

- **Read/Write replica:** Reads and updates Directory information, such as the addition or deletion of objects. This replica should be near the workgroup serviced by that partition. If a Master replica is lost, a Read/Write replica must become the Master. If the first Master comes back online, it will be deleted automatically in deference to the Master with an earlier time stamp.

- **Read-Only replica:** Primarily a backup that speeds information by allowing users to view the information, without allowing any changes.

- **Subordinate Reference replica:** Placed automatically by NDS on a server if the parent Directory partition has either a Master, Read/Write, or Read-Only replica on the server and the child Directory partition does not. Subordinate Reference replicas are maintained by NDS.

In NetWare 4.10, you can manage partitions and replicas with Partition Manager, accessed from the Tools menu of NetWare Administrator. In NetWare 4.11, Partition Manager is still available as a DOS utility (as we'll see later), but the Windows-based work is handled by NDS Manager. You may run NDS Manager on its own, or add the NDS Manager option to your NetWare Administrator Tools menu.

During partition operations, you may see some unknown icons as the synchronization between different Directory databases settles. There is no reason to worry unless this continues until the next day.

During installation, a replica of the partition containing the server's context is added to each new server unless there are already three replicas. Servers with bindery files will get a replica, regardless of how many replicas are there already. Extra partitions or replicas are controlled by the NDS Manager utility (Partition Manager in NetWare 4.10) or the PARTMGR program in DOS.

Partition and Replica Management Guidelines

Here are some guidelines for managing partitions and replicas:

- Make sure you replicate the partition that includes the [Root] object. If this partition dies, your NDS tree is worthless. Make an extra copy or two while you're at it.

- For NDS fault-tolerance, plan for three replicas of each partition. If your network design allows it, keep replica copies in different physical locations.

- Create partitions to group your network users in their natural boundaries. If users from the partition are spread far and wide, move replicas close to them. The closer the replicas are to the workgroup using them, the better.

- Servers that need to run Bindery Services must have either a Master or a Read/Write replica of the partition.

- Changes to the replicas, such as adding or deleting objects or redefining a partition, send little traffic across the network. Only the changed information is sent across the network. However, placing or rebuilding a replica requires the system to copy the entire replica across the network. Enough traffic is generated to impact the users slightly. It's better to leave these operations for low-traffic times if possible. Each object in a replica takes about 1 KB of disk space.

Follow these guidelines, and use your common networking sense, and the management of replicas and partitions will go smoothly. High-speed connections between partitions and replicas, as in a purely local or campus network, will never show a significant performance drop because of replica placement. When you start crossing WANs, especially those with slow connections, pay extra attention to replica and boundary placement.

When You Mess Up NDS

During research for this section, the lab network (GCS-TREE) somehow got quite messed up. Perhaps the fact that I deleted the SYS: volume holding the Master replica of the [Root] partition for the network had something to do with the problem. Kids, do not try this at home, or when folks with tender ears are within shouting distance.

With NetWare 3 there was a well-defined process for restoring the server resource information: You retrieved the bindery files from your backup tape. If your backup tape did not copy the bindery files (i.e., was a cheap backup system), you copied the bindery files from the diskette you created by telling NetWare to back up the entire server to floppy disks, stopping at the first diskette since that one held the three bindery files. Then you hoped you remembered all the network users and printers added since the backup.

The good news with NetWare 4 is that the NDS information is distributed and current. The bad news is that the NDS information is distributed, and it will take awhile to recover from major surgery or ham-fisted management. The Read/Write replicas will eventually propagate the information to the newly installed NDS files on the butchered server. During that time, however, you will do the following:

- Try to make a Read/Write replica a Master replica (using DSREPAIR). The delay will become interminable, and you will try to do the same thing again, then try to force another replica into Master mode.

- Try to reinstall NDS on the afflicted server, getting error messages when you provide the Admin password. Press Alt+F10 to get out of the loop by stopping the installation.

- Try to redo the replica status again.

- Go to the hardware store and decide which sledge hammer will make the best adjustment tool for your servers.

- Notice the replicas are starting to settle down.

- Try again, without success, to resurrect NDS on the afflicted server.

- Read the employment classifieds.

- Actually get NDS installed once again on the less-afflicted server.

- Be amazed at how much of your network returns in good working order.

> *Users want access to their services, and they want them ten minutes ago.*

The key element in this sequence is the time needed for NDS to heal itself. Of course, a busy network is not a relaxed place. Users want access to their services, and they want them ten minutes ago. Reject the urge to do something, especially something drastic. Help your users find ways to get the resources they need. Check the NDS status and use DSREPAIR a time or two (more details on DSREPAIR soon).

If possible, make your mistakes on a weekend, so the system has a chance to settle down before the users appear. Just don't make any social plans for that weekend.

Before starting any work on NDS, take a moment to verify that your partitions and replicas are well-distributed. Keep Master replicas away from the target of any changes. Make a new Master replica if necessary, and give the network time to settle down before the next step. If you don't, you may need my list of colorful adjectives used to describe recalcitrant replicas. E-mail for details, but don't let any children see the list.

Putting NDS Manager on the NetWare Administrator Tools Menu

First, you need to know where to find the program. If you're running Windows 95, run NDSMGR32.EXE in the \PUBLIC\WIN95 directory. NDSMGR16.EXE runs under Windows 3.1x, and it's located in the \PUBLIC directory.

Second, there's a trick to getting NDS Manager to show up in the NetWare Administrator Tools menu. The details are in the NDS Manager Help file, but let me tell you Windows 95 users how to get going:

1. Start the Windows 95 version of NetWare Administrator. Make sure the Save Settings on Exit menu item on the Options menu is checked, and then close the program.

2. Run the REGEDIT.EXE program, the Registry Editor, within Windows 95. (If you've been messing with any Windows 95 clients, you're probably sick of this program already.)

3. Choose KEY_CURRENT_USER\Software\NetWare\Parameters\NetWare Administrator, creating any pieces of this path that aren't there. I had to create the last two levels; you may be luckier than I was.

4. Highlight Snapin Object DLLs WIN95 and open the Edit menu. If this item doesn't appear, open and close the Windows 95 version of NetWare Administrator, then try it again. Be sure you're running the Windows 95 version (check the About dialog box in the program).

5. Choose New, and then select String Value.

6. Type **NDSMGR** and press Enter.

7. While NDSMGR is still highlighted, pick Edit, then Modify.

8. For the Value data, type **NMSNAP32.DLL**. Then choose OK.

When you restart NetWare Administrator, the NDS Manager option should appear on the Tools menu. This didn't work for me the first time, but it did the second. Make sure you run the proper version of NDSMGR for your particular workstation operating system. These changes won't help NDSMGR show up in the Tools menu if you start the 16-bit version of the program, as I did. The only differences between the two versions are in the Help About screens, so be careful.

Taking a look at Figure 10.10, notice how flexible the columns are on the NDS Manager screen. I've rearranged the bottom columns so that they are completely different from the default settings on the top. This allows me to put the information I want first. In this case, I put the little pictures of the servers, showing that the GATEWAY2000 server is the Master replica for all three partitions. How do I know there are three partitions? The top-left window, labeled Partitions, lists three containers. Each container has the small partition icon to its left.

Clicking on the icon containing the lowercase *i* pops open information about the highlighted object. (I thought the icon was for WorkPerfect's Info-Central Personal Information Manager, but this is the nineties, and Novell is recycling.) Figure 10.11 shows information about the [Root] partition.

Notice that the last attempted sync and last successful sync coincide. This is a good feeling, and one you should encourage.

Creating a New Partition

The [Root] is the first partition in your new network. Any new partition from that becomes a child partition. Any new partition from that becomes another child partition, and the middle partition becomes both a parent and a child partition (sort of what you become when you turn your parents into grandparents).

A new partition must consist of a container and its objects, both leaf objects and other containers. The partition replicas remain on the same servers they were on before you made the new partition, but the information for the partition will be moved to the appropriate replica for the new partition.

FIGURE 10.10

Rearranging the management furniture

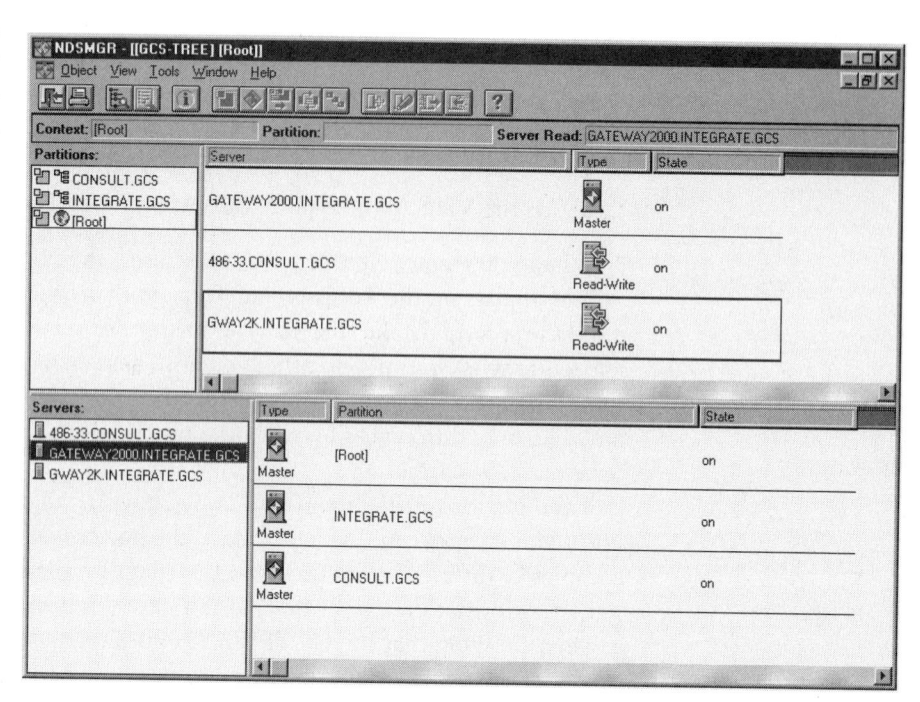

FIGURE 10.11

Checking partition details

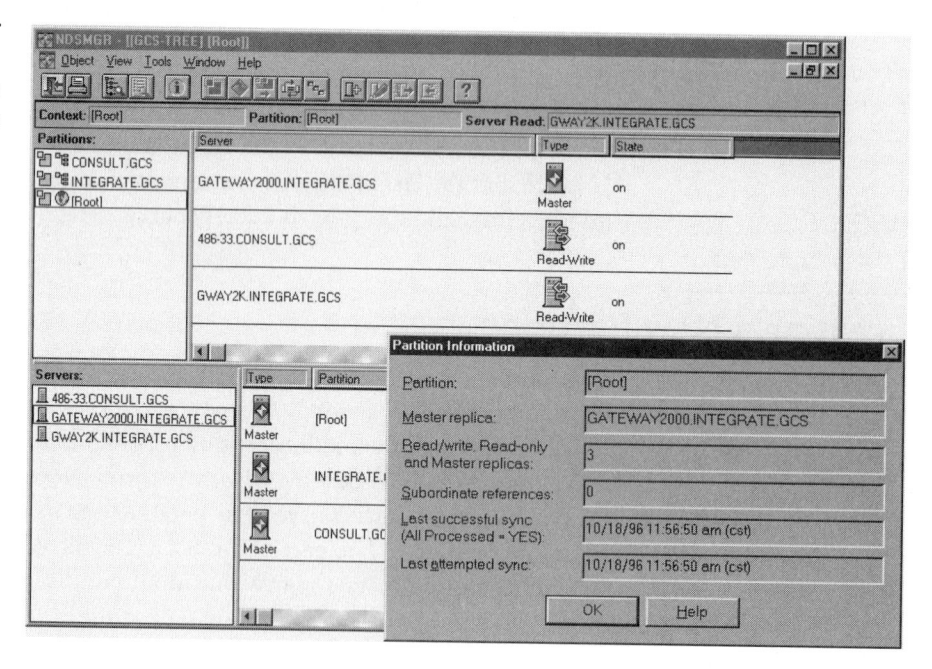

10.8 IN-A-HURRY

Create a Partition

1. Log in to the network as the Admin user or equivalent and start NetWare Administrator.

2. Highlight the container to make a new partition.

3. Start NDS Manager from the Tools menu or as a separate program.

4. In NDS Manager, switch to Tree view mode and highlight the container to make into a new partition.

5. Click on Create as a New Partition and confirm by clicking on Yes in the warning dialog box.

6. Click on Yes in the information box that appears during the partition operation.

7. Refresh the screen to see the new partition icon.

Figure 10.12 shows partition creation about to begin. There is no strain in creating a partition, but large networks may take some time for NDS to become synchronized once again. Your network traffic will increase slightly, since there will be communication between partitions and replicas across the network.

Using the Abort Partition Operation command button that appears after you approve the new partition is usually not a good idea. If you had a sudden attack of conscience and decided giving the programmers in CONSULT their own partition was a bad idea, you could click on the Abort button quickly. But partition operations are so fast on LANs that you probably wouldn't catch the operation in time to stop it.

I wouldn't even try to stop a partition operation unless I realized a WAN link was down. In a case like that, where a WAN break stopped an operation from completing, you would need to abort the partition operation. Otherwise, on local connections with all servers present and accounted for, wait for the partition operation to finish, then undo it, as described in the next section.

After you click on Yes to create the new partition, a nice box labeled Create Partition says that all preconditions have been met, and you may create the partition. This dialog box appears in Figure 10.12. Click on Yes once more, and your partition will be created. Things happen so fast in NetWare 4.11 that you don't even get a warning about how long the operation may take. In a LAN setting, your partition appears before you can read the screen saying the partition is being created.

FIGURE 10.12

Giving the PROGRAMMERS their own partition

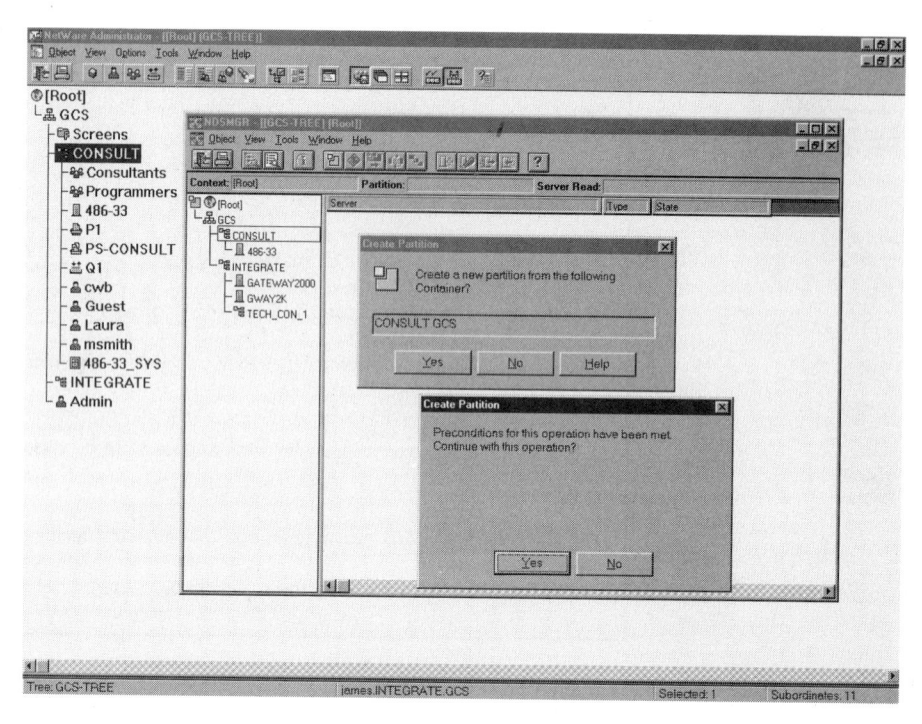

Merging Partitions

10.9 IN-A-HURRY

Merge Partitions

1. Log in to the network as the Admin user or equivalent and start NetWare Administrator.

2. Start NDS Manager from the Tools menu.

3. Locate the child partition that you want to merge back with its parent partition in the NDS Manager browser window.

4. Choose Partition from the Object menu, then select Merge, or highlight the partition and click on the Merge Partition icon on the toolbar, and confirm by clicking on Yes in the dialog box.

5. Refresh the screen to see the new partition alignment.

If you change your mind after creating a new partition, you can easily merge it back with its parent partition. This makes sense if the two partitions serve essentially the same Directory structure and their information is similar. Your choice is only to merge a partition back with its parent partition, not to pick some other partition to merge.

Partitions are not deleted; they are just merged. All the information in one partition is absorbed into the parent partition.

Figure 10.13 shows the dialog box you'll see when you choose to merge partitions. A warning box appears to tell you that this operation may take up to an hour. In large networks with WAN links, merging may take quite a bit of time. The warning dialog box will go away, and things will look like they are finished, possibly before they actually are. Wait an extra minute or two between operations so partitions and replicas don't get confused halfway through the first operation when you start a second one.

Although you can create a partition only while in the hierarchical (Tree) view, you can merge partitions from the flat view, as in Figure 10.13. Once you click on Yes in the Merge Partition dialog box, an informational box appears. This box includes a Cancel command button, if you feel the urge to un-merge immediately.

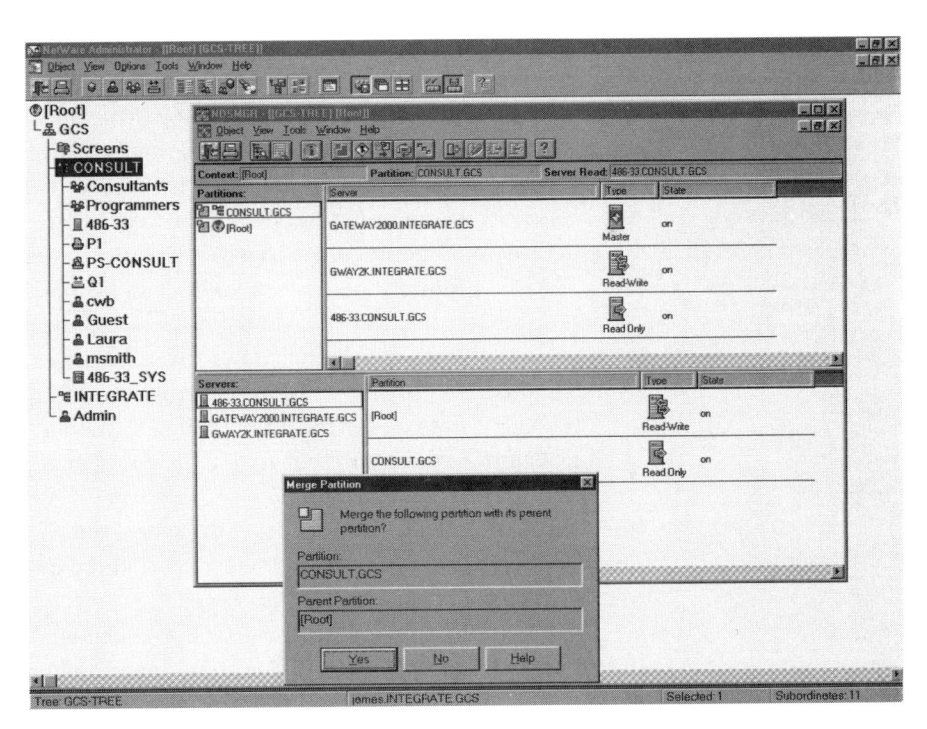

FIGURE 10.13

A child partition returns home to its parent partition.

Viewing or Modifying Replicas

> **10.10 IN-A-HURRY**
>
> **View or Modify a Replica**
>
> 1. Log in to the network as the Admin user or equivalent and start NetWare Administrator.
>
> 2. Start NDS Manager from the Tools menu or as a separate program.
>
> 3. Click on the Replicas button on the right side of the toolbar. Explanation balloons will appear to tell you which icon is which as your cursor touches the icon.
>
> 4. Click on the toolbar buttons to Add Replica, Delete Replica, Change Type, Send Updates, or Receive Updates.
>
> 5. Verify the server name, and the type of replica you wish to add, before clicking on OK.
>
> 6. Click on Close to exit the "finished" dialog box.

Replica management is generally necessary when you make changes to the NDS design. The Partition Replicas dialog box appears after you click on any of the replicas in NDS Manager. This dialog box gives you a look at the replicas for the partition that was highlighted. Figure 10.12 shows a good view of the replica information for the [Root] partition of the GCS network.

Notice here in Figure 10.14 that we're showing the NDS Manager flat view. This is important, as some changes can be made only in the flat view, such as adding a replica. The top window shows the partitions (only [Root] now), and the bottom window shows the status of each server when its name is highlighted. All three types of replicas are on display in Figure 10.14.

The toolbar buttons for the NDS Manager, shown in Figure 10.14, include all the obvious options for replicas: add, delete, change, and update. The display shows that there is one Read-Only replica on server GWAY2. Figure 10.15 shows the Add Replica dialog box that appears when you click on the Add Replica toolbar button, or when you highlight the partition display, click the right mouse button, and choose Change Type.

There are two types of replicas that could be installed on GWAY2K, but I opted for the Read-Only type. The copy operation will take a moment, but

Using NDS Manager to Manage Partitions and Replicas

FIGURE 10.14

Checking the replica status

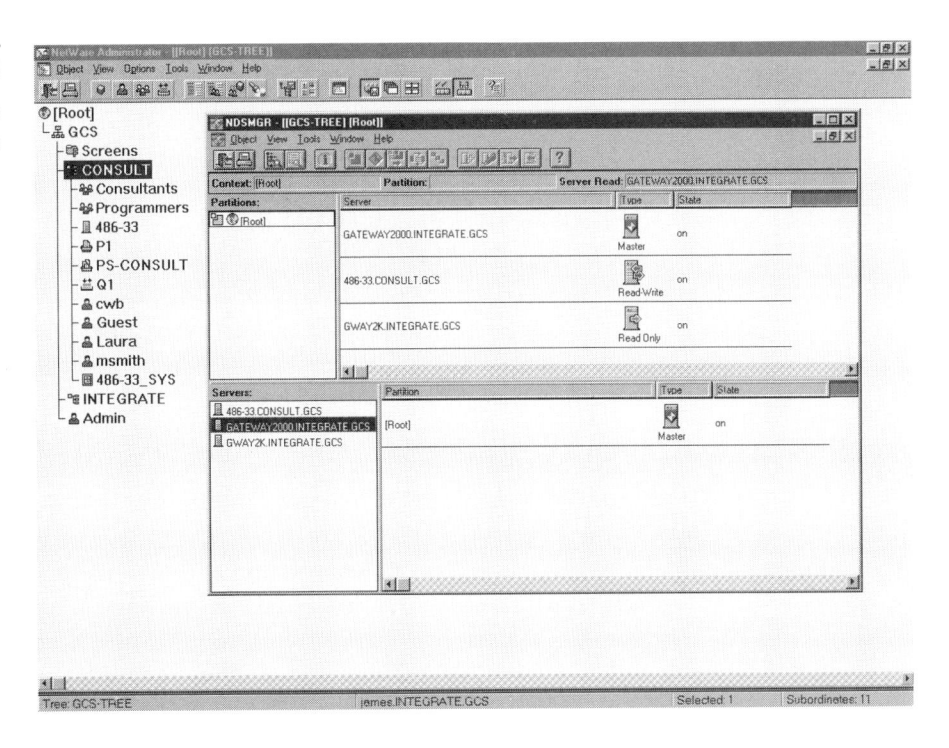

FIGURE 10.15

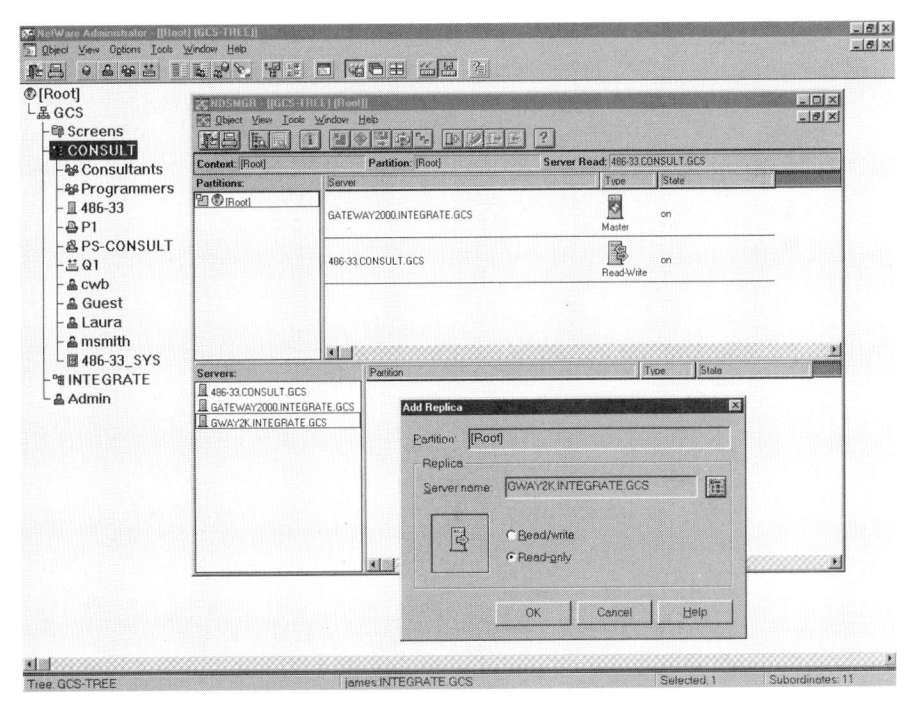

Getting server GWAY2K into the partition replication business

not much longer with a small network and all LAN connections between the servers. If there are WAN links in the path, it will take longer. The more objects in the partition, the more time it will take to add a partition replica.

What if you want to change the replica type? Let's say I realized it would be better to make GWAY2K a Read/Write replica rather than a Read-Only replica. All I need to do is highlight the server name and double-click, or click on the Change Type button. Either way, the dialog box in Figure 10.16 appears.

It really is better to have Read/Write replicas. Read-Only replicas are not recommended, because they can't help re-create your NDS structure in case of damage to parts of the database. When you click on OK in the Change Replica Type dialog box, the replica is immediately changed, with little or no network impact.

When a replica is changed to Master, the current Master replica automatically downgrades to Read/Write. So if you wish to make your Master replica a Read/Write replica, you must do it backwards, and set up the new Master replica first.

When you right-click your mouse button while pointing at a replica, you'll see many choices. If you wish to delete the replica, highlight the Delete menu option, then verify you know what you're doing. The system won't let you

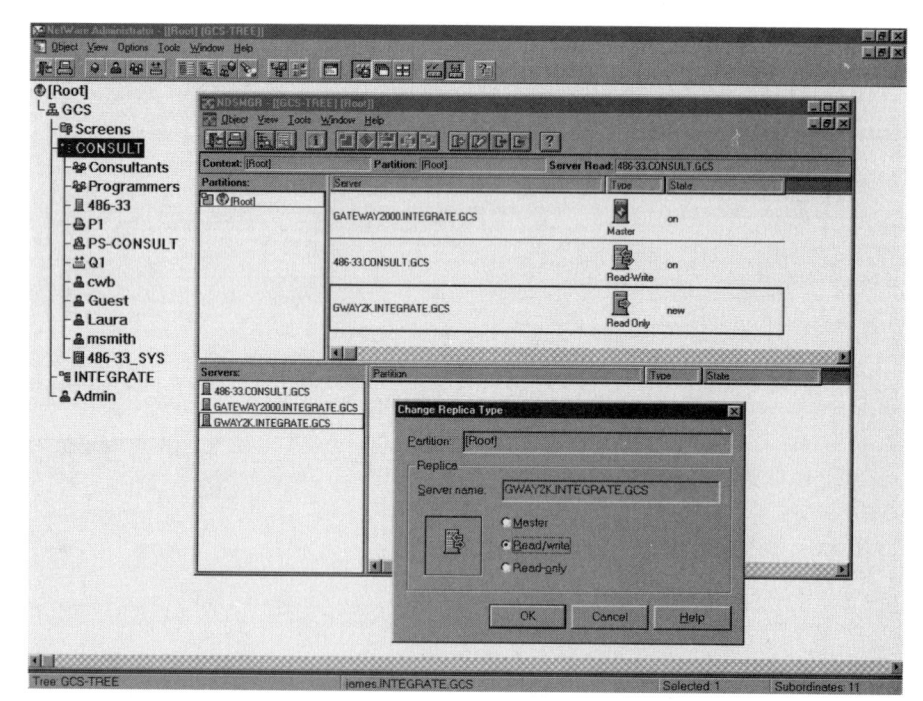

FIGURE 10.16

Changing server GWAY2K's replica from Read-Only to Read/Write delete the Master Replica (it's certainly embarrassing when you kill the Master replica—don't ask me how I know this).

The Update toolbar buttons (the last two on the right, before the question mark icon) depend on the highlighted replica as well. If the replica you have highlighted is the one you want to update with some recent change from another replica, click on the Send Updates command button. If you have a feeling the highlighted replica has a problem and needs to be updated, click on the Receive Updates button. You may also send and receive updates by clicking the right mouse button while pointing to a server. These operations shouldn't be necessary often, but they're handy in case a WAN connection has just been restored.

Viewing Server Partitions

> **10.11 IN-A-HURRY**
>
> **View a Server Partition**
>
> 1. Log in to the network as the Admin user or equivalent and start NetWare Administrator.
>
> 2. Start NDS Manager from the Tools menu or as a separate program.
>
> 3. Highlight the server with the replica of interest.
>
> 4. Double-click on the server name to view the server information, or right-click and choose Information from the menu. This screen is read-only (nothing in the Replica Information box may be changed here).

Let's say we wish to verify that the GWAY2K server is, in fact, now supporting Read/Write replicas for our partition. Plus, we want to know how the server and its replica are doing. That's where the Information button on the toolbar comes in handy.

Switching back to the hierarchical view (I can never make up my mind) and opening the replica display is our first step. When you want information about a server, it really doesn't matter whether the NDS Manager's display on the left is flat or hierarchical. Highlighting one of the server replicas in the main window area is the second step. The final step is to either right-click for the menu and choose Information or to click on the toolbar's Information button. This step pops open what you see in Figure 10.17.

FIGURE 10.17

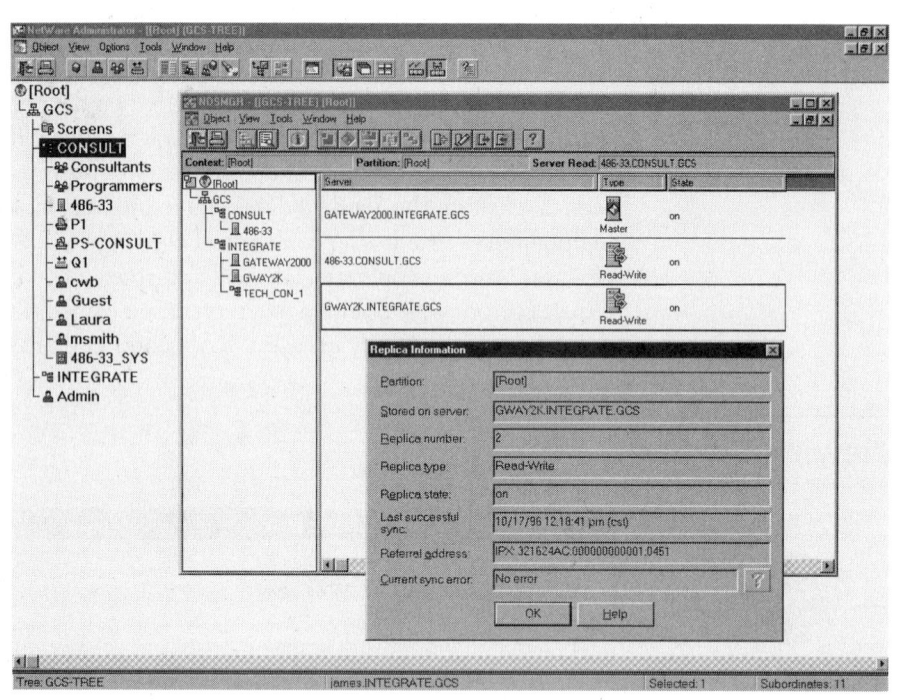

Checking the status of GWAY2K

The information in the Replica Information window is read-only, in case you were thinking of making changes here. But it's so easy to make a change with the new NDS Manager utility—with a right-click or a toolbar choice—that you won't mind that you can't do it here.

Deleting a NetWare Server Object from NDS

Getting rid of a server is serious business. When you press the Delete key, the highlighted server bites the dust, never to rise again. There is no SALVAGE utility to resurrect the server. Gone are all the server's resources, which are now out of reach for all network clients. Still available, thankfully, are all the files and directories on the server volume(s). When (and if) you reinstall NDS on the server, the data will still be there, waiting for your return.

Taking out a server may corrupt your NDS database, so move all partition replicas away from the server before proceeding. If you delete a server holding your only replica, that partition is in deep trouble. There will be a pass-fail test of your tape backup system immediately, which it will most likely fail. If it fails, you must re-create the partition by memory, and by hand.

10.12 IN-A-HURRY

Delete a Server

1. Log in to the network as the Admin user or equivalent.

2. Go to the NetWare server to be deleted and type **DOWN** at the console.

3. Start NetWare Administrator.

4. Start the NDS Manager from the Tools menu or as a separate program.

5. Highlight the server object to be deleted and press the Delete key.

6. Click on Yes to delete.

If you are taking a server out of commission, and have removed all replicas from the server, highlight the server and press the Delete key. You may then see something like the warning shown in Figure 10.18. So, down the server and try once more to delete it.

FIGURE 10.18
You forgot a step before deleting the server.

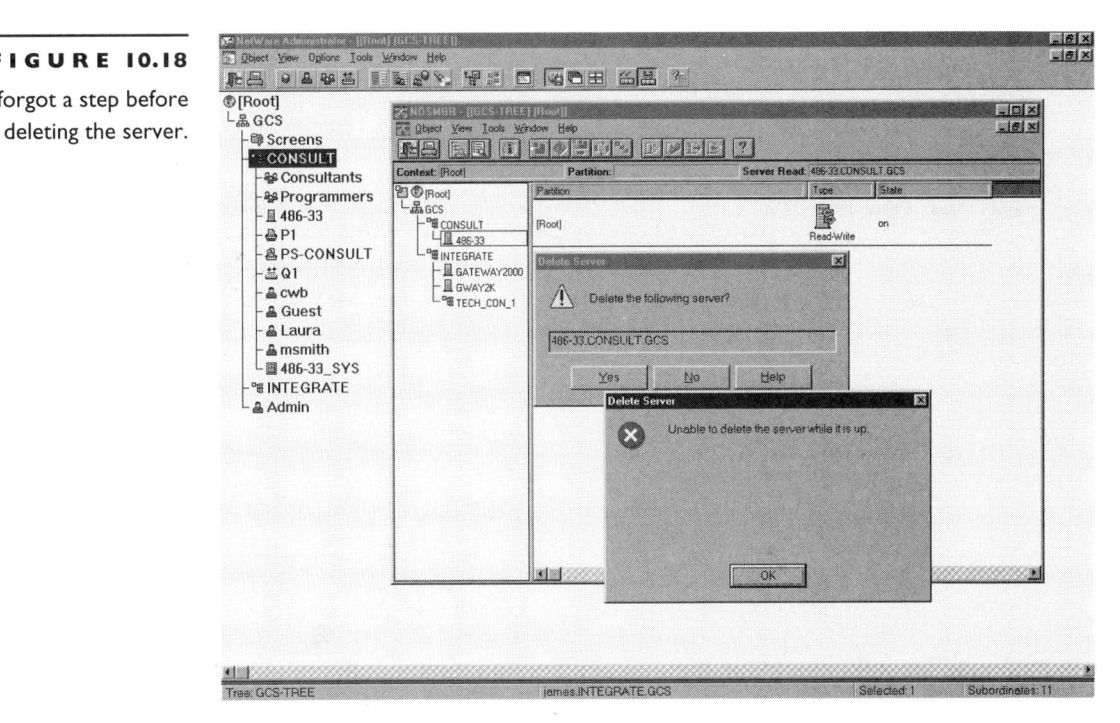

You don't need to delete a server to move the object to another context; just use the techniques described earlier to move the Server object. If you need to move a partition, keep reading.

Moving a Partition (and Its Container)

> **10.13 IN-A-HURRY**
>
> **Move a Partition and Container**
>
> 1. Log in to the network as the Admin user or equivalent and start NetWare Administrator.
>
> 2. Start NDS Manager from the Tools menu, or start it as a separate program.
>
> 3. Highlight the partition to be moved and click on the Move Partition toolbar icon, or click the right mouse button and choose Move from the menu.
>
> 4. Type the new partition location or use the Browser button to move through the NDS tree.
>
> 5. Be sure to check the box to leave an Alias object in place of the moved container.
>
> 6. Click on Yes to move, save, and exit.

When a container is moved, all references in the Directory database for the container are changed. The common name of the container remains the same, but the full name will obviously change to reflect the container's new location in the NDS tree.

The Move Partition button is on the NDS Manager toolbar. You must pick and highlight the partition to move, and it must be the root of an NDS partition, without any child partitions. If there are child partitions, you must merge each of them to the parent partition you plan to move before continuing. This is why you must go through NDS Manager to move a container: The container must be a partition.

Figure 10.19 shows the INTEGRATE Organizational Unit highlighted in NDS Manager. You can still see the partition icon to the left of INTEGRATE within the NDS Manager hierarchical display. CONSULT can't be moved until a new partition is created with that container as the root of the partition. Those users running VLM client files that reference the container in their NET.CFG files will have a problem until you use the NCUPDATE file in the container login script. (NCUPDATE is covered later in this chapter.)

FIGURE 10.19

Threatening to move INTEGRATE.GCS

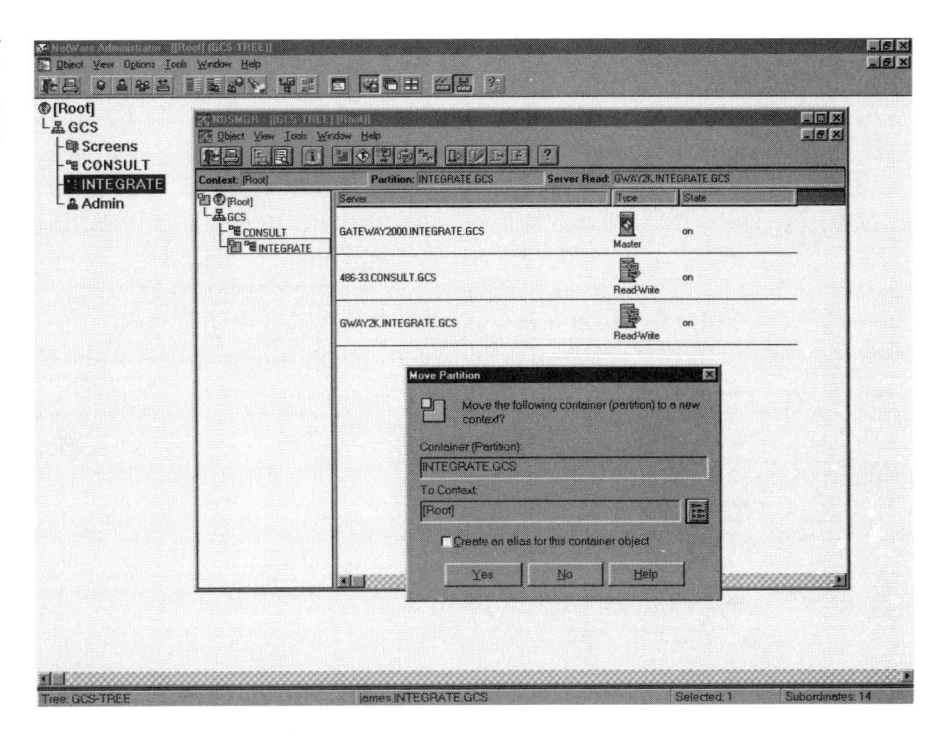

User Management

MOST OF THE information about individual user creation and management is back in Chapter 6. Chapter 7 covers managing users in one type of group or another, including setting up menus and login scripts. What may be called the traditional user management information has already been covered.

But tradition isn't worth much in the 1990s, is it? So we still have a few things worth covering about user management in this chapter.

Using NetWare Accounting

NetWare was the first network operating system to allow accounting. By tracking such details as connect time, disk space used, and service requests to a file server, NetWare accounting moved away from a PC LAN level toward mainframe-type control. Accounting is used by some network administrators to charge back company departments, and by others to track when resources are being used more heavily than in the past.

NetWare accounting is set per server, giving you a way to track the usage of network resources on that server alone. Tracking users of the entire network, through the distributed NDS database, would generate enormous extra network traffic. Since the licenses for NetWare are set per server, accounting is set per server. This may change when the user licensing changes to a network model. I sure wouldn't want to be in charge of making accounting work across a distributed network, however. My guess is that if the user licensing changes, accounting will still track users per resource.

Some companies use this information to charge their network clients for a portion of the server cost, based on a cost value per network resource used. Some companies use this information to track the amount of server usage over time, to see whether usage is growing, shrinking, or staying the same. How you use the information, if at all, is up to you.

Accounting is not mandatory, and it's not necessary to activate accounting to manage any server user or resource. Since accounting does add slightly to the server overhead, some network administrators prefer to charge users by total disk space used, not connect time or disk blocks read and written. Applying charged values generated by the accounting system to users and their departments requires constant attention and maintenance.

The information tracked by the system is displayed by the DOS ATOTAL utility. Many companies use accounting to generate usage levels per server, viewed by the ATOTAL command, without any of the charge-back information per user. The information that is gathered, along with the names of the related command buttons in the Server dialog box, includes:

- Total disk blocks read (Blocks Read)

- Total disk blocks written (Blocks Written)

- Total minutes of connect time (Connect Time)

- Total disk blocks used for storage per day (Disk Storage)

- Total service requests (Service Requests)

Servers that have the accounting feature activated have five extra command buttons in their dialog box, labeled as shown in the list. Servers without accounting do not have these buttons in their dialog box.

User Management

Activating Server Accounting

10.14 IN-A-HURRY

Activate Server Accounting

1. Log in to the network as the Admin user or equivalent and start NetWare Administrator.

2. Double-click on the target server, and then click on the Accounting command button at the bottom of the dialog box.

3. Verify that you wish to start accounting. The server's bindery context must be set for accounting to begin.

Accounting is activated per server, so you must double-click on the particular server in the NetWare Administrator tree diagram. In the Server dialog box, the Accounting command button is the one on the bottom-right. Click on the button, and you will have a choice about starting or stopping accounting, depending on the accounting status (this is a toggle button).

Setting the Charge Rates for Resources

10.15 IN-A-HURRY

Set the Blocks-Read Rate for Server Accounting

1. Log in to the network as the Admin user or equivalent and start NetWare Administrator.

2. Double-click on the target server to open the dialog box, and then click on the Blocks Read command button at the bottom of the dialog box.

3. Click on Add Charge Rate and define a charge if an acceptable one is not listed.

4. Click and drag the cursor across the boxes that define each half-hour slot of the day. Chosen blocks will change to the color of the applied charge.

5. Click on OK to save and exit.

Once you determine that you will charge your users for server resources, you must decide how much to charge them. The user's account balance is kept in cents, so it's easier to use cents as a basis for your charges.

NetWare accounting uses a charge rate that is denoted as a fraction. The charge rate screen will ask for a multiplier (the top number) and a divisor (the bottom number). The multiplier is the amount that will be charged for each unit or resource. For whole cents, place the number of cents over 1, such as 5/1 for a charge of 5 cents for the resource. For fractions, such as 1.5 cents, you must multiply by 10 enough times to make the number a whole number (1.5 x 10 = 15). Then add that 10 to the divisor. If the number is 1.55 cents for some strange reason, multiply by 10 twice to reach 155, then place 100 (10 x 10) in the divisor. For whole cents, the divisor is always 1. For fractions, the divisor is always 100, with a whole number in the multiplier.

The charge rates may vary according to day and time of the week. Setting the rate is always the same, however, no matter how many rates (up to 20) you have for a resource.

Unfortunately, there isn't a database of charge rates. You must define each charge rate in the pages of the Accounting dialog box.

If you want to charge a penny (or any other amount) for each disk block read from this file server, the Blocks Read page of the NetWare Server dialog box is the place to do so. Figure 10.20 shows a two-cent charge for each block read, but only between 9:00 A.M. and 5:00 P.M. during weekdays. Although you can't see the color, green fills the blocks on Saturday and Sunday, when only one-cent per disk read is charged.

The Time and Charge Rate fields, just below the day and week grid, reflect the time and day pointed to by the cursor. Notice the mouse arrow is now pointing to some time on Thursday. The fields let us know we are looking at 2:00 P.M.

Users reading disk blocks from this server during these times will be debited two cents for each disk block read. If you have 64 KB block sizes defined, this won't be too much. A utility of 220 KB will need only three blocks read to load. A 4 KB block size, however, means that same utility will require 55 blocks read. This realization may require you to go back and rethink some of your charge rates. It also means it will be difficult to maintain a stable charge rate across multiple servers with different block sizes.

The other options for accounting are set exactly the same way as in this example. Some managers use the Disk Storage option to tag only one block for the week, such as Monday at 6:00 A.M., to get a single charge for the week. This tracks the use of the resource, but without as much time and trouble involved.

After you've set charge rates, you cannot delete a charge rate that's currently on screen. You can click on the Reset button to cancel the latest charge rate change, but that doesn't work often enough. Your other choice is to cover the offending charge rate with a No Charge rate, effectively blanking out the

User Management

FIGURE 10.20

Checking the charge rate on Thursday at 2:00 P.M.

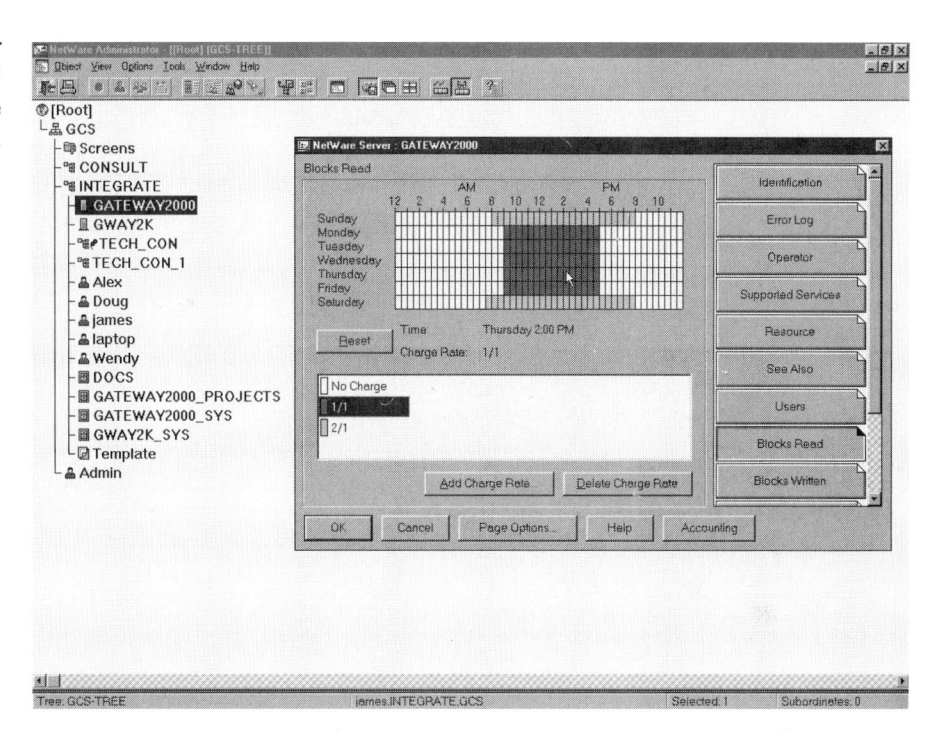

charges. Then you can delete the charge rate. Since no modifications of the charge rates are possible, deletion and re-creation are your only option.

Viewing Accounting Reports with ATOTAL

10.16 IN-A-HURRY

View Accounting Reports with ATOTAL

1. Log in to the network as the Admin user or equivalent.

2. Move your current DOS command line to the SYS:SYSTEM directory of a server with accounting enabled.

3. Type **ATOTAL** from the command line.

4. Read the report on the screen, or pipe the information to a file (for example, ATOTAL > OCTOBER.REP).

Once you start collecting accounting information, there are two things you can do. One is to charge each user's credit balance, which we'll get to next. The other option is to view the totals by day and by week.

This information is not particularly secret, but it's placed in the SYS:SYSTEM directory in a file named NET$ACCT.DAT. This file will grow until you delete it. Here's an example of ATOTAL's display of accounting data:

```
H:\SYSTEM>atotal

ACCOUNTING SERVICES TOTAL UTILITY

10/17/1996:
     Connect time:          99      Server requests:        466
     Blocks read:          148      Blocks written:
     Blocks/day:           399



10/18/1996:
     Connect time:        1717      Server requests:     107333
     Blocks read:        12426      Blocks written:       18863
     Blocks/day:         15771



10/19/1996:
     Connect time:        1742      Server requests:        370
     Blocks read:          111      Blocks written:
     Blocks/day:         24450



Totals for week:
     Connect time:        3558      Server requests:     108169
Press any key to continue ... ('C' for continuous)
```

When used by itself, the ATOTAL information provides a way to track server usage over time. Plotting this information will quickly show server activity. The results will help you to better reallocate resources among servers so that one server won't be overloaded. It is not necessary to set charge rates for users to get the information in this table.

Network-Usage Charges: Friend or Foe?

Personally, I don't care for this accounting business and charge rates on resources. Finding ways to justify the budget for new network technology and keep up with growing demand is a problem for some companies. However, I don't feel that penalizing users for relying on the network to do their job will encourage them to think fondly of the network. What's next, a butt tax for office chairs?

You don't need to charge users to track server usage. I much prefer the server-usage method of justifying network budgets. You can show the usage trend per server, such as connect time or disk reads and writes, is up. If it isn't up, you can blame the old, slow network that server is on, and claim people are avoiding the network because the poor performance is hurting their productivity. Improvements are needed either way.

Claims that charging for resources forces users to keep personal information and games off the network don't wash. It doesn't cost the user money; it just costs the department some of its (funny money) budget. If you force departments to pay for such things as disk space, they're likely to go outside and buy their own hard disks, and possibly even servers.

Our job as network computing providers is not to police what goes across the wire; the department managers must do that. If the employees are slacking off of their work to play games, their performance will suffer and their boss, not you, should investigate. If you allow personal phone callers to leave voice-mail messages at no charge, how can you justify charging for server disk space?

Setting User Account Balances

If accounting is enabled on a server, the users of that server can be assigned a value for each server operation. The screen shown in Figure 10.21 tells you how simple it is to track the server resources consumed by a user.

The Account Balance field shows the remaining credits available for this user. The credits are set on the network resource itself, as described in the previous sections. The Low Balance Limit field shows the credit level that will trigger a warning to the user before the account is disabled. If the Allow

800 Chapter 10 • NetWare 4.1x Administrator Duties and Tools

> ### 10.17 IN-A-HURRY
>
> ### Set the User Account Balance and Low Balance Limit
>
> **1.** Log in to the network as the Admin user or equivalent and open NetWare Administrator.
>
> **2.** Open the User dialog box by double-clicking on the User object name.
>
> **3.** Click on the Account Balance button.
>
> **4.** Click to disable the Allow Unlimited Credit box to enable accounting for the user.
>
> **5.** Set the current Account Balance and the Low Balance Limit.
>
> **6.** Click on OK to save and exit.

Unlimited Credit box is checked, the Account Balance field will show a negative number. This reflects the amount of resources used by that user since accounting was enabled or since the previous number was cleared.

FIGURE 10.21

Accounting for User WENDY

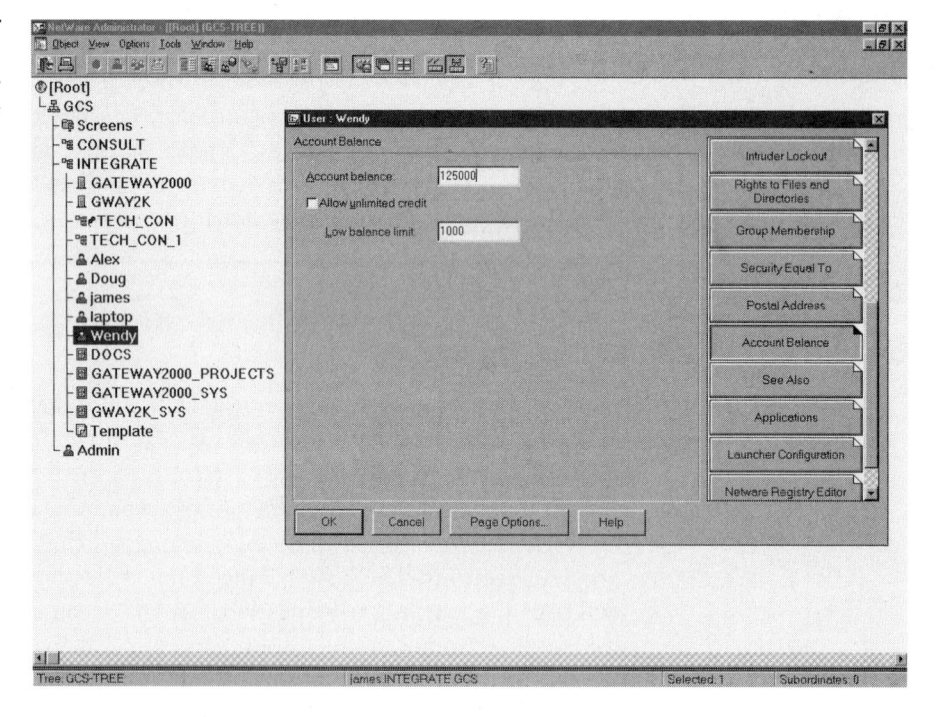

If you wish to track the accounting information for charge-back or overhead calculations, but don't wish to disable users from reaching their network resources, click on the Allow Unlimited Credit box. This will track the information needed for the accounting reports but never lock out users.

Nothing bad happens to the user's information if a user is locked out of the system because of dropping to the level of the Low Balance Limit field. The user will be back in business as soon as an administrator (that means another interruption for you) changes the Account Balance field. Of course, if the person who runs out of credit rates higher than you, and it happens while you're out of town, you may wish you had never activated accounting. Before your boss forces accounting on you, make sure all the possible problems, such as locking users out at the worst possible time, are covered and have an answer waiting.

Limiting User Disk Space

> **10.18 IN-A-HURRY**
>
> **Set the User Disk Space Limit**
>
> 1. Log in to the network as the Admin user or equivalent and open NetWare Administrator.
> 2. Locate the Volume object in the NDS tree, highlight it, and press Enter to open the Volume Information page.
> 3. Click on the User Space Limits command button.
> 4. Use the Browser button to choose the search context.
> 5. Click on Search Entire Tree to check for all volume disk space users, regardless of context.
> 6. Highlight a user and click on Modify to set or change that user's volume space restrictions.
> 7. Click on OK to save and exit.

Here's where you catch the disk hogs, and tie them up if you desire. Setting disk space limits has a much more direct effect than charging back to the department, since the user will personally run out of disk space. The effect of reaching your disk limit is the same as emptying your bank account: no more. The disk will be full as far as that particular user is concerned. This limit is set on a per-volume basis, even more focused than the server.

The capabilities of NDS will allow watching the disk space for users scattered about the network, but that will take quite a bit more development. I would be surprised if some third-party software developer isn't busy at this moment, working on software to query NDS and put this information into a report.

There are some interesting touches in the example shown in Figure 10.22. First, notice the Search Context field is set to [Root], at the top of the network's Organization. This means, when we check the Search Entire Subtree box, we'll get this container and all subcontainers. Since both of our lab Organizational Units are under the GCS container under the [Root], this search catches everyone in the network allowed to use this volume.

FIGURE 10.22

Checking (and potentially clamping) a disk hog

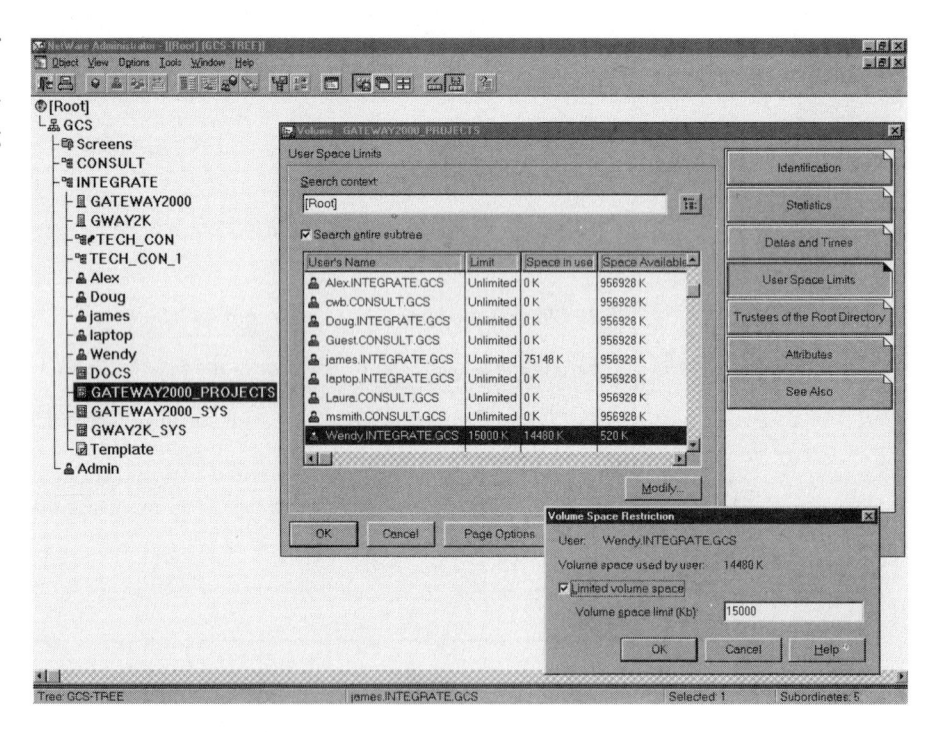

All the disk space numbers are in kilobytes, meaning 1000 of them make a megabyte. The default is to allow all users unlimited disk space, and that works fine for most networks. However, when space is getting tight, taking an inventory of disk space per volume may show a user consuming hundreds of megabytes. The Space in Use column shows the amount of disk space owned by the user, even when that user's space is not limited.

The Space Available column shows the same amount, 956,928 KB, available for everyone. That's because any one person can use that much space, not because all people can use that much space. NetWare makes no space restrictions by default; you must make those changes here. If you don't change the settings, the first ones to fill nearly a gigabyte will get that gigabyte to themselves, and everyone else will go without.

The Volume Space Restriction dialog box opened for our friend Wendy is about to make her available disk space the same as the DOS partition on a file server: 15 MB. When she uses the DIR command anywhere on the GATEWAY2000_PROJECTS volume, it will display the disk space available as 520 KB (15,000 KB — 14,480 KB).

In larger networks, it's much quicker to check one container than to check the current container and all containers below that. However, the query doesn't generate enough traffic to noticeably slow the network, and it's much easier to look at all users of a volume at once.

> *Currently, NetWare provides no way to print this information. Check your dealer for third-party report software that can do this.*

Using UIMPORT to Move Employee Database Records into NDS

UIMPORT (User Import) feeds ASCII data from an existing database into the NDS database. Do you have thousands of students enrolling into your school who need network access? This utility will help you with these tasks:

- Create User objects in the NDS database.
- Update existing User object properties in your NDS database.
- Delete User objects from the NDS database.

There are some considerations, of course, when creating your ASCII file. Every database can create an ASCII file, but the separators used to tell NDS where one record stops and the next record starts can be a problem. If you have punctuation such as commas in your database, you can't use comma-delimited ASCII files. If you do, NDS won't know which comma is for a new record and which is for the last-name and first-name separator. You can use the caret (^) as a separator rather than a comma or question mark.

Once the ASCII file is clean, and you have the records selected, you must tell NDS which of the many properties for the new User objects will be filled in, and which will be skipped and left empty. This is done by the Import Control File. This file can be created by any text editor under DOS, Windows, or OS/2, as long as it will create an ASCII file. There are two types of information in the Import Control File:

- Control parameters that define the characters used in the data file and dictate how the data is updated.

- Field definitions that determine which fields in the NDS database will be given the data.

Control parameters go first, followed by the field definitions. A small Import Control File might look like this:

```
Import control
  Name context=.freshman.students
  Separator=^
  User template=y
Fields
  Last name
  Name
  Telephone
```

Here we are telling the NDS database that the field separator is the caret, and we will apply the Template for the container. The parameters are not case-sensitive, but the format is important. Just like the NET.CFG file, the headings must be flush left, with the entries indented at least one tab or space. (Make it at least two spaces so you don't miss one and cause yourself extra problems.)

Just as when you're creating a new user with NetWare Administrator, two fields are mandatory: the user's login name (Name) and last name (Last Name). If you are updating existing users, only the Name field is mandatory. The fields can be any and/or all properties of a user. The list includes Account Balance, Account Has Expiration Data, Allow Unlimited Credit, Grace Logins Allowed, Group Membership, Home Directory, and every other user information field.

Some of these fields are single-valued, meaning only one bit of information (for example, a name) can be entered. Other fields are multivalued, meaning multiple entries are allowed (for example, Group Membership). Check the manual and the README files for the latest information on the fields and their allowable entries.

You can't have data without a corresponding field definition in the Import Control File. If you have used this utility with an earlier version of NetWare 4, be aware that many of the field names have changed. Check the manual and the README files once again for the latest information.

The syntax for the DOS command is:

```
UIMPORT [control_file] [data_file] [/C]
```

This assumes you have both files in the same directory. If they are not, you'll need to use the full path names for the files. The /C says to write the screen output continuously (without it, you'll be hitting "any key" forever). If you prefer to route the output to a file, use this syntax:

```
UIMPORT [control_file] [data_file] >users\james\uimport.log
```

UIMPORT will take hours to run large files, and will slow your server performance because of the amount of NDS churning required. Run this at night and come in early to repair any server malfunctions that occur. (Nothing should go wrong, of course, but gremlins bite everyone now and then.)

During the first pass or two, you might have some problems getting the separators and field information correct. No automatic program transfer like this works the first time or every time. Using commas as separators guarantees you extra aggravation, because the exported database will contain spurious characters all over the place. If you have a large database to import, first bring in just a few records to get the bugs worked out.

Using NCUPDATE to Configure Non-Client32 Stations

We've spoken several times about the need to update each user's NET.CFG file after moving a container. Novell engineers, not relishing the fall-out if network administrators were forced to update each file by hand, developed the NCUPDATE program.

This utility reads the location of the NET.CFG used to load the VLM programs during client software initialization. Since these client files can (but probably shouldn't) be placed anywhere on the local system, NCUPDATE displays the path on the screen as it updates the client.

Run from the container login script the majority of the time, NCUPDATE needs just a small amount of code to work. Here's an example, assuming we changed the Organizational Unit TECH_CON to TECH_CON_1:

```
IF LOGIN_ALIAS_CONTEXT = Y THEN BEGIN
  MAP INS S1:=GATEWAY2000_SYS:PUBLIC
  #NCUPDATE /NP
  MAP DEL S1:
END
```

The first line quickly checks for one detail: is this person's login container now an Alias rather than the real container? Remember, we need this line to make sure users that connect through a moved container can find their login scripts properly. This does not change any container information that does not relate to login.

Assuming the user does meet the condition, we branch into the next three lines. A mapped drive to a particular PUBLIC directory is set, guaranteeing the user has access to the NCUPDATE program. The second line runs the NCUPDATE utility with the /NP switch. NP means No Prompt, automatically updating the NET.CFG file. If you execute the utility without the /NP switch, the users will have a choice. That's probably not a good idea in this situation. If you give them a choice, you'll need to explain to them why they have a choice and what their options are. It's more efficient here to just change their NET.CFG files automatically.

The MAP DEL S1: disconnects the PUBLIC drive mapped earlier, and END drops out of this little program loop. If you have more lines in the container login script, they would start after the END line. If you don't have any more commands in the container login script, the script ends and the login process continues.

This script should be left in effect long enough to convert all the users. Once all the NET.CFG files have been updated, you can delete the Alias to the new container name (you can update the login script using NetWare Administration or NETADMIN). Then you'll find the last two people that somehow never logged in and had their files updated, because they'll call you and complain that the network is broken.

Remember users in containers subordinate to the newly renamed container. They will need to update their NET.CFG files as well. Make sure all of them are converted before you remove the NCUPDATE code from the container login script.

Besides the /NP option to specify that you don't want to have the program ask permission to update the NET.CFG file, you can use these options:

- NCUPDATE /? from the command line shows the help information but does not execute the program.

- NCUPDATE /VER shows the version number of the file and the files it uses when running but does not execute the program.

Server Management

NETWARE 4.1X HAS moved from the server-bound approach used in NetWare 3 to a network-wide, global approach. But the engines for all this worldliness are still the servers, busily supporting the replicated NDS database, managing the disk drives that make up the volumes, and connecting to the clients across the network cabling.

A Hollywood director would move the viewpoint from the server to the enterprise network, like pulling the camera up and away from a single car to show the entire highway. Soon, however, the focus would come back down to the hero, forcing his car ever faster. In our movie, that hero is you, forcing the server ever faster. If the car dies, the highway backs up, and something bad happens to our hero. If the server dies, the network backs up, and your phone rings with calls from angry users.

Just as the movie hero checks the car gauges, so must you check the gauges of your network. Your primary gauge is the MONITOR.NLM program. Your turbo-booster is the SERVMAN.NLM program, included within the MONITOR program starting with NetWare 4.11. Your toolkit includes DSMERGE.NLM, DSREPAIR.NLM, the DSTRACE function, INSTALL.NLM, and a few other assorted commands.

RCONSOLE for Remote Console Control

Unless you enjoy hunkering down in a small computer room squatting over and around several servers, learn to use the RCONSOLE (Remote Console) utility. This client/server application runs both on the server (REMOTE.NLM and RSPX.NLM) and on your local DOS workstation (RCONSOLE.EXE).

The server part must be started before the client can make a connection. If you have the RCONSOLE.EXE and supporting files on your local workstation, you are not required to be logged in to NDS to run RCONSOLE.

RCONSOLE allows you to:

- Execute all console commands remotely.
- List directories in the NetWare and DOS partitions of the server.
- Edit text files in either the NetWare or DOS partitions of the server.
- Transfer files from your workstation to the server, but not vice versa.
- Down and/or reboot the server.
- Install or upgrade NetWare.

There's nothing you can do at the server console that you can't do with RCONSOLE. Using remote access in this manner allows you to leave the keyboard and monitor off the server, increasing the server's security. Taking care of catastrophic failures will require an attached keyboard and monitor, but most of the time, you'll be fine without them, assuming your server PC boots without a keyboard attached.

Configuring REMOTE at the Server

There are two steps in configuring the server for remote access. You must start the REMOTE program, with or without a password. A password is preferred, and you have an option of using an encrypted password. You must then start either the RSPX.NLM program for access across the network, or AIOCOMX.NLM (or other communication port driver, depending on your server hardware), AIO.NLM, and RS232.NLM. The earlier ACONSOLE.NLM (Async Console) in NetWare 3 has given way to the beefed-up RCONSOLE.

At the server console colon prompt, type

```
LOAD REMOTE <password>
```

and press Enter. Then type

```
LOAD RSPX
```

and press Enter.

Until you encrypt the password, the password you give at the console is the one you must type when making a remote connection. NetWare 4.1*x* no longer allows the Supervisor password to unlock the REMOTE program, so if you want a password, you must specify that password. These commands should be placed at the end of the AUTOEXEC.NCF program so remote access is configured every time the server starts.

For an encrypted password, you must run the REMOTE program and provide your password, letting the system generate the encrypted password. For connection, you must then provide the encrypted password result. (The password *good* came out 0A137773E4AEAFFA3B on my system.) Every time you load REMOTE on that server, you must use the encrypted password. A better idea is to let the system save the command to load the REMOTE program and the encrypted password automatically by placing it in a specially created SYS:\SYSTEM\LDREMOTE.NCF file. Then, rather than typing

```
LOAD REMOTE -E 0A137773E4AEAFFA3B
```

you can type

```
LDREMOTE
```

Since LDREMOTE is a batch file-type program, you don't need the LOAD command. You must then either add the appropriate command to enable LAN or async connections. You can add those commands to the LDREMOTE.NCF program, but if you generate another encrypted password, the new file will overwrite your modified file.

To disable remote connections, you can use the command:

```
REMOTE LOCK OUT
```

This is best done at the physical console, although it does work from a remote connection. Once that remote connection is broken, however, the console remains locked and you can't get back in. To enable remote connections, use:

```
REMOTE UNLOCK
```

RCONSOLE from the Client Side

Once the remote connection software is loaded at the server, the client part is fairly simple. From a DOS prompt, type

```
RCONSOLE
```

and press Enter.

A screen will appear, asking your choice of connection type: Asynchronous or SPX. On LANs, the answer is SPX. A screen similar to Figure 10.23 will appear, listing all the servers answering the broadcast request from the RCONSOLE program.

FIGURE 10.23

The server list for RCONSOLE connections

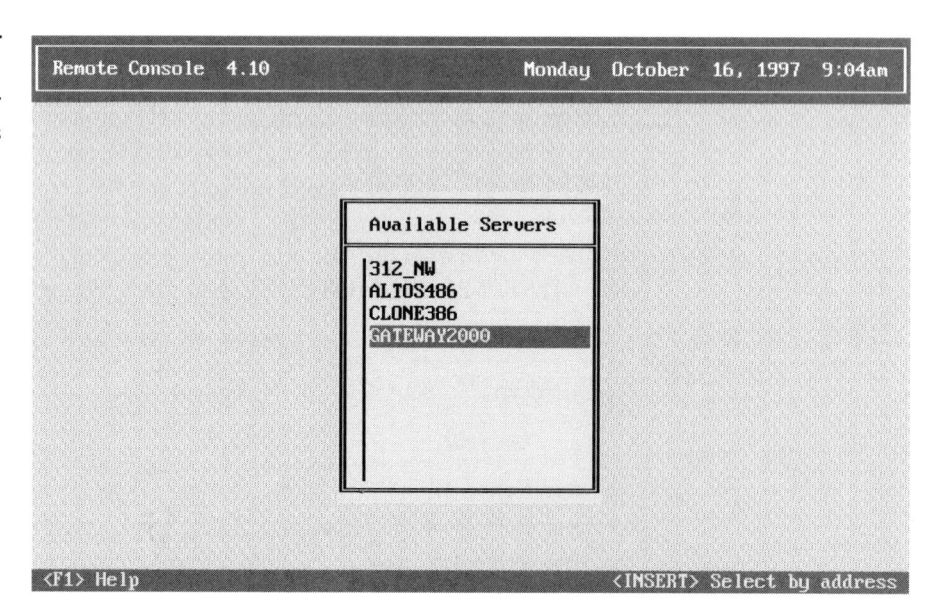

```
Remote Console  4.10                      Monday  October  16, 1997  9:04am




                        ┌─ Available Servers ─┐
                        │ 312_NW              │
                        │ ALTOS486            │
                        │ CLONE386            │
                        │ GATEWAY2000         │
                        │                     │
                        │                     │
                        │                     │
                        └─────────────────────┘




 <F1> Help                                        <INSERT> Select by address
```

Notice there is no mention of containers or contexts with the server names. RCONSOLE bypasses NDS and speaks directly to the server. You can connect directly to a specific server, skipping the pick list in Figure 10.23 by giving its name with the command, as in:

    RCONSOLE GATEWAY2000

Whether you pick from the list or go directly to the server, the next step is to provide the password configured for that server. Type in the password given when you loaded REMOTE on the server, and you will immediately become a remote console.

There are some keystrokes that you need for your remote console work:

Alt+F1   Opens the Available Options menu overlay.

Alt+F2   Exits RCONSOLE.

Alt+F3   Moves to the next server console screen.

Alt+F4   Moves to the previous server console screen.

Alt+F5   Shows the network address of the RCONSOLE workstation.

The Ctrl+Escape combination on the server that opens the Current Screens menu does not work with RCONSOLE. Neither does the Alt+Escape combination to roll through the screens. The up and down arrows to scroll through previously entered commands do, however, work remotely.

RCONSOLE Available Options Menu

Everything you need in RCONSOLE can be done from the Available Options menu called by the Alt+F1 combination. (If you're like me, and have trouble remembering which keystrokes work with which program, write Alt+F1 somewhere on your cubicle wall.)

Figure 10.24 shows the Available Options menu, overlaying the Help screen for the REMOTE console command. Move the highlight bar with the cursor keys and press Enter to activate any menu item.

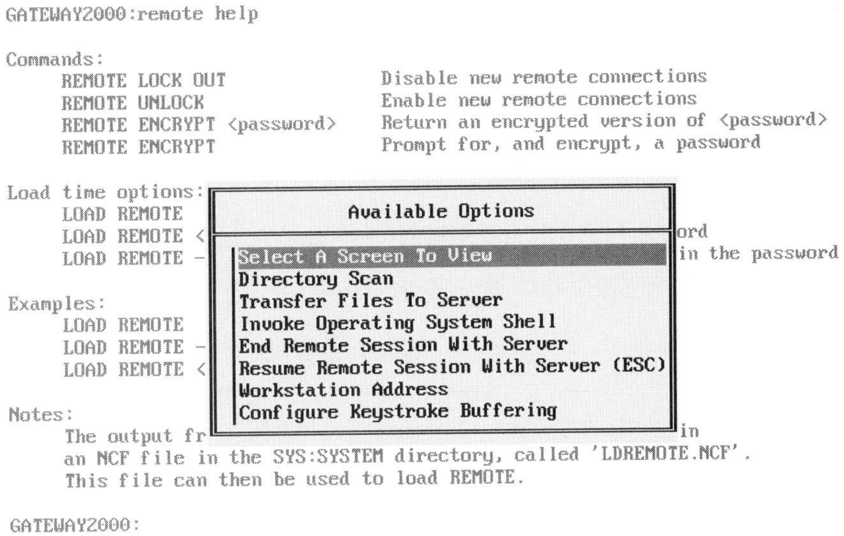

FIGURE 10.24

The RCONSOLE menu

```
GATEWAY2000:remote help

Commands:
    REMOTE LOCK OUT              Disable new remote connections
    REMOTE UNLOCK                Enable new remote connections
    REMOTE ENCRYPT <password>    Return an encrypted version of <password>
    REMOTE ENCRYPT               Prompt for, and encrypt, a password

Load time options:
    LOAD REMOTE
    LOAD REMOTE <            ┌─────── Available Options ───────┐         ord
    LOAD REMOTE -            │ Select A Screen To View         │         in the password
                             │ Directory Scan                  │
Examples:                    │ Transfer Files To Server        │
    LOAD REMOTE              │ Invoke Operating System Shell   │
    LOAD REMOTE -            │ End Remote Session With Server  │
    LOAD REMOTE <            │ Resume Remote Session With Server (ESC) │
                             │ Workstation Address             │
Notes:                       │ Configure Keystroke Buffering   │
    The output fr            └─────────────────────────────────┘         in
    an NCF file in the SYS:SYSTEM directory, called 'LDREMOTE.NCF'.
    This file can then be used to load REMOTE.

GATEWAY2000:
```

The menu items are fairly straightforward. Let's take a quick look at each option:

- **Select a Screen to View:** Opens a submenu of all active console screens. Move the highlight bar to a screen and press Enter to move immediately to that screen.

- **Directory Scan:** Lists the files and subdirectories in any directory on the server, both the NetWare and DOS partitions. To reference the DOS partition, use C:\< *directory name*>.

- **Transfer Files to Server:** Copies files from any local or mapped workstation drive to any directory on any server partition. Long files show the progress of the amazingly slow transfer process.

- **Invoke Operating System Shell:** Exits to the DOS shell, but RCONSOLE takes so much memory this has limited value.

- **End Remote Session with Server:** Disconnects with server (same function as Alt+F2).

- **Resume Remote Session with Server:** Clears the menu off the screen and returns you to the remote connection (same function as Escape).

- **Workstation Address:** Shows the network and local address of your workstation (same function as Alt+F5).

- **Configure Keystroke Buffering:** Normally, each keystroke is sent immediately to the server. Because of async connections, you may wish to control the delivery of your text. The three options are:

  - Keystroke delay (send when keyboard is idle).
  - Manual keystroke send (Alt+F8 to send).
  - On demand buffering (Alt+F9 to enter a buffered command).

Most of the time, you'll use RCONSOLE across the network to connect to a server in your building. You'll connect to the server, check the status of one or more NLMs, check the MONITOR program, and disconnect. If your servers are ten floors up and the elevator is broken, this utility will save you a workout.

Here's a trick to reboot a server remotely, using RCONSOLE:

- Load RCONSOLE and connect to the server in question.
- Move to the console prompt and remove DOS from memory: type **REMOVE DOS**.
- Type **DOWN** to stop the server.
- Reboot by typing **EXIT**.

When DOS is removed from the server memory, the EXIT command forces a reboot. If your server is configured to boot DOS and go straight into NetWare, this system works great. And there are no stairs to climb.

MONITOR Almost Everything

The MONITOR screen is your primary place to check the health of your server. You may only rarely use another server utility. When checking a new server on a new network, use the MONITOR program before you do anything else. Half the time, it will provide the answers to your questions (and if it doesn't, running it gives you some time to think of what to do next).

Many network supervisors leave MONITOR running all the time. After 10 minutes, the snake appears as a screen-saver, blanking the MONITOR display. The snake is an ASCII-graphic creature made of various gray-scale blocks following a bright red head. If you load MONITOR with the L for Lock option, the snake appears in one minute. The longer and faster the snake goes, the busier the network. If you do use the Lock option, the Admin password unlocks the MONITOR screen. The other MONITOR load option is N for no screen-saver at all. In other words, no snake.

> **TIP**
>
> *It's a good idea to check the MONITOR information now and then. Some network managers take screenshots of server-information screens, such as those that show redirected blocks, cache utilization, and processor utilization, to have a benchmark for later reference. You're a busy person; don't believe you can remember your cache utilization statistics from four months ago. Make notes or make screenshots, but keep some record of the health of your network as shown by MONITOR.*

The General Information Screen and What It Means

10.19 IN-A-HURRY

View Server Information with MONITOR

1. Type **LOAD MONITOR** from the console prompt.

2. Press Tab once or twice to get to the Available Options menu.

3. From the Available Options menu, choose the menu option for the utilization data you want to view: Cache, Memory, Processor, or Resource Utilization.

The opening screen of MONITOR holds the most useful information. See Figure 10.25 for a look at the screen from GATEWAY2000.

The GATEWAY2000 server has 32 MB of RAM and a 1600 MB (1.6 GB) hard disk. This equates to 7029 buffers of 4 KB each, of which just over 5000 are usually available. The number fluctuates as NLMs take and return server RAM for various operations.

Note that GATEWAY2000 has almost nothing loaded on it in the way of NLMs. GWAY2K, the identical twin, runs the NetWare Web Server and

FIGURE 10.25
Server secrets unveiled

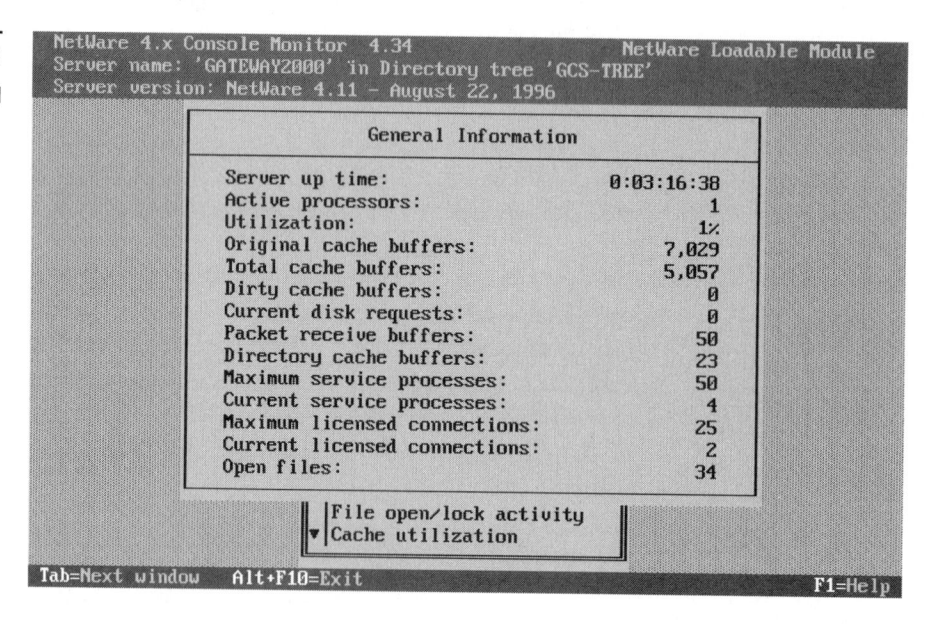

```
NetWare 4.x Console Monitor  4.34                    NetWare Loadable Module
Server name: 'GATEWAY2000' in Directory tree 'GCS-TREE'
Server version: NetWare 4.11 - August 22, 1996

                    ┌─────── General Information ───────┐
                    │ Server up time:          0:03:16:38 │
                    │ Active processors:                1 │
                    │ Utilization:                     1% │
                    │ Original cache buffers:       7,029 │
                    │ Total cache buffers:          5,057 │
                    │ Dirty cache buffers:              0 │
                    │ Current disk requests:            0 │
                    │ Packet receive buffers:          50 │
                    │ Directory cache buffers:         23 │
                    │ Maximum service processes:       50 │
                    │ Current service processes:        4 │
                    │ Maximum licensed connections:    25 │
                    │ Current licensed connections:     2 │
                    │ Open files:                      34 │
                    └─────────────────────────────────────┘
                       │ File open/lock activity │
                       │▼Cache utilization       │
Tab=Next window    Alt+F10=Exit                              F1=Help
```

IPX/IP Gateway, among other things, and has only 3386 of the original 7029 buffers available. See why I tell you to get more memory?

The ALTOS486 server used during the first iteration of this book had a 500 MB disk, but it also had 32 MB of RAM. The original cache buffer number there was 7620, with about 5450 available. NetWare 4.10 is slightly more conservative than 4.11, but not that much.

Server CLONE386, the underpowered server with only 8 MB of RAM and a 312 MB disk that lived out its usefulness just after finishing the 4.10 version of this book, had 1487 original cache buffers, of which only 740 or so were available. (Warning: that server was a test to show it can be done, not an attempt to sell an 8 MB server to unsuspecting users.)

Across the top of the MONITOR screen, the version of the NetWare server (4.11) and of the MONITOR program (4.34) are listed, along with the fact that this is a NetWare Loadable Module, in the upper right. The server name and tree are also listed at the top. The last line in the top information section gives the server operating system version again, along with the date of manufacture. This information will be important as you upgrade pieces of your server operating system over time, and Novell support asks what versions you have.

You expand the General Information window by pressing the Tab key, or waiting just ten seconds. The window will expand itself, covering some of the Available Options menu. Press Tab again (or Escape) to return it to a smaller size.

The fields on the MONITOR General Information screen are described in Table 10.1.

TABLE 10.1 Fields on MONITOR's General Information Screen

FIELD	DESCRIPTION
Server Up Time	Days, hours, minutes, and seconds since the server was started.
Active Processors	The number of CPUs in this server (new with NetWare 4.11).
Utilization	Percentage of time the CPU is busy. This normally hovers under 5%, unless you have NLMs that do active processing, such as gateways and databases.
Original Cache Buffers	The number of 4 KB buffer blocks contained in your server memory minus room for the operating system and DOS. This number is rarely high enough.
Total Cache Buffers	The number of buffers available for file caching after loading all the NLM programs and other server housekeeping programs. This number is never high enough.

TABLE 10.1 (cont.)

Fields on MONITOR's General Information Screen

FIELD	DESCRIPTION
Dirty Cache Buffers	Buffers waiting to be written to a server disk.
Current Disk Requests	Number of disk requests waiting for service.
Packet Receive Buffers	1 KB buffers that hold client requests while the server processes them. The default is 10, but the server allocates more as needed.
Directory Cache Buffers	Buffers dedicated to holding the server directory entries, speeding access to files since the directory need not be read from the disk when a request comes. The server allocates more as needed.
Maximum Service Processes	Largest number of task handlers, or processes, available for servicing client requests. Once the server allocates this maximum number, the number can not be reclaimed. This number can be lowered in SERVMAN or by using a SET command, freeing memory for cache buffers. When there is no more memory to allocate more processes, performance suffers.
Current Service Processes	Current processes available for servicing client requests.
Maximum Licensed Connections	Number of concurrent users licensed for this server, able to use file and print services.
Current Licensed Connections	Number of active users attached to the NetWare server. Unlicensed connections from other network resources that just use NDS but not logged in do not count against your user licenses.
Open Files	Number of files accessed by the server and other clients.

Some of these numbers have a direct impact on server performance. The more memory, the better performance. How much is enough? Superserver manufacturers are advertising the ability to support 1 GB of server RAM. My guess is that 1 GB is enough—for awhile.

If your total cache buffers number is suffering because of many NLMs, you need more memory. The amount of total cache buffers available is probably the quickest indicator of server health and performance.

Cache Utilization

The Available Options menu option to get to the important cache information is labeled, clearly enough, Cache Utilization. Highlight and press Enter, and you will see a screen much like the one shown in Figure 10.26.

The most important indicator for more RAM is the Long Term Cache Hits listing. If this number is below 98%, Novell engineers suggest you add more RAM. (Of course, Novell engineers suggest you add more RAM for almost every problem, but statistically they will be right once in a while.)

Cache use by NetWare is one of the biggest performance advantages of the operating system over its competitors. The cache is a temporary storage area for files read from the disk. Once a file is read from the disk, it stays in the server memory for a time, guessing that you may need that same information again. If you do, then the next request comes from server RAM rather than being read from the disk, saving tremendous amounts of time. It's common to sort a large database from your workstation, and have all of the database file stay in the cache, finishing 20 times faster than reading the file from the disk.

The number is averaged for every cache request since the server has started. It is the most accurate reflection of cache utilization, much better than the Short Term Cache Hits and even the Total Cache Buffers number from the previous screen. After all, if all the file requests are being handled from cache, whatever amount you have must be enough.

FIGURE 10.26

Checking the cache

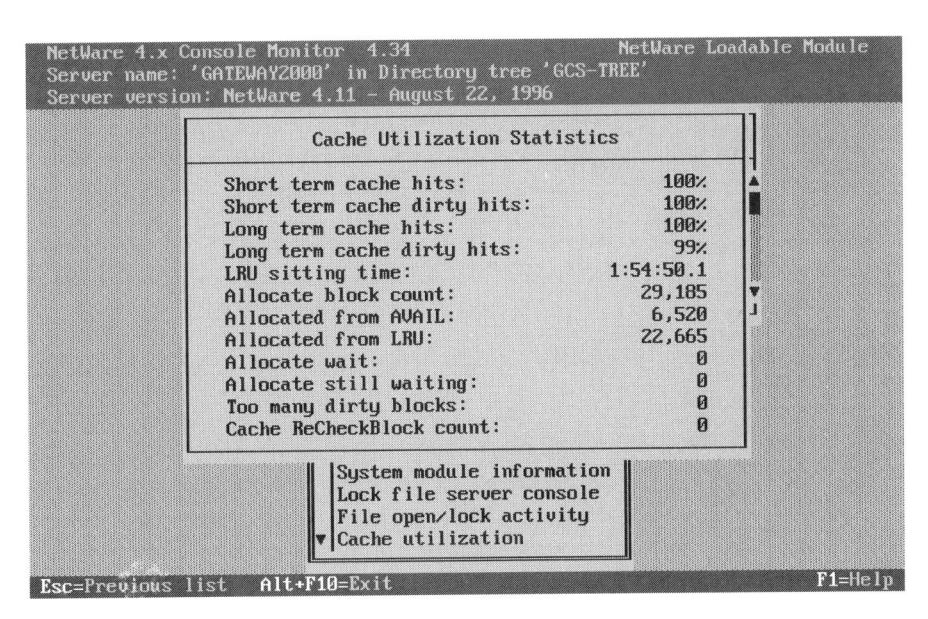

The fields on the Cache Utilization Statistics screen are described in Table 10.2.

TABLE 10.2 Fields on MONITOR's Cache Utilization Screen

FIELD	DESCRIPTION
Short Term Cache Hits	Percentage of disk-block requests serviced by the cache in the last second.
Short Term Cache Dirty Hits	Percentage of disk blocks requested in the last second that were in cache, but changed since being read from the disk.
Long Term Cache Hits	Your trigger to get more memory. Below 98% is failing.
Long Term Cache Dirty Hits	Percentage of disk blocks requested since the server started that were in cache but waiting to be written to the disk.
LRU Sitting Time	Least Recently Used, indicating the age of a block that is the oldest in the LRU list. Higher times are better, indicating there is plenty of memory to service the clients. Time is in days, hours, minutes, and seconds, including tenths.
Allocate Block Count	Total block requests since the server was started.
Allocated from AVAIL	Number of cache-block requests filled by available (not being used) blocks.
Allocated from LRU	Number of cache-block requests filled by blocks from the LRU list of used cache blocks.
Allocate Wait	Instances where a cache request waited while a block from the LRU list was made available. If this number increases regularly, you need more RAM.
Allocate Still Waiting	Number of times the operating system is forced to wait for an LRU block. If less than 7 to 10 minutes, your blocks are being reused too quickly. Add more RAM.
Too Many Dirty Blocks	Number of block-write requests delayed by an overloaded write queue. This can be caused by a busy disk channel. Add more RAM.
Cache ReCheckBlock Count	Times a cache request had to try again because the target block was still being used. If this number is steadily increasing, add more RAM.

As you look over the descriptions in Table 10.2, you should recognize a recurring theme in the recommendations. I hate to sound like a broken record (CD with a tracking error for you kids), but more RAM cures many server ills. The move toward huge disks eats RAM, since directory file cache settings are based on disk size. More applications running on the server take more RAM, since the program must have a segment of RAM in which to run.

The move for companies to replace two or three NetWare 3 servers with one NetWare 4 server means that one server must have the RAM of the earlier three, plus some to support NDS. This is why I advise you to put RAM on every budget request for everything else.

RAM needs go up over time, but not because the software changes. Every server adds disk space and NLMs now and then. Each time you add something, you check the RAM and it doesn't look too bad. Then you add another NLM and another few users, and it doesn't look much worse than it did last time. Unfortunately, your available RAM for file cache is now about half what you had when you started the server the first time. Your server gets gradually slower and flakier until you fix things. And how do you fix things? Add more RAM.

Processor Utilization

Some people worry constantly about the server CPU. Part of this worry comes from competitors, such as Banyan's Vines and Microsoft's NT Advanced Server, who claim that their multiprocessor versions give them an advantage over NetWare's single processor. Unfortunately for Banyan and Microsoft, this isn't necessarily true, especially when you consider the price and performance of these multiprocessor servers versus a single CPU server running NetWare. But to keep up in the RFP (Request For Proposal) checkbox feature war, Novell has released SMP (Symmetric Multi-Processing) NetWare as part of NetWare 4.11. Previously available with NetWare 4.10, but only from the hardware vendors directly, SMP support now comes with every NetWare package.

Most network bottlenecks happen at the disk channel. The server CPU is rarely loaded, unless you are running NLMs on the server that execute as databases and gateways. Even then, people misunderstand the utilization number. When it reaches 100%, things are not going to blow up, the CPU is just working on all barrels. It isn't uncommon to see utilization spike above 100%, because your server processor is probably faster than the benchmark processor used to set the percentages.

820 Chapter 10 · NetWare 4.1x Administrator Duties and Tools

To check the server CPU utilization, choose Processor Utilization from the Available Options menu. You can choose the process or interrupt to view, or press F3 to show CPU utilization for all items.

Figure 10.27 shows a portion of the Processor Utilization screen displaying all processes and interrupts. I loaded the GATEWAY2000 server a bit to get some numbers to jump around. Regardless, notice that the Idle Loop process shows the highest numbers by far.

The columns and the information they represent are:

- **Process Name:** Name of the process or the interrupt number. For instance, Interrupt 10 is the 3C509 Ethernet card in the GATEWAY2000 server.

- **Time:** Time spent executing the code for the process by the CPU. The time for interrupts is the amount of time the CPU spent with the ISR (Interrupt Service Routine) for that interrupt.

- **Count:** The number of times the process ran during the sample period. For interrupts, this is the number of times the interrupt was serviced.

- **Load:** The percentage of the last second the CPU spent on each process or interrupt.

FIGURE 10.27

Viewing processes that affect the CPU

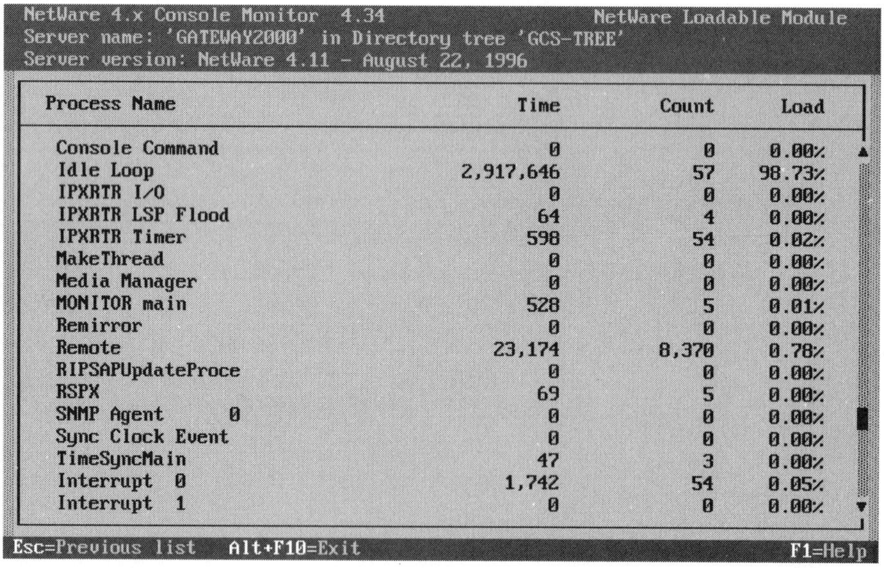

```
NetWare 4.x Console Monitor   4.34              NetWare Loadable Module
Server name: 'GATEWAY2000' in Directory tree 'GCS-TREE'
Server version: NetWare 4.11 - August 22, 1996
```

Process Name	Time	Count	Load
Console Command	0	0	0.00%
Idle Loop	2,917,646	57	98.73%
IPXRTR I/O	0	0	0.00%
IPXRTR LSP Flood	64	4	0.00%
IPXRTR Timer	598	54	0.02%
MakeThread	0	0	0.00%
Media Manager	0	0	0.00%
MONITOR main	528	5	0.01%
Remirror	0	0	0.00%
Remote	23,174	8,370	0.78%
RIPSAPUpdateProce	0	0	0.00%
RSPX	69	5	0.00%
SNMP Agent 0	0	0	0.00%
Sync Clock Event	0	0	0.00%
TimeSyncMain	47	3	0.00%
Interrupt 0	1,742	54	0.05%
Interrupt 1	0	0	0.00%

```
Esc=Previous list    Alt+F10=Exit                              F1=Help
```

These statistics are tracked only while this screen is open. Each interval of time represented on the chart is one second.

You can use the F5 key to tag several of your favorite processes to track, and show them on one concise screen. The last page of the full listing shows the total sample time, overhead required to keep this display updated, and the adjusted sample time (minus the overhead).

Memory Utilization

Available memory is another performance indicator. NLMs use memory as they load, and release it when they unload. Like Microsoft Windows 3.1*x* (and Windows 95, for that matter), however, occasionally some of the memory never gets released. Unlike Windows, NetWare provides an easy way to reclaim that lost memory.

Figure 10.28 shows the detail screen for the IPX NLSP Router. This appears when you choose the Memory Utilization item from MONITOR's Available Options menu, then press Enter on one of the options, although you must use the Tab key to open the window and show all the fields. If you press Escape from this screen, you will see the Allocated Memory for All Modules summary screen. This display shows, strangely enough, all the memory used by all the NLMs on the server.

FIGURE 10.28

Tracking system memory use

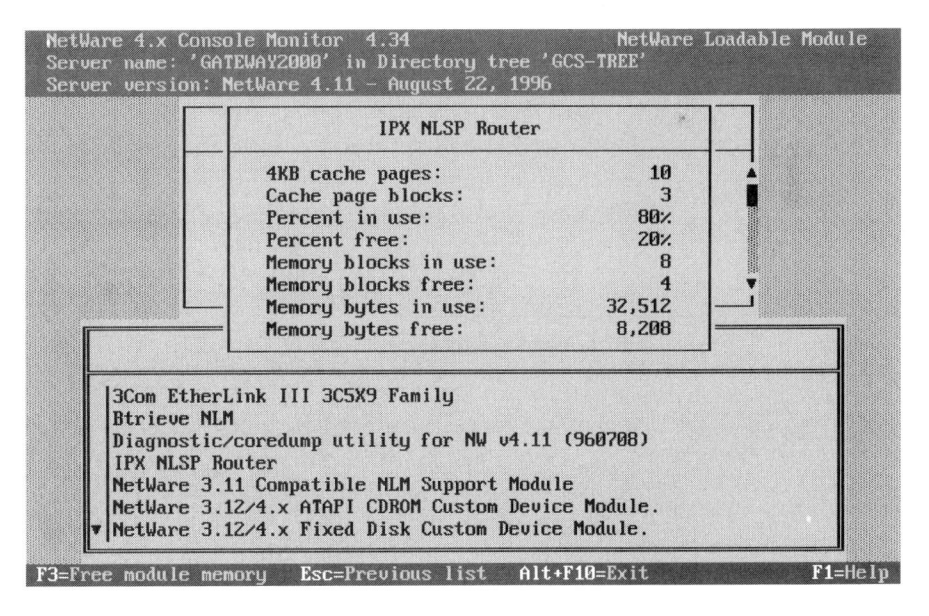

Table 10.3 describes the fields on this screen.

TABLE 10.3	FIELD	DESCRIPTION
Fields on MONITOR's Allocated Memory for All Modules Screen	4KB Cache Pages	Number of 4 KB memory-cache pages available in the memory allocation pool.
	Cache Page Blocks	A cache-block page consists of one, two, or sixty-four 4 KB cache pages (4 KB, 16 KB, 256 KB). This number shows the blocks requested by the system and placed in the allocated memory pool.
	Percent in Use	Percentage of allocated memory.
	Percent Free	Available percentage of allocated memory.
	Memory Blocks in Use	The number of blocks currently used.
	Memory Bytes in Use	Number of bytes currently used.
	Memory Blocks Free	Available memory blocks.
	Memory Bytes Free	Available memory bytes.

Each of the modules listed in the lower box shows the same statistics for its own memory use. When you highlight any one of the system modules, as we did with the NLSP Router, the information in the top window displays module-specific information.

Two memory-release options are explained on the status line at the bottom of the screen: F3 frees memory from the specific module, and F5 frees memory from the entire system. You will find this referred to as "garbage collection" by some, cleaning up the bits of memory strewn here and there. I prefer to think of it as a treasure hunt for more memory.

> *I prefer to think of it as a treasure hunt for more memory.*

Resource Utilization

When you choose Resource Utilization from MONITOR's Available Options menu, the Server Memory Resource Utilization screen appears. Although this screen looks like more server memory information (the main window titled Server Memory Statistics is a good clue), the memory tracked here is used by NLMs only. The operating system forces NLM programs to use a resource tag when they allocate resources, somewhat like tracking books taken from the library. This way, the system can track which module has which memory page.

In Figure 10.29, the top window shows the summary of all server memory with the information displayed two ways. First is the number of bytes allocated to the pool, and second is the percentage of total server memory allocated to the pool.

Table 10.4 describes the fields on this screen.

TABLE 10.4 Fields on MONITOR's Server Memory Resource Utilization Screen	FIELD	DESCRIPTION
	Allocated Memory Pool	Memory reserved for NLM programs. The cache buffer pool allocates memory to NLMs (and hence to this allocated memory pool) dynamically. When the NLM is unloaded, the memory is returned to the cache buffer pool. The Memory Utilization option (see Table 10.3) offers a look at the NLM programs and the memory they have allocated.
	Cache Buffers	The pool of memory currently being used for file caching. This should be the largest pool; if it's less than 50%, consider adding more RAM. If it's below 30%, add more RAM before connections get dropped and the server abends (crashes). This number fluctuates rapidly, depending on NLM usage.
	Cache Movable Memory	Memory directly allocated from the cache buffer pool. It returns to that pool when released. The memory manager of the operating system may move the location of these memory blocks to optimize memory usage, unlike the nonmoveable pool.
	Cache Non-Movable Memory	Used when large blocks of memory are needed. Allocated directly from the cache buffer pool and returned there when released.
	Code and Data Memory	Memory used by the operating system and other NLM programs to store their executable code and data.
	Total Server Work Memory	Sum of the memory pools.

You can use the Tab key, but it doesn't actually expand the data window. The top window border does turn yellow, indicating that it is the active window, but the only thing you can do is press F1 for help.

FIGURE 10.29

Server memory resource utilization

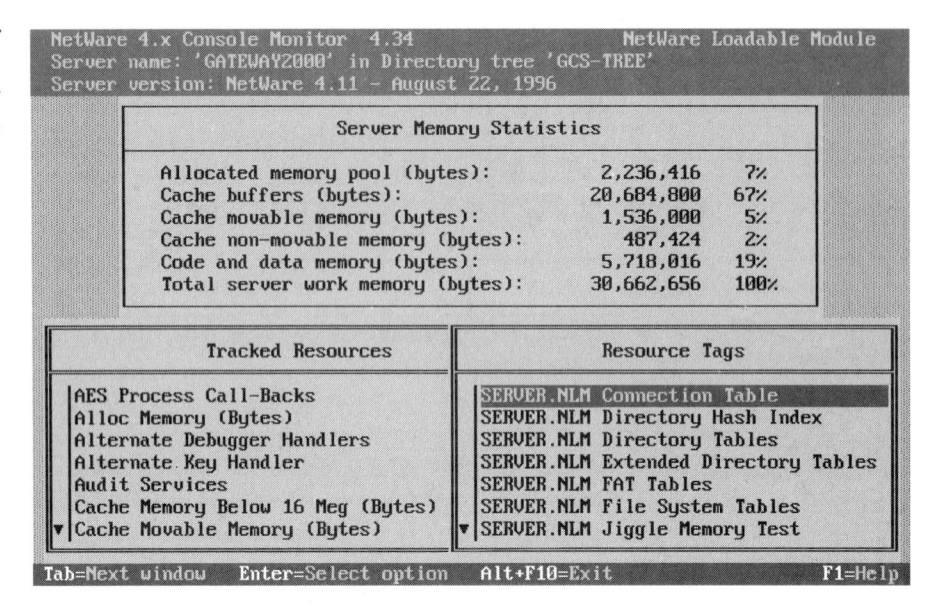

```
NetWare 4.x Console Monitor  4.34                    NetWare Loadable Module
Server name: 'GATEWAY2000' in Directory tree 'GCS-TREE'
Server version: NetWare 4.11 - August 22, 1996

                        Server Memory Statistics
            Allocated memory pool (bytes):      2,236,416    7%
            Cache buffers (bytes):             20,684,800   67%
            Cache movable memory (bytes):       1,536,000    5%
            Cache non-movable memory (bytes):     487,424    2%
            Code and data memory (bytes):       5,718,016   19%
            Total server work memory (bytes):  30,662,656  100%

            Tracked Resources                    Resource Tags
     AES Process Call-Backs              SERVER.NLM Connection Table
     Alloc Memory (Bytes)                SERVER.NLM Directory Hash Index
     Alternate Debugger Handlers         SERVER.NLM Directory Tables
     Alternate Key Handler               SERVER.NLM Extended Directory Tables
     Audit Services                      SERVER.NLM FAT Tables
     Cache Memory Below 16 Meg (Bytes)   SERVER.NLM File System Tables
   ▼ Cache Movable Memory (Bytes)      ▼ SERVER.NLM Jiggle Memory Test

  Tab=Next window    Enter=Select option    Alt+F10=Exit           F1=Help
```

When you highlight an item in the Tracked Resources list and press Enter, the Resource Tags window opens, as you can see in the bottom right of Figure 10.29. The open window refers back to the Cache Movable Memory (Bytes) listing, which is highlighted in pale yellow (sorry, pale yellow is difficult to see in black and white).

Once an item in the Resource Tags list is highlighted, press Enter to see specific details for that resource. The pop-up window tells you two new things: which module allocated that particular resource tag and the memory pool from which it came.

Memory pools are allocated according to a specific memory map, just like your PC but much more reliably than with DOS. The server memory map, from the base of the operating system on, stacks up like this:

Operating system (code and data memory)	Used by the operating system and all NLMs.
Cache nonmoveable memory	Various memory tables, including space for the compression and decompression algorithms.
Cache moveable memory pool	Directory, FAT, connected users, and so on.

Allocation blocks	4 KB blocks set aside for use by NLMs. Each NLM gets its own memory space for loading and for execution. If more space is needed, it's taken from the cache buffers.
Cache buffers	All the leftover memory not needed for everything else. It is used to cache files read from and written to the server disks.

Connection Information

> **10.20 IN-A-HURRY**
>
> **Clear Connections with MONITOR**
>
> **1.** Type **LOAD MONITOR** from the console prompt.
>
> **2.** Choose Connection Information from the Available Options menu.
>
> **3.** From the Active Connections screen, choose the connection to view.
>
> **4.** Choose the Resource Tag to view in detail.

The choices in MONITOR we've covered so far have to do with serious server management. The other seven, taken in order of appearance, may be the ones you use more often. What do you think will happen more often: tracking the memory usage of one NLM or clearing a connection because a user locked up Windows again?

When a user does lock up a program, or leaves for the day with his or her system still connected, the Connection Information screen is the place to take care of the problem. There are ways to see which files are still open, check how long the user has been connected, and disconnect that user, all from your desk.

When you open MONITOR, the default choice of the Available Options menu is Connection Information, which is first in the list. The list is not alphabetical, so Novell engineers obviously felt this was the option you would use the most often.

After opening the Connection Information screen, you will see a list of the active connections. The number to the left of each entry is the connection number, assigned when each user or resource logs in. The names are kept in alphabetical order. Connections with the asterisk in front of the name are NDS connections, not counted against the server license count. They access the NDS database of information on this server, but they don't use the file and

826 Chapter 10 ▪ NetWare 4.1x Administrator Duties and Tools

print resources specific to the server. The Not-Logged-In connection is a user workstation that has not logged in to this server, or has not used a specific resource of this server. Take a look at Figure 10.30 and notice the starred connections versus the normal connections.

To view details of one of the active connections, highlight the connection and press Enter. To delete a connection, highlight it and press Delete. You can choose multiple connections with the F5 key before pressing the Delete key.

The only new feature in this display from several versions back is the addition of the Active Processors entry. Since NetWare 4.11 is the first version from Novell to support multiple processors in off-the-shelf NetWare, there's a reason this line shows up now.

Figure 10.31 shows the information for my workstation. The top window shows connection information. The bottom window, which is partially covered, shows open files. When you first press Enter, the two windows don't overlap. You can press the Tab key to open the information screen.

Table 10.5 describes the fields on the Connection Information screen.

> *On the Connections Information screen, you'll see the term semaphore. A semaphore is an interprocess communication signal used to control access to resources such as multiuser data files. NetWare supervisors never need to worry about semaphores; developers set and control them within programs. NLMs use lots of semaphores.*

FIGURE 10.30

Active connections on GATEWAY2000

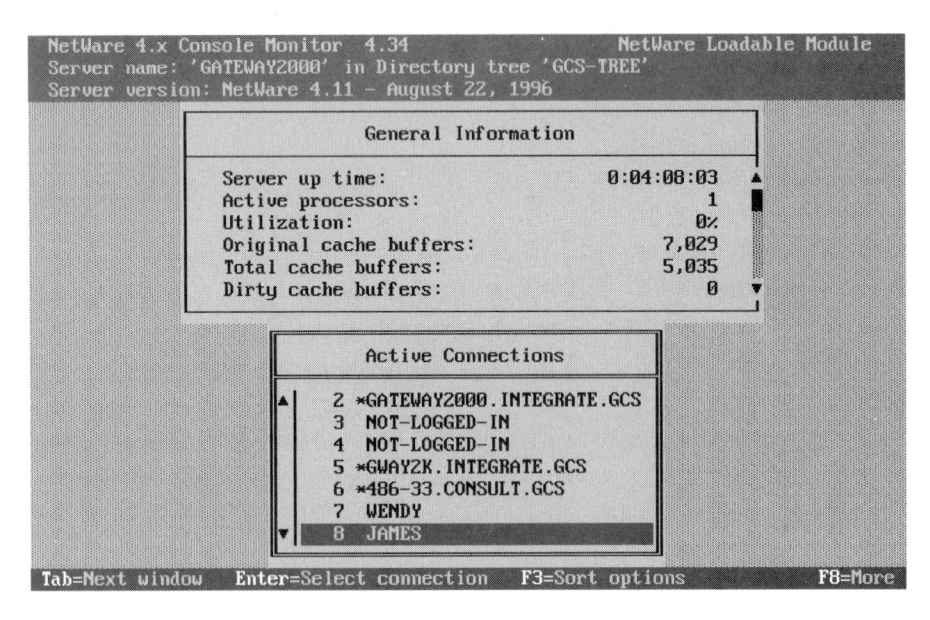

```
NetWare 4.x Console Monitor   4.34                    NetWare Loadable Module
Server name: 'GATEWAY2000' in Directory tree 'GCS-TREE'
Server version: NetWare 4.11 - August 22, 1996

                        General Information
         Server up time:                        0:04:08:03
         Active processors:                             1
         Utilization:                                  0%
         Original cache buffers:                    7,029
         Total cache buffers:                       5,035
         Dirty cache buffers:                           0

                        Active Connections
            2 *GATEWAY2000.INTEGRATE.GCS
            3  NOT-LOGGED-IN
            4  NOT-LOGGED-IN
            5 *GWAY2K.INTEGRATE.GCS
            6 *486-33.CONSULT.GCS
            7  WENDY
            8  JAMES

Tab=Next window    Enter=Select connection    F3=Sort options       F8=More
```

FIGURE 10.31

Checking on my connection

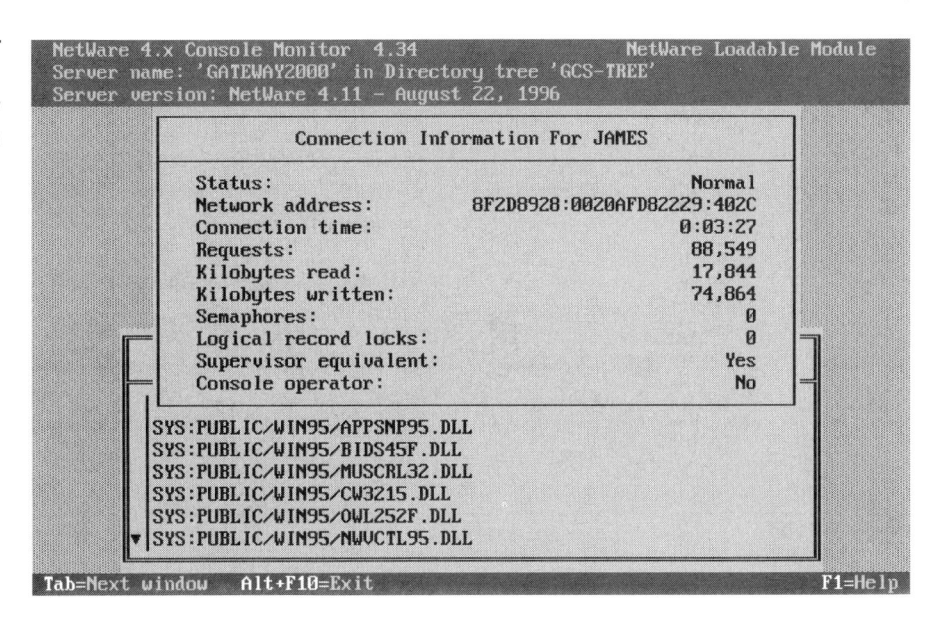

```
NetWare 4.x Console Monitor  4.34            NetWare Loadable Module
Server name: 'GATEWAY2000' in Directory tree 'GCS-TREE'
Server version: NetWare 4.11 - August 22, 1996

              ┌─────── Connection Information For JAMES ───────┐
              │ Status:                                 Normal │
              │ Network address:       8FZD8928:0020AFD82229:402C │
              │ Connection time:                       0:03:27 │
              │ Requests:                               88,549 │
              │ Kilobytes read:                         17,844 │
              │ Kilobytes written:                      74,864 │
              │ Semaphores:                                  0 │
              │ Logical record locks:                        0 │
              │ Supervisor equivalent:                     Yes │
              │ Console operator:                           No │
              └────────────────────────────────────────────────┘
     SYS:PUBLIC/WIN95/APPSNP95.DLL
     SYS:PUBLIC/WIN95/BIDS45F.DLL
     SYS:PUBLIC/WIN95/MUSCRL32.DLL
     SYS:PUBLIC/WIN95/CW3215.DLL
     SYS:PUBLIC/WIN95/OWL252F.DLL
   ▼ SYS:PUBLIC/WIN95/NWVCTL95.DLL

Tab=Next window    Alt+F10=Exit                            F1=Help
```

TABLE 10.5

Fields on MONITOR's Connection Information Screen

FIELD	DESCRIPTION
Status	Possibilities are:
	Not Logged In (client is not authenticated and so does not count against the licensed user count)
	Authenticated (client authorized by NDS but cannot access other resources on the server)
	Normal (authenticated by NDS and currently using a server resource, so this connection counts against the server license count)
	Waiting on a Lock (normal connection waiting for a locked resource, generally a file, to become available)
	Waiting on a Semaphore (normal connection waiting for access to a semaphore-controlled resource)
Network Address	Logical address of the client. Format is *network:node:socket* on the server. The socket number is used to separate server processes or programs in use by each client. The socket number may be the same, or it may be different, depending on the client.
Connection Time	Days, hours, and minutes the user has been connected to this server. If the user isn't logged in to this server, the number will be zero.

TABLE 10.5 (cont.)

Fields on MONITOR's Connection Information Screen

FIELD	DESCRIPTION
Requests	Service requests sent to the server from the client during this connection.
Kilobytes Read	Number of kilobytes read from all the server disks on all volumes during this connection.
Kilobytes Written	Number of kilobytes written to any of the server disks on any volume during this connection.
Semaphores	Number of semaphores in use by the client.
Logical Record Locks	Locks used by the client to restrict access by other users to a file in use by the client.
Supervisor Equivalent	Yes or No, depending on the client's configuration.
Console Operator	Yes or No, depending on the client's configuration.

The bottom window in Figure 10.31 shows the files currently open for the client. The first file opened winds up at the bottom of the list, since all subsequent files appear from the top of the list. If you choose one of the open files and press Enter, another window opens and shows the physical file lock status. More details on file locking will be explained in the "Seeing File Open/Lock Activity" section, coming up in just a bit.

Disk Information

> **10.21 IN-A-HURRY**
>
> **View Disk Information in MONITOR**
>
> 1. Type **LOAD MONITOR** from the console prompt.
> 2. Choose Disk Information from the Available Options menu.
> 3. From the System Disk Drives screen, choose the disk drive to view.
> 4. Press Tab to expand the Drive Information window.
> 5. View the information in the Drive Status window. If you can highlight an item, you can press Enter to display further details about it.

Server Management

When you choose Disk Information from Available Options menu, you enter the disk drive information section of MONITOR. There's not a lot you can change in this section, but it's a great way to check the status of the server drives. One critical item to review is the number of disk blocks used by the Hot Fix feature because of a failing disk. If this number increases slowly, your disk may be failing. If this number increases drastically, perform a backup immediately and buy another disk today.

When you go into this section, you will see each physical disk listed in the System Disk Drivers window. Pressing Enter on any listing will open two windows. The top window shows disk drive statistics, the lower displays disk operations that you can perform. Figure 10.32 shows these two windows, with the top window overlapping the Drive Status title of the lower window. Most of this information for the drive was set during installation and has not changed.

The bottom window, Drive Status, allows modification of some parameters, but they are not normally changed after installation. Table 10.6 describes the fields in the Drive Information window, and Table 10.7 lists those in the Drive Status window.

> *If you have installed disk mirroring, check here regularly. You may not know if the disks are mirroring properly unless you look into this section of MONITOR. I've seen systems where one disk died, but no one knew until we checked the console MONITOR screen.*

FIGURE 10.32

Disk details

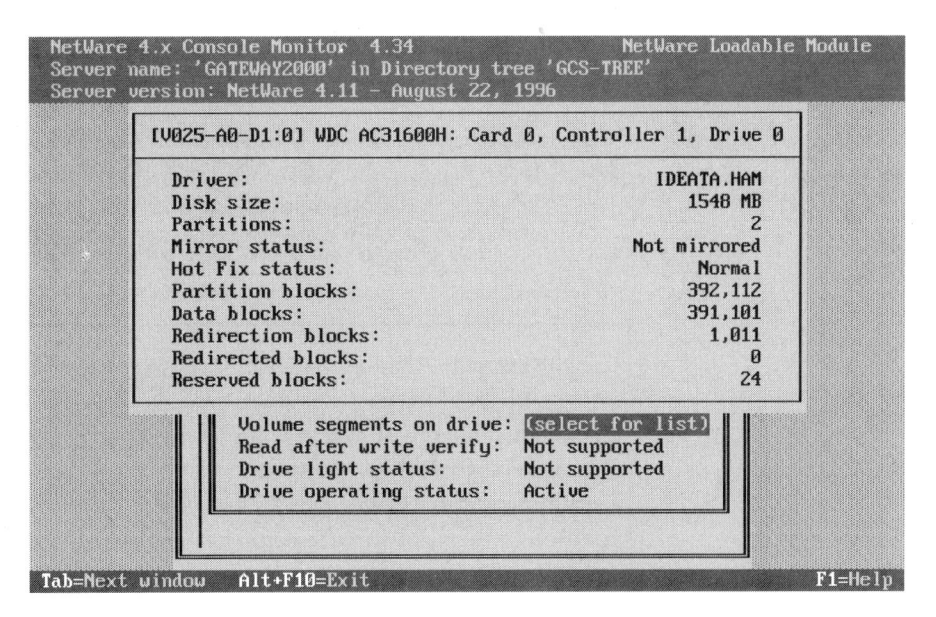

```
NetWare 4.x Console Monitor   4.34              NetWare Loadable Module
Server name: 'GATEWAY2000' in Directory tree 'GCS-TREE'
Server version: NetWare 4.11 - August 22, 1996

    ┌─[V025-A0-D1:0] WDC AC31600H: Card 0, Controller 1, Drive 0─┐
    │                                                             │
    │   Driver:                                       IDEATA.HAM  │
    │   Disk size:                                       1548 MB  │
    │   Partitions:                                            2  │
    │   Mirror status:                              Not mirrored  │
    │   Hot Fix status:                                   Normal  │
    │   Partition blocks:                                392,112  │
    │   Data blocks:                                     391,101  │
    │   Redirection blocks:                                1,011  │
    │   Redirected blocks:                                     0  │
    │   Reserved blocks:                                      24  │
    └─────────────────────────────────────────────────────────────┘
         Volume segments on drive:   (select for list)
         Read after write verify:    Not supported
         Drive light status:         Not supported
         Drive operating status:     Active

Tab=Next window    Alt+F10=Exit                              F1=Help
```

TABLE 10.6 Fields on MONITOR's Drive Information Screen

FIELD	DESCRIPTION
Driver	Software driver used by NetWare to access the disk.
Disk Size	Total size of the disk, including all partitions.
Partitions	Partitions on the disk. Drives with DOS partitions will show 2, as our example does. Nonbootable NetWare drives will show only 1 partition.
Mirror Status	Possibilities are: 　Mirrored (using two disks on one disk controller to double-write everything for fault-tolerance) 　Not Mirrored (a single disk) 　Remirroring (indicates the system is resynchronizing a disk pair)
Hot Fix Status	Normal, to indicate that NetWare's Hot Fix feature (moving information from a bad or suspect section of the disk drive to a known good section) is working properly. If you see anything else here, your disk is probably in trouble and you must take action.
Partition Blocks	Total number of 4 KB disk blocks in the NetWare partition.
Data Blocks	Total number of 4 KB disk blocks available for files and directories.
Redirection Blocks	Total number of 4 KB disk blocks set aside for use with the Hot Fix feature. Information from bad blocks will be moved to these blocks, and the bad block marked as unusable.
Redirected Blocks	Number of bad blocks moved to the redirection area. If this number increases slowly over time, start your budget process for server repair and upkeep. If this number jumps up, back up your system and buy a new disk immediately.
Reserved Blocks	Blocks set aside for system use.

Note that the Read After Write Verify option in the Drive Status window lets you choose between a Software Verify or a Hardware Verify method, or you can disable this function completely. The Hardware Verify method does not catch disk controller errors in most cases. If your disk controller handles everything automatically, think hard before disabling software verification in addition to the hardware routines. The Software Verify routines add very little overhead for the insurance they provide.

Server Management

TABLE 10.7
Fields on MONITOR's Drive Status Screen

FIELD	DESCRIPTION
Volume Segments on Drive	Pressing Enter displays each volume segment for that drive, plus the space for that volume.
Read After Write Verify	Three choices are available if your drive and controller support this option: 　Software Level Verify (device driver software performs the read-after-write verification on the drive) 　Hardware Level Verify (the disk controller hardware performs the read-after-write verification) 　Disable Verify (no read-after-write verification)
Drive Light Status	If you drive and controller support this option, NetWare will flash the drive light so you can verify which physical drive corresponds to the chosen system disk drive.
Drive Operating Status	Should be active, of course. You can choose to deactivate the drive. Obviously, an inactive drive cannot be seen or modified by NetWare.
Removable Drive Mount Status	If your system has a removable drive, the drive's current status: mounted or dismounted.
Removable Drive Lock Status	Must say Unlocked before the removable media can be taken from the system.

LAN/WAN Information

10.22 IN-A-HURRY

View LAN/WAN Information in MONITOR

1. Type **LOAD MONITOR** from the console prompt.
2. Choose LAN/WAN Information from the Available Options menu.
3. From the Available LAN Drivers screen, choose the LAN driver to view.

There are three fields to check on each LAN/WAN driver when giving a network the once over. When you choose LAN/WAN Information from MONITOR's

Available Options menu, you'll see the Available LAN Drivers screen. From there, pick the LAN driver of interest to see details. Figure 10.33 shows the top part of this screen for the 3C509 interface card in the GATEWAY2000 server.

The first fields you want to check are Total Packets Sent and Total Packets Received. These give a good clue to your network health. The statistics are kept from the time the server starts; when it goes down, these numbers are cleared.

The other field to check is No ECB Available Count. No ECB (Event Control Block) means that packets were received by the server, but the server did not have the resources to handle those packets. Usually, the problem is the number of packet receive buffers; use the SET command or SERVMAN utility to increase that number.

The information at the top of the screen shows the version of the driver, the node address of the server, a list of the protocols supported on this board, and the board's network address. Other boards in the server will show similar information, with different addresses.

Although this information is overkill for the typical network, you should appreciate the complexity of the information tracked for each network adapter card. Management software for your network and server uses these values to determine network health.

FIGURE 10.33

More details about the network board than you can really use

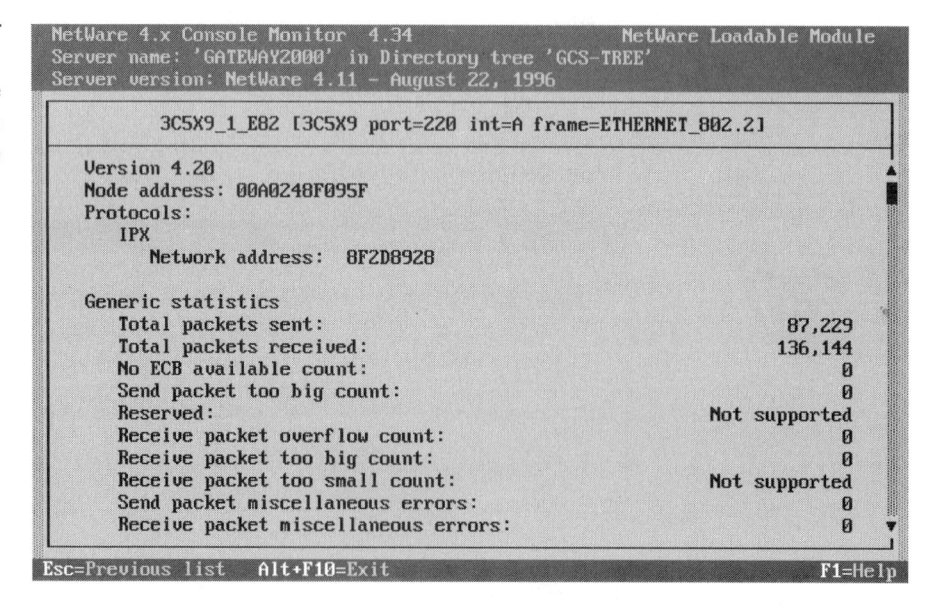

```
NetWare 4.x Console Monitor   4.34                  NetWare Loadable Module
Server name: 'GATEWAY2000' in Directory tree 'GCS-TREE'
Server version: NetWare 4.11 - August 22, 1996

        3C5X9_1_E82 [3C5X9 port=220 int=A frame=ETHERNET_802.2]

   Version 4.20
   Node address: 00A0248F095F
   Protocols:
      IPX
         Network address:   8F2D8928

   Generic statistics
      Total packets sent:                                    87,229
      Total packets received:                               136,144
      No ECB available count:                                     0
      Send packet too big count:                                  0
      Reserved:                                       Not supported
      Receive packet overflow count:                              0
      Receive packet too big count:                               0
      Receive packet too small count:                 Not supported
      Send packet miscellaneous errors:                           0
      Receive packet miscellaneous errors:                        0

Esc=Previous list    Alt+F10=Exit                             F1=Help
```

System Module Information

10.23 IN-A-HURRY

View NLM Information in MONITOR

1. Type **LOAD MONITOR** from the console prompt.

2. Choose System Module Information from the Available Options menu.

3. From the System Modules screen, choose the NLM program to view.

4. Choose an item from the Resource Tags list to see details.

"System modules" is a fancy name for NLM programs running on the server. The System Module Information option on the Available Options menu shows you the list of all NLMs loaded and information about each one.

Figure 10.34 shows the screen several options deep. The Resource Tags list should look familiar. We covered this list a few sections ago, although this viewpoint is not as detailed as the one shown earlier. This screen looks at the memory usage of each NLM, and it allows you to check the resource usage of every NLM.

In Figure 10.34, I have chosen the 3Com driver NLM. The resource tags are displayed in the right window, and the top window has the module name

FIGURE 10.34
Details for every NLM on your system

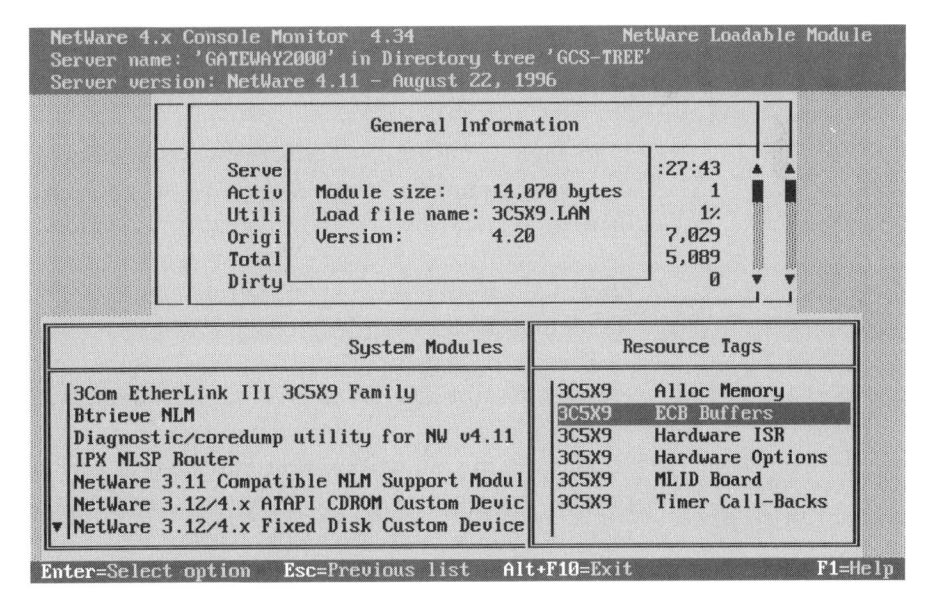

```
NetWare 4.x Console Monitor  4.34                    NetWare Loadable Module
Server name: 'GATEWAY2000' in Directory tree 'GCS-TREE'
Server version: NetWare 4.11 - August 22, 1996

                        General Information
        ┌─────────┬──────────────────────────────────────┬──────────┐
        │ Serve   │                                      │ :27:43   │
        │ Activ   │ Module size:      14,070 bytes       │     1    │
        │ Utili   │ Load file name:  3C5X9.LAN           │     1%   │
        │ Origi   │ Version:          4.20               │ 7,029    │
        │ Total   │                                      │ 5,089    │
        │ Dirty   │                                      │     0    │
        └─────────┴──────────────────────────────────────┴──────────┘

              System Modules                    Resource Tags
   ┌────────────────────────────────────┐ ┌────────────────────────────┐
   │ 3Com EtherLink III 3C5X9 Family    │ │ 3C5X9   Alloc Memory       │
   │ Btrieve NLM                        │ │ 3C5X9   ECB Buffers        │
   │ Diagnostic/coredump utility for NW v4.11 │ │ 3C5X9   Hardware ISR │
   │ IPX NLSP Router                    │ │ 3C5X9   Hardware Options   │
   │ NetWare 3.11 Compatible NLM Support Modul │ │ 3C5X9   MLID Board  │
   │ NetWare 3.12/4.x ATAPI CDROM Custom Devic │ │ 3C5X9   Timer Call-Backs │
   │▼NetWare 3.12/4.x Fixed Disk Custom Device │ │                     │
   └────────────────────────────────────┘ └────────────────────────────┘

   Enter=Select option   Esc=Previous list    Alt+F10=Exit        F1=Help
```

and size. If I now pressed Enter on the 3C5X9 ECB Buffers listing highlighted in the lower-right window, a new window would open and cover the bottom half of the screen. There I would see information about the selected resource tag, the name of the module that allocated the resource tag, the type of resource, and the amount of the resource (memory) used.

Do you have a suspect NLM or two? Do some of your server-based programs go crazy now and then? These screens will give you a chance to track the memory usage of each problem NLM, as well as all the subsidiary NLMs called by the main programs. But don't head to this screen at the first hint of trouble; these things are far down the troubleshooting list. However, they do give you some great ammunition against a vendor saying that its NLM software is perfect, so all the problems must come from another program.

Locking the File Server Console

> **10.24 IN-A-HURRY**
>
> **Lock the File Server Console**
>
> 1. Type **LOAD MONITOR** from the console prompt.
> 2. Choose Lock File Server Console.
> 3. Provide a password, and retype it for verification.
> 4. To unlock the file server console, type the password given to lock the console, or use the Admin password.

With MONITOR's Lock File Server Console option, we address security concerns once again. Knowing that easy access to the server console can cause damage to your network (the villian can disconnect users or take drives offline, not to mention change all the other server parameters), Novell engineers offer a lock for the MONITOR screen. Figure 10.35 shows the system asking for an unlock password.

This option is useful when your server can be reached by many people. Not everyone has the ideal situation of keeping the servers in a locked room. If the console is in a location where you can see it, or if you are using MONITOR remotely from your workstation, you want to be able to see the information or the snake whenever you look in that direction. Taking the keyboard and monitor away is more secure, but that approach may be inconvenient.

FIGURE 10.35
Protecting MONITOR in an unsafe environment

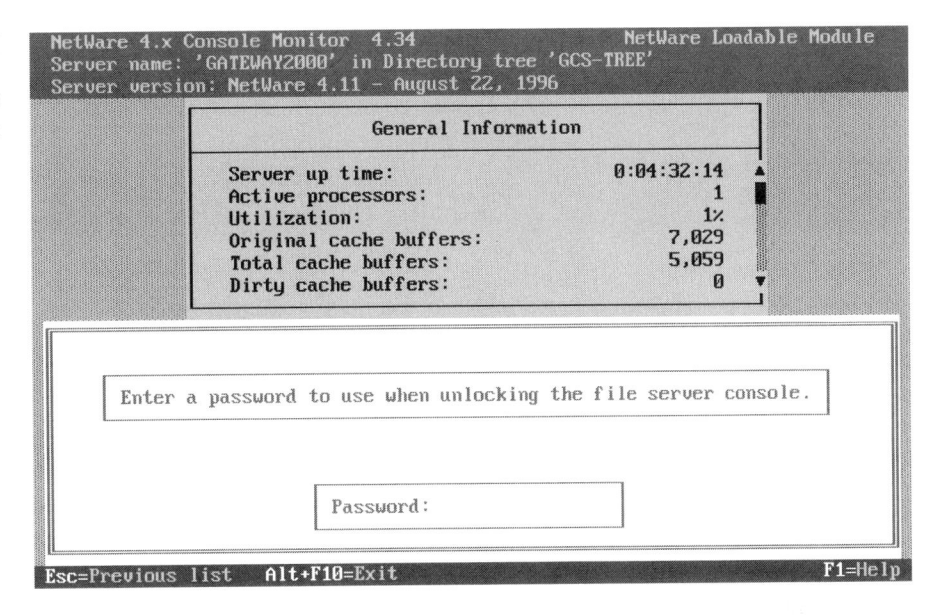

```
NetWare 4.x Console Monitor   4.34                    NetWare Loadable Module
Server name: 'GATEWAY2000' in Directory tree 'GCS-TREE'
Server version: NetWare 4.11 - August 22, 1996

                        General Information
              Server up time:                  0:04:32:14
              Active processors:                        1
              Utilization:                             1%
              Original cache buffers:              7,029
              Total cache buffers:                 5,059
              Dirty cache buffers:                     0


      Enter a password to use when unlocking the file server console.



                             Password:



Esc=Previous list    Alt+F10=Exit                              F1=Help
```

As you can see in Figure 10.35, you can assign a special password to unlock the file server console. When you enter one into the password box, you are asked to retype it to verify. When you are ready to unlock MONITOR, use the password you just entered or the password for the Admin user. (Sorry, but you can't see the rich, dark red and black of the scary password screen.)

In a clever bit of programming, even the RCONSOLE connections are locked when this is used. Now you can leave the display running in your cubicle without fear of someone with malicious intentions getting his or her hands on your server, or just someone clumsily pressing the wrong key.

Seeing File Open/Lock Activity

10.25 IN-A-HURRY

View Files Opened and Locked Activity in MONITOR

1. Type **LOAD MONITOR** from the console prompt.

2. Choose File Open/Lock Activity from the Available Options menu.

3. Use the Select an Entry list to find the specific file, and then choose that file to view the lock information.

The File Open/Lock Activity option on MONITOR's Available Options menu is a companion to the Connection Information screen that shows the files in use by each individual user. Here, you can check on a particular file to see the lock status and which connection number is using the file.

Figure 10.36 shows the end of the file hunt, reaching down to a particular file and seeing those particulars. In this case, it's the NETADMIN.EXE file from the PUBLIC directory.

The information is in two windows. The fields are described in Table 10.8

TABLE 10.8 Fields on MONITOR's File Open/Lock Activity Screen

FIELD	DESCRIPTION
Use Count	Number of connections using this file by having it open, locked, or logged.
Open Count	Number of connections with this file open.
Open For Read	Connections reading this file.
Open For Write	Connections using this file with access to write to the file.
Deny Read	Connections that have opened this file and requested that other stations not have the right to open the file for reading.
Deny Write	Connections that have opened this file and requested that other stations not have the right to open the file for writing.
Open Status	Lock status of the file.
Connection	Number of the connection on the Connection Information screen. Use this to find out who has the file open or locked.
Task	A task number defined by the NLM, and of little use.
Lock Status	Shows whether the file is in use, and how the file is configured (shareable, read-only, etc.).
Log Status	Whether the file activity is logged.

This information is useful when a particular file is giving you problems and you can't track down the user holding the file open or locked. However, it's more common to track the files a user has open in the Connection Information screen.

Server Management

FIGURE 10.36

Checking out who has a file checked out

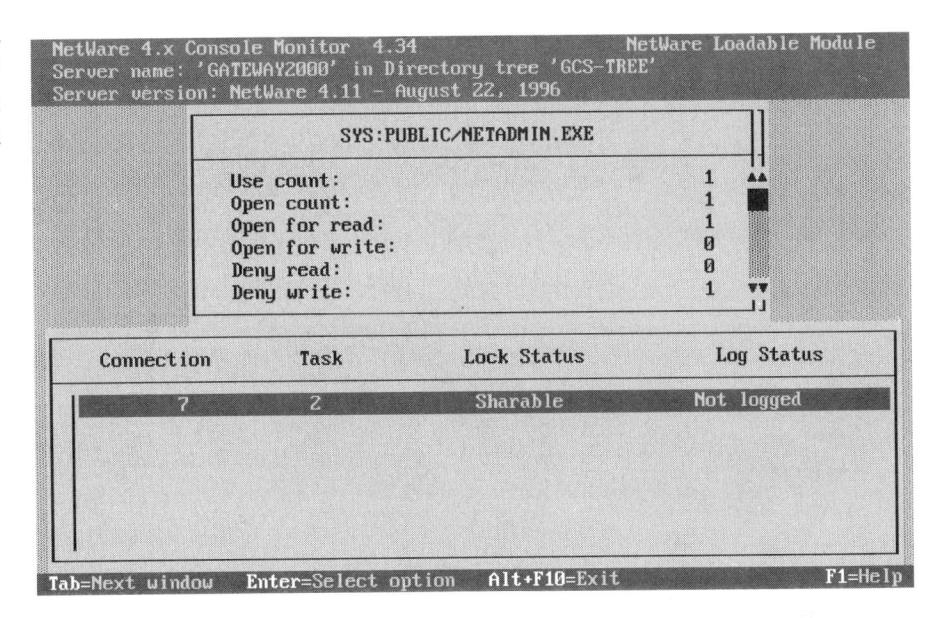

```
NetWare 4.x Console Monitor  4.34              NetWare Loadable Module
Server name: 'GATEWAY2000' in Directory tree 'GCS-TREE'
Server version: NetWare 4.11 - August 22, 1996

              ┌─────────── SYS:PUBLIC/NETADMIN.EXE ───────────┐
              │ Use count:                              1     │
              │ Open count:                             1     │
              │ Open for read:                          1     │
              │ Open for write:                         0     │
              │ Deny read:                              0     │
              │ Deny write:                             1     │
              └───────────────────────────────────────────────┘

     Connection        Task         Lock Status        Log Status
         7              2            Sharable          Not logged



 Tab=Next window    Enter=Select option    Alt+F10=Exit         F1=Help
```

Scheduling Information

10.26 IN-A-HURRY

Set Process Schedule Delays with MONITOR

1. Type **LOAD MONITOR** from the console prompt.

2. Choose Scheduling Information from the Available Options menu.

3. View the load percentage for any process that is taking too much processor time.

4. Highlight the process that needs adjusting and use the + and - keys to increase or decrease the delay.

Here we have another peek deep inside NetWare. Here, you have the ability to help balance the load from an NLM that's a little too greedy with CPU cycles. All the active processes are listed, with the CPU load generated by each. Those that are taking too much time can be toned down.

However, you must make sure the process you are willing to choke down won't be harmed by this decrease in CPU cycles. The users of this process may complain if performance drops. Just because an application takes a lot of CPU cycles to run doesn't mean it's being wasteful. Some applications, such as databases and gateways, require constant attention from the operating system to maintain acceptable performance.

You should discuss problems with a particular NLM with the manufacturer before reducing its CPU time. An upgrade may be in order. You may be able to use this option to cut down the NLM's processing time while you're waiting for delivery of the upgrade.

If this CPU chopping is necessary, you may wish to have it set automatically when the server is rebooted. Check out the utilities list in the DynaText manual for details on using SHCDELAY.NLM, which lets you contain some processes in the AUTOEXEC.NCF file.

Figure 10.37 shows the end of the list. Once you open the Scheduling Information screen, there are several pages of processes, depending on how busy your server is.

FIGURE 10.37

Processing work in detail

```
NetWare 4.x Console Monitor -4.34              NetWare Loadable Module
Server name: 'GATEWAY2000' in Directory tree 'GCS-TREE'
Server version: NetWare 4.11 - August 22, 1996

  Process Name              Sch Delay      Time       Count      Load

  Media Manager                  0            0          0       0.00%
  MONITOR main                   0            0          0       0.00%
  Remirror                       0            0          0       0.00%
  Remote                         0       15,246        262       0.51%
  RIPSAPUpdateProce              0            0          0       0.00%
  RSPX                           0            0          0       0.00%
  SNMP Agent          0          0            0          0       0.00%
  Sync Clock Event               0            0          0       0.00%
  TimeSyncMain                   0           26          3       0.00%

  Interrupts                              36,285        428      1.22%
  Idle Loop                            2,817,332        405     95.02%
  Work                                    89,213        467      3.00%

  Total sample time:                   2,968,650
  Histogram overhead time:                 3,750    ( 0.12%)
  Adjusted sample time:                2,964,900

 +=Increase delay    -=Decrease delay    Esc=Previous list         F8=More
```

The numbers are updated every two seconds. The overhead of this process is shown in the Histogram Overhead Time field at the bottom of the display. The columns on this screen are:

- **Process Name:** Name of the NLM generating the statistic.

- **Sch Delay:** The scheduling delay value for this process. The default is 0, meaning every process gets an equal chance at CPU time. Increasing the scheduling delay slows down this process, giving more time to the other processes. You cannot increase CPU cycles for an individual process, just decrease them. Pressing the + key increases the delay. A value of 2 means the process now gets half as many CPU cycles as a process showing 0. Using the - key moves the number back toward 0.

- **Time:** Time the CPU spent executing for that process or servicing that interrupt.

- **Count:** Number of times the process ran during the sample period.

- **Load:** Percentage of CPU time spent servicing this process or interrupt of the total CPU time. This is your key to tracking which process may be hogging CPU cycles.

SET Command Overview

The SET commands allow you to change almost every server parameter you can imagine. There are well over 100 SET commands, and most of them have from 2 to 1,000,000 options. The possible commands at your fingertips are higher than the United States federal deficit, believe it or not.

There is great power in the SET commands, but it's like a medieval fantasy, when our hero finds a magic sword that can conquer the dragons. Unfortunately, he usually destroys half the town before he learns to manage the power of the sword. Keep that in mind as you look over the SET commands.

Fortunately, the default SET command parameters have been honed over the years to a point where few, if any, changes are needed. Even more fortunate for us, the SERVMAN utility will help make those decisions that are necessary for the SET parameters, as well as for AUTOEXEC.NCF and STARTUP.NCF.

Figure 10.38 shows the server console with the SET command categories. After the list, the help information for SET is displayed, showing the format used by all the SET commands.

FIGURE 10.38

A set of SET categories

```
GATEWAY2000:set
Settable configuration parameter categories
   1. Communications
   2. Memory
   3. File caching
   4. Directory caching
   5. File system
   6. Locks
   7. Transaction tracking
   8. Disk
   9. Time
  10. NCP
  11. Miscellaneous
  12. Error Handling
  13. Directory Services
Which category do you want to view:
GATEWAY2000:
GATEWAY2000:help set
SET [parameter_name] [= parameter_value]
  View or set current operating system parameters.  Most parameters do not need
  to be changed, however they may be configured to fit your situation.
  Example:  set replace console prompt with server name = off

GATEWAY2000:
```

The example given with the Help command is a small detail that wasn't under our control with earlier NetWare versions, but is now. As you can see, the server name is displayed as part of the server console prompt. The command:

```
SET replace console prompt with server name = off
```

overrides the default setting of on. The format, just as shown, is:

```
SET [parameter_name] [=parameter_value]
```

SET commands have long names, as this one illustrates: Mirrored Devices Are Out of Sync Message Frequency. Yes, that's one command, and one long command name.

The following sections provide a quick summary of each of the 13 categories and what types of details are available in each. The complete list of each parameter and all the options that go with it is in Appendix C. As I've said before, and as the manuals and Help screens say, the SET parameters are not something to play with when you're bored by Solitaire. The Help text options on the server are a little sparse, but the full Help screens and other details in SERVMAN make that program worth a close look.

> *I put all the SET command descriptions and details in an appendix for two reasons. One is that SERVMAN does a better job with Help screens and information than the SET commands on the console. The other is that SERVMAN keeps you from needing to type the SET command and parameter at the console prompt. I always make a typo or forget a word when typing the long command, so I prefer SERVMAN (called from within MONITOR in NetWare 4.11).*

Communication Parameters

Communication parameters manage the communication buffers. Of eleven options, four parameters control packet receive buffers, and four control the watchdog.

Packet receive buffers hold data packets in the server's memory while they are being processed. Use MONITOR to view the number of packet receive buffers allocated.

Making sure stations are connected is the job of the watchdog packets. If the client doesn't communicate with the server within a certain time (configurable, of course), the server sends a watchdog packet.

Over another configurable time (59.3 seconds is the default), a default of ten packets is sent to the station. If the workstation doesn't respond to ten minutes of requests, the server assumes the station is disconnected and clears the internal connection for that workstation.

Memory Parameters

The Memory section of eleven commands controls the dynamic memory pool and works with EISA servers for proper memory registration. The two commands you are most likely to use are Register RAM Above 16MB, and Set the Number of Reserved Buffers Below 16MB. Remember these options from the Custom Installation routine? They're the last two options in the Memory section.

File Caching Parameters

Caching is one of the most important parts of NetWare server performance, and the six commands in this section control cache size and behavior. You can set details such as the minimum number of file cache buffers to have on hand when starting the server, or the delay before changed buffers (dirty disk cache buffers) are written to disk. These options are helpful for optimizing the performance of servers that focus on reading or writing information.

Directory Caching Parameters

One way NetWare speeds file access is by keeping the location of recently used files and directories in server RAM as a directory cache. The directory cache buffers are separate from the file cache buffers. When the server starts, 20 cache buffers are set aside for directory caches. Entries stay in the cache for a default of 33 seconds, but can be overwritten if the directory cache buffers can't handle the activity load.

If enough directory cache buffers are allocated for the amount of files on the system, all directory entry tables may be cached in memory. However, the more directory cache buffers, the fewer file cache buffers. You must find a balance between increasing performance through more directory buffers and decreasing performance because of too few file cache buffers.

File System Parameters

There are twenty-three SET commands for the file system, three of which control warnings about almost full volumes. File-purging parameters set how long files must be kept under the Minimum File Delete Wait Times setting, and that affects other files. Since deleted files remain on the disk for a time, the system must calculate how much free space is available by taking deleted but not purgable files into consideration.

File compression has eight parameters to set, including items such as when compression should start, when it must end, and how much disk space a compressed file should save to warrant compression.

Lock Parameters

Three lock parameters control the number of open files per workstation, the number of open files for the system, the number of record locks for each connection, and how many total record locks are supported. The three types of locks are:

- **File locks:** Secure a file or files by a workstation, keeping other stations from accessing any of those files.

- **Physical record locks:** Enforced by the system, and control data access by more than one user at a time. While locked, other users cannot access or change a range of bytes (a record) in a file. When another station tries to access the lock record(s), the system sends an "Access Denied" message.

- **Logical record locks:** Also enforced by the system against multiple-user access. The locking application assigns a name to each section of data that must be locked. Access for other users is checked against the named sections before the application unlocks the section.

Transaction Tracking Parameters

The five transaction tracking parameters help the TTS (Transaction Tracking System) guarantee that a transaction is written completely to disk, or backed completely out again if there is a problem. No harm can come to any record if a failure stops the database; no half-finished transactions will cause a data-integrity problem.

Disk Parameters

Three parameters in the disk area control one part of the Hot Fix feature. Redirection as part of Hot Fix may now occur during a write or read request, or during a read-after-write verification.

- **Write redirection:** The disk sees an error during a write operation. The Hot Fix system writes the data to a redirection block and tags the original block as a problem.

- **Read redirection:** A disk error appears during a read operation. The block is marked bad, and the data in that block is lost unless the disk is mirrored. If there is a mirror disk, the data is read from the second disk and redirects the data to a redirection block on the first disk. This keeps the mirroring intact.

- **Read-after-write redirection:** During the read operation done to verify the data just written, a data mismatch forces the system to mark the block as bad and rewrite the data to a redirection area.

Time Parameters

The two dozen parameters concerned with time synchronization help configure the TIMESYNC.CFG file. Time zone settings, time synchronization to other servers, and time source references are covered as well.

NCP (NetWare Core Protocol) Parameters

Ten parameters help configure NCP details, such as NCP packet particulars and server packet security levels between the workstation and server. For example, you can set the security option for packet signatures (a NetWare exclusive) to guard against counterfeit stations from impersonating authorized stations. The ability to support LIP (Large Internet Packets) is also set here.

Miscellaneous Parameters

This catchall area includes nineteen parameters, including the Replace Console Prompt With Server Name choice we saw earlier. Maximum Service Processes, Allow Unencrypted Passwords, and Automatically Repair Bad Volume illustrate the range of choices in this section.

Error Handling Parameters

Six options control the log files, the size of the log files, and what happens when the log files reach the configured maximum size. For example, you can set the log file size for the volume log, server log, and TTS log (if TTS is enabled).

Directory Services Parameters

Another dozen options for NDS support. These include setting the bindery context, NDS synchronization intervals and restrictions, and time intervals for maintenance processes. Maintenance items include reclaiming disk space and controlling the NDS trace file. This group of SET parameters is new since NetWare 4.0.

Using SERVMAN to Fine Tune Your File Server

The SERVMAN (SERver MANager) utility, introduced with NetWare 4, has become a one-stop control program. Earlier NetWare 4 versions included a means of configuring IPX/SPX, but that has now been folded into INETCFG.NLM with all the other protocol support.

The main screen of SERVMAN is reminiscent of MONITOR. In fact, you can now reach all the server settings by calling the Server Parameters menu choice from the main MONITOR screen. However, you don't get the nifty Server General Information screen, as we see in Figure 10.39.

Server Management **845**

FIGURE 10.39

The SERVMAN opening screen

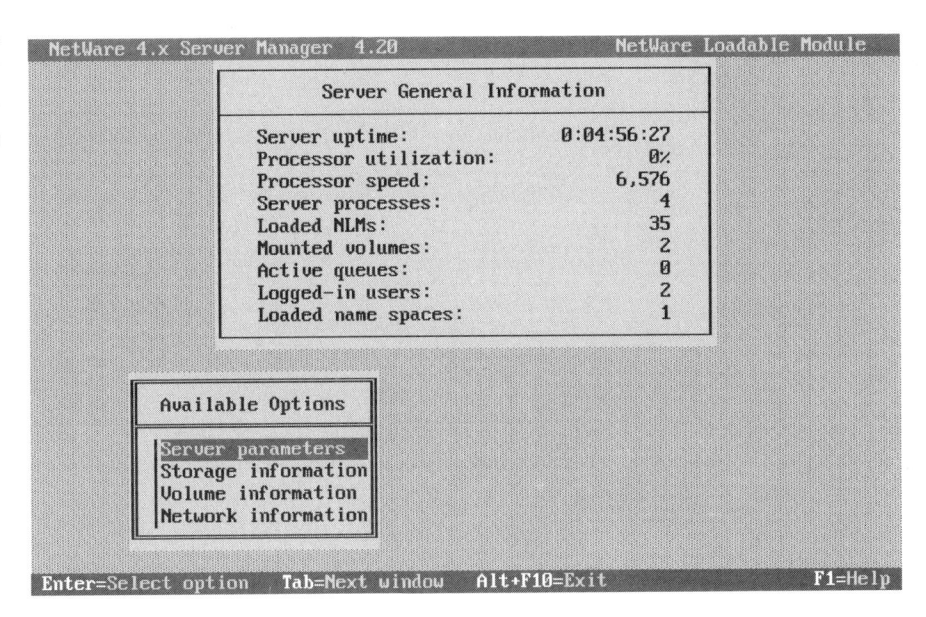

```
NetWare 4.x Server Manager  4.20                    NetWare Loadable Module
                    ┌─────── Server General Information ───────┐
                    │ Server uptime:              0:04:56:27   │
                    │ Processor utilization:              0%   │
                    │ Processor speed:                 6,576   │
                    │ Server processes:                    4   │
                    │ Loaded NLMs:                        35   │
                    │ Mounted volumes:                     2   │
                    │ Active queues:                       0   │
                    │ Logged-in users:                     2   │
                    │ Loaded name spaces:                  1   │
                    └──────────────────────────────────────────┘

              ┌──── Available Options ────┐
              │ Server parameters         │
              │ Storage information       │
              │ Volume information        │
              │ Network information       │
              └───────────────────────────┘

 Enter=Select option   Tab=Next window   Alt+F10=Exit              F1=Help
```

Some information is duplicated, but some is new. As with MONITOR, the information is updated every second. Table 10.9 describes the fields on SERVMAN's opening screen.

The Processor Speed value on SERVMAN's opening screen shows the same thing you see when you type SPEED at the console prompt. For example, server CLONE386, a 33 MHz 80386, had a rating of 322. Server ALTOS486, a 33 MHz 30486, had a rating of 905. The system pictured, a Gateway2000 120 MHz Pentium, has a speed rating of 6576—quite a difference. Of course, network speed is dependent on more than just the processor, but more is always better than less.

TABLE 10.9

Fields on SERVMAN's Opening Screen

FIELD	DESCRIPTION
Server Uptime	Time since the server was started or last booted.
Processor Utilization	Percentage of the CPU clock cycles devoted to network service.
Processor Speed	A NetWare rating based on the CPU type (80386, 30486, Pentium, etc.), clock speed (33 MHz, 50 MHz, 66 MHz, etc.), and memory wait states (0, 1, 2, etc.).
Server Processes	Number of processes active on the server.

TABLE 10.9 (cont.)	FIELD	DESCRIPTION
Fields on SERVMAN's Opening Screen	Loaded NLMs	Modules loaded and running on the server.
	Mounted Volumes	Mounted volumes on this server.
	Active Queues	Queues running on the server.
	Logged-in Users	Connections from users using a server resource.
	Loaded Name Spaces	Active name spaces (DOS, Macintosh, OS/2, NFS, FTAM) on this server.

As with MONITOR, there is an Available Options menu to go along with the informational display. The four options on the SERVMAN menu cover these areas:

- **Server Parameters:** Allows you to view and modify operating system parameter values in the AUTOEXEC.NCF and STARTUP.NCF files. Every SET option is covered here.

- **Storage Information:** Shows details of the server's disk driver, physical disk, and partition information.

- **Volume Information:** Shows details concerning each volume mounted on the server.

- **Network Information:** Displays another view-only screen, this one concerning the physical network.

Copying SET Parameters to a File

Before you start changing anything, it might be wise to do a little CYAWP (Cover Your A** With Paper). Press Enter while the highlight bar is on Server Parameters, opening the menu labeled Select a Parameter Category. This list shows the same 13 items we just reviewed in the SET parameter list. Take a look around if you want, but our goal here is to exit the menu. When you press Escape to close this menu, even without changing a single parameter, an option window opens. Update Options offers you a chance to copy all parameters to a file as the default choice. Take this choice, and place the file anywhere you wish; the suggestion is SYS:\SYSTEM\SETCMDS.CP.

Then 142 SET parameters are written to disk, sort of a State of the Server address. Let's take a look at the first lines of the listing:

```
IPX NetBIOS Replication Option = 2
Maximum Packet Receive Buffers = 100
Minimum Packet Receive Buffers = 50
Maximum Physical Receive Packet Size = 4202
Maximum Interrupt Events = 10
Reply To Get Nearest Server = On
Number Of Watchdog Packets = 10
Delay Between Watchdog Packets = 59.3 Sec
Delay Before First Watchdog Packet = 4 Min 56.6 Sec
New Packet Receive Buffer Wait Time = 0.1 Sec
Console Display Watchdog Logouts = Off
```

There are another 131 of these, detailing all the goods on server GATEWAY2000. Before starting any modifications, it wouldn't hurt to dump this file to disk. Dump it to your local disk, so you can view it if needed after messing up the server so bad the volumes won't mount or the network boards won't talk to the network.

Setting Server Parameters

> **10.27 IN-A-HURRY**
>
> **Set Server Parameters in SERVMAN**
>
> 1. Type **LOAD SERVMAN** from the console prompt, or choose Server Parameters from the MONITOR screen (in NetWare 4.11).
>
> 2. Choose Server Parameters, then the category to view or modify.
>
> 3. Scroll through the parameter listing to see current settings. Help information will be displayed for every choice.
>
> 4. If necessary, reboot the server to allow the new parameter to take effect.

The Server Parameters screen is where you will spend most of your time in SERVMAN. You'll check the status of other areas, but this is where the changes are made. Figure 10.40 shows the first few listings in the Communications Parameters category.

FIGURE 10.40

Setting SERVMAN parameters

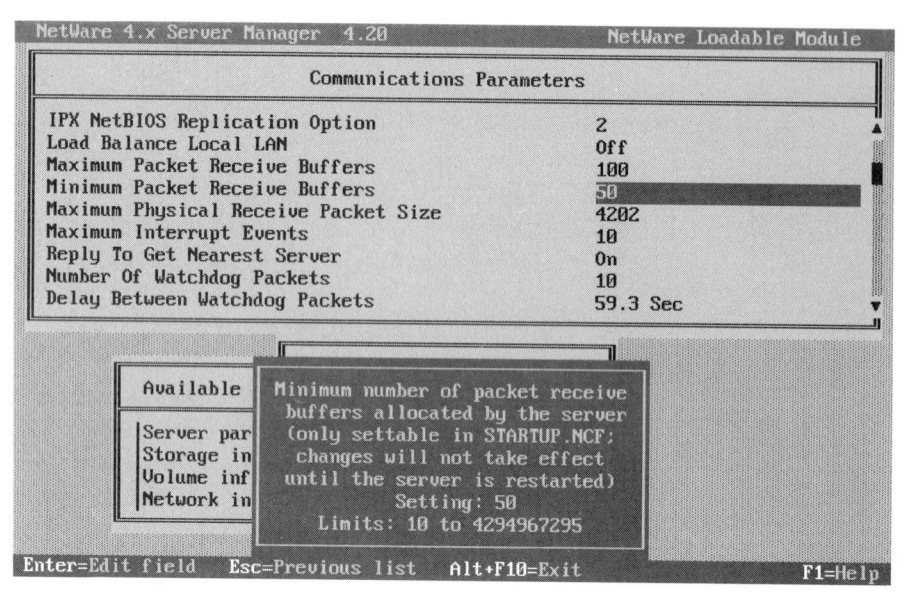

Using SERVMAN is straightforward, although changing numbers on a random basis can prove disastrous and ruin your weekend. Pick a section of the server parameters to modify, and the Help screens will show you everything you need to know. You merely change the value, press Escape to exit the Server Parameters area, and let the system write the information to the proper file. If you need to reboot before the change is effective, the Help screen will tell you.

> There are many ways to look at the same information in NetWare 4.1x. Much of this information can be seen in MONITOR, but not all of it. For example, if you want to see whether file compression is on for this volume, you can check here or in NetWare Administrator, but not in MONITOR.

Viewing Storage Information

The information in SERVMAN about storage devices goes a bit beyond that in MONITOR. See Figure 10.41 for a look at the details of the Western Digital hard disk in GATEWAY2000. You can't change any of the information in this section. Read and enjoy, but don't edit.

FIGURE 10.41

Disk device details

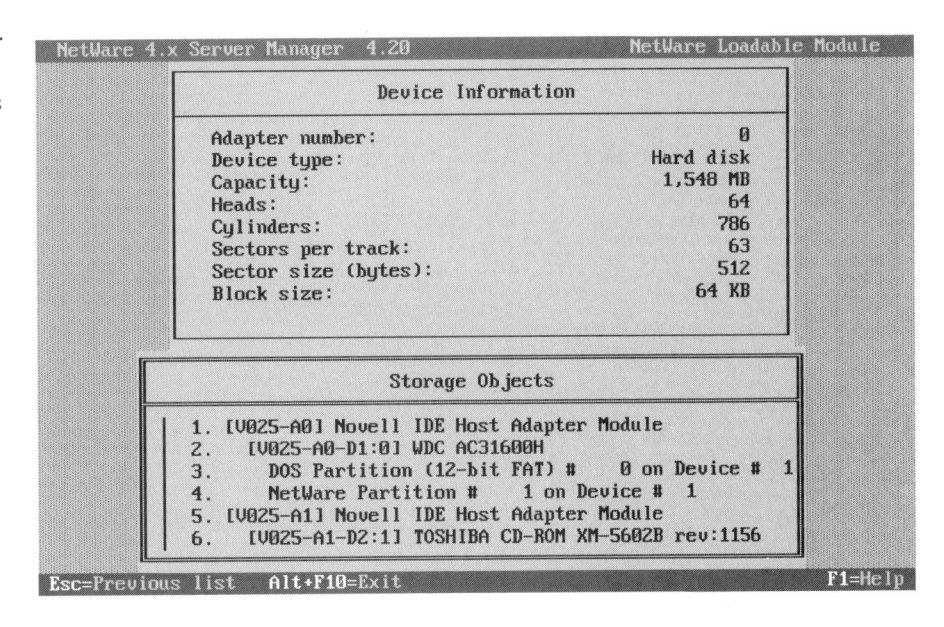

```
NetWare 4.x Server Manager  4.20                    NetWare Loadable Module
                    ┌─────────────── Device Information ───────────────┐
                    │                                                  │
                    │  Adapter number:                              0  │
                    │  Device type:                         Hard disk  │
                    │  Capacity:                             1,548 MB  │
                    │  Heads:                                      64  │
                    │  Cylinders:                                 786  │
                    │  Sectors per track:                          63  │
                    │  Sector size (bytes):                       512  │
                    │  Block size:                              64 KB  │
                    │                                                  │
                    └──────────────────────────────────────────────────┘

                    ┌─────────────────── Storage Objects ──────────────┐
                    │                                                  │
                    │  1. [V025-A0] Novell IDE Host Adapter Module     │
                    │  2.   [V025-A0-D1:0] WDC AC31600H                │
                    │  3.     DOS Partition (12-bit FAT) #    0 on Device #  1
                    │  4.     NetWare Partition #    1 on Device #  1  │
                    │  5. [V025-A1] Novell IDE Host Adapter Module     │
                    │  6.   [V025-A1-D2:1] TOSHIBA CD-ROM XM-5602B rev:1156
                    │                                                  │
                    └──────────────────────────────────────────────────┘
Esc=Previous list    Alt+F10=Exit                              F1=Help
```

10.28 IN-A-HURRY

View Server Information in SERVMAN

1. Type **LOAD SERVMAN** from the console prompt, or choose Server Parameters from MONITOR (in NetWare 4.11).

2. Choose Storage Information, Volume Information, or Network Information. For storage and volume information, next choose the object to view.

3. Press Escape to return to the main SERVMAN menu.

If you're curious, the same level of detail is available about the CD-ROM drives, even though this is the first time Novell has supported IDE CD-ROMs. Go ahead and try it; no one is looking.

Viewing Volume Information

The Volume Information screen in SERVMAN is another display of more information than is available in MONITOR. Figure 10.42 shows the details about the PROJECTS volume in server GATEWAY2000.

FIGURE 10.42

Many volume details

```
NetWare 4.x Server Manager   4.20              NetWare Loadable Module

                    PROJECTS: Volume Information

         File system name:              NetWare 4.0 File System
         Loaded name spaces:                                DOS
         Read only:                                         Off
         Compression:                                        On
         Sub allocation:                                     On
         Sub allocation unit size:                          512
         Migration:                                         Off
         Migrated files:                                      0
         Block size:                                      64 KB
         Sectors per block:                                 128
         Total blocks:                                   16,442
         Free blocks:                                    14,959
         FAT blocks:                                          6
         Freeable limbo blocks:                               0
         Non-freeable limbo blocks:                           0
         Directory size (blocks):                            18
         Directory entries:                               4,608
         Used directory entries:                          3,445
         Extended directory space:                            0

Esc=Previous list    Alt+F10=Exit                          F1=Help
```

> **NOTE**
>
> *If you're worried about overlooking some new information, let me set your mind at ease: There are no changes in these deep details from version 4.10 to 4.11. In fact, I seem to remember these same details from way back in NetWare 3. These foundation technologies change slowly.*

Viewing Network Information

SERVMAN's screen for viewing network information has one unique item: the Get ECB Buffers line. MONITOR does not have this information in this format, although it does list the ECB failures if there are any. Figure 10.43 shows the somewhat meager SERVMAN network listing.

The information is fairly straightforward here. Packets transmitted and received are kept only since the network adapter board was started last, which is usually when the server is rebooted. Unclaimed packets are those using a protocol this server does not support.

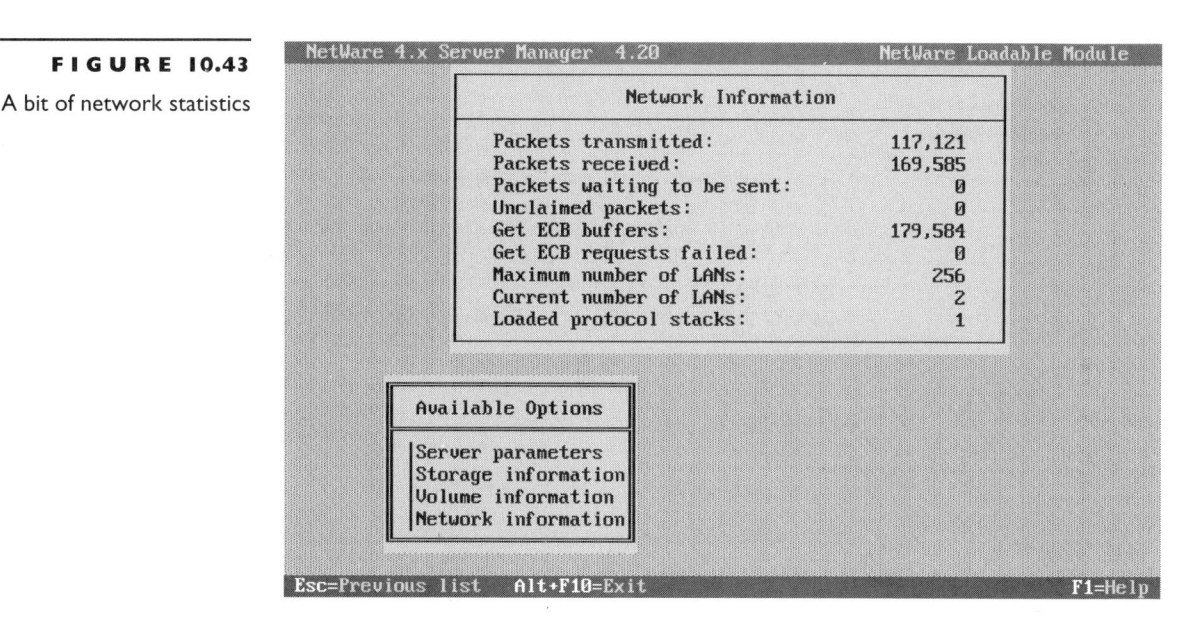

FIGURE 10.43

A bit of network statistics

```
NetWare 4.x Server Manager  4.20                    NetWare Loadable Module

                    ┌─────────────────────────────────────┐
                    │         Network Information         │
                    │                                     │
                    │   Packets transmitted:      117,121 │
                    │   Packets received:         169,585 │
                    │   Packets waiting to be sent:     0 │
                    │   Unclaimed packets:              0 │
                    │   Get ECB buffers:          179,584 │
                    │   Get ECB requests failed:        0 │
                    │   Maximum number of LANs:       256 │
                    │   Current number of LANs:         2 │
                    │   Loaded protocol stacks:         1 │
                    └─────────────────────────────────────┘

                       ┌────────────────────┐
                       │  Available Options │
                       │                    │
                       │ Server parameters  │
                       │ Storage information│
                       │ Volume information │
                       │ Network information│
                       └────────────────────┘

 Esc=Previous list    Alt+F10=Exit                            F1=Help
```

DSTRACE Tracks NDS Synchronization Processes

NetWare's TRACK ON console command has always been helpful. Watching server communications as clients connect to servers, and servers exchange network routing information, gives a nice warm feeling that things are working as they should be.

That same warm feeling is now extended to the NDS communications between servers. The DSTRACE (Directory Services Trace) utility, run from the server console or in SERVMAN, will display server chat concerning NDS. Figure 10.44 is a screen full of (luckily) boring NDS communications.

Notice the nice endings to all the processes:

```
All processed = YES
```

The amount of information sent back and forth in a network this small is minimal. I can see my Thomas Conrad 10BaseT concentrator, with activity display lights across the front, and forcing a synchronization causes no noticeable action on the activity display.

The reasons you may wish to watch such a boring display are:

- To check whether the NDS replicas are finished with a process

- To watch for NDS errors, especially during and/or soon after adjusting or moving NDS objects

FIGURE 10.44

Successful replica synchronizations

```
TE.GCS>
SYNC: Using version 5 on server <CN=GWAY2K>
  SYNC: sending updates to server <CN=GWAY2K>
SYNC: update to server <CN=GWAY2K> successfully completed
SYNC: Start outbound sync with (#=3, state=0, type=1) [01000102]<486-33.CONSULT
.GCS>
SYNC: Using version 5 on server <CN=486-33>
  SYNC: sending updates to server <CN=486-33>
SYNC: update to server <CN=486-33> successfully completed
SYNC: End sync of partition <[Root]> All processed = YES.

(96/10/17 20:57:30)
SYNC: Start sync of partition <INTEGRATE.GCS> state:[0] type:[0]
  SYNC: Start outbound sync with (#=2, state=0, type=1) [040000FB]<GWAY2K.INTEGRA
TE.GCS>
SYNC: Using version 5 on server <CN=GWAY2K>
  SYNC: sending updates to server <CN=GWAY2K>
SYNC: update to server <CN=GWAY2K> successfully completed
SYNC: Start outbound sync with (#=3, state=0, type=1) [01000102]<486-33.CONSULT
.GCS>
SYNC: Using version 5 on server <CN=486-33>
  SYNC: sending updates to server <CN=486-33>
SYNC: update to server <CN=486-33> successfully completed
SYNC: End sync of partition <INTEGRATE.GCS> All processed = YES.
```

NDS-related system messages are numbered -601 through -699 and F966 through F9FE. Not all NDS system messages are bad news, just like regular NetWare system messages. However, you know the old story: No news is good news. If you see system messages that don't clear up as NDS settles down after changes, they are usually error messages. The "System Messages" section of the DynaText documentation describes all the system messages in mind-numbing detail.

To see the NDS synchronization information using DSTRACE, go to the server console or start an RCONSOLE session. At the console prompt, type:

```
SET NDS TRACE TO SCREEN = ON
```

To stop, replace the ON with OFF. (Use the up arrow on the console to repeat the command, then just backspace over the ON to make it OFF.)

If you wish to save this information for your server archives, or send the file to a support person, use this command at the server console:

```
SET NDS TRACE TO FILE = ON
```

The file will be sent to DSTRACE.DBG in the SYS:SYSTEM directory. To write the file elsewhere, type:

```
SET NDS TRACE FILENAME = path\filename
```

When you feel there is enough information in your file, repeat the TRACE TO FILE command, adding OFF. If you don't stop it, the file will wrap at about 500 KB. Old information will be overwritten with new information as long as the log file is open.

As with most log files, not everything is written faithfully to the log. If your log and screen information looks good, but things are still strange, trust your feelings rather than the log file.

DSREPAIR Means Directory Services Repair

If you read the computer magazines, you know that distributed database technology is fraught with peril for database vendors. Trying to manage database pieces spread across multiple computers is beyond the ability of most commercial database vendors today. Part of the problem is the learning curve for database designers just starting to investigate using the network as a constant, reliable communications platform to tie all the database pieces together.

Novell has a considerable head start over database vendors in the network communications area. Servers have been negotiating with each other across the network since 1986. And as we saw with the DSTRACE utility, the NDS database must keep things synchronized through regular cross-network communication.

But things can still go wrong. Some customers (and network administrators as well) can tear up a ball bearing with a powder puff. When the unlucky object of these attentions is the NDS database, DSREPAIR will put things right once again.

DSREPAIR works on a single server database at a time. There is no option to repair all the databases from remote servers in one operation from one server console. You can, however, easily run DSREPAIR on multiple servers sequentially using RCONSOLE.

Here's what DSREPAIR can do for you:

- Repair the local database. The DS.NLM file on a server will be addressed by the DSREPAIR utility.

- Repair the local replicas. Examine and repair replicas, replica rings, and server objects. You can also verify each replica has the same data as the others.

- Search for local database objects. A browser function helps you locate and synchronize objects in the local database.

- Analyze the servers in each local partition for synchronization problems. View errors and list the partition name, server name, synchronization time, and errors with error codes.

- Write replica details to a log file. Detailed information about local partitions and servers is made available to check for database damage. If the local server has a wrong address for a remote server, you can check that here.

- Create a dump file of a damaged database. A compressed file is dumped, so you must use DSREPAIR to work with the file.

- Check the remote server ID list. Verify identification numbers for all remote servers and change those numbers as necessary.

Some NDS problems are less serious than others, and your Directory may continue to function. However, if you see a message saying that the server can't open the local database, go directly to DSREPAIR and start to work. Reinstalling the NDS database from a tape backup is more trouble, and that backup is probably slightly out of date. Try DSREPAIR before anything else.

Now that you know what DSREPAIR can do, here's what it can't do:

- Repair a remote NDS database.

- Recover Unknown objects that do not have the mandatory object properties.

DSREPAIR looks a lot like all the other NetWare utilities. Its opening screen shows the current version in the top-left corner above the name of the tree and server being examined. The bottom of the screen shows helpful keystroke information and a brief description of the highlighted menu choice. Figure 10.45 shows the opening menu of DSREPAIR.

The menu options are:

- **Unattended Full Repair:** Most of your work in DSREPAIR will be quick and simple, accomplished with this menu choice. In fact, if you start DSREPAIR and press Enter, your Directory will probably be back in shape in just a few seconds. Then you can press Enter again after reading the results of the operation, and press Escape to exit DSREPAIR altogether.

FIGURE 10.45

Preparing to repair the NDS database with DSREPAIR

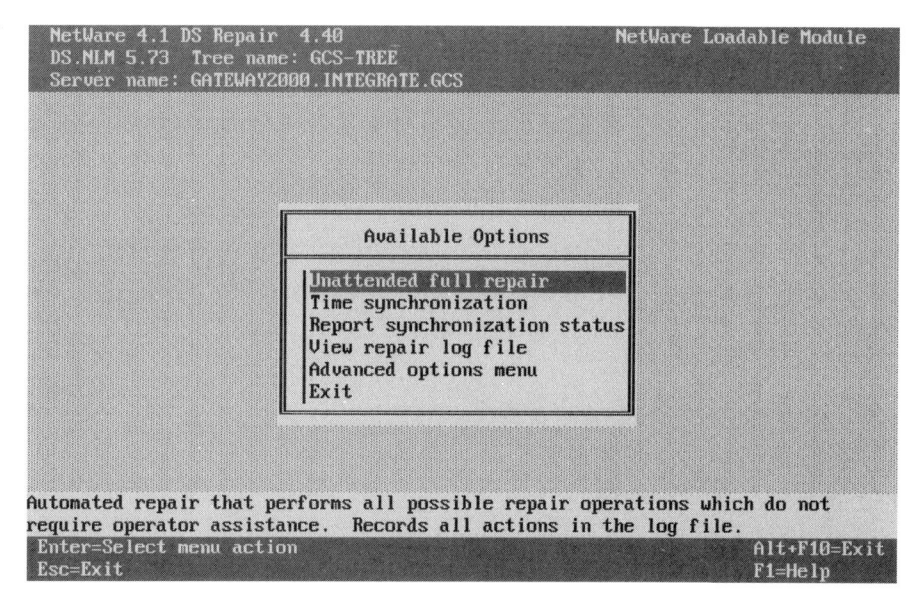

```
NetWare 4.1 DS Repair  4.40                    NetWare Loadable Module
DS.NLM 5.73  Tree name: GCS-TREE
Server name: GATEWAY2000.INTEGRATE.GCS


                         ┌─── Available Options ───┐
                         │ Unattended full repair  │
                         │ Time synchronization    │
                         │ Report synchronization status │
                         │ View repair log file    │
                         │ Advanced options menu   │
                         │ Exit                    │
                         └─────────────────────────┘


Automated repair that performs all possible repair operations which do not
require operator assistance.  Records all actions in the log file.
 Enter=Select menu action                                     Alt+F10=Exit
 Esc=Exit                                                     F1=Help
```

- **Time Synchronization:** Contacts every server in the local database and checks NDS and time synchronization details. If this server holds a replica of the [Root] partition, every server in the tree will be polled. Each server will be listed with its DS.NLM version, type of replica code, time source, whether time is synchronized, and the difference in time to the remote server. This process starts immediately when this option is selected, and the results are written to the DSREPAIR.LOG file.

- **Report Synchronization Status:** Determines whether the NDS tree is healthy by checking the synchronization status of each replica on each server. You must provide the Admin name and password to start this function. A log entry is added to the DSREPAIR.LOG file.

- **View Repair Log File:** Shows the entire DSREPAIR.LOG. file, allowing you to view all entries. The log file is controlled with the Log File Configuration option in the Advanced menu.

- **Advanced Options Menu:** Opens another menu allowing you to manually perform each of the automatic repairs done by the first menu option. The Advanced options give you more power and flexibility, as well as more potential for disaster. Use them carefully.

- **Exit:** Exits DSREPAIR, with a chance to cancel by entering No or pressing the Escape key.

Running the Unattended Full Repair

> **10.29 IN-A-HURRY**
>
> **Repair the NDS Database Automatically with DSREPAIR**
>
> 1. Type **LOAD DSREPAIR** from the console prompt.
>
> 2. Choose Unattended Full Repair (the default), and press Enter to start the repair operation.
>
> 3. Press Enter after reading the automatic repair results to view the log.
>
> 4. Press Escape to return to the main DSREPAIR menu.

When you press Enter on this first option, you won't be asked to verify your choice or to provide any information. The option is labeled "Unattended" and means just that. Press Enter, and the repair starts immediately.

During the repair process, the NDS database must be closed for obvious reasons. Just like any database record, if the file can be written to while it's being overhauled, dangerous things can happen.

Because the locking of the directory database will inconvenience users, it stays locked the shortest time possible. Repair of the GATEWAY2000 server took seven (yes, 7) seconds. Obviously, a small network with no real problems will take less time than a large network with a reason to use DSREPAIR.

Figure 10.46 shows the DSREPAIR process under way. The lines whiz by so quickly you can't read any of them during the process. The whizzing stops a time or two, but not long enough to consider the pause as a breakdown in the process. Although the display in the upper-right corner shows no errors, seven minor errors of no consequence to anything except the database were found and listed in the log file.

The bottom of the screen shows three interesting options:

F2=Options Menu	Shows the DSREPAIR Options menu.
F3=Pause the screen	Stops the screen and repair so you can examine the process.
Esc=Stop repair	Abandons the repair and returns to the menu.

FIGURE 10.46

Repair work in progress

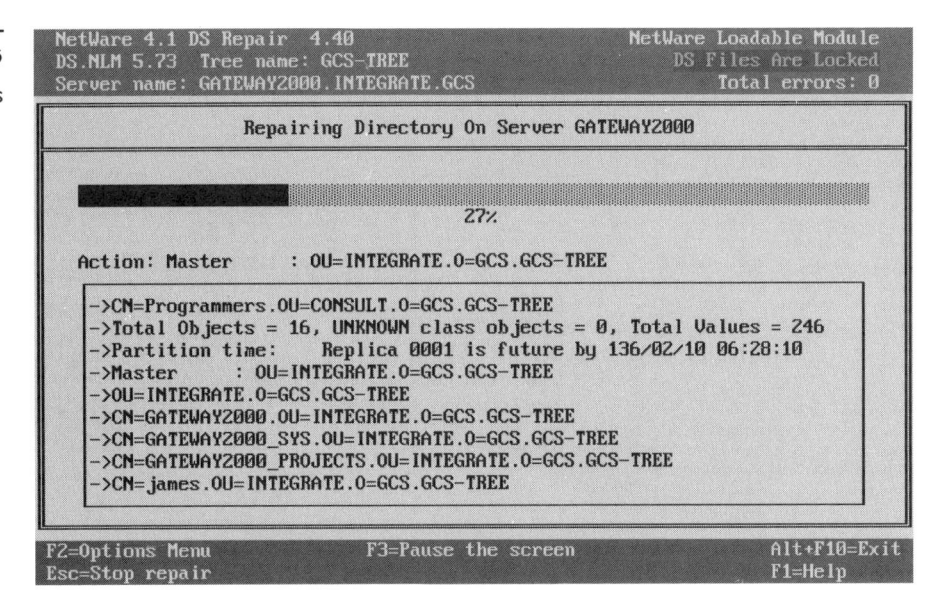

```
NetWare 4.1 DS Repair  4.40                        NetWare Loadable Module
DS.NLM 5.73   Tree name: GCS-TREE                    DS Files Are Locked
Server name: GATEWAY2000.INTEGRATE.GCS                    Total errors: 0
┌──────────────────────────────────────────────────────────────────────────┐
│                 Repairing Directory On Server GATEWAY2000                │
│                                                                          │
│   ████████████████                                                       │
│                                27%                                       │
│                                                                          │
│   Action: Master        : OU=INTEGRATE.O=GCS.GCS-TREE                    │
│                                                                          │
│   ┌──────────────────────────────────────────────────────────────────┐   │
│   │ ->CN=Programmers.OU=CONSULT.O=GCS.GCS-TREE                       │   │
│   │ ->Total Objects = 16, UNKNOWN class objects = 0, Total Values = 246│ │
│   │ ->Partition time:    Replica 0001 is future by 136/02/10 06:28:10│   │
│   │ ->Master        : OU=INTEGRATE.O=GCS.GCS-TREE                    │   │
│   │ ->OU=INTEGRATE.O=GCS.GCS-TREE                                    │   │
│   │ ->CN=GATEWAY2000.OU=INTEGRATE.O=GCS.GCS-TREE                     │   │
│   │ ->CN=GATEWAY2000_SYS.OU=INTEGRATE.O=GCS.GCS-TREE                 │   │
│   │ ->CN=GATEWAY2000_PROJECTS.OU=INTEGRATE.O=GCS.GCS-TREE            │   │
│   │ ->CN=james.OU=INTEGRATE.O=GCS.GCS-TREE                           │   │
│   └──────────────────────────────────────────────────────────────────┘   │
└──────────────────────────────────────────────────────────────────────────┘
F2=Options Menu          F3=Pause the screen              Alt+F10=Exit
Esc=Stop repair                                           F1=Help
```

> **NOTE**
>
> *Little of what zooms by is helpful to a network administrator. But what great technical names: external synchronizer and attribute definitions are some of the functions that scroll by. I can almost hear Scotty now, yelling over the warp engines, "Cap'n, I canna keep the External Synchronizer up much longer! Our Attribute Definitions are blown!"*

Using the Advanced Options Menu and Submenus

If the automatic full repair procedure doesn't fix your Directory problem, the Advanced Options menu is the next choice. You have little to lose at this point. Alternatively, your next step after the unattended repair is to restore from tape, or to delete the local database and copy it from another server. You might as well try a few advanced options before searching through the tape library.

Figure 10.47 shows the Advanced Options menu that appears as a submenu to the opening DSREPAIR program. The look is consistent to what you've seen before, including the identification information on the top and the help information at the bottom of the screen.

Remember that each of these options locks the Directory database. No one can be authenticated by NDS on this server during that time, since the database will be unavailable.

FIGURE 10.47

Serious DSREPAIR tools

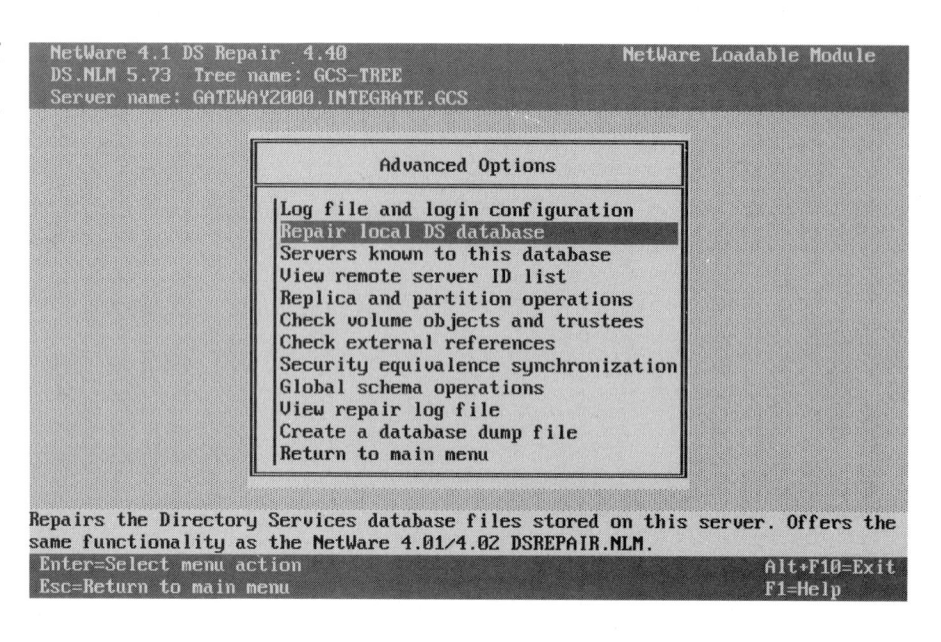

```
NetWare 4.1 DS Repair  4.40                         NetWare Loadable Module
DS.NLM 5.73  Tree name: GCS-TREE
Server name: GATEWAY2000.INTEGRATE.GCS

                    ┌─────────── Advanced Options ───────────┐
                    │ Log file and login configuration        │
                    │ Repair local DS database                │
                    │ Servers known to this database          │
                    │ View remote server ID list              │
                    │ Replica and partition operations        │
                    │ Check volume objects and trustees       │
                    │ Check external references               │
                    │ Security equivalence synchronization    │
                    │ Global schema operations                │
                    │ View repair log file                    │
                    │ Create a database dump file             │
                    │ Return to main menu                     │
                    └─────────────────────────────────────────┘

Repairs the Directory Services database files stored on this server. Offers the
same functionality as the NetWare 4.01/4.02 DSREPAIR.NLM.
Enter=Select menu action                                        Alt+F10=Exit
Esc=Return to main menu                                         F1=Help
```

> **NOTE**
>
> *The electronic documentation (DynaText) didn't have the latest information about DSREPAIR and DSMERGE in the NetWare 4.10 package, because the software wasn't completely finished by the documentation deadline. Unfortunately, documentation at this level isn't included with NetWare 4.11, either. If you've reached this point, take the time to read through the following descriptions of each option on the Advanced Options menu. If you're going to try and rescue a Directory before calling in the tape restore program, you might as well know what you're getting into. This is cheaper than calling per-incident support, and tech support will tell you to try these same things.*

LOG FILE AND LOGIN CONFIGURATION The default DSREPAIR log file, which will be created automatically for you, is SYS:SYSTEM\DSREPAIR.LOG. If you wish to delete the log file, here is one place to do so. Figure 10.48 shows the process in progress.

The first field, Current File Size, cannot be changed here. The Reset the Log File? option, to delete the current log file, is the first choice you have. Pressing Enter by accident as you go into this submenu may teach you the value of the Salvage option in FILER.

The option to log output to a file of your own choosing is the same as is available in DSTRACE, but with a more complete capture of information. This file will be helpful if your Directory gets so messed up that you need help from Novell support technicians. A copy of this file can be sent for their

FIGURE 10.48

Combo screen: Log file configuration and directory login

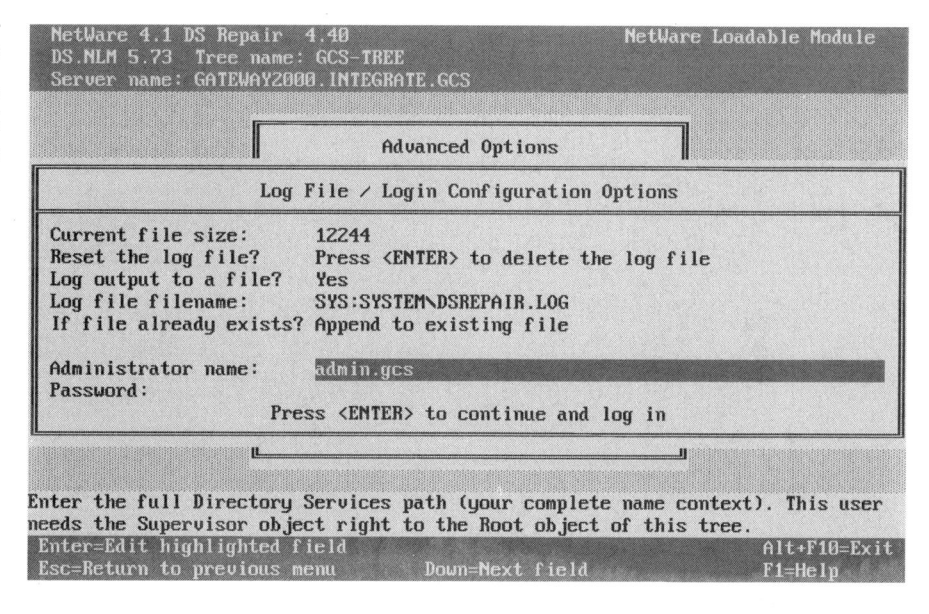

```
NetWare 4.1 DS Repair  4.40                      NetWare Loadable Module
DS.NLM 5.73   Tree name: GCS-TREE
Server name: GATEWAY2000.INTEGRATE.GCS

                         ┌─────────────────────┐
                         │   Advanced Options  │
        ┌────────────────┴─────────────────────┴────────────────┐
        │         Log File / Login Configuration Options        │
        │  Current file size:      12244                         │
        │  Reset the log file?     Press <ENTER> to delete the log file
        │  Log output to a file?   Yes
        │  Log file filename:      SYS:SYSTEM\DSREPAIR.LOG
        │  If file already exists? Append to existing file
        │
        │  Administrator name:     admin.gcs
        │  Password:
        │           Press <ENTER> to continue and log in
        └───────────────────────────────────────────────────────┘

Enter the full Directory Services path (your complete name context). This user
needs the Supervisor object right to the Root object of this tree.
Enter=Edit highlighted field                              Alt+F10=Exit
Esc=Return to previous menu       Down=Next field         F1=Help
```

perusal. You may rename the log anything you wish, or leave the default name. If the named log file already exists, you can append or overwrite the file. If you don't want to specify the log file, a temporary one will be created during repair operations. This will be shown to you after the repairs are finished.

To continue, you must provide the Admin user's name and password. The name and password will be authenticated by the NDS database before you can save your log file changes.

REPAIR LOCAL DS DATABASE This option does much of the same work as the Unattended Full Repair option on the main menu, with a few extra choices. One important distinction is that this option performs the repairs on a temporary file set, and you have the opportunity to back out before the temporary files become permanent. Figure 10.49 shows the choices you'll be able to make.

Here are the questions and what your answers mean:

- **Pause on errors?:** If Yes, you will be forced to press Escape or Tab with every error. This could get tedious. The first time through, say No.

- **Validate mail directories?:** Mail directories are not required by NDS; those were necessary in NetWare 3 for storing login scripts. If you have mail directories for an e-mail program built like the old bindery mail system, make sure this is Yes. If you have users who access the server

FIGURE 10.49

NDS database repair options

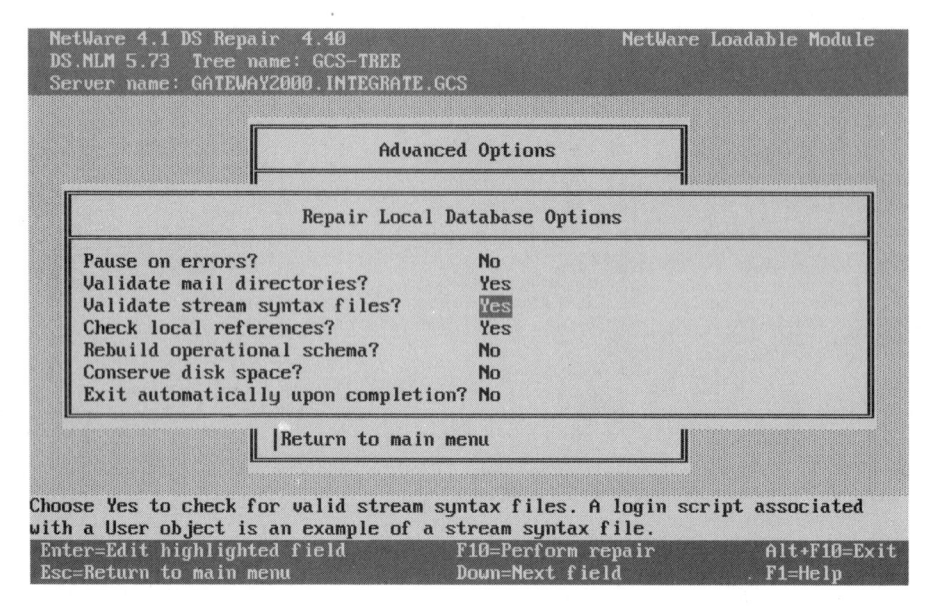

```
NetWare 4.1 DS Repair  4.40                      NetWare Loadable Module
DS.NLM 5.73  Tree name: GCS-TREE
Server name: GATEWAY2000.INTEGRATE.GCS

                        ┌─────────────────────┐
                        │  Advanced Options   │
                        └─────────────────────┘
         ┌──────────────────────────────────────────────────┐
         │          Repair Local Database Options           │
         ├──────────────────────────────────────────────────┤
         │  Pause on errors?                    No          │
         │  Validate mail directories?          Yes         │
         │  Validate stream syntax files?       Yes         │
         │  Check local references?             Yes         │
         │  Rebuild operational schema?         No          │
         │  Conserve disk space?                No          │
         │  Exit automatically upon completion? No          │
         ├──────────────────────────────────────────────────┤
         │              Return to main menu                 │
         └──────────────────────────────────────────────────┘

Choose Yes to check for valid stream syntax files. A login script associated
with a User object is an example of a stream syntax file.
Enter=Edit highlighted field        F10=Perform repair         Alt+F10=Exit
Esc=Return to main menu             Down=Next field            F1=Help
```

through Bindery Services, they will need their login directories for login scripts as well.

- **Validate stream syntax files?:** Stream syntax files, like login scripts, are a type of object property. These are stored in a special reserved area of the SYS: volume, along with the NDS database. Orphaned stream syntax files are tagged and deleted.

- **Rebuild operational schema?:** Do this only under orders by Novell technical support; it's rarely needed. The operational schema is the schema required for basic operation of NDS, making it very messy if rebuilt unnecessarily.

- **Conserve disk space?:** If disk space is tight, this option will save some bytes. However, you lose a good chance to recover a database if you're too stingy with the bytes. Leave this set to No.

- **Exit automatically upon completion?:** If you know enough or are so incurious as to not care what happens with the rebuild, change this to Yes. Otherwise, leave it alone. Even if you don't know a lot about how NDS works, you will be able to understand some of the log files and explanations given at the end.

After you've answered these questions, press F10 to perform the repair.

SERVERS KNOWN TO THIS DATABASE Here we can fine-tune the local NDS database per server, and see what the local server knows about the remote servers. Each of the known servers is listed, with its status and its local ID. See Figure 10.50 for a look at the server display as seen from GATEWAY2000.

FIGURE 10.50

Know thyself, and thy fellow servers in the NDS database.

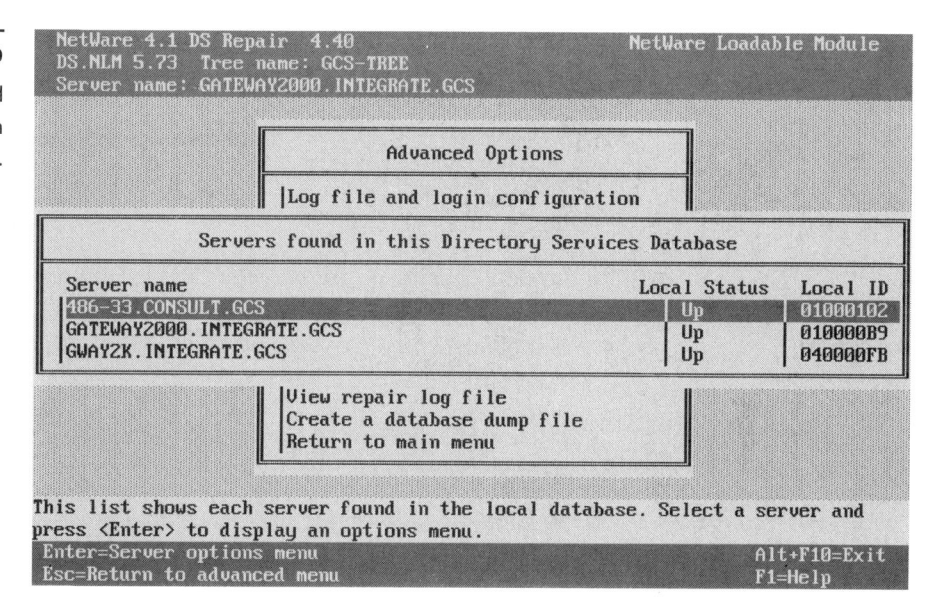

```
NetWare 4.1 DS Repair  4.40                      NetWare Loadable Module
DS.NLM 5.73   Tree name: GCS-TREE
Server name: GATEWAY2000.INTEGRATE.GCS

                    ┌─────────────────────────────────────┐
                    │         Advanced Options            │
                    │ Log file and login configuration    │
        ┌───────────┴─────────────────────────────────────┴────────────┐
        │       Servers found in this Directory Services Database      │
        │ Server name                          Local Status   Local ID │
        │ 486-33.CONSULT.GCS                   Up             01000102 │
        │ GATEWAY2000.INTEGRATE.GCS            Up             010000B9 │
        │ GWAY2K.INTEGRATE.GCS                 Up             040000FB │
        │                                                              │
        │              ┌───────────────────────────────┐               │
        │              │ View repair log file          │               │
        │              │ Create a database dump file   │               │
        │              │ Return to main menu           │               │
        └──────────────┴───────────────────────────────┴───────────────┘
This list shows each server found in the local database. Select a server and
press <Enter> to display an options menu.
 Enter=Server options menu                                     Alt+F10=Exit
 Esc=Return to advanced menu                                   F1=Help
```

The information imparted in this screen is easy to understand. The three servers listed are those in the NDS database of GATEWAY2000. Each server, according to the local database, is up. The local ID for each server is listed.

It's possible for a server to be listed as up on this screen but really be down. It's possible to go the other way, with a server really active though shown as down here. Once the servers exchange some information, the display will match reality.

Pressing Enter while highlighting any of the listed servers opens up a new menu, named Server Options. The action occurs immediately after you press Enter, so if you're unsure, check the Help screens first by pressing F1.

The Server Options menu has these choices:

- **Time Synchronization and Server Status:** Contacts every server in the local database and requests time and NDS information. If this server contains a replica of [Root], it will poll every server in the tree. The information presented here is exactly like that shown from the main DSREPAIR menu choice of Time Synchronization.

- **Repair All Network Addresses:** There needs to be an entry for each remote server in the local SAP tables. These tables match the remote server object's IPX network address and the address in the replica. If the addresses don't match, the RNA (Repair Network Address) function updates the local tables. If there is no name for an SAP address entry for a remote server, there is little else to be done.

- **Repair Selected Server's Network Address:** Same as above, but with the highlighted server only.

- **Update Schema on All Servers:** Checks all known remote servers to make sure the schema (the rules that define the NDS tree and database) is the NetWare 4.1*x* version. This option checks all servers known to this local Directory database.

- **Update Schema on the Selected Server:** Same as above, but for the highlighted server only.

- **View Entire Server's Name:** Shows the full distinguished server name for the highlighted server; for example, GATEWAY2000.INTEGRATE.GCS.

VIEW REMOTE SERVER ID LIST Each server (and, in fact, every object) has a unique identifier on each remote server. This submenu shows the IDs for the remote servers as tracked by the local server database, and this server's ID as known on the remote servers. Figure 10.51 shows an example of this list.

The Local ID to Remote ID List window shows the two remote servers known to our local server. You can also see, at the right end of the window, their IDs and the local GATEWAY2000 server's IDs on the remote systems.

Pressing Enter on either of the two known remote servers pops open the Remote Server ID Options menu. The three options are:

- **Verify All Remote Server IDs:** Checks the remote server IDs on the list. Repairs those that need it, and deletes any that are incorrect.

- **Verify Selected Remote Server ID:** Same as above for the highlighted remote server.

- **Delete the Selected Remote Server ID:** Checks the selected remote server ID. Repairs it if necessary; deletes it if incorrect.

Server Management **863**

REPLICA AND PARTITION OPERATIONS This innocent-looking entry hides multiple submenus and powerful processes. Figure 10.52 shows the first of the submenus. After you choose this option, the Replicas Stored on This Server box opens, showing all the replicas on our local server. In Figure 10.52, you can see the box in the background.

FIGURE 10.51
Matching remote server IDs here and there

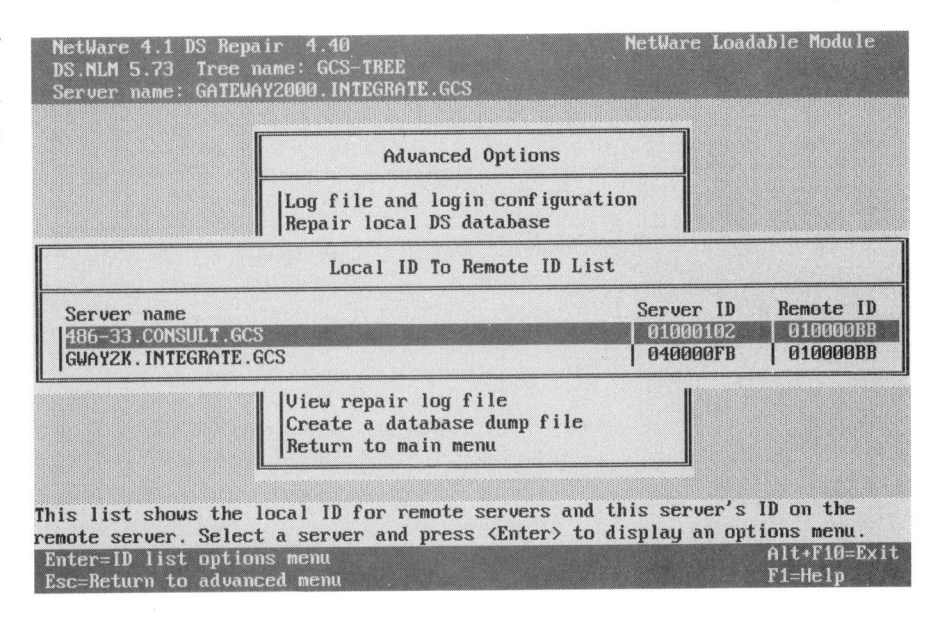

```
NetWare 4.1 DS Repair   4.40                    NetWare Loadable Module
DS.NLM 5.73  Tree name: GCS-TREE
Server name: GATEWAY2000.INTEGRATE.GCS

                    ┌─── Advanced Options ───┐
                    │ Log file and login configuration │
                    │ Repair local DS database │
         ┌────────── Local ID To Remote ID List ──────────┐
         │ Server name                  Server ID   Remote ID │
         │ 486-33.CONSULT.GCS           01000102    010000BB │
         │ GWAY2K.INTEGRATE.GCS         040000FB    010000BB │
         │                                                   │
         │       View repair log file                        │
         │       Create a database dump file                 │
         │       Return to main menu                         │
         └───────────────────────────────────────────────────┘
This list shows the local ID for remote servers and this server's ID on the
remote server. Select a server and press <Enter> to display an options menu.
 Enter=ID list options menu                        Alt+F10=Exit
 Esc=Return to advanced menu                       F1=Help
```

FIGURE 10.52
Specific replica options for GATEWAY2000

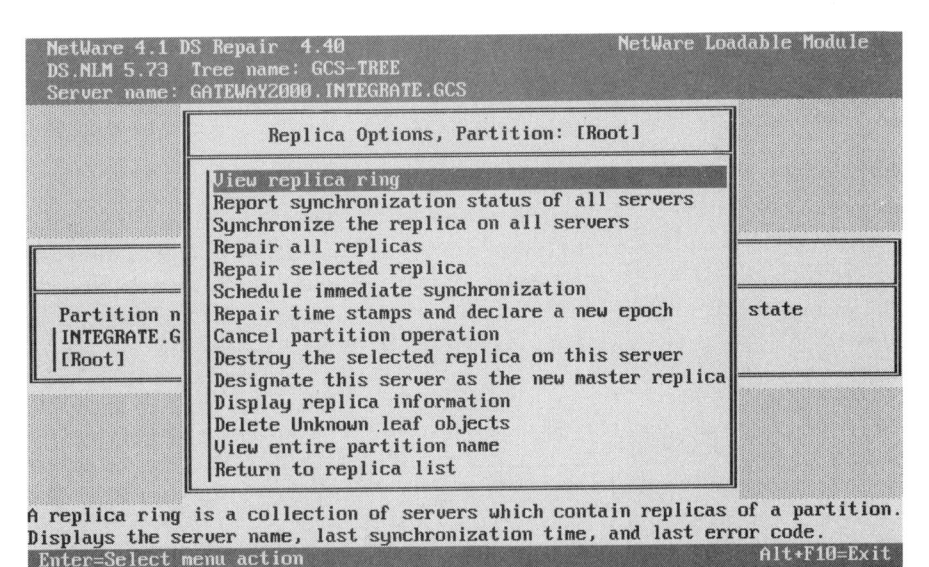

```
NetWare 4.1 DS Repair   4.40                    NetWare Loadable Module
DS.NLM 5.73  Tree name: GCS-TREE
Server name: GATEWAY2000.INTEGRATE.GCS

              ┌──── Replica Options, Partition: [Root] ────┐
              │ View replica ring                          │
              │ Report synchronization status of all servers │
              │ Synchronize the replica on all servers     │
              │ Repair all replicas                        │
              │ Repair selected replica                    │
              │ Schedule immediate synchronization         │
   Partition n│ Repair time stamps and declare a new epoch │ state
   INTEGRATE.G│ Cancel partition operation                 │
   [Root]     │ Destroy the selected replica on this server │
              │ Designate this server as the new master replica │
              │ Display replica information                │
              │ Delete Unknown leaf objects                │
              │ View entire partition name                 │
              │ Return to replica list                     │
              └────────────────────────────────────────────┘
A replica ring is a collection of servers which contain replicas of a partition.
Displays the server name, last synchronization time, and last error code.
 Enter=Select menu action                          Alt+F10=Exit
 Esc=Return to replica list                        F1=Help
```

The first menu option, View Replica Ring, brings up a new term: *replica ring*. As you can read on the lower part of the screen, a replica ring is basically a group of replicas within a partition. Remember all the copies of replicas you can spread everywhere? These functions help keep those coordinated and functional.

You're not missing anything interesting in the background box, which explains that the INTEGRATE.GCS partition on this server holds a Read/Write replica type and it is On.

See Table 10.10 for descriptions of the options on the main Replica Options menu.

TABLE 10.10 Options on DSREPAIR's Main Replica Options Menu

OPTION	DESCRIPTION
View Replica Ring	Brings up a box labeled Servers That Have Replicas of This Paritition. Choose a server to see another submenu of choices.
Report Synchronization Status of All Servers	Runs a quick report and details time synchronization status of partitions.
Synchronize the Replica on All Servers	Reads the table of remote servers and replicas on the local server, and forces all servers to synchronize with all other servers.
Repair All Replicas	Checks the replica information on each remote server defined in the local Directory database tables and make any modifications necessary. If the local database hasn't been repaired in the last 30 minutes, repair that before trying this option.
Repair Selected Replica	Same as above, for one highlighted replica rather than all.
Schedule Immediate Synchronization	Provides a good way to force synchronization, especially if you're watching the DSTRACE screen and are tired of waiting.
Repair Time Stamps and Declare a New Epoch	Must be performed only on the Master replica. Time stamps are placed on objects when they are modified or created, and they must be unique. This option provides a new point of reference in all replicas, so that they are all updated to match the Master replica.
Cancel Partition Operation	Stops the partition operation on the selected replica, if the process hasn't gone too far.

TABLE 10.10 (cont.) Options on DSREPAIR's Main Replica Options Menu	OPTION	DESCRIPTION
	Destroy the Selected Replica on This Server	Last-ditch effort to scratch the problems with this replica: Blow it away, and hope the other replicas can provide the information necessary to rebuild this replica.
	Designate This Server as the New Master Replica	If the original Master replica is damaged or lost, this option makes this replica the Master replica. If the old Master replica comes back from a hardware failure, there will be two Master replicas, causing some confusion until the synchronization checks and forces the issue by deleting the original Master replica.
	Display Replica Information	Writes a full replica report to the DSREPAIR.LOG file, including replica ID, time stamps, full names of replicas and servers, replica types, and status flags. It's helpful for technical support.
	Delete Unknown Leaf Objects	Under supervision of Novell technical support folks, allows you to get rid of unknown leaf objects that may be causing problems.
	View Entire Partition Name	Shows the entire partition name, regardless of its length.
	Return to Replica List	Backs up one menu (sames as pressing Escape).

These operations force repairs and synchronizations while writing full details to the log file. These options provide a rifle approach, as opposed to the shotgun approach of the Unattended Full Repair option.

As with VREPAIR in past NetWare versions, you may need to perform some operations several times. While the replica and partition information is updated throughout the network, small errors here and there may be magnified, or they may not appear until later in the process. So don't expect any of these options to be able to work magic and quickly fix your problem. Things take longer when working across a distributed network, and this is no exception.

Choosing the View Replica Ring choice, the first one on the Replica Options menu, brings up another box. This one is labeled Servers That Have Replicas of This Partition. In our case, all three servers have replicas of this partition.

Highlight the server and replica type of your choice, and still another new menu appears: Replica Ring Options. Here we have nothing but actions, with no pause for reflection. If you've come down this many levels in your server operating system, you might as well go for it. These are your choices:

- **Report Synchronization Status on the Selected Server:** Gathers partition details on specific server and replica.

- **Synchronize the Replica on the Selected Server:** Same as above for a single, highlighted replica.

- **Send All Objects to Every Replica in the Ring:** This may create high network traffic. All other replicas are relabeled as new replicas, and the old replicas are destroyed. The host server sends a new copy of the replica to the remote servers that had their old replicas deleted. Modifications made to the now-deleted replicas that didn't have time to get back to the host replica are gone.

- **Receive All Objects from the Master to This Replica:** Again, this may create high network traffic. The reverse of the above. The old replica is marked deleted, and any objects are deleted. The host server replica is replaced by the Master remote replica.

- **Remove This Server from the Replica Ring:** If a server has been eliminated from the tree, or no longer contains the referenced replica, you may need to go ahead and delete this server's references in the replica ring. You should do this only under the guidance of Novell technical support.

- **View Entire Server Name:** Another look at the server name, for those servers with names that can't fit in the small box of text in the earlier menu.

- **Return to Servers with Replicas List:** Backs up one menu (same as pressing Escape).

> **WARNING**
> *The Remove This Server from the Replica Ring option can cause you endless grief. Novell technical support people should be leading you through this, so you'll stand a good chance of making it through unscathed. If you're doing this on your own, be prepared to rebuild the NDS information on this server, either by copying a replica and hoping everything comes back, or re-creating the database by hand. If you're down here this deep, you may want to think of calling in the Calvary.*

SECURITY EQUIVALENCE SYNCHRONIZATION One major reason to upgrade your NetWare 4.02 and earlier servers to NetWare 4.1x is reflected here. The Equivalent to Me property was not in the earlier NetWare 4 versions. Consequently, those NDS databases can't support this feature in NetWare 4.1x.

The Equivalent to Me property was added to make synchronizing security equivalent objects faster and more reliable. This is such a sensitive option you must provide the administrator name and password before starting the process. Figure 10.53 shows the screen and the two options to set before continuing. The figure shows the default settings for these options.

If the Security Equals flag is set to Yes, you are prompted whenever another object shows up in the first object's Security Equals property, and contains an equivalence that does not list the first object in the Equivalent to Me property. You are then offered the choice to update or delete the Equivalent to Me field or do nothing.

When set to No, the Security Equals property is accepted as correct, and the Equivalent to Me property is updated automatically.

GLOBAL SCHEMA UPDATE The schema consists of the rules governing objects and their relationships to NDS. It's important to have all servers on the same schema. Think of the schema as somewhat like the NDS program that tracks and controls all the objects. Having all servers on the same version of the program is smart, and it's also necessary. Figure 10.54 shows your choice in the submenu.

The first step in the upgrade looks at known servers in the tree and checks their schema version. If it's current, nothing happens, and the next server is

FIGURE 10.53
Setting security scan options

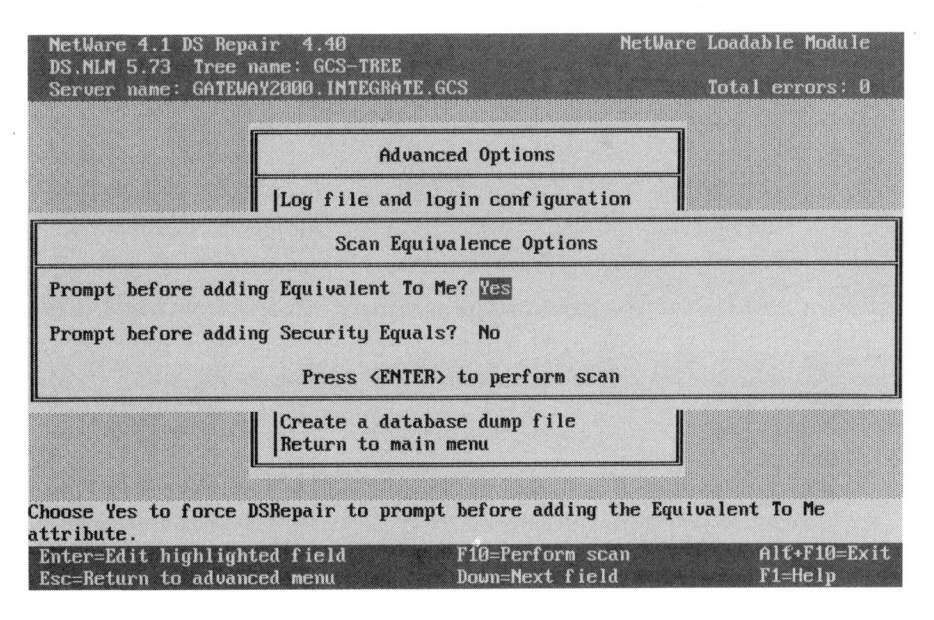

FIGURE 10.54

Choosing your global schema update procedure

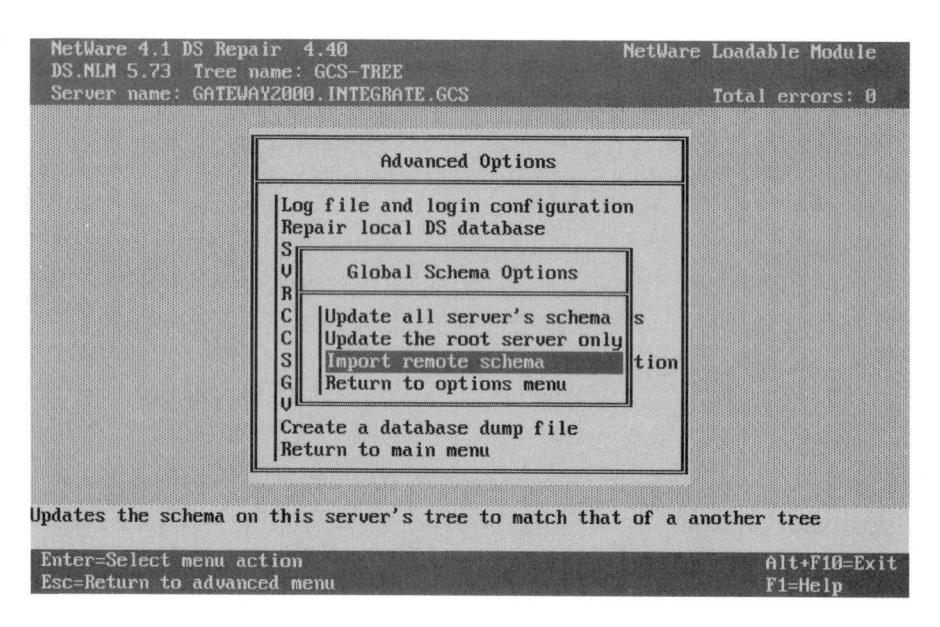

```
NetWare 4.1 DS Repair  4.40                      NetWare Loadable Module
DS.NLM 5.73  Tree name: GCS-TREE
Server name: GATEWAY2000.INTEGRATE.GCS                   Total errors: 0


                         ┌─────Advanced Options─────┐
                         │Log file and login configuration
                         │Repair local DS database
                         │S
                         │U ┌────Global Schema Options────┐
                         │R │
                         │C │Update all server's schema   │s
                         │C │Update the root server only  │
                         │S │Import remote schema         │tion
                         │G │Return to options menu       │
                         │U └─────────────────────────────┘
                         │Create a database dump file
                         │Return to main menu
                         └──────────────────────────┘

Updates the schema on this server's tree to match that of a another tree

Enter=Select menu action                                      Alt+F10=Exit
Esc=Return to advanced menu                                   F1=Help
```

checked. Why would Novell engineers put a choice here, when the Help screen for the choice admits there will be network errors if all servers aren't up to the same level?

The answer is that this is placed here for servers that were down or having an NDS problem when the updates were done. If at all possible, don't do any NDS maintenance unless all servers are up and running.

New versions of DSREPAIR released after NetWare 4.10, available on NetWire, allow schema updates between multiple NDS trees. Your evidence of this new option, now officially part of NetWare 4.11, is in Figure 10.54. Notice that you have the option of importing a remote schema from another tree. This wasn't possible with earlier versions of NetWare 4.

VIEW REPAIR LOG FILE The DSREPAIR.LOG file keeps track of every result from every procedure run against the NDS on this server. Figure 10.55 shows parts of some different operations.

> *NetWare 4.10 allowed you to edit this file, but they've changed this feature in NetWare 4.11. I've discovered that I can't edit this file in any way, shape, or form. I've tried editing it through the DSREPAIR advanced menu, and can't do it. I've tried using a text editor on the log file, after closing DSREPAIR, and I still can't do it.*

FIGURE 10.55

Viewing (but not editing) the DSREPAIR log file

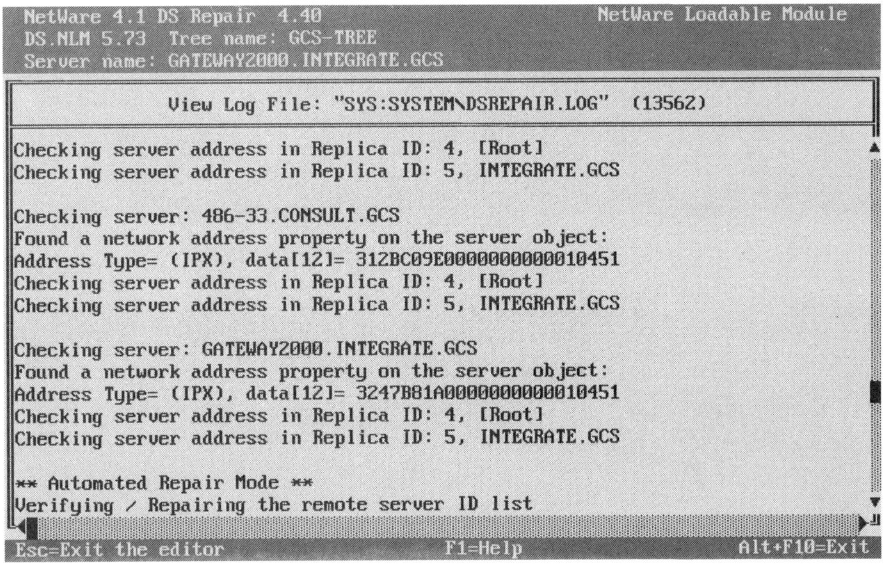

```
NetWare 4.1 DS Repair  4.40                    NetWare Loadable Module
DS.NLM 5.73  Tree name: GCS-TREE
Server name: GATEWAY2000.INTEGRATE.GCS
┌─────────────── View Log File: "SYS:SYSTEM\DSREPAIR.LOG"  (13562) ───────────────┐
│Checking server address in Replica ID: 4, [Root]                                 │
│Checking server address in Replica ID: 5, INTEGRATE.GCS                          │
│                                                                                 │
│Checking server: 486-33.CONSULT.GCS                                              │
│Found a network address property on the server object:                           │
│Address Type= (IPX), data[12]= 312BC09E00000000000010451                         │
│Checking server address in Replica ID: 4, [Root]                                 │
│Checking server address in Replica ID: 5, INTEGRATE.GCS                          │
│                                                                                 │
│Checking server: GATEWAY2000.INTEGRATE.GCS                                       │
│Found a network address property on the server object:                           │
│Address Type= (IPX), data[12]= 3247B81A00000000000010451                         │
│Checking server address in Replica ID: 4, [Root]                                 │
│Checking server address in Replica ID: 5, INTEGRATE.GCS                          │
│                                                                                 │
│** Automated Repair Mode **                                                      │
│Verifying / Repairing the remote server ID list                                  │
└─────────────────────────────────────────────────────────────────────────────────┘
Esc=Exit the editor              F1=Help                           Alt+F10=Exit
```

When you're finished viewing this file, press Escape and select to save the log file under the same name, or just exit.

CREATE A DATABASE DUMP FILE The Novell support team can make sense out of your dump file, if you send them one. The file is compressed, so looking at it yourself does no good. Since security is important to many customers, the file format keeps prying eyes from being able to easily read your Directory database. If not for security, why would the dumped file be almost five times larger than the ASCII log file?

You have a choice about dump file placement. The only restriction is that it be placed on a NetWare volume. Figure 10.56 shows the path name redirection option box.

If a dump file is there already, you may change the name or the path. The dump file zooms to disk, and before you know if it's started or not, the success screen tells you to press Enter and head back into the menu system once again.

Believe it or not, we are finished wandering in the world of partitions, replicas, schemas, and Directory databases. At least, we are for awhile. Once you choose the Return to Main Menu option or press Escape, you're out of the Advanced Options section. Back at the main menu, you'll see that we're out of DSREPAIR altogether.

FIGURE 10.56

Place your dump file where you want it.

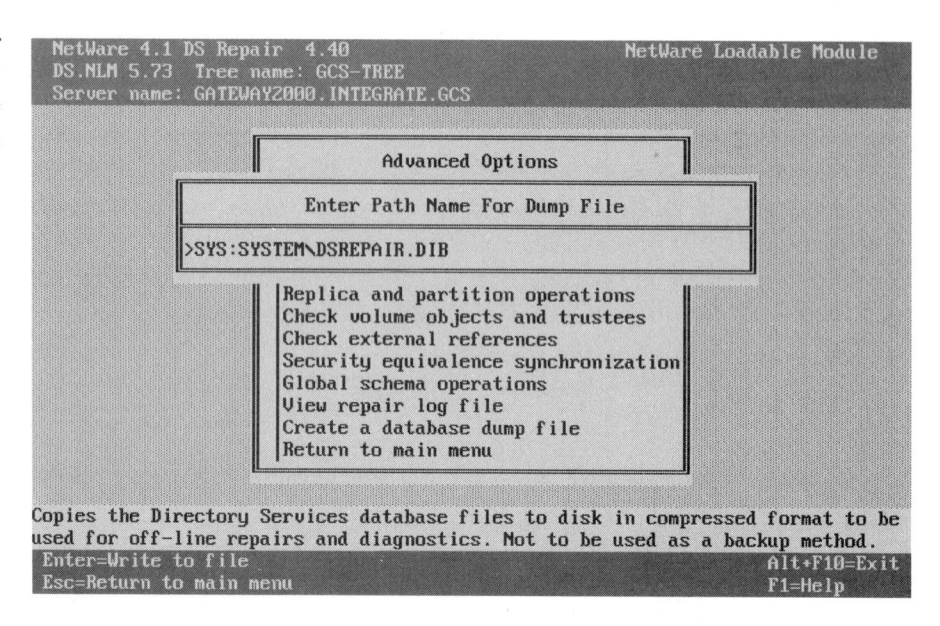

```
NetWare 4.1 DS Repair   4.40                        NetWare Loadable Module
DS.NLM 5.73   Tree name: GCS-TREE
Server name: GATEWAY2000.INTEGRATE.GCS

                    ┌─────────────────────────────────────┐
                    │          Advanced Options           │
                    ├─────────────────────────────────────┤
                    │    Enter Path Name For Dump File    │
                    ├─────────────────────────────────────┤
                    │>SYS:SYSTEM\DSREPAIR.DIB             │
                    └─────────────────────────────────────┘
                         │Replica and partition operations │
                         │Check volume objects and trustees│
                         │Check external references        │
                         │Security equivalence synchronization│
                         │Global schema operations         │
                         │View repair log file             │
                         │Create a database dump file      │
                         │Return to main menu              │

Copies the Directory Services database files to disk in compressed format to be
used for off-line repairs and diagnostics. Not to be used as a backup method.
 Enter=Write to file                                        Alt+F10=Exit
 Esc=Return to main menu                                    F1=Help
```

Using a Graphical DSREPAIR

> **10.30 IN-A-HURRY**
>
> **Use DSREPAIR from NDS Manager**
>
> **1.** Log in as Admin or equivalent and open NDS Manager.
>
> **2.** Highlight a partition in the upper-left window.
>
> **3.** Click on the Partition Continuity toolbar button (in the middle group, the far-right icon, showing three descending boxes).
>
> **4.** Highlight the server to be repaired.
>
> **5.** Click on the Repair Local Database toolbar button.

Hidden within NDS Manager is a fully graphical, almost complete copy of DSREPAIR. Novell managers haven't made much noise about this utility, but they should: this is pretty cool.

Figure 10.57 shows the DSREPAIR window you can get to from NDS Manager. If you can squint at the middle section of toolbar icons in the background NDS Manager window, you may be able to see the far-right icon of that group is three boxes arranged diagonally. On your own system, you'll see they are three different colors, making a nice transition effect. Since they are representing Partition Continuity, the transition is important.

The foreground window carries the label, appropriately enough, of Partition Continuity. You can't see the proper name, because I have the cursor pointing at the DSREPAIR icon. Notice the top status line says "Run DSRepair on the selected server."

Why would you use the console DSREPAIR if this version is here? Because the console version is more complete, and may work on systems too crippled to support users. Besides, the more you use the console version, the more you appreciate the graphical option.

FIGURE 10.57

DSREPAIR goes Hollywood.

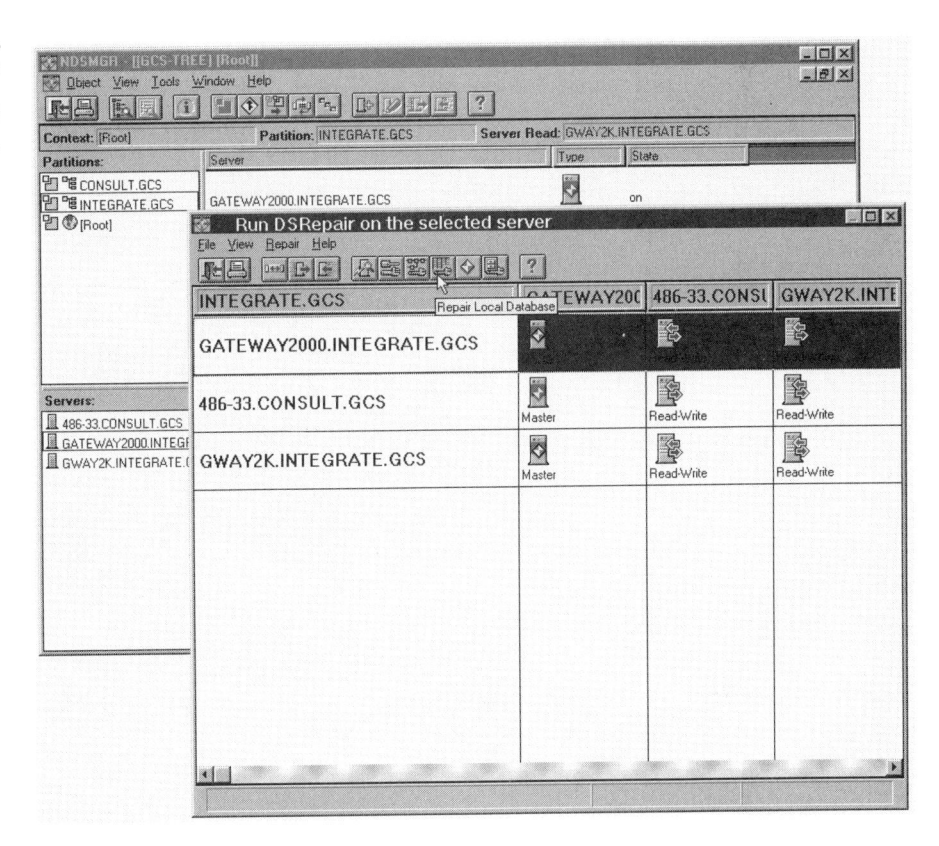

Running DSREPAIR functions from NDS Manager provides the same log file as the console version. You also have a choice of saving the log to an external file right on the viewing window. While DSREPAIR is running, the standard screens and repair details fly by on the server console in question, but, as you can see in Figure 10.58, the NDS Manager program stays graphical.

You can see the Save As command button on the bottom window in Figure 10.58. If you have young eyes, you can read the warning telling you that running DSREPAIR requires closing of the partition and so on.

The other icons within the Partition Continuity windows of NDS Manager allow you to:

- Close the active window (DSREPAIR).

- Print partition information.

FIGURE 10.58

DSREPAIR warning and resulting log within NDS Manager

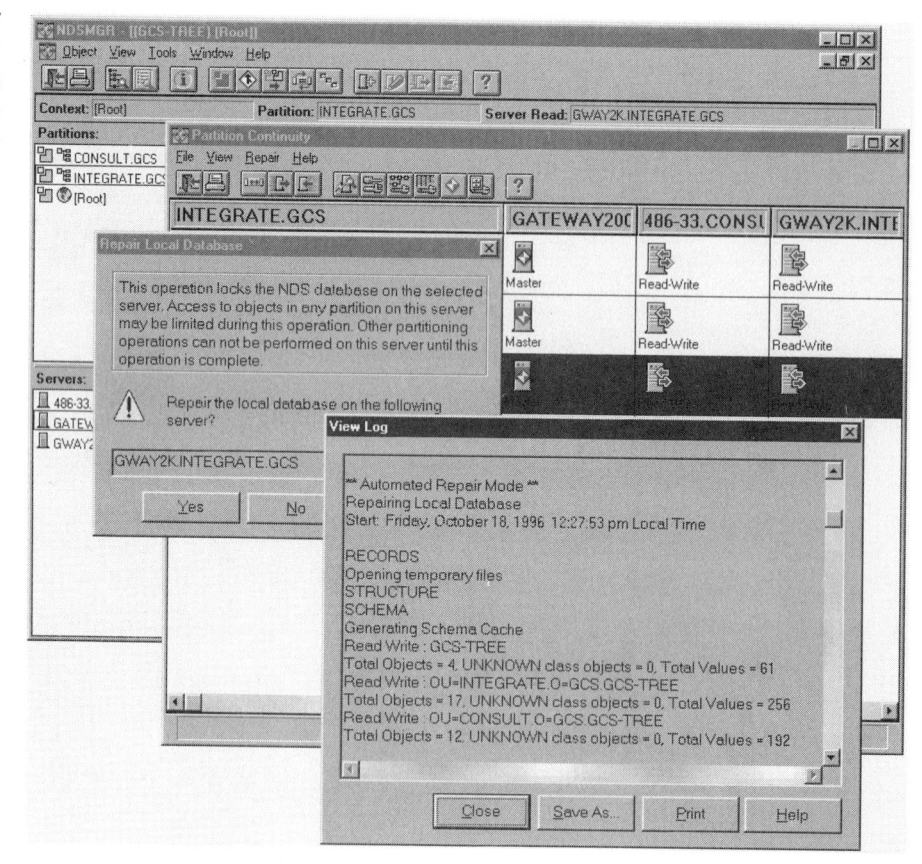

- Schedule an immediate synchronization of the highlighted partition.
- Send replica updates from the highlighted replica to all others.
- Update the highlighted server's replica from the Master replica.
- Check remote server IDs on the highlighted server.
- Repair a single replica.
- Repair network addresses on the selected server.
- Run DSREPAIR on the selected server.
- Reassign the current replica to be the Master replica.
- Repair volumes and trustees on a selected volume.

As you can see, there a few items missing from the NDS Manager version that you can do in the console version of DSREPAIR, but the main options are available. You may never have to mess with DSREPAIR if you're lucky.

> **TIP** *There are a few more fun things hiding in NDS Manager, and you should take some time to check it out yourself. The Help screen includes hundreds of error codes and their meanings, which is worth the price of admission all by itself. Not that you should expect to see error codes, but the only thing worse than seeing an error code at night is seeing one the morning your trip out of town starts. At least this way, you'll know what the error is quickly, and you may be able to fix it without taking a later plane.*

Using DSMERGE for NDS Tree Management

Companies with large networks often assume they need multiple NDS trees to handle their network design. Part of this feeling is misguided security, and part is a misunderstanding of how well the Organizations and Organizational Unit containers do their jobs.

After the company has multiple trees, the network managers realize it's difficult for users to see or take advantage of resources outside their own tree. With the first version of NetWare 4, the ability to merge two trees into one wasn't included. This caused some consternation.

Novell engineers developed a DSMERGE (Directory Services Merge) program. Using information gained at customer sites during DSMERGE development, the program was improved up until the last minute. Consequently, the documentation is lagging behind the software once again.

WARNING *The* Supplement to Introduction to NetWare NDS *booklet, was included in version NetWare 4.10, but not in 4.11. While using DSMERGE, and in fact any of the DS repair software mentioned, check the context-sensitive Help screens before every operation. What you think you're about to do, and what you may be doing, could be different.*

DSMERGE allows you to prune and graft your tree at the highest level imaginable: [Root]. This is not used to move containers or partitions (use NetWare Administrator for these functions). The program only works with two trees at one time. Your players in this tree drama are:

- **Local source tree:** The tree that will be folded into another tree. Start the operations from the server holding the master replica of this tree's [Root] partition.

- **Target tree:** The eventual new tree, with your local source tree folded in. The target tree name will be the same of the new tree.

Here are some details you should know before starting a DSMERGE operation:

- DSMERGE does not change container names or contexts within containers. The merged objects are retained. The file system is not touched at all, except for changed names of containers holding the volumes.

- The [Root] of the target tree becomes the new [Root] for objects in the source tree. Tree names for all servers and other objects in the source tree are changed to reflect their new tree name.

- During the merge, all replicas of the [Root] partition are removed from servers in the local tree. After the merge, the local tree replica is replaced by a replica of the combined trees.

Figure 10.59 shows the opening screen of the DSMERGE program. You see there are not many options, and the listings are straightforward.

The prerequisites are fairly stiff before a DSMERGE operation. If you think about it, there's nothing more extensive you can do to your NDS network. Every object in your source tree will be changed, and many of your target tree objects will require some adjustment. Here are the prerequisites:

- No active network connections are allowed. Close all connections on both trees. If there are users around who may try to login, disable login on all affected servers.

FIGURE 10.59

Major tree surgery upcoming

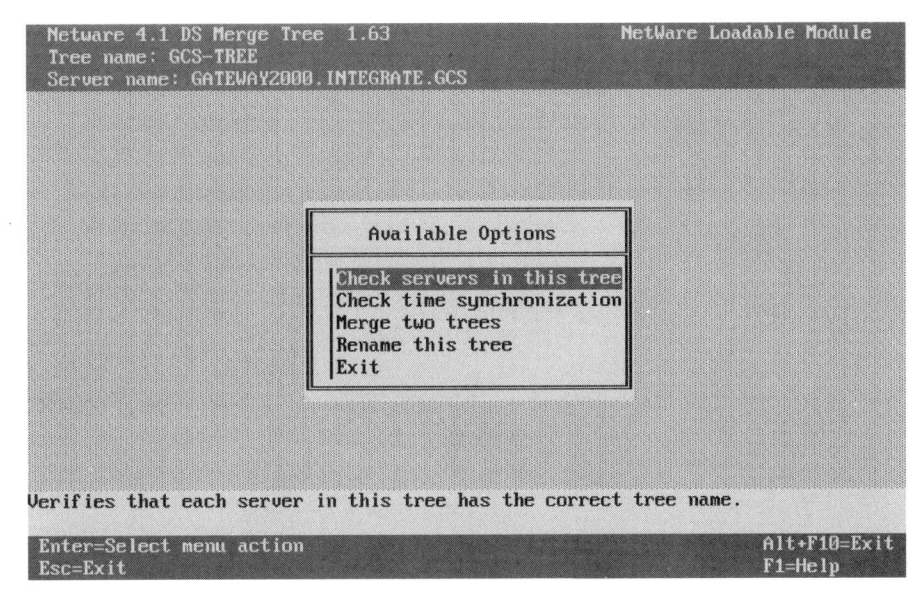

```
Netware 4.1 DS Merge Tree   1.63                NetWare Loadable Module
Tree name: GCS-TREE
Server name: GATEWAY2000.INTEGRATE.GCS




                        ┌──────Available Options──────┐
                        │ Check servers in this tree  │
                        │ Check time synchronization  │
                        │ Merge two trees             │
                        │ Rename this tree            │
                        │ Exit                        │
                        └─────────────────────────────┘




 Verifies that each server in this tree has the correct tree name.

 Enter=Select menu action                              Alt+F10=Exit
 Esc=Exit                                              F1=Help
```

- No leaf or Alias objects are allowed in the [Root] of the local source tree. Delete or move any Alias or leaf objects in the [Root] before starting. Give the Directory time to digest those changes.

- No similar names are allowed at the top of both trees. You may have identical container objects in both trees if they are not immediate subordinates of [Root]. The immediate container sets their identification. The full distinguished name will let your users tell the difference between ACME.ACCTNG.P1 and ACME.MFG.P1.

- NDS must be the same version on both trees. Upgrade all pre-4.11 servers that have a replica of the [Root] object, but be prepared to upgrade all servers. Having all servers running the same version will eliminate some problems and make management less complicated. It's worth the time to get every server on the same version before starting your network redesign.

- All servers must be up and running in both trees. If WAN links are involved, verify the servers on the remote side of the link. Technically, only those servers containing a replica of the [Root] must be up, but any down servers will delay the total integration of the two trees. It's best to have every server running.

- Schema on both trees must be the same. Any products installed on one tree that modify the schema must be installed on the other tree before merging.

- Time reference must be the same. Verify that each server in both trees is synchronized within ten seconds of the other. If both trees have either a Reference or Single Reference time server, change one of them to a Secondary or Primary time server. All servers in both trees should then reference the same time source.

- The two trees must have different names. If both trees have the same name, one must be renamed before starting DSMERGE.

You start DSMERGE from a server console or RCONSOLE session. Although you don't log in as the Admin user at the console or through RCONSOLE, you will need the Admin passwords for both trees. At the console colon prompt, type:

```
LOAD DSMERGE
```

Now you've reached DSMERGE's Available Options menu. These choices are described in the following sections.

Checking the Servers in This Tree

Before you start merging trees here and there, all the servers must be up, running, and current on their software versions. The first option on the DSMERGE menu is Check Server in This Tree. Press Enter to scan the tree and list all servers. Figure 10.60 shows the results of this check on my lab network.

What is this telling us? First, the servers are up, and they are in the tree where they belong. If the field shows an error or a status of down, check that before proceeding with the merge operation. The same goes if you see DS Locked, meaning the NDS database is probably still trying to digest some earlier change.

The worst news is if a server has an exclamation point in front of the name, as in:

```
!486-33
```

If this is the case, fix that server's problem before attempting the merge.

FIGURE 10.60

Servers in the tree, awaiting DSMERGE

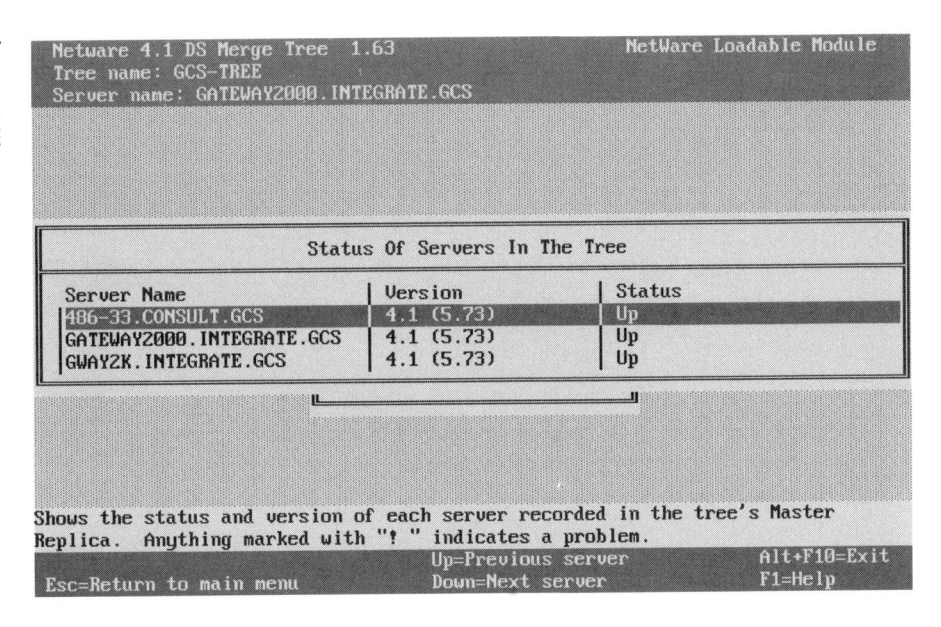

```
NetWare 4.1 DS Merge Tree  1.63                NetWare Loadable Module
Tree name: GCS-TREE
Server name: GATEWAY2000.INTEGRATE.GCS


                     Status Of Servers In The Tree
         ┌─────────────────────────────┬──────────────┬──────────┐
         │ Server Name                 │ Version      │ Status   │
         ├─────────────────────────────┼──────────────┼──────────┤
         │ 486-33.CONSULT.GCS          │ 4.1 (5.73)   │ Up       │
         │ GATEWAY2000.INTEGRATE.GCS   │ 4.1 (5.73)   │ Up       │
         │ GWAY2K.INTEGRATE.GCS        │ 4.1 (5.73)   │ Up       │
         └─────────────────────────────┴──────────────┴──────────┘


Shows the status and version of each server recorded in the tree's Master
Replica.  Anything marked with "!" indicates a problem.
                                    Up=Previous server        Alt+F10=Exit
Esc=Return to main menu             Down=Next server          F1=Help
```

Checking Time Synchronization

> **10.31 IN-A-HURRY**
>
> **Check Time Synchronization with DSMERGE**
>
> **1.** Type **LOAD DSMERGE** from the console prompt.
>
> **2.** Choose Check Time Synchronization.
>
> **3.** Check the server name, time server type, whether it's synchronized, and the time difference.
>
> **4.** Press Escape to return to the menu.

Synchronize your watches is a cliché of spy movies and comedies spoofing them, but it makes sense here. NDS relies on time stamps to control the database; events in dispute are settled by examining the time stamps. The merge may not continue if time is not properly configured on all involved servers.

When you press Enter on the Check Time Synchronization menu choice, a progress bar displays the query process to all servers. After all servers have responded to the NDS query, the server name and information are displayed. Figure 10.61 shows the screen with this information.

FIGURE 10.61

This tree is on time.

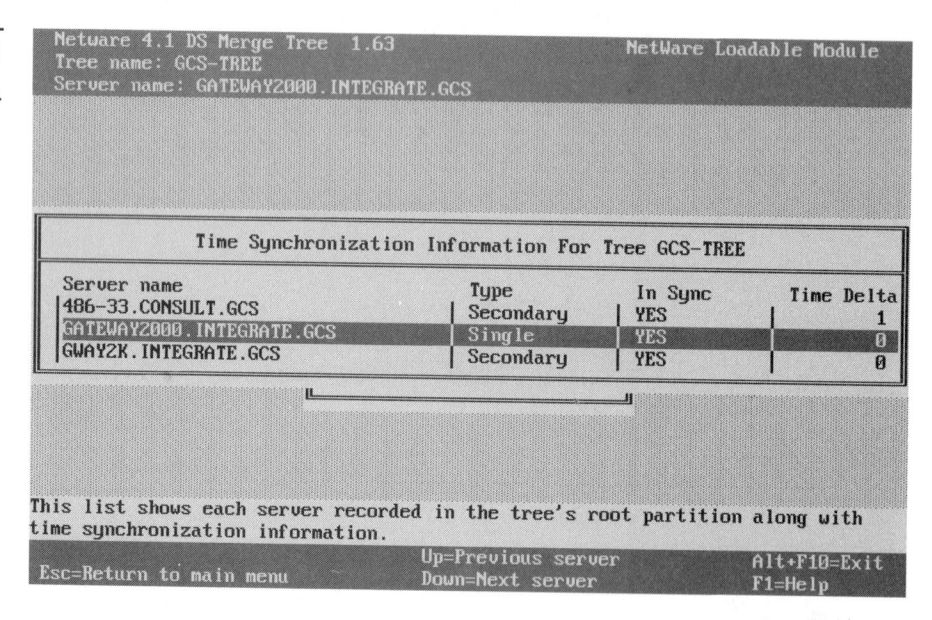

```
Netware 4.1 DS Merge Tree   1.63                        NetWare Loadable Module
Tree name: GCS-TREE
Server name: GATEWAY2000.INTEGRATE.GCS


            ┌─────────── Time Synchronization Information For Tree GCS-TREE ───────────┐
            │ Server name                    │ Type       │ In Sync │ Time Delta │
            │ 486-33.CONSULT.GCS             │ Secondary  │ YES     │     1      │
            │ GATEWAY2000.INTEGRATE.GCS      │ Single     │ YES     │     0      │
            │ GWAY2K.INTEGRATE.GCS           │ Secondary  │ YES     │     0      │
            └──────────────────────────────────────────────────────────────────────────┘

 This list shows each server recorded in the tree's root partition along with
 time synchronization information.
                              Up=Previous server             Alt+F10=Exit
 Esc=Return to main menu      Down=Next server               F1=Help
```

The first column shows the names of all servers in the tree. The second column shows the type of time server each is running. In our example, GATEWAY2000 is a Single Reference server, advertising the time, and 486-33 and GWAY2K both listen for time information. They are all in sync, and the time variance between the servers is zero, or less than two seconds, except for 486-33, which has a slightly larger variance, but nothing drastic.

Just because this screen looks good doesn't mean your time troubles are over. The report here does not check which time servers are referring to which time source. The time arrangement for the new, merged tree must be planned and configured before merging. If the other tree has a Single Reference time server, as is GATEWAY2000, one of the two must be downgraded to a Secondary or Primary time server before the merge.

Merging Two Trees

10.32 IN-A-HURRY

Merge Trees with DSMERGE

1. Type **LOAD DSMERGE** from the console prompt.
2. Choose Merge Two Trees and press Enter.
3. Provide the Admin name and password for the local tree.
4. Choose the target tree from the list and provide the Admin name and password for that tree.
5. Press F10 to start the merge.

When you select Merge Two Trees, the tree name for your local source tree will be filled in automatically. The full administrator's name, not just Admin, must be placed in the next field. The password is required, obviously. Figure 10.62 shows this screen being filled out.

FIGURE 10.62

Authenticating Admin users in both trees

```
Netware 4.1 DS Merge Tree  1.63                    NetWare Loadable Module
Tree name: GCS-TREE
Server name: GATEWAY2000.INTEGRATE.GCS



                            Merge Trees Information

   Source tree:          GCS-TREE
   Administrator name:   admin.gcs
   Password:             *****

   Target tree:          (Press <Enter> for a tree list)
   Administrator name:
   Password:



The source tree will be merged into the target tree. Press <Enter> to select a
target tree from a list.
   Enter=Edit this field          F10=Perform merge           Alt+F10=Exit
   Esc=Return to main menu        Down=Next field             F1=Help
```

If the target tree name you want isn't on the list that appears when you press Enter, press the Insert key and provide the network address of any server in the target tree. To get that address, type **CONFIG** at the server console prompt, and make a note of the IPX internal network number. That address will enable your local server to latch onto the target tree.

The Admin user password is required for the target tree as well. When all this is filled out, press F10 to perform the merge. The time the merge will take will vary depending on the size of the network, but it will be longer than when you organized the partitions earlier.

Renaming Trees

> **10.33 IN-A-HURRY**
>
> **Rename a Tree with DSMERGE**
>
> **1.** Type **LOAD DSMERGE** from the console prompt.
>
> **2.** Choose Rename This Tree.
>
> **3.** Provide the Admin name and password for the tree.
>
> **4.** Type the new name and press Enter.

Although you should give serious thought to naming your tree before you finish the installation, names do change at times. Merging a small tree into a large tree is the most efficient method, but you may prefer the name of the small tree. Your company or division may change names, necessitating a change of your network. You can change the name of a tree here. The physical process of changing the tree name is not difficult.

We covered tree naming in Chapter 3, but here's a refresher of the rules, which are a bit more restrictive than those for a regular object:

- Must be 32 characters or less

- May only include A–Z and 0–9; _ and - (underscore and dash), but not multiple adjacent underscores

- Cannot start or end with an underscore

After starting DSMERGE on the server console or RCONSOLE session, select the Rename This Tree option. You must then type the Admin name and password before you can type the new name. Figure 10.63 shows this process in progress.

FIGURE 10.63

A new tree name soon

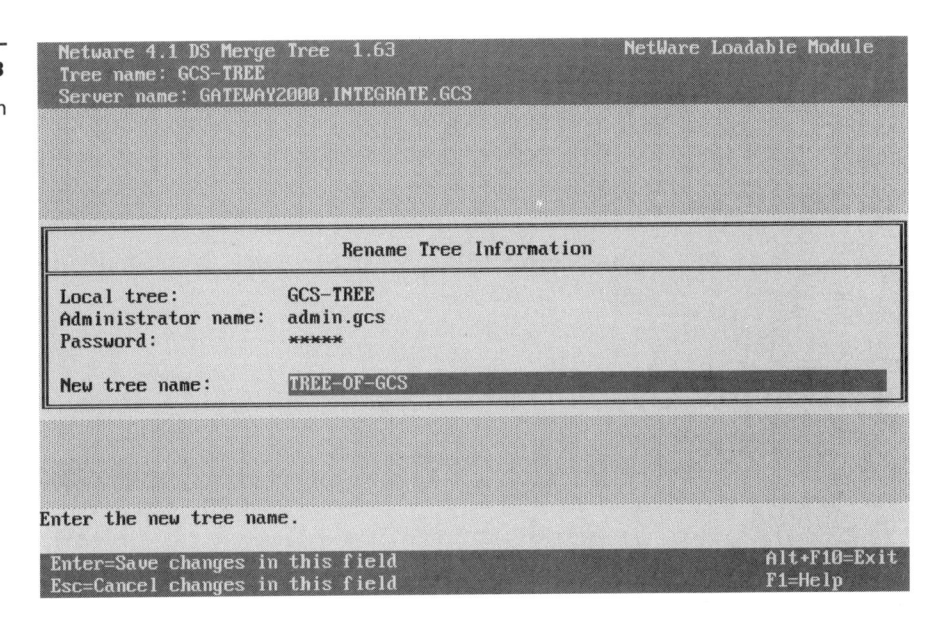

```
Netware 4.1 DS Merge Tree  1.63                    NetWare Loadable Module
Tree name: GCS-TREE
Server name: GATEWAY2000.INTEGRATE.GCS



                        ┌─────────────────────────────────────────┐
                        │         Rename Tree Information         │
                        ├─────────────────────────────────────────┤
                        │ Local tree:          GCS-TREE           │
                        │ Administrator name:  admin.gcs          │
                        │ Password:            *****              │
                        │                                         │
                        │ New tree name:       TREE-OF-GCS        │
                        └─────────────────────────────────────────┘


Enter the new tree name.

Enter=Save changes in this field                          Alt+F10=Exit
Esc=Cancel changes in this field                          F1=Help
```

After you press F10, it will take a few minutes to replicate the new tree name across the network. Don't do any other administrative tasks during that time, since NDS will be busy and may behave slightly odd during the process. Remember, if you change the tree name, you'll need to reset bunches of application references on all your user workstations. Make sure you really, truly, want to rename a tree before doing so.

Exiting and Cleaning Up

After you're finished with DSMERGE (choose Exit on the menu, and say Yes to Exit DSMERGE?), there are some things that you'll need to do immediately. Whether you merged trees or renamed one or two, a lot of users are suddenly lost in the woods, unable to find their favorite tree.

The bad news: NET.CFG files must be changed to reference the new PREFERRED TREE name. NCUPDATE won't help you here, because there is no leftover Alias object to trigger the LOGIN_ALIAS_CONTEXT feature in the login script. Of course, if you went from two trees to one, the PREFERRED TREE line may not be needed at all. If there's only one tree, there's no reason for the PREFERRED TREE statement. For Client32 systems, remember that the Preferred Tree field is in the Networking Properties screen, not in the NET.CFG file.

One more bit of administrivia: When merging multiple trees, the first tree's Admin user will lose all rights. Say you have Tree A merging into Tree B. No problem; both Admin users are fine. Say you now merge Tree B into Tree C. Problem: Admin from the original Tree A finds itself without rights. The Admin from either old Tree B or new Tree C must manually grant rights again to Admin A.

Installing Additive Server Licenses

10.34 IN-A-HURRY

Install an Additional License on a NetWare Server

1. Type **LOAD INSTALL** from the console prompt.

2. Choose License Option from the menu.

3. Insert the license diskette into the appropriate server drive and press Enter.

4. Move to the console prompt (press Alt+Escape on the console or Alt+F3 in RCONSOLE to cycle forward through all open screens).

5. Type **VERSION** to verify the new license count.

6. Move back to the INSTALL screen and exit by pressing Escape.

This process, new in NetWare 4.10 and continued in 4.11, allows you to add the number of user licenses per server you need, but not more than you need. Earlier NetWare versions required you to choose the number of concurrent users as one number: 5, 10, 20, 50, 100, 250, 500, or 1000 users. Obviously, if you needed 105 users, you wasted a lot of licenses.

Options for Novell included moving to a client-licensing arrangement. However, this turns out to be more unfair than a server license. It's common for NetWare users to have a 50-user license, but have 65 users. The trick is that only 50 are ever logged in at any one time. If you forced each user, even those that only connect to a particular server once a month, to buy a client license, the extra cost for the company wouldn't be trivial.

So NetWare 4.1*x* has additive licensing, often called "bump disks" for multiuser software. Now if a company has 105 clients, it can buy one license for 100 users, and another for 5 users. That covers the total needs, while still buying licenses in bulk rather than one at a time.

Commonly Used Console Commands

This section contains the eight commands typed at the console most often. The command frequency was determined by pure happenstance: I asked some friends which console commands they used, if any. These came up more than any other, but each network and network administrator is different.

The "top eight" are described in the following sections, in alphabetical order, not ranked in importance.

Displaying a Network List

The DISPLAY NETWORKS command lists all networks and network IDs known to the server's internal router. Figure 10.64 shows an example.

FIGURE 10.64
Result of the DISPLAY NETWORKS command

```
GATEWAY2000:display networks
   00000001   0/1         312BC09E   1/2         321624AC   1/2         3247B81A   0/1
   8F2D8928   0/1
There are 5 known networks.
GATEWAY2000:
```

The first number is the external network number of recognized networks. One of these numbers belongs to every server adapter card, as well as every configured protocol on every adapter card. The three physical servers in the lab generate five known networks, even though none have more than one network adapter card.

The second number indicates how far away the other network is. The first number of what looks like a fraction is the number of hops to the remote network. The second number is the time in ticks (about 1/18th of a second) required to send a packet to that address.

Displaying a Server List

The DISPLAY SERVERS command shows servers in the network. Figure 10.65 shows an example of the result of DISPLAY SERVERS.

FIGURE 10.65

Result of the DISPLAY SERVERS command

```
GATEWAY2000:display servers
   00C0110003FA  1   486-33        1   486-33        1   GATEWAY2000   0
   GATEWAY2000   0   GCS-TREE      1   GCS-TREE      0   GCS-TREE      0
   GCS-TREE      1   GWAY2K        1   GWAY2K        1   GWAY2K-GW     1
   PS-CONSULT    1
There are 13 known services.
```

The server name is shown. The number afterwards is the number of hops between your server and the referenced server. Your server always shows 0 hops.

Each NetWare 4.1x server advertises at least two services: file service and NDS service. Print servers show up as servers in this display, as do NDS trees. Notice that the IPX/IP Gateway shows up as a server also (GWAY2K-GW).

Shutting Down the Server

The DOWN command writes information in the server cache to disk, closes files, updates directory entry tables and file allocation tables, and shuts down the server in an orderly manner.

When you use DOWN, warnings are sent to each connected workstation, then you'll see a message saying that it's safe to reboot or power off the server.

Using Exit to Unload NetWare

EXIT unloads NetWare from server memory after the server is down. When you use EXIT, you'll end up at the DOS prompt from the server DOS partition. EXIT removes NetWare memory and applications from the server, making the unit a DOS machine once more.

If restarting your server is the goal, you may type

```
RESTART SERVER
```

after using DOWN. This saves the steps of using EXIT and then running the SERVER.EXE program from the DOS partition.

Listing NLMs

The MODULES command lists all loaded NLM programs, along with version information. Figure 10.66 shows an example of the result.

FIGURE 10.66

Using the MODULES command

```
GATEWAY2000:modules
NBI.NLM
    NetWare Bus Interface
    Version 1.44    July 2, 1996
    Copyright 1996 Novell, Inc.  All rights reserved.
NWPA.NLM
    NetWare 3.12/4.x NetWare Peripheral Architecture NLM : NBI Aware.
    Version 2.31    July 1, 1996
    Copyright 1991-96, Novell, Inc.  All rights reserved.
IDEATA.HAM
    Novell IDE/ATA/ATAPI Host Adapter Module
    Version 1.21    July 2, 1996
    Copyright 1991-96, Novell, Inc.  All rights reserved.
IDECD.CDM
    NetWare 3.12/4.x ATAPI CDROM Custom Device Module.
    Version 1.00    June 18, 1996
    Copyright 1994-96, Novell, Inc.  All rights reserved.
IDEHD.CDM
    NetWare 3.12/4.x Fixed Disk Custom Device Module.
    Version 1.20    June 18, 1996
    Copyright 1992-96, Novell, Inc.  All rights reserved.
<Press ESC to terminate or any other key to continue>
```

This list normally takes several pages, and the modules don't seem to appear in any particular order. However, they are listed in the order loaded. When modules are unloaded, they leave a slot open for the next module. If no free slots exist, later modules are appended to the end of the list.

Dates of modules can become critical when chasing stubborn problems. Rest assured, whatever date you have on your system modules, at least two will be out of date already (or at least that will be the problem according to technical support).

Tracking RIP and SAP Information

TRACK ON displays RIP and SAP tracking information sent between servers on the console screen. Figure 10.67 shows an example of the result.

FIGURE 10.67

Using TRACK ON to track routing information

```
SAP Tracking Screen
                                                              IN [000000
01:00C0110003FA]  5:48:04      00C0110003FA  1
IN [00000001:00C0110003FA]  5:49:04      00C0110003FA  1
IN [00000001:00C0110003FA]  5:50:03      00C0110003FA  1
IN [00000001:00C0110003FA]  5:51:03      00C0110003FA  1
IN [8F2D8928:0020AFD82229]  5:51:43      Send All Server Info
OUT [8F2D8928:0020AFD82229]  5:51:43     GWAY2K-GW           1
IN [00000001:00C0110003FA]  5:52:03      00C0110003FA  1
IN [00000001:00C0110003FA]  5:53:03      00C0110003FA  1
IN [00000001:00C0110003FA]  5:54:03      00C0110003FA  1
IN [00000001:00C0110003FA]  5:55:02      00C0110003FA  1
IN [00000001:00C0110003FA]  5:56:02      00C0110003FA  1
IN [00000001:00C0110003FA]  5:57:02      00C0110003FA  1
IN [00000001:00C0110003FA]  5:58:02      00C0110003FA  1
IN [00000001:00C0110003FA]  5:59:02      00C0110003FA  1
IN [00000001:00C0110003FA]  6:00:01      00C0110003FA  1
IN [00000001:00C0110003FA]  6:01:01      00C0110003FA  1
IN [00000001:00C0110003FA]  6:02:01      00C0110003FA  1
IN [00000001:00C0110003FA]  6:03:01      00C0110003FA  1
IN [8F2D8928:0020AFD82229]  6:03:19      Get Nearest Server
OUT [8F2D8928:0020AFD82229]  6:03:19     Give Nearest Server
GWAY2K
<Use ALT-ESC or CTRL-ESC to switch screens, or any other key to pause>
```

This display has now been split into an SAP and RIP screen. Earlier versions had both RIP and SAP on the same screen, but growth changed that setup. Two screens keep the information from scrolling by so fast, which was a problem in a busy network.

Each packet is labeled IN if the server is receiving information, and OUT if the server is broadcasting information. Servers also receive and respond to connection requests from clients attempting to log in to a server. These requests show up as Get Nearest Server requests and Give Nearest Server responses. Clients looking to log in will send a packet labeled Get Nearest Server, and the server will send its name and address in a packet labeled Give Nearest Server.

The first line shows a packet coming in to the server, on network 00000001 from address 00C0110003FA, at 5:49:04. Most other packets are coming from the same location. Notice that SAP information broadcasts once each minute or so.

This is server GWAY2K, and you can see at the end of the screen that a request for information came in, and the response was provided in less than a second.

To turn off this display, use the TRACK OFF command.

Turn TRACK ON when you can't understand why a client is unable to log in to a particular server. While watching the console screen, either directly or through RCONSOLE, have the user log in again. The activity of the server, assuming that the server can even see the client, will help you isolate the problem.

Listing Version Information

Use VERSION to list the NetWare operating system license information. Figure 10.68 shows an example of the information the command shows.

FIGURE 10.68

Using VERSION to see license information

```
GATEWAY2000:version
Novell NetWare 4.11   August 22, 1996
(C) Copyright 1983-1996 Novell Inc.
All Rights Reserved.
Patent Pending -- Novell Inc.

OEM Identification:  1
Maximum Number of License Connections:  25
Installed Licenses:
Serial Number    Connections    License Type    Version    Expiration
20466007         25             WEB/CONN        4.11       NONE
```

This shows the NetWare version, with the date stamp, which is useful when you're checking for needed upgrades or patches. The most important part of the command result is the number of license connections on the server, and installed licenses. NetWare 4.10 shows a license chain of all additive licenses on the server, listed in order. NetWare 4.11 lists installed licenses that are controlled by NetWare License Services.

Listing Volume Information

VOLUMES shows mounted volumes on the server, including CD-ROM volumes. Figure 10.69 shows an example of the result.

FIGURE 10.69

Using VOLUMES to see server volumes

```
GATEWAY2000:volumes
Mounted Volumes            Name Spaces              Flags
  SYS                        DOS                    Cp Sa
  PROJECTS                   DOS                    Cp Sa
GATEWAY2000:
```

The Name Spaces section shows DOS here, but includes Mac, NFS, and OS/2 when those name spaces are supported on the volume. Name spaces are set per volume, not per server.

The Flags column shows volume characteristics: Cp means compressed, Sa means block suballocation, and Mg means data migration is enabled (which isn't the case for the volumes shown in Figure 10.69).

Managing Protocols and Remote Server Access with INETCFG

The INETCFG (InterNETworking CONfiguration) utility is the focal point of all protocols on your server. The LOAD and BIND commands in the AUTOEXEC.NCF file, configured when you installed your server, can be moved under control of INETCFG. This makes it possible to configure multiple protocols in this one utility. Figure 10.70 shows the opening menu for INETCFG.

FIGURE 10.70

Opening menu for protocol and other network configurations. This version comes with the IPX/IP Gateway, and includes some extras.

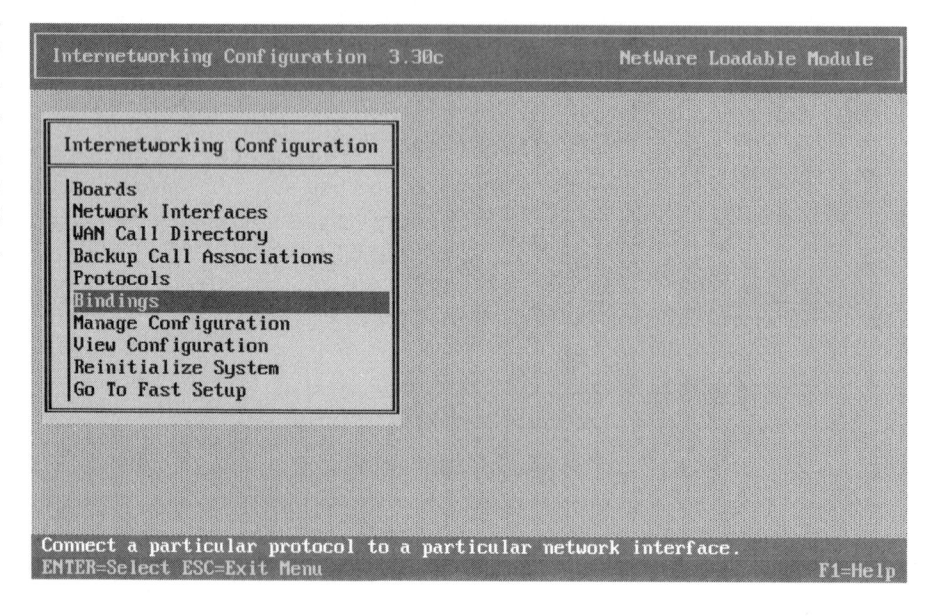

```
Internetworking Configuration   3.30c              NetWare Loadable Module

    ┌─ Internetworking Configuration ─┐
    │ Boards                          │
    │ Network Interfaces              │
    │ WAN Call Directory              │
    │ Backup Call Associations        │
    │ Protocols                       │
    │ Bindings                        │
    │ Manage Configuration            │
    │ View Configuration              │
    │ Reinitialize System             │
    │ Go To Fast Setup                │
    └─────────────────────────────────┘

Connect a particular protocol to a particular network interface.
ENTER=Select  ESC=Exit Menu                                  F1=Help
```

The menu options work as follows:

- **Boards:** Adds a new hardware network board or modifies the hardware parameters of an existing board.

- **Network Interfaces:** Configures WAN boards, if you have one in your server. Don't use this menu item for LAN boards.

- **WAN Call Directory:** Specifies connection parameters for remote site connections.

- **Backup Call Associations:** Allows you to add, modify, or delete backup call numbers for remote site connections.

- **Protocols:** Enables and configures protocols for your server.

- **Bindings:** Links protocols to network interfaces.

- **Manage Configuration:** Sets up SNMP parameters, exports copies of your configuration to disk, imports them back from a disk, enables remote access to the server, and edits the AUTOEXEC.NCF file.

- **View Configuration:** Displays the commands used by INETCFG to set the network configuration of your server. The submenu breaks down the presentation various ways, so you can check just one section or get an overview of the entire configuration.

- **Reinitialize System:** Makes your newly configured settings the active settings (new with NetWare 4.11).

- **Go to Fast Setup:** Starts a streamlined set of menus for basic configuration details (new with NetWare 4.11).

When you first run INETCFG, the LOAD and BIND statements are moved from your AUTOEXEC.NCF to a special file under control of INETCFG exclusively. These files should not be edited directly or interfered with in any manner:

- AURP.CFG
- TCPIP.CGF
- IPXSPX.CFG
- NLSP.CFG

- NETINFO.CFG
- INITSYS.NCF (new with NetWare 4.11)

INETCFG offers one-stop protocol shopping for your server. This program configures the network boards, sets up different protocols, and hooks them to the proper boards.

NetWare has a great history of support for the Macintosh computer. Novell was the first network operating system vendor to support AppleTalk, and is now supporting Macintosh systems over IPX as well. As an example of the importance of Macintosh support to Novell, the installation program offers a chance to support AppleTalk. Turn to Chapter 13 for the entire Macintosh and NetWare story. That chapter includes the installation and configuration details necessary to support Macintosh clients.

Just as important to Novell as AppleTalk, TCP/IP also has a switch for support during server installation. Whether you set that switch or not, you'll need some TCP/IP details to configure this protocol on your NetWare server. You'll find those details in Chapter 14, where we discuss integrating NetWare Unix hosts, along with Internet connections.

Configuring IPX

10.35 IN-A-HURRY

Configure IPX with INETCFG

1. Type **LOAD INETCFG** from the console prompt (or RCONSOLE).
2. Choose Boards to verify the initial setup done during installation.
3. Choose Network Interfaces to verify the initial setup done during installation.
4. Choose Protocols to open the Protocol Configuration menu.
5. Choose IPX to set any advanced options.
6. Press Escape twice to return to the main menu.

IPX is the workhorse protocol for 99.9 percent of all NetWare networks. Although it's now possible to run a NetWare server without IPX by using NetWare/IP, there's little reason to do so. Supporting a second protocol doesn't interfere with the server's ability to maintain IPX support. And as we've seen, IPX is well-suited for the LAN, providing excellent performance without requiring any management, installation, or configuration time.

The default IPX configuration doesn't add any extra bells and whistles. Figure 10.71 shows the entry screen behind the Protocols and IPX menu choices. If you wish to set advanced options, you may do so here by enabling the Advanced IPX option. If you don't enable Advanced IPX, there isn't a single active field in this or the next screen.

There are a few options in Expert Configuration Options you will want to check into. The Expert Configuration Options choices aren't particularly complex, either. Take a look at Figure 10.72, which appears when you press Enter on the Expert Configuration Options field.

This screen also provides NLSP options. This is the NetWare Links Support Protocol, a feature introduced in NetWare 4.10 that replaces RIP and SAP. See Chapter 18 for information about using NLSP. The other fields on the IPX Expert Configuration screen that you can configure include:

- **Get Nearest Server Requests:** Accepts or ignores packets requesting the name of the nearest server. These are usually clients trying to login. The default is to accept.

FIGURE 10.71

Advanced IPX is still fairly simple.

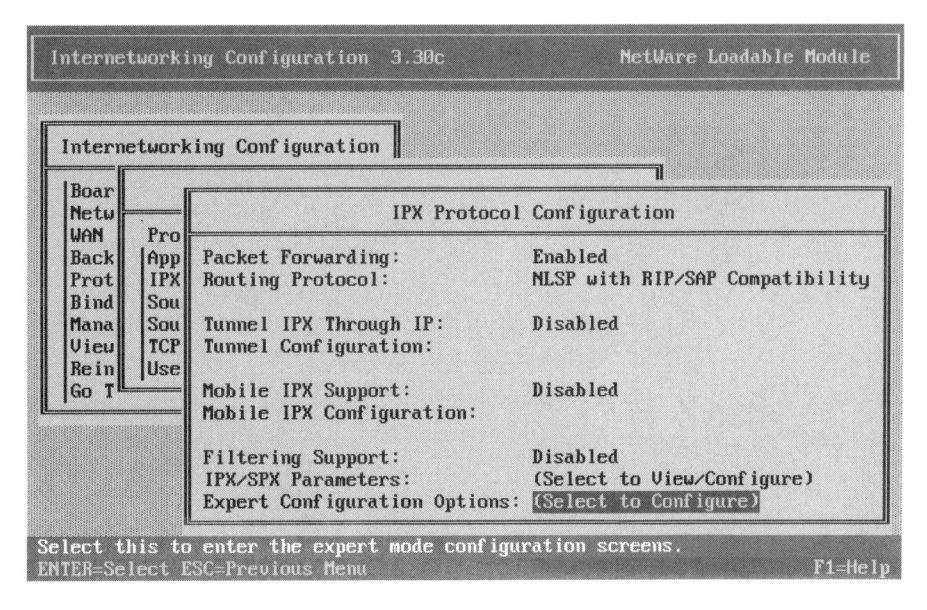

FIGURE 10.72

Expert IPX defaults and explanations

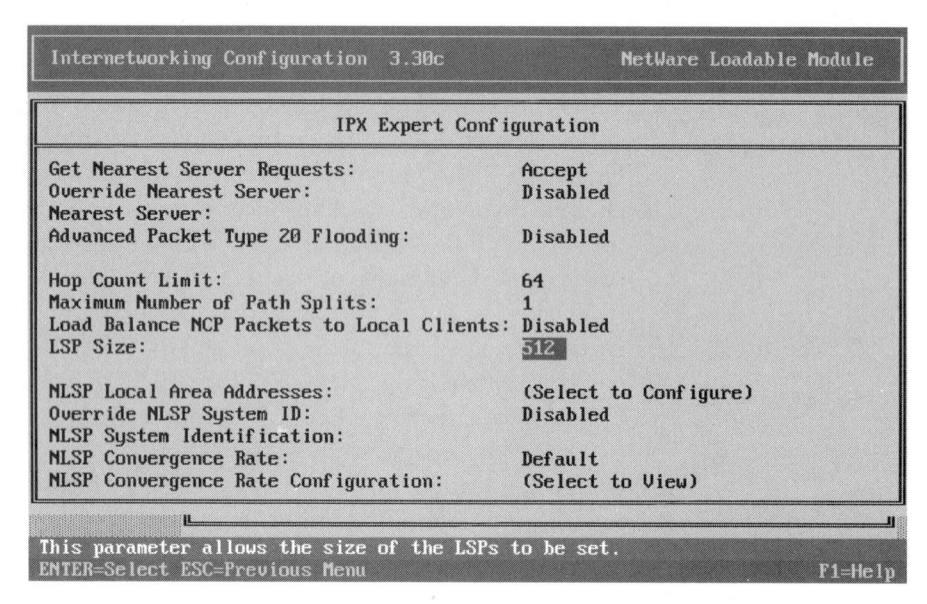

```
Internetworking Configuration  3.30c          NetWare Loadable Module

                         IPX Expert Configuration
  Get Nearest Server Requests:         Accept
  Override Nearest Server:             Disabled
  Nearest Server:
  Advanced Packet Type 20 Flooding:    Disabled

  Hop Count Limit:                     64
  Maximum Number of Path Splits:       1
  Load Balance NCP Packets to Local Clients: Disabled
  LSP Size:                            512

  NLSP Local Area Addresses:           (Select to Configure)
  Override NLSP System ID:             Disabled
  NLSP System Identification:
  NLSP Convergence Rate:               Default
  NLSP Convergence Rate Configuration: (Select to View)

This parameter allows the size of the LSPs to be set.
ENTER=Select ESC=Previous Menu                          F1=Help
```

- **Override Nearest Server:** When enabled, responds to Get Nearest Server packets with the name of another server. This is useful with Novell's MPR (MultiProtocol Router), which can't accept more than one connection. If enabled, the previous field allows you to name the server to send in response to the Get Nearest Server query. The default is disabled.

- **Advanced Packet Type 20 Flooding:** Support for NetBIOS (IPX Type 20) packet routing and propagation. This may place multiple NetBIOS packets on some legs of the network. For NetWare network, any NetBIOS packets are too many. Avoid them if possible.

- **Hop Count Limit:** The number of routers (or other NetWare servers) a packet can go through before being killed. Although this sounds harsh, the reasoning is sound; if a packet goes through too many servers and routers, it must be lost. Packets, being male, hate to ask for directions (and actually can't if they want to). Novell recommends setting this value to the maximum diameter of your network, up to 16 hops (127 if you have enabled NLSP).

- **Maximum Number of Path Splits:** Sets the number of equal-cost paths NLSP will consider when forwarding packets. Be aware that paths set to equal cost, but that have unequal speed, may cause IPX problems due to packets arriving at "inopportune" times. In other words, don't count two paths equal in cost unless they're roughly equal in performance.

- **Load Balance NCP Packets to Local Clients:** NetWare 4.11 allows load balancing from the server, meaning faster performance and maximized high-performance links rather than slower connections.

- **LSP Size:** Least Sized Packet, in bytes, which can't be larger than your minimum frame size for all types of frames enabled.

More detailed IPX information is available in IPXCON, which we'll cover soon. Keep in mind, the level of configuration we have just covered is not necessary for the vast majority of networks.

Configuring RCONSOLE Parameters

> **10.36 IN-A-HURRY**
>
> **Configure RCONSOLE with INETCFG**
>
> 1. Type **LOAD INETCFG** from the console prompt (or RCONSOLE).
> 2. Choose Manage Configuration, and then choose Configure Remote Access to This Server.
> 3. Enable Remote Access, and provide an appropriate password.
> 4. Enable RCONSOLE Connection.
> 5. Press Escape twice to return to the main menu.

Remote access to your server means more than just RCONSOLE, although that utility is used the majority of the time. If you have Unix systems on your network, you can run RCONSOLE from any terminal that supports vt100 emulation. This is the XCONSOLE program, and the Unix protocol support is Telnet. This screen also allows you to install software from a remote server.

As we did in the RCONSOLE section earlier, we must load both REMOTE.NLM and RSPX.NLM. This can also be done through INETCFG. As you can see in Figure 10.73, we have enabled remote access and provided a password. Following my instructions earlier, this password is longer than six characters, and includes numeric characters as well.

894 Chapter 10 • NetWare 4.1x Administrator Duties and Tools

FIGURE 10.73
Configuring the server side of RCONSOLE

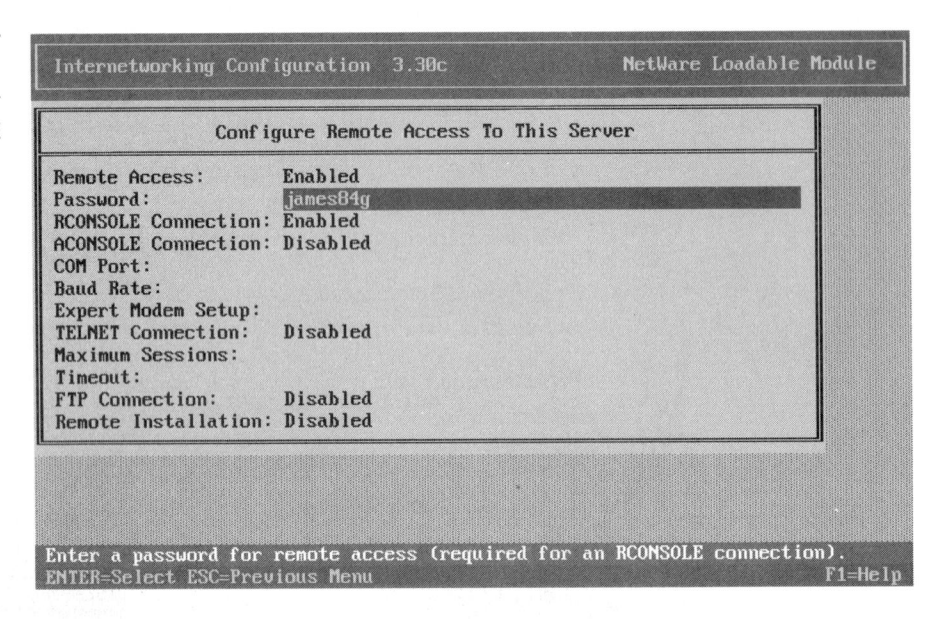

```
Internetworking Configuration  3.30c          NetWare Loadable Module

            Configure Remote Access To This Server
  Remote Access:        Enabled
  Password:             james84g
  RCONSOLE Connection:  Enabled
  ACONSOLE Connection:  Disabled
  COM Port:
  Baud Rate:
  Expert Modem Setup:
  TELNET Connection:    Disabled
  Maximum Sessions:
  Timeout:
  FTP Connection:       Disabled
  Remote Installation:  Disabled


  Enter a password for remote access (required for an RCONSOLE connection).
  ENTER=Select ESC=Previous Menu                                    F1=Help
```

> **WARNING**
>
> *Notice that the password for RCONSOLE is not hidden here, as it is for user passwords. Just another reason to keep the server away from curious hands and eyes. Anything that can be done at the console can be done through RCONSOLE, making this a security hole you must keep plugged.*

Configuring ACONSOLE Parameters

Remote access through a modem directly to the server was a great innovation in the middle 1980s, but seems to be less important today. For one thing, resetting the COM port when the modem locks up requires a server reboot. Managers try to minimize these reboots, but modems have a mind of their own. Another reason this has fallen out of favor is the wide availability of remote control software for PCs, allowing a user to remotely control a station on the network. This station can certainly run RCONSOLE, so that if the modem locks and a reboot is necessary, it happens to a workstation rather than to the server.

If you need a modem connection to the server, INETCFG provides a place to set it up. You use the same screen as you do for RCONSOLE configuration. Figure 10.74 shows the new ACONSOLE information configured.

10.37 IN-A-HURRY

Configure ACONSOLE with INETCFG

1. Type **LOAD INETCFG** from the console prompt (or RCONSOLE).

2. Choose Manage Configuration, then Configure Remote Access to This Server.

3. Enable Remote Access, and provide an appropriate password (if a password hasn't already been defined).

4. Enable ACONSOLE Connection.

5. Set the COM port, baud rate, and any Expert Modem Setup parameters, as necessary.

6. Press Escape twice to return to the main menu.

FIGURE 10.74 Multiple remote-access options to this server

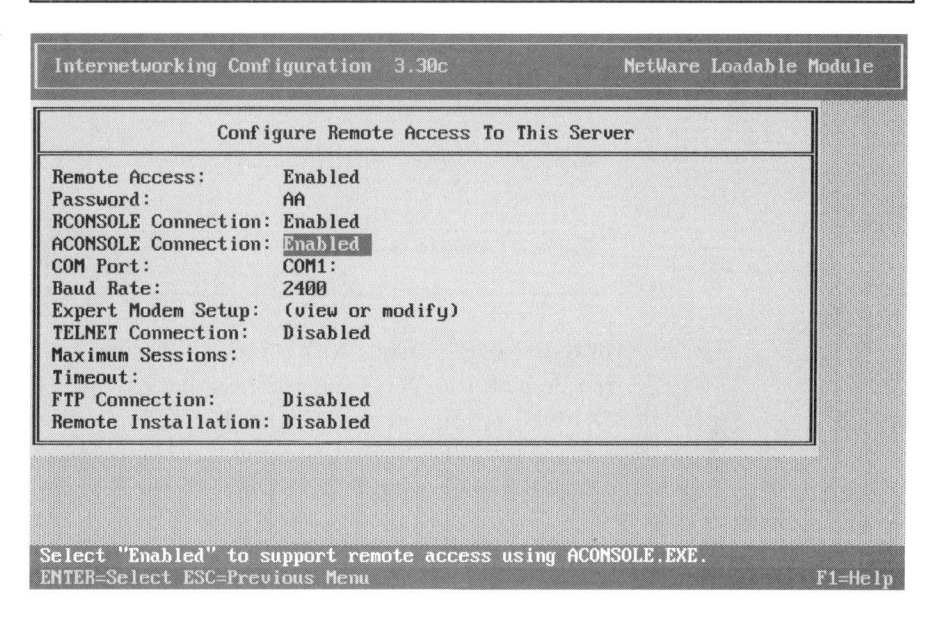

```
Internetworking Configuration   3.30c              NetWare Loadable Module

                    Configure Remote Access To This Server
   Remote Access:        Enabled
   Password:             AA
   RCONSOLE Connection:  Enabled
   ACONSOLE Connection:  Enabled
   COM Port:             COM1
   Baud Rate:            2400
   Expert Modem Setup:   (view or modify)
   TELNET Connection:    Disabled
   Maximum Sessions:
   Timeout:
   FTP Connection:       Disabled
   Remote Installation:  Disabled


Select "Enabled" to support remote access using ACONSOLE.EXE.
ENTER=Select  ESC=Previous Menu                              F1=Help
```

The only options for server COM ports are COM1 and COM2. The modem Baud Rate options are 2400, 4800, and 9600. (Since modems are cheap today, get a 9600 model, if you can still find one this slow; 9600 is the limit of the server connection.) Yes, the default really is 2400; I told you this was an old utility. The screen painting in ACONSOLE is not at all optimized, and the color palette takes longer than you think to transmit. If you have particular modem initialization parameters to set, the Expert Modem Setup option will let you type in all you want.

Activating ACONSOLE requires RS232.NLM to be loaded in the AUTOEXEC.NCF file. This NLM controls the COM port for the modem.

Viewing Advanced IPX Statistics with IPXCON

> **10.38 IN-A-HURRY**
>
> **View IPX Protocol Details with IPXCON**
>
> 1. Type **LOAD IPXCON** from the console prompt (or RCONSOLE).
> 2. View the packet statistics on the opening screen.
> 3. For more details, choose IPX Information, and then choose Detailed IPX Information.
> 4. For IPX internal router statistics, choose the Circuits, Forwarding, and Services options.
> 5. Press Escape to exit.

For those never satisfied with standard information, IPXCON should satiate your desire for numbers and numbers that have little value in normal networks. IPXCON, as you can see in Figure 10.75, duplicates some of the information from the MONITOR program, but the menu hints at so many more numbers.

Useful functions of IPXCON include the following:

- Monitor IPX routers and network segments.
- View IPX router and network segment status.
- View all IPX packet paths.
- Locate the IPX routers on your complete network.
- Monitor remote IPX routers running NetWare IPX router software.

FIGURE 10.75
Tracking the packets as they whiz by

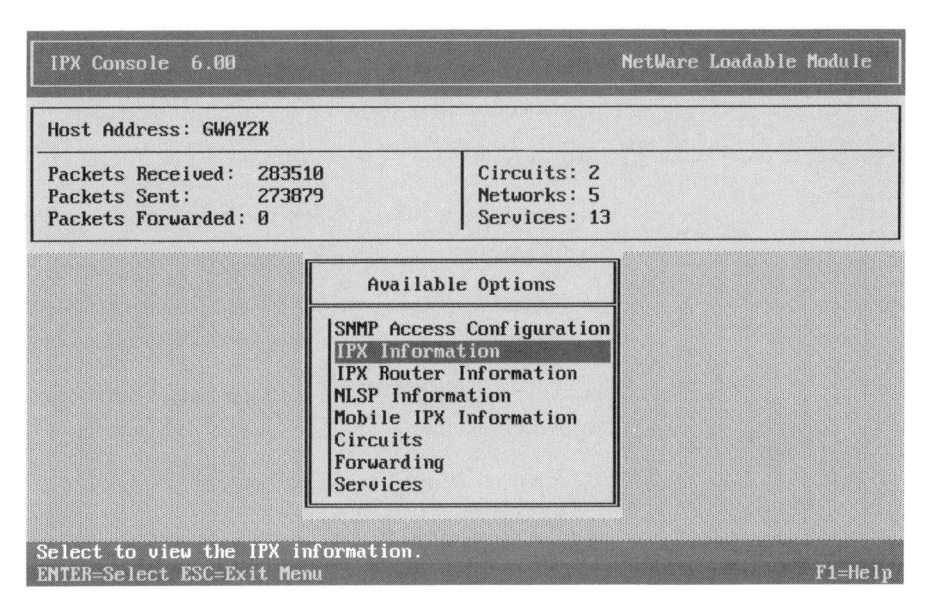

```
IPX Console  6.00                              NetWare Loadable Module

Host Address: GWAY2K

Packets Received:  283510        Circuits: 2
Packets Sent:      273879        Networks: 5
Packets Forwarded: 0             Services: 13

                    Available Options
                    SNMP Access Configuration
                    IPX Information
                    IPX Router Information
                    NLSP Information
                    Mobile IPX Information
                    Circuits
                    Forwarding
                    Services

Select to view the IPX information.
ENTER=Select ESC=Exit Menu                              F1=Help
```

These options aren't of much interest if you have a small network with just a few servers, all in one location. If you have a large internetwork, however, knowing details about the status and throughput of your IPX routers will become more and more important to you.

Using NetSync

NetSync lets you manage NetWare 3.1*x* servers as part of your NDS network. While it doesn't make a NetWare 3.1*x* server into a NetWare 4.1*x* server, it makes it manageable by NetWare Administrator and all your other familiar NetWare 4.1*x* tools. Some of the features are:

- Synchronize NetWare 3.1*x* users and groups with a NetWare 4.1 server bindery context.

- Manage NetWare 3.1*x* users and groups using NetWare Administrator and NETADMIN.

- Move NetWare 3.1*x* print services to a NetWare 4.1*x* server, and consolidate multiple print servers into one.

- Users of NetWare 3.1x servers can easily attach and use any other NetWare 3.1x network resource with a single login (limited by proper trustee rights, of course).

Who needs this? Companies that:

- Can't move all the NetWare 3.1x servers to NetWare 4.1x servers at one time.

- Have critical software not yet compatible with NetWare 4.1x, but need the NetWare 4.1x management advantages.

- Are running NetWare Name Services software and can't yet migrate all servers in the NNS (NetWare Name Service) domain to NetWare 4.1x.

Companies should avoid NetSync if:

- You have only NetWare 4.1x servers.

- You don't want to move NetWare 3.1x users and groups into the NetWare 4.1x global Directory.

- You are moving all NetWare 3.1x servers to NetWare 4.1x servers in a fairly short time span.

NetSync Overview

NetSync works by having the NetWare 4.1x server absorb the NetWare 3.1x server's bindery. One NetWare 4.1x server can control a cluster of 12 NetWare 3.1x servers. All servers become part of the container where the NetWare 4.1x server existed before starting NetSync. The Bindery Services for the NetWare 4.1x server is normally, but doesn't need to be, set to the same container. Life is easier if all these things match, however.

NetSync NLMs run on all NetWare servers that are part of the NetSync cluster. The NLMs handle the communication between servers, and allow the NetWare Administrator and NETADMIN programs to control access to the NetWare 3.1x servers.

WARNING

The SYSCON program will not work properly in this environment; you must use NetWare Administrator or NETADMIN for all user changes. If you use SYSCON, the change will be made only on the NetWare 3.1x server, and that server will then be out of sync with the Directory database. When you try SYSCON, the system will warn you about your potential mistake, but it won't stop you.

The host NetWare 4.1x server distributes all the bindery objects that are created from the incoming bindery information during the installation throughout the NDS database. Objects that affect the NetWare 3.1x server are downloaded to it, but they stay synchronized to the NDS database. If a NetWare 3.1x server goes down, any missing Directory changes to the NetWare 4.1x server bindery context are downloaded to keep the database current, once the 3.x server returns to the network. Each NetWare 3.1x server keeps a copy of this cluster bindery, or *super-bindery* as Novell likes to call it.

The files to control the NetWare 3.1x cluster are placed on the host server in a newly created directory named SYS:SYSTEM\NETSYNC. This makes a convenient place to copy the necessary files from the host NetWare 4.1x server to each NetWare 3.1x server that joins the group. Files for the host server required to run NetSync are placed in the SYS:SYSTEM area, as you would expect for NLMs.

Installation on the NetWare 4.1x Server

There are several things that must be taken care of before installation. First of all, duplicate user names may be a problem. If the name on both systems is for the same person, things should work. If there are two different LAURA users on two different NetWare 3.1x servers, you must rename one of them before continuing.

Make sure the bindery context you plan to use is settled. It's easiest to use the bindery context for the NetWare 4.1x host server for the NetSync cluster. After you start NetSync and connect the NetWare 3.1x servers into the cluster, you cannot change the bindery context.

To start the process, on the NetWare 4.1x server that will be the host server for the NetSync cluster, type

```
LOAD NETSYNC4
```

Take a look at the file name: NETSYNC4. I always type NETSYNC and wonder why it won't work. The name is NETSYNC4 because there is a corresponding NETSYNC3 program for the NetWare 3.1x server.

Once you load the NLM on the NetWare 4.1x host server, the screen in Figure 10.76 appears. Since we are at the beginning of the process, there isn't much to see except some directions.

We must prepare the way for the NetWare 3.1x servers by setting up the NetWare 4.1x server that will be the host. Starting the NETSYNC.NLM program

FIGURE 10.76

Starting the NetSync process for the first NetWare 3.1x server

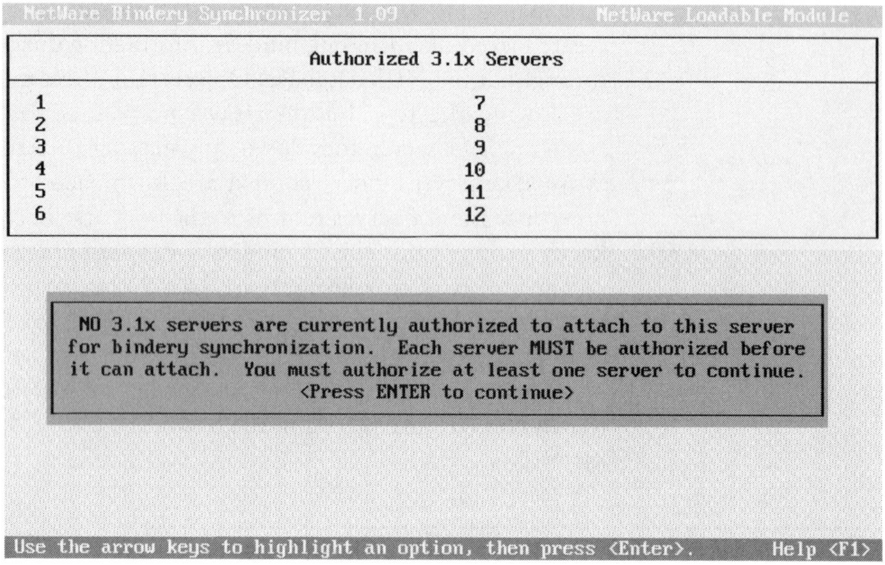

copies the files to the proper directory for later transfer to the NetWare 3.1x server. The process also sets up the log files to track the NetWare 3.1x servers we will add soon.

Pressing Enter, as the instruction box in Figure 10.76 tells us, opens an information box for details about our first NetWare 3.1x server. We must provide the name of the server, a password for NetSync, and decide if we want to install the files on the NetWare 3.1x server. The last option asks if we wish to copy the NetWare 3.1x bindery to the NetWare 4.1x host server. The default for both questions is Yes. Figure 10.77 shows this entry box.

For the first time, we can see some of the NetSync options in the Options menu. As usual, there is a log file. The Log File Options choice offers a chance to view, delete, control the amount of information on the log screen, and set the maximum size of the log file.

The password will be used twice: once here, and once from the NetWare 3.1x server when finishing the connection from that end. The suggestion is not to use the same password as used by the Admin or SUPERVISOR, since this could pose a security leak. (Seems to me, once someone had your Admin password, playing with NetSync would be low on the skulduggery list.) If you forget the password before you connect from the NetWare 3.1x side, you will need to delete the server from the list and reauthorize it with a password you can remember.

FIGURE 10.77

Identifying the first NetWare 3.1x server for our cluster

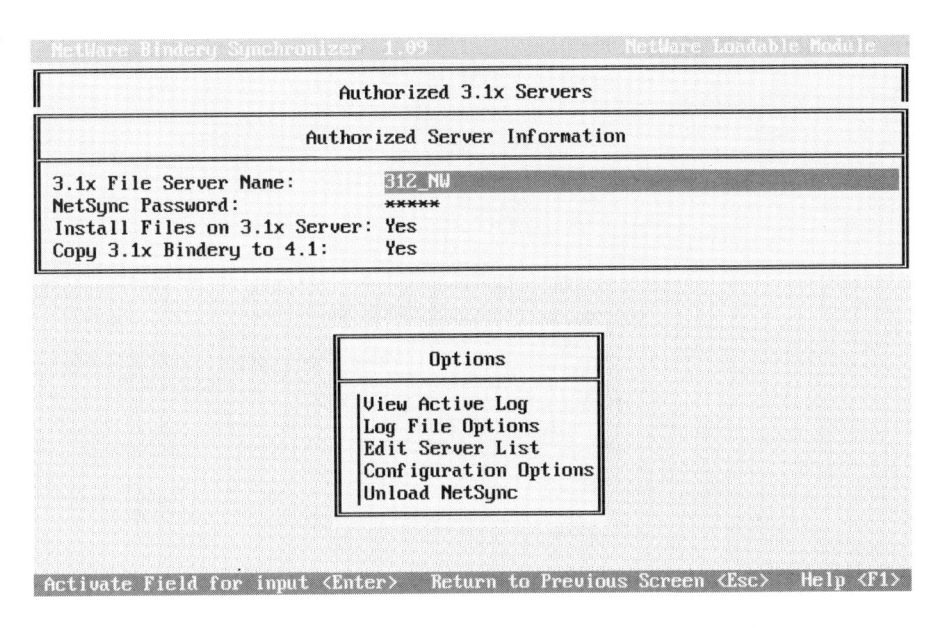

```
╔═ NetWare Bindery Synchronizer 1.09 ═══════════════ NetWare Loadable Module ═╗
║                         Authorized 3.1x Servers                              ║
╠══════════════════════════════════════════════════════════════════════════════╣
║                        Authorized Server Information                         ║
║   3.1x File Server Name:       312_NW                                        ║
║   NetSync Password:            *****                                         ║
║   Install Files on 3.1x Server: Yes                                          ║
║   Copy 3.1x Bindery to 4.1:    Yes                                           ║
║                                                                              ║
║                          ┌──────── Options ─────────┐                        ║
║                          │ View Active Log          │                        ║
║                          │ Log File Options         │                        ║
║                          │ Edit Server List         │                        ║
║                          │ Configuration Options    │                        ║
║                          │ Unload NetSync           │                        ║
║                          └──────────────────────────┘                        ║
║                                                                              ║
╚═ Activate Field for input <Enter>    Return to Previous Screen <Esc>  Help <F1> ═╝
```

When this information is correct, pressing Escape starts the file-copy process to the new member of our NetSync cluster. You must provide a user name and password for someone on the NetWare 3.1x server with rights to the SYS:SYSTEM and SYS:PUBLIC directories. The easiest option is to provide the SUPERVISOR and that password. Figure 10.78 shows the file-copy process under way to our 312_NW server.

Notice some of the file commands going by. Do you see the Renaming statements? This shows the SYSCON program on server 312_NW being renamed so people can't use it accidentally. If you try to use SYSCON, a batch file will warn you not to, but will let you do it anyway.

New versions of many files are loaded to the NetWare 3.1x server, but this does not make this server a NetWare 4.1x server. You don't have file compression, block suballocation, or NDS in a real way. You have an approximation of some of the advantages of NetWare 4.1x, but this is no replacement for an upgrade.

Once the file-copy process is finished (and it's fairly quick), you have only a few more questions to answer. Both servers have the option of loading their respective NETSYNC.NLM programs upon server startup. This is a good idea. Once you start with NetSync, you must continue.

FIGURE 10.78

Preparing a NetWare 3.1x server to fold into NDS

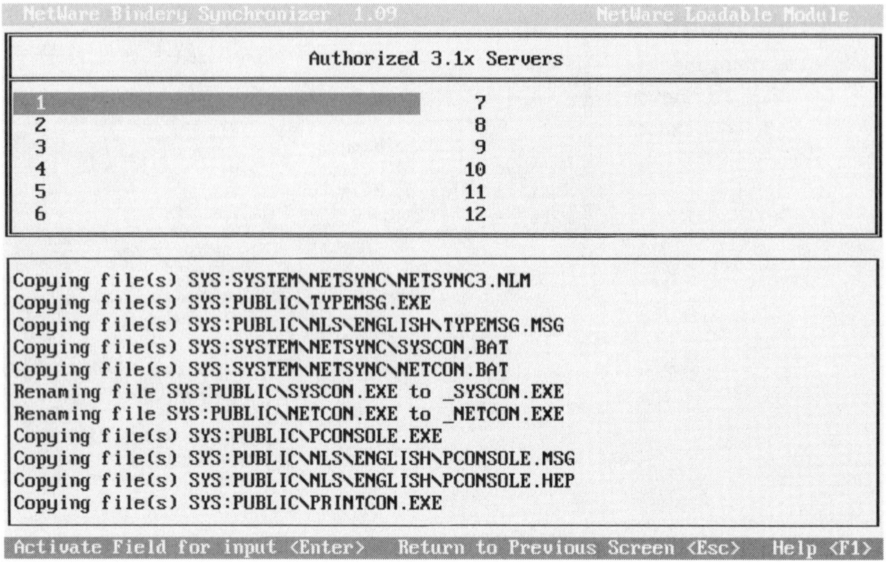

```
NetWare Bindery Synchronizer  1.09                    NetWare Loadable Module

                         Authorized 3.1x Servers
  1                                          7
  2                                          8
  3                                          9
  4                                         10
  5                                         11
  6                                         12

Copying file(s) SYS:SYSTEM\NETSYNC\NETSYNC3.NLM
Copying file(s) SYS:PUBLIC\TYPEMSG.EXE
Copying file(s) SYS:PUBLIC\NLS\ENGLISH\TYPEMSG.MSG
Copying file(s) SYS:SYSTEM\NETSYNC\SYSCON.BAT
Copying file(s) SYS:SYSTEM\NETSYNC\NETCON.BAT
Renaming file SYS:PUBLIC\SYSCON.EXE to _SYSCON.EXE
Renaming file SYS:PUBLIC\NETCON.EXE to _NETCON.EXE
Copying file(s) SYS:PUBLIC\PCONSOLE.EXE
Copying file(s) SYS:PUBLIC\NLS\ENGLISH\PCONSOLE.MSG
Copying file(s) SYS:PUBLIC\NLS\ENGLISH\PCONSOLE.HEP
Copying file(s) SYS:PUBLIC\PRINTCON.EXE

Activate Field for input <Enter>   Return to Previous Screen <Esc>   Help <F1>
```

Figure 10.79 shows the Include Load Commands option for server 312_NW. The default is Yes. A similar screen for the cluster host server will appear shortly.

The last screen informs us that the installation was successful. As you would expect, some NLMs have changed. Before the software can be installed on the NetWare 3.1x server, you must reboot the server. Figure 10.80 shows this warning.

This finishes the installation for server 312_NW. The process must be repeated for all other NetWare 3.1x servers to be part of the cluster.

Installation on the NetWare 3.1x Server

To begin the installation on your NetWare 3.1x server, first reboot that server. This makes sure all the new NLMs are loaded as they should be. If you asked for NetSync to start automatically, you will see a screen much like Figure 10.81.

Your NetSync password goes here. If you mistype it, you must then specify the NetWare 4.1x host server before you can try the password again.

If your NetWare 3.1x server was part of an NNS domain, you will see a screen asking if you want to remove the server from the domain. You can't be in both NNS and NDS, so say Yes to move forward with the NDS cluster installation. Print queues, if you had some under NNS, will need to be modified.

FIGURE 10.79

Making NetSync a part of every startup

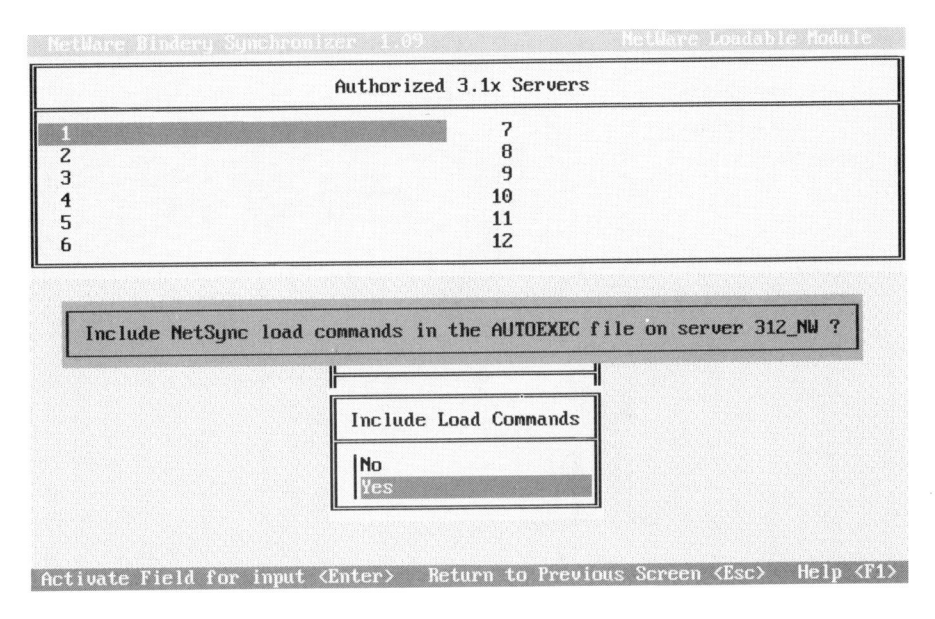

FIGURE 10.80

Final instructions before the installation is finished

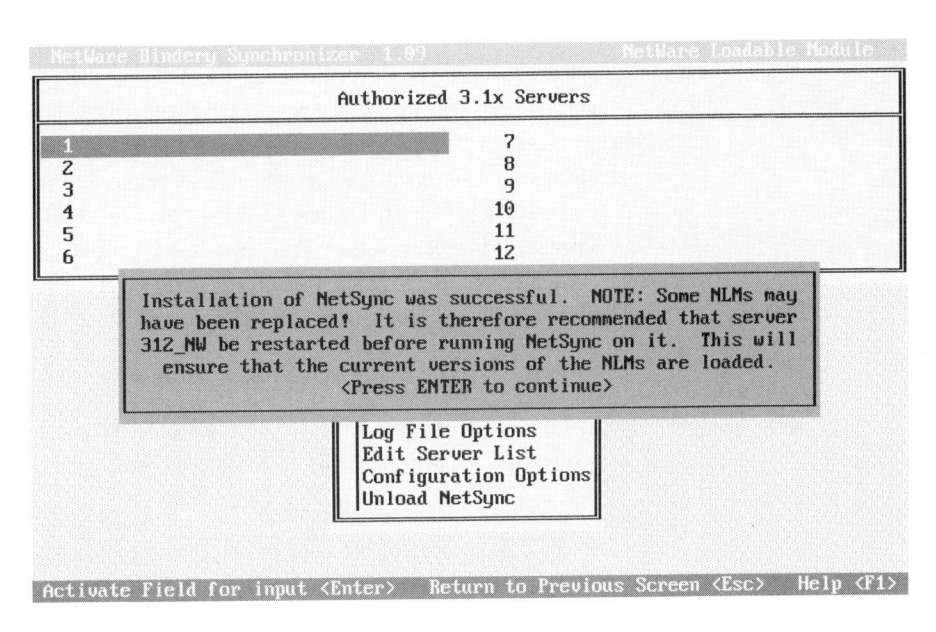

FIGURE 10.81

Continuing the installation from the NetWare 3.1x side

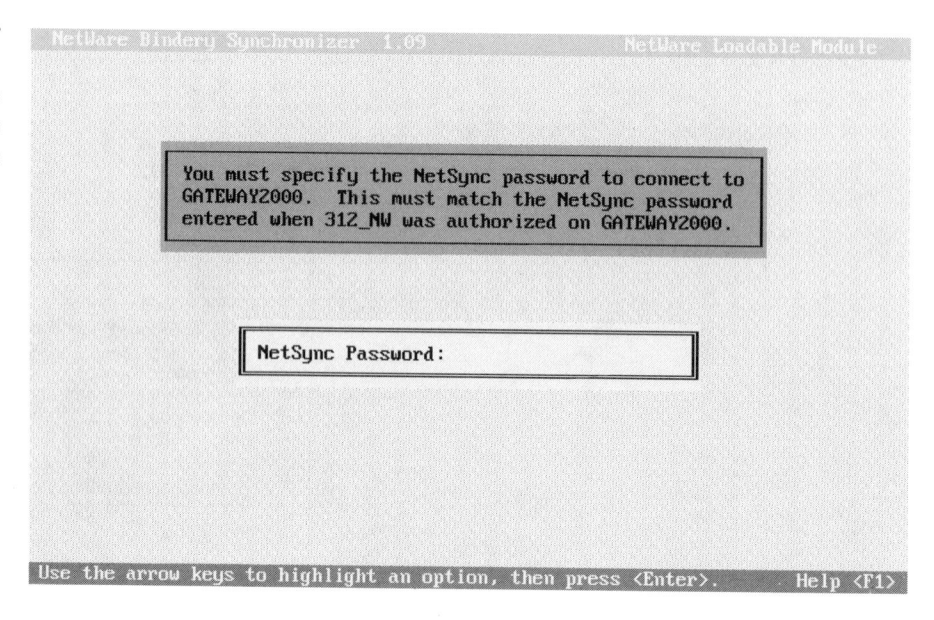

```
NetWare Bindery Synchronizer 1.09                    NetWare Loadable Module

           ┌──────────────────────────────────────────────┐
           │ You must specify the NetSync password to connect to │
           │ GATEWAY2000. This must match the NetSync password   │
           │ entered when 312_NW was authorized on GATEWAY2000.  │
           └──────────────────────────────────────────────┘



                    ┌─────────────────────────────────┐
                    │ NetSync Password:               │
                    └─────────────────────────────────┘




 Use the arrow keys to highlight an option, then press <Enter>.    Help <F1>
```

When you tell the system which NetWare 4.1x server you wish to connect to each time, your installation is finished. Print files and other user information is transferred and massaged into NDS in the background. The look of success is the menu on the NetWare 3.1x server. See the NetSync screen on the console of 312_NW in Figure 10.82.

The Log File Options screen is open in Figure 10.82. I didn't show it on the NetWare 4.1x side, but the submenu is the same on both sides. The Options menu includes the following choices:

- **View Active Log:** A scrolling console screen of NetSync events.

- **Log File Options:** Enable the log file, delete the log file, or choose the amount of information and the maximum size of the log file.

- **Configuration Options:** Whether to delete NetSync configuration data, and the delay in seconds between watchdog packets between this server and the NetWare 4.1x cluster host. The default is 300 seconds (5 minutes).

- **Move a Print Server:** Decide whether to move a print server up to the NetWare 4.1x cluster host for it to control. You can keep this name or give it a new name on the cluster host. If you change the name to an existing NetWare 4.1x print server, the information in this print server will be merged into the one on the cluster host.

FIGURE 10.82

Netsync running on the NetWare 3.1x server

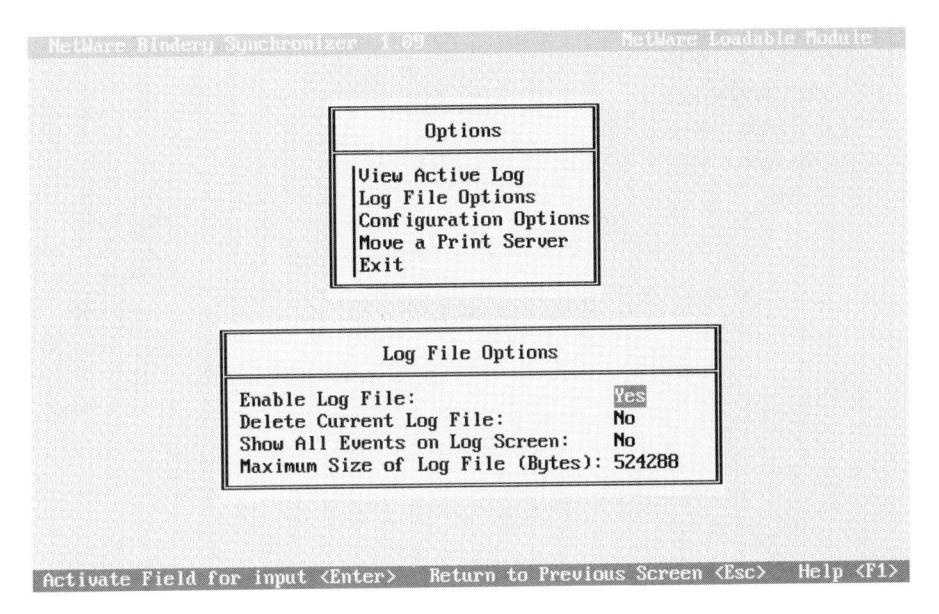

Maintenance of the NetSync Cluster

If we revisited the main NetSync screen on our NetWare 4.1x host server, we could see the name of 312_NW listed in the number one spot. There is an asterisk by the name, indicating that server is synchronized to the NetSync cluster.

Maintenance is fairly normal with NetSync objects. Users must be handled like any other NDS object. The resources of the NetWare 3.1x server are not available to NDS, because they are just bindery objects represented in NDS. See Figure 10.83 for an example.

Any changes made to objects on 312_NW from the NetWare 3.1x side of the cluster will not be updated into the NDS database, unless you do a full upload from the 3.1x server again, causing lots of network traffic. All changes in the NDS database will automatically be replicated into NetWare 3.1x.

NetSync is a one-way system. The NetWare 3.1x users gain access to NDS and all the resources available there. They do still count against the user license count of the servers they connect to, both NetWare 4.1x and NetWare 3.1x.

NDS users can't reach the resources of the NetWare 3.1x servers. For that, you must upgrade the servers, so they can be a full partner in the NDS world.

FIGURE 10.83

All 312_NW's users are now NDS objects, but the server is not.

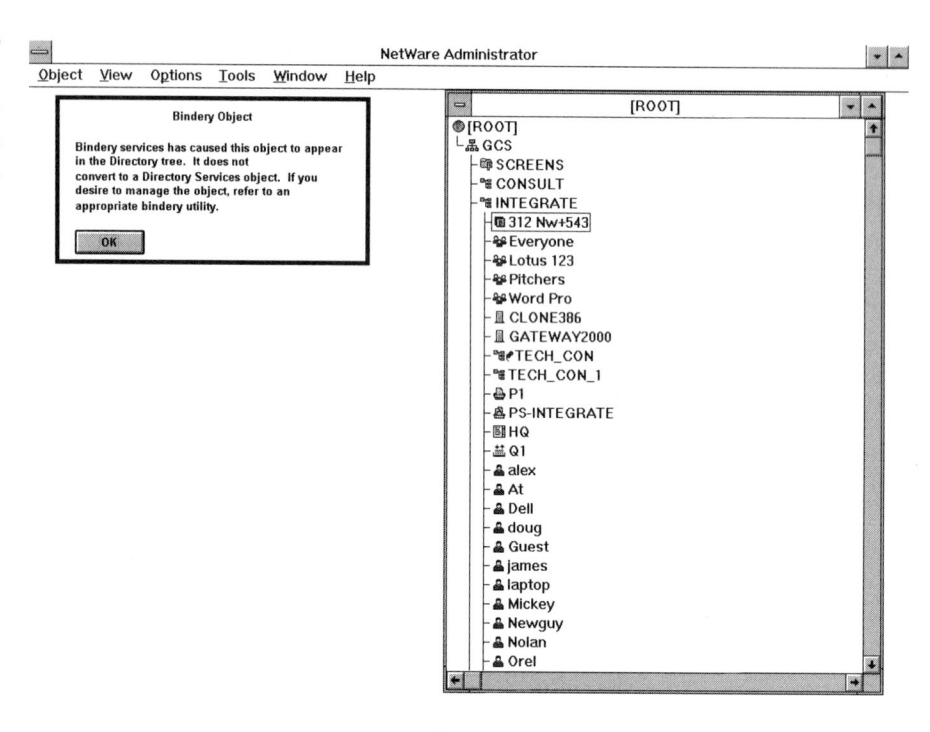

NDS Administration with DOS Tools

USING THE DOS tools NETADMIN and PARTMGR in NDS is a bit of a kludge. One of the main selling points for NetWare 4.1*x* is the graphical administration capability. The system is designed to use the NetWare Administrator program, enabling drag-and-drop capabilities, easy window resizing, and the rest of the GUI advantages.

Of course, SYSCON is not part of NetWare 4.1*x*, meaning that DOS administrators would lose their tool for managing users if a SYSCON replacement wasn't available. NETADMIN is that tool, but it's different than SYSCON.

PARTMGR is a different story. There is no analog to PARTMGR in NetWare 3.*x*, because PARTMGR handles NDS partitions and replicas. No NDS before, no DOS utility before. (The fact that PARTMGR is included at all is a bit of a surprise to me.)

> *If you are still managing NetWare from a DOS workstation, it's time you upgraded. You may skip Windows 95 if you wish and go straight to Windows NT or OS/2 (at least for a while), but a GUI is in your future. Do you honestly believe Novell engineers will spend as much time enhancing the DOS management programs as they invest in NetWare Administrator? I don't either.*

If you skipped the information earlier in this chapter about the rights needed to perform administrative functions, go back and take a quick look. Sneak a look at the screens for NetWare Administrator while you're there. They make your work easier and quicker than their DOS utility counterparts can.

Starting and Moving Around in NETADMIN

The NETADMIN.EXE program is copied to the SYS:PUBLIC directory during server installation. After you have a drive mapped to SYS:PUBLIC, you can run NETADMIN by typing the name at a DOS prompt.

The opening NETADMIN screen offers just a few choices, fewer than SYSCON did for earlier NetWare versions. Figure 10.84 shows the opening screen.

FIGURE 10.84
The NETADMIN opening screen

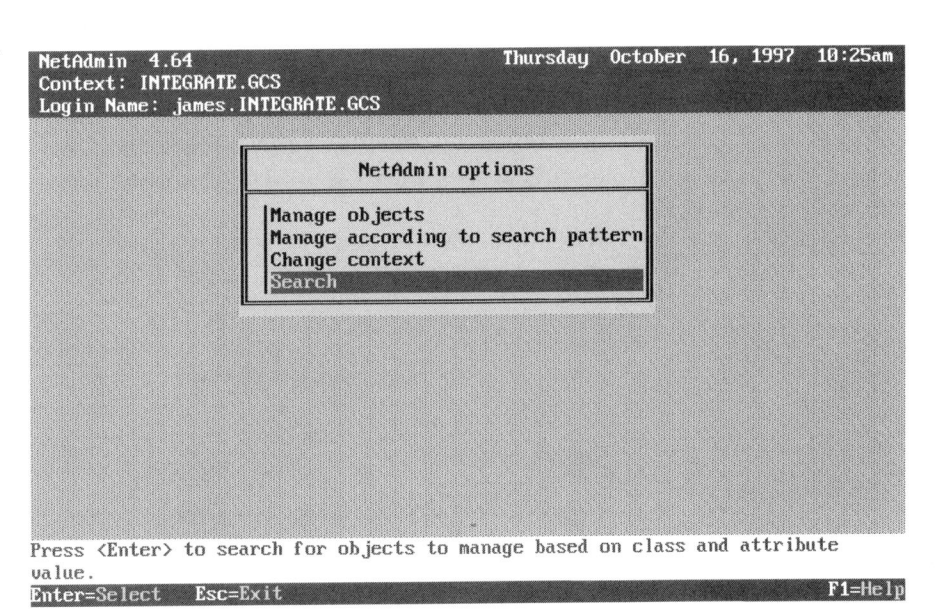

The options work as follows:

- **Manage Objects:** Lets you create, move, or rename objects, as well as edit object properties. This is the most common choice when starting NETADMIN.

- **Manage According to Search Pattern:** Sets filters for searches, to limit the number of objects viewed at one time. You may choose to see only User objects, for instance. The pattern stays until you change it or exit NETADMIN.

- **Change Context:** Moves to another context for management purposes. You can easily change contexts from the Object, Class screen in NETADMIN.

- **Search:** Lets you look for a specific object or object class in the container of your choice.

The context is always listed in the upper-left corner of the NETADMIN screen. If you want to move to another context, choose Change Context from the menu. An Enter Context text box opens, asking for your preferred context. If you don't know that context, press Insert. The ubiquitous Object, Class browser screen opens, ready for you to move the highlight bar and press Enter wherever you desire to make your new context.

The Object, Class screen appears everywhere, filled with the appropriate objects. It's the same as the Select Object dialog box in NetWare Administrator. Unfortunately, in NETADMIN, I can't move the Object, Class screen out of the way of the other screen information. Figure 10.85 shows the Object, Class screen open at the beginning of a Manage Objects search. It shows all the objects of NetWare 4.1x in the INTEGRATE.GCS context.

Every Object, Class screen is a variation on this one. If you choose Change Context from the opening menu, you see this screen showing only containers to move to. If you have set the search pattern so only User objects appear, the screen will show only User objects.

Creating Container Objects

Figure 10.86 shows the creation of the Organizational Unit TECH_CON_2. There's no need for a mailbox or User Template for a container. Why is User Template in NETADMIN when it's not in NetWare Administrator anymore? I told you the DOS tools lag behind in the upgrades.

10.39 IN-A-HURRY

Create a Container Object with NETADMIN

1. Log in as Admin or equivalent.

2. Type **NETADMIN** at the DOS prompt.

3. Choose Manage Objects.

4. Choose the container to hold the new container object by moving through the browser screen.

5. Highlight the container and press F10.

6. Press Insert and choose an object class from the list. Unless you're at [Root], your only choice is Organizational Unit.

7. Press Escape to return to the main menu.

FIGURE 10.85

Your only good look at the Object, Class browser screen in this section

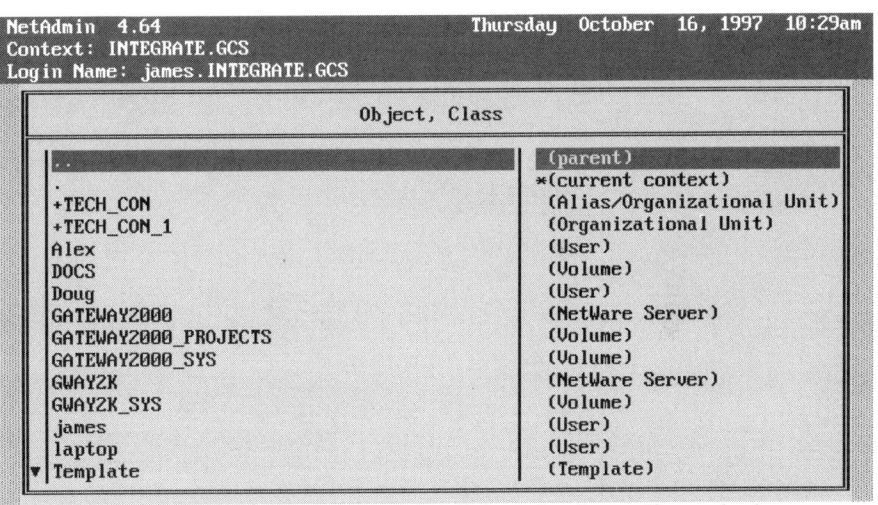

```
NetAdmin 4.64                           Thursday  October  16, 1997  10:29am
Context: INTEGRATE.GCS
Login Name: james.INTEGRATE.GCS

                            ┌─────── Object, Class ───────┐
                            │ ..                  │ (parent)                    │
                            │ .                   │ *(current context)          │
                            │ +TECH_CON           │ (Alias/Organizational Unit) │
                            │ +TECH_CON_1         │ (Organizational Unit)       │
                            │ Alex                │ (User)                      │
                            │ DOCS                │ (Volume)                    │
                            │ Doug                │ (User)                      │
                            │ GATEWAY2000         │ (NetWare Server)            │
                            │ GATEWAY2000_PROJECTS│ (Volume)                    │
                            │ GATEWAY2000_SYS     │ (Volume)                    │
                            │ GWAYZK              │ (NetWare Server)            │
                            │ GWAYZK_SYS          │ (Volume)                    │
                            │ james               │ (User)                      │
                            │ laptop              │ (User)                      │
                            ▼ Template            │ (Template)                  │

Press <F10> to select the parent object, <Enter> to change the context.

Enter=Change context/Select   F10=View or edit   F5=Mark   Ins=Add   Alt+F1=More
```

FIGURE 10.86

Creating an Organizational Unit

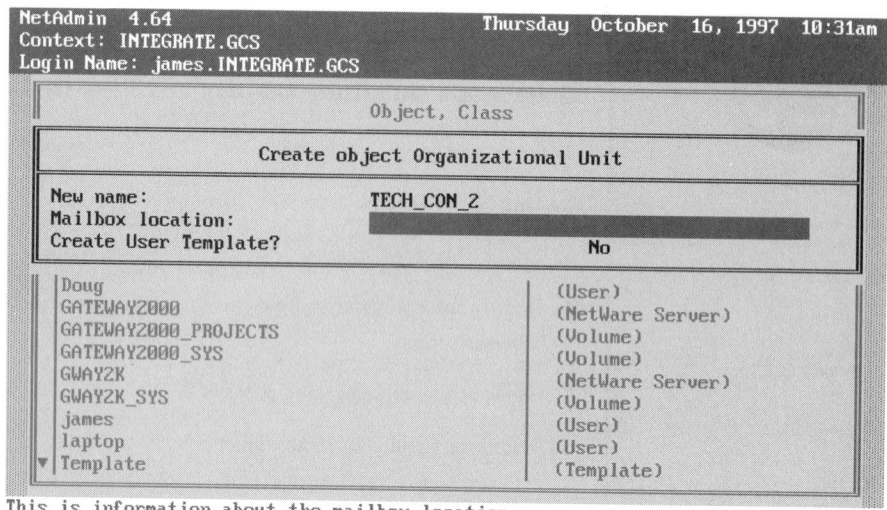

```
NetAdmin  4.64                           Thursday  October  16, 1997  10:31am
Context:  INTEGRATE.GCS
Login Name:  james.INTEGRATE.GCS
┌─────────────────────────────────────────────────────────────────────────┐
│                              Object, Class                              │
├─────────────────────────────────────────────────────────────────────────┤
│                     Create object Organizational Unit                   │
│                                                                         │
│   New name:                      TECH_CON_2                             │
│   Mailbox location:                                                     │
│   Create User Template?                              No                 │
│                                                                         │
│   │Doug                                    │(User)                      │
│   │GATEWAY2000                             │(NetWare Server)            │
│   │GATEWAY2000_PROJECTS                    │(Volume)                    │
│   │GATEWAY2000_SYS                         │(Volume)                    │
│   │GWAY2K                                  │(NetWare Server)            │
│   │GWAY2K_SYS                              │(Volume)                    │
│   │james                                   │(User)                      │
│   │laptop                                  │(User)                      │
│ ▼ │Template                                │(Template)                  │
└─────────────────────────────────────────────────────────────────────────┘
This is information about the mailbox location.

Enter=Accept    F10=Save    Esc=Exit                              F1=Help
```

Setting Intruder Detection

10.40 IN-A-HURRY

Set Intruder Detection for a Container Object with NETADMIN

1. Log in as Admin or equivalent.

2. Type **NETADMIN** from the DOS prompt.

3. Choose Manage Objects.

4. Highlight the container that needs intruder detection and press F10.

5. Choose View or Edit Properties of This Object, and then choose Intruder Detection.

6. Enable Detect Intruders, and then set the log in and lock out times.

7. Press F10 to save and exit.

8. Press Escape to return to the main menu.

Every container should have intruder detection active. Figure 10.87 shows the settings for the newly created TECH_CON_2 container. Notice how much more restrictive the settings are here compared with the NetWare Administrator settings back in Figure 10.4.

FIGURE 10.87

Getting tough with intruders

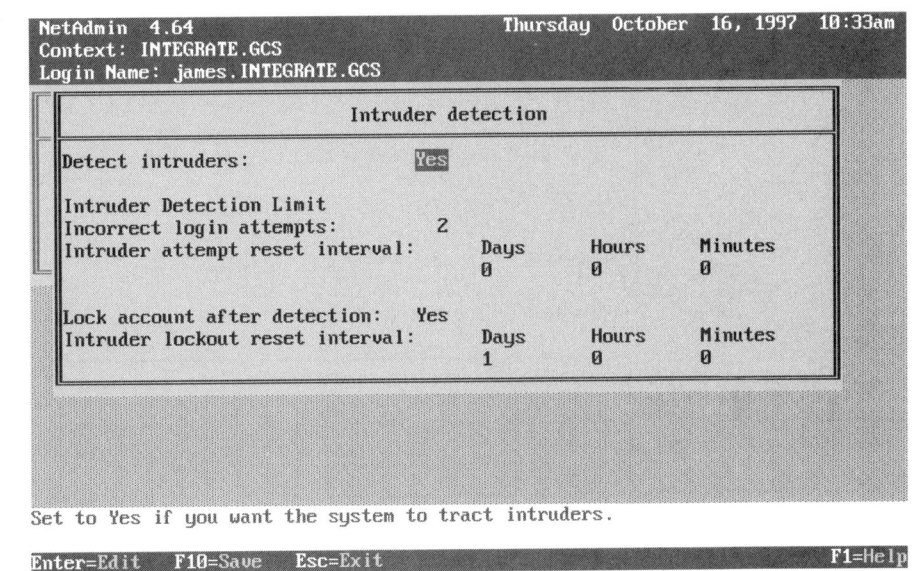

```
NetAdmin  4.64                          Thursday  October  16, 1997  10:33am
Context: INTEGRATE.GCS
Login Name: james.INTEGRATE.GCS

                         Intruder detection

Detect intruders:                Yes

Intruder Detection Limit
Incorrect login attempts:         2
Intruder attempt reset interval:        Days      Hours     Minutes
                                         0          0          0


Lock account after detection:   Yes
Intruder lockout reset interval:        Days      Hours     Minutes
                                         1          0          0




Set to Yes if you want the system to tract intruders.

Enter=Edit    F10=Save    Esc=Exit                              F1=Help
```

Creating Leaf Objects

The process for creating any leaf object is just like creating a user, more or less. There are only a few mandatory fields. The full explanations of naming restrictions and other details for creating users in NETADMIN are in Chapter 6. Figure 10.88 is a quick reminder of how this looks inside NETADMIN.

10.41 IN-A-HURRY

Create a Leaf Object with NETADMIN

1. Log in as Admin or equivalent.

2. Type **NETADMIN** from the DOS prompt.

3. Choose Manage Objects.

4. Highlight the container to hold the new leaf object and press Enter.

5. Press Insert, choose the leaf object to create, and press Enter.

6. Provide the information in the mandatory fields. The other fields are optional.

7. Press F10 to save and exit.

8. Press Escape to return to the main menu.

FIGURE 10.88

Moving day, but no packing

```
NetAdmin  4.64                                Thursday  October  16, 1997  10:37am
Context: TECH_CON_2.INTEGRATE.GCS
Login Name: james.INTEGRATE.GCS
┌─────────────────────────────────────────────────────────────────────────────┐
│                              Object, Class                                   │
│                           Create object User                                 │
│  Login Name:           Kim                                                   │
│  Last name:            Wimpsett                                              │
│  Mailbox location:                                                           │
│  Create a home directory?                      Yes                           │
│  Copy the User Template object?                No                            │
│                                                                              │
│  --- Home Directory Information ---                                          │
│  Volume object name:   GATEWAY2000_PROJECTS.                                 │
│  Path on volume:       \Kim                                                  │
│                                                                              │
└─────────────────────────────────────────────────────────────────────────────┘
Enter the new name for this object.
Enter=Accept    F10=Save    Esc=Exit                                  F1=Help
```

Managing Objects

As with NetWare Administrator, you can move, rename, and search for objects with NETADMIN.

Moving Objects

> **10.42 IN-A-HURRY**
>
> **Move an Object with NETADMIN**
>
> 1. Log in as Admin or equivalent.
> 2. Type **NETADMIN** from the DOS prompt.
> 3. Choose Manage Objects.
> 4. Highlight the container holding the object to move and press Enter.
> 5. Choose the object to be moved, and then choose Move from the Actions for Object menu.
> 6. Provide the new context. Press Insert and use the Object, Class screen to browse if necessary to find the new context, then highlight that context and press F10.
> 7. Press F10 to save and exit.
> 8. Press Escape to return to the main menu.

Let's say we made a mistake and put Kim in the wrong place. Since Kim probably doesn't want to be in the wrong place, we must move her.

With NETADMIN, the time is spent finding the object to move, not necessarily moving that object. We must drill down until we are directly managing the object to be moved. Once we have that object in hand, so to speak, we can choose the Move option from the object's Actions menu. The Move Object box shows you where the object is now, and you fill in where you want the object to be. Figure 10.89 shows us about to move Kim to the proper context.

Again, pressing Insert opens the Object, Class browser screen. If you know precisely where you wish to move the object, you can type the information.

Either way, pressing F10 saves the information and starts the move. A message warning you that the process may take up to 60 seconds appears, but it usually doesn't take that long.

Renaming Objects

One good thing about NetWare 4.1*x*: similar operations happen in similar ways. The process of renaming an object is almost exactly the same as moving the object.

10.43 IN-A-HURRY

Rename an Object with NETADMIN

1. Log in as Admin or equivalent.

2. Type **NETADMIN** from the DOS prompt.

3. Choose Manage Objects.

4. Highlight the container holding the object to rename and press Enter.

5. Choose the object to be renamed, and then choose Rename from the Actions for Object menu.

6. Type the new name for the object.

7. Choose whether to save the old name or not.

8. Press F10 to save and exit.

9. Press Escape to return to the main menu.

FIGURE 10.89

Moving day, but no packing

```
NetAdmin 4.64                          Thursday  October  16, 1997  10:40am
Context: TECH_CON_2.INTEGRATE.GCS
Login Name: james.INTEGRATE.GCS

          ┌─────── Actions for User: Kim ───────┐
     │Vi│  ┌──────────────── Move Object ────────────────┐
     │Re│  │                                             │
     │Mo│  │ Old Context:    TECH_CON_2.INTEGRATE.GCS    │
     │De│  │ New Context:    TECH_CON_1.                 │
     │Vi│  │                                             │
     │View or edit the trustees of this object │

                  Enter the new context for this object.
     Enter=Edit   F10=Save   Esc=Exit                            F1=Help
```

The only question is whether to save the old name. If the answer is Yes, the old name will remain listed in the Other Names field in the Identification screen. If it's a container you're renaming, you have the option of leaving an Alias behind.

Searching for Objects

> **10.44 IN-A-HURRY**
>
> **Search for Objects with NETADMIN**
>
> 1. Log in as Admin or equivalent.
> 2. Type **NETADMIN** from the DOS prompt.
> 3. Choose Search from the main menu.
> 4. Choose the context to begin the search.
> 5. Choose to search all subordinate containers, or just the current container.
> 6. Choose the class of object to search for.
> 7. Choose the property to search. The list will vary depending on the object you select. Entries will be alphabetical.
> 8. If necessary, choose a logical operator and a value.
> 9. Press F10 to save and exit.
> 10. Press Escape to return to the main menu.

The search process is helpful, and it lets us save queries we like to use later. Once you have the information filled out, and have tried the search to make sure it works, you can save it. We're doing that in Figure 10.90.

Each of the fields in the Search screen can be browsed. You can knock yourself out with the Insert key, pulling up the Object, Class screen. Each field has plenty of options, so you can narrow down your search as tightly as you wish.

When the search is finished, the results window holds those objects that match your criteria. From there, you may press Enter on any object and do with it what you will. After you're finished doing what you will, you may then choose Search again from the main menu, and you'll find your last search parameters in place. If you change contexts while working with an object, the current context will be listed. Otherwise, all is as you left it.

FIGURE 10.90

Saving the query for a security check

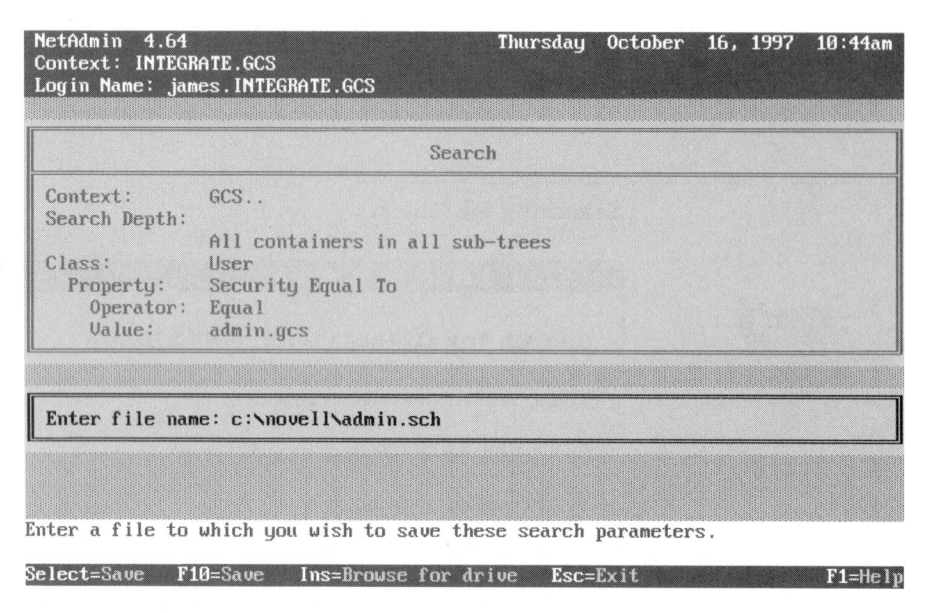

```
NetAdmin 4.64                           Thursday October 16, 1997 10:44am
Context: INTEGRATE.GCS
Login Name: james.INTEGRATE.GCS

                                Search
   Context:        GCS..
   Search Depth:
                   All containers in all sub-trees
   Class:          User
     Property:     Security Equal To
     Operator:     Equal
     Value:        admin.gcs


   Enter file name: c:\novell\admin.sch



Enter a file to which you wish to save these search parameters.

Select=Save   F10=Save   Ins=Browse for drive   Esc=Exit        F1=Help
```

If you like the results of your search, you can press F4 and save the search parameters into a file. The file must have an extension of SCH, as you can see in Figure 10.90. When you want to search again, press F2 to restore the saved parameters. If you have several saved sets, you can pick the one you wish to use.

Using the Partition Manager in DOS: PARTMGR

The DOS version of NDS Manager is PARTMGR. Stored in the SYS:PUBLIC directory, it wouldn't be a bad idea to move the program to SYS:SYSTEM or somewhere less available.

All the features of NDS Manager are in PARTMGR. The rules for handling partitions and managing replicas of partitions are described in detail with the NDS Manager section, earlier in the chapter.

Creating New Partitions

To create a new partition, run PARTMGR, choose Manage Partitions, select the container, and press F10. The selected container will be created as a new partition. The partition will be split from the parent partition, which is in the parent container. The new partition will be named after the container that holds it.

NDS Administration with DOS Tools 917

> ### 10.45 IN-A-HURRY
>
> **Create a Partition with PARTMGR**
>
> 1. Log in as Admin or equivalent.
> 2. Type **PARTMGR** at the DOS prompt.
> 3. Choose Manage Partitions from the main menu.
> 4. Move through the browser screen to the container you wish to hold the new partition.
> 5. Highlight the container and press F10.
> 6. Answer Yes to "Do you want to create a new partition?"

Figure 10.91 shows this screen where the decision is made to create a new partition. As the top-left corner of the PARTMGR screen tells us, this is the CONSULT container, and we're reading the GWAY2K.INTEGRATE replica. The new partition, if we agree to create it, will be CONSULT.

It will take time for the partition to be created. After it's created, you may wish to think about spreading around a copy or two of the replica for safekeeping.

FIGURE 10.91
Creating the CONSULT partition

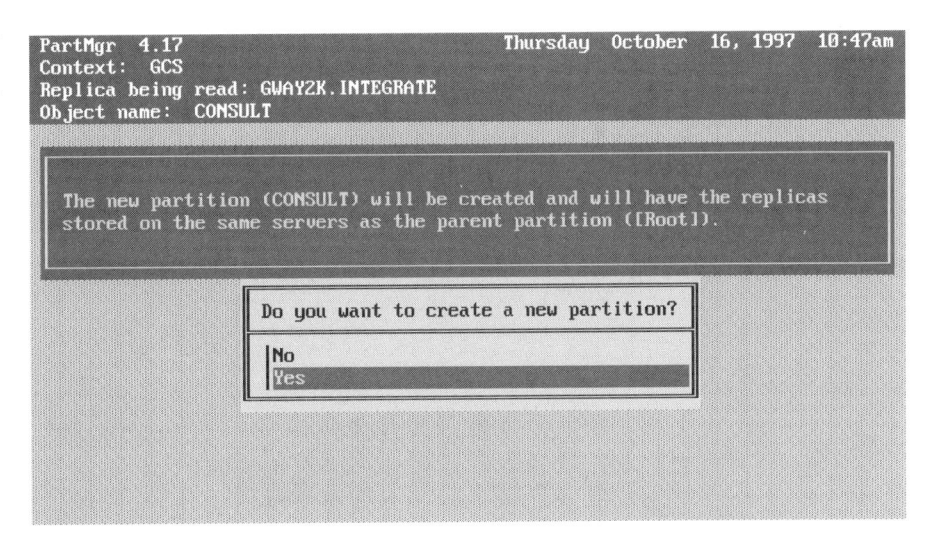

```
PartMgr  4.17                            Thursday  October  16, 1997  10:47am
Context: GCS
Replica being read: GWAY2K.INTEGRATE
Object name:  CONSULT

    ┌────────────────────────────────────────────────────────────────┐
    │ The new partition (CONSULT) will be created and will have the  │
    │ replicas stored on the same servers as the parent partition    │
    │ ([Root]).                                                      │
    └────────────────────────────────────────────────────────────────┘

                      ┌─ Do you want to create a new partition? ─┐
                      │ No                                       │
                      │ Yes                                      │
                      └──────────────────────────────────────────┘

Esc=Cancel   Enter=Select                                          F1=Help
```

Viewing or Modifying Replicas

> ### 10.46 IN-A-HURRY
>
> **View or Modify a Replica with PARTMGR**
>
> 1. Log in as Admin or equivalent.
> 2. Type **PARTMGR** at the DOS prompt.
> 3. Choose Manager Partitions from the main menu.
> 4. Move through the browser screen to a partition.
> 5. Highlight the partition and press F10.
> 6. Press Enter to view, modify, or delete a partition.

To work with replicas in PARTMGR, choose Manage Partitions. In the browser screens, any container that's labeled a partition has at least one replica. To view those replicas, press F10 on those containers. You'll see the Replicas Stored on Server window, as shown in Figure 10.92. The replicas and their type are listed.

FIGURE 10.92

Storing replicas on the GATEWAY2000 server

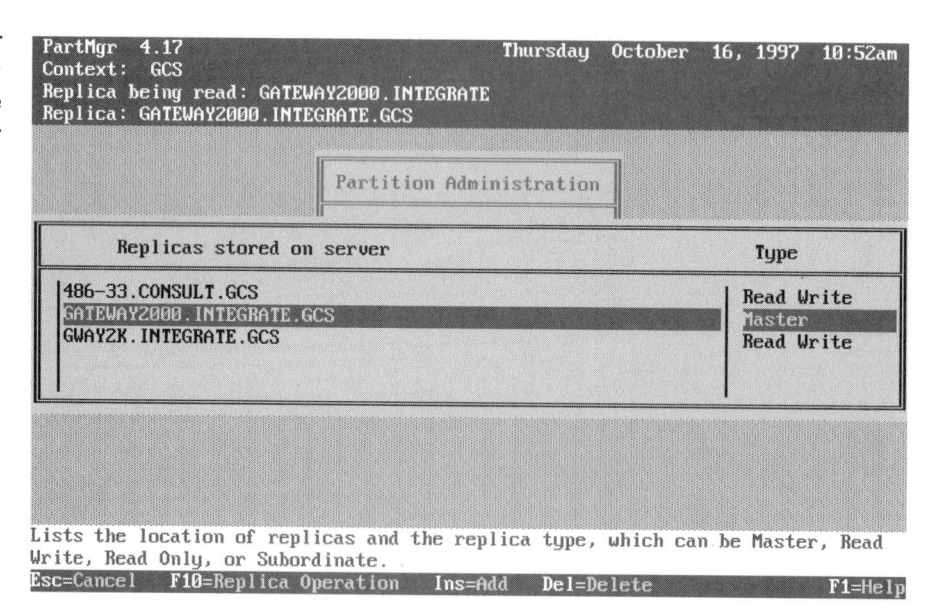

```
PartMgr  4.17                              Thursday  October  16, 1997  10:52am
Context:  GCS
Replica being read: GATEWAY2000.INTEGRATE
Replica: GATEWAY2000.INTEGRATE.GCS

                        ┌─────────────────────────┐
                        │  Partition Administration │
                        └─────────────────────────┘

        Replicas stored on server                              Type
    ┌──────────────────────────────────────────┐  ┌──────────────┐
    │ 486-33.CONSULT.GCS                       │  │ Read Write   │
    │ GATEWAY2000.INTEGRATE.GCS                │  │ Master       │
    │ GWAY2K.INTEGRATE.GCS                     │  │ Read Write   │
    └──────────────────────────────────────────┘  └──────────────┘

Lists the location of replicas and the replica type, which can be Master, Read
Write, Read Only, or Subordinate.
Esc=Cancel    F10=Replica Operation    Ins=Add    Del=Delete         F1=Help
```

Once you highlight a replica and press Enter, a Replica Management screen opens. There are three choices:

- **Change Replica Type:** Moves from the current replica type to Master, Read/Write, or Read-Only.

- **Send Updates to Other Replicas:** The currently displayed replica sends its information to the other replicas on the other partitions. This may create a fair bit of network traffic. This is handy if one replica becomes damaged, or you want new information on the current replica to be sent out to update all the other replicas.

- **Receive Updates from Master Replica:** The current replica will be overwritten with the contents of the Master replica. Like the Send Updates option, this is useful if there is damage to the current replica.

If you have something more drastic in mind, the status line at the bottom of Figure 10.92 offers you a chance to delete the replica (using the Delete key). You can also press Insert to create a new replica.

Starting Accounting with NETADMIN

10.47 IN-A-HURRY

Enable or Modify Server Accounting with NETADMIN

1. Log in as Admin or equivalent.
2. Type **NETADMIN** at the DOS prompt.
3. Choose Manage Objects from the main menu.
4. Move through the browser screen to find the server for which you want to enable accounting and press Enter.
5. Choose View or Edit Properties of This Object, and then choose Accounting.
6. Set charge rates for any desired services.
7. Buy green eyeshades and an adding machine.
8. Press Escape to save and exit.

Compare the image of Figure 10.93 to that of Figure 10.20. This is another good example of the value of a GUI in management.

Each of the accounting functions is listed in this menu. All the charges you wish to set are available, although they're hard to read. Part of the problem is the time scale. The screen shown in Figure 10.93 can't cover 24 hours in a graph as does NetWare Administrator. Believe it or not, both these screens are showing the same information.

You'll find descriptions of charge rates and the like back with the figure we just spoke of, Figure 10.20, in the section titled "Set the Blocks-Read Rate for Server Accounting." Although I'm against charging for server resources and network bandwidth, it's possible to do from this screen.

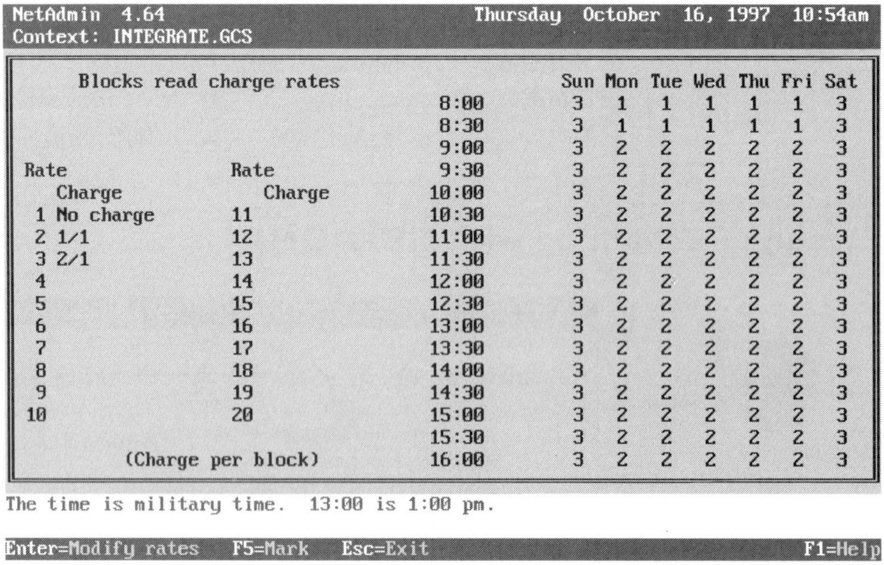

FIGURE 10.93

Hard to read, but charges are set for disk blocks read

Superb Supervision

YOU DON'T ADMINISTER a network, you administer people. Please don't forget that fact. Your users are not computers, they are people. The network is just a tool the people use to do their jobs. I've mentioned

Supervisor Overload

After reading this huge chapter, you may have the wrong idea of what a network administrator should do on a daily basis. The Admin shouldn't fiddle with the server parameters everyday; the Admin should look for ways to improve how the network supports the users in their jobs. The confusion arises because fiddling with server parameters is often necessary to provide the best server platform for the network users. Just don't let the server become the focus of your network attentions.

There are many details to understand and control when managing a network. Don't feel bad that you can't remember all of them. No one knows every option for NetWare without referring to a book, the online documentation, or support sources such as the Novell Web page or NetWire. People who astound you with some arcane command parameter you never heard of are more likely to have just used that parameter than they are to be some kind of network genius.

Part of your network management success will be based on your mastery of the server. A much bigger part of your success will be based on how you handle the users. As tempting as it is, enforcing arbitrary rules on the network just to make you life easier won't solve your problems with the users.

This gets into a tough area for all network managers: How to control the network without constraining the users. How do you balance the desires of your management to limit areas of product support without telling some users to throw away what they're using and replace it with an approved product? You can't, at least not always. When something like this happens, explain the necessity of supporting products with excellent network integration rather than stand-alone products. Make the rules sound reasonable, not arbitrary.

Some users will always be disappointed by any management decision, and your decisions as the network administrator will have the same initial response. Explain how the rules were developed to help the network, rather than punish the users. Everyone feels picked on (or dumped on) now and then, so listen to the concerns your users have with any pending network decisions. Once the decision is made, explain again to the disappointed users how the decision was made, and why it wasn't made to single them out.

The more you communicate with your network users, the easier your job will become. The more the users understand why the network is the way it is, the fewer complaints you will have. The fewer complaints you have, the more time you have to think ahead rather than deal with the crisis of the moment. The more time you have to think ahead, the smoother your network will run, grow, and embrace new technologies. It's nice to see a feedback loop turn out to be positive for a change, isn't it?

this before, but some of you don't believe me. Let me restate: your job is to help the users.

Does this make you a doormat, subservient to every weird whim of any user? Not at all. The users on a network are similar to diners in a fine restaurant: the network is there to serve, but certain rules of conduct apply. Proper dress (decorum) are necessary if the diners (users) wish to be served. Politeness is important. Tips are appreciated.

It's easy to get bogged down in the technical details of administering a network, but those details obscure the people on the network. Which do you think your boss would prefer: a network tweaked to the last bit where the users feel left out, or an acceptable network with users that feel like owners of the network?

My friend Stan has a good example of bad network management, and the moral is "keep your opinions to yourself." A user bought a flimsy (though name brand) laptop and had a problem. The tech told the customer the problem came because the laptop was crap.

The customer pointed out that the technical department approved the purchase. In fact, Stan's boss had done so. The problem did turn out to be hardware, because the laptop is the low-priced entry system and the docking station didn't work. Put yourself in that tech's shoes: did mouthing off to the user fix the problem? No. Did it make the tech look stupid, since his department approved the purchase? Yes. Is the user a friend of the network support department today? Not on your life; imagine the stories of support department stupidity swirling around the water cooler and fax machine.

When you have a team of technical personnel, make sure all the members know their place in the team, and that their place makes the best use of their abilities. Don't put an irresponsible person in charge of critical backup operations. Bad things will happen sooner rather than later.

Unfortunately, you will never catch up with all that your job requires of you. It's mathematically impossible to cover every possible variable for every possible user, especially when those users want entirely different, contradictory support. Then there is the conflict between your network clients, who want everything possible to make the network faster and more fun, and your boss, who wants to spend less money.

The best chance you have to succeed in a conflict-ridden environment like this is to have your own idea of what the network should be. Your vision, if articulated to your boss and your clients, can bridge the gap between what your boss will pay for and what your clients need. If there is a vacuum, and you have no clear idea of your network, everyone will feel free to force the

> *Does this make you a doormat, subservient to every weird whim of any user?*

network into what they want. In that case, I just hope what they want is something you can 1) provide and 2) live with comfortably.

Before I grew into computers, I worked for a manufacturer. At trade shows, people would come to the booth and ask, "Why don't you have this feature?" It would bother me, because everyone wants the product to make people happy. But I couldn't add every suggestion; the unit price would triple. We were making a low-end, entry product, not the top of the line.

Finally, I came up with a response. After a person asked about a new feature, I said, "That's a good idea. How much would you be willing to pay for that?" Most of the time, the response was the same: "Nothing." Those suggestions I disregarded. I listened to the people with ideas they were willing to pay for.

When a department begs to have a new network wrinkle, ask the same question: How much are you willing to pay for this? That weeds out most of the suggestions right there.

CASE STUDY

MiniCo: NetWare 4.1x Administrator Duties and Tools

MINICO HAS 3 servers, 75 users, and one location.

Managing Your Network with a Plan

CONSIDERATIONS

The goals:

- Develop and distribute network information to the users.
- Train the users on the new network.
- Develop an internal plan for network growth.
- Project network needs two years in the future.

DECISION

Get the network up now, and worry about the rest later.

EXPLANATION

Caught in the time trap, Alexander von Thorn (the Distribution Manager who is also the lead network manager) had little time to "woo" network users to their new way of working. Training for the users was disorganized and ad-hoc; no reference material was made available. MiniCo has no idea what the network will be doing two years from now.

Supervisor Functions and the Necessary Rights

CONSIDERATIONS

The choices:

- Set up workgroup administrators to help with the network.
- Let a single administrator handle the whole network.

DECISION

Do not set up special workgroup administrators.

EXPLANATION

MiniCo's network is small enough to have a single administrator, Alexander. Jim Lewczyk (a programmer) and Scott Elyard (the Sales Manager) help out, but more as full administrators rather than subadministrators with specific areas of responsibility.

MINICO CASE STUDY, CONTINUED

Installing NetWare Administrator

CONSIDERATIONS

The goals:

- Install NetWare Administrator on each support person's workstation.
- Give the administrators training in the use of NetWare Administrator features.

DECISION

All three administrators for MiniCo had NetWare Administrator installed on their system, but none received training.

EXPLANATION

Alexander, Scott, and Jim all have NetWare Administrator loaded on their workstations, and all three have authority over the entire network. No training was ever received, so the three users often stumble upon alternative ways to perform certain administrative tasks.

NDS Administration with NetWare Administrator

CONSIDERATIONS

The choices:

- Use NetWare Administrator for NDS tasks.
- Use NETADMIN for NDS tasks.

DECISION

Use NetWare Administrator for NDS administrative procedures.

EXPLANATION

Alexander likes NetWare Administrator better than NETADMIN, so he uses the Windows 95 program for most administrative functions. He finds it easy to create and manage users and objects with the GUI.

Using NDS Manager to Manage Partitions and Replicas

CONSIDERATIONS

The goals:

- Plan the network partitions for fault-tolerance.
- Manage the placement of replicas across the network.

DECISION

Keep the network a single partition, with replicas on all servers.

EXPLANATION

Three servers is the safe minimum to hold replicas of any one partition. MiniCo's default installation provided for a single partition with replicas on each server. No one has had the time to investigate any necessary changes, so it's a good thing the design works well for the company.

MINICO CASE STUDY, CONTINUED

User Management

CONSIDERATIONS

The options:

- Use NetWare accounting.
- Employ mass-import utilities during installation.

DECISION

Don't use accounting. Set up each user individually.

EXPLANATION

MiniCo has no desire to track the disk or CPU usage for charge-backs or growth planning. User setup utilities were not considered necessary for the network installation process.

Server Management

CONSIDERATIONS

The possibilities:

- Use RCONSOLE and MONITOR to manage the server.
- Modify any SET parameters for server customization.
- Use DSTRACE to track NDS activity.
- Use DSMERGE to manage multiple NDS trees.
- Manage server license counts.

DECISIONS

Use RCONSOLE rarely, MONITOR even less, and don't change the default SET parameters. Don't use DSTRACE or DSMERGE or worry about license counts.

EXPLANATION

The three servers are in their own room, which would encourage the use of RCONSOLE. However, Alexander always feels more comfortable touching the server, so he uses the server console almost exclusively. Since he doesn't use RCONSOLE, and he can't see the servers, MONITOR doesn't help. He has not seen any reason to change SET parameters from their default settings.

With such a small network (only three servers), MiniCo has no reason to worry about NDS synchronization and performance. The license count hasn't changed since installation.

NDS Administration with DOS Tools

CONSIDERATIONS

The choices:

- Use NETADMIN and PARTMGR.
- Use NetWare Administrator and NDS Manager for network management.

DECISION

Avoid the DOS tools.

EXPLANATION

No one at MiniCo had any attachment to NETADMIN and PARTMGR, because these utilities were not part of the NetWare 3.*x* package. All administration is done using NetWare Administrator and NDS Manager.

CASE STUDY

MegaCorp: NetWare 4.1x Administrator Duties and Tools

MEGACORP HAS 50 servers, 2500 users, and 5 locations.

Managing Your Network with a Plan

CONSIDERATIONS

The goals:

- Develop and distribute network information to the users.
- Train the users on the new network.
- Develop an internal plan for network growth.
- Project network needs two years in the future.

DECISION

Prepare and distribute network help information, provide training for all network users, have IS (Information Services) personnel track long-term network technologies.

EXPLANATION

Each user had organized, classroom training before they were moved to NetWare 4.1x, and each class attendee received one page of network help instructions. The special tech support number for network problems was listed at the top of the page.

Two IS managers are assigned to the job of tracking new network technologies that may impact MegaCorp. These managers evaluate new products and extrapolate network needs, based on current usage patterns and applications under development that will add more network traffic.

Supervisor Functions and the Necessary Rights

CONSIDERATIONS

The choices:

- Use subadministrators from the department.
- Allow only IS personnel to manage the network.

DECISION

Use subadministrators in the department whenever possible, with IS supervision.

EXPLANATION

MegaCorp's Central IS department is large enough to handle all the network chores, but subadministrators are used whenever possible. This serves several goals: It gives the departments

MEGACORP CASE STUDY, CONTINUED

a feeling of ownership, it provides quicker tech support response for the department's users, and it encourages the departments to help Central IS improve the network. Everyone wins.

Installing NetWare Administrator

CONSIDERATIONS

The goals:

- Install NetWare Administrator on each support person's workstation.
- Give the administrators training in the use of NetWare Administrator features.

DECISION

All the administrators and subadministrators have NetWare Administrator installed on their system. Every support person has received training in the program.

EXPLANATION

Training for the administrators, even the departmental administrator assistants, was an important consideration for MegaCorp. Everyone with any network supervisory functions has NetWare Administrator and has received training for the utility.

NDS Administration with NetWare Administrator

CONSIDERATIONS

The choices:

- Use NetWare Administrator for NDS tasks.
- Use NETADMIN for NDS tasks.

DECISION

Use NetWare Administrator for all NDS functions.

EXPLANATION

MegaCorp had no prior sentimental attachment to SYSCON, so NETADMIN does not look more familiar than NetWare Administrator.

Using NDS Manager to Manage Partitions and Replicas

CONSIDERATIONS

The goals:

- Plan the network partitions for fault-tolerance.
- Manage the placement of replicas across the network.

DECISION

Each network has multiple partitions, with at least three replicas of each. Servers in HQ serve as replicas for the outlying networks to ease management chores and conserve WAN bandwidth.

EXPLANATION

Partition and replica planning was part of the preinstallation research done by MegaCorp. Each network has multiple partitions with critical data copied between servers for on-line backup. Each partition has a replica in HQ to ease management.

If there were no replicas at HQ, the entire login process would happen across the WAN. With a

MEGACORP CASE STUDY, CONTINUED

Read/Write replica at HQ, the administrators can log in to the partition at HQ, then let any NDS changes filter across the WAN link back to the other servers supporting the partition. NDS synchronization takes much less bandwidth than NDS manipulation; MegaCorp's method relies on the WAN for NDS synchronization only.

User Management

CONSIDERATIONS

The possibilities:

- Use NetWare accounting.
- Employ mass-import utilities during installation.

DECISION

Track usage through accounting, but not for charge-back purposes. Use every user setup utility available.

EXPLANATION

MegaCorp uses the accounting functions to track the use of network resources, but departments are not charged for network usage. The company wants to encourage network use, so disk space is plentiful for each user and no barriers are put on the network to discourage usage.

Since so many users had to be installed at one time, Central IS personnel made heavy use of the UIMPORT utility. Building the user database was something that could be done before the network arrived, and tested on the pilot installation. This planning saved days of testing and reworking during the installation project.

Server Management

CONSIDERATIONS

The possibilities:

- Use RCONSOLE and MONITOR to manage the server.
- Modify SET parameters for server customization.
- Use DSTRACE to track NDS activity.
- Use DSMERGE to manage multiple NDS trees.
- Manage server license counts.
- Monitor and adjust IPX parameters.
- Configure RCONSOLE.

DECISIONS

Use RCONSOLE constantly. Keep MONITOR running on every server screen. Modify SET parameters based on the server's primary job function. Monitor DSTRACE regularly, especially from Central IS. Adjust server license counts as user load changes. IPX performance is monitored, and sometimes adjustments are made to IPX parameters. RCONSOLE is configured with secure passwords and used constantly. Upgrade all servers so that there is no reason to use NetSync.

EXPLANATION

RCONSOLE allows one Central IS technician to manage many servers quickly, especially those across the WAN links. MONITOR is on display on each server, so it's the first screen that appears when RCONSOLE starts.

MEGACORP CASE STUDY, CONTINUED

Many servers have been adjusted with the SET parameters. The most common modifications are to improve either the read or write performance of appropriate servers. Performance profiles for various server functions are posted in the Central IS technical support database.

Central IS personnel take log snapshots now and then for the historical server record. The single-tree design of Mega_Tree eliminates any current need for DSMERGE (but DSMERGE was used with the pilot network to familiarize the network administrators with the utility).

As projects grow and then wind down in the user departments, Central IS is regularly called upon to modify license counts for some servers. The ability to add and subtract licenses was one big advantage of NetWare for a company as dynamic as MegaCorp.

Verifying driver and network hardware choices by checking IPX statistics is part of the normal monthly routine at MegaCorp. Some IPX parameters, mostly those having to do with timing synchronization with remote servers, have been modified.

RCONSOLE is used constantly. ACONSOLE is not used, since routers connect all network locations.

NDS Administration with DOS Tools

CONSIDERATIONS

The choices:

- Use NETADMIN and PARTMGR.
- Use NetWare Administrator and NDS Manager for network management.

DECISION

Use NetWare Administrator and NDS Manager.

EXPLANATION

MegaCorp wanted graphical management utilities. No Central IS person prefers any DOS utility over the corresponding graphical option.

Providing Applications for Your Network Clients

CHAPTER

AS MUCH FUN as network utilities are, sometimes you must provide applications for your network clients. Your network might need to support a single multiuser application for all the users or many different applications for every user. The normal case, fortunately, is for most users to share the core applications. Specific projects will require different software, but the majority of your users will need access to the same programs.

Some might go as far as to suggest that providing applications is the primary reason for the network. I think that is a bit shortsighted, since I prefer to believe the network is sharing information rather than just programs. But trying to follow the paths of applications begetting information begetting sharing the information begetting using the information in new applications can make one dizzy. Suffice it to say that applications are bound into everything that happens on the network.

Applications have changed over the years, but not enough. Early PC applications were hard-pressed to do a good job supporting a single user on a dual-floppy PC or single hard drive. Each printer was tied directly to the computer. The needs for multiple configuration files, remote printer control, dispersed applications, and data directories never arose.

Today, even the smallest freeware program must understand how to install to remote server hard disks and run with separate data and applications directories. If it does not, we throw it away in disgust. Shareware programs routinely support multiple print queues, shared files, and NetWare-controlled record locking. It looks like the application software developers are far ahead of the network.

But those looks are deceiving. Many commercial applications lag behind the capabilities of shareware. It's all too common to run into software that expects to be installed onto a local hard disk. Multiple printers? Forget it. Record locking, shared documents, and network awareness are still dreams for some software companies.

Be prepared for the new wave of "client/server" applications: Web server systems. Using IntranetWare as a basis, software companies are scrambling to move applications of all sorts to a Web model. This doesn't necessarily bode well in the short run for NetWare, since Novell is new to the Web server game, and companies don't yet understand the advantages of using a NetWare server as a Web server platform. That will change, however, as users shuffled off to Web applications start realizing how slow other Web servers are, and they begin demanding the performance NetWare provides.

Application Categories

NOVELL'S FORMER APPLICATION group (now the Corel WordPerfect Suite 7) divided applications into three categories: network-aware, network-enabled, and network-integrated.

Network-aware applications are programs that can run on the network, but do not use any special network features. They cannot use messaging or other communication options.

Network-enabled applications are programs that run well on the network, but use proprietary solutions for services such as messaging and user authorization. These application services, such as the user database in an e-mail program, cannot be shared with other applications. This approach is wasteful because it adds extra cost to each program, services aren't shared (often even between applications by the same company), and the cost of managing all these different systems is high. Do you want to add a new user to the network database, then to the e-mail, scheduling, and database user lists?

Network-integrated applications are excellent choices for the modern network. They do not have the shortcomings of network-aware or network-enabled applications. They provide good communication and collaboration features. Also, they are well-integrated into the advanced services of the network operating system, such as the user Directory database. This makes them easier to manage, keeping down the cost of ownership.

This is a long way from some applications available in the mid-1980s, which I called network-hostile. They hard-coded drive C: into the installation program. Almost as bad were the programs stored on the server hard disk that required a single license floppy at the workstation to start, but were sold as multiuser. Does that make sense? The evolution of applications is like the leap in medicine from leeches to modern antibiotics.

Unfortunately, almost all PC LAN applications are stuck in level two, network-enabled. We can't really blame the software developers, however. The tool they need to share communication channels and the user database is, in fact, a better user database. NDS provides a strong global directory with extensions available for developers. Now the smart developers are moving to take advantage of these features with applications that are integrated into the network.

An example of this integration was the ability of WordPerfect 6.1 to control the NetWare print queue from within the application. If a user wishes to check the job status, or cancel the print job with another word processor, the proper NetWare utility must be opened outside the word processor. With WordPerfect 6.1, this happens with the click of a button. In WordPerfect 7, even more network savvy touches are evident.

Another good example of network-enabled control is the ability for software to store the bulk of the application on a server, requiring minimum disk space on the workstation. Keeping individual configuration files for the software on the individual workstation is acceptable, but it's better to keep configuration files on the server. Having them under control on the server allows the network administrator to change and update those files quickly and easily. Keeping them on the server also helps protect them from user mistakes.

Trends in Distribution, Metering, and Licensing

THE THREE AREAS for application improvement when used on a network are:

- The distribution of applications and subsequent updates
- Metering application use
- Licensing to guarantee software vendors that their programs are being used legally

Novell is one of the active participants in this improvement, but it isn't the only company making advances.

Novell's NetWare Navigator product is a management tool that provides ways to manage applications across your network, no matter how large your network may be. A single manager from a single control console can organize and execute application installation and updates. NetWare Navigator can handle applications installed on servers or individual workstations.

The first company that shipped a product of this kind for PC LANs was Frye Computer Systems with their SUDS (Software Update and Distribution System) product. There are now more than a dozen similar products.

Good products provide a script facility, as well as the ability to schedule updates, run them without an operator, and support both DOS and MS Windows programs. The program should be able to make updates based on hardware type and the particular machine, and be able to check software versions before updating.

The distribution of software to workstations is always going to be difficult, because users still have this strange idea that the computer on their desk is theirs. I know it says "personal computer," but the personal part diminished a bunch when the users connected to the network. You will need to work with some users to make sure the configurations on the systems don't get too wild, or you'll need to update 30 percent by hand rather than just 10 percent if your update software works well. You'll never get 100 percent of anything to work properly in the computer business. If you think you did, you just overlooked something.

Metering and licensing are two parts of the same coin. Metering tracks which software is being used and by whom. Licensing works with metering to set the usage levels of software products. Most metering software shows usage by concurrent users, which is what most software vendors track. Good metering software will also provide reports of application usage after the fact.

The LSAPI (Licensing Service Application Programming Interface) has been developed by Novell, Gradient, IBM, and Microsoft. This specialized API (Application Programming Interface, a way software vendors write programs that other programs can access) provides a common interface for developers to manage execution of their products by electronic license certificates. A management system add-on will soon be able to control and monitor software usage. You'll even be able to track applications launched from a network client's hard disk, if the workstation is logged in to the network at the time. Look at Novell's own NetWare Licensing Services, included in NetWare 4.11, as the next step in this continuing trend.

These advances, and more to come, show improvement in the handling of network applications. It wasn't so long ago that companies had to keep

> *I know it says "personal computer," but the personal part diminished a bunch when the users connected to the network.*

closets full of single-user applications, such as Lotus 1-2-3, because the vendor didn't provide a network license. Now, a major application without network pricing and licensing is, thank goodness, an anomaly.

Application Server Guidelines

LIKE EVERYTHING ELSE about your network, the directory structure for your applications is unique. The setup for your applications will be based on your preferences, the preferences of your users, and most of all, the dictates of your application. We'll go over some guidelines for your directory structure, but don't get upset when you must bend the rules to fit your situation.

The most important guideline is this: Keep your application programs separate from your data. Many network administrators keep their applications on one volume and let the users keep their data on another volume. For example, the database application is on volume SYS:, and the data controlled by that database is on VOL1.

This guideline makes good sense in almost every case. Most important, if you mingle the applications and the data, something will happen to one or the other. If users have Delete rights for a data directory in the same directory structure as the application programs, something will be erased. It shouldn't happen, but it will.

If your tape backup system is unable to capture everything in one tape, it may be able to back up the data in one tape if it is separated from the application programs. Separating the data and programs also means you need to back up only the SYS: and/or application volumes when something changes.

Although it's possible (with most tape software) to choose which directories are copied in a backup operation, it's easier to back up a volume. Your backup parameters take more time to set up and are more prone to errors if you must thread in and around your directories to cover everything.

Take a look at Figure 11.1 for a simple example of separating your data from your programs. This uses the GATEWAY2000 system, with one 500 MB disk divided into two volumes.

The SYS: volume holds all the applications. In this case, the example is the PerfectOffice network installation from WordPerfect (now the Corel

FIGURE 11.1

A simple but effective method for separating your application programs from your data

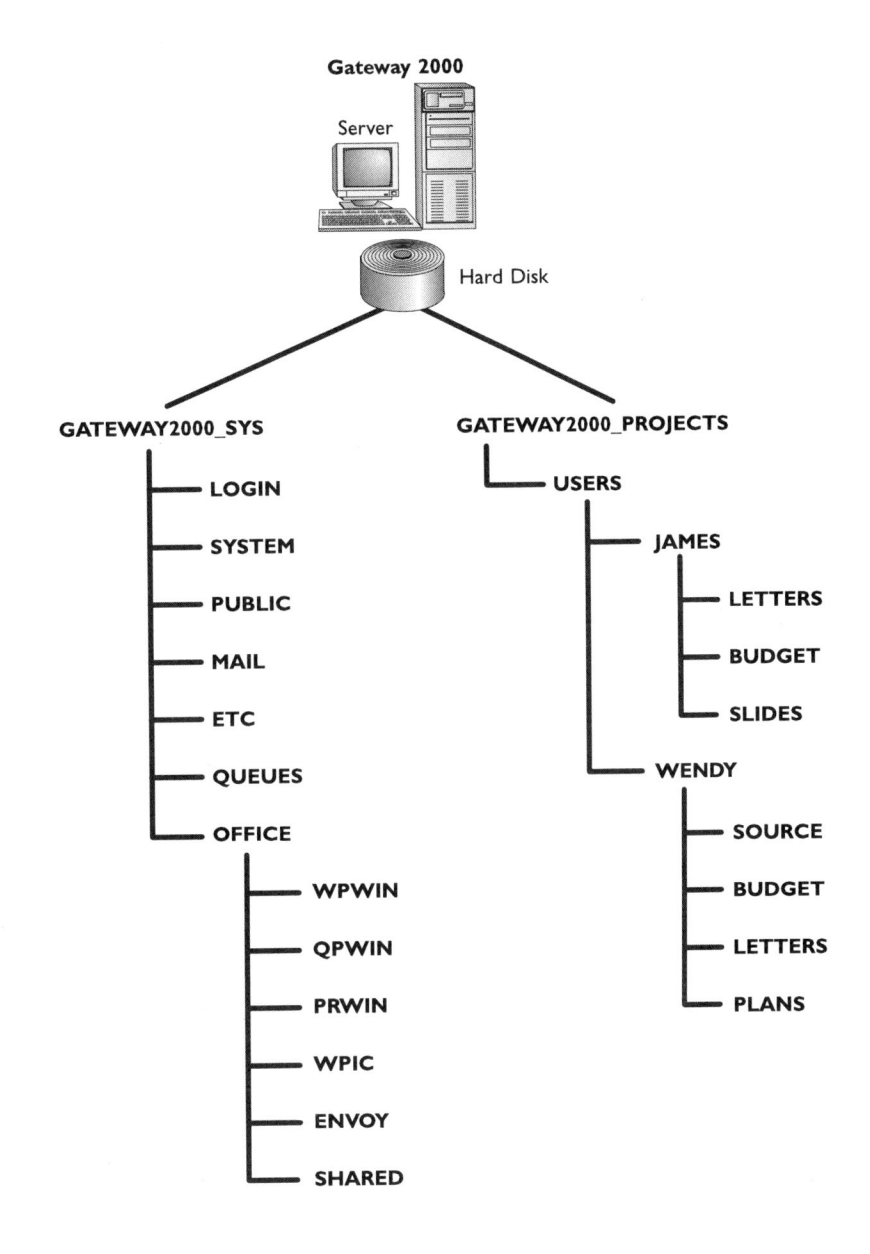

```
Gateway 2000
Server
Hard Disk

GATEWAY2000_SYS
    ├── LOGIN
    ├── SYSTEM
    ├── PUBLIC
    ├── MAIL
    ├── ETC
    ├── QUEUES
    └── OFFICE
            ├── WPWIN
            ├── QPWIN
            ├── PRWIN
            ├── WPIC
            ├── ENVOY
            └── SHARED

GATEWAY2000_PROJECTS
    └── USERS
            ├── JAMES
            │       ├── LETTERS
            │       ├── BUDGET
            │       └── SLIDES
            └── WENDY
                    ├── SOURCE
                    ├── BUDGET
                    ├── LETTERS
                    └── PLANS
```

WordPerfect Suite 7). You can see the NetWare system directories on GATEWAY2000_SYS, and the final directory on the list is OFFICE. Under OFFICE are the directories for WordPerfect for Windows, Quattro Pro for Windows, Presentations 3.0 for Windows, WordPerfect Info Central, Envoy (the document-sharing technology), and a directory for shared information and configuration files.

If you have lots of applications (which we really don't here), you will be better off with a separate volume. Calling a volume APPS, for instance, makes several things easier. All drive mapping can point to the same volume, so it's easy to remember. It also adds one more level of separation for your tape backup process.

In our example, the PROJECTS volume holds the USERS directory. This is where all the home directories are automatically placed when a new user is created. In Figure 11.1, you can see the directories for JAMES and for WENDY (of course, your network will have more than two users—this is just to give you the idea).

Since these are home directories, users can organize them any way they wish. Your users' home directories will be around the jobs they must deal with in their workday. I may have directories named LETTERS, BUDGET, and SLIDES (for presentations). Wendy may have SOURCE for source code files, BUDGET, LETTERS, and PLANS for new databases under development.

When the end of the day rolls around and it's time for backup, the most important volume is PROJECTS. The valuable data is there, where people are creating and using information. If space is tight on the tape for the backup, the SYS: volume could be skipped most of the time. Application files and the NetWare system files change rarely. It may seem like you need a software upgrade every day, but it's not really true.

It's not unusual to go a step farther down this road, and keep the applications and data files on separate servers. In our example, the SYS: volume may be that of ALTOS486, while GATEWAY2000_PROJECTS is the volume for the data and user directories. The advantage of this method is that it adds a bit of server fault-tolerance. If the application server has a problem, the data is still safe. If the data server goes down, users can still work with their applications and temporarily store data files on their local disks.

Figure 11.2 shows this arrangement in NetWare Administrator browser windows. ALTOS486_SYS is on the left, with the OFFICE subdirectory highlighted. You can see the program subdirectories within. The other window shows GATEWAY2000_PROJECTS, with my user subdirectory indicated.

This arrangement also helps balance the load on servers a bit. If your server handles both the applications and the data files, there will be quite a bit of traffic. Multiply this scenario by the number of applications serving the users on your network, and you can imagine the traffic load. The ability of NetWare 4.1*x* to support large numbers of concurrent users makes it tempting to load the server with all sorts of application and data directories. Let's see if

FIGURE 11.2

Applications here; data there

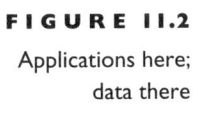

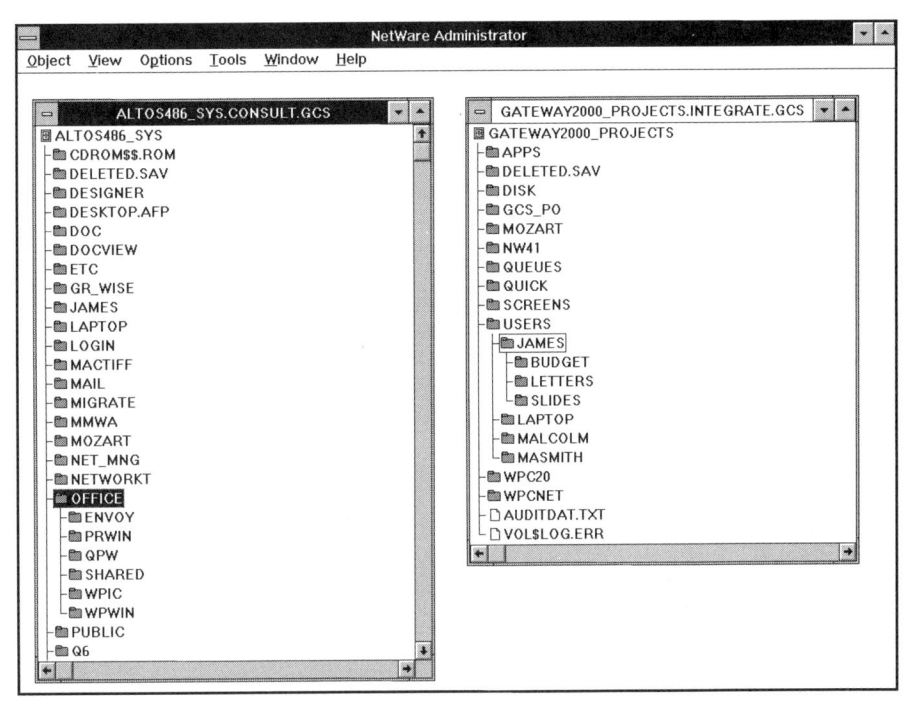

there are ways to maximize performance by splitting applications and data among different servers and optimizing each server to the assigned task.

Improving Disk-Write Performance

The default values provided by Novell for NetWare servers balance the reading and writing functions. Parameters you change to make disk writes faster tend to slow down file reads, and vice versa. This is the technological equivalent of not being able to have your cake and eat it, too. However, if you can dedicate one server to a majority of disk writes (like the server holding the data directories), you can tilt the balance to your advantage.

You can check the need to increase the server's concurrent write performance by comparing the number of dirty cache buffers (those that are changed and need to be written to disk) to the total number of cache buffers. Look in the MONITOR screen under General Information. If the number of dirty cache buffers is over 70 percent of the total cache buffers, you can improve server performance by changing these parameters. (See Chapter 10 for more on using MONITOR.)

> ### 11.1 IN-A-HURRY
>
> **Use SERVMAN to Improve Disk-Write Performance**
>
> 1. Start SERVMAN, either by typing **LOAD SERVMAN** from the console prompt (in NetWare 4.10 and 4.11) or from within MONITOR (in 4.11).
>
> 2. Choose Server Parameters, then select File Caching.
>
> 3. Highlight Maximum Concurrent Disk Cache Writes and increase the number from 50 (the default) to 100.
>
> 4. Press Escape twice to reach the Update Options menu and choose Update AUTOEXEC.NCF and STARTUP.NCF Now. Press Enter to verify the update.
>
> 5. From the Available Options menu, choose Server Parameters, then Directory Caching.
>
> 6. Highlight Dirty Disk Cache Delay Time and increase the time from 3.3 to 7 seconds.
>
> 7. Press Escape, then choose Directory Caching.
>
> 8. Highlight Dirty Directory Cache Delay Time and increase the time from 0.5 to 2 seconds.
>
> 9. Highlight Maximum Concurrent Directory Cache Writes and increase the number from 10 (the default) to 25.
>
> 10. Press Escape twice to reach the Update Options menu and choose Update AUTOEXEC.NCF and STARTUP.NCF Now. Press Enter to verify the update.
>
> 11. Press Escape to exit SERVMAN.

You can use the SET parameters from the server console prompt, but SERVMAN is easier to handle. With NetWare 4.11, you can launch SERVMAN from within MONITOR. With both 4.10 and 4.11, you can start SERVMAN from the server console prompt (at the physical console or by using RCONSOLE) by typing:

```
LOAD SERVMAN
```

The range of Maximum Concurrent Disk Cache Writes is 10 to 4000. Your best course is to increase the number to 100, then check the performance under load the next day. You may increase the number again, but I don't suggest radically changing a setting without checking the effects of the change on all the other settings.

SERVMAN will change the settings immediately, and give you the chance to set those changes in the appropriate startup file. This means you don't need to reboot the server for these changes to take effect. If you do save the changes (and you should), the settings will be remembered when the server is rebooted.

Move back through the menu choices until you reach the Dirty Disk Cache Delay Time setting. This sets the amount of delay before changed disk blocks are written to disk. Low numbers write more frequently, but write fewer changed blocks. Forcing the system to wait a few extra seconds means more write requests are serviced more efficiently. This doesn't slow down your application, because when the file buffers accept the file-write request, the application continues on.

The Dirty Directory Cache Delay Time works the same way for the directory cache tables. Since directory listings are kept in file-cache RAM while current, changes must be regularly written to disk. Saving the write for a bit longer makes for more efficient writes, but also slightly increases the danger of directory entry table corruption. Move from the default of 0.5 seconds to 2 seconds. Figure 11.3 shows this parameter selected and ready to be changed.

The Maximum Concurrent Directory Cache Writes setting increases the number of the aforementioned directory cache writes that can happen at one time. Move the number from 10 to 25 for a test. This does impact the performance of directory cache reads, so watch this setting.

FIGURE 11.3

Cleaning up dirty directory caching

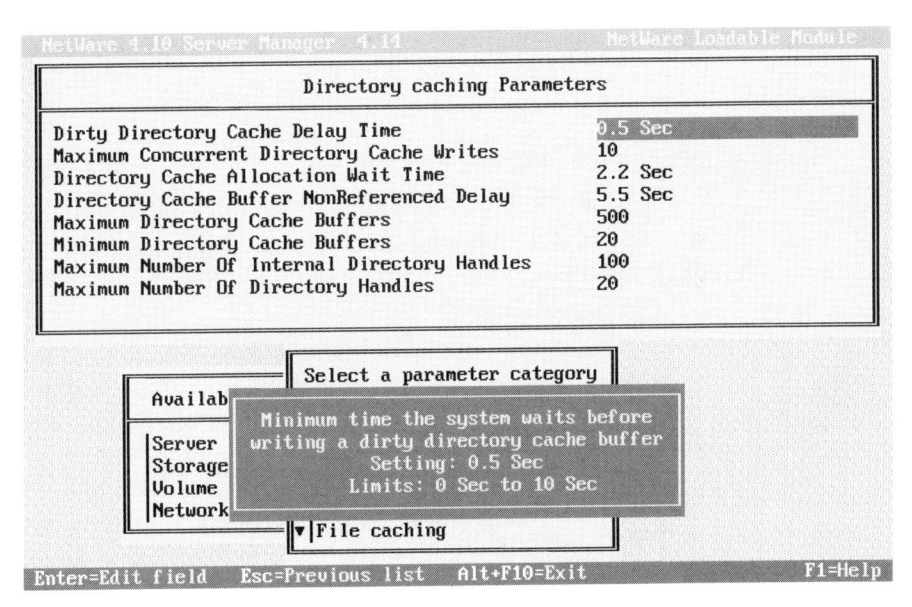

Improving Disk-Read Performance

> ### 11.2 IN-A-HURRY
>
> **Use SERVMAN to Improve Disk-Read Performance**
>
> 1. Start SERVMAN, either by typing **LOAD SERVMAN** from the console prompt (in NetWare 4.10 and 4.11) or from within MONITOR (in 4.11).
>
> 2. Choose Server Parameters, then select File Caching.
>
> 3. Highlight Maximum Concurrent Disk Cache Writes and decrease the number from 50 (the default) to 10.
>
> 4. Press Escape to reach the Categories menu, and choose Directory Caching.
>
> 5. Highlight Maximum Concurrent Directory Cache Writes and increase the number from 10 (the default) to 5.
>
> 6. Highlight Directory Cache Buffer Nonreferenced Delay and change it from 5.5 seconds (the default) to 60 seconds.
>
> 7. Press Escape to reach the Categories menu, and then choose File System.
>
> 8. Scroll down to Turbo FAT ReUse Wait Time and change the value from 5 minutes, 29.6 seconds (the default) to 600 seconds (10 minutes). Use seconds to set the value.
>
> 9. Press Escape twice to reach the Update Options menu and choose Update AUTOEXEC.NCF and STARTUP.NCF Now. Press Enter to verify the update.
>
> 10. Press Escape to exit SERVMAN.

Remember, the cache both giveth and taketh away.

The flip side of making your data files server write faster is making your application files server read faster. The way to do this is to force the system to keep directory cache buffers longer and slow down the number of disk writes. Remember, the cache both giveth and taketh away.

After loading SERVMAN and getting to the File Caching menu choice in the Server Parameters menu, find Maximum Concurrent Disk Cache Writes. Change this value from the default of 50 to 10, reducing the number of write operations executed concurrently. If you read the previous section, you know this is one of the values we increased to make writes go faster. Now we're flipping that coin and using this parameter to limit write time to make more time for disk reads.

The next move is to change Maximum Concurrent Directory Cache Writes from the default of 10 down to 5. This again limits the number of write operations, and it is in direct contrast to improving disk-write performance. (See Figure 11.3 for an example of this SERVMAN screen.)

The Directory Cache Buffer Nonreferenced Delay value specifies the length of time a directory cache buffer can stay in memory. The higher the number, the longer a directory cache buffer is considered valid and reusable. File access causes more directory cache buffers to be opened to keep up. The more directory cache buffers you have active, the faster the files are found when requested.

After you've changed the Directory Caching parameters, press Escape and choose File System from the Categories menu. Find Turbo FAT ReUse Wait Time and increase it to 600 seconds.

Turbo FAT ReUse Wait Time is particularly helpful with large database files. A turbo FAT (file allocation table) index is built when an accessed file has more than 64 FAT entries. This speeds up performance with large files, which are often database files that use sequential record listings (and similar features) and constantly access the same FAT entries.

The Turbo FAT ReUse Wait Time value refers to how long the turbo FAT index remains active and in memory after the indexed file is closed. The longer the file stays available, the quicker subsequent file access is. Forcing the files to stay available a full ten minutes almost doubles their default availability.

As always, you must write these changes to the AUTOEXEC.NCF and STARTUP.NCF files if you want to have them available after the server reboots. Let SERVMAN do it for you, and you won't need to worry about getting the syntax right with a SET command.

Consolidating Application Licenses

If your workgroups have only a single server and are spread too far apart to use a central server, you have no option for tuning as we just discussed. Worse, you may need to buy many small licenses for network applications rather than one large license. It's more expensive to buy 10 packages, each supporting 10 users, than one package to support 100 users.

But, if your one-server workgroups are all on the same network, the advantages of NetWare 4.1*x* may help you in a way you might not have considered. With earlier versions of NetWare, the one-server workgroup made sense because of the high management overhead of mapping each user to several different servers. It was done all the time, of course, but tracking user LKG across six servers meant six times the work as leaving the user on one server. With NDS, however, you can track user LKG across as many servers as you want, with a single login. Even more important for your social life, this can be done with a single administration step.

Let's go over an example considering three departments: Accounting, Graphics, and Legal. Each has 30 users. Each department has specific software licensed for those 30 users. But what about the general applications that these 90 users need? Why buy three network versions of Paradox, if all 90 users need access to Paradox? We know the Legal department needs access to the legal database, but doesn't everyone need a word processor? Why buy three separate licenses?

Figure 11.4 shows one way to share the load and save some money. The Accounting users must access the Solomon accounting package, but no one else cares about that. So they have a 30-user license for Solomon. The 30 users in the Graphics department need CorelDRAW, and the 30 users in the Legal department need access to the Legal database. Nothing unusual here. Then there is the question of buying three licenses each for a word processor, database, and e-mail package (one each for every department).

But the horizontal applications can be shared easily. Everyone needs word processing, so the Legal department server holds a 100-user license of WordPerfect. This lets all users in all three departments have access to one network copy of WordPerfect, rather than three separate ones. The same scenario is repeated on the Graphics department server, where the e-mail application is stored. Accounting also helps out by hosting the Paradox database, again with a 100-user license.

With NetWare 3.*x*, you would need to create and manage each user in each department on three different servers. With NetWare 4.1*x*, the users can connect to the Directory Services database and be granted access to their job-specific applications and the horizontal applications: one login, three servers, six applications.

As we've seen in Chapters 4, 6, and 7, there's no reason each department can't be its own Organizational Unit. The three departments could also be one large Organizational Unit with three separate groups. Either option, or some other arrangement you may come up with, is perfectly acceptable.

FIGURE 11.4
Coordinating server application licenses

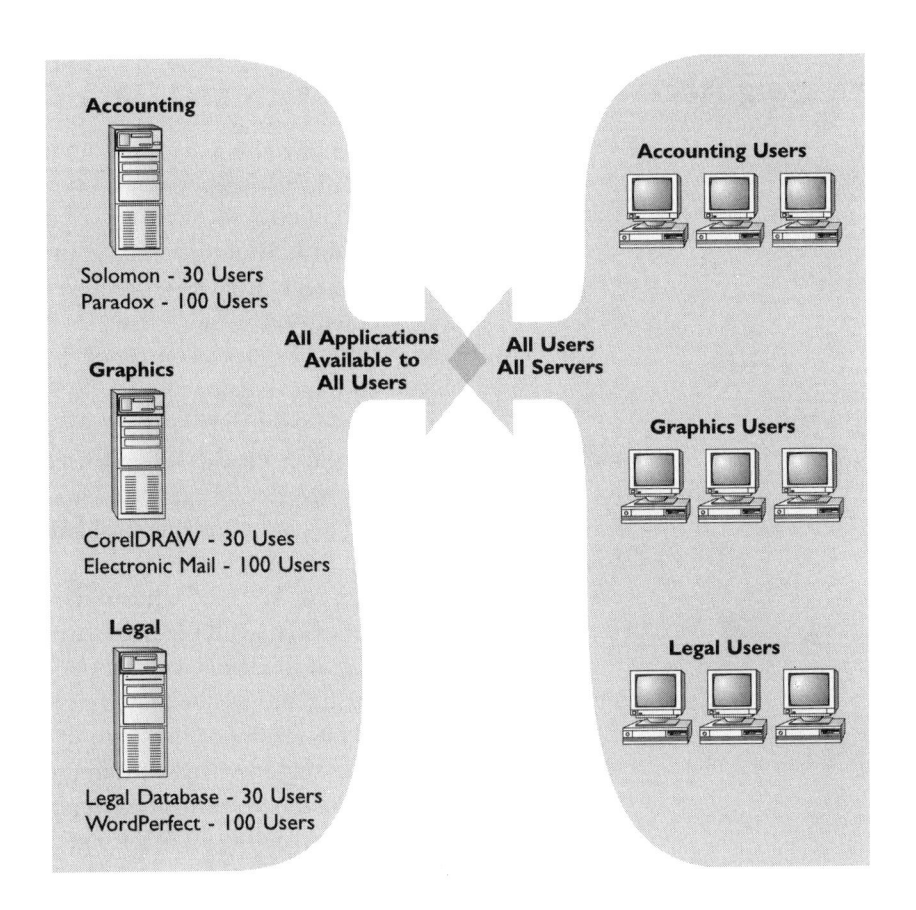

Accounting
Solomon - 30 Users
Paradox - 100 Users

Graphics
CorelDRAW - 30 Uses
Electronic Mail - 100 Users

Legal
Legal Database - 30 Users
WordPerfect - 100 Users

All Applications Available to All Users

All Users All Servers

Accounting Users

Graphics Users

Legal Users

Access Rights for Application Directories

THE DEFAULT RIGHTS for all users to new directories are Read and File Scan (for servers in the same container as the user). This allows everyone to see the directories but not take any action in those directories. The primary action we want to avoid is a user accidentally deleting a file or two hundred. And, as we discussed in Chapter 9, the first step in virus control is keeping users (and hence viruses) from modifying executable files.

Managing Access Rights in Application and Data Directories

Keeping our application programs separate from the data generated by those programs forces us to manage the access rights separately. This time, multiple management steps are a good thing. We want all users to have enough rights to read and execute the application programs, but not to be able to make other file-system changes. Data directories require that appropriate users have full user rights, which I consider Read, Write, Create, Erase, and File Scan. These rights allow the users as much control over the directory on the server as they have on their own hard disks.

The model for these settings is the NetWare system itself. The PUBLIC directory contains all the utility files for users. Every user has access to PUBLIC, and must have the ability to find and run each program there. However, since this is a system directory, you don't want anyone to change the files by deleting them or modifying the access rights. As PUBLIC provides Read and File Scan rights to everyone, so should you provide those rights to the application programs.

Applications differ, of course, and the final determination must be made by the application programs. If the installation routine demands more rights, such as the ability to Create and Delete temporary files in the application directories, you have no choice but to make those changes. But it will be worth a few minutes of testing to see if you can create and delete the temporary files elsewhere. Often, you can satisfy an application's need for a place to work with temporary files with this DOS setting:

```
SET TEMP=C:\TEMP
```

If you make use of the power users in a department to function as administrative helpers, check their rights to these application directories. They will often need full file access and control rights to administer the applications. This also means they should be made virus-aware, since they have both the ability (file rights) and attitude (let's load this new utility and see if it helps) to introduce a virus to the network.

Setting Rights to an Application Directory

Applications do a good job of creating directories and distributing their files (sometimes all over the place), but they don't set rights for your users. You must do this, but because of rights inheritance, you need only adjust the top of the application's directory structure.

11.3 IN-A-HURRY

Grant Rights to Application Directories

1. As the Admin user or equivalent, start NetWare Administrator.

2. Highlight the directory to set user or group rights.

3. Click the right mouse button to open the submenu and choose Details.

4. Click on the Trustees for this Directory button.

5. Click on Add Trustees to open the Select Object dialog box.

6. Highlight the user, group, or container that needs rights to the application directory, and click on OK.

7. Check the appropriate access rights (Read and File Scan are suggested).

8. Click on OK to save and exit.

The recipient of these rights may be an individual user, several users, a group, a container, several groups or containers, or the entire network. Since the PerfectOffice directory is our example, and it contains horizontal applications used by everyone, the example here is for the entire network to be granted access.

Figure 11.5 shows the OFFICE subdirectory chosen in the ALTOS486_SYS volume. The dialog box for the directory shows the [Public] object being granted trustee rights to Read and File Scan the OFFICE directory. As you can see in the display, the ENVOY, PRWIN, QPW, SHARED, WPIC, and WPWIN subdirectories are directly under the OFFICE directory. Everyone will also have the same Read and File Scan rights to these subdirectories.

In the lower-right corner of Figure 11.5, you can see the Effective Rights dialog box, which I opened to illustrate the exact rights available. The Effective Rights dialog box isn't updated until you save the rights assignment settings and open the same view again.

More details for granting trustee rights to various network users and groups are discussed in Chapter 7.

FIGURE 11.5

Granting [Public] the right to use OFFICE

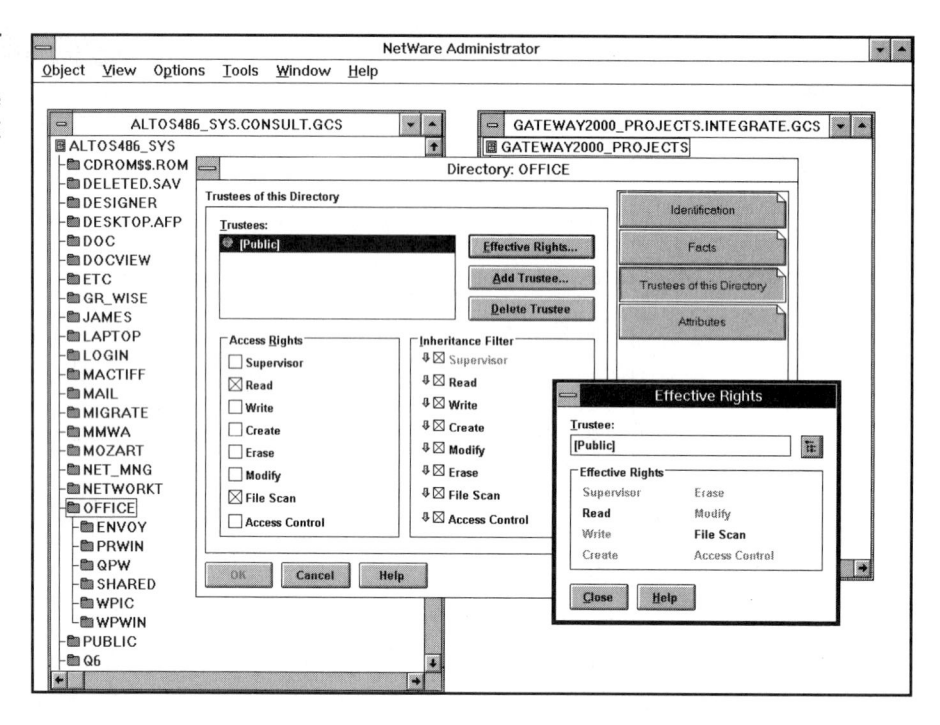

Protecting Application Programs and Data Files

YOUR APPLICATION PROGRAMS must be protected from a variety of disasters. Some of these you have control over; some you don't. Those that you have control over include:

- Accidental deletion
- Intentional deletion
- Users allowed access to these files
- Concurrent program users as per the license agreement

Some of the disasters over which you have less control, or no control at all, include:

- Server or disk failure
- Catastrophe
- Application and data theft
- Software updates

We looked at a way to stop the authorized users from accidentally (or intentionally) deleting files in the previous section. That method applies to the users and their rights to access the files. There is also a way to give the files themselves some self-defense mechanisms. The attributes (often called flags) that can be given to directories and files are described in Chapter 9, which covers network security. Check back to Tables 9.3 and 9.4 for complete lists of both types of attributes.

All these attributes (except Execute Only, in NetWare 4.10) can be changed by someone with the Modify right. That is why the manual strongly cautions you about granting the Modify right to any nonsupervisory users.

Several of these attributes provide excellent self-defense for your files and directories. The most common flag used to protect files is Read Only. When a file is marked Read Only/Shareable, multiple concurrent users can read and execute the program, but none of them may delete, rename, or write to the file.

File Attributes as a Safety Device

11.4 IN-A-HURRY

Set File Attributes with FLAG

1. Log in as the Admin user or equivalent and move to the directory where the file attributes need to be changed.

2. Type **FLAG** to check the current file status.

3. Type **FLAG *.* RO** to set the file to Read Only.

4. Type **FLAG** to check the current file status and verify the attribute has been applied.

If you're familiar with the DOS ATTRIB command, the FLAG command should look familiar. DOS files have a Read Only switch as well. There is more reason to use this type of file protection in a shared environment.

Although it's not technically necessary to move to the directory where the files need to be set, it's easier and safer for me. I check the status of the files before continuing, just in case the files have already been flagged Read Only (RO). See Figure 11.6 for the FLAG Help screen and an example. The example on the bottom of the screen adds the extra /FO to specify files only in this directory. It's a bit extra, but using this option will keep you from making mistakes.

Officially, the manual recommends you use FILER or NetWare Administrator to set your file attributes. The only problem with those two options is that they take longer to set attributes for groups of files. You can work with multiple files at a time with FILER and with the version of NetWare Administrator that comes with NetWare 4.11 (but not with the one in NetWare 4.10), but I think it's much easier to do this with FLAG.

If you don't believe me, check out this next example. Using FILER, I moved down through the volumes to this directory. Since there are many files I wanted to set as RO, I used the F6 key to mark a pattern. The pattern was *.*, since I wanted to mark all the files. Unfortunately, that marks all the directories in the Directory Contents box as well. Take a look at Figure 11.7 and check out the situation.

FIGURE 11.6

The result of typing FLAG /? /FO

```
FLAG                    File Attributes Help                    4.15

Syntax:   FLAG [path [+|-]attribute(s)] /FO

              File Attributes                        Status Flags
              ---------------                        ------------
      Ro   Read-only              Rw   Read-write       Co   Compressed
      H    Hidden                 Sy   System           Cc   Can't compress
      P    Purge                  A    Archive-needed   M    Migrated
      Di   Delete-inhibit         Ri   Rename-inhibit
      Sh   Shareable              T    Transactional
      Ci   Copy-inhibit           X    eXecute-only
      Dm   Don't migrate          Ic   Immediate compress
      Dc   Don't compress         Ds   Don't suballocate
      ALL  ALL                    N    Normal

      For example, to:           Type:
          Give files on drive Z:
          Read-only attribute         FLAG Z:*.* RO /FO
```

[Novell DOS] G:\SCREENS\41>

FIGURE 11.7

Multiple files are marked in FILER, but this required multiple keystrokes

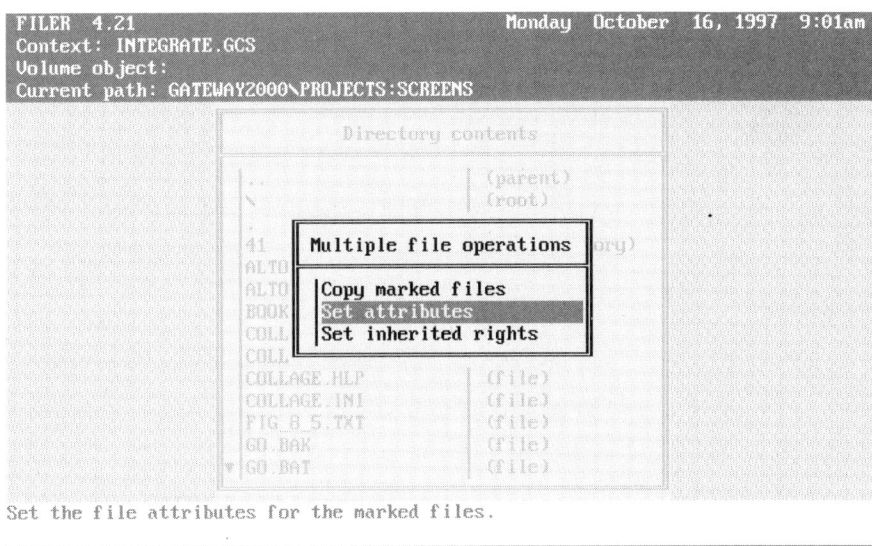

```
FILER 4.21                                    Monday  October  16, 1997  9:01am
Context: INTEGRATE.GCS
Volume object:
Current path: GATEWAY2000\PROJECTS:SCREENS

                          ┌─────── Directory contents ───────┐
                          │ ..                      (parent)  │
                          │ \                       (root)    │
                          │ 41   ┌─ Multiple file operations ─┐
                          │ ALTO │                            │
                          │ ALTO │ Copy marked files          │
                          │ BOOK │ Set attributes             │
                          │ COLL │ Set inherited rights       │
                          │ COLL └────────────────────────────┘
                          │ COLLAGE.HLP            (file)     │
                          │ COLLAGE.INI            (file)     │
                          │ FIG_8_5.TXT            (file)     │
                          │ GO.BAK                 (file)     │
                        ▼ │ GO.BAT                 (file)     │
                          └───────────────────────────────────┘
Set the file attributes for the marked files.

Enter=Select   Esc=Escape                                             F1=Help
```

When I pressed Enter to start the multiple file operation, an error message appeared, declaring that I couldn't use the marked parent directory in multiple operations. So I moved the highlight bar to the top of the box, pressed the F5 key to unmark the parent directory, and tried again. This time, the error message said that multiple operations are not allowed on the current directory. Then, after all this, I got the menu choice you see in Figure 11.7. That's why I prefer FLAG.

Changing Directory and File Ownership

The process for changing file and directory ownership is similar to changing file and directory rights. This time, let's use NetWare Administrator for the task.

Why would you want to change the owner of a file or directory? Two reasons come to mind. One is to make tracking the evolution of the network clearer to whomever follows you in your present job. If the owner of a questionable file or directory is Bob, the future administrator has no idea if Bob was a user or an administrator. If the owner is Admin, there's no question.

The second reason to change file ownership applies to those companies that allocate disk space to users. When Bob creates a directory and copies files there, as in a typical software installation, all that file space counts against his budget. That's not fair to good old Bob, so you should change the file's owner value to Admin.

11.5 IN-A-HURRY

Modify Directory and File Ownership

1. Log in as the Admin user or equivalent and start NetWare Administrator.
2. Highlight the directory or file to be modified in the browser window.
3. Click the right mouse button and choose Details.
4. Click on the Facts button.
5. Click on the Browser button on the right end of the Owner field.
6. Choose the owner from the Select Object dialog box and click on OK.
7. Click on OK to save and exit.

Figure 11.8 shows the screen in NetWare Administrator to set the owner of the OFFICE directory from JAMES to Admin. Although you can name the owner of files and directories, one does not influence the other. After changing the directory's owner, you must then change the owner for all the files in the directory. You can't tag multiple files; each must be done individually.

You cannot type the name of the owner in the field. You must click on the Browser button at the end of the field to get to the Select Object dialog box. This prevents any typos that could cause confusion, and makes sure the entire owner's name, including context, is correct.

Changing Ownership with FLAG

The same trick we used in FILER to change the rights on multiple files (shown back in Figure 11.7) doesn't work to change the owner of multiple files and directories. However, good old FLAG does the trick with a fistful of files at once. For example, to change all the files in the current directory to have Admin as the owner, from the command line, type:

```
FLAG *.* /name=Admin
```

No muss, no fuss.

If you're curious as to who owns which files, just typing **FLAG** at the DOS prompt will list the file name, DOS and NetWare attributes, status, and owner. Subdirectories in the current directory will be listed with their owners as well. You can see why I think FLAG is a great utility.

FIGURE 11.8

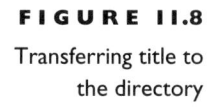

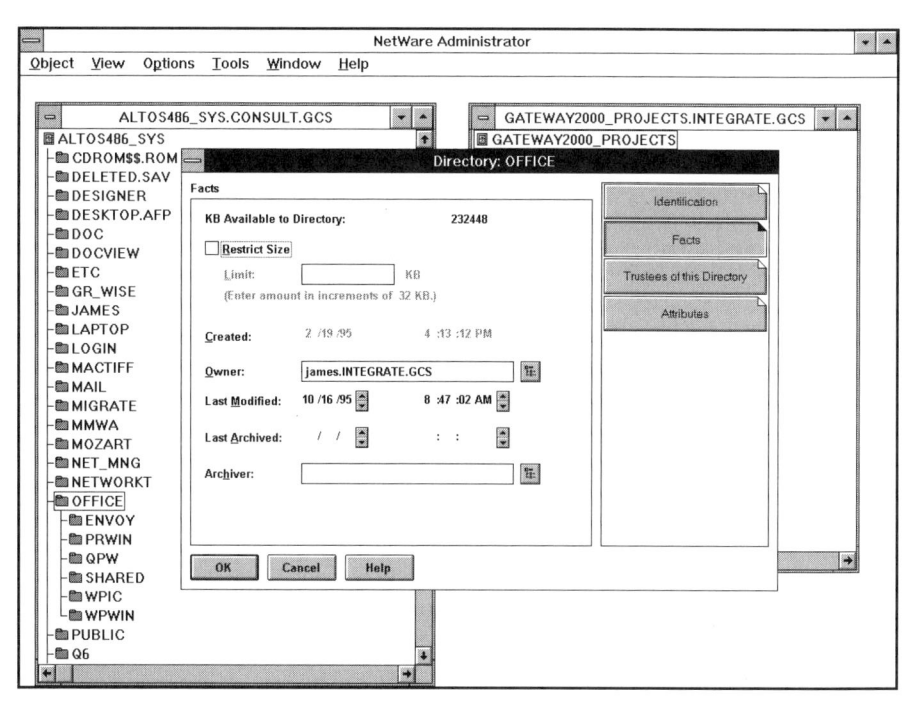

Transferring title to the directory

Modifying File Rights with the Rights Command

The RIGHTS command allows you to view or modify the rights of a group or user to files, directories, and volumes. We are speaking of file and directory rights only; this has nothing to do with NDS. The command-line program is quick, available, and only slightly cryptic.

The syntax is:

```
RIGHTS path [[ + | - ] rights] [/option...] [/? | /VER]
```

where:

- The *path* specifies the path to the file, directory, or volume in question. A path is always necessary.

- The + or – (plus sign or minus sign) is used to add or delete the specified rights.

- The *rights* refers to one or more directory and file rights.

- The *option* ... is the place to list command modifiers.
- The /? option displays the Help screen.
- The /VER option displays the RIGHTS version.

Most of the time, you can give rights to a user that has no rights in a certain directory. The quick method is:

```
RIGHTS SYS:OFFICE\WPWIN R W C E F /NAME=MASMITH
```

This grants user MASMITH the rights to Read, Write, Create, Erase, and File Scan in the \OFFICE\WPWIN directory of the SYS: volume. The options used with RIGHTS are listed in Table 11.1. See Table 11.2 for a quick review of the abbreviations used for file and directory rights.

TABLE 11.1 RIGHTS Command Options

OPTION	FUNCTION
/C	Scrolls continuously, usually so fast you can't read anything
/F	Displays the IRF (Inherited Rights Filter)
/I	Displays the trustee and group rights for a user for a directory, including where the inherited rights come from
/NAME	Specifies the user or group name
/S	Shows subdirectories
/T	Displays trustee assignments

TABLE 11.2 Abbreviations for File and Directory Rights

ABBREVIATION	RIGHT
A	Access Control to change trustee rights and assignments
ALL	All rights except Supervisor (not a good idea, since this includes Modify and Access Control)
C	Create (and Write)
E	Erase
F	File Scan
M	Modify names of files and directories; change file attributes

TABLE 11.2 (cont.)

Abbreviations for File and Directory Rights

ABBREVIATION	RIGHT
N	No rights (not Normal, as with FLAG)
R	Read (and Open)
REM	Remove a user or group as a trustee
S	Supervisor
W	Write (and Open)

The following are the operational rules for RIGHTS (rights always have rules, you know):

- With + (plus) you add rights to existing rights.

- With – (minus) only the mentioned rights are deleted.

- You can add and delete rights in one command, but carefully group the add commands and keep them separate from the delete commands.

- When you detail rights without a + or –, listed rights replace all existing rights.

- A path is always necessary. To specify your current directory, use a period (.).

- Wildcards are acceptable.

Let's look at an example. To add rights to the current directory for user LAPTOP, the sequence shown in Figure 11.9 took place.

FIGURE 11.9

Checking rights with RIGHTS

```
I:\SCREENS\41rights . rwcef /name=laptop

GATEWAY2000\PROJECTS:\SCREENS<F255>
Directories                        Rights

41                                 [ RWCE F ]

Rights for one directory were changed for laptop
```

The command was given from the \SCREENS\41 directory, but it was still necessary to reference the current directory by using the period, or rather the dot, for the current directory. Rights added were Read, Write, Create, Erase, and File Scan. The user was LAPTOP. Don't forget and think that /NAME is where you put the name. Remember it's /NAME=, and you fill in the name after the equal sign.

Another fun project is figuring out where a user or group has rights in the NDS tree. Neither NETADMIN or NetWare Administrator show the inherited rights chain. If you stay in those programs, you must keep checking rights in each parent directory.

The command line comes through once again. Check the sequence shown in Figure 11.10.

FIGURE 11.10

Adding rights with RIGHTS

```
H:\RIGHTS SYS:\OFFICE\WPWIN /NAME=DOUG /I<F255>

Name=Doug
Path                                              Rights

ALTOS486\SYS:\<F255>

    Inherited Rights Filter:                      [        ]

    Inherits from above:                          [        ]

    ----------
    Effective Rights=                             [        ]

ALTOS486\SYS:\OFFICE<F255>

    Inherited Rights Filter:                      [SRWCEMFA]

    Inherits from above:                          [        ]

    Effective Rights =                            [ R    F ]

ALTOS486\SYS:\OFFICE\WPWIN

    Inherited Rights filter:                      [SRWCEMFA]

    Inherits from above:                          [ R    F ]

    Effective Rights =                            [ R    F ]
```

The command is straightforward. We want to know what rights DOUG has in the \OFFICE\WPWIN directory and where they come from. The results are in three blocks: root, \OFFICE, and \OFFICE\WPWIN.

In root, user DOUG has no rights. That's to be expected. In \OFFICE, there are still no rights for DOUG, but the IRF is shown. Nothing is blocked, but since he had no rights in the parent directory, he has nothing to inherit. However, we have granted DOUG Read and File Scan rights to use the \OFFICE directory, so he can use the PerfectOffice programs. These show up as effective rights.

In \OFFICE\WPIN, his rights are the same. The IRF allows all rights to come from above, so he still has Read and File Scan rights. He has not been granted any special rights to this subdirectory, so he has the same rights here as in the parent directory.

This is an easy example, because we granted everyone the rights to the PerfectOffice applications. Many subdirectory rights structures aren't so easy to track, and rights seem to appear by magic. In those cases, the RIGHTS command will clear up the mystery.

Using RIGHTS from a security point of view is covered in Chapter 9. In Chapter 12, you'll find RIGHTS from the user's point of view.

Application Administration Tricks

> *Don't think of tricks as in cheating, but tricks as in a clever way to circumvent small irritations.*

PERHAPS *TRICK* HAS the wrong connotation for this section. We aren't pulling rabbits out of hats, but we would like to make life as easy as possible for the network clients. Don't think of tricks as in cheating, but tricks as in a clever way to circumvent small irritations.

One customer of mine has a subdirectory named COMMON, where everyone on the network has full rights. This makes for a low-tech bulletin board, where anyone can put a file for one or more other employees to use. There is no guarantee that the file won't be out-of-date, so it's not the most reliable means of collaboration, but they make it work. Everyone understands the limitations of sharing in this manner and works with each other.

Another customer has become fond of search drives for company budget and word processing templates. The directories are set up like the PUBLIC directory, with the files set to ROS (Read Only/Shareable). All files used must be saved in a different directory, of course. But when the wording changes in some contract paragraph, the network administrator places the changed file in the shared CONTRACTS directory in place of the superseded file. Now that all users have been trained to always pull their boilerplate paragraphs from this directory rather than an old contract, changes are available quickly and reliably for everyone.

Drive Mapping Techniques

There are a couple of nice tricks with the MAP command that you might find useful. If your users have local hard disk directories to be searched before the network drives should be searched, use a command like:

```
MAP INS S16:=GATEWAY2000_SYS:PUBLIC
```

This maps S16 rather than S1 for the first search drive, placing the MAP drives after all the existing search drives set by the PC's PATH statement. Using just MAP without the INS command puts this search-drive reference in the first position of the DOS environment space, overwriting what is there already. When you exit the network, the overwritten PATH commands will not be replaced. Using INSERT in the MAP command avoids this problem.

If you have placed all the Windows 3.1x files on the PC, putting network search drives before the Windows directory will create extra, and unnecessary, network traffic. Worse, it will slow response for the user. The exception is the PUBLIC directory; you may want to use MAP INS S1 to place all the NetWare utilities at the forefront of the PATH statement.

If you have several drives to map, use the S16 drive setting for each. The first one will be drive Z:, then drive X:, and so on. The next lowest search number is assigned with each subsequent mapping.

Mapping drives to volumes in other contexts is easy, once you remember the Alias objects for the volumes from different contexts. I always forget to set up an Alias the first time when mapping a volume from a server in another context. Of course, when I test the login script and see the error messages, I slap my forehead and say, "D'oh!" Then I explain to the customers looking over my shoulder how that was a lesson for them, so they would always remember to use the Alias object. (Most of them fall for it.)

The other option is to use Directory Map objects. These work like Alias objects, but they should be created only once and placed in a high container for everyone to reference easily. We'll get to that information in just a bit.

From the command line, erasing a drive mapping is simple. Type:

```
MAP DEL H:
```

and you're finished.

If you prefer to make a new mapping for drive H: without deleting the previous mapping, you'll get a question prompt. When you map a local drive letter (A: through E: are normally set aside for DOS) to a network drive, you'll also get a question prompt. Just a quick check to remind you that if you redirect drive C: to the network, you won't be able to see your own hard disk until you delete the mapping.

Mapping a Fake Root

The MAP ROOT command was developed as a response to problems with network-unaware applications in the early days. Many programs expected to be placed on the local hard disk, from the root of the hard disk. They refused to install to a subdirectory. A fake root drive was needed.

So Novell added the MAP ROOT option to help fool those applications. For example, to set drive F: to look like the root of my private home directory, I can type:

```
MAP ROOT F:=GATEWAY2000_PROJECTS:USERS\JAMES
```

Any old-fashioned applications will happily install there, thinking they are in fact at the root of the hard disk. You can abbreviate the ROOT to just R in the command if you wish.

Another advantage, especially for home directories like this, is that the volume subdirectory designated as the ROOT becomes the highest directory that drive letter can see. In the example, the DOS CD .. command to move to the parent directory would not work to move to the USERS directory. Some companies use MAP ROOT for this feature alone, even if all their applications understand network directory installation.

OS/2 handles all drive mappings as a fake root. Consequently, applications expect their executable files to be placed there, and the need for ROOTs continues.

Using Directory Maps

A Directory Map object is a leaf object that refers to a directory on a volume, somewhat like an Alias object. Any directory can be used as the object that is referenced by the Directory Map. These may be used in login scripts and from the command line.

A Directory Map is helpful when you have applications that you upgrade regularly, or other situations where you want a single point of reference to a directory that changes. When change inevitably comes, you only need to change the directory reference in the Directory Map object, not in every login script.

For example, one of my customers (like many other companies) uses the WordPerfect word processor (I myself have used WordPerfect since version 4.2). When WordPerfect 6.1 came out, superseding WordPerfect 6.0a, the administrator didn't want to automatically delete the 6.0a version at the site. So we installed version 6.1 on a new volume. Was this a disaster, changing all the various references to reflect the new location of WordPerfect? Not at all. Changing the Directory Map object, referring to the new WordPerfect version in its new location, allowed us to reference WordPerfect as always, but have it point to the new location.

See Figure 11.11 for a reminder of creating a Directory Map object. The browser window on the left shows the location of WordPerfect 6.1 from the PerfectOffice suite. The window on the right shows the location of the Directory Map to be created as the reference point.

FIGURE 11.11

Referencing WordPerfect

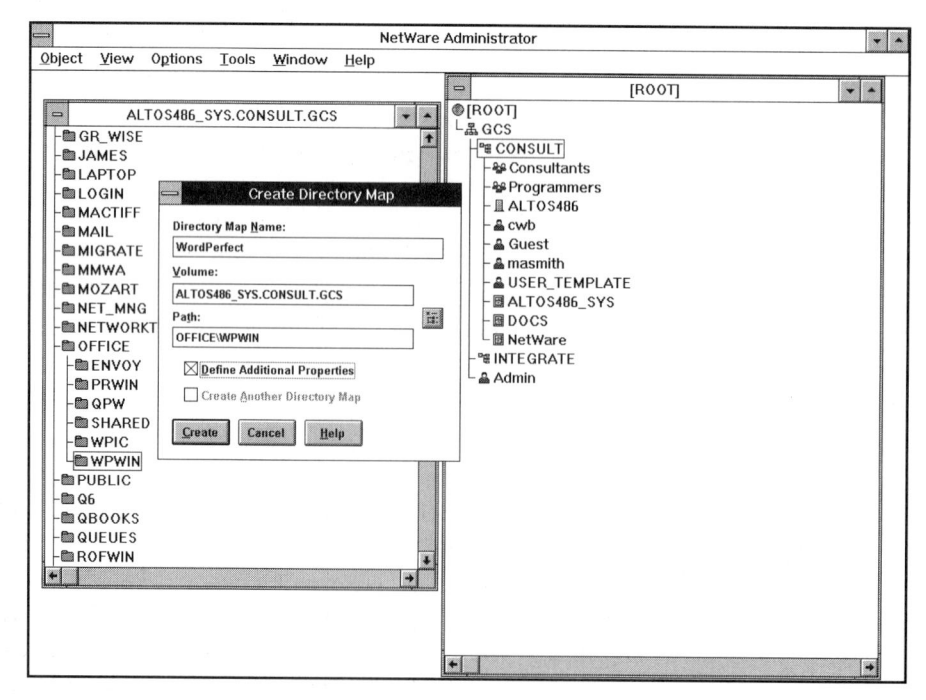

Some Application Guidelines

FORTUNATELY, THE UNDERSTANDING of networks among software developers is growing, and has been for several years. With more applications than ever available, custom-fitting each to a network would be impossible. But several trends have pushed software into being more network-friendly.

First, Windows 3.1x provides a means for thousands of the products released over the last few years to work on the network by accepting the foundation provided by Microsoft. You might argue there are better foundations for the software industry (like those used by our friends in the Unix community), but better a well-known foundation than nothing.

Second, Novell has been steadily providing software support for third-party vendors from the beginning. Over the years, application growth for NetWare networks has been tremendous. There are now more applications built to run over Novell's IPX/SPX protocol than any other, including TCP/IP.

The big news here is Novell's increasing support for Java and JavaWare. While the NetWare server supports Java while running the NetWare Web Server, code is being written to run Java applications directly on the server in conjunction with NLMs. In fact, the Java interpreter will likely be an NLM which will support Java applications. This feature wasn't close enough to finished to be included in NetWare 4.11, but look for it early in 1997.

The good part of all this is that applications will get more network-aware over the coming years. The bad part is that the new features of applications, including sound and video components, will require more robust networks and increased throughput. Looks like job security for NetWare administrators to me.

Microsoft Windows

Microsoft's Windows program has become the standard for Intel-powered desktop computers, just as NetWare has become the standard network to connect those computers. Windows of various flavors and NetWare must work together smoothly.

Unfortunately, the burden of making Windows behave on the network falls to Novell, since Microsoft is busy trying to sell its own networking products. The good part of this has been that it forced Novell to develop client software for Windows that is far better than the software Microsoft provides.

Windows 3.1x

Discussions abound whether to place the Windows application components on the server or leave them on the local hard disk. The good points of putting them on the server are that it saves disk space on local drives, it makes Windows upgrades easier, it's more secure from user accidents, and it's easier to share groups of applications. The negative points are that it increases network traffic, causes some application installation hassles, and forces you to delete Windows from newly purchased PCs.

Software cost doesn't enter into this argument. Microsoft provides no network license for Windows version 3.1. Every user must have a full copy of the program to be legal. Microsoft's Windows for Workgroups version 3.11 does have network licenses available, however.

The slim majority opinion favors running Windows 3.1x from the server. There is a caveat, however. The local configuration files are stored best on a local machine, and more important, the local hard disk is used for the swap file. Running the temporary memory workspace back to the server tremendously increases network traffic.

Just because the majority prefers to run Windows 3.1x from the server doesn't mean you should. It doesn't make sense to delete a working copy of Windows 3.1x from new computers. Laptop users can't argue this; they must run Windows locally. Personal applications can be configured for users of the network version, but it's always easier for the users to control their own desktop. It may not be easier for you as the administrator, but that's another story.

Use the SETUP /A option from the Windows 3.1x installation disks to load the program files to a shared directory on the server. You should label this shared directory something like WIN_NET, WINSHARE, WINPROG, or WINAPPS. If you use the SYS:\APPS structure, you would wind up with SYS:\APPS\WIN_NET for the program files. After copying the files, mark them all Read Only and Shareable using the FLAG command. This will keep the files from being deleted accidentally, and stop anyone from putting a configuration file in this directory by mistake.

Each NetWare client that needs to receive a copy of Windows 3.1x, or that will upgrade its local copy, should run SETUP from that WIN_NET directory. If the station will run Windows 3.1x from the local hard disk, just the straight setup is used. If the station will run the bulk of the Windows programs from the server, the SETUP /N (for network) command should be given.

With SETUP /N, individual configuration files are copied to the local station. This makes it easy to set up the \TEMP directory and the local disk file used as part of the virtual memory feature. Each user running Windows 3.1x from the server must have a search drive pointing to the shared MS Windows files, such as:

```
MAP INS S16:=SYS:\WIN_NET
```

If you already had NetWare 4.1x client files installed on the PC before Windows 3.1x was installed, you will need to reinstall those NetWare client files. The NetWare Windows support files aren't copied to the local machine if Windows isn't already present. The client file installation program takes care to check with you before overwriting network configuration files.

You can have Windows' 3.1x group files that can be shared by everyone on the network. After creating a group on your Windows station using Program Manager, copy the file with the GRP extension to the shared Windows directory. This lets everyone see that GRP file, but first you must edit the PROGMAN.INI file on each station. Under the [Group] heading, add the name and network location of the GRP file, as in:

```
[Groups]
Group11=\\ALTOS486_SYS:\WINFILES\SCHEDULE.GRP
```

This brings up an interesting point with Windows 3.1x: drive letters. Windows 3.1x warns you each time you set up a network application stored on the server. It's as if Windows 3.1x is trying to tell you that the network isn't reliable, so you should store everything locally. With many Windows 3.1x users sharing your network, the login scripts must be consistent so each program icon looking to drive N: will find the appropriate executable file. Windows 3.1x gets even weirder than usual when the drive mapping isn't consistent.

Another caution: your clients must log in to NetWare before starting Windows 3.1x. This is obviously the case for those using the shared network version, but also important for those running Windows 3.1x from a local hard disk. (But an exception is that you can use NWUSER to make your drive mappings and printer connections after Windows 3.1x is started.)

Figure 11.12 shows the NetWare version of the network Control Panel information. The NetWare client software replaces the rather weak Windows utility. Figure 11.12 shows all the options available to support the NetWare client within Windows 3.1x.

964 Chapter 11 • Providing Applications for Your Network Clients

FIGURE 11.12

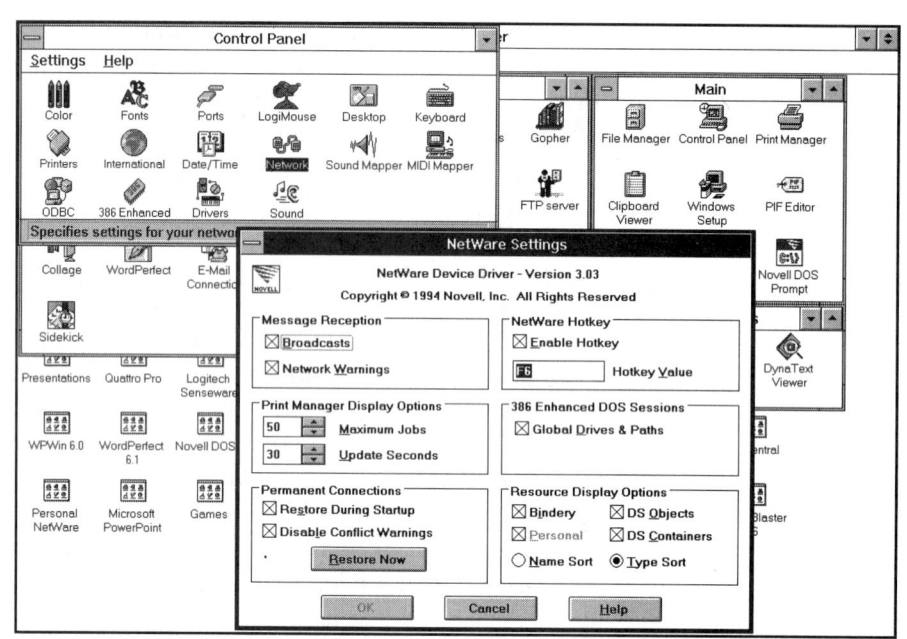

NetWare Settings utility for Windows 3.1x

If you wondered about Novell's sense of humor, click on the Novell logo in the upper-left corner. If you have a sound board, you'll hear a Max Headroom voice stuttering, N–N–NetWare.

The options on the screen work as follows:

- **Message Reception:** Turns on or off the receipt of broadcasts and network warnings on this workstation.

- **Print Manager Display Options:** Sets the number of jobs to display in the Print Manager screen, and how often to update that display.

- **Permanent Connections:** If you have permanent connections set in NWUSER, these boxes tell the system to restore those connections and whether to disable any drive or printer conflict warnings.

- **NetWare Hotkey:** Specifies the hotkey assigned to the NetWare User utility. If you assign F6, the default, then you just need to press F6 while in any Windows application, and the utility will start.

- **386 Enhanced DOS Sessions:** Decides whether drive connections will be consistent across all DOS and Windows applications.

- **Resource Display Options:** Checked boxes show those types of objects: Bindery, DS (Directory Services) Objects, and DS Containers. The Personal choice, for Personal NetWare, is gray, because I didn't have the PNW NetWare protocol loaded in my NET.CFG file.

This same display can be reached through the NetWare User Tools program in NetWare 4.10 (sorry folks, this neat utility isn't in NetWare 4.11). We'll do exactly that in the next chapter, where we let the users do some of the work.

Windows 95

All this goes out the window (literally) when we start discussing Windows 95. Microsoft has made it nearly impossible to run Windows 95 from a server; many system files demand to be local. To compound the hassle, Windows 95 is impossible to install across the network by downloading a set configuration to an empty disk. This was tricky but possible with Windows 3.1x.

You may hear of people devising complicated scripts to copy the Windows 95 files into the proper places in the proper ways without going through the official download and installation process, but none I've heard about save enough time to make up for the retrofits necessary on the machines that don't accept the downloaded files gracefully.

Why is downloading a Windows 95 installation impossible? We can't blame Microsoft entirely, because some of the problem comes from the Plug-and-Play technology users have been demanding. Your operating system must be tightly tied to your hardware if Plug and Play has a prayer, and Windows 95 took that to heart. Yes, there may be ways to support Plug and Play yet still support downloaded systems, but then we get to the problem of long file names. How do you copy directory names like "Program Files" to a DOS-only hard disk? This can't be done. Give up trying to mass-install Windows 95, because life is too short to waste banging your head against the Microsoft wall.

You can, however, use a NetWare CD-ROM drive as the source drive for a workstation Windows 95 installation or upgrade. Copying the files across the network will probably be faster than any but the speediest local CD-ROM drives. The only caution is to make sure that the CD-ROM drive is available for application upgrades and Windows modifications after the initial installation. Anytime you add something to a Windows 95 system, you probably will need the CD-ROM drive once again. See Appendix A for some suggestions for upgrading clients to Windows 95 and NetWare's Client32.

GroupWise E-mail and Group Scheduling

One of the quickest benefits of a network is e-mail. I remember installing NetWare/86 back in about 1986 for a small company with all their offices down one long hallway. That made it easy to run the Ethernet Thinnet cable down one side and back up the other. Amazingly, the simple e-mail system Novell included at the time with NetWare became a big hit. A company with the offices down one hallway cut their hall traffic in half, because of e-mail.

This has been the trend everywhere. E-mail and messaging are a couple of the primary goals for new Internet users. WordPerfect Library, as it was known in the early days, provided more than just messaging: there was scheduling, e-mail, and a notebook database.

Reincarnated as GroupWise version 4.1 with the release of NetWare 4.10, this is still the leading product in most magazine reviews, especially those that recognize the extra added attractions GroupWise includes beyond basic e-mail. GroupWise 5 came out with NetWare 4.11; Novell kept GroupWise when it sold the rest of the WordPerfect applications to Corel.

Like many programs, GroupWise is catching up to NDS. The installation routine is in DOS, and it doesn't read NDS. After the first two users are configured, however, the Bindery Services files provide the names and details about network clients.

As an example of NDS flexibility, I installed the GroupWise applications in ALTOS486_SYS:, and the GroupWise post office on GATEWAY2000_PROJECTS. This follows my preferred pattern of putting static files on SYS: volumes and growing files on non-SYS: volumes. Figure 11.13 shows the initial installation screen. I entered only the first network drive; the installation program did the rest.

The choice of where to put the post office modules comes up later. These directories hold all the mail and other information going between network clients. These directories can grow, and they probably will, as people start to notice how much quicker and easier it is to schedule a meeting electronically than it is to leave voice mail all over the building.

FIGURE 11.13

GroupWise setup in progress

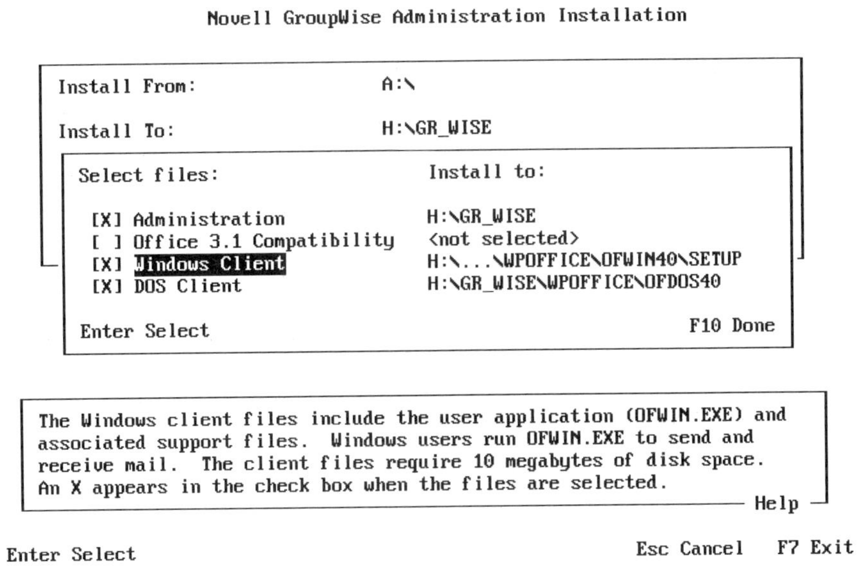

```
            Novell GroupWise Administration Installation
   ┌─────────────────────────────────────────────────────────────┐
   │ Install From:              A:\                              │
   │                                                             │
   │ Install To:                H:\GR_WISE                       │
   │   ┌─────────────────────────────────────────────────────┐   │
   │   │ Select files:              Install to:              │   │
   │   │                                                     │   │
   │   │   [X] Administration       H:\GR_WISE               │   │
   │   │   [ ] Office 3.1 Compatibility  <not selected>      │   │
   │   │   [X] Windows Client       H:\...\WPOFFICE\OFWIN40\SETUP │
   │   │   [X] DOS Client           H:\GR_WISE\WPOFFICE\OFDOS40   │
   │   │                                                     │   │
   │   │ Enter Select                              F10 Done  │   │
   │   └─────────────────────────────────────────────────────┘   │
   └─────────────────────────────────────────────────────────────┘

   ┌─────────────────────────────────────────────────────────────┐
   │ The Windows client files include the user application (OFWIN.EXE) and │
   │ associated support files.  Windows users run OFWIN.EXE to send and │
   │ receive mail.  The client files require 10 megabytes of disk space. │
   │ An X appears in the check box when the files are selected.  │
   │                                                       Help  │
   └─────────────────────────────────────────────────────────────┘

 Enter Select                                     Esc Cancel    F7 Exit
```

Unlike some vendor's software, GroupWise supports DOS and Windows clients. In fact, it supports several Unix and Macintosh clients as well; these products are the most cross-platform e-mail systems available.

The client setup allows you to download the programs to your local drive or to keep most of them on the network. For this application (and every Windows application except Windows 95), I prefer to keep the programs on the host servers. Figure 11.14 shows the client setup screen for the Windows software. The network disk space used is only for configuration files in the \WINDOWS subdirectory. The impact is nearly nothing, but you still risk being unable to run the program if the server is down.

You can have a single post office on one server that takes care of all your local network clients, or you may spread the post offices out a bit. GroupWise has several communications packages to connect networks together and exchange mail and scheduling information. Worldwide networks have been set up over dial-up phone lines. When you get that many people involved in that many places, things can get a bit sticky, but the horsepower is here for you to run a business worldwide.

Remote GroupWise clients have their own software, installed on traveling or remote office computers. The local post office coordinates your stationary and traveling messages and databases. It's a major pain to go on a trip, answer

FIGURE 11.14

Choose your GroupWise setup options

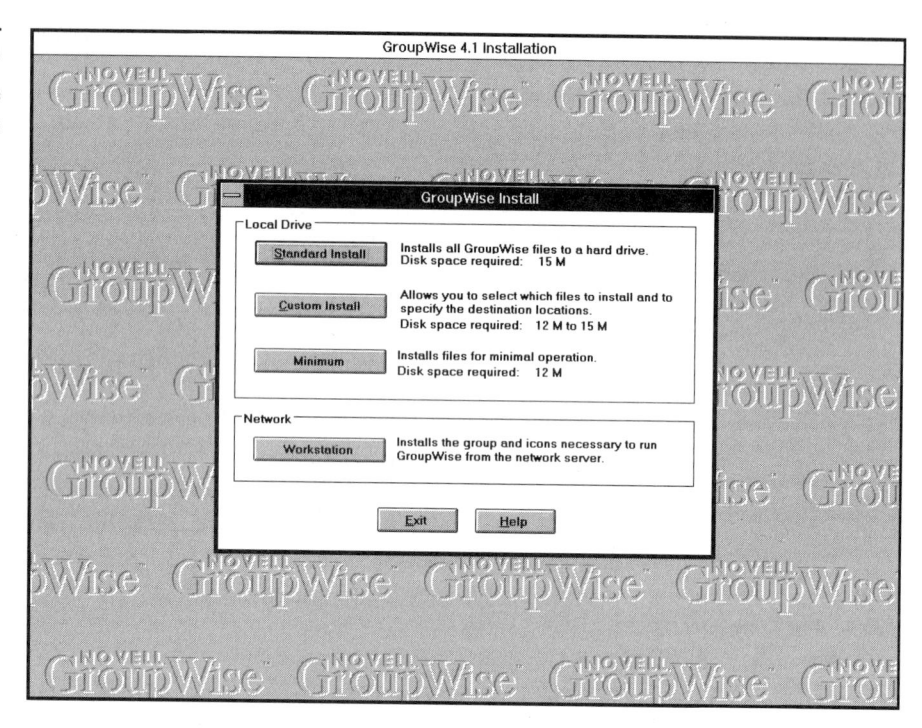

e-mail and set schedules, then return home to a desktop system a week behind. Transferring files here and there and trying to remember which file went with which message is time-consuming and frustrating. With GroupWise, however, you just log in at the office, and the database is synchronized for you. It's painless, quick, and efficient. Some might call it a miracle.

WordPerfect and PerfectOffice

The combination of WordPerfect, the world's most installed word processor (if you don't count EDLIN and EDIT for various DOS versions), Quattro Pro, InfoCentral, and Presentations make up the PerfectOffice suite. The Professional version includes the Paradox database and AppWare. If your system already has GroupWise installed, the PerfectOffice installation will see that and take advantage of it. In WordPerfect 6.1, the Send menu option is right below Print. When you click on Send you have two options, one of which starts GroupWise. This tight coupling is continued with GroupWise 5 and WordPerfect Suite 7.

Like other Novell products, the preferred method of installation is from a CD-ROM. For this system, I installed PerfectOffice to ALTOS486_SYS, again putting static (those that won't grow) application files on the SYS: volume. As does GroupWise, PerfectOffice has the option to install the program files to a server and copy just a few files to a workstation. Figure 11.15 shows the PerfectOffice workstation installation screen.

There is a bit more of a disk penalty with PerfectOffice than with GroupWise, because the InfoCentral application copies more than 3 MB of personal database information. There are ways to share the data you collect in your InfoCentral PIM (Personal Information Manager), but you start with some personal files.

There are several interesting networking features of PerfectOffice, besides the goodies we discussed at the start of the chapter. The spelling checker and thesaurus are common across all applications, as are the File Open screens. With proper Read Only and File Scan access to the application files and everyone using their own home directories, information can be shared safely without someone overwriting the only copy of the latest contract.

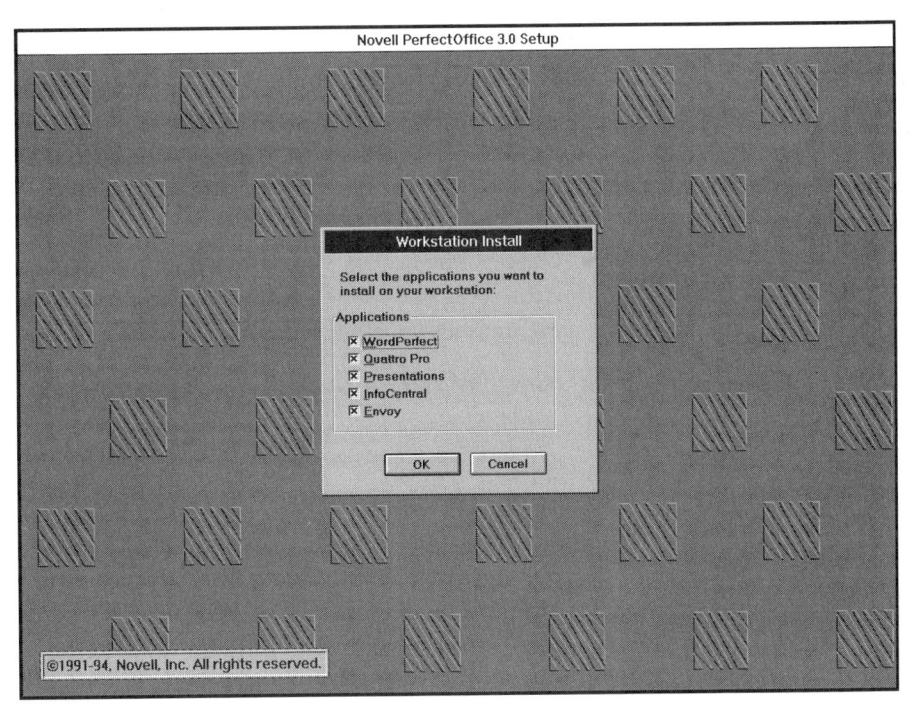

FIGURE 11.15

Pick your productivity tool

Most of the common files, such as the speller, thesaurus, and common DLL files, are in the \OFFICE\SHARED\WPC20 directory. Individual configuration files are stored on the network in the \OFFICE\SHARED\WPCNET directory.

When shared directories are used to store files, WordPerfect knows which files are open and being used. If you wish to open a document that is already open, you will receive a warning to that effect. You cannot save the file back with the same name, because that would overwrite any changes made by the person with the file open when you opened the file. Not bad—a word processor that handles file locking more intelligently than some databases.

General Application Hints

Don't let some manual rework your network plan without a fight.

There's no better advice than to read the manuals for multiuser applications that will be installed on your network. However, you must read the instructions with a level of skepticism and wariness. Many programs provide the bare rudiments of network installation details, and it's up to you to fill in the gaps of their network knowledge. Let's go over some quick rules and guidelines. Remember, it may be multiuser software, but it's your network. Don't let some manual rework your network plan without a fight.

Here are some general tips relating to applications on your network:

- Install all applications as the Admin user. It keeps the ownership straight, and there are some programs that look for the SUPERVISOR or Admin user, not an equivalent.

- Observe the license restrictions on all software. To do otherwise is stealing. If you fudge, bad karma will cause your server to crash the evening before your vacation.

- When possible, provide drive mappings for applications. Since most new applications run under Windows, organize your volumes so each volume is referenced by its own drive letter. This makes the group setups within Windows much easier.

- Smart network programs allow the use of UNC (Universal Naming Convention) path names. When PerfectOffice installs WordPerfect and Presentations as network workstation clients, those applications reference the server and volume, not a drive letter. This saves letters, and enables you to change server names by leaving an alias in NDS. Rather than a path of H:\OFFICE\WPWIN\WPWIN.EXE, the WordPerfect command line in the Windows 3.1x command line properties box shows \\ALTOS486\SYS\OFFICE\WPWIN\WPWIN.EXE.

- Feel free to use the MAP ROOT command to fool stupid programs that demand a root directory.

- Directory Map objects can help ease installation problems or hard-to-find subdirectories.

- Flag application directories Read Only and Shareable (if appropriate).

- Make groups for each set of users that needs an application. Feel free to have a WP group, a Presentations group, a 1-2-3 group, and all the rest.

- Assign Read and File Scan rights to these application groups for their respective applications.

- Be sensitive when things look unreasonable; dig deeper. WordPerfect won't let you set the initial font on a network printer, but it will let you set this on the same printer if you say it's a stand-alone printer. Does that make sense? Actually, yes. You don't want each user resetting the printers every which way. What looks stupid at first is really clever programming.

New with 4.11: NetWare Application Launcher

NEW WITH NETWARE 4.11 is the NetWare Application Launcher, or NAL, another TLA (Three Letter Acronym). Novell engineers have been fussing with NAL since the beginnings of NetWare 4.0, and it seems they've finally gotten the program going.

What is NAL? Simply put, it's a way for you to provide a network interface to all applications. Any application stored on a NetWare server can be referenced through NAL rather than directly by each user, and the application can be configured on each user's Windows front end. If you thought you were clever for figuring out a good way to store Windows 3.1x program groups on a server, you'll love NAL and the flexibility and control it gives you.

Configuring Application Objects

> **11.6 IN-A-HURRY**
>
> **Configure an Application Object to Use with NAL**
>
> 1. Log in as Admin or equivalent and open NetWare Administrator.
> 2. Highlight the container to hold the application object.
> 3. Press Insert, or click the right mouse button and click on Create.
> 4. Choose the appropriate Application object for the software.
> 5. Provide the application icon title.
> 6. Type in the path, or use the Browse button to set the path to the application file.
> 7. Set any necessary environment settings or other configurations.
> 8. Save the Application object.

First, you must create an "Application object" for you to control. This is nothing more than a shortcut to an application's main executable file on a server. The fun part comes when you realize you can control the program's initialization, drive letters, and printer ports. You can also add scripts to run before the application starts, add scripts to run after the application closes, and even add descriptions and contact names.

> **TIP**
>
> *If you want to really jab one of your co-workers, put his or her name as primary support for some application that person hates, such as listing a tech who hates graphics as the contact for Microsoft PowerPoint and Corel WordPerfect Presentations. Ha ha, what a fun time everyone will have, except that one poor soul getting all those calls!*

There's quite a bit of documentation concerning how to get NAL software loaded into your NetWare Administrator application. Since the online documentation contradicts the NetWare Administrator Help screens, I'm at a loss about which to follow. All the tools necessary were installed automatically within NetWare Administrator in my copies, although there's no entry in the Tools menu option. This looks like another instance where the programmers are ahead of the technical writers, so don't worry about it. Your system should automatically include the necessary tools. If not, trust the Help screens more than the online documentation.

The NAL.EXE and NAL95.EXE programs must be in \PUBLIC for your users to reach them. By the names, you can tell that different programs are used, depending on whether your client software is 16-bit or 32-bit. The documentation gives the "minimum" requirements for client usage, but if your clients are running Windows of some flavor, they're ready to go.

Pick a container to hold the Application object. This can be any container, either an Organization or Organizational Unit, dedicated to holding applications or full of all sorts of things. In Figure 11.16, notice that I put the object in my main GASKIN Organization container. You can put yours anywhere, but placing the applications in a different container may make management a bit easier. Any NDS client can have access to the application, once the support person acting as applications manager has been instructed to add that user to the approved list.

Highlight the container to hold the new Application object, and press Insert. If you prefer, you can click the right mouse button and choose Create

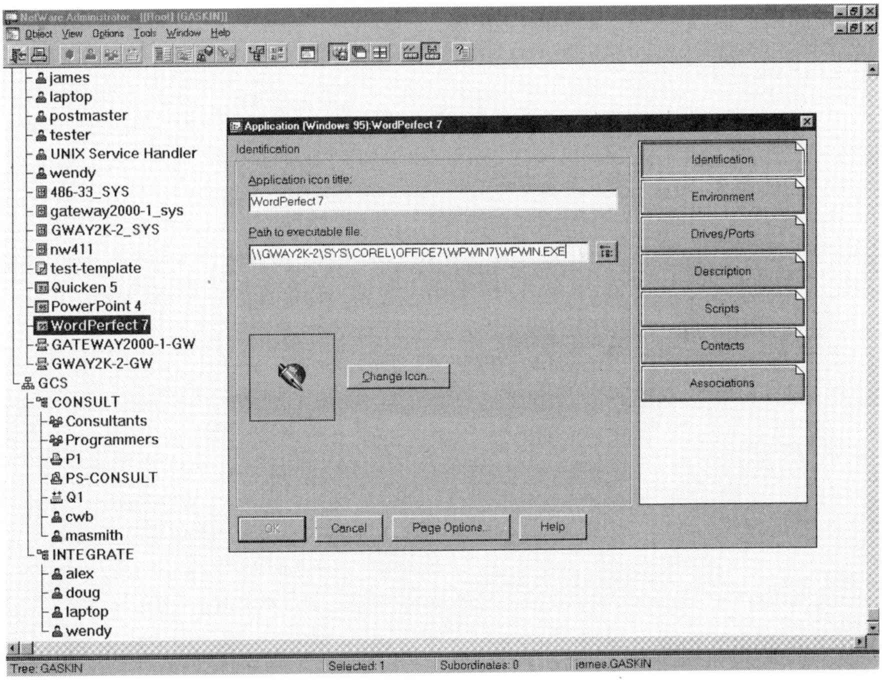

FIGURE 11.16

Naming, setting the path, and choosing the icon for WordPerfect 7 from the menu. Scroll down the New Object dialog box until you come to the proper Application object description. There are four options, covering DOS, Windows 3.1x, Windows 95, and Windows NT. (OS/2 applications are under consideration, but the declining market share for the IBM operating system makes it simple to stop with the current four options.) Double-click on the application type you prefer, and the Create Object dialog box will appear.

You are asked for a name and the path to the executable file. A Browser button is included, making it simple to search around and find the application you want if you don't remember the path. Two checkboxes offer you a choice to define additional properties or create another application. This dialog box should be familiar to you, and the smart choice is to define more properties.

Now we get to Figure 11.16, after mentioning it three paragraphs back. I have created the WordPerfect 7 application, saved it, and am now modifying the application properties. This path was chosen so you could see the application name highlighted on the left tree listing, along with the Application object dialog box on the right.

> **NOTE**
>
> *New in the NetWare 4.11 version of NetWare Administrator is the ability to decide which command buttons will be displayed down the right side of the dialog boxes. Since the Application object dialog box doesn't have enough pages to fill the slots, there's no reason to change the defaults.*

Above the WordPerfect 7 object already created, you can see the Quicken 5 and PowerPoint 4 Application objects. The physical locations of the executable files mean little to NAL, as you'll see.

In Figure 11.16, notice the other command buttons running down the right side of the WordPerfect 7 window. Identification is the page showing in the figure. Let's go over what the other pages contain.

Environment

The Environment page allows certain program parameters, but nothing directed toward changing the network environment. Yes, the title may be a bit misleading here. This page holds a list of any command-line parameters for the application, and it sets the working directory. Checkboxes for Run Minimized and Clean Up Network Resources are also on this page. The default is no to the first, and yes to the second.

Drives/Ports

Here's where you may get into some fancy management. If the application being configured needs extra drive letters mapped, or printer connections set, this is the page you want to visit.

In Figure 11.17, you can see I've mapped the next drive (which will change for different users, of course) to the directory above the primary executable file. Since Corel's WordPerfect Suite 7 uses quite a few shared utilities between applications, this mapping may come in handy.

If I needed two or three drive letters mapped, as may be necessary with a few strange applications, NAL configuration allows me to map to those drives. And the good part comes when you realize that using these mappings means your individual and container login scripts don't need to mention these drives. Only the NAL configuration needs to be changed if you move a few applications to different volumes.

The second part of the screen is devoted to supporting odd printer configurations. You can see from the first pick box under Port that I have made a

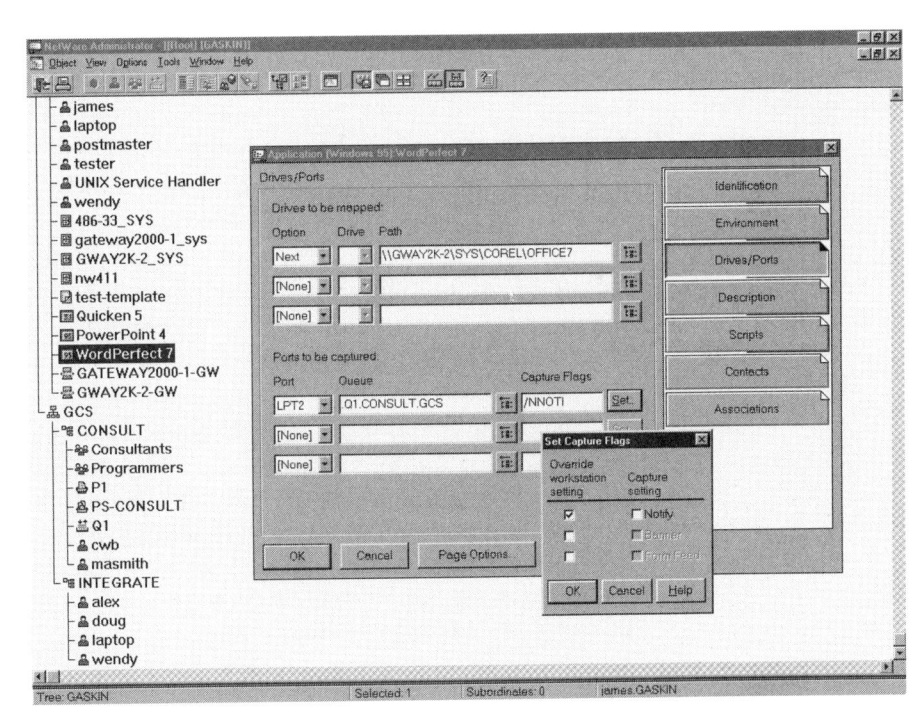

FIGURE 11.17

Drives, ports, and printer configuration changes

connection for LPT2. Why would you set up this connection? Perhaps you want LPT1 to be captured to the regular laser printer for text output, but a few people need access to a color printer. Mapping extra printer connections for everyone wouldn't be efficient, but making this one change in the NAL configuration provides the same functions in a fraction of the time.

Notice that in Figure 11.17, I have told this application to override the normal print queue configuration and to provide notification to the print user. Since this printer isn't the users' normal printer, they may feel better when getting a reminder to pick up their printing at a different place than usual. This is just another considerate touch that makes you the friend of all users, right?

> *This is just another considerate touch that makes you the friend of all users, right?*

Description

For users unfamiliar with the application presented by NAL, this page tells them whatever you decide to add about the application. Far be it for me to suggest that your users may be asked to use applications for which they have no training, but that happens sometimes. More likely, you are providing the users some extra information, such as the location of extra reference material. Or, perhaps you could list the name of the VP who cut the training budget to the bone.

Scripts

This is an interesting option. Scripts written here can execute before and after the application. Drive mappings and printer port configurations can be changed with these scripts. The page is dull, with two blank text boxes filling the left side of the dialog box. The top box is labeled Run before Launching, and the bottom box is Run after Termination.

It would be nice if the documentation included some details about these scripts, but alas, it does not. The best place to check for more information is the Help menu choice from the main NetWare Administrator screen. At the bottom is an option for Frequently Asked Questions and Answers, which is your best bet for finding information. Perhaps this Help screen is produced after all the others, which is why this one includes more details.

Scripts follow the idea of login script commands, so refer back to the login script details earlier in this book, or break down and check the online documentation. Until then, follow this syntax for mapping a drive:

```
\\server\volume\path
```

Follow this syntax for capturing a printer port:

```
\\server\queue_name
```

Unless you have no choice, use the Drives/Ports option instead of Scripts. Scripts, especially those that require experimentation, make me nervous. More important, they tend to take longer.

Contacts

Here's your place to have fun. Assuming your users actually read these screens when you provide them, the next command button offers a space to put contact names. Using the Add command button pops open the Select Object dialog box, allowing you to cruise your directory in search of just the right patsy, er, contact. Highlight the user best suited for this honor, and click on OK to forever link this tech support person with this application. Users can see these names, but not modify or delete them.

Associations

No, this isn't the place to put "Elks" and "Shriners" for your users to see. This is actually the second most important command button of all in this dialog box.

Figure 11.18 shows the method of adding user associations to the application configuration, so that those users may activate the applications using NAL. As an example of the cross-context nature of NAL, notice I'm adding MASMITH to the list of approved users, along with everyone in the GASKIN container.

If they had have asked me, I would have said that "Authorized Users" was a better command button label than "Associations," but they didn't ask me. Think of this button as associating some users with some applications, and the label will make a bit more sense. Not enough sense, but at least it will help you remember.

Until you add users, groups, or containers to the Associations page, no users may access your applications through NAL. Each application must be configured separately, even though users without authority may see the application in the NAL group, taunting them. Depending on the version of software the client is running, and any improvements Novell makes during the shipping process, users may not see an application unless they have the rights to run that application. That's the plan, anyway.

FIGURE 11.18

Approved list for the NAL applications

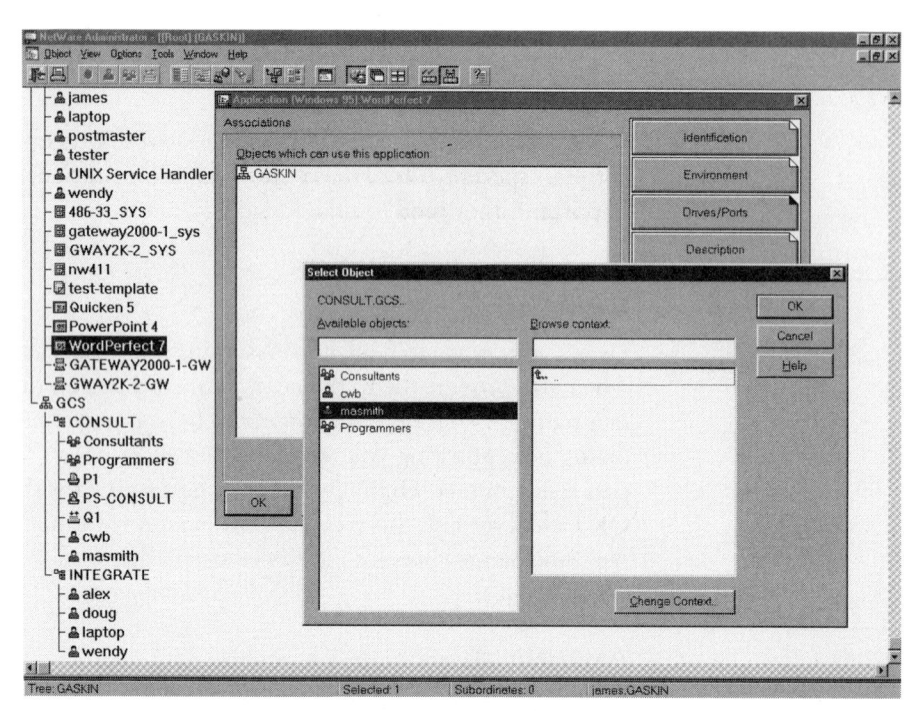

The Client Side of NAL

What does all this work look like to the client? Surprisingly clean and friendly. Once the user runs the appropriate NAL program (there are different versions for Windows 3.1*x* and Windows 95), a small box strongly representative of a Windows 3.1*x* program group pops open. The users merely double-click on the application they wish to run, and it does. If you have something amiss in your application configuration, the users won't get an error message, but the program won't run either. There's no message for the users if they try to run an application they are not authorized to run.

Figure 11.19 shows the dialog box open, with three applications: Eudora Pro, Quicken 5, and WordPerfect 7. Each of these applications are available to me, but only once I run the appropriate NAL program from the server.

What about all those details we just went through filling out? The users may see these when they check the properties of each Application object. As you can see in Figure 11.19, all the information we set is echoed to users when they request

FIGURE 11.19

Your choices for one-click application launching

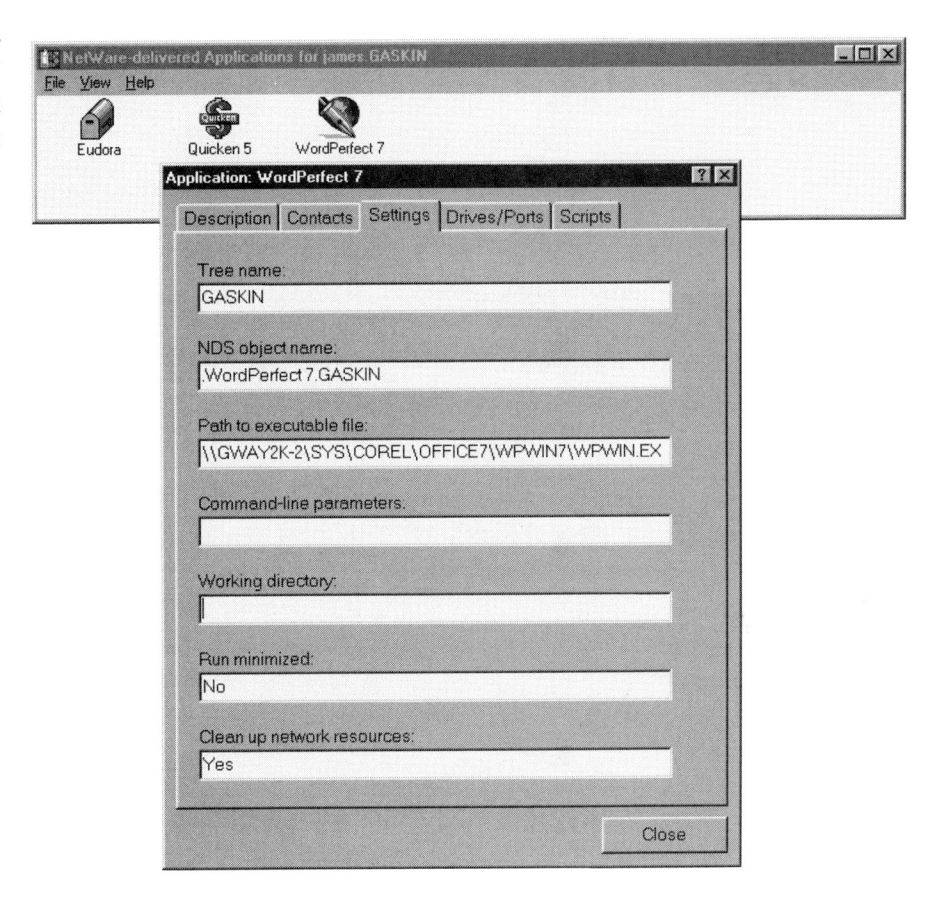

more details by clicking on the appropriate tab. This screen is read-only, so users can't get excited and add themselves to any application lists.

NAL will make a difference in your network, if you let the program help you rather than fight you. Of course, third-party products such as Dashboard 95 from Quarterdeck and Norton Commander from Symantec have made a few dollars by reorganizing the Windows interface into something different. Not all systems have improved the interface enough to throw out Windows, but this way you don't need to spend any money to find out if you like the idea or not. Since all the parts for NAL come included with IntranetWare, you may save your company some time and money without using your own limited budget.

Application Aggravation

'M SENSITIVE TO the wails from software developers about how hard it is to keep track of all the different network types and write their software to fit. I really am. But I also have some marketing advice for these developers: grow up, get clever, and grab market share.

NetWare customers want applications to run better with NetWare than they do on a stand-alone computer. Guess what, the good programs do. As a network administrator, you can tell companies that do a good job with networked applications that you appreciate their hard work. You can also tell those companies that don't do a good job you aren't interested in buying poorly written software.

How about this slogan: If you don't network, I don't buy. Think that will get their attention?

CASE STUDY

MiniCo: Providing Applications for Your Network Clients

MINICO HAS 3 servers, 75 users, and one location.

Application Categories

CONSIDERATIONS

The goals:

- Define existing applications as network-hostile, network-neutral, or network-aware.
- Replace network-hostile applications.
- Rewrite internal applications to better utilize the network.

DECISION

Use the network as an extension of each user's hard disk.

EXPLANATION

Only the accounting application was network-aware before the network was expanded to support the entire company. Alexander von Thorn (the Distribution Manager who is also the lead network administrator) made Group-Wise available to everyone for the scheduling and project management tools, along with his NetWare 4.11 upgrade.

Trends in Distribution, Metering, and Licensing

CONSIDERATIONS

The possibilities:

- Track all applications for concurrent usage.
- Distribute applications and/or upgrades through an automated network procedure.
- Audit compliance with software licensing requirements.

DECISION

Walk around and check the applications in use.

EXPLANATION

Many companies new to networking take a casual attitude toward software use on the network. This works, because users usually have their own software on their own hard disk, so the applications are legal. However, it's usually not efficient and results in more software cost and more management headaches, which can be avoided by tracking software usage.

Application Server Guidelines

CONSIDERATIONS

The goals:

- Separate applications and data.
- Customize servers to handle either read or write activity.

MINICO CASE STUDY, CONTINUED

DECISION

Keep the data on one volume, and the applications on another.

EXPLANATION

Initially, Alexander had lumped many applications and data files in the same directories, which made it impossible for him to set file attributes at the directory level. Everyone had full access. Now the few applications on the MiniCo network are loaded on the SYS: volumes of each server. The data files, including users' home directories and print queue spool files, are held on the other volumes of the SUPPORT_1 and SALES_1 servers, and sometimes on the user's personal hard disk. The server ACCT has a single 500 MB volume, dedicated to the accounting software. All of the NetWare 4.1x defaults were accepted on the servers.

Access Rights for Application Directories

CONSIDERATIONS

The choices:

- Set as limited rights as possible to application directories.
- Don't bother changing any rights.

DECISION

Allow all users Read Only and File Scan rights.

EXPLANATION

Once Alexander discovered that everyone in each container had free reign over the server volumes in those containers, he studied the RIGHTS command a bit more. Now users have Read Only and File Scan rights, which are all that are necessary on application directories. In the data directories, users have Create, Erase, and Write rights.

Protecting Application Programs and Data Files

CONSIDERATIONS

- Set minimal file attributes.
- Don't bother setting any file attributes.

DECISION

Use file attributes to keep application files safe.

EXPLANATION

After realizing the problem with all users having too much power, Alexander was careful to go back and make all executable files on the network Read Only. This gives extra protection against user accidents.

Application Administration Tricks

CONSIDERATIONS

The possibilities:

- Investigate and use fake root drive mappings.
- Use Directory Map objects.

DECISION

Just set up the applications so that people can use them; worry about "tricks" later.

MINICO CASE STUDY, CONTINUED

EXPLANATION

MiniCo's network, thrown up rather quickly because of the time crunch, has no "tricks" involved. Since few network applications are available, Alexander set up only a single Directory Map object for the existing copies of WordPerfect 6.1 for Windows in use. Now he knows that the Directory Map object for the upgraded version of WordPerfect Suite 7 will be easy to set up.

Some Application Guidelines

CONSIDERATIONS

The goals:

- Examine the network load to support Windows over the network.
- Design the most efficient application support through search drive mapping.

DECISION

Leave Windows on everyone's home system.

EXPLANATION

When MiniCo purchases some new network applications, they will be shared properly over the network. The first goal, however, was just to share disk space and printers. That goal was met easily. Alexander is looking ahead, but hasn't gotten approval for more applications at this time.

New with 4.11: NetWare Application Launcher

CONSIDERATIONS

- Use NAL for applications.
- Configure each person's desktop for appropriate applications.

DECISION

Configure each desktop system.

EXPLANATION

Many of the users already had their Windows 3.1x systems configured for their primary applications. The RoadTrip users already had their applications loaded on each individual hard disk. There was no need to reinvent the application wheel, so Alexander just left it all alone.

CASE STUDY

MegaCorp: Providing Applications for Your Network Clients

MEGACORP HAS 50 servers, 2500 users, and 5 locations.

Application Categories

CONSIDERATIONS

The goals:

- Define existing applications as network-hostile, network-neutral, or network-aware.
- Replace network-hostile applications.
- Rewrite internal applications to better use the network.

DECISION

Upgrade or rewrite all applications to take advantage of NetWare 4.11.

EXPLANATION

Realizing half the value of the network is better management, control, and efficiency, MegaCorp dedicated Central IS to making the software as network-friendly as possible. Programmers started reworking internal applications months before NetWare 4.11 was installed, and they tested their rewrites on the pilot network.

A strong push for company-wide software culminated in the choice of Corel WordPerfect Suite 7 for productivity and GroupWise for messaging of all kinds. Small pockets of other software were left in some locations, but Central IS will stop support of these applications by the end of the year.

Trends in Distribution, Metering, and Licensing

CONSIDERATIONS

The possibilities:

- Track all applications for concurrent usage.
- Distribute applications and/or upgrades through an automated network procedure.
- Audit compliance with software licensing requirements.

DECISION

Place SofTrack from ON Technology on every NetWare 4.11 server that provides applications to users.

EXPLANATION

Large companies can't afford to buy "extra" software to stay within licensing requirements, and they can't afford to use illegal software. This tightrope requires them to manage and monitor software usage across the network.

MEGACORP CASE STUDY, CONTINUED

MegaCorp chose SofTrack, one of the earliest NetWare application tracking utilities, now sold by ON Technology. Written by John McCann, SofTrack allows companies to share licenses between servers, pool suite applications under the same license count, specify priority levels of user access to software, monitor usage by department, and report when usage reaches configurable thresholds. This software supports DOS, Windows 3.1*x* and 95, OS/2, and Macintosh users.

Application Server Guidelines

CONSIDERATIONS

The goals:

- Separate applications and data.
- Customize servers to handle either read or write activity.

DECISION

Separate (but with redundancy) applications and data volumes. A few servers have been tuned.

EXPLANATION

MegaCorp likes to save money, but considers it more important to ensure network reliability and application availability. Applications are stored on different servers than the data, and some servers are tuned to their respective reading or writing tasks. Not every department and application suite can be organized this way, but statistics are kept to track the performance of tuned and default servers to see if the extra tuning is worthwhile. So far, the results show some improvement.

Access Rights for Application Directories

CONSIDERATIONS

The choices:

- Set as limited rights as possible to application directories.
- Don't bother changing any rights.

DECISION

Allow all users Read Only and File Scan rights.

EXPLANATION

As planned during installation, each user has Read Only and File Scan rights to the application directories. Every application in use functions with these restrictions, and the management overhead to correct "accidents" is almost nil.

Protecting Application Programs and Data Files

CONSIDERATIONS

The choices:

- Set minimal file attributes.
- Check file ownership to keep users under preset storage limits.

DECISION

Set the minimum possible file attributes to protect the files.

EXPLANATION

Part of the installation routine for every application is to change the file attributes to Read

> **MEGACORP CASE STUDY, CONTINUED**
>
> Only. Management felt that the Read Only attribute and user controls made a higher level of protection unnecessary.
>
> Each user must follow storage guidelines, and location IS personnel check the server volumes periodically. When necessary, file ownership is changed so users won't have their storage budget eaten up by software they are not totally responsible for using.
>
> ### Application Administration Tricks
>
> **CONSIDERATIONS**
>
> The possibilities:
>
> - Investigate and use fake root drive mappings.
> - Use Directory Map objects.
>
> **DECISION**
>
> Use every possible technique to make the users more comfortable on the network.
>
> **EXPLANATION**
>
> Directory Maps, fake root mappings, and creative search drive mappings were planned into the network. Every "trick" that makes life easier for the users was used. Central IS doesn't care if a user knows the name of a server, just as long as that user knows \\APPS\WPWIN will find the WordPerfect 6.1 for Windows application.
>
> ### Some Application Guidelines
>
> **CONSIDERATIONS**
>
> **THE GOALS:**
>
> - Examine the network load to support Windows 3.1x over the network.
> - Store Windows 95 and Windows NT client software on each local system.
> - Design the most efficient application support through search drive mapping.
>
> **DECISION**
>
> Load Windows 3.1x across the network, and put the swap space on the local drive. Windows 95 configurations demand to be on the local hard drive, and they were left on the local systems.
>
> **EXPLANATION**
>
> Because of the uncertainty of the timing for their upgrade from Windows 3.1x to Windows 95 for many of their clients, MegaCorp technicians didn't want to revisit their 2500 workstations and rework Windows 3.1x. The network setup option was used, with the swap file and the particular INI files placed on the local workstation.
>
> Search drive mappings are changed when necessary to better support the users. Rearranging a search drive listing can save megabytes of disk queries across the network.

MEGACORP CASE STUDY, CONTINUED

Windows 95 upgrades were handled across the network, but required a technician at each workstation. Microsoft makes it nearly impossible to support Windows 95 clients from a shared network directory, so MegaCorp didn't waste much time trying to force the issue. New desktop systems purchased since the introduction of Windows 95 had that operating system preloaded by the vendor.

New with 4.11: NetWare Application Launcher

CONSIDERATIONS

- Use NAL for applications.
- Configure each person's desktop for appropriate applications.

DECISION

Use NAL whenever possible, including for all new applications.

EXPLANATION

Centralized control is vital when 2500 individuals are involved. The default use of NAL for all new applications gradually converted all applications used on a regular basis. How? Whenever there was an upgrade, the new versions somehow wound up in NAL rather than on individual desktop systems. This was done so smoothly that the users never realized what was happening; they just knew upgrades happened more easily and more regularly.

Teaching Your Clients to Use the Network

CHAPTER 12

FIRST, A REMINDER: your clients don't like the network as much as you do. They don't like computers as much, either. Hardware and software either bore or terrify them. Don't take it personally.

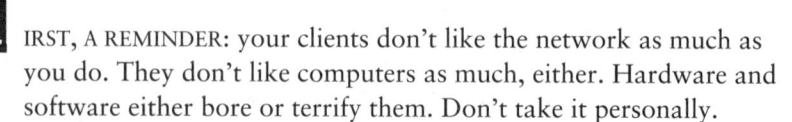

You may teach, but you can't make them all learn. Some will learn and do well. Those are your future power users. Others will learn enough to do their job, and even figure out a few things on their own. This group will be the bulk of your user community. A few will regard computerization as a modern version of the biblical plague of locusts, and will never learn enough to go beyond basic skills. If your company didn't require employees to use computers before you added the network, expect one or two people to quit their jobs rather than learn how to do something new. As grim as it may sound, this is normal.

To prepare for this, you and your management must plan how to handle the user community. Change is stressful, and changing to NetWare 4.1x—even though this network runs better and is easier to use than what you had before—might stress some people.

Preparing the User Community

YOUR MANAGEMENT HAS some questions to answer. First of all, what are the top three client issues?

These issues will be a major part of the reason for the new network or the network upgrade. What of value to the users will this new system provide? See if you can get the answers in order of importance. Let's start with the most important reason for the system.

Is providing the users an easy graphical interface the most important reason? How about increasing disk space? Maybe combining several departments onto one server?

The top user priority for the new system will guide you in presenting the network to your users. If a graphical interface is important, because all your workstations now support Windows 95, don't spend time showing people the command-line tools or NETUSER. If disk space is the hook, tell users about the home directories and room for more archived files and online information. If several departments are moving to the same server, or just the same container, show how much easier finding and using network resources are with NetWare 4.1*x*.

The worst case is learning your boss had no user benefit in mind when the new network was approved. Be prepared for the users to gripe and complain as you change their system for no tangible benefit. Better yet, quickly figure a benefit, and show the users how their situation has improved. This isn't cynical, it's making the best of a bad situation.

Now that your boss has weaseled out of the first question, here's another: What's the proposed ratio of user training compared to support staff responsibilities? The more training the users have, the fewer support headaches for you and your compadres. Less user training, more headaches. No training, order aspirin by the pound.

Remind your boss that there are several kinds of training to be discussed. Network training is obvious, since you're installing a new system. How much network training? Here are some of your options:

- Send everyone on the new system out for training.
- Have a trainer come in and teach everyone.
- Send a few users out for training.
- Have a trainer come and teach a few users.
- Train one person from each department yourself.
- Throw everyone to the network wolves.

Unfortunately, the last choice is often the first choice. I wish I could tell you this has never happened, but users are thrown into new systems all the time. If this happens at your place, you have my condolences.

Remember, we haven't talked about application training yet. Nor have we mentioned desktop operating system training. You can't expect the users to understand the NDIR command if they don't know how to use the DOS DIR command. The more computer training of any kind your network clients have, the better off they (and you) are.

Imagine a pie chart. The complete pie is your goal. The more training for the users, the less staff time filling the rest of the chart. More training, less support staff needed. More training, higher office productivity, and a bonus for your boss. Maybe you should explain things that way.

> **The Client's View of Your Network**
>
> There's a famous old map from the middle ages, charting what little knowledge people had of the world. The coastline of Europe was not too bad, but after about 100 miles of ocean, no one knew anything. With a dramatic flair, the mapmaker wrote this at the edge: "Beyond here, there be monsters."
>
> Most of your users don't have a good idea what the network is, where it is, or how it works. That's why, when you point out the file server sitting under a table, they're disappointed. Something that causes as much trouble as a network should be big and complicated-looking. Perhaps downsizing companies should buy mainframe facades, with little motors keeping the big tape reels jerking along. That would impress people.
>
> Your network clients see only their computer and their printer when they look at the network. The rest of the network is something strange, and as far as some users are concerned, filled with monsters.

Clients and the NDS Tree

The idea of inheritance never occurred to your users, unless a rich relative was ill.

Object-oriented views of the world have been rare. NetWare 4.1*x* is probably the first object-oriented program that will get wide distribution.

I know network management stations have used objects for years, as have a few programmers. The trade magazines are full of object-oriented, client/server, user-friendly, fault-tolerant, Information Superhighway stories, but the typical NetWare client doesn't read those stories. The idea of inheritance never occurred to your users, unless a rich relative was ill.

This will require you to present the new network landscape to your users in ways that directly help their daily activities. You should talk about the NDS tree, and how it works, but the moment you see symptoms of the MEGO (My Eyes Glaze Over) disease, you should stop. Go straight to hands-on help with the tools they need to do their work. After a bit, you will see that the users are able to stand more explanation before their eyes roll up in their heads, and you will gradually teach them more than you ever thought possible. But don't rush it.

Go over the analogies and illustrations used earlier in this book for examples. Make up your own examples that apply to your business to supplement what's in this book and the manuals.

Use examples of physical items, like describing the NDS tree as a hallway, with Organizations as big rooms off the main hallway, and Organizational Units being smaller rooms off the larger rooms or smaller hallways. [Root] can be the building lobby, with all hallways running from there. Leaf objects such as users and printers and servers are things placed in various rooms. See Figure 12.1 for this example.

FIGURE 12.1

Making the virtual tangible

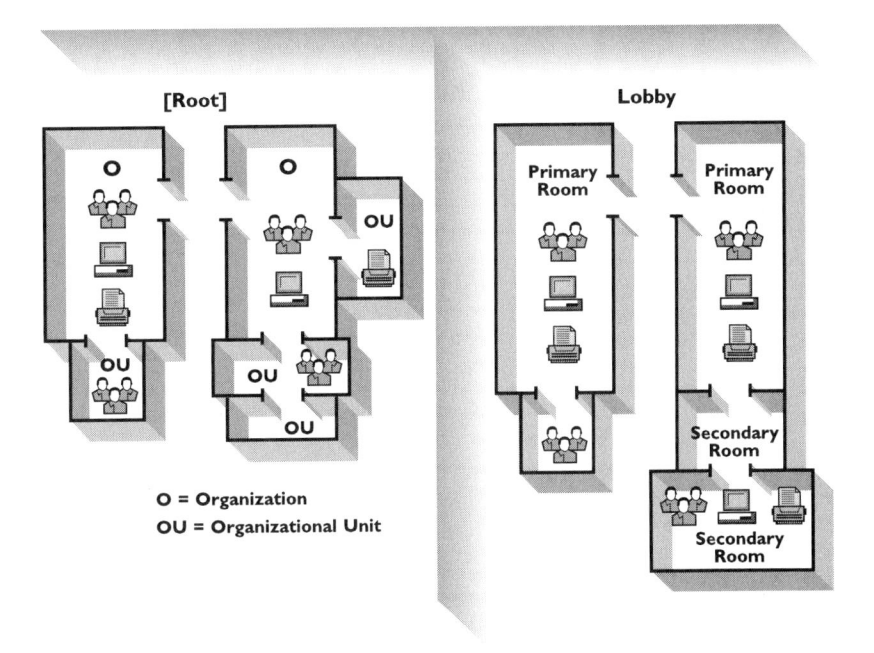

On the left, we have the NDS tree. The [Root] object is at the top of everything, with Organizations leading from it. There can be many Organizations, of course, but here we show two. The Organizational Units can be contained only within Organizations or other Organizational Units; they cannot be installed in the [Root].

On the right, we have a lobby representing [Root], supporting the primary rooms. Only the primary rooms open from the lobby. Secondary rooms branch off the primary rooms, and often a secondary room supports attached secondary rooms of its own. As with Organizational Units, a secondary room may actually hold more than a primary room. Think of the anteroom leading to a ballroom as an example of this.

Icons for people, groups, computers, and printers are scattered around both drawings. It's easy to imagine real people and other objects in a real room. The same arrangement, with people and their supporting equipment, have the same look when placed in Organizations and Organizational Units. After all, Organizations and Organizational Units are just containers, as are rooms.

Using CX to Change Your Context

As a person moves from one large room through the lobby to another large room and into a smaller room, so can a person's location in the NDS tree move around. What if the people in the real rooms knew some shortcuts? Is it possible to go directly from one secondary room to another secondary room, without passing through the primary room or lobby? With a secret tunnel, you can. Hotels do it all the time, with the service hallways hidden behind the ballrooms and meeting rooms.

The NDS tree allows this same jumping from one place to another. Although not as exciting as secret tunnels, the CX command provides the same quick movement from one place to another.

The CX command (used from the command line) by itself tells you the current context. When you use it with its parameters, CX allows you to change containers and to show the contents of your current container and all others in your tree. Syntax is important, because the CX command does more than the DOS CD command it's often compared to. Just as you use CD to move to a certain directory to start an application, you can use CX to move to the proper context to begin your login process.

Let's take a look at the parameters of CX:

CX *new context*	Moves to the named new context.
CX /VER	Provides the version of the program, and lists the subordinate programs necessary for execution.
CX /?	Displays the two-page Help screen.

A few rules are worth mentioning here. First of all, CX is similar to CD, but also to DIR, because you can see objects below you, as well as change contexts. If you have spaces in object names (legal but sometimes a problem), you must use underscores (_) in place of the spaces, or wrap the name in quotation marks.

There are a variety of options available with CX, which are listed in Table 12.1.

TABLE 12.1 CX Utility Options

OPTION	FUNCTION
CX [*new context*] /R	Moves to [Root] (like the CD \ command moves to the system root).
CX [*new context*] /T	Lists containers below the current or named context, including subordinate containers.
CX [*new context*] /CONT	Lists containers below the current or named context in a vertical list without subordinate containers.
CX [*new context*] /A	Includes all objects.
CX [*new context*] /C	Sets continuous scroll through output.

You will probably use this utility quite a bit at the beginning of your NDS explorations. You probably used the CD command all the time to figure out where you were on a NetWare server, or the pwd (Print Working Directory) command in Unix to figure out where you were in a Unix file system. This will be no different. Eventually, you'll know where you are, and you'll cut down your usage quite a bit. You may become so familiar with the graphical management and user tools that you won't use the command line much for any NetWare task.

Now for some examples. If you wished to see your context before you log in, you would type and see a result similar to:

```
C:\>CX
integrate.gcs
```

To move back to [Root], the command and result are:

```
CX /R
[Root]
```

In Directory tree-speak, the single dot (period) refers to the parent context. This is the opposite of the function of the dot in a DOS directory tree, which means the current directory. (See if you can learn that before I did, which was after about ten mistakes.) For example, the command to move up one context level from INTEGRATE.GCS and the result are:

```
CX .
gcs
```

Yes, you must put a space between the command and the period.

To move from [Root] to INTEGRATE.GCS, the command is:

```
CX INTEGRATE.GCS
```

If you are starting this movement from CONSULT.GCS, however, be sure to remember the beginning period before your intended destination. This tells the NDS tree you are referencing the context from the [Root], just as if you changed DOS directories by typing CD \NWCLIENT. The beginning backslash tells the system to move from the root. With NDS, that signal is the dot (period).

To show all the containers in the current context, type:

```
CX /CONT
```

To see everything from your context on down, including all leaf objects, type:

```
CX /T /A
```

If you want to see everything from [Root] on down, place /R as the first option in the above command.

Some users won't ever catch on to this, which is one reason I suppose MS Windows sells so well. The CX command is useful, but not mandatory, when exploring your NDS tree.

NetWare User Tools: One-Touch Convenience in NetWare 4.10

THE BEST FRIEND your Windows 3.1*x* users will have is the NetWare User Tools program, officially called NWUSER.EXE. This program exists in two different places. The NWUSER.EXE program is loaded to the \WINDOWS\SYSTEM directory when NetWare client files are installed. It's also built into the NETWARE.DRV file, placed in the same directory.

There are two versions, because the file is called in two different ways. Most often, it's called with a touch of the F6 key. However, that default may be disabled if an application requires the F6 key, and you can't (or don't want to) find another hotkey for the program. For instance, Microsoft's Visual Basic program demonstration calls the NetWare User Tools program and locks it like a miser's safety deposit box. If this is the case, you can add the program to any Windows 3.1*x* group and call it by the double-click method.

NetWare User Tools first appeared in Personal NetWare, the peer-to-peer networking product that replaced NetWare Lite. Since then, Novell has added a couple of polished edges, but the program has remained fundamentally the same.

This is a good thing, this remaining the same. Personal NetWare is aimed at small workgroups without any network experience and without an on-site administrator. The simplicity of NetWare User Tools belies its sophistication and ability to function in all NetWare environments. With NetWare User Tools, you can see and make use of every level of NetWare resources, from Personal NetWare desktop servers, to NetWare 3.*x* servers, to NetWare 4.10 enterprise networks.

Why Doesn't NetWare 4.11 Have NetWare User Tools?

You'll notice that I refer to "NetWare 4.10" in this section about the NetWare User Tools program. Why? Because Novell executives, in another decision that indicates the air in Provo is too thin to provide enough oxygen to the brain, have left NetWare User Tools out of NetWare 4.11.

(continued on next page)

> When I tried to run an earlier version of NWUSER.EXE, a message box told me to use the Windows 95 Network Neighborhood equivalent functions. With all due respect to Network Neighborhood, NetWare User Tools is better than what Microsoft provides. Besides that, the hotkey came in handy on a regular basis.
>
> There's a small chance that Novell executives will relent and upgrade NetWare User Tools to work with Windows 95. There's a small chance my favorite numbers will win Lotto Texas soon. I hope the first chance happens, if the second chance can't. Having NetWare User Tools back would be some small consolation for buying more losing Lotto tickets.
>
> Until the happy day that NetWare User Tools returns, I'll make do with Network Neighborhood. Those of you with NetWare 4.10 servers should read the details about NetWare User Tools. We'll talk about performing these functions using Network Neighborhood later in the chapter. I grouped them at the end to make all the functions for Windows 95 network clients easier to find. But I still feel cheated, and NetWare User Tools is still missed.

Logging in from NetWare User Tools

You can log in to NetWare from the NetWare User Tools program. While in the program, if you select any resource from a server you are not already logged in to (but after all the NetWare client software has been run), the Login to NetWare dialog box will appear. Figure 12.2 shows this login dialog box for a NetWare 3.12 server.

When you highlight a server and click on the Map command button, or drag the server from the Resources list into the Connections list, the Login to NetWare dialog box appears. This is a quick and straightforward login method.

You have a choice of connecting as a guest or as a registered user. Since I am already logged in to several other servers, the system guesses I wish to log in to this server as user JAMES. If this is so, I need only provide a password and click on OK or press Enter. The connection happens behind the scenes, and the server moves from the Resources list to the Connections one.

This is technically more of an attach than a login. You don't run a login script when you log in with NetWare User Tools. To make up for the lack of a login script, the program gives you the option to make permanent drive mappings and printer connections with NetWare User Tools. We'll discuss those options in a bit.

FIGURE 12.2

Log in graphically

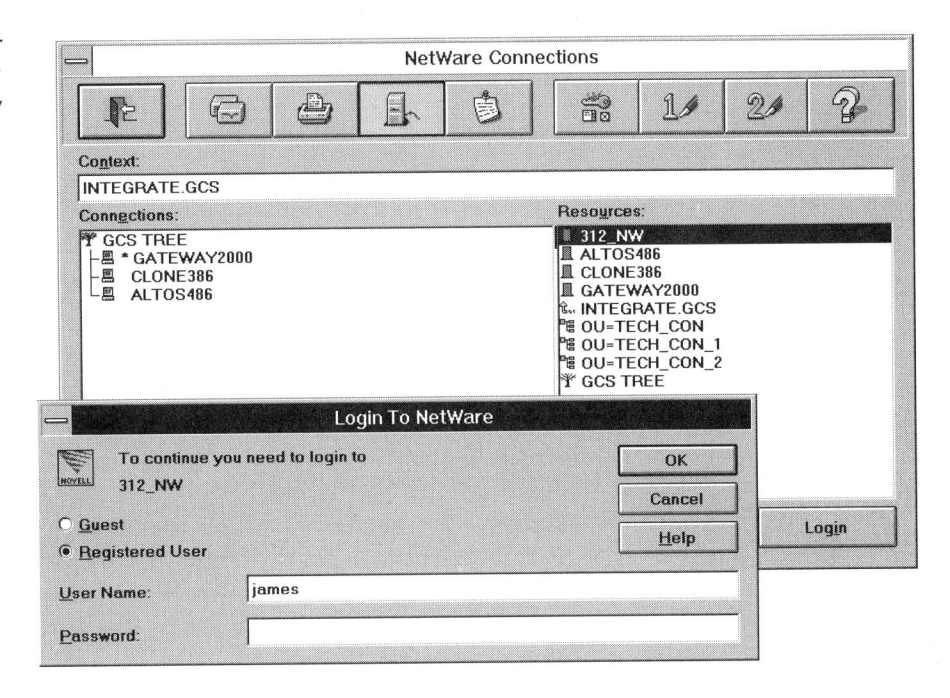

Using the Keyboard in NetWare User Tools

For the mouse-impaired, there is a complete set of alternative key combinations to run NetWare User Tools. Table 12.2 shows the keystrokes to activate each option in the NetWare User Tools program.

TABLE 12.2

NetWare User Tools Keyboard Commands

FUNCTION	KEY COMBINATION
Exit	Alt+X or Escape
NetWare Drive Connections	Alt+D
NetWare Printer Connections	Alt+P
NetWare Connections	Alt+C
NetWare Send Messages	Alt+M
NetWare Settings	Alt+S

TABLE 12.2 (cont.)
NetWare User Tools Keyboard Commands

FUNCTION	KEY COMBINATION
NetWare User Tools for Windows Help	Alt+H
User-Defined Button 1	Alt+1
User-Defined Button 2	Alt+2

Each key combination works from any screen in NetWare User Tools. The bottom-left corner of the program has a two-line information window that displays the name and key combination for each command button when you run your cursor over the button. The icons on the top row are called the toolbar, although I tend to call them icons.

> **TIP**
>
> *For those of you that have sound cards, the dragging of objects from one side of NetWare User Tools to the other activates the N–N–NetWare sound effect. The N–N-N part starts when you click and start dragging the object. The N-NetWare finish comes when you drop the object. If this clever but distinctive sound becomes annoying to you or others located near you, use the command buttons rather than the drag-and-drop method. So far, the buttons remain mute.*

Enabling the Hotkey for NetWare User Tools

> **12.1 IN-A-HURRY**
>
> **Enable or Disable the Hotkey for NetWare User Tools in NetWare 4.10**
>
> 1. Start Windows 3.1x after installing the NetWare client files and open the Control Panel.
> 2. Double-click on the Network icon (the one that looks like a printer cable).
> 3. In the NetWare Hotkey section in the upper-right corner, check the Enable Hotkey box.
> 4. Change from the default of F6 if necessary (try F6 first).
> 5. Click on OK to save and exit.

If you must add the hotkey, change the hotkey, or disable the hotkey, this is one place to do so. When you install the NetWare client software on a system with Windows 3.1x, you should check that this F6 hotkey doesn't interfere with any other program's usage of this key. Most of the time, there's no problem.

The NetWare client software adds some pizzazz to the typical Windows 3.1x network connections screen. We will see this same screen later, and get here much more pleasantly. The version called from within NetWare User Tools is also fancier.

We'll cover all the different features you see here in Figure 12.3 sooner or later. Right now, concentrate on the upper-right corner of the NetWare Settings dialog box. The Enable Hotkey box is checked, and F6, the default hotkey, is shown in the text field.

You can set any key as the hotkey by pressing that key. If the name of the key you pressed appears in the field, it is legal for use as the hotkey. This may result in some inappropriate keys, such as Backspace, Page Up, or NumLock, to be placed in this field by accident. Be careful.

Once the hotkey is either enabled or disabled as per your choice, click on OK to save and exit. Your choice becomes active immediately.

> *Sound board alert: If you wish to hear N–N–NetWare without dragging and dropping resources, click on the NetWare logo in the upper-left corner.*

FIGURE 12.3

Setting the NetWare User Tools hotkey through Windows 3.1x

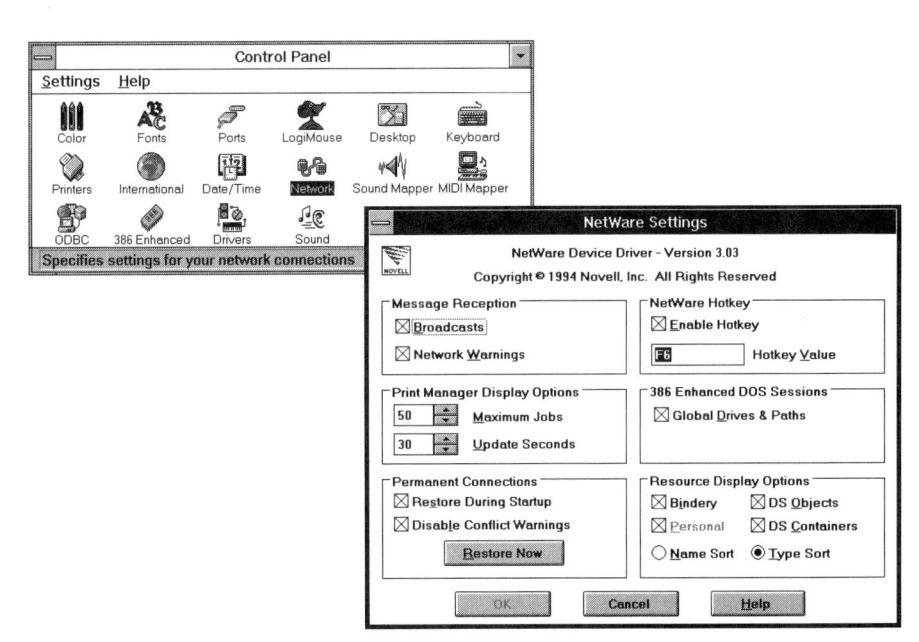

Mapping Drives

> **12.2 IN-A-HURRY**
>
> **Map Drives with NetWare User Tools in NetWare 4.10**
>
> 1. While in Windows 3.1*x*, start NetWare User Tools.
>
> 2. Click on the command button in the top row next to the Exit button. The icon shows two external hard drives.
>
> 3. Drag a volume from the Resources list and drop it on a drive letter, or highlight a drive letter and a volume and click on Map.
>
> 4. If you are overwriting an existing mapping, or mapping to a local drive, you will be asked to verify your intent.
>
> 5. Press Escape or click on the Exit button.

Forget the MAP command-line utility. Mapping drives with NetWare User Tools is quicker, graphical, and immune to typos. If you are running Windows 3.1*x*, this is the way to map drives. These drive mappings will be global, including DOS boxes under Windows 3.1*x*, if you have the Global Drives & Paths box checked in the NetWare Settings dialog box. See Figure 12.3 in the previous section—the box to check is under the NetWare Hotkey section. The default is to have global settings.

The first job is to locate the drive resource (meaning volume or directory) you wish to map. The Resources list works like all the other browse windows in NetWare 4.10. If you are looking in one context, you see that context only. If you double-click on a context, you change to that context. You can easily run up and down the NDS tree using NetWare User Tools.

The drag-and-drop method shows a little drive icon being pulled to the Drives list on the left side of the NetWare User Tools window. If you move the drive somewhere you can't legally drop it, the international circle-and-crossbar symbol covers the drive icon. See Figure 12.4 to witness the flying drive about to be dropped onto an empty drive letter.

After you see the volume you wish to use, you may want to "map root" a drive to a particular directory. If so, double-click on the volume name to open the directory listings. Double-click on as many directory names as you need to

FIGURE 12.4

Mapping a NetWare 4.10 volume with NetWare User Tools

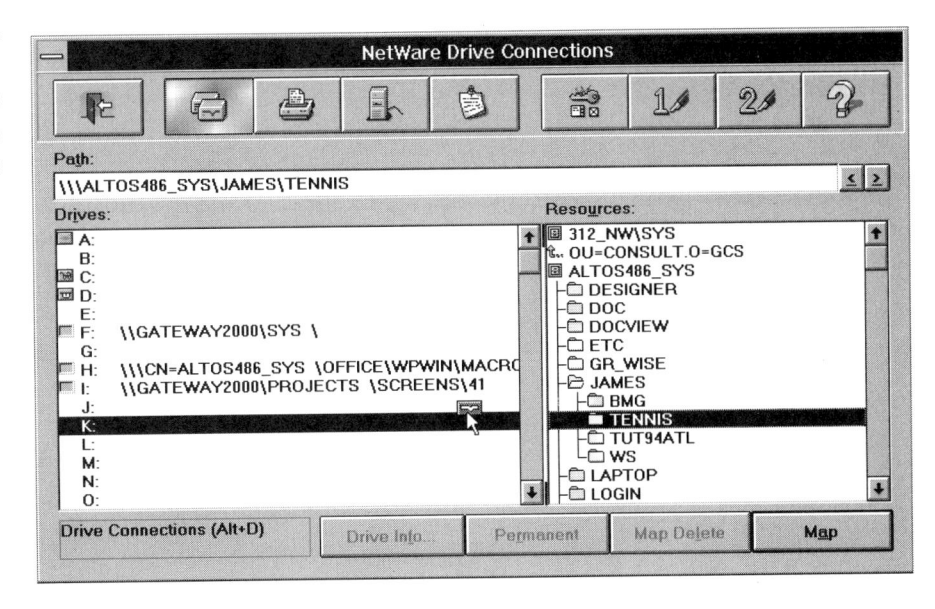

drill down to the subdirectory for your mapping operation. When you find it, drag that particular directory to your desired drive letter.

Notice the directory path displayed in the Path text box. Here I'm mapping the K: drive to Personal Tennis Coach, a shareware program from MSR Software in San Francisco. (It tracks tennis matches and gives tips, but still hasn't cured my topspin backhand from going into the net more often than not.) The chosen directory will be set up as a map root drive, making it impossible to move up the directory structure.

You can adjust the map root directory if you wish. See the right and left arrows at the end of the Path text box? Using these buttons, you can adjust the fake root setting for that drive letter. As you click on the arrows, notice that a space appears between directories in the Path text box. Where this space is shows where the fake root is set. You must click on the Map command button to force these settings into effect.

As you change location within directory structures, those changes are reflected in the NetWare User Tools display. After all, this is only a graphical front-end to the MAP command. All the MAP features you would expect are here, but they can be run with a mouse rather than a keyboard.

The Drive Info command button at the bottom of the NetWare User Tools window is a quick way to show your rights in a directory. When a mapped drive is highlighted, showing the path in the path display, the Drive Info button becomes active. Then you can either click on the button or double-click on the mapped drive. Either way, something along the lines of Figure 12.5 will appear.

FIGURE 12.5

Checking your rights the graphical way

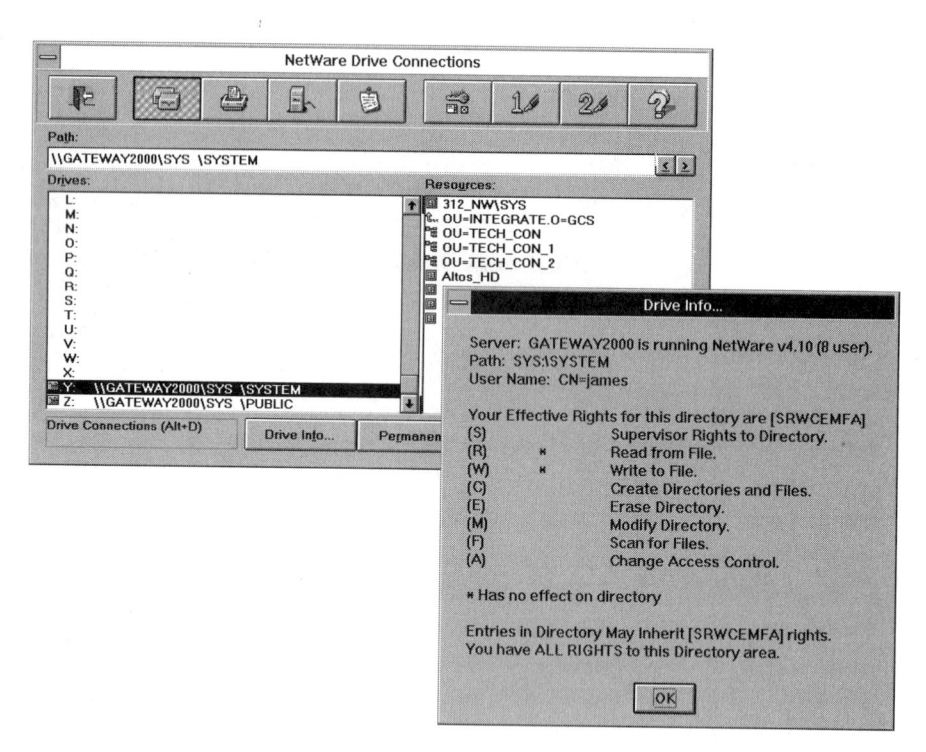

All rights are displayed here, but the appropriate ones for non-supervisor users will appear in a smaller window. The information at the top of the Drive Info window provides the following information:

- Server name where the volume supporting the mapped drive resides

- NetWare version

- Number of current users (it seems to indicate the number of licensed users, but it really doesn't)

- The path of the directory of the rights being displayed

- The user's name

There are two other quick details to check in the NetWare Drive Connections window. First, notice the icons to the right of Drives Y and Z. See the little eyeglasses? Those indicate search drives. In Figure 12.4, Drive A's icon is supposed to resemble a floppy drive. Drive C also has the eyeglasses, because it is another search drive.

Drive D is my favorite. It looks like it's sticking out its tongue, doesn't it? That's really a CD-ROM drive, and the tongue is a CD-ROM disk. Who says pictures never distort reality?

Making Drives Permanent

> **12.3 IN-A-HURRY**
>
> **Make a Drive Mapping Permanent with NetWare User Tools in NetWare 4.10**
>
> 1. While in Windows 3.1x, start NetWare User Tools.
>
> 2. Click on the Drives Connection button in the top row next to the Exit. The icon is two external hard drives.
>
> 3. Highlight the drive mapping to make permanent and click on the Permanent command button at the bottom of the dialog box. (Notice the change in the icon to the left of the drive letter.)
>
> 4. Press Escape or click on the Exit button.

Mapping a drive permanently through NetWare User Tools works only after you start Windows 3.1x, because the permanent drive mapping is added to the WIN.INI file. The permanent drives are added to the [Network] section. The global drives setting makes sure this is carried through to the DOS boxes, however. All the WIN.INI manipulation is handled for you automatically.

I prefer to log in to the system and set the initial drives through the various login script options, and use this feature only for changing and adding drive mappings. The reason for my preference is that this NetWare User Tools feature doesn't handle search drives.

Figure 12.6 shows our TENNIS subdirectory highlighted once again. Take a close look at the icon to the left of Drive K. See the little dark line going through and dipping down for a bit? That's supposed to represent a network cable connecting to this drive letter. A similar icon is used for network drive letters in File Manager.

Permanent drive maps aren't permanent in any real way, since they're so easy to change. If you get tired of a permanent drive, just highlight the drive and click on the Map Delete command button. This takes away the network drive icon and erases the setting from your WIN.INI file.

FIGURE 12.6

Mapping a permanent TENNIS drive

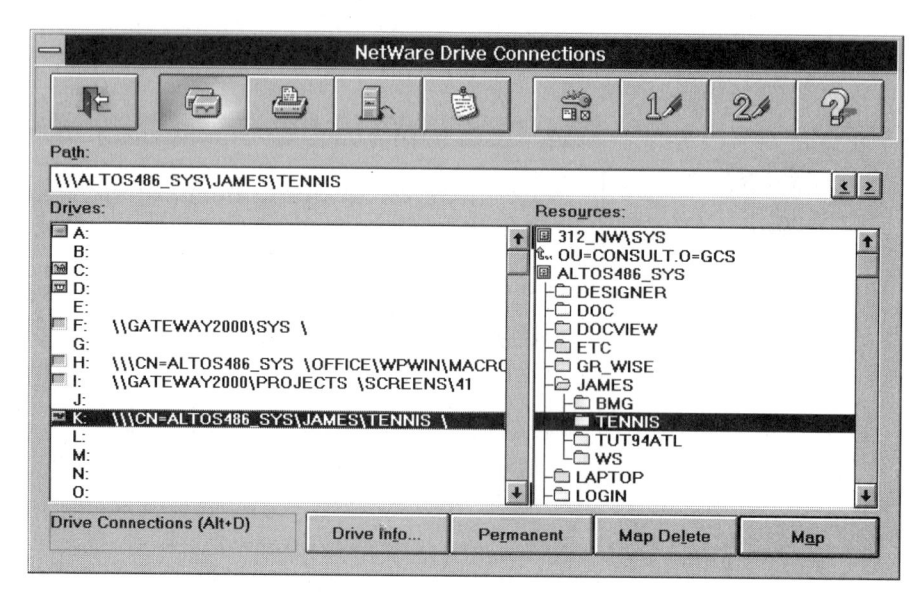

Controlling Printing

Just as the drive mapping function in NetWare User Tools made me swear off the MAP command, so has the printing feature weaned me from CAPTURE. There are quite a few command-line options that can be used when connecting to a new printer, and NetWare User Tools simplifies making these specifications.

The printer icon on the top line of command buttons is a lot more intuitive than the button for network drives (why is there an icon for a heartbeat monitor?). When you click on the printer icon, the NetWare Printer Connections face of NetWare User Tools appears. Take a look at Figure 12.7 for the opening shot.

12.4 IN-A-HURRY

Set Up Network Printing with NetWare User Tools in NetWare 4.10

1. While in Windows 3.1x, start NetWare User Tools.

2. Click on the Printer command button (with the printer icon) in the top row.

3. Find the network printer you wish to use in the Resources list. Move up and down the NDS tree if necessary.

4. Drag the printer or print queue to use over to the appropriate LPT port and drop it there, or highlight the desired printer or print queue and the LPT port and click on the Capture command button.

5. Set any LPT settings necessary.

6. Press Escape or click on the Exit button.

FIGURE 12.7

Dropping a printer

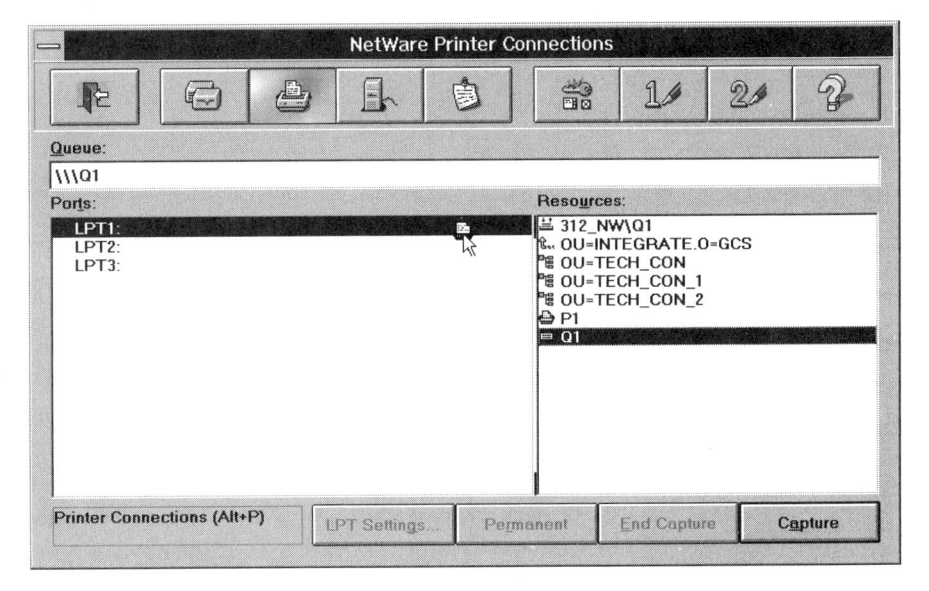

The process for setting up a printer connection is just like that for mapping drives. Everything in NetWare User Tools is fairly consistent (almost like the programmers actually paid attention to the needs of the users).

You can drag-and-drop the printer or print queue onto the LPT port. Clicking on the printer, the LPT port, and then the Capture button works just as well. Choosing either the printer or the print queue gives the same result.

To delete a print connection, use the same dragging-and-dropping or button-clicking procedures. You can just drag an existing printer connection and drop it back into the Resources list to disconnect (the CAPTURE / ENDCAP command). You can also highlight your printer connection and click on the End Capture button.

Making Printer Connections Permanent

> **12.5 IN-A-HURRY**
>
> **Make a Printer Connection Permanent with NetWare User Tools in NetWare 4.10**
>
> 1. While in Windows 3.1x, start NetWare User Tools.
>
> 2. Click on the Printer command button in the top row.
>
> 3. Highlight the captured printer connection to make permanent.
>
> 4. Click on the Permanent command button at the bottom of the window. (Notice the new printer icon to the left of the printer port.)
>
> 5. Press Escape or click on the Exit button.

Once again, a user has an easy way to make a permanent connection to a network resource without bothering the network administrator. As with making a permanent drive connection, just highlight the captured printer or print queue and click on the Permanent command button. The information is again written automatically to the WIN.INI file. It's available in DOS, but only after you start Windows 3.1x. Figure 12.8 shows a permanent printer connection.

Disconnecting a permanent printer is simple: Highlight the printer and click on End Capture. The WIN.INI file is modified, and the next time you start Windows, the printer you removed won't be configured.

FIGURE 12.8

A printer icon for a permanent printer connection

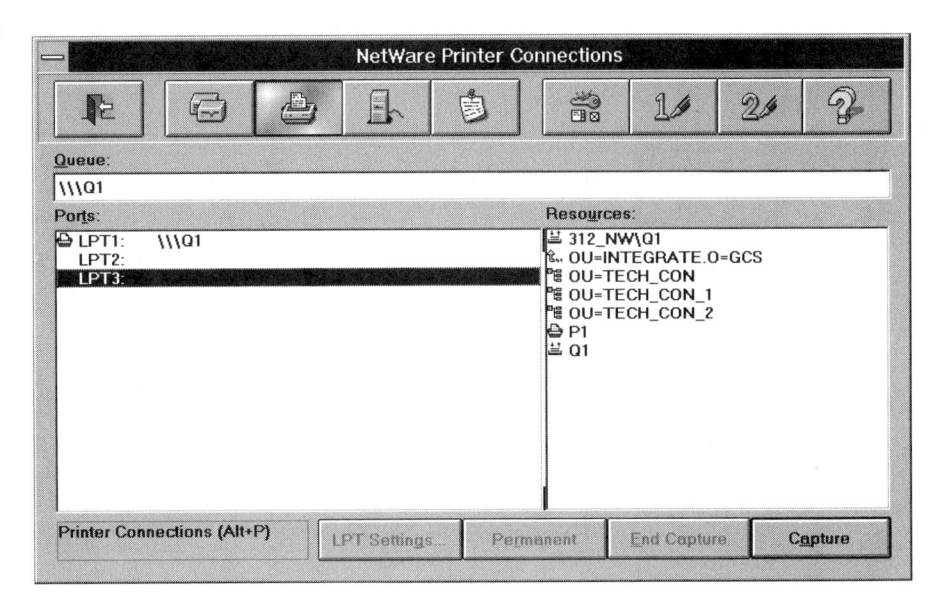

When you make a printer permanent, the LPT settings in place at the time you mark it permanent are kept. If you change the printer settings, you should use End Capture to disconnect the printer, then recapture it to make the new settings permanent. See the next section for information about adjusting the printer settings.

Adjusting Printer Settings

> **12.6 IN-A-HURRY**
>
> **Adjust the LPT Settings with NetWare User Tools in NetWare 4.10**
>
> 1. While in Windows 3.1x, start NetWare User Tools.
>
> 2. Click on the Printer command button in the top row.
>
> 3. Highlight the captured printer connection to adjust and click on the LPT Settings command button to open the NetWare Settings for LPT dialog box.
>
> 4. Change the print job settings as necessary, and then click on OK to exit the dialog box.
>
> 5. Press Escape or click on the Exit button.

When you capture a printer using NetWare User Tools, the printer settings are taken from the default print job configuration details. If you don't have a print job configuration, you will need to manually change all the print settings.

The NetWare Settings for LPT dialog box contains all the printing details any user is likely to need. You will be familiar with many of these settings if you struggled along with me in Chapter 8. Figure 12.9 shows the NetWare User Tools NetWare Settings for LPT dialog box. Table 12.3 describes the checkboxes and settings.

FIGURE 12.9
More printing choices for the user

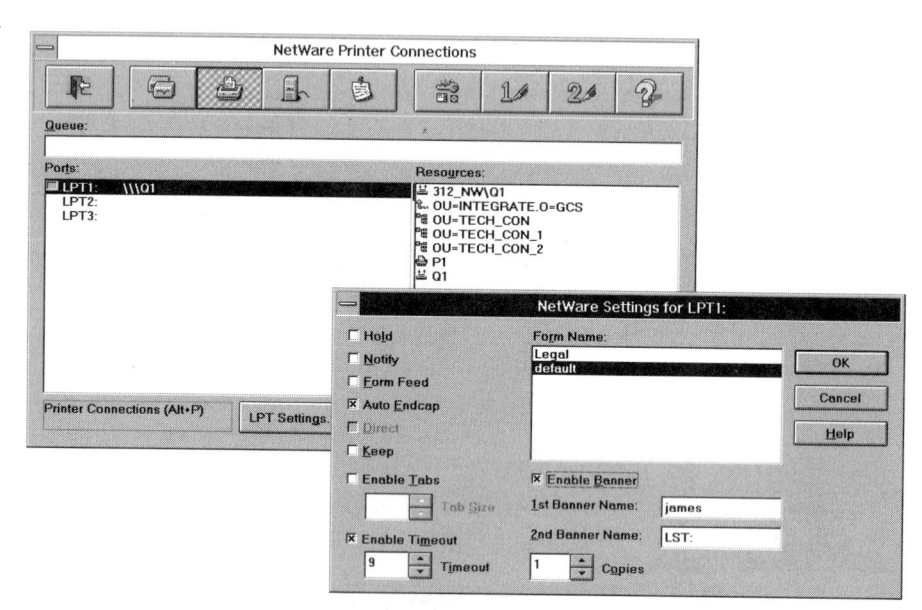

TABLE 12.3
Options in the NetWare User Tools NetWare Settings for LPT Dialog Box

OPTION	FUNCTION
Hold	Holds jobs in the print queue until you're ready to resume printing. Checking this box holds the jobs, and unchecking this box releases the jobs.
Notify	Tells the system to notify the user when the job is either finished or has a problem. This notification does not include printer notifications for offline, out of paper, and the like.

TABLE 12.3 (cont.) Options in the NetWare User Tools NetWare Settings for LPT Dialog Box

OPTION	FUNCTION
Form Feed	Inserts a blank page between print jobs. Usually, this isn't needed, because most applications can handle network printing.
Direct	For Personal NetWare only, bypasses the print queue for local print jobs if no other print jobs are waiting.
Keep	Holds jobs in the print queue after being printed. This allows you to easily reprint jobs without resubmitting them to the queue. When you uncheck the box, any remaining print jobs held in the queue are deleted.
Enable Tabs	Sets the number of spaces in a tab if your application does not have a print format feature. (If it doesn't, replace the application; this is a command from the old days and should never be necessary today.)
Enable Timeout	Holds the print queue open for the specified number of seconds (maximum of 1000) to wait for more application output. This helps with applications that don't send a specific end print job notice to the print queue. After the specified time passes with no extra print characters, the queue will assume the job is finished and start the printing process.
Form Name	Allows you to pick which of the available printer forms (if defined) you wish to use.
Enable Banner	Specifies whether a banner page will be printed at the start of each print job.
1st Banner Name	Specifies the name on the banner page. The default is the user name.
2nd Banner Name	Specifies the second name on the banner page. The default is LST:.
Copies	Lets you increase or decrease the number of copies of each print job printed. The maximum is 255.
Auto EndCap	Sends print jobs to a network printer or file when you exit or enter an application. This is useful if you want to hold the printing of several files until you exit the application.

> **NOTE:** The Hold checkbox in the NetWare User Tools NetWare Settings for LPT dialog box actually allows you to hold jobs in the print queue and release them when you're ready to resume printing. The number in the Maximum Jobs field, under Print Manager Display Options in the NetWare Settings dialog box (Figure 12.3), sets the maximum number of jobs that can be displayed, not held.

These local settings for each particular user override any settings for the defined print job configuration. As mentioned in the previous section, to keep these settings for your subsequent sessions, you must make the printer with these settings a permanent printer. Otherwise, you must reset any of these options each time you log in.

Printers captured during a work session with NetWare User Tools will use the default settings. All but two of the settings shown in Figure 12.9 are the defaults. The exceptions are settings for Enable Timeout (the default is not enabled) and Form Feed (the default is to use a form feed).

Is Windows 3.1x Printing Configured Properly?

12.7 IN-A-HURRY

Configure Windows 3.1x for Fast Network Printing

1. While in Windows 3.1x, open the Control Panel.
2. Open the Printers dialog box and check the Use Print Manager box.
3. Click on the Connect command button.
4. Choose the LPT port to configure, and check the Fast Printing Direct to Port box.
5. Click on OK, then click on Close, and then close the Control Panel.
6. Open the Print Manager utility.
7. From the Options menu, choose Network Settings and verify that both boxes are checked.
8. Close all programs and groups.

We're cramming in two Windows 3.1x print control programs on one screen. After all, what's the use of having the ability to open several programs at once if you don't use it? Figure 12.10 shows all the Windows programs ready for us to optimize for network printing.

FIGURE 12.10

Windows 3.1x network printing support options

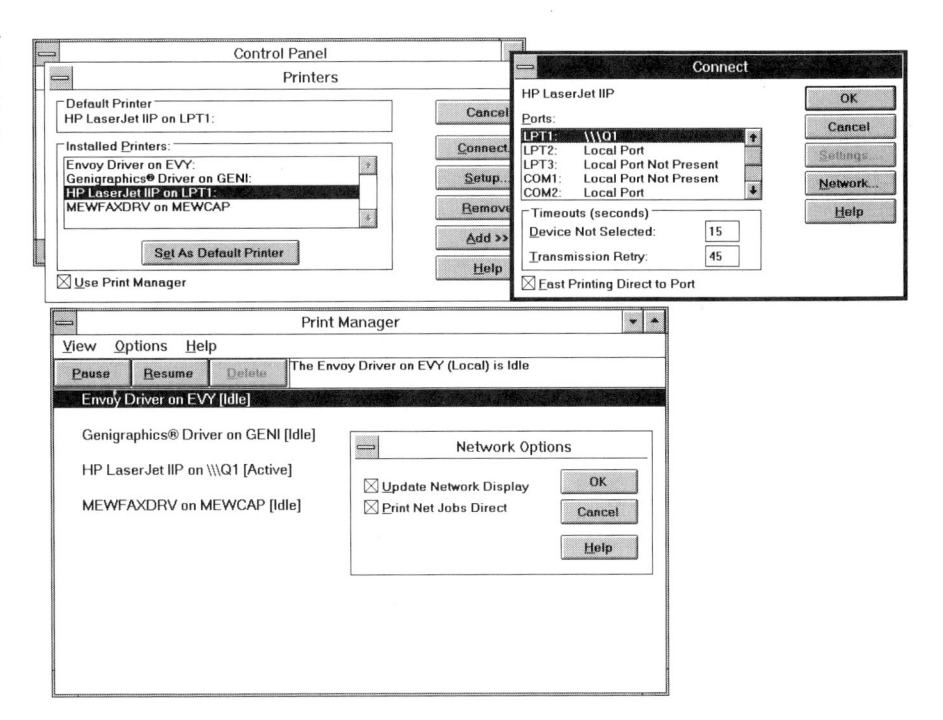

Let's go over the choices we need to make and the reasons for those choices. First of all, although it looks contradictory to use the Print Manager program, it's necessary. Since NetWare has such great print queue support, why would you want to organize a print queue on your workstation just to feed a better print queue on the network? You don't, but we must enable Print Manager so we can bypass it properly. Aren't computers logical?

After checking the box to use the Print Manager program, click on the Connect command button. This opens the Connect dialog box, where we need to check the LPT ports and check the Fast Printing Direct to Port box. The LPT port highlighted should match the LPT printer or queue connection defined in NetWare User Tools. You can call NetWare User Tools by clicking on the Network command button in this dialog box. That command button opens the NetWare Printer Connections window we worked with in the previous sections.

The Fast Printing option bypasses MS DOS interrupts and sends the print job directly to the network print queue, speeding things up considerably.

The next step is to use the Print Manager utility to finish our configuration. If we didn't check the box for Print Manager back in the first Printers dialog box, we couldn't open the program now.

Once in Print Manager, open the Options menu and choose Network Settings. The dialog box you see in the middle of Figure 12.10 offers two checkboxes, and we want them both checked.

The first, Update Network Display, keeps the local print system information current. The second, Print Net Jobs Direct, bypasses the Print Manager. Print Manager works fine for locally attached printers, but using it to track network print jobs consumes extra resources and gives no advantage.

Now you know how to configure Windows 3.1x printing in order to bypass most of it. Is this clean and logical? No, but nothing about printing is clean and logical. Better printer options are coming, thankfully, as network printers are getting smarter and will soon be able to participate fully in NDS.

NetWare Connections (Servers)

12.8 IN-A-HURRY

Make NetWare Server Connections with NetWare User Tools in NetWare 4.10

1. While in Windows 3.1x, start NetWare User Tools.

2. Click on the NetWare Connections button (the tall server case icon) in the top row.

3. Double-click on the NetWare server or container object to use.

4. If necessary, log in to the server to make the resources available.

5. To check server information, click on the NetWare Info command button.

6. To set or change your password to the highlighted server (or tree, if you are logged in to a tree), click on the Set Pass button.

7. To log out of the highlighted server, click on the Logout button.

8. Press Escape or click on the Exit button.

The NetWare Connections window of NetWare User Tools may be the first place you should go before doing anything new. If you aren't connected to the necessary servers or containers, you won't have access to the network resources you need. Use this screen to connect to different NDS trees and servers.

If you try to use a network resource from a server that requires you to log in, the login screen will pop up automatically (as in Figure 12.2 earlier in the chapter), and your name will be listed as the user name. If you wish to log in as a guest rather than a registered user, you have that option. You can log in to the following objects:

- Organization

- Organizational Unit

- NetWare Server

- Bindery Server

Remember, this login is more like an attach; you don't run a login script. Most users log in before starting Windows 3.1*x*. The NET.CFG has a place under the NetWare DOS Requester section to set your starting context, preferred tree, and preferred server if you wish. Although you don't log in to a server in NetWare 4 as in NetWare 3.*x*, you can ask for a particular server to handle your login request, such as the server holding the master replica of the NDS database.

To attach to more than eight servers concurrently, check your NET.CFG file. It must have a line stating

```
CONNECTIONS=number
```

in the NetWare DOS Requester section. Fill in the required number of connections, up to the limit of 50.

Figure 12.11 shows the NetWare Connections window of NetWare User Tools, along with the results of pressing the NetWare Info command button. GATEWAY2000 is the head server in the network, at least for me at this time.

Your network resources are in the right list, and your current connections are on the left. The command buttons across the bottom do the following:

- **NetWare Info:** Shows server and network details for the object highlighted in the Connections list. The information will include:

    The NetWare version of the server

    Your login name

FIGURE 12.11

Checking NetWare Info for a server

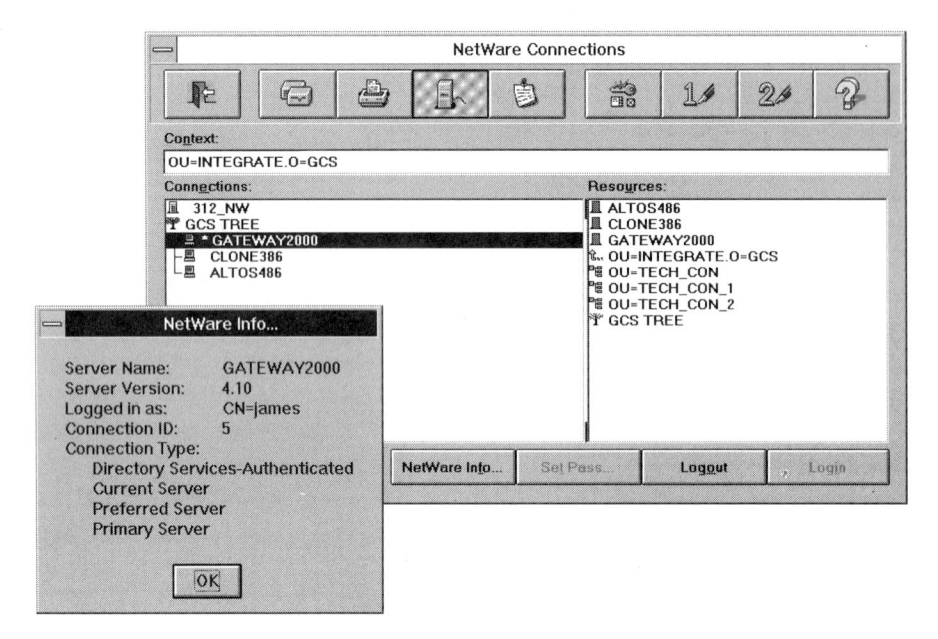

*[Screenshot of NetWare Connections window showing Context: OU=INTEGRATE.O=GCS, a Connections list (312_NW, GCS TREE, *GATEWAY2000, CLONE386, ALTOS486), and a Resources list (ALTOS486, CLONE386, GATEWAY2000, OU=INTEGRATE.O=GCS, OU=TECH_CON, OU=TECH_CON_1, OU=TECH_CON_2, GCS TREE). A NetWare Info dialog displays: Server Name: GATEWAY2000; Server Version: 4.10; Logged in as: CN=james; Connection ID: 5; Connection Type: Directory Services-Authenticated, Current Server, Preferred Server, Primary Server.]*

Your connection number on that server

Whether the connection is Directory Services, Personal NetWare, or Bindery

If this is your primary connection

If this is your preferred connection (from NET.CFG)

If this is your current connection

- **Set Pass(word):** Sets or changes your password for the highlighted NDS object. You will be asked to type the old password, type the new password, and retype the new password.

- **Logout:** Logs out of the highlighted object in the Connections list.

- **Login:** Logs in to the resource highlighted in the Resources list.

Notice the Login button at the bottom of the NetWare Connections window. In Figure 12.11, it's gray, meaning inactive. If you move the highlight bar up and down the Resources list, the Login button will become active for the server objects where you can log in.

The asterisk by the GATEWAY2000 name indicates that server is my current connection. You can change the current connection by highlighting a different server, holding down the Ctrl key, and double-clicking on the new server. Your view of network resources may change, depending on the information contained in your current server.

The information line just below the top icons now shows the context of your view of NDS. As you click on the different containers in the Resources list, the context shown will reflect your changes. You may think you've lost some servers if you change your context and don't expand it to show all the resources.

Sending Messages

> **12.9 IN-A-HURRY**
>
> **Send Messages with NetWare User Tools in NetWare 4.10**
>
> 1. While in Windows 3.1x, start NetWare User Tools.
>
> 2. Click on the Send Message button (with the note pinned to a wall).
>
> 3. Type the message in the Message text area just below the icons. (Up to 255 characters are allowed for other NDS clients; 58 characters for messages to bindery users.)
>
> 4. Select the single user or group to receive your message in the Resources list. (Click on a command button to Show/Hide Groups or Show/Hide Users if you can't see your intended recipient.)
>
> 5. Click on the Send button.
>
> 6. Press Escape or click on the Exit button.

The command-line SEND utility is still available, but remembering the syntax and the proper user names can be difficult for casual network users. That's why this little note utility in NetWare User Tools is so handy.

One of the improvements from the NetWare User Tools early days in Personal NetWare is in the Message section. With earlier versions of NetWare User Tools, the Send command button was always active in this screen. It was easy to highlight the message recipient, click Send to tell the system what to do, and then see the verification notice telling you that a blank message was sent with your name attached. Now, the Send button isn't active until at least one character has been typed in the message space. See Figure 12.12 for a common use for these quick messages.

FIGURE 12.12

An important corporate question

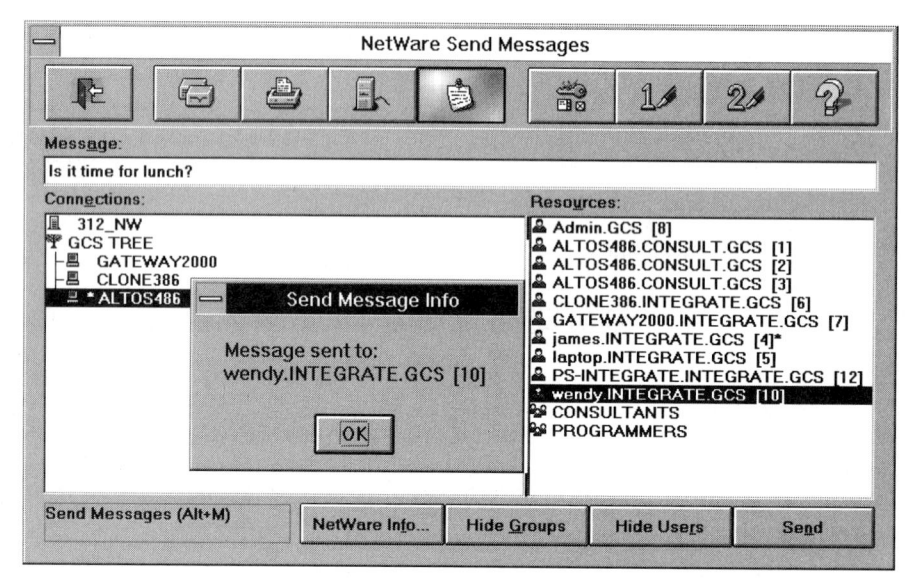

[Screenshot of NetWare Send Messages window with message "Is it time for lunch?" and Send Message Info dialog showing "Message sent to: wendy.INTEGRATE.GCS [10]"]

Only logged-in users are included in the message Resources list, for obvious reasons. This is not a store-and-forward e-mail system—it's a quick note. Another improvement in this version of NetWare User Tools, however, is that when you get a second message before you clear the first one off the screen, the second message queues up and delivers itself when able. Before, the second message would just bounce off into oblivion.

You can't choose multiple users or groups from the Resources list as message recipients. However, you can send the same message to another user or group, then another, and so on. When you close NetWare User Tools, the text is cleared. If you want to resend your message, do it right away.

In large networks, the two new command buttons across the bottom of the screen—Hide Groups and Hide Users—are useful. Both buttons are toggles, so if it says Hide Users now, clicking on it will change the button to Show Users. Depending on the state of these buttons, the Resources list will be full of some combination of groups and users, either showing or not. Yes, you can hide everything.

> *One of the quirks of an object-oriented system appears in Figure 12.12: Servers and server connections are treated like user connections. There's no difference between one object and another at most levels of the operating system, so here we have strange things like users and printers showing up, ready to be invited to lunch.*

Message recipients in Windows 3.1*x* get a typical message box, right in the middle of their screen. They must click on OK to clear it. DOS users see the message in reverse video on the top line of their displays. They must press Ctrl+Enter to clear the message. DOS systems stop dead until the message is cleared.

If you wish to avoid messages locking up your computer while you're not around, you can turn off broadcasts through the NetWare Settings dialog box in NetWare User Tools, which is the subject of the next section.

Managing NetWare Settings

> **12.10 IN-A-HURRY**
>
> **Set the Hotkey and Other NetWare Settings with NetWare User Tools in NetWare 4.10**
>
> 1. While in Windows 3.1*x*, start NetWare User Tools.
> 2. Click on the NetWare Settings button (the one with the burning key).
> 3. Change the settings as necessary.
> 4. Click on OK to save and exit.

Back in Figure 12.3, we checked our hotkey settings through Windows 3.1*x*. Figure 12.13 shows the same information, but reached through a different method. NetWare settings are as close as a click away anytime you're in NetWare User Tools.

You may notice that the main NetWare User Tools window still shows all the message-sending information. The icon is still pushed in. Why? Because the NetWare Settings screen is an overlay of NetWare User Tools, not one of the functions. Novell engineers were nice enough to place an easy hook to the NetWare Settings screen here, so you don't need to go through Windows as we did earlier.

FIGURE 12.13

NetWare Settings in a fancier window

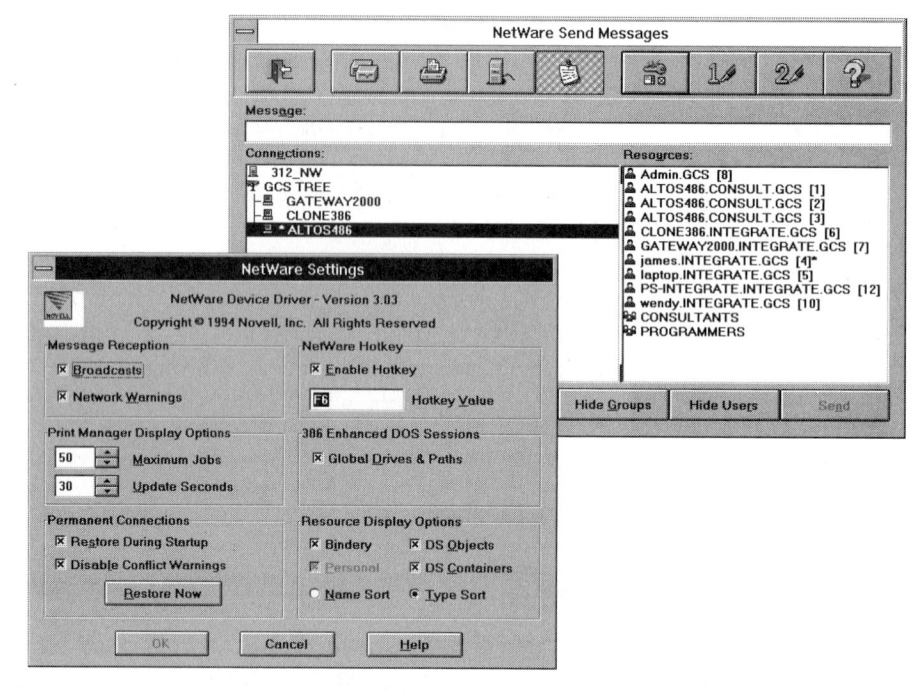

The options here work as follows:

- **Message Reception:** Check Broadcasts to receive broadcasts from the server and users, including messages from other users (sent via the SEND utility or NetWare User Tools). Check Network Warnings to show network messages during client software loading. These messages must be cleared before the loading can continue.

- **Print Manager Display Options:** Set Maximum Jobs to indicate how many print queue jobs to display, from 1 to 250 (the default is 50). This limits only the display of print jobs in the queue, not the number of print jobs. Update Seconds sets the number of seconds, from 1 to 65, between updates of the Print Manager display list (the default is 30).

- **Permanent Connections:** Check Restore During Startup to write the permanent drive and printer connections to the WIN.INI file. If this isn't checked, all settings stay only for the session. After changing this setting, you must exit and restart Windows for your change to take effect.

Disable Conflict Warnings turns off the messages displayed when permanent drives and printers are in the way of login settings. Rather than asking if you wish to overwrite the existing mappings with those from the permanent connections settings, the permanent settings automatically win the conflict. Click on the Restore Now button to restore all permanent connections written to the WIN.INI file (if passwords are necessary, the login screen will appear).

- **NetWare Hotkey:** Check Enable Hotkey to allow F6 or another key to start the NetWare User Tools program from the NETWARE.DRV file. Otherwise, you must start the application from the icon in a Windows 3.1*x* group. The Hotkey Value box shows the key combination set for the hotkey (if enabled).

- **386 Enhanced DOS Services:** Global drive mappings are those consistent between Windows 3.1*x* and DOS box sessions. Any new mapping in a DOS box becomes available to Windows and vice versa. When the Global Drives & Paths checkbox is checked, all drives mapped anywhere are available everywhere. When it isn't checked, each Windows application and DOS box may have different drive mappings. The settings when Windows starts are passed to each new DOS box. This applies only if you're running Windows 3.1*x* in 386 Enhanced mode. You must exit and restart Windows for this change to take effect.

- **Resource Display Options:** Each checked box in this section controls the display of network resources inside NetWare User Tools. When checked, they will be displayed.

    Bindery shows bindery resources (NetWare 3.*x* server resources).

    Personal shows Personal NetWare shared desktop resources.

    DS Objects shows NDS objects (servers, printers, users, and so on).

    DS Containers shows NDS containers (such as Organizations and Organizational Units).

- **Type Sort/Name Sort:** Type Sort (the default) shows objects arranged by type. Name Sort arranges them by name. Using Type Sort keeps all the printers with other printers and volumes with volumes.

Customizing NetWare User Tools User-Defined Buttons

> **12.11 IN-A-HURRY**
>
> **Add Your Own Application Hotkey to NetWare User Tools in NetWare 4.10**
>
> **1.** While in Windows 3.1x, start NetWare User Tools.
>
> **2.** Click on a User Defined command button (with the red pen marking 1 or 2).
>
> **3.** Type the program name, with its path, in the Command Line text box.
>
> **4.** To edit a button, while in NetWare User Tools, press Alt+1 or Alt+2.
>
> **5.** Click on OK to save and exit.

Since NetWare User Tools is available anytime and anywhere in Windows 3.1x with a keypress or double-click, Novell did us a favor and put two user-definable buttons on the top row of icons. These buttons are easily modified (another improvement over the initial release of NetWare User Tools with Personal NetWare).

Figure 12.14 shows the two buttons redefined. Button 1 is now SideKick, developed by Borland and now owned by Simplify Software. Button 2 is now E-Mail Connection, a multiple-system, e-mail front-end from ConnectSoft. Since both applications have their own icons, NetWare User Tools puts those icons here automatically.

Any executable MS Windows program can be listed on these buttons. To revise one of the buttons, just press Alt+1 or Alt+2 while in NetWare User Tools. This will bring up the User Defined Path dialog box, as shown in Figure 12.14. Here, you can delete or edit the command line. If the command is deleted, the original icon reappears on the modified button.

You cannot start a second instance of one of the user-defined programs from NetWare User Tools. If you try, an error message will appear, but no harm will be done.

FIGURE 12.14

Checking the command to start E-Mail Connection (button 2)

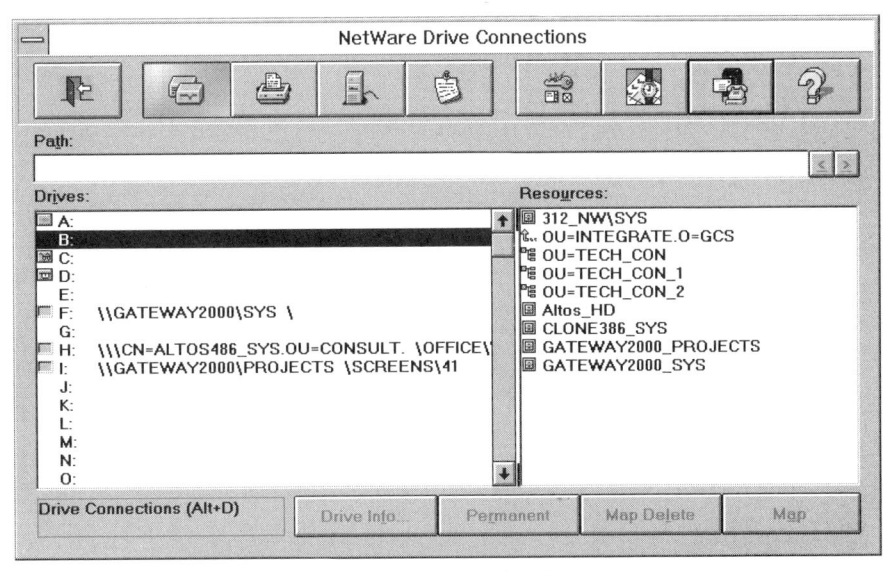

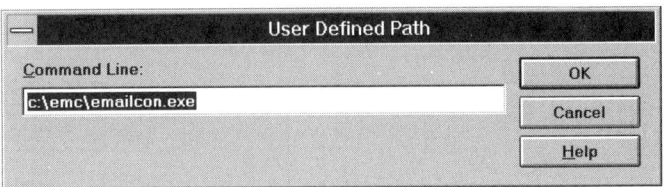

The Graphical Help Display

12.12 IN-A-HURRY

Using the NetWare User Tools Help System in NetWare 4.10

1. While in Windows 3.1x, start NetWare User Tools.

2. Click on the last icon in the toolbar, the large yellow question mark.

3. Wherever the cursor changes from an arrow to a hand, you can click for extra information.

4. Click on OK to exit.

In developing an end-user tool for the smallest companies, NetWare User Tools designers obviously spent some time thinking about the Help system. These are not the usual tepid Windows 3.1*x* Help screens.

Help is more graphical in NetWare User Tools than in any other program I use. As you can see in Figure 12.15, the graphic re-creates the program. Anywhere the cursor turns from an arrow to a hand, you can click and discover more help.

FIGURE 12.15

The colorful graphical Help screen reduced to black and white

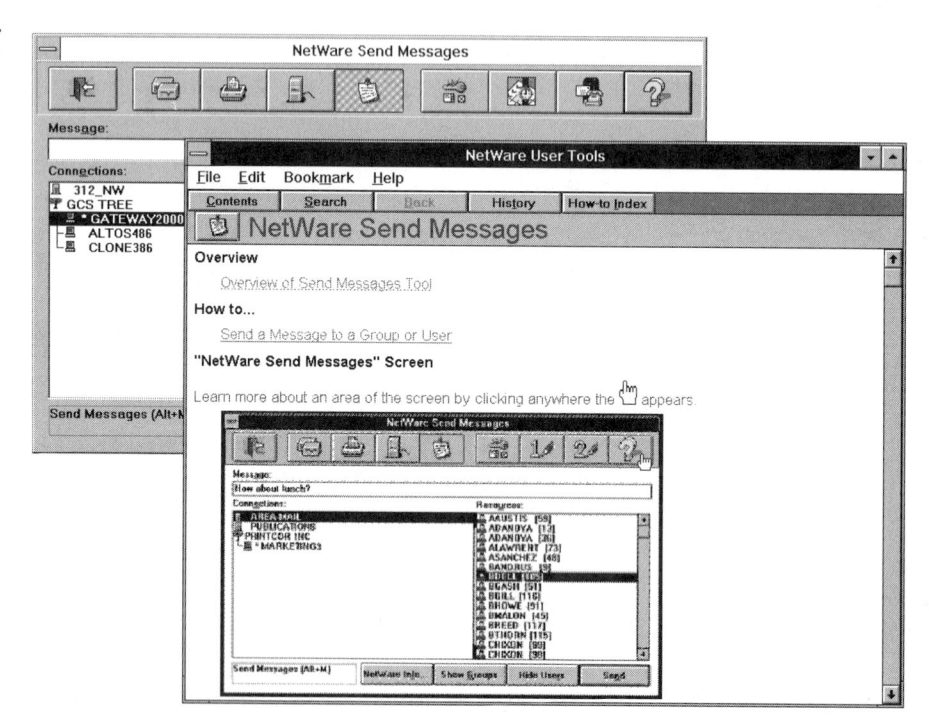

The title NetWare Send Messages is in bright red, the faint text lines are in green, and all the colors of NetWare User Tools itself are re-created within the Help system. Look closely, and you'll see my cursor, now a hand, right by the yellow question mark.

The command buttons in the Help system do the following:

- **Contents:** Displays a colorful rendition of the toolbar icons, each with an explanation. The mutating cursor clues you in that each icon has its own Help screen, and you reach that screen by clicking on the image, not in a list of words.

- **Search:** Displays the standard Windows 3.1*x* Search dialog box, where typing the first few letters jumps to the keyword in a scrolling list.

- **Back:** Moves back to the previous Help screen.

- **History:** Displays a standard Windows 3.1*x* Help screen history list, with previous screen titles listed in order.

- **How-To Index:** Displays a hypertext list of NetWare User Tools functions and features.

NETUSER for DOS Users

OFFICIALLY, NETUSER IS NetWare User Tools for DOS. But since that would be confusing after just covering NetWare User Tools, and since all the DOS users must type NETUSER each time they want to start this program, we'll call it NETUSER.

If you are familiar with the SESSION program from NetWare 3.*x*, you will see a few changes in NETUSER. Of course, the largest changes were made to take NDS into account. The other big change is the inclusion of some print options that weren't in SESSION. This new version also seems to get a bit more information on the screen at times.

> *Never underestimate the power of the command line.*

NetWare 4.11 includes no changes whatsoever to NETUSER, so if you're upgrading from NetWare 4.10, your DOS users won't have anything new to learn. I have a feeling the program wasn't upgraded because of declining DOS usage rather than program perfection, but one can never tell. NETUSER does work, and work well, even when the graphic utilities have a problem or two. Never underestimate the power of the command line.

The NETUSER program is installed in the SYS:\PUBLIC directory with the other NetWare utilities. Each user should automatically have access to this program. To start the program from the DOS prompt, users type:

    NETUSER

There are no startup options.

Figure 12.16 shows the opening NETUSER screen. The top two lines show the user's current context, as well as the NETUSER version, the date, and the time.

FIGURE 12.16

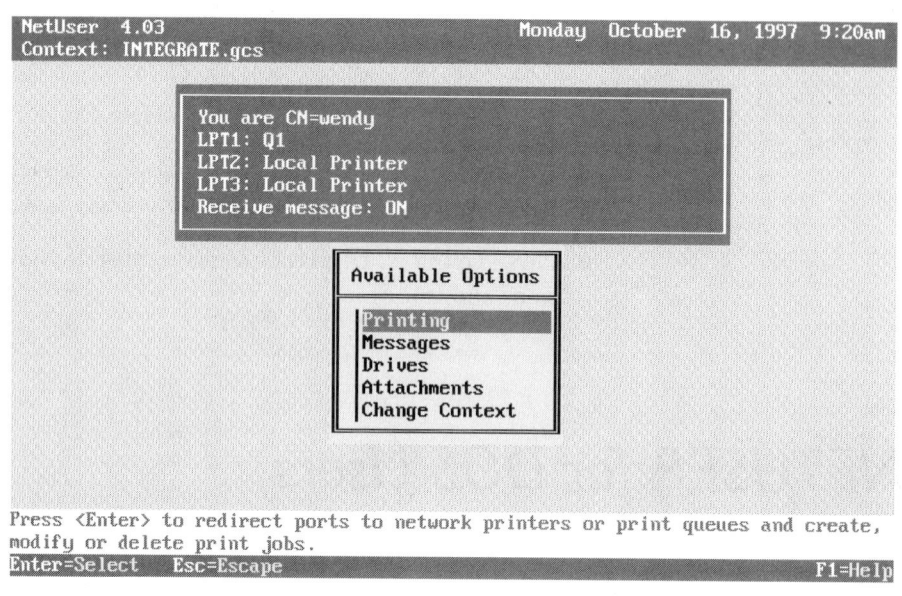

Opening of NETUSER

```
NetUser  4.03                                    Monday  October  16, 1997  9:20am
Context: INTEGRATE.gcs

            You are CN=wendy
            LPT1: Q1
            LPT2: Local Printer
            LPT3: Local Printer
            Receive message: ON

                          Available Options
                          Printing
                          Messages
                          Drives
                          Attachments
                          Change Context

Press <Enter> to redirect ports to network printers or print queues and create,
modify or delete print jobs.
Enter=Select    Esc=Escape                                              F1=Help
```

The first information box solves your identity crisis: You are CN=. CN is Common Name, another label for leaf object, another name for user. That's you, or whomever you pretended to be when you logged in to the network.

Your printing situation is summed up here, as well as your willingness to accept messages from fellow users. Each of the three available LPT ports shows whether it's set for local or network printing. The Receive Message line shows either ON or OFF, depending on your current setting.

The menu of Available Options covers the same ground as NetWare User Tools, but not so completely or conveniently. Unlike the easy movement through your NDS tree supported by NetWare User Tools using the mouse, NETUSER relies on a text representation with too little information displayed at any one time. Users are more likely to be confused by NETUSER than by NetWare User Tools.

Configuring Printing

There is something missing in this printing section: the ability to view or change your print job configuration settings. Unlike NetWare User Tools, NETUSER does not provide an option to modify details such as the banner,

12.13 IN-A-HURRY

Use Printing Controls in NETUSER

1. From a DOS prompt, type **NETUSER**.

2. Choose Printing from the Available Options menu (highlight it and press Enter).

3. Choose which of the available ports you want to configure.

4. To check or change print jobs, choose Print Jobs in the next Available Options menu.

5. To change printers, choose that option in the next Available Options menu. Choose the printer or print queue to capture from the pick list that appears.

6. Press Alt+F10 (or Escape several times) to open the Exit? menu, then press Enter to exit.

---

timeout, number of copies, and other options. When you capture a printer with NETUSER, you must accept the print job configuration you are dealt. Figure 12.17 shows the print system option, with a look at how LPT2 and LPT3 display network and local printing assignments.

If you wish to unhook an LPT port from a network printer, highlight the port and press the Delete key. A menu asking if you wish to disable the port appears, and you should answer yes. The wording is misleading; rather than disabling the port, you are changing it back to local output.

You capture a printer or change an existing printer the same way. The Change Printers option shows the available printers and print queues for your current context. If you wish to capture printers from another context, press the Insert key. A skinny field asking you to enter the context will appear. Since you don't want to type this information, press Insert again, and the familiar Object, Class browser screen appears. You can climb around your NDS tree looking for the printer of your choice.

Checking on print jobs opens the same information screen as you get using PCONSOLE to check on print jobs for a print queue. Print jobs in this screen can be modified (changed or deleted) by only the owner or a queue operator.

FIGURE 12.17

Checking printing with NETUSER

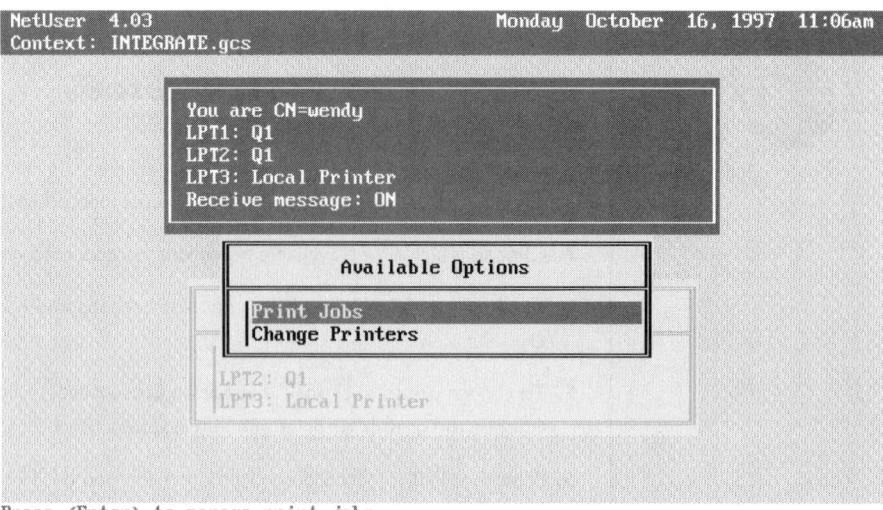

Sending and Receiving Messages

12.14 IN-A-HURRY

Send Messages with NETUSER

1. From a DOS prompt, type **NETUSER**.

2. Choose Messages from the Available Options menu.

3. To turn off message receipt on your station, set Receive Message to OFF.

4. To send a message, choose the users or groups for your messages (use the F5 key to choose multiple recipients), type the message (up to 58 characters for a DOS workstation; 255 characters to an MS Windows one) in the text box and press Enter to send it.

5. Press Alt+F10 (or Escape several times) to open the Exit? menu, and then press Enter to exit.

The message feature has what may be the only advantage of NETUSER over NetWare User Tools. With this utility, you can send a message to multiple recipients, rather than sending the same message several times. The shortcoming here is that your message can only be routed within your context. When you change the context, the message you previously typed and sent is gone when you return. You'll need to type the message all over again. So this is a time-saving feature only if your recipients are in one context.

Figure 12.18 shows the process of sending a message to a group of users (or several groups). Use the F5 key to tag multiple groups to receive your message. The window to list users is a bit larger, since there are more users to see than groups (usually).

FIGURE 12.18

Reminding the active network users about more work

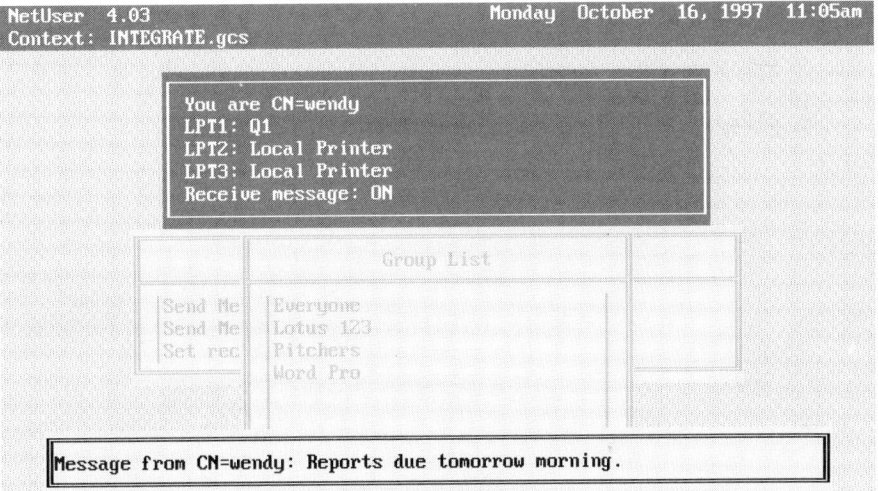

The message will appear only to active network users. While NetWare 4 allows messages to be queued at active stations, there is no queue for intended recipients that are not connected to the network. If you must send a message to everyone, use e-mail that people check regularly.

The status of your system to receive broadcast messages is displayed in the top information box. This NETUSER choice is the same as the choices in the

NetWare Settings dialog box (back in Figure 12.13) about receiving broadcasts and network warnings. If your choice here is NO, nothing will be received.

When you first choose Messages from the Available Options menu, you have a choice of using Directory Services or Bindery mode. Bindery mode uses the same server-centric naming as NetWare 3.*x*. You are asked to choose a NetWare server you are attached to, and then you can send messages to users attached to that server. However, Bindery Services under NetWare 4 will show all the attached users with the full contexts of their names. It will also show their login times.

Mapping Drives and Checking Your Rights

> **12.15 IN-A-HURRY**
>
> **Manage Drives with NETUSER**
>
> 1. From a DOS prompt, type **NETUSER**.
> 2. Choose Drives from the Available Options menu, then choose Drive Mapping or Search Mapping.
> 3. Press Enter on a network drive to see your rights in that directory.
> 4. Press F3 on a network drive to change your directory.
> 5. Press Insert to map a new drive letter.
> 6. Press Delete on a network drive to delete that drive mapping.
> 7. Press Alt+F10 (or Escape several times) to open the Exit? menu, and then press Enter to exit.

There are two functions behind the Drives menu choice: Drive Mapping and Search Mapping. Both work almost exactly the same way.

The keystrokes you can use for handling drive mappings are listed across the help area at the bottom of the screen, but not in all screens. Worse, they wrap onto two screens. Table 12.4 lists them for you in one place.

Figure 12.19 shows the process of adding a new drive mapping. Or is it modifying a drive mapping? It doesn't matter; they both look the same. Pressing Insert opens the Select Directory box, which comes up blank. To see

NETUSER for DOS Users

TABLE 12.4 NETUSER Drive Mapping Keystrokes

KEY	FUNCTION
Enter	Displays drive information or your rights in the highlighted directory.
Insert	Adds a new drive mapping.
Delete	Deletes a drive mapping.
F3	Changes a drive mapping.
F5	Marks multiple drives.
F7	Unmarks marked drives.
F4	Toggles between Directory Services and Bindery Services display styles.

your choices, use the Insert key to open a pick list of available volumes, supported by both NetWare 4.x and NetWare 3.x servers. To move outside your context, choose Additional Volume Objects or Additional Servers; both options open the Object, Class browser screen once again. Feel free to move up and down the NDS tree looking for the volume to map.

FIGURE 12.19 Using the pick lists when mapping drives

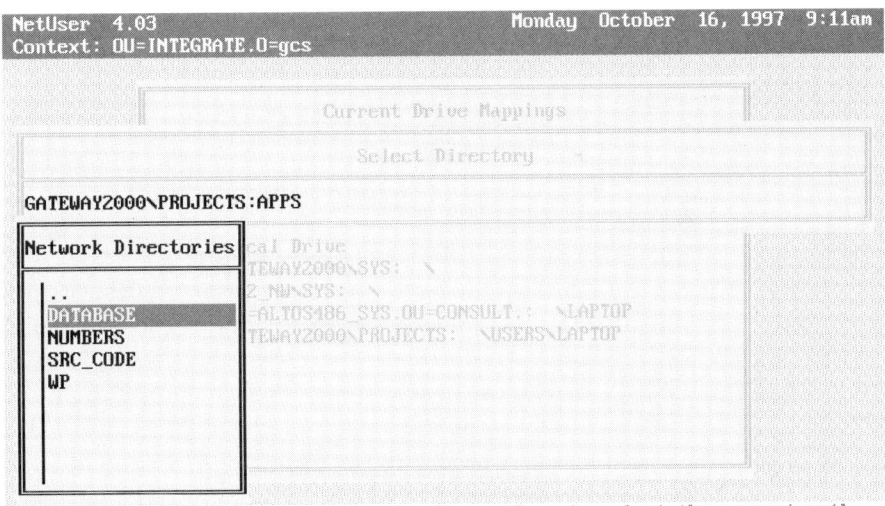

Once you decide on the volume, the Network Directories pick list opens, letting your cruise up and down the NDS tree for that particular volume. As the instructions suggest in Figure 12.19, you can highlight the directory you want and press Escape to move the directory name to the upper line with the volume name. When the path looks the way you want it, press Enter. You will be prompted to make this a map root drive, so choose Yes if this is correct.

The other option in this submenu is to check your rights. Place the highlight bar on any drive mapping and press Enter. A list of effective rights will appear on the right side of the screen. You can only observe your rights in this screen; you cannot change them.

Setting Attachments and User Details

> **12.16 IN-A-HURRY**
>
> **View and Set User Details with NETUSER**
>
> 1. From a DOS prompt, type **NETUSER**.
>
> 2. Choose Attachments from the Available Options menu, then choose a server from the list that appears.
>
> 3. From the Available Options menu, choose Login Script, Password, or Server Information.
>
> 4. Press Alt+F10 (or Escape several times) to open the Exit? menu, and then press Enter to exit.

By choosing Attachments from the first NETUSER menu, and then selecting Login Script, users can change their own login scripts, if they have the rights to do so. By choosing Password, they can change their passwords, again if they have that right. Users can always check server information. Figure 12.20 shows the menu where they choose which of these three options they want to use.

As you can see in the background, this information is organized by server. This may be slightly confusing to some users, since the same login script and password are available on multiple servers. It's really available through NDS replication on multiple servers, but that may be a fine point for some users.

FIGURE 12.20

User login script and password options

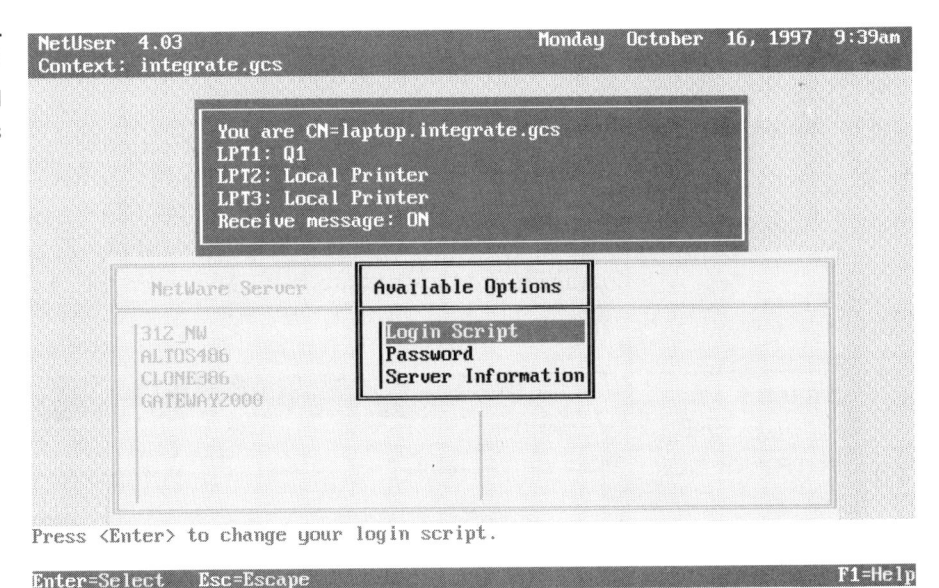

```
NetUser  4.03                              Monday  October  16, 1997  9:39am
Context: integrate.gcs

          You are CN=laptop.integrate.gcs
          LPT1: Q1
          LPT2: Local Printer
          LPT3: Local Printer
          Receive message: ON

              NetWare Server        Available Options
              312_NW                Login Script
              ALTOS486              Password
              CLONE386              Server Information
              GATEWAY2000


Press <Enter> to change your login script.

Enter=Select   Esc=Escape                                         F1=Help
```

Changing Your Context

> ### 12.17 IN-A-HURRY
>
> **Change your Context through NETUSER**
>
> 1. From a DOS prompt, type **NETUSER**.
>
> 2. Choose Change Context from the Available Options menu, then type in the new context or press Insert to open the Object, Class screen.
>
> 3. Press F10 on the name of the context, or the single dot (current context) line to move to your desired context.
>
> 4. Press Alt+F10 (or Escape several times) to open the Exit? menu, and then press Enter to exit.

Users that prefer pick lists to change contexts rather than the rather raw CX utility can use NETUSER to move about. When you choose Change Context from the menu, you can type in the context, or just press Insert to open the Object, Class browser screen. Figure 12.21 has another look at our old browser friend.

Forget the Enter key as a means of selection here. The Enter key moves you into or out of contexts. If I were to press Enter where the highlight bar is in Figure 12.21, I wouldn't make INTEGRATE.GCS my current context; I would only open INTEGRATE.GCS and show the containers inside. Only containers are shown, since that's all we can take advantage of in this utility.

FIGURE 12.21

Moving from GCS to INTEGRATE.GCS

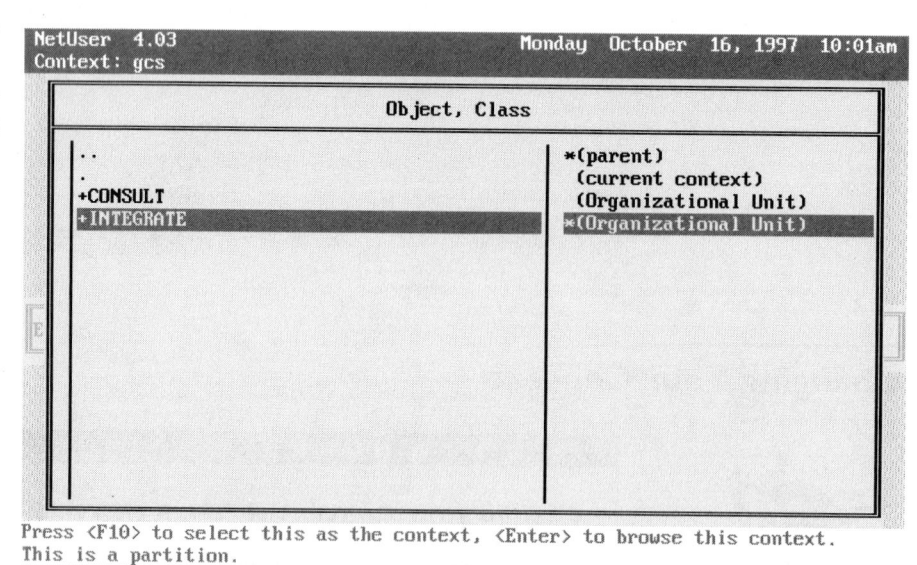

```
NetUser  4.03                                Monday  October  16, 1997  10:01am
Context: gcs
                        ┌─────────── Object, Class ───────────┐
                        │ ..                    *(parent)      │
                        │ .                     (current context)│
                        │ +CONSULT              (Organizational Unit)│
                        │ +INTEGRATE            *(Organizational Unit)│
                        │                                      │
                        │                                      │
                        │                                      │
                        │                                      │
                        └──────────────────────────────────────┘
 Press <F10> to select this as the context, <Enter> to browse this context.
 This is a partition.
 Enter=Change context    F10=Accept context    Esc=Exit             F1=Help
```

When you're happy with the context, you can do one of two things. You can press F10 on the name of the context, as the bottom-line instructions suggest. You may also press Enter, move into the new context, and press Escape to back out. When you press Escape, you're offered a chance to save your current context. Since that was the idea all along and you just hit the wrong key, you might as well say yes.

Configuring Printing from the Command Line with CAPTURE or NPRINT

TODAY, NETWORK-AWARE applications handle printing quickly, easily, and reliably. The applications automatically route printing to the proper printer, follow the directions you set in the applications as far as copies and banner pages, and ensure a printout. These are wonderful, but they are too few. Far too many applications act as if printing was something new to computers.

Because of this, the CAPTURE command is almost as important as it was back in the early days of NetWare. Using CAPTURE allows an application to blindly treat the printer as a dedicated device, because NetWare takes care of the printing details. This works, but it means you, as the administrator, must set up lots of extra printing information (see Chapter 8). It also requires the user to understand enough about printing to occasionally produce some printed pages without your direct intervention.

The CAPTURE utility fools applications into thinking they are spitting print information out of a parallel port, but the data is captured and routed across the network into a NetWare print queue. Only parallel printers can be captured. Both the NetWare Requester for DOS and the NetWare Requester for OS/2 work with the CAPTURE command. If you have an application that uses a serial port, use the DOS MODE command to redirect from the serial to the parallel port.

NPRINT replaces the DOS PRINT command for network use. This command is used for existing files that must be printed, not for application output.

Because so many applications are ignorant of network printing, the CAPTURE and NPRINT utilities have a ton of options. NetWare 4 has added the ability to print using a print job configuration from anywhere in your network (assuming you have the proper authority). You may also now use these utilities in reference to a printer, not a print queue, although print queue references are certainly still acceptable.

Both CAPTURE and NPRINT have excellent Help screens available. It's common to check the help information the first dozen times you use either program, until you memorize the commands that work for you.

Using CAPTURE

CAPTURE must be run before an application is started. The goal is to CAPTURE all print output to a specific, predefined print job configuration, or provide all the CAPTURE details on the command line. If a print job configuration exists, any command-line options will take precedence.

Table 12.5 shows some sample tasks and the syntax used to accomplish those tasks.

TABLE 12.5 CAPTURE Command Syntax

SAMPLE TASK	SYNTAX
Capture to network printer P1	CAPTURE P=P1
Capture to print queue Q1	CAPTURE Q=Q1
End a capture	CAPTURE EC or CAPTURE ENDCAP
Hold the print job in the queue	CAPTURE HOLD
List the printing parameters for the job to be printed	CAPTURE D
Redirect printer output to a file	CAPTURE CR=*filename*
Redirect printer output to a printer	CAPTURE P=*printername* (same as an initial CAPTURE)
Use print job configuration Color	CAPTURE J=COLOR
View online help	CAPTURE /? or CAPTURE ?
View all online Help screens	CAPTURE /? ALL
View help for the Banner option	CAPTURE /? B
View current CAPTURE settings	CAPTURE SH, CAPTURE SHOW, or CAPTURE /SH

> *To end a capture, use CAPTURE EC or CAPTURE ENDCAP. ENDCAP is no longer a separate utility.*

Before typing a new CAPTURE command, it's always smart to check for any existing CAPTURE parameters. The CAPTURE /SH command displays something similar to what you see in Figure 12.22.

FIGURE 12.22

Results of the CAPTURE /SH command

```
[Novell DOS] H:\>capture /sh

LPT1  Capturing data to print queue Q1.CONSULT.gcs
    Notify:           Disabled
    Automatic end:    Enabled
    Timeout count:    9 seconds
    Name:             (None)
    Form feed:        Disabled
    Banner:           (None)
    Keep:             Disabled
    Copies:           1
    Tabs:             No conversion
    Form:             default
    User hold:        Disabled

LPT2  Capturing is not currently active.

LPT3  Capturing is not currently active.

[Novell DOS] H:\>
```

Here we see the exact same CAPTURE parameters as in the last section where we talked about NetWare User Tools printing parameters. Check back to Figure 12.9 for a graphical presentation of these same parameters.

Most applications limit their print output to LPT1. If you have applications that can print to other LPT ports, you can take advantage of that fact with the CAPTURE command. When you use the CAPTURE command for a parallel port besides LPT1, you must specify that port in the command. To redirect output to LPT2, with a 9-second timeout and no form feed, the command would be:

```
CAPTURE LPT2 Q=Q1 TI=9 NFF
```

Since both the form feed (NFF means No Form Feed) and the timeout (TI=9 means TImeout in 9 seconds) differ from the defaults, they must be mentioned specifically. The default is for a form feed, but not a timeout.

In the CAPTURE command illustrated just now, the TI=9 and NFF are options. Table 12.6 summarizes the CAPTURE options.

TABLE 12.6
CAPTURE Command Options

OPTION	USAGE	FUNCTION
All	ALL	Used with EC to stop CAPTURE from all LPT ports.
AutoEndcap	AU	Default. Holds the captured data until the application is closed, then submits the print jobs.
Banner	B=*text*	Specifies the text in the lower half of the banner page, limited to 12 characters. Text with spaces must be enclosed in quotation marks (as in "Wendy's Report"). If not specified, the printer port will be listed in the lower half of the banner page. See NB.
Cancel	CA	Used with EC to cancel any remaining printer data that was captured.
Cancel and EndCap	ECCA	Stops the CAPTURE utility and dumps any captured data.
Copies	C=*number*	Default of 1. Can range up to 65,000.
Create	CR=*path* and *filename*	Creates a file for the print data, allowed only with the TI, AU, or NA options. Not available with OS/2.
Details	D	Lists similar information as SH, but provides more, including print job configuration and print job owner.
End Capture	EC	Stops the data capture to the specified port, or LPT1 if no specification is given.
Form	F=*name* or *number*	Default of form 0. Specifies which predefined form will be used. PRINTDEF or NetWare Administrator is used to define print forms.
Form Feed	FF	Default. Pushes a blank page out of the printer at the end of a print job to position a blank page for the next print job. Often redundant, since most applications now give a form feed to eject paper from page printers. See NFF.
Help	/?, ?, /H	General help information. /ALL lists all Help screens.
Hold	HOLD	Sends jobs to the print queue, but doesn't print them until the hold is released. Use either PCONSOLE or NetWare Administrator to release the print jobs.

TABLE 12.6 (cont.) CAPTURE Command Options	OPTION	USAGE	FUNCTION
	Job Configuration	J=name	Names the print job configuration to use for this CAPTURE session. If a default configuration exists and no other is named, the default will set the printing parameters. This also works to specify a print job configuration from outside the current or parent context.
	Keep	K	Forces the NetWare server to keep all captured data, and print that data, if your workstation hangs or disconnects during a print capture. The default is to delete the captured information. This is needed on rare occasions, such as for lengthy print sessions.
	LPT port	L=number or LPTx	The local port to be captured; necessary if not the default of LPT1. You can modify NET.CFG to support up to nine printer ports.
	Name	NAM=text	Name (12 characters or less) for the top of the banner page. User name is the default.
	No AutoEndCap	NA	Stops the print job from being closed and sent to the printer when you exit your application, making it available for more information. An EC must be issued to move this to the printer, if a TI value has not been set.
	No Banner	NB	Suppresses the banner page. See Banner.
	No Form Feed	NFF	Eliminates the form feed at the end of a print job. See FF.
	No Notify	NNOTI	Stops a message from being sent from the print server to the user indicating print success. Not the same as general printer information for the print server operators. Default is NNOTI enabled.
	No Tabs	NT	Default. Specifies tab characters, and all other nontext characters, will be passed to the printer. Same as byte stream setting. Use this all the time unless forced to change.

TABLE 12.6 (cont.)
CAPTURE Command Options

OPTION	USAGE	FUNCTION
Notify	NOTI	Sends the user a message at print job completion.
Printer	P=*name*	Used to specify the printer to send the CAPTURE output to. Same as Q=, but P and Q can't be used together.
Queue	Q=*name*	Used to specify the print queue to send the CAPTURE output to. Same as P=, but P and Q can't be used together.
Server	S=*name*	For bindery queues, to specify the proper NetWare server. Not needed with the NDS print system.
Show	SH	Informational display of CAPTURE settings.
Tabs	T=*number*	Specifies the number of spaces to replace the tab character within print jobs. The range is 1 to 18 characters.
TimeOut	TI=*number*	TI=0 is the default. You can set 0 to 1000 seconds for the print queue to wait after last print data to consider the print job finished and send it to the printer. If printouts are interspersed with each other or disappear, increase this value.
Version	/VER	Captures version information, including support files needed to run this utility.

The most common place to find the CAPTURE command is in a login script. By setting the details for all applications to print across the network before the user even connects to the network, much of the user confusion and hassle is eliminated. With more and more users working inside MS Windows, the command-line CAPTURE utility is giving way to the Printer Connections screen in NetWare User Tools.

Using NPRINT

While CAPTURE is used to support printing from within applications, NPRINT is used to print existing files from the command line. This command is similar to

Configuring Printing from the Command Line with CAPTURE or NPRINT

the DOS PRINT command. It's often used to print a small text file, such as an AUTOEXEC.BAT file, to test a printer.

The syntax for NPRINT differs slightly from CAPTURE, but the two commands share most syntax and options. Unlike CAPTURE, NPRINT commands must reference an existing file name, and that file name must immediately follow NPRINT. The syntax is:

```
NPRINT filename [P=printername | Q=queuename] [/option…]
```

To print the file C:\AUTOEXEC.BAT, the command would likely be:

```
NPRINT C:\AUTOEXEC.BAT P=P1 NB NFF
```

Handier than the DOS PRINT command, NPRINT allows you to specify multiple file names without resorting to wildcards. So if you're looking for information on a particular machine, you can use this command:

```
NPRINT C:\AUTOEXEC.BAT,C:\CONFIG.SYS P=P1 NB NFF
```

Just keep the file names separated by commas and you'll be fine. Table 12.7 shows some sample NPRINT tasks and the syntax used to perform them.

TABLE 12.7 NPRINT Command Syntax

SAMPLE TASK	SYNTAX
NPRINT CHAP1.TXT to network printer P1	NPRINT CHAP1.TXT P=P1
NPRINT CHAP1.TXT to print queue Q1	NPRINT CHAP1.TXT Q=Q1
Print five copies of a file with no banner	NPRINT CHAP1.TXT P=P1 C=5 NB
Hold the print job in the queue	NPRINT CHAP1.TXT Q=Q1 HOLD
List the printing parameters for the job to be printed	NPRINT CHAP1.TXT Q=Q1 D
Use print job configuration Color	NPRINT CHAP1.TXT J=COLOR
View online help	NPRINT /? or NPRINT ?
View all online Help screens	NPRINT /? ALL
View help for the Banner option	NPRINT /? B

These examples should remind you of those for the CAPTURE utility. Most are the same. The NPRINT options are the same as the CAPTURE options, with minor differences.

With NPRINT, you have no options to stop, start, or cancel a CAPTURE session, nor one to print to a file. You already have a file with NPRINT; it may be that same file you spooled to disk with CAPTURE.

The two options new to NPRINT are:

- **Copies (C=*number*)**: Specifies the number of copies to make of the named file. The default is 1; the range is 1 to 65,000.

- **Delete (D)**: Automatically deletes the file after printing is finished. The default is not to delete the file.

Some final NPRINT notes:

- The default is to include a banner page and form feed, just as with CAPTURE. You must override these defaults with each use of NPRINT unless your default print job configuration is used, or you name a print job configuration in the command line.

- Printer definitions can only be referenced with the J=*print job configuration name* option. Use PRINTDEF to define any new print job configurations needed.

- You can now specify the printer name rather than the queue name.

- NPRINT *filename* works with the default print job configuration and printer.

Setting Up Remote Printers

NEW WITH NETWARE 4, the NPRINTER.EXE program replaces RPRINTER.EXE. NPRINTER allows the workstation or server to support printers controlled by print servers running on other servers. Printers defined as Manual Load or Remote need the NPRINTER program loaded for them.

> **NOTE:** With Windows 95 workstations, you use NPTWIN95. See Chapter 8 for details.

As you might expect, this new program runs faster and jumps higher than the old one. Some of the advantages include:

- Gives higher performance—more print data through the workstation to the printer
- Runs under Windows 3.1*x*
- Runs on OS/2 workstations
- Less RAM needed from the workstation
- Loads from an interactive utility or the command line

The NPRINTER.EXE program has improved partly because of the improvements in port-driver technology from Novell. In NetWare 4, the software to run the printer port at the server is now separate from the print server software (PSERVER.NLM and NPRINTER.NLM). When PSERVER loads a printer that specifies Auto Load (Local), the NPRINTER.NLM is loaded at the server automatically. Since the administrator doesn't need to load it specifically, you may have missed this. The NPRINTER.NLM handles just the interface between the print server and the parallel port hardware in the physical file server. The NPRINTER.EXE program works the same way for a workstation.

Loading the NPRINTER menu program on the workstation provides a quick way to check the settings and verify your configuration. The first thing that shows up is a pick list with all the active print servers listed. If the print server that will support this remote printer isn't listed here, you may want to press F4 and look at the world in DS Printer Object Mode. This is a fancy way of saying you can press Insert to browse through the Object, Class screen for the printer.

Either way, the next choice is whether this printer is parallel or serial. Parallel printers provide better performance and easier configuration, but serial printers are also supported. Whichever you choose, you must provide some more details. For a parallel printer, you define the port (LPT1), the interrupt (polled mode without an interrupt is best, and nearly mandatory for PCs running Windows 3.1*x*), and the buffer size in kilobytes. The default buffer is 3 KB, and you can move it up to 60 KB. However, the more buffer space, the more CPU time stolen by the NPRINTER program. If this is a dedicated print server, load up the buffer. If not, don't.

Serial printers need to know the serial port number, the interrupt (or polled mode again), the buffer size, and the baud rate (9600 is the default; the range is 300 to 38,400). Standard serial questions such as stop bits, data bits, and parity follow. If you try to use a higher speed than 9600, make sure your serial port supports the higher speed. If not, your printouts will suffer.

Once you answer these configuration details, you're finished. Press Enter, and the printer is active as a system printer. The amount of RAM stolen with the default settings is about 5500 bytes. This is not bad, and the printer doesn't noticeably drag the system too far down too often.

The batch file method works well, once you verify your settings with the menu-driven program. Here's an example of a statement to load NPRINTER and service a printer named COLOR in the INTEGRATE.GCS container:

```
NPRINTER .COLOR.INTEGRATE.GCS
```

This statement, for safety's sake, gives the entire printer name for the NDS context. You may be able to use just the printer name; try it and see.

NPRINTER has several options, which are listed in Table 12.8.

TABLE 12.8 NPRINTER Command Options

OPTION	FUNCTION
NPRINTER /s	Shows the status of loaded NPRINTERs (up to 7 may be active on one workstation: 3 parallel and 4 serial).
NPRINTER /u	Unloads the last loaded NPRINTER.
NPRINTER /? or /H	Shows the Help screen.
NPRINTER /T=# (1–9)	Changes the timing interval of printer service. Higher number gives priority to other workstation tasks beside NPRINTER.
NPRINTER /b=# (3–60)	Specifies the number of print buffers.
NPRINTER /VER	Shows the version of NPRINTER and files required to support the program.

NPRINTER is a good use for older PCs that can't handle Windows 3.1*x* well. A dedicated PC print server should keep up with a standard eight-page-a-minute laser printer. If you load the NPRINTER program and the support file on the local hard drive, you don't even need to log in to the network; IPX support from the client file startup procedure will be enough. Rather than running the LOGIN program, run NPRINTER instead.

Other Handy User Command-Line Utilities

NOT ALL COMMAND-LINE utilities are due for an early death. Perhaps it's just a sentimental feeling from a long-time NetWare person, but I'm glad that some commands will live forever from the command line.

Why? They're quick, that's why. If you run MS Windows all the time, you can still pop open a DOS box now and then and run a command-line utility faster than you can load the graphical version of the same utility. With the global paths and drive mappings set in MS Windows, you can check any problem with an application with a command-line utility while the application is still asking if you want to retry.

Checking Your Access with RIGHTS

The RIGHTS utility provides the quickest way for a user to check a problem with an application that refuses to run. Many times, you get an error message that mentions you don't have the rights to run a program, but sometimes you get something cryptic that makes little or no sense. Just type

```
RIGHTS
```

from the command line and you may have the answer to your question.

The result of the raw RIGHTS command might be this:

```
ALTOS486\SYS:
Your rights for this directory: [ ]
```

Or it might be something like what you see on the screen in Figure 12.23.

This is nicer than what you get with NetWare User Tools sometimes. If you check a directory where you have no authority, the answer may be "You have NO RIGHTS in this directory." The emphasis on NO RIGHTS just seems a bit cruel, even if true.

Take a quick look at the user's RIGHTS in a directory when that user complains that a program won't work. This is especially important when new applications are installed, and someone may fall through the cracks of authorization.

FIGURE 12.23

Results of the RIGHTS command

```
[Novell DOS] H:\LAPTOP>rights
ALTOS486\SYS:\LAPTOP
Your rights for this directory:  [SRWCEMFA]
    Supervisor rights to directory.         (S)
    Read from a file in a directory.        (R)
    Write to a file in a directory.         (W)
    Create subdirectories and files.        (C)
    Erase directory and files.              (E)
    Modify directory and files.             (M)
    Scan for files and directories.         (F)
    Change access control.                  (A)

[Novell DOS] H:\LAPTOP>
```

Checking File Attributes with FLAG

When a user can't perform an operation, after you use RIGHTS to check for authorization, use FLAG. The results of FLAG *.EXE may be something like what is shown in Figure 12.24.

As you can see from the results of the FLAG command in the LOGIN directory, a user complaining that the CX.EXE program can't be deleted can now be shown why this is so. Read Only files can't be deleted until the file attributes are changed. If user ALEX checks his RIGHTS, he may find he doesn't have the ability to modify files. Without this ability, he can't change the CX.EXE from Read Only to Read Write, which would allow him to delete the file. (Of course, you may ask him why he is trying to do such a thing in the first place.)

FIGURE 12.24

Results of FLAG *.EXE

```
[Novell DOS] H:\LOGIN>flag *.exe

Files          = The name of the files found
Directories    = The name of the directories found
DOS Attr       = The DOS attributes for the specified file
NetWare Attr   = The NetWare attributes for the specified file or directory
Status         = The current status of migration and compression for a file
                 or directory
Owner          = The current owner of the file or directory
Mode           = The search mode set for the current file

Files                DOS Attr NetWare Attr          Status Owner         Mode
--------------------------------------------------------------------------------
LOGIN.EXE            [Ro----] [----ShDi--RiDc----]         .ALTOS486.C...  0
NLIST.EXE            [Ro----] [----ShDi--RiDc----]         .ALTOS486.C...  0
TYPEMSG.EXE          [Ro----] [----ShDi--RiDc----]         .ALTOS486.C...  0
MAP.EXE              [Ro----] [----ShDi--RiDc----]         .ALTOS486.C...  0
CX.EXE               [Ro----] [----ShDi--RiDc----]         .ALTOS486.C...  0

[Novell DOS] H:\LOGIN>
```

In Chapter 9, we spoke of FLAG and how it helps you manage the security of your network. The problems users complain about are not generally in system directories such as this one, but in shared directories and their own home areas. After some applications were loaded, someone (probably you, being efficient) changed the EXE files from Read Write to Read Only. This has done the job it was supposed to: it keeps the files from being deleted by accident. Now, the user has come to you, and he or she must make a strong case for deleting files before you rework the file attributes.

Getting File, Directory, and Volume Information with NDIR

Just as NPRINT is the network version of DOS PRINT, NDIR is the network version of DOS DIR. However, NDIR is much more powerful than its DOS counterpart. NDIR allows you to:

- View all file information (date, size, owner, attributes, and archive).
- View all directory information (date, size, owner, attributes, and archive).
- View volume information.
- Sort the file, directory, or volume information according to creation date, owner, file or directory attributes, and the like.

The NDIR command syntax is:

```
NDIR [path] [/option…] [/? | /VER]
```

The *path* is a path leading to the information you want to view. Include the volume, directory, or file name. Replace */option* with any available option. As usual, the /? option brings up online help, and /VER shows the version number of the utility and the files it uses to execute.

The path must be listed in the format of *directory\filename* using the backslash. The options must use the slash (/). You can use several options, but they must be separated by spaces. Wildcards are allowed as you would expect with a DIR-type command, but so are multiple file names. As with NPRINT, list file names separated by a comma.

Don't be ashamed if you can't memorize the options for NDIR and utilize every trick it offers. Nobody can. Everyone remembers the options they like and looks up the rest. You shouldn't feel embarrassed if your first NDIR command is always the help listing (/?); mine is.

Using FILER for File Management

THE FILER UTILITY runs at a workstation and helps the users manage files and directories. There are no NDS functions in FILER. There are some administrator-type functions involved, however.

Is FILER a better DOS file manager than other file management utilities? No, but it does some of the same functions. All DOS and MS Windows file management utilities will offer easier ways to manipulate files and directories than FILER, but none are guaranteed to handle all the NetWare extended attributes.

Figure 12.25 shows FILER's opening screen. You can see that it is a typical NetWare utility. The utility version is listed, as is the context and current path.

FIGURE 12.25

Finally, the FILER

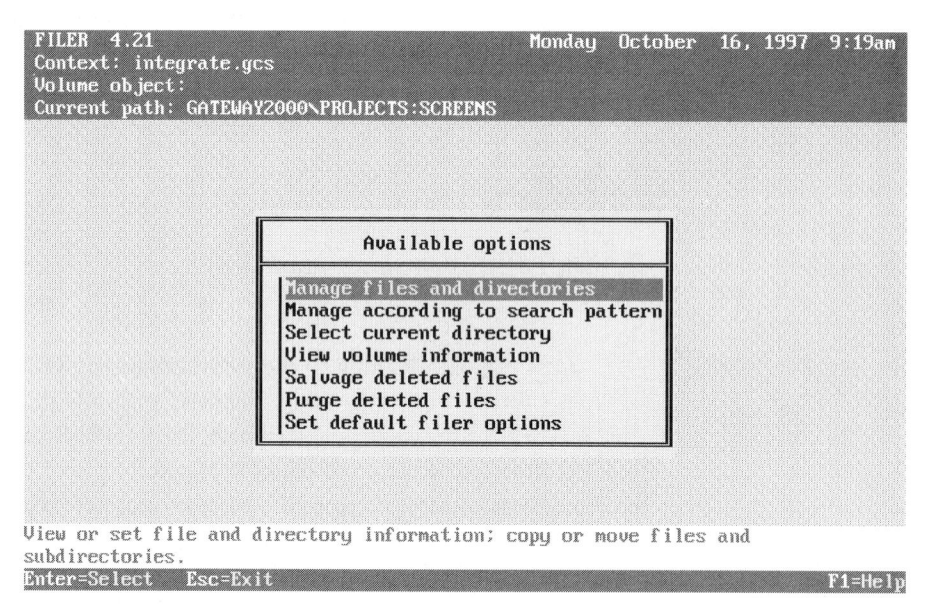

```
FILER 4.21                              Monday  October  16, 1997  9:19am
Context: integrate.gcs
Volume object:
Current path: GATEWAY2000\PROJECTS:SCREENS




                          ┌─────────Available options─────────┐
                          │ Manage files and directories      │
                          │ Manage according to search pattern│
                          │ Select current directory          │
                          │ View volume information           │
                          │ Salvage deleted files             │
                          │ Purge deleted files               │
                          │ Set default filer options         │
                          └───────────────────────────────────┘



View or set file and directory information; copy or move files and
subdirectories.
Enter=Select   Esc=Exit                                         F1=Help
```

The bottom line always shows your optional keystrokes for certain functions. These keys come and go, depending on which screen is up at the time. Table 12.9 shows all the keystrokes you can use in FILER.

Using FILER for File Management

TABLE 12.9 FILER Keystrokes	KEY	FUNCTION
	Enter	Selects for movement up or down the directory tree. Pressing Enter on a subdirectory makes the subdirectory your current directory rather than enabling you to set directory or file attributes.
	Escape	Moves back a screen (not up a directory).
	F10	Selects for taking actions on the selected item. If you want to change directory attributes, highlight the directory and press F10.
	F3	Modifies file or directory names.
	F5	Marks multiple items.
	F6	Marks a pattern (such as *.exe).
	F8	Unmarks a marked pattern.
	Delete	Deletes the highlighted item.
	Insert	Adds a new item.
	F1	Shows the Help screen.

Let's go through all the menus and submenus of FILER and see which features are the most useful.

Managing Files and Directories

The file and directory management section of FILER is a good place to spend most of your time, since the primary reason to use FILER is to deal with files and directories (aren't you glad Novell didn't name this utility DIRECTORYR?). Figure 12.26 shows the results of choosing Manage Files and Directories from the main menu.

Here is the order for all FILER object lists, always in this arrangement:

.. (parent)   Press Enter here to move up a directory level.

\ (root)   Press Enter here to move to the root of the volume.

. (current)   Press Enter or F10 here to view and/or set current directory information.

FIGURE 12.26

Checking out the GroupWise Post Office Directory

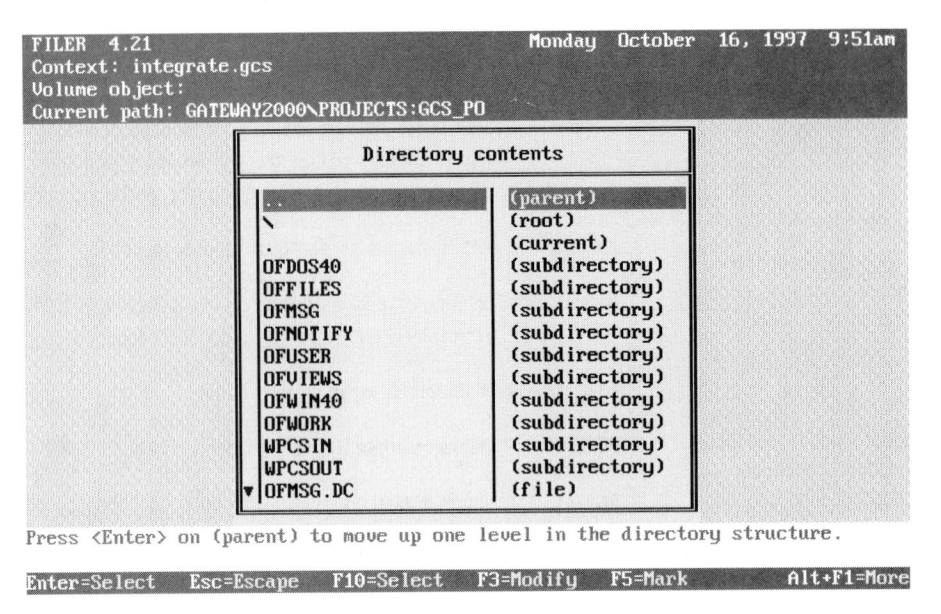

```
FILER  4.21                                Monday  October  16, 1997  9:51am
Context: integrate.gcs
Volume object:
Current path: GATEWAY2000\PROJECTS:GCS_PO

                        ┌─── Directory contents ───┐
                        │ ..          (parent)     │
                        │ \           (root)       │
                        │ .           (current)    │
                        │ OFDOS40     (subdirectory)│
                        │ OFFILES     (subdirectory)│
                        │ OFMSG       (subdirectory)│
                        │ OFNOTIFY    (subdirectory)│
                        │ OFUSER      (subdirectory)│
                        │ OFVIEWS     (subdirectory)│
                        │ OFWIN40     (subdirectory)│
                        │ OFWORK      (subdirectory)│
                        │ WPCSIN      (subdirectory)│
                        │ WPCSOUT     (subdirectory)│
                        │▼OFMSG.DC    (file)        │
                        └──────────────────────────┘
Press <Enter> on (parent) to move up one level in the directory structure.

Enter=Select   Esc=Escape   F10=Select   F3=Modify   F5=Mark        Alt+F1=More
```

| OFDOS40 (subdirectory) | Press Enter here to move into the subdirectory, or F10 to open the Subdirectory Options menu. |
| OFMSG.DC (file) | Press Enter or F10 to open the File Options menu. |

As the list of function keys reminds you, pressing F3 on any subdirectory or file allows you to change the name. If you try this on the current directory or higher, an error message tells you no.

Pressing F10 while highlighting any subdirectory opens the Subdirectory Options menu. The menu choices and the functions they perform are:

- **Copy Subdirectory's Files:** Copy these files to another subdirectory. A text window opens, asking for the destination directory. Pressing Insert opens a browser screen showing all NDS volumes and local drives.

- **Copy Subdirectory's Structure:** Copy the files and all subdirectories to a new subdirectory, duplicating the structure. The browser screen is available, making it easy to choose any NDS volume or local drive.

- **Move Subdirectory's Structure:** Move the contents of the directory, including subdirectories and files. A different browser screen is available, since the system assumes you are moving the structure within the same volume. All other volumes are available.

- **Make This Your Current Directory:** Press Enter to move into the subdirectory, making it your current directory. This is the same as pressing Enter on the directory name without the help of this menu.

- **View/Set Directory Information:** View and or set directory information such as owner name, creation date/time, directory attributes, trustees, and rights.

- **Rights List:** View the type and rights of this directory's trustees.

Deleting a Subdirectory

> **12.18 IN-A-HURRY**
>
> **Delete NetWare Subdirectories with FILER**
>
> 1. From a DOS prompt, type **FILER**.
> 2. Choose Manage Files and Directories (highlight it and press Enter).
> 3. Highlight the subdirectory to delete and press the Delete key.
> 4. Decide if you wish to delete the files only, or the entire subdirectory structure.
> 5. Verify you wish to delete the files, or the entire structure.
> 6. Press Alt+F10 (or Escape several times) to open the Exit? menu, and press Enter to exit.

Deleting a subdirectory from FILER is handy. Unlike DOS, FILER allows you to delete subdirectories that are not empty. If you press Delete on any subdirectory, you get two menus before the system allows you to trash a subdirectory. Figure 12.27 shows the process of deleting a subdirectory and the warning messages you must go through.

Although the MS Windows File Manager program also deletes directories full of files, many DOS versions do not. For a long time, FILER was the only option for dumping multiple directories without painfully going through each directory and deleting the files by hand.

As we'll soon see, FILER includes a salvage feature in case you've deleted the wrong directory. You must have the rights necessary to delete the files and directories, of course. The FILER program doesn't bypass file system rights.

FIGURE 12.27

Double-check before deletion

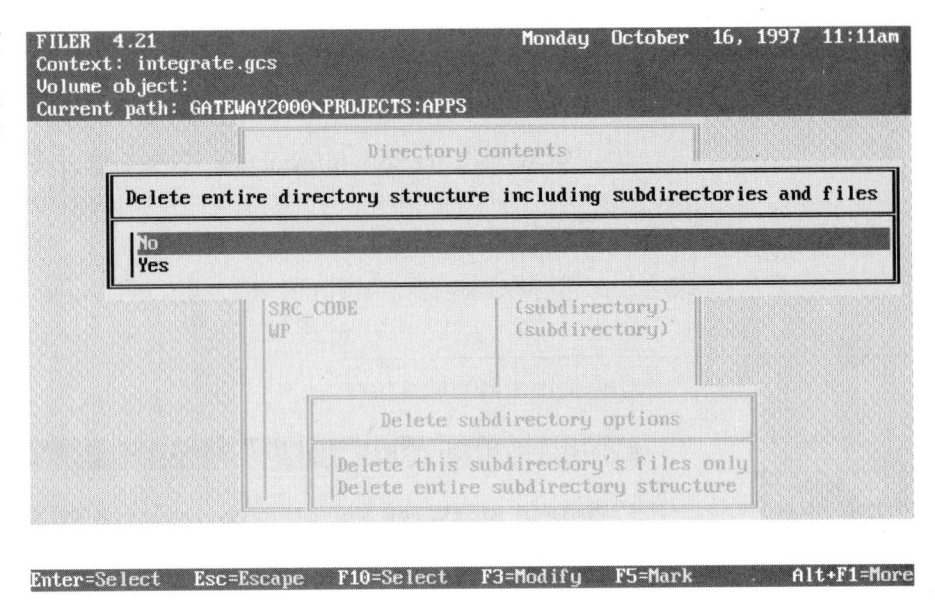

```
FILER 4.21                                    Monday  October  16, 1997  11:11am
Context: integrate.gcs
Volume object:
Current path: GATEWAY2000\PROJECTS:APPS

                           Directory contents
  ┌─────────────────────────────────────────────────────────────────────┐
  │ Delete entire directory structure including subdirectories and files│
  ├─────────────────────────────────────────────────────────────────────┤
  │ No                                                                  │
  │ Yes                                                                 │
  └─────────────────────────────────────────────────────────────────────┘
         SRC_CODE                    (subdirectory)
         WP                          (subdirectory)

                        Delete subdirectory options
                     Delete this subdirectory's files only
                     Delete entire subdirectory structure


Enter=Select    Esc=Escape    F10=Select    F3=Modify    F5=Mark    Alt+F1=More
```

The flip side of this coin is creating a new subdirectory. Not nearly so dramatic, for this function, all you need to do is press Insert. A text box will open, asking for the directory name. A valid DOS name is required.

Refining Search Parameters

Unlike many DOS utilities, FILER has the ability to refine your search parameters, including exclusions. The default pattern is *.*, for including everything. You can use *.exe or A*.* or *. for directories only. When you choose Manage According to Search Pattern from FILER's Available Options menu, all of these options are available:

- Exclude directory patterns
- Include directory patterns
- Exclude file patterns
- Include file patterns
- File search attributes; hidden or system file attributes
- Directory search attributes; hidden or system directory attributes

These settings will stay in place until you change them. The search options are often handy when you are searching through huge volumes of files and directories.

Selecting the Current Directory

FILER's Select Current Directory option is more than just another way to move to a subdirectory. When you press Enter on this menu choice, a Current Directory Path text box opens. When you press Insert, the Volumes browser screen opens, showing you all available volumes on your network. Use this to skip to another entire volume, server, or both.

Viewing Volume Information

12.19 IN-A-HURRY

View NetWare Volume Information with FILER

1. From a DOS prompt, type **FILER**.

2. Choose View Volume Information.

3. Choose Statistics to see total size, space remaining, and compression information.

4. Choose Features to see volume type, block size, name spaces, and installed features.

5. Choose Dates and Times to see creation dates and times, owner, last modified time, and last archived time.

6. Press Alt+F10 (or Escape several times) to open the Exit? menu, and press Enter to exit.

One of my favorite old NetWare utilities was VOLINFO. This volume information command-line utility opened a comparison screen showing server volume total space and available space in kilobytes. Unfortunately, VOLINFO is one of the many utilities that have been replaced.

A consolation for this loss is the View Volume Information menu option in FILER. As you can see in Figure 12.28, more than just a few details about your current volume are available.

FIGURE 12.28

Volume stats for GATEWAY2000 _PROJECTS

```
FILER 4.21                                    Monday  October  16, 1997  11:48am
Context: integrate.gcs
Volume object:
Current path: GATEWAY2000\PROJECTS:GCS_PO
```

Volume statistics		
Total space in KB(1024 bytes):	354,304	100.00%
Active space used:	124,128	35.03%
Deleted space not yet purgeable:	0	0.00%
Space remaining on volume:	230,176	64.97%
Maximum directory entries:	19,968	
Directory entries available:	7,800	39.06%
Space used if not compressed:	489,438	
Total space compressed:	145,488	
Space saved by compressing data:	343,950	70.27%
Uncompressed space used:	-21,360	

`Esc=Escape`   `F1=Help`

> **NOTE**
>
> *The FILER display far surpasses the information from VOLINFO, but I still miss the old utility. When I force change, change is good. When change is forced on me, I grump. Can you honestly tell me you don't do the same?*

Novell should run this screen as an advertisement for file compression. Take a look at these totals: nearly 344 MB of disk space saved by compression in a 354 MB volume. This is better than 50 percent file compression.

Of course, I should admit that this volume holds the copy of the NetWare CD-ROM disk. The files there haven't been used, so they've been packed well over time. But it's still impressive, don't you think? Show this to your boss as a reason for NetWare 4.1*x*.

Salvaging Deleted Files

Another command-line utility from earlier NetWare versions that bit the dust is SALVAGE. Similar to DOS salvage programs, the SALVAGE utility found and resurrected files and directories. Now this capability is incorporated into FILER.

> ### 12.20 IN-A-HURRY
>
> **Salvage Files with FILER**
>
> **1.** From a DOS prompt, type **FILER**.
>
> **2.** Choose Salvage Deleted Files.
>
> **3.** Choose View/Recover Deleted Files to recover files from any directory.
>
> **4.** Choose Salvage From Deleted Directories to recover files from a deleted directory.
>
> **5.** Choose Set Salvage Options to see the sort order of salvageable files.
>
> **6.** Press Alt+F10 (or Escape several times) to open the Exit? menu, and press Enter to exit.

When a NetWare user, or the NetWare system, deletes a file or directory, the file is not gone. It's merely marked as deleted. As long as space is available, these files are not overwritten by new files. If the file hasn't been overwritten (and the deleted files have not been purged), that file is salvageable.

If you don't want it to be possible for deleted files to be salvaged, you can use a SET command to have them purged immediately (Immediate Purge of Deleted Files). See Appendix C for a list of SET commands.

Figure 12.29 shows the salvage screen for the GroupWise directory. Since I installed the utility, my name is listed as owner for all these files. If you look where the highlight bar is, you can see the start of the salvageable file display. Pressing Enter on any directory will move you into that directory and repeat the display for salvageable files there.

The salvage sort options include:

- Sort list by file name
- Sort list by file size
- Sort list by deletion date
- Sort list by the person who deleted the file

FIGURE 12.29

Resurrecting files

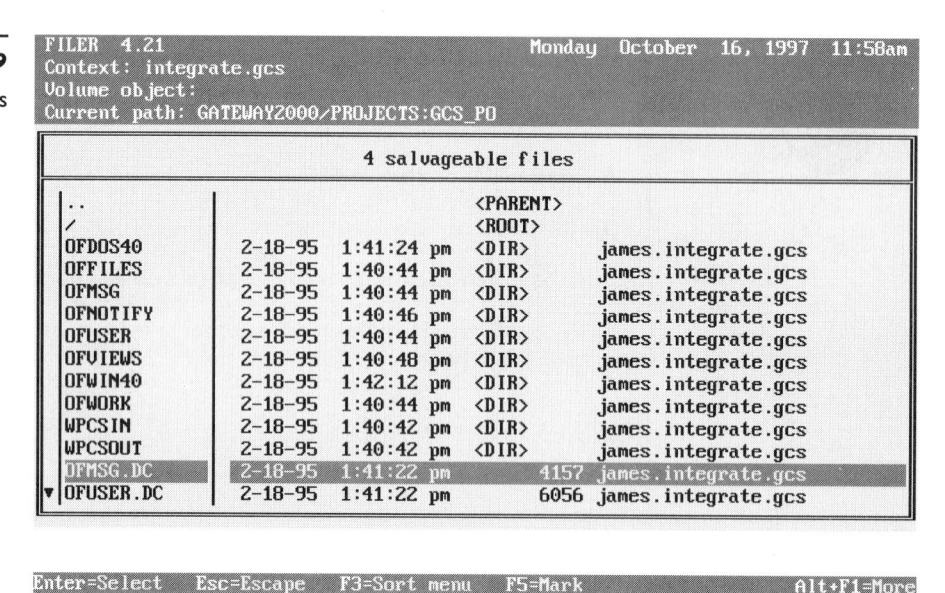

```
FILER 4.21                                    Monday October 16, 1997 11:58am
Context: integrate.gcs
Volume object:
Current path: GATEWAY2000/PROJECTS:GCS_PO

                        4 salvageable files
  ..                              <PARENT>
  /                               <ROOT>
  OFDOS40      2-18-95  1:41:24 pm  <DIR>     james.integrate.gcs
  OFFILES      2-18-95  1:40:44 pm  <DIR>     james.integrate.gcs
  OFMSG        2-18-95  1:40:44 pm  <DIR>     james.integrate.gcs
  OFNOTIFY     2-18-95  1:40:46 pm  <DIR>     james.integrate.gcs
  OFUSER       2-18-95  1:40:44 pm  <DIR>     james.integrate.gcs
  OFVIEWS      2-18-95  1:40:48 pm  <DIR>     james.integrate.gcs
  OFWIN40      2-18-95  1:42:12 pm  <DIR>     james.integrate.gcs
  OFWORK       2-18-95  1:40:44 pm  <DIR>     james.integrate.gcs
  WPCSIN       2-18-95  1:40:42 pm  <DIR>     james.integrate.gcs
  WPCSOUT      2-18-95  1:40:42 pm  <DIR>     james.integrate.gcs
  OFMSG.DC     2-18-95  1:41:22 pm           4157  james.integrate.gcs
▼ OFUSER.DC    2-18-95  1:41:22 pm           6056  james.integrate.gcs

Enter=Select   Esc=Escape   F3=Sort menu   F5=Mark              Alt+F1=More
```

Purging Deleted Files

If resurrecting files bothers you, you can slam that coffin door shut. Like the PURGE command-line utility, FILER's Purge Deleted Files menu option deletes all the deleted but not forgotten files.

You have just a few choices here. First, you can purge files based on a wildcard setting, such as *.exe and the like. You also have a choice to purge only the current directory, or all subdirectories as well. Running this from the command line works the same way. Starting at the root of a volume will purge all files for all subdirectories.

Setting Default FILER Options

Operational choices, such as confirmation before deleting files, are set with FILER's Set Default Filer Options menu choice. There are eight Yes/No questions to answer. Let's go down the list and the default settings:

- **Confirm deletions:** No. Forces the confirmation of each file to be deleted with FILER. If you have multiple files selected or are deleting a directory, this confirmation process is painful.

- **Confirm file copies:** No. Confirms once for all copies.

- **Confirm file overwrites:** Yes. Requires a choice for every file copy that overwrites a file of the same name.

- **Preserve file attributes:** Yes. Keeps extended attributes, such as for OS/2 files, during the copy process.

- **Notify if name space information is lost:** No. If the extended attribute can't be kept, and the attributes are set to NORMAL, no warning is issued.

- **Copy files sparse:** No. Does not keep extended file attributes when you copy files from an OS/2 system.

- **Copy files compressed:** No. When compressed files are copied, uncompresses them before saving them to their destination.

- **Force files to be copied compressed:** No. If Yes, forces files to stay in compressed mode, even if they are being moved to a media that doesn't support compression.

Finding Help

> *No, you appear stupid when you ignore help while struggling with a problem.*

HELP IS ALWAYS important in life. Sometimes you need help when you least expect it.

NetWare is complex and powerful. This means your users (and you) will need help on a regular basis. Does it make you appear stupid when you ask for help? No, you appear stupid when you ignore help while struggling with a problem.

Novell has several avenues of help available. The NetWire Forum on CompuServe (GO NETWIRE) has been running for years, and there are many forum areas with messages, questions, and answers. Many Novell technical support people answer the questions on NetWire, sometimes officially and sometimes not.

Those with Internet access will find the same Novell-supplied information, plus a bit more, on Novell's WWW (World Wide Web) Server. The URL (Uniform Resource Locater) is http://www.novell.com from any Web browser. There is Lynx support for those Unix systems without a graphical interface.

Chapter 12 • Teaching Your Clients to Use the Network

FTP (File Transfer Protocol) is supported from the same server as the Web server, with a mirror site in Germany. Try ftp.novell.com or ftp.novell.de for a list of files and information available for downloading. When using anonymous FTP, make sure you give anonymous as the user name, and your entire Internet address (for example, jgaskin@onramp.net) as your password.

Comp.sys.novell is a non-moderated newsgroup on the Internet. The traffic is heavy (100+ messages a day) and comes from all over the world. Since there's no moderator or sub-newsgroups, everything is currently piled into one big heap. You may be assured, however, that the messages you will see come from some of the most technically savvy folks in PC networking.

Getting Command-Line Help

Of course, long-distance, detailed help is often less important than immediate help. That's why NetWare has provided a Help screen for every command-line utility and the complete set of manuals on disk.

You just need to type the command name with a question mark to receive a page or more of help information. For example, Figure 12.30 shows the result of typing MAP /?.

FIGURE 12.30
Specific help quickly

```
MAP                           General Help                          4.12

Purpose: To assign a drive to a directory path.
Syntax:  MAP [option | /VER] [search:=[drive:=]] | [drive:=] [path] [/W]

To:                                                     Use:
  Insert a search drive.                                  INS
  Delete a drive mapping.                                 DEL
  Map the next available drive.                           N
  Make the drive a root directory.                        R
  Map a drive to a physical volume on a server.           P
  Change a regular drive to a search drive                C
  or a search drive to a regular drive.
  Display version information                             /VER
  Do not change master environment.                       /W

For example, to:                                        Type:
  Map the next available drive                            MAP N FS1/SYS:LOGIN
  to the login directory on server FS1
  Map drive W: as a search drive                          MAP S16:=W:=APPS:WP
  to the WP directory

[Novell DOS] F:\>
```

Some Help screens go on for multiple pages (NLIST and NDIR, for example), but many are just one screen. All utilities have help available in this manner.

The NetWare programs such as FILER and PCONSOLE have context-sensitive help available within the program. The traditional F1 key opens the Help screen everywhere in all NetWare utility programs.

Using the DynaText Electronic Manuals

Remember the problems I listed with paper as a technology exchange medium back in Chapter 8? Novell has taken these comments to heart (okay, they did this independently of me) and now releases all documentation electronically with NetWare 4.1x.

Manuals are fine, but they are difficult to share. If a person borrows your manual, you can't use that same manual unless you're looking over that person's shoulder—not too practical. Ever take a manual home, then forget to bring it back? Ever lose a manual? Ever go through six manuals trying to find the notes you made on one page? These problems are eliminated with the DynaText manuals provided with your NetWare operating system.

One of the paper manuals provided in your NetWare box is *Installing and Using Novell Online Documentation*, with 54 interesting pages. Instructions are included to run the documentation from:

- A workstation hard disk
- A server hard disk
- A workstation CD-ROM drive
- A NetWare server CD-ROM drive set up as a NetWare volume

You can run several of these systems at one time. Setting up the documentation on a stand-alone workstation is recommended if this is your first NetWare 4.1x installation. This gives you a chance to read the manuals before you start your installation.

Since we covered installing the documentation to a server volume using the INSTALL program in Chapter 3, let's concentrate on putting the manuals on a local system. The examples used here involve Windows 3.1x workstations. Instructions for Macintosh and UnixWare users are in the red manual (titled *Installing and Using Novell Online Documentation*). Instructions for Windows 95 workstations are in the section titled "DynaText and Windows 95," coming up in a bit.

Installing the Documentation to a Hard Disk

Take the CD-ROM disk labeled as the 4.1*x* Online Documentation and place it in an installed CD-ROM drive. If you have NetWare 4.10, you will then find the label on the directory for the CD-ROM disk is really NW410DOC_A instead of NW410DOC as the manual says (in NetWare 4.11, it's labeled correctly as NW411DOC). That's no problem here, but it will be if you're reading this before you install your server. If you later make the CD-ROM documentation disk its own volume, this name change is important.

Set your language using the command:

```
SET NWLANGUAGE=ENGLISH (or FRANCAIS, ITALIANO, DEUTSCH,
    ESPANOL)
```

Do not place a space between NWLANGUAGE, the equal sign, and your chosen language. This should be in the workstation's AUTOEXEC.BAT file already if you installed the client files.

You will need about 60 MB for the documentation files themselves, and another 6 MB for the viewer files. If you wish to install only the viewers locally and put the books themselves on a file server, replace the destination disk drive letter. The command to copy the documentation to a hard disk is:

```
XCOPY D:\DOC\ENGLISH\*.* C:\DOC\ENGLISH /S
```

There are two assumptions at work here. First, that your CD-ROM drive is labeled drive D:, but that's a fairly safe bet. Second, that English is your language of choice. Replace ENGLISH with another language if desired.

If you are installing these files to a server volume, you may wish to use the NCOPY command rather than DOS XCOPY. This method works only with the CD-ROM, because the electronic books are stored in a compressed format on the floppy disks. In that case, you must use the INSTALL procedure from the server.

You may also install documention as an extra product using the INSTALL program from the console screen. Personally, I prefer to use XCOPY because it seems faster (even though it probably isn't), and I hate to complicate installations by adding everything in the world to the server right off the bat.

Installing and Configuring the DynaText Viewer for Windows 3.1*x*

No matter where you have the electronic books themselves, you can run the DynaText viewer from your local hard disk or from the network volume where the manuals are installed. This is necessary if you are reading the manuals from the CD-ROM disk in your local CD-ROM drive. This enables you to read the documentation if the server, or your connection to the server, is impaired.

There are two copy operations that are necessary. Again, we're listing drive D: as the CD-ROM drive and drive C: as the local hard drive.

```
XCOPY D:\DOCVIEW\DTAPPWIN\*.* C:\DOCVIEW\DTAPPWIN /S
XCOPY D:\DOCVIEW\DTDATWIN\*.* C:\DOCVIEW\DTDATWIN /S
```

The total space taken with these operations is just under 6 MB. These viewer files are now configurable on your system, and the executable files are on your local hard disk. Now to configure things, open Windows 3.1*x*, choose File, then Run from the Program Manager main menu. Browse and select:

```
\DOCVIEW\DTAPPWIN\DTEXTRW.EXE
```

List \DOCVIEW\DTAPPWIN as the working directory. Pick an icon from the list available after clicking on the Change Icon button.

Next, move this file to your \WINDOWS subdirectory:

```
\DOCVIEW\DTAPPWIN\DYNATEXT.INI
```

Finally, using a text editor, finish the COLLECTION line in DYNATEXT.INI with:

```
D:\DOC\$NWLANGUAGE\NW41=NetWare 4.1 Manuals
```

Close Windows and reboot to make sure the SET command was issued properly and that the paths to your newly installed files are in the right places.

The first operation above, making a new item for your Windows 3.1*x* Desktop, must be done for each user who needs access to the electronic documentation. Reference the copy of the program on the server disk, and you won't need to copy any files to each workstation.

You don't need to specify a drive letter for this; the UNC (Universal Naming Convention) works fine. My path listing for this is:

```
\\ALTOS486\SYS\DOCVIEW\DTAPPWIN\DTEXTRW.EXE
```

This works well for supporting a large group of users that all have different desktop configurations.

Reading the Manuals from a Local CD-ROM Drive

It's possible to list both the local and server-based manual collections. This allows you to read the server-based manuals to keep that slight speed edge, while having a local source in case you can't reach the server. The trick here is in the COLLECTION line in DYNATEXT.INI.

The line where you list your collections is a bit like a PATH statement. You can have more than one collection listed, like your PATH may reference several directories. The syntax is even the same: at the end of one collection detail, put a semicolon and keep going.

Check Figure 12.31, and notice I have two sets of NetWare 4.1 electronic manuals available. One is on my local CD-ROM drive, and the other is on the server ALTOS486. In the upper-left corner of the main screen, you can see the two collections. The highlighted version is on the server; the other is in my local CD-ROM drive. They are the same, but I've named them differently so I can tell them apart.

FIGURE 12.31

The online manual to install the online manuals

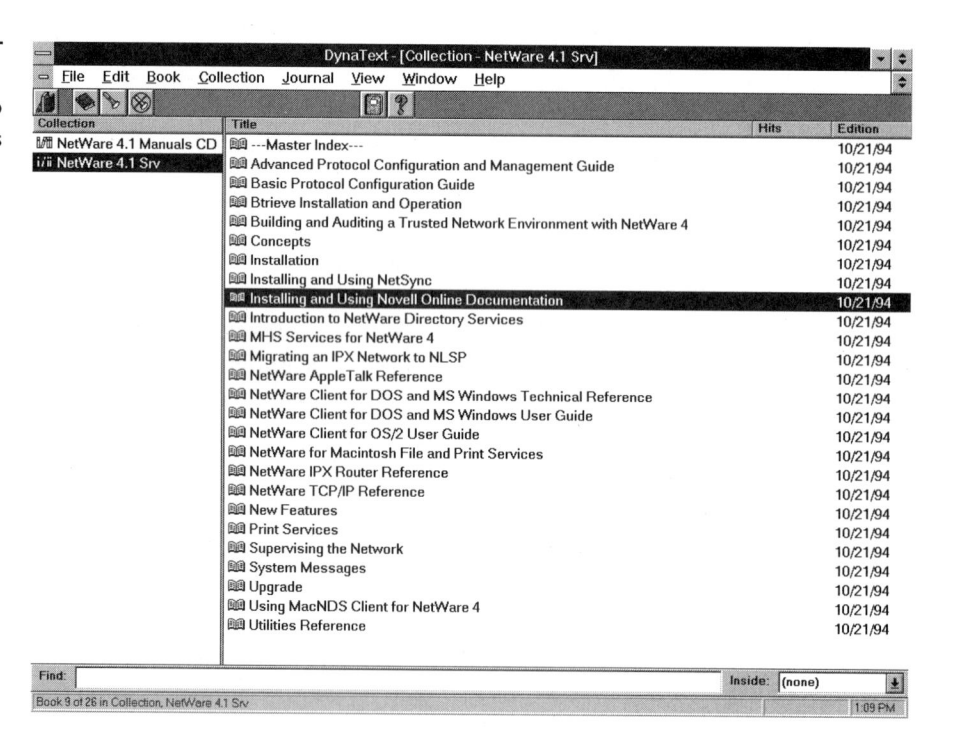

Performance from the local CD-ROM isn't too bad actually. I expected it to be 25 percent worse, but a long scrolling operation within one of the manuals took 90 seconds from the server, and only 95 seconds from the local CD-ROM. I believe the network version loads faster, so I prefer that version.

This lets you keep the ability to read your manuals without the network server whenever you have the CD-ROM disk loaded. If you want to have something else in your CD-ROM drive, you'll have the manuals from the server to read. If the disk is not in the CD-ROM drive when you start the program, nothing shows. The program assumes your path is wrong, since the manuals aren't where you said they would be. No harm done.

Using and Searching the Manuals

Figure 12.31 shows the opening screen of the manuals. You can open any book by double-clicking or highlighting the book and clicking on the book icon beside the flashlight. Yes, it's a graphical viewpoint, with screenshots and diagrams represented in DynaText just as in your paper manuals.

The powerbar across the top may be moved down the sides or to the bottom. The icons work as follows:

- The stack of books represents collections.
- The single book opens the highlighted volume.
- The flashlight starts a search.
- The canceled flashlight cancels a search.

Figure 12.32 shows a volume open. The volume chapters are listed down the left side. Each chapter with a little plus sign in the box has chapter headings to view within the chapter. Click on the plus box, as I did on Chapter 3, and the chapter headings appear. Click on any line on the left side, and the text will quickly appear on the right side.

In the right window, you see the text just as you see it in the manuals, with two improvements. First, you can reduce the text to see more at one time. Second, when you click on an underlined topic, as shown in the topic box, you are quickly whisked to that page.

Little camera icons denote graphics. Double-click on one of these to open a graphic, which can be scaled and printed. The other icon you'll see is a small table, which presents a table, surprisingly enough. These tables can also be printed.

FIGURE 12.32

Reading a DynaText chapter in Windows 3.1

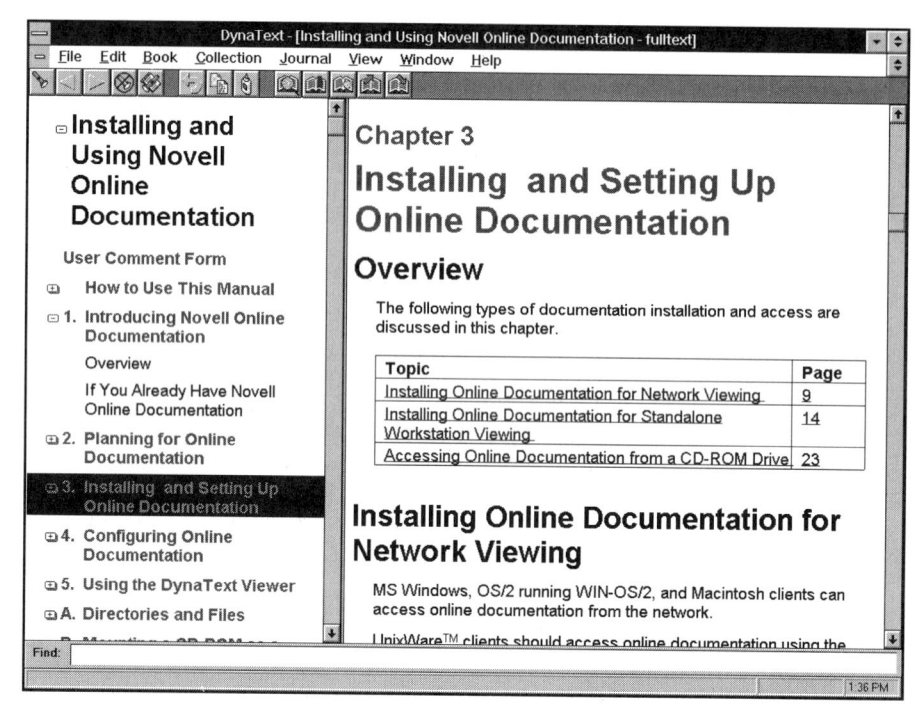

The bottom-left corner shows Find and a long text box. The system performs a wide range of searches, counting and highlighting the occurrence of each bit of found text. When you are in one book, the search is restricted to that book. From the opening screen (Figure 12.31), your search will cover every word of the documentation.

DynaText and Windows 95

What's the future of DynaText now that HTML (Hypertext Markup Language), a subset of SGML (Standard Generalized Markup Language, used by DynaText), is so popular? In other words, will Web clients be used as the documentation viewer instead of the special DynaText program?

Probably, but not until NetWare 4.2 or so. Since HTML is a subset of SGML, everything in the documentation would need to be redone, which will take quite a bit of time. There's a small chance Web browsers will offer SGML viewers sometime, especially with the feature-race underway between Netscape and Microsoft, but I don't think that will answer our documentation problems. Just realize that now that DynaText is finally working correctly, with a special configuration program and simple maintenance, it's time to replace the program. Such is the way of the computer world.

Figure 12.33 shows the same page as Figure 12.32, but the viewer is running in Windows 95, and the documentation has been upgraded slightly. The upgrade didn't include instructions for Windows 95 installation, so I'll take care of that little detail in the next section.

FIGURE 12.33

Reading a DynaText chapter with Windows 95

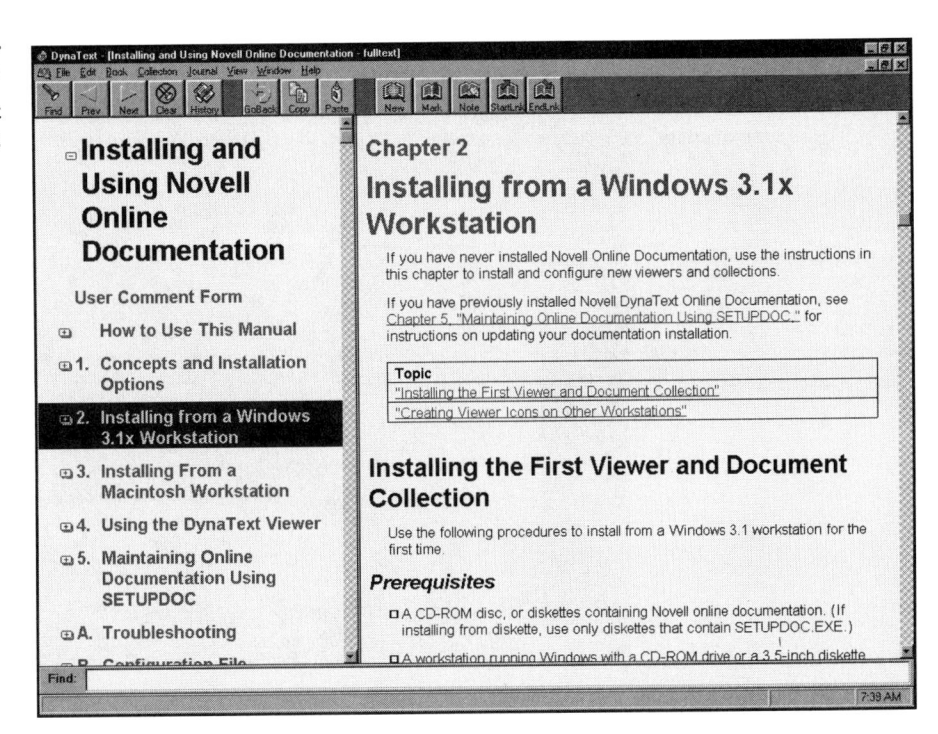

Running the SETUPDOC Program

As the instructions in Figure 12.33 describe, the SETUPDOC program is the key to installing DynaText, configuring the viewers, and upgrading existing online documentation. Everything springs from the one program, which is more convenient than in prior versions.

Run the SETUPDOC program directly from the CD-ROM, or, heaven forbid, from the diskettes. I'm somewhat surprised diskettes are still an option for installing NetWare 4.11, but I certainly hope you aren't cursed by such an installation.

Figure 12.34 shows the opening screen of SETUPDOC, with the distracting background from Novell (which, unfortunately, I can't delete). The shot is taken from Windows 95, but the variance between the view of Windows 3.1 and Windows 95 documentation is amazingly small.

FIGURE 12.34

A much needed DynaText control utility

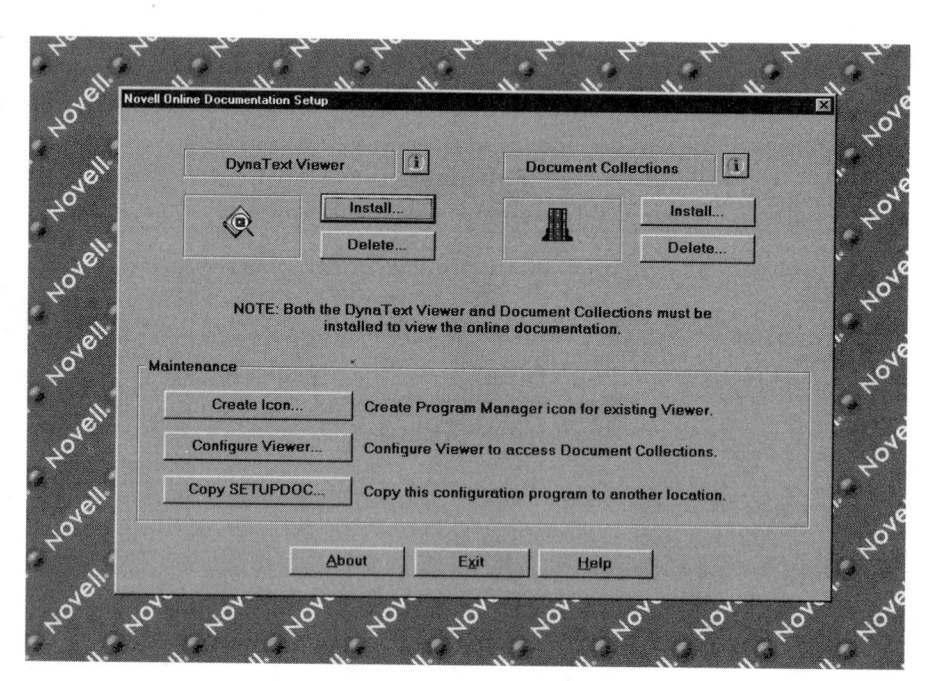

Your initial installation will consist of clicking on the Document Collections to install, waiting for the more than 60 MB of files to be copied, and then installing the viewer. Each step in the process allows full control over each chapter in each DynaText book.

Some products from Novell developed specifically for NetWare 4.11 will install the documentation files automatically. The viewer must always be installed directly on the workstation, however, so the workstation can receive a configuration file or two to manage the icon and rights to the documentation.

The viewer program itself stays with the rest of the documentation, but various workstation configuration files are changed in important (and we hope accurate) ways to facilitate viewing.

There are options to configure different groups with varying access levels to the documentation, but that seems like a lot of extra work for little advantage to me. I can't understand why you would want to limit access to documentation. Is users taking time to learn about the network a bad thing? Grant everyone access to all documentation and be done with it.

The option to install the documentation and viewer on individual workstations still exists. If you are reading this chapter before installing NetWare for your company, it will help you to place the documentation on your own station. Not only can you read the official (but dry and much more boring than this) documentation before getting started, but you'll also have a way to view the troubleshooting information when your server is down.

Windows 95 Network User Support in NetWare 4.11

WINDOWS 95 CHANGES the rules for your NetWare connection in many ways. We've talked about a few of those ways already, and we'll talk about more later. This section will focus on the ways that Windows 95 built-in client network utilities have eliminated the need for NetWare User Tools (at least in the minds of some Novell vice president).

TIP

I can't begin to explain Windows 95 fully in this section, nor would I want to attempt such a feat. Instead, I'll refer you to The Expert Guide to Windows 95 *by Mark Minasi (published by Sybex). There is no shortage of Windows 95 books on the shelves, but I'm assuming you're past the initial learning curve and need some detailed, behind-the-scenes information. Minasi provides that in his book.*

Do not make the mistake of enabling Windows 95's NetWare emulation software. Microsoft, ever eager to bust Novell's chops, now emulates (but didn't license) the NCP codes necessary to look like a NetWare 3.1x server.

Microsoft engineers, at least with the early versions of Windows 95, didn't do a good enough job, and much corporate confusion resulted.

This section of the book is strictly about using Windows 95 workstations as network clients. When we talked about printing, I mentioned sharing Windows 95-controlled printers as a replacement for NPRINTER, but that's as much Windows 95 networking as I like to use. Any more will only cause problems; peer-to-peer networks require different management procedures and user training than do server-centric networks such as NetWare.

The good news is that Windows 95 is a much better network client than Windows 3.1. Features many network managers have prayed for are included. You'll find concurrent multiple protocol support, graphical interfaces for the network protocol configuration screens, and enough multitasking support to make life almost bearable as a network client. Windows 95 isn't the ultimate desktop client, but it's better than what we've had since NetWare started.

Several functions we discussed earlier with NetWare User Tools are worth examining quickly with a Windows 95 client. Let's start with the age-old search for identity.

> The good news is that Windows 95 is a much better network client than Windows 3.1.

WhoAmI and NetWare Information

12.21 IN-A-HURRY

Use Network Neighborhood in Windows 95

1. Double-click on the Network Neighborhood icon.

2. Right-click on one of the servers or the NDS tree icon.

3. Click on WhoAmI, Logout, Authenticate, Login to Server (or NDS Tree, if you clicked on the tree icon), or Send Message.

Combining the command-line program WHOAMI and the NetWare information provided by NetWare User Tools, Windows 95 and Client32 covers almost the same amount of information. As with many upgrades, progress brings advantage and disadvantages.

Compare Figure 12.35 with the earlier Figure 12.11. Figure 12.35, running under Windows 95, requires the use of Network Neighborhood to see the information previously provided by a NetWare utility.

FIGURE 12.35

User Tools information via Network Neighborhood

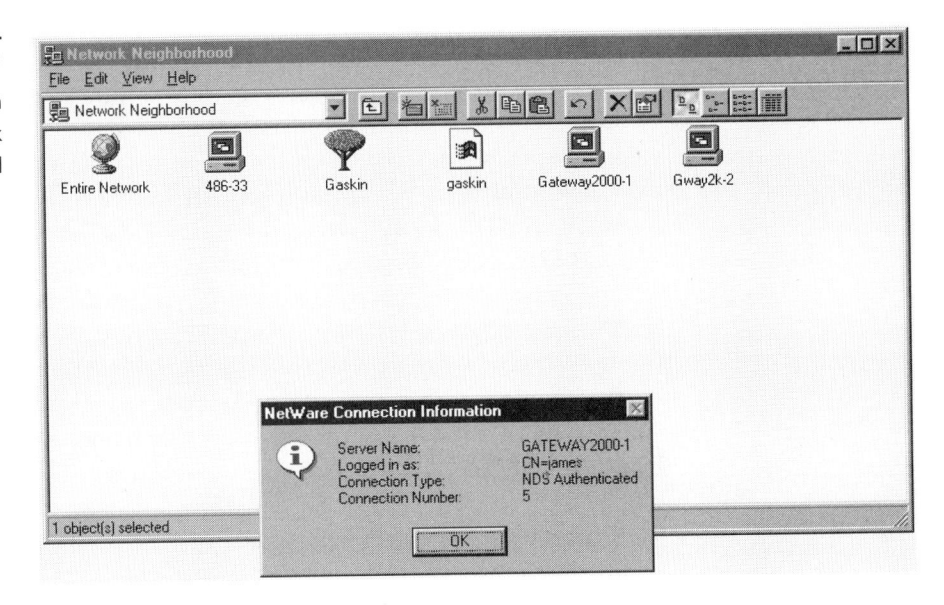

You reach this point by double-clicking on the Network Neighborhood icon on the Desktop. Once the Network Neighborhood application is open, highlight one of the servers or the NDS tree icon with a right mouse click. The drop-down menu includes WhoAmI, Logout, Authenticate, Login to Server (or Login to NDS Tree, if you clicked on the tree icon), and Send Message. Figure 12.35 is the result of clicking on the WhoAmI menu option.

> **NOTE**
>
> *Why Microsoft believes a messy computer desktop to mirror my messy physical desktop is an improvement, I'll never know. I wanted my computer to help me get organized, and I found out it's just as sloppy about leaving things laying around as I am. Looks like I paid thousands of dollars to become virtually messy, when I can be physically messy for free. Oh well, such is progress.*

While you receive the important information about your user name and primary server from Network Neighborhood, you don't get quite as much detail as you did from NetWare User Tools back in Figure 12.11. I did learn that I was NDS authenticated and connection number 5. The connection information doesn't do a user much good, but this is an easy way for you, the network administrator, to discover a user's connection number if you must clear a hung connection (assuming that the Windows 95 workstation isn't the one causing the hung connection, of course).

Sending Messages within Network Neighborhood

Since Windows 95 offers rudimentary peer-to-peer network functions, you would expect that users have the ability to send messages to other workstations. Offered as a DOS command-line option since the beginning of NetWare, SEND is reincarnated once again under Client32.

Hiding within the same menu structure as WhoAmI is the Send Message option. Figure 12.36 shows this feature under Windows 95, with the new logo and all.

After sending this message to one of the available, logged-in network clients, a results screen appears on the sender's workstation. The screen, lacking in graphical interest, shows the target user name, the connection number, and

FIGURE 12.36

Modern communications

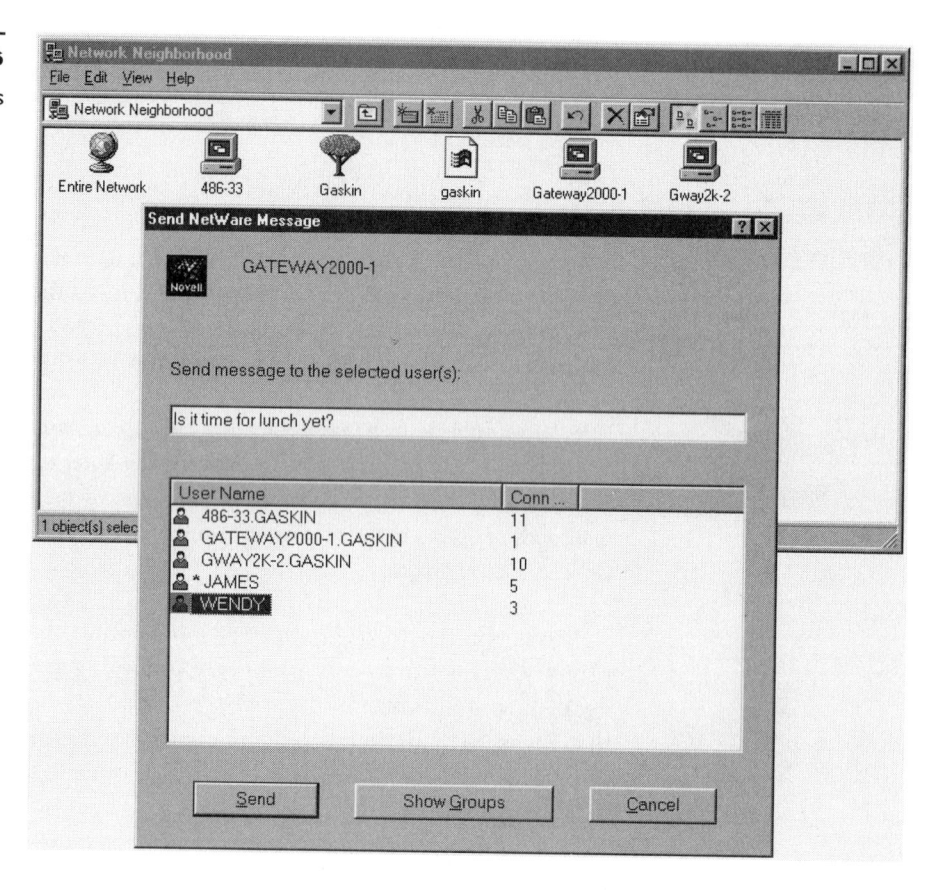

the status of the message. Status is a bit high-falutin' for a column heading, since the message is either "Sent" or "Not Sent," depending on whether the person has elected to block incoming messages.

Is this a valuable network feature? I suppose that if you were too lazy to pick up the phone and dial the interoffice number but energetic enough to open Network Neighborhood, type the message, find the person, and click on the Send command button, this would be helpful. Of course, the phone gives you the option of leaving a voice-mail message. At least the NetWare 4 operating system started queuing the SEND messages, rather than dropping them into the bit bucket if the person already had one message sitting uncleared on the screen or enabled the CASTOFF command to reject messages. If you're too young too understand what a "bit bucket" is, ask someone with a few wrinkles, but ask respectfully.

Messages on the receiver screen must be manually cleared. If your message target is calculating some huge spreadsheet or reformatting a database when the message arrives, he or she will need to stop working and clear the message before continuing. You can only hope that your message is more important than the work it interrupted.

Logging in from Network Neighborhood

On the surface, the ability to log in from within Network Neighborhood doesn't make any sense. If you don't activate all the network connections when you start Windows 95, how will Network Neighborhood know about your network?

Be that as it may, there are reasons to log in after Windows 95 is up and running. You may have a special login script set up on a particular server, such as for a "backup" user defined to operate the tape backup system for the network. You may have needed to close a DOS box because some program blew up, and now you want to reestablish your original network configuration. You may want to log in as a different person entirely to test some portion of the network configuration.

No matter what the reason, it's possible to log in from within Windows 95. Actually, the best way to do this is to open the Start menu, go to the Novell Client32 menu option, and run the official NetWare Login program used during the Windows 95 boot process. Why? Because the Network Neighborhood is designed for Windows NT Server networks, and it doesn't always give the proper network names.

Figure 12.37 shows the regular Novell NetWare Login dialog box, the same one you see at the beginning of the Windows 95 boot process. The login process will proceed the same from here as it does during the initial Windows 95 boot sequence. Universal drive mappings will replace the existing mappings unless you specifically instruct the program otherwise.

FIGURE 12.37

Login here if you wish

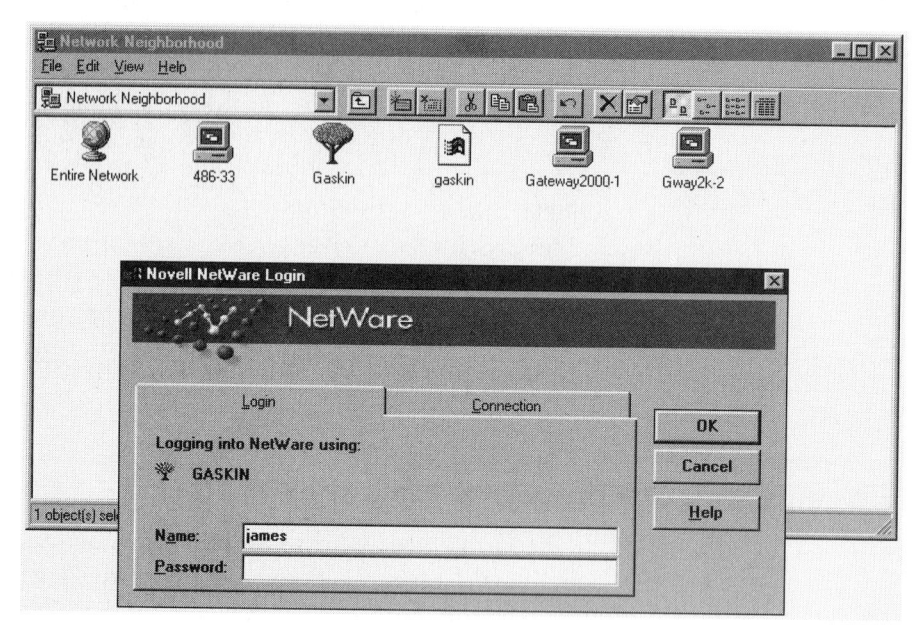

> **NOTE**
>
> Want to see how devious Microsoft can be? Take a look at the upper-left corner of the dialog box, right before the word "Novell." See the little Microsoft flag? That's hard-coded into the dialog box, and OEMs such as Novell are powerless to change it. No matter how much OEMs modify the code they're given, they can't get rid of the Microsoft flag flying right before the OEM's product name. How curious.

Mapping Drives from Windows 95

Here's where we find the mysteries of Windows 95 clash with the complexities of NetWare 4.1x, which can cause a real problem: how to get rid of old NDS items that have wormed their way into the fabric of Windows 95. In particular, several servers that have been renamed, or have not been part of the network for quite some time, still exist in the fevered imagination of Windows 95 Network Neighborhood, at least when you try to map a new network drive.

Officially, the little drive icon on the status bar, second to the right of the display box showing "Network Neighborhood," will allow you to map drives. This is the equivalent (supposedly) of the NetWare User Tools function shown back in Figure 12.4. Not only do we not have the ease of drag-and-drop operation so joyfully employed in NetWare User Tools, but now we don't even have the correct server list to view. That's right, we have wrong servers on display. Yes, the Refresh option on the View menu has been employed, several times. The workstation was rebooted. The user was logged in to each different server shown in the main Network Neighborhood box. The results, however, were always what you see in Figure 12.38, and were always wrong.

FIGURE 12.38

Map drives, but be careful of ghost servers

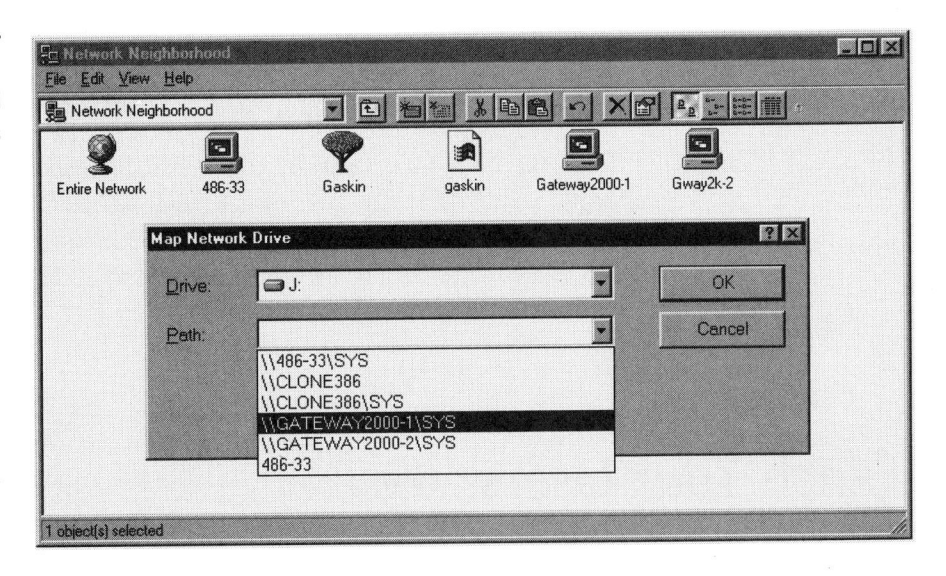

Clone386 was used for the first iteration of this book, and while it still technically works, the idea of upgrading a 386/33 with only 8 MB of RAM gives me the willies. I guess I'm just getting too old to fight cranky servers, but Clone386 remains unplugged, and was never upgraded from NetWare 4.10 to NetWare 4.11.

GATEWAY2000-2 was the first name I gave to my second Gateway2000 server, on loan from the Gateway2000 company for the book revision. While it made sense to call the two new servers GATEWAY2000-1 and -2, many icons and text boxes shortened the server names, eliminating the differences between the two servers. That's why I removed NDS from GATEWAY2000-2 and reinstalled the system as GWAY2K-2. While not as accurate as the earlier name, at least the two server names are different in all circumstances. I hope this extra effort makes the nice Gateway2000 people happy.

The third name, 486-33 without the \\ to mark it as from the UNC format, has me stumped. I can't figure where Windows 95 got this information, but there it is.

What's the moral of this story? Complicated systems take time to settle down, and NetWare 4.11 and Windows 95 aren't quite there yet. I'm not happy that Novell executives voted to dump NetWare User Tools, but the need for a solid Windows 95 client no doubt outweighed any sentimental value for the old NetWare User Tools utility. It's a shame, but that's progress.

Printing Doesn't Live Here Anymore

Unlike NetWare User Tools, Network Neighborhood doesn't include any functions to modify network printer assignments. Choose your network printing options from within the Print menu option in your application. You may certainly feel free to look back at Chapter 8 if you missed the network printing choices covered in that chapter.

Teach Your Users Well

EACH USER HAS a job to do. Each job requires information and interaction. Your network is the conduit between the two. This does not gain the network, or even you, any respect.

When the users are unhappy, it's usually a management failure. Resources must be planned and deployed to support the users. If those resources, particularly your time and any necessary equipment, aren't available, the users get even more unhappy.

The animosity isn't personal, and isn't deep. While it is aggravating, it's understandable. You get aggravated with your boss because tools you need aren't provided, don't you? When the network tool is not available, it's natural for the users to get mad at you, and it's safer for them than getting mad at their boss.

Track your user complaints. Half or more of the complaints will be caused by something the users should know. The fact that they don't know has more to do with management priorities than user stupidity or apathy. Management's lack of priorities and support for you and your department will cause you more problems indirectly than any user will directly.

CASE STUDY

MiniCo: Teaching Your Clients to Use the Network

MINICO HAS 3 servers, 75 users, and one location.

Preparing the User Community

CONSIDERATIONS

The goals:

- Understand NDS concepts and explain them to your users.
- Train the users on the new network.
- Prepare "shortcuts" pages with helpful hints for the users.

DECISION

Tell each user some details when that user's system is connected to the network.

EXPLANATION

Not having the time or budget for a full training program, MiniCo executives decided that Alexander von Thorn (the Distribution Manager who is also the lead network administrator) could cover the important details for each user as he went along. Although Alexander understood the network fairly well by this time, a slapdash network introduction in the middle of the workday isn't enough.

More important, the lack of user training and prepared materials told the employees of MiniCo that Jack Mingo (the company President) wasn't 100 percent behind the new network. Most just figured it was because Alexander and Bill (the Judge) Quick (the Operations Manager) convinced him to go with NetWare rather than the new Macintosh server. The fact that only three people, including Jack, use a Macintosh is what really decided the issue, of course.

NetWare User Tools: One-Touch Convenience in NetWare 4.10

CONSIDERATIONS

The goals:

- Set the hotkey for easy access to NetWare User Tools.
- Teach users the program.

DECISION

Show Windows 3.1x users NetWare User Tools during their quick NetWare one-on-one orientation.

EXPLANATION

Because the network wasn't planned ahead well enough, time prevented organized training on NetWare User Tools and the development of help materials for the users. Alexander, and

MINICO CASE STUDY, CONTINUED

helpers Jim Lewczyk (Programmer), Greg Oire (Marketing Manager), and Scott Elyard (Sales Manager) showed each Windows 3.1x user NetWare User Tools as the first option to use when adjusting the network connection.

NETUSER for DOS Users

CONSIDERATIONS

THE CHOICES:

- Explain NETUSER to all users.
- Show only the DOS users how to use NETUSER.

DECISION

Explain NETUSER to DOS-only users.

EXPLANATION

The few users that used DOS primarily were shown NETUSER and how it worked. Since MiniCo is heavily slanted to Windows 3.1x and moving to mostly Windows 95, however, the explanations were short and somewhat incomplete.

Configuring Printing from the Command Line with CAPTURE or NPRINT

CONSIDERATIONS

The choices:

- Provide an explanation of command-line printing.
- Try to keep users from using the print command-line utilities.

DECISION

Discourage users from using the command-line utilities.

EXPLANATION

Since training time was short or nonexistent, MiniCo tried to steer users away from command-line utilities and toward NetWare User Tools, Network Neighborhood, or NETUSER. Because these interactive programs handle so many of the user's needs, there is little reason to spend much time explaining command-line utilities.

Setting Up Remote Printing

CONSIDERATIONS

The goals:

- Check which users have laser printers attached to their stations.
- Make most of these remote system printers.

DECISION

Use NPRINTER from DOS and Windows 3.1x workstations, and NPTWIN95 from the Windows 95 workstations.

EXPLANATION

NPRINTER is free with NetWare, saving the cost of third-party print servers. The new version of NPRINTER takes little RAM from the workstation and less CPU time as well (although it's still noticeable, so a few users complain).

The reliability of NPRINTER connections is sometimes suspect. Users often forget and turn their systems off when they leave, meaning a

> **MINICO CASE STUDY, CONTINUED**

system printer attached to their workstation is turned off as well.

Similar problems exist with the NPTWIN95 program and its control of access to locally attached printers. One of these days, Alex will see an ad for a print server at just the right time, and he will move most users away from workstation-attached printers.

Other Handy User Command-Line Utilities

CONSIDERATIONS

The choices:

- Explain the use of RIGHTS, FLAG, and NDIR to the users.
- Let the users figure out what they need and how to use it themselves.

DECISION

Briefly show users the RIGHTS, FLAG, and NDIR commands during NetWare instruction.

EXPLANATION

RIGHTS, FLAG, and NDIR are useful command-line utilities, but more useful for administrators than users. Nonetheless, when Alexander and helpers remembered, they showed these to the users. Most users promptly forgot the reasons for, and details of, these commands.

Using FILER for File Management

CONSIDERATIONS

The choices:

- Train users on FILER.
- Tell users to use Windows File Manager or Windows Explorer instead.

DECISION

Skip FILER and recommend Windows File Manager or Windows Explorer.

EXPLANATION

The DOS FILER utility has some advantages for administrators, but not many uses for users running MS Windows. FILER was felt to be less friendly than other options for the users. Besides that, teaching all the options available in FILER would take longer than Alexander and helpers had time for during the quick "here's NetWare" talk each new user received.

Finding Help

CONSIDERATIONS

The possibilities:

- Explain command-line help options.
- Allow users to access the DynaText online documentation.

DECISION

Quickly mention command-line help. Set up DynaText for users as needed.

EXPLANATION

During the quick NetWare overview for each user, command-line help options (the /? parameter) were explained. Of course, not knowing the available command-line options slowed down the users quite a bit.

DynaText access must be configured for each Windows user, or planned during the installation. Being rushed, MiniCo didn't add DynaText automatically. Each user that shows a need for online documentation is granted

> **MINICO CASE STUDY, CONTINUED**

access. The administrators are the primary users of the documentation.

Windows 95 Network User Support in NetWare 4.11

CONSIDERATIONS

The choices:

- Teach users how to use Windows Explorer and Network Neighborhood.
- Let the users figure it out themselves.

DECISION

Give the Windows 95 users an even quicker NetWare orientation than the one for the other users.

EXPLANATION

Windows 95 users were given even less network training, since the Microsoft utilities Windows Explorer and Network Neighborhood were supposed to be simple enough for any user to figure out. Alex finally had to help a few people, but graphical interfaces to the network did cut down on training time.

CASE STUDY

MegaCorp: Teaching Your Clients to Use the Network

MEGACORP HAS 50 servers, 2500 users, and 5 locations.

Preparing the User Community

CONSIDERATIONS

The goals:

- Prepare the user community with preinstallation information.
- Develop and prepare user materials for postinstallation reference.
- Provide a half-day training class for each department the week of their changeover.
- Place IS personnel in each converted department the first two days after the conversion to answer questions.

DECISION

Prepare users, train users, reassure users, and make this conversion a success.

EXPLANATION

Coming from a network with only DOS user and management tools, MegaCorp looked at the NetWare $4.1x$ installation as a benefit to all users. The network was presented as being easier to use, easier to navigate, and easier to customize than the previous network.

Each department was given hands-on training the week of the changeover. The lag between training and setting up the new network should be as short as possible. Training someone two months ahead of time is of little value.

Materials were available to the newly converted departments before and after the upgrade to NetWare. IS personnel were placed in the converted departments after the move to NetWare $4.1x$, to reassure users and provide immediate help for any questions. At least a few IS people stayed for two days, but the number of questions and stress caused by the change dwindled rapidly.

NetWare User Tools: One-Touch Convenience in NetWare 4.10

CONSIDERATIONS

The goals:

- Ensure the NetWare User Tools hotkey is available for each Windows $3.1x$ user.
- Prepare a help sheet for NetWare User Tools.
- Spend time teaching the utility in the NetWare upgrade class.

DECISION

Present NetWare User Tools as the best, and easiest, user-to-NetWare connection for Windows $3.1x$ users.

MEGACORP CASE STUDY, CONTINUED

EXPLANATION

MegaCorp was impressed with NetWare User Tools from the beginning. The flexibility, power, and ease of use of the utility made it a staple of the MegaCorp NetWare training.

Each user was given a help sheet, explaining the functions of NetWare User Tools, along with the types of network "housekeeping" it provides. A few users asked to have this utility placed in their Windows Startup group, so it was the first thing they saw when starting their workstation.

NETUSER for DOS Users

CONSIDERATIONS

The choices:

- Explain NETUSER to all users.
- Show only the DOS users how to use NETUSER.

DECISION

Present NETUSER to DOS users only. For those users, prepare a help sheet for NETUSER and briefly cover NETUSER during user training. Reiterate the basics of NETUSER to DOS users immediately after the NetWare 4.1x transition.

EXPLANATION

The trend toward GUIs, especially MS Windows, has almost eliminated the DOS users from MegaCorp. The small percentage of DOS users were given help sheets on NETUSER. All the IS personnel were familiar with the program. Users with Windows 3.1x who still used DOS software on occasion were encouraged to use NetWare User Tools rather than NETUSER.

Configuring Printing from the Command Line with CAPTURE or NPRINT

CONSIDERATIONS

The goals:

- Mention CAPTURE and NPRINT during user training.
- List the most popular options on the user's help sheet.
- Cover how to get detailed help for all command-line utilities in training classes and on the help sheet.

DECISION

Spend little time on command-line utilities, but tell the users how to get help and information. Refer users to graphical NetWare tools rather than to their equivalent command-line options.

EXPLANATION

Many users have learned computers after Windows became the interface standard, and they don't know anything about command-line utilities. The number of users needing command-line utilities in general, and CAPTURE and NPRINT in particular, was estimated to be fairly low. Brief explanations were given during the user training. Most of the short time was spent showing how to get help for all command-line utilities (with the \? parameter). A mention was put on the help sheet each user received.

Windows clients of all types were shown how to find and utilize network printers through the graphical interfaces. The users who do the most printing have personal laser printers, simplifying printing in their cases.

MEGACORP CASE STUDY, CONTINUED

Setting Up Remote Printing

CONSIDERATIONS

The choices:

- Evaluate the use of NPRINTER and NPTWIN95 in the network.
- Use third-party print servers rather than NPRINTER or NPTWIN95.

DECISION

Use third-party print servers.

EXPLANATION

Although NPRINTER and NPTWIN95 worked fine during the pilot network phase, MegaCorp decided to use third-party print servers for printing support. Relying on users to remember to leave their computers on was one worry, as was the possible impact on the workstation's performance.

Print servers, especially those internal to the printer as offered for HP LaserJets, provide much higher throughput than NPRINTER or NPTWIN95. Many print servers now support TCP/IP as well as IPX/SPX for NetWare, meaning they have great value in multiprotocol situations.

Other Handy User Command-Line Utilities

CONSIDERATIONS

The choices:

- List the RIGHTS, FLAG, and NDIR utilities on the help sheet.
- Train the users on these utilities.

DECISION

Mention, but don't demonstrate, these utilities during training. Place them on the help sheet.

EXPLANATION

MegaCorp felt users gain little advantage with these command-line utilities over functionality of MS Windows or other utilities. No users are authorized to change their own rights, so the RIGHTS command does the user little good. The same story holds true for file attributes and FLAG. With more friendly directory utilities in MS Windows and on the network, NDIR was deemed somewhat superfluous.

Using FILER for File Management

CONSIDERATIONS

The choices:

- Train users on FILER.
- Tell users to use another file management utility instead.

DECISION

Skip FILER.

EXPLANATION

The DOS FILER utility program was once the most powerful network file management tool available. Over the years, however, other utilities added many of the same features in a graphical format.

Users were shown that MS Windows File Manager and Norton Commander for Windows work on network drives. Using familiar utilities on the new network made the transition less wrenching for MegaCorp users.

MEGACORP CASE STUDY, CONTINUED

Finding Help

CONSIDERATIONS

The possibilities:

- Explain command-line help options.
- Allow users to access the DynaText online documentation.

DECISION

Place command-line utilities on the help sheet. Allow all users access to the DynaText online documentation.

EXPLANATION

Although the use of command-line utilities is not encouraged, they were listed on the help sheet each NetWare user received as part of training. During NetWare client installation, each user was set up to use the DynaText online documentation.

There was some debate whether users needed access to the full set of online NetWare documentation, but the decision was made to allow the access. No harm could come from the users learning more about the network, and the easy access made the department power users and subadministrators better able to support their users.

Windows 95 Network User Support in NetWare 4.11

CONSIDERATIONS

The goals:

- Ensure that Network Neighborhood works properly on all Windows 95 systems.
- Prepare a help sheet for Windows 95 applications for NetWare.
- Spend time teaching the Windows 95 utilities in the NetWare upgrade class.

DECISION

Present the built-in Windows 95 tools as the easiest user-to-NetWare connection for those users. However, discourage drive mapping through Network Neighborhood.

EXPLANATION

Each Windows 95 user was given a help sheet, explaining the functions of NetWare functions available in Network Neighborhood and Windows Explorer. Windows 95 users were somewhat envious of the Windows 3.1x users' access to NetWare User Tools, but Network Neighborhood and Windows Explorer provide the same functionality, if not the same concise interface.

The administrators did issue one caveat: When trying to map drives through Network Neighborhood, users may see NDS items that actually no longer exist, such as servers that have since been renamed or that have not been part of the network for quite some time.

Integrating NetWare with Other Operating Systems

PART 3

CHAPTER 13

Using Macintoshes with NetWare 4.1x

NOVELL WAS THE first desktop LAN company to support Apple's Macintosh computer. First released in December 1988, NetWare's support for Apple networking became the preferred high-performance server operating system for Macintosh networks.

Building on that early lead, NetWare 4.1x now makes the Macintosh a full citizen of NDS. MacNDS client software uses the IPX protocol to connect Macintosh clients directly to native NetWare 4 servers. The native Macintosh interface now takes advantage of all NetWare server and NDS functions.

NetWare for Macintosh software (a group of NLM programs included with NetWare) provides these capabilities:

- Macintosh users can share files with non-Macintosh users.

- Macintosh users can send print jobs to NetWare queues.

- Non-Macintosh users can send print jobs to AppleTalk printers on AppleTalk networks.

Don't get too excited by that first point; the Macintosh is still a completely different computer from the PC. You can share files between Macintosh systems and non-Macintosh systems, but this only helps when the applications on each client can read and understand the file's structure. There is no magic translator built into NetWare that enables a Macintosh to run PC software or vice versa. However, many application programs are realizing the value of a common file format, regardless of the client operating system.

> **The Coming of the Common File Format**
>
> WordPerfect was the first major software vendor to guarantee that an application file from one client could be used by any other WordPerfect client on any other platform.
>
> The state of desktop computing interoperability when WordPerfect made this cross-platform file sharing a reality was dismal. Clients supported by WordPerfect included the TI PC, the Victor 9000, the DEC Rainbow, and the AT&T 6300, each with its own unique version of DOS. The idea of connecting WordPerfect's first platform, Data General, or any Unix systems in a meaningful way was essentially impossible.
>
> The world is a much more integrated place today. Many of the major software applications have a common file format, or they have the ability to read and write other file formats without needing a separate conversion step. So the easy connection of Macintosh, OS/2, Unix, and PC clients to a NetWare 4 network makes even more sense today than in the mid-1980s.

Macintosh Networking Crash Course

IF YOU ARE a PC person faced with Macintosh networking decisions, you need a bit of background. A grip on your patience won't hurt, either. Macintosh systems have a different approach to networking, but all the systems will work together.

Let's get a few basic terms under control. Everyone likes it better when outsiders learn the lingo, and Macintosh networking lingo is different than NetWare terminology.

- **AppleTalk:** The proprietary protocol suite from Apple Computer that provides a peer-to-peer network architecture. Ease of installation is a moot point; AppleTalk is standard on every Macintosh. Each device on the network must have a unique address within the range set for the network.

- **AppleTalk node:** An addressable device on a network, such as a computer, printer, or server.

- **AppleTalk stack:** The suite of AppleTalk protocols that supports functions such as file and print services.

- **AppleTalk internetwork:** Two or more AppleTalk networks connected by AppleTalk router(s). The routers and supporting protocols are necessary to find machines on the other sides of routers.

- **AppleTalk zone:** A logical grouping of nodes. Any grouping is allowed, much like an Organizational Unit in NetWare. The zones often are grouped as Organizational Units, collecting nodes and network resources by geographical area, departmental use, or function.

- **AppleTalk router:** Hardware and/or software that connects AppleTalk networks so all nodes in each network can find and use resources from the other network.

- **AppleTalk Phase 2:** Released in 1989. Some new services were added, and some old services were extended. Some of the advantages include support for more than 254 nodes per network and for up to eight AppleTalk networks connected by the AppleTalk internet router.

- **Extended AppleTalk network:** An AppleTalk network that supports Phase 2 extensions, such as zone lists and network ranges. Novell documentation often refers to this as an *extended network*.

- **Non-extended AppleTalk network:** An AppleTalk network that does not support Phase 2 extensions.

AppleTalk, EtherTalk, and TokenTalk and the Seven Layers of OSI

A nicely layered protocol, AppleTalk fits well into the OSI (Open Systems Interconnection) network model. Let's take a look at this from the bottom up, and remember the discussions in the first chapter about IPX and TCP/IP as we go through these layers now.

At the physical and data-link layers (1 and 2):

- Ethernet—ELAP (EtherTalk Link Access Protocol), which is Apple's version of 10 MBps Ethernet. Phase 1 is modeled on Ethernet 2.0 (different than Ethernet 802.3). Phase 2 is modeled after Ethernet 802.3. This is now the default network connection for Macintosh computers made after 1989.

- FDDI—FLAP (FDDITalk Link Access Protocol), which is Apple's implementation of the 100 MBps FDDI (Fiber Distributed Data Interface) networking standard.

- TokenTalk—TLAP (TokenTalk Link Access Protocol), which is Apple's support for both the 4 MBps and 16 MBps Token Ring from IEEE 802.5 and IBM respectively. Only Phase 2 supports TokenTalk.

- LocalTalk— LLAP (LocalTalk Link Access Protocol), which is Apple's 230 KBps network for AppleTalk, shipped with every Macintosh since the original unit. The cable is UTP, with RS-422 connectors or small DIN connectors.

- Serial (RS-422)—ARAP (AppleTalk Remote Access Protocol), which is for remote connections over a serial line, over a modem.

At the network layer (3):

- AARP (AppleTalk Address Resolution Protocol), which maps network addresses to physical addresses.

- DDP (Datagram Delivery Protocol), which prepares packets for the network.

At the transport layer (4):

- RTMP (Routing Table Maintenance Protocol), which is a mechanism for routers to exchange information concerning routes and building each router's connection table. Internetworks use RTMP constantly.

- AURP (AppleTalk Update Routing Protocol), which is similar to RTMP, but sends updates only after a network change.

- AEP (AppleTalk Echo Protocol), which is similar to TCP/IP *ping*. It bounces packets off another node to ensure data can be transmitted.

- ATP (AppleTalk Transaction Protocol), which provides reliable request and response for transaction reliability.

- NBP (Name Binding Protocol), which connects device names with network addresses. It is transparent to the user and to the Macintosh Chooser application.

At the session layer (5):

- ADSP (AppleTalk Data Stream Protocol), which sets a full-duplex data connection between two nodes for reliable delivery.

- ASDSP (AppleTalk Secure Data Stream Protocol), which provides extra security for ADSP.

- ZIP (Zone Information Protocol), which associates zone names with network addresses and uses queries to maintain the network information when new zones are added. ZIP provides a means of finding a particular node in a large internet.

- ASP (AppleTalk Session Protocol), which adds reliability to ATP.

- PAP (Printer Access Protocol), which allows Macintosh clients to connect to print services on the network.

At the presentation and application layers (6 and 7):

- AFP (AppleTalk Filing Protocol), which is an application-level protocol to allow file and printer sharing.

- PostScript, which displays and prints output language.

You should be able to see many similarities between TCP/IP and IPX/SPX and AppleTalk. The original LocalTalk network for Macintosh systems had too little horsepower to be much more than a printer-sharing network, but EtherTalk and TokenTalk have made the Macintosh a contender in the corporate market.

Macintosh Network Addresses and Zones

Each AppleTalk network is assigned a unique number, and each node in that network refers to that number. Packets addressed to a node must provide both the network and node addresses, in the format:

```
network#.node#
```

The network number is two bytes; the node number is only one.

When a node connects to an AppleTalk network, a number is assigned for the node number. The station remembers that number and tries to use it again the next time the station connects to the network. If the station can't use the same number, it will look for the next available number to use.

The network numbers are a little more involved. The advance in Phase 2 allows each network multiple network numbers for a single network. Each network number can support up to 253 network nodes.

The network range for extended networks is expressed as two numbers, such as 1000 to 1010. These numbers in the range must be unique. Another network cannot use the same range or overlap any of the first network's address. You multiply the number of addresses in the range, in this case 10, by the 253 allowable addresses for nodes, for a possibility of 2530 individual nodes. There is no limit to network range, but you should keep the size down to maintain performance.

AppleTalk routers must always connect networks with different numbers. Therefore, a network can't come back around and route to itself by accident or connect to networks with conflicting network numbers. AppleTalk bridges must connect network segments with the same number range.

A *zone* is more a group than a physical limitation. Although the name zone implies a geographical area, any node may belong to many zones, or not belong to any zone. The zones may cross network boundaries and contain nodes from many networks. The name used is usually indicative of the zone's function, such as ACCOUNTING, SALES, or GRAPHICS. Zones are used quite often by the Chooser and other applications to organize devices into groups for easy reference. Zones also tend to have a server as part of the zone. The zone acts as a top-level organizer in the Chooser.

A zone list may contain up to 255 zone names. One zone is configured as the default zone. New workstations connecting to the network send an NBP broadcast request. A router will continue broadcasting the packets and even forward them to another zone name if necessary.

The DynaText documentation does a good job explaining AppleTalk. In fact, there's an entire volume labeled "NetWare AppleTalk Reference." More important for you, however, is that the Chooser and the Macintosh will probably do fine if you just stand out of their way. This is what happens:

- Your Macintosh sends out NBP request packets (similar to a NetWare client sending "get nearest server" packets when starting).

- Routers send the NBP requests to networks associated with the selected zone name. These requests will be sent to other networks as necessary.

- Routers directly connected to network associated with the selected zone broadcast the NBP request to every node in the zone.

- Services in the selected zone send NBP reply packets to the original Macintosh. The service name of available resources are displayed in the Chooser.

The network range for AppleTalk Phase 1 is a single number (for example, 12-12). NetWare for Macintosh supports AppleTalk Phase 1. But if your systems were bought within the last few years, AppleTalk Phase 2 is probably all you need to worry about.

Installing Macintosh Server Software

BEFORE YOU INSTALL Macintosh server software, NetWare 4.1x must be up and running on the file server that will support Macintosh clients. Above and beyond the amount of server resources necessary to support your disk space and concurrent users, another ration of RAM is needed for the Macintosh NLMs. Here's the official version of required memory resources:

- 1 MB for NLMs, but subtract 500 KB if BTRIEVE is already loaded on your server.
- 12 KB per active AFP session.
- 10 KB per Macintosh connection.
- 20 KB per ATPS (AppleTalk Print Services) print server.
- 20 KB per ATPS spooler.
- 10 KB per concurrent ATPS spooler user.
- 20 KB per ATXRP (AppleTalk eXtender Remote Printer) printer.

The important numbers are the 1 MB for the NLMs and the 10 KB for each Macintosh on the network. Throw in a handful of RAM for each printer and print user, and you need at least 2 MB no matter how few Macintosh clients you have. If you have more than 50 Macintosh clients and three or four printers, you're well over the 2 MB mark, which probably means a minimum of 4 MB additional server RAM. Remember, RAM makes the world go 'round, or at least makes your network go 'round faster. If you need to support Macintosh clients, make the department with the Macintoshes throw some server memory into the deal.

> *Remember, RAM makes the world go 'round, or at least makes your network go 'round faster.*

Let's get some of the official business out of the way. The NLMs are loaded (and function) by server, not by network. The support for Macintosh file names is done by volume, not by server. Since NetWare for Macintosh is now included in all copies of NetWare 4.1x, no extra purchase is necessary.

The user limit of each server can be all PC clients, all Macintosh clients, all OS/2 clients, or any combination up to the limits of your license. But remember that NetWare 4.1x now uses "cumulative" licensing. If you have 50 users already, and 8 Macintosh clients want to join the party, you only need to buy another NetWare license for 10 users. With previous versions, you were required to bump your license to the next level, which was 100 users.

Be aware that Macintosh systems almost always use the frame type ETHERNET_SNAP (Sub-Network Access Protocol, a variant of an 802.2 packet). This frame type is not normally used with PCs and Unix systems, so it may not be configured on any of your server network interface boards. The NetWare for Macintosh installation instructions *do not* specifically tell you to use the ETHERNET_SNAP frame type.

> **WARNING**
>
> *If you assume the frame type will be added automatically, as I did, or that the Macintosh will see the 802.3 or 802.2 frame types, you will waste a day trying to figure out why the Chooser in the Macintosh client doesn't see any zones or your NetWare server. This warning comes from personal experience. You may configure MacIPX a different way, but it's difficult to get your first Macintosh connected to gain access to the Macintosh client files until you get your frame type under control.*

Preparing for Macintosh Server Installation

If you have skipped to this point from the initial server installation description in Chapter 3, welcome. You may skip the upcoming list of details. If you are adding Macintosh support to an existing NetWare 4.1x server, this list is for you:

- Gather the NetWare installation media, whether the CD-ROM or the (ugh) diskettes. If you have copied the installation files to a server hard disk, verify the path to that location and any Admin passwords necessary.

- Verify that the Macintosh systems are physically connected to a functioning network.

- Go to the server console for the soon-to-be Macintosh host server. Or, if you can, use the RCONSOLE program from your desk.

- Either disconnect all other NetWare users from the server or at least warn them that the server will go down during the installation.
- If you are integrating an existing Macintosh network, get a list of all zones and network numbers.

Loading the NLMs

> **13.1 IN-A-HURRY**
>
> **Start the NetWare for Macintosh Installation**
>
> 1. Type **LOAD INSTALL** at the server console (or through RCONSOLE).
> 2. Choose Product Options, then Install NetWare for Macintosh.
> 3. Select the source of the NetWare files, and change the file PATH if necessary.
> 4. Choose Install NW-MAC.
> 5. Make your choices in the Final Installation Options menu and press Enter to continue.

Unlike many of the earlier administrative functions run from the workstation, there are no immediate supervisor passwords to type when you start the NetWare for Macintosh installation. Let this be an example for us: the server's security is partly dependent on physical security. In other words, the server is safer if people can't get there. If you do have a keyboard and monitor on the server, you should have a console password and lock the console whenever you're finished. The same warning goes for the remote access program RCONSOLE: You should have a different password for the console than for the Admin or equivalent user.

To begin installing NetWare for Macintosh, start at the server console's colon prompt by typing:

```
LOAD INSTALL
```

The main Installation Options menu will appear. Our choice for now is the Product Options (other optional installation items) option. Highlight this line and press Enter. You will see the screen shown in Figure 13.1, where I've highlighted the Macintosh installation option.

FIGURE 13.1

Starting the Macintosh support installation routine

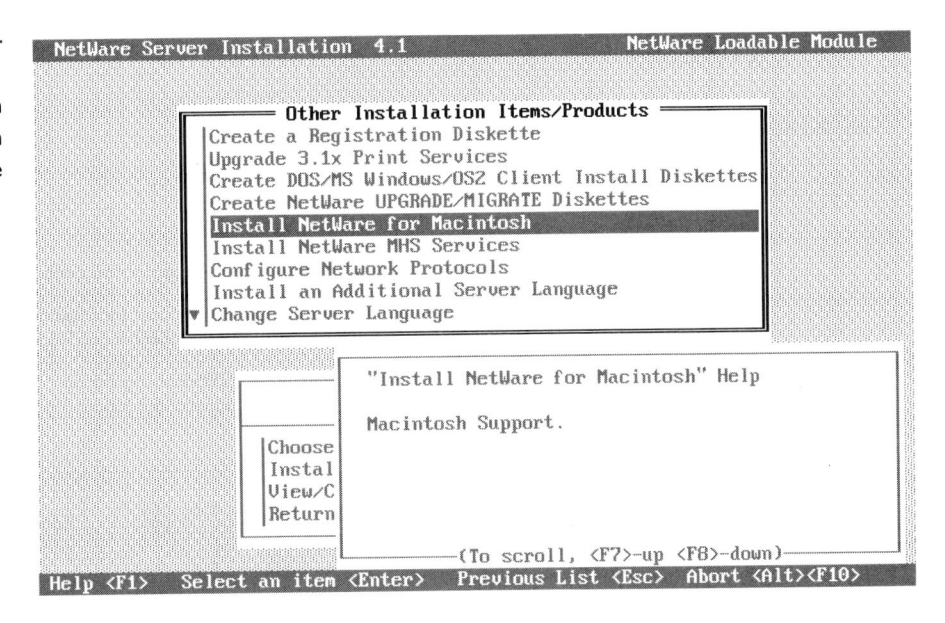

```
╔═ NetWare Server Installation 4.1 ════════════ NetWare Loadable Module ═╗

       ╔═══════ Other Installation Items/Products ═══════╗
       │ Create a Registration Diskette                  │
       │ Upgrade 3.1x Print Services                     │
       │ Create DOS/MS Windows/OS2 Client Install Diskettes │
       │ Create NetWare UPGRADE/MIGRATE Diskettes        │
       │ Install NetWare for Macintosh                   │
       │ Install NetWare MHS Services                    │
       │ Configure Network Protocols                     │
       │ Install an Additional Server Language           │
       ▼ Change Server Language                          │
       ╚═════════════════════════════════════════════════╝

              ╔══════════════════════════════════════════╗
              ║ "Install NetWare for Macintosh" Help     ║
              ║                                          ║
              ║ Macintosh Support.                       ║
              ║ Choose                                   ║
              ║ Instal                                   ║
              ║ View/C                                   ║
              ║ Return                                   ║
              ║                                          ║
              ║         ─(To scroll, <F7>-up <F8>-down)─ ║
    Help <F1>  Select an item <Enter>   Previous List <Esc>   Abort <Alt><F10>
```

The next screen will ask for the source of the Macintosh support files that will be installed to the server. If you are loading the files from a local CD-ROM, as I am in this example, you must verify that fact. If you are loading the files from another path, such as a local or remote hard disk, you must verify that location and provide the same to the installation program. You must provide a login name and password for the remote system. Figure 13.2 shows this installation step in NetWare 4.10. In NetWare 4.11, the installation program will show

NW411:\PRODUCTS\NW411\INSTALL\IBM\DOS\XXX\ENGLISH\

as the source directory. Notice that the system knows we wish to install the English files, because the server is set for English as the primary language.

After you press the Enter key to verify the location of the installation files, a small file-loading process starts and finishes almost before you know what happened. The installation progress thermometer bar loads on the screen, but zips by quickly. You are then offered a screen with two choices: Cancel Installation or Install NW-MAC. Since we've just started, it seems a shame to stop now, so highlight Install NW-MAC and press Enter.

More files are copied, but without the thermometer bar. The files go by quickly, but you will notice many printer-support files as they whiz by.

FIGURE 13.2

Specifying the source for Macintosh installation files

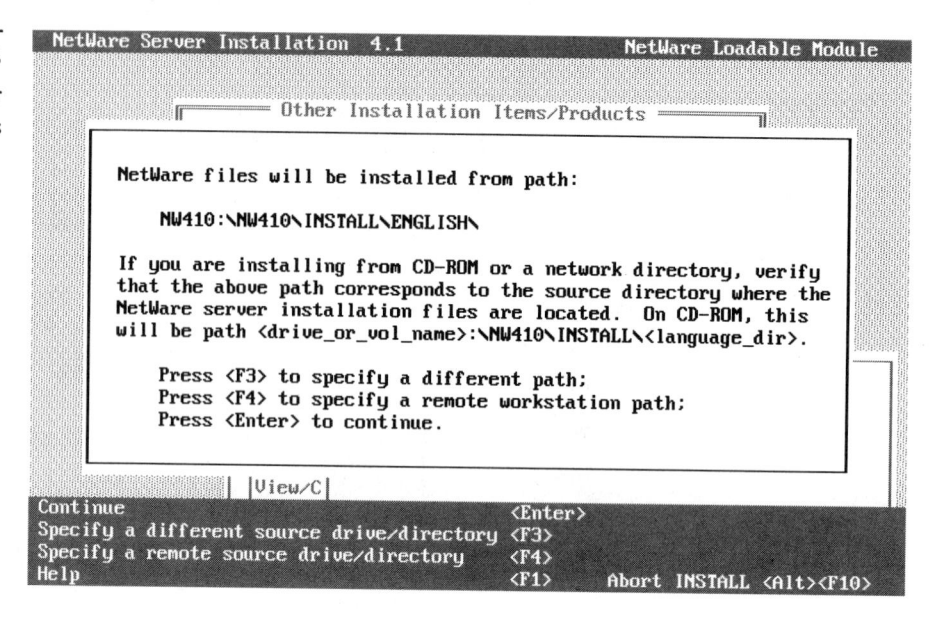

```
╔═ NetWare Server Installation 4.1          NetWare Loadable Module ═╗

              ┌──────── Other Installation Items/Products ────────┐
              │                                                    │
              │ NetWare files will be installed from path:        │
              │                                                    │
              │    NW410:\NW410\INSTALL\ENGLISH\                  │
              │                                                    │
              │ If you are installing from CD-ROM or a network directory, verify │
              │ that the above path corresponds to the source directory where the │
              │ NetWare server installation files are located. On CD-ROM, this │
              │ will be path <drive_or_vol_name>:\NW410\INSTALL\<language_dir>. │
              │                                                    │
              │     Press <F3> to specify a different path;       │
              │     Press <F4> to specify a remote workstation path; │
              │     Press <Enter> to continue.                    │
              │                                                    │
              └────────────────── View/C ─────────────────────────┘
Continue                                              <Enter>
Specify a different source drive/directory            <F3>
Specify a remote source drive/directory               <F4>
Help                                                  <F1>    Abort INSTALL <Alt><F10>
```

If you are reinstalling NetWare for Macintosh, or upgrading from an earlier version, there are two choices of interest. The file-transfer process will stop, and you will be asked if you wish to:

```
Overwrite file SYS:\SYSTEM\NW-MAC\ATPSCON\NBPTYPE.DEF?
```

This file contains the database of printer models used by the printer control program ATPSCON. If you have customized some printer model information previously, and agree to overwrite this file, the information will be lost and an empty file put in its place.

Immediately after the NBPTYPE.DEF question comes a similar one for the file EXTMAP.DAT. This file contains a list of extension mappings. If you have previously used this file, don't overwrite it, or your earlier work will be lost.

The Final Installation Options screen appears, as shown in Figure 13.3. There are four options that must be set before continuing:

- **Select volumes to add the Macintosh name space:** Macintosh file names are much more intelligent than the limited 8.3 format used by DOS and MS Windows 3.*x*. The special files controlling the file name access and name mapping between Macintosh users and non-Macintosh users happens per volume. The fact that Macintosh names are supported on one volume on a server has no effect on any other volume on that same server.

FIGURE 13.3

Final, but this doesn't include configuration

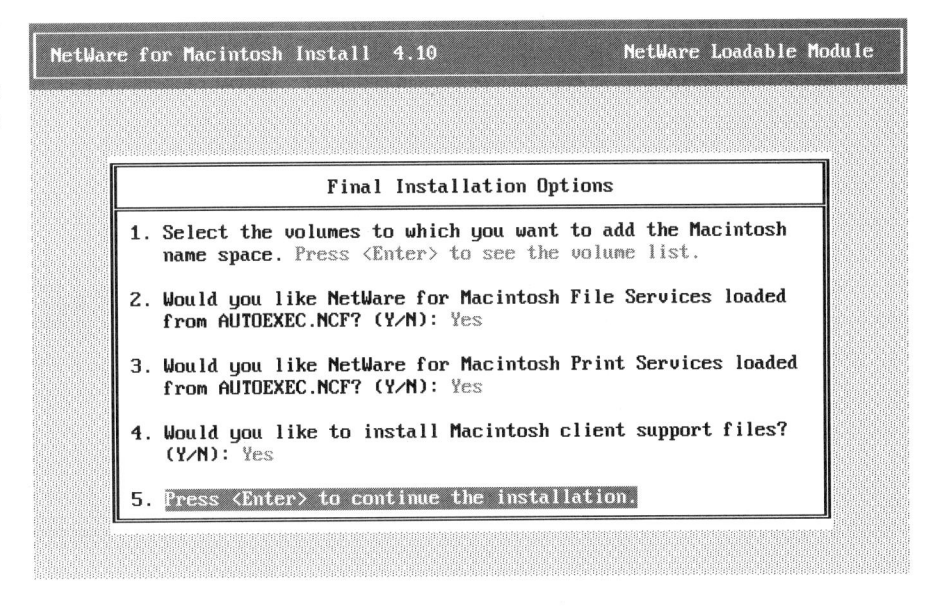

```
NetWare for Macintosh Install  4.10              NetWare Loadable Module

                    ┌─────────────────────────────────────────────┐
                    │           Final Installation Options        │
                    ├─────────────────────────────────────────────┤
                    │ 1. Select the volumes to which you want to add the Macintosh
                    │    name space. Press <Enter> to see the volume list.
                    │
                    │ 2. Would you like NetWare for Macintosh File Services loaded
                    │    from AUTOEXEC.NCF? (Y/N): Yes
                    │
                    │ 3. Would you like NetWare for Macintosh Print Services loaded
                    │    from AUTOEXEC.NCF? (Y/N): Yes
                    │
                    │ 4. Would you like to install Macintosh client support files?
                    │    (Y/N): Yes
                    │
                    │ 5. Press <Enter> to continue the installation.
                    └─────────────────────────────────────────────┘
```

- **Start Macintosh File Services from AUTOEXEC.NCF:** The default for this is actually No. If the server crashes, Macintosh files are not handled gracefully and may need some desktop repair. If the server reappears and Macintosh clients connect before the desktop repair is done, there may be some problems. However, we will see later how to modify the startup command for the file services to repair any desktop damage immediately when the server starts. With that protection, this option may safely be set to Yes.

- **Start Macintosh Print Services from AUTOEXEC.NCF:** Same type question as before, but less damage will occur if the user reconnects to a newly revived server. Go ahead and change this to Yes as well.

- **Install Macintosh client support files?:** The MacNDS program and others will be copied to the server in the \PUBLIC\CLIENT\MAC directory as self-extracting archive (SEA) files. This is a good thing to say Yes to.

Once the four choices are considered and made, highlight option 5 and press Enter to continue. Then, as if that isn't enough, you will be asked to verify that you do, in fact, wish to continue. Highlight Yes and press Enter here, as well.

The configuration immediately follows installation, but we're going to separate things. This makes sense for the times you may return to modify your AppleTalk stack after installation. See Figure 13.4, whose options match the headings of the next few sections. We'll work our way down the list. If you're doing the initial installation, just keep going.

FIGURE 13.4

Installation is technically done. Configuration is beginning.

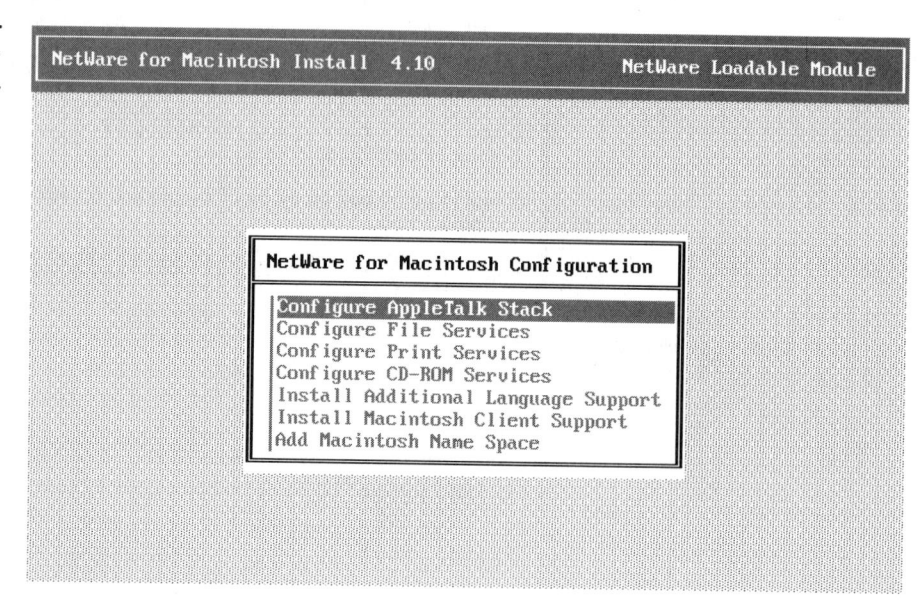

```
NetWare for Macintosh Install   4.10            NetWare Loadable Module




                     ┌─────────────────────────────────────┐
                     │  NetWare for Macintosh Configuration │
                     ├─────────────────────────────────────┤
                     │ Configure AppleTalk Stack           │
                     │ Configure File Services             │
                     │ Configure Print Services            │
                     │ Configure CD-ROM Services           │
                     │ Install Additional Language Support │
                     │ Install Macintosh Client Support    │
                     │ Add Macintosh Name Space            │
                     └─────────────────────────────────────┘
```

Configuring the AppleTalk Stack

> **13.2 IN-A-HURRY**
>
> **Configure the AppleTalk Protocol Stack**
>
> **1.** Type **LOAD INSTALL** at the server console (or through RCONSOLE).
>
> **2.** Choose Product Options, then View/Configure/Remove Installed Products under Other Installation Actions.
>
> **3.** Choose NW-MAC v4.11 NetWare for Macintosh 4, then Configure AppleTalk Stack.
>
> **4.** Work through the seven items on the Internetworking Configuration menu.
>
> **5.** Press Escape to exit.

Although the configuration screen comes up during the NetWare for Macintosh installation process, it's really the INETCFG (InterNETworking ConFiGuration) program. If you prefer, you can reach this screen by typing LOAD INETCFG from the server console prompt.

The seven Internetworking Configuration menu items are:

- **Boards:** Add, delete, and configure interface boards. For each board in the server, configure the board name, interrupt, I/O base address, node address (to override the setting on the interface board), number of retries to redo a failed transmission, memory base address if used by the board, and a space for a comment.

- **Network Interfaces:** Configure the network interfaces on configured boards. If there is more than one board, this screen allows you to choose the board to make future modifications on.

- **WAN Call Directory:** Add, delete, and modify WAN call destinations. This item is used only if a WAN driver is installed in the server.

- **Protocols:** Configure the network layer protocols such as IPX, TCP/IP, and AppleTalk. Allows you to view the enabled or unconfigured protocols on the server. For AppleTalk, choose to configure AppleTalk and set the details in the AppleTalk Configuration screen.

- **Bindings:** Connect a particular protocol to a particular network interface. Opens the Configured Protocol to Network Interface Binding screen, allowing you to connect a protocol to an interface.

- **Manage Configuration:** Configure other server information not included above. Set SNMP (Simple Network Management Protocol) details, export or import the configuration to a diskette, configure the remote access profile for this server, and edit the AUTOEXEC.NCF file.

- **View Configuration:** View in read-only mode the various configuration commands used in the AUTOEXEC.NCF and INETCFG.NCF files. You can also view the console log.

Several of these options are of no use in setting up AppleTalk. Let's go through the ones that we need now.

The Boards and Network Interfaces Options

If you have more than one network adapter in the server, you must choose which one to use. That happens in the Network Interfaces menu item. If that's your situation, choose the board that will connect to the network with the Macintosh computers.

The Protocols Option

Figure 13.5 shows the submenu that appears when you choose Protocols from the Internetworking Configuration menu.

Along with AppleTalk and IPX, the other choices on the Protocol Configuration menu are:

- **Source Route End Station:** Enables the Source Routing Router (ROUTE.NLM) program for Token Ring and/or FDDI network adapters.

- **TCP/IP:** Sets the details for TCP/IP protocol support on this server. (See Chapter 14 for details.)

- **User-Specified Protocol Load List:** A place to load miscellaneous NLM files to perform other functions not covered with the previous choices.

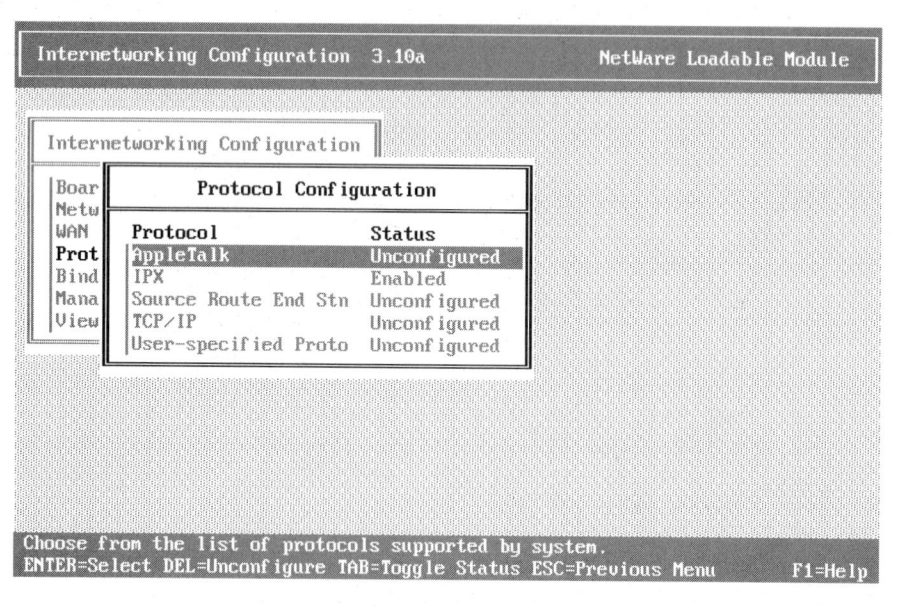

FIGURE 13.5
Preparing to configure the AppleTalk protocol

Now you need all the AppleTalk zone and network number information you gathered before starting. The DynaText volume titled "NetWare AppleTalk Reference" has an excellent in-depth description of AppleTalk routing. Included are three examples of AppleTalk network configurations as guides for your network setup. Three tables present the descriptions and options for three different network setups. Figure 13.6 shows the middle configuration described by the NetWare electronic documentation.

FIGURE 13.6

The middle-road AppleTalk configuration

```
Internetworking Configuration  3.10a                    NetWare Loadable Module

                          ┌─────── AppleTalk Configuration ───────┐
      Internetwor         │                                        │
      ┌────────┐          │ AppleTalk Status:         Enabled      │
      │ Boar   │          │ Packet Forwarding:        Enabled ("Router")│
      │ Netw   │          │ Type of Packet Forwarding: Phase 2     │
      │ WAN    │ Pro      │ DDP Checksum:             Disabled     │
      │ Prot   │ App      │                                        │
      │ Bind   │ IPX      │ Static Routes for On Demand Calls:     │
      │ Mana   │ Sou      │ Static Routes Configuration:           │
      │ View   │ TCP      │                                        │
      │        │ Use      │ Tunnel AppleTalk through IP (AURP): Disabled │
      └────────┘          │ AURP Configuration:                    │
                          │                                        │
                          │ Filtering Support:        Enabled      │
                          │ Internal Network:         Enabled      │
                          │ Network Number:                (decimal)│
                          │ Network Zone(s) List:   (Select to View/Configure)│
                          │ Expert Configuration Options:          │
                          └────────────────────────────────────────┘
AppleTalk zones associated with this network.
ENTER=Select  ESC=Previous Menu                              F1=Help
```

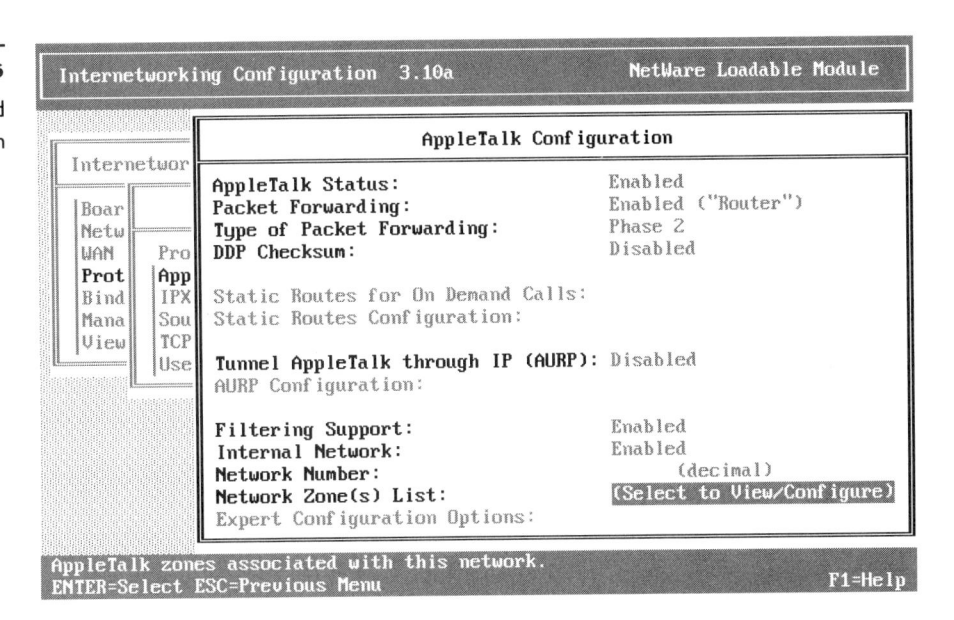

Table 13.1 shows the default settings and options for these fields.

TABLE 13.1

AppleTalk Configuration Fields

FIELD	DESCRIPTION
AppleTalk Status	Starting state. If this setting is Enabled, AppleTalk will activate during system startup. Disabled leaves the configuration intact but not active. The default is Enabled once you open this screen.
Packet Forwarding	Decides whether the server acts like a Macintosh workstation (end node) or a router. If it acts like a router, nodes can access services on other networks. The default is Disabled (end node).

TABLE 13.1 (cont.) AppleTalk Configuration Fields

FIELD	DESCRIPTION
Type of Packet Forwarding	NetWare for Macintosh is a Phase 2 router, but will work with Phase 1 routers if your network dictates. Transition forced Phase 2 restrictions to comply with Phase 1 routers, particularly limiting the network range to one (4-4, not 4-6) and a single zone name. This only appears if Packet Forwarding is Enabled. The default is Phase 2.
DDP Checksum	DDP (Datagram Delivery Protocol) is used to deliver packets between nodes on different subnetworks. This setting depends on your settings for existing nodes and routers. The default is Disabled.
Static Routes for On-Demand Calls	Listing of particular addresses to contact when demanded.
Static Routes Configuration	Route addressing and location details.
Tunnel AppleTalk through IP (AURP)	AURP (AppleTalk Update Routing Protocol) uses a link-state algorithm to determine routes through an internetwork. AURP allows you to connect separate AppleTalk networks through an TCP/IP tunnel, similar to IP Tunnel for NetWare. TCP/IP must be fully configured before AURP can be activated and configured. The default is Disabled.
Filtering Support	Allows you to filter AppleTalk using the FILTERCFG program. The default is Disabled.
Internal Network	Allows the server to support AppleTalk applications. When this is Enabled, applications can choose between having the application get an address on the internal network or one of the bound LAN interfaces. The default is Disabled.
Network Number	Sets the internal network number to a unique number for your AppleTalk network. The range is 1 to 65,279.
Network Zone(s) List	Zone name(s) with 1 to 32 characters, including any printable characters and embedded spaces. Type the zone name(s) as used in your network. The case you use in typing the name is the case that will be displayed on the Macintosh nodes later. You will need to set one of the zones as the default zone.
Expert Configuration Options	Name of the vendor providing AppleTalk over X.25 on the other peer. The options are Novell, Cisco, and Other.

Installing Macintosh Server Software 1105

When you make your choices and press the Escape key, you will have a chance to write all the changes made in this screen into a configuration file. But the protocol won't do you any good until it's bound to a network interface card. That's what the Bindings option lets you do.

The Bindings Option

Figure 13.7 shows where the AppleTalk protocol is bound to a network interface. In our example, it's to the Thomas-Conrad TC5043-T 10BaseT Ethernet card that uses the NE2000 driver supplied by Novell. Although it's an ISA card sitting in an EISA bus in ALTOS486, it works fine (although not at the highest level the EISA bus can support).

We reached this point by choosing the Bindings choice back on the Internetworking Configuration menu. This is where you return after saving the earlier AppleTalk configuration information.

If one of the previously configured IPX protocol frame types does not include ETHERNET_SNAP, configure that before starting the AppleTalk protocol configuration. Press the Insert key at the Configured Protocol to Network Interface Bindings screen, in the background in Figure 13.7. The menu doesn't say if you have ETHERNET_SNAP configured, so you must check each IPX protocol interface already defined for this frame type.

FIGURE 13.7
Adding AppleTalk to the protocol mix

```
Internetworking Configuration 3.10a            NetWare Loadable Module

  Internetworking Configuration
       Configured Protocol To Network Interface Bindings
            Binding NetWare AppleTalk to a LAN Interface
  Network Interface:                       NE2000_1

  Network Range and Zone configuration:    Define here (Seed)
  Network Range/Number:                    5-5
  Zone(s) List:                            (Select to View/Configure)

  Provide Application through this Interface:
  Applications Zone Name:


Configure Net Range and Zones if this is a seed router.  Hit F1 for more help.
ENTER=Select  ESC=Previous Menu                                        F1=Help
```

Once the ETHERNET_SNAP detail is taken care of, press Insert again to add the AppleTalk protocol bindings. The Network Range and Zone Configuration field needs the same information provided in the last section, in our case a seed router because this is the first AppleTalk router on our network. The Network Range/Number field needs a different number than the 10 we used previously. The 10 was used as an internal network number, this is for external use. The Zone(s) List field works the same way: type in the zone name you provided earlier (GCS1 in our example). Then press the Escape key twice to return to the Internetworking Configuration menu once again.

The Manage Configuration and View Configuration Options

The penultimate choice on the Internetworking Configuration menu offers a way to manage the configurations. Currently, we don't need to edit the AUTOEXEC.NCF, because the INETCFG program moves the protocol and bindings part of the AUTOEXEC.NCF to another file (NETINFO.CFG in SYS:ETC), which is reached only by the INETCFG program. The last choice, View Configuration, offers a chance to see all your newly configured INETCFG commands. You may peruse them in a group, or separated into LAN, WAN, Protocol, and Protocol Bind Commands submenus. When you're finished perusing, press Escape.

You will be warned that changes made in the INETCFG program are not active until the system is rebooted. This makes sense, because all the changes happen in the AUTOEXEC.NCF file and other startup files like INETCFG.NCF. Select Yes to Exit Configuration. And remember, you must reboot for anything new to happen.

Configuring File Services

> **13.3 IN-A-HURRY**
>
> **Configure the AppleTalk File Services**
>
> 1. Type **LOAD INSTALL** at the server console (or through RCONSOLE).
> 2. Choose Product Options, then View/Configure/Remove Installed Products under Other Installation Actions.
> 3. Choose NW-MAC v4.11 NetWare for Macintosh 4, then Configure File Services.
> 4. Use the Detailed Configuration submenu to set User Access Information.
> 5. Press Escape to exit.

The Configure File Services menu choice hides the AFPCON (AppleTalk File Protocol CONfiguration) program, just as the AppleTalk stack setup hides the INETCFG program. You can go directly to this menu by typing

    LOAD AFPCON

at the server console prompt.

This menu option handles more than you might think. You might assume it has something to do with file and directory access. It really controls how the users interact with the system and gain access to the AFP server software running on the NetWare 4.1*x* server. See Figure 13.8 for an example of this screen.

FIGURE 13.8
Setting Macintosh client access parameters

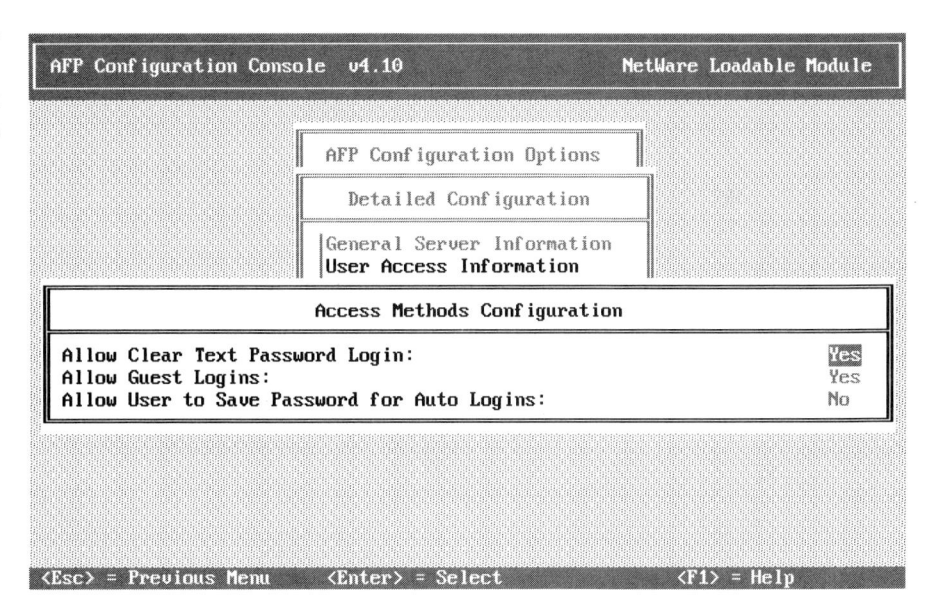

```
AFP Configuration Console  v4.10            NetWare Loadable Module



                           ┌─────────────────────────────┐
                           │  AFP Configuration Options  │
                           ├─────────────────────────────┤
                           │     Detailed Configuration  │
                           ├─────────────────────────────┤
                           │ General Server Information  │
                           │ User Access Information     │
    ┌──────────────────────┴─────────────────────────────┴──────────────────┐
    │                    Access Methods Configuration                       │
    ├───────────────────────────────────────────────────────────────────────┤
    │ Allow Clear Text Password Login:                                  Yes │
    │ Allow Guest Logins:                                               Yes │
    │ Allow User to Save Password for Auto Logins:                      No  │
    └───────────────────────────────────────────────────────────────────────┘



 <Esc> = Previous Menu     <Enter> = Select            <F1> = Help
```

Once you've reached the Access Methods Configuration screen, by choosing User Access Information from the Detailed Configuration submenu, use these settings as a starting point:

Allow Clear Text Password Login	Yes
Allow Guest Logins	Yes
Allow User to Save Password for Auto Logins	No

The disadvantage of allowing users to save their passwords in the Chooser for faster login is the security hole it leaves. Using automatic passwords is a bad idea for any system.

In the next submenu, Performance Enhancements, you have the chance to change the following fields:

- **Set Maximum Number of AFP Connections:** A number between 1 and the maximum server user count.

- **Use Filename Extension Mappings:** Yes if you wish to have the type and creator of a file mapped to applications to be launched for the file.

- **Use AFP Estimated Offspring Count:** Yes to estimate, rather than actually count, the number of files and subdirectories in a directory. This can save time.

- **Use NetWare Cache Control Algorithm:** Yes to let AFP decide when to write file changes to the disk, rather than letting the Macintosh operating system flush the cache buffers.

- **Set Finder Accelerator Max Cache Percentage:** Percentage of available memory (0 to 5 percent) for the Finder Accelerator to use. 0 is disabled. The more memory used, the higher the chance of dragging down the server performance.

- **Add Allow AFP to Report Volume Size Greater than 2 Gigabytes:** Do you have volume sizes greater than 2 GB? If not, the default is null.

As mentioned earlier, the user count of a NetWare 4.1*x* server can consist of both PC and Macintosh users, all mingled together. If your server has a limit of 250 users, you may allow 250 Macintosh clients to use that server's resources. If your network is split evenly between PC and Macintosh folks, you may set a top limit of 125 for Macintosh users. This will guarantee that PC users have a chance at the other 125 user slots. OS/2 and Unix clients figure into this equation, as well.

The last option in the AFP Configuration Options menu is Maintenance and Status. This allows you to shut down or restart the AFP server. It also allows a check of the volume information, showing the volume name, whether the Desktop Status is okay, and if AFP is currently supported. This is read-only information, so you can't make changes here, but it's nice to have a place to verify some settings.

Configuring Print Services

> **13.4 IN-A-HURRY**
>
> **Configure the AppleTalk Print Services**
>
> 1. Type **LOAD INSTALL** at the server console (or through RCONSOLE).
> 2. Choose Product Options, then View/Configure/Remove Installed Products under Other Installation Actions.
> 3. Choose NW-MAC v4.11 NetWare for Macintosh 4, then Configure Print Services.
> 4. Log in as the Admin user and provide the password.
> 5. Use the appropriate menu for the print system job of interest.
> 6. Press Escape to exit.

As with the other installation choices, choosing Configure Print Services opens another NLM management program disguised as a submenu item. This time, the lucky program is ATPSCON (AppleTalk Print Services CONfiguration). You can go directly to this program by typing

```
LOAD ATPSCON
```

at the server console prompt.

NetWare for Macintosh allows you to keep printing separate for Macintosh and non-Macintosh users. You may also allow PC users to print to Macintosh printer, or vice versa. Let's take a quick look at the vice versa option and make a NetWare printer available to the Macintosh users.

Move to the Configure Spoolers choice on the Configuration Options menu in ATPSCON. After pressing Enter, you are presented with the configured spoolers or an empty screen. Pressing Insert will open the Spooler Parameters screen, as shown in Figure 13.9.

You can fill in every field except Spooler's AppleTalk Type. The information in that field is filled in by the program, which looks at the printer model information and translates that into as close a match as possible for the Macintosh client.

FIGURE 13.9

Making NetWare printers available to Macintosh clients

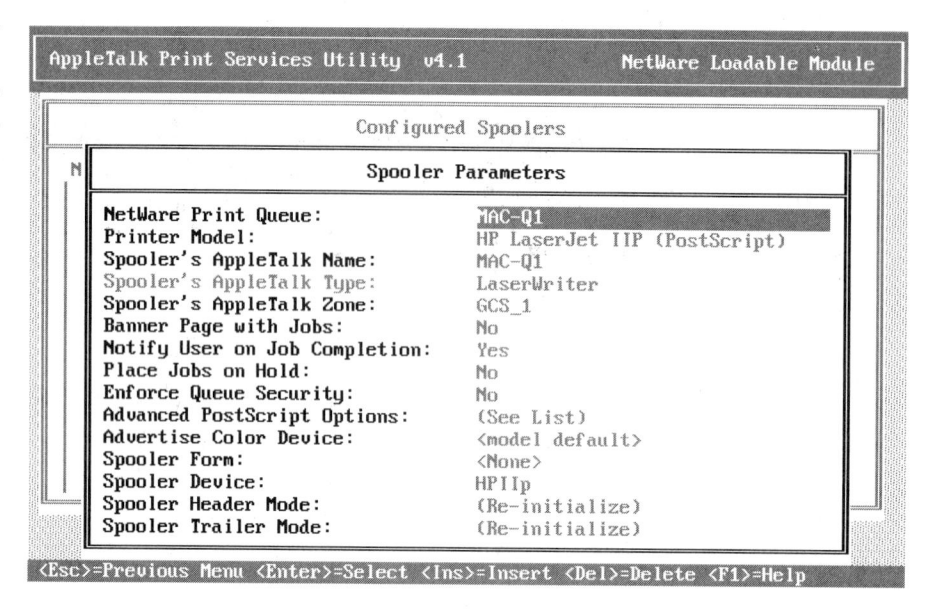

```
AppleTalk Print Services Utility  v4.1            NetWare Loadable Module

                        Configured Spoolers
                        Spooler Parameters

    NetWare Print Queue:            MAC-Q1
    Printer Model:                  HP LaserJet IIP (PostScript)
    Spooler's AppleTalk Name:       MAC-Q1
    Spooler's AppleTalk Type:       LaserWriter
    Spooler's AppleTalk Zone:       GCS_1
    Banner Page with Jobs:          No
    Notify User on Job Completion:  Yes
    Place Jobs on Hold:             No
    Enforce Queue Security:         No
    Advanced PostScript Options:    (See List)
    Advertise Color Device:         <model default>
    Spooler Form:                   <None>
    Spooler Device:                 HPIIp
    Spooler Header Mode:            (Re-initialize)
    Spooler Trailer Mode:           (Re-initialize)

<Esc>=Previous Menu <Enter>=Select <Ins>=Insert <Del>=Delete <F1>=Help
```

Many of the fields on this screen are based on the setup we've been doing, such as the Spooler's AppleTalk Zone name. Other options, such as Banner Page with Jobs and Spooler Form, work the same as they do for any other NetWare printer.

One curious setting is the Place Jobs On Hold field. If it isn't set to No, ATPS (AppleTalk Print Services) places all print jobs on either user hold or operator hold. Nothing will print unless someone clears this using PCONSOLE or the MS Windows print queue utility.

Another choice you can use when managing your Macintosh and non-Macintosh printing system is the Quick Configuration Lookup option. For example, you can use it to find all the Generic PostScript printers in zone GCS_1. When integrating an existing Macintosh network into the NetWare world, this lookup feature can be handy.

You will find that Macintosh print services under NetWare still have a few quirks. The following objects will appear in NDS, as you would expect:

- Print queues created in ATPSCON or PCONSOLE

- Printers specified in PCONSOLE

- Print servers created in PCONSOLE

The following items remain rooted in the Macintosh world, and don't appear as NDS objects:

- Printers specified in ATPSCON
- Print servers defined in ATPSCON
- Spoolers defined in ATPSCON

This is a good time to appoint one of the Macintosh power users a "Mac-Admin" helper. If you don't have a Macintosh system yourself, some printing problems will be difficult for you to handle. A helper in the Macintosh user community will save you considerable time and trouble.

> ### A Brief History of Macintosh Printing
>
> The Apple Macintosh, shipped in 1984, provided the first completely graphical computer and printer combination. At the time, Unix systems had a few large, expensive PostScript laser printers that attached to the network. DOS computers, however, were far behind the graphics race. Graphics printing at that time generally consisted of drivers to print drivers to Epson 9-pin, dot-matrix printers.
>
> Ever wonder why the Macintosh developed and dominated the desktop printing market? The graphical screen was one reason, but the contest between PostScript laser printing and a DOS dot-matrix printout was more lopsided than the elephant versus the peanut.
>
> The contest between DOS and Macintosh printing is even today. DOS machines have PostScript printers, and the market-leading LaserJet using HP's PCL (Printer Control Language) produces outstanding printouts. Print drivers on the workstation must specify the supported PDL (Page Description Language), either PostScript or some version of PCL. Applications today handle this fairly well.

Keeping Printer Types Straight

Printers usually support either PostScript or PCL (Printer Control Language), but a few now support both. If your Macintosh users have an existing printer or three, they will have no problem using those printers. Whether they wish to share those printers with the rest of the network is a different story. If they do share, PC applications will have more problems with PostScript than the Macintosh systems. You might make only one PostScript printer available to the PC users that really need access.

With dual-mode printers, make sure you define your PRINTDEF job descriptions to reset the printer back to PostScript after every print job. A header mode and trailer mode should be defined for each spooler associated with that dual-mode printer. The online documentation dedicates Appendix B in the "NetWare for Macintosh File and Print Services" volume to configuring some specific printers.

NetWare includes three Apple PDFs (Printer Definition Files) plus a generic PostScript PDF. PRINTDEF uses these PDFs to create printer-specific print job configurations. You can take advantage of dual PDL-mode printers, as well as dual paper trays and duplex printing features.

> *Refer to Chapter 8 for general NetWare printing information and setup. The "NetWare for Macintosh File and Print Services" volume in the DynaText documentation includes an even dozen chapters describing NetWare support of Macintosh to NetWare and NetWare to Macintosh printing services.*

NetWare for Macintosh, when installed, creates six directories on the SYS volume of the server where the NetWare for Macintosh services are installed. The directories are SYS:\NW-MAC and the five subdirectories:

- FONTS
- PPDS
- PSUTILS
- SETUP
- ATPSCON

The PPDS directory includes the 36 PPD (PostScript Printer Definition) files that appear as the defaults in ATPSCON. Another 3 MB worth of PPD files are included, in compressed format, on the diskette NWMAC-2 of the Macintosh client files. These are version 4.0 DOS format PPD files usable by NetWare for Macintosh print services.

The PKUNZIP program is included to unzip the files. To unzip all the files and make them available to the ATPSCON program, move to the SYS:\SYSTEM\NWMAC\PPDS directory. Copy the PPD.ZIP file to your current directory, then type:

```
PKUNZIP PPD
```

Three megabytes of disk space is a small price to pay for having several dozen specific printer files available to ATPSCON at all times.

The PSUTILS subdirectory includes nine PostScript utilities that may be used by both Macintosh and DOS workstations to configure PostScript printers. The details are in Appendix A of the "NetWare for Macintosh File and Print Services" documentation volume.

Configuring CD-ROM Services

> **13.5 IN-A-HURRY**
>
> **Support HFS CD-ROM Disks on the NetWare Server**
>
> 1. Type **LOAD INSTALL** at the server console (or through RCONSOLE).
>
> 2. Choose Product Options, then View/Configure/Remove Installed Products under Other Installation Actions.
>
> 3. Choose NW-MAC v4.11 NetWare for Macintosh 4, then Configure CD-ROM Services.
>
> 4. Configure the HFS CD-ROM options.
>
> 5. Press Escape to exit.

NetWare for Macintosh automatically supports the Macintosh-standard HFS (Hierarchical File System) CD-ROM disks. The following features are provided:

- All workstations on the network can share data stored on a CD-ROM disk.

- The CD-ROM disk will be mounted as a NetWare for Macintosh volume.

- HFSCD.NLM copies data from the CD-ROM disk to the server volume when files are opened to speed access to the data.

- Data not accessed in a configurable amount of time is purged from the index kept on the hard disk. Data exceeding the defined volume space for the CD-ROM data will be removed from the index as well.

- Removed files remain in the volume directory, allowing access through the volume to the CD-ROM disk.

- The HFSCDCON.NLM program provides configuration and management utilities.

As you can guess, the HFSCDCON program is loaded when the Configure CD-ROM Services choice is made from the NetWare for Macintosh Configuration screen. HFS is the standard Macintosh data structure for files and folders (directories).

RTDM (Real Time Data Migration) between the NetWare volume and the CD-ROM disk is handled by the RTDM.NLM program, loaded automatically when the other CD-ROM support files are loaded. When a Macintosh client opens a CD-ROM file, RTDM.NLM copies the file to a NetWare volume, using the volume like a giant file cache. This greatly improves the access times to the files.

There are five options on the HFS CD-ROM Options menu:

- **Disk List:** Shows the active HFS CD-ROM disks on this server. If you have more than one, highlight the one you are curious about and press Enter to display its current status.

- **Manual Migrator Start:** File migration is normally done once a day automatically, but this option forces the migration.

- **Migrator Status:** Shows the status of the file-migration process.

- **Setup:** Shows the configuration screen for the NFSCD.NLM file-migration process.

- **Exit:** Unloads the HFSCDCON program but leaves the NFSCD.NLM running on the server.

Figure 13.10 shows the Setup screen for the migration process. This is the screen shown by the Setup menu choice.

The file-control fields are Automatic Scan Default Path and NetWare Volume Space Limits. The first requires a directory on a Macintosh name-space-enabled volume. The second sets in megabytes the amount of space for the on-disk CD-ROM data cache. When you have a default scan path set, you can then turn on the Automatically Scan Discs setting.

The migration Start Hour uses 0 as the default, meaning midnight. The Stop Hour may be set at any time, but listing another 0 allows the migration to finish without interruption. If a backup is scheduled and the migration list becomes large, this setting allows you to stop the migration before the backup begins.

FIGURE 13.10

Controlling CD-ROM disk file migration details

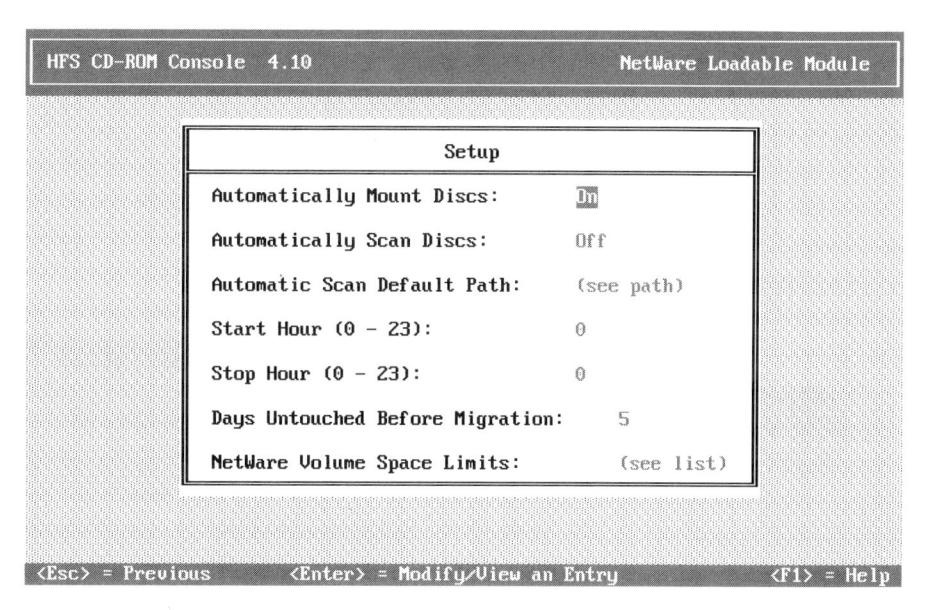

```
HFS CD-ROM Console 4.10                        NetWare Loadable Module

                            Setup
            Automatically Mount Discs:      On
            Automatically Scan Discs:       Off
            Automatic Scan Default Path:    (see path)
            Start Hour (0 - 23):            0
            Stop Hour (0 - 23):             0
            Days Untouched Before Migration: 5
            NetWare Volume Space Limits:    (see list)


     <Esc> = Previous      <Enter> = Modify/View an Entry      <F1> = Help
```

Installing Additional Language Support

13.6 IN-A-HURRY

Add Languages for Macintosh Clients

1. Type **LOAD INSTALL** at the server console (or through RCONSOLE).

2. Choose Product Options, then View/Configure/Remove Installed Products under Other Installation Actions.

3. Choose NW-MAC v4.11 NetWare for Macintosh 4, then Install Additional Language Support.

4. Define the path to the additional language files.

5. Press Enter to save and exit.

The Install Additional Language Support option on the NetWare for Macintosh Configuration menu helps you copy the needed language files from the NetWare 4.1*x* distribution CD-ROM disk to the server.

You are presented with a disk drive letter and expected to supply a path to the language files. If they are on a CD-ROM disk on the server, put either the DOS drive letter for the CD-ROM or the volume name. If you are running the CD-ROM disk from your workstation and using this menu through RCONSOLE, you can set that disk drive letter as well.

Installing Macintosh Client Support

13.7 IN-A-HURRY

Add Client Files for Macintosh Clients

1. Type **LOAD INSTALL** at the server console (or through RCONSOLE).

2. Choose Product Options, then View/Configure/Remove Installed Products under Other Installation Actions.

3. Choose NW-MAC v4.11 NetWare for Macintosh 4, then Install Macintosh Client Support.

4. Check the client support language to be installed by pressing Enter.

5. Press Escape to copy the files to the server.

There are a few Macintosh client files necessary to make your Macintosh client a full NetWare NDS participant (less than the number of files necessary for DOS and MS Windows clients). The files are copied to the \PUBLIC\CLIENT\ MAC\ENGLISH directory. (In NetWare 4.10, all the Macintosh client files are contained in one self-extracting archive file labeled MacNDS.sea, which is copied to the \PUBLIC\MAC\ENGLISH directory.) The files are:

- **MacNCP:** Enables you to specify a preferred user name, NDS tree, and Directory context for NDS logins. Also enables or disables the receipt of messages.

- **NetWare UAM:** NetWare User Authentication Method (NetWare UAM) software provides NetWare NDS password encryption for the Macintosh workstation. The NetWare UAM is required on all Macintosh workstations that will access servers on which clear-text and guest logins are disabled.

- **MacIPX:** Enables a Macintosh to communicate on the network using the IPX/SPX family of protocols and is required by MacNCP to access NDS for authentication on a NetWare 4 network. AppleTalk (usually over EtherTalk or TokenTalk) is used to access the AFP server software on the NetWare host server.

- **AppleShare 3.5 or 7.1:** If your Macintosh uses a version of AppleShare older than version 3.5 or 7.1, the Installer installs the updated version.

- **NetWare Aliases:** The NetWare Aliases extension enables you to create an alias to folders and files on NetWare volumes. You can store this alias on your workstation and use it to quickly log in to a server and open a frequently used file or other service.

Once the compressed file is placed on the server volume, any Macintosh connecting to the server can reach the directory and execute the file. Even if the Macintosh client connects with Bindery Services, the directory is still accessible and the file will execute and place the proper Macintosh client files in the proper places.

We'll cover the details about the client side of the server/client connection in the section titled "Installing Macintosh Clients," coming up shortly.

Adding the Macintosh Name Space

> **13.8 IN-A-HURRY**
>
> **Add the Macintosh Name Space to Volumes**
>
> 1. Type **LOAD INSTALL** at the server console (or through RCONSOLE).
>
> 2. Choose Product Options, then View/Configure/Remove Installed Products under Other Installation Actions.
>
> 3. Choose NW-MAC v4.11 NetWare for Macintosh 4, then Add Macintosh Name Space.
>
> 4. Check the volume that needs to support the Macintosh name space.
>
> 5. Press Escape to install the Macintosh name space support.

During the initial installation, you picked the volume(s) needing Macintosh name space support. Refer to Figure 13.3, the first option. If you skipped that step then, or need to add Macintosh support to another volume or two, you can use the Add Macintosh Name Space choice on the NetWare for Macintosh Configuration menu. (Adding name spaces used to be somewhat thrilling and unpredictable, but now it's boring.) Highlight the Add Macintosh Name Space menu item and press Enter. The volumes without Macintosh name space support on the current server will be listed. Press Enter to check the box for each volume to be modified, and press Escape to exit the pick list screen and add the name space support. That's it.

If SYS: is the volume getting the Macintosh name space support, the MAC.NAM program will be set to load automatically when the server comes up. The MAC.NAM program is on the NetWare boot disk, in the main directory with the other startup files (such as STARTUP.NCF).

If other volumes have the name space configured, the startup programs may not be able to find the MAC.NAM program. Once the SYS: volume becomes active, the server startup directory is no longer seen; the DOS partition of the server is not available to the NetWare server software. Make life simple by copying the MAC.NAM program to the SYS:SYSTEM directory if it has not already been placed there by the installation program. Once there, it will always be found whenever you try to start the Macintosh name space on any volume for that server.

> **WARNING**
>
> *Do not add Macintosh support to a volume that is nearly full, because there won't be room to add the extra overhead for the file name translation. Also, do not add Macintosh support to a volume supporting only one or two Macintosh clients if you can avoid it. The performance impact will be higher than if you moved a few extra directories to a volume that already supports the Macintosh.*

Installing Macintosh Clients

ONCE YOU HAVE your Macintosh client workstation connected to good cabling, the AppleShare program in Chooser will automatically see the NetWare server and defined zones. If you have several zones, check each one until the server you wish to use appears. If there is only a single zone defined, you won't see any zones mentioned in the Chooser.

Installing Macintosh Clients **1119**

> ### 13.9 IN-A-HURRY
>
> **Set Up Macintosh Clients**
>
> 1. Verify that the Macintosh client is connected to the network where the newly Macintosh-aware server lives.
>
> 2. Open the Chooser and double-click on AppleShare, then choose the NetWare server.
>
> 3. Type a login name and password if necessary.
>
> 4. You'll see a list of volumes that support the Mac name space. Double-click on the SYS: volume.
>
> 5. When the red filing cabinet appears (with the little 4 indicating NetWare 4), double-click on it.
>
> 6. Restart your machine. Verify the files and their placement on your Macintosh client.

Click on the server name, then on OK. The dialog box to log in to the server will appear (you can't log in to NDS, because you don't have the NDS software yet). You must provide a name of a user on that server. Before going any farther, give that user full rights to the \PUBLIC\CLIENT\MAC\ENGLISH directory (in NetWare 4.10, the \PUBLIC\MAC\ENGLISH directory).

When you're connected, open the red filing cabinet labeled with the name of the NetWare server. You'll see a message similar to the one shown in Figure 13.11 in NetWare 4.10, but not necessarily in 4.11. Remember when you had the chance to change the name the server broadcasts to the Macintosh clients? This is the name you will see now.

In NetWare 4.10, the procedure is a bit more complex. The display will open with the root directory. Drill down through PUBLIC, MAC, and the chosen language (ENGLISH for our example) until you see the MacNDS.sea program. This self-extracting archive file will place the NetWare client files wherever you wish. Place them on the file server. Then you'll need to extract the files to the folder where you put MacNDS.sea.

Start the Installer program. This is where rubber meets road, and client files get parceled to their proper places on your Macintosh client. After installation, your workstation must be rebooted.

Between the Guide Menu and the time display will be a barren tree. That's NetWare NDS before you log in. You will log in to the particular file server holding the Macintosh name space volume, but only under Bindery Services. Click on the NDS tree, and provide your NDS name and password.

FIGURE 13.11

The server recognizes the Macintosh client in NetWare 4.10.

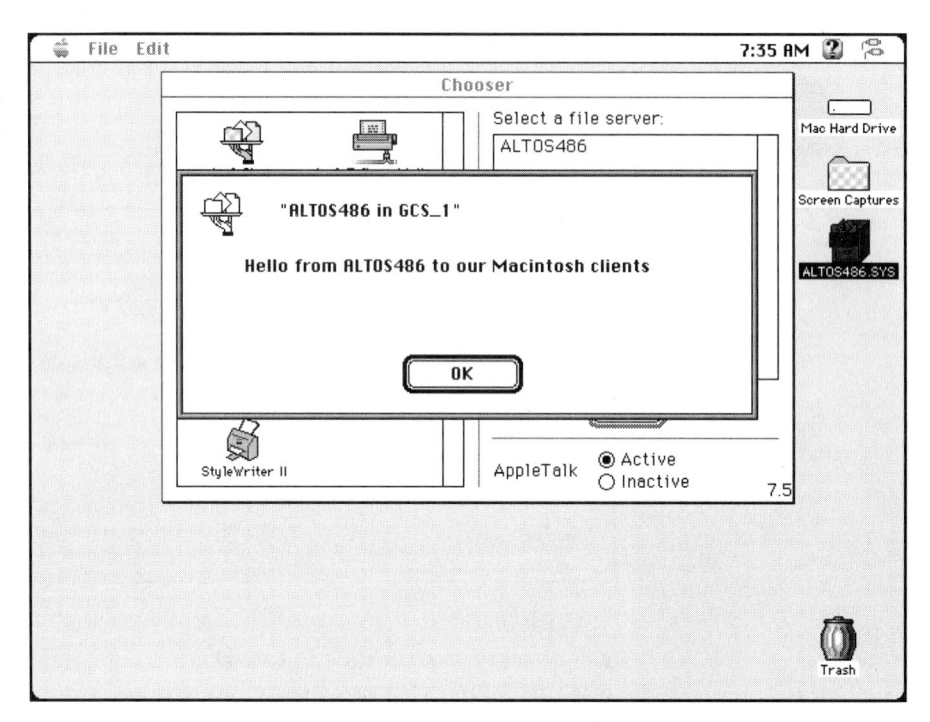

The tree will grow leaves and turn green faster than spring in time-lapse photography for a TV commercial. Once the tree is green, you are a full member of NetWare NDS, just like any misguided MS Windows bigot.

Navigating through NDS

YOU MAY NEED to explain some of the basic NetWare 4.1x ideas to the Macintosh group, especially when they hit NDS. (In NetWare 4.10, you'll see the MacNCP window.) The Directory Tree field, if you have a single-tree network, will always be filled in correctly. If you have multiple trees, you can click on the Find button in the NetWare Client References screen to see the Available Trees window. All known trees are listed, but there's another chance to find even more trees by clicking on the Remote button. The window you'll see shows your available servers on the left side, with the NDS trees known to that server on the right.

The next field, Directory Context, shows the current context for the Macintosh client. You can change this by typing a new context. In NetWare 4.11, you can also select a new context from the pop-up list.

Directory Services Login Name is exactly what you would expect. The user name configured for the Macintosh will be listed automatically, or you may change it here and connect again.

File and print services for Macintosh systems still require the AppleTalk File Protocol loaded on the NetWare server. At this time, no vendor (including Novell) has rewritten the entire Macintosh interface and applications for NCP (NetWare Core Protocols).

Novell is making progress, however. All the Macintosh utilities with NetWare 4.11 show the new, "ball-sy" logo.

Helping Macintosh and PC Users Work Together

MANY PC PEOPLE like to harangue Apple people for their arrogance. Do they suppose no one in the PC side of computing has an ego? I can point them to, oh, at least three or four PC company executives and/or owners with egos the size of small cities. At least a couple of these people have egos the size of small countries.

Besides, if your ideas really are better than everyone else's, are you arrogant or just truthful? The first Macintosh came loaded with friendliness before user interface meant anything to anyone. The existing systems at that time had no user interface; there was an empty screen daring you to guess what to do. Whether the Apple design crew developed the interface themselves, or borrowed the ideas from our friends at PARC, is not part of this discussion. That's a whole other book.

The problem, of course, comes when either someone else trumps your idea, or you have a new idea that's not better, just different. Can you objectively

> *Besides, if your ideas really are better than everyone else's, are you arrogant or just truthful?*

look at your idea and the competing ideas and honestly judge between them? Sadly, history answers no to that question. Worse, some people start to reject ideas simply because their company didn't develop them, refusing to take advantage of advancing technology.

So it happened with Apple. The science of human/computer interfacing has caught up to Apple. The price/performance computing curve passed it long ago.

The next generation of Apple products will not display the leap-of-technology brilliance that was exemplified by the early Macintosh. Apple is now bound to, of all companies, IBM in the PowerPC development process. The Macintosh operating system successor will be partly designed by IBM and Motorola and who knows who else.

If this level of corporate ego can work together, you can support Macintosh and PC people on your network. While it's fun to sling names back and forth (MacIdiot! Windoze!) that doesn't help get our work done. More important, it doesn't help your users, regardless of their computer type, get their work done. And that's the idea here, remember?

IntranetWare: NetWare, Intranets, and the Internet Combined

CHAPTER 14

I CAN ALMOST SEE your puzzled expression, looking down at this page. What is IntranetWare, and why should I care? IntranetWare is NetWare 4.11 with lots of extra cool things, and you should care because IntranetWare represents the future—not just Novell's future, but your networking future.

It's no secret that the Internet has captured the imagination of the world. Your network users are bugging you about getting to the Internet on one side, and sales and marketing are hollering for you to get them a Web server on the other. Luckily for you, IntranetWare makes all the Internet connections you need, both as a client of Internet resources and as a provider of those resources.

Earlier excitement over Unix for client/server applications has given way to hysteria over the Internet. The reason Novell relabeled NetWare as IntranetWare was to reflect the inclusion of Internet-inspired technology. First among these advancements are improvements in Web servers and Web clients from minimal graphic interface into an entire industry onto themselves. Combining the values of Web servers, Web clients, and easy IPX-to-IP translation is what IntranetWare is all about.

It's important to realize that all the options in this chapter dedicated to reaching the Internet work equally well for reaching local Unix systems. In fact, you can use one IPX/IP gateway and reach local Unix hosts, remote company Unix hosts, and Internet hosts of all kinds, all at the same time.

Comparing NetWare and Unix

ONCE ESOTERIC AND stuck in academia, Unix has become the biggest news in the "open" computer industry. *Open systems* has many definitions—probably two definitions for everyone you ask. My short answer to "what is open systems?" is only three words: Unix on Ethernet.

This answer is a bit glib and incomplete, although it's impossible to find an open system that doesn't support Unix and Ethernet. It's also impossible to find a system running Unix over Ethernet that wouldn't fit everyone's description of open systems, so perhaps my three-word answer is just as good as the answers proposed by all those vendor committees.

"Unix on Ethernet" leaves out NetWare, which is certainly a problem. Perhaps a better indication of what is open and what isn't is the ability of a system to connect to other systems. Regardless of what we call open and proprietary, there is a strong need for NetWare to connect to and work with Unix, on any network transport.

The name "Unix" is now a trademark of X/Open, a group of vendors formed in 1984 to ensure Unix is open, available, and consistent. This came about because Novell gave that trademark to X/Open in 1994 after buying USL (Unix Software Laboratories) in 1993. Novell "owned" Unix for a time, but has turned the trademark over to a neutral body, X/Open, to guarantee the Unix name implies meeting standards of openness and quality.

A Short History of Unix and the Internet

Let's take a quick look back in history to see how Unix got where it is, and how the Internet grew to dominate the news.

Unix, like NetWare, was developed by a few people with some clear goals. Unlike NetWare, Unix was not a commercial product for the first decade. It was used, and enhanced, by an ever-growing number of programmers, designers, and users.

Ken Thompson is generally credited with developing Unix in 1969, with Dennis Ritchie heading the list of other important contributors. You C programmers should certainly know the name of Dennis Ritchie. The story is that Ken Thompson wrote Unix in August 1969 while his wife and newborn baby were visiting relatives for two weeks. Unix booted just before they returned. I wonder where we would be today if the family returned early.

While together at Bell Labs, Thompson, Ritchie, and others were part of a team of companies writing MULTICS (MULTIplexed Information and Computing System) for a GE 645 mainframe computer. Bell Labs dropped out, but Thompson *et al* continued for a very important reason: they had written a game called Space Travel.

Since MULTICS was no longer available and the GE mainframe was gone, Thompson and Ritchie rewrote the program on an available DEC PDP-7. Continuing on,

(continued on next page)

they then wrote the earliest Unix for that same box. Called UNICS at the time, the name was a play on the name MULTICS, since it originally tried to do only one thing at a time for one user, unlike the multiuser and complex MULTICS. Just think, the history of computing has been forever changed by bad punsters.

Bell Labs got interested officially when Unix was ported to a larger DEC PDP-11/20 and some text-processing capabilities were added. By 1972, the second edition of the *Unix Programmer's Manual* mentioned that more than the current ten computers were soon expected to run Unix. In 1973, the kernel was rewritten in C by Thompson and Ritchie, and the step up from assembler made things much more portable. The spread of Unix was under way.

One way to spread an operating system is through communication. The "Network Working Group" met in the summer of 1969 in Snowbird, Utah, for the first committee meeting discussing what would become the Internet. Paul Baran of the RAND Corporation had written multiple papers in the early 1960s describing ways computers could communicate. The government, trapped in the throes of the Cold War, wanted a way to distribute computer intelligence. Single sites were vulnerable to the (inevitable, they thought) missile attack from the Communists. Spreading computers around the country would eliminate that single point of failure.

The first remote login happened in late 1971, from MIT. A year later, at the International Conference on Computers and Communications in Washington, DC, the public was treated to a demonstration.

TCP/IP started its development trip in late 1972. Since DARPA (Defense Advanced Research Projects Agency) was funding the work, military considerations such as satellite transmissions, missed packets, support for data and voice, and communicating between heterogeneous systems were part of the design criteria. Nothing tied TCP/IP to Unix until January 1, 1983, when all Internet systems were forced to use TCP/IP or unplug from the Internet. From that day, people have confused Unix and TCP/IP.

DNS (Domain Name Service) was developed in the early 1980s by Paul Mockapetris at USC. The number of Internet hosts doubled (from 500) the next year, and for several more years after that.

(continued on next page)

Not officially in the computer business until divestiture in 1984, AT&T didn't offer a commercial version of Unix until 1982. By the mid-70s however, Unix was being offered to universities for a minimal fee by Bell Labs. Generations of students are credited with both improving the various flavors of Unix and carrying those flavors with them into the commercial world. One school, the University of California at Berkeley, made enough changes and improvements to start the popular BSD (Berkeley Software Distribution) strain of Unix.

The USL SVR4 (System Five Release 4) source code released by USL is the "official" Unix reference code. AT&T controlled the source code until Novell bought USL; UnixWare was the retail product based on the reference source code released by Novell. SCO has since bought the UnixWare software license and code from Novell, and they, along with HP, are in charge of advancing the operating system. Good luck, folks, and hurry.

Other Unix versions of note are SunOS and Solaris, from Sun Microsystems. These versions run on the SPARC (Scalar Processor ARChitecture) microprocessor, developed by Sun and Intel microprocessors. XENIX was developed by SCO (Santa Cruz Organization) for Intel processors in the middle 1980s, and sold by Microsoft. At one time in the late 1980s, the largest provider of Unix systems was Radio Shack, whose stores were selling their own hardware with the Microsoft XENIX software.

All companies walk the tightrope between compatibility with the definition of Unix and special features they include to attract customers. IBM's AIX (Advanced Interactive eXecutive) version of Unix is a bit different from HP's HP/UX and DEC's OSF/1 and so on. Some companies, like Sun, have bought the source code from USL outright, and will continue to go their own way. They will no longer license the reference code.

Much is made of the multiple Unix flavors by DOS and some NetWare users, trying to cast doubts on the viability of a technology with so many strains. Please be advised that this is a natural outgrowth of development for a technology not controlled by a single entity. Also be advised that the flavors of Unix show more common points than do NetWare versus LAN Manager versus Banyan VINES. Going from one Unix to another is less confusing than going from one network operating system to another; common heritage does offer some advantages.

The Internet first felt the glare of the world spotlight on November 1, 1988, when the "Worm" clogged the Internet to the point of collapse. Back into the darkness went the Internet, until early 1994 when the first World Wide Web client to reach the public, Mosaic, turned the text-only Internet into a colorful, graphical, hyperactive consumer toy. Easy access, via the Web, meant millions of new customers. Now the Internet is called the "Information Superhighway" by politicians looking for votes, and businesses looking for bucks.

Let's take a look at some of the differences between Unix on the left and NetWare on the right:

UNIX	NETWARE
Preemptive	Not preemptive
Shaped by a large community of researchers and committees	Developed by Novell
Available on a wide range of processors, including Intel	Available on Intel processors (Processor-Independent NetWare demonstrated in 1994 but later dropped)
Several multiprocessor versions	Multiprocessor versions released in mid-1995
Virtual memory (RAM and disk considered valid workspace)	Real memory
Daemons	NLMs (NetWare Loadable Modules)
Distributed file systems available (NFS, AFS, RFS)	No distributed file systems
Transport protocol: TCP/IP	Transport protocol: IPX/SPX

I wrote in the first edition that both processor-independent NetWare and multiprocessor NetWare would be taken for granted by the release of NetWare 4.11. I'm batting .500—SMP NetWare is bundled free with NetWare 4.11, but the PIN (Processor Independent NetWare) project has been shelved.

The first edition reflected Novell executive's guarantee that Unix and NetWare would meld before 1997. Not only will Unix and NetWare go their own ways, but Novell dumped the responsibility of Unix onto SCO and HP. Many feel this act, last in a long string of stupid Unix moves by various Unix vendors, would ensure Windows NT dominance starting in 1997. It's hard to argue with that last statement, as NT eats into the market share of both NetWare and Unix.

Distributed file systems have been a hallmark of Unix since late 1984, when Sun released NFS (Network File System). Nothing in the DOS, Macintosh, or OS/2 worlds compares to NFS, which combines local and remote file systems transparently without drive mapping. The remote file systems just plug into your directory structure; there's no difference to the user. Distributed file systems are to file handling what directory services like NDS are to network user management. Expect to see some interesting file-system improvements in NetWare over the next few years.

Of course, TCP/IP is the network language of Unix and open systems. While IPX/SPX is the primary protocol for NetWare, NetWare/IP now allows complete communication between a NetWare client and NetWare server over IP without any IPX involved. All services for NetWare clients are available. We'll see more of this later in this chapter, and we'll also discuss Novell's IPX/IP Gateway included in the IntranetWare bundle.

Unix (for NetWare People)

First of all, Unix is a multitasking, multithreaded operating system. It was built from the ground up as a multiuser (in fact, multiprogrammer) operating system. It is more complex than NetWare, because it does more things.

Why do we care about this? Because the Internet is run by Unix systems. If you want to get to a Web server, the chances of that server running Unix are better than 9 out of 10. The more you know about Unix and TCP/IP, the more you know about the Internet.

The more you know about Unix and TCP/IP, the more you know about the Internet.

One big difference between NetWare and Unix is where the programs are processed. With NetWare, all application processing is done at the client PC or Macintosh. With Unix, all application processing is done at the host. This is now complicated by the growing client/server software industry. The X Windows system in Unix allows cooperative processing, as do many of the NetWare NLM programs available.

Unix utilizes preemptive scheduling, a fancy name for priorities. Certain system functions can interrupt other functions. This allows scheduled jobs to begin, and also allows system functions to perform necessary procedures, regardless of what else the system is doing. NetWare does not have this, and that is one of the reasons your Unix friends look down on NLMs. Novell engineers hesitate to make NetWare look more like Unix this way, because servicing file requests in a certain amount of time is an important performance boost for NetWare over other PC LAN operating systems. Delaying file service for system overhead would negate some of that performance advantage.

This is why NetWare will never be a real-time system, as some Unix variants are. Real-time systems must guarantee that certain functions will happen at exact time intervals, and NetWare can't guarantee that.

Everything in Unix Is a File

You'll hear your Unix friends talk about "files" in strange ways. In Unix, everything can be considered a file. Any real file on a disk we're used to, but the keyboard and monitor as files? That's right. That's what *stdin* and *stdout* refer to: your keyboard (STanDard IN) and monitor (STanDard OUT), respectively.

The three types of files are called ordinary files, directories, and special files. Ordinary files and directories are much the same as those in DOS, although we would be more historically correct to say that files and directories in DOS are much like those in Unix. These can be ASCII (text) files or binary, just as in DOS.

A directory is a directory, again just as in DOS. Directories can include files and subdirectories. The nesting of subdirectories within directories was quite an innovation for DOS in its day. If you remember, IBM and Microsoft ignored that idea in DOS 1.0 and did not permit subdirectories. When hard disks became available, so did subdirectories (in a later DOS version).

Now for the weird part: Unix considers a physical device as a *special* file. Any part of the hardware system and all peripherals can be treated as a file. What DOS considers devices and names directly, Unix considers special files. Any target of output and source of input will be referred to as a file. It's a strange concept, but if you can get your arms around it, you'll see the enormous flexibility it offers. Any file or device (in the DOS sense) can be directed to any other file or device. Output from anything can become input to anything.

Unix is case-sensitive, unlike DOS and NetWare. If you try to execute the file named calendar by typing **Calendar**, it won't work. The file ABC is not abc or Abc or ABc and so on. This will cause us some trouble when we start trying to link Unix and NetWare files, so start thinking literally now.

Even more literally, Unix has never had the lousy naming convention DOS is still stuck with: the 12345678.123 (eight.three) file name limitation. The file name income.december.93 is a legal Unix file name, but remember it will be a different file than income.December.93 (capitalization, remember?).

Daemons as NLMs

To quote *Peter Norton's Guide to Unix* by Peter Norton and Harlan Hahn (Bantam Books), "The most exotic inhabitants of the Unix universe are the daemons. A daemon is a process that executes in the background in order to be available at all times." Perhaps this is exotic to DOS-only people, but NetWare folks are used to NLMs.

From Stan Kelly-Bootle's *Understanding Unix* (Sybex), "The spelling indicates that such processes are amiable spirits rather than evil demons. Daemons run ceaselessly in the background performing various essential tasks." This again sounds much like NLMs.

Don't carry this too far, because there is a difference between a daemon and a background process in Unix. A background process is a user-initiated program running actively in the background, usually applications, utilities, or administrative tools. Any application running on the NetWare server itself must be an NLM. While a load-monitoring program for NetWare must be an NLM, in Unix it will just be an application running in the background.

Since NetWare doesn't have these user background processes available, it uses NLMs. Unix uses only a few daemons at one time, and the rest are background processes. Any Unix users can spawn background processes and go about their business. NetWare users can't start NLMs, unless they have console privileges.

The NetWare and Unix Kernels

Both NetWare and Unix have core programs that run all other programs. In NetWare, it's the SERVER.EXE program. In Unix, it's the kernel (often named Unix or VMUnix in the root directory).

Experienced NetWare administrators are more familiar with kernels than the Unix people might imagine. The earlier NetWare versions required painful configuration of every detail before a new NET$OS.EXE program was created. The process of making and linking the new NET$OS.EXE program was really relinking a kernel, but called by another name.

Today, the kernels of both NetWare and Unix try to be more separate from the hardware and software additions that are part of every installation. But both perform the same function: They control everything that goes on everywhere.

Networking, Print, File, and User Services Differences

While NetWare *is* networking to PC LAN people everywhere, Unix was networking long before. In fact, the whole DOS excitement over "client/server" computing is laughable to Unix people raised on distributed file systems and the Internet spanning the world. Allow your Unix friends a smirk or two when they see some DOS hyperbole concerning the "new world" of distributed computing.

NetWare networking is different from Unix networking. NetWare has always been a client-to-server network scheme; Unix is primarily peer-to-peer. To confuse us now, NetWare has Personal NetWare peer-to-peer networking for DOS and Windows clients. For further confusion, many Unix networks have an NFS server providing file services for a group of workstations in exactly the same manner NetWare provides services for its clients. Just another example showing any system can be improved by incorporating good ideas from other systems.

The differences between NetWare and Unix networking are in the weakness of the DOS client in PC LAN systems, and the relative structure of the Unix networking world. In the world of NetWare client server networking, the DOS (and Mac and OS/2) clients are much weaker than their Unix counterparts. This throws much of the weight in the client/server model toward the NetWare server. That server has performed well and is getting better, but the feeling has never been one of sharing among equals. Rather, it's always been a feeling of the weak client needing the services of the strong server.

The structure of the Unix world has come through collaborative standards efforts. The entire Internet building process, with the RFC (Request For Comment) procedure building consensus among competitors, is a world model of success. The resulting protocols have provided means to connect diverse equipment and software from multiple vendors in a reliable fashion, without allowing one vendor to block the process as so often happens in the DOS world.

In the Unix world, each machine is both a client and a server within the network. In fact, a stand-alone machine functions on a client and server model as well. This is a difficult concept for DOS users to accept, and those DOS users that can't accept it will never understand Unix. Some of the goals for products such as Windows NT, supposedly both a client and server in a peer-to-peer network, are trying to break "new" ground for PCs that was broken two decades ago by Unix systems.

In the real world, sharing Unix services among machines takes the mutual consent of both partners. The print server system, for instance, must give the print client permission to use that service. Permissions and configurations must be made on both ends of the transaction. In NetWare, only the server needs to grant permissions.

Philosophical Differences

For several years, I maintained that Unix was losing its philosophy while NetWare was gaining one. Now, the tide of computing has shifted, and I'm not sure if this is true anymore.

Unix has invaded the corporate world in a big, big way. The "downsizing" trend from mainframes was made possible by Unix systems, not PCs. The flip side of that trend is "upsizing" PC applications, even network applications, to a Unix system for the increased horsepower and manageability. Who is pushing all these changes? You are, and your users.

I'm beginning to believe the philosophy of Unix and NetWare has given way to the philosophy of the users: we want everything available everywhere. Of course, this idea may be giving way to the Web idea of any client to any server at any time.

Five years ago, it was simple to shrug your shoulders in despair when asked to merge information from two different systems into one report. Today, no excuse will get you out of creating that report. Data is data, regardless of where it lives, and it must be available to all authorized users. This chapter will help you make Unix systems available to your NetWare clients, and vice versa.

Networking Pioneers

Unfortunately, connecting NetWare to Unix involves more than adding some NetWare server names to the /etc/hosts table on your Unix systems. Questions range from what kind of connector goes on the cable to how to manage file formats on different systems. Every piece of every system has a corresponding, but different, piece on the other system.

Fortunately for the NetWare world, Unix people solved most of the tough problems before the IBM PC ever saw the light of day. By 1981, when the PC was introduced late in the year, networking was old hat to our friends who were building what has become the Internet. Gaze on some history (from *Internet System Handbook* by Daniel C. Lynch and Marshall T. Rose, editors; Addison Wesley Publishing):

1969	Researchers and private sector representatives meet for the first time in Snowbird, Utah to start design of what became the Internet. The group became known as the Network Working Group.
1971	First e-mail between two BBN (Bolt Beranek and Newman) programmers.
1971, October	The Network Working Group meets at MIT, where logins to remote systems are successful.

(continued on next page)

1972, October	First public demonstration of the network at the International Conference on Computers and Communications (ICCC) in Washington, DC.
1973-74	TCP/IP is designed.
1983, January 1	TCP/IP is mandated as the only protocol to run over the Internet.

Those involved with Unix networking in general and the Internet in particular may take a bow. Those coming from the world of NetWare and DOS owe your Unix friends a pat on the back sometime soon. Perhaps lunch would be a nice gesture, as well.

The next time you despair of connecting that Macintosh to that file server, think of trying to connect an SDS Sigma 7, SDS 940, IBM 360/75, and a DEC PDP-10 in 1971. Maybe those pioneers really did have it rough, although it seems to get rougher with each retelling.

NetWare TCP/IP Support

WE SPOKE OF TCP/IP in Chapter 1 during an overview of protocols supported by NetWare. With Novell's TCPIP.NLM, NetWare servers can become limited players in the world of TCP/IP. With the addition of NetWare NFS Services, that same NetWare server can suddenly become a major Unix player. Unix systems can use NetWare services, and NetWare clients can read and write Unix host files and print to Unix printers without changing a single byte on the local client workstations.

Even more fun, TCP/IP support provides the foundation for all the IntranetWare services—Web applications, FTP clients, and e-mail programs. Applications developed for use on the Internet expect TCP/IP support, either by running the TCP/IP protocol suite on the computer in question, or by using a gateway to convert IPX packets to TCP/IP packets for travel on the Internet or to hosts supporting TCP/IP. Internal company hosts, such as mid-range Unix systems and even traditional SNA mainframes, that support TCP/IP are often reached by terminal emulation programs running over TCP/IP.

There are three important pieces to Novell's TCP/IP support:

- The TCPIP.NLM and associated programs (included in NetWare 4.1*x*)
- NetWare/IP (included in NetWare 4.1*x*)
- NFS Services for NetWare (optional)

The inclusion of the NetWare Web Server and FTP Server in IntranetWare makes the server-based TCP/IP support more important than ever. After all, if you offer a Web server to the world, the Internet will beat a path to your door with TCP/IP, not IPX.

Before we see the details of NetWare's TCP/IP support, perhaps we should provide a quick TCP/IP foundation.

TCP/IP Overview

Figure 1.12 in Chapter 1 shows the TCP/IP protocol suite, the collection of smaller protocols that are grouped together when someone says "TCP/IP." The primary TCP/IP protocol suite components, along with their functions, are listed in Table 14.1.

TABLE 14.1 TCP/IP Protocol Suite Components

PROTOCOL	FUNCTION
IP (Internet Protocol)	Provides unreliable internetwork routing of datagrams.
ICMP (Internet Control Message Protocol)	Reports errors and responses to queries about remote conditions. It's an integral part of IP.
ARP (Address Resolution Protocol)	Maps an Internet address to a physical network address.
RARP (Reverse Address Resolution Protocol)	Maps a physical network address to an Internet address.
TCP (Transmission Control Protocol)	Provides reliable, connection-oriented delivery between clients. It uses full-duplex connections.
UDP (User Datagram Protocol)	Provides unreliable, connectionless packet-delivery service between clients over IP.

TABLE 14.1 (cont.)	PROTOCOL	FUNCTION
TCP/IP Protocol Suite Components	Telnet	Provides remote terminal connection services.
	FTP (File Transfer Protocol)	File transfer protocol between hosts. It carries ASCII, binary, and EBCDIC file formats.
	SMTP (Simple Mail Transfer Protocol)	Rules for exchanging ASCII e-mail between different systems.
	RIP (Routing Information Protocol)	Protocol that keeps a list of reachable networks for Internet packets.
	DNS (Domain Name System)	Hierarchical naming scheme with domain subnames separated by periods.

Some of these protocols stand alone with NetWare 4, and some are included within other components such as the TCPIP.NLM program. Pieces that are needed are loaded automatically; you don't need to worry about an extra dozen NLMs.

For a good overview of TCP/IP, check out the "NetWare TCP/IP Reference" in your DynaText documentation. There's also a "Basic Protocol Configuration Guide" and an "Advanced Protocol Configuration and Management Guide" that contain more details.

What Is TCP/IP and How Does It Work?

Developed by the Defense Advanced Research Projects Agency (DARPA) to connect dissimilar computers across a common network, TCP/IP has become the foundation of open networking. The ARPAnet, initially used as a means of communication between government and academic researchers, has become the Internet. The task of applying the WAN protocols of the TCP/IP protocol stack to the local network is moving faster than the reverse project of adding local protocols to the WAN. This means TCP/IP is the standard networking protocol suite for companies large and small.

(continued on next page)

> TCP/IP is resilient because it's a packet-switched network that was built at a time when reliable network connections were science fiction, not computer room fact. Each large file is divided into small segments called packets. The file's contents, as packets, can be routed across multiple, different networks and reassembled at the receiving end. TCP/IP protocols define these packets, including a packet destination, packet length, type of packet, and instructions telling computers how to receive and retransmit the packets.
>
> Interestingly enough, in today's climate of worrying about multimedia applications running over data networks, TCP/IP was developed to support voice packets as well as data packets.
>
> The IP part of TCP/IP is much like Novell's IPX. It provides a non-guaranteed delivery method for packets across the network. The protocol is labeled non-guaranteed because it relies on a higher-level protocol to handle retransmissions in case of an error. With IPX, the higher-level protocol is NCP (NetWare Core Protocol); for IP, it's TCP.

DNS (Domain Name System)

DNS has been the organizing force behind the ever-expanding world of networking. NFS systems use DNS to locate other network resources. DNS provides host to IP address mappings, locating computers on an internetwork. The DNS name space is divided into domains. Each domain controls all local host information in a central location, called a *name server*. Information is available to all network members in a client/server relationship.

The domain name space is an inverted tree, as is NDS. The top point, called the *root domain*, may branch into multiple domains to define a group of network clients that may or may not be located together physically. DNS defines the Internet, by grouping the worldwide network into seven top-level domains:

- com   Commercial organizations. Example: novell.com (Novell, Inc.)
- edu   Educational organizations. Example: berkeley.edu (U.C. Berkeley)
- gov   Government organizations. Example: nasa.gov (NASA, the National Aeronautics and Space Administration)
- mil   Military organizations. Example: army.mil (U.S. Army)

net   Networking organizations. Example: nsf.net (NSFNET)

org   Nonprofit organizations. Example: eff.org (Electronic Frontier Foundation)

int   International organizations. Example: nato.int (NATO, the North Atlantic Treaty Organization)

There are seven primary name servers on the Internet to resolve DNS name queries. Each name server may delegate responsibility for a segment to another name server. The higher-level name servers track the lower-level name servers so queries may be directed to the proper system.

> **NOTE**
>
> *Discussions are in progress within the Internet community to add many more top-level domains. Why? With only two primary domains for commercial users (com and net), all the good names in those domains are taken. As with 800 telephone numbers, companies want their names as part of the address, in as short a form as possible. The problem comes from the Internet naming authority's habit of ignoring trademarks when authorizing names. This leads to situations where small Internet-savvy computer companies get assigned domain names that are the same as major commercial trademarks. The lawyers will fight about this for a few more years.*

DNS information is contained in *resource records* holding host information about the domain. Different records include different information. The NetWare UNICON (UNIx CONsole) utility can automatically create and delete the proper records on the name servers.

The *master name server* contains the official database of name and address information for each domain. Changes must be made to this database.

For reliability and load-balancing, DNS supports read-only replicas of the database to reside on secondary servers. These are similar to NDS replicas. The secondary servers automatically query the master name server periodically. Each domain should have at least one replica.

Because of the size and complexity of some networks, specialized name servers help speed performance of name resolution. Cache-only servers hold discovered addresses after they have been discovered, so subsequent requests for addresses on that remote network can be resolved quickly. A *forwarder* performs this job exclusively for remote networks.

NIS (Network Information Services)

NIS is another distributed database that provides common information for network use, such as user and group information. Originally developed by Sun, this service was first called "Yellow Pages," before the phone company got involved.

Similar to NDS, NIS uses the database of users and groups to validate access to network resources, especially NFS. The tables of information are called *NIS maps*, which are controlled by the master NIS server.

The NIS domain is controlled by this NIS server. NIS domains consist of local network connections only and generally cover a single network. The domain names are flat, rather than hierarchical as in DNS, and the rules for these names are not as strict. Each domain must have a unique name. NIS and DNS domains may overlap, but it's not necessary.

There are *replica servers* for NIS (just as in NDS) for fault-tolerance, but the databases are all read-only. Called *slaves* in NIS, these subordinate systems periodically query the master server for updates. The UNICON utility in NetWare NFS Services is able to force replication if enough changes have been made.

In fact, UNICON can handle both standard and custom NIS maps. Through the interactive menus, you can handle all management tasks without resorting to editing configuration files by hand. Figure 14.1 shows the UNICON main menu.

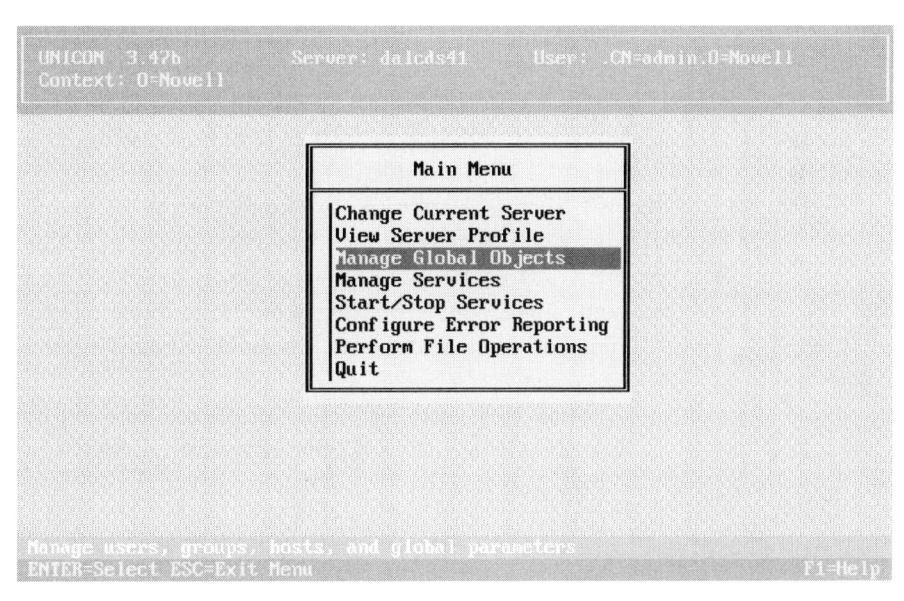

FIGURE 14.1
UNICON main menu

IP Addresses

You might expect to see "TCP/IP Addresses" as the subhead here, but IP is correct. TCP/IP address means the same thing in most circles, but it's not technically correct.

An IP address has four bytes, separated by periods: XX.XX.XX.XX. These decimal numbers break down into ones and zeros by the time they get to the network itself, and those ones and zeros are important when we look at an address.

Each address consists of two parts: the network portion, which specifies the network, and the host portion, which identifies the node (computer). The ratio between available network addresses and host addresses decides which class of network address we have.

The differentiation between network numbers is based on the beginning bits of the address. This helps performance in routing by allowing routers to look at the fewest possible bits of each address that zooms by.

Class A IP addresses consist of 1 byte (of four) of network number, and 3 bytes (of four) of host numbers. There are 126 Class A network addresses, because networks 0 and 127 are reserved.

In dotted-decimal notation, the Class A address range is 1 through 126 (1.h.h.h–126.h.h.h). There are only a few Class A addresses, but each Class A network can have more than 16 million hosts.

Class B addresses have 2 bytes of network portion and 2 bytes of host portion. There are about 16,000 Class B networks (128.h.n.n through 191.h.n.n). Each Class B network may have more than 65,000 computers.

Class C addresses (192.n.n.h through 223.n.n.h) consist of a 3-byte network portion followed by 1-byte of host portion. There can be about 2 million Class C networks, but only 254 nodes can be in each.

The Class A addresses are long gone, as you would expect with so few to go around. The Class B addresses are also strictly limited. Class C addresses are available, but with only 254 nodes available per Class C network, most companies require multiple network addresses. This makes for messy subnetting, and wasted addresses, since not every network that needs its own address has exactly 254 nodes.

Your network number must be unique for every node. If not, strange things happen on your network, since duplicate addresses will cause confusion in the network protocols.

Subnetwork Masks

Subnetting allows a complex local network to be seen as a single network from the outside. One network can be divided into two or more smaller network for the following reasons:

- Multiple media—to connect Token Ring and Ethernet segments, or remote networks.

- Reduce congestion—more nodes per network means more traffic. Segmenting the network keeps local traffic local, reducing overall congestion.

- Isolate networks for troubleshooting—having several smaller networks greatly reduces the chance that a single failure somewhere can take down the entire network.

- IP address space—dividing a Class A or B address over smaller subnetworks makes efficient use of your available network addresses.

Each subnetwork behaves as if it were an independent network, and the users have no extra configuration in regular use. Routing between nodes on different subnetworks is transparent. A routing table is maintained for each node or router.

A subnetwork divides the host address portion of the IP address into two parts, just as the IP address is split into network and host sections. Rather than *<network address><host address>*, the new division looks like *<network address> <subnetwork address> <host address>*.

The middle portion, the subnetwork address, depends on the subnetwork mask to split the numbers properly, giving the desired number of subnetworks containing the right number of hosts. The more subnetworks you have, the fewer hosts can be in each.

Your Unix or Internet administrator will give you the proper subnet mask to use. If you put the wrong number in, nothing will work, so make sure you copy the number correctly. Your subnet mask, if simple, will be something like 255.255.255.0, or FF.FF.FF.00 (same number, different format). If your network design is more complicated, you may have a series of subnet masks for various servers, such as 255.255.255.192 or 255.255.255.224. These subnet masks are used when subnetting your network into two or six smaller networks. Be careful when copying and typing these numbers.

Subnet Secrets

Of all the problems in networking, TCP/IP subnet design and numbering are one of the worst. NetWare folks new to TCP/IP feel stupid when trying to understand subnets and subnet masks for the first time. Don't feel stupid, feel normal. TCP/IP folks are still struggling with these same addressing problems.

> **NOTE** *After years of trying to fake subnet addressing, I finally did the research and came up with exactly which subnet masks go with which network addresses. We don't have the time to go into all the reasons why and wherefore these network numbers work, but you can do the research if you wish. The best freely available information I've seen on TCP/IP subnetting is on 3Com's Web site (http://www.3com.com) in its White Paper on TCP/IP addressing issues. Look it up, but be warned it's pretty involved and often complicated. After all, this is a complicated subject.*

The problems come when splitting a single Class C address containing 254 usable IP addresses into two or more subnetworks. This often happens at a NetWare file server, acting as router. Here's the cheat sheet; don't ask about the details unless you have the time to get deep into IP arithmetic, which makes new math look old.

If you need two subnetworks rather than the one Class C network, you may have a maximum of 62 uniquely numbered nodes in each network. More networks equal fewer nodes per network. The number of nodes per network doesn't equal 254 because, to get two usable networks, you must create four total networks. You can't use the first and last networks in the series, because they include the numbers 0 and 255, which are used by the system and reserved for use by your network. To get six usable networks of thirty usable IP addresses, you create eight networks and ignore the first and last ones, leaving six usable networks.

Following these addresses (substituting your own Class C address for the one here), your network subnets will function properly. If you ignore these numbers and create your own, they won't work, I promise. I've been there. Here's the information for two subnetworks:

Subnet mask: 255.255.255.192

First usable network IP address starts at 204.251.122.64
Address range of 204.251.122.65–126

Second usable network IP address starts at 204.251.122.128
Address range of 204.251.122.129–190

Here's the information for six subnetworks:

Subnet mask: 255.255.255.224

Network #1 address: 204.251.122.32
Address range of 204.251.122.33–62

Network #2 address: 204.251.122.64
Address range of 204.251.122.65–94

Network #3 address: 204.251.122.96
Address range of 204.251.122.97–126

Network #4 address: 204.251.122.128
Address range of 204.251.122.129–158

Network #5 address: 204.251.122.160
Address range of 204.251.122.161–190

Network #6 address: 204.251.122.192
Address range of 204.251.122.193–222

You may notice that the addresses 63, 95, 127, 159, 191, and 223 are missing in this discussion. That is because these are addresses that are reserved for use by the system.

Keep this page close at hand if you're setting up subnetworks. If your network is connecting to the Internet, and your Internet service provider talks about cider ("CIDR", or Classless Inter-Domain Routing), use the network numbers you're given. Each IP address on the Internet at any one time must be unique, so making up your own addresses generally leads to either a nonfunctional network or disaster. Neither is fun.

NetWare TCP/IP Components

The TCPIP.NLM program suite includes the following NLM and database files:

- NetWare TCP/IP NLM file (TCPIP.NLM)
- Simple Network Management Protocol NLM file (SNMP.NLM)
- SNMP Event Logger NLM file (SNMPLOG.NLM)

- TCP/IP Console NLM file (TCPCON.NLM)
- IP Static Route Configuration NLM file (IPCONFIG.NLM)
- Sample Internet database files (HOSTS, NETWORKS, PROTOCOL, and SERVICES)
- ICMP Echo NLM files (PING.NLM and TPING.NLM) for diagnostics
- BootP Forwarder NLM file (BOOTPFWD.NLM)
- IP Filter Support (IPFLT.NLM)
- IP Tunnel (IPTUNNEL.LAN)

The TCP/IP NLM files are loaded into the SYS:SYSTEM directory during installation. The Internet database files are installed in the SYS:ETC\SAMPLES directory.

NetWare TCP/IP supports both Novell and third-party applications. Third-party products are supported through the TLI (Transport Layer Interface) used by the AT&T-developed STREAMS or the BSD 4.3 Sockets interface. Figure 14.2 shows how the software pieces plug together.

Since the Unix and Internet folks in your organization will want to know the depth of NetWare's TCP/IP support, let's go down the list of services. Table 14.2 summarizes NetWare's TCP/IP support services.

TABLE 14.2 NetWare's TCP/IP Support Services

SERVICE	FUNCTION
TCP/IP Application Support	Provides a transport interface for higher-level network services, such as NetWare NFS. Both TCP and UDP transport services are provided.
IP Routing	Forwards IP traffic from one network to another. Novell's TCP/IP software supports link state, distance vector, and static routing.
RIP (Routing Information Protocol)	Uses the distance-vector algorithm for routing operations and decisions. Most TCP/IP networks still use RIP.
OSPF (Open Shortest Path First)	Uses the link-state algorithm for routing operations and decisions.
EGP (Exterior Gateway Protocol)	Exchanges routing information between IP internetworks controlled by different entities.

NetWare TCP/IP Support 1145

TABLE 14.2 (cont.)
NetWare's TCP/IP Support Services

SERVICE	FUNCTION
Static Routing	Manually configures routes, dictating the routers used to reach remote destinations. Static routing may be used exclusively or in addition to dynamic routing protocols.
Router Discovery	Used by routers to advertise their presence on a network, similar to the way NetWare servers use SAP to announce themselves.
Subnetwork Support	Networks can be divided into subnetworks to lower traffic levels and simplify management. However, subnetting TCP/IP is much more difficult than adding new networks to a NetWare network.
Variable Subnetwork Support	NetWare 4.1x allows different size subnetworks through support of variable-length subnet masks.
Subnet Zero	Support for OSPF and RIP II routing protocols. These protocols include the subnetwork mask and are not confused between the zero subnetwork and the natural network.
Directed Broadcast	A broadcast sent to all hosts on a particular IP network or subnetwork, often used to find or announce services.
BOOTP Forwarding	BOOTstrap Protocol is used by some systems to discover their IP address and sometimes load other operating information, such as their operating system. This is similar to the "Get Nearest Server" packet sent by NetWare clients as they attempt to log in. The questioning host broadcasts a BOOTP request; routers may either block these requests or pass them to the appropriate network if the BOOTP server is on another network. Four different BOOTP servers may be referenced.
TCP/IP Network Management with SNMP	Simple Network Management Protocol is the most popular TCP/IP management protocol. All the Unix-based management systems use SNMP as their primary protocol.
Internetworking Configuration Utility	INETCFG is the menu-driven utility we've seen when setting up AppleTalk. INETCFG replaces the LOAD and BIND commands in the AUTOEXEC.NCF file and provides interactive menus for configuration.
Permanent Connections	Links to other systems may be configured during initialization to stay up continually. If the line drops, the connection is automatically retried for reconnection.

FIGURE 14.2

TCP/IP support in a NetWare server

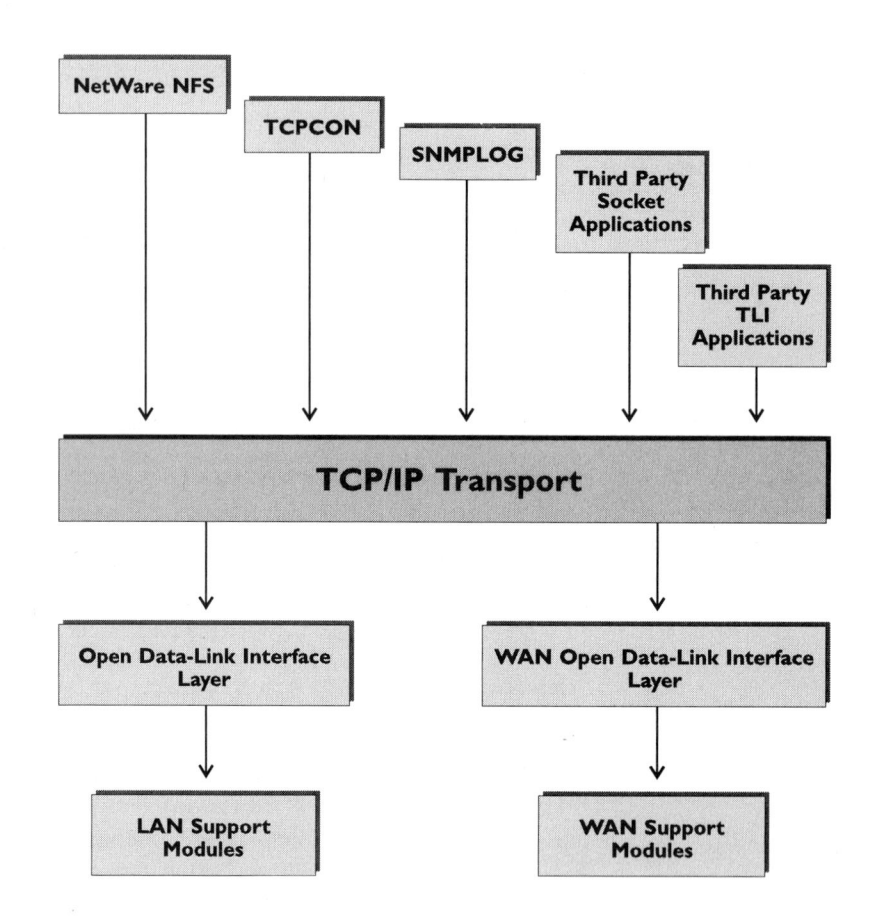

[Diagram: NetWare NFS, TCPCON, SNMPLOG, Third Party Socket Applications, and Third Party TLI Applications all feed into TCP/IP Transport, which connects to Open Data-Link Interface Layer (→ LAN Support Modules) and WAN Open Data-Link Interface Layer (→ WAN Support Modules).]

Don't let the list in Table 14.2 make you nervous. Most of your work will be done within INETCFG, and you won't need to worry about loading the right NLM at the right time. The TCP/IP system modules will take care of that themselves.

Installing TCPIP.NLM

The steps for installing TCPIP.NLM look more involved than they actually are. The big trick here is to remember to BIND the new IP protocol to a network interface board. It doesn't happen automatically, and it won't happen until you reboot the server or type the LOAD and BIND statements at the console. It's better to reboot, so you can make sure everything works as it should.

14.1 IN-A-HURRY

Activate TCP/IP Support

1. Type **LOAD INETCFG** from the server console (or over RCONSOLE).

2. Choose Protocols, then TCP/IP from the Protocol Configuration menu. (It will say Unconfigured if you have not set up TCP/IP.)

3. To accept the default settings, press Escape and answer Yes to the prompt.

4. Press Escape and choose Bindings.

5. Choose the protocol-to-interface binding where you wish to add TCP/IP and press Insert.

6. Highlight TCP/IP and press Enter twice.

7. Provide the unique IP address for the server, and either accept or change the sub-network mask. This mask must match that of your IP network.

8. Press Escape and save, and then choose View Configuration from the main menu.

9. Check All INETCFG Commands to ensure the LOAD TCPIP and BIND IP statements have been written into the file.

10. Press Escape to exit.

11. Reboot the server to check the installation and load the IP protocol support.

The necessary files for TCP/IP support are installed on the network automatically. If you get confused and check the INSTALL program, thinking TCP/IP is a new product to install, you'll find there is no entry for that. Go to the console or use RCONSOLE and start the INETCFG program.

Running the INETCFG utility will copy your protocol information from the AUTOEXEC.NCF file to INITSYS.NCF and NETINFO.CFG. The first file is the only file created with NetWare 4.10, but NetWare 4.11 adds the second as well. This additional file is about the only real change between the two versions, and you won't need to change a thing yourself, since the system deals with this file. You must move these protocol statements to these new files, or you can't install TCP/IP on the server.

For standard TCP/IP support, there are two critical pieces of information: the IP address for your NetWare server and the subnetwork mask being used by the network. If you don't have these two fields configured properly, your network will blow up and you'll be wounded by the shrapnel. Okay, the TCP/IP network administrator(s) will come and yell at you. Neither is pleasant.

First we must install TCP/IP support, which is done through the TCP/IP Protocol Configuration screen (choose Protocols from the main menu, then TCP/IP from the Protocol Configuration menu). As you can see in Figure 14.3, the default information covers most of what you'll need.

The most common change to make from the defaults is to make this server an IP router. The second field asks this question, although it's less direct than it could be. If you enable IP Packet Forwarding, a setting will be changed in the LOAD command for TCP/IP. What we have in Figure 14.3 will generate a LOAD command like this:

```
LOAD Tcpip RIP=Yes Forward=No
```

We're not finished yet. We must BIND the TCP/IP protocol to one of our network interface cards. This is done through the Bindings menu choice. When you choose Bindings, you'll see an entry for each frame type you have set for each network interface card you have in this server. If you have Ethernet of some kind, you may have four frame types (Ethernet 802.3, Ethernet 802.2, Ethernet_II, and Ethernet SNAP). However, if you have only one interface card in your server, there's no way to make a wrong choice.

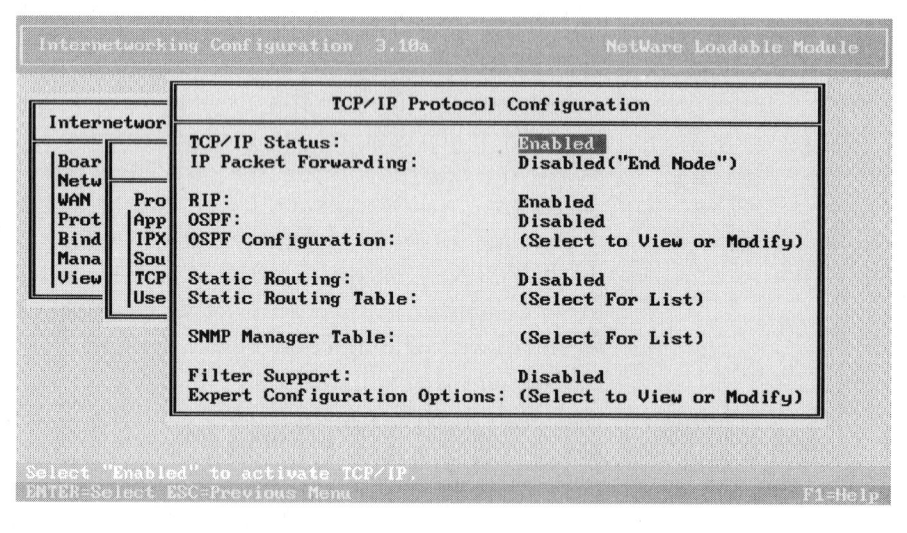

FIGURE 14.3

Default TCP/IP support

A listing shows IPX in the Protocol column of the Configured Protocol To Network Interface Binding screen, reached by choosing Bindings from the main menu. If you press the Insert key in this box, a new box will appear with a list of configured protocols. Because we have enabled TCP/IP (in Figure 14.3), TCP/IP is listed as an enabled protocol. Choose TCP/IP, and you'll see the screen shown in Figure 14.4.

The first field is the network interface we chose to reach this point. The Local IP Address field and the one after it are the important ones. For the address, you must supply a unique IP address that will be tied to this interface of this server. This is not a host address, separate from the network. The IP address really specifies both a host and network connection, although most hosts have a single interface and so a single address. If you add a second IP connection on the same server, you'll need a second IP address.

Ask your company's TCP/IP network administrator for the address for your server. The administrator will also know the subnetwork mask for the network. If the address is wrong, strange things will happen, and at least one other network host will have a problem. If the subnetwork mask is wrong, consequences range from you not seeing the network to serious network router confusion.

Press Escape to save this information and exit, which brings you back to the main menu once again. Choose the final option, View Configuration, to check on what we've done.

FIGURE 14.4

Setting the IP address and subnetwork mask

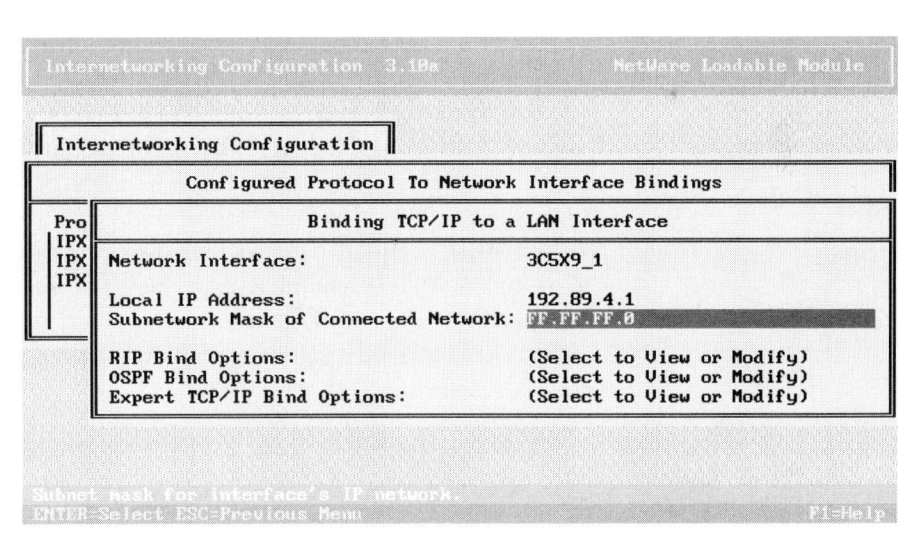

```
┌─────────────────────────────────────────────────────────────────────┐
│ Internetworking Configuration  3.10a          NetWare Loadable Module│
│                                                                      │
│ ┌─ Internetworking Configuration ─┐                                  │
│ │         Configured Protocol To Network Interface Bindings          │
│ │ ┌───┐┌──────────────────────────────────────────────────────────┐  │
│ │ │Pro││           Binding TCP/IP to a LAN Interface              │  │
│ │ │IPX││                                                          │  │
│ │ │IPX││ Network Interface:              3C5X9_1                  │  │
│ │ │IPX││                                                          │  │
│ │ └───┘│ Local IP Address:               192.89.4.1               │  │
│ │      │ Subnetwork Mask of Connected Network:  FF.FF.FF.0        │  │
│ │      │                                                          │  │
│ │      │ RIP Bind Options:              (Select to View or Modify)│  │
│ │      │ OSPF Bind Options:             (Select to View or Modify)│  │
│ │      │ Expert TCP/IP Bind Options:    (Select to View or Modify)│  │
│ │      └──────────────────────────────────────────────────────────┘  │
│                                                                      │
│ Subnet mask for interface's IP network                               │
│ ENTER=Select  ESC=Previous Menu                              F1=Help │
└─────────────────────────────────────────────────────────────────────┘
```

The first option, All INETCFG Commands, shows all the LOAD and BIND commands that the INETCFG program has pulled out of the AUTOEXEC.NCF file. This is what we want, although you may focus more narrowly if you wish. Figure 14.5 shows the newly changed configuration for GATEWAY2000, now ready for TCP/IP.

FIGURE 14.5

LOAD and BIND everything.

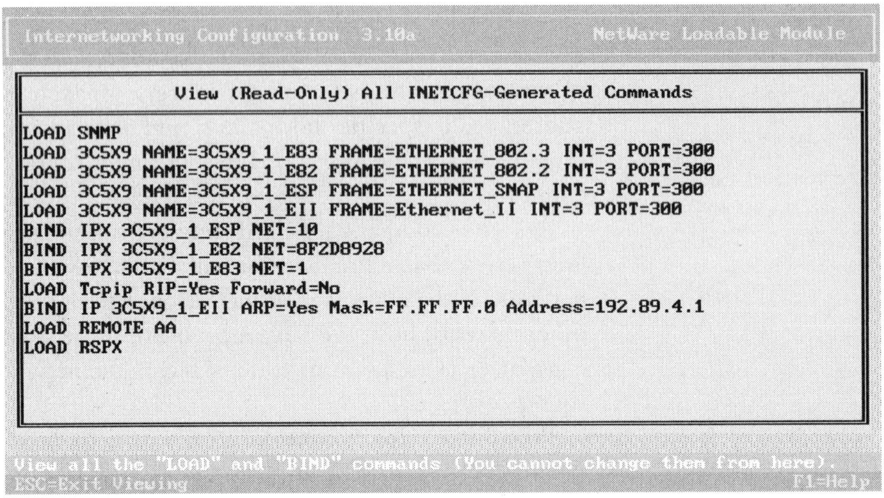

```
Internetworking Configuration   3.10a              NetWare Loadable Module

            View (Read-Only) All INETCFG-Generated Commands
LOAD SNMP
LOAD 3C5X9 NAME=3C5X9_1_E83 FRAME=ETHERNET_802.3 INT=3 PORT=300
LOAD 3C5X9 NAME=3C5X9_1_E82 FRAME=ETHERNET_802.2 INT=3 PORT=300
LOAD 3C5X9 NAME=3C5X9_1_ESP FRAME=ETHERNET_SNAP INT=3 PORT=300
LOAD 3C5X9 NAME=3C5X9_1_EII FRAME=Ethernet_II INT=3 PORT=300
BIND IPX 3C5X9_1_ESP NET=10
BIND IPX 3C5X9_1_E82 NET=8F2D8928
BIND IPX 3C5X9_1_E83 NET=1
LOAD Tcpip RIP=Yes Forward=No
BIND IP 3C5X9_1_EII ARP=Yes Mask=FF.FF.FF.0 Address=192.89.4.1
LOAD REMOTE AA
LOAD RSPX

View all the "LOAD" and "BIND" commands (You cannot change them from here).
ESC=Exit Viewing                                                    F1=Help
```

The first line, LOAD SNMP, came about when TCP/IP was loaded. You may configure that a bit more if you wish; check out Chapter 18 for details.

The fourth LOAD 3C5X9 command line shows a frame type of Ethernet_II, which is the default for TCP/IP support. The following three BIND commands add IPX to all frame types except Ethernet_II, since this frame type was just added for TCP/IP support.

The LOAD Tcpip line follows the information in Figure 14.3, where we said to enable TCP/IP, enable RIP, but don't forward the RIP packets. That's why we see RIP=Yes but Forward=No.

The next line is the result of the information we provided in Figure 14.4. Let's dissect the line:

```
BIND IP 3C5X9_1_EII ARP=Yes Mask=FF.FF.FF.00
   Address=192.89.4.1
```

BIND IP 3C5X9_1_EII says that we're binding the IP protocol to the interface card using the Ethernet_II frame type. Since we have only a single interface card in GATEWAY2000, the same card supports all the interfaces, protocols, and frame types.

ARP=Yes says we do want to use Address Resolution Protocol. This came from our support of RIP, since ARP is needed by RIP.

Mask=FF.FF.FF.00 tells the system about the subnetwork mask for this network. This value should match all other hosts and routers. Your systems may use 255.255.255.0 as a subnet mask instead.

Address=192.89.4.1 sets the local IP address. By local, I mean for this Ethernet connection on this file server. This address must be unique on your network. If your network is connected to the Internet, the InterNIC (Internet Network Information Center) has already provided your TCP/IP network administrator with a specific range of addresses. The address you type here must be from that list, or you'll cause someone on the Internet some real grief.

Later changes are made in the same INETCFG menu items. You can edit any of the fields in any of the last three figures without a problem, but you should work with the TCP/IP network administrator for your network. Some of these options are amazingly obtuse. My favorite is whether or not you should enable RIP Poison Reverse. Isn't that a great question? Poison reverse is an improvement in RIP to eliminate router loops by sending a packet back through a route with a flag indicating this route is to be avoided.

> *My favorite is whether or not you should enable RIP Poison Reverse.*

Using XCONSOLE

The name XCONSOLE is a bit misleading. By all rights, you would expect that a remote X Windows server could peruse this NetWare server's CONSOLE screen in graphics mode. Unfortunately, that's not quite right.

XCONSOLE supports a remote X station running the standard NetWare CONSOLE command, but it's still ASCII graphics or worse. Even on a high-resolution X screen, we effectively give a VT100-level terminal emulation to the remote X station. (It would be better if the X client used a VT100 Telnet connection to reach the NetWare server, to avoid the disappointment.)

The value of XCONSOLE is for larger companies that have Unix-based management consoles. Keeping a DOS client handy just to run RCONSOLE can be a problem, so Novell engineers developed XCONSOLE. With this addition (which first appeared in NetWare 3.11), remote Unix management stations could easily manage NetWare servers using a VT100 emulation. It's not real pretty, but it works.

Using the IPTUNNEL Transport

> ### 14.2 IN-A-HURRY
>
> **Activate IPTUNNEL**
>
> **1.** Type **LOAD INETCFG** from the server console (or over RCONSOLE).
>
> **2.** Choose Boards from the main menu.
>
> **3.** Choose the board with TCP/IP support and press Insert.
>
> **4.** Choose IPTUNNEL from the Available Drivers list.
>
> **5.** Name the board, give the peer server address, and give the local address.
>
> **6.** Press Escape to save, and choose Bindings from the main menu.
>
> **7.** BIND IPX to the IPTUNNEL driver.
>
> **8.** Press Escape to save and exit.
>
> **9.** Reboot the server to check the installation and load the IPTUNNEL module.

For a few companies, this feature was the big news behind NetWare 3.11: the first appearance of the TCP/IP utilities. At least one company, famous but unnamed in Novell presentations, pushed the deployment of IPTUNNEL. Why? The service company that supported that company's WAN charged an even $500,000 for every protocol. IPTUNNEL has saved that company more than $2,000,000.

As you might guess, IPTUNNEL encapsulates IPX/SPX packets inside TCP/IP packets. This is done so routers and other devices that don't support IPX can still carry NetWare traffic. The primary use is to describe two NetWare servers as partners and let them act as IPX routers across an IP network.

Go through INETCFG as we did to set up TCP/IP. IPTUNNEL must be attached to a board that has TCP/IP configured and running. Figure 14.6 shows the primary IPTUNNEL configuration screen.

The highlight bar is on the crucial bit of information: the peer address. This is the NetWare server on the remote side of the TCP/IP network that will receive the encapsulated IPX packets. Once the packets are received, they will be stripped out of the TCP/IP envelopes and sent on their way as normal IPX packets.

FIGURE 14.6

Tunneling to the peer IP address

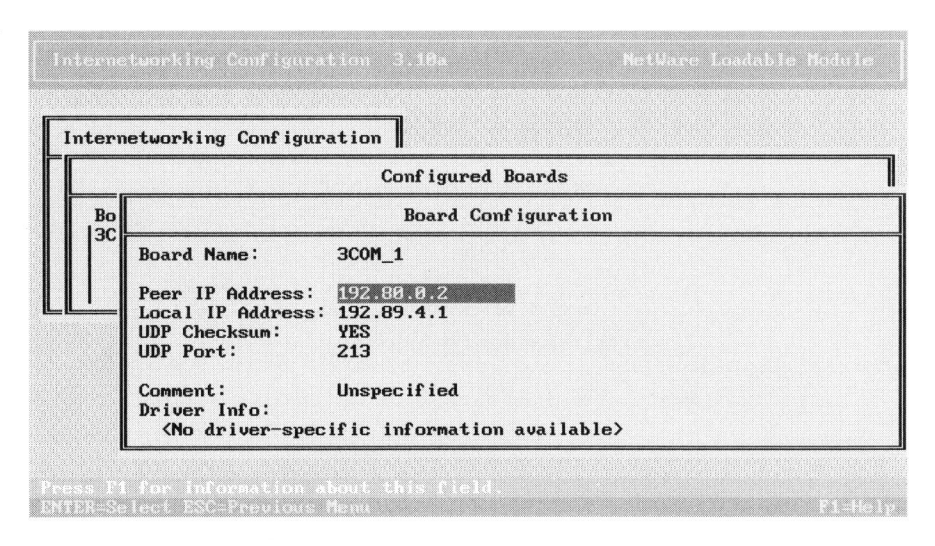

```
Internetworking Configuration    3.10a              NetWare Loadable Module

┌─ Internetworking Configuration ─┐
│ ┌──────── Configured Boards ─────────────────────────────────┐
│ │ Bo  ┌──────────── Board Configuration ────────────────────┐
│ │ 3C  │
│ └──   │  Board Name:     3COM_1
│      │
│      │  Peer IP Address:  192.80.0.2
│      │  Local IP Address: 192.89.4.1
│      │  UDP Checksum:     YES
│      │  UDP Port:         213
│      │
│      │  Comment:          Unspecified
│      │  Driver Info:
│      │     <No driver-specific information available>

Press F1 for information about this field
ENTER=Select  ESC=Previous Menu                              F1=Help
```

Multiple peer servers can be listed. The easiest way to do so is to repeat this procedure, placing the new peer address. Check the INETCFG commands screen to make sure the commands are listed properly.

Using NetWare/IP

FOR SOME CUSTOMERS, using TCP/IP for communications between servers wasn't enough. What about using TCP/IP for communications between NetWare clients and servers? In other words, can we do away with IPX altogether? The quick answer is yes, we can.

TCP/IP has some wonderful benefits:

- Support—more system support across more systems than any other protocol.

- Great WAN protocol—the defacto remote networking protocol suite.

- Free—with every Unix operating system, TCP/IP is included as part of the networking software.

- Size and speed—small and fast on PCs. Low-overhead Windows protocol stacks are getting faster than ever.

To be fair, let's look at the disadvantages of TCP/IP:

- Installation is painful. Addressing issues and the configuration necessary on every client make TCP/IP much more difficult to administer than IPX/SPX.

- Network routing is complicated. Configuration must be done carefully to avoid problems.

- TCP/IP is free with Unix systems, but not with PCs. PC TCP/IP cost ranges from $100 to $400 per client, although Microsoft is now including minimal TCP/IP support in Windows 95/NT as part of the operating system.

- Application support is limited. Few programs write to desktop TCP/IP protocol stacks, although the rampant spread of Web clients and other Internet-inspired applications expect to find TCP/IP.

Realistically, you might figure that people would want to avoid TCP/IP with a list like this. However, TCP/IP is the language of love in open systems, so LAN operating systems are working to get TCP/IP support. Even though IPX wins hands-down in a LAN performance contest, TCP/IP is the protocol of choice for some companies. To support those companies, Novell developed NetWare/IP. Unless your situation demands a TCP/IP network only, however, there's no advantage to using NetWare/IP rather than IPX.

A set of NLMs and client software for NetWare 3 and NetWare 4, NetWare/IP provides an almost complete replacement for IPX. The only exception is for those programs that use NetBIOS network discovery broadcasts, such as a few management applications. These will not work because the UDP broadcast limitations can't support the broadcasts required by NetBIOS to discover network information. Other NetBIOS programs do work, however.

NetWare/IP includes the same TCP/IP transport components used by Novell's LAN WorkPlace for DOS. The use of a single TCP/IP protocol for multiple purposes is an advantage to large companies faced with managing thousands of users.

Customers using NetWare/IP have reported the following benefits:

- It allows NetWare to run in an IP-only environment. Companies standardized on TCP/IP can still provide NetWare services for their users.

- Existing NetWare applications are supported. All applications written for NetWare's IPX protocol function exactly the same when used with NetWare/IP.

- It reduces costs. Running two protocols is more expensive than running and supporting a single protocol. Users with NetWare/IP can keep a single set of tools for TCP/IP, and train their users on a single protocol. Routers and other network components often charge extra for two protocols.

- There is an easy, phased transition from IPX to an IP network. The NetWare/IP gateway connects IP and IPX clients together transparently. Customers can move from IPX to NetWare/IP as quickly or slowly as they wish.

TCP/IP uses DNS as a lookup service to supply names and addresses to network clients. NetWare/IP supports DNS for NetWare/IP clients by creating a NetWare/IP domain. This domain must be a subdomain of an existing DNS domain, and it cannot have subdomains itself.

This DNS requirement is not a problem, since NetWare/IP customers have large TCP/IP network and host installations already. If they didn't, they wouldn't want to use NetWare/IP. NetWare servers must provide the specialized DNS needs of NetWare/IP clients. This is done via a set of NLMs.

Any size NetWare/IP domain can be created and managed, but generally local systems are kept local. One server is designated as the DNS server, or an existing Unix DNS server may also be used.

DNS translates network names (128.32.134.5) into more readable names (sjf-nwip.novell.com). There are seven main name servers on the Internet, and each domain name uses the format of *machine.subdomain.domain*, but you may have more subdomains. It is impossible to tell a machine name from a subdomain name.

The critical part of server support for NetWare/IP is performed by the DSS (Domain SAP Server). The DSS holds one logical database, which stores and distributes IPX SAP information to NetWare/IP servers. Secondary DSS servers may be set up for fault-tolerance, but only one primary DSS can exist per NetWare/IP domain. The DSS server may be the same as the DNS server, which may be the same as the NetWare/IP server.

When a NetWare server boots, it sends a SAP broadcast throughout the rest of the network. When a NetWare/IP server boots, it sends a SAP record directory to its nearest DSS using UDP. Every 5 minutes (configurable), the information is refreshed.

Other processes on the NetWare/IP server, such as NDS and print servers, use the same modified SAP packets to the DSS server for advertising purposes. By sending packets directly to the servers, broadcasts are avoided and network traffic is lessened.

How do NetWare/IP clients see and use regular NetWare servers? That's the job of the NetWare/IP Gateway, which is a different product from the NetWare IPX/IP Gateway we will discuss later. The NetWare/IP Gateway is a server that bridges the gap between a NetWare/IP domain and the regular NetWare network. NetWare/IP clients go through the gateway and see the rest of the network without a problem. NetWare clients running IPX can see and use resources from the NetWare/IP servers through the gateway. The gateway works when supporting both local and remote servers over a WAN link.

There is a slight performance penalty, as well as some increased RAM overhead on VLM stations, imposed by NetWare/IP. The NWIP.COM and TCPIP.COM programs add about 32 KB of RAM overhead to non-Client32 workstations. Both will run from upper memory (if you have any available).

The server disk space impact is around 2 MB needed from the SYS volume. Extra RAM needed is 710 KB plus 440 bytes for each NetWare/IP active client.

How NetWare/IP Works on the Non-Client32 Client

That's the plan, but sometimes real life gets in the way.

With all the talk lately of modular programming, you might think replacing IPX with TCP/IP would be a quick matter of swapping this piece of software for that piece. That's the plan, but sometimes real life gets in the way.

When NetWare was developed, much of the functionality of NetWare's ease of use for network setup and use depended on features in IPX. Consequently, IPX is tightly integrated into NetWare utilities like MAP, NDIR, FILER, and the rest. IPX provides functions that are not available with TCP/IP. Re-creating those functions took some time and some cleverness.

Part of the complaints TCP/IP people have about IPX has to do with the regular use of SAP (Service Advertising Protocol) broadcasts. The TCP/IP people have a point; regular broadcasts of all servers advertising themselves is a problem with slow WAN links. But remember, IPX was developed as a local protocol, where bandwidth is freely available and there are no long WAN delays to cause problems.

Service advertising in NetWare replaces all the name service and address configuration problems in TCP/IP. This information in TCP/IP networks must be gained by querying name servers through preconfigured default gateways. All this configuration must be done before a TCP/IP node can participate in the network.

SAP is primarily what makes NetWare workstations so easy to configure and install. When a new workstation comes into a NetWare network, there are no name servers to query, no gateways to know, and no host tables to read. Have you ever had to configure a NetWare client before logging in to the network? Not a bit. The workstation address is the interface card address, and the network number is set by the server and advertised.

The client part of NetWare/IP replaces the IPX parts with specific IP software. A little slice of software called the IPX Far Call Interface inside the IPXODI.COM program maintains compatibility with all versions of IPX. This ABI (Application Binary Interface) accepts application requests for network service and connects them to the Open Data-link Interface (ODI) for transmission across the network. Figure 14.7 shows this client software.

FIGURE 14.7

The normal NetWare client software

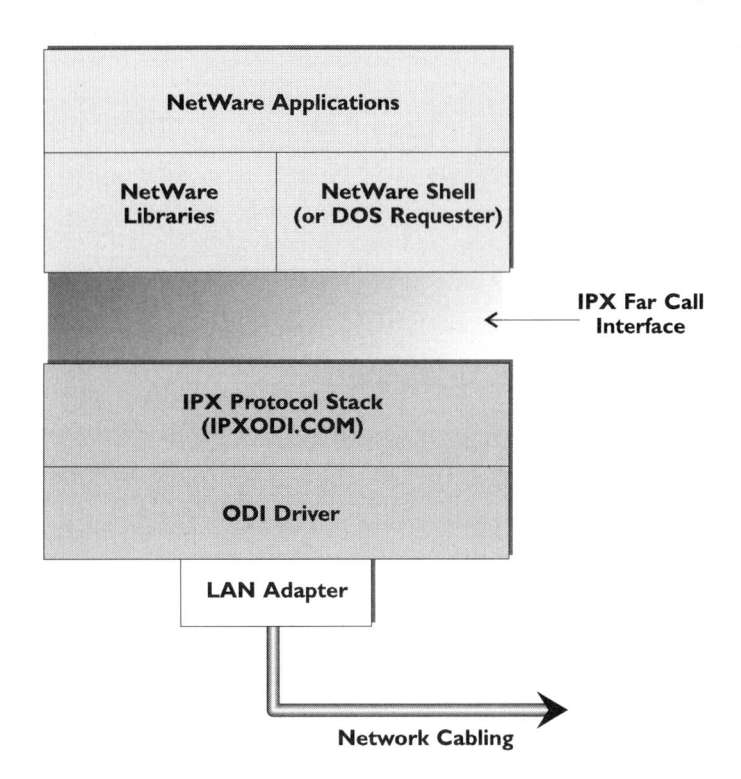

All this is transparent to the user, of course. In fact, the IPX Far Call Interface was rarely mentioned before it needed to be replaced for NetWare/IP.

With NetWare/IP, two software pieces must take the place of the IPXODI.COM program. The first is NWIP.EXE, which provides the IPX Far Call Interface emulation layer. This shields the NetWare applications from knowing that this workstation is different from any another NetWare client.

The second piece of software is the TCP/IP protocol stack itself, contained in the TCPIP.EXE program. This does the work of IPXODI.COM in routing the applications across the network. In this case, however, the protocol used is TCP/IP rather than IPX. Figure 14.8 shows the newly converted client software.

There is a correction to make here. Many people have taken exception to the fact that Novell uses UDP/IP (User Datagram Protocol/Internet Protocol) rather than TCP/IP. Why? TCP/IP requires dedicated connections and forces

FIGURE 14.8

The NetWare/IP client software

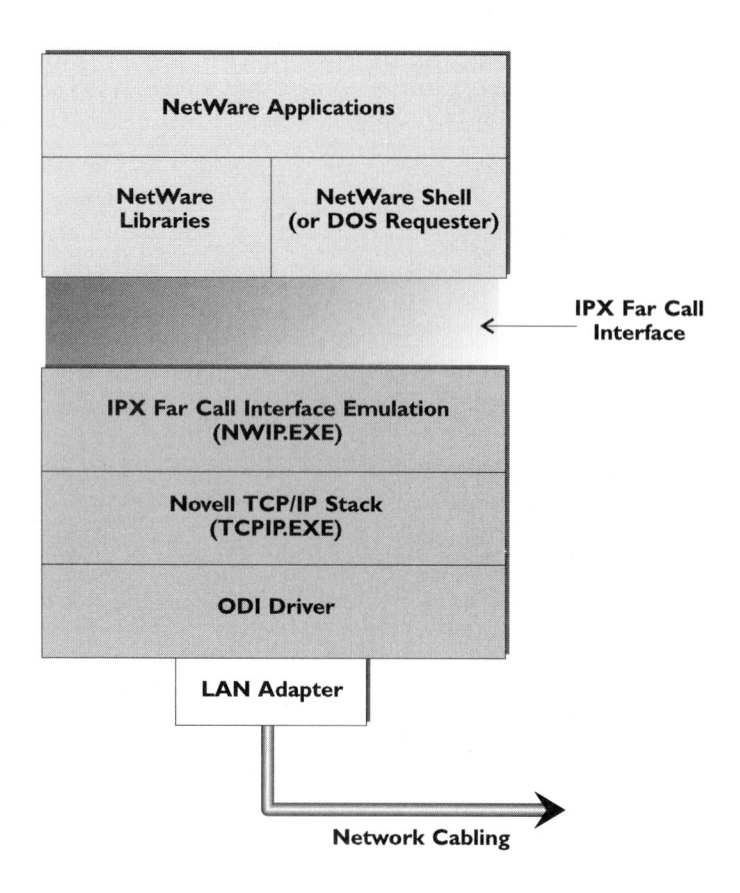

the network itself to guarantee delivery. UDP works exactly like IPX: it makes a best-effort delivery attempt, but higher-level protocols are tasked with the delivery guarantee.

Is UDP good enough to rely on for NetWare/IP? I guess so, since all NFS connections ride across UDP. The big advantage of UDP is the lack of hard connections between client and host, lessening overhead. Dropped connections cause little concern to either side.

Some of the features of the client software that make up NetWare/IP are:

- Support for the Windows Socket Interface version 1.1 known as Winsock.

- Support for most common APIs for running TCP/IP applications under DOS and any version of MS Windows.

- Support for up to 64 TCP and 32 UDP sockets.

- IP communications supported on up to four client ODI interfaces.

- ARP (Address Resolution Protocol) used to prevent duplicate IP addresses.

- Network media supported includes Ethernet, Token Ring, FDDI, ARCnet, IBM Broadband, and asynchronous serial lines using both SLIP (Serial Line Interface Protocol) and PPP (Point to Point Protocol).

- IP configuration via ASCII text file, BOOTP, or RARP (Reverse Address Resolution Protocol).

- IP network test utilities including SNMP.

- NetBIOS over TCP/IP support.

Client32 and NetWare/IP Client Software

The difference between Client32 and earlier VLM-based clients supporting NetWare/IP is night and day. Client32, especially when used with the more advanced memory model in Windows 95, supports NetWare/IP easily. All you need to do is click on two checkboxes during installation. If you remember our discussion of Client32 installation in Chapter 5, you'll recall that the Client32 Installation Additional Options screen (Figure 5.13) offers a checkbox for TCP/IP, and a second checkbox for NetWare/IP that becomes active if the TCP/IP box is checked.

Performance of NetWare/IP has traditionally been about 10 percent slower than IPX, but that gap is narrowing. Of course, some say that Client32 has slowed down the performance of clients to the point that NetWare/IP doesn't impose a performance penalty. My tests showed that running Client32 over NetWare/IP transport protocol was about even with Client32 running over IPX.

Installing and Using NetWare/IP

As always, there are a few tricks to remember when installing NetWare/IP. If you're an experienced NetWare administrator, you'll be used to some of these quirks. If you're coming from the Microsoft or Unix networking worlds, you'll get sick of the DOS-based C-Worthy interface Novell continues to use a decade after it became tired looking.

Let me provide a road map of my last NetWare/IP installation:

1. Follow the NetWare/IP product installation routine.
2. Blow up.
3. Read the NetWare/IP documentation from the NetWare CD-ROM.
4. Attempt to repair the installation per the documentation recommendations.
5. Erase everything and start over.
6. Configure TCP/IP on the server.
7. Reboot to start TCP/IP on the server.
8. Configure DNS Server.
9. Initialize the DNS master database.
10. Configure DSS Server.
11. Configure NetWare/IP Server.
12. Rename the NetWare/IP domain from gaskin.com (default) to nwip.gaskin.com.
13. Reboot the server to activate the new settings.
14. Start DNS Server.

15. Start DSS Server.

16. Start NetWare/IP Server.

17. Install the client.

18. Communicate between the client and server over TCP/IP.

Well, it's not the cleanest installation, but it finally worked.

Novell's instructions and process leave quite a bit to be desired in this area. If Novell executives carry through on their promise to make NetWare's primary transport TCP/IP in the summer of 1997, replacing IPX/SPX, they should work overtime to improve the installation and configuration screens.

Before you begin the process of installing NetWare/IP, make sure the TCP/IP NLMs are loaded and running on your server. The NetWare/IP installation routine offers you a chance to configure TCP/IP during the NetWare/IP installation, but it won't work. Install, configure, and test TCP/IP before taking the next step.

Yes, I know, I should have read the documentation and filled out all the worksheets before starting the installation. That's true, but if you and I both did that, neither one of us would have this book, would we?

Services included with NetWare/IP are the DNS Server, DSS Server, NetWare/IP Server, NetWare-to-UNIX Print Gateway, and the XCONSOLE Server (vt100 terminal support to configure the NetWare server console over TCP/IP). The NetWare/IP Server depends on the DSS Server, and either a NetWare DNS name server or an external name server referenced in the configuration files.

Configuring and Initializing DNS

From the UNICON utility main menu, choosing Manage Services shows the "Running Services," but it does not include the DSS. Why? DSS is configured through the NWIPCFG utility. Why there and not here? I haven't a clue.

If you choose to manage DNS, a new menu appears showing Administer DNS, Initialize DNS Master Database, and Save DNS Master to Text Files. When you choose to administer DNS, another menu appears, offering Manage Master Database, Manage Replica Databases, Link to Existing DNS Hierarchy, Query Remote Name Server, and Disable DNS Service. Here we verify that NetWare/IP works with existing DNS systems, or we can just receive information from external name servers.

Under Manage Master Database, there are menu choices for Manage Data, Delegate Subzone Authority, and Delegate Subzone by IP Authority. This is the seventh menu level from the top (just in case you're counting or dropping bread crumbs to find your way home).

Subzones can be assigned to others to manage, which is especially useful in geographically dispersed networks. The site administrator can do most of the work, and a central administrator can check by using the Change Current Server menu choice from UNICON's main menu.

The most important step in Manage Services is to Initialize DNS Master Database. This is well hidden, but important. This step must be taken before the NetWare/IP server will start. You are free to modify and configure your DNS entries at will on this screen.

Configuring DSS and NetWare IP

From the UNICON main menu (Figure 14.1), you can choose Manage Services, then NetWare/IP. You might think you should load NWIPCFG to configure NetWare/IP the first time, just as I guessed. Oops, it won't work that way. In UNICON, choose Manage Services, then Manage NetWare/IP to configure your DSS first, then configure your NetWare/IP server.

On the NetWare/IP Administration menu, bypass Configure NetWare/IP Server and Delete NetWare/IP Server Configuration to pick Configure Primary DSS. The opening window asks you to name the NetWare/IP domain. The default will be your DNS domain; that will be wrong. Add *nwip* to the beginning to differentiate between the two. My DNS domain gaskin.com had to be changed to nwip.gaskin.com before the NetWare/IP Server would load. Luckily, no children were within earshot as I figured this out.

> Luckily, no children were within earshot as I figured this out.

Figure 14.9 shows a screen from UNICON. You can see the NetWare/IP domain, and the DNS domain is listed at the bottom of the screen. The look and feel of NetWare/IP server management is consistent with all other NetWare server utilities.

The other options on this menu are for the primary DSS host name and for a unique IPX network number for your new virtual network segment supporting NetWare/IP. The Help screen for the primary DSS host name says this name must be "fully qualified," as if it meant the NDS fully qualified name. That won't work, because in this case, Novell wants the DNS qualified name (gateway2000-1.gaskin.com)—another potential hang-up poorly explained.

FIGURE 14.9

Configuring the NetWare/IP server

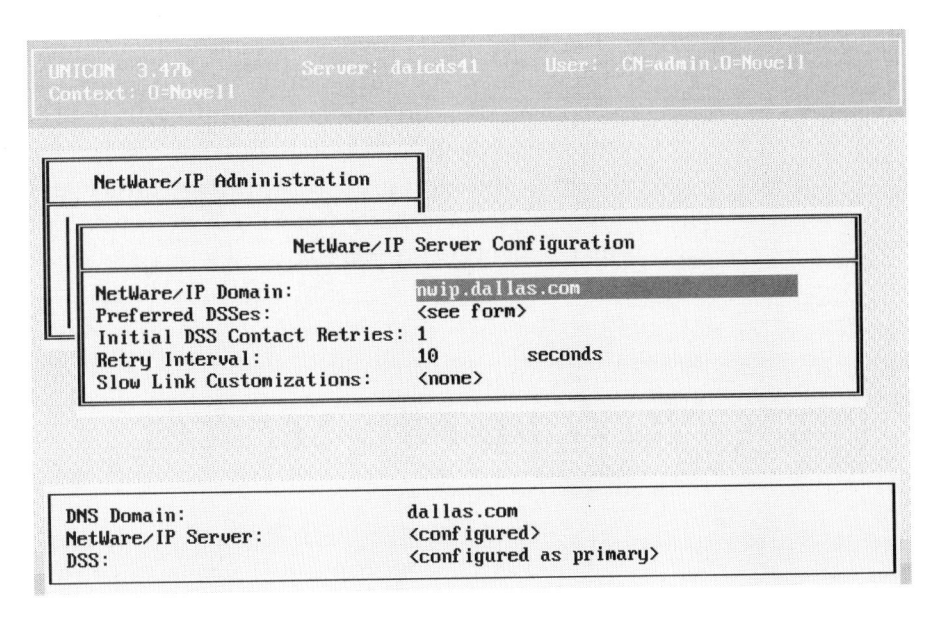

```
UNICON  3.47b                 Server: dalcds41        User: .CN=admin.O=Novell
Context: O=Novell

┌─ NetWare/IP Administration ──────────────────────────────────────────┐
│   ┌─ NetWare/IP Server Configuration ──────────────────────────┐     │
│   │ NetWare/IP Domain:          nwip.dallas.com                │     │
│   │ Preferred DSSes:            <see form>                     │     │
│   │ Initial DSS Contact Retries: 1                             │     │
│   │ Retry Interval:             10        seconds              │     │
│   │ Slow Link Customizations:   <none>                         │     │
│   └────────────────────────────────────────────────────────────┘     │
│                                                                      │
│     DNS Domain:            dallas.com                                │
│     NetWare/IP Server:     <configured>                              │
│     DSS:                   <configured as primary>                   │
└──────────────────────────────────────────────────────────────────────┘
```

Now, back to the Configure NetWare/IP Server menu option. Here you set the name of the NetWare/IP domain (again), the preferred DSSs (IP address or host name of one to five DSS systems), contact retry numbers, and intervals between attempts. Slow Link Customizations allows time padding for slow remote connections, so the connections won't timeout. The setting to make this server a gateway between your NetWare/IP clients and NetWare IPX clients is here, but the default is No. Since most networks are a mixture of both protocols, at least two of your NetWare/IP servers should forward information. Multiple gateways automatically load balance requests, with the least busy server taking each new request as it comes.

The second option on the NetWare/IP Administration menu is Delete NetWare/IP Configuration. Don't be embarrassed if you must delete this at least once to start over. I did.

Once your configuration is done, you can return to the UNICON main menu (press Escape until you return there) and start NetWare/IP. Now, finally, it should work. Your only sign of success is a lack of failure messages and, on the server console, a message saying "NetWare/IP Server is initialized and functional." NetWare/IP maintains it's own Pkernel screen, but this rarely shows anything interesting.

To sum up, NetWare/IP is valuable to a few companies with special requirements. If your management isn't demanding a network with TCP/IP and nothing else, don't mess with NetWare/IP. It takes more time, more server configuration, and more client setup than regular NetWare, for no advantage outside the transport protocol. Remember, you need TCP/IP support at the NetWare server to run the NetWare Web Server, but not NetWare/IP support from the clients to the server.

Running NetWare NFS Services

THE INCLUSION OF the TCP/IP protocol in NetWare 3.11 servers changed the open systems community's view of NetWare. Suddenly, the race was on to make NetWare servers regular members of TCP/IP networks. With the addition of NetWare NFS, NetWare NFS Gateway, and FLeX/IP, any NetWare server could perform Unix-type functions as just another system on the network. A complete set of SNMP software ensures existing management consoles can support the NetWare server.

With the release of NetWare 4.10, the NFS products were repackaged into one product with multiple options. NetWare NFS Services contains all the functions included in the previous three products. A subset product, NetWare UNIX Print Services 2.1, NetWare 4 Edition, includes bidirectional printing, FTP, TFTP, SNMP, and NIS and DNS integration. Because of the integration of name services such as DNS and NIS, only NetWare 4.1x can support these new products.

Let's go down the list of important areas included in NetWare NFS Services.

Managing NFS Services

All NFS Services administration is handled by UNICON. UNICON runs at the console, like MONITOR or INETCFG, and it works perfectly well over RCONSOLE as well.

You can see the main screen of UNICON back in Figure 14.1. In that figure, the Manage Global Objects option is highlighted. This option handles managing users, groups, hosts, and global parameters.

XCONSOLE is also available for remote management. The ability to manage NetWare servers remotely using standard management consoles is particularly important with NFS Services. Companies with large Unix installations (the market for NFS Services) will almost always have SNMP management systems in place.

Managing Name Services

As we mentioned earlier, Unix systems have two different name services available, DNS and NIS. NetWare NFS Services supports either or both. You can set up your NetWare server as the master name server, or use an existing DNS or NIS server.

NIS Server software provides a centralized database of common user and group information. This software can manage Unix systems as well as NetWare servers.

DNS Server provides a centralized database of host-to-address mappings. This software can also manage existing Unix systems as well as NetWare servers.

Figure 14.10 shows a server profile screen. Pay particular attention to the IP addresses you see.

FIGURE 14.10

Server profile within UNICON

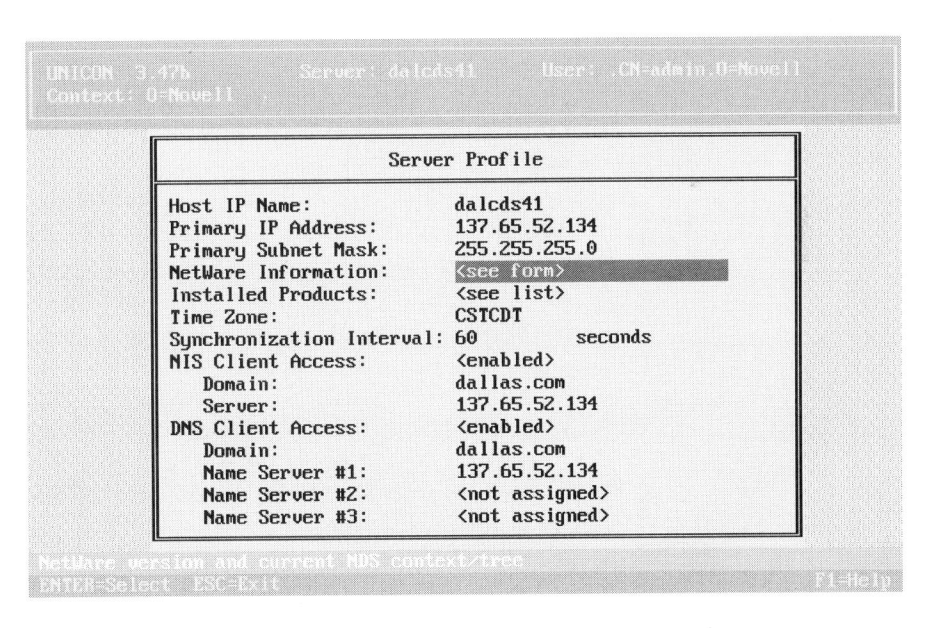

```
UNICON  3.47b              Server: dalcds41         User: .CN=admin.O=Novell
Context: O=Novell

                          ┌─────────── Server Profile ───────────┐
                          │                                      │
                          │ Host IP Name:          dalcds41      │
                          │ Primary IP Address:    137.65.52.134 │
                          │ Primary Subnet Mask:   255.255.255.0 │
                          │ NetWare Information:   <see form>    │
                          │ Installed Products:    <see list>    │
                          │ Time Zone:             CSTCDT        │
                          │ Synchronization Interval: 60  seconds│
                          │ NIS Client Access:     <enabled>     │
                          │   Domain:              dallas.com    │
                          │   Server:              137.65.52.134 │
                          │ DNS Client Access:     <enabled>     │
                          │   Domain:              dallas.com    │
                          │   Name Server #1:      137.65.52.134 │
                          │   Name Server #2:      <not assigned>│
                          │   Name Server #3:      <not assigned>│
                          └──────────────────────────────────────┘

NetWare version and current NDS context/tree
ENTER=Select  ESC=Exit                                          F1=Help
```

The top line lists the name of this server, dalcds41. The IP address for this server is next.

Notice that both NIS Client Access and DNS Client Access are enabled. Take a good look at the address of the server listed in both sections. It's the same as the NetWare server.

This shows that a NetWare name server can support DNS and NIS clients at the same time. While I don't figure many existing networks will throw away their Sun name server systems, it's nice that NetWare is able to manage any system.

Setting Up File Sharing

NFS (Network File System) is the run-away best-selling method of sharing files in the Unix community. There are a few alternatives, and a move afoot to upgrade NFS, but it's the big game in town.

Unlike NetWare, NFS systems act as both clients and servers. Some large NFS networks have dedicated servers, but even with a dedicated server, it's quite simple to share files between systems. So to package Novell's NFS server product (NetWare NFS) and client product (NetWare NFS Gateway) separately in the past was deemed a bit odd by some Unix folks.

There are four parts of the File Sharing module:

- **NFS Server:** Supports NFS clients use of the NetWare server files. Properly authenticated NFS clients can read and write files directly on a NetWare server, just like any other NetWare client. The NFS Name Space is used to support the longer file names used by the (mostly) Unix clients.

- **NFS Gateway:** Allows NetWare clients to read and write remote NFS file systems exactly as if they were another NetWare volume. NetWare security is added to that of the NFS system sharing its file system, so NetWare clients can be restricted by NetWare before they ever reach the NFS system.

- **Lock Manager:** Provides file locking between NetWare and NFS as much as possible. NFS locks are advisory, not absolute as those of NetWare. PC NFS client software often ignores any NFS locking information. People that expect NFS to control file access and locking, as NetWare does, will be disappointed.

- **NetWare NFS Daemon (NWNFSD):** Supports PC systems using an NFS product developed for DOS or MS Windows access to the NetWare file system as an NFS client. No configuration or setup is necessary.

There's quite a bit of setup to match the NFS and NetWare systems when file sharing is involved. Figure 14.11 shows a screen for setting up an NFS file system as a remote volume for NetWare client use.

FIGURE 14.11

NetWare as an NFS client

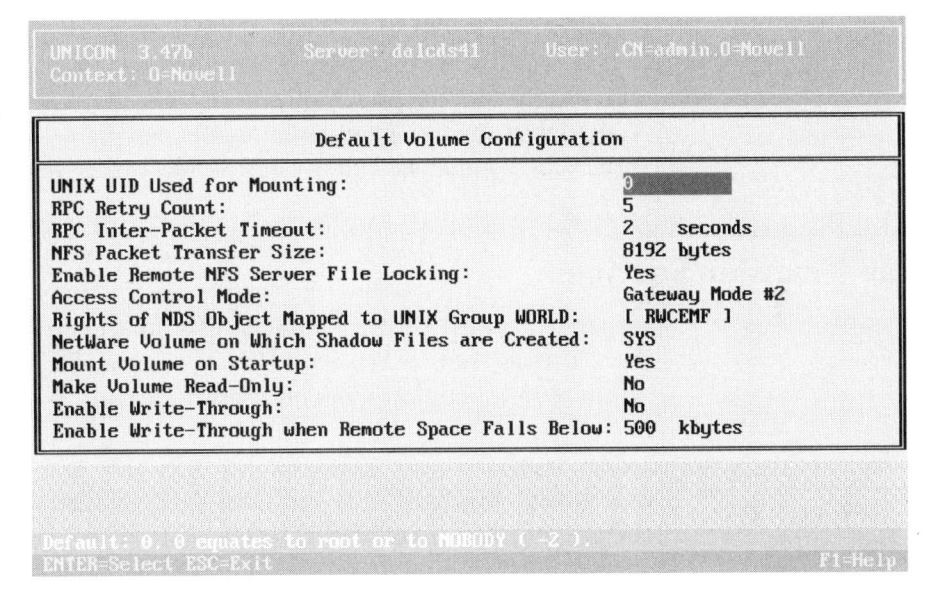

```
UNICON  3.47b            Server: dalcds41       User: .CN=admin.O=Novell
Context: O=Novell

                    ┌─────────── Default Volume Configuration ───────────┐
                    │ UNIX UID Used for Mounting:                  0     │
                    │ RPC Retry Count:                             5     │
                    │ RPC Inter-Packet Timeout:                    2     seconds
                    │ NFS Packet Transfer Size:                    8192  bytes
                    │ Enable Remote NFS Server File Locking:       Yes   │
                    │ Access Control Mode:                         Gateway Mode #2
                    │ Rights of NDS Object Mapped to UNIX Group WORLD:  [ RWCEMF ]
                    │ NetWare Volume on Which Shadow Files are Created: SYS
                    │ Mount Volume on Startup:                     Yes   │
                    │ Make Volume Read-Only:                       No    │
                    │ Enable Write-Through:                        No    │
                    │ Enable Write-Through when Remote Space Falls Below: 500  kbytes
                    └────────────────────────────────────────────────────┘

Default: 0. 0 equates to root or to NOBODY ( -2 ).
ENTER=Select ESC=Exit                                              F1=Help
```

There are several interesting things to examine on this screen. The UNIX UID (User ID) tells the remote host who the NetWare server is. If the NetWare server is not allowed to mount the file system, we won't get attached.

Notice in the middle of the screen, the line Rights of NDS Object Mapped to UNIX Group WORLD shows typical NetWare rights to a file system. That's exactly what we have as far as NetWare clients are concerned. The NetWare server has full file-access rights, so all clients have the same unless specifically restricted.

The Shadow Files are a directory listing of the remote NFS server's file system kept on the NetWare server. By keeping the files local, time for directory queries is cut dramatically. The listings are synchronized at a configurable interval.

NFS Gateway is my favorite product of the Unix and NetWare integration suite. Need Unix file access for a hundred NetWare clients? This does the job, without changing a single setting on a single NetWare workstation.

Setting Up Printing

There are two printing components: Unix-to-NetWare printing, and NetWare-to-Unix printing. As mentioned earlier, cross-platform printing support is available as a subset.

NetWare users can access printers attached to Unix systems (or any system) running the lpr (line printer) protocol. Unix clients using the same protocol can print to any NetWare system printer configured to support the remote print jobs. Figure 14.12 shows one of the printing setup menus.

File Transfer Services

Separate from NFS, simple file sharing is done in the Unix and TCP/IP world by FTP (File Transfer Protocol). This is a staple of the Internet, and the way a client retrieves or places files on a server system.

FIGURE 14.12
Sharing NetWare queues with Unix systems

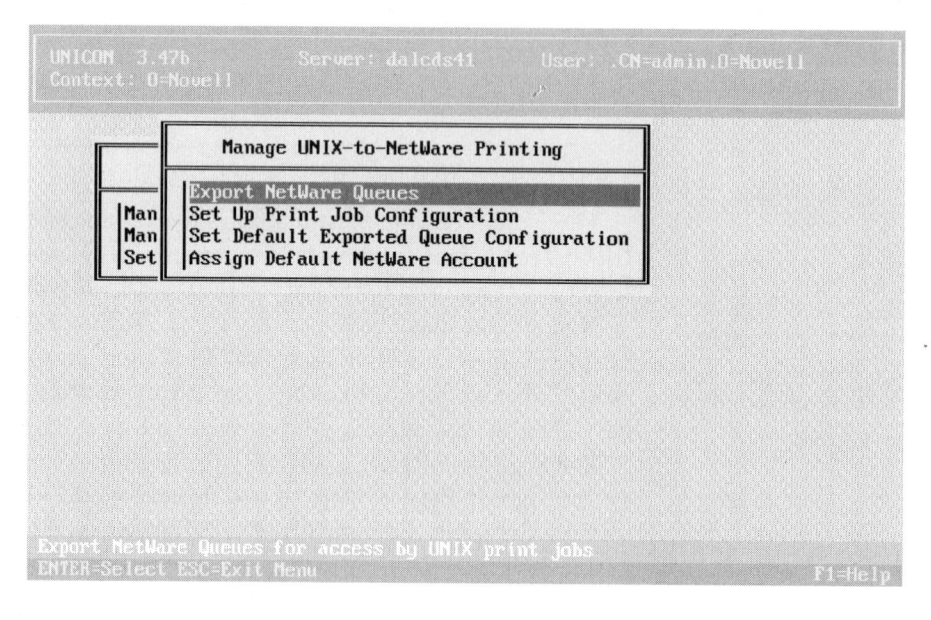

NetWare's FTP Server allows TCP/IP clients to access and transfer files from the NetWare server. This is not NFS, where files are read and written directly on the server, but strictly a transfer process. If you're familiar with NetWire and getting patches from a CompuServe library, FTP is similar.

TFTP (Trivial File Transfer Protocol) is newly added to the NetWare NFS Services bag of tricks. TFTP requires no password, login procedure, or authentication. Who would use this in today's world of hacker paranoia? E-mail servers, for one. Automated file transfer programs for another. It is used, and Novell's support for TFTP has been important to many customers.

Figure 14.13 shows the Available Services menu, just blocking the Running Services list. Notice that TFTP is not loaded, but FTP is showing in the background Running Services window.

FIGURE 14.13

Available NetWare-to-Unix services

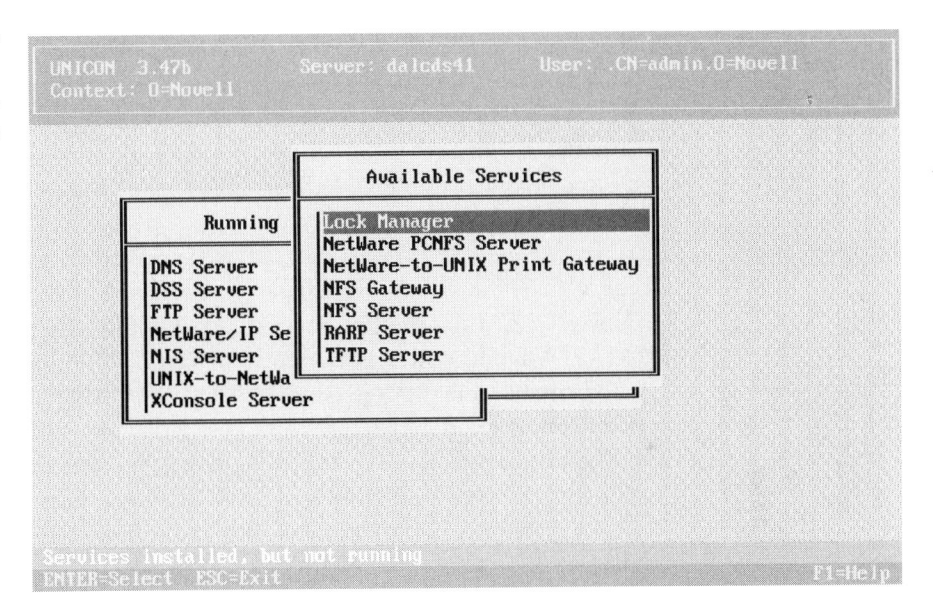

You may also notice that the NetWare-to-UNIX Print Gateway is not active, but you can see in the background that the UNIX-to-NetWare process is running. Each of these modules is exactly that, a module, and you may run all or one or any combination.

One Product, Two Names: NIAS and/or NetWare IPX/IP Gateway

INTERNET HYSTERIA CAUGHT Novell somewhat by surprise. During early 1996, Novell developers were working on their own gateway to convert IPX traffic into TCP/IP for a trip onto the Internet. There are a dozen other companies making these products. Some third-party gateways run on the NetWare server, while others run on Windows NT, Unix, OS/2, or specialized turn-key hardware systems.

About the middle of 1996, Novell executives realized the Internet was a bigger deal than they imagined, and Novell was consequently far behind. Since the internal local network was being called the "intranet" when utilizing such Internet touches as Web servers and standardized e-mail protocols, a light bulb flashed over the heads of Novell executives. Thus, the NetWare Internet Access Server (NIAS) was bundled, along with the Web Server, Multi-Protocol Router (MPR), NetWare/IP, and NetWare 4.11 itself, into IntranetWare and released in October 1996.

Earlier in 1996, Novell released its InnerWeb Publisher product, including the Web Server and an IPX/IP gateway licensed from Quarterdeck. When Novell started shipping its own gateway with InnerWeb, the name changed to NIAS. When the gateway became a product within IntranetWare, the name suddenly became the NetWare IPX/IP Gateway. Novell documentation can't make up its mind, either.

Before going into the installation details, let's take a quick look at the components that make an IPX-to-IP gateway work. There are two parts to every gateway: some software at the client, and software and (usually) hardware at the server.

At the client, Internet applications such as Netscape expect to find a program from the Winsock (WINdows SOCKets) family. The application, although officially a "TCP/IP" application, communicates only with Winsock, letting Winsock handle the transfer protocol details. By "spoofing" TCP/IP in the special Winsock, the NetWare IPX/IP Gateway makes Netscape and other Internet applications believe they are running on TCP/IP rather than IPX.

IPX carries the application packets from the client to the server. During this time, the application still believes TCP/IP is involved.

The server software takes care of the critical function of converting IPX data packets, received from the clients, into TCP/IP packets. The second half of the Winsock program, the TCP/IP portion, takes over at the server. Using the TCP/IP address of the gateway, the packet flies out to the Internet, and the application is none the wiser about IPX being involved.

Each packet going out the gateway adds a port number to the IP address. This allows the gateway to track which returning packet belongs to which NetWare client. On the far end, the Internet resource doesn't know or care that the ultimate packet recipient is running on IPX rather than TCP/IP.

Installing the NetWare IPX/IP Gateway

> **14.3 IN-A-HURRY**
>
> **Install the IPX/IP Gateway**
>
> 1. Have TCP/IP support active and verified on each NetWare server that you want to make a gateway.
>
> 2. Place the CD-ROM disk labeled "Internet Access Server 4" in the server's CD-ROM drive.
>
> 3. Type **LOAD INSTALL** at the server console.
>
> 4. Choose Product Options, and then select Install a Product Not Listed.
>
> 5. Mount the CD as a volume if possible (performance is much better) by typing **LOAD CDROM** and **CD MOUNT NIAS4**.
>
> 6. Press F3 and enter NIAS4\NIAS\INSTALL.
>
> 7. Select Install Product from the new screen.
>
> 8. Choose the server to become the gateway, and follow the rest of the installation directions.

Like NetWare/IP, the NetWare IPX/IP Gateway is installed as an extra product through the INSTALL server utility. The only real prerequisites for the installation are that TCP/IP support be active on the NetWare server in question and that you know the IP address of any external router that will support your IPX/IP Gateway.

When you start INSTALL, you want to pick either the IPX/IP Gateway or NIAS, depending on what Novell finally decides to put on the CD-ROM. If neither of these is listed in your product option window, choose Install a Product Not Listed and press Enter.

You'll have it easier than I did, no doubt. The early version required me to put the full path of D:\NIAS\INSTALL rather than just change the CD-ROM drive letter. By the time you get the product, the root index of the CD-ROM disk should have all the products listed.

Depending on whether you have your CD-ROM drive mounted as a NetWare volume (something I don't normally suggest), you'll need to say where the files are located. If you don't have the CD-ROM drive mounted as a volume, the system will warn you that there is a possible conflict between the CD-ROM drive and the keyboard. One would hope this would have been taken care of with the upgrade to NetWare 4.11, but evidently not. Although it's possible to hang the keyboard, I never have had this problem during this operation. The superstitious among you should cross your fingers when you press Enter, just for good luck.

> *The superstitious among you should cross your fingers when you press Enter, just for good luck.*

The next window offers you a chance to Install Product or Display Log File, as well as Exit. This choice is new with NetWare 4.11. Display Log File shows a log file kept of all products installed to this server. It's handy, but not necessary now. Choose to Install Product and continue.

Another new touch to NetWare 4.11 is the ability to install to multiple servers or to a single remote server, at one time. This is indicated by a screen labeled Install to Servers, which shows the current server. Pressing the Insert key allows you to pick other servers as well, assuming each of them has already loaded the RSPAWN.NLM program supporting this new feature.

Say Yes to start the installation. You're asked then if you want to install the configuration files to the server. Since the default is No, and unless you have previously configured an IPX/IP Gateway and exported the configuration details, accept the default and keep going.

License issues rear their head once more, as the server waits patiently for your license diskette. Feed it, and the file-copy process starts automatically, whether you want it to or not.

The familiar File Copy Status screen gets to work next. The IPX/IP Gateway files, from the Internet Portal file group (a third name for the product?) are copied first, and they whiz by. The MPR files take much longer. Why the MPR files? You may need to connect to the Internet via a connection supported through your NetWare server, meaning you will need the MPR files. Check the MPR section later in this chapter if you plan to place your communication boards in the server. Or, you could save yourself some potential trouble, and use an external router connected to your Internet provider rather than ask your server to perform multiple jobs.

Other files are included in the copy process, most notably new client files. Why? Because the IPX/IP Gateway adds some extra features to the client software, including the Winsock programs necessary for the Internet applications to function through the gateway. To utilize Winsock, a special version of Netscape 2.0*x* is included. You'll also get a new INETCFG utility, so you can configure some of these new protocol-dependent server applications.

> **NOTE**
>
> *I would show you some screens from the installation process, but, frankly, they're all pretty dull and you've seen them before. What's one more File Copy Status screen among friends?*

The fun of configuration happens in the updated INETCFG utility. Two new menu options at the bottom of the main menu, Reinitialize System and Go to Fast Setup are the immediate differences. The first new option makes all changes active, and the second offers a simplified menu system useful for basic configuration details. Perhaps soon these options will be in the INETCFG shipped with "regular" NetWare 4.11, or at least a mid-course patch update.

Configuration for the IPX/IP Gateway happens several menus deep (what a surprise). From the front menu, choose Protocols, then TCP/IP. Toward the bottom of the screen, choose IPX/IP Gateway Configuration. This opens the screen on display in Figure 14.14.

There's not much to do here, because the heavy lifting was done when you installed TCP/IP on the server. That's why the DNS addresses and domain name show up.

Let's go down the list of important things on this screen. First, you must enable the IPX/IP Gateway. Press Enter, then choose Enable, because the default is Disabled.

Client logging tracks details of client activity. Tracked are the service, the client, and the time period. IPXGSTAT.LOG in the SYS: directory is the log file name. Following that logic, the next option is to see the full gamut of information (still not very much, as you'll notice when you see it), just errors, or warnings and errors.

The next option, Access Control, is fairly important. With access control enabled, the system administrator may limit access to the gateway on a per-user basis. If you leave this option disabled, all NetWare clients with the proper Winsock and other client software can get to the Internet. This is not in the best interest of your company, believe me. Wasted time is only the first

FIGURE 14.14

Configuring your gateway to the Internet

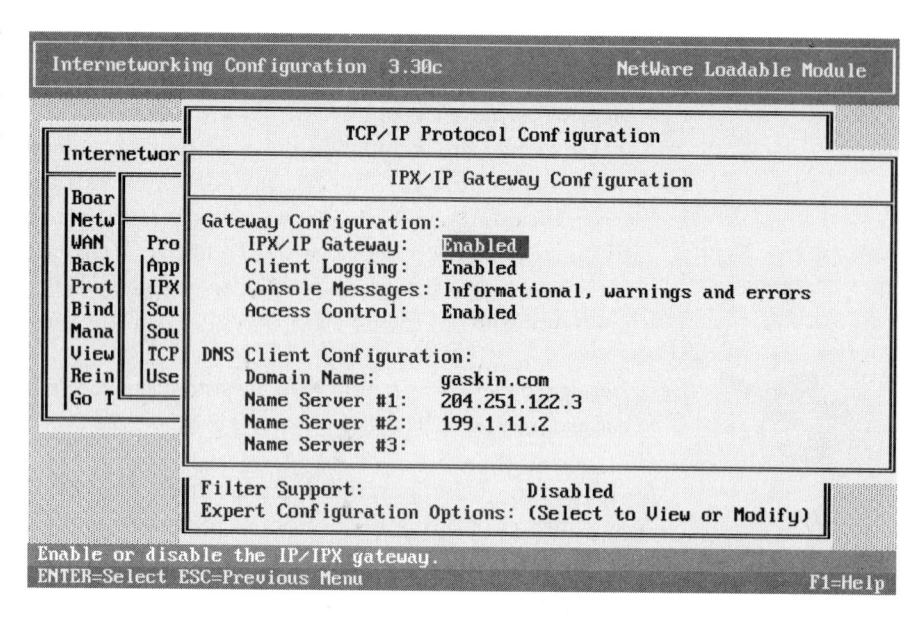

```
Internetworking Configuration 3.30c              NetWare Loadable Module

           ┌─────────────── TCP/IP Protocol Configuration ───────────────┐
  Internetwor│
  ┌──────────│────────── IPX/IP Gateway Configuration ──────────────────│
  │ Boar     │
  │ Netw     │ Gateway Configuration:
  │ WAN  │Pro│   IPX/IP Gateway:      Enabled
  │ Back │App│   Client Logging:      Enabled
  │ Prot │IPX│   Console Messages:    Informational, warnings and errors
  │ Bind │Sou│   Access Control:      Enabled
  │ Mana │Sou│
  │ View │TCP│ DNS Client Configuration:
  │ Rein │Use│   Domain Name:         gaskin.com
  │ Go T │   │   Name Server #1:      204.251.122.3
  └──────│   │   Name Server #2:      199.1.11.2
         │   │   Name Server #3:
         │   │
         │   │ Filter Support:                  Disabled
         │   │ Expert Configuration Options:    (Select to View or Modify)
         └───└──────────────────────────────────────────────────────────┘
  Enable or disable the IP/IPX gateway.
  ENTER=Select  ESC=Previous Menu                                  F1=Help
```

problem. Anyone in your company downloading pornography or stolen software puts the entire company at risk for criminal and civil legal problems.

DNS information has come from earlier installation of the TCP/IP software. In fact, GATEWAY2000-1 is now running both the IPX/IP Gateway and NetWare/IP. Although completely contradictory, both applications are running fine.

In case you're wondering, in my copy of NetWare 4.11, the software we just installed is referred to as the IPX/IP Gateway, as you can see from Figure 14.14. However, if you run the INSTALL utility and select View/Configure/Remove Installed Products, you'll see "NetWare Internet Access Server v4.0," big as life.

One last chore must be done, although I believe the installation routine should have taken care of this step. We must tell the NetWare Administrator program we have some new management routines, so we can control the IPX/IP Gateway.

Find \WINDOWS\NWADMN3X.INI for NetWare 4.11 systems, and go to the heading [Snapin Object DLLs WIN3X]. Add the line

```
ipxgw3x.dll=ipxgw3x.dll
```

at the beginning of the list entries.

For NetWare 4.10 systems, find the program \WINDOWS\NWADMIN.INI and the [Snapin Object DLLs] heading. Add the line

```
dll=c:\novell\client32\gwadmin.dll
```

to the list of entries. Save the file before starting your version of NetWare Administrator.

Tracking Clients and Managing Your IPX/IP Gateway

Now that the server is going (after you reboot, of course), the clients need support. If you were wavering on using Client32 or not, and you want the IPX/IP Gateway, your decision has just been made for you. If you want this gateway, you should run Client32.

Way back in Chapter 5, Figure 5.13, we saw the new Client32 installation program's screen. The last checkbox on the screen was for the IPX/IP Gateway. When that box is checked, the proper files are downloaded to the client, including various Winsock versions for 16-bit and 32-bit application support. WINSOCK.DLL supports 16-bit applications, and WSOCK32.DLL, surprisingly enough, does the job for 32-bit programs.

Windows 95 includes its own TCP/IP stack, including Winsock. In fact, you may have a problem keeping the Novell Winsock program, because Microsoft considers Winsock a critical system file and keeps a copy in the \WINDOWS\SYSBCKUP directory. Now and then, Windows 95 discovers that the Winsock in the \WINDOWS directory is not its own Winsock, and copies the "official" Winsock from the hidden \WINDOWS\SYSBCKUP directory into \WINDOWS, overwriting the Winsock you really need. The only way I've found to stop that from happening is to copy the Winsock version you want over the "official" one in the hidden SYSBCKUP directory.

There's one more step necessary at the client: enabling the IPX/IP Gateway for that workstation. The SWITCHER program supports the desire for some users to use the IPX/IP Gateway at times, and to use Microsoft's TCP/IP Winsock at other times. Figure 14.15 shows the checkbox to activate the Novell Winsock for the first time on a client. This screen should appear the first time you use the Client32 software including the IPX/IP Gateway client additions. If it does not, and your gateway doesn't work correctly, run the \NOVELL\CLIENT32\GWSWITCH.EXE program and make your selection.

If you have several gateways on your network, you will be asked to choose your preferred gateway. If one is down, another will allow access, so you may provide fault tolerance without going to any extra trouble.

FIGURE 14.15

Switching to the IPX/IP Gateway

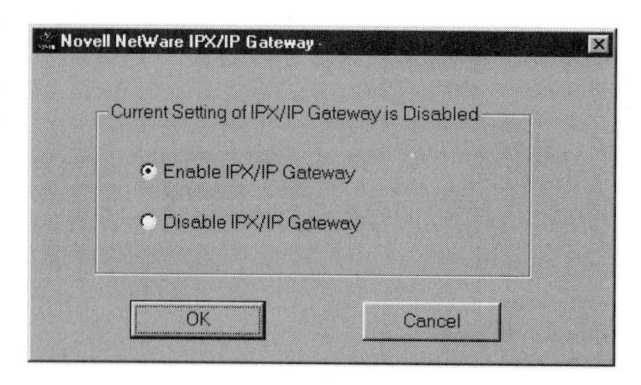

Time for an application? How about a Novell version of Netscape?

During the IPX/IP Gateway installation, copies of Netscape for 16-bit and 32-bit clients are installed on the server. The IPX/IP Gateway comes with a full license for Netscape for each network user, so all clients may have access to the software.

Installation is simple: Run the SETUP program from either the \NETSCAPE\16 or the \NETSCAPE\32 directory, depending on your client type. The SETUP program copies the files and handles the configurations for you. There is no option (in the version I have, at least) to share the Netscape application from a server.

A Short Security Lesson

Personally, I see no reason to activate the TCP/IP protocol on a Windows 95 workstation. When you have an all IPX network, such as all NetWare clients communicating with NetWare servers, the IPX/IP Gateway provides a complete security firewall against Internet intruders. Since the Internet uses only TCP/IP, hackers can use only TCP/IP hacking tools, and TCP/IP stops at the IPX/IP Gateway. Your internal NetWare network is invisible to outsiders, since there are no stations running TCP/IP inside your network to be exploited.

But James, you say, isn't your gateway server vulnerable? After all, it's on the Internet, and it's running TCP/IP.

True, your gateway server is running TCP/IP and is on the Internet. Even if you use an external router for your Internet connection, as I do with my Ascend Pipeline 50 ISDN router, outsiders can see through your router to your gateway host server. Your server does have an IP address, so it is visible to the Internet. This explains how your NetWare server can run the Web Server software and be visible to Web clients on the Internet.

Is this a security problem? Absolutely not. None of the applications that have given Unix hosts their reputation for poor security are on your NetWare server. Sendmail? Nope. \etc\passwd? Nope. Once a hacker gets to your server, the tools that person has to attack security holes will not find any holes.

There are no Unix host applications running on your system, either. The popular Unix daemons (background system processes, similar to NLMs) to exploit include Telnet, rlogin, and FTP. None of these applications run on the NetWare IPX/IP Gateway, meaning there are no security breaches. If you activate the FTP server portion of the Web Server, you control access. Even if you allow complete access to anonymous clients, the FTP program is different from the ones running on Unix hosts, and hackers can't do any particular damage to it.

Your IPX/IP Gateway provides excellent security. There is no need to add an expensive and management-intensive firewall, *unless you have TCP/IP nodes on your internal network*. If you have even one computer running its own TCP/IP protocol stack, a firewall is necessary.

Yes, Microsoft's TCP/IP protocol stack that is installed automatically when you load the Internet Explorer from the Plus! Pack falls into the dangerous area. Any Windows 95 client, or Windows NT client for that matter, can easily load TCP/IP, even if the user doesn't mean to. Then what happens to the safety and security profile of your network? It's gone. For this reason, don't allow any Windows 95 or NT clients to load their own TCP/IP protocol stack, unless you have a separate firewall active between your network and the Internet.

Personally, I feel Microsoft is being almost fraudulently flip by encouraging Internet access over TCP/IP from desktop systems without mentioning the security situation. Since Windows 95 and NT clients have the ability to function as peer servers, any information on that machine and any server resource they have access to become vulnerable. So, not only do these local TCP/IP systems allow intruders, they make them welcome by displaying the resources of your entire network.

I'll repeat: Don't let even one Windows 95 or NT client run the TCP/IP protocol stack on a local machine unless you have a secure firewall in place. Anything less vastly increases your chances of explaining to management why the company's secret sales projections are now displayed across the Internet.

Controlling Gateway Client Access

> ### 14.4 IN-A-HURRY
>
> **Set Up Client Access to the IPX/IP Gateway**
>
> 1. Open NetWare Administrator as the Admin or equivalent user.
> 2. Highlight the user, group, or container to modify and press Enter.
> 3. Page down through the command buttons until the IPX/IP Gateway Service Restrictions button appears, and then click on that button.
> 4. Make your changes, and click on OK to save and exit.

Remember when we checked on the IPX/IP Gateway configuration screen in INETCFG to enable access control? Here's what you gain:

- Control over when your clients can reach the Internet
- Control over what they can see when they get there

Why would you restrict access? Aren't all your co-workers adults? Sure they are, but they are adults tempted to waste time on the Internet and unclear on the rules concerning intellectual property, copyright infringement, and pornography in the modern age. I won't attempt to go into all the legal, ethical, and personnel decisions facing companies on the Internet (not in a book about NetWare, anyway); let's just say that the Internet offers more temptation than some people can resist.

Figure 14.16 shows the new snap-in modules to NetWare Administrator to control IPX/IP Gateway access. Remember the extra file editing you did just a bit ago? Here's the payoff for that work.

By the window ID on the top left, you can see I've created a new user named Laura. She will have Internet access, but not all night. The longer people stay at the office, the more temptation there is to "relax" with the Internet for a few minutes. Since many activities some folks consider relaxing lean toward the "leisure" areas of the Internet, closing the IPX/IP Gateway at 10:00 P.M. will help discourage inappropriate activities.

The default for this screen is the top choice, Inherited Default Access. This flows down the NDS tree, so if you set rights for an Organization, those rights will flow down to the Organizational Units within that Organization.

FIGURE 14.16

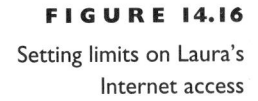

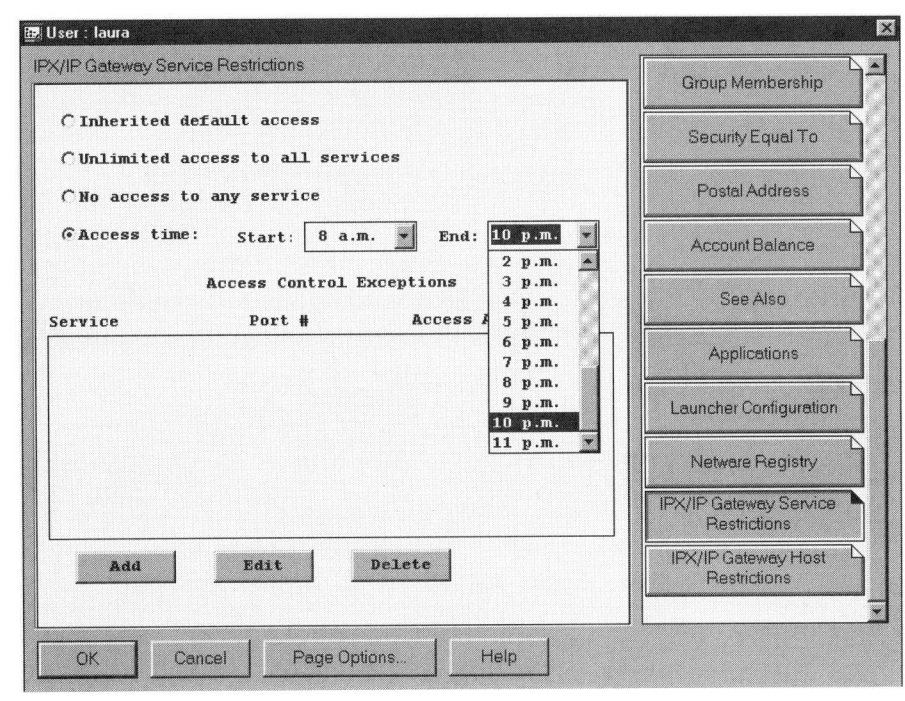

Setting limits on Laura's Internet access

Why is there a choice marked No Access to Any Service? This works just like disabling an account while a person is on vacation. If you don't want to delete the user, or delete all the user's configuration details, you can leave the configuration in place and block access. What if Laura says she didn't do something you accused her of doing on the Internet? Most likely, someone else has learned her account's password. Give her another account, and block the old Laura account. Then teach her about protecting her password from her co-workers.

As it stands, Laura has access until 10:00 P.M. You can see the drop-down list box, offering choices beyond the default 8:00 A.M. to 5:00 P.M. time slot.

The next step in controlling access is to limit the ability of a user to use certain applications. Depending on your company's acceptable use policy that defines Internet access and behavior, some users may be allowed to use a Web client but not other Internet applications.

Figure 14.17 shows this exact situation: We're going to block Laura's ability to read newsgroups by blocking NNTP (Network News Transport Protocol) until after hours. While this would make more sense on a group or Organization level, let's keep Laura as our example.

FIGURE 14.17

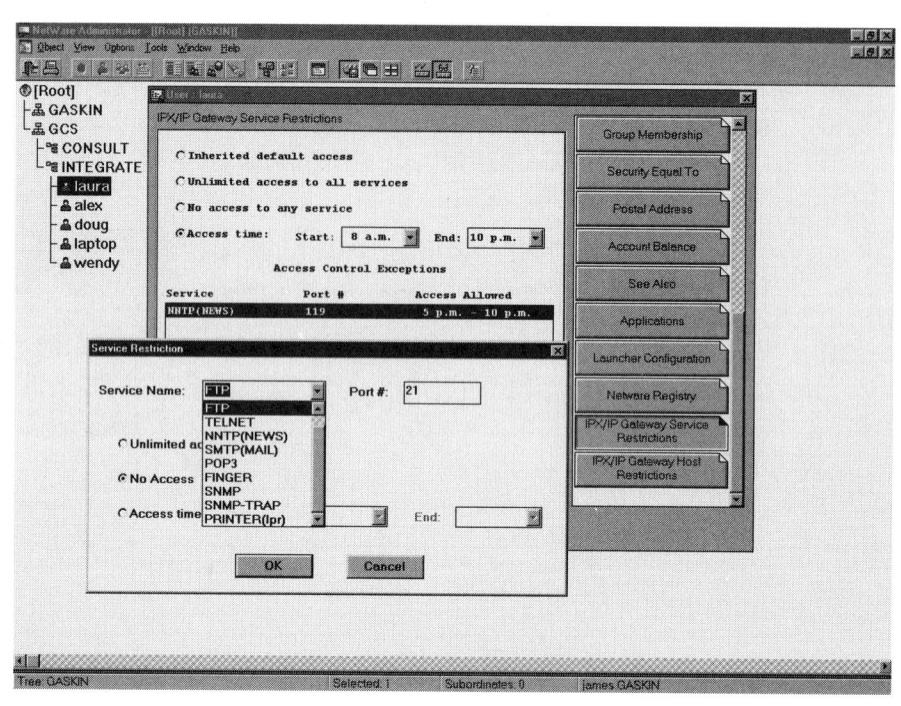

More limits on Laura

[figure: NetWare Administrator screen showing IPX/IP Gateway Service Restrictions and Service Restriction dialog with Service Name dropdown listing FTP, TELNET, NNTP(NEWS), SMTP(MAIL), POP3, FINGER, SNMP, SNMP-TRAP, PRINTER(lpr)]

Just above the foreground window you see the Service box, which was empty in Figure 14.16. Notice I have blocked Laura from using any NNTP-based applications except between 5:00 P.M. and 10:00 P.M. The Service name is NNTP, which NetWare Administrator graciously identifies as News. The Port number is the software programming location used by news servers and news readers. The Access Allowed column shows when Laura may read newsgroups.

The foreground window, Service Restrictions, shows how the selection process works. Although the command buttons are blocked in this view, you can see in Figure 14.16 that your three options are Add, Edit, and Delete. The Service Restrictions box appears when you click on Add; a slightly different box appears without the Service Name selection list when you choose Edit.

You can see the selection list for Service Name covers quite a few Internet application protocols. The Port number box is filled in automatically for you, depending on the service chosen. If you want to block a specific port number not attached to a service, you may do so.

One Product, Two Names: NIAS and/or NetWare IPX/IP Gateway

Choices for blocking allow Unlimited Access (in case her profile is different from that of the group), No Access, and Access Time. In the case of FTP, highlighted in Figure 14.17, we're allowing Laura no FTP access at any time. Copying software from the Internet leads to virus problems at best, and copyright infringement charges at worst. It's best to let only your most trusted power users and network support personnel download files.

Most management teams worry about the time employees spend perusing inappropriate Web sites. If your boss has these fears, soothe them with Figure 14.18.

The second new page in NetWare Administrator is named IPX/IP Gateway Host Restrictions. As you can see, we're setting limits on Alex. Of course, you may set the limits on more than one person at a time.

When you click on the Add button, the Host Restriction box opens. You must know the IP address of hosts to be restricted, which is somewhat painful. Some other Internet gateways provide a lookup function, allowing you to put in the host name and receive the host IP address. Perhaps Novell will add this feature in the next version.

Once you put the IP address in the field, the IPX/IP Gateway will check the Internet for that site and provide the name in the main window. You can see

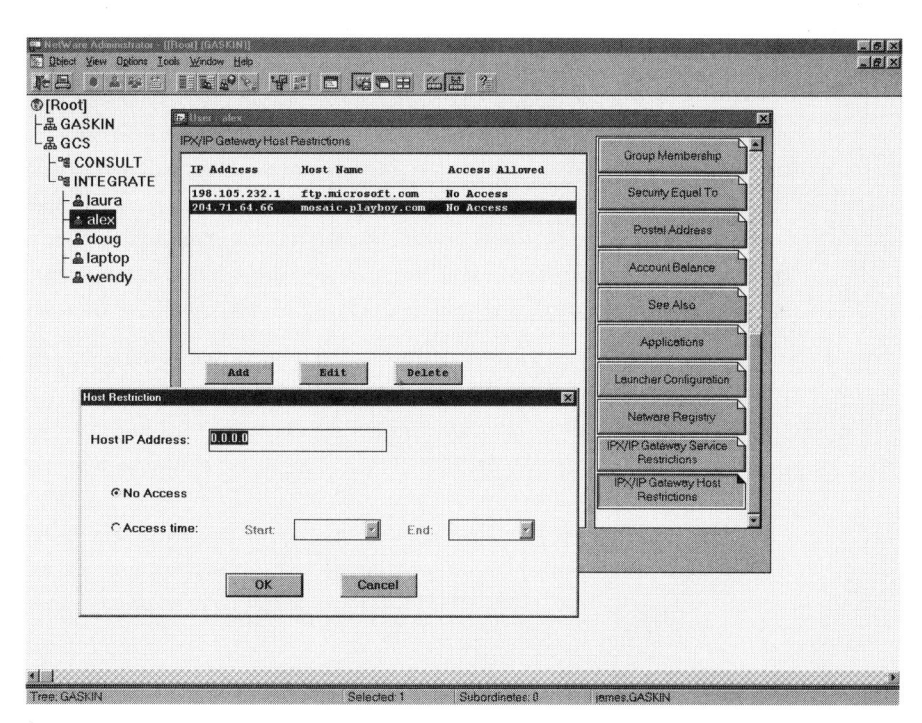

FIGURE 14.18

Internet hosts Alex can't visit

we've set Microsoft's FTP server as off-limits to our network. The second restriction is playboy.com (this is such a popular example that Playboy should have to pay for this much publicity). If you know the Internet, you know Playboy has no monopoly on content inappropriate for the workplace. Since your boss may not know that, I added this example rather than one that truly goes into the area of pornography by the definitions of most communities.

If you click on the Edit button, you can change the access times, but not much else. You can also change the setting from an access time range to no access.

Why You Should Use the IPX/IP Gateway

Does the IPX/IP Gateway provide you with any real benefits? Absolutely. Anyone attempting to connect NetWare clients to the Internet who doesn't investigate a few of the NetWare-to-Internet gateways available is doing a disservice to himself or herself, as well as to the NetWare clients.

IP address management has been mentioned here and there, but take it from me, it's not an exciting occupation. Do you want to track one more unique number for every workstation and every other TCP/IP device on your network? That's what you're facing with TCP/IP stacks on each workstation.

Windows 95 and NT clients may have TCP/IP provided free, but your existing Windows 3.1x clients don't. Beyond that, Windows 95 and NT clients come with the TCP/IP stack, but no applications. Want Internet e-mail, a news reader, or an FTP program? Yes, the Internet Explorer provided from Microsoft can provide some of those functions, but they aren't as good as some of the other TCP/IP applications available. Many gateways come with application suites, and Novell provides Netscape. Just Netscape alone does a better job than Internet Explorer (at least in my opinion), and it's free with the IPX/IP Gateway.

Don't underestimate the value of controlling your clients when they connect to the Internet. The restrictions offered by Novell's IPX/IP Gateway aren't as good as some, but they're better than nothing. You must manage and control your users, if for no other reason than reducing your chances of employee lawsuits. Some users will feel uncomfortable with material found on the Internet, and the company becomes liable in many cases when that material finds its way onto your NetWare server. Putting some access controls in place, even if they're not done well, at least supports the idea that management is trying to control the users.

(continued on next page)

> Novell's IPX/IP Gateway provides the minimum access control features. Check one of the Web search engines for NetWare-to-Internet gateways and see how many other options turn up. There are about a dozen other vendors, all of whom make products comparable to, or better than, the Novell offering.
>
> Finally, security becomes another issue. Firewalls are expensive and complicated, but you receive excellent protection by using a gateway pushing TCP/IP out to the Internet, while pushing IPX to the NetWare clients. Just avoid any TCP/IP systems within your own network. No security holes make for more sleep and less worry wrinkles.

Running the NetWare Web Server

HERE'S THE SECOND shoe dropping along with the IPX/IP Gateway: the Web Server. Novell released the Web Server as part of the InnerWeb Publisher earlier in 1996, but without the IPX/IP Gateway, NetWare clients using the IPX protocol couldn't use the Web Server. Now, every client can see and use the NetWare Web Server whether it uses the Internet or not.

Why would you want a Web server but not the Internet? That's the whole idea behind the intranet: to revolutionize your LAN with Web client to Web server protocols and interaction. In fact, Novell says the intranet has three important components: the LAN, a Web server, and Web clients.

The "Web client" portion of the preceding sentence deserves special consideration. Much of the value in the Web protocols concerns any server supporting any desktop. If you're a long-time NetWare user, you're used to seeing all important desktop operating systems supported by NetWare. We've already covered clients running DOS, Windows 3.*x*, Windows 95, Windows NT, and we'll soon discuss OS/2 clients.

Most of the computer world is far behind Novell in client support. Microsoft has the market cornered with Windows of various flavors, but can't take the lead in the Web client market because Internet Explorer is available only for Windows clients. Netscape offers Windows clients, but also offers Unix clients of every flavor, as well as Macintosh clients. Microsoft may leverage its operating system monopoly into a leading market share for Internet Explorer on Windows, but it will never capture the rest of the client market without expanding beyond its own desktop environments.

The Web client is becoming the real "desktop" for computer users, and Novell users are no exception. Putting Web software on your NetWare server makes it easy to share the files on that server with any client capable of running Web client software. The Web Server has full support for the following:

- R-CGI (Remote Common Gateway Interface), which allows developers to create external processes that can communicate with external servers, such as a TCP/IP host or Unix server. Of course, other NetWare servers may be used, as well as the local server hosting the Web Server software.

- L-CGI (Local Common Gateway Interface), which communicates with processes running as NLMs on the local file server.

- BASIC and PERL scripts.

- Java applications.

With these features, along with the NetWare Web Server's blazing file performance figures, a company with no NetWare in the building could well rationalize a NetWare Web Server purchase. After all, not everyone wants to learn Unix in order to get a high-performance Web server. Some people may even prefer not to learn Windows NT, the other major Web server option, especially since NetWare outperforms Windows NT in independent tests.

Novell's Web Server is based on the HTTP server developed by NCSA (National Center for Supercomputing Applications, developers of the first commercial Web client, Mosaic). The basics of Web services are covered, since the foundation of the product is the pioneering developer of the Web itself.

There is no reason for me, a non-Webmaster, to try and explain all the details of Web server configuration and maintenance. Scores of Web books are crowding the bookstore shelves, often pushing fine and valuable network books to the background (grumble, grumble). But let's at least take the time to get the Web Server installed and working, so your Webmaster (whether you or someone else) can start typing those HTML codes to present content in a meaningful way.

> *Before you start arguing about whether the NetWare Web Server makes the grade, let me inform you that several national computer trade magazines have reviewed the Web Server 2.5, which is the version released with the InnerWeb Publisher. Many of the reviews felt the NetWare Web Server performance and ease of use warranted attention from potential Web sites everywhere, even if the site had no other NetWare software installed. With the Web Server, Novell finally has an application server that runs faster and jumps higher than Windows NT. What a nice change.*

Installing the Web Server

> **14.5 IN-A-HURRY**
>
> **Install the Web Server**
>
> 1. Install and verify TCP/IP support on the server to become a Web server.
>
> 2. Type **LOAD INSTALL** at the server console.
>
> 3. Choose Product Options, select Choose an Item or Product Listed Above, and then press Enter.
>
> 4. Choose Install NetWare WEB Server v2.51 and press Enter.
>
> 5. Provide the source of the Web Server files (your primary NetWare CD-ROM disk) or a copy of the NetWare installation files copied to another server.
>
> 6. Read the README.TXT file when asked (no, really, read one for a change).
>
> 7. Provide a decent Web Server password to finish the installation.
>
> 8. Reboot your server and become an Internet content provider.

Even if you bought the NetWare 4.11 package only, not the IntranetWare bundle, you still get the NetWare Web Server. This reflects more on Novell executive's last-minute decisions to separate the intranet components into the IntranetWare bundle than it does Novell largesse. Either way, the Web Server is included and ready to go to work.

As Figure 14.19 shows, your server must already have TCP/IP loaded and configured. This makes sense; the primary function of Web servers is to provide content on the Internet. Reaching the Internet means running TCP/IP. Even if you run your Web Server software for internal use exclusively, adding TCP/IP won't cause a problem.

Part of the reason the Web Server wasn't separated from the NetWare 4.11-only package is that the Web Server is part of the Product Options main menu of the INSTALL utility. Taking out this product would require more juggling and testing than Novell had time to complete. But this also makes installation a snap. Simply load INSTALL from the server console, choose Product Options, highlight Install NetWare Web Server v2.51, and press Enter.

FIGURE 14.19

The first step to Internet publishing

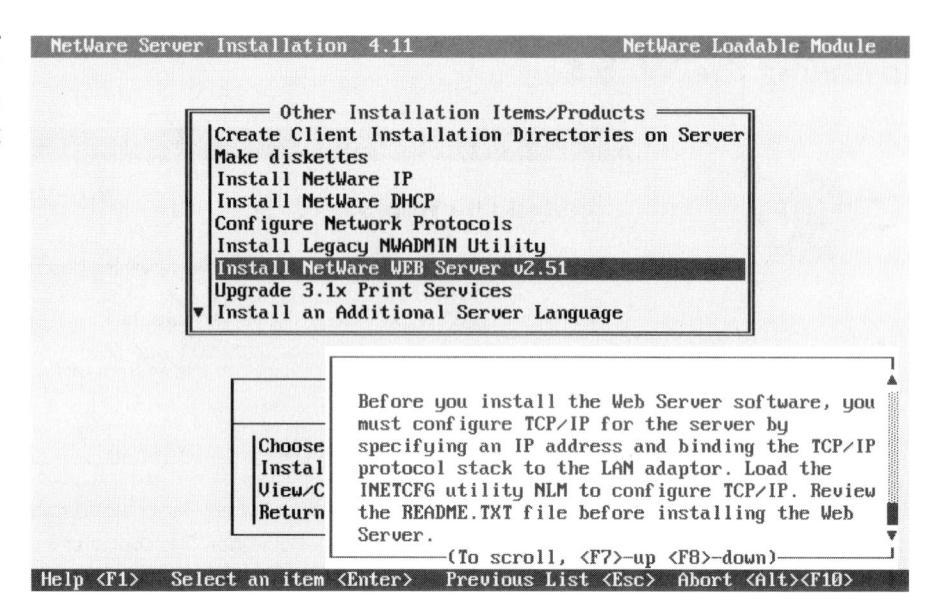

```
NetWare Server Installation  4.11                    NetWare Loadable Module

                ┌──────── Other Installation Items/Products ────────┐
                │ Create Client Installation Directories on Server  │
                │ Make diskettes                                     │
                │ Install NetWare IP                                 │
                │ Install NetWare DHCP                               │
                │ Configure Network Protocols                        │
                │ Install Legacy NWADMIN Utility                     │
                │ Install NetWare WEB Server v2.51                   │
                │ Upgrade 3.1x Print Services                        │
                ▼ Install an Additional Server Language              │
                └────────────────────────────────────────────────────┘
                          ┌────────────────────────────────────────────────┐
                          │ Before you install the Web Server software, you│
                          │ must configure TCP/IP for the server by        │
                  Choose  │ specifying an IP address and binding the TCP/IP│
                  Instal  │ protocol stack to the LAN adaptor. Load the    │
                  View/C  │ INETCFG utility NLM to configure TCP/IP. Review│
                  Return  │ the README.TXT file before installing the Web  │
                          │ Server.                                        │
                          └──────(To scroll, <F7>-up <F8>-down)────────────┘
 Help <F1>   Select an item <Enter>   Previous List <Esc>   Abort <Alt><F10>
```

The first screen asks for the source of the files. Since the Web Server is on the primary NetWare 4.11 CD-ROM, put the CD-ROM in the server CD-ROM drive. The default location is drive D:, which corresponds to most CD-ROM drives on most computers. If this matches your setup, press Enter and go forward. If not, press F3, provide the correct drive letter, and press Enter.

The CD-ROM and keyboard warning jumps up next. Press Enter once again and continue.

Files fly by, since there aren't that many files necessary to run the Web Server, believe it or not. No current word processor could exist with these few files, but then the Web Server doesn't include a spelling checker, either.

A warning box appears, asking you to read the README.TXT file. Might as well press Enter and glance at it. That way, if something goes wrong, you have a fighting chance of remembering you ignored vital information in the README.TXT file, and you'll go back and check it.

When you finish with the README.TXT file, the files that have been copied to the NetWare server are configured and sent to their proper locations. The Web Server creates its own directory structure under the WEB directory on the SYS: volume, and only files inside the WEB hierarchy are available to Web clients. This keeps your other NetWare files safe from prying eyes using Web clients.

You are asked for a Web Server password. Choose one at least five characters long, including numbers and letters. Web server passwords tend to attract attention from miscreants, so make yours as strong as possible.

After you provide a password and retype it, more files will fly about, and you will be instructed to down and restart your NetWare server. After doing so, the Web Server 2.51 will load automatically.

The \WEB subdirectory contains the following files after installation:

- README
- CONFIG
- DOCS
- LCGI
- MAPS
- SAMPLES
- SCRIPTS
- LOGS

Yes, the README.TXT file is the same one you should have looked at during installation. If you have a problem, here's the first place to look. You could even take the daring step of reading the file before you need it. Just be sure no one is looking when you act proactively like this, or you'll get a bad reputation.

The CONFIG directory includes basic Web system configuration files. Included is the HTTP.CFG file, showing your password in encrypted format, safe from prying eyes. The IP address of the Web Server is stored in that file as well, which the installation routine picked up from the TCP/IP configuration files.

Configuring and Managing the Web Server

WEBMGR.EXE, the official name for the Web Server Manager, is copied to the \PUBLIC directory during installation. If you're afraid a user will find the utility and cause trouble, you may certainly try moving the file or adding a stronger password.

14.6 IN-A-HURRY

Use the Web Manager Utility

1. Log in to the network as the Admin user or equivalent.
2. Run the WEBMGR.EXE program from the \PUBLIC directory.
3. Click on the Open icon, and give the location of the configuration files for the Web Server to be managed.
4. Click on each page tab and modify settings as necessary.

Everything for Web Server configuration and management happens in WEBMGR. Figure 14.20 shows the opening screen for the WEBMGR program, after specifying which Web Server to open from the File menu.

FIGURE 14.20

Managing Web Server the graphical way

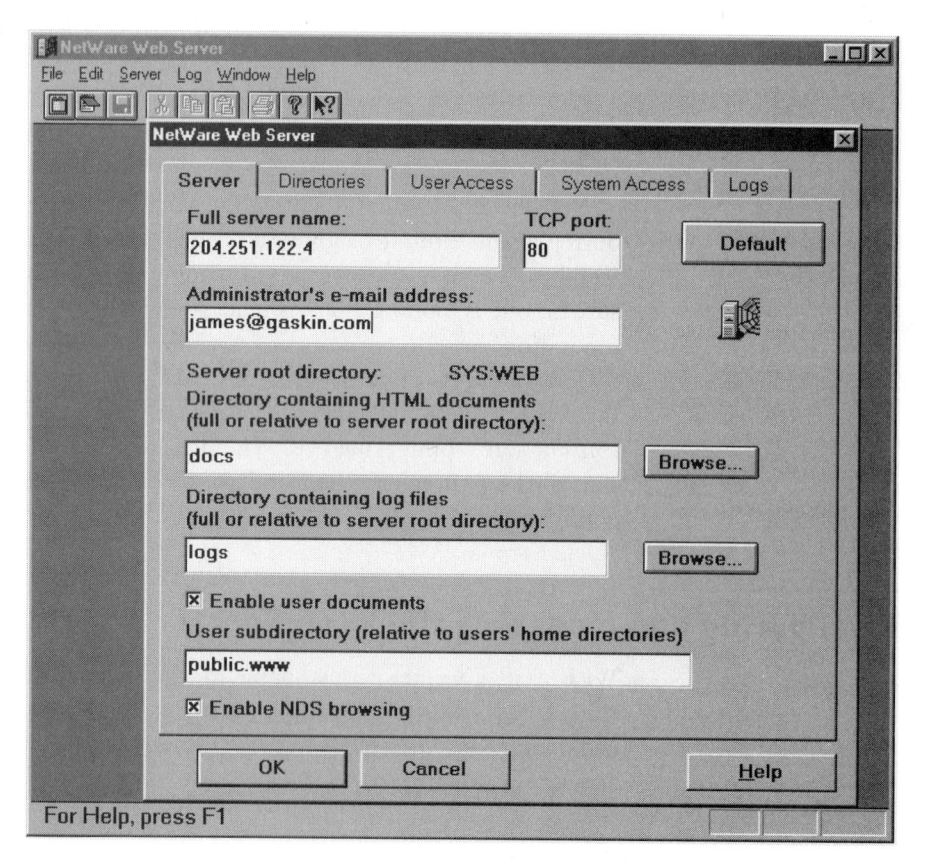

The first screen provides administrative details, such as the server name (or IP address, as supplied here) and the e-mail address to list for comments on the Web pages. Other fields show the default directory locations for HTML documents, logs, and user documents. Authorized users may create their own Web pages and directory structures under the \WEB hierarchy.

Enable NDS Browsing is the label on the last checkbox on the screen. When checked, this feature allows Web clients to see your NDS structure by viewing http:\\your-server-name\nds and wandering about. Is the Web interface better than NetWare Administrator? No, but it may be more efficient across a WAN connection. At this point, the fact that you can view the NDS structure with a Web client makes up for the fact you can't yet do anything useful with this interface.

The next tabbed page, Directories, sets the locations of all the various scripts, image maps, and indices used by same. The defaults work well, although you can make any changes you wish. Remember, any user's personal Web pages will be created under this same file hierarchy, so changing the defaults doesn't make too much sense, at least at the beginning. Save the experiments for your second Web site, not your first.

If your Web Server is connected to the Internet, the default setting allows all Web clients access to the Web documents. This makes sense: If you didn't want people to see your Web site, you wouldn't put the Web Server system on the Internet, would you?

The User Access page sets the most important part of your Web site: Who can see it? You have quite a bit of flexibility; you can set who sees what for documents, maps, and images. Figure 14.21 shows this page, in brilliant shades of gray.

Of course, there are things behind the scenes you may not want to share with the world. More to the point, in an intranet situation, Web sites may be dedicated to specific users or departments. Having everyone browse the personnel manual in electronic format is one thing, but allowing the entire employee population to peruse R&D files could create problems.

The checkbox labeled All Valid Users, in the middle-right portion of the screen, disables the pick list named Authorized Users. If the checkbox stays blank, as in Figure 14.21, authorized users are allowed access to only the directory or service listed.

Logs brings up the rear of the tabbed pages, and rather dull stuff holds sway on this screen. You may set log file size, whether log files roll or not, and how many old logs files are kept. If, of course, you wish to keep any old log files at all.

FIGURE 14.21

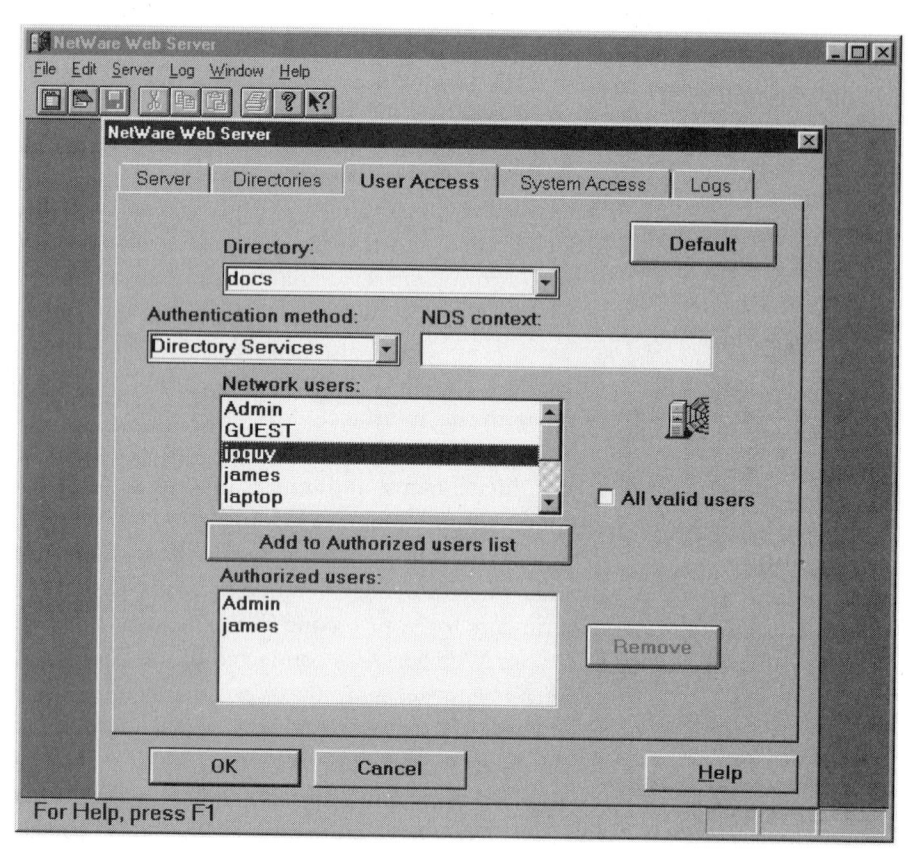

Setting Web access

For the last screenshot and wrap-up of these new IntranetWare features, let's take a look at what the Web Server actually looks like. Yes, just as with all the other good Web server packages, the default Web page available right out of the box does look good. In fact, Novell cleverly put all of its documentation right on the demonstration page. Once you get this far, you have lots of help getting farther. Figure 14.22 shows what I mean.

I hope you can read all the fine print here in Figure 14.22. Java applets are included. Various sample scripts take your name, feed version numbers at the touch of a button by performing a query in the background, and connect you with the Novell home page if necessary.

FIGURE 14.22

Out-of-the-box Web success

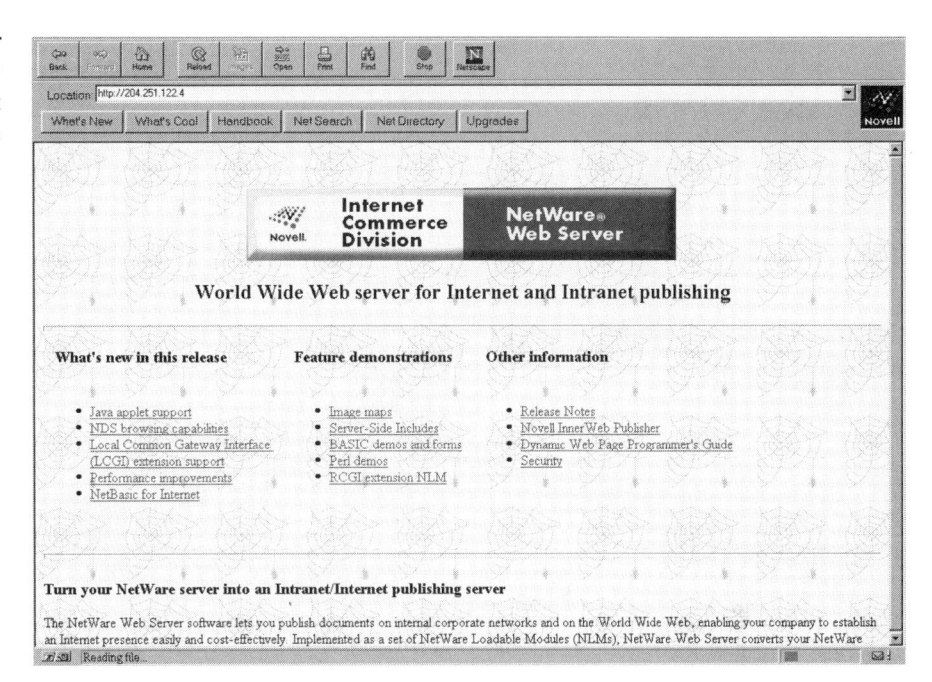

> *This is one of the better canned server demonstrations I've seen included with a Web server, but I already mentioned that I'm not a Web guru by any stretch. Does this give a real Webmaster enough material to start with? I think so, not that my opinion here counts for much. But authors of various articles and reviews all say that Web Server does a good job and presents files faster than they ever imagined, so I'm not the only reviewer impressed.*

Check into the fourth disk of your IntranetWare installation CD-ROM set if you want to add the FTP Server software for your Web Server. If so, you'll be forced to install the Unix-to-NetWare (and vice versa) printer gateways, but that may help your situation a bit. If you want to install only the FTP Server, let the installation program do what it wants, and then delete the LOAD file references for the printer gateway later.

These pieces form the heart of the IntranetWare bundle now superseding NetWare 4.11 by itself. Does the combination of NetWare/IP, the NetWare IPX/IP Gateway, and the Web Server make a powerful Internet and intranet statement? Yes. With these systems, your existing NetWare network components, including servers, printers, workstations, application software, and extra utilities, are the backbone of an intranet network to rival the best system from the world's largest companies. After all, they often must reinvent portions of their network, and IntranetWare carefully preserves your existing investment. All told, this system works well, works fast, and works cheap (the price is the same for IntranetWare as for just NetWare 4.11, remember?).

Using the Multi-Protocol Router

THE MULTI-PROTOCOL Router, or MPR version 3.1 (now counted as a separate product for NetWare servers), claims heritage from the earliest NetWare server that supported two network interface cards. Way back then, in about 1986, Novell called its connecting service a "bridge," but it wasn't. We old-timers learned that the hard way, when the first Token Ring boards couldn't connect systems on two different network segments through the Novell server. Novell then admitted the "bridge" was really a router, meaning the server software made the segment addressing choices based on protocol addresses rather than physical addresses.

Everyone else in the computer biz did it the opposite way, of course, by claiming the company's products had more features than they really did have. Novell, following the contrarian path, claimed to have fewer features.

So, you can see that Novell engineers have had a decade of experience in routing protocols. The routing protocol software still runs in the NetWare server whenever you add a second, third, or fourth network interface card. Novell has taken that feature, beefed it up, and added what it has learned with the NetWare Connect product to make what you now see as the MPR. The IPX/IP Gateway, the FTP Server, and the MPR make the difference between IntranetWare and regular NetWare 4.11.

What can you do with the MPR? Make a complete, private WAN between your network and other branches. Does your company have remote branches? Are you connected to them across a telecommunications link? If so, you probably paid anywhere from $2,500 to $10,000 for the box connected to the phone line. You can replace that box connected to your phone line with a NetWare server and MPR. Even if you bought a brand new, small server for the operation, you will come out ahead. Check it out.

Installing the MPR

The DynaText documentation describes the installation procedures as if you had a separate CD-ROM labeled "NWMPR31." In my IntranetWare package, that's not the case. However, the MPR is loaded each and every time I load the IPX/IP Gateway, even though I make no reference to the product. I guess Novell is just being efficient, since many folks using the IPX/IP Gateway will use the services of the MPR.

So, since I can't find the files matching the installation procedures in the documentation, I suppose you should install the IPX/IP Gateway to get the MPR installed. I know that works, and you have a choice of not activating your IPX/IP Gateway if you don't want to, yet still keep the MPR.

Refer back to the installation section for the IPX/IP Gateway (or Novell Internet Access Server, if you prefer). When it comes time to configure the MPR, come back here. I'll wait.

Configuring the MPR

This information will be necessarily spotty and incomplete. I'm not taking the sleazy way out (really, I'm not; I can configure WAN devices, I promise), but your equipment and situation will vary so much from everyone else's that a single configuration description will never apply to everyone. All I can promise is that you'll get even more familiar with INETCFG. I don't consider that a blessing.

The first step is to LOAD INETCFG from the server to become MPR-enabled. You can run the MPR on dedicated NetWare Runtime, to separate the routing functions from normal office LAN functions. That isn't necessary, but it makes some people feel safer. You may certainly run the MPR system on any NetWare 4.1*x* server you like, but I would suggest you pick a lightly used server. There will be times the server must come down and back up to reset WAN boards, and you don't want to inconvenience any more users than necessary.

Start in INETCFG by configuring your new network board. When you open the Boards menu option and press Insert to add a new board, you'll see many boards with drivers already installed inside NetWare. The vast majority are LAN boards, of course, but a few WAN boards are stuck here and there. Press the Insert key once more if you have your own board and drivers to add.

Name your board, set the interrupt, I/O base address, and memory base address in the next window, labeled Board Configuration. You will likely see quite a bit of text under the Driver Info heading, since these boards are more unusual in a NetWare installation than your basic Ethernet board. Reading this information will save you time later, so do so.

Once the MPR is configured and a protocol bound to the board (yes, I'm skipping a bit here), go back to the main INETCFG menu and choose the Reinitialize System option. If your board works, you will be congratulated. If your board conflicts with other boards, go back to your board documentation and try it again.

Novell engineers, understanding the situation, even put the technical support 800 number for DigiBoard International in their board driver information text. Start this during regular business hours, so you at least have a chance to get some technical support if you have problems. Besides, we haven't even talked about your CSU/DSU and the hassles of working with the telephone company. And, guess what, we won't.

You, TCP/IP, the Internet, and the Web

PERHAPS I'M THE wrong one to say this, since I wrote my first book on connecting NetWare networks to Unix systems, but connecting Unix and NetWare can be important for many companies. I certainly think it's important, but I'm biased.

Like it or not, Unix became the shining example of "open computing" in the middle 1980s. Much of the communication gains made by the Internet community were based on the sharing of standards and information between Unix and TCP/IP product vendors.

Each system has its own quirks and weirdness. You probably feel more comfortable with NetWare than with Unix, so you may feel Unix is as odd as fish riding bicycles. If you talk to a Unix person, however, you may find they think NetWare is just some kind of super DOS. This isn't right, but more important, it shows you that two intelligent people can each have a lot to learn.

More exciting, many intelligent people today believe Unix has somehow disappeared. After all, you don't hear much about Unix anymore, because of all the noise about the Internet.

Guess what? The Internet runs on Unix. All those Web servers? The majority are Unix systems. FTP servers? Unix. Routers? Unix. E-mail servers? Unix. My guess says that 90 percent or more of Internet servers of any type run on Unix.

Understanding Unix will give you a foundation that applies to every other operating system and to the Internet. Is this like saying that learning Latin in high school makes English more clear? Yes, but it's more than that. People don't speak Latin anymore, but they speak Unix all the time.

Although TCP/IP networking has become somewhat divorced from Unix because of the Internet's popularity, all the stuff you've learned about Unix is still important. After all, when you peel up the Internet and Web veneer, you find Unix almost every time.

MiniCo and MegaCorp Revisited: The Internet Angle

We left MiniCo and MegaCorp at the end of Part II, when we were finished with the networking chores that apply to nearly every network. But we'll look in on them one last time, to see how they're handling their Internet connections.

Finally, MiniCo and MegaCorp agree almost completely on their approach to a technology area: Web Server. The only differences are the number of Web servers installed, the speed of Internet connections, heavy use of company-only servers by MegaCorp, and the quality of presented material. For once, when budget constraints don't rule the equation, MiniCo actually races ahead of MegaCorp.

Both MiniCo and MegaCorp decided to use the Web Server version 2.51 included with IntranetWare for their Web site foundations.

As per their habit, MegaCorp managers laid out the design criteria, organized a committee to study the problem, and developed a plan of implementation. This took four months, including the time spent sending programmers to Web programming classes.

MiniCo's President, Jack Mingo, as per his habit, told Alexander von Thorn (the main network administrator) to look into it and see what he could do. With the addition of RoadTrip Productions, Alexander had a good resource. He asked Loren MacGregor, the RoadTrip Webmaster, to see if he could work up something for them.

(continued on next page)

Although Loren had no formal HTML or other Web programming experience, his general programming background and his affinity for graphic design bloomed with this project. Taking the book catalogs from both MiniCo and RoadTrip, along with author photos and biographies, Loren set out to see what type of Web presence he could develop.

Within a week, Loren had the NetWare Web Server up and running, with an excellent design and content presentation. Every book from both companies, including Loren's own *Weddings That Pay for Themselves* workbook, had at least one screen's worth of information.

As small publishers, MiniCo and RoadTrip forged alliances with a few of the bookstores running a strong Web presence. Links from the bookstore Web servers to MiniCo's site provided much more depth and information about the books they published than the bookstores had time to develop themselves.

By the time the MegaCorp administrators put copies of their paper-based catalogs and annual report on the Internet, their competitors had received two awards for Web site excellence. MegaCorp's site received 90 percent less traffic than their competitors. In fact, MegaCorp received fewer hits than MiniCo.

The tale of the two companies and their Internet connections is not much different. MegaCorp studied the value of the NetWare IPX/IP Gateway versus placing TCP/IP on each workstation. After three months, and the writing of a twelve-page Acceptable Use Policy, MegaCorp decided on a third-party NetWare-to-Internet gateway that provided more logging and filtering options than did the Novell IPX/IP Gateway.

MiniCo just loaded the IPX/IP Gateway and started surfing. Everyone was told, "*Work* on the Internet when using company equipment on company time." A two-page Acceptable Use Policy was developed over the first few weeks, but employee understanding of the goals and regular management reinforcement of the "work while at work" attitude guaranteed no person became addicted to the Internet or downloaded inappropriate material.

This story shows that money and strict management don't always win the race. Sometimes, great opportunities present themselves, such as the Internet and Web services. The first group to recognize great value often gains an edge over those who worry and analyze too long. Of course, knowing the difference between the next trend and the next fad requires intuition that can be managed and mandated.

Installing and Configuring OS/2 Clients

CHAPTER 15

How would you like a network client operating system that runs 32-bit software, has complete memory protection (so one multitasking application can't bother any other application), and that connects to NetWare 2.*x*, 3.*x* and 4.*x* servers? As a bonus, this network client runs almost all MS Windows and DOS applications. For a few dollars extra, you can get a full set of Internet software in the same box.

OS/2, especially the version 3.0 labeled "Warp" by amazingly unrestrained IBM marketers, is this client operating system. With the NetWare client software, your OS/2-powered computer can do all the above, and more.

Everything you need for OS/2 clients is included in the NetWare 4.1*x* box. This is a good thing, because the folks at IBM committed a huge blunder (in my opinion, anyway) when they released OS/2 Warp without the NetWare client software as part of the basic package. (The corporate environment is where IBM has made its money, and the company ignored the majority of corporate desktop clients when it left out NetWare.)

Luckily for IBM, someone at Novell picked up that dropped ball, at least in NetWare 4.1*x*. There has been some aggravation in supporting OS/2 and NetWare in the past, but now everyone seems to be following the same road map. If you have some OS/2 clients to support (that's why you're reading this, right?), you have probably been checking with NetWire and Novell's Web Server regularly to get the latest client files. With the help of that support and this chapter, you have a good chance of keeping your OS/2 network clients satisfied.

> **The Future of OS/2**
>
> I'm ready for something to replace Windows 3.1 as the default desktop. At first, I was unsure whether that should be Windows 95, Windows NT, or OS/2. Making DOS the foundation of your desktop operating system in today's multitasking world will always be limiting. But now I think that it's time to move onto either Windows NT or OS/2.
>
> Unfortunately, OS/2 may suffer the same fate as BetaMax: technically superior but completely out-marketed. Of course, if everyone that likes OS/2 buys it rather than caving in to marketing hype, OS/2 will thrive. Are you OS/2 fans persuasive enough to talk all your friends into trying OS/2 rather than waiting for the next fancy operating system promised by Microsoft?
>
> In almost every way, OS/2 is better than Windows or Windows NT. OS/2 provides outstanding multitasking performance for a desktop operating system, and it's now rock-solid. However, for every copy of OS/2 in the field, there are ten copies of MS Windows or some variation. That Microsoft lead over IBM has only lengthened as Windows 95 and Windows NT 4.0 hit the streets.
>
> "You can't fight City Hall," they say, but it's easier to fight City Hall than it is to turn the tide of overwhelming market share. Personally, I think UnixWare Personal Edition makes a great "universal desktop" operating system—even better than OS/2, especially in mixed Unix and NetWare networks. Too bad SCO, now in control of UnixWare, seems to have no interest in pursuing the Personal Edition of UnixWare to the corporate desktop. Too bad Microsoft will likely squelch alternatives to the corporate desktop with its double-barreled dose of Windows 95 and Windows NT (with the Windows 95 interface).

OS/2 Installation Options

SIMILAR TO THE DOS and MS Windows client software, the OS/2 client software can be installed in two ways: from diskettes or from the NetWare CD-ROM platter. Across the network client installations don't work with OS/2, because there is too much client information needed to make a quick "net boot" disk.

Requirements for the OS/2 Station

Check your OS/2 documentation for more details, but here are the minimum requirements for OS/2 workstations to function as NetWare clients:

- An IBM PC or compatible with a minimum 386 (SX or DX) microprocessor
- Hard disk with 3 MB of storage available for NetWare Client for OS/2 software
- 8 MB of RAM
- A high-density diskette drive
- A supported network adapter board
- A VGA monitor
- A mouse or similar pointing device

> *Any choice of pointing rodent will probably work fine.*

Now for the real-world adjustments: minimum 486/50 with 12 MB RAM and lots of empty space on the hard disk (if not for NetWare, than for some other OS/2 applications). OS/2 Warp comes packaged on CD-ROM now, so a CD-ROM drive will make your life easier. A standard VGA monitor will drive you to distraction; get at least an 800 × 600 monitor with 256 colors. Any choice of pointing rodent will probably work fine. OS/2 Warp is much less picky about machine hardware than earlier versions.

This list is likely to be revised whenever IBM finally makes OS/2 a valid operating system on its PowerPC product line. The client requirements for horsepower and disk space will probably increase, mainly because client requirements always go up.

It goes without saying that you should make the intended NetWare client a functioning OS/2 workstation before you start adding anything else to it. OS/2 Warp's installation program is pretty slick, especially with the CD-ROM version. But test everything you can under OS/2 before you start adding NetWare to the mixture. Even better, spend some time trying to get a grip on the differences between OS/2 Warp and MS Windows, because there are a few (hundred) differences.

Copying the OS/2 Client Diskettes for NetWare 4.10

> **15.1 IN-A-HURRY**
>
> **Make OS/2 Client Diskettes from the CD-ROM in NetWare 4.10**
>
> **1.** Load the NetWare 4.10 CD-ROM in the local OS/2 workstation CD-ROM drive.
>
> **2.** Prepare six blank, formatted 3.5-inch diskettes.
>
> **3.** Change to the \CLIENT\OS2 directory on the NetWare CD-ROM disk.
>
> **4.** Type **MAKEDISK** *drive_letter:*.
>
> **5.** Follow the instructions and feed the diskettes into the drive.
>
> **6.** Label the diskettes as instructed.

The manual explains how you can also create the OS/2 client diskettes from the file server using the INSTALL command, but that is just as slow as making DOS diskettes. If you have any choice in the matter, use the MAKEDISK program from the CD-ROM.

The DynaText documentation also explains how to make these client diskettes across the network, if the NetWare CD-ROM is mounted as a volume. This works after you get an OS/2 station connected to the network as a client. That's possible, just as it is with DOS, but much more trouble. Your best bet is to install from the NetWare CD-ROM.

NetWare 4.11 doesn't include the MAKEDISK program. With OS/2 clients under NetWare 4.11, use the installation from the CD-ROM by placing the NetWare 4.11 CD-ROM disk in the local OS/2 CD drive and running the INSTALL program.

The MAKEDISK program is in the \CLIENT\OS2 directory on the NetWare 4.10 CD-ROM disk. You simply run the program and follow the instructions for putting the diskettes into the drive. The labeling for the diskettes goes this way:

- WSOS2_1
- WSOS2_2

- WSOS2_3
- WSOS2_4 (NetWare 4.11)
- WSDRV_1
- OS2UTIL_1
- OS2DOC_1
- Extra drivers from Novell or third parties (NetWare 4.11)

Please label them, so you don't copy over the fourth diskette by accident. And label them all, because if you leave the label off of one of them, I guarantee that it will be separated from the others.

Installing OS/2 Client Software from Diskettes

> **15.2 IN-A-HURRY**
>
> **Install OS/2 Client Software from Diskettes**
>
> 1. Load the first diskette of the client set, WSOS2_1, into a floppy drive on the OS/2 machine.
> 2. Click on the icon in the appropriate drive icon on the desktop (drive A: for our example).
> 3. In the Drive A - Tree View window, click on the drive A: icon.
> 4. In the Drive A - Icon View window, double-click on the INSTALL.EXE icon.
> 5. Read the "Welcome to the NetWare Installation program" information.
> 6. From the Installation menu, choose Requester on Workstation.
> 7. Set the appropriate target and source drive and path.
> 8. Allow the program to configure the CONFIG.SYS file and copy the files.
> 9. Choose your network driver file, just as you did with the DOS workstations.
> 10. Set your level of DOS, MS Windows session support, and IPX/SPX settings.

If this OS/2 machine has a CD-ROM drive and you are using NetWare 4.10, skip ahead to the next section, "Installing OS/2 Client Software from the NetWare CD-ROM Disk." It's quicker and easier. NetWare 4.11 users have only the diskette or upgrade options.

After you have your fistful of diskettes, and the network adapter board is installed in your OS/2 machine, you're ready to get connected. Feed the first diskette, labeled WSOS2_1, into the floppy drive. Start clicking and mousing about, reading everything you can.

Unlike the typical NetWare client installation procedure, the defaults for OS/2 client installation will set up your machine without any IPX or MS Windows support. You will want to turn IPX on and make it global, and add MS Windows support. If you plan to run RPRINTER from this machine, you also need to add the SPX protocol, so choose to add "optional" protocols during installation.

This procedure assumes you don't have a version of NetWare on this OS/2 machine already. If the workstation does have another version of NetWare, your best bet is to boot your system and bypass the loading of any network drivers. If you're already running the NetWare client software when you run the installation, the new version should install over the old and copy open files over to a special subdirectory. When you reboot, the system will make the adjustments and copy the new files to their proper places. (However, I don't always trust automated procedures, so I can't suggest you do this—I'll only tell you that it's possible and works most of the time.)

Figure 15.1 shows the opening of the Drive A: - Icon View window. INSTALL.EXE is second from the right in this window.

Slick and clean, isn't it? The NWUNPACK.EXE file is the OS/2 version of the file of the same name for DOS. The MS Windows libraries are on the WSOS2 diskette, and they will be installed next.

Figure 15.2 shows the "Welcome to the NetWare Installation program" information screen. Much can happen from this screen, during the first installation or when you are modifying a setting or two later.

The second menu choice in the menu bar across the top of the screen, Configuration, is the best way to edit your NET.CFG file. The only Utilities menu option is for configuring ODINSUP, for those users who need both NetWare and LAN Server protocol support on their workstation.

No, I don't know why the OS/2 NetWare client software directory that is created during the installation is labeled NETWARE instead of NWCLIENT, as in DOS machines. That would make things more consistent, wouldn't it?

FIGURE 15.1

A graphical installation in progress

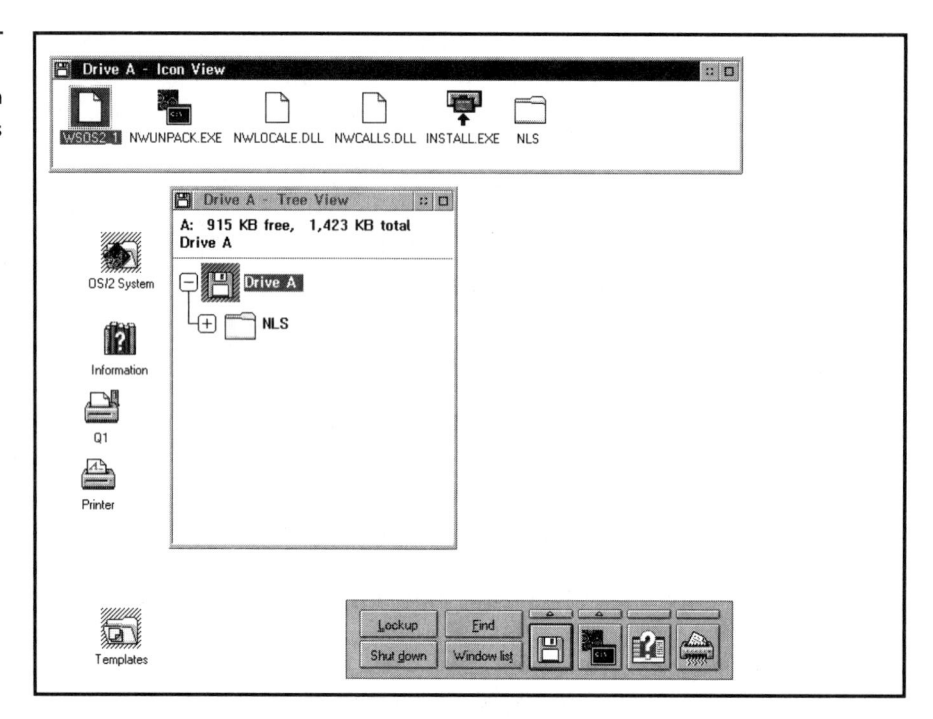

FIGURE 15.2

The main installation program for OS/2 clients

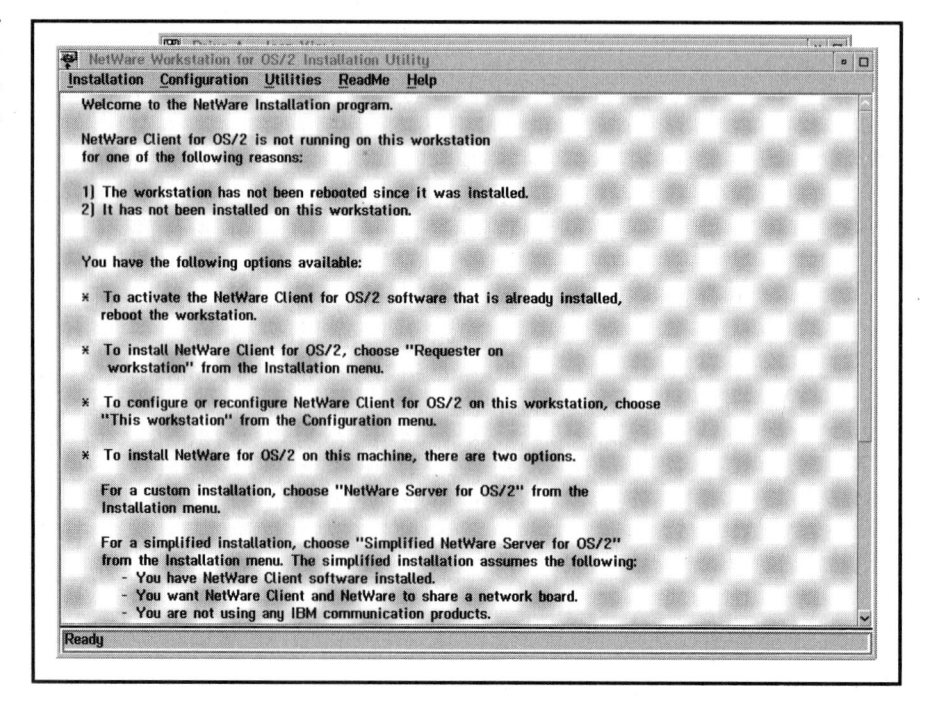

Skip to the section titled "Configuring the OS/2 Client" for more on NET.CFG file setup.

For some help in setting up the network interface card for your OS/2 system, take a look at Chapter 5, which covers connecting PC clients. The process isn't exactly the same, but the philosophy and background information is close enough to be helpful.

Installing OS/2 Client Software from the CD-ROM Disk

15.3 IN-A-HURRY

Install the OS/2 Client Software from the CD-ROM

1. Load the NetWare CD-ROM in the CD-ROM drive on the OS/2 workstation.
2. Click on the OS/2 System icon to open the Drives - Icon View window.
3. Click on Drive D (the CD-ROM drive) to open the Drive D - Tree View window.
4. Click on the Client folder, then on the OS/2 folder in the Client - Icon View window.
5. Click on the INSTALL.EXE program icon in the OS2 - Icon View window.
6. Read the "Welcome to the NetWare Installation program" information.
7. From the Installation menu, choose Requester on Workstation.
8. Set the appropriate target and source drive and path.
9. Allow the program to configure the CONFIG.SYS file and copy the files.
10. Choose your network driver file, just as you did with the DOS workstations.
11. Set your level of DOS, MS Windows session support, and IPX/SPX settings.

Here we have another exclusive—more information that isn't in the manual. I didn't find this method until after I loaded the NetWare client software on the GATEWAY2000 server, now masquerading as an OS/2 workstation. Take a quick look at Figure 15.3 so you can follow along with the plan.

FIGURE 15.3

Installing OS/2 client support directly from the CD-ROM disk

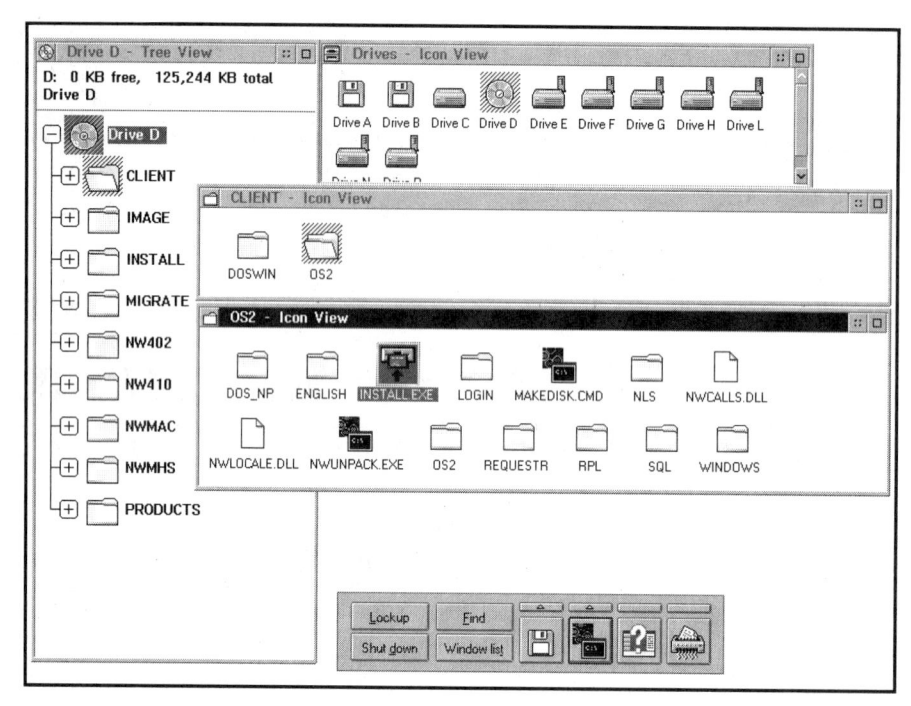

This figure shows four open windows, and they appeared in this order:

- Drives - Icon View
- Drive D - Tree View
- Client - Icon View
- OS2 - Icon View

We started from the OS/2 System folder open on the desktop, as shown earlier in Figure 15.1 (the System folder is that shaded icon on the left side of the Drive A - Tree View window in that figure). When you open the folder by double-clicking on it, one of your options is the Drives folder. (Yes, OS/2 also calls everything folders rather than directories.)

Once you get to the INSTALL.EXE program, everything proceeds the same as it does with the diskettes, as described in the previous section, except that it goes a little more quickly and without the floppy shuffle. As you may have noticed, there are all sorts of network drives in the Drives - Icon View window. These are represented by the low, flat hard drive box with a tower server in the background.

Configuring the OS/2 Client

THE NET.CFG FILE isn't loaded automatically on OS/2 clients. That's the bad news. The good news is that configuring NET.CFG is much easier with the installation program in OS/2 than it is with the tools for DOS and MS Windows workstations.

Figure 15.4 shows the NET.CFG step of the installation program with the NET.CFG file ready to save. Notice the various parts of the window offering help and examples, including the tip that "You can cut and paste text from the help window."

The list in the upper-left, labeled NET.CFG Options, shows each possible NET.CFG option. The upper-right box, labeled Current NET.CFG File Contents, holds the NET.CFG file as it is being created or modified. When this window opens, this section is blank.

The information in the bottom section changes, depending on the command button pressed on the far right. The current information is an example

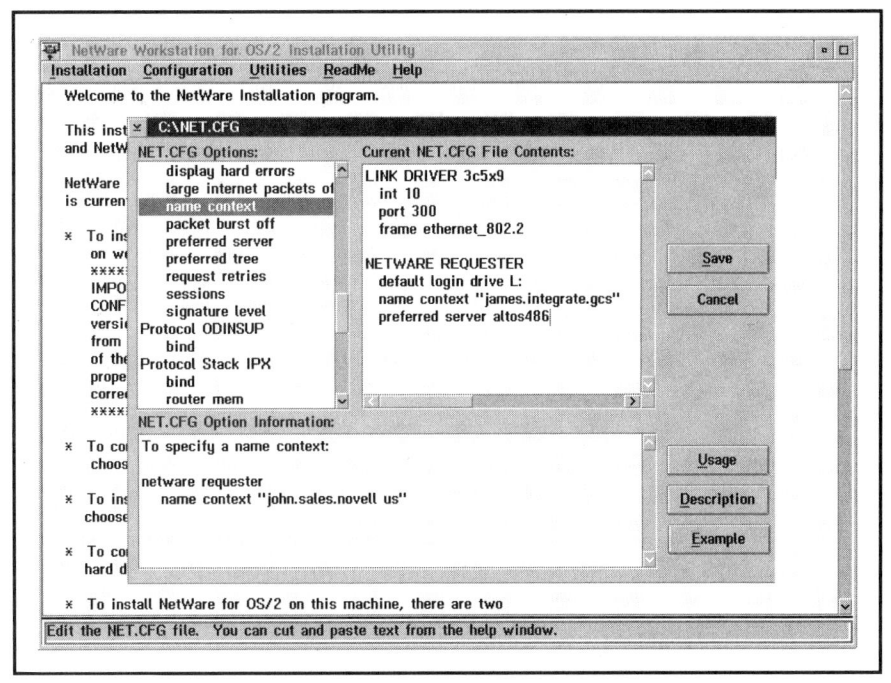

FIGURE 15.4

NET.CFG the OS/2 way

of the "name context" option. You can see that name context is highlighted in the NET.CFG Options list above.

You can use this installation routine for configuring the NET.CFG file during installation, as well as after NetWare is installed if you need to make changes.

If you prefer to edit with an OS/2 text editor, look for NET.CFG in the root directory, not in the directory with the other client files. As with the NET.CFG file in DOS, make sure there is a hard return at the end of the last line, or the line will be ignored.

Troubleshooting the NET.CFG file is the same for OS/2 as it is for DOS clients:

- Verify that the frame type used in the client is the same as that on the server.
- Verify that the network cabling is working.
- Verify that the server is up and able to support new clients.
- Check your typing (there is no spelling checker in the NET.CFG installation editor).

New with NetWare 4.11 is the NET.CFG option Disconnect On, listed under the NetWare Requester section. With this option, the machine starts without starting the client. Why would you want to do this? It's handy for those laptop users out there, who don't want to listen to error beeps as the network files can't find the network while the laptop is away from the office.

While the client doesn't start, the client software and drivers are loaded into memory. When you're ready to connect to the network, type NWSTART at the OS/2 command prompt or click on the NWSTART file name. Type NWSTOP to end the session using the active network client.

Connecting to a Server

WHEN NET.CFG WORKS properly, your login sequence will be similar, but not exactly the same, as with DOS machines. Most important, there are no search drives used in OS/2. All the search functions are handled by a combination of PATH, LIBPATH, and DPATH settings in the CONFIG.SYS file.

Finding OS/2 Utilities

Drive P: is the standard drive that OS/2 uses to point to the \PUBLIC directory. The default login script for OS/2 contains the line:

```
MAP P:=SYS:PUBLIC
```

This works in combination with the P:\OS2 setting in your PATH statement. The combination points drive P: to the OS2 subdirectory under \PUBLIC. That is the location of OS/2 versions of all the necessary utilities kept in the regular \PUBLIC directory for DOS and MS Windows users.

However, your mapping for drive P: is to the \PUBLIC directory. If you change drive letters on the OS/2 command line to drive P: and execute a program, it will execute the DOS version in the \PUBLIC directory, not the OS/2 version in the \PUBLIC\OS2 directory. If you run the same utility from any other drive letter, the proper OS/2 utility will be executed.

Logging in from OS/2 Clients

Drive L: is the default drive for the LOGIN directory when the system comes up. You should log in from the OS/2 command line. In the NET.CFG file, you can add information, such as your name context and preferred tree (if you have more than one tree on your network), so a user can log in with just his or her name; the user won't need to type the entire name, including all containers.

As with DOS and MS Windows, you can make connections with the NetWare User Tools program, but that utility will only attach the user to the server, not log in.

When you use your own login name to test the OS/2 login, you will likely discover two things:

- As mentioned earlier, OS/2 does not support search drives.

- The EXIT command followed by a text string is not supported.

The OS/2 Display

After you're connected to a server, you'll notice two new icons: one for Novell and one for the network. In Figure 15.5, you can see Novell and Network icons in the upper-left corner of the screen. Both are shaded, meaning they're open.

FIGURE 15.5

OS/2's view of NetWare

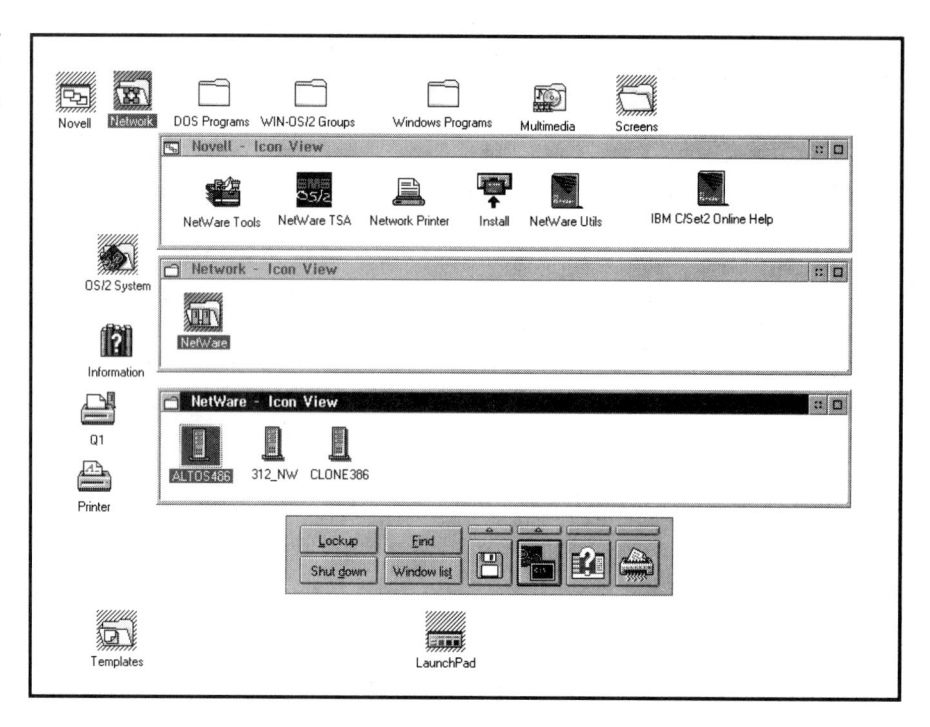

The top, skinny window is the Novell - Icon View window. The icons represent the following:

- **NetWare Tools:** NetWare User Tools program, OS/2 version.

- **NetWare TSA:** NetWare Target Service Agent, to allow the hard drive on this machine to be backed up by SBACKUP or another program using SMS (Storage Management Services).

- **Network Printer:** Controls NPRINTER on this station, allowing an attached printer to become a NetWare system printer.

- **Install:** The Installation program (see Figure 15.2, shown earlier).

- **NetWare Utils:** Help information about the NetWare utilities available for OS/2.

- **IBM C/Set2 Online Help:** The OS/2 chapter of the DynaText online documentation (in native OS/2 Help file format), placed on the OS/2 machine for easy reference.

The middle window, Network - Icon View, comes from OS/2, using NetWare's NWWORKER.DLL file. The NetWare folder is in there by itself because I have not connected this system to any other networks. If it were connected to other networks, they would have folders here as well.

The bottom window, NetWare - Icon View, shows the NetWare servers available. (Remember, GATEWAY2000 has transmogrified into this OS/2 client, which is why it doesn't show up in this window.)

Double-clicking on a server icon displays the available volumes and print queues. Figure 15.6 shows server ALTOS486 on display.

Notice the label on our new, vertical skinny window: \\ALTOS486\SYS - Tree View. Where have we seen that naming convention? That's right, it's the UNC (Universal Naming Convention), which allows us to connect to servers without using a mapped drive letter. OS/2 seems to be with the program here.

When you double-click on the volume icon, you'll see the directories of the volume, again organized as folders. Files are displayed as pages. To see queue status, double-click on the queue icon. This shows the standard status information, such as print jobs in the queue.

FIGURE 15.6

Graphical server information

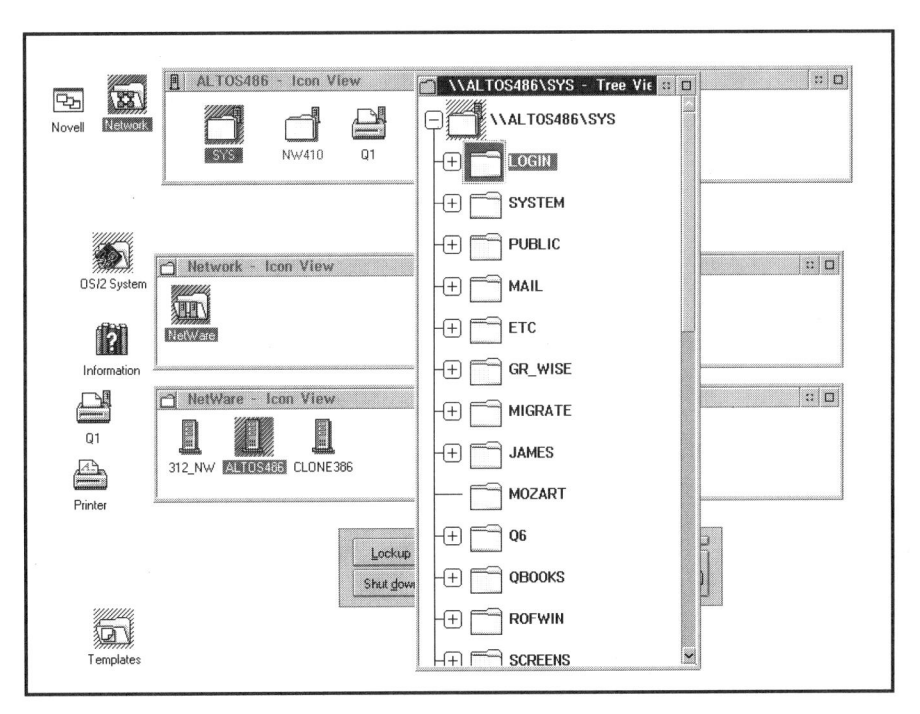

Using the NetWare User Tools Program in OS/2

NETWARE USER TOOLS is perhaps a bit better in OS/2 than it is in MS Windows. The only disappointment to me is the lack of a hotkey, but the OS/2 Window List (displayed with the Ctrl+Escape key combination) seems slightly easier to use than in MS Windows, so the hotkey isn't quite so important.

Figure 15.7 shows the NetWare Tools window (the OS/2 version leaves off the "User" part of the name in OS/2). Take a quick look around the window. Notice you can display more than one service at a time: both Disk Drives and Printer Ports windows are open, which is not possible in the MS Windows version. More windows can fit here if you wish.

FIGURE 15.7

The NetWare (User) Tools program in OS/2 in NetWare 4.10

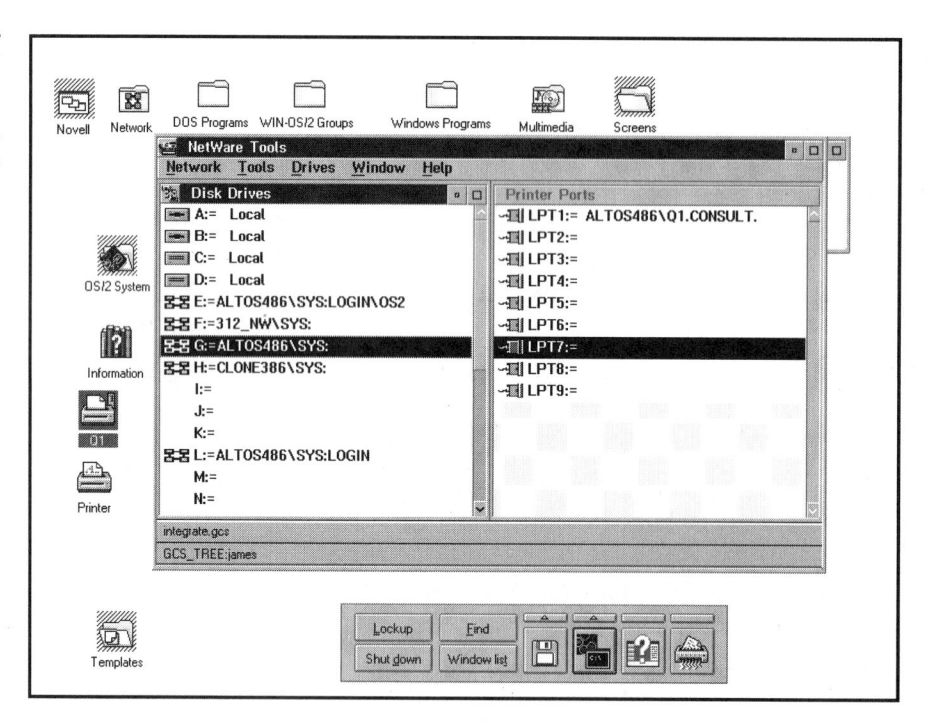

The bottom-left corner of the window shows the current context (integrate.gcs), the tree (GCS_TREE), and the user name (james). All this information is available automatically.

The diagrams for connected drives and the like are a bit different here than in the MS Windows version. Notice that the icon for drive D:, the CD-ROM drive, doesn't try to show a picture of the CD; it looks like any other hard drive. My DOS login script gets slightly confused here with OS/2, because CONFIG.SYS doesn't support the LASTDRIVE setting. That is the reason that drive E: shows up as the LOGIN drive, which normally appears as drive F:. Nice how the system knew to move to the OS/2 subdirectory under LOGIN, isn't it?

On the right side of the window, nine printer ports are available. Supporting this many printer ports is possible under MS Windows, as we saw earlier, but OS/2 provides this support automatically. (Imagine the paper you could waste with nine printers at your beck and call!)

Figure 15.8 shows the same NetWare Tools program, with a feature that is not in the MS Windows version: a user list display.

All the users in the tree are displayed, whether they're connected or not. (Why IBM and/or Novell thought we would be happy seeing ourselves represented as a smiley face, I have no idea. Do these people think computers are funny?)

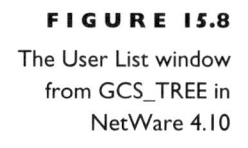

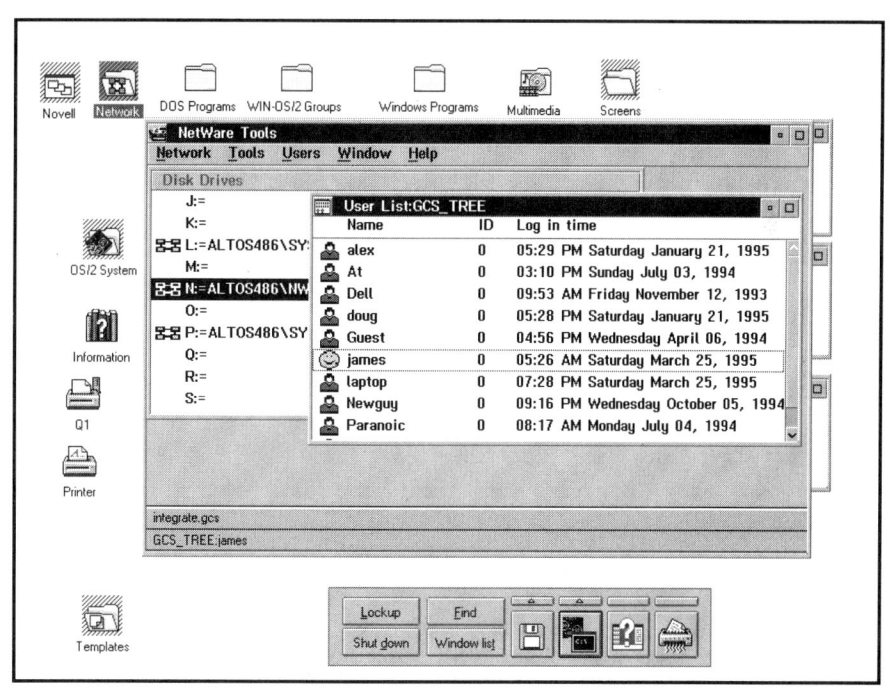

FIGURE 15.8

The User List window from GCS_TREE in NetWare 4.10

Take a look at the menu bar across the top of the NetWare Tools program. Did you notice that in Figure 15.7 the menu after Tools is Drives, but in Figure 15.8 it's Users? This menu option will change, depending on the active tool. The choices in the Tools menu are:

- **Disk Drives:** Displays drive mapping information.

- **Printer Ports:** Displays printer ports and shows all printer redirections in use.

- **Servers:** Shows available servers.

- **Directory Tree:** Shows the NDS tree, and allows you to move up and down in the tree.

- **User Lists:** Lists all users defined on the system, by allowing you to choose a server or tree name. (The display in Figure 15.8 shows all the users in the tree.)

- **Print Queues:** Displays available print queues and allows you to attach to one if you wish.

Any or all of these windows may be opened in combination and tiled or cascaded within the NetWare Tools windows. The more, the messier, of course, but it is nice to have an option to see two things at once. To show available resources from any of these windows, try pressing the Insert key, or check under the menu items at the top of the window.

One last look here at NetWare Tools for the printing system. Figure 15.9 shows the process of capturing a print queue under OS/2.

This matches the window you see with the LPT Settings command button in NetWare User Tools under MS Windows, but with two small differences (besides the automatic availability of nine printers):

- There is no Time Out setting as such in OS/2; use the settings for the printer port directly, or just trust the system. (OS/2 software vendors must have figured out printing a bit better than their DOS and MS Windows counterparts.)

- In the OS/2 version, you have a chance to change your print job configuration with every captured printer. This provides extra flexibility that is not available in the MS Windows version. (Perhaps some of these minor improvements will make it into the next MS Windows release.)

FIGURE 15.9

A familiar print capture screen

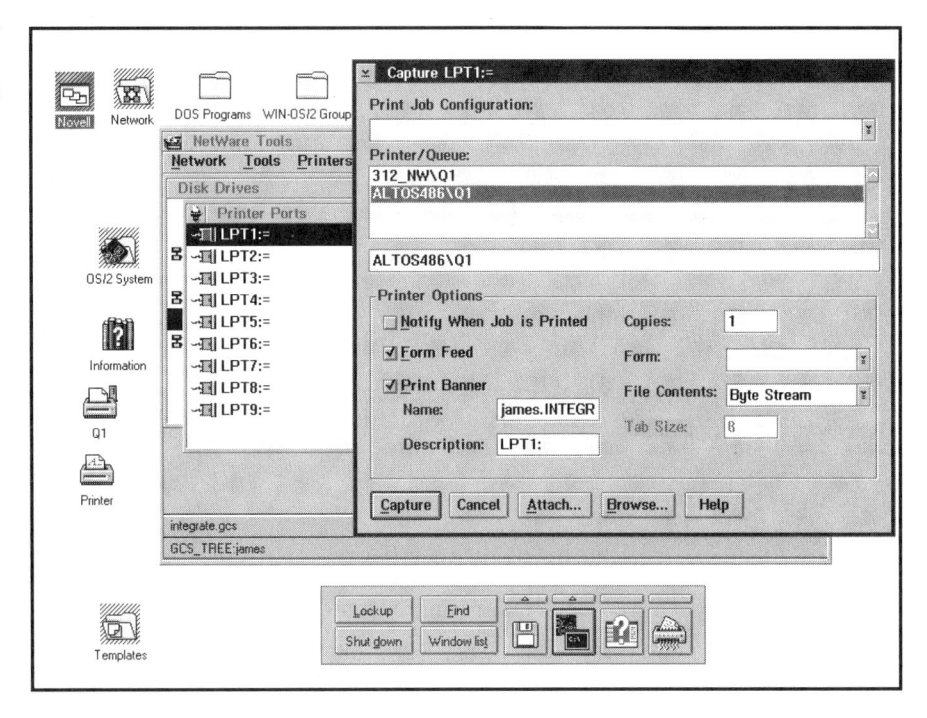

The only new features within NetWare 4.11's OS/2 support are a window showing servers and trees on your network. I'm sorry to say that the additions make no real improvement in the OS/2 client support.

For more information about using NetWare User Tools, see Chapter 12.

Running NetWare Administrator from an OS/2 Workstation

NETWARE ADMINISTRATOR FOR NetWare 4.10 is not an OS/2 program, but it can run from OS/2 workstations, although it requires a little extra setup. Specifically, we must create a diskette labeled VLMBOOT to support NetWare Administrator on OS/2 workstations. You may not run the 32-bit NetWare Administrator program from within OS/2, because that version of the program requires the Client32 software. Effectively, the days of using an OS/2 workstation for NetWare management are over, but we'll leave this information here for those with NetWare 4.10 systems. Remember, if you're now upgraded to NetWare 4.11, your OS/2 station is out of the network management business.

You can create this diskette in two ways: from the server using the INSTALL program (not recommended) or from the original NetWare CD-ROM on a DOS workstation. The second method is faster and easier. You can use it if you have easy access to a DOS machine with a CD-ROM drive or if you have the CD-ROM disk mounted as a NetWare volume. You can't do this from an OS/2 workstation, however; it must be done from the server or a DOS workstation.

From the root of the CD-ROM, type:

```
INSTALL
```

This opens the Installation screen, offering three choices:

- NetWare Server Installation
- DOS/Windows Client Installation
- Create Diskettes

Since we've already done the first two, let's try door number three, Monty. Figure 15.10 shows the results of that choice.

Choosing Create Diskettes takes you to a bare screen informing you of the need for one diskette. Later, it will demand that the diskette be formatted and blank, so be ready (although it will work with disks that are not blank or formatted, don't push your luck). Choose the drive letter (A: or B: most likely), and watch as the system reads from the disk image file and then writes that information.

While you're watching, prepare a label that says "NetWare Client for OS/2 VLMBOOT" for this diskette. The copy process places COMMAND.COM, AUTOEXEC.BAT, CONFIG.SYS, and VLMBOOT files on the disk, along with directories \NWDOS, \NWCLIENT, and \VLMDLL, full of assorted support files. (The \NWDOS comes from the fact that the machine creating this floppy is running Novell DOS 7; your system may give a different directory name.)

Back at your OS/2 workstation, close all MS Windows programs and start the INSTALL program from the NetWare folder. From the Configuration menu, choose VLM Boot Setup, and put the diskette in your first floppy drive. When you start the VLM Boot Setup process, name the drive where the disk is and click on OK.

FIGURE 15.10

A critical link in the chain for OS/2 workstations to support NetWare Administrator in NetWare 4.10

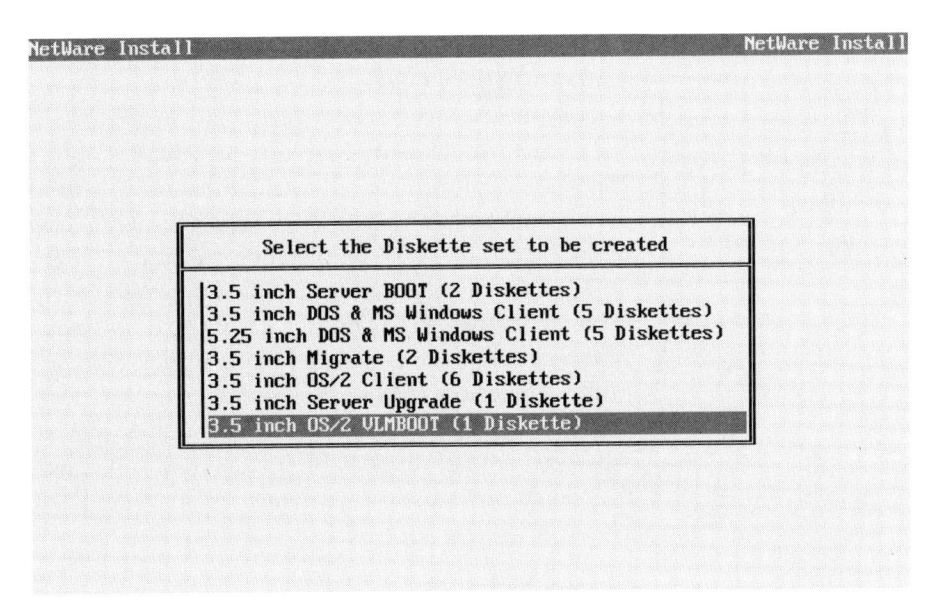

```
NetWare Install                                          NetWare Install



          ┌──────────────────────────────────────────────────┐
          │        Select the Diskette set to be created     │
          ├──────────────────────────────────────────────────┤
          │ 3.5 inch Server BOOT (2 Diskettes)               │
          │ 3.5 inch DOS & MS Windows Client (5 Diskettes)   │
          │ 5.25 inch DOS & MS Windows Client (5 Diskettes)  │
          │ 3.5 inch Migrate (2 Diskettes)                   │
          │ 3.5 inch OS/2 Client (6 Diskettes)               │
          │ 3.5 inch Server Upgrade (1 Diskette)             │
          │ 3.5 inch OS/2 VLMBOOT (1 Diskette)               │
          └──────────────────────────────────────────────────┘
```

Disks will churn a bit, then you'll have the chance to create a NetWare VLM boot image file, which you should do. After that, and after you reboot your system, an icon on the desktop will now be labeled VLMBOOT. Double-clicking on this icon opens a true DOS box. From there, your easiest route is running MS Windows, and then running the NetWare Administrator program from the \PUBLIC directory of one of your attached servers.

OS/2 for NetWare Managers

I'M UNDECIDED ABOUT OS/2. I prefer UnixWare. It's easier to connect to NetWare, it runs Unix and X-Windows programs, and Unix is the ultimate 32-bit operating system available today. At least, according to many of the people I know (including the one in the mirror). Being that UnixWare is just about out of the running since SCO has taken it and hidden it under a bushel basket, that leaves Windows 95 and Windows NT. Heresy though it may be,

> *Heresy though it may be, I'm getting used to the Windows 95 interface, and I feel more comfortable than with OS/2.*

I'm getting used to the Windows 95 interface, and I feel more comfortable with it than with OS/2.

Do you have OS/2 clients that need access to NetWare 4.1x, including being full citizens of NetWare Directory Services? No problem. Should you, as the NetWare administrator, go to any extra trouble to use OS/2 as your primary management station? No. There aren't enough advantages for the extra effort under NetWare 4.10, and the door is closed on that option for NetWare 4.11.

What does this mean for the future of OS/2 versus Unix versus Windows NT versus Windows 95? Microsoft has won the desktop interface wars, unless Netscape can pull a David and Goliath trick with even longer odds than the historical version. IBM shows every sign of distancing itself from OS/2 in the near future, and IBM spokespeople can't even muster any enthusiasm now when saying their support for OS/2 is solid and committed and eternal. At least they could pretend; perhaps acting lessons would help.

Installing NetWare 4.1x Server for OS/2

CHAPTER 16

YOU MAY WONDER why Novell would go to the trouble to make NetWare 4.1x run as an application under OS/2. Is it because OS/2 provides better file and print performance than the NetWare run-time operating system? No. Perhaps it's because OS/2 servers provide better security? No. How about because OS/2 is the most popular platform for corporate computing? No.

Then why? It's for companies with lots of branch offices, with a few computers in each, that still need the performance and security of a NetWare server, but can't afford to dedicate an expensive server machine in each office. Think about a small branch of a bank or retail operation; three or four computers will handle that office's needs. But add an expensive, dedicated PC server in each of 2000 branch banks or florist shops, and the price zooms upward.

This option is reminiscent of the old days of NetWare 2.x with its nondedicated server version. The good news is that NetWare Server for OS/2 version 4.1x performs far better than NetWare 2.x ever did. In fact, NetWare Server for OS/2 is surprisingly stable and performs better than I expected.

Overview of NetWare Server for OS/2

THOUSANDS OF COMPANIES have standardized their networks based on NetWare, and thousands of commercial and custom applications require a NetWare server to manage file access. This trend has been building for years, and shows no signs of stopping anytime soon.

When an application expects to find a NetWare server, a NetWare server better be there. Personal NetWare does a good job in small installations such as this, but does not offer the performance, security, and programming options available with "regular" NetWare. NetWare Server for OS/2 provides the programming environment of regular NetWare, but also provides the cost savings of supporting both a client workstation and the server on one PC—a stout PC, of course, but only one PC nonetheless.

Advantages of NetWare 4.1x Server for OS/2

With this stout PC, the company deploying NetWare Server for OS/2 gains a triple-threat box:

- NetWare 4.1x server

- OS/2 workstation capable of supporting OS/2, MS Windows, or DOS applications

- A communications server

You can see why a company with a few small, remote branches would appreciate the convenience and cost savings provided by NetWare Server for OS/2: one box, many functions. If your company needs to support multiple small installations, NetWare Server for OS/2 is worth a look.

Are you worried about retraining your NetWare users for NetWare Server for OS/2? You shouldn't be; the client and server parts of NetWare Server for OS/2 look exactly like those of NetWare 4.1x. They should, since both programs come on the same CD-ROM. That's right, the same NetWare file, print, directory, security, management, routing, and messaging you get with NetWare 4.1x also comes with NetWare Server for OS/2. There is no difference between the two systems besides the presence of OS/2 as a foundation for NetWare services.

Your network clients will see the same NetWare 4.1x server utilities we have discussed throughout the book. All the client software is included in the package, since the client software is the same as for NetWare 4.1x running on a dedicated NetWare server. If you wish to support Macintosh or Unix clients, everything you need is included.

This may give some of you a moment's hesitation. To support Macintosh or Unix clients, multiple NLMs must be run on the file server. Part of the limitation with NetWare for Unix (originally called Portable NetWare) is the inability to run NLMs. This means that NLMs are not available on OS/2 servers, right?

Wrong, NLMs run fine on NetWare Server for OS/2. The reason NLMs are not available for NetWare for Unix systems is because the NLM compiler demands an Intel processor to run the NLMs. All OS/2 machines must have Intel processors, so NLMs run perfectly well on NetWare Server for OS/2.

> Are you worried about retraining your NetWare users for NetWare Server for OS/2?

Server Requirements

The minimum hardware requirements for the machine running NetWare Server for OS/2 are:

- 386 or better processor
- 16 MB of RAM
- 150 MB hard disk, with an 80 MB free partition for NetWare
- A network interface board
- A CD-ROM drive for installation of the default CD-ROM distribution disk

As usual, the minimums are barely worth listing. A 386 machine today will hardly run OS/2 Warp, much less an add-on NetWare server. Make a low-end Pentium the minimum hardware level.

The 16 MB of RAM is way too little, as well. This gives 8 MB of RAM for OS/2, and 8 MB for NetWare. As you'll soon see, it's possible to install and run NetWare Server for OS/2 on a system of this size, but performance takes a serious impact. If you are installing across the network, 2 MB more of RAM must be available to run the CLIB.NLM and STREAMS.NLM that support remote network connections for servers.

The 150 MB of disk space breaks down into 50 MB or so for OS/2, and 80 MB of "free" space for NetWare. Be careful here—free space doesn't mean empty space on the hard disk; it means a separate partition that is unformatted and unnamed.

If you guess, as I did, that "free" space means open space, and that NetWare Server for OS/2 uses the OS/2 file system to write to any open space on the disk, you will be mistaken. You will also need to reformat and reinstall your OS/2 system, and start your NetWare Server for OS/2 installation all over again. Any valuable data on the OS/2 client must be backed up before starting this routine, of course.

If you plan to install the NetWare DynaText electronic documentation, make another 60 MB of hard disk available. None of these numbers leave room for any data, so add up the megabytes necessary to hold your information before buying your hard disk.

Both the OS/2 client and NetWare server can share the same network interface board. There's no reason to install a second interface card just to add NetWare to the system. If you plan to share the interface board, install the OS/2 NetWare client software before installing the server software. Both services can also share the same CD-ROM drive, if the CD-ROM is supported by a SCSI controller with proper drivers for OS/2, which are compatible with NetWare, and you use the CDROMSHR.DSK disk driver.

One last note: Give the server to the least active user. By this, I mean the user that is on the computer the least, or runs the least demanding application. Heavy use of the NetWare software will impact the performance of all OS/2 applications, and heavy use of the local applications on the system will slow the network performance. It's best if the application part of the server is used as little as possible, so the network performs as well as possible. The server tuning and CPU sharing work well, however. If the network is not being used, your OS/2 applications will zip along as always. If no OS/2 applications are demanding lots of horsepower, there will be no noticeable drag on the NetWare server's performance.

A more realistic minimum machine for supporting the NetWare Server for OS/2 would be:

- Pentium processor
- 32 MB of RAM
- 500 MB hard disk
- A high-performance (EISA or PCI) network interface board
- A CD-ROM drive supported by a SCSI controller

An installation option allows you to install the NetWare Server for OS/2 on a machine that is not configured as a NetWare client. This doesn't make much sense, because the whole point here is to use a single machine as both a workstation and NetWare server. Be aware that unless your OS/2 workstation is a NetWare client as well as a server, you won't be able to see any of the applications or data on the server portion of the hard disk.

Officially, OS/2 version 2.1 or greater is required. Our NetWare for OS/2 server is the same Gateway 2000 machine that was the OS/2 Warp version 3 with DOS and MS Windows application support (in the previous chapter). The Bonus Pack software is included in the box, but wasn't loaded on the system.

No one at Novell could tell us if NetWare Server for OS/2 would work on a Warp system, but we tried it anyway. I'm happy to report there wasn't a single problem with either the installation or continued operation of the Warp system acting as the host for the NetWare operating system.

Installation Options

NETWARE SERVER FOR OS/2 installs in two pieces:

- An OS/2 graphical installation program that connects NetWare to the OS/2 host computer
- The NetWare Custom Installation procedure (explained in Chapter 2)

The process is amazingly similar to installing any other NetWare server operating system. The initial differences are all based on the fact that OS/2 is up and running on the server computer when you start the installation. When you install the system to a dedicated NetWare server, the run-time operating system handles the hardware driver interfaces. You never realize there's a difference; it's all part of the installation routine. Here, you notice a difference, because OS/2 handles the hardware driver interfaces.

The early installation steps of fitting disk and LAN drivers for the server machine are done in OS/2, along with the location of NetWare server system files. Once these steps are out of the way, installation proceeds in the same way that is does for any NetWare server.

Installing from a CD-ROM

16.1 IN-A-HURRY

Install NetWare Server for OS/2 from the CD-ROM

1. Place the CD-ROM disk in the drive.
2. Move to that drive letter (usually D:).
3. Type **INSTALL**.
4. If asked, choose your server language.
5. Choose NetWare Server Installation (the system will know that this is an OS/2 host).
6. Continue with the NetWare installation procedures.

Installation Options | 1225

To install from the CD-ROM, place the NetWare CD-ROM disk in the CD-ROM drive for the OS/2 client to be upgraded to a NetWare Server for OS/2. Change to the CD-ROM drive, usually D:, and type:

    INSTALL

The manual says a menu of language choices will appear; that didn't happen for my system, because I have the English-only version. If you see the language menu, pick your choice from the offered English, Deutsche, Italiano, Español, or Francais.

On my system, a text menu appeared offering three choices:

- NetWare Server Installation
- OS/2 Client Installation
- Create Diskettes

The first choice doesn't mention that the server installed is NetWare Server for OS/2, but it is. The text menu choices are all for OS/2, because the program that is running is INSTALL.CMD, not INSTALL.BAT for DOS machines (which is in the same directory). Choose NetWare Server Installation and press Enter, then skip ahead to the "NetWare Installation Steps" section.

Installing from a Remote Network Installation

> **16.2 IN-A-HURRY**
>
> **Install NetWare Server for OS/2 across the Network**
>
> 1. Use the OS/2 NetWare client software to mount the remote CD-ROM drive, or find the INSTALL.CMD file at the top of the directory structure copied from the CD-ROM to a NetWare server disk.
>
> 2. Type **INSTALL**.
>
> 3. If asked, choose your server language.
>
> 4. Choose NetWare Server Installation (the system will know that this is an OS/2 host).
>
> 5. Continue with the NetWare installation procedures.

As with a dedicated NetWare server, you can install your server across the network. The main advantage of network installation is speed. Using a remote server as a source for the network files allows the remote server to feed the files from the disk cache, which is much faster than the local CD-ROM disk.

This method also offers the assurance that your network connection is configured properly and all drivers are loaded correctly. Otherwise, you won't be able to see and use the remote NetWare server. The remote server may be a dedicated server or another NetWare Server for OS/2 machine.

If you are loading the network from a CD-ROM mounted as a NetWare volume, map a drive to that volume. If you are loading the network from a set of files copied from the CD-ROM to a server hard disk, map a drive to the server directory that holds the INSTALL.CMD file.

After you've mapped the appropriate drive, from the OS/2 command prompt, type:

    INSTALL

You will either see the language menu choice or go straight to the menu offering you three installation choices, as described in the previous section. Choose NetWare Server Installation, and you're on your way.

You can also install NetWare Server for OS/2 from floppy diskettes. But if you're using NetWare Server for OS/2, you're obviously much too smart to install NetWare of any kind from a huge stack of floppy diskettes.

Choosing Your Installation Method

The same Installation screen used to install your OS/2 client software, as we did in the previous chapter, is the starting point for installing NetWare Server for OS/2. Figure 16.1 shows this screen, with the Installation menu open.

The three server installation choices you have on the menu work as follows:

- **NetWare Server for OS/2:** Runs the Custom Installation method.

- **Simplified NetWare Server for OS/2:** Runs the Simplified Installation method.

- **Upgrade NetWare Server for OS/2:** Upgrades existing NetWare Server for OS/2 software.

FIGURE 16.1

Starting the NetWare Server for OS/2 installation process

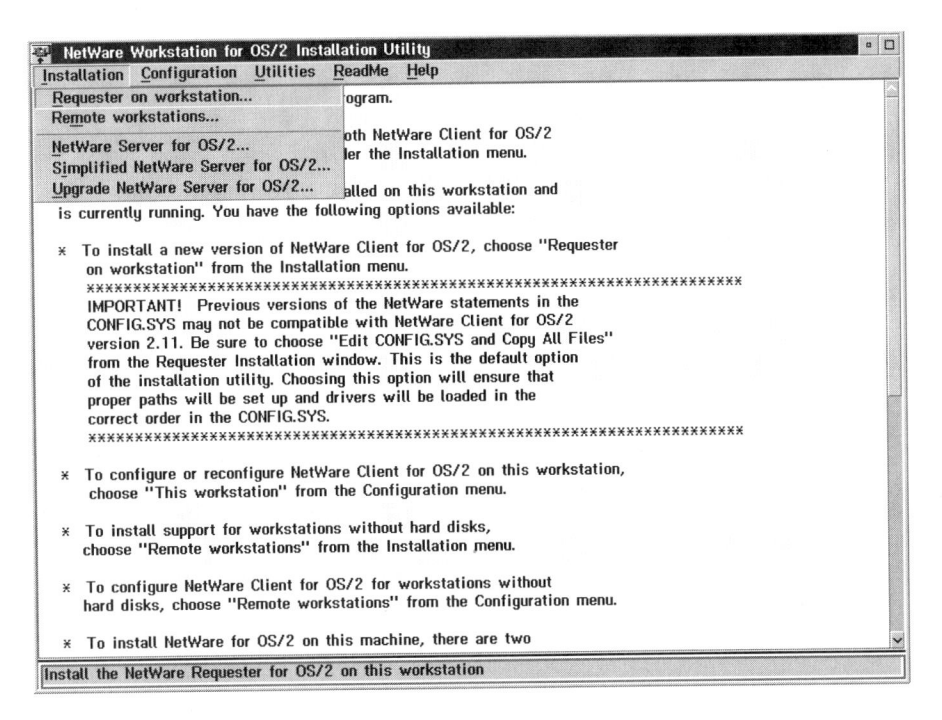

Simplified Installation

16.3 IN-A-HURRY

Use the Simplified Installation Option for NetWare Server for OS/2

1. Choose Simplified NetWare Server for OS/2 from the Installation menu.

2. Set the target directories for the server and driver files.

3. Give your server a name.

4. Exit the installation utility and reboot the system.

5. Continue with the NetWare installation (see Chapter 3).

The results of the Simplified NetWare Server for OS/2 installation are much like those of the Simple Installation choice for dedicated NetWare:

- The system will have client and server software installed.
- The client and server software will share a network board and use the default settings.
- No IBM communication protocols will be used; only IPX/SPX and TCP/IP.
- A randomly generated IPX internal network number and other server default choices are acceptable.
- The hard disk will not be mirrored or duplexed.
- There will be a single NetWare volume per disk.
- The installation routine will automatically update the CONFIG.SYS, NET.CFG, AUTOEXEC.NCF, and STARTUP.NCF files.
- There is a single container for all NDS objects.

If you have a single-server network, and this is the server, the Simplified choice is the right one. If your network is a small branch office that is connected by a WAN link to a larger corporate network, you will need to choose the NetWare Server for OS/2 installation (which is the same as the Custom Installation for dedicated NetWare) in order to manage the NDS portions of your installation routine.

NetWare Server for OS/2 Installation Steps

Here's the road map for the NetWare Server for OS/2 installation routine:

- Prepare the disk drive (if necessary).
- Set the destination directories for files.
- Determine drivers for the shared network board.
- Name the server.
- Reboot.

> **16.4 IN-A-HURRY**
>
> **Use the NetWare Server for OS/2 Option for Installation**
>
> 1. Choose NetWare Server for OS/2 from the Installation menu.
> 2. Set the target directories for server and driver files.
> 3. Choose whether to share a network board between the client and server.
> 4. Provide the server name, IPX internal network number, and other details.
> 5. Exit the installation utility and reboot.
> 6. Load a LAN driver for your network board.
> 7. Configure the disk for NetWare.
> 8. Continue with the NetWare installation (see Chapter 3).

These are the steps performed under control of OS/2. You'll use the graphical interface, but mostly you'll be typing or verifying text, so there are no real advantages to the graphical format.

The first thing to do is configure your disk drive. If you mistakenly set up a partition that is listed as "unknown" rather than "free," as I did, you must delete and re-create the partition. You will then have the option of supporting HPFS (High Performance File System) or something else. Choose HPFS unless you were specifically told not to by your boss. If the Boot Manager is not yet configured, you may need to stop and do that now, as well.

> *The Boot Manager is handy if you have multiple systems installed. If not, you can set the delay timing to just a few seconds, so the system will continue automatically. For more information about the Boot Manager (and other OS/2 features), look in your OS/2 manual or refer to Peter Dyson's excellent book,* Mastering OS/2 Warp *(published by Sybex).*

Next, you must set the destination directories for your files: one directory for server files and one for the driver files. The defaults are C:\NWSERVER and C:\NETWARE, respectively. Make any necessary adjustments for your drive letter (in case C:\ isn't the one you have for your local hard disk). Unless you have a good reason to change file locations, it's a good idea to leave the default directory locations as they are.

Your next step is to choose the appropriate network protocols for your installed network interface board. The protocols supported by NetWare are listed. Avoid the IBM protocols if the server isn't running in an IBM network. If you plan to support TCP/IP and AppleTalk, the option is here (in the NetWare Server for OS/2 Installation only, not in the Simplified Installation).

Then it's time to name your server. The standard NetWare naming rules apply. I renamed the Gateway 2000 machine from GATEWAY2000 to GATEWAY-OS2, as you will soon see.

The last step is to reboot the system. When you return, you'll be back in the typical NetWare installation routine.

NetWare Installation Steps

After rebooting your system, you will automatically continue on with the NetWare installation. If something goes wrong, move to the \NWSERVER directory on your OS/2 system and type:

```
NWINSTAL
```

Your installation routine will continue with the standard NetWare installation screens and routine. Your system will officially be a NetWare server, since this is the INSTALL program running from the server console. Check back in Chapter 3 for details on the NetWare installation choices and options.

Operation of NetWare Server for OS/2

How does your OS/2 system look when running NetWare? Take a look at Figure 16.2, and notice the two extra items in the Novell group and the option highlighted in the Window List.

The contents of the Novell group are the same as with the OS/2 client software (described in the previous chapter), with two additions: PMMon and NetWare Server for OS/2. You can probably guess that the highlighted icon in the Novell group, NetWare Server for OS/2, is the most important new addition. If the server is not loaded, double-clicking on this icon will load the server software and start the server. (If the server is already loaded when you double-click, you'll see a message telling you just that.)

FIGURE 16.2

Indications of a NetWare server on this OS/2 machine

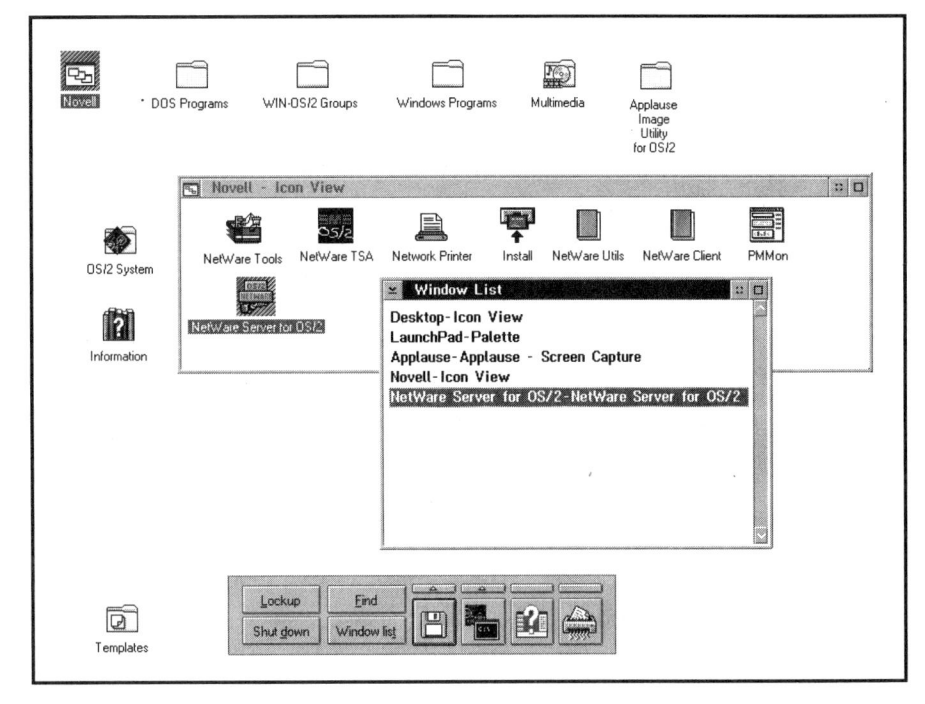

You can also start the server from the command line by typing this command from any command prompt (assuming your hard disk is C:):

```
C:\NWSERVER\NWOS2
```

There are no NetWare settings to change in the program's object properties under OS/2. If you switch to the NetWare Server for OS/2 screen, as is about to happen in the Window List of Figure 16.2, you will see the standard full-screen server console NetWare 4.1x uses everywhere.

There are four NLMs you should *not* install:

- DOMAIN.NLM, the NLM to manage memory, does not work with NetWare Server for OS/2. All memory management is handled by the OS/2 operating system.

- NPRINTER.EXE is an NLM that you can still use from the workstation NetWare client side of the OS/2 machine, but shouldn't. If you want to have a printer attached directly to the system, use the NPRINTER.NLM program from the NetWare Server for OS/2 console.

- VGADISP.NLM, which is used to display Japanese characters on a console monitor screen, isn't needed, because OS/2 handles any Japanese characters that will be displayed.

- MONITOR.NLM technically runs and won't cause a problem, but the MONITOR utility isn't aware of the CPU cycles taken by the OS/2 host system. This causes inaccurate information to be displayed. Use the PMMon (Performance Monitor) utility from within OS/2 instead of MONITOR. (Unfortunately, PMMon doesn't include a screen saver, as MONITOR does.)

Do you need more proof that the NetWare Server for OS/2 looks just like a regular NetWare server?

All the other NLMs work as they should on NetWare Server for OS/2. Be aware of memory limits, however, since OS/2 takes up a big chunk of memory.

Do you need more proof that the NetWare Server for OS/2 looks just like a regular NetWare server? Take a look at Figure 16.3, and see if you can tell the difference between this and any other NetWare volume. I can't.

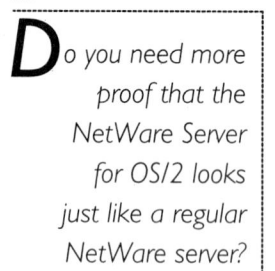

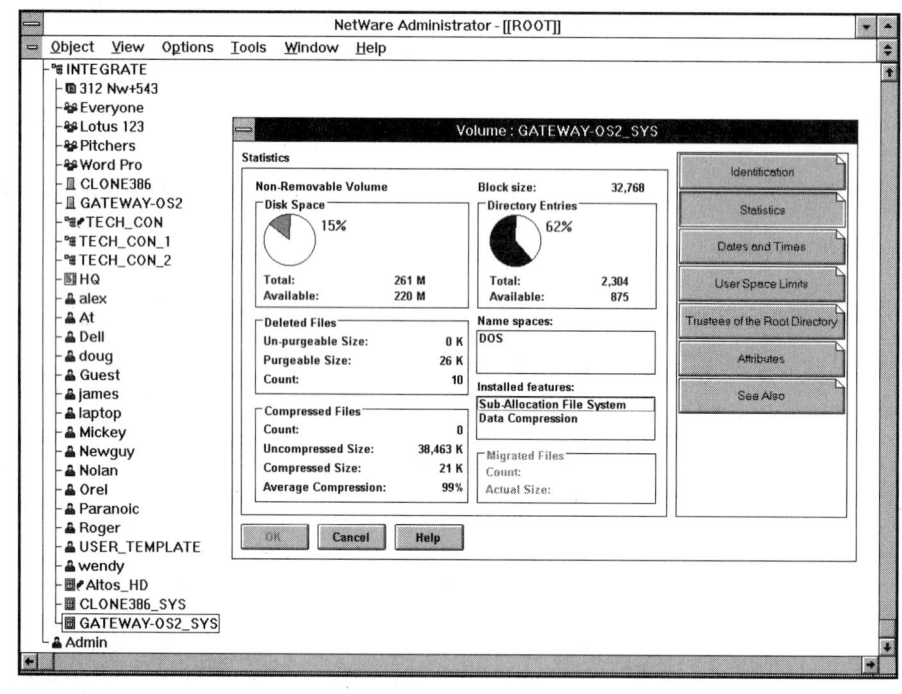

FIGURE 16.3

The particulars of GATEWAY-OS2_SYS

Using the Performance Monitor Program

TRACKING PERFORMANCE OF your NetWare Server for OS/2 is the province of PMMon, or Performance Monitor. This program's graphical display shows some of the same information as the MONITOR NLM, and does so in a clear graphical format. Figure 16.4 shows GATEWAY-OS2's statistics.

FIGURE 16.4
PMMon showing current and historical activity levels

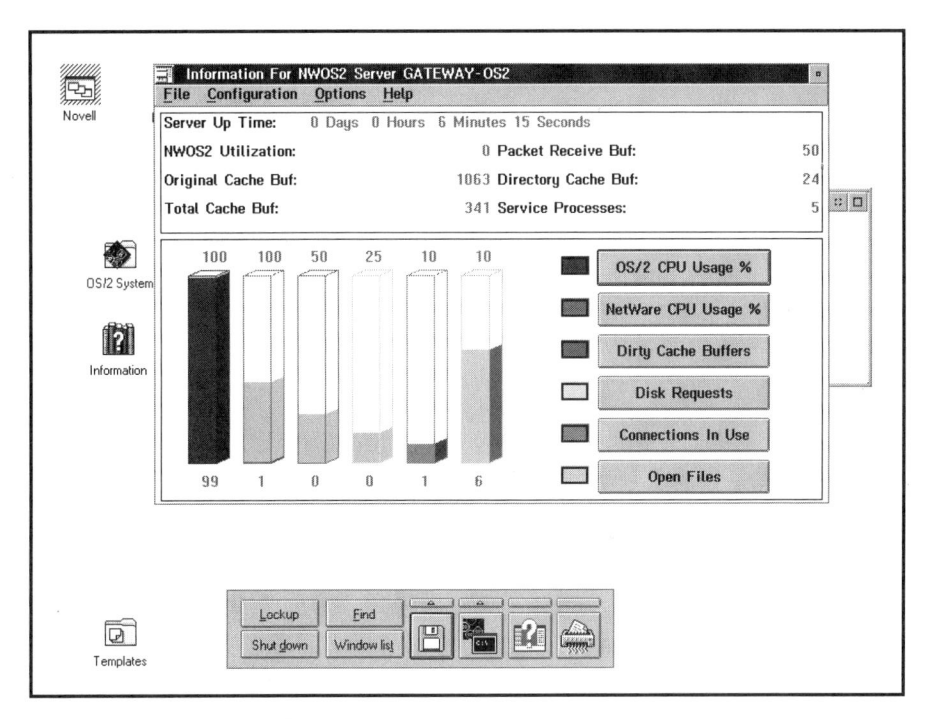

The stacked-bar in the graph on the far left corresponds to the top button on the right, the second-to-the-left stacked-bar corresponds to the second button on the right, and so on. The colors and the ranges you can set for each measurement are shown in Table 16.1.

TABLE 16.1 Options for PMMon Settings

SETTING	COLOR	RANGE
OS/2 CPU Usage %	Blue	100 (Maximum)
NetWare CPU Usage %	Red	100 (Maximum)
Dirty Cache Buffers	Brown	1–9999
Disk Requests	Cyan	1–9999
Connections In Use	Purple	1–9999
Open Files	Green	1–9999

The dark color on the three bars reflects current levels (OS/2 CPU Usage, Connections In Use, and Open Files). The levels of the other bars are light gray on the screen, indicating the highest point reached by that measurement during the current reporting period. These marks are known as *watermarks*, and you can choose whether or not to display them for each bar.

You can't make any adjustments to the CPU Usage bars, except for the option of showing the watermark or not. There is only 100% CPU usage available, and the number must be divided between OS/2 and NetWare.

The other values do have ranges, and you can set the display range for each of them (see Table 16.1). The number at the top of each bar shows the high point you've chosen to display.

For all the values with ranges, you have the option of scaling the display automatically. This allows the graph to more accurately reflect values on a busy server. For instance, the Disk Requests number is currently set to 25 in the example shown in Figure 16.4. When the Scale Automatically box is checked in the Disk Requests dialog box (which appears when you click on the Disk Requests button), the scale will be incremented by the number originally set each time the maximum display number is reached. If a busy spurt hits the network, and disk requests go over the first setting of 25, the bar will then show 50 units. Another increase will bump the scale to 75. However, the setting doesn't return to the lower scale on its own; you must reset it for a lower setting.

Managing Memory Allocation

There are two ways to manage the memory divided between OS/2 and the NetWare server: manual and automatic. The default is automatic, and it's a good idea to leave the settings alone until your system has some history.

Figure 16.5 shows the Memory Sharing dialog box. I changed the Sharing Mode to Manual so the numbers in the bottom part of the dialog box would become active and show up in the screenshot.

FIGURE 16.5
Forced memory equality

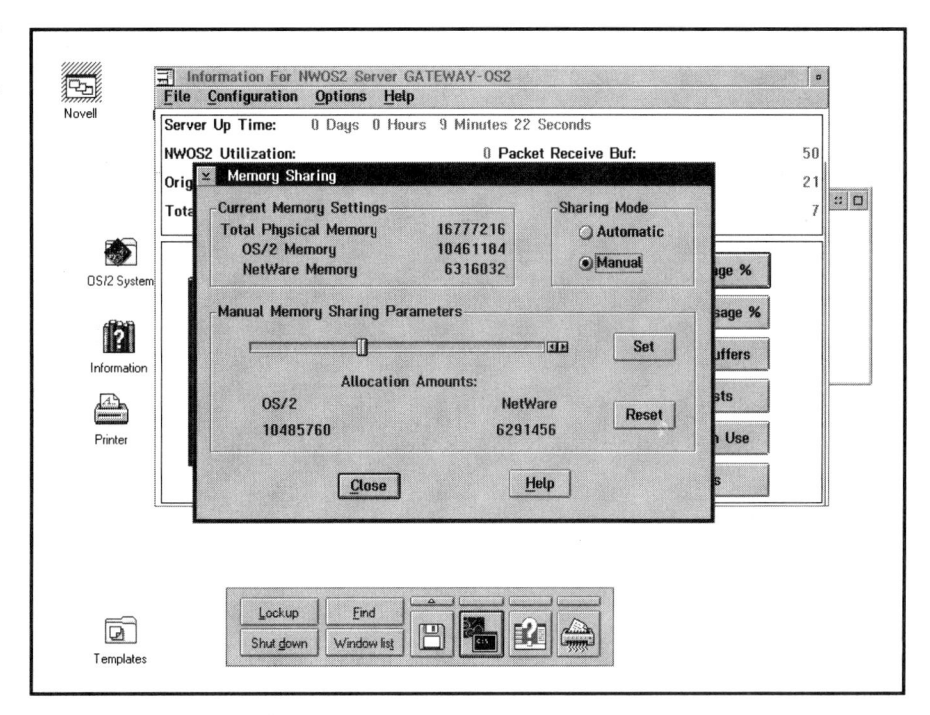

You can see by the numbers that the guidelines of 8 MB for both OS/2 and NetWare are a generalization. The numbers shown on the screen are those the system set automatically; I didn't change the ratio when I clicked on the Manual button. I would never have tried to run NetWare in as little as 6.3 MB of RAM.

When Sharing Mode is set to Automatic, these numbers will adjust as the systems are used. When the network server application is used heavily, memory will be borrowed from the OS/2 side to increase network performance. The opposite is true when the workstation is pushed hard and the network is loafing.

In the Memory Sharing dialog box, you can adjust the memory allocation ratio. To make changes, set Sharing Mode to Manual, and then slide the knob or click on the arrows at the end of the slide.

Performance Tuning

You can also adjust ten preset levels of performance for the NetWare Server for OS/2. Figure 16.6 shows the ten levels available, designated as choices 1 through A. This list is found in the Configuration menu, under (cleverly enough) Performance Tuning.

The higher the number, the more horsepower allocated to NetWare. The lower the number, the more horsepower allocated to OS/2. The number that came up by default on my system is Level 5.

FIGURE 16.6

Setting performance levels for NetWare

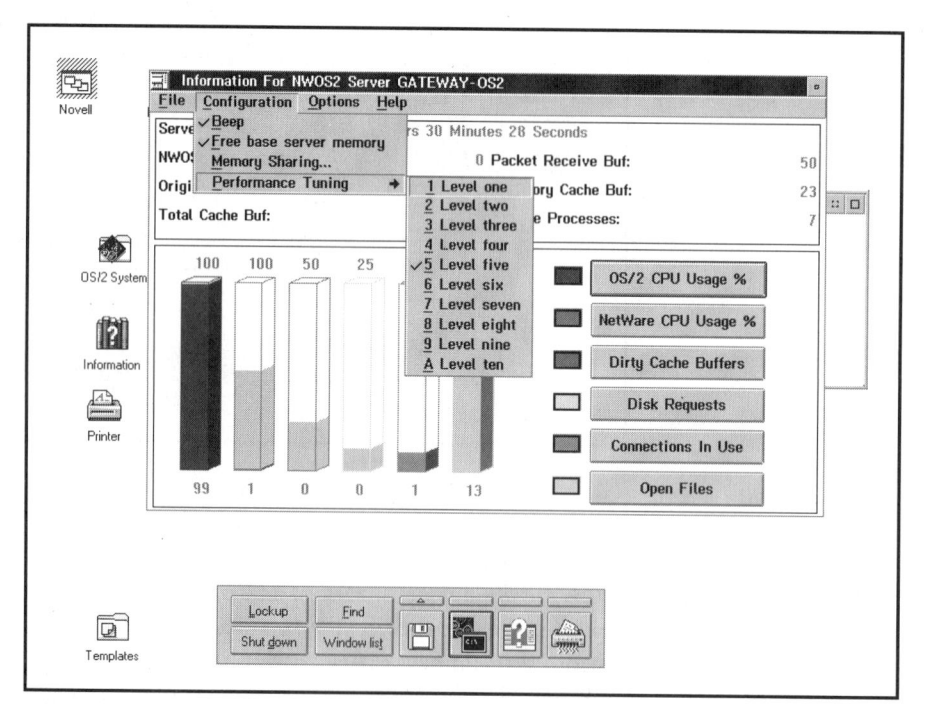

A quick performance test with the Level 5 setting showed about what I expected: Tests that relied on cache buffer performance were slower on the NetWare Server for OS/2 than on the other systems, even CLONE386. What was the reason for this? The answer is lack of memory in the OS/2 server. Remember, less memory is available to NetWare under the OS/2 operating system than in a regular NetWare server.

However, tests that didn't rely on memory showed GATEWAY-OS2 to be the fastest server by just a little bit. I would expect this, since the Pentium processor and faster bus speed should win if the lack of cache memory doesn't influence the test.

What was the result? With enough memory, NetWare Server for OS/2 works surprisingly well. You may not like the idea of nondedicated NetWare, but the performance will be better than acceptable.

One last note: See the option in the Configuration menu for Free Base Server Memory? Unfortunately, this doesn't mean free memory is available. It means, if you select this option, that the NetWare memory will be released to OS/2 when the NetWare server is stopped. The default is No, meaning NetWare memory will be kept separate from OS/2 memory and saved until the NetWare server is restarted.

Special NET.CFG Parameters

There are eight parameters within the NET.CFG file that can be used to set details about the server's performance levels. This special section looks like this:

```
NETWARE FOR OS/2
    PERFORMANCE TUNING number
    INITIALIZATION SCREEN DELAY number
    BASE SERVER MEMORY number
    REMOVE BASE SERVER MEMORY
    ALLOCATE MEMORY value
    AUTOMATIC MEMORY SHARING value
    MAXIMUM SERVER MEMORY number
    BLOCK ALLOCATION SIZE number
```

The parameter descriptions and allowable settings are listed in Table 16.2.

TABLE 16.2 NET.CFG File Parameters for NetWare Server for OS/2

PARAMETER	DESCRIPTION
PERFORMANCE TUNING	Same as Performance Tuning in the Performance Monitor program. The range is 1 to 10. The default is 8 (or 9).
INITIALIZATION SCREEN	Number of seconds the NetWare Server for OS/2 information shows on the screen when OS/2 boots. The range is 0 to 180. The default is 8 seconds.
BASE SERVER MEMORY	Number of megabytes of memory reserved for the NetWare server software. The range varies. The default is 4 MB.
REMOVE BASE SERVER	Makes NetWare server memory available to OS/2 when the NetWare server is taken down. This parameter is active if listed. The default is No (not listed in NET.CFG).
ALLOCATE MEMORY	Requests that memory allocated for the NetWare server software be above or below 16 MB. This is left over from an earlier version of NetWare for OS/2 that had a problem with memory over 16 MB, so you won't need this command with NetWare 4.1x for OS/2.
AUTOMATIC MEMORY SHARING	The default for this parameter is On, meaning that the system sets the balance of memory allocation between NetWare and OS/2.
MAXIMUM SERVER MEMORY	Maximum number of megabytes allowed for the NetWare server software. The range for this setting varies.
BLOCK ALLOCATION SIZE	Sets the number of memory pages in each block of system memory OS/2 releases to NetWare. One memory page is equal to about 4 KB of memory. The range is 4 to 1024. The default is 8.

Surprisingly Stable

OS/2 HASN'T TAKEN over the world, but it provides a decent platform for a network operating system. Both Microsoft and IBM have released their respective versions of LAN Manager on an OS/2 platform. Now, Microsoft has migrated its LAN to a Windows NT server, but IBM is going forward with OS/2 as the platform of choice.

Neither operating system platform has the performance, stability, and technical history of NetWare, of course, but we can't hold that against them.

In the coming years, we'll see more platforms that support file and print services for desktop clients. Already, some servers can even imitate NetWare servers, as do those that use the File and Print Services for NetWare offered by Microsoft. Unix systems regularly support NetWare server applications, some of which are licensed from Novell and some of which have been developed independently.

Obviously, NetWare Server for OS/2 has been developed by Novell and is real NetWare. That much we've seen in this chapter. What the last paragraph tells us is that NetWare file and print services are now being cloned by all manner of companies, with and without Novell's permission.

A network consists of more than just file and print services. Those services may have been enough five years ago, but today, a real network must also supply directory management, routing, printing, messaging, and security services. What was good enough five years ago pales beside the advantages of NDS.

Taking Advantage of Special Network Features

PART 4

Installing and Using NetWare 4.1x SFT III for Complete Fault-Tolerance

CHAPTER 17

ONE DREAM OF all network managers is "never having to say you're sorry" for a down network. Many networking system vendors promise you ways to reduce the chance and duration of downtime, but only Novell comes close to guaranteeing network uptime. NetWare 4.1x SFT (System Fault Tolerant) Level III places two separate servers on your network, each active and up-to-date on every network transaction. If one server fails, the network continues as if nothing had happened.

In the large system world, Tandem Computers pioneered this concept by placing two of each system component in each computer system. This works, but it requires proprietary systems that cost more than off-the-shelf systems, since the proprietary systems are more complicated. The software to make both sides of the system run as one computer is a bit more complicated, as well. The payoff is the highest possible availability.

Novell took the approach of linking two off-the-shelf systems and tying them together with software and a special interface card between the two units. This allows customers to acquire any level of hardware performance they wish, while still having the option of adding complete fault-tolerance to their network server. In other words, if you need only medium horsepower but high availability, you can buy two medium-powered servers and link them together. If you need a high-horsepower server, you can buy two high-end servers and link those together. Your costs are controlled by your performance needs, not a proprietary system markup.

NetWare 4.1x SFT III is now a much better server than the earlier SFT III versions. This new fault-tolerant system now supports TCP/IP at the server, just like any other NetWare 4.1x system (see Chapter 14 for TCP/IP details). AppleTalk support for Macintosh clients works exactly as described back in Chapter 13.

Overview of NetWare SFT III

WE'LL BEGIN WITH an overview of how SFT works with NetWare 4.1x. We'll look at the hardware, processes, and files involved. But first, let's get the definitions of SFT out of the way:

- **SFT Level I, Hot Fix:** Moves hard disk data from bad locations on the disk to other locations. This prevents data from being lost to a bad spot on the disk. Redundant FATs (file allocation tables) and DETs (directory-entry tables) significantly reduce the chance of losing important disk directory information due to a single bad block anywhere.

- **SFT Level II, Disk Mirroring or Duplexing:** Disk mirroring runs two hard disks from the same disk controller. Each bit written to one hard disk is written to the other. If one disk stops, the other disk continues without a problem. Disk duplexing runs different disks on different disk controllers within the server. If one controller stops, the other pair continues without a problem. The TTS (Transaction Tracking System) is the other important data-safety feature of Level II.

- **SFT Level III, Server Mirroring:** Taking the next step, server mirroring runs two different servers but remains synchronized during every network operation. If the primary server fails due to a hardware problem on that server, the secondary server picks up and maintains all network connections and operations in less than one second. Users are unaware of the network server switch.

Each SFT level includes the capabilities of the lower levels. For example, SFT Level II includes SFT Level I automatically. All three SFT levels are included in your standard NetWare 4.1x distribution CD-ROM, although you need an SFT license diskette to activate the SFT Level III software.

Figure 17.1 shows how the two identical SFT III servers are connected to each other and to the network. Notice that each server has its own network interface card, connected to the network cabling like any other network node or server. Each system must be able to communicate with the network directly to support clients and to send messages between the mirrored servers themselves.

FIGURE 17.1

Connecting mirrored servers to the network and to each other

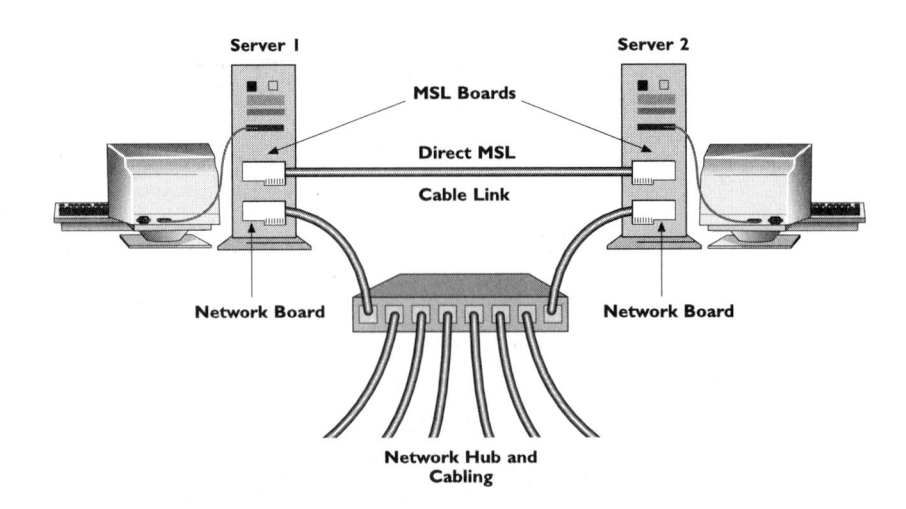

The MSL (Mirrored Server Link) adapters are special, high-speed boards cabled directly to each other. There are seven different makers of MSL adapters:

- Digital Equipment Corporation (DEC)
- Madge
- Microdyne
- Plaintree Systems
- Thomas Conrad Corporation
- SysKonnect
- Vinca

MSL board brand names, supported buses, and phone numbers are included in the DynaText online documentation, in the chapter about NetWare 4.1*x* installation. Your NetWare dealer should be aware of new products in the SFT III market as they become available.

Some of these boards use coax cable to connect the two systems, and some use fiber-optic cable. Coax systems, such as the 100 Mbps TCNS board from Thomas Conrad (one of the earliest makers of boards at this speed), are less expensive than their fiber-optic system counterparts. Fiber-optic cabling offers you the opportunity to separate mirrored servers by up to 40 kilometers (about 25 miles), in case you wish to place the mirrored servers in different buildings for the ultimate in disaster prevention.

The hardware of the two servers should be as identical as possible, but SFT III will work with servers that are not exactly the same. In these cases, the configuration of the lowest level server will limit the capabilities of the more powerful server. In other words, if you have 32 MB of RAM in one server but 48 MB of RAM in the second, only the first 32 MB of RAM will be used by NetWare in the second server. Make life easy for yourself by buying identical servers for SFT III.

How does this work? SFT III has two components: the MSEngine (Mirrored Server Engine) and the IOEngine (Input/Output Engine). Let's take a look at each of these components and some of the other details that make SFT III work.

Roles of the MSEngine and the IOEngine

The MSEngine handles the nonphysical processes. These include the NetWare file system, print queue management, and NDS.

There is only one MSEngine per mirrored pair of servers. This is the "server" the clients see. The file system, network receive buffers, and print queue management system are maintained in the MSEngine. NLMs that do not directly address hardware can also be loaded in the MSEngine; NLMs that do need direct hardware access must be loaded on each physical server. NLMs suitable for the MSEngine include the ever-present MONITOR and PSERVER, along with such heavy-duty applications as the ORACLE database NLMs. If one of the physical servers fails, the MSEngine continues.

During a switchover from the primary server to the secondary server, the MSEngine is responsible for active network processes. This means it must:

- Keep open files open.

- Retry file requests that did not reach the receive buffers when the switchover occurred.

- Keep print requests in the print queue active and ready to print after the switchover.

- Retry print requests that did not reach the print queue when the switchover occurred.

- Hold print requests in the queue if the designated printer was attached to the now inactive physical server.

The IOEngine handles physical processes, such as the network connection, disk I/O, hardware interrupts, routing, and device drivers. Both the primary and secondary SFT III servers have their own IOEngine, although they share the MSEngine.

> *Remember, in the computer world today, virtual is often more important than physical.*

NetWare clients see the IOEngine as a standard NetWare server or router. The primary server will advertise as the best route. If something happens, the secondary server will advertise as the best route.

IOEngines are not mirrored; each runs on one of the physical servers. NLMs and other processes that must connect directly to hardware are therefore run on each system and not mirrored. You must install the applications on both physical servers. Your application license agreement is not violated by this; IOEngine applications are seen as one virtual server, even if they are loaded on two physical servers. Remember, in the computer world today, virtual is often more important than physical.

Control and Startup Files for SFT III Servers

Control and startup files for SFT III servers are different, and they may apply to the MSEngine or IOEngine, but not both. These files include:

- IOSTART.NCF (one for each IOEngine) resides on each machine's DOS partition. This file holds the IOEngine name, IPX internal network number, disk and MSL drivers, IOEngine SET parameters, and load instructions for some NLMs.

- MSSTART.NCF resides in the DOS partition of each machine (two identical files) in the startup directory with the MSERVER.EXE program. It holds MSEngine commands used after the servers are mirrored, but before the SYS: volume is mounted. This is the only location for some SET parameters.

- MSAUTO.NCF is stored in SYS:SYSTEM. It contains MSEngine commands after the servers are mirrored and the SYS volume is mounted. These commands include startup details for NDS, time services, name and IPX internal network number, loading details for MSEngine NLMs, and most other mirrored server NLMs.

- IOAUTO.NCF resides in the DOS partition or SYS: volume. This file (one for each IOEngine) loads network drivers, binds network protocols, and handles details for NLMs that require an active MSEngine and the SYS: volume, such as backup and printing NLMs.

These files are executed in the order listed above, and they are created during the installation process. You can edit them by going through the INSTALL program or through the EDIT utility on a server console.

SFT III Server Log Files

Both the IOEngine and the MSEngine have console displays on each server. Unfortunately, you can't show more than one screen at a time. Use the Ctrl+Esc key combination to display active screens on the console, and type the number of the screen you wish to view (or Alt+Esc to toggle between screens).

Because you can't see both screens at one time, the log files are more important than ever when debugging a server problem involving SFT III servers. Besides the CONLOG file, which we discussed in Chapter 10, there are three SFT III-specific error log files in the SYS:SYSTEM directory:

- IO$LOG.ERR tracks the activity of both IOEngines.

- SYS$LOG.ERR tracks the MSEngine's activity.

- MSSTATUS.DMP shows status dumps of engine states and synchronization and communication information after a failure.

The IOEngines in each machine regularly send "Are you there?" packets to each other across the regular network. This verifies that the LAN boards are up and running. The rest of the server-to-server communications travel across the MSL channel.

Installing SFT III

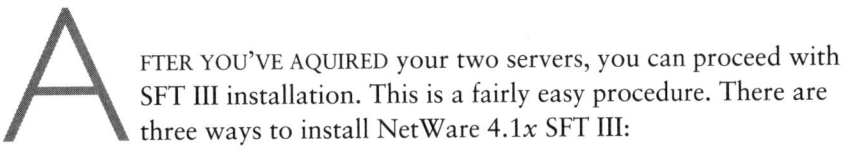

AFTER YOU'VE AQUIRED your two servers, you can proceed with SFT III installation. This is a fairly easy procedure. There are three ways to install NetWare 4.1x SFT III:

- Upgrade an existing NetWare 4.1x server to SFT III and add the second server.

- Upgrade an existing NetWare 2.x, 3.x or 4.x server to NetWare 4.1x, then configure the second server.

- Upgrade an existing NetWare 3.11 SFT III mirrored pair of servers.

Server Requirements

When you're drafting the purchase order for your servers, remember that you can avoid any potential problems by using two identical servers. Here are the server requirements for SFT III:

- Computer with a 386, 486, or Pentium processor
- Minimum of 16 MB of RAM in each server

Yes, the manual says 20 MB minimum for NetWare 4.11, but the SFT III portion isn't updated to match. Use more RAM no matter what.

- Minimum 125 MB hard disk (practical minimum 500 MB)
- Identical monitors and monitor boards (both VGA, for example, not one VGA and one EGA)
- CD-ROM drive and drivers supported as a DOS device in the primary server
- A 3.5-inch diskette drive in each server
- MSL boards connecting the two servers with appropriate cabling
- The same brand and version of DOS in both servers

The hard disk storage is important for both servers, since the NetWare partitions in each must be the same size. The disks in each server can be different sizes (although you can't use part of the larger disk), but the NetWare partitions must match (or they won't mirror to the disk in the other server). Always make the server with less RAM server number one for installation purposes. If the disks don't match, make the NetWare partition sizes match. The extra space on the larger disk will be unusable with SFT III.

You must also have the NetWare 4.1x CD-ROM and NetWare 4.1x SFT III License diskette. Speaking of diskettes, you'll need three blank ones to help start up the second mirrored server. You might as well format those now.

NetWare 4.1x should be installed on one, but not both, servers. The SFT III installation will copy the appropriate files to the second server.

All drivers for various hardware pieces, especially those for the MSL boards, should be gathered together before starting. Little in life is more frustrating than stopping a new installation project before it really gets started. Missing the right drivers is a great way to derail your installation train.

> *Missing the right drivers is a great way to derail your installation train.*

New Installations

> **17.1 IN-A-HURRY**
>
> **Install a New NetWare 4.1x SFT III Server**
>
> 1. Boot the first server under DOS and load the NetWare CD-ROM.
> 2. Type **INSTALL** and choose NetWare Server Installation, then NetWare SFT III Installation, then Convert NetWare 4.1x to SFT III.
> 3. Name your server (the MSEngine only; the IOEngines will be named by the system).
> 4. Assign IPX internal network numbers to the MSEngine and the two IOEngines. Each must be unique (accept the defaults).
> 5. Specify the directory path for your DOS partition files (accept the default).
> 6. Copy the files to the DOS partition.
> 7. Load the first of three blank diskettes and copy files to each as directed.
> 8. Choose the MSL driver or drivers.

Although there are three means of installing NetWare SFT III, as listed just a bit ago, there are actually only two ways to do this practically. If you have an existing NetWare server you wish to make into an SFT III server, it must first be upgraded to NetWare 4.1x. (See Appendix A for information about moving your NetWare 2.x, 3.x, or 4.x server up to NetWare 4.1x.) Therefore, the process for installing NetWare SFT III on an older NetWare server version is really the same as installing it on a NetWare 4.1 server, but with an extra step at the beginning. That step may take a few days to complete, depending on how old your NetWare server is, but we'll count it as a single step anyway.

Once your NetWare server is up to version 4.1x, we can start. The DynaText documentation goes into great detail about this installation, in the "Installation" chapter appropriately enough. To show how easily NetWare SFT III actually installs, Novell placed a single-page help sheet in the manual box.

Once the MSL drivers are loaded and the IOEngine is started, you can take the newly loaded floppy disks to your second server.

Installing NetWare 4.1x SFT III on the Paired Server

> **17.2 IN-A-HURRY**
>
> **Install SFT III on the Paired Server**
>
> 1. Place the first of the three newly created floppy disks in the server floppy drive.
> 2. Type **INSTALL**, and feed the other diskettes as directed.
> 3. Create the NetWare partition, being careful to make the partition the exact same size as the one on the first server.
> 4. Set up the disk mirroring between the two servers.

When the disks become mirrored, all the software on the first system is copied to the second server. There is no reason to copy the files yourself, since the 100 Mbps link between the two servers can transport the files much faster than a CD-ROM drive can.

After the disks are mirrored, you're finished with the installation. Just remember the systems are not truly "synchronized" until the disk mirroring is finished.

Upgrading Existing NetWare SFT III Systems

> **17.3 IN-A-HURRY**
>
> **Upgrade an Existing NetWare SFT III System**
>
> 1. Load the NetWare CD-ROM drive and type **INSTALL**.
> 2. Select NetWare 4.1x SFT III installation, and then choose Upgrade Current SFT III to SFT III 4.1x.
> 3. Specify your location for the DOS partition files (accept the default).
> 4. Copy the files from the CD-ROM to the DOS partition.
> 5. Load the first of three blank diskettes and follow the upgrading instructions.

Upgrading an existing NetWare 3.11 SFT III system is a bit easier than creating a new mirrored pair of servers, as described in the previous section. Take notice of some of the more extensive server requirements for NetWare 4.1x over NetWare 3.11. You may find your servers need a bit more RAM to handle NDS and file compression, neither of which was available in NetWare 3.11.

The process for the upgrade is similar to the process for the procedure described in the previous section, with a few different menu choices. Obviously, you'll pick Upgrade Current SFT III to SFT III 4.1x in the menu rather than the choice to convert a NetWare 4.1x server to SFT III.

You'll need the same set of three blank diskettes, and any updated MSL drivers. The installation program doesn't always upgrade existing drivers properly; check your startup files to make sure new drivers are installed. Your existing drivers will probably work without a problem, but if new drivers are available, you should install them.

After you have the three newly loaded diskettes in hand, go to the second server. Put the first floppy in that server's floppy drive and type:

```
INSTALL
```

Then insert the other diskettes as directed. Next, create the NetWare partition. Make sure it is the exact same size as the partition on the first server. Finally, set up the disk mirroring between the two servers.

Living with NetWare SFT III

MY FRIEND BOB works for a company that was an alpha tester for NetWare 4.10 SFT III, primarily because that company has 18 NetWare 3.11 SFT III server pairs in operation. Each server in the production environment has 256 MB of RAM and more than 70 GB of disk storage. The company is, without a doubt, a "serious" user of NetWare. The management hopes to run NetWare 4.10 SFT III with 1 GB of RAM.

Bob used the Thomas Conrad TCNS cards for all the NetWare 386 SFT III server pairs. Since then, the company has started a migration to FDDI (Fiber Distributed Data Interface), so now the company is testing the SysKonnect FDDI MSL boards. This allows them to split server pairs between buildings, something their need for uptime demands. They want the servers to be separated widely enough that the mirrored server would be safe and able to continue processing if a disaster occurred in one of the buildings.

One advantage of NetWare 4.1x SFT III is the better support of TCP/IP. This is important to Bob, since his company has quite a few Unix systems in production.

Be careful during the new server installation procedure. If something goes wrong during the file conversion and copying processes, you can't easily recover and start over. The changed files must be put back in their original state. If this happens to you, take comfort (what little comfort you can) in the fact that the problem is not you, it's the installation procedure.

Upgrading NetWare 3.11 SFT III to NetWare 4.1x SFT III servers works much better. The installation routines take over just as they should, and add some new tricks. When the DOS portion of the installation finishes, the IPX drivers load, and you lose your DOS connection when the drivers take control of the card. When Bob got to this point, the system asked him if he wanted to continue the same connection that was cut off earlier. When he said yes and provided his password for authentication, the installation routine started back exactly where it left off.

NetWare 4.1x SFT III does not guarantee 100 percent uptime; nothing can guarantee that. Because of the memory synchronization between systems, the SFT III version of NetWare 4.10 seems to Bob to be slightly more susceptible to abends (ABnormal ENDs, an old term for crashes) than regular NetWare 4.10. This is actually because NetWare 4.1x SFT III checks memory more rigorously than does regular NetWare 4.1x. Undetected parity errors show up during the memory mirroring process. In regular NetWare 4.1x, these errors would show up later as an NMI (Non-Maskable Interrupt) error.

The primary and secondary servers will switch back and forth more often than you expect. If the primary server has a glitch, the other server (almost) always continues, becoming the primary server. When the original primary server reboots itself, it synchronizes to catch up with all network activity during its downtime. After the synchronization is complete, it then becomes the secondary server.

If all goes well, no one ever knows about this server switching. However, the system is vulnerable during the switchover. The more switchovers, the more possibility of disaster. Since Bob's company prices their downtime extremely high, any potential for downtime is disturbing.

> *NetWare 4.1x SFT III does not guarantee 100 percent uptime; nothing can guarantee that.*

As you realize, nothing short of celestial intervention can guarantee 100 percent uptime. However, NetWare 4.1x SFT III goes farther than any other PC network system to reach that uptime figure.

Tolerant Thoughts

ONCE AGAIN, WHAT was once magic is now mundane. Third parties offer ways to maximize server uptime, including shadow servers and disk-mirroring. Disk systems are more reliable, and it's easier to buy a RAID system today than ever before. The new RAID 5 subsystems have redundant power supplies and fans, and allow the replacing of dead drives while the system is up and supporting users.

Novell's own technological advances make SFT III less important for some users. The single login procedure for users spreads the user database between multiple servers. If your regular server is unavailable, you can still log in easily. You lose the files attached to that server, but the rest of the network is just as available as it always was. If a server goes down, however, you are still likely to lose any work that was not saved to the server (it would be saved under SFT III).

Speaking of "files attached to that server," developers are now working on clustering technology that separates the disk subsystems from any one server. Imagine a network with disk subsystems directly on the network cable rather than tied to a server. Imagine any server reading or writing any file on any disk in any subsystem, across the network. Is this magic?

No, it's old technology. DEC did this a decade ago with its VAX clusters. Clustering is on its way to PC networks, for two reasons:

- The PC and network operating systems are getting strong enough to support it.

- PC users demand ever-higher data availability.

I can see a future where all services are distributed across the network, and no mirrored server pairs are involved. Any server can support any user in reaching any file on any disk system. This is one of the future capabilities of NDS. Did you really think NDS was just an easier way to log in and manage users?

Using the NetWare 4.1x Enhancements

CHAPTER 18

NOVELL IS SPENDING tens of millions of marketing dollars to convince users just like you that NetWare 4.1x is the best value for your network dollar. Part of Novell's problem is its earlier success; NetWare 3.x works well for millions of customers worldwide. You may have NetWare 3.x running in your company. So, what do you say when your boss asks you whether it's time to upgrade? Tough one, isn't it? If your boss is technically inclined, you can explain the values of NDS, which is truly a wonderful advance in the world of desktop networking. However, if your boss isn't particularly technical, the charms of NDS will fall on deaf ears.

This pinpoints what I think is a weakness in the Novell marketing slant: It seems that all Novell's eggs are placed in the NDS basket. I think NDS is great (and I hope you feel the same way after all these pages), but NetWare 4.1x has plenty more to offer than just Directory Services.

The other important addition in NetWare 4.11 is the entire IntranetWare bundle of products. Since the Web Server, IPX/IP Gateway, and NetWare/IP are all included in the IntranetWare package, we won't call them "enhancements," but rather important components of the base system. That's why we covered them back in Chapter 14. The Multi-Protocol Router is another feature we covered in Chapter 14.

Each section of this chapter will highlight an enhancement of NetWare 4, and NetWare 4.1x in particular. Some of these will be features, and some will be benefits. These are my definitions: a *feature* is something the system does; a *benefit* is something positive you get from that feature.

I organized the topics in this chapter roughly in order of how valuable I feel these features are to the greatest number of users. However, each network is unique. What turns you on may leave the network manager in the next building cold. Hot features—the ones that provide real benefits—tend to change over time. What you care little about today may become very important when it solves a problem for you tomorrow.

File Compression: Buy One Disk, Get Two Disks' Worth of Space

MY FRIENDS AT Novell report that file compression is the most exciting feature to small customers with limited financial resources. Larger customers, with limited administrator resources, tend to be more excited about NDS. I guess that covers the spectrum; everyone has either too little money or too little time (or both).

I guess that covers the spectrum; everyone has either too little money or too little time (or both).

File compression has these characteristics:

- Automatically enabled on all NetWare volumes
- Activated by volume, directory, or file
- Able to get better than 2:1 compression on some files
- Can be set to compress files after any amount of time you wish
- Can be archived (but the files must be restored to a volume that supports compression)

On volumes that have been upgraded from earlier NetWare versions, file compression is set to On by default. Earlier NetWare 4 versions left compression Off, but now it's enabled unless you specify otherwise.

The File Compression Process

Files are compressed in the background, and the compression is handled by an internal NetWare 4.1*x* operating system process. The file compression process goes this way:

- The system verifies compression is enabled on the volume.
- The system verifies compression is enabled in the directory and for the file to be compressed.
- The file to be compressed is examined.

- If more than 2 percent of the disk space will be saved (the setting for the amount of disk space is configurable) by compressing the file, the compression process begins by creating a temporary file describing the original file.

- The compressed file is checked for errors.

- If the file verifies correctly, the original and compressed files are swapped (the original becomes the temporary file and is purged as needed for space).

If an error occurs or there is a power failure, the file compression process is stopped, and the compressed file won't replace the original file. In other words, the original file is kept and no compression is performed until the next pass.

You have these choices about how file compression is handled:

- Files can be decompressed the first time they are read.

- Files can be decompressed the second time they are read within a set time limit.

- Files can stay compressed.

The options allow you to keep active files from being compressed, eliminating the extra overhead to read a compressed file and maximizing throughput.

Compression is much more intensive than decompression, so the compression time should be scheduled during a period where there is no network activity, such as midnight. You can enable file compression on a volume anytime. You can suspend (disable) compression with a SET command or by using the SERVMAN utility. Novell engineers recommend that you leave compression On at the volume level, and then selectively turn Off compression at the file or directory level using SERVMAN.

> **WARNING**
>
> *If you do disable file compression, when you turn it back on, many files may need compressing all at once. Schedule this procedure carefully to avoid impacting your server performance.*

Checking File Compression Status

> ### 18.1 IN-A-HURRY
>
> **Check File Compression Statistics**
>
> 1. Open NetWare Administrator and highlight the volume to check.
> 2. Right-click on the volume and choose Details.
> 3. Click on the Statistics command button on the right side of the dialog box.

NetWare Administrator provides an easy way to check the status of compressed files. Yes, you could check compression statistics under DOS with NETADMIN, but then you don't get the cute little pie charts. You can see these charts in the example shown in Figure 18.1.

FIGURE 18.1

Statistics for volume ALTOS486_SYS

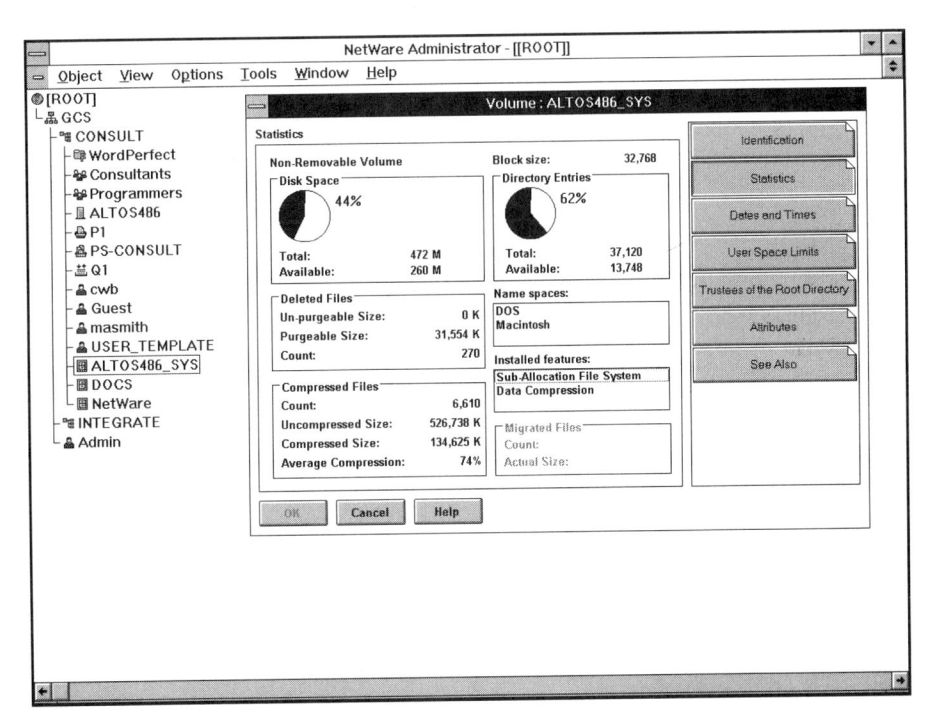

Is compression worthwhile? Take a look at the numbers on the screen in Figure 18.1. There are only 472 MB available on the volume (shown as the total under the first circle graph to the left). Under the Compressed Files heading in the bottom-left corner, notice the uncompressed size of the files on this volume is listed as 526,738 K. Do you count an extra 54 MB of files on this volume that wouldn't be there with NetWare 3.*x*? So do I. See why Novell says you can get up to 63 percent extra disk space by using file compression?

File Compression Management

These are the only reasons to disable compression for a volume:

- There's too little memory in the server to support the compression overhead (CLONE386, used in many examples in this book, has compression disabled).

- All files are active data files, and production speeds demand the best possible performance.

If these reasons don't apply to your situation, you should use compression on each volume.

There are two steps in compression management:

- Enable a volume to support compression. This is automatically set to On during the creation of the volume.

- Activate compression per volume, directory, or file.

Generally, compression is enabled and activated per volume, but you can turn compression off without reworking your volume. Then no more compression will take place on that volume until you turn compression back on.

The default setting is to compress a file after seven days of inactivity. If that doesn't work for you, adjust it to any interval you wish. Check Chapter 2 for the details on setting compression options during initial volume setup.

Improved Performance of Peripheral Devices

EVER ALERT FOR more TLAs (Three Letter Acronyms), Novell has now developed NPA (NetWare Peripheral Architecture). NPA makes it easier to add and support different storage devices and their associated controllers. There are two levels to the NPA: one for the controller board in the system and the other for the device attached. This is all handled by the NWPA.NLM file loaded during the initial server boot sequence.

The Media Manager is a database built into NetWare that tracks all peripheral storage devices and media attached to the server. In earlier NetWare versions, the single interface between the NetWare operating system and the hardware was a DSK file (a device driver file with the DSK extension). No matter how many devices were connected to one host adapter board in the server, only one DSK file could be used to connect the systems.

As you might guess, today's modular world demands more layers in between the operating system and the hardware. More is better in this case because several layers make it easier to upgrade the driver for one storage device without messing up another storage device. The new layers are:

- **HAM (Host Adapter Module):** Driver controlling the host adapter hardware. Each HAM is adapter-specific, and may be supplied by either Novell or the third-party manufacturer of the adapter. HAM drivers route requests across the bus to the specific adapter required.

- **HAI (Host Adapter Interface):** Programming hooks (APIs) within the NPA that provide a means of communication between the HAM and the Media Manager.

- **CDM (Custom Device Module):** The storage device component software that handles details with the HAM. CDMs are normally supplied by the device manufacturer, although common ones are supported directly by NetWare. One CDM must be loaded for each physical device; for example, you'll need four CDMs for four devices attached to one HAM. To set this up during installation, you will need to use the Custom Installation routine.

- **CDI (Custom Device Interface):** APIs within the NPA that provide a means of communication between the CDMs and the Media Manager.

> *As you might guess, today's modular world demands more layers in between the operating system and the hardware.*

Are these new modules worthwhile? Yes, especially as more vendors get with the NetWare 4.1*x* development program. If everyone making storage devices follows the rules laid out in the NetWare development guidelines, storage devices of all kinds will be less trouble to install, and they will provide higher performance. Even if the third-party vendors don't do their part, this modular technique allows Novell engineers to make improvements more easily than ever before.

Block Suballocation Saves Even More Space

A BLOCK IS THE smallest amount of disk space that can be allocated on a NetWare volume. Block size is assigned by the installation program for each volume, but you can change the default. The smaller the block size, the more memory required of the operating system. For that reason, some network managers override the installation suggestions and use the maximum block size, 64 KB, for servers with limited RAM.

Block suballocation combines overflow file fragments from several files in a single disk block. If a 65 KB file is copied to a volume with 64 KB blocks, two blocks are required. That one file takes away almost twice the disk space necessary. If this happened with earlier NetWare versions, you were just out of luck—and out of disk space sooner than you should be.

With NetWare 4.1*x*, however, block suballocation places 512-byte pieces of files in a block with other overflow file pieces. Our 65 KB file suddenly takes only 65 KB of disk space: 64 KB for one block, and two 512-byte pieces in another block with other overflow files. This is just another way to stretch your disk drive dollar, courtesy of NetWare 4.1*x*.

MHS: Novell's Messaging Services for NetWare 4.10 Only

MESSAGING IS ONE of the seven services Novell feels must be part of the modern network operating system (along with file, print, directory, security, routing, and management services). NetWare's MHS (Message Handling Service) is clearly named to reflect its function in providing messaging as a service. Its job is to allow users to communicate across the network, using messaging services such as e-mail, shared calendars, and shared task lists.

NetWare 4.11 does not support MHS. Why not? Part of the reason for Novell to purchase WordPerfect was the technology included within WordPerfect Office. Renamed GroupWise, the message-handling technology in GroupWise 5 (the current release as this is written) provides all manner of connection options for NetWare networks. See your Novell reseller for GroupWise information.

How MHS Works

MHS is a store-and-forward electronic-messaging service. Third-party vendors follow MHS specifications set forth in the SMF (Standard Message Format) version 71 document for NDS systems. Older products were written to use the bindery files, and you should upgrade those products if you now have NetWare 4.10 in place.

MHS supports all message-enabled applications. With the increased importance of connecting to the Internet and sharing information across a WAN, messaging will become a critical need for many companies.

MHS includes the following pieces:

- **Messaging server:** A NetWare server with MHS loaded and installed. The messaging server name will follow that of the server supporting MHS.

- **Distribution List objects:** Leaf objects created to use as shortcuts when sending e-mail.

- **Message Routing Group object:** A message routing group is a set of messaging servers that communicate with each other across the network for message-transfer purposes. This group will be created automatically during MHS installation. The current version of MHS supports a single message routing group only.

- **Mailboxes:** The physical locations for MHS users to receive e-mail and other information.

- **External Entity objects:** Leaf objects that represent non-NDS objects, or have been imported into NDS for some reason. These objects are often used for remote messaging addresses.

- **Postmaster:** The user granted the authority necessary to modify the messaging server, assign mailboxes to objects, and modify or delete mailboxes.

- **Postmaster General:** The designated user (normally Admin) who controls the Messaging Group object and other postmasters.

- **Gateway:** A separate, optional program that connects your MHS system to another service, such as a fax server, another e-mail application, or the Internet.

Now included as part of the NetWare 4.10 distribution software, NetWare MHS handles all the functions listed above for your local network. Connections to remote networks need the addition of Global MHS (GMHS), the optional software module that connects to the outside world. Contact your Novell reseller for information about GMHS.

You will notice many third-party programs require MHS to be up and running on your server. Electronic messaging-enabled packages of all types will need MHS. If you need just basic e-mail for your local network, Novell now fulfills that need.

With MHS in NetWare 4.10, you will notice an improvement in those third-party applications that use MHS: the messaging database is the same as the NDS database. You no longer need to manage duplicate databases and reconcile user changes on the server and on the e-mail software.

FirstMail: Free E-mail Returns to NetWare 4.10 Only

It wasn't much, but it was free.

Early NetWare versions (2.*x* and before) always included a DOS e-mail program. It wasn't much, but it was free. I believe Novell left it out of the operating system about the time NetWare 3.0 was released. At this time, e-mail was a growing software area, and Novell was actively pushing developers to write for MHS, so I suppose the company dropped their own e-mail package to further that goal. But I think that was a mistake, because most users bought real e-mail software once they realized the limitation of the free e-mail included with NetWare. The result was that a lot of small companies couldn't test the value of e-mail without spending thousands of dollars for one of the third-party packages available.

The good news is that Novell has once again included a basic e-mail package, called FirstMail, in NetWare 4.10. I believe this is smart. Big companies buying NetWare 4.10 will already have a corporate standard for e-mail. FirstMail is nice, but it is only substantial enough for small companies limited to a single, local network. Once again, companies that haven't used an e-mail package can test the technology without investing buckets of money on a third-party product.

Unfortunately, FirstMail did not make it into NetWare 4.11. For local e-mail, look to GroupWise from your Novell reseller. Why did Novell drop FirstMail from NetWare 4.11? More poor marketing advice is the only answer I can give you.

Configuring FirstMail

> **18.2 IN-A-HURRY**
>
> **Set Up FirstMail Mailboxes in NetWare 4.10**
>
> 1. As the Admin user or equivalent, open NetWare Administrator, and then open the server messaging group.
> 2. Click on Users, and then click on the Add button.
> 3. Click on each user who needs a mailbox (hold down the Ctrl key to select multiple users).
> 4. Click on OK.

Since FirstMail is installed automatically when MHS is installed, there's nothing extra to do on your NetWare server to install FirstMail. There is one thing to configure, however. To use the program, the users need FirstMail mailboxes.

You can set this up through NetWare Administrator. Open the server messaging group and add mailboxes for everyone. Click on Users and then the Add button to open the Select Object dialog box. Hold down the Ctrl key and click on all the users that will be in the mail system (probably everyone). Click on OK, and you're finished with the system configuration chores.

Running FirstMail

To run FirstMail, DOS users just type at any DOS prompt:

```
MAIL
```

This loads the MAIL.EXE program in \PUBLIC.

MS Windows users must create a new program icon for WMAIL.EXE, found in the \PUBLIC directory of their messaging server. There are some niceties you may wish to add, such as address books and the like, but don't get carried away. If you want high-function e-mail, you must look beyond FirstMail. Be prepared for your users to gripe that FirstMail doesn't do all the things they read about in the magazines, such as get mail from the Internet and the like.

In Figure 18.2, you can see a message being created in the MS Windows client software. The only change made is the check mark in the Copy Self box, which stores a copy of the message in the user's own folder.

Notice the address laptop@integrate.gcs is in the To field. The DynaText manuals sometimes indicate you should use the server name for the address, which is not correct when using NDS. With NDS, you never directly reference a file server. The documentation says different things in different places, so be careful.

Look closely at the button bar below the menu. The buttons make it easy to send a message, open your mail, open a message-storage folder, and handle mail in other ways. A press of the F1 key provides help for your users.

The DOS counterpart of Figure 18.2 can be seen in Figure 18.3. The opening screen allows you to choose menu options with a single keystroke, but it's rather plain. Nothing fancy here—just an e-mail message.

Take a look at the bottom of the screen in Figure 18.3 to see some of your options for received mail in the DOS version. You can save the message to a folder (Move) as well as delete, copy, forward, reply, or print. Yes, your users may print lots of e-mail at the beginning, until they start to trust their electronic system and the personal folders they have installed.

Is FirstMail the best free e-mail you can get? No, but it's the best free e-mail that comes in the box with the NetWare operating system.

FIGURE 18.2

Basic e-mail in MS Windows

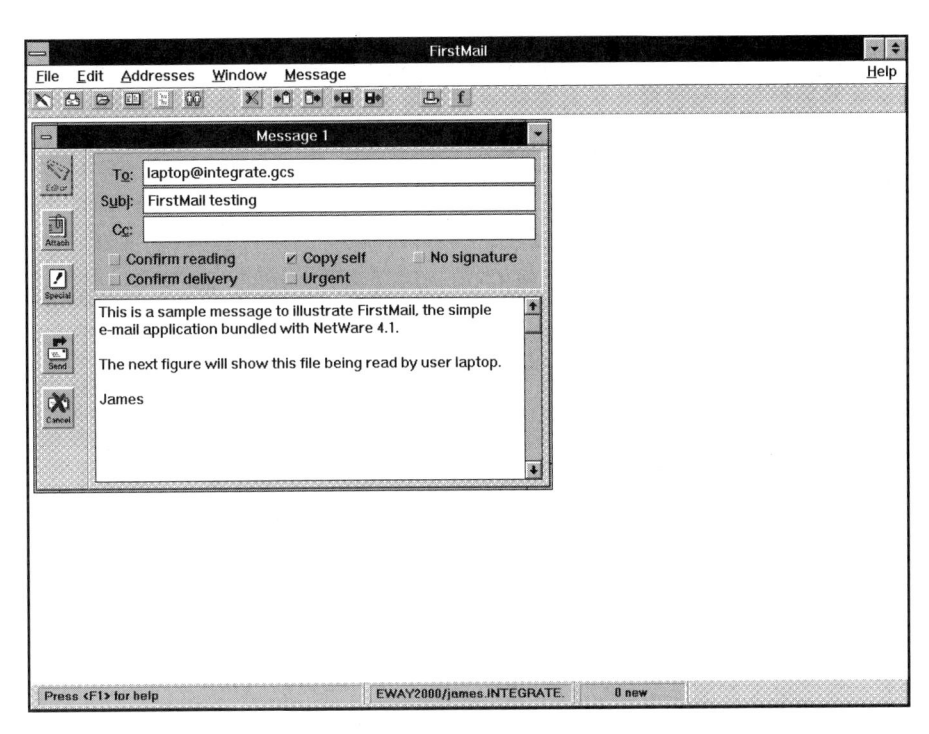

FIGURE 18.3

The DOS mail reader screen

New Server Memory Management Techniques

SERVER MEMORY IN earlier NetWare versions was split into five different segments, often called *pools*. A flat memory model is always better and easier to use, however, so Novell engineers changed to this method in NetWare 4. Now, when programs leave little bits of memory stranded, they can be collected. Before, the stranded memory gradually took up so much space the server crashed.

The problem with a flat memory space is that ill-behaved programs can write to memory addresses controlled by other programs. This causes the second program to crash. If the bad program overwrites some of the area used by the NetWare operating system, your server crashes.

NetWare 4 has the ability to run two sets of memory: the OS memory domain and the OS_PROTECTED memory domain. These domains are created by the DOMAIN.NLM utility.

Using the DOMAIN.NLM Utility to Load Suspect NLMs

The DOMAIN.NLM utility must be loaded from your STARTUP.NCF file before all other modules. The DOMAIN.NLM will automatically load NWTIL.NLM and NWTILR.NLM, so make sure these files are in the SYS:SYSTEM directory with DOMAIN.NLM.

When you reboot the server and load DOMAIN.NLM in the STARTUP.NCF file, the OS and OS_PROTECTED memory domains are created. Each ill-behaved (or suspect) NLM is loaded by typing:

```
DOMAIN=OS_PROTECTED
LOAD suspect.NLM
```

To change back to the OS memory domain, at the console prompt, type:

```
DOMAIN=OS
```

When should you do this, and with which NLMs? The NLMs that ship with NetWare are guaranteed to behave. Likewise, third-party NLMs certified by Novell are guaranteed to behave. If you develop your own NLMs, or are working with custom NLMs that have not been certified by Novell, run them on a lab server or in a protected domain until you know how they behave.

There are several more options with the DOMAIN.NLM utility, so consult your online documentation. Check your new NLM program to see if it supports the necessary cross-domain function calls necessary before running it in the OS_PROTECTED domain.

Server Self-Tuning for Better Performance (and How to Improve It)

The flat memory model in the NetWare 4 server operating system allows processes that need more memory to be assigned more memory. This happens automatically, without any intervention on your part.

Each time the server is restarted, the settings that were adjusted during operation are set back to the defaults. You can change the defaults to more accurately reflect the performance profile of your server after it has had time to tune itself. The tuning happens fairly quickly, but not as quickly as it would have if the right values were in place when the server started.

Check the MONITOR screen on a regular basis to get an idea of your performance profile during heavy network traffic sessions. Make a note of those settings. Then go back to Chapter 10 and check out how to use the SERVMAN utility, so you can change as many SET parameters as necessary. Take a look at Chapter 11 to see some suggestions for optimizing your server for certain operations.

SMS: *Storage Management Services and SBACKUP*

ONE OF THE new management capabilities of NetWare is SMS (Storage Management Services). The SMS system is independent of the backup and restore hardware and the file systems (DOS, OS/2, Macintosh, MS Windows, or Unix) being backed up. SMS describes the architecture provided by NetWare to support reliable cross-platform backup and restore procedures. It's up to the product manufacturers to implement SMS (and many of them do).

SIDF (System Independent Data Format) describes a common way for data to be read and written from media. Normally, a backup tape made with a Mountain product is worthless when loaded into a Cheyenne tape unit. However, companies that follow the SIDF guidelines can read and write any other SIDF-compliant tape or optical disk.

The SIDF Association is working with other standards organizations, such as ANSI (American National Standards Institute), ECMA (European Computer Manufacturers Association), and ISO (International Standards Organization), to ratify SIDF as a true industry standard. Although SIDF began as part of Novell's SMS strategy, the idea of cross-platform backup media is too valuable for one company alone, and Novell has turned over SIDF to the SIDF Association.

Components of SMS

SMS NLM programs and other software include:

- SBACKUP.NLM, which is the backup software utility that provides backup and restore functions.

- SMDR (Storage Management Data Requester), which manages communications between SBACKUP and TSAs (Target Service Agents).

- SMSDI (SMS Storage Device Interface), which manages communications between SBACKUP and storage devices and media.

- Device drivers (IDE.DSK, TAPEDAI.DSK, AHAnnnn.DSK), which handle the physical and mechanical operations of storage devices. They act on commands passed through SMSDI from SBACKUP.

- NetWare Server TSAs (such as TSA410), which manage communications asking for data from SBACKUP to the NetWare server holding the data. They then return the data through SMDR to SBACKUP, which passes it to the physical device.

- Database TSAs (such as TSANDS), which manage communications between the server hosting SBACKUP and the database on the server hosting the data, then back through the SMDR to SBACKUP.

- Workstation TSAs (such as TSADOS and TSAOS2), which manage communications between the SBACKUP host server and the workstation holding the data to be backed up.
- WSMAN (Workstation Manager), which manages a list of workstations available to be backed up. The workstations send "I'm alive" packets on a regular basis.

> **Backup Solutions**
>
> If you have a new network, your dealer should have provided a backup solution for your servers when the system was installed. Not having a reliable file backup system is beyond imprudent, it is sheer folly. If you are setting up your system yourself without the help of a dealer, go directly (do not pass GO, do not collect $200) to a reseller or dealer and buy a tape backup system before another sunset.
>
> One of my favorite third-party backup and restore systems is Legato Networker (from Legato Systems in Palo Alto, California), primarily because it uses SMS, backs up multiple systems at one time, and supports both NetWare and Unix systems during the same tape backup. Other companies are providing many of these same features. One of the highest backup rates belongs to the NetFRAME DataJET (Milpitas, California): 100 MB a minute, or 12 GB per hour, under the right conditions.
>
> Look around for a tape backup system, both hardware and software, that protects your network data well enough to make you comfortable. SBACKUP works, but it's only one small part of Novell and NetWare. Other companies, such as Legato Systems, focus completely on new and better ways to protect data.

Using SBACKUP

SBACKUP works only when it is run by the Admin or equivalent user. Because the tape system must have access to all the files on the network, the user who runs SBACKUP is a security risk.

The Novell documentation lists seven vendors of SBACKUP-compliant hardware. More are being added; check with your NetWare resellers for their recommendations.

SBACKUP is similar to FirstMail; it's a good basic system, but has few of the bells and whistles most companies want from their backup systems.

Backing Up NetWare 4.1x

SMS standards are almost a requirement now for backup product vendors. They must meet these standards in order to properly back up and restore NetWare 4.1x information. However, there is a difference between backing up NetWare 4.1x data and backing up NDS.

The additions in NetWare 4.1x that affect backup systems include extra attributes and flags on the files. Data compression is a new trick for NetWare, so the backup system must understand and handle compressed and noncompressed files without a hiccup.

NDS is a different story altogether (at least it is when speaking of multiple servers on a network). There are no database files with special attributes to back up. The NDS database is replicated across multiple network servers. If there is a problem with NDS on a server, the last thing you should do is restore some NDS files from a backup tape.

The active replicas on other servers in your network will copy their NDS information to your problem server over time. Several management tools available in NetWare Administrator allow you to move or copy replica information. From the server console, DSREPAIR offers several ways to rebuild or copy a damaged NDS database on one server. When a server suffers a catastrophic failure, rebuild NDS through these methods if at all possible.

> *If you want confirmation you're not as prone to stupidity as I am under stress, look back in Chapter 10 and read about when I deleted the SYS: volume holding the master replica of [Root] for my network. Believe it or not, I recovered the network without restoring a tape backup of NDS. If I can resurrect NDS after deleting the main replica, you can resurrect NDS as well.*

If none of the above methods work, reinstall NDS, then go back through the previous suggestions to force other servers to update your problem server with the latest NDS changes. DSREPAIR is probably the best place to start resynchronizing the NDS database information. Almost anything is better than restoring NDS from tape.

HSM: Hierarchical Storage Management for More Storage Space

HAVING A HIGH-CAPACITY storage system is like being rich: you know what it's like, but you're not there yet. With Novell's HSM (Hierarchical Storage Management) software, you may win the lottery and have all the storage space (sorry, not money) you can stand. The only (minor) downside is the hierarchical part: we've split storage into several levels:

- **Online:** Instant information retrieval, with the information stored on hard disks in the server.

- **Near online:** Storage with a few seconds (less than a minute) delay, using optical disks for storage.

- **Offline:** Storage that requires several minutes or more to retrieve, since the tape storage units must be found and loaded into the tape drive.

Even automated tape systems are slower than those for optical disks, and tape access is slower than that of optical disks as well.

These information-storage strategies have long been used with mainframe and Unix systems. Novell didn't invent them, but NetWare is the first desktop network operating system to support any type of HSM.

The migration plan developed for files is based on how often the files are accessed. A common time limit is 90 days. If a file in a designated volume or directory is not accessed in 90 days, it can be migrated (moved) to the optical disk system. If the file is not accessed in 90 more days, it may then be migrated to a tape storage system. If the file is then needed, it must be read from the tape and de-migrated back to the server.

The best time limits to set for file migration depend on the system in use. Many customers take some time to discover the right migration times. Making the migration time too long won't save you enough disk space. Making the time too short will cause files to go back and forth to and from the hard disk, clogging your system and making everyone unhappy.

Part of the reason for HSM systems is the disparity between the cost of storing a megabyte of information on a hard disk versus an optical disk versus a tape cartridge. Some of these numbers are being skewed by the plummeting price of hard drive storage. Hard disk space that used to cost several dollars a megabyte a few years ago is now down to 10 cents a megabyte in some configurations. That's close to optical disk and tape cartridge prices, although tape will always be the cheapest.

The system Novell uses to move information between the server hard disks and an optical jukebox is called HCSS (High Capacity Storage System), and it's the usable part of the HSM technology. HCSS was developed to work with HP (Hewlett-Packard) jukeboxes and compatible systems. Check with your NetWare reseller for other systems that are being certified by Novell as time goes on.

HCSS, as deployed in NetWare, hides the migration and de-migration of files from the user. Certain volumes (not SYS:) may be designated as HCSS volumes. They must contain at least 10 percent of the storage space of the attached optical jukebox. This ensures enough space for files being moved to and from the optical disks.

When you create the HCSS volume, you can set File Compression and Block Suballocation to Off or On (it's your decision). Data Migration must be set to On.

Any block size is allowable. If you turn on Block Suballocation, however, make the block size 64 KB.

There are several pieces that make a successful HCSS deployment. You must add the jukebox to the server managing the system (adding RAM, of course), load the HCSS NLM programs, and configure a workstation to manage HCSS.

A workstation's NWADMIN.INI file must be modified to snap in the HCSS management DLLs (Dynamic Link Libraries). Only one workstation (probably yours) is required to make these additions. Once the system is modified, HCSS will show up in the Tools menu in NetWare Administrator.

NLSP: Improved Routing for Your WAN

AS WE SAW in the chapters concerning protocols (Chapters 1 and 14), Novell's IPX/SPX takes a lot of abuse from some people. People who don't understand why the protocol generates so much traffic over low-bandwidth WAN links complain about IPX/SPX. But rather than blame IPX/SPX, you must really blame RIP (Routing Information Protocol), SAP (Service Advertising Protocol), and NCP (NetWare Core Protocol) for the overhead traffic.

Novell has develop NLSP (NetWare Link Services Protocol) to replace RIP and SAP. Loaded as an NLM program on NetWare 3.11 and above, NLSP provides the following advantages over RIP and SAP:

- **Improved routing:** RIP-based routers know about only the next router, not the network. NLSP knows the layout of the entire network, and lets routers make more intelligent choices when routing traffic.

- **Reduced network overhead:** Routers using RIP periodically broadcast their entire routing table to keep other RIP devices up-to-date. While these broadcasts keep all routers in sync, they are broadcast whether the network changes or not. NLSP systems send broadcasts only when the network changes (the link state changes). Rather than using general broadcast packets, NSLP uses multicast packet addresses, meaning only routers need to pay attention to these broadcasts. All other network devices can safely ignore the multicast NLSP packets.

- **Low WAN overhead:** NetWare servers send a SAP broadcast every 60 seconds, containing their entire service database. NLSP eliminates SAP packets by sending broadcasts only when a service changes. Unlike SAP, NLSP uses a reliable packet that contains both IPX network and services information.

- **Faster data transfer:** IPX header compression is used by NSLP to reduce packet sizes across WAN links. NLSP also supports load balancing between parallel paths. If more equal-cost paths exist between network nodes, NLSP can support as many parallel paths as you allow, or you may disable load splitting.

- **Parallel paths:** NLSP supports two or more paths between two network nodes. This is impossible under the spanning-tree routing used in traditional Ethernet networks, as an example. Using multiple paths between NLSP nodes (often called load splitting) provides fault-tolerance and higher performance.

- **Increased reliability:** NLSP regularly checks all links for the data integrity of the link. When a link fails, NLSP quickly switches to an alternate link. It then updates the network routing diagrams stored in each node, informing all devices of the change in connection status.

- **Lower CPU usage:** RIP and SAP broadcast sending and receiving require a fair amount of routing overhead in the host computer. NLSP cuts down this overhead because of the reduced need for broadcasts. Link state protocols like NLSP do take more time to figure the best packet routes than RIP, but this overhead is small compared with the RIP broadcast overhead.

- **Better support for larger NetWare networks:** Packets using RIP may go through only 15 hops between their source and destination addresses; NSLP supports up to 127 hops. This allows bigger networks automatically, even before you add the growth of network nodes possible through NLSP's hierarchical addressing. NLSP can easily support thousands and thousands of networks and servers.

- **Superior manageability:** NLSP uses a standardized management interface based on SNMP (Simple Network Management Protocol). A single NLSP router can provide the network manager with a complete network topology map.

- **Backward-compatible:** NLSP and RIP-based routers can easily exist on the same network. Your RIP-to-NLSP conversion can proceed in phases, and you don't even need to reboot NetWare servers and routers after enabling NLSP.

- **Support for multiple networking media:** NLSP provides end-to-end data delivery over Ethernet, Token Ring, and point-to-point links. Any media supported by a NetWare server will support NLSP, including the drivers for the NetWare server.

- **Optional link-cost assignment:** You can manually assign a cost to each NLSP link and allow NLSP to choose the most efficient path for each packet. A NetWare server/router may be designated as more expensive than a dedicated router. When available, NLSP will route packets across the dedicated router, using the NetWare server/router only as a backup. For WAN links, a T1 line would be designated as less expensive than a 56 KB connection, making NLSP automatically route packets across the high-speed link if possible.

In a smaller, purely local network, the RIP and SAP overhead is not a concern. In a mixed LAN/WAN environment, you have an incentive to activate NLSP, especially if your WAN links are not high-speed. If you have a large, local network with multiple routers, you may gain an advantage by adding NLSP to support more than 15 hops between source and destination addresses. Very large local networks (with more than 400 different network numbers) must be segmented into NLSP routing domains in a hierarchical design.

Before converting your network to NLSP, check out the *NetWare Link Services Protocol In-Depth* booklet from Novell. Your dealer can order one.

NLSP information is provided in the "IPX Upgrade" part of the DynaText information. Adding the IPX upgrade, including NLSP, to a pre-NetWare 4.1*x* server is covered in this section, as well.

SNMP: A Management Solution

SNMP (SIMPLE NETWORK Management Protocol) is widely used for TCP/IP networks and Unix hosts. Because of this, many people mistakenly believe SNMP is a TCP/IP-only management solution. This is not true.

The developers made sure SNMP was transport-protocol neutral. As management becomes more critical to PC networks, SNMP systems will become available for IPX-only networks. The only restriction today is marketing, not technology.

SNMP for the NetWare 4.1x Server

Since NetWare 4.1x is object-oriented, the idea of SNMP managing objects rather than computers and printers should not cause you any mental strain.

Network and object details for SNMP are kept in a MIB (Management Information Base) file. Since NetWare 4.1*x* is object-oriented, the idea of SNMP managing objects rather than computers and printers should not cause you any mental strain.

Each device to be managed runs a small bit of software called the SNMP Agent. The Agents monitor certain functions depending on the device hosting them. When some event happens, the Agent sends a message to a predetermined address. The SNMP management console software collects these traps and uses them to monitor the health of the network.

The NetWare server can easily run the SNMP Agent software, and that capability is included in the TCP/IP software. You can add TCP/IP support without SNMP, but if you're in an enterprise network with SNMP management consoles, your servers deserve to be monitored.

> ### A Bit of SNMP History
>
> SNMP was developed by four gentlemen over dinner in Monterey, California, in March 1987. Two of the gentlemen were working in universities, and the other two worked for a leading Internet service provider. Being engineers, the group developed the SGMP (Simple Gateway Monitoring Protocol) in two months.
>
> By August 1988, SNMP (the spiffed-up subsequent protocol that improved upon SGMP) was a reality. The protocol details were officially declared an Internet draft standard, meaning they were completed, implemented, and under production at several companies.
>
> In April 1989, SNMP became recommended, making it the de facto operational standard for managing TCP/IP networks and internetworks. More than 30 vendors displayed products at the InterOp trade show in San Jose, California, in October 1989. SNMP had officially become "The Protocol" when speaking of network management.
>
> In enterprise networks, SNMP is still The Protocol, and shows no signs of slowing down. Although SNMP was developed to be small enough to run in an IBM XT (at least, the Agent part), it isn't used on many PC-only networks. This probably won't change anytime soon. Most of the serious management consoles for SNMP are Unix systems, and they are designed and priced for large networks, not for small and medium LANs.
>
> Now in the wings is SNMP version 2, adding some capabilities and security to SNMP. Unfortunately, the two SNMP camps are fighting about security details, so the IETF has yet to release an official SNMP version 2. NetWare server and client software will be compatible with any updated SNMP management consoles that support SNMP version 2; management is too important for companies to drop the ball at the start of a new version.

Management consoles are most often Unix workstations with special software. The most popular management software is by Sun and HP. These systems may cost close to $100,000 when fully configured; overkill for a NetWare-only network. However, if you have a graphical management package for your wiring concentrators, you have a subset of an SNMP management console.

SNMP.NLM handles the Agent chores for SNMP management consoles, and also helps control the TCP/IP module for the TCPCON.NLM utility. The community name used during SNMP message authentication must be provided before SNMP starts. The default community name is public, used for read-only SNMP activities. Therefore, no SNMP management console can change any parameter on the NetWare server.

You can configure three community name options in INETCFG:

- **Monitor Community:** Determines which SNMP management consoles can read this information.

- **Control Community:** Determines which SNMP management consoles can write (change) this information.

- **Trap Community:** Designates where traps will be sent (management consoles to inform of changes).

Each option in INETCFG has three choices:

- Any community can access the server (read or write).

- No community can access the server.

- Only specified communities may have access.

There is a default option, which leaves read authority for the public community.

If you are going to activate SNMP, you should go directly to your Unix system administrator and work out the details. There's no NetWare-only SNMP packages, so this isn't something you get into just as a lark. If you start SNMP, you must have a large network with active network management.

While NetWare Management Systems (NMS) can make use of SNMP clients, check the installation of NMS before you add SNMP to the server. With a NetWare-only network, there is no need for the SNMP overhead.

SNMP Options in NET.CFG for NetWare Clients

NetWare clients may be SNMP Agents, just like the NetWare server. To the SNMP management console, both machines are just Agents holding different information.

Here are the files that were copied to each PC's \NWCLIENT directory during the NetWare client installation process:

- HRMIB.EXE, which is the Host Resources manager application that collects information about DOS client workstations on the network.

- HRMIB.INI, which is the configuration file for HRMIB.EXE.

- MIB2IF.VLM, which is MIB-II (Management Information Base version 2) and provides interface groups support.

- MIB2PROT.VLM, which provides MIB-II TCP/IP groups support.

- WSASN1.VLM. which is the ASN.1 (Abstract Syntax Notation One) translation module. ASN.1 provides the syntax for transferring information between systems that may or may not use different encoding systems.

- WSDRVPRN.VLM, which is the print information collection file for tracking print mappings and captured printers.

- WSREG.VLM which is the registration module for the SNMP management console.

- WSSNMP.VLM, which is the desktop SNMP module, including MIB-II System and SNMP groups support.

- WSTRAP.VLM, which is the Trap module.

- STPUDP.COM, which is the Transport Provider module for UDP/IP.

- STPIPX.COM, which is the Transport Provider module for IPX.

If these files were not copied during installation, or have been erased since, you must add them before activating SNMP. If you get them from the NetWare CD-ROM, be sure to use the NWUNPACK.EXE program to decompress the files rather than copy them.

You'll need to edit the NET.CFG file on each workstation that will run the SNMP Agent software. These files must be listed in this order for SNMP Agent software to work:

```
NETWARE DOS REQUESTER
  VLM = WSSNMP.VLM
  VLM = WSTRAP.VLM
  VLM = WSREG.VLM
  VLM = WSASN1.VLM
  VLM = MIB2IF.VLM
  VLM = WSDRVPRN.VLM
  VLM = MIB2PROT.VLM
```

There are many desktop SNMP NET.CFG parameters that can be set. These were not covered back in Chapter 5 with the other NET.CFG parameters, because they're so specialized. If you are planning to use SNMP on your

NetWare clients, study the parameters in the DynaText chapter titled "NetWare Client for DOS and MS Windows Technical Reference."

Client32 stations hide the complexities of workstation SNMP configuration within their network settings. For Windows 95 stations, open the Networking Control Panel, click on Add, click on Service, and then click on Novell. From there, you can pick from one of several SNMP options. All the gory SNMP details are here, but presented a bit more elegantly than with pre-Client32 systems.

Exciting Enhancements

SOME OF THE enhancements listed in this chapter are part of the core NetWare 4.1*x* product, and some are highly specialized and of interest to only a few customers. File compression is the most popular of all enhancements, since you get something (more space for files) for almost nothing (some server RAM).

If you don't use any of the extra enhancements, such as HSM or SNMP, don't feel bad. Most NetWare users don't take advantage of these technologies.

But don't you feel smart using an operating system with more horsepower than you'll ever need? Too many NetWare competitors offer the opposite; horsepower is promised, but the release date of these features keeps fading into the distant mists of the future.

It's a common statement that most users leave 80 percent of their application programs unexplored. In other words, the users are happy using only 20 percent of the product's power. NetWare doesn't use that ratio; more like 70 percent of the power is used by everyone, with 30 percent reserved for those with special needs. Few, if any, customers ever need more PC LAN features and horsepower than NetWare delivers.

Troubleshooting Your Network

CHAPTER 19

NO MATTER HOW carefully you plan, how carefully you build your network, and how carefully you train your users, things will go wrong. In fact, things going wrong is a normal part of your network. When things don't go wrong, you should worry.

When something on the network is not working properly, you must change hats from strategic thinker to ambulance driver. Even if the problem is not much of a problem to the network as a whole, the affected user needs to be reassured. Psychology is important. When users have a problem, they don't want to hear it isn't a big problem. They want to hear that you understand their problem and are working to fix that problem. They will be reasonable (most of the time) if you acknowledge their distress ("I feel your pain") and inform them of your actions to resolve the problem.

A Troubleshooting Scene

Let's look at a troubleshooting situation as a scene from a movie, or, more appropriately, a sitcom.

SCENE: Irate user that can't boot his computer to the network.

YOU: "What's the problem?"

USER: "Your stupid network is broken." User registers disgust and waves an arm toward the defunct computer.

YOU (sitting at computer): "Your hard disk seems to be dead."

This is the time many network managers try to defend their network, pointing out that the user's problem is caused by and limited to the user. Your "stupid" network had nothing to do with this problem. However, resist this urge. The user is angry, and will now be embarrassed. Anything you say in defense of the network will be seen by the user as 'rubbing my nose in it.'

(continued on next page)

> YOU: "Let me configure a boot floppy, so you can get logged in to the network. We'll order a new hard disk for you, and I'll let you know when it arrives so we can install it at your convenience."
>
> USER: "Thanks for your prompt attention to this matter. I apologize for disparaging the network, but I was upset by this disk failure. Please forgive me. Allow me to buy lunch today in apology."
>
> ACTION: Glowing sunshine warmly colors the scene. Birds sing. Flowers bloom. Theme music swells.
>
> Perhaps this is a bit far out, even for Hollywood. But the idea of not defending your network against an angry user is a good one. Angry people often need to blow off steam, and you're a good target. You aren't the boss, so you can't fire them. You aren't an immediate co-worker, so the user won't be embarrassed every morning afterward. You are a fairly safe target for the user's anger. Anything you say in defense of your network, or that insinuates that the problem is self-caused, will only make the user angrier. This is a "no-win" situation for you, at least in the short-term.
>
> This doesn't make you a doormat. The network administrator's favorite fable is "The User Who Cried Wolf" for good reason. You will soon learn which users howl the loudest with the smallest problems. When several problems arrive at once, as they often do, you may safely put these users at the bottom of the help list. After all, you have already documented your multiple quick responses, right? How can they complain if they were served quickly many times, and only served slowly when a larger network crisis appeared? Well, they will complain, but no one will listen to them, because you have documentation. That's the beauty of CYAWP (Cover Your A** With Paper).

General Troubleshooting Tips

WHAT CHANGED? THIS is my first question when a problem appears. Something almost always changes. Computer hardware has gotten so reliable that it's rare to find outright physical failures. Disk drives still wear out and power supplies still die, but hardware failure will not be a problem at the top of your list of aggravations.

Chapter 19 • Troubleshooting Your Network

> *I contend that you don't manage a network, you manage network changes.*

I contend that you don't manage a network, you manage network changes. If nothing is changing, there's no troubleshooting to do. When nothing changes, you can focus on the future and try to keep up with your computer trade magazines. When you're adding people and users and software and hardware, there will always be something to fix.

There are, however, occasions where a hardware component does cause your problem, even if it isn't a component failure. How about someone moving a wiring concentrator plug from a UPS to a wall plug? When the power blips and takes your concentrator offline, is that a component failure? Yes, but no. Something changed, and you can't blame that on component failure.

Many network managers have developed a "Top Ten" list of troubleshooting or prevention tips. Rather than stopping at ten, here's all I could find, think of, or steal. Let's start with preventative measures.

Prevention Tips

- Have your management decide on a downtime "comfort level."

The faster you want to resurrect the network, the more money you must spend in preparation. A maximum of a few minutes of downtime can be guaranteed by using NetWare SFT III (System Fault Tolerance, level III) and having backup hardware for every system wiring component. Downtime will stretch to several hours if you have some, but not all, of your replacement equipment available. Downtime will stretch to a day or more if you rely completely on outside resources.

- Have your management decide which users must get back to work first.

In case of a serious network problem, you may be able to support only a few users. Which users will those be?

- Know what you have.

Inventory all your network hardware and software. How else will you buy spare parts and get updated replacement drivers?

- Expect everything and everyone to let you down.

If you expect the worst, you're prepared for anything. You're also pleasantly surprised almost all the time, since the worst rarely happens.

- Anything that can fail, will fail.

Be prepared for any LAN component to fail, be stolen, or be tampered with.

- Know your component failure profiles.

On a server, failures are likely to be (in order): disks, RAM, network adapters, or the power supply. The same applies to a workstation, but only one user is inconvenienced.

- Balance your network to eliminate as many single points of failure as possible.

Many network administrators spread every workgroup across two wiring concentrators, so one failure won't disable an entire department. You can also spread a group's applications across multiple servers, which is easy to do with NetWare 4.

- Spend the money necessary to back up your system every night.

The quickest way to recover from corrupt or lost data files is by using a complete backup made the night before.

- Test your backup and restore software and hardware.

How long does it take to completely restore a volume with your backup hardware and software? You can't bring a replacement hard disk online until the restored files are in place.

- Duplicate system knowledge among the administrative staff.

If a person, even you, is the single point of failure, take precautions. I know you feel you're always there, but do you want to come back from your honeymoon to replace a disk drive? Start some cross-training.

- Your suppliers will let you down sometime, somehow.

Support organizations have problems, too. Don't bet the ranch on your dealer stocking a replacement drive they "always" have. If you must have one without fail, have it on your shelf.

- Find sources of information before you need them.

Check out NetWire on CompuServe, Novell's Web Server on the Internet, and participate in NetWare-oriented bulletin board services and Internet newsgroups. The more you know, and the more places you can go for information in a hurry, the better off you are.

- Document everything far more than you think necessary.

Write down everything about your network, then fill in the blanks. Assume your manager must recover the network while you're on your honeymoon. Will your documentation provide the manager with enough information? If some or all of your documentation is stored electronically, reprint the information after every substantial change and store the paper in a safe location.

- Keep valuable network information in a safe.

Your password, some backup tapes, boot diskettes, software licenses, proof of purchase forms, and a copy of your network documentation should be in a safe, literally. Only network administrators and your manager should have access to this safe.

- Make your network as standardized as possible.

Hardware and software consistency is not the hobgoblin of small minds; it's the savior of the harried administrator. Consistent CONFIG.SYS, AUTOEXEC.BAT, and NET.CFG files make life easier. It may be impossible to keep them consistent, but try. Find a good network adapter card and stick with it. Make as few different MS Windows desktop arrangements as you can.

- Make a detailed recovery plan in case of a partial or complete network disaster and test your recovery plan.

Companies with workable recovery plans stay in business after a disaster. Those with no recovery plans are rarely in business two years after the disaster. But you'll never be sure the plan works until the plan is tried. Do you want to try the plan after office hours in a test, or while the CEO is looking over your shoulder? Test the plan, as well as the people involved in that plan.

- Put step-by-step instructions on the wall above every piece of configurable equipment.

Every server, gateway, or communications box should have a complete operational outline on the wall above the equipment. It must cover all steps necessary for a computer novice to take the system down and/or bring the system back up. Large companies with a night support staff will find this particularly useful.

Tips for Solving Problems

Network problems can be both physical (cable) and virtual (protocols). This makes troubleshooting more fun than normal.

No matter how prepared you are, something will go wrong. It's nothing personal—it's just life. When faced with a problem, the following hints may be of some help.

- What changed?

I said this at the beginning, but it's worth repeating. When there's a problem, 99 percent of the time, somebody changed something somewhere. Scientists have disproved the idea of "bit rot," where software that did work goes sour and mutates into software that doesn't. However, it's common for workstation software to be pushed beyond its capabilities or to be modified by new applications. But that is a change, isn't it?

- When you hear hoofbeats, look for horses before you look for zebras.

Check the simple things first; hoofbeats are more likely to come from horses than from zebras, at least in Texas where I'm writing this. Is the plug in the wall? Is the power on? Is the monitor brightness turned up (I once drove across town in a snowstorm to turn up the brightness on a Unix system monitor). Is this the right cable? Is the cable plugged in on both ends? Is a connection loose? You get the idea—nothing is too simple to verify before going on to the next step.

- Isolate the problem.

Does this problem happen with other machines? With this same user name? Will this system work on another network segment? Will the server talk to another workstation?

- Don't change something that works.

If you change a configuration parameter, and that doesn't fix the problem, change the parameter back to what it was. The same goes for hardware. No use introducing new variables from new hardware or software while you're still trying to find the problem.

Let me say this again: if you change something and it doesn't fix your original problem, change it back. It may look okay now, but you will more often than not mess up more than you fix if you change things all over the place.

- Check your typing.

Typos in the configuration files will cause as much of a problem as the wrong command. Your software won't work well if your path includes \WINCOWS rather than \WINDOWS.

- Read the documentation.

Equipment documentation may not be good enough, but it's better than nothing. Print out the README files from the installation disks and keep the printout with the manuals. It's much easier for manufacturers to put crucial manual modifications in the README file than in the manual.

- Look for patches.

Check NetWire or the Novell Web Server for files to update your troublesome hardware. Call the vendor of third-party products for new drivers for network adapters and drive controllers.

- Refer back to previous trouble logs.

Keep a log of problems and solutions for your network. Even a new problem may be related to an old problem you solved before.

- Trust, but verify, everything a user tells you.

People interpret the same events different ways. What is unnoticed by a user may be a crucial bit of information for you. If a user tells you a screen looks a certain way, take a look for yourself.

- Call your NetWare dealer early in the process.

Buying your NetWare hardware and software from a local dealer gives you the right to call and ask for help. This is especially true during and just after installation. If you have a good relationship with your dealer, the support people should answer specific questions (such as, "Does this network adapter have a different driver when used in the server?") without charge. Be prepared to pay for support if your questions are open-ended ("Why doesn't this server talk to the workstation?") or you request a technician to come and look at your system.

- Check out an NSE Pro (Network Support Encyclopedia, Professional Volume) CD-ROM.

Tons of information is on every disk. Patches, white papers, compatibility reports, and tips of all kinds are there if you look.

- Call Novell technical support.

It's better to spend the money on 1-800-NETWARE than leave your network down a second day. But don't call until you've gone through the documentation, NetWire, and all local support resources. It's embarrassing to find out the solution is in the manual during a paid support call.

- Do things methodically, one by one.

Don't make a "brilliant" leap of deductive reasoning; that's a high risk/high reward procedure. Las Vegas casinos are rich because suckers play long odds. Keep following the plan, and don't try to be a hero.

Learning Your Network's Normal Operation

DO YOU KNOW what your car sounds like when it's working properly? Do you know the beeps and buzzes your computer makes as it boots? Do you know how your body feels as you struggle out of bed?

Of course you do. You know these things from regular repetition. More important, you know that when one of those sounds or feelings is not right, something needs to be checked out.

Your network is the same way. You must learn how it is when it's normal, so you can quickly tell when it isn't normal.

Tracking the Details

Several obvious things help you track the details of your network's normal operation.

Paper, in this case network documentation, is more necessary than you may imagine. You have about two thousand items to remember for every user. If you have lots of users, learn to write down everything, or every day will be a rough day.

An activity log is vital to managing large networks. This doesn't need to be fancy, just consistent. If you do it on paper, you should regularly put it in a database to organize and comment on the results of each action. Having it available on the system makes it easier for other administrators to share.

Help Desk software is becoming inexpensive enough for small- and medium-sized companies. By tracking every support call from users, you maintain a single database with all trouble calls listed, cataloged, and indexed. Most important, this type of software tracks and shares the little, but aggravating, configuration details for many software packages that cause your network problems. If you have more than two network managers, you can benefit from Help Desk software.

Networks are often judged harshly by old mainframers, since a station or printer or two may be unavailable at any one time. To some, especially those that wish to cast aspersions on your network, this will count as "downtime" and be held against you. Don't let them define downtime to fit their terms. In fact, let's define downtime and another type of network time:

- **Downtime:** Time a network service or resource is unavailable to any user.

- **Crosstime:** Time when a service object, such as a printer, is down, but the user has easy options to use comparable services.

If a server is down, but all users can log in through NDS, they are not down. The few users that need access to volumes on the down server do suffer downtime; everyone else suffers crosstime. Routing to another printer in place of your normal printer is not downtime; it's crosstime.

> *Routing to another printer in place of your normal printer is not downtime; it's crosstime.*

You should track the times that resources are down, but you must put this information into context. If you have ten servers, and one server is down for one day, your servers are 90 percent available that day. If that is the only down day in a 30-day month, the monthly total for server availability is 99.67 percent available (299 available server days divided by 300 possible server days). This is very acceptable, even to mainframe bigots.

> **TIP** *If the mainframe people give you too much trouble, ask for their remote-access uptime. It's usually lousy. They'll blame it on the phone lines, but just laugh and walk away.*

Of the 2000 details you must track for users, about 1950 are tied up with their workstations, especially if they run MS Windows. Don't feel bad if you never feel in control of MS Windows on your network. There are no built-in network or management controls, and every software vendor feels free to rewrite every configuration file. Unraveling Christmas tree lights out of the wadded ball you left them in last year is easier than debugging some of these INI files.

Regardless of the hassle factor, some baseline must be made of your workstations, servers, and network in general. You might want to check some of the third-party server management software available, but you can also monitor your network fairly well with the tools NetWare provides.

Tracking Normal Server Performance

It's easy to ignore the server when it's running as it should. You have so many other little problems, such as printers that act strangely and users who behave even more strangely, that you leave the server alone.

Although it is easy not to pay attention to the server, it isn't advisable. You must spend a few minutes now and then checking on the server when it's running well so you'll have some idea what it should look like under normal circumstances. Believe me, when it's down, and you can't figure out why, you'll wish you had a few screenshots and configuration files saved in a notebook on your desk (hint, hint).

The MONITOR Program

MONITOR is your best bet for tracking server performance during the day. Many network managers leave this screen on all the time. Even the snake-like screen saver indicates server activity. The longer and faster the snake gets, the more server activity going on.

Using the MONITOR program, four important performance indicators are easily seen from the General Information screen:

- **Utilization:** Shows how much CPU time is being spent servicing the network. This is half of the network load, with disk activity being the other half. If this number regularly stays over 50% for more than a minute or two at a time, you need more horsepower. It's possible for this number to run over 100%, so don't overreact if you see 103% utilization sometime.

- **Total Cache Buffers:** The lower this number, the slower file performance will be. If less than half of your cache buffers are in the Total category, get more RAM.

- **Current Service Processes:** This number indicates outstanding read requests. When a read request comes in but there is no way to handle it immediately, a service process is created to perform the read ASAP. Too few cache buffers will run this number up. With plenty of RAM but increasing service processes, you need disk channel help. Upgrade the controller or disk, or move high-load applications to another server.

- **Packet Receive Buffers:** These hold packets from workstations until they can be handled by the server. These buffers will be allocated as needed, but a gradually higher number indicates the server isn't keeping up with the load.

Figure 19.1 shows the MONITOR main screen, with the General Information window open to show all statistics. You can press Tab to shrink or expand this window. Shrink it to use the Available Options menu.

FIGURE 19.1

The standard server performance check

```
NetWare 4.10 Console Monitor   4.12              NetWare Loadable Module
Server name: 'ALTOS486' in Directory tree 'GCS_TREE'
Server version: NetWare 4.10 - November 8, 1994

                     ┌──────── General Information ────────┐
                     │ Server up time:             0:02:00:19 │
                     │ Utilization:                       21% │
                     │ Original cache buffers:          7,617 │
                     │ Total cache buffers:             5,693 │
                     │ Dirty cache buffers:                 0 │
                     │ Current disk requests:               0 │
                     │ Packet receive buffers:             50 │
                     │ Directory cache buffers:            33 │
                     │ Maximum service processes:          40 │
                     │ Current service processes:          12 │
                     │ Maximum licensed connections:        5 │
                     │ Current licensed connections:        2 │
                     │ Open files:                         21 │
                     └──────────────────────────────────────┘
                       │ Lock file server console  │
                       │ File open/lock activity   │
                     ▼ │ Cache utilization         │

Tab=Shrink data window    Alt+F10=Exit                         F1=Help
```

> **NOTE**
>
> *There is an interesting note about the screen shown in Figure 19.1. Do you see the Directory Cache Buffers entry, showing 33? After about one minute of uptime, this number increased to 50. Just a bit of server self-tuning information. You can set this parameter using the SERVMAN utility; details are back in Chapter 10.*

The other screen you may leave open in MONITOR is the Cache Utilization Statistics view. You can see the Cache Utilization menu choice at the bottom of Figure 19.1. If the Long Term Cache Hits figure stays above 90%, you have a server well configured for file service.

You should take a few screen snapshots of your server's MONITOR screen now and then. Using RCONSOLE makes this easy (old-timers used to scratch the numbers in stone tablets, since there was no way to capture a server console screen to a printer before RCONSOLE). Make a few of these screenshots for each server now and then, with a notation of the date and time. (See Chapter 10 for information about using RCONSOLE.) Connections and open files are shown at the bottom of the window. Both of these are good load indicators for referencing the server activity.

Server Log Files

Three server log files are created automatically by NetWare, and one more is optional:

- SYS$LOG.ERR contains file server errors and general status information. This log file is stored in the \SYSTEM directory and can be viewed with NetWare Administrator, NETADMIN, or any file viewer.

- VOL$LOG.ERR shows volume errors and status information. This file is stored in the root of each volume and can be viewed with a file viewer.

- TTS$LOG.ERR has information about TTS (Transaction Tracking System). This file is stored in the root of each volume with TTS active and can be viewed with a file viewer.

- CONSOLE.LOG keeps a copy of all console screen messages. It is started by this line in the AUTOEXEC.NCF file: LOAD CONLOG. This log file is stored in the \SYS:ETC directory and can be viewed using INETCFG or with a file viewer.

The SYS$LOG.ERR is normally checked using the NetWare Administrator program, but this viewer can't show a long log file. The beginning of the log file will not be shown, on the assumption that you are more interested in immediate history. If you wish to see the entire log file, use a text viewer.

Figure 19.2 shows the log file for ALTOS486 displayed in NetWare Administrator. The second command button on the right of the dialog box opens this view. Scroll bars are available in horizontal and vertical directions.

Notice that items that are not normally considered errors are tracked in this file. The first entry shows that GATEWAY2000 is unreachable for some reason, but ALTOS486 can't tell why. The second entry shows that

FIGURE 19.2

Errors and server information

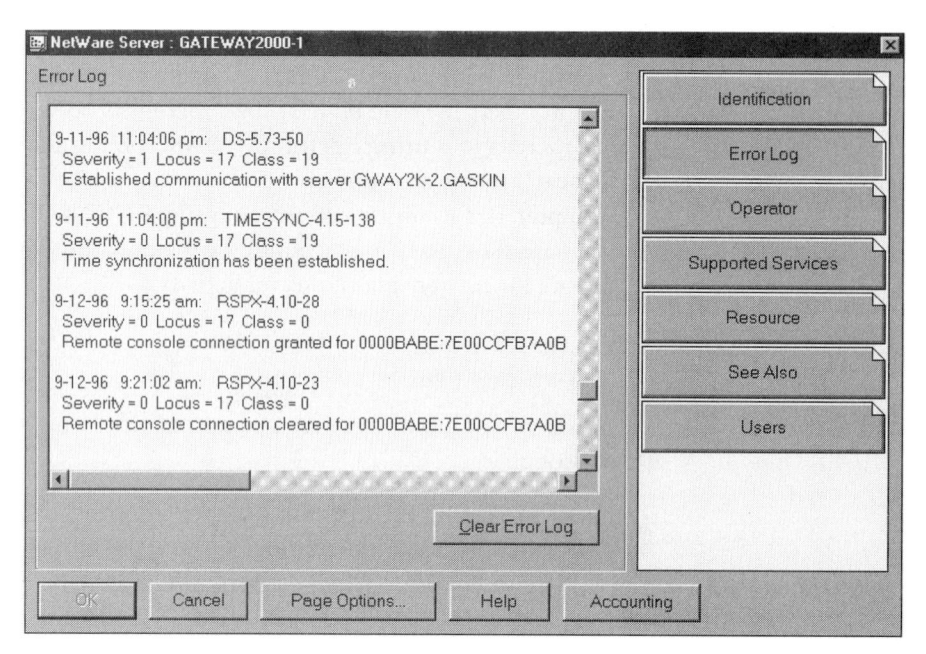

![NetWare Server: GATEWAY2000-1 Error Log window showing:

9-11-96 11:04:06 pm: DS-5.73-50
Severity = 1 Locus = 17 Class = 19
Established communication with server GWAY2K-2.GASKIN

9-11-96 11:04:08 pm: TIMESYNC-4.15-138
Severity = 0 Locus = 17 Class = 19
Time synchronization has been established.

9-12-96 9:15:25 am: RSPX-4.10-28
Severity = 0 Locus = 17 Class = 0
Remote console connection granted for 0000BABE:7E00CCFB7A0B

9-12-96 9:21:02 am: RSPX-4.10-23
Severity = 0 Locus = 17 Class = 0
Remote console connection cleared for 0000BABE:7E00CCFB7A0B]

CLONE386 is now talking to ALTOS486, and the last full entry shows that GATEWAY2000 is on speaking terms as well.

The middle entry acts more like a typical log file notation: a remote console session has been granted for a station at the listed address. If these connections appear from a station you aren't familiar with, check it out. This will either show a security violation, or more likely, that you ran RCONSOLE from a different station than usual.

The volume log, VOL$LOG.ERR, is created automatically and stored in the root of each volume. There are no special ways to reach this log, but you won't need to read it often. Figure 19.3 shows an example volume log in the life of a lab server. It's up, it's down, it's up, it's down, it's up....

You can see there are several errors listed, but all were fixed automatically during the mounting process. Since this is a lab server and subject to harsh treatment, I'm not surprised to see a few errors here and there. Most of your volume log will look like this yo-yo—up, down, up, down. It may stretch over several years, since many volumes stay mounted for months at a time.

FIGURE 19.3

Volume log

```
LIST         73      180       09/24/96 06:25 ♦ VOL$LOG.ERR
Volume SYS dismounted on Sunday, September 1, 1996  11:21:42 am.

Volume SYS mounted on Sunday, September 1, 1996  11:22:20 am.

Volume SYS mounted on Tuesday, September 3, 1996   2:26:29 pm.
Volume mount had the following errors that were fixed:
Problem with file CONSOLE.LOG, length extended.
Problem with file CONSOLE.LOG,  old length = 0, new length = 65536

Volume SYS dismounted on Monday, September 9, 1996   7:53:31 pm.

Volume SYS mounted on Monday, September 9, 1996   7:54:09 pm.

Volume SYS dismounted on Monday, September 9, 1996  10:15:59 pm.

Volume SYS mounted on Monday, September 9, 1996  10:16:34 pm.

Volume SYS dismounted on Monday, September 9, 1996  11:04:34 pm.

Volume SYS mounted on Monday, September 9, 1996  11:05:06 pm.

Volume SYS dismounted on Tuesday, September 10, 1996   6:58:24 am.

Command>                                  Keys: ↑↓→← PgUp PgDn  F10=exit F1=Help
```

The last automatic log file, TTS$LOG.ERR, is activated only on those servers where TTS is enabled. If TTS is started, the log is started. Those servers without TTS enabled will not have the log file.

TTS guarantees transactions are completely finished or completely undone back to the pre-transaction state. The log file lists times and data file names rolled back because of an incomplete transaction. This file won't have much inside it, except a time and date stamp of when TTS was started or shut down. These times will match those in the volume log.

CONSOLE.LOG is a bit different. It keeps a copy of all console messages that normally scroll by quickly as the server boots. Figure 19.4 shows a part of the CONSOLE.LOG file.

This viewer is in the INETCFG utility, loaded at the server console. The steps are:

- Type **LOAD INETCFG** at the console or through RCONSOLE.

- Choose View Configuration.

- Choose Console Messages.

FIGURE 19.4

Console comments in a file

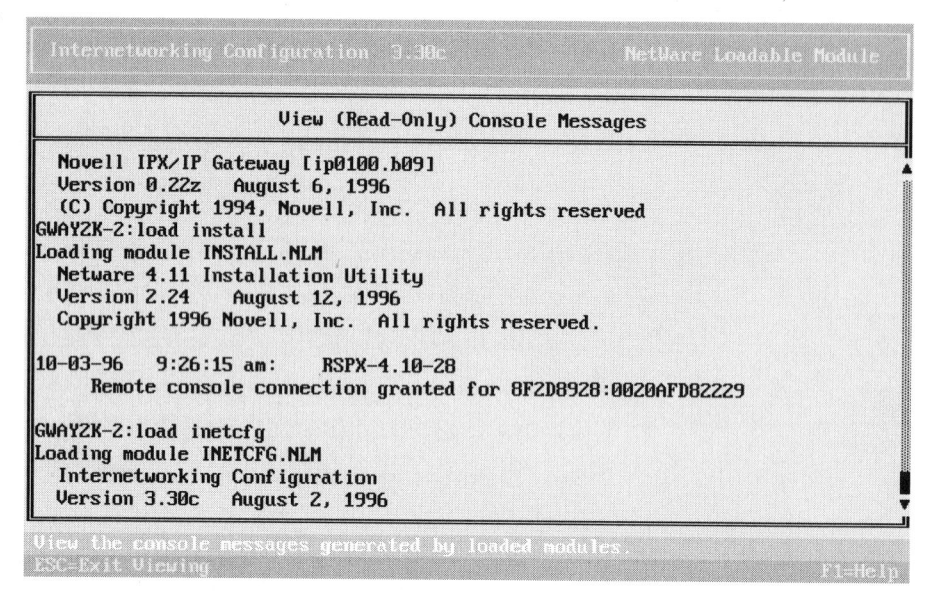

```
Internetworking Configuration  3.30c              NetWare Loadable Module

                    View (Read-Only) Console Messages

  Novell IPX/IP Gateway [ip0100.b09]
  Version 0.22z    August 6, 1996
    (C) Copyright 1994, Novell, Inc.  All rights reserved
 GWAY2K-2:load install
 Loading module INSTALL.NLM
    Netware 4.11 Installation Utility
    Version 2.24    August 12, 1996
    Copyright 1996 Novell, Inc.  All rights reserved.

  10-03-96    9:26:15 am:       RSPX-4.10-28
      Remote console connection granted for 8F2D8928:0020AFD82229

 GWAY2K-2:load inetcfg
 Loading module INETCFG.NLM
    Internetworking Configuration
    Version 3.30c    August 2, 1996

 View the console messages generated by loaded modules
 ESC=Exit Viewing                                              F1=Help
```

As the screen in Figure 19.4 says, the log is shown read-only. You can open the log in the \SYS:ETC directory with a file viewer if you wish. You can also use a text editor to make notes about the log process before you print the log for safekeeping.

Making Configuration File Copies

Printing logs for safekeeping is a good idea. Having a clean server boot record may come in handy someday when you're trying to re-create a load sequence for a long list of NLMs.

The log files we just mentioned are easy to find and print. There are a couple of other quick options, as well. Figure 19.5 shows the option to copy all SET parameters to a file.

The SERVMAN utility offers a chance to copy all parameters to a file every time you leave the Select a Parameter Category menu of the Server Parameters option. When you choose to copy all parameters to a file, the SETCMDS.CP file is copied to the SYS:\SYSTEM directory. That location is the default, but you can change that path. Once the file location is chosen, every SET command is listed with the current setting.

FIGURE 19.5

Take advantage of this offer

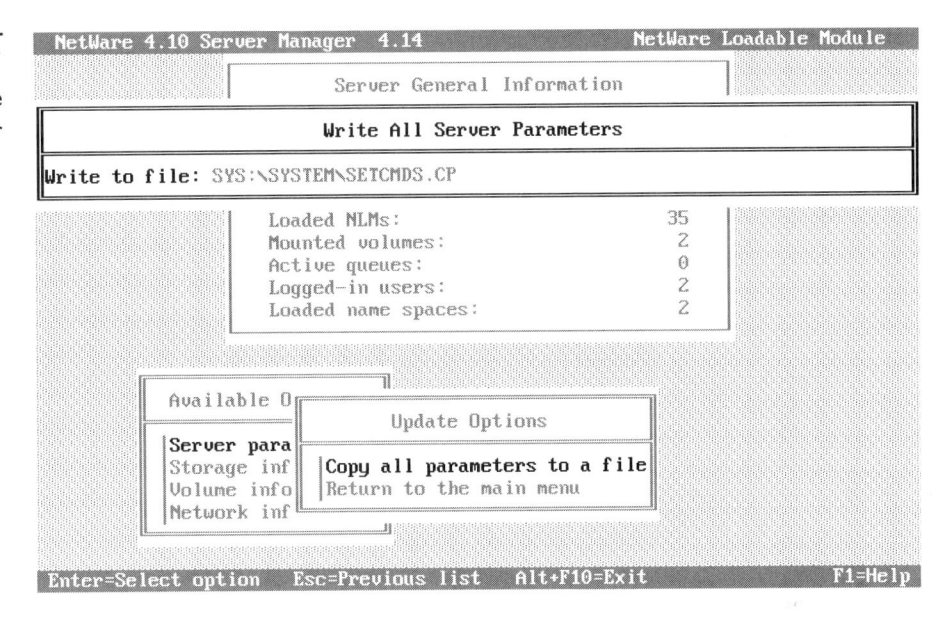

```
NetWare 4.10 Server Manager   4.14                    NetWare Loadable Module
                          Server General Information
                       Write All Server Parameters
 Write to file: SYS:\SYSTEM\SETCMDS.CP

                       Loaded NLMs:          35
                       Mounted volumes:       2
                       Active queues:         0
                       Logged-in users:       2
                       Loaded name spaces:    2


              Available O
                              Update Options
              Server para
              Storage inf  Copy all parameters to a file
              Volume info  Return to the main menu
              Network inf


 Enter=Select option    Esc=Previous list    Alt+F10=Exit          F1=Help
```

There isn't any help information in this file, and the file is over 5 KB of ASCII text, but it's good to have. Some of the SET parameters can be a real problem if they are incorrect. Having a clean copy of the parameters for each of your servers is handy if a problem should arise.

The AUTOEXEC.NCF file is kept in the \SYS:SYSTEM directory. It's easy to find, so you have no excuse not to make a quick printout of it every time it changes. Put it in the server notebook. Keep the old ones, so you can return to a former configuration if necessary.

The easiest way to get a copy of STARTUP.NCF is while the server is down. This file is kept in the \NWSERVER directory of the DOS partition by default. You may have placed it in a different directory during installation, but I asked you not to at the time. So look in \NWSERVER first. If it is there, copy it to floppy disk and print it later. Your alternative is to look at it in the INSTALL program (choose NCF File Options, then Edit STARTUP.NCF File). From there, you can print the screen.

If you have used the INETCFG utility to manage your protocols, the AUTOEXEC.NCF file will have all the protocol statements commented out with the number sign (#). There is a message telling you to check the INITSYS.NCF and NETINFO.CFG files in the \SYS:ETC directory. There is also a warning in the message not to edit those files directly, but to use the INETCFG utility. However, you can certainly print these files and put the printouts in your server notebook.

Tracking Normal Workstation Details

An easy place to check the performance of a workstation is through the MONITOR screen on a server. When you choose Connection Information and press Enter on the user connection name, a screen similar to the one shown in Figure 19.6 will appear.

FIGURE 19.6

A healthy, active workstation connection

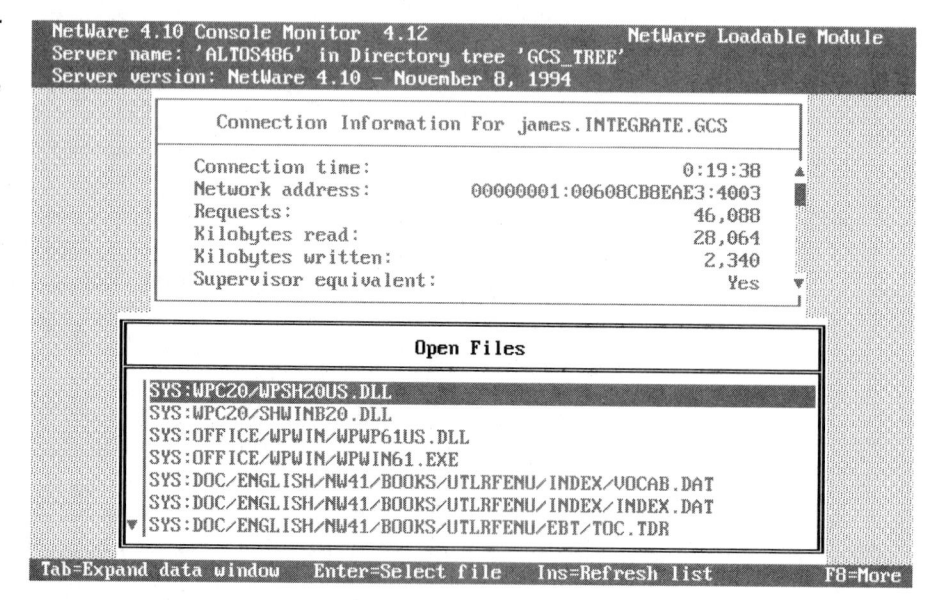

```
NetWare 4.10 Console Monitor   4.12                  NetWare Loadable Module
Server name: 'ALTOS486' in Directory tree 'GCS_TREE'
Server version: NetWare 4.10 - November 8, 1994

              Connection Information For james.INTEGRATE.GCS
              Connection time:                           0:19:38
              Network address:           00000001:00608CB8EAE3:4003
              Requests:                                   46,088
              Kilobytes read:                             28,064
              Kilobytes written:                           2,340
              Supervisor equivalent:                         Yes

                                  Open Files
       SYS:WPC20/WPSH20US.DLL
       SYS:WPC20/SHWINB20.DLL
       SYS:OFFICE/WPWIN/WPWP61US.DLL
       SYS:OFFICE/WPWIN/WPWIN61.EXE
       SYS:DOC/ENGLISH/NW41/BOOKS/UTLRFENU/INDEX/VOCAB.DAT
       SYS:DOC/ENGLISH/NW41/BOOKS/UTLRFENU/INDEX/INDEX.DAT
       SYS:DOC/ENGLISH/NW41/BOOKS/UTLRFENU/EBT/TOC.TDR

Tab=Expand data window    Enter=Select file    Ins=Refresh list       F8=More
```

What does this tell us? Well, first, if you see the user's name on the connection list, the network connection must be in fairly good shape. The connection time is listed, as is the number of requests made from the workstation to the server. The resulting kilobytes read and written are shown, and these three numbers are updated in real time.

The second window shows open files, and again, this number is updated in real time. If you press Enter on a file name, the record lock information window will pop up. If the user stops an application or otherwise closes files, those changes will appear immediately in the window.

Go back to Chapter 5 for details about workstation installation and setup. For this section, we're assuming the workstation did work at one time and has now developed a problem.

During installation of each workstation or shortly thereafter, it's a good idea to make a copy of the three primary configuration files for PC workstations running DOS or Windows 3.1x: AUTOEXEC.BAT, CONFIG.SYS, and NET.CFG. You may want to make a quick batch file that copies these three files to the HOME subdirectory for each user.

Another option is to copy the files to bootable floppies. This makes it easy to connect each station to the server in case of a hard disk failure. For the boot floppies, put the proper adapter driver on the diskette, along with the VLM files. Label each diskette with the workstation identification number. You may need to re-create some of the hard disk directory structure so the AUTOEXEC.BAT file works properly, or you can wait and do it by hand if (or when) the time comes. Do not let the user keep this diskette; bad things will happen to it. Keep a diskette holder for all of these disks in your area.

Yes, these workstation diskettes are just one more thing to keep track of, but they will come in handy. As these diskettes start piling up, your urge to develop and enforce a standard workstation configuration will grow.

The NET.CFG File

The NET.CFG file (installed in the \NWCLIENT directory by default) controls the interaction between the network hardware and software and your DOS, MS Windows, or OS/2 workstation. Installation details should have been taken care of already, but sometimes new network servers or new software packages cause problems.

If you have the same adapter in each workstation, the NET.CFG file may be mass-produced and copied to each station during installation. Remember to check the PREFERRED TREE settings if you have more than one tree. The name context must be tracked, as well as any other modifications you use in your network configuration.

Client32 software running under Windows 95 only rarely uses a NET.CFG file. Client32 software running on a DOS or Windows 3.1x system will still have this file, however.

Protecting Workstations Against MS Windows Program Problems

Windows of any flavor is a royal pain to manage. Configuration files are scattered through at least two (and sometimes more) directories. Mysterious DLL (Dynamic Link Library) files, program code pieces that are used by every

Windows application, are scattered everywhere as well. When you think everything is working fine, something blows up. If you reboot MS Windows less than twice a day, you're doing well.

Moving to Windows 95 hasn't helped as much as I had hoped. The best we can get is rebooting every two days rather than twice a day as with Windows 3.1*x*, but DOS is still the foundation of Windows 95. Windows NT is the only non-DOS dependent operating system available from Microsoft. While the Redmond Rowdies are pushing to make Windows NT the new standard by adding the Windows 95 GUI to a stouter foundation, that has yet to happen. Besides, the inertia of millions upon millions of Windows 3.1*x* system users will drag down networks until the next century.

One handy tip is to keep all the INI, GRP, and DAT files on every Windows 3.1*x* system backed up to a separate directory. On my system, I have a SAVE.BAT file in the \WINDOWS directory. The file contents are:

```
copy c:\windows\*.ini c:\windows\save
copy c:\windows\*.grp c:\windows\save
copy c:\windows\*.dat c:\windows\save
```

Running this before each software installation gives me a fighting chance against some of the poor installation procedures I've seen. The DAT files, especially REG.DAT, help MS Windows keep track of programs that are registered with the MS Windows system. If the REG.DAT file is damaged, you'll have problems. You should have a backup copy.

Running most of the MS Windows program files from the server helps control some of the random catastrophes, but not all of them. Each user will constantly add some little MS Windows program, and you won't know until it destroys something and prevents that user from connecting to the network. Then you'll get that plaintive call, along with the vow that he or she hasn't added anything to the system (and you'll also believe that the cow jumped over the moon).

There's little we can do to stop MS Windows from being changed constantly. All we can do is try to make it easy to recover from whatever weird program clobbered the system this time. Some self-defense tactics include:

- Keep the Windows applications on the server.
- Keep the INI and GRP files on the server whenever possible.
- Remind the users that Windows needs to be rebooted now and then.

> *All we can do is try to make it easy to recover from whatever weird program clobbered the system this time.*

- Provide as complete a set of productivity tools as possible. Having e-mail, group scheduling, word processing, fax software, database, PIM (Personal Information Manager), spreadsheet, and modem utilities available as a shared server resource eliminates 90 percent of the ill-behaved applications that users want to add themselves.

- Make sure the swap file is installed on each local hard disk, not across the network.

A swap file is a technique used by the MS Windows virtual memory system to increase program work space by considering part of the hard disk as just like RAM. The performance is much slower, of course, but at least the programs don't crash for lack of work space.

- Set FILES=30, BUFFERS=30, and FILE HANDLES=80 as a minimum in an MS Windows workstation's CONFIG.SYS file.

Tracking Normal Network Performance

When Network General released their Sniffer products in the late 1980s, I worked for a company that sold them. Every customer I visited had the same question: How busy is my network? At the time, Sniffers cost between $15,000 and $32,000 and came in a Compaq 286 luggable that weighed more than 20 pounds.

People still want to know how busy their network is, but they don't need to spend thousands of dollars unless they want special protocol decoders and intelligent network analyses. If you just want to see how many packets are whizzing through your network, and which stations are generating those packets, software-only traffic monitors are readily available.

Novell makes LANalyzer, an MS Windows-based system that has a long history. The product has a wonderful gas gauge display that shows activity in easily understood formats. It's well worth checking out.

My favorite products of this kind are from Triticom, a small company in Eden Prairie, Minnesota. Products include network monitors that just show traffic levels, named EtherVision, TokenVision, and ArcVision. All these cost less than $500. The company also sells software-only protocol analyzers, the LANdecoder series, for around $1,000. If you have a LANalyzer, you might want to get the DecodesPLUS product, which adds protocol decoding capability to LANalyzer, from Triticom.

The opening screen of EtherVision is shown in Figure 19.7. The highlight is on the Test Cable option, which allows this station to check the cable integrity. (Of course, on an Ethernet 10BaseT network, cable faults are not the problem they are with coax cable, but it's handy to have a quick way to test cables.)

FIGURE 19.7

Software network monitoring ready to go

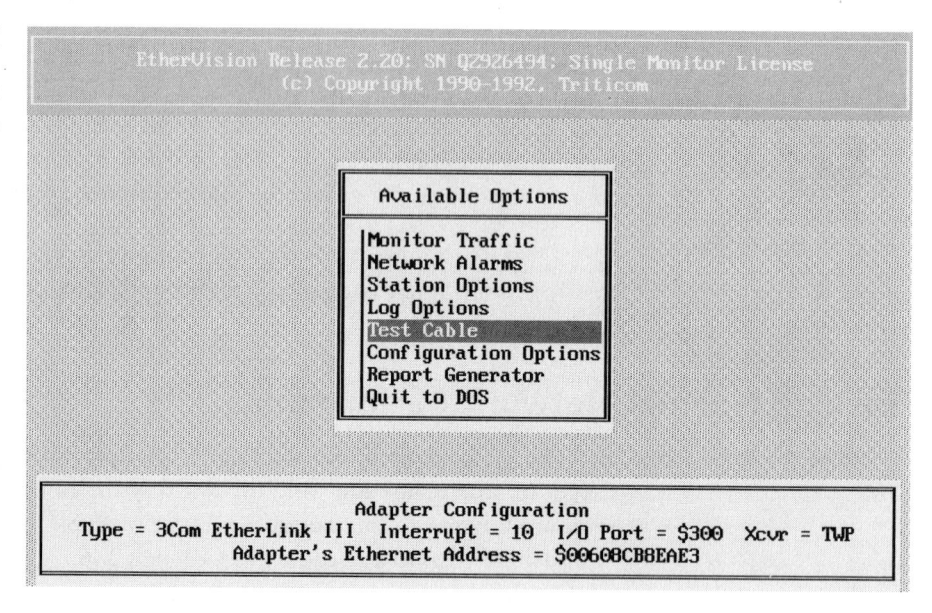

```
EtherVision Release 2.20: SN Q2926494: Single Monitor License
              (c) Copyright 1990-1992, Triticom

                    Available Options
                    Monitor Traffic
                    Network Alarms
                    Station Options
                    Log Options
                    Test Cable
                    Configuration Options
                    Report Generator
                    Quit to DOS

                   Adapter Configuration
  Type = 3Com EtherLink III   Interrupt = 10   I/O Port = $300   Xcvr = TWP
              Adapter's Ethernet Address = $006008CB8EAE3
```

There are two screens of great interest in EtherVision for normal network monitoring. First of all, you want to get some idea of how busy the network is during normal times. Second, you may want to know which workstations are sending packets to which servers.

Figure 19.8 shows the opening traffic monitor screen, with one change made from the default view. Rather than showing the number of packets sent from each address listed, I changed the display to show the percentage of total network traffic generated by each listed computer.

The bottom section of the window shows summary information. It shows that there are five stations generating packets, and there have been 1953 total packets sent in this capture session, totaling just over a megabyte. Of these packets, 22 have been broadcasts. The load is 2 frames per second, with a peak of 253 frames per second, and another peak of 5 broadcast packets in one second. This capture has been going on less than a minute and a half.

Learning Your Network's Normal Operation 1307

FIGURE 19.8

Percentage of total network traffic generated by each node

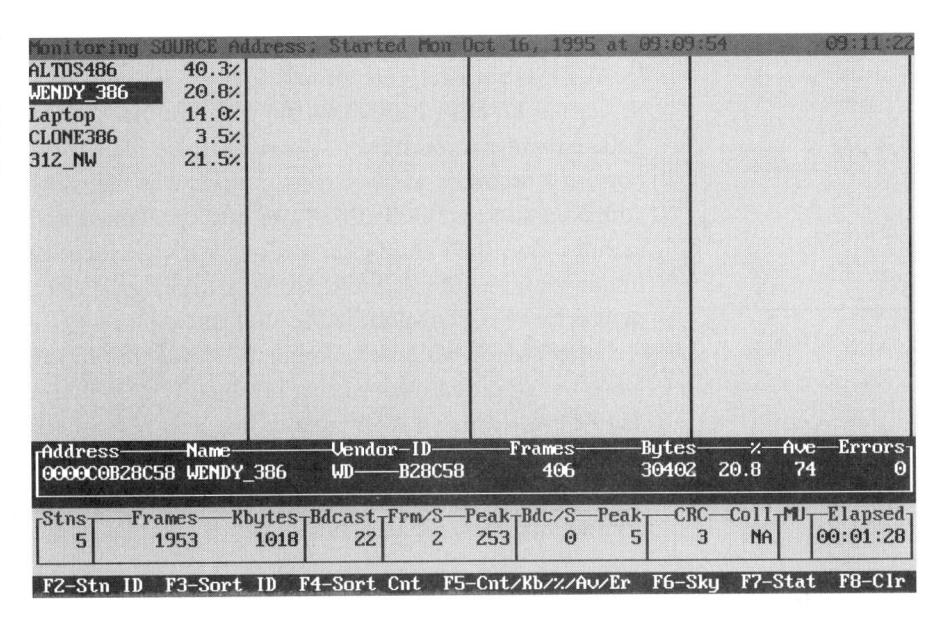

```
Monitoring SOURCE Address: Started Mon Oct 16, 1995 at 09:09:54        09:11:22
ALTOS486    40.3%
WENDY_386   20.8%
Laptop      14.0%
CLONE386     3.5%
312_NW      21.5%




  Address-------Name-------Vendor-ID-------Frames-----Bytes-----%---Ave--Errors
  0000C0B28C58 WENDY_386   WD----B28C58      406      30402    20.8  74     0
 Stns--Frames---Kbytes-Bdcast-Frm/S--Peak-Bdc/S--Peak---CRC---Coll-MU-Elapsed
   5    1953    1018      22     2    253     0     5     3    NA    00:01:28
  F2-Stn ID  F3-Sort ID  F4-Sort Cnt  F5-Cnt/Kb/%/Av/Er  F6-Sky  F7-Stat  F8-Clr
```

Do you know which servers each workstation sends packets to, and how many packets? That information is available with the touch of the Enter key. After highlighting the computer listed as WENDY_386, I pressed Enter. The display shown in Figure 19.9 is the result.

FIGURE 19.9

Who knows where the packets go? EtherVision

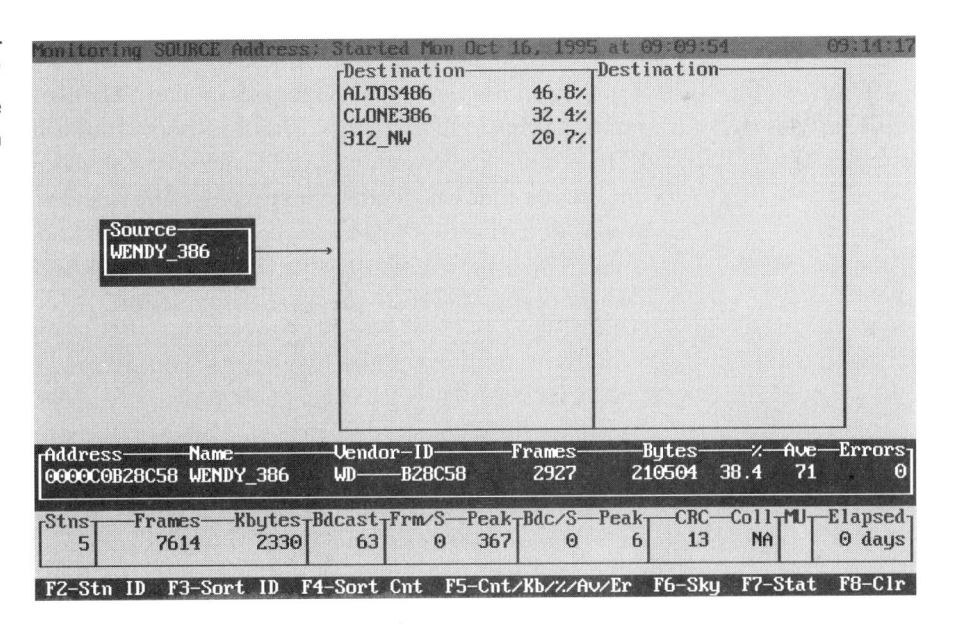

```
Monitoring SOURCE Address: Started Mon Oct 16, 1995 at 09:09:54        09:14:17
                         Destination----     Destination
                         ALTOS486    46.8%
                         CLONE386    32.4%
                         312_NW      20.7%


         Source
         WENDY_386  ──────▶




  Address-------Name-------Vendor-ID-------Frames-----Bytes-----%---Ave--Errors
  0000C0B28C58 WENDY_386   WD----B28C58     2927     210504    38.4  71     0
 Stns--Frames---Kbytes-Bdcast-Frm/S--Peak-Bdc/S--Peak---CRC---Coll-MU-Elapsed
   5    7614    2330      63     0    367     0     6    13    NA    0 days
  F2-Stn ID  F3-Sort ID  F4-Sort Cnt  F5-Cnt/Kb/%/Av/Er  F6-Sky  F7-Stat  F8-Clr
```

The traffic display is clear: 46.8 percent of packets from WENDY_386 go to ALTOS486, 32.4 percent to CLONE386, and the balance to 312_NW. Server GATEWAY2000 is working on another project during this test.

The name for the station is just a display alias for the address shown in the bottom-left corner of the screen. A table translates between hexadecimal addresses such as 0000C0B28C58 and the name I assign. The Vendor ID listing shows the manufacturer along with the identifying part of the address. In our example, 0000C0 is the vendor code for Western Digital adapters, now owned by SMC, continuing the WD tradition.

Other companies make competitive software-only analyzers, including Novell's LANalyzer. Some other products I'm familiar with are Intel's LANDesk and FTP Software's LANWatch. EtherPeek, TokenPeek, and LocalPeek from The AG Group do the same job from a Macintosh platform. Network General still carries the high-end lead banner (a personal feeling, not based on exhaustive testing), but there is plenty of competition in that price range.

Component Failure Profiles

THAT'S AN UGLY phrase, "component failure," but it does happen. Your job as network administrator includes figuring out what will fail when and how to fix it quickly.

Guide to Managing PC Networks by Steve Steinke, with Marianne Goldsmith, Michael Hurwicz, and Charles Koontz (published by Prentice-Hall PTR) is a book about managing PC networks of all kinds. This book includes one section that has details of expected faults in a mythical network. The graphs don't list exact percentages, but I can guess fairly well. What are the causes of network downtime? In order, these are the reasons for downtime and the percentage each item is responsible for:

47%	Cabling or physical infrastructure
20%	Servers
13%	Drivers, network operating system
13%	Improper configuration

3%	Routers
2%	Hubs
2%	Wide-area links

Do you believe these numbers? I would like to see the data behind these statistics, because I would bet cable problems cause more than half of the network downtime. Some studies rate cabling as the cause of 90 percent of network downtime, but those studies are paid for by people who are selling either high-grade cable or physical plant management products. See the section about cabling problems later in this chapter for some tips.

One area this doesn't address is users, since they aren't a component that will fail. However, they will cause plenty of downtime, one way or the other.

Part of the relatively low failure rate for cabling may be explained by the next chart in the book, named "Causes of Cabling Fault Events on a Mythical Network." Once again, here are my estimates of the percentages:

88%	Coax Ethernet
8%	Token Ring
4%	10BaseT Ethernet

These numbers I do believe without question. Anyone who has ever crawled under desk after desk looking for the loose BNC thin Ethernet connector that is causing the network problems is a strong advocate for 10BaseT Ethernet. Fortunately, none of the popular cabling schemes being promoted today are a shared-bus system like coax Ethernet.

On the server itself, the breakdown of breakdowns goes this way:

69%	Disk drives
18%	RAM
11%	Network interface boards
2%	Power supply

This listing makes sense. The two highest failure rates belong to the only moving part (disk drive) and the part most sensitive to overheating (RAM). However, it isn't only heat that will cause RAM to stop a server. The cause can be voltage fluctuations, components running beyond their specifications, or just plain component failure.

Common Workstation Problems and Solutions

YOU WILL HAVE more problems from users running MS Windows than from DOS, Macintosh, Unix, or OS/2 users. But you knew that already, didn't you? Primarily, MS Windows presents the most problems because it's the most popular platform, and also because it must track the most variable hardware and software resources.

> **NOTE**
> *Novell support actually had a disproportionate amount of tech support people dedicated to OS/2 during the rollout of NetWare 4.10. But IBM's fading desktop fortunes have changed that for NetWare 4.11.*

Some problems and solutions are common to all PC workstations. Again, we're assuming a workstation was working, then developed a problem. Questions about installation are covered in the appropriate chapters about that workstation type.

The following sections cover the most common workstation problems and provide some suggestions for solving them.

Workstation Can't Connect to the Server

- Check the workstation cable to the wall.

Many patch cables that run between the workstation and the wall plug have been kicked out of their sockets. Others have been rolled over by a desk chair one too many times.

Check that the plug for the patch cable is plugged into on the wall. My friend Greg Hubbard says all 10BaseT Ethernet cards should have a speaker. That way, when you plug the Ethernet card into a phone plug, you'll hear the dial tone and realize your mistake. (Of course, if your phone still uses RJ-11 jacks, the ones that are smaller than 10BaseT RJ-45 connectors, this won't be a problem.)

Check the link between the wall plug and the wiring closet. Has anyone added cabling anywhere in that part of the building? It's common for new cabling installation to bump and loosen old cabling.

Is the port on your wiring concentrator working? Switch the problem connection with a known good connection into a known good port.

- Check the frame type.

Has the NET.CFG file on the workstation been amended? Is this workstation now trying to reach a new server? The default frame type for Personal NetWare and some early versions of NetWare 4 was not Ethernet 802.3. Since NetWare has used that frame type since the beginning of time, many managers forget to check frame types.

- Verify the login name and password.

Wrong login names or passwords will obviously prevent a user from connecting to the server. If the user can't remember his or her password, change it immediately.

- Check for a locked account.

With intruder detection, stations may be locked out of the network after a configurable number of unsuccessful login attempts. When a user comes to you with a password problem, check to see if the account is locked.

- Verify that all the workstation files were loaded properly.

Error messages go by fast, and sometimes they are missed by users. Changes in the workstation may use some heretofore network memory.

- Make sure the network adapter is seated properly.

Adding a card to one slot often loosens cards in other slots. Remember that a card can look well-seated from outside the case, but actually be disconnected. Patch cables, when tugged on, can loosen network adapters.

- Check any routers, bridges, and hubs.

WAN links are much less reliable than LAN links. If you're trying to reach a remote network service, always assume the WAN link is at fault before changing anything at the workstation.

WAN links take longer, and some workstations may time out before reaching the remote server and getting authenticated properly. Increase the SPX timeout value.

Routers, both local and remote versions, sometimes get flaky on one port or another. Test other connections running through the same router in the same manner. You may need to check the router and reset a port.

Wiring hubs rarely fail, but they sometimes become unplugged. They also are liable to run out of space, and the wiring plan gets reworked on the fly to add another station or two. When this happens, your station my be left out of a concentrator altogether.

- Reboot the workstation.

This can't hurt, and you'll be amazed at what a reboot can fix.

Workstation Can't Use an Application

- Find out what changed at the workstation.

Some new utility may have changed the AUTOEXEC.BAT or CONFIG.SYS file. A new MS Windows application may have modified a necessary INI file.

- Check the user's rights.

Does the user have the trustee rights to run the application? If you assign trustee rights to the directory and not the file, this shouldn't be much of a problem. This is usually a problem with new applications, because few applications handle setting the rights for the users properly. Make sure to check all the application directories created by the installation. It is becoming common to place some directories for the same application on the same level of the directory tree, rather than placing all the directories under one main directory. You may need to grant rights to another directory or two so the user has rights to use some of the application files in the oddly placed directory.

Be careful after upgrading an application. The rights will probably be the same in the existing directories, but a new directory or two is often added during an upgrade. You'll need to grant trustee rights to that directory as well.

- Check the flags.

Most applications should have flags set to Read Only and Shareable. Data files will be marked Shareable and Write, but the application must support multiple-user file access.

Upgraded applications will need to be checked, since new files in the new version will probably not have the proper flags set. Verify your tape-restore procedure, since some vendors don't copy the extended file attributes NetWare uses to set the flags. An application that was Read Only when backed up may become Normal (Read, Write, Erase, and so on) after being restored by tape. If someone then accidentally erases some files, the application won't work.

- Check the user's current directory.

Many users never understand the drive redirection used by NetWare. When you ask where a problem is for them, they'll say, "drive K." Make sure drive K: still points to the same subdirectory. New users are especially vulnerable to changing directories within a drive mapping without realizing what they've done.

- Check the application's need for installing at the volume root.

Some applications demand to be placed in the root directory. Others don't, but have a limit of how deep they can be installed in a directory structure. Some say they can be installed anywhere, but references to other directories are based on indexing from the root of the directory. You will need to use fake root mapping if any of these problems occur.

- Check the DOS environment space.

MS Windows workstations need at least 512 bytes, double the DOS standard of 256 bytes. Users connecting to lots of network resources concurrently may need even more. Check the SHELL command in CONFIG.SYS.

- Does the application need NetBIOS?

Some applications, even on NetWare, still require NetBIOS. Check that out, and load NetBIOS on a test workstation. If NetBIOS is used and has worked before, verify the workstation is loading NetBIOS properly. Workstation changes may have ruined some necessary client files.

If NetBIOS is needed, set up batch files so NetBIOS can be loaded and then unloaded after the application is exited. No use wasting more RAM than you need to for NetBIOS.

- Verify that the application files are not mangled and that the application isn't missing some files.

If an application is corrupted, you must reinstall it. In an MS Windows application, the DLL files may be missing or some users may be picking up old versions of them through poor search mapping.

- Check for file handles and SPX connections.

Database programs in particular often eat lots of file handles. Check the application's documentation in the off chance the writers have done their job and listed this information. Verify that the number of file handles in NET.CFG matches the number in CONFIG.SYS.

- See if the application directory looks empty.

This means that the user doesn't have rights to the directory. Check the rights of the container or group for the user before making a change for one user alone.

Workstation Shows "Not Enough Memory" Errors

- Check to see what has changed.

If a working network client suddenly has too little memory, something has changed. Check drivers and other TSR (terminate-and-stay-resident) programs in the workstation.

Move all network drivers and other TSRs to high memory if possible. With MS DOS, run the MEMMAKER program after all network client files are loaded. Rerun MEMMAKER after every change to the workstation client files.

- Check the DOS environment space.

MS Windows workstations need at least 512 bytes, double the DOS standard of 256 bytes. Users connecting to many network resources concurrently may need even more. Check the SHELL command in CONFIG.SYS.

- Unload sneaky resident programs.

Some applications, such as fax and e-mail programs, sometimes leave little notification programs, or utilities to fax from within your application on workstations. These can take up memory without explaining their presence to the user.

- Modify the VLM load files.

If this workstation doesn't need BIND support, don't load that VLM. You may also go through and select to load just the VLM components needed for your network.

- Beware of the network client software upgrade.

New driver and client files often require more room than the previous versions. You may wish to postpone an upgrade for some users that are critically short of memory. Make a note of those stations in your network logs.

- Beware of new video boards.

Video boards and network interface cards often fight over particular memory location in PCs.

- Beware of new monitors.

High-resolution monitors can force a video board to a higher resolution requiring more memory. Then the upper memory for a network driver won't be available, forcing the driver to load low. Then you have "RAM Cram." Run MEMMAKER after any new hardware or software is added to a workstation.

MS Windows Doesn't Work Right

- Find out what has changed.

Everything in MS Windows affects everything else. Users are constantly adding utilities, screen savers, and wallpaper, all of which can mess up something else.

Sometimes, the user is not at fault. Demo software under MS Windows now often adds DLL files, modifies crucial INI and GRP files, and loads more fonts into the local MS Windows system. Did anyone ask for this? No. Do you need to fix it? Yes.

Believe me, something has always changed in MS Windows. As much as you're tempted, you can't always blame Microsoft for this. Every application vendor has its problems, and some problems aggravate MS Windows more than others.

Get a good uninstall program for MS Windows. Many applications, even when they uninstall themselves, don't clean up behind themselves very well.

Windows 95 is better, as the application guidelines now require an uninstall program. Programmers don't always follow that advice, of course, being programmers. However, what Microsoft giveth, Microsoft taketh. Windows 95 hides what's going on "under the covers" more than Windows 3.1*x* did. Check out *The Expert Guide to Windows 95* by Mark Minasi (from Sybex) for more detailed help than you'll find in the manuals.

- Restart MS Windows daily.

Microsoft has not yet stopped the memory leaks within MS Windows. Applications regularly leave fewer resources available after they unload. MS Windows doesn't need to leak, but careless programming is everywhere. You have the same problems with NLMs on the NetWare server.

About half of the single 64 KB data block feeding DOS underneath MS Windows is used by MS Windows itself. Every application takes a chunk of that remaining data block. This is why the Memory Setting entry in About Program Manager (available from the Help option of the Program Manager screen) can show more than 16 MB available, while applications say no memory is available.

The critical number in MS Windows is for the System Resources value. When MS Windows starts, this value should show above 80%. When it dips below 30%, save your work regularly. At about 8%, printing will stop. Closing and restarting MS Windows reclaims those lost resources.

Check System Resources before and after loading an application for an idea of the application's resource needs. Then check again after the application is unloaded. It's likely that you'll have fewer resources than when you started.

- Check to see if the user has logged in from the wrong workstation.

Shared MS Windows files on the server make great sense and save time for administration, but they are dependent on the right workstation configuration. If a user logs in from a different workstation, details such as the permanent swap file will be different on the different machine.

- Check for new fonts.

Many applications add special fonts to MS Windows. Each font loaded takes memory and slows performance. If your workstations have less than 8 MB of RAM, pare down the fonts. One font family can take enough resources away for an application to have trouble where it didn't have trouble before.

- Don't use wallpaper if memory is critical.

Wallpaper may take just enough memory to cause trouble in RAM-deficient systems. Until you can add more memory or upgrade the workstation, strip out all nonfunctional pieces of MS Windows.

One Aggravating Example

Installation isn't the only problem with MS Windows. Some programs thoughtfully provide uninstall procedures, which I heartily endorse. However, they can get out of hand.

One program deleted the NWCALLS.DLL file from the \WINDOWS\SYSTEM directory. This file, along with NWNET.DLL and NWLOCALE.DLL, determines your MS Windows computer's ability to see NDS. If one of these files is missing, you can't see NDS, which makes the NetWare Administrator program display rather sparse.

What is the solution? Use the NWUNPACK.EXE program in the \CLIENT\DOSWIN directory of the NetWare 4.1 CD-ROM, or the \PUBLIC\CLIENT\DOSWIN directory on the NetWare 4.11 CD-ROM. Or use the same file in the \PUBLIC\CLIENT\DOSWIN directory of your file server if you have the client support files copied to the server under the \PUBLIC directory. Use this command:

```
NWUNPACK NWCALLS.DL_ C:\WINDOWS\SYSTEM
```

Replace NWCALLS.DL_ with the appropriate file if a different one is missing from your directory (the underscore means it's still compressed). The NWUNPACK program is used by the installation routine. It uncompresses the files, placing them where you specify. Run it, and boom, NDS will be visible again.

Printing Problems

- Verify the proper printer or print queue is captured properly.

With NetWare User Tools, it's easy for users to drag-and-drop the wrong printer by accident. Verify the chosen printer is the correct printer. It's best to use a login script to assign the default printers for your network.

- Check the print job configuration.

If you have multiple print job configurations, verify the proper one is still used by the user. This is something else that is easy to change by accident with NetWare User Tools. Under Windows 95, verify these settings through the Printers Control Panel (Properties).

- Check the printer hardware.

Is the printer plugged into the print server? Can other users print to this printer? Is the proper paper and font cartridge (if used) in place?

- Check which page description language was used in the print job.

Sending PostScript output to a non-PostScript printer is a guarantee of problems and the need to reset the printer. Do the users understand the different types of printers they have available and how to send print jobs to those printers?

- Stop the 20-second print screen hangup.

When the Shift-Print Screen key combination is pressed on a network workstation without a local printer, about 20 seconds goes by until DOS gives up on the local printer. Until then, the station appears dead. If this is a problem for some users, add this line to the NET.CFG file:

```
LOCAL PRINTERS=0
```

> **NOTE**
> *There seems to be a problem with the Notification setting for printers under NetWare Administrator. Several times, I have been unable to stop notifications from printers by using the tools in NetWare Administrator. However, PCONSOLE always stops the incessant notifications about a turned-off printer.*

Common Server Problems and Solutions

LET ME SUMMARIZE the NetWare manuals' advice on server problems: add more RAM. The manuals provide quite a bit more help than that, of course, but more RAM is a constant mantra for NetWare servers. I have regularly suggested you add RAM whenever possible, and take this as another polite request. Save yourself the headache; get more RAM.

As servers support more users, more RAM is necessary. As more NLMs are loaded, more RAM is necessary. More disk space means more RAM.

Some applications, such as the NetWare NFS Services, demand a ton of RAM on their own (20 to 24 MB of RAM just for NFS Services). More insidious is the RAM-creep of little programs and utilities that gradually eat your available cache buffers until you reach rock bottom.

Your servers are the core of the network. Server hardware is not a place to save a few pennies. When your boss complains about the cost of quality components in the server, amortize the cost across all potential server users. The more users you expect to support, the less investment per user a quality server will require. And this isn't just sales talk. Your server is an investment in the knowledge-sharing infrastructure necessary to propel your company into the future.

NetWare is a resilient operating system, and server hardware is more reliable today than ever before. Even before you start considering mirrored or duplexed disk drives or a completely fault-tolerant SFT III system, off-the-shelf computer components work faster and longer today than ever before. However, this is of little comfort as you stand before a dead server, with the howling mob at your back. Problems do happen. You must learn to manage these problems before and after they occur.

However, this is of little comfort as you stand before a dead server, with the howling mob at your back.

Server Availability: A Management Decision

Your management decides how available your servers will be. Your job is to maintain service to the agreed-upon level. How available is that?

The quick answer is 7 × 24, meaning seven days a week, and every hour of the day. Do you need this? Think about the answer. When will you do maintenance? Must you keep the system available during tape backup? How will you add a new disk drive to a server?

Guarantee your network will be available normal business hours. If you have no one in the office at 3:00 A.M., why does the network need to be available? Would it be reasonable for your network to be generally available, but with no guarantees, after 7:00 P.M. and before 7:00 A.M.?

Every system needs maintenance. If your network must be up overnight, pick one window of time on the weekends or during an evening for maintenance. Network management demands accessibility to the servers, including taking them down now and then.

> **WARNING**
>
> *If you work in a large company, network-hostile mainframe bigots will track every minute a server is down. They will point to the fact that your network is unavailable more time than the mainframe. Remember, mainframes don't need to shut down to add new disks. I hope your situation isn't this bad, but such hostility happens in some companies. Mainframers are feeling a bit unloved lately (with good reason, perhaps) and will spend a lot of energy to discredit the networks that are replacing them. Be prepared.*

The Hardware Scale and the Costs

Even if your network consists of one server and fifteen users, management personnel must decide how much availability they are willing to pay for. Nothing is certain with computers, but the more guaranteed uptime translates into more cost.

Figure 19.10 is a rough detail of servers, extra components, and enhancements. Going up the hardware scale provides both reliability and performance. Going up the hardware scale also increases costs, as shown in the figure.

FIGURE 19.10
More bang for more bucks

Estimated Costs	Network Servers, Components, and Enhancements
$50,000	Superservers (NetFrame, Tricord)
$20,000	Servers on Steroids (Compaq, HP, Acer, AST, etc.)
$15,000	SFT III with PC Servers
$12,000	RAID Storage Systems
$8,000	PC Server Models (dual-power supplies, more disk drives, EISA or PCI slots, larger RAM capacity, ECC RAM)
$5,000	Add Mirrored or Duplexed Drives
$3,000	Desktop PCs as Dedicated Servers
$1,000	Peer-to-Peer Networks

Any chart showing dollars in the computer business is suspect, since prices generally fall. Those prices that don't fall reliably, such as the cost of memory chips, tend to gradually fall with occasional spikes to weaken the hearts of purchasing managers everywhere. Hard drives are now selling for 50 cents a megabyte. Even more incredible is seeing gigabyte drives in the video game store for any price, much less prices that were science fiction only a few years ago.

The ascending hardware listing is explained this way:

- **Peer-to-peer networks:** Low cost, low numbers of users supported comfortably. This is the wrong book for you if you want information about peer-to-peer networks, but they are inexpensive.

- **Desktop PCs as dedicated servers:** Common choice for low-end servers. Desktop PCs don't have as much space for hard disks or RAM. Power supplies are sometimes inadequate for multiple disk drives.

- **Add mirrored or duplexed drives:** Disk mirroring (two drives, one controller) and disk duplexing (two drives, two controllers) improve performance and provide protection against a single disk failure stopping your server. With the dropping cost of hard drives, it's hard to justify trusting your network to a disk drive as a single point of failure.

- **PC Server models:** Extra space for drives, more RAM, and beefier power supplies help these systems look and act more like servers. Always in a tower case, these systems look more expensive and rugged, making management happier with the investment.

- **RAID storage systems:** RAID (redundant array of independent disks) systems go farther to eliminate the disk as a point of failure and add performance. These systems are often able to swap hard drives while the server is running, eliminating downtime due to a bad disk.

- **SFT III with PC Servers:** Using SFT III and two stout servers practically guarantees continuous uptime and protection from a single point of failure anywhere in the server room.

- **Servers on steroids:** Companies such as Compaq, HP, Acer, and AST (among others) are filling the gap between PC Servers and superservers. Diagnostic software and hardware offer a level of control and management unattainable with regular PC servers. Many of these systems now offer multiple processors, boosting horsepower even higher if your software is able to use the extra CPUs.

- **Superservers:** NetFrame and Tricord stake out the highest end, with servers built more like mini-mainframes than PCs. These servers use high-speed internal buses and better memory, management, and diagnostics, beyond even those servers on steroids. These systems provide the ultimate server available today, at the ultimate price.

The further up the scale you go, the more money you must invest in your network. This extra investment buys peace of mind and better performance. The decision on the proper amount of investment for your network must be made by management. See if you can find a subtle way to remind the people making the decisions that you can't get a Rolls Royce for a go-cart price.

Operating System and RAM Problems

The following are typical operating system and RAM problems and some solutions to try.

- Abend messages

An abend (ABnormal END) is a system shut down due to an internal error of some sort. The best course of action after an abend is to write down the abend error message number, and look it up in the System Messages section of the DynaText documentation. Reboot the server, then check for sufficient RAM. Verify current versions of NLMs and drivers. If new hardware or software has been added, restart the server without the new component as a test. If all else fails, you may need to reload the operating system, but that doesn't happen often.

- Users can't see server.

Check the frame type in use. Multiple frame types are easily supported, but both clients and servers must use a common frame type in order to communicate.

Check the LOAD and BIND statements to make sure nothing has changed. Some third-party utilities may un-BIND or un-LOAD drivers during installation or by accident. Driver errors may also cause a network interface card to disconnect.

- Server can't see users or other servers.

Again, check the frame type in use. Also check the LOAD and BIND statements. Check that SAP (Service Advertising Protocol) is active and not disabled.

Verify network numbering of internal and external network numbers for the server. Driver errors may also cause a network interface card to disconnect.

- Server goes up and down for no reason.

Check the power supply. This fails more often in a server than you might think. If your server UPS isn't doing the job, low voltage may cause the power supply to reset the computer motherboard. You should have a dedicated circuit for all your server equipment. Also, keep the cleaning crew from using AC plugs in the server area. I once saw a cleaning crew unplug servers to power the vacuum cleaners.

> *I once saw a cleaning crew unplug servers to power the vacuum cleaners.*

Freeing Server Memory Temporarily

As I've said many times before, the main thing to do when you're low on RAM is to buy more RAM quickly. Here are some suggestions for freeing some server memory temporarily (until you can add more memory to the server):

- Type **REMOVE DOS** or **SECURE CONSOLE** to release the DOS memory in the server for file cache.

- Forcibly purge files with FILER or NetWare Administrator to free the directory entry table space.

- Unload NLM programs that are not needed, such as MONITOR (often left up).

- Dismount volumes that are not being used (this suggestion is straight from the manual, as if you have extra disks hanging off your server that no one needs).

- Turn off block suballocation and specify a 64 KB block size on volumes. This requires the volume to be reinitialized, meaning all data on the volume must be backed up and restored. This measure saves RAM but is a lot of trouble, takes the server off line for quite a while, and runs a slight risk of losing data. However, you might try it if you need to add a new volume with the smallest RAM impact possible. This method does use quite a bit more disk space, especially if you turn off file compression to save that RAM as well.

- Move volumes from this server to a different server with more RAM.

Disk Errors

For volume dismounts and other disk problems, try the following:

- If you have an external disk subsystem, verify the power is on and the cables are still connected.

- Check for error messages on the console. Ordinary disk errors will force a volume to dismount.

- Verify settings for the controller and driver combination.

- Check for increased numbers of Hot Fix redirection areas used. Increasing Hot Fix numbers generally indicate your disk is dying and should be replaced. The manual offers instructions on increasing the Hot Fix redirection area; I say dump the drive or at least reformat it and start all over.

- Run VREPAIR on the volume. This loads from the console, and if your SYS volume is having a problem, you will need to reference the file on the DOS partition or the floppy. Run VREPAIR at least twice each time you use it.

- Load INSTALL and choose Disk Options, then Perform Surface Test, then the drive to check. You should try to run the nondestructive test first, but be aware that this takes hours and your server will be unavailable this entire time. If a bad block is found, the disk test will shut down. Your last option before throwing the disk away is to reformat the disk and restore the software. You do have a current backup, right?

Running out of disk space is a problem you don't want to have. Don't let this sneak up on you. If it happens to your SYS volume, the server usually shuts down. Even if it isn't your SYS volume, it still causes extra work and other hassles.

Check your volume space regularly. To produce a quick report on your current volume, use the command:

```
NDIR /VOL
```

This replaces the VOLINFO command from NetWare 3.*x*. Figure 19.11 shows the command and result for the ALTOS486 SYS volume.

FIGURE 19.11

Good space left, good compression

```
[Novell DOS] H:\LAPTOP>ndir /vol
Statistics for fixed volume ALTOS486/SYS:
Space statistics are in KB (1024 bytes).

Total volume space:                           483,488   100.00%
Space used by 9,449 entries:                  211,424    43.73%
Deleted space not yet purgeable:                  224     0.05%
                                              -------  -------
Space remaining on volume:                    272,064    56.27%
Space available to laptop.INTE...:            272,064    56.27%

Maximum directory entries:                     37,120
Available directory entries:                   15,508    41.78%

Space used if files were not compressed:      429,173
Space used by compressed files:               119,840
                                              -------
Space saved by compressing files:             309,333    72.08%

Uncompressed space used:                       91,584

Name spaces loaded: MAC

[Novell DOS] H:\LAPTOP>
```

When space becomes a serious concern, type **PURGE** for each volume. If the command-line PURGE doesn't clear enough space, use FILER or NetWare Administrator to purge the deleted files still taking up directory entry table space. Change the Minimum File Delete Wait Time SET parameter to 0 so that files can be purged immediately. This stops them from being kept whole and salvageable on the volume. You can also start deleting files, or moving them to another volume or server.

Cabling Problems

AS MENTIONED EARLIER in this chapter, cabling causes lots of network problems. Vendors of new cable will describe real horror stories of old cable and the problems it caused. Introduce those vendors to your boss.

As was also mentioned earlier in this chapter, coax Ethernet causes more than 20 times the number of network outages than are caused by 10BaseT Ethernet. Log your time spent chasing cable problems for two weeks, and

> **For Coax Ethernet or ARCnet Users**
>
> If you have coax Ethernet, or worse, ARCnet, you no doubt turned to this troubleshooting chapter quickly. Let me tell you what you may or may not want to hear: upgrade. Dump the old stuff and get into the 1990s.
>
> You have been told this several times before. You know this is necessary every time you crawl under a desk to check a BNC connector. You know coax ages, gets brittle, and breaks time after time. You just need to convince your management.
>
> Put the boss's secretary on the worst coax leg of your network. This isn't dishonest, but it is in your self interest. Every time you go up to the executive area to fix the network (again and again), be sure you know how much it will cost to replace the coax Ethernet with 10BaseT Ethernet.
>
> Per-port cost of 10BaseT concentrators is $30 or less for plain vanilla products. There are several product options at this price; ask your NetWare dealer. Micro transceivers that will convert the AUI (Attachment Unit Interface) 15-pin plug to 10BaseT wiring cost $30 or less each as well. If you have any volume to speak of, you should be able to convert each coax user for about $50. Remember that number when you're crawling under the secretary's desk, and repeat it to the boss when you emerge.

then figure out the cost of those problems in your time alone. This is especially effective if your company is faced with a need to hire more network technicians. Replacing the cable will probably keep down your head count.

The first step when your network is having problems is to check all cables to make sure they are plugged in. Don't laugh. Cables that aren't plugged in never work. Here are some other suggestions for avoiding cable problems:

- Find a cable contractor you like, and stick with that contractor. Cabling consistency counts for a lot. If you find a cabling contractor that does good work, tests the cables with digital equipment, and offers a good warranty, you're lucky. Don't switch contractors for a few cents per foot.

- Buy quality cable. Cheap cable is good for telephones, but not for data networks. High-speed systems in development now will push quality cable, and will quickly overload cable not up to par. Buy the best cable (Level 5) now, and you're covered for the foreseeable future.

- Declare a truce with any hostile telecom folks in your company. Some companies have telecom and datacom departments that are openly hostile. If your company is that way, I'm sorry. Go to management and request a meeting with all parties involved. If you can get over your differences, you will find that the telecom folks can be a great help.

- Verify cable distances, especially on new runs. All UTP (unshielded-twisted pair) cable networks have a length limit, usually 100 meters (300 feet plus a little). Going slightly beyond that limit will cause random problems. Going far beyond that limit will stop the connection entirely. There are third-party products that extend the cabling distance over UTP. Buy one of those, or just add a powered wiring concentrator to help cover the extra distance.

- Take care to avoid interference for your cable runs. Strong interference will blitz your cable and disrupt your network. Did you ever hear stories about networks that always went down at dusk? The cable was routed by a light switch. When that light was turned on, the cable interference overloaded the network and blocked all the packets.

- Provide UPS systems for all powered wiring components. In a blackout, your server and your desktop machine will likely continue on battery power. But if the wiring concentrator is powerless, how will you connect to the server from your workstation?

Tell Your Boss: Prior Planning Prevents Poor Performance

EVERY DECISION MADE during the design and implementation of your network impacts the performance and reliability of that network. Some of these choices are easy to evaluate: a fast Pentium-based server will perform better than a low-end 486 system. Other design choice ramifications don't appear until something has blown up, taking your network and peace of mind with it.

Keep in mind crosstime (as opposed to downtime) and explain the idea to your management. The option to support network clients through alternative servers and other resources is a sign of network flexibility, not fallibility.

Building fault-tolerance for your network is more work and more money. It's also the only way to guard against downtime. Mirrored or duplexed disk drives are a quick, easy example. If one drive dies, the other one keeps going without missing a beat. Try that in a server with a single disk.

What can your boss do to help the troubleshooting process? Provide money for training (you and your users). Provide network analysis and management tools. Provide spare parts.

The best your boss can provide is a reasonable atmosphere. High expectations are met with high resources. Low resources lead to low results. Your management must make the decision on how important the network is, and then provide resources accordingly.

In a typical company, management will try to force high expectations from low resources. That's possible for a time, especially if you're smart and work hard. However, one day the lack of spare parts and support tools will catch up to you. Your network will be down for at least one day. Your boss will try to blame you. Don't let that happen; point to the empty shelf labeled spare parts. Keeping a copy of your rejected proposals for network upgrades won't hurt, either.

Appendices and Glossary

Upgrading, Migrating, and Windows 95 Client Installation Support

APPENDIX A

MANY OF THE buyers of NetWare 4.11 will be current NetWare customers. That has been the case with previous NetWare upgrades, and it will be the case in the future. Once you're a NetWare customer, you tend to remain a NetWare customer (much to Microsoft's, IBM's, and Banyan's chagrin).

Being a NetWare customer doesn't mean you automatically upgrade with every NetWare release. This causes Novell engineers some problems, because they must support users back on NetWare 2.*x*, as well as those running NetWare 4.10. This wide range of supported NetWare versions has created several upgrade options, which are the subject of this appendix.

Options for Upgrading Your Server

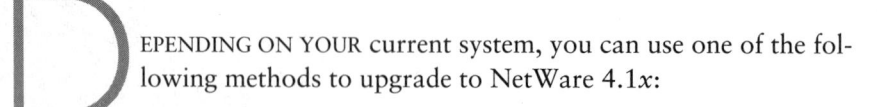

DEPENDING ON YOUR current system, you can use one of the following methods to upgrade to NetWare 4.1*x*:

- **The NetWare 4.1 Installation program:** The INSTALL.NLM program offers an easy way to upgrade your NetWare 3.1*x* or NetWare 4.0*x* server to NetWare 4.1*x*. With this option, there is little difference between upgrading and installing a new server.

- **Across-the-Wire migration:** The MIGRATE utility, running on a DOS client workstation, copies bindery information and server data between the NetWare 2.1*x*, NetWare 2.2, or NetWare 3.1*x* server to the new NetWare 4.1*x* server. The data on the older NetWare server is only copied; not changed. Bindery entries are migrated to NDS objects. For NetWare 3.*x* systems moving up to NetWare 4.11, you can use the File Migrate option in NetWare Administrator and the DS Migrate utility.

- **Same-Server migration:** The MIGRATE utility (or the File Migrate option and the DS Migrate utility for NetWare 3.x to 4.11 upgrades) again helps to convert bindery information from the earlier NetWare version to NetWare 4.1x. Data on the server is deleted and must be restored from a backup device.

- **In-Place Upgrade:** In a two-step process, the 2XUPGRDE.NLM utility maintains the server data while reformatting NetWare 2.1x or NetWare 2.2 disk partitions. When that process is finished, the resulting NetWare 3.1x server and partition are ready to upgrade to NetWare 4.1x using the NetWare 4.1 Installation program.

Let me say this for the first of many times: no matter how you upgrade your server, make at least two (2) copies of all data that will be migrated. Any information of value on the earlier version of NetWare that you wish to use under NetWare 4.1x should be backed up to tape or rewritable optical disks. Doing both would be an excellent safety measure.

Am I paranoid? Yes, always, especially about server disk operations. You should make a backup before doing any operation that affects a server disk. Converting to a new version of NetWare is no different: back up or be sorry. That's such a good line, let's say it again: back up or be sorry.

Okay, back to your options for upgrading. Which of these routes makes the most sense for your situation? Let's see if we can figure out a nice matrix that gives upgraders some guidance.

Let's label the matrix From NetWare Version, Hardware (same or different), and Recommendation.

FROM NETWARE VERSION	HARDWARE (SAME OR DIFFERENT)	RECOMMENDATION
NetWare 2.x	Same (are you sure?)*	In-Place upgrade Same-Server migration
	Different	Across-the-Wire migration
NetWare 3.x	Same (are you sure?)*	Same-Server migration
	Different	Across-the-Wire migration
NetWare 4.0x	Same	NetWare 4.1 Installation program

	Different	Across-the-Wire migration
Another network operating system	Same or Different	Across-the-Wire migration Same-Server migration

*Are you sure that you want to use the same hardware? See the section "Before You Upgrade Your Server, Think Again" for cautions.

Remember, there are two pieces to your upgrade: the bindery information (in the case of NetWare 2.*x* and NetWare 3.*x*) and the data on the server. The NDS modules are upgraded by the NetWare 4.0*x* to NetWare 4.1 Installation program.

Before You Upgrade Your Server, Think Again

I want to make a distinction between upgrading your network operating system to NetWare 4.1*x* and upgrading your existing physical server to NetWare 4.1*x*. The first is usually a good idea; the second is often not.

When you bought your old server, say the server now running NetWare 3.11, you bought the best hardware you could afford. If you're lucky, and price wasn't an option, you got a serious server with lots of RAM, a big hard disk, and as fast a processor as possible (486/50 was a popular model at the time). The serious server likely had an EISA (Extended Industry Standard Adapter) bus, or perhaps it was an IBM model using a MicroChannel bus. Today, unfortunately, this setup hardly makes a good workstation.

Look what has happened to each of your server's features:

- **RAM:** 16 MB used to be plenty for a server, now that amount is barely adequate for a workstation running anything more powerful than Windows 3.1*x*. Retail PCs often come with 32 MB of RAM; your server should start there and increase RAM quickly.

- **Hard disk:** 1 GB was a big disk for early NetWare 3.*x*. Today, PCs bought at office supply stores and WalMart have 1 GB (and larger) hard disks.

- **Hard disk controller:** SCSI (Small Computer Systems Interface) controllers were the rage as NetWare 3.*x* became popular. Today, SCSI-2 and Fast and Wide SCSI multiply the throughput of your SCSI adapter. EIDE (Enhanced IDE) drives and controllers have broken the 512 MB disk-size barrier and offer great speed and throughput.

- **486 processor:** NetWare 3.x ran well on a 486, even on a processor slower than 50 MHz. However, the number of NLMs has grown, and more pressure is put on the server processor than ever before. Your power users would be insulted to get a new PC with "only" a 486 processor. A medium to fast Pentium processor is necessary for any server supporting more than a workgroup. Pentium Pro servers are priced attractively enough now to warrant serious consideration.

- **EISA or MicroChannel bus:** MicroChannel has been officially stopped by IBM; no other vendors seriously supported it. EISA is still going strong, although low-cost servers often have only ISA slots. PCI (Peripheral Component Interconnect) bus slots and corresponding adapters are strong entrants into the server bus race, and provide the throughput necessary for the 100 Mb Ethernet adapters becoming more and more popular.

- **CD-ROM drive:** Does your old server have a CD-ROM drive? Bet it doesn't.

What does all this mean? Your old server is underpowered today. Upgrading the server would probably take too much money, especially if your motherboard doesn't support high-capacity RAM modules. Your old disk controller is outdated, so just getting a bigger disk won't help enough. Besides, new servers are becoming more affordable as disk prices plummet and the cost of Pentium processors are forced lower by their new processor competitors.

Face it, your old server needs to be retired.

Of course, you must read this with your particular situation in mind. If you have a 486/50 with 16 MB RAM, 500 MB hard disk and an ISA network adapter supporting 20 nonpower users, your server has some life left. That configuration is still adequate for a workgroup server.

But if this same server is expected to support 100 users or several extra NLM programs, such as network management utilities or databases, you will be disappointed. Your boss will be even more disappointed, because people will complain. If this matches your situation more than the one described in the previous paragraph, you do need to kiss your old server good-bye.

What can you do with it? If your server is the same configuration (or close) as the example, it will work fine as a workstation. Any of your users would be happy to get this system, since at least a few of them are still running MS Windows on a 386 PC.

If your server has a ton of RAM (more than 32 MB), try and spread that RAM around. Similar systems in your organization, bought about the same time as your server, will be able to use that RAM to move from 4 MB up to a minimum of 8 MB or better yet, 16 MB. With Windows 95, every PC workstation needs a practical minimum of 16 MB of RAM. Oh, you say, that isn't what the literature says? What a surprise—"enthusiastic" marketing literature. Windows NT Workstation demands even more RAM.

How Data Migrates

The first thing to do before migrating your data from an old server to a nice, new NetWare 4.11 server is to back up your data. Then back up that same data again, preferably with a different type of device so any errors in your hardware or software won't mess up two backups. If you do two backups with the same hardware and software, you will reproduce any error made during the first backup in the second backup.

Of course, if you are migrating to new server hardware, you'll have less fear and paranoia about your backup. If both the old and the new replacement server are up and running, any migration glitch is merely inconvenient rather than catastrophic. But even in the two-server scenario, you aren't absolved from the need to back up the original server. (Remember, back up or be sorry.)

Before any data-file migration, there are some things you must do in preparation for the big move:

- Delete unneeded files. No sense in taking old worthless files to your nice, new server. If you wish to consolidate some directories, the time to do so is before the migration.

- Pare down any long directory names to the 8.3 DOS format. NetWare 2.*x* allowed 14-character directory and file names, but those longer names are not supported in NetWare 4.11. If you have any long directory names, change them before the migration. Macintosh and OS/2 long file names are supported under the proper name space volumes in NetWare 4.11.

- Make sure no directory structures are deeper than 25 levels. Deep directory structures are not my favorites anyway, but the migration utilities are limited to 25 directory levels. If you have directory structures deeper than 25 levels, change them before the migration.

- Run BINDFIX before migrating. BINDFIX will clean up the trustee rights and mail subdirectories of deleted users.

Options for Upgrading Your Server 1337

The migration utility allows you to choose which volumes to migrate. You can migrate all volumes or different volumes to different NetWare 4.11 servers. You may wish to move files on one NetWare 2.*x* or 3.*x* server to several different NetWare 4.11 servers. Any upgrade or other change is a good time to reorganize your network.

Use the MIGRATE utility to move from NetWare 2.*x* or 3.*x* servers, or from other network operating systems. NetWare 4.11 provides the File Migrate option in NetWare Administrator, and you should use this option for NetWare 3.*x* systems moving up to NetWare 4.11, because you're more likely to use the DS Migrate utitility to model your NDS structure.

DS Migrate is a new utility, based on the Preferred Systems DS Standard management product, that helps organize NetWare 3.*x* bindery information into NDS format before migration. Part of the NetWare Administrator management program, DS Migrate runs from the Tools menu. A Windows 95 management station is required when using DS Migrate. A separate File Migrate option resides on the same menu list, and the pair of utilities work better than the single-step MIGRATE utility.

Migration is primarily a euphemism for backup and restore, as far as the data files go. Most upgrade choices require you to rework the hard disk when you're staying on the same physical server. Even if the migration utility doesn't require you to repartition the hard disk, NetWare 4.11 wants a larger DOS partition than earlier NetWare versions. This alone may force you to rework your hard disk when the migration utility doesn't. This is why I recommend that you clean up the old volumes and back them all up twice, no matter what your migration plan is.

How Passwords Migrate

Surprise: Passwords don't migrate from NetWare version 3.*x* and earlier to NetWare 4.11. Novell says this is because anyone tapping the wire could see the unencrypted passwords during the upgrade, so this is a security measure. More likely, it's a security measure to make everyone come up with a new password on the new system, in the hopes that the new password will be more secure than the old one. If you're moving from NetWare 4.0*x* to NetWare 4.11, your passwords will be okay. Otherwise, all the users must reset their passwords.

The migration process will, depending on your instructions, provide (or not) for passwords during the migration. A list of the passwords will be written to the ASCII file NEW.PWD on the upgraded system. Your choices for password assignments on the new system are:

- No passwords. No passwords are required the first time each user logs in. However, the users must provide a password during the first login (if their accounts require them to use a password, which is definitely a good idea).

- Assign users a random but unique password. All users except SUPERVISOR are assigned a system-generated password. These passwords are stored in the NEW.PWD file. The network administrator must provide the passwords to the users before they can log in to the system. Users may continue with this assigned password or change it whenever they wish (if you have granted them the authority to change their passwords).

- All users receive the same password. The same password is assigned to all the new system users who had a password on the old system. The password is stored in the NEW.PWD file, and must be provided to each user before he or she can log in to the new system.

How File Attributes Migrate

The advantage of using the migration utility with NetWare-approved backup systems is the retention of all NetWare file attributes. If a file on a NetWare 3.x server is marked as Read Only and Shareable, it will transfer to the new system as Read Only and Shareable.

There are several new file attributes to consider: compression and migration attributes. The migration attribute does not concern the migration from one NetWare version to another, but the migration from the server hard disk to an offline data storage facility.

After your run the migration utility, you must manually go through the files and directories on the NetWare 4.11 system and set any compression attributes. Don't trust the migration utility to properly set the compression attributes on the new files. Manually check each volume and directory after migration to ensure the attributes are set the way you want them to be.

Upgrading Bindery Information

Since NetWare 3.x servers have become the workhorse for most corporate networks, migrating the bindery information is critical. It's one thing to re-create the security profile for a dozen users after a migration, but quite another to recreate thousands of security profiles.

The two largest areas of concern are the trustee rights and login scripts. Much of the work will be done for you by the migration utility, but you will (again) be forced to verify that the rights have been transferred properly.

Login scripts will require a bit more work. The user login scripts are transferred in two steps: the NetWare 3.x user login scripts are copied to the new NetWare 4.11 server in two files: UIMPORT.CTL and UIMPORT.DAT.

After the migration, use the UIMPORT utility on the NetWare 4.11 server to transfer the bindery information into NDS in NetWare 4.11. (The UIMPORT utility is described in Chapter 10.)

System login scripts are not migrated. These have been replaced in NetWare 4.11 by Container login scripts. Since there may be several Container login scripts on every NetWare 4.11 server, the earlier System login script has no direct correlation in NetWare 4.11.

User login scripts are transferred, but no corrections are made. The new names of servers and the changed directory structure will not be reflected in the transferred login scripts. You must manually make these changes in all login scripts.

Special care should be given to directory paths in the new system. The volume names are probably the same in the NetWare 4.11 server as the older NetWare server in a one-to-one server upgrade. However, many companies use the upgrade as a chance to combine several older servers onto one new server or change the location of files and directories to reflect their new network design. In these cases, volumes will have new names and/or servers. These changes must be made in the login scripts.

With NetWare 3.x, multiple servers were available through the ATTACH command. NetWare 4.11 doesn't use the ATTACH command; NDS makes it easy to connect one user to many NetWare servers. All NetWare 3.x-specific login commands must be updated. The tables are in the DynaText electronic manuals in the "Upgrade" volume.

Printing Migration

NetWare 4.11 print servers can handle up to 256 printers, meaning (you guessed it) that your printing system will probably change during the upgrade process. There are two utilities to help you migrate your printing system: PUPGRADE.NLM and MIGPRINT.EXE. MIGPRINT works with Across-the-Wire migrations; PUPGRADE is used for Same-Server migrations.

MIGPRINT moves printers, print queues, print job configurations, and print servers into your NetWare 4.11 Directory tree from NetWare 2.x or NetWare 3.x servers. Once the print system is migrated, you will need to manually adjust the system details for your new NetWare 4.11 environment. You will have the option to move the print queue volume from SYS: to a different volume on the NetWare 4.11 server.

PUPGRADE works only for NetWare 3.x servers moving to NetWare 4.11. This utility is run on the new NetWare 4.11 server after other migration duties are completed. PUPGRADE upgrades the PRINTCON and PRINTDEF databases. The transferred printer and print servers will be upgraded for NetWare 4.11 as well.

Read about PUPGRADE in the "Printing" volume of the DynaText electronic manuals. MIGPRINT is in the DynaText "Upgrade" volume.

Where to Go from Here

THE FIRST PLACE you should go from here is to telephone your NetWare reseller and buy a new server rather than upgrading your old server.

The only exceptions are when upgrading from an earlier version of NetWare 4.0x to NetWare 4.11, or when you are placing the upgraded server into a light-duty situation. If you're coming from NetWare 3.x or NetWare 2.x, your server is almost certainly too old and slow and limited in memory to make a satisfactory medium- or high-duty NetWare 4.11 server.

But since your budget or your boss (or both) may restrict your ability to buy the hardware you know you need, we must push onward. Right or wrong, you've got to get a system up and running.

NetWare 4.11 no longer includes the physical red *Upgrade* manual. You must install the DynaText documentation and read through that carefully. There are lots of little "gotchas" hiding in the upgrade process, such as the restrictions when moving from an IDE NetWare 3.x server to NetWare 4.11 (you can't add a DOS partition to the drive when moving to NetWare 4.11).

Chapter 2 provides the hardware requirements for a good NetWare 4.11 server, and starts you on the road to installing that server. Chapter 3 concerns installing NDS on a single server in a new NetWare 4.11 network. If you're reading this appendix, you'll probably be doing exactly that—installing a first NetWare 4.11 server. Go to Chapter 4 to learn more about NetWare Directory Services.

Turn to Chapter 6 and read about login scripts, Container scripts, and the other new ways to organize and manage groups of users. NetWare Administrator (mentioned everywhere, but detailed in Chapter 10) may be a shock after years of using SYSCON, but I think you'll grow to like the program.

Upgrading Clients to Windows 95 and NetWare's Client32

AS YOUR NETWORK clients upgrade to Windows 95, you'll learn the pain (and overtime) of configuring large groups of new clients. Adding to the pain is the normal pain of upgrading any Windows version to any other Windows version. If you see we're stacking pain on top of pain, you're right.

Novell and Microsoft provide batch update utilities. Both promise great results, and Microsoft provides the INSTALL /A for Windows 95 just as it did for Windows 3.*x*. However, your life will be filled with frustration if you blindly believe, and follow, the provided instructions.

The first problem comes when you learn that Client32 doesn't allow shared network directories of Windows 95 files. You must place a complete version of Windows 95 on each workstation planning to use Client32. Sorry.

The next headache begins when you take a look at the involved setup procedure in the Help files under Novell Client32 in Windows 95. There's quite a long, involved process of configuration file building and modifying before you're ready to roll. I don't know about you, but long configuration processes never work the first time for me. Even the Help screens admit that the configuration process takes a while, which translates into a guarantee of real-world problems.

Let's take stock: Microsoft's NETSETUP won't work without modification, because we can't share Windows 95 executable files when running Client32 software. Novell's MSBATCH bypasses that problem, but is long, involved, and so new at the release of NetWare 4.11 that the only MSBATCH information resides in the NetWare Client32 Help screens on a Windows 95 station. That's right—I can't find MSBATCH anywhere in DynaText. Does that give you a good feeling?

Of course, Novell rectifies that problem a bit by providing TID (Technical Information Document) 2905964 on the Novell Web server (http://www.novell.com). You are also encouraged to search for MSBATCH on the Web server to get the latest information.

Realistically, you'll never install or upgrade a system to Windows 95 and Client32 without sitting at that station and modifying installation instructions for that particular machine. Besides, if the automated installation actually worked correctly, you would still need to go to that station and verify settings and configuration details. One more question: Do you want the user to do an installation by him or herself, without you being involved? I didn't think so. You'll need to be at each upgraded workstation for awhile, so you might as well block out the time now.

The Daniel Foo Shih Chieh Installation/Upgrade Method

Daniel Foo is a nice gentleman in Singapore who bought a copy of the first version of this book. In fact, he bought it twice. It was so heavy (almost as heavy as what you're holding) that he bought a second copy so he wouldn't need to carry the book back and forth to work on the bus.

He sent me a note talking about the book, which I certainly appreciate. He then sent questions concerning printing problems, and upgrading Windows 95 stations under his care. Over time, he became involved in various newsgroups struggling with Windows 95 and Client32 interaction.

Since Daniel has dozens of systems to upgrade and test, he has been trying every thing he could find. The following method, derived through suggestions and trial and error, has worked the best for him. This system assumes you already have Windows $3.1x$ on the workstation and that you have a network link. That's the situation for Daniel's systems, and I bet that's the situation for most of yours as well.

First, my words of caution: Verify all is working on the upgrade target. Verify a current backup is available for any information the user considers valuable on that machine. The one system you trust to work correctly will crash, just as the user says, "Oh, by the way, I have the only copy of the marketing project on that hard disk." Don't tempt the fates: Back up your systems.

Don't use the NETSETUP or INSTALL /A options for Windows 95. Rather, copy the contents of the Windows 95 CD-ROM to a server hard disk in a special directory. Get everything. Sure, it's over 600 MB, but you just upgraded your server, remember? You should have room to spare.

Also copy the Novell Client32 for Windows 95 files to the same server. Put them in their own directory, separate from the \PUBLIC\CLIENT\WIN95 files placed on the server by the NetWare 4.11 installation process.

On the PCs to be upgraded, make a new directory with two subdirectories: C:\MASTERS, with subdirectories CLIENT32 and WIN95. Copy the \WIN95 directory from the Windows 95 CD-ROM on the server to the appropriate directory, and copy all Client32 files to their temporary home.

Yes, this takes some disk space. However, any system about to move up from Windows 3.1*x* to Windows 95 needs *lots* of open disk space, so a temporary 50 MB or so shouldn't hurt anything.

Daniel starts the PC upgrade process by coping the PCs startup files to CONFIG.SY1 and AUTOEXEC.BA1. You can tell immediately Daniel has done this before, because he doesn't use an extension that other upgrade programs use, such as .OLD and the like. However, you can name the files whatever you like, just be sure to protect yourself.

Next, remove all the real mode drivers and set parameters, leaving a skeleton AUTOEXEC.BAT and only the C:\DOS\HIMEM.SYS statement in the CONFIG.SYS file. You must keep HIMEM for Windows 3.1*x* to run. Of course, Windows won't run well (no snide comments here), but we don't care right now.

After rebooting the system, start Windows 3.1*x*, error messages notwithstanding. Run C:\MASTERS\WIN95\SETUP and stand back. If Windows 95 doesn't recognize the hardware in the computer, add real mode drivers as necessary and start again.

Verify Windows 95 runs and acknowledges all appropriate system hardware. Then run C:\MASTERS\CLIENT32\SETUP and stand back once more.

Connect to your NetWare server and verify login scripts and NDS control. Then apply the Client32 patches from the server and verify those before leaving the user to play Solitaire running in 32 bits.

Oh, yes, you can delete the C:\MASTERS directory and subdirectories then. However, with the reliability of Windows 95, having complete local regeneration capabilities might not be too bad. Daniel may have a great idea for regular maintenance, just as he and the other contributors on the newsgroups developed a great upgrade method.

Upgrades Always Have a Hangup

THERE ARE LOTS of problems the manuals don't warn you about, of course. Whatever you think is adequate for your data backup procedures is probably not adequate. Go back and add one more backup or file copy of critical files.

Whatever time you have budgeted for the upgrade and changeover, increase the time. Double it if possible; more time will be needed than you imagine.

It isn't your fault (or mine) if it takes you longer to upgrade your existing system than you thought it would. You upgraders have some information to "unlearn." Administrators new to NetWare 4.11 start without the baggage of remembering how things used to be, and getting confused when NetWare 4.11 is different than the NetWare version they are using now.

Read the case studies, and notice the problems MiniCo had with its network installation. Why did those guys have problems? They didn't plan, and they rushed. There is a happy ending, but there is extra pain and aggravation as well.

Life is tough enough; don't make it harder by rushing into NetWare 4.11 before you check out the terrain. Every hour spent planning your upgrade or new installation will repay you tenfold in making your network a positive experience for your network users.

How NetWare 4.1x Differs from Earlier Versions

APPENDIX B

NOVELL'S NETWARE HAS been the leader in local-area networking for more than a decade. But this is the computer business, where the leader yesterday can be a follower tomorrow. Can we still say NetWare is the leading network operating system, even with all the competitors busily working to catch up and pass NetWare?

Yes, we can say NetWare is still the leader, in both market share and product features. Novell engineers always aim to make networking easier for people trying to get their work done.

Would it surprise you if I said there were as many NetWare dealers as 7-11 stores? Wrong. There are *twice* as many NetWare dealers as 7-11 stores. You should not have trouble finding a place to buy NetWare.

Of course, you may still be having trouble convincing your (shortsighted) boss to finally approve the purchase of NetWare 4.1*x*. If so, read on.

Advantages of NetWare over Other Network Operating Systems

NOVELL ENGINEERED NETWARE first and foremost to provide users access to files. Early on, the shared hard disk concept was forced by the high cost of mass storage. Later, as hard disk storage prices dropped, file sharing became important as a way to share information.

With more than a decade of improvements, NetWare provides file access faster, but with more control than any other network operating system. The file-caching scheme developed in the early days has consistently given better performance than mere hard drive improvements.

The use of cache buffers keeps important server resources in RAM. When one user reads a file, the file stays in server memory. If that same user, or another user, needs a piece of that file again, he or she gets immediate access. Server RAM is much faster than even the fastest hard disk.

Another cache improvement pioneered by Novell was the "hashing" of directory information. Novell uses some of the cache memory in the server for a complete list of each file on the hard disk and the physical location of those files. This cache eliminates the time spent in reading the directory off the hard disk. When a file is requested, the first physical movements of the hard disk drive heads are to the file, not to the directory to ask directions for the file location.

These are examples of NetWare's advanced control of server memory. All the caching in the world runs out sooner or later, of course, and the hard disk must be used. Once again, NetWare engineers have been thinking of improvements for more than a decade.

Early hard disks were large, slow, and expensive. The IBM XT originally shipped with a 10 MB hard disk, and people wondered if they would ever fill it up.

One way Novell turbo-charged hard disk access was through "elevator seeking." Elevators go all the way up, then all the way down. This reaches all the waiting riders in the most efficient manner.

Hard disks, however, service file requests in the order they are received. When taken to extreme, this leads to "thrashing," where the heads whip back and forth. Back when I started, the disks were so big and heavy the server would rock back and forth unless it was on a solid table.

By queuing up the hard disk requests (possible because of the directory hashing), NetWare engineers implemented elevator seeking for the file server hard disk. Rather than service requests in the order received, NetWare accesses files in the direction the disk heads are already moving. Figure B.1 illustrates how elevator seeking works.

These technical advantages give NetWare a performance advantage over competing networks. One other important success factor for Novell has been the developers' philosophical approach to the networking business.

Ray Noorda, president of Novell from 1983 to 1994, rescued Novell Data Systems from bankruptcy in the early 1980s and turned it into Novell, Inc. An important goal for Mr. Noorda was to grow the networking business, not just Novell. Following the old adage that "a rising tide raises all boats," Noorda pushed Novell to support every interface card and computer on the market. Alliances were made and technical information was shared between other companies that were, to all appearances, rivals of Novell. An example is

FIGURE B.1
Elevator seeking services files in order of location

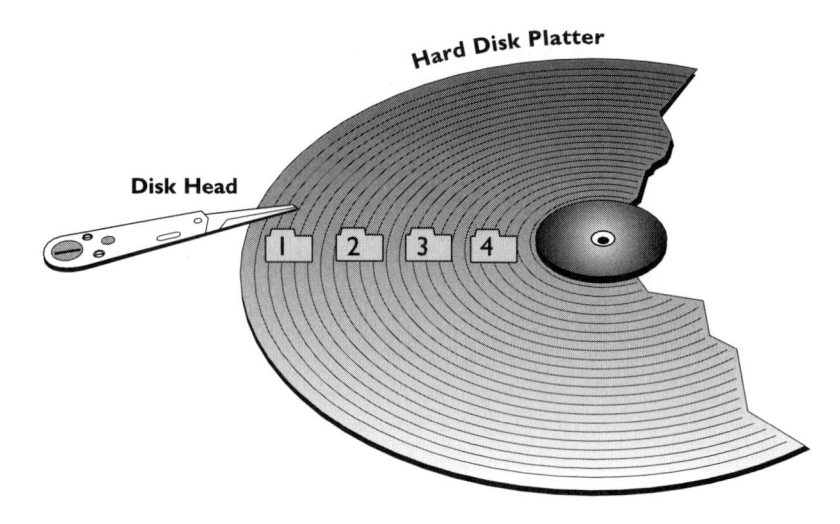

Hard Disk Platter

Disk Head

1 2 3 4

Order of File Request: 4213
Order of File Service: 1234

Novell's strong support of 3Com's outstanding Ethernet cards, even while 3Com was selling a competing network operating system.

The term Noorda used was "co-opetition," a combination of cooperation and competition. For the world of PCs and PC networking, this was amazing. Don't expect your Unix friends to be impressed, however. The Internet was grown and developed in exactly the same way, except the entire Unix and WAN industries share information—not a bad model.

Advantages of NetWare 4.1x over NetWare 3.x

NETWARE 3.X IS THE world's leading network operating system. Whether you count total server licenses, clients supported, third-party support, or dollars invested by clients, NetWare 3.x tops every measurement. Millions of users every workday rely on one or more NetWare 3.x servers.

Designed to be the best departmental network operating system, NetWare 3.x has succeeded. But between the time NetWare 3.0 premiered in 1989 and today, the world of networking has grown tremendously.

Where NetWare 3.x was built for the department, the world now demands an "enterprise-wide" network solution. Companies that used to depend on the mainframe to offer information to geographically dispersed locations now demand that capability from their network operating systems.

Customers demand more from their servers today. Some of the requirements demanded now were impossible for even the largest mainframe 20 years ago. Requirements today include:

- Servers that support a thousand concurrent users
- Servers that support many thousands of potential users
- Support for DOS, MS Windows, OS/2, Macintosh, and Unix clients
- Internet connections and access control
- Applying Internet-based technologies to internal networks
- Improved WAN performance
- Multiple language support on one server
- Automatic hard disk compression
- Ability to communicate with mainframe and Unix systems

Some of the features needed by large corporations are supported by NetWare 3.x. But consider this analogy: Although a DC-10 can carry groups of people through the air, the Concorde designers applied new thinking to the requirements and revolutionized jet travel with more speed and style. NetWare 4.1x also improved upon NetWare 3.x by adding both new technology and new ways of helping users reach their networking goals. Here is a summary of some of the features NetWare 4.x offers to improve your network and their advantages for your users:

- File compression and block suballocation stretch your disk drive investment.
- NLMs (NetWare Loadable Modules) in protected mode reduce server downtime and provide multiple language support.

- With NDS (NetWare Directory Services), users have a global view of the network rather than a server-centric view.

- New and enhanced server and workstation utilities are provided for both DOS and Windows users, including new 32-bit utilities for Windows 95/NT.

- The NetWare client software includes workstation support for DOS and MS Windows, OS/2, Macintosh, and Unix clients. Single network login allows users access to an enterprise network after authentication.

- The NetWare Web Server provides an easy way to create an intranet and to provide information on the Internet.

- The server installation procedures include the Simple Installation and Custom Installation options, and the upgrade utilities ease migration to NetWare 4.1*x*.

- NetWare Server for OS/2 runs the NetWare operating system under OS/2 for smaller sites, especially branch offices of larger companies.

- New features and enhancements to NetWare print services allow more flexible printing.

- SMS (Storage Management System), SNMP (Simple Network Management Protocol), and TSA (Target Service Agent) add sophisticated control of disk storage, network management, and client/server backup.

- HCSS (High-Capacity Storage System) adds an optical disk library, called a jukebox, to the NetWare server.

- Packet Burst Protocol and Large Internet Packets speed WAN connections. Multiple protocols are supported in the client and server. NLSP (NetWare Link Support Protocol) provides better routing, and the MPR (Multi-Protocol Router) adds full WAN control to your NetWare server.

- The new online documentation, viewable by any Windows client, includes functions for searches and adding public or private note attachments.

Your Choice: DOS or Windows Management Utilities

When Novell started, networking management of competitor's products meant command-line utilities and cryptic text files. Novell provided a clean and fairly straightforward utility interface. It was DOS, of course, since this happened in the early 1980s.

The interface has served Novell well over the years. It's a model for many third-party vendors who make their screens look as much like NetWare as possible. The DOS interface (called the C-Worthy interface, named after the compiler used) is now even cleaner and more informative than before.

If you prefer DOS, you will be greeted by the familiar C-Worthy interface with some upgrading. See Figure B.2 for a look at the new Volume Statistics screen now inside the FILER administration utility.

But it's still DOS, and some people don't like that as much as Windows. That alone is a good reason to move to Windows, but even more important is that the handling of objects works better with a GUI (graphical user interface). Since NetWare 4.1*x* is now object-oriented and flexible, the drag-and-drop capabilities provided by Windows ease management tasks more than ever. And the Client32 platform running on Windows 95 makes 32-bit utilities a reality. More horsepower on the management workstation means better performance.

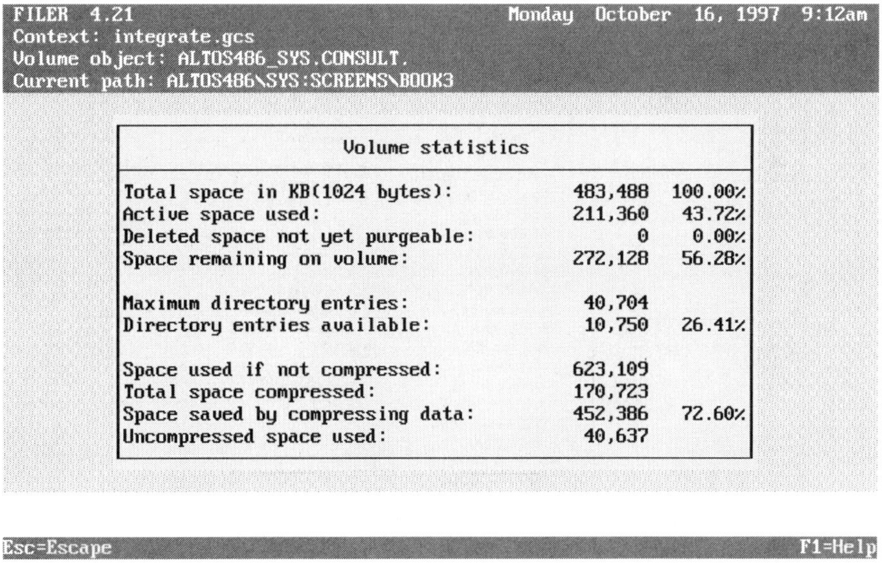

FIGURE B.2

The DOS look and feel of NetWare administration

```
FILER 4.21                                    Monday October 16, 1997  9:12am
Context: integrate.gcs
Volume object: ALTOS486_SYS.CONSULT.
Current path: ALTOS486\SYS:SCREENS\BOOK3

                        ┌─────────────────────────────────────────┐
                        │           Volume statistics             │
                        ├─────────────────────────────────────────┤
                        │ Total space in KB(1024 bytes):  483,488  100.00%│
                        │ Active space used:              211,360   43.72%│
                        │ Deleted space not yet purgeable:      0    0.00%│
                        │ Space remaining on volume:      272,128   56.28%│
                        │                                                 │
                        │ Maximum directory entries:       40,704         │
                        │ Directory entries available:     10,750   26.41%│
                        │                                                 │
                        │ Space used if not compressed:   623,109         │
                        │ Total space compressed:         170,723         │
                        │ Space saved by compressing data: 452,386  72.60%│
                        │ Uncompressed space used:         40,637         │
                        └─────────────────────────────────────────┘

Esc=Escape                                                          F1=Help
```

With full graphics at every step, the NetWare Administrator program under Windows shows more information more quickly than possible with the DOS-based utilities. Notice in Figure B.3 how the information concerning the ALTOS486_SYS volume is clearer than that shown in Figure B.2.

Similar options exist for the users, but an extra twist has been thrown in. Where the users had no DOS or Windows system available in NetWare 3.x, they have both starting in NetWare 4.0. NETUSER is an extension of the DOS C-Worthy interface used for the management utilities. With NETUSER, even the newest user can easily attach to network printers, send messages, and change their drive mappings.

The corresponding Windows 3.1x program is NetWare User Tools. This is even easier for users to navigate. Once you enable its hotkey, you can call the NetWare User Tools program from anywhere within Windows 3.1x with the touch of the F6 key (or another key you assign). Users can "mouse about," dragging and dropping for printer control, sending and receiving messages, and drive mapping. In NetWare 4.11, only the Windows 3.1x users still have NetWare User Tools, since Windows 95 comes with Network Neighborhood.

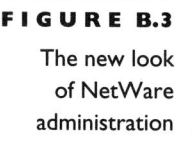

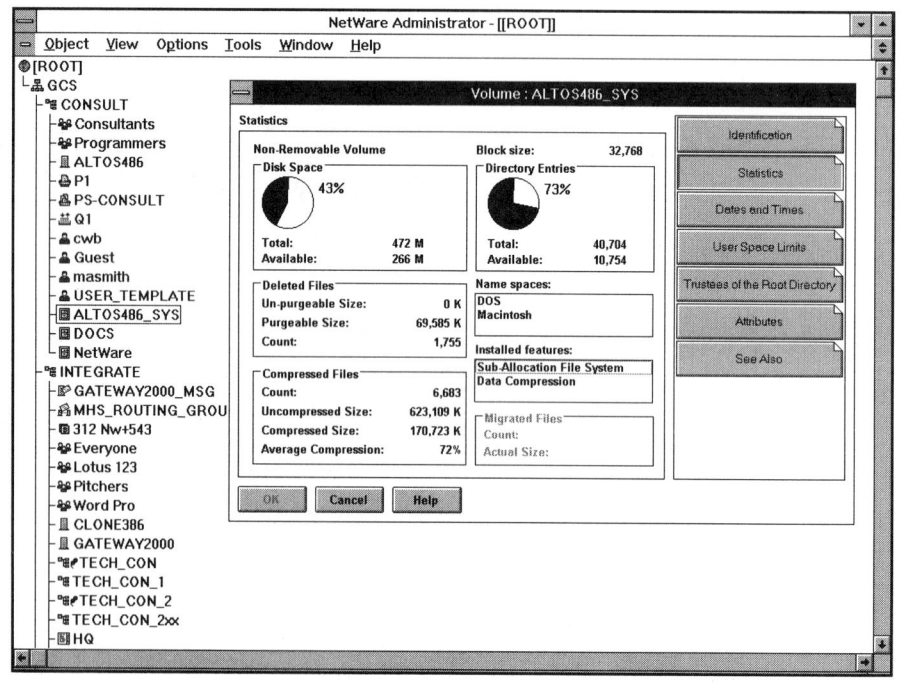

FIGURE B.3

The new look of NetWare administration

Windows 95 clients perform the same functions within Network Neighborhood or Windows Explorer. The Client32 additions to Windows 95 even allow users to map drives and configure printers, all from their Windows 95 desktop.

File Compression and Other File System Enhancements

No matter how much disk space you have, you will run out one day. That's a guarantee in the computer business. Now that "feature-bloat" and "code creep" have pushed standard word processors to requiring more than 35 MB of space, that day will come sooner than you imagine. Your budget may not be ready.

Applying the techniques learned in providing file compression in Novell DOS 7 and packing installation programs onto fewer diskettes, NetWare 4.0 premiered the first file server background compression. Unlike the compression program you may have on your own computer disk, this system is optimized for the file server. For your desktop system, the scales are balanced for good on-the-fly compression and decompression.

Software developers have choices to make during product development. There's no free lunch in software development; the code that crunches the files down the best takes longer to decompress the files. Conversely, the code that expands files the fastest doesn't get the best compression ratio.

Your desktop system uses software written to crunch the file as well as it can in the time allotted. But it can't crunch too much, because then the file retrieval would be slower when you need it later. So you get a compromise.

On the NetWare server, other options are available. There's no need to worry about crunching the file in real time, for several reasons. Since the server has enough disk space to support many people, the file compression is not mandatory the instant you save the file. Because the system is shared, you may be saving a file at your desk that the person in the next cubicle is busy opening. No sense in wasting server CPU cycles crunching and expanding the same file at the same time, is there?

NetWare engineers developed software that focuses on reducing file opening time. When people want a file, they want it now. Besides, NetWare has a reputation to protect when it comes to file service, and quick response to file requests is an important part of that reputation.

File compression is done by another set of software, separate from the file expansion software. Two important details optimize performance. First, you can set the delay (in days) for a file to be untouched before being compressed from 0 (zero) days (immediate compression) and 100,000 days (obviously a joke unless you plan on checking back in 273 years). The default is 7 days before compression.

After choosing your compression delay, you can choose how you will deal with compressed files that are read by a user or application. You can always leave them in compressed mode, you can always leave them in uncompressed mode, or you can cheat. The third option is to leave the file compressed if it's only read one time in the seven days, but leave it uncompressed if it's read twice in that time period. Figure B.4 shows the duality of file compression.

FIGURE B.4

File compression: read in haste, compress at leisure

Compression

Dedicate plenty of CPU horsepower.
Run compression at midnight when the server is not busy.

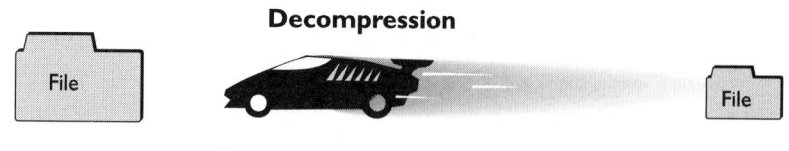

Decompression

Use as little CPU horsepower as possible, since files will be read during the workday.

One quick note about another space-saving feature: suballocation of disk blocks. Suballocation (which is not undersea ship deployment for the Navy) allows NetWare to have large blocks of data (up to 64 KB in one block), which speeds file retrieval. But if you save a 64.5 KB file, another entire 64 KB block is needed, of which 63.5 KB is wasted. NetWare 4.1x allows suballocation of the disk block size, down to 512 bytes, and groups these leftover file pieces in one large block. Suballocation allows our 63.5 KB file to take one 64 KB disk block and one 512-byte section of a second block. This approach is much more efficient.

Server Performance

File servers are getting bigger and faster, almost as fast as our demands on them are growing. Two recent PC innovations are supported by NetWare 4.1*x* to increase the workload your server can handle.

First, NetWare 4.1*x* supports the PCI (Peripheral Component Interconnect) bus developed by Intel. PCI cards communicate directly with the CPU in either 32 or 64 bits at a time. Bus-mastering PCI cards can perform some tasks concurrently with the CPU for even greater time savings.

Second, NetWare 4.1*x* takes advantage of the 4 MB page feature of the Intel Pentium processor. The more server memory that can be handled in one operation, the better, and the Pentium allows control of 4 MB at a time under certain circumstances. NetWare 4.1*x* provides some of those circumstances. If you were wondering if a Pentium file server was worth the extra money, keep this in mind.

Memory Management

Memory used to be segmented into five "pools" in NetWare 3.*x*. After studying the NLMs on the market, however, Novell engineers learned that a single, flat memory space provides both better performance and easier memory allocation routines. "Garbage collection" routines, which are programs that find released but unused bits of memory and gradually work them back into the system, work better in this memory model as well.

Another memory improvement is segmented memory areas to store unknown or suspect NLM applications. Memory in computers is divided into four rings, from 0 (the closest to the CPU) to 3. Ring 3 memory leaves gaps between applications and protects the Ring 0 application memory space from interruption.

With new or suspect NLMs in Ring 0, your server can be slowed or even stopped by an NLM not behaving properly. Placing these NLMs elsewhere greatly reduces the chance of the rogue NLM affecting the rest of the server.

There is a slight performance penalty for Ring 3 operations. Some network administrators place all new NLM applications in Ring 3 for a few weeks. If there are no problems, they can move them into the trusted memory area with all the other well-behaved NLMs. This offers a way to protect your server and still provide the best possible performance.

Server Self-Tuning

While running, the server software constantly adjusts the memory available, directing extra memory where it will do the most good. This shows in all the variable settings in the MONITOR.NLM program, which runs on the server console.

The good part is that the system tunes itself, but the bad part is that it will not remember those settings the next time you reboot the server. The settings will gradually move back to the most efficient levels once again, but you can help them along.

Check the MONITOR screen and make a note of items that affect performance, such as the number of directory cache buffers. The range is between 20 to 4000, with a default of 500. If your server shows a number far from the default, especially toward the low end, use SET command parameters (see Appendix C) in your AUTOEXEC.NCF file or SERVMAN (see Chapter 10) to place the buffers at this value on server startup. This puts your server into a more efficient mode immediately.

Advantages of NetWare 4.1x over NetWare 4.0

THERE ARE MANY improvements in NetWare 4.1*x* over NetWare 4.0, but most people focus on the ones concerned with NDS. In NetWare 4.1*x*, NDS is more flexible, easier to install, and easier to reconfigure.

For the first time, the Macintosh is a complete NetWare citizen. MacNDS gives Macintosh users access to NDS. There is a way to run NetWare 4.1*x* on an OS/2 server, which reduces the number of machines needed for remote offices and small networks.

Confused? Need help? The new DynaText electronic documentation has the answers.

Directory Service Improvements

No matter how well you plan, your company structure changes. With the new tools for NDS, it won't be difficult to change your network to match.

NDS Manager provides a graphical environment for many normal NDS chores. This utility may be called from within the NetWare Administrator Tools menu, or as a program on its own.

Also in the new tools department is DSMERGE, an NLM that works at the highest levels of your NDS structure. DSMERGE allows you to check the servers in your tree, change the name of trees, merge two trees together, and check the time synchronization between the servers.

To help to pull your NetWare 3.x servers into the NDS fold, Novell provides NetSync. This NetWare Bindery Synchronizer allows you to manage a NetWare 3.x server as part of your NDS tree. Up to 12 NetWare 3.12 servers can be managed from any one NetWare 4.12 server. One great advantage of NetSync means that the "cluster" of NetWare 3.x servers looks like one server to the users. One login procedure per cluster per customer.

New Installation Options

If your network is small, some of the power of NDS is no advantage to you. If you won't get all the power, why should you go through the configuration?

With NetWare 4.1x you can choose either Simple or Custom NDS installation. With the Simple Installation, the software will automatically create a single-level NDS structure with the name of your organization (or whatever name you choose) the same as the name of your tree. This works well if your network has less than 10 servers and 500 users. It also installs a single protocol, IPX/SPX. When you add a second server to an existing Simple network, the installation program will allow you to add the second server into the existing NDS.

A Custom Installation allows more NDS flexibility during the process. If your network has multiple servers, multiple protocols, and/or multiple locations, the Custom route is for you.

The physical act of installation is now easier. You can install from a CD-ROM attached to the server, from a CD-ROM anywhere on the network, from another file server (if it has a copy of much of the CD-ROM), or from floppy disks.

New NDS Configuration Options

The NWADMIN (or more officially, NetWare Administrator for Windows) and NETADMIN programs have new features. You may now, with NetWare 4.1x, see and administer multiple trees.

NDS Manager allows you to move a container, change and manage partitions and replicas, and perform many of the DSREPAIR functions. You will be surprised at how much you can manage without ever leaving Windows 95.

In both NWADMIN and NETADMIN, a new Rename Subtree option is available. This option allows you to rename a container object.

If you do move a container, the NCUPDATE program may be of interest. This utility updates users' NET.CFG files when they log in. A new name context for each user can be provided to keep up with the wandering container.

NetWare Client for Macintosh: MacNDS

Novell was the first company to support the Macintosh computer in PC networking. With NetWare 4.1*x*, it's the first to integrate the Macintosh fully into the same directory space as the PC clients.

MacNDS uses the toolkits developed by Novell to provide IPX/SPX support for the Macintosh. The NetWare tools and interfaces that people in the PC world are comfortable with now exist inside the native Macintosh interface.

NetWare Server for OS/2 Options

Companies with small remote offices have a difficult time providing all the services necessary to the remote office. At headquarters, users have access to NetWare and the IBM host without problems. The remote offices need the same resources, but have difficulty.

When you amortize an SNA (Systems Network Architecture) gateway over five or six dozen users, the cost per user is minimal. When you amortize a remote SNA gateway for a remote office over six users, the cost per user is prohibitive. The same goes for providing office productivity tools on a NetWare server.

This scenario is the reasoning behind NetWare Server for OS/2. Using a nondedicated OS/2 machine, NetWare, OS/2 applications, and mainframe access can be provided to the remote office users. Combining all three functions onto one machine lowers the cost per user. It's still not as low as when amortized over dozens of users, but it's better than it was.

New in NetWare 4.1*x* are better OS/2 and NetWare memory management techniques. If your OS/2 and NetWare server spends most of its time serving NetWare, you can now allocate more memory to the NetWare process. If more time is spent providing mainframe access, push more resources that way.

Printing Enhancements

Counting on the ability of smarter printers, Novell has unveiled NetWare Distributed Print Services (NDPS). Using the network for two-way communications between printers and servers will make better printing decisions easier for users.

Printer Agents will combine the functions of print queue, print server, and spooler into one technology. Although released after 4.11, NDPS will help prepare networks for the day when printers anywhere on the Internet are addressable as NetWare system printers.

Printing control and management have been enhanced in NetWare 4.1x over earlier NetWare 4 versions by the new utility NetSync. Primarily used to treat a cluster of NetWare 3.x servers as a small NDS system, NetSync also connects NetWare 3.x print queues to one or more NetWare 4.1x print servers.

A second new feature is the Print Layout Page option in the print server information. With one click, you can see a graphic diagram of that server's print queues, printers, and print jobs in the queue.

New Storage and Backup Options

No one has enough storage, whether we're talking closets or network disk space. HCSS (High-Capacity Storage System) helps add storage space by adding jukebox systems of optical media into the NetWare file system of the server. Users treat the optical media the same way they do any other server volume, using the same software and commands.

In NetWare 4.1x, multiple drives are supported in a jukebox. Improvements mean more efficient jukebox information retrieval, and less time spent in importing the information into the NetWare file system. Customization is now possible, with the new parameters you can set for HCSS.

The big news in the backup world for the last year has been the growing support for SIDF (System Independent Data Format). Any SIDF-compliant tape hardware and software can read tapes made by another SIDF-compliant system.

Large, growing companies often have a problem with archival information. When your old tape backup hardware wears out, the replacement system usually has a different format and larger size. The tapes of important information from a year or two before are suddenly no longer usable. SIDF addresses this problem for companies, as well as allowing them to transport tapes between different manufacturer's equipment.

NetWare Peripheral Architecture

Novell has always supported more server hardware than any other network vendor. Keeping that lead is the purpose behind NPA (NetWare Peripheral Architecture).

NetWare drivers are now separated into two parts: HAM (Host Adapter Module) and CDM (Custom Device Module). The HAM drives the host adapter hardware (the card in the server). The CDM drives any hardware devices attached to that adapter.

This was done in the past with a single .DSK file. That advantage of NPA is scalability. Before, any hardware change required a new driver file, which could present problems with other installed devices. With NPA, all you need for new hardware is the CDM for that particular new piece of equipment.

DynaText: Read About Documentation

ElectroText has been transformed into DynaText. Several improvements have been made, not the least of which is that DynaText runs faster and jumps higher than ElectroText. You have heard that before about "new, improved" software, but it's true this time.

ElectroText was limited to Windows readers; DynaText has support for Macintosh users in your network. The graphics inside translate into the same picture on all platforms.

A new innovation for Novell electronic documentation is "sticky-notes" for the online manuals. These can be either public or private.

C2 Level Security Rating

Although rarely used in corporate America, the C2 Security rating is a big deal if you work with the military or other government agencies. The co-author of the *Orange Book*, a security ratings bible, now works for Novell. Tell that to your boss if you get questioned about Novell's level of security awareness. Then tell your boss to quit putting the system password on a sticky note on the monitor.

IntranetWare Additions to NetWare 4.11

NOVELL HAS DONE the amazing: added extra functionality for the same price. The IntranetWare version of NetWare 4.11 offers all the features of NetWare 4.11 we've just covered, plus the following enhancements.

Web Server Version 2.51

Sold separately as part of the InnerWeb Publisher package, the Web Server does technically come in the box with NetWare 4.11, but truly belongs to IntranetWare. If you're not involved with the Internet, you may wonder what all the fuss is about. Let me tell you.

Web servers, and the Novell Web Server in particular, rely on a standardized client and server communications protocol called HTTP (HyperText Transfer Protocol). Web servers provide information in small pieces that the client, no matter what operating system, formats and presents based on the browser software running on the client.

Most of the information provided by Web servers are documents. Well, what's the best network operating system in the world for providing files to intelligent clients quickly and reliably? That's right, NetWare.

Web Server 2.51 includes the ability to connect to remote hosts, remote NetWare servers, local NetWare servers, and most databases running on TCP/IP hosts. Easy script language samples provided by Novell make your Web experience simple and straightforward, even if you're new to the Web world.

Even more exciting, the Web Server relies on NDS for security. Authorized clients may browse NDS through their Web clients, viewing your entire network directory structure in HTML look and feel.

IPX/IP Gateway

If you think you've found a fly in the network ointment because the Web Server supports TCP/IP clients, and NetWare users run over the IPX protocol, Novell is one step ahead of you. The IPX/IP Gateway, sold earlier with the InnerWeb Publisher as NIAS (Novell Internet Access Server), handles the IPX-to-IP conversion necessary for NetWare clients to use Internet, and intranet, resources.

Part of the IPX/IP Gateway software runs at the client and is bound into Client32. This portion of the gateway software intercepts application requests for the TCP/IP network, such as when Netscape wants to find a new Web server, and "spoofs" the application into believing the client software is TCP/IP. Then, the second part of the Gateway software on the NetWare server does the actual converting of the packet format. On the return trip, the port number, assigned by the Gateway to outgoing packets, provides the means to locate the proper NetWare client who requested the packet in the first place.

NDS controls allow you to select which NetWare users may use the Gateway, and when during the day they are allowed to use it. Going further, you may restrict access to some Internet applications, such as newsgroups, while allowing access to other Internet resources, such as Web servers. All this configuration happens in the NetWare Administrator utility.

Netscape Client Software

The IPX/IP Gateway includes a fully licensed version of Netscape version 2.01, modified by Novell for use with NetWare. You'll see the snazzy *N* logo with the receding balls indicate Web progress, and have the Novell home page information available at the start of each session. Not the "shareware" or "crippled-ware" version, this Netscape comes fully functional and licensed for all your concurrent users.

NetWare/IP

If your company is one of the few that has converted to TCP/IP for all internal and external network communications, you'll be happy to hear that NetWare/IP has been improved for IntranetWare. Now at version 2.2, NetWare/IP provides the local TCP/IP protocol stack components needed for complete client-to-server communication over TCP/IP rather than IPX.

MPR (Multi-Protocol Router)

The final extra piece of IntranetWare is the MPR. Also a separate product not long ago, MPR now works with your IPX/IP Gateway for connection to your Internet service provider, or in a traditional way for communication to your telecommunication connections. You may list multiple call locations, allowing backup connections to your remote offices.

How the Global Directory Helps Users

YOU, MY READER friend, are an unusual person. You not only understand computers, you like them. You like working with them and playing with them.

Unfortunately, some people believe computers are just tools to use as a means of producing other work. I know that seems strange, but it's true.

One consequence of this attitude on the part of computer users is a low tolerance for computer interaction. These people refuse to learn how a computer system works. They have this idea that the computer should support them, not the other way around.

This type of user is the biggest beneficiary of NDS. Users no longer need to remember server names, volume names, print queue and print server names, or anything else of a technical nature. With the new client software for both DOS and MS Windows, users can see and connect to resources without having a clue where these things are physically located.

Many administrators copied login scripts and user names between NetWare 3.x servers so the users could automatically attach to multiple servers. This is no longer necessary. While this looks like a much better benefit for you than the users, it does help them.

When resources are added (a new color laser printer, for example), users can use them immediately, without waiting for you to configure a dozen different server user lists. Advertise the new Printer object, and all users can see and use it at their whim.

The client programs included with NetWare 4.1x help computer-phobic users. A single network view is available through both DOS and Windows, where all the network resources appear. Even the most cantankerous users will be forced to admit everything they need is within easy reach.

NetWare 4.1x SET Commands

APPENDIX C

THIS APPENDIX DESCRIBES each of the SET commands and parameters, which are grouped in 13 categories:

- Communications
- Directory caching
- Directory Services
- Disk
- Error handling
- File caching
- File system

- Locks
- Memory
- Miscellaneous
- NCP (NetWare Core Protocol)
- Time
- Transaction tracking

Communications SET Commands

```
IPX NetBIOS Replication Option = 2
```

NetBIOS replicated broadcasts must be handled in a special way. The options are 0 = not replicate them, 1 = use the old method of replication, 2 = use the new method of replication, or 3 = use method 2 but don't replicate them over WAN links.

```
Maximum Interrupt Events = 10
```

A thread switch occurs when one process gives way to another. If a thread-switch request is ignored for too long, service for most users will bog down. By setting a limit on the number of interrupt events, such as handling IPX routing requests, you guarantee the server rotates clock cycles to all processes. The range for this setting is 10 to 1,000,000.

```
Maximum Packet Receive Buffers = 100
```

As an example of NetWare 4.1*x* scaling up to support a larger user population, the high end of this setting was 2000 in NetWare 4.0; now it's up to 4000. The low end is 50. In a busy network, 100 won't be enough. Check the MONITOR display to see how many packet receive buffers are being used. Then set close to that number at startup, using SERVMAN. A good rule of thumb is to provide 10 packet receive buffers for every workstation connected.

```
Minimum Packet Receive Buffers = 50
```

The minimum packet receive buffers will be increased as the system realizes the need. However, if you see "No ECB Available Count" as the server is booted, you need to increase this setting. No ECB (Event Control Block) means that packets were received by the server, but the server did not have the resources to handle that packet. The range for this setting is 10 to 2000. This value should be less than the Maximum Packet Receive Buffers setting.

```
New Packet Receive Buffer Wait Time = 0.1 Sec
```

Setting a time before allocating new packet receive buffers eliminates creating buffers for spurious traffic or a network error. The range is .1 second to 20 seconds. Leave the default if your have an EISA bus master board in your server.

```
Maximum Physical Receive Packet Size = 4202
```

This setting indicates the largest packet that can be accommodated by the MLID driver. This command must be in the STARTUP.NCF file (reboot the server to put your changes in effect). The default should be fine for Token Ring and Ethernet systems. The range is 618 to 24682.

```
Reply to Get Nearest Server = On
```

When clients start their network software, they send a broadcast requesting a server to answer them and start the login process. A fast server may use up all of its connections if it answers every request. Setting this to Off will keep the server from answering the broadcast, but it will still respond to direct requests.

```
Number of Watchdog Packets = 10
```

Watchdog packets check each connection that stops responding to the server. This parameter sets how many checks will be made before disconnecting an unresponsive client. The range is 5 to 100. Disconnecting frees a connection for another licensed user, and helps when users turn off their systems without logging out and returning their license to the pool.

```
Delay Between Watchdog Packets = 59.3 Sec
```

This setting specifies the delay before the server sends the second and subsequent watchdog packets. The range is 9.9 seconds to 10 minutes, 26.2 seconds.

```
Delay Before First Watchdog Packet = 4 Min 56.6 Sec
```

This sets the delay before the server sends the first watchdog packet to an unresponsive client. The range is 15.7 seconds to 14 days.

```
Console Display Watchdog Logouts = Off
```

When this is set to On, it displays every watchdog termination on the server console (and attached RCONSOLE stations) and beeps. It's handy if your network is having connection problems, but it's annoying if things are normally in good shape.

Directory Caching SET Commands

```
Dirty Directory Cache Delay Time = 0.5 Sec
```

This parameter sets the minimum time before a dirty (changed) directory cache buffer is written to the disk. Longer delay times give slightly better performance, but increase the chances of corrupted directory entry tables. The range for this setting is 0 to 10 seconds. A setting of 0 is not advised, since it slows performance.

```
Maximum Concurrent Directory Cache Writes = 10
```

Concurrent writes aren't actually concurrent, unless you have multiple drives. The idea is to group write requests for each sweep of the disk head across the disk platters. The range for this setting is 5 to 50. Higher numbers make for more efficient writes but less efficient reads, and vice versa.

```
            Directory Cache Allocation Wait Time = 2.2 Sec
```

   Directory cache buffers take memory away from file cache buffers. Directory cache requests will be ignored for the time listed. The range is .5 second to 2 minutes. If the setting is too low, more file cache buffers than necessary will be converted. If the setting is too high, the system is sluggish in servicing client requests. If a performance increase isn't seen in the first 15 to 20 minutes after the server starts, decrease this parameter slightly.

```
         Directory Cache Buffer Nonreferenced Delay = 5.5 Sec
```

   Nonreferenced delay is the time a directory cache goes without being used. The range for this setting is 1 second to 5 minutes. The longer this time, the more likely the directory cache is to have a file request already loaded. The shorter the time, the fewer directory cache buffers are needed, and the more file cache buffers supported.

```
               Maximum Directory Cache Buffers = 500
```

   This indicates the maximum number of directory cache buffers allowed. The range for this setting is 20 to 4000. For servers that are low on memory, reduce this value, sacrificing some file search speed to support other processes. Reboot to return memory to the pool.

```
               Minimum Directory Cache Buffers = 20
```

   Use MONITOR to view the number of directory cache buffers the system allocates after being in operation for awhile. Set the minimum number about 20% below that. The range for this setting is 10 to 2000. If the system needs more directory cache buffers, they will be added. Remember that unused directory cache buffers are not returned to the memory pool.

```
         Maximum Number of Internal Directory Handles = 100
```

   The number of directory handles available to the system speeds up access rights for NLMs using connection zero. Each time the NLM needs a directory handle, one will be assigned, up to the limits of this setting. The range is 40 to 1000.

```
            Maximum Number of Directory Handles = 20
```

   This setting is similar to the one for internal directory handles, but for users rather than NLMs. The range is 20 to 1000.

Directory Services SET Commands

```
NDS Trace to Screen = Off
```

When set to On, this parameter displays NDS events on the server console screen.

```
NDS Trace to File = Off
```

When set to On, this parameter sends NDS events to a trace file. The default file is SYSTEM\DSTRACE.DBG, but that can be changed when starting the NDS log file. The maximum size of the trace file is limited to about 500 KB, after which new information overwrites the oldest.

```
NDS Trace Filename = SYSTEM\DSTRACE.DBG
```

This is the default value for the NDS trace file mentioned previously. The maximum path length for name is 255 characters.

```
NDS Trace File Length to Zero = Off
```

This deletes the contents, but not the file, of the NDS trace file. To use this setting, you must also set the NDS Trace to File parameter On, because the trace file must be open for this to function.

```
NDS Client NCP Retries = 3
```

This sets the retry level for NetWare to try and reconnect an NDS connection. This is the time spent waiting for your system to return to your control after a cable is disconnected, or a server you were using is lost. The range for this setting is 1 to 20. Shorter timeouts come with a lower number, but a large, busy network needs a higher number. A setting of 4 to 6 should be plenty for a large network with congestion problems and the possibility of servers being disconnected.

```
NDS External Reference Life Span = 192
```

External references are local IDs assigned to remote users when they access another server. This parameter specifies how long to track that reference before letting the system delete it. The range for this setting is 1 to 384 hours.

```
NDS Inactivity Synchronization Interval = 30
```

This sets the amount of time between NDS synchronizations if no NDS changes force action. When changed, this value forces a synchronization. The range is 2 to 1440 minutes. If your network must replicate across a WAN, make this time longer (4 to 6 hours).

```
NDS Synchronization Restrictions = Off
```

When this parameter is set On, the server will synchronize only with NDS of the same DS.NLM version as this server. You must specify the version if setting the restrictions to On. For example, the GATEWAY2000 server's DS.NLM is version 4.63, so you might allow it to synchronize with versions 4.61 and 4.62. Your setting would be On,461,462. You can check the DS.NLM version by typing MODULES at the server console.

```
NDS Do Not Synchronize With = On, 290, 291, 296, 332,
463, 477
```

When set to Off, this allows system DS.NLMs to synchronize with all other versions of NDS. Setting this to On blocks the synchronizing with the versions listed.

```
NDS Servers Status = Up/Down
```

This forces all servers to recognize the setting for all objects in the local name database as Up or Down. If a server is up but the system recognizes it as down, use this setting to mark all servers up. This will override the local status for the remote server and pull things into line with the other servers.

```
NDS Janitor Interval = 60
```

The janitor process cleans up unused records, reclaims disk space, and purges objects flagged as deleted. A change here forces the janitor process to execute and follows by executing again at the new time interval. The range for the interval is 1 to 10,800 minutes.

```
NDS Backlink Interval = 780
```

A backlink indicates that an object in a replica has an ID on a server where the replica doesn't exist. This setting forces a backlink consistency check, followed by regular checks at the specified interval. The range for the interval is 2 to 10,800 minutes.

```
Check Equivalent to Me = Off
```

Turning this On enforces checking the new Equivalent to Me attribute upon user authentication.

```
Bindery Context = OU=INTEGRATE.O=GCS
```

This specifies one or more containers to list as a bindery context when providing Bindery Services. Up to 16 contexts may be listed, separated by semicolons. You must have a replica of the container you specify in the same context. The maximum length for the name is 255 characters.

Disk SET Commands

```
Enable Disk Read After Write Verify = On
```

Don't disable this portion of Hot Fix if you have a single disk. If your disks are mirrored and reliable, you can gain extra speed by setting this to Off. Disable this for disks and drivers that perform their own read-after-write verification to avoid doing this verification twice. This setting affects disks loaded after the parameter is changed; put it in your STARTUP.NCF file for regular use.

```
Remirror Block Size = 1
```

This sets the size of the information block transferred during partition remirroring. The setting range is 1 to 8, in 4 KB increments; for example, 1 = 4 KB, 2 = 8 KB, and 8 = 32 KB.

```
Concurrent Remirror Requests = 4
```

In cases of multiple physical disks supporting one mirrored volume, a limit can be placed on the number of remirroring operations active at any one time. This comes into play when mirrored disks are replaced after failure or when they are upgraded. The range for this setting is 2 to 32.

```
Mirrored Devices Are Out of Sync Message Frequency = 30
```

This checks for out-of-sync devices at this interval. The range is 5 to 9999, in minutes.

```
Sequential Elevator Depth = 8
```

This sets the number of sequential elevator requests for the Media Manager. The range is 0 to 4,294,967,295.

```
Ignore Disk Geometry = Off
```

This allows creation or modification of nonstandard and otherwise unsupported partitions.

```
Enable IO Handicap Attribute = Off
```

This deals with a new attribute that allows some devices to inhibit read requests. Set this to On only at the direction of the equipment manufacturer.

Error Handling SET Commands

```
Server Log File Overflow Size = 4194304
```

This sets the maximum file size for the SYS$LOG.ERR. The range for this setting is 65,536 to 4,294,967,295.

```
Server Log File State = 1
```

This parameter specifies what happens when the SYS$LOG.ERR file grows larger than the set limit. The settings are 0 = do nothing, 1 = delete the log file, and 2 = rename the log file.

```
Volume Log File Overflow Size = 4194304
```

This sets the maximum file size for the VOL&LOG.ERR. The range for this setting is 65,536 to 4,294,967,295.

```
Volume Log File State = 1
```

This parameter specifies what happens when the VOL$LOG.ERR file grows larger than the set limit. The settings are 0 = do nothing, 1 = delete the log file, and 2 = rename the log file.

```
Volume TTS Log File Overflow Size = 4194304
```

This sets the maximum file size for the TTS%LOG.ERR. The range for this setting is 65,536 to 4,294,967,295.

```
Volume TTS Log File State = 1
```

This parameter specifies what happens when the TTS$LOG.ERR file grows larger than the set limit. The settings are 0 = do nothing, 1 = delete the log file, and 2 = rename the log file.

```
                Enable Deadlock Detection = Off
```

This is a special SMP setting used for debugging some NLMs.

```
                Auto Restart After Abend Delay Time = 2
```

This sets the minutes before a server suffering an abend will automatically go all the way down and reboot. The range is 2 to 60 minutes.

```
                Auto Restart After Abend = 1
```

This allows you to enable or disable the server auto restart function. The settings are 0 = ignore the abend situation, 1 = let the system decide to keep going or reboot, and 2 = reboot with every abend. If you do set the automatic reboot, check your ABEND.LOG now and then in the SYS:SYSTEM directory to see if you've had abends.

File Caching SET Commands

```
                Read Ahead Enabled = On
```

During sequential file access, such as reading block number one of a large file, NetWare assumes you are going to read block two, three, four, and so on. When this parameter is set to On, the system reads these blocks ahead of the actual read request from the application. This can greatly improve access time, because when the actual read request does come in, the next disk block is already in RAM, waiting.

```
                Read Ahead LRU Sitting Time Threshold = 10 Sec
```

This setting tells NetWare that if the cache LRU (Least Recently Used) time is below the set time, do not perform the read-ahead block feature. The range for this setting is 0 seconds to 1 hour.

```
                Minimum File Cache Buffers = 20
```

File cache buffers are made of server RAM that isn't needed for other functions. If memory is short, and other processes request extra memory, this setting specifies the fewest file cache buffers the system will allow. The range is 20 to 1000. If this number is too high for your server RAM, other processes may fail because of lack of available memory.

```
Minimum File Cache Report Threshold = 20
```

If your memory runs down and you reach your Minimum File Cache Buffers setting, you'll see the message "Cache memory allocator exceeded minimum cache buffer left limit." If you want to see a warning before that happens, set this parameter above 0 (zero). The range is 0 to 1000. Each number here adds to the Minimum File Cache Buffers number. With the two default settings, you'll be warned when the file cache buffers are down to 40.

```
Maximum Concurrent Disk Cache Writes = 50
```

Watch the number of dirty cache buffers in MONITOR. If the number set here is above 70% of total cache buffers, meaning more cache buffers are waiting for a write operation than anything else, increase this parameter. This allows more write requests to be packaged for a disk sweep. The range for this setting is 10 to 4000. A lower number helps your read performance; a high number helps the write performance.

```
Dirty Disk Cache Delay Time = 3.3 Sec
```

Similar to the Maximum Concurrent Disk Cache Writes setting, this setting also helps create better write performance. This specifies how long a write request that does not fill a cache buffer should be held before forcing a write to disk. If you have many small writes in your system, increase this number. The range for this setting is 0.1 second to 10 seconds.

File System SET Commands

```
Minimum File Delete Wait Time = 1 Min 5.9 Sec
```

Files deleted are not gone until purged. This is a wonderful feature, especially when you immediately realize you have deleted drive F: when you meant drive A:. The parameter here says a file must be salvageable at least this long, even when the volume is full and users have no new space. If there's plenty of room on the volume, a file may be salvageable for weeks. The range for this setting is 0 seconds to 7 days.

```
File Delete Wait Time = 5 Min 29.6 Sec
```

The first setting in this section defines the minimum wait time; this setting is for the normal wait time, and the same situation applies. If the file is deleted but there is plenty of room on the volume, it will not be purged for quite a while. When the volume finally fills of regular and purgeable files, the oldest purgeable files are erased first. The range for this setting is 0 seconds to 7 days.

```
Allow Deletion of Active Directories = On
```

Can a directory be deleted when another connection has a drive mapped to it? Your choice, but the default is yes (On).

```
Maximum Percent of Volume Space allowed for Extended
    Attributes = 10
```

This parameter is checked when the volume is mounted, this setting specifies how much space is to be available for extended attribute files. These files are for the Macintosh, OS/2, UNIX, FTAM, and all non-DOS file types. The range for this setting is 5 to 50. If you change this setting, the volume won't know until it's remounted.

```
Maximum Extended Attributes per File or Path = 16
```

This sets the limit of extended attributes per file or directory. It applies to all server volumes. The range for this setting is 4 to 512.

```
Maximum Percent of Volume Used by Directory = 13
```

This sets the portion of the volume that can be set aside as directory space. The range for this setting is 5 to 50.

```
Immediate Purge of Deleted Files = Off
```

When this setting is On, all files are purged immediately when deleted. Keep this Off for your own peace of mind.

```
Maximum Subdirectory Tree Depth = 25
```

This setting is checked upon booting only. Since some DOS applications can't go deeper than 10 directory levels, lowering this number won't hurt. The range is 10 to 100 subdirectories. The default allows up to 25 subdirectories—more than a sane person can keep track of.

```
Volume Low Warn All Users = On
```

If you turn this Off so that you won't be warned when the volume is almost full, you will need to check the volume levels every day, or buy a great big hard disk.

```
      Volume Low Warning Reset Threshold = 256
```

If you have 4 KB blocks, 256 blocks (the default) as the low warning reset threshold is only 1 MB, which is much too little. The range for this setting is 0 to 100,000 blocks, and it applies to all volumes in the server. Set it to start warning you at about 10% free space or even more. If a new application cranks up and generates lots of data, you may hit the wall quickly. The sooner you know, the better.

```
      Volume Low Warning Threshold = 256
```

This specifies the lower threshold of warning for lack of disk space. The range for this setting is 0 to 1,000,000, and it applies to all volumes in the server. Each volume that has a different block size will have a different alarm threshold. Keep the level (set with this parameter and Volume Low Warning Reset Threshold) at 10% or above.

```
      Turbo FAT Re-Use Wait Time = 5 Min 29.6 Sec
```

Turbo FATs (file allocation tables) are lists of disk blocks that make up a single large file. When a program is accessed that contains more than 64 FAT entries, a turbo FAT index is created. The longer this stays in memory, the faster the reopening if the large file is accessed again quickly. The range for this setting is .3 seconds to 1 hour, 5 minutes, 54.6 seconds. If you reopen the same large file after a predictable delay, increase this setting. But realize that this increase will come at the expense of the next large file opened, since released memory goes to index the next large file.

```
      Compression Daily Check Stop Hour = 6
```

File compression can take plenty of CPU time, so this parameter forces compression to stop. This is a 24-hour clock, so the range is 0 (midnight) to 23 (1:00 P.M.). If you have lots of file compression activity, make sure it's stopped before the workday load begins on the server. Files that aren't compressed one day keep their flags, and are compressed the next.

```
      Compression Daily Check Starting Hour = 0
```

The flip side of stopping compression (with Compression Daily Check Stop Hour) is when to start compression. Using the same 24-hour clock (0 to 23, for midnight to 1:00 P.M.), this parameter sets the compression start time. You may wish to start and finish compression before a backup, for instance. This setting will be written into STARTUP.NCF if you wish.

```
      Minimum Compression Percentage Gain = 2
```

This sets the minimum benefit a file must receive from compression. The range for this setting is 0 to 50%. This setting may be placed in STARTUP.NCF.

```
Enable File Compression = On
```

This specifies whether compression is suspended per server. Each volume is configured to support compression. If compression is suspended, immediate compress requests will be queued until compression is once again allowed.

```
Maximum Concurrent Compressions = 2
```

Multiple volumes can be compressed concurrently, up to eight at a time.

```
Convert Compressed to Uncompressed Option = 1
```

This setting tells the system how to handle a compressed file that has been uncompressed to read. The settings are 0 = leave the file in compressed mode, 1 = leave compressed unless it's read again within a definable time period, or 2 = always leave uncompressed.

```
Decompress Percent Disk Space Free to Allow Commit = 10
```

To prevent uncompressed files from filling the volume, a percentage of the volume may be kept free to hold newly uncompressed files. The range for this setting is 0 to 75%. When files are written to, they stay uncompressed.

```
Decompress Free Space Warning Interval = 31 Min 18.5 Sec
```

If there is insufficient disk space for files to remain uncompressed when they should be, a warning is issued. This setting specifies how often you should be interrupted by that warning. The range for this setting is 0 seconds to 29 days, 15 hours, 50 minutes, 3.8 seconds.

```
Deleted Files Compression Option = 1
```

This setting specifies whether or not to compress deleted files. The settings are 0 = don't compress, 1 = compress the next day (giving them time to be purged), or 2 = compress deleted files immediately.

```
Days Untouched Before Compression = 14
```

This setting specifies how long a file must be untouched before the compression flag is set. The range for this setting is 0 (compress immediately) to 100,000 days (ridiculous, but numerically easy to calculate).

```
Allow Unowned Files to Be Extended = On
```

Setting this parameter to On specifies that orphaned files (whose owner has been lost or deleted) can be modified.

Locks SET Commands

```
Maximum Record Locks per Connection = 500
```

This sets how many record locks one workstation can use at a time. Check this value in the MONITOR screens. The range for this setting is 10 to 100,000.

```
Maximum File Locks per Connection = 250
```

This sets how many files one workstation can use at one time. Again, check MONITOR to see the open files per workstation. OS/2 workstations may need more. The range for this setting is 10 to 1000.

```
Maximum Record Locks = 20000
```

This specifies the total record locks for the system to handle. Some database applications use an enormous number of record locks. The range for this setting is 100 to 400,000. If the application generates errors, increase this number. But be aware that increasing this number does take memory and CPU cycles to track.

```
Maximum File Locks = 10000
```

This sets the maximum number of open and locked files controlled by the operating system. Check MONITOR to see the number of open files during peak times. The range for this setting is 100 to 100,000.

Memory SET Commands

```
Allow Invalid Pointers = Off
```

Invalid pointers can be allowed to cause a nonexistent memory page to be mapped in with a single notification. The default is not to allow this.

```
Read Fault Notification = On
```

This tells the system whether or not to send notification of emulated read page faults to the console and the error log.

```
Read Fault Emulation = Off
```

This tells the system whether or not to emulate a memory page that isn't present during a read.

```
Write Fault Notification = On
```

This specifies whether or not the console and error log are notified when the system tries to write to a nonexistent memory page.

```
Write Fault Emulation = Off
```

This chooses whether or not to emulate a write operation for a memory page that isn't present.

```
Garbage Collection Interval = 15
```

This specifies how often the system should attempt to collect garbage free memory. The range for this setting is 1 to 60 minutes.

```
Number of Frees for Garbage Collection = 5000
```

This sets the number of memory-release operations before a garbage collection can occur. The range for this setting is 100 to 100,000.

```
Minimum Free Memory for Garbage Collection = 8000
```

This sets the minimum free bytes necessary before collecting the free memory. The range for this setting is 1000 to 1,000,000.

```
Alloc Memory Check Flag = Off
```

This chooses whether or not to check the allocated memory nodes for corruption.

```
Auto Register Memory Above 16 Megabytes = On
```

This must be set in STARTUP.NCF if you have a server with more than 16 MB of RAM (and I hope you do). It will automatically add memory to the server's control in EISA machines with more than 16 MB (older EISA systems will have trouble with this). Boards and disk adapters in AT bus systems, or those with online DMA (direct memory access), should set this parameter to Off.

```
Reserved Buffers Below 16 Meg = 200
```

This is another STARTUP.NCF parameter. Drivers unable to access memory above 16 MB will need buffers available below the 16 MB limit. The range for this setting is 8 to 300.

Miscellaneous SET Commands

```
Sound Bell for Alerts = On
```

This sets the console to beep or not when an alert appears.

```
Replace Console Prompt with Server Name = On
```

This places the server name to the left of the console prompt.

```
Alert Message Nodes = 20
```

This sets the number of nodes, such as network management software stations, that can receive alert messages from the server. The range for this setting is 10 to 256.

```
Worker Thread Execute in a Row Count = 10
```

This sets the number of times the system scheduler may consecutively start new work before allowing other existing threads to run. The range for this setting is 1 to 20.

```
Halt System on Invalid Parameters = Off
```

When an invalid parameter is detected, by default, the system displays an alert and attempts to continue. If you set this parameter to On, the system will halt when it encounters an invalid parameter.

```
Upgrade Low Priority Threads = Off
```

When set to On, this parameter forces the system to allow low-priority threads, such as file compression, to run at the regular priority level. Some NLMs can dominate the system, leaving out the low-priority processes.

```
Display Relinquish Control Alerts = Off
```

If a module uses the processor for more than 0.4 second without passing control back to the scheduler, a message can be sent to the console. If you are writing NLMs or testing new ones, you may wish to set this to On to get all the feedback you can.

```
Display Incomplete IPX Packet Alerts = On
```

Another debugging tool, this setting tells the system to send an alert message when an incomplete IPX packet is received.

```
Display Old API Names = Off
```

When NLMs are loaded, this sets whether or not the console should display the number of older API calls still used by the NLM. When debugging or upgrading, this is helpful. The old APIs still work, but not as quickly as the new ones. Contact your NLM vendor for an upgrade if these alerts appear when the parameter is set to On.

```
Developer Option = Off
```

When you set this to On, it helps debugging by providing more error messages and more detail about those messages. Verbose error messages will be the norm if this is set to On.

```
Display Spurious Interrupt Alerts = On
```

Spurious interrupts usually indicate a serious problem in the making for your server hardware. One board generally causes the problem, and should be isolated and replaced. In some cases, a driver update will solve the problem.

```
Display Lost Interrupt Alerts = On
```

Another indication of a potential hardware problem is a lost interrupt, where a device requests service through an interrupt but drops the request before the CPU can respond. Isolate and replace the offending hardware.

```
Pseudo Preemption Count = 10
```

This sets the number of times threads may make read and write calls before being forced to allow other processes access to the CPU. This forced release of control is called *pseudo preemption*, and may be set everywhere or for particular NLMs. The range for this setting is 1 to 4,294,967,295.

```
Global Pseudo Preemption = Off
```

This specifies whether or not all threads are set for pseudo preemption.

```
Minimum Service Processes = 10
```

This sets the minimum number of service processes allowed without waiting for the set New Service Process Wait Time amount.

```
Maximum Service Processes = 50
```

If more than 20 requests for disk I/O are delayed, increase this number. The range for this setting is 5 to 100. If necessary, add more RAM to the server. Check the MONITOR Service Processes values to track this information. The more concurrent requests to be handled by the server (the heavier the load), the more service processes needed.

```
New Service Process Wait Time = 2.2 Sec
```

This sets the delay before creating a new service process after a request. The range for this setting is 0.3 to 20 seconds.

```
Automatically Repair Bad Volumes = On
```

If a volume fails to mount, this parameter tells the system whether to start VREPAIR automatically (On) or not (Off).

```
Enable SECURE.NCF = Off
```

This adds extra security levels to comply with new C2 Security ratings. This setting concerns running SECURE.NCF during server boot.

```
Allow Audit Passwords = Off
```

This allows audit passwords for the wretched little auditors trying to make your life miserable.

```
Allow Unencrypted Passwords = Off
```

Encrypted passwords prevent a network capture program, such as a protocol analyzer, from seeing a user's password by encrypting the password between the client and the server. Older NetWare versions did not support this. If you have older systems, you may need to set this to On. You should try copying the newer files to the older servers.

NCP SET Commands

```
NCP File Commit = On
```

Some NetWare-aware programs prefer to force files to write to disk before receiving confirmation of the success of the write. Normal files are placed in the cache, and the cache responds to the application with verification, even though the file hasn't actually been placed on the disk. The default setting of On allows this forced writing.

```
Display NCP Bad Component Warnings = Off
```

Poorly written programs may not handle NetWare system calls properly. This setting allows (On) or prevents (Off) alert messages from going to the console.

```
Reject NCP Packets with Bad Components = Off
```

Badly structured NCP packets may be rejected or accepted. The default setting (Off) is to accept them.

```
Display NCP Bad Length Warnings = Off
```

Size parameter exceptions generate alert messages, and this parameter offers the chance to display these (On) or not (Off).

```
Reject NCP Packets with Bad Lengths = Off
```

This specifies whether or not NCP packets that generate size parameter exceptions should be accepted or rejected. The default is to accept them (Off).

```
Maximum Outstanding NCP Searches = 51
```

Generally, one connection can generate only one directory search. A few programs can support multiple search operations and may cause directory problems. If so, increase the default value. The range for this setting is 10 to 1000.

```
NCP Packet Signature Option = 1
```

NCP packet signatures are a security feature that uses embedded identification in the packets to guarantee identity. The values and their definitions for the server are 0 = no packet signatures, 1 = packet signatures at the request of the client, 2 = packet signatures if the client can and wants to (but don't force them), or 3 = force packet signatures. Packet signatures use CPU resources and slow performance on both ends of the network transactions. Few situations require this level of security.

```
Enable IPX Checksums = 1
```

This setting specifies how to use IPX checksums (number for each packet calculated based on the packet contents and interpreted at the receiving end to guarantee packet integrity). The settings are 0 = no checksums, 1 = checksum if enabled at the client, or 2 = checksums required.

```
Allow Change to Client Rights = On
```

This sets whether or not a job server such as a print queue or fax server can assume the rights of the client for NCP packet signatures. Some programs can't function without setting this to On. Setting this to Off prevents packet forgery through a job server of some type.

        Allow LIP = On

LIP (Large Internet Packets) overcome the traditional 512-byte packet size NetWare was limited to because of ARCnet support. Any router in the network path of a packet forced the use of small packets. When set to On, and all intermediate routers and servers support large packets, the normal packet size will be used for the entire journey.

Time SET Commands

        TIMESYNC Add Time Source = *server*

This specifies the name of the server to use as a time source.

        TIMESYNC Configuration File = SYS:SYSTEM\TIMESYNC.CFG

This sets the location of the TIMESYNC.CFG file. You can have a maximum of 255 characters in the full path name.

        TIMESYNC Configured Sources = Off

This specifies the time sources for this server to listen to. When this is set to On, the server ignores SAP time sources and listens only to those sources listed in the TIMESYNC.CFG file.

        TIMESYNC Directory Tree Mode = On

This specifies SAP packet use in the NDS tree for time synchronization. When it is set to On, time synchronization ignores SAP packets from outside the NDS tree. If it is Off, the server will accept packets from any time source on the network. Don't set this parameter to Off if SAP is set to On, or time synchronization could be corrupted.

        TIMESYNC Hardware Clock = On

When this is set to On, Primary and Secondary servers set the hardware clock, and Single Reference and Reference servers take their time for the hardware clock at the start of each polling interval. When this is set to Off, this server uses an external time source, such as a radio clock.

    TIMESYNC Polling Count = 3

This sets the number of time packets to exchange while setting the time during polling. The range for this setting is 1 to 1000.

    TIMESYNC Polling Interval = 600

This setting is for the long polling interval for the time. The range for this setting is 10 to 2,678,400 seconds (31 days). All servers in the same tree must use the same setting.

    TIMESYNC Remove Time Source = server

This deletes the named server as a time source. The server name can be a maximum of 48 characters.

    TIMESYNC Reset = Off

Set this parameter to On to force the TIMESYNC.NLM to reset selected internal values and clear the configured server list. The setting will automatically change back to Off.

    TIMESYNC Restart Flag = Off

Setting this to On reloads the TIMESYNC.NLM without rebooting the server.

    TIMESYNC Service Advertising = On

When this is set to On, it allows the Single Reference, Reference, and Primary time sources to advertise using SAP. Secondary time services do not advertise.

    TIMESYNC Synchronization Radius = 2000

This sets the maximum variance for time synchronization. The range for this setting is 0 to 2,147,483,647 milliseconds. Less than 2 seconds will cause problems because of the randomness of PC clock crystals. A wider margin may cause problems for some time-critical applications.

    TIMESYNC Time Adjustment = +hh:mm:ss/-hh:mm:ss/AT date time

This setting schedules a time adjustment from a Single, Reference, or Primary time server. It corrects time errors across the network. If you don't set a time to start the adjustment, it will happen in six polling cycles or one hour from the entry time. You can set this as +*hh:mm:ss*, –*hh:mm:ss* or AT *date time*. The command can contain a maximum of 99 characters. Type CANCEL to erase a previously scheduled adjustment.

```
TIMESYNC Time Source = server
```

This specifies the server to be a time source. The server name can be a maximum of 48 characters. If no server name is given, you will see a display of the configured server list.

```
TIMESYNC Type = Secondary
```

This specifies the default time source. The other option is Single.

```
TIMESYNC Write Parameters = Off
```

This specifies whether the TIMESYNC Write Value parameters should be written to the configuration file. The default is not to write these parameters to the file (Off).

```
TIMESYNC Write Value = 3
```

This specifies which parameters are written by the TIMESYNC Write Parameters option. The settings are 1 = write internal parameters only, 2 = write configured time sources only, or 3 = write both parameters and configured time sources.

```
Time Zone = No Time Zone
```

This sets the string for the time zone, consisting of the abbreviated time zone name, the offset from UTC, and the abbreviation used with daylight saving time.

```
Default Time Server Type = Secondary
```

This specifies the time synchronization server type. The setting can be Secondary, Primary, Reference, or Single, with a maximum of 50 characters. It can be overridden by other time parameters.

```
Start of Daylight Saving Time = (monthname dayname
    daynumber)
```

This sets the local date and time for the change to daylight saving time. Both start and end times must be set before the date is accepted. You can use any single date and time or time rules enclosed in parentheses, as in Start of

Daylight Saving Time = (APRIL SUNDAY FIRST 2:00:00 AM). The maximum length is 79 characters.

```
End of Daylight Saving Time = (monthname dayname
daynumber)
```

This sets the local date and time for the end of daylight saving time. Both start and end times must be set before the date is accepted. You can use any single date and time or time rules enclosed in parentheses, as in End of Daylight Saving Time = (OCTOBER SUNDAY LAST 2:00:00 AM). The maximum length is 79 characters.

```
Daylight Saving Time Offset = None
```

When used, this parameter forces UTC time to be based on local time. You can set it to any time amount.

```
Daylight Saving Time Status = Off
```

This shows whether daylight saving time is in effect. This setting has no affect on the local time.

```
New Time with Daylight Saving Time Status = Off
```

When set to On, this parameter automatically adjusts the local time by subtracting or adding the daylight saving time offset value.

Transaction Tracking SET Commands

```
Auto TTS Backout Flag = On
```

When this parameter is set to On, it automatically answers all prompts and performs any necessary TTS backout procedures upon booting the server. This must be set in STARTUP.NCF if used.

```
TTS Abort Dump Flag = Off
```

This sets whether transactional backout data is written to a log file. If On, the information is saved to TTS$LOG.ERR. The file can later be printed or viewed.

```
Maximum Transactions = 10000
```

This sets the concurrent transactions for the entire system. The range for this setting is 100 to 10,000.

```
TTS Unwritten Cache Wait Time = 1 Min 5.9 Sec
```

This sets the maximum amount of time a block of transactional data can be delayed in a cache buffer. Some blocks must be written before others can finish and be written themselves. If the maximum time limit is passed, write requests are held until the unfinished block is written to disk. The range for this setting is 11 seconds to 10 minutes, 5.9 seconds.

```
TTS Backout File Truncation Wait Time = 59 Min 19.2 Sec
```

This sets the amount of time TTS backout file allocated blocks remain available. The range for this setting is 1 minute, 5.9 seconds to 1 day, 2 hours, 21 minutes, 51.3 seconds.

Recommended Reading

APPENDIX D

THE BOOKS LISTED here are those that I used as references while writing this book. I've included brief descriptions, so you can get an idea of whether you will benefit from reading these books (in addition to the one you're holding in your hands now, of course).

General Reading

Guide to Managing PC Networks, Steve Steinke (Prentice Hall, 1995).
How Local Area Networks Work, David R. Kosiur and Jonathan Angel (Prentice Hall, 1995).

Both of these books are about networking in general. If you (or some of your staff) are new to networking, these books can help you understand the history and fundamentals of networking.

Manager's Guides

LAN Survival–A Guerrila Guide to NetWare, Deni Connor and Mark Anderson (AP Professional, 1994).

This book includes information for network administrators in a NetWare environment. It covers all versions of NetWare.

A Manager's Guide to Multivendor Networks, John Enck (Professional Books, 1991).

This guide is excellent for managers who need comparative information about PC networks, standards, and large-system options (such as DECnet and SNA).

LAN Protocol Handbook, Mark A. Miller (M&T Books, 1990).
Here you'll find detailed information about all the protocols you might use, as well as some you probably will never use.

Novell's Guide to Managing Small NetWare Networks, Kelley J.P. Lindberg (Novell Press, 1993).
Aimed at smaller networks (fewer than 100 users) and the NetWare 2.*x* and NetWare 3.*x* market, this guide is still valuable. Many of the administrative functions in NetWare 3.*x* are similar to those in NetWare 4.*x*. If you have a mixed NetWare environment, this is a good book to have.

Toubleshooting NetWare Systems, Logan G. Harbaugh (Sybex, 1996).
This book is exactly what its title says. It presents and solves problems for all NetWare versions and all NetWare clients.

Internetworking Guides

Internetworking with TCP/IP–Principles, Protocols, and Architecture, Douglas Comer (Prentice Hall, 1988).
I have the first edition, but later editions of this book are available. It includes everything you need to know about TCP/IP and all the protocols that make up the TCP/IP suite.

The Simple Book–An Introduction to Management of TCP/IP-based Internets, Marshall T. Rose (Prentice Hall, 1991).
This is *the* book of SNMP (where the "Simple" comes from in the title). If you have SNMP (Simple Network Management Protocol) management somewhere on your network, you need this book.

Internet System Handbook, Daniel C. Lynch and Marshall T. Rose, editors (Addison Wesley, 1993).

Dan Lynch (founder of InterOp) and Marshall Rose (see the previous listing for one of the many accomplishments in Marshall's career) persuaded most of the Internet pioneers to write down the details of each section of the Internet. Protocols, applications, history, and futures are all covered. It isn't a "user" book for the Internet, but an excellent background and manager's book.

Novell's Guide to Integrating Unix and NetWare Networks, James E. Gaskin (Novell Press, 1993).

My first book—what can I say?

OS/2 Information

Mastering OS/2 Warp–The OS/2 Warp Bible, Peter Dyson (Sybex, 1995).

Everything you could want to know about OS/2, especially the Warp version. I found this book very helpful when I set up the OS/2 client.

Windows 95 Help

The Expert Guide to Windows 95, Mark Minasi (Sybex, 1996).

Serious advanced help for those cursed with supporting large numbers of Windows 95 workstations.

The Windows 95 Resource Kit, Microsoft Press (Microsoft Press, 1995).

All the details that should have been in the manual or the Help screens. Luckily, they only charge you an extra $50; they could have asked for more if the Justice Department wasn't watching.

Networking Reference Books

Novell's Dictionary of Networking, Peter Dyson (Novell Press, 1994).
The Network Press Encyclopedia of Networking, Werner Feibel (Sybex, 1996).

This dictionary contains nearly 2000 terms, covering all parts of the networking world. The encyclopedia has thousands of more terms, with diagrams, illustrations, and long explanations. These books are essential to the tech support library.

Network Support Encyclopedia (NSE), Novell Staff (Novell, new updates monthly).

The NSE CD-ROM includes thousands of Novell documents and support information. Novell's patches and drivers are included, as well as troubleshooting information, compatibility testing results, and all Novell product manuals. A must-have for any serious tech support department.

LAN to WAN Interconnection, John Enck and Mel Beckman (McGraw-Hill, Inc., 1995).

An excellent reference that contains information about all available LAN and WAN topologies, options, and details. If you have more than a single cable-type network, this book is for you. When your boss wants to know how any LAN or WAN system could be attached to your network, pull this book off your shelf and get up to speed.

Internet Books

NetWare to Internet Gateways, James E. Gaskin (Prentice Hall, 1996).

Yes, that's me again. If you want to get to the Internet, be my guest. There are a dozen ways to get there, not including the IPX/IP Gateway that Novell now offers. (If you have a NetWare 3.x system that you want to use as a gateway, the new Novell product leaves you out; it supports only NetWare 4.11.) The CD-ROM that comes with the book includes six vendors' products for Internet gateways running on NetWare servers, Windows NT, OS/2, and Unix hosts.

Corporate Politics and the Internet: Connection Without Controversy, James E. Gaskin (Prentice Hall, 1996).

Yes, that's me yet again. Assuming you took my advice and examined the NetWare-to-Internet gateways, you now have a new problem: The lawyers have invaded the Internet. My book covers all the legal, ethical, and personnel decisions a company must make when connecting to the Internet. Help for Internet clients, Internet service providers, and Web server managers is included.

Civilizing Cyberspace, Stephen Miller (Addison Wesley, 1995).

If you're interested in any of the social, governmental, and philosophical changes wrought in our society by the Internet, this is the book for you. Much is here to agree and disagree with, but when you finish reading it, you'll have a better grip on the social costs of the Internet.

Glossary of Terms

A

abend

For ABNormal ENDing; a computer crash.

Access Control List (ACL)

A NetWare Directory Services (NDS) object property that allows other objects to access the object, including object and property rights. The ACL also includes the Inherited Rights Filter (IRF).

Access Control right

The right to change trustee assignments and/or the Inherited Rights Filter (IRF) of a file or directory.

accounting

The accounting process, when engaged, tracks network resources used by clients. (NetWare 4.1*x* accounting is discussed in Chapter 10.)

ACL

See *Access Control List*.

ACU

See *Automatic Client Upgrade*.

Add or Delete Self right

The property right that specifies whether a trustee can add or remove itself as a value of that property.

address

A unique identifier on the network, most often the number assigned to the network card by the manufacturer. *Address* may also refer to memory location in an operating system.

Other addresses becoming newsworthy now include IP addresses (204.251.122.48), which are identifiers for systems on the Internet or other TCP/IP (Transmission Control Protocol/Internet Protocol) networks. e-mail addresses use the *domain name* after the @ sign, such as james@gaskin.com.

Address Resolution Protocol (ARP)

The IP (Internet Protocol) protocol that provides the physical address when only the logical address is known.

addressing, disk channel

SCSI (Small Computer Systems Interface) hardware identification number, 0 to 7.

addressing space

Supported RAM under the NetWare 4.1*x* operating system. The limit of 4 GB is theoretical, not practical, since no server hardware supports 4 GB of RAM today.

Admin object

The practical equivalent to SUPERVISOR in earlier versions of NetWare. The only User object defined during installation, Admin has the rights to create and manage objects. (See Chapter 10 for related information.)

AFP

See *AppleTalk Filing Protocol*.

AFP Server object

A specialized server leaf object that represents an AppleTalk Filing Protocol (AFP) server.

Alias object

A leaf object that represents an object in a different location in the Directory tree. Using Alias objects, one object (such as a NetWare volume) can appear to be in several containers at one time, thus enabling users in each container to easily locate and use the original object. (See Chapter 4 for related information.)

AppleShare software

Macintosh software that provides file and print services in an AppleTalk network.

AppleTalk Filing Protocol (AFP)

The Macintosh version of file sharing services.

AppleTalk protocols

Specifications for the AppleTalk network, such as LAP (Link Access Protocol), LLAP (LocalTalk LAP), and ELAP (Ethernet LAP). Other AppleTalk protocols include ASP (Appletalk Session Protocol), DDP (Datagram Delivery Protocol), NBP (Name Binding Protocol), PAP (Printer Access Protocol), RTMP (Routing Table Maintenance Protocol), and ZIP (Zone Information Protocol). (See Chapter 13 for related information.)

application

A software program, which may or may not use the available network resources.

archive

To save files to a longer-term, but slower-access, media than the hard disk. Archive normally refers to optical disks or magnetic tape.

Archive Needed attribute

A NetWare extended file attribute indicating that the file has changed since the last backup.

ARP

See *Address Resolution Protocol.*

attach

To attach is to make a connection between the workstation and a NetWare server. (The ATTACH command used in earlier NetWare versions in login scripts is not valid in NetWare 4.1x.)

attributes

Extended bits after the file name describing file-specific operating system characteristics. Attributes are often called *flags* in NetWare. Attributes include Read Only, Write, and Compressed.

NetWare's extended file attributes (often called *flags*) can be set to aid in security. Listing a file as Read Only, for instance, makes it less possible for a user to accidentally delete the file or for a virus to change that file.

audit

The ability of a user, defined as an auditor, to monitor, but not change, network events and records. In NetWare 4, this is done through the AUDITCON program utility. (See Chapter 9 for related information.)

AUDITCON

A NetWare 4 utility that allows a non-supervisory user to monitor network activity, but that user cannot modify any network settings or files. (See Chapter 9 for details.)

authentication

A security procedure that verifies that a NetWare Directory Services (NDS) user has permission to use the network service requested. NetWare 4.1*x*'s authentication is based on the public key encryption system, and it is extremely reliable and safe.

AUTOEXEC.NCF

The script of commands used by a NetWare server when booting and setting up the NetWare environment. This file is similar in purpose and organization to the AUTOEXEC.BAT file of a personal computer. (See Chapter 3 for related information.)

Automatic Client Upgrade (ACU)

A method to upgrade Novell client software during the login process, powered by four different executable programs called during the login script. This method is handy for mass upgrades when your client population uses consistent workstation configurations.

automatic rollback

A security feature of TTS (Transaction Tracking System) that, when engaged, guarantees a database transaction is completed. If the network, client, or server fails during a TTS transaction, the database is returned to the state existing before the transaction started.

B

backup

A copy of hard disk information made to a tape system, optical disk, or another hard disk. A backup is used more often to recover from accidents than from catastrophes. (See Chapter 1 for related information.)

backup host/target

A *backup host* is a NetWare server with attached storage (tape, hard disk, or optical disk). A *backup target* can be any workstation, server, service, or third-party device with the TSA (Target Service Agent) utility loaded.

bindery

A security database controlling user privileges in earlier NetWare versions. NetWare 4 uses NetWare Directory Services (NDS).

Bindery object

A leaf object that represents an object unidentified by NDS (NetWare Directory Services), placed in the Directory tree by an upgrade or a migration process. (See Chapter 4 for related information.)

Bindery Queue object

A leaf object that represents a bindery print queue in the Directory tree.

Bindery Services

A NetWare 4 feature that mimics bindery databases for software that requires the bindery of earlier NetWare versions. Many existing third-party print servers, for example, require Bindery Services. (See Chapter 4 for related information.)

binding/unbinding

Binding is initiating protocol-support software for a network board. *Unbinding* is removing protocol-support software from a network board. (See Chapter 2 for related information.)

block

The smallest unit of disk space controlled by the NetWare operating system. Size ranges from 4 KB to 64 KB. Smaller blocks require more server memory. The best utilization is achieved by using the 64 KB block size with block suballocation.

block suballocation

A process that divides one block into 512-byte units that store fragments of other files. This greatly reduces the amount of disk space required, especially when many small files are stored on the disk.

boot files

Files that control the operating system parameters and configuration when the system starts. For example, AUTOEXEC.NCF for NetWare servers is a boot file.

BOOTCONF.SYS

A remote boot image file for diskless workstations. Avoid using this file if at all possible.

BOOTP (BOOTstrap Protocol)

Early configuration protocols used by TCP/IP (Transmission Control Protocol/Internet Protocol) systems to provide IP address and other configuration details to diskless workstations. Enough code was placed in a chip on the system motherboard to find the BOOTP server and request information. Superceded by *DHCP*.

bridge

A powered network device that connects two or more network segments and passes packets based on physical addresses only. Routers use protocol-supplied addresses.

Browse right

The object right that allows users to see Directory tree objects.

browse

Using the Browse right to navigate up and down the Directory tree.

Btrieve

Software using key-indexed records for high performance. The company that developed Btrieve was owned by Novell for many years (but no longer), so many applications expect to find the Btrieve utility running on NetWare servers.

buffer

Memory area set aside to hold temporary data until the data can be accepted by either the workstation or network.

C

cabling system

Physical wires supporting your network. (See Chapter 1 for related information.)

cache buffer

A server memory buffer that improves performance by keeping recently used files in server memory.

cache buffer pool

The total amount of memory available for server cache operations. The cache buffer pool is used to cache volume FATs (file allocation tables), volume directory tables, recently used files, directory names, and FAT indexes for large files. (See Chapter 11 for a description of adjusting cache buffers to optimize either reading or writing files.)

cache memory

Another name for a *cache buffer* or *cache buffer pool*.

caching

Directory caching is a NetWare technique of keeping directory names in server memory for quicker access, rather than reading the directory from the disk.

File caching is caching recently used files in server RAM to speed file reading and operations.

Can't Compress attribute

A flag indicating a file can't be compressed.

channel

A logical memory connection point between workstation memory and hard disk controllers. *Channel* also refers to a pathway through a communications medium, such as a channel on a multiplexer, or the B (bearer) and D (data) channels on an ISDN (Integrated Services Digital Network) line.

client

A machine that uses any of the network services provided by a network server. In NetWare, clients may be DOS, MS Windows, OS/2, Macintosh, or Unix systems.

Client32

New client software upgrade that takes advantage of 32-bit technology and expanded memory availability, developed primarily for Windows 95 and Windows NT. In NetWare 4.11, Client32 can also be used for DOS and Windows 3.1*x* clients.

CMOS RAM

Complementary Metal Oxide Semiconductor RAM (random-access memory), used for storing system configuration information. CMOS RAM is supported by a battery to retain information when the system is turned off or unplugged.

communication protocol

Rules governing the sending and receiving of data between two machines. (See Chapter 1 for related information.)

Compare right

The property right granting the ability to compare values to those of another property.

Compressed attribute

A file attribute declaring the file's compression status.

Computer object

An optional leaf object that represents a computer on the network in the Directory tree.

configuration

Details concerning the physical or software components of a system, and how each is instructed to work with the other pieces of the system.

connection number

A NetWare server-assigned number for each workstation, print server, process, or application that requires a server connection. The connection numbers are assigned on a first-come, first-served basis.

Container login script

A login script in NetWare 4 that affects all users in the container. This replaces the System login script in NetWare 3. Container login scripts are optional. When they are used, they execute before Profile and User login scripts. (See Chapter 7 for related information.)

container object

An object that can contain other objects within the Directory tree.

context

Shorthand to represent the specific container of an object within the Directory tree. (See Chapter 4 for related information.)

controller address

A unique number for each controller board in a disk channel.

controller board

Hardware that connects the computer to other devices, such as hard disks, tape systems, or optical jukeboxes.

Copy Inhibit attribute

A Macintosh-specific file attribute that prevents a file from being copied.

Country object

A container object, which must be directly under the [Root] object in the Directory tree, that defines the country for a specific part of your network. The Country object is not mandatory in NetWare 4, but it is necessary for connecting to external networks that rely on X.500 directory services.

Create right

A file-system right that allows new files and subdirectories to be created. The Create right is necessary for file salvage. Create is also used in NetWare Directory Services (NDS) as an object right.

cylinder

A concentric, distinct area on a hard disk for storage. The more cylinders in a disk, the greater its storage capacity.

D

DARPA

Defense Advanced Research Projects Agency. Expanded name from the original ARPA in the early 1970's to reflect the source of early Internet development money.

data fork

The Macintosh file part that contains user-specified data.

data migration

The movement of inactive files from migration-enabled NetWare volumes to another near-online or offline storage format. (See Chapter 18 for related information.)

data protection

In NetWare, duplicate file directories and the process of moving data from bad blocks to known good blocks.

To protect data location information, NetWare 4.1*x* uses duplicate DETs (directory-entry tables) and FATs (file allocation tables) to provide fault-tolerance on the hard disk. Having copies of each of these tables reduces the risk of loss due to a bad block or two.

To protect data against surface defects, NetWare 4.1*x* uses the following methods:

- *Read-after-write verification*: Verifying every bit written to the disk before the copy is erased from server RAM (NetWare default).

- *Hot Fix*: Separate area of the hard disk used to copy data from bad blocks on the disk. The bad block is then marked as bad so no other data will be written there.

- *Disk mirroring*: Placing data on two disks connected to the same controller.

- *Disk duplexing*: Placing data on two identical disks connected to two separate controllers.

data set

SBACKUP (NetWare 4.1*x*'s backup software utility) information.

DCB

See *disk coprocessor board*.

DDP (Datagram Delivery Protocol)

See *AppleTalk protocols*.

default drive

The current disk drive used by a workstation, indicated by the drive prompt.

default server

The server that responds to a workstation's "Get Nearest Server" request when the user first starts the login process. In earlier NetWare versions, the default server name was often specified in the NET.CFG file on the workstation. NetWare Directory Services (NDS) has replaced the need for the default server destination with the default *context*.

Delete Inhibit attribute

A file attribute that prevents file deletion.

Delete right

A NetWare Directory Services (NDS) object right that allows users to delete files or Directory tree objects.

delimiter

A symbol or character that differentiates between commands, parameters inside commands, or records. Common delimiters are comma (,), period (.), slash (/), backslash (\), hyphen (-), and colon (:).

demigration

An HCSS (high-capacity storage system) method of moving a file back from the jukebox to the server (after migration) when requested.

destination server

The target server in NetWare 4 server migration.

DET

See *directory-entry table*.

device driver

Software that connects a system's operating system to the system's hardware, such as a disk or network controller.

device numbering

A unique identification number or address used to identify network devices. The number may be a physical address, device code, or logical number determined by the operating system.

device sharing

Allowing more than one person to use a device, and a great excuse for a network. Shared devices include hard disks, printers, modems, fax servers, tape backup units, and communication gateways.

DHCP (Dynamic Host Configuration Protocol)

A protocol update of *BOOTP*. Used to provide IP address and other configuration details from a central server to connected workstations. Novell's DHCP ships with NetWare 4.11 as part of TCP/IP (Transmission Control Protocol/Internet Protocol) support.

Directory/directory

The *Directory* is the database supporting the hierarchical structure of NetWare Directory Services (NDS), the upgrade from the bindery.

A *directory* is a file-system organization method. A directory may contain both files and other directories.

directory and file rights

Authority to modify directories and files.

directory entry

A NetWare operating system basic unit of file-system control, including the file or directory name, owner, date and time of last update (files), and physical location of the first data block on the hard disk.

directory-entry table (DET)

Basic information concerning files, directories, directory trustees and other entities per volume are tracked in the directory table. Maximum entries per directory table is 2,097,152, since each of the 65,536 maximum directory blocks per volume can each hold 32 entries. A directory entry is 32 bytes long.

Directory management request

A NetWare Directory Services (NDS) database modification method, including new Directory partitions and replica management.

Directory Map object

A leaf object similar to an Alias object in that it represents another object in another context in the Directory tree. This object is used mostly with login script MAP commands to represent the locations for common applications. (See Chapter 4 for related information.)

directory path

A complete file-system specification, including the server name, volume name, and the name of each directory ending in the file name.

directory rights

Attributes that allow access to directories.

Directory Services

The distributed security and network-resource-locating database released with NetWare 4 to replace and upgrade the bindery. This database works on the network level, not per server.

Directory Services request

A user or an administrator request to the Directory database to read or modify the database contents. There are three types of requests:

- *Directory-access requests* are user requests to create, modify, or retrieve objects.

- *Directory-access control requests* are administrator requests to allow access rights to the Directory database for users.

- *Directory-management requests* are administrator requests to manage the physical Directory database, such as to perform partitioning operations.

directory structure

The filing system of volumes, directories, and files that the NetWare server uses to organize data on its hard disks. (See also *file system*.)

Also, a directory structure is the hierarchical structure that represents how partitions are related to each other in the Directory database. (See also *Directory tree*.)

Directory tree

Container objects and all the leaf objects that make up the hierarchical structure of the NetWare Directory Services (NDS) database. Also known as an *NDS tree*.

disk controller

A hardware device (interface card) that connects the computer with the disk drive. The disk controller translates signals for file manipulation from the operating system into physical movement of the disk drive heads to find the requested file location.

disk coprocessor board (DCB)

An early hardware disk controller with a microprocessor to off-load storage operations from the main server microprocessor to improve disk performance. This method has been replaced by speedier disk-storage options.

disk driver

Software that connects the NetWare operating system to the disk controller. The four Novell-supplied disk drivers are ISADISK.DSK (ISA disks), IDE.DSK (IDE disks), PS2ESDI.DSK (ESDI controllers in an IBM MicroChannel Architecture system), and PS2SCSI.DSK (SCSI controllers in an IBM MicroChannel Architecture system). Third-party vendors often supply their own disk drivers.

NetWare 4.1x now uses the Media Manager, a database that tracks storage devices and associated media attached to a server. This is part of the NWPA (NetWare Peripheral Architecture). Components include the HAM (Host Adapter Module), which is adapter-specific; the HAI (Host Adapter Interface), providing software programming interfaces; the CDM (Custom Device Module), device-specific for the storage device; and the CDI (Custom Device Interface), the programming interface for the storage device.

disk duplexing

Two controllers supporting two hard drives, each written with the same information. If either disk or controller fails, the system continues without interruption.

disk format

Hard disk preparation to allow the disk to receive information. The disk format depending on the operating system.

disk interface board

See *disk controller*.

disk mirroring

Two drives, supported by one controller, each written with the same information. If either disk fails, the system continues without interruption.

disk partition

A hard disk section treated by the operating system as if it were a separate drive. With NetWare, each disk can have more than one partition, and volumes can span multiple partitions.

disk subsystem

An external hardware housing holding one or more disk, tape, or optical drives. The disk subsystem is connected to the NetWare server via cable to the controller board.

DMA (dynamic memory access)

A method of transferring information from a device such as a hard disk or network adapter directory into memory without passing through the CPU. Because the CPU is not involved in the information transfer, the process is faster than other types of memory transfers. The DMA channel must be unique for each device.

DNS (Domain Name Service)

Developed in the early 1980s to automate the previously manual editing of host files on Internet-connected systems. DNS allowed the number of hosts to double each year, and is still the directory service in use on the Internet and the Web.

Don't Compress attribute

A file attribute that prevents the operating system from compressing the file.

Don't Migrate attribute

A file attribute that prevents the operating system from migrating the file.

DOS client

A NetWare client running DOS (and/or MS Windows).

DOS device

A mass storage unit supporting the DOS disk format. It is used by UPGRADE and SBACKUP (NetWare 4.1x's backup software utility).

drive

A *physical drive* is a physical mass storage device that supports the reading and writing of data. A *logical drive* is a network disk directory addressed as a separate drive with a drive-letter prompt.

drive mapping

The process of assigning various network disk directories as separate drives, each with a unique drive letter. (Chapter 12 explains local, network, and search drive mappings from the user's point of view.)

driver

Software that connects the NetWare operating system to physical devices, such as drive controllers and network interface boards.

DSREPAIR

A server-run NetWare Loadable Module (NLM) program that repairs and corrects problems with the NetWare Directory database. With DSREPAIR, records, schema, bindery objects, and external references can be repaired, modified, or deleted. (See Chapter 10 for details.)

DSS (Domain SAP Server)

NetWare software running on a NetWare/IP-enabled server to track the information normally distributed via IPX (Internetwork Packet eXchange) SAP (Service Advertising Protocol) broadcasts. Since TCP/IP (Transmission Control Protocol/Internet Protocol) networks dislike broadcasts, NetWare/IP clients must query the DSS for network configuration details, such as the nearest server during login.

dynamic configuration

The ability of NetWare to allocate resources from available server processes first, and to allocate new processes if an available process fails to answer the request in a timely manner.

dynamic memory

Memory chips that require constant electrical current to hold the information written to them. Dynamic memory is used for RAM.

dynamic memory access

See *DMA*.

E

effective rights

A user's access rights to a file, directory, or object based on the combination of trustee assignments, inherited rights, Group object rights, and any security equivalence. NetWare calculates a user's rights before every action.

Effective rights are based on a combination of the following:

- The object's direct trustee assignments to the directory or file in question
- Any inherited rights from parent directories
- Rights to the object gained from being a member of a group with trustee rights to the object or file/directory
- Rights from a listing in a User object's security equivalence list

Embedded SCSI

A hard disk drive with a SCSI (Small Computer Systems Interface) controller built into the hard disk logic.

Erase right

The authority to delete files or directories.

Ethernet configuration

The Ethernet standard followed by network connections. NetWare 4.1x supports four Ethernet configurations:

- Ethernet 802.3: Raw Ethernet frame, used as the default for NetWare 3.x and earlier
- Ethernet 802.2: NetWare 4.x default frame type
- Ethernet II: Frame type for TCP/IP, AppleTalk Phase I, and DECnet
- Ethernet SNAP (Subnetwork Address Protocol): Frame type for AppleTalk Phase II

Execute Only attribute

A file attribute in NetWare 4.0 and 4.10 that prevents the file from being copied. Use this sparingly; it's difficult to change this attribute.

F

fake root

A NetWare function that has applications accept a subdirectory as the root of the drive. Network-aware applications don't require tricks such as the fake root.

FAT

See *file allocation table*.

fault-tolerance

A means of protecting data by providing data duplication on multiple storage devices. (See also *System Fault Tolerance*.)

Also, distributing the NetWare Directory database among several servers to provide continued authentication and access to object information should a server go down. (See also *replica*.)

file allocation table (FAT)

The DOS index that tracks disk locations of all files and file fragments on the disk partition. NetWare uses the DOS FAT, accessed from the directory-entry table (DET). Files that exceed 64 blocks are listed as a *turbo FAT*, and indexed with all FAT entries for that particular file. This speeds access to the complete file.

file compression

A method of replacing repeating characters in a file with shortened characters, reducing the file length. NetWare 4.1*x* supports file compression, enabled by volume, directory, or file.

file indexing

NetWare's means of indexing FAT entries for better performance while accessing large files. Any file larger than 64 blocks is indexed automatically.

file locking

The process of limiting access to a file so the first user or application can modify the file before a second user or application makes changes.

file name extension

The three characters after the period in DOS file names.

FILER

A workstation utility that allows both users and supervisors to manage the file system on NetWare servers. (See Chapter 10 for details.)

file rights

The authority over what can be done to a file. (See Chapters 9 and 11 for related information.)

File Scan right

The authority to see the files and directories with the DIR and NDIR commands.

file server

A machine used to run the network operating system. Referred to as the NetWare server when speaking of a machine running the NetWare operating system.

file sharing

An operating system feature that allows more than one user concurrent access to a file.

file system

The overall data organization on the hard disk, tracking each file in its specific hierarchical location. NetWare supports file systems across volumes, directories, subdirectories, and files. (See Chapter 1 for related information.)

File Transfer Protocol

See *FTP*.

flag

Another name for file attributes in NetWare.

FLAG

A utility program that allows you to view or modify the extended NetWare attributes of files on NetWare volumes. (See Chapter 10 for details.)

frame

A packet-format specification. NetWare supports Ethernet 802.3, Ethernet 802.2, Ethernet II, Ethernet SNAP, Token Ring, and Token Ring SNAP frames.

FTP (File Transfer Protocol)

IP (Internet Protocol) protocol that specifies rules for file exchange between two systems.

FTP Server

Server software included with IntranetWare that allows remote clients to place and retrieve files from the server, generally over the Internet. Only a few limited FTP (File Transfer Protocol) commands, such as PUT file and GET file, are supported by any FTP server or client. Most FTP servers allow anonymous users, similar to the traditional Novell GUEST user, to have access to some files without needing a password. The majority of Internet file distribution happens through FTP servers and anonymous clients.

G

gateway

A link between two or more networks allowing dissimilar protocols to communicate. See also *IPX/IP Gateway*.

Group object

A leaf (not container) object listing one or more User objects in the Directory tree. Whatever access is granted to the Group object is passed to all User objects within the group. (See Chapter 7 for related information.)

H

handle

A computer system pointer that specifies a resource or feature. For example, a system may use file handles, device handles, and directory handles.

hard disk

A magnetic storage device that uses rigid platters turning at high speeds.

Hardware Specific Module (HSM)

See *Open Data-link Interface (ODI)*.

hashing

An index file in server memory calculating each file's physical address on the hard disk. By skipping the sequential disk directory reads, file operations can be serviced much more quickly.

HBA

See *host bus adapter*.

HCSS

See *high-capacity storage system*.

hexadecimal

An alphanumeric numbering system that uses 0 through F to represent 0 through 15, as follows: A=10, B=11, C=12, D=13, E=14, F=15.

Hidden attribute

A file attribute that prevents a file from being seen with the DOS or OS/2 DIR command. It also prevents the file from being copied or deleted.

high-capacity storage system (HCSS)

A file-manipulation system that moves files from the server hard disk to optical disks in a jukebox.

Migration is the method of moving a file from the server to the jukebox. *Demigration* is when the migrated file is moved back to the server hard disk when it is requested. The file path name remains the same as far as the user is concerned, no matter where the file is physically located.

HCSS uses a directory table on the server hard disk to track the directory contents on different jukebox optical disks. Each jukebox can have more than one HCSS directory, and all optical disks can be assigned to one HCSS directory, or grouped within several directories. (See Chapter 18 for related information.)

home directory

A user's private area on the server hard disk. The user has full control over the home directory. (See Chapter 1 for related information.)

hop count

The number of network routers a packet passes through. NetWare allows only 16 hops between the packet source and destination. NSLP (NetWare Link Service Protocol) supports up to 127 hops.

host

A mainframe, traditionally. *Host* is also used to indicate an SBACKUP (NetWare 4.1*x*'s backup utility) server.

host bus adapter (HBA)

A disk controller with enough intelligence to speed disk access. NetWare handles up to five host adapter channels, each supporting four controllers per channel and eight drives per controller.

Hot Fix

A NetWare data-protection method that moves data from disk blocks that appear to be defective to a safe, reserved area. The suspect disk area is marked and not used again. The default redirection area is 2 percent of the disk partition's space.

HSM (Hardware Specific Module)

See *Open Data-link Interface (ODI)*.

hub

A physical wiring component that splits or amplifies the signal. The word *hub* is generally used with ARCnet cabling; *concentrator* is used in Ethernet 10BaseT, MAUs (media access units), and Token Ring.

I

identifier variable

A login script variable. For example, the identifier variable LOGIN_NAME is replaced with the login name supplied by the user when logging in. (See Chapter 7 for related information.)

Immediate Compress attribute

The file-system attribute that specifies files are to be compressed as soon as possible.

Indexed attribute

The status flag indicating the file is now indexed as a turbo FAT (file allocation table) for quicker access.

INETCFG.NLM

Internetworking Configuration. Utility used to enable TCP/IP (Transmission Control Protocol/Internet Protocol) on the server, and configure your IPX/IP Gateway. Run from the console by typing LOAD INETCFG.

Inherited Rights Filter (IRF)

The list of changes in a user's inherited file access rights as the user moves down the file directory tree. The IRF only revokes rights. You must have the Write property right to the Access Control right to a file or directory to change the IRF.

To allow flexibility in file systems and NDS design, there must be a way to lock some users out of areas below areas where they have access. The IRF blocks rights by revoking rights at directories or containers. This allows the network supervisor to freely grant access to higher levels, thereby saving time by granting rights to many people at once, while retaining the ability to lock users out of sensitive areas. An example is allowing everyone rights to the \ACCOUNTING directory, but using the IRF to limit access to \ACCOUNTING\PAYROLL.

internetwork

Two or more smaller networks that communicate with each other through a bridge, router, or gateway. Also called an *internet*.

interoperability

Support for one user to use resources from two or more dissimilar networks. Advances such as ODI (Open Data-link Interface) and TCP/IP (Transmission Control Protocol/Internet Protocol) support in the server make interoperability easier, but not automatic.

intranet

Your local network infused with Internet technology. For most companies, this means Web servers and clients used for connections within the company network, rather than outside to the Internet. IntranetWare supports this function well, and the fact that your existing LAN may become an intranet with the addition of some Web Server software just shows how smart you were to install NetWare in the first place.

IntranetWare

Novell's bundle that includes the operating system (NetWare 4.11), the Web Server, NetWare/IP, the Multi-Protocol Router (MPR), and the IPX/IP Gateway (Novell Internet Access Server). The name emphasizes the value of your existing NetWare network, now infused with Web and Internet technologies.

IP (Internet Protocol)

Part of the TCP/IP (Transmission Control Protocol/Internet Protocol) protocol suite similar to IPX (Internetwork Packet eXchange) in that it makes a best-effort attempt to deliver packets, but does not guarantee delivery. TCP is required for that step, as SPX (Sequenced Packet eXchange) is required in NetWare.

IP Address

The 4-byte address, which must be unique in the entire Internet if connected, that identifies host network connections. Normally seen in the dotted-decimal format, such as 204.251.122.12. Internet committees oversee IP address coordination and distribution.

IPX (Internetwork Packet eXchange)

The Novell-developed and XNS (Xerox Network Services) derived protocol used by NetWare. Addressing and routing for IPX is handled by NetWare, unlike the corresponding functions in TCP/IP (Transmission Control Protocol/Internet Protocol).

IPX external network number

The unique network number that identifies a single network cable segment. The IPX (Internetwork Packet eXchange) network is defined by a hexadecimal number of from one to eight digits (1 to FFFFFFFE). A random number is assigned during installation, or the installer can specify the external network number.

IPX internal network number

The unique network number that identifies a NetWare 4 server. Each server on a network must have a unique IPX (Internetwork Packet eXchange) internal network number. A random number is assigned during installation, or the installer can specify the internal network number for each server.

IPX internetwork address

A 12-byte number (24 hexadecimal characters) made up of three parts: a 4-byte IPX (Internetwork Packet eXchange) external network number, a 6-byte node number (derived from the interface card's unique address), and a 2-byte socket number.

IPX/IP Gateway

Generically, any software that converts datagrams from IPX (Internetwork Packet eXchange) to IP (Internet Protocol). There are at least a dozen vendors that sell IP translation gateways, most of which are focused on the NetWare market.

Specifically, the name of Novell's IP translation software running under NetWare 4.11 and included as part of IntranetWare. See also *Novell Internet Access Server*.

IPXODI (Internetwork Packet eXchange Open Data-link Interface)

The client software module that accepts data from the DOS requester, attaches a header to each data packet, and transmits the data packet as a datagram.

IRF

See *Inherited Rights Filter*.

J

jukebox

A clever play on the old musical device, since a jukebox for NetWare is a device holding multiple optical disks, which plays one or more at a time, as requested by the operating system. Capacity for jukeboxes ranges from two disks and one reader to hundreds of disks and a dozen readers.

L

LAN (local-area network)

A network connected by physical cables, such as within a floor or building.

LAN driver

Software in the server and workstation that interfaces the physical network board to the machine's operating system.

Large Internet Packet (LIP)

The NetWare 4.1x feature that allows packets going through routers to have more than 576 bytes. The small packet size was a limitation of ARCnet packets, and NetWare defaulted to the small size in case ARCnet was on the other side of the router. Because the use of ARCnet is dwindling, this restriction has been lifted.

leaf object

A NetWare Directory Services (NDS) object that can't contain other objects. Examples are users, volumes, printers, and servers.

Link Support Layer (LSL)

The client and server software between the LAN drivers and the communications protocols. The LSL allows more than one protocol to share a network board.

LIP

See *Large Internet Packet*.

loadable module

An executable file with the extension NLM (for NetWare Loadable Module) that runs on the server. NLMs can be loaded and unloaded without taking down the server.

local-area network

See *LAN*.

log in

The process by which a user requests and receives authentication from the operating system, and is then able to use network resources.

Login scripts configure details such as printer setup and drive assignments.

LOGIN directory

SYS:LOGIN, a default NetWare directory, created during installation. The directory contains LOGIN and NLIST utilities to support users who are not yet authenticated.

login restrictions

User restrictions that control certain network security parameters. Login restrictions include the workstation a user is allowed to log in from, the time of day, and whether the user is allowed to have more than one active connection to the network. (See Chapter 9 for related information.)

login security

An aspect of NetWare security. The NetWare supervisor establishes login security by using the LOGIN command to control who can access the network. Users must be authenticated by Net-Ware Directory Services (NDS) by use of the login name and the correct password (although they are optional, passwords are strongly recommended). Passwords travel between the client and server in encrypted mode, so network protocol analyzers cannot capture any passwords.

login script

An ASCII text file that performs designated commands to configure the users' workstation environment. The login scripts are activated when the user executes the LOGIN command.

Container login scripts set general parameters for all users in a container, and execute first. *Profile login scripts* also set parameters for multiple users, but only for those users that specify the Profile script. This script executes after the Container script. User login scripts set parameters for individual users, and are the least efficient for administrators to use. (See Chapter 7 for related information.)

log out

To disconnect from the network (erasing all mapped drives). The LOGOUT command does not remove the NetWare client software from workstation memory.

LSL

See *Link Support Layer*.

M

Macintosh client

A NetWare desktop client using a Macintosh computer. By enabling the NetWare for Macintosh software included as part of NetWare 4.1*x*, Macintosh clients can become a full partner in the network. (See Chapter 13 for details.)

MAIL directory

SYS:MAIL is a default NetWare directory, created by the system during installation. Earlier NetWare versions stored each user's login script in his or her personal mail directory; now login scripts are a property of the User object. Users created under NetWare 4 don't get personal mail directories.

major resource

TSA (Target Service Agent) data that is regarded as a group by SBACKUP (NetWare 4.1*x*'s backup software utility). An example is a server and volume on that server.

MAP

A command-line utility that checks drive assignments and allows users to modify those assignments. The login script MAP command is used to assign drive letters to directory paths during the login process.

Media Manager

NetWare functions that abstract backup storage device control, allowing applications to address different storage devices without using device-specific drivers.

memory

A computer's internal storage under control of the operating system, generally called RAM (random-access memory) in desktop computers. The storage and retrieval speed of RAM is more closely matched to that of the CPU than any other system storage.

memory allocation

Segmenting RAM (random-access memory) for specific purposes such as disk caches, extended memory, and application execution space. NetWare 4 has replaced the five memory allocation pools with a single, more efficient memory pool.

memory protection

An operating system control function that allows you to lock NetWare Loadable Modules (NLMs) in a memory domain called OS_PROTECTED where the NLM can't access memory used by other NLMs or the operating system.

message packet

A packet, which is a basic unit of transmitted network information.

message system

The set of APIs (Application Program Interfaces) running on top of IPX (Internetwork Packet eXchange) which facilitate messages between nodes on the network.

MHS (Message Handling Services)

Early (NetWare 2.*x* through 4.10) e-mail integration and coordination software. MHS provided a standard means of connecting disparate e-mail systems. The focus on Internet technologies, including the IntranetWare products, has moved the e-mail world to Internet standards, leaving MHS behind.

Migrated attribute

A NetWare file indicator showing whether a file has migrated through HSM (Hierarchical Storage Management) off the server hard disk.

migration

The process of moving bindery and other data from earlier NetWare servers, or a different network operating system, to NetWare 4. Part of an HCSS (high-capacity storage system) method of moving a file from the server to the jukebox (*migration*) and, when requested, back to the server hard disk (*demigration*).

minor resource

TSA (Target Service Agent) data category recognized by SBACKUP (NetWare 4.1*x*'s backup software utility). Minor resources are located below major resources; for example, a directory under a volume.

MLID (Multiple Layer Interface Driver)

See *Open Data-link Interface (ODI)*.

Modify bit

A status file attribute that indicates whether the file has been changed since the last backup. This bit is used by backup systems such as SBACKUP to know which files to protect when a partial backup is used.

Modify right

Authority to change file or directory names or attributes.

MONITOR

The utility that displays the primary server information screen. MONITOR tracks the state of the server and, to a lesser extent, the state of the network. As a NetWare Loadable Module (NLM), it executes only at the server. (See Chapter 10 for details.)

MSM (Media Support Module)

See *Open Data-link Interface (ODI)*.

Multi-Protocol Router (MPR)

Expansion of Novell's long-time ability to route multiple protocols through the NetWare server operating system. Sold separately for awhile, MPR is now included with IntranetWare. Any currently available WAN connection, up through T1 lines, may be controlled by WAN boards in a NetWare server running the MPR software.

multiserver network

A physical network with more than one server. Internetworks have more than one network connected by a router or gateway.

N

name context

Context; the location of an object in an NDS (NetWare Directory Services) tree.

name space

The ability of a NetWare volume to support files from non-DOS clients, including Macintosh, OS/2, FTAM (Open Systems Interconnect), and Unix (NFS) systems. Each client sees files on the file server in its own file format. A Macintosh client will see a file as a Macintosh file, while an OS/2 user will see that same file as an OS/2 file.

Name space support is enabled per volume. NLMs with an extension of NAM are loaded to provide the file name translations. The ADD NAME SPACE command is necessary for each volume, after the appropriate name-space NLM is loaded (for example, LOAD NFS, then ADD NAME SPACE). This process creates multiple entries for each file in the name space of the volume's file system.

Name spaces cannot be removed without using the VREPAIR utility, or by deleting the volume and creating a replacement volume without the name space.

NBP (Name Binding Protocol)

See *AppleTalk protocols*.

NCP

See *NetWare Core Protocol*.

NCP Packet Signature

The NetWare security feature that allows each workstation to add a special "signature" to each packet going to the server. This signature changes with every packet, and this process makes it nearly impossible for another station to pretend to be a station with more security privileges.

NDIS (Network Driver Interface Specification)

A process similar to ODI (Open Data-link Interface) that allows a workstation to support multiple protocols over one network interface card. This was developed by 3Com, Microsoft, and Hewlett-Packard and released before Novell released the ODI drivers. ODINSUP (ODI NDIS Supplement) supports NDIS drivers under ODI when necessary.

NDS

See *NetWare Directory Services*.

NDS Manager

New graphical utility included with NetWare 4.11 and IntranetWare which includes parts of the older Partition Manager client application and the DSREPAIR console NLM application. All partition and replica operations, except major repairs, are supported by NDS Manager.

NETBIOS.EXE

The client networking file that emulates NetBIOS, the peer-to-peer network application interface used in IBM or IBM-inspired networks. The INT2F.COM file is necessary when the NETBIOS.EXE file is used.

NET.CFG

The client workstation boot file that contains configuration and setup parameters for the client's connection to the network. This file functions like the DOS CONFIG.SYS file, and is read by the machine only during the startup of the network files. (See Chapter 5 for related information.)

NETSYNC3/NETSYNC4

The two utility programs for NetWare 3 and NetWare 4 servers, respectively, that allow NetWare 3 servers to be managed by NetWare Directory Services (NDS). (See Chapter 10 for details.)

NetWare Administrator

The primary program for performing NetWare 4.1x supervisory tasks. This application is fully graphical, and it can be executed from within MS Windows or OS/2. (See Chapter 10 for details.)

NetWare Application Launcher (NAL)

The new utility for managing applications presented to NetWare clients. The NetWare Administrator defines which applications are available for the users, and provides an icon group for the users. Different startup and shutdown scripts may be used for extra application control. NAL uses the Universal Naming Conventions (UNC), reducing the need for more drive letters and their attendant management.

NetWare Client32

See *Client32*.

NetWare Core Protocol (NCP)

The NetWare presentation layer protocol and procedures used by a server to fulfill workstation requests. NCP actions include manipulating files and directories, changing the Directory, printing, and opening programming connections (*semaphores*) between client and server processes. The process of starting and stopping a connection between the workstation and server is indelicately called creating and destroying a service connection.

NetWare Directory database

Sometimes abbreviated by Novell documentation as NDD, the NetWare Directory database stores and organizes all objects in the Directory tree. The objects are stored in a hierarchical structure, mimicking the hierarchical arrangement of NetWare Directory Services (NDS) itself.

NetWare Directory Services (NDS)

A NetWare 4-specific database that maintains information on, and access to, all network resources for all network clients. NDS replaces the bindery in earlier NetWare versions. The database in NDS is distributed and replicated among multiple servers for fault-tolerance and high performance. Network resources controlled by NDS include users, groups, printers, volumes, and servers.

NDS allows access to network resources independent of the server holding those resources. With the bindery, each user was required to know the server responsible for each network service. NDS allows users to access resources without knowing the server responsible for those resources.

Users no longer establish a link to a single server in order to log in. Users are authenticated (logged in and verified) by the network itself through NDS. The authentication process provides the means for the client to communicate with NDS, as well as to check the security profile of each user. (See Chapters 3 and 4 for related information.)

NetWare DOS Requester

Client software for DOS and MS Windows computers. The DOS Requester replaces the earlier NetWare shell software. Modules of the DOS Requester provide shell compatibility for applications.

Rather than intercept all software function calls before they reach DOS, as the shell did, the DOS Requester works with DOS. When DOS requires a network service, it passes the function call to the NetWare DOS Requester. (See Chapter 5 for related information.)

NetWare/IP

Server modules and client software product that replaces IPX (Internetwork Packet eXchange) as the transport protocol between NetWare clients and NetWare servers. Requires multiple NLMs (NetWare Loadable Modules) and new client software. Gateways between the IPX and IP (Internet Protocol) networks allow NetWare clients from either side to see and use the resources of the other network.

NetWare Licensing Services (NLS)

A new NDS (NetWare Directory Services) and management feature that tracks application use to ensure that you have enough valid licenses for the number of concurrent users for each application. This feature has been available from third-parties in the past, but it makes sense for Novell to include more application management features along with the NetWare Application Launcher (NAL).

NetWare Link Service Protocol

See *NLSP*.

NetWare Loadable Module (NLM)

A program that executes at the NetWare server. NLM programs are loaded at the command line, by one of the configuration programs, such as AUTOEXEC.NCF, or by another NLM.

There are four types of NLMs in NetWare 4:

- Disk drivers (DSK extension) control the hard disk and other mass-storage devices.

- LAN drivers (LAN extension) control the network interface boards in the server.

- Name space NLMs (NAM extension) add non-DOS file name support to a volume.

- Utilities or applications (NLM extension) execute at the server for client support, for management, or to provide applications to users.

NetWare NFS Services

The collection of NetWare Loadable Modules (NLMs) that allows a NetWare server to participate in Unix networks as both an NFS (Network File System) client and server. Additional features are bidirectional printing between Unix and NetWare, and FTP (File Transfer Protocol) server capabilities for the NetWare server. (See Chapter 14 for related information.)

NetWare operating system

The operating system developed by Novell in the early 1980s to share centralized server resources with multiple clients. The seven important features of the NetWare operating system are directory, file, print, security, messaging, management, and routing services. NetWare currently owns the majority market share among all PC-based network operating systems. More than a million new computers a month become NetWare clients worldwide.

NetWare partition

A disk partition on a server hard disk under control of NetWare.

NetWare Requester for OS/2

NetWare Requester software for OS/2 clients that provides the same NetWare client functions as those provided by the NetWare DOS Requester. (See Chapter 15 for related information.)

NetWare Runtime

A specialized version of the NetWare operating system that allows only a single concurrent client. This is used most often as a platform for communications or application servers that provide their own user authentication. NetWare Runtime servers support all NetWare NLMs (NetWare Loadable Modules), both from Novell and from third-party vendors.

NetWare server

An Intel-based PC running the NetWare operating system. A software NetWare server is created in Unix systems running the NetWare for Unix product available from a number of third-party vendors. To the NetWare client, the Unix-hosted NetWare server is exactly like any other NetWare server.

Servers for NetWare 3 are always dedicated machines. NetWare 4 servers can only be non-dedicated when running on an OS/2 host machine; otherwise, they are also dedicated. (For the list of server requirements, see Chapter 2.)

NetWare server console operator

A user authorized by the Admin or equivalent supervisory personnel to run server and print server software. Standard management tasks, such as print server loading and unloading or checking a file server using the MONITOR.NLM, can be done by console operators.

NetWare Server object

A leaf object representing a NetWare server in the Directory tree.

NetWare Tools/NetWare User Tools

The Windows 3.1x-based graphical user utility provided with NetWare 4.10. NetWare User Tools (NWUSER) allows any user to see available network resources, map drives, add or change printing assignments, and send messages.

NetWire

The online information service accessed through CompuServe. Marketing and product information (propaganda) is available, as are patches, fixes, and helpful technical support files.

All the information in NetWire on CompuServe is also included in Novell's Internet offerings: ftp.novell.com or http://www.netware.com.

network backbone

A special network generally connecting only specialized devices such as servers, routers, and gateways. The backbone is a separate cabling system between these devices, isolating the backbone from regular client/server traffic.

network board

An interface card, or NIC (network interface card in earlier NetWare-speak) that fits into a workstation or other network device and connects the device to the cabling system.

network communication

Data exchanged in packet format over a defined network.

Network Driver Interface Specification

See *NDIS*.

network interface card (NIC)

A network board, card, or adapter (choose your term) that connects a device with the network cabling system. More recent Novell documentation favors "network board" rather than NIC or adapter; other companies and references are less restrictive.

network node

An intelligent device attached to the network. Traditionally, nodes are servers, workstations, printers, routers, gateways, or communication servers. However, other devices, such as fax machines, copiers, security systems, and telephone equipment may be considered network nodes.

network numbering

A unique numbering scheme to identify network nodes and separate network cable systems. IPX (Internetwork Packet eXchange) automatically adds the node number for the client, while the server installation process sets the network cable segment number (IPX external network number) and the address of the server (IPX internal network number). TCP/IP (Transmission Control Protocol/Internet Protocol) networks require the installer to set and maintain all network addresses.

network printer

A printer attached to either the network cabling, file server, or workstation that is usable by any network client.

network supervisor

A traditional term for the person responsible for the network, or a portion thereof (subadministrator). Also called the network administrator. Truly, a hero for the modern age.

Network Support Encyclopedia (NSE)

The CD-ROM based information resource including patches, fixes, drivers, bulletins, manuals, technical bulletins, compatibility testing results, press releases, and product information.

Produced by Novell, the NSE is available by subscription by calling 1-800-NETWARE.

NETX

The VLM (Virtual Loadable Module) under the client DOS Requester that provides backward-compatibility with the older versions of the NetWare shell.

NIAS

See *Novell Internet Access Server*.

NIC

See *network interface card*.

NIS (Network Information Services)

A distributed database that provides common information for network use, such as user and group information. Similar to NDS (NetWare Directory Services), NIS uses the database of users and groups to validate access to network resources, especially NFS. The tables of information are called *NIS maps*, which are controlled by the master NIS server.

The NIS domain is controlled by this NIS server. NIS domains consist of local network connections only and generally cover a single network. The domain names are flat, rather than hierarchical as in DNS (Domain Name Service), and the rules for these names are not as strict.

NLM

See *NetWare Loadable Module*.

NLS

See *NetWare Licensing Services*.

NLSP (NetWare Link Service Protocol)

A new routing protocol designed by Novell that exchanges information about the status of the links between routers to build a map of the internetwork. Once the network map is built, information is transferred between routers only when the network changes.

RIP (Router Information Protocol), the previous method for routers to exchange information, requires regular broadcasts that add network traffic. Using NLSP reduces routing traffic across WAN links.

NLSP does use RIP to communicate with NetWare clients.

node number

Similar to a network number, a node number generally refers to a client machine only. Under NetWare, node numbers are based on the unique, factory-assigned address (Ethernet and Token Ring) or the card's configurable address (ARCnet and Token Ring cards supporting LAA, or Locally Administered Addresses).

Normal attribute

The default setting for NetWare files, indicated by a specific file-system attribute.

Novell Internet Access Server (NIAS)

The server software module that translates data requests from a client running on IPX (Internetwork Packet eXchange) to TCP/IP (Transmission Control Protocol/Internet Protocol) for connection to the Internet or TCP/IP host.

There are two pieces to this technology: one at the client and one at the server. The client software includes a special version of Winsock that "spoofs" the TCP/IP client software, such as Netscape, into believing the client is running the TCP/IP protocol stack. In reality, only IPX is running at the client.

The server portion of the Winsock software converts the data transport protocol from IPX to IP for connection to the TCP/IP systems. Outgoing packets are assigned port numbers in addition to the IP address of the NIAS, which is shared by all systems. Incoming packets, identified by their port numbers, are routed back across IPX to their original stations.

NSE

See *Network Support Encyclopedia*.

O

object

Any distinct, separate entity; in NetWare 4.1*x*, a NetWare Directory Services (NDS) database entry that holds information about a network client or another resource. The categories of information are called *properties*. For example, a User object's mandatory properties are login name and last name. The data in each property is called its *value*.

NetWare 4.1*x* network objects include users, printers, servers, volumes, and print queues. Some of these are physical; some are virtual, like the print queue and groups of users. Container objects help manage other objects.

Leaf objects, such as users, printers, volumes, and servers, are the end nodes of the Directory tree. Containers (called *branches* in some other systems) are Country, Organization, and Organizational Unit objects. A container object can be empty. Leaf objects can't contain any other objects.

Object names consist of the path from the root of the Directory tree down to the name of the object. The syntax is *object.container.container.root*. There may be one or more containers in the middle section.

Typeless names list just the names (as in JAMES.INTEGRATE.GCS). Typeful names list the designators as well (as in CN=JAMES.OU=INTEGRATE.O=GCS). An advantage of NetWare 4.1*x* over earlier versions of NetWare 4 is that it allows the constant use of typeless names.

object rights

Rights granted to a trustee over an object. An example is the Create object right for a container object, which allows the trustee to create new objects in that container.

ODI

See *Open Data-link Interface*.

ODINSUP

For Open Data-link Interface/Network Driver Interface Specification SUPport, this strained acronym refers to the interface that allows both ODI and NDIS protocol stacks to exist on a single network interface card.

Open Data-link Interface (ODI)

Novell's specification, released in 1989, that details how multiple protocols and device drivers can coexist on a single network interface card without conflict. The ODI specification separates device drivers from protocol stacks. The biggest advantage of ODI over NDIS is speed and size; ODI routes packets only to the appropriate frame type, rather than to all frame types as in NDIS. The major components of the ODI architecture are:

- *Multiple Layer Interface Driver (MLID)*: A device driver that manages the sending and receiving of packets to and from a physical (or logical) network. Each MLID is matched to the hardware or media, and is therefore unique.

- *Link Support Layer (LSL)*: The interface layer between the protocol stacks and the device driver. Any driver may communicate with any ODI-compliant protocol stack through the LSL.

- *Media Support Module (MSM)*: The interface of the MLIDs to the LSL and the operating system. This module handles initialization and run-time issues for all drivers.

- *Topology-Specific Module (TSM)*: The software layer that handles a specific media type, such as Ethernet or Token Ring. All frame types are supported in the TSM for any media type supported.

- *Hardware-Specific Module (HSM)*: The software layer that handles adapter startup, reset, shutdown, packet reception, timeouts, and multicast addressing for a particular interface card.

open systems

Technically, a goal of guaranteed interoperability between disparate operating systems. Marketing has recast this term to mean any system that can be coerced to communicate with TCP/IP (Transmission Control Protocol/Internet Protocol). Realistically, open systems utilize Internet and Web technologies to support any client connecting to any server.

optical disk

A high-capacity disk storage device that writes or reads information based on reflecting laser light for bits, rather than reading magnetic fluctuations as on a standard hard or floppy disk. Disks may be read-only (a CD-ROM), read-once (a WORM, for Write Once Read Many), or fully rewritable.

optical disk library

A jukebox, which is an optical disk reader with an autochanger that mounts and dismounts optical disks as requested.

Organization object

The container object below the Country object and above the Organizational Unit object in an NDS (NetWare Directory Services) tree. Organization objects can contain Organizational Unit objects and leaf objects. (See Chapter 4 for related information.)

Organizational Role object

In an NDS (NetWare Directory Services) tree, a leaf object that specifies a role within an organization, such as Purchasing Manager or Workgroup Leader. The Organizational Role object usually has special rights, and these rights tend to rotate among different users as job responsibilities change. (See Chapter 4 for related information.)

Organizational Unit object

The container object below the Organization object in an NDS (NetWare Directory Services) tree. The Organizational Unit object can contain other Organizational Unit objects or leaf objects. (See Chapter 4 for related information.)

OS/2 client

A computer running NetWare client software for the OS/2 operating system. OS/2 clients can perform the same user and administrative operations that DOS or MS Windows workstations can perform. (See Chapter 15 for details.)

P

packet

A block of data sent across the network; the basic unit of information used in network communications. Service requests, service responses, and data are all formed into packets by the network interface card driver software before the information is transmitted. Packets may be fixed or variable length. Large blocks of information will automatically be broken into appropriate packets for the network and reassembled by the receiving system.

Packet Burst Protocol (PBP)

The NetWare version of TCP/IP's (Transmission Control Protocol/Internet Protocol's) *sliding windows*. Rather than send one packet to acknowledge the receipt of one packet, PBP acknowledges multiple packets at one time. This improves the performance of NCP (NetWare Core Protocol) file read and writes, especially across WAN connections.

NetWare 3.1 requires additional NLMs (NetWare Loadable Modules) loaded at the server and some configuration at the client. NetWare 4.1x has PBP built into both server and client software automatically.

packet receive buffer

The memory area in the NetWare server that temporarily holds arriving data packets. These packets are held until the server can process the packets and send them to their proper destination. The packet receive buffer ensures the server doesn't drop arriving packets, even when the server is heavily loaded with other operations.

Paging

A NetWare 4 performance feature that takes advantage of the Intel 80386 and 80486 processor architecture to group memory into 4 KB blocks of RAM. The NetWare operating system assigns memory locations in available 4 KB pages, then uses a table to allow the noncontiguous pages to appear as a logical contiguous address space.

PAP (Printer Access Protocol)

See *AppleTalk protocols*.

Parent directory

In a file system, the directory immediately above any subdirectory.

Parent object

An object that holds other objects. In NetWare Directory Services (NDS), an Organization is a parent object for all included Organizational Unit and leaf objects.

parity

A simple form of error checking in communications.

partition

In a hard disk, a section treated by the operating system as an independent drive. For example, there are DOS and NetWare partitions on a server hard disk.

In NetWare Directory Services (NDS), a partition is a division of the NDS database. A partition consists of at least one container object, all the objects therein, and all the data about those objects. A partition is contained in a replica. Partitions contain only NDS information; no file-system information is kept in a partition.

Partitions are useful for separating the Directory to support parts of the network on different sides of a WAN link. Multiple partitions are also advised when the network grows to include many servers and thousands of NDS objects. More partitions keep the NDS database closer to the users and speed up lookups and authentication.

The [Root] object at the top of the Directory tree is the first partition created during installation. New partitions are created with the NDS Manager (NetWare 4.11), NetWare Administrator (NetWare 4.10), or PARTMGR utility. Each partition must contain contiguous containers. The partition immediately toward the [Root] of another is called that partition's *parent*. The included partition is referred to as the *child* partition.

password

The most common security measure used in networks to identify a specific, authorized user of the system. Each user should have a unique password. NetWare 4.1*x* encrypts the login passwords at the workstation and transmits them in a format only the NetWare server can decode. (See Chapter 9 for password guidelines.)

path

The complete location of a file or directory, listed from the root of the drive through each directory and subdirectory and ending with the file names.

PBP

See *Packet Burst Protocol*.

PCONSOLE

The DOS utility that allows supervisors to control the NetWare printing system. With PCONSOLE, printers, print queues, and print servers can be created, modified, assigned, and deleted. (See Chapter 8 for details.)

physical memory

The RAM (random-access memory) in a computer or server.

port

A *hardware port* is the termination point of a communication circuit, as in parallel port.

A *software port* is the memory address that specifies the transfer point between the microprocessor and a peripheral device.

power conditioning

The methods used to protect electronic equipment from power fluctuations. Power conditioning can work by suppressing, isolating, or regulating the electric current provided to that equipment. (See Chapter 1 for related information.)

Primary time server

The NetWare 4 server that provides time information to Secondary time servers and workstations. Primary time servers must synchronize time with at least one other Primary or Reference time server. (See Chapter 3 for related information.)

print device

Any device that puts marks on paper or plastic, such as a laser, dot-matrix, or inkjet printer or a plotter. NetWare's defined print device files have a PDF extension and can be configured by using the NetWare Administrator or PRINTDEF utility. (See Chapter 8 for related information.)

print device mode

The sequence of printer commands (or print functions, control sequences, or escape sequences) that control the appearance of the printed file. Print device modes can define the style, size, boldness, and orientation of the typeface. Modes are set by using the NetWare Administrator or PRINTDEF utility. (See Chapter 8 for related information.)

print job

Any file in a print queue waiting to be printed. Once the print server forwards the print job to the printer, the print job is deleted from the queue. (See Chapter 8 for related information.)

print job configuration

Characteristics that define how a job is physically printed, rather than how the printed output looks on the page. For example, a print job configuration may specify the printer the print job will be printed on, the print queue the print job is sent through, the number of copies to print, and the use of a banner page. (See Chapter 8 for related information.)

print queue

The directory on a volume that stores print jobs waiting for printer assignment. In NetWare 4.1x, the print queue directory may be stored on any volume. Earlier NetWare versions (and NetWare 4 servers in bindery mode) limit the print queue to the SYS: volume. Print queue capacity is limited only by disk space. Print queues can be created by using either the NetWare Administrator or PCONSOLE utility. (See Chapter 8 for related information.)

print queue operator

A user with additional authority to manage the print queue. Print queue operators can edit the status of print jobs, delete print jobs, change the service mode, or modify the print queue operational status. This is an excellent job for subadministrators. (See Chapter 8 for related information.)

print queue polling time

The interval between print server status checks of the print queue for jobs. Users can modify the time period.

print server

In a NetWare server, the PSERVER.NLM software that moves print jobs from the print queue to the appropriate network printer. NetWare print servers can service up to 255 printers and associated print queues.

  Third-party print servers are small hardware devices that connect directly to the network cabling and support one or more printers remote from the file server. Printing performance is increased by using remote print servers rather than printers attached to the file server itself.

Print Server object

The leaf object that represents a network print server in the Directory tree.

print server operator

A user granted extra authority to manage a print server. Rights include the ability to control notification lists, supported printers, and queue assignments.

printer

Any device that puts marks on paper or plastic, such as a laser, dot-matrix, or inkjet printer or a plotter. A network printer can be attached to the file server or an external print server. In NetWare Directory Services (NDS), Printer objects are independent of the Print Queue and Print Server objects.

printer definition

The control characters, specific to the printer model, that interpret the commands to modify printed text. (See Chapter 8 for related information.)

printer form

A print system option that allows users to specify which type of paper (letter, legal, memo, and so on) to use for any print job. Each defined printer form is given a unique name and number between 0 and 255. Printer forms may be specified in the print job configuration or with the command-line printer utilities NPRINT and CAPTURE. The mounted form must match the requested form, or the print job won't print.

Printer object

The leaf object representing a physical printer on the network in the Directory tree.

privilege level

The rights granted to users or groups by the NetWare Administrator program. These rights set the level of network access for that user or group.

Privilege level also refers to the microprocessor access level determined by the Intel architecture for 80386 and higher microprocessors. Four levels are defined: 0 through 3. NetWare uses the 0 and 3 levels. These levels, also known as *protection rings*, are controlled by the NetWare memory domains. The OS_PROTECTED domain, used for ill-behaved or suspect NLMs (NetWare Loadable Modules), provides memory protection for the server's other NLMs and operating system memory.

Profile login script

A special type of login script that can be applied to several users with identical login script needs. Profile login scripts are not mandatory. They execute after the Container login script but before the User login script. (See Chapter 7 for related information.)

Profile object

The special leaf object that represents the Profile login script in the Directory tree.

prompt

An on-screen character (or characters) that awaits your input. Examples are the DOS prompt, the OS/2 prompt, and the colon prompt of the NetWare server console.

property

A piece of information, or characteristic, of any NetWare Directory Services (NDS) object. For example, User object properties include login name, last name, password restrictions, and similar information.

property rights

Rights to read, create, modify, or delete properties of a NetWare Directory Services (NDS) object.

protected mode

The mode in 80286 and higher Intel processors that supports multitasking and virtual memory management. This is the mode that processors use by default. They switch to real mode only when forced to emulate the earlier 8086 processor functions. In protected mode, 80286 processors can address up to 16 MB of memory. 80386 and higher processors can address up to 4 GB of memory.

protection ring

See *privilege level*.

PUBLIC directory

One of the NetWare system directories created during installation. PUBLIC stores NetWare utilities and files for use by all clients. The default login script for DOS users maps a search drive to SYS:PUBLIC, with Read and File Scan rights granted automatically.

public files

Files kept in the SYS:PUBLIC directory, placed there during NetWare installation. These include all command-line utilities, help files, and printer definition files.

Public trustee

A special NetWare 4 trustee, used only for trustee assignments. It allows objects in NetWare Directory Services (NDS) that don't have any other rights to have the effective rights granted to the [Public] trustee. This works similarly to the user GUEST or group EVERYONE in earlier NetWare versions. [Public] can be created and deleted, just like any other trustee. The Inherited Rights Filter (IRF) will block inherited rights for the [Public] trustee.

Rather than use the [Public] trustee to grant rights to large groups of objects, it's more secure to grant those rights only to a container object. The difference between the two options is that rights granted to a container object are only passed to those objects in the container, while [Public] rights go to all objects.

Purge attribute

The file-system attribute that allows the NetWare operating system to completely erase a directory or file that has been deleted.

R

RAM (random-access memory)

The main system memory in a computer addressed by the operating system. RAM is used for the operating system, applications, and data. The memory is dynamic, and the information contained in RAM is cleared when power is discontinued.

RCONSOLE (Remote Console)

The NetWare utility that echoes the server console to a DOS workstation. This ability is also included in the NetWare Administrator program under the Tools drop-down menu.

Any function that can be done at the server console can be done via RCONSOLE. Before running RCONSOLE, however, the server must have the following commands in the AUTOEXEC.NCF file, or they must be entered at the colon prompt:

```
LOAD REMOTE password
LOAD RSPX
```

read-after-write verification

The method used by NetWare to guarantee the integrity of data written to the hard disk. After data is written to the disk, it is compared to the data still held in memory. If it matches, the memory is cleared. If the data does not match, the hard disk block is marked as "bad" and the Hot Fix feature redirects the data to a known good block in the Hot Fix Redirection area.

Read Only attribute

The file-system attribute indicating that the file can be read, but not modified, written to, or deleted.

Read right

The file-system right that allows a user to open and read files. When used with property rights, the authority to read the values of the property.

real mode

The 8086 emulation mode in 80286, 80386, and 80486 Intel processors. Real mode is limited to 1 MB of RAM address, as the 8086 itself is limited, and no multitasking is possible. Contrast this with *protected mode*.

record locking

The operating system feature that prevents more than one user from modifying a record or file at the same time.

recursive copying

Copying the complete contents of a directory or directory structure, using the recursion property that enables a subroutine to call itself. For example, XCOPY and NCOPY use recursive copying to copy all files in a directory structure.

Red Horde

Nickname for Novell, Inc., the leading PC LAN vendor, as well as the 32,000 NetWare resellers worldwide.

Reference time server

A NetWare 4 server that provides the network time to Primary and Secondary time servers and workstations. (See Chapter 3 for related information.)

remote boot

The process of booting a workstation from the files on a NetWare server rather than from a local drive.

remote workstation

A personal computer linked to the LAN by a router or through a remote asynchronous connection. Remote workstations can be either stand-alone or part of another network.

Rename Inhibit attribute

The file-system attribute that prevents a file or directory from being renamed.

Rename right

The authority for an object to change the name of an object. This technically changes the Name property.

replica

A copy of a NetWare Directory Services (NDS) partition, used to eliminate a single point of failure, as well as to place the NDS database closer to users in more distant parts of the network. There are three types of replicas that can be managed:

- *Master replica*: The primary replica, created during installation. A Master replica of the [Root] partition is stored in a hidden directory on the SYS: volume of the first file server installed.

- *Read/Write replica*: Used to read or update the database. Actions such as adding or deleting objects or authenticating users are handled by the Read/Write replicas. There should be at least two Read/Write replicas for each partition, to ensure that the Directory will function if one or two of the servers that hold replicas are unavailable.

- *Read-Only replica*: The least powerful replica, used to access or display NDS database information, but unable to support changes. (Read-Only replicas are generally not very useful.)

Subordinate Reference replicas are maintained by the system. They cannot be modified by a user (even the supervisor).

Replica synchronization is the process of a partition's replicas exchanging information to stay up-to-date. When a change is made to one replica, the synchronization process guarantees all other replicas obtain the same information as soon as it is practical.

resource fork

A Macintosh-specific file portion that contains Macintosh-specific windows and icons, as well as the file resources.

resource tag

An operating system function call that tracks NetWare server resources. Screens and memory allocated for various tasks, as well as the memory resources used by NetWare Loadable Modules (NLMs), must be tracked so the resources can be made available to the operating system once the NLMs are stopped or no longer require the resource.

resources

Technically, any part of the network, including cabling, concentrators, servers, gateways, and the like. Practically, resources are the components on a network that are desired by the network clients. Under this definition, resources tend to be server volumes, gateways, printers, print queues, users, processes, and the security options of a network.

restore

The opposite of back up. To replace a file or files from the backup media onto the server hard disk. This is done when the file or files on the server hard disk have been erased or corrupted by accident (most commonly) or when an entire disk's worth of files needs to be replaced after a disk failure.

ribbon cable

Flat cable with each conductor glued to the side of the other conductors rather than twisted around each other. This type of cable is used most often for internal disk and tape drive connections.

rights

Privileges granted to NetWare users or groups of users by the Admin user (or equivalent). These rights determine all operations the user can perform on the system, including reading, writing, creating, deleting, and modifying files and directories.

Trustee assignments grant rights to specific directories, files, or objects. An object with a trustee assignment to a directory, file, or another object is called a *trustee* of that directory, file, or object.

Each object maintains a list of which other objects have rights to the object in the ACL (Access Control List) property.

Directory rights apply to the directory in the NetWare file system to which they are assigned, as well as to all files and subdirectories in that directory. Rights can be reassigned, or the Inherited Rights Filter (IRF) may remove some of the rights passing down the file-system directory tree. These rights are part of the file system only, and have no relevance to NetWare Directory Services (NDS) objects.

The following types of rights apply to a NetWare 4.1*x* network:

- *File rights* apply to only the file to which they are assigned. Trustees may inherit file rights from the directory containing the file.

- *Object rights* apply to only NDS objects. These rights do not affect the properties of the object, just the object itself.

- *Property rights* apply to only the properties of NDS objects. These rights may be assigned to each property, or a default set of rights may be assigned to all properties.

A trustee must have the Access Control right to a directory or file before granting directory or file rights to other objects. A trustee must have the Write, Add or Delete Self, or Supervisor right to the ACL property of the object before granting other objects property or object rights to the object.

Rights flow downhill. By granting trustee rights to the top level of a directory, the trustee has the same rights to all files and subdirectories. The two ways to change inheritance are to reassign rights or use the Inherited Rights Filter (IRF) to block the rights. Inheritance applies equally to the file system and to the objects in the Directory tree. (See Chapter 9 for more details.)

RIP

See *Router Information Protocol.*

root container

The topmost container in a Directory tree partition. The partition and replicas are named after the applicable root container.

root directory

The topmost directory level in a directory structure. The root directory is the volume in NetWare, and all directories are subdirectories of their volume.

[Root] object

The topmost object in a Directory tree. The purpose of the [Root] object is to provide an access point to different Country and Organization objects. Rights granted to the [Root] object are granted to the entire Directory tree. The [Root] object holds no information; it merely acts as a reference point.

router

An intelligent device that connects two or more networks. A router sends packets from one network to another network, based on the address contained in the protocol rather than the physical address listed at the beginning of the packet. Router functions are included in NetWare servers, or may be stand-alone workstations or specialized computers developed for high-speed routing operations.

Since routers use the address in the protocol portion of the packet, they are able to connect different cabling topologies. This is how a NetWare server can contain up to four different network boards and send all packets to their proper destinations.

Routers are often connected to high-speed modems to support geographically separated networks. These devices are sometimes referred to as *remote routers*.

Router Information Protocol (RIP)

The protocol based on TCP/IP (Transmission Control Protocol/Internet Protocol) that maintains a table of reachable networks and calculates the difficulty in reaching a specific network based on the number of intervening routers (referred to as the *hop count*). Workstations can query the nearest router to locate the least hop count route to a distant network by broadcasting a request packet.

RIP has a reputation for creating lots of network traffic based on the periodic broadcast packets containing all current routing information. These packets help in keeping the routing tables of all routers in the internetwork synchronized. Broadcasts are also sent when a network configuration change is detected, such as when a new router is added or a router goes offline.

RTMP (Routing Table Maintenance Protocol)

See *AppleTalk protocols*.

S

salvageable files

Files that have been deleted by a user or application but are still tracked by NetWare. The NetWare 4.1*x* FILER utility shows the list of salvageable files and will recover files if they have not been overwritten on the server disk.

If the directory that contained a deleted file was also deleted, the file is saved in a system directory labeled DELETED.SAV in the volume's root directory.

Deleted files can be purged, eliminating any chance of salvage. If the NetWare server runs out of available allocation blocks on the volume, it will start purging files to make room for new files. The files are deleted on a first-deleted, first-purged basis.

SAP

See *Service Advertising Protocol*.

SBACKUP

A software utility that provides the means for NetWare backup and restore operations.

schema

NDS (NetWare Directory Services) database design components, hidden from direct manipulation. Vendors writing applications to utilize NDS may modify and expand the schema, such as when the IPX/IP Gateway adds new objects to the NDS database.

SCSI (Small Computer Systems Interface)

Pronounced "scuzzy," SCSI is the industry standard that sets guidelines for connecting peripheral storage devices and controllers to a microprocessor. SCSI defines both the hardware and software requirements for the connections. The wide acceptance of the SCSI standard makes it easy to connect any disk or tape drive to any computer.

SCSI bus

Another name for the SCSI (Small Computer Systems Interface) interface and communications protocol. Make sure connected devices are properly terminated and addressed.

SCSI disconnect

A feature in NetWare 4 that allows communications with SCSI (Small Computer Systems Interface) disks to be more efficient by informing the disk to be ready for upcoming I/O (input/output) requests.

SDI

See *Storage Device Interface*.

search drive

A designated drive used by the operating system to look for a requested file that is not found in the current directory. Search drives allow users working in one directory to access application and data files in other directories. NetWare 4.1x allows up to 16 search drives per user, normally defined in one or more login scripts.

search mode

A specification used to tell a program how to use search drives when looking for a data file. When an EXE or COM file requires support files, the file-open request is made through the operating system. This request may or may not specify a path to the support files. When a path is specified, that path is searched. If no path is specified, the default directory is searched first. If the files are not found, the NetWare client software uses the search mode of the executable file to determine whether or not to continue looking in the search drives.

Secondary time server

A NetWare 4.1x server that requests and receives time information from another server, then provides that time information to requesting workstations. (See Chapter 3 for related information.)

security

The operating system controls used by the network administrator to limit user access to the network's resources. The six categories of security are *login security, trustees, rights, inheritance, attributes,* and *effective rights*. (See those entries and Chapter 9 for related information.)

security equivalence

A property of User objects that grants the rights to the object listed as equivalent to the rights the original object has to all other objects. Security equivalence is a quick way to give the same access privileges to two or more objects.

Being a member of a group list gives a user the same trustee rights as those granted to the Group object. The same security equivalence is granted to all users listed in the occupant list of an Organizational Role object.

Each object also receives an "implied" security equivalence to its own container. If the container is granted the Supervisor right to a volume, all users in that container will also have the Supervisor right to that volume.

semaphore

A file-locking and control mechanism to facilitate control over the sharing of files. Semaphores with byte value 0 allow file sharing; byte value 1 locks the file while in use. Semaphores are also used to limit the concurrent number of users for applications. When the user count is reached, the semaphore blocks any more users from gaining access until a current user closes the file.

Sequenced Packet Exchange (SPX)

The part of NetWare's transport protocol suite that guarantees packet delivery at the protocol level. The use of a check on each packet not only guarantees that the packet reaches its destination, but that it arrives intact.

If an SPX packet is not acknowledged within a specific amount of time, SPX retransmits the packet. In applications that use only IPX (Internetwork Packet eXchange), the application program is responsible for ensuring packets are received intact.

Because of the guaranteed nature of SPX, this protocol is often used for backup systems based in workstations.

serial port

A hardware port. IBM PC and compatible computers generally come with COM1 and COM2, which transmit data one bit at a time. Serial ports are primarily used for a modem or a mouse on the workstation. In the past, these ports were used on file servers for serial printers. Today, most printers are parallel printers, so it's rare to see a serial printer attached to a file server.

serialization

The process of branding each NetWare operating system with a unique serial number to prevent software piracy. If two NetWare servers discover (through non-filterable broadcasts) that both are using software with the same serial number, copyright violation warnings are shown at the server console and each connected workstation.

server

A *NetWare server* is a PC providing network resources through the use of the NetWare operating system.

A *print server* is a device that routes print jobs from a print queue and sends them to a printer. The print server may be software in a file server or workstation, or a stand-alone unit attached to the network cabling. The NetWare Directory Services (NDS) object that represents this device is referred to as a Print Server object.

A *time server* is a NetWare server that provides time to network clients and is capable of providing time for other servers. All NetWare 4 servers are time servers of some type (Primary, Secondary, Single Reference, or Reference).

A *Web server* is a software system based on HTTP communications to send HTML-enabled documents to Web client systems. Novell's Web Server 2.51 is included with IntranetWare.

server console

The information screens for the NetWare server operating system. Monitoring traffic levels, setting configuration parameters, loading additional software (NetWare Loadable Modules, or NLMs), and shutting down the server must be done at the server console.

The physical keyboard and monitor on the file server are the primary server console. The RCONSOLE utility allows a DOS session on a network client to echo the server screen and redirect keyboard input across the network.

server protocol

An inaccurate shorthand method of referring to NCP (NetWare Core Protocol). (NCP is used on more devices than just the server.)

Service Advertising Protocol (SAP)

The NetWare protocol that allows servers of all types to broadcast their available services across the network. Routers and other NetWare servers receive and track these broadcasts to keep their router information tables up-to-date.

NetWare clients begin each login process by broadcasting a "Get Nearest Server" SAP packet. The first server that responds will become the server the workstation attaches to before continuing the login process.

Because of the traffic generated by SAP, most WAN routers now offer the capability of filtering SAP broadcasts. SAP filtering can also be activated on the NetWare 4 server.

SERVMAN

The server-based utility that provides an interactive-front end to NetWare 4.1*x*'s SET commands. SERVMAN configures the AUTOEXEC.NCF, CONFIG.SYS, and TIMESYNC.CFG files through the traditional NetWare menu interface. (See Chapter 10 for details.)

SFT

See *System Fault Tolerance*.

Shareable attribute

The file-system extended attribute for NetWare that allows more than one user to access the file concurrently.

short machine type

A short (four letters or less) identifier specified in the NET.CFG file. The default is IBM. The short machine type is used specifically with overlay files, such as IBM$RUN.OVL for the DOS windowing utilities.

Single Reference time server

A NetWare 4.1*x* server that provides time to workstations and Secondary time servers. The Single Reference name comes from the fact that a server so designated is the single source of time for the network. This is the default for the first server in a Directory tree. (See Chapter 3 for related information.)

SMS

See *Storage Management Services*.

socket

The destination point within an IPX (Internetwork Packet eXchange) packet on a network node. The socket number is part of an IPX internetwork address. Many sockets, such as those used by NCP (NetWare Core Protocol), are reserved by Novell. Third-party developers may also reserve socket numbers by registering their intentions with Novell.

source routing

The IBM method of routing data across multiple networks by specifying the route in each frame. The end stations determine the route through a discovery process supported by source-routing bridges or routers.

There are two types of source routing:

- In *single-route broadcasting*, designated bridges pass the packet between source and destination, meaning only one copy of each packet arrives in the remote network.

- In *all-routes broadcasting*, the packet is sent through all bridges or routers in the network. This results in many copies of the same frame arriving at the remote network—as many frames as there are bridges or routers.

source server

The server supplying the data and bindery files to a NetWare 4 destination server during an Across-the-Wire upgrade.

sparse file

A file with at least one empty block, often created by databases. Some operating systems will write any file to disk in its entirety, even if only 12 bytes, starting at byte 1,000,001, were written. NetWare copies only the last block to disk, tracking the application's request and saving time and disk space.

The NCOPY utility will not copy sparse files unless forced to with the /f option.

SPX

See *Sequenced Packet Exchange*.

STARTUP.NCF

The first of two boot configuration files on a NetWare server. The STARTUP.NCF file primarily loads and configures the disk driver and name space support. Some SET parameters may also be set through this file.

station

Usually, station is short for *workstation*, but it can refer to any intelligent node connected to the network.

Storage Device Interface (SDI)

SBACKUP (NetWare 4.1*x*'s backup software utility) routines that are used to access various storage devices. If more than one storage device is attached to the host server, a list of all devices is supplied by SDI.

Storage Management Services (SMS)

NetWare services that support the storage and retrieval of data. SMS is independent of file systems (such as DOS, OS/2, Unix, or Macintosh) and the backup and restore hardware.

SMS NLMs and other software modules that run on NetWare servers include:

- SBACKUP: Provides backup and restore capabilities.

- SMDR (Storage Management Data Requester): Sends commands and information between SBACKUP and Target Service Agents (TSAs).

- Storage Device Interface: Sends commands and information between SBACKUP and the storage devices.

- Device drivers: Control the mechanical operation of storage devices and media under orders of SBACKUP.

- NetWare-server TSAs: Send requests for SBACKUP-generated data to the NetWare server where the data resides, then return requested data through the SMDR to SBACKUP.

- Database TSAs: Send commands and data between the SBACKUP host server and the database where the data to be backed up resides, then return the requested data through the SMDR to SBACKUP.

- Workstation TSAs: Send commands and data between the SBACKUP host server and the station where the data to be backed up resides, then return the requested data through the SMDR to SBACKUP.

- Workstation Manager: Accepts "I am here" messages from stations available for backup. It keeps the names of these stations in an internal list.

STREAMS

The common interface between NetWare and transport protocols that need to deliver data and requests for services to NetWare. STREAMS makes protocols, such as IPX/SPX, TCP/IP, SNA, and OSI transport protocols, transparent, allowing services to be provided across internetworks.

NetWare can install the protocols of your choice (if your applications support these protocols), and the service to the user will be unchanged.

NetWare 4 STREAMS and related NLMs are:

- STREAMS.NLM: The STREAMS application interface routines, the utility routines for STREAMS modules, the log device, and a driver for ODI (Open Data-link Interface).

- SPXS.NLM: Access to the SPX (Sequenced Packet eXchange) protocol from STREAMS.

- IPXS.NLM: Access to the IPX (Internetwork Packet eXchange) protocol from STREAMS.

- TCPIP.NLM: Access to the TCP (Transmission Control Protocol) and UDP (User Datagram Protocol) protocols from STREAMS.

- CLIB.NLM: Function library required by some NetWare Loadable Modules (NLMs).

- TLI.NLM : The API (Application Program Interface) that sits between STREAMS and applications.

subdirectory

A directory contained within another directory in a file system.

subnetwork

Term for a network that is part of a larger network and connected by a router. From the outside, the subnet identity is hidden, and only the main network is visible, making addressing simpler.

subnet mask

IP address technique used to differentiate between different TCP/IP (Transmission Control Protocol/Internet Protocol) networks. Each client must have a subnet mask, so it will know its exact network address range. The format is in dotted decimal. The most common subnet mask is 255.255.255.0.

Supervisor right

The file-system trustee right that conveys all rights to directories and files. The Supervisor object right grants all access privileges to all objects, and all rights to the property when speaking of property rights.

Misuse of the Supervisor right may be the single largest security hole in many networks. Grant Supervisor privileges rarely.

surface test

A hard disk test that scans for bad blocks. The NetWare INSTALL program offers two surface tests: destructive and nondestructive. These may be run in the background on a dismounted hard disk so you can keep the server up, but the server performance will be impacted. And although the nondestructive test works the vast majority of the time, it's best to never perform hard disk operations until the disk has a fresh backup or two.

synchronization

Replica synchronization is the process of ensuring Directory partition replicas contain the same information as that of the other replicas in the partition.

Time synchronization is the process of ensuring all servers in a Directory tree agree on the time.

System attribute

The file-system attribute that specifies file or directories are only to be used by the operating system.

SYSTEM directory

The directory created during installation on each server that contains the NetWare operating system files. Also included are NetWare Loadable Modules (NLMs), the AUTOEXEC.NCF file, and many of the NetWare utilities used by the Admin user to manage the network. The name of this directory is SYS:SYSTEM and should not be changed.

System Fault Tolerance (SFT)

A process of protecting information on the server by providing multiple storage devices. If one storage mechanism fails, the data will be safe on the alternate storage device. This may range from duplicated FAT (file allocation table) entries all the way to completely redundant server hardware. (See Chapter 17 for details.)

System login script

In NetWare 3, the login script that affected all users on the server. In NetWare 4, the System login script has been replaced by the Container login script.

T

tape backup unit

A tape drive that copies information from hard disks to tape.

target

Any device on the network with local storage that needs to be backed up that is running the TSA (Target Service Agent) software. The target may be the same server that holds the backup system, or it may be another server or a workstation.

During the merger of two Directory trees, the tree that retains its tree name and [Root] partition is called the *target tree*.

Target Service Agent (TSA)

Software that processes and organizes data movement between the target and the SBACKUP (NetWare 4.1*x*'s backup software utility) process on the host.

TCP/IP (Transmission Control Protocol/Internet Protocol)

The primary, industry-standard suite of networking protocols, and the only protocol allowed on the Internet since 1983.

TCP/IP is built upon four layers that roughly correspond to the seven-layer OSI model. The TCP/IP layers are process/application, host-to-host, internet, and network access.

NetWare TCP/IP refers to the collection of NetWare Loadable Modules (NLMs) that add support for TCP/IP onto the NetWare server. Routing can be enabled, as can RIP (Router Information Protocol) to support that routing. One advantage of TCP/IP support in the NetWare server is the ability for IPX (Internetwork Packet eXchange) packets to travel across a TCP/IP-only network by using IP (Internet Protocol) tunneling.

The NetWare TCP/IP suite of protocols is a necessary foundation for all NFS (Network File System) products from Novell. The NetWare TCP/IP suite provides both the 4.3 BDS Unix socket interface and the AT&T Streams TLI (Transport Layer Interface).

With the release of IntranetWare, the TCP/IP support at the NetWare server becomes even more important. The Web Server relies on TCP/IP to communicate with the Internet and intranet clients. NetWare IPX clients using the IPX/IP Gateway require TCP/IP at the gateway server to provide the TCP/IP protocol stack necessary for connection to TCP/IP hosts, either locally or on the Internet.

Telnet

Internet protocol providing terminal emulation to remote systems using TCP/IP. All TCP/IP applications today use fancier emulations, but basic Telnet functionality provides the foundation for them all.

termination

The process of placing a specific resistor at the end of a bus, line, chain or cable to prevent signals from being reflected or echoed, causing transmission problems. Typical devices that need terminating resistors include hard disk drives and SCSI (Small Computer Systems Interface) devices.

TFTP (Trivial File Transfer Protocol)

Subset of the FTP suite, used without any security measures such as passwords. Rarely used by people today, but a mainstay of automated file transfer functions, such as e-mail message transfer.

time synchronization

The method of guaranteeing that all servers in a Directory tree report the same time. Any NetWare Directory Services (NDS) function, such as a password change or renaming of an object, requires an NDS time stamp.

The *time stamp* is the unique code that includes the time and specifies an event. The NDS event is assigned a time stamp so the order of events may be recounted.

NDS uses time stamps to do the following:

- Establish the order of events (such as object creation and partition replication).

- Record "real-world" time values.

- Set expiration dates on accounts, passwords, and other items.

The time server software specifies each NetWare 4 server as either a Single Reference, Primary, Reference, or Secondary time server. (See the individual entries for more information.)

Time source servers must find each other. The two ways to do so are SAP (Service Advertising Protocol) and custom configuration. Primary, Reference, and Single Reference servers use SAP to announce their presence on the network by default. Primary and Reference time servers also use SAP packets to determine which other servers to poll in order to determine the network time. Secondary time servers use SAP information to pick a time server to reference. SAP is easy to install and works without regard to the network layout. It does create a small amount of network traffic.

Alternatively, you can set up a custom configuration. Specific time servers that a particular server should contact may be listed. You can also specify that a server should ignore SAP information from other time sources, and that it shouldn't advertise its presence using SAP.

The network supervisor retains complete control of the network time environment using this method. However, the custom configuration method does require extra planning and installation time.

topology

The physical layout design of network components, such as cables, workstations, servers, and concentrators.

There are three design options when planning your network topology:

- *Star network*: End nodes are connected directly to a central concentrator but not to each other. Used for ARCnet and 10BaseT Ethernet.

- *Ring network*: All nodes are cabled in a ring; a workstation's messages may need to pass through several other workstations before reaching the target station or server. Used by IBM's Token Ring network and followers.

- *Bus network*: All nodes are connected to a central cable (called a *trunk* or *bus*). The electrical path of a 10BaseT Ethernet network is really a bus.

Transaction Tracking System (TTS)

A standard, configurable feature on NetWare 4 servers that protects database applications. By "backing out" of any incomplete transactions resulting from a network failure, the system guarantees to return the database to the state that it was in before the interrupted transaction.

Transactional attribute

The file-system attribute that indicates that TTS (Transaction Tracking System) is protecting this file.

trustee

A User or Group object that has been granted access to an object, a file, or a directory. This access-granting method is called a *trustee assignment*, which says, "This user can access this object, directory, or file in the following ways." The following relate to trustees:

- Trustee list: Kept by each directory, file and object, the trustee list includes those objects that can access the object, file, or directory. The trustee list is kept in the object's ACL property.

- Trustees of groups: Rather than granting trustee rights to multiple objects one at a time, they can be granted to a group of users. Trustee assignments granting access for the group enable each individual user to have the same trustee rights as the group.

- [Public] trustee: A special case that grants the trustee rights of [Public] to all users. Users who try to access an object, directory, or file without explicit rights still have the rights granted to the [Public] trustee.

Rights are the access levels allowed an object to a directory, file, or object. Trustee assignments grant to an object the rights to other objects. Assign the right to the trusted object, not the trustee. For example, to grant LAURA the right to delete a Print Queue object, make LAURA a trustee of the Print Queue object, not the Print Queue object a trustee of LAURA.

TSA

See *Target Service Agent*.

TSA resources

Categories of data created by each TSA (Target Service Agent). These may be either major resources or minor resources, depending on the TSA.

TSM (Topology Specific Module)

See *Open Data-link Interface*.

TTS

See *Transaction Tracking System*.

turbo FAT index table

The special FAT (file allocation table) index file created when a file exceeds 64 blocks and the corresponding number of FAT entries. NetWare creates the turbo FAT index to group all FAT entries for the file in question. This turbo FAT index allows a large file to be accessed quickly.

typeful name

The complete NetWare Directory Services (NDS) path name for an object, including the container specifiers. An example is CN=JAMES.OU=INTEGRATE.O=GCS. This was the default in earlier versions of NetWare 4.

typeless name

The complete NetWare Directory Services (NDS) path name for an object, excluding the container specifiers. An example is JAMES.INTEGRATE.GCS.

U

UIMPORT

A DOS utility for adding user names and details into NetWare Directory Services (NDS) from an external database. The information must be placed in ASCII format. (See Chapter 10 for details.)

unbinding

Stopping and removing a communication protocol from LAN drivers and the network board.

Unicode

A 16-bit character code, defined by the Unicode Consortium, that supports and displays up to 65,536 different unique characters. With Unicode, multiple language characters can be displayed with a single code. Unfortunately, not every character created using a given code page will display correctly on a workstation using a different code page. Different Unicode translation tables are needed when you change code pages.

All objects and their attributes in the NetWare Directory Services (NDS) database are stored as Unicode representations. Clients use only a 256-character code page made of 8-bit characters.

These Unicode files are necessary for each language and translation table:

- 437_UNI.033: Translates the specific code page to Unicode.

- UNI_850.033: Translates Unicode to the specific code page (page 437, supporting English, French, and German, among others).

- UNI_MON.033: Handles the proper display of upper and lowercase letters.

The Unicode pages and translations are one of the reasons you must define a country code for different locales.

UNICON

Short for UNIx CONsole, UNICON is the server utility used to configure and manage NetWare/IP.

uninterruptible power supply (UPS)

A power backup system every server should have. The UPS maintains power to an attached device when source AC power is disrupted.

There are two types of UPS:

- An online UPS monitors the power going through the unit. The power goes through the internal battery that feeds power to the protected device. These systems are more expensive, but do an excellent job of smoothing out rough power before providing power to the end device.

- An offline UPS monitors the power line and becomes activated when the power drops. There is a tiny lag before the UPS can kick in completely.

NetWare 4.11 includes UPS serial port support, which allows you to connect your UPS directly into the server's serial port.

Unix client

A NetWare client running the Unix operating system. Originally, Novell's Unix hopes were pinned to UnixWare, but Novell has now sold that product to SCO and HP, both of whom promise to continue the strong ties of UnixWare to NetWare. Other Unix systems are starting to provide better NetWare integration for their clients, including the ability for the Unix client to use IPX/SPX as its transport protocol. (See Chapter 14 for related information.)

Unknown object

The leaf object that represents an object that NetWare Directory Services (NDS) can't identify. The object is either corrupted or is an object that has become unstable after a partitioning operation. If this is the case, the Unknown object will become known as the partitioning settles down, after a few minutes. If the Unknown object remains, delete it.

unloading

Using the command (UNLOAD) that stops NetWare Loadable Modules (NLMs) and removes them from NetWare operating system memory.

upgrade

The process of converting your network operating system from an earlier version of the operating system to a more current version. Many customers will upgrade from NetWare 3.*x* to NetWare 4.*x*, just as most customers upgraded from MS Windows to Windows 95.

Migration refers to the process of upgrading NetWare 2.*x*, 3.*x*, or another network operating system to NetWare 4 using one of the following two methods:

- The Across-the-Wire upgrade transfers the network information from an existing server to an existing NetWare 4 server on the same network.

- The Same-Server method upgrades the network information on the same server hardware.

The In-Place upgrade method is a three-step process that converts NetWare 2.1*x* or 2.2 to NetWare 3.1*x* using the SERVER.EXE program. Then you continue the upgrade to NetWare 4 from NetWare 3.*x*. With an In-Place upgrade, you begin with a file system upgrade. Then you install the new operating system, giving you a NetWare 3.1*x* file system. This has not upgraded the system and public files on SYS: volume SYS yet. Finally, you can complete the upgrade to NetWare 4.

UPS

See *uninterruptible power supply*.

UPS monitoring

The connection between a NetWare server and an attached UPS (uninterruptible power supply) that allows the NetWare server to know when the UPS becomes active after power has been lost.

When the UPS becomes active, the system sends a signal to the NetWare server, and the server notifies users of the backup power situation. A timeout may be specified, giving the users time to close their files and log out. When the time expires (and the power has not returned), the NetWare server closes all open files and shuts itself down properly.

User login script

The login script specific to the user and the environment set up for that user. Examples are specific drive mappings for particular users or an extra printer connection for a special job. User login scripts execute after the Container and Profile login scripts. Adding the NO DEFAULT option in a Container script bypasses the User login scripts.

User object

The leaf object in NetWare Directory Services (NDS) that signifies a person on the network. The following are important when dealing with User objects:

- The login name is the name the user logs in with, and it is mandatory.

- You may assign a user to Group objects, meaning the user inherits the rights assigned to that group.

- Home directories are the user's personal space on the server hard disk. It's easiest to group all the home directories in one directory, or one volume if there is a large number to support.

- Trustee rights are the user's rights to access specific directories and files (other than those assigned by the system).

- Security equivalence is the quick way to give one user the same rights as another user.

- User login scripts are the configurable setup script for individual users. Login scripts for individual users will take much of your management time; avoid them if possible.

- Print job configurations are printing templates assigned to containers, or available for any user to specify when necessary.

- Account management options are available for workgroup administrators to perform some network supervisory jobs without being granted full Supervisor status. You may grant the Supervisor object right to one user to manage other User objects and fulfill specific functions, such as checking and updating user addresses and phone numbers.

- User account restrictions are the quickest security control for all users. Restrictions can be placed on everything from the time of day users have access to the system, to the number of bytes they may use on the server hard disk.

user template

A feature that allows a new User object to inherit default property values based on predefined information. This speeds the creation of many users at one time, especially if these users share details such as account restrictions, locations, fax numbers, and so on.

utilities

Programs, usually small, that have a specific purpose and add specific functionality to an operating system. NetWare 4 utilities are included for DOS, MS Windows, and OS/2 clients.

Utilities that execute on the server and are listed as NetWare Loadable Modules (NLMs) are run from the console colon prompt. Examples of NLMs are MONITOR, PCONSOLE, and SERVMAN. The server NLMs add LAN drivers, disk drivers, name space support, and other low-level network utilities to the NetWare operating system.

Workstation utilities execute on a client workstation and are COM or EXE files.

UTP (unshielded twisted-pair)

Cable with two or more pair of wires twisted together and wrapped with a plastic sheath. Each individual wire is twisted around its mate; the more twists, the less interference.

Originally used for telephone wiring, UTP is now the LAN wire of choice. Various grades of cable run from the low end (Level 1 is awful; Level 3 is telephone wire) to the high end (Level 5), supporting high-speed data transmissions.

V

Value-Added Process (VAP)

First-generation NetWare Loadable Modules (NLMs) that run on NetWare 2.*x*.

Virtual Loadable Module (VLM)

The modular, executable client program that connects each DOS workstation with the NetWare server. There are many VLMs called by the VLM.EXE program, some adding new NetWare client features, and others ensuring backward-compatibility.

There are two types of VLMs: *child VLMs* and *multiplexor VLMs*. Child VLMs support particular implementations of a logical grouping. For instance, there is a child VLM for each NetWare server type:

- NDS.VLM: NetWare Directory Services (Net-Ware 4) servers
- BIND.VLM: Bindery-based servers (prior to NetWare 4)
- PNW.VLM: NetWare desktop-based servers (Personal NetWare)

Multiplexor VLMs are the multiplexing modules that route network calls to the proper child VLM.

VLM

See *Virtual Loadable Module*.

volume

A logical grouping of physical hard disk storage space. A NetWare volume is fixed in size and is the highest level in the NetWare directory structure, similar to the DOS root directory. Each volume is represented by a Volume object in the Directory.

A NetWare 4 server can support as many as 64 volumes. These volumes may be divided logically on a single hard disk, be a single volume per hard disk, or be a single volume spanning multiple hard disks.

The first, and only mandatory volume, is labeled SYS:, and it includes the NetWare system and client support files. Other volumes can have names between 2 and 15 characters in length.

A volume must be "mounted" by NetWare, and this is the sequence:

- The volume becomes visible to the operating system.
- The volume's FAT (file allocation table) is loaded into memory. Each file block of data takes up one entry in the FAT. Because of this, volumes with a smaller block size require more server memory to mount and manage.
- The volume's DET (directory-entry table) is loaded into memory.

volume definition table

The table that tracks volume-segment information, including volume name, volume size, and the volume segments on various server hard disks. The volume definition table is required for each NetWare volume, but it is created by the system during volume initialization.

Volume object

The leaf object that represents a volume on the network in the Directory tree. The Volume object's properties store information concerning the NetWare server holding the physical volume and the volume name.

volume segments

The physical division of a volume. A volume may be composed of up to 32 volume segments, and the maximum number of volume segments on a single NetWare disk partition is 8.

Volumes can have multiple physical segments spanning multiple hard disks. This allows you to create large volumes, with NetWare maintaining the volume definition table to track all the segments. Be aware that if one drive of a volume fails, the entire volume must be re-created. For this reason, some networks prefer to stick with a one-disk, one-volume philosophy.

W

wait state

The period of time a microprocessor does nothing but wait for other processes. For instance, slow memory forces many wait states on a fast CPU.

wait time

The number of seconds the UPS (uninterruptible power supply) will wait before signaling to the attached NetWare server that normal power is lost. The NetWare server then sends a message to all workstations warning their users to log out.

WAN (wide-area network)

A network that communicates over a long distance across non-physical media, such as public or private telephone lines, satellites, or microwaves. Traditionally, a WAN includes modems connecting different LANs (local-area networks) across leased telephone lines.

watchdog

Packets sent from the server to make sure a workstation is still connected. More watchdog packets are sent until the workstation responds or the server clears that connection.

Web Manager

The WEBMGR.EXE program that is installed during Web Server installation in NetWare 4.11. This allows a Windows client to configure and modify settings on Web Server systems.

Web Server

A software system based on HTTP communications to send HTML-enabled documents to Web client systems. Novell's Web Server 2.51 is included with IntranetWare, and works extremely quickly, as you might expect. After all, Novell sets the speed standards for file service in the LAN world, why not in the Web world as well? End of commercial.

wide-area network

See *WAN*.

Winsock

Short for WINdows SOCKets, Winsock software is the result of a vendor group meeting in 1991 to provide a single, standard application platform separate from the underlying network transport protocol. The top part of the Winsock software residing on a client machine interfaces with a TCP/IP application, such as Netscape. The bottom part of Winsock interfaces with the TCP/IP protocol stack on the machine, regardless of the TCP/IP developer.

workstation

A personal computer connected to a NetWare network. The term *workstation* may also refer to a Unix or OS/2 machine. Synonyms are client, station, user, or end node.

Write right

The file-system right that allows a user to open and write to files.

The property right that allows a user to add, change, or remove any values of the property.

X

XCONSOLE

A utility included with server TCP/IP (Transmission Control Protocol/Internet Protocol) support that allows a remote vt100 or equivalent terminal or terminal emulation program to run RCONSOLE.

XON/XOFF

The handshaking protocol that negotiates the sending and receiving speeds of transmitted data to ensure no data is lost.

X/Open

A group formed by competing/cooperating vendors in 1984 to ensure standards were fair to all companies, not dictated by market share. As Unix has waned in public consciousness, so has X/Open. Novell granted the UnixWare name and reference code technology to X/Open in 1994 for continued sharing of Unix standards.

Z

ZIP (Zone Information Protocol)

See *AppleTalk protocols*.

zones

An arbitrary group of nodes on an AppleTalk internetwork. Zones divide large internetworks into manageable groups. Clients can only belong to one zone at a time, and that zone is determined automatically when that node connects to the network.

Zones have names up to 32 characters in length. In a network without routers, the zone is invisible to all clients. In a network with routers, the zone names are converted to addresses by the NBP (Name Binding Protocol) and the ZIP (Zone Information Protocol).

A Zone Information Table is maintained by each router. A NetWare server can act as a router for AppleTalk.

Index

Note to the Reader:

First level entries are in **bold**. Page numbers in **bold** indicate the principal discussion of a topic or the definition of a term. Page numbers in *italic* indicate illustrations.

Numbers and Symbols

4 MB page feature of Pentium processors, 1355
10BaseT networks. *See* Ethernet networks
100BaseT (Fast Ethernet) networks, 13
100BaseVG networks, 13–14
* (asterisk)
   in Group object names, 450, 468
   in User object login names, 358, 400
\ (backslash)
   in Group object names, 450, 468
   in User object login names, 358, 400
^ (caret), as delimiter in user databases, 804
: (colon)
   in Group object names, 450, 468
   in User object login names, 358, 400
, (comma)
   in Group object names, 450, 468
   in User object login names, 358, 400
- (hyphen), in server names, 134
% (percent sign), in login script identifier variables, 496–497
 # (pound sign)
   # login script command, 492
   in AUTOEXEC.NCF file, 1301
? (question mark)
   in Group object names, 450, 468
   in User object login names, 358, 400
/ (slash)
   in Group object names, 450, 468
   in User object login names, 358, 400
_ (underscore)
   in Group object names, 450, 468
   in organization names, 140
   in server names, 134
   in User object login names, 358, 400

A

A (Add or Delete Self) property right, 686, **1398**
A (Archive Needed) file attribute, 680, **1399**
Access Control (A) directory right, 672
Access Control (A) file right, 674, 954
Access Control List (ACL) object property, 686–687, 751, **1398**, **1433**
access rights. *See* rights; security; trustees
ACCM Link Driver parameter in NET.CFG file, 311
ACCOMP Link Driver parameter in NET.CFG file, 311
accounting, **1398**
   in NETADMIN program, **919–920**, *920*
     user account balance setup, 431, *432*
   in NetWare Administrator, 374–376, **793–801**
     activating server accounting, 795
     examples, **926**, **929**
     setting charge rates for resources, 795–797, *797*, *799*
     setting user account balances and low balance limits, 799–801, *800*
     user account balance setup in NetWare Administrator, 374–376, *375*
     viewing accounting reports with ATOTAL, 797–798
ACONSOLE program, **894–896**, *895*, **930**
Active Connections screen, MONITOR program, **825–828**, *826*
adapters. *See* network interface cards (NICs)
Add or Delete Self (A) property right, 686, **1398**
adding. *See also* installing
   hotkeys in NetWare User Tools, 1022, *1023*
   Macintosh name space to volumes, 1117–1118
   Print Queue objects to Printer object's list, 567, *568*
   print queue operators

adding—AppleTalk printer settings

    in NetWare Administrator, 554–557, *557*
    in PCONSOLE, 627–628
  print queue users
    in NetWare Administrator, 558–560, *559*
    in PCONSOLE, 626–627, *627*
  Print Server object password in PCONSOLE, 616–617
  Print Server object users and groups in NetWare Administrator, 583–585, *584*
  print server operators
    in NetWare Administrator, 585–586, *586*
    in PCONSOLE, 615–616
  print server users and groups in PCONSOLE, 614, *615*
  print servers for print queues in PCONSOLE, 628–629
  Printer object, 577–578, *578*
  protocols during installation, 102–103, *102*
  User objects to Group objects, 454–457, *455*, 471, *472*
addresses, 1398
  in ARCnet networks, 19
  for Ethernet network cards, 6
  I/O port addresses for network interface cards, 71, 265
  IP addresses, **1140, 1413**
  LAAs (locally administered addresses), 9–10
  memory addresses for network interface cards for PC clients, 265
  read-only memory (ROM) addresses, 71–72
ADMIN User object, 131, 1398. *See also* User objects
  and assistant network administrators, 456–457
  creating User objects, 351–352
  naming, 140, 147, *148*
  versus NetWare 3.x SUPERVISOR, **669,** 730–731, 735
  NetWare Administrator security management and, 690
  NetWare Directory Services (NDS) security and, 683
  print queue operator assignment, 556–557, *557*
  [Root] object and, 208
  selecting password for, 140, 147, *148*
  and User object management, 444–445
  workgroup administrators and, **752–753**
administrators, 740–753, 920–930, **1422.** *See also* DOS utilities; NETADMIN; NetWare Administrator
  administrator overload, **921**
  assistant network administrators, **456–457**
  management's network slogans, 744–746
  MegaCorp example, **927–930**
  MiniCo example, **924–926**
  network planning, **741–750**
    examples, **924, 927**
    planning for the future, 743–744
    selling the plan to users, 749–750
    selling the plan to your boss, 746–749
  recommended reading, **1392–1393**
  security and, **728–729**
  supervisory functions and rights, **750–753**
    examples, **924, 927–928**
  workgroup managers, **752–753**
Advanced Options menu, DSREPAIR program, 857–869
  Create a Database Dump File option, 869, *870*
  Global Schema Options screen, 867–868, *868*
  Local ID to Remote ID List screen, 862, *863*
  Log File/Login Configuration Options screen, 858–859, *859*
  Repair Local Database Options screen, 859–860, *860*
  Replica and Partitions Operations options, 863–866, *863*
  Replica Ring Options submenu, 865–866
  Security Equivalence Synchronization option, 866–867, *867*
  Servers Known To This Database option, 861–862, *861*
  Servers That Have Replicas of This Partition screen, 865
  View Repair Log File option, 855, 868–869, *869*
AFP (AppleTalk Filing Protocol), 42–43, 44, 1092
AFP (AppleTalk Filing Protocol) Server objects, 220, **1398**
AIO printer settings
  in NetWare Administrator, 570, 573–574
  in PCONSOLE, 633, 635
Alias objects, 210, 219–220, **1399**
ALL directory attribute, 678
ALL file attribute, 680, 954
All Property Rights trustee assignment, 751
Allocated Memory for All Modules screen, MONITOR program, 821–822, *821*
ALTERNATE Link Driver parameter in NET.CFG file, 311
anti-virus protection, 678, 717–719, 733, 737
AnyLAN networks, 13–14
AppleTalk printer settings. *See also* Macintosh computers
  in NetWare Administrator, 570, 573
  in PCONSOLE, 633, 635

AppleTalk protocols—attributes 1453

AppleTalk protocols, 42–43, 44, 1089–1092, 1399.
    See also Macintosh computers; protocols
    AppleTalk Filing Protocol (AFP), 42–43, 44, 1092
    binding to network interface cards, 1105–1106, *1105*
    configuring AppleTalk protocol stack, 1100–1106
    EtherTalk protocol, 42, 1090
    IPX/SPX protocol and, 42–43
    LocalTalk protocol, 42, 1091
    TokenTalk protocol, 42, 1091
application-centric file systems, 22–24, *23*
applications, 932–987, 1399
    administration tricks, **957–960**
        drive mapping techniques, *958–959*, **1408**
        examples, **982–983**, **986**
        mapping fake ROOTs, *959*, **1409**
        using Directory Map objects, 218, *959–960*, *960*, **1406**
    application server guidelines, **936–944**
        consolidating application licenses, 943–944, *945*
        examples, **981–982**, **985**
        improving disk-read performance with SERVMAN, 942–943
        improving disk-write performance with SERVMAN, 939–941
        separating applications from data files, 936–939, *937*, *939*
    distribution, metering, and licensing trends, **934–936**, *981*, *984–985*
    guidelines, **961–971**
        examples, **983**, **986**
        general tips, 961, 970–971
        Novell GroupWise e-mail and group scheduling, 966–968, *967*, *968*
        Windows 3.1x, 961–965, *964*
        Windows 95, 965–966
        WordPerfect and PerfectOffice, 968–971, *969*
    LSAPI (Licensing Service Application Programming Interface), 935
    MegaCorp example, **984–986**
    MiniCo example, **981–983**
    NetWare Application Launcher (NAL), **971–979**, **983**, **987**, **1419**
        Associations page, 977, *978*
        client side of, 978–979, *979*
        Contacts page, 977
        creating and configuring Application objects, 972–977, *973*

Description page, 976
Drives/Ports page, 975–976, *975*
Environment page, 974
examples, **983**, **987**
Scripts page, 976–977
network-aware, network-enabled, and network-integrated applications, **933–934**, *981*, *984*
protecting applications and data files, **948–957**, **1404**
    changing directory and file ownership, 951–953, *953*
    examples, **982**, **985–986**
    setting file attributes with FLAG command, 679–683, *682*, 949–951, *951*, *952*, **1046–1047**, *1046*, 1078, 1082, **1410**
    viewing and changing file rights with RIGHTS command, **953–957**, *955*, *956*, **1045**, *1046*, 1078, 1082
rights for application directories, **945–947**
    examples, **982**, **985**
    managing rights in application and data directories, 946
    setting, 946–947, *948*
troubleshooting workstation problems with, **1312–1314**
Archive Needed (A) file attribute, 680, 1399
ARCnet networks, 18–20, *19*, 1326
Arc Vision software, 1305
ASCII files, importing user databases into NDS as, 803–805
assistant network administrators, 456–457
Associations page, in NetWare Application Launcher, 977, *978*
asterisk (*)
    in Group object names, 450, 468
    in User object login names, 358, 400
asynchronous I/O (AIO) printer settings
    in NetWare Administrator, 570, 573–574
    in PCONSOLE, 633, 635
AT&T, and Unix development, 1125–1126
ATM (Asynchronous Transfer Mode) networks, 17, 18
ATOTAL program, 797–798
ATTACH login script command, 492, 1339, 1399
attributes, 677–683, 1399. *See also* security
    directory attributes, **678–679**
    examples, **731**, **736**
    file attributes
        setting with FLAG command, 679–683, *682*, 949–951, *951*, *952*, **1046–1047**, *1046*, 1078, 1082, **1410**

identification and operator attributes for Print Queue objects, 552–554, *553*
NDS trees and, 206
AUDITCON program, 719–726, 1399–1400. *See also* security
   examples, **733, 738**
   performing audits, 723–725, *724*
   setting auditor passwords, 722–723
   starting, 720–721, *722*
   viewing audit reports, 725–726, *726*
AUTHEN PAP Link Driver parameter in NET.CFG file, 311
AUTO LARGE TABLE parameter in NET.CFG, 297
AUTO RECONNECT parameter in NET.CFG, 297
AUTO RETRY parameter in NET.CFG, 298
AUTO.VLM file, 296
AUTOEXEC.BAT file
   @CALL statement, 283
   for PC clients, 283
   SCSI conflict problems and, 97–98
   for server boot disk, 80
   for server installation boot disk, 73, 74–75
   SET NWLANGUAGE= statement, 177
   starting server automatically at startup, 95–96
AUTOEXEC.NCF file, 1400
   BIND command, 102–103
   copying, 1301
   editing during NDS installation, **153–154**, *154*
   INETCFG and, 889–890
   network protocol configuration settings, 171–174, *172, 173, 174*
   pound sign (#) in, 1301
   SET BINDERY CONTEXT= statement, 246
   SET commands in, *95*, 153, 154, *154*, 1356
Available LAN Drivers screen, MONITOR program, 831–832, *832*
Available Options menu, RCONSOLE program, 811–813, *811*
AVERAGE NAME LENGTH parameter in NET.CFG, 298

B

B (Browse) object right, 685, 1401
background processes, in Unix, 1130–1131
backing up NetWare 4.1x, 1271–1272, **1273–1274**, 1400. *See also* tape backup systems

backslash (\)
   in Group object names, 450, 468
   in User object login names, 358, 400
base I/O port addresses, for network interface cards, 71, 265
BAUD Link Driver parameter in NET.CFG file, 311
BIND parameter in NET.CFG file, 317
BIND RECONNECT parameter in NET.CFG, 298
BIND.VLM file, 295
bindery, 1400. *See also* leaf objects
   leaf objects and, 214–215
   upgrading to NetWare 4.1x, 1338–1339
   why bindery emulation may be necessary, 245–246
Bindery and Bindery Queue objects, 221–222, 1400
Bindery mode in PCONSOLE, 607
Bindery Services, 244–250, 1400–1401. *See also* NetWare Directory Services
   bindery context and, **244**
   examples, **254, 258**
   how Bindery Services works, 244–245
   installing, 246–247, *247*
   maintaining, 249–250
   NDS trees and, 246, 247–249, *248, 249*
   Simple Installation method and, 247–249, *248, 249*
   and using resources from another tree, 246
   why bindery emulation may be necessary, 245–246
binding, 1401
   AppleTalk to network interface cards, 1105–1106, *1105*
   IPX protocol to network interface cards, 102–103
block suballocation, 114, 1264, 1354, 1401
boards. *See* network interface cards
books. *See* recommended reading
booting servers
   creating server installation boot disk, 72–75
   from floppy disks, 79–81
   from hard disk drives, 76–78, *76, 77*
bottom-up NDS tree design, 230–232, *233, 234*
bridges, 35, 1401
BROADCAST RETRIES parameter in NET.CFG, 298
BROADCAST SEND DELAY parameter in NET.CFG, 298
BROADCAST TIMEOUT parameter in NET.CFG, 298
Browse (B) object right, 685, 1401
Browser windows in NetWare Administrator, 694–695, *694*, 756–757, *757*

C

C (Compare) property right, 686, 1402
C (Country) container objects, 210, 222, **1403**
C (Create) directory right, 672, **1403**
C (Create) file right, 674, **1403**
C (Create) object right, 685, **1403**
C2 level security rating, 1360
cabling, **1402**
    for ARCnet networks, 19, *19*
    fiber-optic cabling, 12
    installing
        examples, 50, 53–54
    STP (shielded twisted-pair) cabling, 12, 16
    Token Ring versus Ethernet networks, 10–11
    troubleshooting, **1325–1327**
    UTP (unshielded twisted-pair) cabling, 1447
        Fast Ethernet networks and, 13
        FDDI networks and, 16
        installing, 31–32
        Token Ring versus Ethernet networks and, 10–11
        wiring closets and, 33–34, *33*
CACHE BUFFER SIZE parameter in NET.CFG, 299
CACHE BUFFERS parameter in NET.CFG, 298
Cache Utilization Statistics screen, MONITOR program, **817–819**, *817*
CACHE WRITES parameter in NET.CFG, 299
caches. *See also* memory
    cache buffers, 1347, **1402**
    directory caching SET commands, 842, 940–943, *941*, **1368–1369**, **1402**
    file caching SET commands, 841, **1374–1375**, **1402**
@CALL statement, in AUTOEXEC.BAT, 283
CAPTURE command
    examples, **1077**, **1081**
    print job configuration, 370, 371, 645, 648
    printing configuration, 1006, **1035–1040**, *1037*
    printing system and, 533–534
cards. *See* network interface cards
caret (^), as delimiter in user databases, 804
carrier sense multiple access/collision detect (CSMA/CD) access method, 5–6, 13
case sensitivity
    in Group object names, 449–451, 468
    in NetWare versus Unix, 1130
    in User object names, 357, 400
case studies. *See* MegaCorp; MiniCo
CDI (Custom Device Interface), 1263–1264

CDM (Custom Device Module)
    CDM drivers, 98–100
CD-ROM drives. *See also* disk drives; floppy disks; hard disk drives
    configuring for Macintosh servers, 1113–1114, *1115*
    creating OS/2 client disks from NetWare 4.10 CD-ROM, 162–164, *163*, 1201–1202
    installing NetWare 4.1x Server for OS/2 from, 1224–1225
    installing NetWare
        from remote CD-ROMs mounted as volumes, 87–88
        from server-based CD-ROMs, 81, 82–83, 84–86
    installing non-Client32 client software from, 279–280, 281–282
    installing OS/2 client software from, 1205–1206, *1206*
    NetWare requirements, **68–69**
    reading DynaText online documentation from, 1062–1063, *1062*
    SCSI conflict problems, 68–69, 97–98
central processing units (CPUs)
    NetWare requirements, 60–61
    Pentium 4 MB page feature, 1355
CERT (Computer Emergency Response Team), 666
changing. *See also* converting; editing; modifying
    contexts
        with CX command, 241, 994–996
        with NETUSER, 241, 1033–1034, *1034*
        with NetWare User Tools, 241
    default server language, 176–177, *177*
    directory and file ownership, 951–953, *953*
    file rights with RIGHTS command, 953–957, *955*, *956*
    Hot Fix utility settings, 105
    hotkeys and other NetWare settings with NetWare User Tools, 1019–1021, *1020*
    login scripts with NETUSER, 1032, *1033*
    LPT printer settings with NetWare User Tools, 1009–1012, *1010*
    passwords with NETUSER, 1032, *1033*
    print jobs in PCONSOLE, 620–623, *620*, *621*
    print queue status in PCONSOLE, 624–625, *624*
    Print Server object description in PCONSOLE, 616, *617*
    Print Server object password in PCONSOLE, 616–617
    print server operators in PCONSOLE, 615–616
    print server users and groups in PCONSOLE, 614, *615*
    printer status in NetWare Administrator, 591–594, *592*
    volume segment size, 108–111, *109*, *110*, *111*

Check Servers In This Tree option, DSMERGE program, 876, *877*
Check Time Synchronization option, DSMERGE program, **877–878**, *878*
CHECKSUM parameter in NET.CFG, 299
child partitions, 777
child VLMs, **275–276**
choosing. *See* selecting
Ci (Copy Inhibit) file attribute, 680, **1403**
classes of objects, **205**
clearing. *See* deleting
Clearinghouse protocol, 36
Client32 clients, **326–338**, 1402. *See also* PC clients
    connecting DOS and Windows 3.1x clients to networks, **331–334**
    examples, **341–342**, **345–346**
    installing for DOS and Windows 3.1x systems, **327–331**, *328*, *329*
    installing for Windows 95 systems, **326–327**, **334–338**, *336*, *337*
    NetWare IPX/IP Gateway and, **1175**
    NetWare/IP protocol on, **1159–1160**
    upgrading clients to, **1341–1343**
clients. *See* Macintosh computers; OS/2; PC clients; User objects; user utilities; users; workstations
collision detection, **5–6**, 13
colon (:)
    in Group object names, 450, 468
    in User object login names, 358, 400
comma (,)
    in Group object names, 450, 468
    in User object login names, 358, 400
commands. *See also* DOS utilities
    CAPTURE
        examples, **1077**, **1081**
        print job configuration, 370, 371
        printing configuration, 1006, **1035–1040**, *1037*
        printing system and, 533–534
    console commands, **883–888**. *See also* server management
    DISPLAY NETWORKS, **883–884**, *883*
    DISPLAY SERVERS, 884, *884*
    DOWN, 884
    EXIT, **884–885**
    MODULES, 885, *885*
    TRACK ON, **886–887**, *886*
    VERSION, 887, *887*
    VOLUMES, **887–888**, *888*

CX, 241, **994–996**
FLAG, **679–683**, *682*, **949–951**, *951*, 952, **1046–1047**, *1046*, 1078, 1082, **1410**
Help for, **1058–1059**, *1058*
login script commands, **491–494**
    # command, 492
    ATTACH, 492, 1339, 1399
    COMSPEC, 492
    EXIT, 493
    FIRE PHASERS, 493
    IF...THEN, 493
    MAP, 485, **490–491**, 494, **1416**
    PAUSE, 494
    SET, 494
    WRITE, 494, **496–497**
MAP
    in Default login scripts, **490–491**
    login scripts and, 485
    mapping drives, **958–959**
    Windows 3.1x and, 963
MAP ROOT, 959
menu script commands, **512–517**
    control commands, **515–517**
    EXEC, 515
    GETx, **516–517**
    ITEM, **514–515**
    LOAD, 516
    MENU, **513–514**
    organizational commands, **513–515**
    SHOW, 516
NDIR, **1047**, 1078, 1082, **1324**, *1325*
NPRINT
    examples, **1077**, **1081**
    print job configuration, 370, 371, 645, 648
    printing files from command line, 1035, **1040–1042**
    printing system and, 534
NVER, **263–264**, 334
RIGHTS
    changing file rights, **953–957**, *955*, *956*
    viewing rights, 1045, *1046*, 1078, 1082
SET commands, **839–844**. *See also* server management
    in AUTOEXEC.NCF file, 95, 153, 154, *154*, 1356
    communication parameters, 841, **1366–1368**
    directory caching parameters, 842, **940–943**, *941*, **1368–1369**, 1402
    directory services parameters, 844, **1370–1372**

commands—Container login scripts

disk parameters, 843, 1372–1373
error handling parameters, 844, 1373–1374
file caching parameters, 841, 1374–1375, 1402
file system parameters, 842, 1375–1378
installation options, 95
lock parameters, 842–843, 1379
memory parameters, 841, 1379–1380
miscellaneous parameters, 844, 1381–1383
NCP (NetWare Core Protocol) parameters, 844, 1383–1385
options during NetWare installation, 95
SERVMAN and, 95, 839–841, 1356
SET BINDERY CONTEXT= statement, 246
SET NWLANGUAGE= statement, 176, 276–277
in STARTUP.NCF file, 95, 151–152
time parameters, 843, 1385–1388
transaction tracking parameters, 843, 1388–1389
VOLINFO, 1324
communication SET commands, 841, 1366–1368
comp.sys.novell newsgroup, 1058
Compare (C) property right, 686, **1402**
Complete Encyclopedia of Networking (Feibel), 664–665, 1395
compression. *See* file compression
CompuServe NetWire Forum, 1057, **1422**
Computer Emergency Response Team (CERT), 666
Computer objects, 219
COMSPEC login script command, 492
CONFIG.SYS file
SCSI conflict problems and, 68–69, 97–98
for server installation boot disk, 73–74
configuring, 1403
ACONSOLE parameters with INETCFG, 894–896, *895*
AppleTalk protocol stack for Macintosh servers, 1100–1106
Application objects in NetWare Application Launcher, 972–977, *973*
CD-ROM services for Macintosh servers, 1113–1114, *1115*
file services for Macintosh servers, 1106–1108, *1107*
FirstMail program, 1267–1268
IPX protocol with INETCFG, 890–893, *891*
Macintosh clients for NDS, 1118–1120, *1120*
Multi-Protocol Router, 1193–1194
NetWare IPX/IP Gateway, 1173–1175, *1174*
network interface cards for Macintosh servers, 1102

non-Client32 clients with NCUPDATE, 805–807, 1358
OS/2 clients, 1207–1208, *1207*
print jobs in NetWare Administrator, 602–605, *603*
Print Queue objects in NetWare Administrator, 552–564
protocols during NDS installation, 171–174, *172, 173, 174*
RCONSOLE from client, 809–811, *810*
RCONSOLE with INETCFG, 893–894, *894*
REMOTE at server, 808–809
Web Server, 1187–1192, *1188, 1190, 1191*
Windows 3.1x for fast network printing, 1012–1014, *1013*
CONN.VLM file, 295
connecting
DOS and Windows 3.1x Client32 clients to networks, 331–334
mirrored servers, 1245–1246, *1246*
with NetWare User Tools
to NetWare servers, 1014–1017, *1016*
to network printers, 1006–1008, *1007*
to network printers permanently, 1008–1009, *1009*
OS/2 clients to servers, 1208–1211, *1210, 1211*
Connection Information screen, MONITOR program, 825–828, *826, 827*
CONNECTIONS parameter in NET.CFG, 299
console commands, 883–888. *See also* commands; server management
DISPLAY NETWORKS, 883–884, *883*
DISPLAY SERVERS, 884, *884*
DOWN, 884
EXIT, 884–885
MODULES, 885, *885*
TRACK ON, 886–887, *886*
VERSION, 887, *887*
VOLUMES, 887–888, *888*
console versus default server language settings, 177
CONSOLE.LOG file, 1297, 1299–1300, *1300*
consolidating application licenses, 943–944, *945*
Contacts page, in NetWare Application Launcher, 977
Container login scripts, 1403. *See also* login scripts
creating or editing with NETADMIN, 508–509, *509*
creating or editing with NetWare Administrator, 506
example, 499–502, *499*
migrating, 1339

container objects, 131, 205, **1403**. *See also* NetWare Directory Services (NDS); objects
  container rules for objects, **213–214**, *214*
  Country (C) container objects, 210, 222, **1403**
  creating
    in NETADMIN, **908–909**, *909*, *910*
    in NetWare Administrator, **762–765**, *763*, *764*
    moving partitions and their containers, **792**, *793*
    Organization (O) container objects, 211–212, 445, **1425**
    Organization Unit (OU) container objects, 212–213, 445, **1425–1426**
    [Root] object and, 208–209, *209*
contexts, 131, 238–243, **1403**. *See also* NetWare Directory Services (NDS)
  bindery context, **244**
  changing
    with CX command, 241, **994–996**
    with NETUSER, 241, **1033–1034**, *1034*
    with NetWare User Tools, 241
  distinguished names, 238
  examples, **253**, *257*
  For your information screen, 140–141, *141*
  how to use to your advantage, **242–243**
  importance of, **239–241**, *239*
  logging in and, 242–243
  naming the Organization and Organizational Units, 139–140, *139*, 148–150, *149*, *150*
  relative distinguished names, 240
  selecting ADMIN name and password, 140, 147, *148*
  setting up user's "home" context, 243
  settings for additional servers, **147–150**
  settings for first NetWare server, **138–141**, *139*
  typeless versus typeful name formats, 238, **1443–1444**
control files, for NetWare 4.1x SFT III, 1248
controlling client access to NetWare IPX/IP Gateway, **1178–1183**, *1179*, *1180*, *1181*
converting. *See also* changing
  menu scripts from previous NetWare versions, 520
Copy Inhibit (Ci) file attribute, 680, **1403**
copying
  AUTOEXEC.NCF file, 1301
  server configuration files, 1300–1301, *1301*
  SET parameters to files, 846–847
  STARTUP.NCF file, 1301
COUNTER Link Driver parameter in NET.CFG file, 311

Country (C) objects, 210, 222, **1403**. *See also* container objects
CPUs (central processing units)
  NetWare requirements, 60–61
  Pentium 4 MB page feature, 1355
CRCs (cyclical redundancy checks), 718
Create (C) directory right, 672, **1403**
Create (C) file right, 674, **1403**
Create (C) object right, 685, **1403**
Create a Database Dump File option, DSREPAIR program, 869, *870*
creating. *See also* defining; designing NDS trees; planning
  Application objects in NetWare Application Launcher, 972–977, *973*
  container objects
    in NETADMIN, 908–909, *909*, *910*
    in NetWare Administrator, 762–765, *763*, *764*
  DOS partitions for booting servers from hard disk drives, 76–78, *76*, *77*
  DOS, Windows, OS/2 client install disks, 162–164, *163*
  Group objects
    with NETADMIN, 466–469, *468*
    with NetWare Administrator, 447–451, *449*, *450*
  home directories
    with NETADMIN, 351, 352, 401–404, *402*, *403*, *404*
    with NetWare Administrator, 351, 352, 359–361, *360*
  installation floppy disks, 81, 83–84, 86–87
  leaf objects
    in NETADMIN, 911–912
    in NetWare Administrator, 767–769, *768*, *769*
  login scripts with NETADMIN, **415–416**, **507–510**
    Container login scripts, 508–509, *509*
    Profile login scripts, 509, *510*
    User login scripts, 509–510, *510*
    for User object setup, 415–416, *417*
  login scripts with NetWare Administrator, **377–379**, **505–507**
    Container login scripts, 506
    Profile login scripts, 506–507
    User login scripts, 507
    for User object setup, 377–379, *378*

NetWare Administrator icon in Windows 3.1x, 753–755
OS/2 client disks from NetWare 4.10 CD-ROM, 162–164, *163*, 1201–1202
partitions
    during NetWare installation, 103–104, *104, 105*
    in NDS Manager, 781–783, *782*
    with PARTMGR, 916–917, *917*
pilot systems for NetWare Directory Services, 224–225
print devices in PRINTDEF, 639
Print Queue objects in NetWare Administrator, 545–548, *546, 547*
printer forms
    in NetWare Administrator, 594–596, *595*
    in PRINTDEF, 644–645, *644*
registration disk, 159–161, *161*
server installation boot disk, 72–75
UPGRADE/MIGRATE disks, 164
User objects with NETADMIN, **395–437**
    account balance tracking, 431, *432*
    basic User object creation, **397–400**, *398, 399*
    detail settings, **405–413**
    e-mailbox setup, 408–409, *409*
    environment information, 407–408, *407*
    examples, **440, 442**
    foreign e-mail addresses and aliases, 410–411
    group membership setup, 351, 352, 418, *419*
    home directory setup, 351, 352, 401–404, *402, 403, 404*
    identification information, 405–406, *406*
    intruder lockout setup, 429–430, *430*
    login names, 400
    login restriction setup, 421–423, *422*
    login scripts, 351, 352, 415–416, *417*
    login time restriction setup, 426–427, *427*
    network address restrictions, 427–428, *429*
    password restrictions, 423–425, *424*
    postal address information, 411–412, *412*
    Profile script editing, 421
    related information tracking, 413, *414*
    rights to files and directories setup, 434–437, *436*
    security configuration, **413–437**
    security equivalence setup, 351, 352, 419–420, *420*
    user reference information, 413, *414*

volume space restriction setup, 432–433, *434*
User objects with NetWare Administrator, 352–395
    account balance tracking, 374–376, *375*
    basic User object creation, **354–358**, *356, 357*
    detail settings, **358–376**
    e-mailbox setup, 366–367, *367*
    environment information, 364–366, *365*
    examples, **439, 441–442**
    foreign e-mail addresses and aliases, 368–369, *369*
    group membership setup, 351, 352, 384–385, *385*
    home directory setup, 351, 352, 359–361, *360*
    identification information, 362–364, *362*
    installing client software and NetWare Administrator, **353–354**
    intruder lockout setup, 391, *393*
    login names, 357–358
    login restriction setup, 379–381, *380*
    login scripts, 351, 352, 377–379, *378*
    login time restriction setup, 387–389, *388*
    network address restrictions, 389–390, *390*
    password restrictions, 381–384, *382*
    postal address information, 373, *374*
    print job configuration, 352, 370–373, *371*
    related information tracking, 376, *377*
    rights to files and directories setup, 391–395, *393, 394*
    security configuration, **376–395**
    security equivalence setup, 351, 352, 386, *387*
User Templates with NETADMIN, 483–484
CSMA/CD (carrier sense multiple access/collision detect) access method, 5–6, 13
currency formats, 175
Custom Device Interface (CDI), 1263–1264
Custom Device Module (CDM)
    CDM drivers, 98–100
Custom Installation method, 91–121. *See also* NetWare 4.1x installation
    adding protocols, 102–103, *102*
    automatic server startup option, 95–96
    block suballocation on volumes, 114, **1264**, 1354, **1401**
    changing Hot Fix settings, 105
    changing volume segment size, 108–111, *109, 110, 111*
    copying server files to DOS partition, 93–94, *94*

creating NetWare disk partitions, 103–104, *104, 105*
data migration option, 114–115
disk configuration, 103–106
disk driver installation, 96–100, *96*
disk mirroring and duplexing options, 105–106, **1404, 1407**
file compression settings for volumes, 113–114
file name format options, 94–95
internal IPX network number setting, 93, **1414, 1422**
keyboard mapping options, 94–95
LAN driver installation for network interface cards, 100–101, *101*
monolithic (.DSK) versus NPA (NetWare Peripheral Architecture) drivers, 98–100, 1263–1264, 1360
naming the server, 92–93
naming volumes, 112
saving volume changes, 115
SET command options, 95
troubleshooting SCSI conflict problems, 68–69, 97–98
volume block size options, 112–113
volume management options, **106–115**, *108*
CX command, 241, 994–996
cyclical redundancy checks (CRCs), 718

D

D (Delete) object right, 685, **1404**
daemons, in Unix, **1130–1131**
.DAT extension, 512
DATA ECB COUNT parameter in NET.CFG file, 324
data files
   managing rights in data directories, **946**
   protecting, **948–957, 1404**
      changing directory and file ownership, 951–953, *953*
      examples, **982, 985–986**
      setting file attributes with FLAG command, 679–683, *682*, 949–951, *951*, 952, **1046–1047**, *1046*, 1078, 1082, **1410**
      viewing and changing file rights with RIGHTS command, 953–957, *955*, *956*, **1045**, *1046*, 1078, 1082
   separating applications from, 936–939, *937*, *939*
data migration, **1404, 1417**
   creating UPGRADE/MIGRATE disks, 164
   enabling, 114–115
   in upgrading to NetWare 4.1x, **1336–1337**

datagrams, 37
date formats, 175
Daylight Savings Time (DST) adjustments, 137–138, *137*
Dc (Don't Compress) directory attribute, 678, **1407**
Dc (Don't Compress) file attribute, 680, **1407**
decentralizing management of printing services, 548
DecodesPLUS software, 1305
Default login scripts, 486–487, 489–491
defining. *See also* creating; designing NDS trees
   print modes in NetWare Administrator, 600–601, *601*
Delete (D) object right, 685, **1404**
Delete Inhibit (Di) directory attribute, 678, **1404**
DELETED directory, 24
deleting
   Group object trustees, 463–464
   NetWare Directory Services (NDS), **184–187**
      examples, **194, 197**
      from multiple-server networks, 187, *188*
      from one-server networks, 185–187, *186*, *187*
      warnings, 185, *186*, *187*
   NetWare (NCP) Server objects from NDS, 790–792, *791*
   print devices in NetWare Administrator, 596–597, *598*
   Print Queue objects from Printer object's list, 567, *568*
   print queue operators
      in NetWare Administrator, 554–557, *557*
      in PCONSOLE, 627–628
   print queue users
      in NetWare Administrator, 558–560, *559*
      in PCONSOLE, 626–627, *627*
   Print Server object users and groups in NetWare Administrator, 583–585, *584*
   print server operators
      in NetWare Administrator, 585–586, *586*
      in PCONSOLE, 615–616
   print server users and groups in PCONSOLE, 614, *615*
   print servers for print queues in PCONSOLE, 628–629
   purging deleted files, 1055, 1325
   recovering deleted files with FILER, 1054–1055, *1056*, **1434**
   subdirectories with FILER, 1051–1052, *1052*
   User objects from Group objects, 454–457, *455*, 471, *472*

delimiters, 1405
    caret (^) in user databases, 804
departmental NDS tree design, 230–232, *233*, *234*
describing printing Feature properties in NetWare Administrator, 576, *577*
Description page, in NetWare Application Launcher, 976
designing NDS trees, 223–227, 230–238. *See also* planning
    departmental, workgroup, user-location, or bottom-up design, 230–232, *233*, *234*
    distributed organization chart with a WAN or mixed design, 236–238, *237*
    goals for, 223–224
    versus implementing, 227
    organizational, user function, or top-down design, 233–236, *235*, *236*
    physical versus logical design phases, 225–226, 232, *233*, *234*
    for users, 226
device drivers. *See* drivers
Di (Delete Inhibit) directory attribute, 678, 1404
DIAL Link Driver parameter in NET.CFG file, 312
DIRECT Link Driver parameter in NET.CFG file, 312
directories, 1405. *See also* file systems; FILER
    changing directory ownership, 951–953, *953*
    directory attributes, **678–679**
    hashing directory information, 1347
    home directories, 23-24, **1412**
        creating with NETADMIN, 351, 352, 401–404, *402*, *403*, *404*
        creating with NetWare Administrator, 351, 352, 359–361, *360*
    subdirectories, **1439**
        deleting with FILER, 1051–1052, *1052*
    system directories, 24–25
    in Unix, **1130**
    and upgrading to NetWare 4.1x, 1339
    viewing directory information with NDIR command, 1047, 1078, 1082, **1324**, *1325*
Directory, 1405. *See also* NetWare Directory Services
    NDS trees and, 206
directory caching SET commands, 842, 940–943, *941*, 1368–1369, 1402
Directory Map objects, 218, 959–960, *960*, **1406**
directory rights, 1405, 1433. *See also* file system security; rights; security; trustees
    for application directories, 945–947

    examples, 982, 985
    managing rights in application and data directories, 946
    setting, 946–947, *948*
changing directory ownership, **951–953**, *953*
for Group objects
    modifying in NETADMIN, 475–477, *476*, *477*
    modifying in NetWare Administrator, 460–463, *462*
managing directory trustees with FILER, 709–711, *711*
managing with NetWare Administrator, 693–702, *694*
supervisory functions and, 750
for User Objects
    modifying in NETADMIN, 434–437, *436*
    modifying in NetWare Administrator, 391–395, *393*, *394*
Directory Services. *See* NetWare Directory Services (NDS)
Directory Services Merge. *See* DSMERGE
Directory Services Repair. *See* DSREPAIR
directory services SET commands, 844, 1370–1372
Directory Services Trace (DSTRACE) program, 851–853, *852*, 926, 929
Directory trees, 222–238, 1406. *See also* DSMERGE; leaf objects; NetWare Directory Services; [Root] object
    attribute information and, 206
    Bindery Services and, 246, 247–249, *248*, *249*
    creating pilot systems, 224–225
    departmental, workgroup, user-location, or bottom-up design, 230–232, *233*, *234*
    designing versus implementing, 227
    designing for users, 226
    Directory schema and, **206**
    distributed organization chart with a WAN or mixed design, **236–238**, *237*
    examples, **253**, **256–257**
    goals for NDS tree design, 223–224
    inheritance information and, 206
    merging, 879–880, *879*
    naming for first NetWare server, 133–134, *135*
    naming standards, 227–230
    organizational, user function, or top-down design, **233–236**, *235*, *236*
    physical versus logical design phases, **225–226**, 232, *233*, *234*
    selecting for additional servers, 142–144, *143*
    subordination and, 206
    teaching users about, **992–994**, *993*

using resources from another tree, **246**
using single versus multiple trees, **142**, *143*
disabling F6 hotkey in NetWare User Tools, **1000–1001**, *1001*
disk caches
   cache buffers, 1347
   directory caching SET commands, 842, 940–943, *941*, **1368–1369**, **1402**
   file caching SET commands, 841, **1374–1375**, **1402**
disk compression. *See* file compression
disk drivers, 1406–1407
   installing, **96–100**, *96*
disk drives, 1408. *See also* CD-ROM drives; partitions; volumes
   block suballocation, 114, **1264**, **1354**, **1401**
   booting servers from, **76–78**, *76*, *77*
   Disk Information screen in MONITOR program, **828–831**, *829*
   disk mirroring and duplexing options, 105–106, **1404**, **1407**
   disk SET commands, 843, **1372–1373**
   drivers, 96–100, *96*, **1406–1407**
   Drives/Ports page in NetWare Application Launcher, **975–976**, *975*
   elevator seeking and, 1347, *1348*
   ESDI disk controllers and drives, 64
   floppy disk drives, 69
   IDE disk controllers and drives, 64
   installing DynaText online documentation, 1060
   mapping, **1408**
      mapping fake ROOTs, **959**, **1409**
      with NETUSER, **1030–1032**, *1031*
      with NetWare User Tools, **1002–1005**, *1003*, *1004*
      permanently with NetWare User Tools, **1005–1006**, *1006*
      from Windows 95, **1072–1074**, *1073*
   NetWare requirements, **63–66**
   NetWare superiority and, **1346–1347**, *1348*
   preparing for NetWare installation, **76–78**
      for booting servers from floppy disks, 79–81
      for booting servers from hard disk drives, 76–78, *76*, *77*
      examples, **124–125**, *127*
   RAID disk systems, **65–66**, *1320*, 1321
   SCSI disk interfaces and drives, **64–65**
   ST506 disk controllers and drives, 63

troubleshooting server disk errors, 1324–1325, *1325*
user disk space restriction in NETADMIN, **432–433**, *434*
user disk space restriction in NetWare Administrator, **801–803**, *802*
display monitors, NetWare requirements, 69–70
DISPLAY NETWORKS console command, 883–884, *883*
DISPLAY SERVERS console command, 884, *884*
displaying. *See* viewing
distinguished names, 240–241
distributed organization chart with a WAN or mixed NDS tree design, 236–238, *237*
distributing applications, 934–936, 981, 984–985
Distribution List objects, 221
DMA Link Driver parameter in NET.CFG file, 312
DMA settings, for network interface cards, 71, 266
DNS (Domain Name System), 1137–1138
DOC directory, 24–25
documentation. *See* DynaText online documentation
Domain Name System (DNS), 1137–1138
DOMAIN.NLM utility, **1270–1271**
Don't Compress (Dc) directory attribute, 678, **1407**
Don't Compress (Dc) file attribute, 680, **1407**
Don't Migrate (Dm) directory attribute, 678, **1407**
Don't Migrate (Dm) file attribute, 680, **1407**
DOS. *See also* Macintosh computers; Microsoft Windows; OS/2; Unix
   connecting Client32 clients to networks, 331–334
   creating client install disks for, **162–164**, *163*
   installing Client32 clients, **327–331**, *328*, *329*, 341–342, 345–346
   TCP/IP protocol for, 41
DOS menus. *See* menu scripts
DOS NAME parameter in NET.CFG, 299
DOS partitions
   copying server files to, **93–94**, *94*
   creating, **103–104**, *104*, *105*
   creating for booting servers from hard disk drives, 76–78, *76*, *77*
   versus volumes, **103**
DOS Requester. *See* NetWare DOS Requester
DOS utilities. *See also* commands; NETADMIN; PCONSOLE
   ACONSOLE program, **894–896**, *895*, 930
   ATOTAL program, **797–798**
   AUDITCON program, **719–726**, **1399–1400**

examples, **733, 738**
performing audits, 723–725, *724*
setting auditor passwords, 722–723
starting, 720–721, *722*
viewing audit reports, 725–726, *726*
DSMERGE program, **873–882**
   Check Servers In This Tree option, 876, *877*
   Check Time Synchronization option, 877–878, *878*
   examples, **930**
   exiting and cleaning up, 881–882
   Merge Two Trees option, 879–880, *879*
   Rename This Tree option, 880–881, *881*
DSREPAIR program, **779–780, 853–873, 1408**
   Advanced Options menu, 855, **857–869**, *858*
   graphical version in NDS Manager, **870–873**, *871, 872*
   repairing NDS corruption, **779–780**
   Report Synchronization Status option, 855
   Time Synchronization option, 855
   Unattended Full Repair option, 854, 856–857, *857*
DSTRACE program, **851–853**, *852, 926, 929*
FILER program, **709–713, 1048–1057, 1410**
   deleting subdirectories, 1051–1052, *1052*
   examples, **1078, 1082**
   keyboard shortcuts, 1048–1049
   managing directory or file trustees, 709–711, *711*
   managing IRFs (Inherited Rights Filters), 712–713, *713*
   purging deleted files, 1056, 1325
   recovering deleted files, 1054–1055, *1056*, **1434**
   searching for files and directories, 1052–1053
   selecting current directory, 1053
   setting default options, 1056–1057
   viewing volume information, 1053–1054, *1054*
FirstMail program, **1267–1268**
   running, 1268, *1269*
   setting up mailboxes, 1267–1268
INETCFG program, **171–174, 888–896**
   ACONSOLE parameter configuration, 894–896, *895*
   installing NetWare TCP/IP support (TCPIP.NLM), 1146–1151
   IPX configuration, 890–893, *891*
   Multi-Protocol Router configuration, 1193–1194

network protocol configuration, 171–174, *172, 173, 174*
   RCONSOLE parameter configuration, 893–894, *894*
   SNMP (Simple Network Management Protocol) and, 1281
   viewing CONSOLE.LOG file, 1297, 1299–1300, *1300*
IPTUNNEL program, 1152–1153, *1153*
IPXCON program, 896–897, *897*
IPXODI.COM program, 266–267, 273–274, **1414**
LSL.COM (Link Support Layer) program, 266–267, 268, **1425**
MAKEDISK.BAT program, 280–281
MENUCNVT program, 520
MENUMAKE program, 520
MIGPRINT program, 1339–1340
MONITOR program, **813–839, 1417**
   Active Connections screen, 825–828, *826*
   Allocated Memory for All Modules screen, 821–822, *821*
   Available LAN Drivers screen, 831–832, *832*
   Cache Utilization Statistics screen, 817–819, *817*
   Connection Information screen, 825–828, *826, 827*
   Disk Information screen, 828–831, *829*
   examples, **926, 929**
   File Open/Lock Activity option, 834–835, *835*
   General Information screen, 814–816, *814*
   LAN/WAN Information option, 831–832, *832*
   Lock File Server Console option, 834–835, *835*
   Memory Utilization option, 821–822, *821*
   Processor Utilization screen, 819–821, *820*
   Resource Utilization option, 822–825, *824*
   Scheduling Information screen, 837–839, *838*
   Server Memory Statistics screen, 822–825, *824*
   server self-tuning and, 1271, 1356
   System Module Information screen, 833–834, *833*
   tracking server performance, **1295–1297**
   troubleshooting and, *1296*
NCUPDATE program, 805–807, 1358
NetSync program, **897–905, 1419**
   installing on NetWare 3.1x servers, 902–904, *903*
   installing on NetWare 4.1x servers, 899–902, *900*
   maintaining NetSync objects, 905, *906*

NETUSER program, **1025–1034.** *See also*
  NetWare User Tools
  changing contexts, 241, 1033–1034, *1034*
  changing login scripts and passwords, 1032, *1033*
  examples, **1077**, **1081**
  mapping drives, 1030–1032, *1031*
  printing controls, 1026–1027, *1027*
  sending and receiving messages, 1028–1030, *1029*
  viewing rights, 1032
  viewing server information, 1032, *1033*
NMENU.BAT program, **511–513**
NPRINTER program, **535**, **536**, **1042–1044**, 1077–1078, 1082
PARTMGR program, **777–778**, **916–919**
  creating partitions, 916–917, *917*
  examples, **926**, 930
  viewing or modifying replicas, 918–919, *918*
PRINTCON program, **645–648**, **657**, **661**
  creating and editing print job configurations, 645–648, *646*
  examples, **657**, **661**
  selecting default print job configuration, 648
PRINTDEF program, **638–645**, **657**, **661**
  creating and modifying print devices, 639–640
  creating and modifying printer forms, 644–645, *644*
  editing print devices, 639–640, *640*
  examples, **657**, **661**
  exporting print devices, 642–643, *643*
  importing print devices, 641–642, *642*
  print mode definition, 640–641, *641*
RCONSOLE program, **649–650**, **807–813**, **1431**
  Available Options menu, 811–813, *811*
  configuring from client, 809–811, *810*
  configuring with INETCFG, 893–894, *894*
  configuring REMOTE at server, 808–809
  examples, **926**, 929
  viewing printer status at print server console, **649–650**, *649*, 657–658, 662
SALVAGE program, 1054
SBACKUP program, 1272, **1273–1274**, **1435**
security utilities, **709–714**
  examples, **732**, **737**
  managing directory or file trustees with FILER, 709–711, *711*

managing IRFs (Inherited Rights Filters) with FILER, 712–713, *713*
managing property and object rights with NETADMIN, 713–714, *715*
SERVMAN program, **844–850**, **939–943**, **1437**
  copying server parameters, **1300–1301**, *1301*
  Directory Caching Parameters screen, 940–943, *941*
  improving disk-read performance, 942–943
  improving disk-write performance, 939–941
  installing Bindery Services, 246–247, *247*
  Network Information screen, 850, *851*
  opening screen, 844–846, *845*
  Server Parameters screen, 846–848, *848*
  SET commands and, 95, 839–841, 1356
  Storage Objects information screen, 848–849, *849*
  Volume Information screen, 849–850, *850*
SESSION program. *See* NETUSER program
UIMPORT program, 803–805, 1338–1339, **1444**
VREPAIR program, 1324
XCONSOLE program, 1151
dot-matrix printers, 531–532, *531*
DOWN console command, 884
drive mapping, 958–959, 1408. *See also* disk drives
  mapping fake ROOTs, **959**, **1409**
  with NETUSER, 1030–1032, *1031*
  with NetWare User Tools, 1002–1005, *1003*, *1004*
  permanently with NetWare User Tools, 1005–1006, *1006*
  from Windows 95, 1072–1074, *1073*
drivers, 1405, 1406–1407, 1408
  CDM drivers, 98–100, 1263, 1360
  HAM drivers, 98–100, 1263, 1360
  hard disk drivers, 96–100, *96*, **1406–1407**
  installing disk drivers, 96–100, *96*
  LAN drivers, **1414**
    installing for network interface cards, 100–101, *101*
    loading ODI LAN drivers for PC clients, 286–288, *286*, *287*, *288*, *289*
    MONITOR program Available LAN Drivers screen, 831–832, *832*
    for PC clients, 266–267, 268–273
  Link Driver options in NET.CFG file, **310–315**
  MLID (Multiple Link Interface Driver), 269, **1425**
  monolithic (.DSK) versus NPA (NetWare Peripheral Architecture) drivers, 98–100, 1263–1264, 1360
  NWPA.NLM driver, 99, 1263

drives. *See* CD-ROM drives; disk drives; floppy disks; hard disk drives
Drives/Ports page, in NetWare Application Launcher, 975–976, *975*
.DSK (monolithic) drivers, 98–100, 1263–1264, 1360
DSMERGE program, 873–882. *See also* server management
    Check Servers In This Tree option, 876, *877*
    Check Time Synchronization option, 877–878, *878*
    examples, **930**
    exiting and cleaning up, 881–882
    Merge Two Trees option, 879–880, *879*
    Rename This Tree option, 880–881, *881*
DSREPAIR program, 779–780, 853–873, 1408. *See also* server management
    Advanced Options menu, **855,** 857–869
        Create a Database Dump File option, 869, *870*
        Global Schema Options screen, 867–868, *868*
        Local ID to Remote ID List screen, 862, *863*
        Log File/Login Configuration Options screen, 858–859, *859*
        Repair Local Database Options screen, 859–860, *860*
        Replica and Partitions Operations options, 863–866, *863*
        Replica Ring Options submenu, 865–866
        Security Equivalence Synchronization option, 866–867, *867*
        Servers Known To This Database option, 861–862, *861*
        Servers That Have Replicas of This Partition screen, 865
        View Repair Log File option, *855,* 868–869, *869*
    in NDS Manager, 870–873, *871, 872*
    repairing NDS corruption, 779–780
    Report Synchronization Status option, 855
    Time Synchronization option, 855
    Unattended Full Repair option, 854, 856–857, *857*
DST (Daylight Savings Time) adjustments, 137–138, *137*
DSTRACE program, 851–853, *852,* 926, 929
duplexing disk drives, 105–106, 1404, 1407
DynaText online documentation, 1059–1067. *See also* Help
    AppleTalk documentation, 1093
    DSREPAIR and DSMERGE and, 858
    installing, 158–159, 178–181, *179, 180, 181, 182,* 1060
    installing and configuring viewer for Windows 3.1x, 1060–1061
    installing and configuring for Windows 95, 1065–1067, *1066*
    Multi-Protocol Router installation, 1193
    navigating and searching, 1062–1064, *1064*
    print migration documentation, 1340
    reading from CD-ROM drives, 1062–1063, *1062*
    SETUPDOC program, 1065–1067, *1066*
    in Windows 95, 1064–1065, *1065*

E

E (Erase) directory right, 672, **1409**
E (Erase) file right, 674, 954, **1409**
ECB COUNT parameter in NET.CFG file, 324
editing. *See also* changing; modifying
    AUTOEXEC.NCF file during NDS installation, 153–154, *154*
    INSTALL.CFG file for non-Client32 client installation, 277–278
    login scripts with NETADMIN, 415–416, 507–510
        Container login scripts, 508–509, *509*
        Profile login scripts, 421, *509, 510*
        User login scripts, 509–510, *510*
        for User object setup, 415–416, *417*
    login scripts with NETUSER, 1032, *1033*
    login scripts with NetWare Administrator, **377–379, 505–507**
        Container login scripts, 506
        Profile login scripts, 506–507
        User login scripts, 507
        for User object setup, 377–379, *378*
    print devices in PRINTDEF, 639–640, *640*
    STARTUP.NCF file during NDS installation, 151–153, *152*
effective rights, 1408–1409. *See also* rights
    in NetWare Administrator, 672
electronic manuals. *See* DynaText online documentation
elevator seeking, 1347, *1348*

e-mail. *See also* Message Handling Service
   FirstMail program, **1267–1268**
      running, 1268, *1269*
      setting up mailboxes, 1267–1268
   foreign e-mail addresses and aliases
      for Group objects in NetWare Administrator, Group objects, 459–460
      for User objects in NETADMIN, 410–411
      for User objects in NetWare Administrator, 368–369, *369*
   GroupWise guidelines, **966–968**, *967*, *968*
e-mailbox setup
   in FirstMail program, 1267–1268
   for Group objects with NETADMIN, 472–473
   for Group objects in NetWare Administrator, 457–459, *458*
   for User objects in NETADMIN, 408–409, *409*
   for User objects in NetWare Administrator, 366–367, *367*
enabling
   data migration, 114–115
   F6 hotkey in NetWare User Tools, 1000–1001, *1001*
Encyclopedia of Networking (Feibel), 664–665, 1395
environment information
   in NETADMIN, 407–408, *407*
   in NetWare Administrator, 364–366, *365*
Environment page, in NetWare Application Launcher, 974
EOJ parameter in NET.CFG, 300
Erase (E) directory right, 672, **1409**
Erase (E) file right, 674, 954, **1409**
erasing. *See* deleting
error handling SET commands, 844, 1373–1374
ESDI disk controllers and drives, 64
ETC directory, 24
Ethernet networks, 4–7, 10–11, **1409**. *See also* networks
   CSMA/CD (carrier sense multiple access/collision detect) access method and, 5–6, 13
   Fast Ethernet networks (100BaseT), **13**
   MAC (Media Access Control) specifications, 13
   MiniCo example, **49**
   network interface card (NIC) addresses, 6
   switched Ethernet networks, 7, *8*
   versus Token Ring networks, 5, 10–11, *11*
   troubleshooting, **1325–1326**
EtherTalk protocol, 42, 1090

EtherVision software, 1305–1308, *1306*, *1307*
examples. *See* MegaCorp; MiniCo
EXCLUDE VLM parameter in NET.CFG, 300, 310
EXEC menu script command, 515
Execute Only (X) file attribute, 681, **1409**
executing. *See* running; starting
EXIT console command, 884–885
EXIT login script command, 493
exiting
   DSMERGE, 881–882
   NETADMIN, 396
exporting
   print devices in NetWare Administrator, 598–599, *599*
   print devices in PRINTDEF, 642–643, *643*
extensions. *See* filename extensions
External Entity objects, 221

F

F (File Scan) directory right, 672, **1410**
F (File Scan) file right, 674, 954, **1410**
F6 hotkey, in NetWare User Tools, 1000–1001, *1001*
fake ROOTs, 1409
   mapping, *959*
Fast Ethernet networks (100BaseT), 13
fault-tolerance, 1409. *See also* NetWare 4.1x SFT III
FDDI (Fiber Distributed Data Interface) networks, 16
Feibel, Werner, 664–665, 1395
fiber-optic cabling, 12
file attributes, 677–683, **1399.** *See also* security
   directory attributes, **678–679**
   examples, **731**, **736**
   identification and operator attributes for Print Queue objects, 552–554, *553*
   migrating, **1338**
   NDS trees and, 206
   setting with FLAG command, 679–683, *682*, 949–951, *951*, *952*, **1046–1047**, *1046*, 1078, 1082, **1410**
file caching SET commands, 841, 1374–1375, **1402**
file compression, 113–114, **1259–1262**, 1353–1354, **1410**
   managing, 1262
   settings for volumes, 113–114
   viewing file compression statistics, 1261–1262, *1261*
file formats
   for PC and Macintosh computers, 1089
   SIDF (System Independent Data Format), 1272, 1359

file name format options, 94–95
File Open/Lock Activity option, MONITOR
  program, **835–836**, *837*
file rights, **1405, 1410, 1433**. *See also* file system
  security; rights; security; trustees
  changing file ownership, **951–953**, *953*
  for Group objects
    modifying in NETADMIN, **475–477**, *476*, *477*
    modifying in NetWare Administrator, **460–463**,
      462
  managing with NetWare Administrator, **693–702**,
    694
  supervisory functions and, 750
  for User Objects
    modifying in NETADMIN, **434–437**, *436*
    modifying in NetWare Administrator, **391–395**,
      393, *394*
  viewing and changing with RIGHTS command,
    953–957, *955*, *956*, **1045**, *1046*, 1078, 1082
File Scan (F) directory right, 672, **1410**
File Scan (F) file right, 674, 954, **1410**
file servers. *See* servers
file sharing in NetWare NFS Services, **1166–1168**,
  1167
file system security, 669, **670–677**, 770–771. *See also*
  directory rights; file rights; security; trustees
  examples, **731, 735**
  guidelines for, 677
  hidden protection, 670
  inheritance, 670–671, 687, **688**
  IRFs (Inherited Rights Filters), 671, 673, **674–677**,
    675, **676, 1413**
    managing with FILER, 712–713, *713*
    object and property rights and, 687–**688**
  [Public] trustees, 671, 751, **1430**
  stacking and subtracting rights, **676**, *676*
file system SET commands, 842, 1375–1378
file systems, 22–25, **1410**. *See also* directories; FILER
  examples, **49, 52–53**
  home directories and, 23–24
  NetWare 4.1x enhancements to, **1353–1354**, *1354*
  NetWare system directories, 24–25
  in NetWare versus Unix, 1130, 1131–1132
  user-centric versus application-centric systems,
    22–24, *23*
  viewing file information with NDIR command,
    1047, 1078, 1082, **1324**, *1325*
File Transfer Protocol (FTP), **1410**

FTP sites for NetWare Help, 1058
  in NetWare NFS Services, 1168–1169
file trustees, managing with FILER, 709–711, *711*
filename extensions, **1410**
  .DAT, 512
  .DSK, 98–100, 1263–1264, 1360
  .LAN, 100–101, *101*
  .SRC, 512
FILER program, 709–713, 1048–1057, **1410**. *See also*
  user utilities
  deleting subdirectories, 1051–1052, *1052*
  examples, **1078, 1082**
  keyboard shortcuts, 1048–1049
  managing directory or file trustees, 709–711, *711*
  managing IRFs (Inherited Rights Filters), 712–713,
    713
  purging deleted files, 1056, 1325
  recovering deleted files, 1054–1055, *1056*, **1434**
  searching for files and directories, 1052–1053
  selecting current directory, 1053
  setting default options, 1056–1057
  viewing volume information, 1053–1054, *1054*
files
  copying SET parameters to, 846–847
  in Unix, 1130
finding
  files and directories with FILER, 1052–1053
  objects with NETADMIN, 915–916, *916*
  objects with NetWare Administrator, 773–776,
    775
  topics in DynaText online documentation,
    1062–1064, *1064*
FIO.VLM file, 295
FIRE PHASERS login script command, 493
FIRST NETWORK DRIVE parameter in NET.CFG,
  300
FirstMail program, 1267–1268. *See also* Message
  Handling Service
  running, 1268, *1269*
  setting up mailboxes, 1267–1268
FLAG command, 679–683, *682*, 949–951, *951*, 952,
  1046–1047, *1046*, 1078, 1082, **1410**
flags. *See* attributes
floppy disk drives, 69
floppy disks. *See also* CD-ROM drives; disk drives;
  hard disk drives
  booting servers from, **79–81**
  copying installation files from, 81, 83–84, 86–87

installing non-Client32 client software from, 280–282
installing OS/2 client software from, 1202–1205, *1204*
For your information screen, 140–141, *141*
FORCE FIRST NETWORK DRIVE parameter in NET.CFG, 300
foreign e-mail addresses and aliases
for Group objects in NetWare Administrator, Group objects, 459–460
for User objects in NETADMIN, 410–411
for User objects in NetWare Administrator, 368–369, *369*
foreign language settings, 175–177
changing default server language, 176–177, *177*
console versus default server language settings, 177
installing additional server languages, 175–176
for Macintosh clients, 1115–1116
for non-Client32 PC clients, 276–277
forward slash (/)
in Group object names, 450, 468
in User object login names, 358
forwarders in TCP/IP protocol, 1138
4 MB page feature of Pentium processors, 1355
FRAME Link Driver parameter in NET.CFG file, 312
freeing server memory temporarily, 1323
FTP (File Transfer Protocol), 1410
FTP sites for NetWare Help, 1058
in NetWare NFS Services, 1168–1169

G

General Information screen, MONITOR program, 814–816, *814*
GENERAL.VLM file, 295
GETx menu script command, 516–517
Global Message Handling Service (GMHS), 368
Global Schema Options screen, DSREPAIR program, 867–868, *868*
GMHS (Global Message Handling Service), 368
going to. *See* navigating
granting trustee rights. *See also* security; trustees
to groups or users, 699–702, *700*, *701*
between multiple objects, 705–708, *706*, *707*, *708*
between objects with drag-and-drop, 702–705, *704*
to volumes or directories, 696–699, *697*, *698*
Greenwich Mean Time (GMT) adjustments, 137–138, *137*

%GREETING_TIME login script identifier variable, 497
group membership setup
in NETADMIN, 351, 352, 418, *419*
in NetWare Administrator, 351, 352, 384–385, *385*
Group objects, 216, 445–478, 1411. *See also* objects; User objects
creating with NETADMIN, **466–469**, *468*
creating with NetWare Administrator, **447–451**, *449*, *450*
group scheduling with GroupWise software, **966–968**, *967*, *968*
and managing users and resources, 445–446
MegaCorp example, **526**
MiniCo example, **523**
modifying with NETADMIN, **469–478**
e-mailbox setup, 472–473
identification information, 469–471, *470*
member lists, 471, 472
rights to files and directories, 475–477, *476*, *477*
See Also page (related resource information), 474
trustees, 477–478, *478*
modifying with NetWare Administrator, **451–466**
e-mailbox setup, 457–459, *458*
foreign e-mail addresses, 459–460
identification information, 451–453, *452*
member lists, 454–457, *455*
rights to files and directories, 460–463, *462*
See Also page (related resource information), 465–466, *465*
trustees, 463–464, *464*
naming, 450, 468
GroupWise guidelines, 966–968, *967*, *968*
Guide to Managing PC Networks (Steinke), 1308–1309, 1392
Guide to Unix (Norton and Hahn), 1130
guides. *See* recommended reading

H

H (Hidden) directory attribute, 679, **1411**
H (Hidden) file attribute, 680, **1411**
Hahn, Harlan, 1130
HAI (Host Adapter Interface), 1263

HAM (Host Adapter Module)
   HAM drivers, 98–100
HANDLE NET ERRORS parameter in NET.CFG, 300
hard disk drives, 1411. *See also* CD-ROM drives; floppy disks; partitions; replicas; volumes
   block suballocation, 114, **1264**, 1354, **1401**
   booting servers from, **76–78**, *76*, *77*
   Disk Information screen in MONITOR program, 828–831, *829*
   disk mirroring and duplexing options, 105–106, **1404**, **1407**
   disk SET commands, 843, 1372–1373
   drivers, 96–100, *96*, **1406–1407**
   Drives/Ports page in NetWare Application Launcher, 975–976, *975*
   elevator seeking and, 1347, *1348*
   ESDI disk controllers and drives, 64
   IDE disk controllers and drives, 64
   installing DynaText online documentation, 1060
   mapping, **958–959**, **1408**
      mapping fake ROOTs, **959**, **1409**
      with NETUSER, 1030–1032, *1031*
      with NetWare User Tools, 1002–1005, *1003*, *1004*
      permanently with NetWare User Tools, 1005–1006, *1006*
      from Windows 95, 1072–1074, *1073*
   NetWare requirements, **63–66**
   NetWare superiority and, **1346–1347**, *1348*
   preparing for NetWare installation, 76–78
      for booting servers from floppy disks, 79–81
      for booting servers from hard disk drives, 76–78, *76*, *77*
      examples, **124–125**, *127*
   RAID disk systems, **65–66**, *1320*, *1321*
   SCSI disk interfaces and drives, 64–65
   ST506 disk controllers and drives, 63
   troubleshooting server disk errors, 1324–1325, *1325*
   user disk space restriction in NETADMIN, **432–433**, *434*
   user disk space restriction in NetWare Administrator, **801–803**, *802*
hardware interrupts (IRQs), for network interface cards, 70–71, 264
Hardware Specific Module (HSM), 269, **1425**

hashing, 1411
   directory information, 1347
HCSS (High Capacity Storage System), 1276, 1359, **1411–1412**
Help, 1057–1067. *See also* user utilities
   command-line Help, 1058–1059, *1058*
   DynaText online documentation, **1059–1067**
      AppleTalk documentation, 1093
      installing, 158–159, 178–181, *179*, *180*, *181*, *182*, 1060
      installing and configuring viewer for Windows 3.1x, 1060–1061
      installing and configuring for Windows 95, 1065–1067, *1066*
      navigating and searching, 1062–1064, *1064*
      print migration documentation, 1340
      reading from CD-ROM drives, 1062–1063, *1062*
      SETUPDOC program, 1065–1067, *1066*
      in Windows 95, 1064–1065, *1065*
   examples, **1078–1079**, *1083*
   in NetWare Administrator, 761
   in NetWare User Tools, 1023–1025, *1024*
HFS CD-ROM drives, on Macintosh computers, 1113–1114, *1115*
Hidden (H) directory attribute, 679, **1411**
Hidden (H) file attribute, 680, **1411**
hidden protection, 670
home directories, 23–24, **1412**. *See also* directories
   creating with NETADMIN, 351, 352, 401–404, *402*, *403*, *404*
   creating with NetWare Administrator, 351, 352, 359–361, *360*
Host Adapter Interface (HAI), 1263
Host Adapter Module (HAM), 1263, 1360
   HAM drivers, 98–100
Hot Fix utility, **1404**, **1412**
   changing settings during installation, 105
hotkeys in NetWare User Tools. *See also* keyboard shortcuts
   adding, 1022, *1023*
   changing, 1019–1021, *1020*
   enabling or disabling F6 hotkey, 1000–1001, *1001*
HSM (Hardware Specific Module), 269, **1425**
HSM (Hierarchical Storage Management) software, **1275–1276**
hyphen (-), in server names, 134

I

I (Index) file attribute, 680, **1412**
I/O port addresses, for network interface cards, 71, 265
IBM. *See also* OS/2
   ATM25 networks, 18
   PROFS (Professional Office System) e-mail system, 368, 459, 473
   SNA (Systems Network Architecture)
      SNADS (SNA Distributed Services) e-mail system, 368, 459, 473
   TCP/IP protocol and, 41
Ic (Immediate Compress) directory attribute, 679, **1412**
Ic (Immediate Compress) file attribute, 680, **1412**
icons
   creating NetWare Administrator icon in Windows 3.1x, 753–755
   in OS/2 client login screen, 1209–1211, *1210*, *1211*
IDE disk controllers and drives, 64
identification information
   for Group objects
      in NETADMIN, 469–471, *470*
      in NetWare Administrator, 451–453, *452*
   for Print Queue objects in NetWare Administrator, 552–554, *553*
   for User objects
      in NETADMIN, 405–406, *406*
      in NetWare Administrator, 362–364, *362*
identifier variables in login scripts, 496–497, **1412**
IDP (Internet Datagram Protocol), 35
IETF (Internet Engineering Task Force), 667
IF...THEN login script command, 493
Immediate Compress (Ic) directory attribute, 679, **1412**
Immediate Compress (Ic) file attribute, 680, **1412**
implementing versus designing NDS trees, 227
importing
   employee database records into NDS with UIMPORT, 803–805, 1338–1339, **1444**
   print devices in NetWare Administrator, 596–597, *598*
   print devices in PRINTDEF, 641–642, *642*
Index (I) file attribute, 680, **1412**
INETCFG program, 171–174, 888–896
   ACONSOLE parameter configuration, 894–896, *895*
   installing NetWare TCP/IP support (TCPIP.NLM), 1146–1151
   IPX configuration, 890–893, *891*
   Multi-Protocol Router configuration, 1193–1194
   network protocol configuration, 171–174, *172*, *174*
   RCONSOLE parameter configuration, 893–894, *894*
   SNMP (Simple Network Management Protocol) and, 1281
   viewing CONSOLE.LOG file, 1297, 1299–1300, *1300*
inheritance. *See also* security
   NDS trees and, 206
Inherited Rights Filters (IRFs), 671, 673, **674–677**, *675*, *676*, **1413**. *See also* rights
   managing with FILER, 712–713, *713*
   object and property rights and, 687–688
InnerWeb Publisher. *See* NetWare IPX/IP Gateway; NetWare Web Server
INSTALL.CFG file, editing for non-Client32 client installation, 277–278
INSTALL.EXE program, installing non-Client32 client software with, **282–290**, *283*
installing. *See also* adding
   additional server languages, 175–176
   additional server licenses, 882–883
   Bindery Services, 246–247, *247*
   cabling, **31–34**, *33*, 50, 53–54
   Client32 clients, **326–338**
      connecting DOS and Windows 3.1x Client32 clients to networks, 331–334
      for DOS and Windows 3.1x systems, 327–331, *328*, *329*
      examples, 341–342, 345–346
      for Windows 95 systems, 326–327, 334–338, *336*, *337*
   DOS and Windows 3.1x client software, examples, 340, 344–345
   DynaText online documentation, 158–159, 178–181, *179*, *180*, *181*, *182*, 1060
   language support for Macintosh clients, 1115–1116
   Message Handling Service (MHS), 168–171, *170*
   Multi-Protocol Router, 1193
   NetSync program
      on NetWare 3.1x servers, 902–904, *903*
      on NetWare 4.1x servers, 899–902, *900*

NetWare 4.1x Server for OS/2, **1224–1230**
  from another network server, 1225–1226
  from CD-ROM, 1224–1225
  installation steps, 1228–1230
  selecting an installation method, 1226–1230, *1227*
  server requirements, 1222–1223
  Simplified Installation method, 1227–1228
NetWare 4.1x SFT III, **1249–1253**
  new installations, 1251–1252
  server requirements, 1250
  upgrading NetWare 3.11 SFT III systems, 1252–1253
NetWare Administrator, **353–354, 753–755**
  examples, *925, 928*
  on Windows 3.1x systems, 353–354, 753–755
  on Windows 95 systems, 354, 755
NetWare IPX/IP Gateway, 1171–1173, 1176
NetWare for Macintosh client software, **1118–1121**
  Macintosh client defined, **1416**
  navigating NDS, 1120–1121
  setting up clients for NDS, **1118–1120**, *1120, 1358*
NetWare for Macintosh server software, 165–167, **1094–1118**
  adding Macintosh name space support to volumes, 1117–1118
  adding Macintosh name space to volumes, 1117–1118
  binding AppleTalk to a LAN interface, 1105–1106, *1105*
  CD-ROM services configuration, 1113–1114, *1115*
  configuring AppleTalk protocol stack, **1100–1106**
  file services configuration, 1106–1108, *1107*
  installing additional language support for clients, 1115–1116
  installing Macintosh client support, 1116–1117
  loading NLMs, 1096–1100, *1097*
  network interface card and network interface configuration, 1102
  preparation, 1095–1096
  print services configuration, 1109–1113, *1110*
  protocol configuration, 1102–1105, *1102, 1103, 1105*

NetWare TCP/IP support (TCPIP.NLM), 1146–1151
NetWare/IP protocol on servers, 1160–1164, *1163*
non-Client32 client software, **276–291**
  attaching to networks for the first time, 290–291
  from CD-ROMs, 279–280, 281–282
  completing the installation, 289–290, *289, 290*
  editing INSTALL.CFG file, 277–278
  from floppy disks, 280–282
  loading ODI LAN drivers, 286–288, *286, 287, 288, 289*
  MAKEDISK.BAT program and, 280–281
  from network servers, 278–279, 281
  running INSTALL.EXE program, **282–290**, *283*
  Target Service Agent (TSA) configuration for Storage Management Services (SMS), *285, 285*
  Windows 3.1x configuration, 284–285, *284*
  workstation language setting, 276–277
online documentation and viewers, 158–159, 178–181, *179, 180, 181, 182,* 1060–1061
OS/2 client software, **1199–1206**
  from CD-ROM, 1205–1206, *1206*
  creating OS/2 client disks from NetWare 4.10 CD-ROM, 162–164, *163,* 1201–1202
  from floppy disks, 1202–1205, *1204*
  workstation requirements, 1200
third-party products, 182–183, *183*
Web Server, 1185–1187, *1186*
installing NetWare 4.1x, 56–130
  copying installation files, **81–88**
    examples, **125, 127–128**
    from floppy disks, 81, 83–84, 86–87
    from NetWare volumes, 84–87
    from remote CD-ROM drives, 87–88
    from remote CD-ROMs mounted as NetWare volumes, 87–88
    from remote server's network installation area, 81, 84–87
    from server-based CD-ROMs, 81, 82–83, 84–86
  Custom Installation method, **91–121**
    adding protocols, 102–103, *102*
    automatic server startup option, 95–96
    block suballocation on volumes, 114, **1264**, 1354, **1401**
    changing Hot Fix settings, 105

installing NetWare 4.1x—installing NetWare Directory Services (NDS)

changing volume segment size, 108–111, *109, 110, 111*
copying server files to DOS partition, 93–94, *94*
creating NetWare disk partitions, 103–104, *104, 105*
data migration option, 114–115
disk driver installation, 96–100
disk mirroring and duplexing options, 105–106, **1404, 1407**
file compression settings for volumes, 113–114
file name format options, 94–95
internal IPX network number setting, 93, **1414, 1422**
keyboard mapping options, 94–95
.LAN driver installation for network interface cards, 100–101, *101*
monolithic (.DSK) versus NPA (NetWare Peripheral Architecture) drivers, 98–100, 1263–1264, 1360
naming the server, 92–93
naming volumes, 112
saving volume changes, 115
SET command options, 95
troubleshooting SCSI conflicts, 68–69, 97–98
volume block size options, 112–113
volume management options, **106–115**, *108*
disk drive preparation, **76–78**
for booting servers from floppy disks, 79–81
for booting servers from hard disk drives, 76–78, *76, 77*
examples, **124–125**, *127*
INSTALL.NLM program, **88–89**, *88, 90*
versus installing NetWare 4.0, **1357**
MegaCorp example, **126–128**
MiniCo example, **123–125**
NetWare license software installation, **115–119**
copying NetWare files, 117–118, *118*
installing additional server licenses, 882–883
listing NetWare license information, 887, *887*
from remote servers, 116–117, *117*
selecting optional files to install, 118–119, *119, 120*
pre-installation processes, **72–81**
creating server installation boot disk, 72–75
preparing disk drives for NetWare, 76–81, *76*
server requirements, **58–72**
CD-ROM drives, 68–69
CPUs, 60–61

examples, **123–124, 126–127**
floppy disk drives, 69
hard disk drives, 63–66
IDE disk controllers and drives, 64
IRQ, DMA, I/O port settings and ROM addresses, 70–72
monitors, 69–70
network interface cards (NICs), 66–68, *67*
RAID disk systems, 65–66
RAM, 62–63
SCSI disk interfaces and drives, 64–65
Simple Installation method
Bindery Services and, 247–249, *248, 249*
disk driver installation, 96–100
and hard disk configuration, 103
.LAN driver installation, 100–101, *101*
naming the server, 92–93
protocol installation and, 102–103
troubleshooting SCSI conflicts, 97–98
Unix utilities and, 91
installing NetWare Directory Services (NDS), 120, **130–197**
deleting NetWare Directory Services, **184–187**
examples, **194, 197**
from multiple-server networks, 187, *188*
from one-server networks, 185–187, *186, 187*
warnings, 185, *186, 187*
for first NetWare server, **130–141, 151–157, 192–197**
context settings, **138–141**, *139*
copying files to new servers, **154–155**, *155*
editing AUTOEXEC.NCF file, **153–154**, *154*
editing STARTUP.NCF file, **151–153**, *152*
For your information screen, 140–141, *141*
installation completion, 157, *157*
MegaCorp example, **195–197**
MiniCo example, **192–194**
naming NDS tree, 133–134, *135*
naming the Organization and Organizational Units, 139–140, *139*
NetWare 4.11 new products and installations, 188–190, *189, 190*
selecting ADMIN name and password, 140
selecting your time zone, 136, *136*
terms defined, **131**
time setting adjustments, 137–138, *137*
time setting considerations, 135

installing NetWare Directory Services (NDS)—IntranetWare **1473**

installing servers into existing 4.1 networks, 141–150
    context settings, **147–150**
    examples, **193**, **195–196**
    naming the Organization and Organizational Units, 148–150, *149*, *150*
    selecting ADMIN name and password, 147, *148*
    selecting NDS trees, 142–144, *143*
    time synchronization settings, 144–147, *145*
    using single versus multiple NDS trees, 142, *143*
NDS trees and
    naming for first NetWare server, 133–134, *135*
    selecting for additional servers, 142–144, *143*
    using single versus multiple trees, 142, *143*
Other Installation Items/Products screen, **156–183**
    Change Server Language option, 176–177, *177*
    Configure Network Protocols option, 171–174, *172*, *174*
    Create DOS/MS Windows/OS2 Client Install Diskettes option, 162–164, *163*
    Create NetWare UPGRADE/MIGRATE Diskettes option, 164
    Create a Registration Diskette option, 159–161, *161*
    examples, **193–194**, **196–197**
    Install an Additional Server Language option, 175–176
    Install NetWare for Macintosh option, 165–167, *166*, *167*, *168*
    Install NetWare MHS Services option, 168–171, *170*
    Install Online Documentation and Viewers option, 158–159, 178–181, *179*, *180*, *181*, *182*
    Install a product not listed option, 182–183, *183*
    Upgrade 3.1x Print Services option, 161–162
INT7A parameter in NET.CFG file, 325
INT64 parameter in NET.CFG file, 317, 325
Intel Pentium processors, 1355
internal IPX network numbering, 93, **1414**, **1422**
international settings, **175–177**
    changing default server language, 176–177, *177*
    console versus default server language settings, 177
    installing additional server languages, 175–176
    language settings for Macintosh clients, 1115–1116

language settings for PC clients, 276–277
Internet, 40. *See also* IntranetWare; TCP/IP protocol; Unix
    comp.sys.novell newsgroup, 1058
    FTP (File Transfer Protocol), **1410**
        FTP sites for NetWare Help, 1058
        in NetWare NFS Services, 1168–1169
    Novell Web site, 1057
    recommended reading, **1395–1396**
Internet Datagram Protocol (IDP), 35
Internet Engineering Task Force (IETF), 667
internet packets, 35, 37, **1426**
internetworking guides, **1393–1394**
internetworks, 1413
interrupt (IRQ) settings, for network interface cards, 70–71, 264
IntranetWare, 1153–1164, 1170–1196, 1361–1362. *See also* Internet; NetWare 4.11; TCP/IP protocol; Unix
    Multi-Protocol Router (MPR), **1192–1194**, **1362**, **1418**
        configuring, 1193–1194
        installing, 1193
    Netscape client software, 1362
    NetWare IPX/IP Gateway, **1170–1183**, **1196**, **1361–1362**
        advantages of, 1182–1183
        Client32 and, 1175
        configuring, **1173–1175**, *1174*
        controlling client access to, **1178–1183**, *1179*, *1180*, *1181*
        examples, **1196**
        installing, **1171–1173**, 1176
        security, **1176–1177**, 1183
        setting up clients for, **1175–1176**, *1176*
        TCP/IP protocol and, 1170–1171, 1175, 1176
        Winsock program and, 1170, 1175
    NetWare/IP protocol, **1153–1164**, **1362**, **1420**
        on Client32 clients, 1159–1160
        installing on servers, 1160–1164, *1163*
        on non-Client32 clients, 1156–1159, *1157*, *1158*
    Web Server, **1183–1192**, **1195–1196**, **1361**, **1448**
        configuring and managing, **1187–1192**, *1188*, *1190*, *1191*
        examples, **1195–1196**
        installing, **1185–1187**, *1186*
        NetWare 4.11 and, 1185

intruder lockout setup
    in NETADMIN, 429–430, *430*, 910–911, *911*
    in NetWare Administrator, 391, *393*, 765–767, *766*
IO$LOG.ERR file, 1249
IOAUTO.NCF file, 1248
IOEngine in NetWare 4.1x SFT III, 1247–1248
IOSTART.NCF file, 1248
IP addresses, 1140, **1413**
IPADDR Link Driver parameter in NET.CFG file, 312
IPATCH parameter in NET.CFG file, 317
IPTUNNEL program, 1152–1153, *1153*
IPX options in NET.CFG file, 316–318
IPX PACKET SIZE LIMIT parameter in NET.CFG file, 318
IPX RETRY COUNT parameter in NET.CFG file, 318
IPX SOCKETS parameter in NET.CFG file, 318
IPX/SPX protocol. *See also* NetWare IPX/IP Gateway; NetWare/IP protocol; protocols
    binding IPX protocol to network interface cards, 102–103
    IPTUNNEL program and, 1152–1153, *1153*
    IPX configuration with INETCFG program, 890–893, *891*
    IPX defined, **1413**
    IPX network numbering, 93, **1414**, **1422**
    Macintosh computers and, 42–43
    NetWare Core Protocol (NCP) and, 36–39, *38*
    SPX defined, **1436**
    viewing IPX statistics with IPXCON, 896–897, *897*
IPXCON program, 896–897, *897*
IPXNCP.VLM file, 296
IPXODI.COM program, 266–267, 273–274, **1414**
IPXODI options in NET.CFG file. *See also* NET.CFG; PC clients
IRFs (Inherited Rights Filters), 671, 673, **674–677**, *675*, *676*, **1413**. *See also* rights
    managing with FILER, 712–713, *713*
    object and property rights and, 687–688
IRQ Link Driver parameter in NET.CFG file, 312
IRQ settings for network interface cards, 70–71, 264
ITEM menu script command, 514–515

K

Kelly-Bootle, Stan, 1131
kernels in NetWare and Unix, 1131
keyboard shortcuts. *See also* hotkeys
    in FILER program, 1048–1049
    in NETADMIN, 396
    in NetWare User Tools, 999–1000
keyboards, mapping, 94–95

L

LAAs (locally administered addresses), 9–10
LAN drivers, 1414. *See also* drivers
    installing for network interface cards, 100–101, *101*
    loading ODI LAN drivers for PC clients, 286–288, *286*, *287*, *288*, 289
    MONITOR program Available LAN Drivers screen, 831–832, *832*
    for PC clients, 266–267, 268–273
LAN/WAN Information option, MONITOR program, 831–832, *832*
LANalyzer software, 1305
LANdecoder software, 1305
language settings, 175–177
    changing default server language, 176–177, *177*
    console versus default server language settings, 177
    installing additional server languages, 175–176
    for Macintosh clients, 1115–1116
    for PC clients, 276–277
LANs (local area networks). *See* networks
LARGE INTERNET PACKETS parameter in NET.CFG, 300
laser printers, 532
L-CGI (Local Common Gateway Interface), 1184
leaf objects, 131, 205, **214–222**, **1415**. *See also* Group objects; objects; Print Queue objects; Print Server objects; Printer objects; User objects
    AFP (AppleTalk File Protocol) Server objects, 220, **1398**
    Alias objects, 210, 219–220, **1399**
    bindery and, 214–215
    Bindery and Bindery Queue objects, 221–222, **1400**
    Computer objects, 219
    creating
        in NETADMIN, **911–912**
        in NetWare Administrator, **767–769**, *768*, *769*
    Directory Map objects, 218, 959–960, *960*, **1406**
    Distribution List objects, 221
    External Entity objects, 221
    Message Routing Group objects, 220
    Messaging (MHS) Server objects, 220
    naming, 215

leaf objects—login scripts 1475

in NETADMIN, **911–916**
  creating, 911–912
  moving, 913, *914*
  renaming, 913–915
  searching for, 915–916, *916*
in NetWare Administrator, **767–776**
  creating, 767–769, *768, 769*
  moving, 770–771, *771*
  renaming, 772–773, *773*
  searching for, 773–776, *775*
NetWare (NCP) Server objects, **217**, 790–792, *791*, **1421**
NetWare Volume objects, 217
Organizational Role objects, 218, 446, **1425**
Profile objects, 219
[Root] object and, 215, *215*
Unknown objects, 222, **1445**
Legato Networker software, 1273
licenses
  application licensing trends, **934–936**, 981, 984–985
  consolidating application licenses, 943–944, *945*
  installing additional server licenses, 882–883
  listing NetWare license information, 887, *887*
  LSAPI (Licensing Service Application Programming Interface), 935
  NetWare license software installation, **115–119**
    copying NetWare files, 117–118, *118*
    from remote servers, 116–117, *117*
    selecting optional files to install, 118–119, *119, 120*
Link Driver options in NET.CFG file, 310–315
LINK STATIONS Link Driver parameter in NET.CFG file, 313
Link Support Layer (LSL.COM) program, 266–267, 268, **1425**
Link Support options, in NET.CFG file, 315–316
LIP START SIZE parameter in NET.CFG, 301
LISTEN Link Driver parameter in NET.CFG file, 313
listing NetWare license information, 887, *887*
LOAD CONN TABLE LOW parameter in NET.CFG, 301
LOAD LOW CONN parameter in NET.CFG, 301
LOAD LOW IPXNCP parameter in NET.CFG, 301
LOAD LOW REDIR parameter in NET.CFG, 301
LOAD menu script command, 516
loadable modules. *See* NetWare Loadable Modules; VLMs
local area networks (LANs). *See* networks
Local Common Gateway Interface (L-CGI), 1184
Local ID to Remote ID List screen, DSREPAIR program, 862, *863*
LOCAL PRINTERS parameter in NET.CFG, 301
locally administered addresses (LAAs), 9–10
LocalTalk protocol, 42, 1091
LOCK DELAY parameter in NET.CFG, 302
Lock File Server Console option, MONITOR program, 834–835, *835*
LOCK RETRIES parameter in NET.CFG, 302
lock SET commands, 842–843, 1379
Log File/Login Configuration Options screen, DSREPAIR program, 858–859, *859*
log files
  in DSREPAIR program, 855, 858–859, *859*, 868–869, *869*
  server log files, 1249, 1297–1300, *1298, 1299, 1300*
logging in
  to NetWare 4.10 from NetWare User Tools, 997–998, *999*
  to NetWare from Windows 95 clients, 1071–1072, *1072*
logical design phase for NDS trees, **225–226**, 232, *233, 234*
LOGIN directory, 24–25
login names
  in NETADMIN, 400
  in NetWare Administrator, 357–358
login restrictions, 1415
  login time restriction setup
    in NETADMIN, 426–427, *427*
    in NetWare Administrator, 387–389, *388*
  in NETADMIN, 421–423, *422*
  in NetWare Administrator, 379–381, *380*
login scripts, 377–379, 415–416, 485–510, 1415–1416. *See also* menu scripts; User objects
  capitalization in, 496–497
  changing with NETUSER, **1032**, *1033*
  commands, **491–494**
    # command, 492
    ATTACH, 492, 1339, 1399
    COMSPEC, 492
    EXIT, 493
    FIRE PHASERS, 493
    IF...THEN, 493
    MAP, 485, 490–491, 494, **1416**
    PAUSE, 494
    SET, 494
    WRITE, 494, 496–497

Container login scripts, **1403**
   creating or editing with NETADMIN, 508–509, *509*
   creating or editing with NetWare Administrator, 506
   example, 499–502, *499*
   migrating, 1339
creating or editing with NETADMIN, **415–416, 507–510**
   Container login scripts, 508–509, *509*
   Profile login scripts, 509, *510*
   User login scripts, 509–510, *510*
   for User object setup, 415–416, *417*
creating or editing with NetWare Administrator, **377–379, 505–507**
   Container login scripts, 506
   Profile login scripts, 506–507
   User login scripts, 507
   for User object setup, 377–379, *378*
Default login scripts, 486–487, 489–491
editing with NETUSER, **1032**, *1033*
identifier variables, **496–497, 1412**
LOGIN.EXE command switches, 495–496
login security, **692–693**, *693*, **716**
MegaCorp example, **527**
migrating to NetWare 4.1x servers, **1339**
MiniCo example, **523–524**
order of execution for, **487**
preventing changes to by users, **692–693**, *693*, **716**
Profile login scripts, 486–487, 488–489, 498, **1429**
   creating or editing with NETADMIN, 509, *510*
   creating or editing with NetWare Administrator, 506–507
   example, 502–503, *502*
System login scripts, **1440**
   migrating, 1339
User login scripts, 486–487, 489, 498, **1446**
   creating or editing with NETADMIN, 509–510, *510*
   creating or editing with NetWare Administrator, 507
   example, 504–505, *504*
   migrating, 1339
login time restriction setup
   in NETADMIN, 426–427, *427*
   in NetWare Administrator, 387–389, *388*
%LOGIN_NAME login script identifier variable, 497
LONG MACHINE TYPE parameter in NET.CFG, 302

low balance accounting limits, 799–801, *800*
lowercase
   in Group object names, 450, 468
   in login scripts, 496–497
   in User object names, 357, 400
LPT printer settings, changing with NetWare User Tools, 1009–1012, *1010*
LSAPI (Licensing Service Application Programming Interface), 935
LSL.COM (Link Support Layer) program, 266–267, 268, **1425**

M

M (Modify) directory right, 672, **1417**
M (Modify) file right, 674, 954, **1417**
MAC (Media Access Control) specifications, 13
%MACHINE login script identifier variable, 497
Macintosh computers, 1088–1122. *See also* DOS; Microsoft Windows; OS/2; PC clients; Unix; workstations
   adding Macintosh name space to volumes, 1117–1118
   AppleTalk printer settings
      in NetWare Administrator, 570, 573
      in PCONSOLE, 633, 635
   history of Macintosh printing, 1111
   installing NetWare for Macintosh client software, **1118–1121**
      Macintosh client defined, **1416**
      navigating NDS, 1120–1121
      setting up clients for NDS, **1118–1120**, *1120*, 1358
   installing NetWare for Macintosh server software, **165–167, 1094–1118**
      adding Macintosh name space support to volumes, 1117–1118
      binding AppleTalk to network interface cards, 1105–1106, *1105*
      CD-ROM services configuration, 1113–1114, *1115*
      configuring AppleTalk protocol stack, **1100–1106**
      file services configuration, 1106–1108, *1107*
      installing additional language support for clients, 1115–1116
      installing Macintosh client support, 1116–1117
      loading NLMs, 1096–1100, *1097*
      network interface card and network interface configuration, 1102

preparation, 1095–1096
print services configuration, 1109–1113, *1110*
protocol configuration, 1102–1105, *1102, 1103, 1105*
Macintosh networking, **1089–1094**
AppleTalk Filing Protocol (AFP), 42–43, 44, 1092
AppleTalk protocol, 1089–1092, **1399**
EtherTalk protocol, 42, 1090
IPX/SPX protocol and, 42–43
LocalTalk protocol, 42
network addresses and zones, 1092–1094, **1449**
TokenTalk protocol, 42
MAGIC Link Driver parameter in NET.CFG file, 313
mail. *See* e-mail; Message Handling Service
MAIL directory, 24–25, **1416**
MAKEDISK.BAT program, 280–281
management. *See* administrators
MAP command
in Default login scripts, 490–491
login scripts and, 485
mapping drives, 958–959
Windows 3.1x and, 963
MAP ROOT command, *959*
mapping
drives, **958–959, 1408**
with NETUSER, 1030–1032, *1031*
with NetWare User Tools, 1002–1005, *1003, 1004*
permanently with NetWare User Tools, 1005–1006, *1006*
from Windows 95, 1072–1074, *1073*
fake ROOTs, **959, 1409**
keyboards, 94–95
master name servers, in TCP/IP protocol, 1138
Master replicas, 777, **1432**
MAX FRAME SIZE Link Driver parameter in NET.CFG file, 313
MAX TASKS parameter in NET.CFG, 302
Media Manager database, 1263, **1416**
Media Support Module (MSM), 269, **1425**
MegaCorp case studies. *See also* MiniCo case studies
applications, 984–986
Group objects, 526
Internet tools, 1195–1196
login scripts, 527
menu scripts, 528

NetWare Directory Services (NDS), 255–258
NetWare Directory Services (NDS) installation, 195–197
NetWare installation, 126–128
network administration, 927–930
network planning, 52–54, 927
network printing, 659–662
PC clients, 343–346
security, 734–738
User object creation, 441–442
User Templates, 526–527
user training and utilities, 1080–1083
MEM Link Driver parameter in NET.CFG file, 313
member lists. *See also* Group objects
editing in NETADMIN, 471, *472*
editing in NetWare Administrator, 454–457, *455*
memory, 1416. *See also* caches
freeing server memory temporarily, 1323
memory addresses for network interface cards for PC clients, 265
memory SET commands, 841, 1379–1380
MONITOR program
Memory Utilization option, 821–822, *821*
Server Memory Statistics screen, 822–825, *824*
RAM, 1430
NetWare requirements, 62–63
read-only memory (ROM) addresses, 71–72
server memory management, **1270–1271, 1355–1356**
DOMAIN.NLM utility, 1270–1271
managing memory allocation with Performance Monitor, 1235–1236, *1235*
MONITOR Allocated Memory for All Modules screen, 821–822, *821*
in NetWare 4.1x versus NetWare 3.x, **1355**
server self-tuning, 1271, 1356
troubleshooting
server RAM problems, 1318–1319, 1322–1323
workstation "not enough memory" errors, 1314–1315
menu scripts, 511–520. *See also* login scripts
converting menus from previous NetWare versions, 520
examples, 517–520, *518*, 524, 528
menu script commands, **512–517**
control commands, **515–517**
EXEC, 515

GETx, 516–517
ITEM, 514–515
LOAD, 516
MENU, 513–514
organizational commands, **513–515**
SHOW, 516
NMENU.BAT program and, 511–513
running, 511–512
MENUCNVT program, 520
MENUMAKE program, 520
menus in NetWare Administrator, 757–761
Help menu, 761
Object menu, 757–758
Options menu, 759
Tools menu, 760, 780–781
View menu, 758–759
Window menu, 760–761
merging
NDS trees, 879–880, *879*
partitions, 784–785, *785*
Message Handling Service (MHS), 168–171, 1265–1268, 1417
FirstMail program, **1267–1268**
running, 1268, *1269*
setting up mailboxes, 1267–1268
installing, **168–171,** *170*
Messaging (MHS) Server objects, 220
MESSAGE LEVEL parameter in NET.CFG, 302
Message Routing Group objects, 220
MESSAGE TIMEOUT parameter in NET.CFG, 303
messages
sending and receiving with NETUSER, 1028–1030, *1029*
sending and receiving with NetWare User Tools, 1017–1019, *1018*
metering applications, 934–936, 981, 984–985
MHS. *See* Message Handling Service
MIB2IF.VLM file, 296
MIB2PROT.VLM file, 296
microprocessors
NetWare requirements, 60–61
Pentium 4 MB page feature, 1355
Microsoft Windows 3.1x. *See also* DOS; Macintosh computers; NetWare Administrator; NetWare User Tools; OS/2; Unix
configuring for fast network printing, 1012–1014, *1013*
configuring for PC clients, 284–285, *284*

connecting Client32 clients to networks, 331–334
creating client install disks for, 162–164, *163*
creating NetWare Administrator icon, 753–755
guidelines for, **961–965,** *964*
installing Client32 clients, **327–331,** *328*, *329*, 341–342, 345–346
installing and configuring DynaText viewer, 1060–1061
installing NetWare Administrator, 353–354, 753–755, 925, 928
MAP command and, 963
protecting workstations against Windows problems, 1303–1305
TCP/IP protocol version for, 41
USING WINDOWS 3.0 parameter in NET.CFG file, 325
workstations and Windows problems, 1315–1317
Microsoft Windows 95. *See also* DOS; Macintosh computers; NetWare Administrator; OS/2; Unix
creating client install disks for, 162–164, *163*
DynaText online documentation, 1064–1065, *1065*
guidelines for, **965–966**
installing
Client32 clients, 326–327, **334–338,** *336*, *337*, 341–342, 345–346
and configuring DynaText online documentation, 1065–1067, *1066*
NetWare Administrator, 354, 755, 925, 928
recommended reading, **1394**
TCP/IP protocol version for, 41
Windows 95 clients, **326–327, 1067–1074,** **1303–1305, 1315–1317**
examples, **1079, 1083**
installing Client32 clients, **334–338,** *336*, *337*
logging in from Network Neighborhood, 1071–1072, *1072*
mapping drives from Windows 95, 1072–1074, *1073*
printing and, 1068, 1074
protecting against problems, 1303–1305
sending messages within Network Neighborhood, 1070–1071, *1070*
troubleshooting, **1315–1317**
upgrading to, **1341–1343**
viewing connection information, 1068–1069, *1069*
MIGPRINT program, 1339–1340

migrating, 1417, 1445. *See also* upgrading
    data migration, 1404
        creating UPGRADE/MIGRATE disks, 164
        enabling, 114–115
        in upgrading to NetWare 4.1x, **1336–1337**
    file attributes, 1338
    login scripts, 1339
    passwords, 1337–1338
    print services, 1339–1340
    trustee rights, 1339
MiniCo case studies. *See also* MegaCorp case studies
    applications, 981–983
    Group objects, 523
    Internet tools, 1195–1196
    login scripts, 523–524
    menu scripts, 524
    NetWare Directory Services (NDS), 252–254
    NetWare Directory Services (NDS) installation, 192–194
    NetWare installation, 123–125
    network administration, 924–926
    network planning, 49–51, 924
    network printing, 655–658
    PC clients, 339–342
    security, 730–733
    User object creation, 439–440
    User Templates, 523
    user training and utilities, 1076–1079
MINIMUM TIME TO NET parameter in NET.CFG, 303
Mirrored Server Link (MSL) adapters, 1246, *1246*
mirrored servers, 1245–1246, *1246*
mirroring disk drives, 105–106, 1404, 1407
miscellaneous SET commands, 844, 1381–1383
mixed NDS tree design, 236–238, *237*
MLID (Multiple Link Interface Driver), 269, **1425**
Modify (M) directory right, 672, **1417**
Modify (M) file right, 674, 954, **1417**
modifying. *See also* changing; editing
    Group objects with NETADMIN, **469–478**
        e-mailbox information, 472–473
        identification information, 469–471, *470*
        member lists, 471, *472*
        rights to files and directories, 475–477, *476*, *477*
        See Also page (related resource information), 474
        trustees, 477–478, *478*
    Group objects with NetWare Administrator, **451–466**
        e-mailbox information, 457–459, *458*
        foreign e-mail addresses, 459–460
        identification information, 451–453, *452*
        member lists, 454–457, *455*
        rights to files and directories, 460–463, *462*
        See Also page (related resource information), 465–466, *465*
        trustees, 463–464, *464*
    print devices in PRINTDEF, 639–640
    print queue job list in NetWare Administrator, 560–564, *561*, *562*
    printer forms in NetWare Administrator, 594–596, *595*
    printer forms in PRINTDEF, 644–645, *644*
    Printer objects in NetWare Administrator, 568–574, *569*, *572*
    replicas
        with NDS Manager, 786–789, *787*, *788*
        with PARTMGR, 918–919, *918*
    User Objects
        in NETADMIN, 434–437, *436*
        in NetWare Administrator, 391–395, *393*, *394*
    User Templates, 484, *485*
modules. *See* NetWare Loadable Modules; VLMs
MODULES console command, 885, *885*
MONITOR program, 813–839, 1417. *See also* server management
    Active Connections screen, 825–828, *826*
    Allocated Memory for All Modules screen, 821–822, *821*
    Available LAN Drivers screen, 831–832, *832*
    Cache Utilization Statistics screen, 817–819, *817*
    Connection Information screen, 825–828, *826*, *827*
    Disk Information screen, 828–831, *829*
    examples, **926**, **929**
    File Open/Lock Activity option, 835–836, *837*
    General Information screen, 814–816, *814*
    LAN/WAN Information option, 831–832, *832*
    Lock File Server Console option, 834–835, *835*
    Memory Utilization option, 821–822, *821*
    Processor Utilization screen, 819–821, *820*
    Resource Utilization option, 822–825, *824*
    Scheduling Information screen, 837–839, *838*
    Server Memory Statistics screen, 822–825, *824*
    server self-tuning and, 1271, 1356
    System Module Information screen, 833–834, *833*
    tracking server performance, **1295–1297**
    troubleshooting and, *1296*

monitors, NetWare requirements, 69–70
monolithic (.DSK) drivers, 98–100, 1263–1264, 1360
moving
    employee database records into NDS with UIMPORT, 803–805, 1338–1339, **1444**
    leaf objects in NetWare Administrator, 770–771, *771*
    objects in NETADMIN, 913, *914*
    partitions and their containers, 792, *793*
moving to. *See* navigating
MPR. *See* Multi-Protocol Router
MRU Link Driver parameter in NET.CFG file, 314
MS Windows. *See* Microsoft Windows
MSAUTO.NCF file, 1248
MS-DOS. *See* DOS
MSEngine, in NetWare 4.1x SFT III, 1247–1248
MSL (Mirrored Server Link) adapters, 1246, *1246*
MSM (Media Support Module), 269, **1425**
MSSTART.NCF file, 1248
MSSTATUS.DMP file, 1249
Multiple Link Interface Driver (MLID), 269, **1425**
multiplexor VLMs, 275–276
Multi-Protocol Router (MPR), 1192–1194, 1362, 1418. *See also* IntranetWare
    configuring, 1193–1194
    installing, 1193

N

N (Normal) directory attribute, 679, **1423**
N (Normal) file attribute, 681, *955*, **1423**
NAL. *See* NetWare Application Launcher
NAME CONTEXT parameter in NET.CFG, 303
name servers, in TCP/IP protocol, 1137–1138
name services, in NetWare NFS Services, 1165–1166, *1165*
name space support, 1418
    adding Macintosh name space to volumes, 1117–1118
Named Pipes parameters, in NET.CFG file, 322–323
naming. *See also* renaming
    ADMIN User object, 140, 147, *148*
    file name format options, 94–95
    Group objects, 450, 468
    leaf objects, 215
    NDS trees, 133–134, *135*
    objects, 204
    the Organization and Organizational Units, 139–140, *139*, 148–150, *149*, *150*
    servers, 92–93

User objects, 357–358, 400
volumes, 112
naming standards, in NDS trees, **227–230**
NAUN (nearest active upstream neighbor), 9
navigating
    DynaText online documentation, 1062–1064, *1064*
    NETADMIN, 907–908, *907*
    NetWare Administrator, 756–757, *757*
    NetWare Directory Services in Macintosh clients, 1120–1121
NCP (NetWare Core Protocol), 1419. *See also* protocols
    IPX/SPX protocol and, 36–39, *38*
    NCP SET commands, 844, 1383–1385
    NetWare (NCP) Server objects, **217**, 790–792, *791*, **1421**
NCUPDATE program, 805–807, 1358
NDIR command, 1047, 1078, 1082, **1324**, *1325*
NDPS (NetWare Distributed Print Services), 652–653
NDS. *See* installing NetWare Directory Services; NetWare Directory Services
NDS Manager, 776–792, 870–873. *See also* NetWare Administrator; NetWare Directory Services; PARTMGR program
    adding to NetWare Administrator Tools menu, 780–781
    creating partitions, 781–783, *782*
    deleting NetWare (NCP) Server objects from NDS, 790–792, *791*
    DSREPAIR utility in, 870–873, *871*, *872*
    examples, **925**, 928–929
    merging partitions, 784–785, *785*
    moving partitions and their containers, 792, *793*
    partition and replica management guidelines, 778
    repairing NDS corruption, 779–780
    viewing and modifying replicas, 786–789, *787*, *788*
    viewing server partitions, 789–790, *790*
NDS.VLM file, 296
nearest active upstream neighbor (NAUN), 9
NET.CFG file, 1419
    DOS and Windows 3.1x client configuration, **291–325**
        core NetWare 4.1x VLMs, **295–296**
        examples, **340**, 345
        INSTALL.CFG file and, 277
        Link Driver options, 310–315

Link Support options, 315–316
Named Pipes parameters, 322–323
NetBIOS parameters, 319–322
NetWare DOS Requester option, 295–297
NetWare DOS Requester parameters and settings, 297–310
non-core NetWare 4.1x VLMs, **296–297**
Protocol IPX option, 316–318
Protocol ODINSUP option, 323–324
standard options for typical clients, **291–294**
TBMI2 options, 324–325
setting parameters with Performance Monitor, **1237–1238**
setting up user's "home" context, 243
SNMP options for NetWare clients, **1281–1283**
troubleshooting and, **1303**
updating after DSMERGE changes, 882
updating with NCUPDATE, 805–807, 1358
NETADMIN program, 906–916. *See also* DOS utilities; NetWare Administrator
  accounting feature
    user account balance setup, 431, *432*
  container object creation, **908–909**, *909*, *910*
  examples, **926, 930**
  Group object creation, **466–469**, *468*
  Group object modification, **469–478**
    e-mailbox setup, 472–473
    identification information, 469–471, *470*
    member lists, 471, *472*
    rights to files and directories, 475–477, *476*, *477*
    See Also page (related resource information), 474
    trustees, 477–478, *478*
  intruder detection setup, **429–430**, *430*, **910–911**, *911*
  login script creation or editing, **415–416, 507–510**
    Container login scripts, 508–509, *509*
    Profile login scripts, 509, *510*
    User login scripts, 509–510, *510*
    for User object setup, 415–416, *417*
  navigating, **907–908**, *907*
  object management, **911–916**
    creating leaf objects, 911–912
    moving, 913, *914*
    renaming, 913–915
    searching for, 915–916, *916*
  printing functions and, 538

property and object rights management, **713–714**, *715*
starting, **907**, *907*
User object creation, **395–437**
  account balance tracking, 431, *432*
  basic User object creation, **397–400**, *398*, *399*
  detail settings, **405–413**
  e-mailbox setup, 408–409, *409*
  environment information, 407–408, *407*
  examples, **440, 442**
  foreign e-mail addresses and aliases, 410–411
  group membership setup, 351, 352, 418, *419*
  home directory setup, 351, 352, 401–404, *402*, *403*, *404*
  identification information, 405–406, *406*
  intruder lockout setup, 429–430, *430*
  login names, 400
  login restriction setup, 421–423, *422*
  login scripts, 351, 352, 415–416, *417*
  login time restriction setup, 426–427, *427*
  naming, 400
  network address restrictions, 427–428, *429*
  password restrictions, 423–425, *424*
  postal address information, 411–412, *412*
  Profile script editing, 421
  related information tracking, 413, *414*
  rights to files and directories setup, 434–437, *436*
  security configuration, **413–437**
  security equivalence setup, 351, 352, 419–421, *420*
  volume space restriction setup, 432–433, *434*
User Templates, **483–484**
  creating, 483–484
  modifying, 484, *485*
NetBIOS parameters, in NET.CFG file, 319–322
Netscape client software, 1362
NetSync program, 897–905, 1357, 1419. *See also* server management
  installing on NetWare 3.1x servers, 902–904, *903*
  installing on NetWare 4.1x servers, 899–902, *900*
  maintaining NetSync objects, 905, *906*
NETUSER program, 1025–1034. *See also* NetWare User Tools; user utilities
  changing contexts, 241, 1033–1034, *1034*
  changing login scripts and passwords, 1032, *1033*
  examples, **1077, 1081**
  mapping drives, 1030–1032, *1031*

printing controls, 1026–1027, *1027*
sending and receiving messages, 1028–1030, *1029*
viewing rights, 1032
viewing server information, 1032, *1033*
NetWare, history of, **20–22**
NetWare 3.x. *See also* NetSync; NetWare 4.1x, upgrading to
  ATTACH command, 492, 1339, 1399
  bindery, **1400**
    leaf objects and, 214–215
    upgrading to NetWare 4.1x, 1338–1339
    why bindery emulation may be necessary, 245–246
  installing NetSync on 3.1x servers, 902–904, *903*
  versus NetWare 4.1x, **1348–1356**
    DOS versus Windows management utilities, 1350–1353, *1351*, *1352*
    file compression and other file system enhancements, 1353–1354, *1354*
    memory management, 1355
    server performance, 1355
    server self-tuning, 1271, 1356
    SUPERVISOR versus ADMIN User object, 669, 730–731, 735
  upgrading 3.1x Print Services, 161–162
  upgrading NetWare 3.11 SFT III systems, 1252–1253
NetWare 4.0, 21
NetWare 4.10, 22. *See also* NetWare User Tools
  creating OS/2 client disks from CD-ROM, 162–164, *163*, 1201–1202
  FirstMail program, **1267–1268**
    running, 1268, *1269*
    setting up mailboxes, 1267–1268
  logging into from NetWare User Tools, **997–998**
NetWare 4.11. *See also* IntranetWare
  FirstMail program and, 1267
  NDPS (NetWare Distributed Print Services), 652–653
  NetWare Application Launcher (NAL), **971–979, 983, 987, 1419**
    Associations page, 977, *978*
    client side of, 978–979, *979*
    Contacts page, 977
    creating and configuring Application objects, 972–977, *973*
    Description page, 976
    Drives/Ports page, 975–976, *975*
    Environment page, 974
    examples, **983, 987**
    Scripts page, 976–977
  NetWare User Tools and, **997–998**
  new products and installations, 188–190, *189*, *190*
  security improvements, 726–727
  Web Server and, 1185
  Windows 95 user support, **1067–1074, 1303–1305, 1315–1317, 1341–1343**
    examples, **1079, 1083**
    installing Client32 clients, **334–338,** *336*, *337*
    logging in from Network Neighborhood, 1071–1072, *1072*
    mapping drives from Windows 95, 1072–1074, *1073*
    printing and, 1068, 1074
    protecting against problems, 1303–1305
    sending messages within Network Neighborhood, 1070–1071, *1070*
    troubleshooting Windows 95 clients, **1315–1317**
    upgrading clients to Windows 95, **1341–1343**
    viewing connection information, 1068–1069, *1069*
NetWare 4.1x, 1346–1363. *See also* NetWare 4.11
  backing up, 1271–1272, **1273–1274, 1400**
  history of, **22–23**
  installing NetSync on 4.1 servers, 899–902, *900*
  listing license information, 887, *887*
  logging into from NetWare User Tools, 999
  versus NetWare 3.x, **1348–1356**
    DOS versus Windows management utilities, 1350–1353, *1351*, *1352*
    file compression and other file system enhancements, 1353–1354, *1354*
    memory management, 1355
    server performance, 1355
    server self-tuning, 1271, 1356
    SUPERVISOR versus ADMIN User object, 669, 730–731, 735
  versus NetWare 4.0, **1356–1360**
    DynaText online documentation, 1360
    installation options, 1357
    MacNDS client for Macintosh, 1358
    NetWare Directory Services improvements, 1356–1358
    NetWare Peripheral Architecture (NPA), 98–100, 1263–1264, 1360

NetWare Server for OS/2 options, 1358
 printing enhancements, 1359
 storage and backup options, 1359
versus other network operating systems, **1346–1348**, *1348*
versus Unix, **1124–1134**
 C2 level security rating, 1360
 case-sensitivity, 1130
 daemons, background processes, and NLMs, 1130–1131
 directories and files in Unix, 1130
 NetWare and Unix kernels, 1131
 networking, print, file, and user services differences, 1131–1134
 philosophical differences, 1132–1133
upgrading to, **1332–1344**
 migrating data, 1336–1337
 migrating file attributes, 1338
 migrating passwords, 1337–1338
 migrating print services, 1339–1340
 migrating trustee rights and login scripts, 1339
 upgrade method options, 1332–1334
 upgrading Bindery information, 1338–1339
 versus upgrading server hardware, **1334–1336**, 1340

NetWare 4.1x installation, 56–130
 copying installation files, **81–88**
  examples, **125**, **127–128**
  from floppy disks, 81, 83–84, 86–87
  from NetWare volumes, 84–87
  from remote CD-ROM drives, 87–88
  from remote CD-ROMs mounted as NetWare volumes, 87–88
  from remote server's network installation area, 81, 84–87
  from server-based CD-ROMs, 81, 82–83, 84–86
 Custom Installation method, **91–121**
  adding protocols, 102–103, *102*
  automatic server startup option, 95–96
  block suballocation on volumes, 114, **1264**, 1354, **1401**
  changing Hot Fix settings, 105
  changing volume segment size, 108–111, *109*, *110*, *111*
  copying server files to DOS partition, 93–94, *94*
  creating NetWare disk partitions, 103–104, *104*, *105*
  data migration option, 114–115
  disk driver installation, 96–100
  disk mirroring and duplexing options, 105–106, **1404**, **1407**
  file compression settings for volumes, 113–114
  file name format options, 94–95
  internal IPX network number setting, 93, **1414**, **1422**
  keyboard mapping options, 94–95
  LAN driver installation for network interface cards, 100–101, *101*
  monolithic (.DSK) versus NPA (NetWare Peripheral Architecture) drivers, 98–100, 1263–1264, 1360
  naming the server, 92–93
  naming volumes, 112
  saving volume changes, 115
  SET command options, 95
  troubleshooting SCSI conflicts, 68–69, 97–98
  volume block size options, 112–113
  volume management options, **106–115**, *108*
 disk drive preparation, **76–78**
  for booting servers from floppy disks, 79–81
  for booting servers from hard disk drives, 76–78, *76*, *77*
  examples, **124–125**, *127*
 INSTALL.NLM program, **88–89**, *88*, *90*
 MegaCorp example, **126–128**
 MiniCo example, **123–125**
 versus NetWare 4.0 installation, 1357
 NetWare license software installation, **115–119**
  copying NetWare files, 117–118, *118*
  installing additional server licenses, 882–883
  listing NetWare license information, 887, *887*
  from remote servers, 116–117, *117*
  selecting optional files to install, 118–119, *119*, *120*
 pre-installation processes, **72–81**
  creating server installation boot disk, 72–75
  preparing disk drives for NetWare, 76–81, *76*
 server requirements, **58–72**
  CD-ROM drives, 68–69
  CPUs, 60–61
  examples, **123–124**, **126–127**
  floppy disk drives, 69
  hard disk drives, 63–66
  IDE disk controllers and drives, 64
  IRQ, DMA, I/O port settings and ROM addresses, 70–72

monitors, 69–70
network interface cards (NICs), 66–68, *67*
RAID disk systems, 65–66
RAM, 62–63
SCSI disk interfaces and drives, 64–65
Simple Installation method
    Bindery Services and, 247–249, *248*, *249*
    disk driver installation, 96–100
    and hard disk configuration, 103
    LAN driver installation, 100–101, *101*
    naming the server, 92–93
    protocol installation and, 102–103
    troubleshooting SCSI conflicts, 97–98
    Unix utilities and, 91

NetWare 4.1x for Macintosh. *See also*
    Macintosh computers
installing client software, **1118–1121**
    Macintosh client defined, **1416**
    navigating NDS, 1120–1121
    setting up clients for NDS, **1118–1120**, *1120*, *1358*
installing server software, **165–167, 1094–1118**
    adding Macintosh name space support to volumes, 1117–1118
    adding Macintosh name space to volumes, 1117–1118
    binding AppleTalk to a LAN interface, 1105–1106, *1105*
    CD-ROM services configuration, 1113–1114, *1115*
    configuring AppleTalk protocol stack, **1100–1106**
    file services configuration, 1106–1108, *1107*
    installing additional language support for clients, 1115–1116
    installing Macintosh client support, 1116–1117
    loading NLMs, 1096–1100, *1097*
    network interface card and network interface configuration, 1102
    preparation, 1095–1096
    print services configuration, 1109–1113, *1110*
    protocol configuration, 1102–1105, *1102*, *1103*, *1105*

NetWare 4.1x Server for OS/2, 1220–1232, 1358. *See also* OS/2 clients
advantages of, 1221, 1358
installing, **1224–1230**
    from another network server, 1225–1226
    from CD-ROM, 1224–1225
    installation steps, 1228–1230
    selecting an installation method, 1226–1230, *1227*
    server requirements, 1222–1223
    Simplified Installation method, 1227–1228
operation of, **1230–1232**, *1231*, *1232*
Performance Monitor (PMMon), **1233–1238**
    managing memory allocation, 1235–1236, *1235*
    performance optimization, 1236–1237, *1236*
    setting NET.CFG parameters, 1237–1238

NetWare 4.1x SFT III (System Fault Tolerant Level III), 1244–1255
control and startup files, 1248
cost of, *1320*, 1321
effectiveness of, 1253–1255
installing, **1249–1253**
    new installations, 1251–1252
    server requirements, 1250
    upgrading NetWare 3.11 SFT III systems, 1252–1253
MSEngine and IOEngine and, 1247–1248
server log files, 1249
SFT defined, **1245**

NetWare Administrator, 1419. *See also* DOS utilities; NETADMIN; NetSync; server management
Browser windows, 694–695, *694*, 756–757, *757*
creating NetWare Administrator icon in Windows 3.1x, 753–755
file compression statistics, **1261–1262**, *1261*
Group object creation, **447–451**, *449*, *450*
Group object modification, **451–466**
    e-mailbox setup, 457–459, *458*
    foreign e-mail addresses, 459–460
    identification information, 451–453, *452*
    member lists, 454–457, *455*
    rights to files and directories, 460–463, *462*
    See Also page (related resource information), 465–466, *465*
    trustees, 463–464, *464*
installing, **353–354, 753–755**
    examples, 925, 928
    on Windows 3.1x systems, 353–354, 753–755
    on Windows 95 systems, 354, 755
login script creation or editing, **377–379, 505–507**
    Container login scripts, *506*
    Profile login scripts, 506–507

User login scripts, 507
    for User object setup, 377–379, *378*
menus, **757–761**
    Help menu, 761
    Object menu, 757–758
    Options menu, 759
    Tools menu, 760, 780–781
    View menu, 758–759
    Window menu, 760–761
navigating, 756–757, *757*
NDS Manager, **776–792, 870–873**
    adding to Tools menu, 780–781
    creating partitions, 781–783, *782*
    deleting NetWare (NCP) Server objects from NDS, 790–792, *791*
    DSREPAIR utility in, **870–873**, *871*, *872*
    examples, **925, 928–929**
    merging partitions, 784–785, *785*
    moving partitions and their containers, 792, *793*
    partition and replica management guidelines, 778
    repairing NDS corruption, 779–780
    viewing and modifying replicas, 786–789, *787*, *788*
    viewing server partitions, 789–790, *790*
NetWare Directory Services (NDS) administration, **761–776**
    creating container objects, 762–765, *763*, *764*
    creating leaf objects, 767–769, *768*, *769*
    examples, **925, 928**
    moving leaf objects, 770–771, *771*
    renaming leaf objects, 772–773, *773*
    searching for objects, 773–776, *775*
    setting intruder detection, 765–767, *766*
Partition Manager, **777–778**
printing management, **542–605, 656, 660**
    AIO printer communication settings, 570, 573–574
    AppleTalk printer communication settings, 570, 573
    examples, **656, 660**
    parallel printer communication settings, 571–572, *572*
    print job configuration management, 602–605, *603*
    print mode definition, 600–601, *601*
    print queue assignments, 554–555, *555*
    print queue job list management, 560–564, *561*, *562*
    Print Queue object configuration, **552–564**
    Print Queue object creation, 545–548, *546*, *547*
    Print Queue object identification and operator attributes, 552–554, *553*
    print queue operator management, 554–557, *557*
    print queue user list management, 558–560, *559*
    Print Server audit log management, 586–589, *588*
    Print Server object assignment changes, 581–583, *582*
    Print Server object configuration, **578–589**
    Print Server object creation, 550–552, *551*
    Print Server object identification information, 579–581, *580*
    Print Server object user and group management, 583–585, *584*
    print server operator management, 585–586, *586*
    printer device exporting, 598–599, *599*
    printer device importing or deleting, 596–597, *598*
    printer Feature property descriptions, 576, *577*
    printer forms management, 594–596, *595*
    Printer object configuration, **564–578**
    Printer object configuration modification, 568–574, *569*, *571*
    Printer object creation, 548–549, *550*
    Printer object identification information, 565–566, *566*
    Printer object See Also page, 577–578, *578*
    Printer object tie-in with print queues, 567, *568*
    printer problem notification setup, 574–576, *575*
    printer status viewing and modification, 591–594, *592*
    printing system layout diagram, 589–591, *590*
    Quick Setup feature, 543–544
    serial printer communication settings, 570, 573
    Unix printer communication settings, 570, 573
running from OS/2 workstations, **1215–1217**, *1217*
security management, **690–708**
    ADMIN User object and, 690
    Effective Rights listings, 672

examples, 732, 736–737
granting trustee rights between multiple objects, 705–708, 706, 707, 708
granting trustee rights between objects with drag-and-drop, 702–705, 704
granting trustee rights to groups or users, 699–702, 700, 701
granting trustee rights to volumes or directories, 696–699, 697, 698
managing directory and file rights, **693–702**, *694*
managing object or property rights, **702–708**
opening Browser windows, 695, 756–757, *757*
preventing login script changes by users, 692–693, *693*
[Public] object rights, 690–691
revoking property rights, 692–693, *693*
[Root] object default property rights, 691, 694, *694*
User object trustee default property rights, 691, 694, *694*
user management, 793–807
   accounting overview, 793–794, 799
   activating server accounting, 795
   examples, **926**, **929**
   moving employee database records into NDS with UIMPORT, 803–805, 1338–1339, **1444**
   setting charge rates for resources, 795–797, *797*, 799
   setting user account balances and low balance limits, 799–801, *800*
   setting user volume space restriction, 801–803, *802*
   updating NET.CFG with NCUPDATE, 805–807, 1358
   viewing accounting reports with ATOTAL, 797–798
User object creation, 352–395
   account balance tracking, 374–376, *375*
   basic User object creation, **354–358**, *356*, *357*
   detail settings, **358–376**
   e-mailbox setup, 366–367, *367*
   environment information, 364–366, *365*
   examples, **439**, **441–442**
   foreign e-mail addresses and aliases, 368–369, *369*
   group membership setup, 351, 352, 384–385, *385*
   home directory setup, 351, 352, 359–361, *360*

identification information, 362–364, *362*
intruder lockout setup, 391, *393*
login names, 357–358
login restriction setup, 379–381, *380*
login scripts, 351, 352, 377–379, *378*
login time restriction setup, 387–389, *388*
naming, 357–358
network address restrictions, 389–390, *390*
password restrictions, 381–384, *382*
postal address information, 373, *374*
print job configuration, 352, 370–373, *371*
related information tracking, 376, *377*
rights to files and directories setup, 391–395, *393*, *394*
security configuration, **376–395**
security equivalence setup, 351, 352, 386, *387*
User Template creation, **480–483**, *481*, *482*
NetWare administrators. *See* administrators
NetWare Application Launcher (NAL), 971–979, 983, 987, 1419. *See also* applications
   Associations page, 977, *978*
   client side of, 978–979, *979*
   Contacts page, 977
   creating and configuring Application objects, 972–977, *973*
   Description page, 976
   Drives/Ports page, 975–976, *975*
   Environment page, 974
   examples, **983**, **987**
   Scripts page, 976–977
NetWare Connections window. *See* NetWare User Tools
NetWare Core Protocol (NCP), 1419. *See also* protocols
   IPX/SPX protocol and, 36–39, *38*
   NCP SET commands, 844, 1383–1385
   NetWare (NCP) Server objects, **217**, 790–792, *791*, **1421**
NetWare Directory Services (NDS), 120, 130–197, 200–258, 1398, 1405, 1419–1420. *See also* objects
   ADMIN User object
      creating User objects, 351–352
      naming, 140, 147, *148*
      versus NetWare 3.x SUPERVISOR, 669, 730–731, 735
      NetWare Administrator security management and, 690

NetWare Directory Services (NDS) security and, 683
print queue operator assignment, 556–557, *557*
[Root] object and, 208
selecting password for, 140, 147, *148*
and User object management, 444–445
workgroup administrators and, **752–753**
advantages of, **201–202**, 252, **255–256**
backing up, **1274**, **1400**
Bindery Services, **244–250**, **1400–1401**
    bindery context and, **244**
    examples, **254**, **258**
    how Bindery Services works, 244–245
    installing, 246–247, *247*
    maintaining, 249–250
    NDS trees and, 246, 247–249, *248*, *249*
    Simple Installation method and, 247–249, *248*, *249*
    and using resources from another tree, 246
    why bindery emulation may be necessary, 245–246
container objects, **131**, **205**, **1403**
    container rules for objects, **213–214**, *214*
    Country (C) container objects, 210, 222, **1403**
    Organization (O) container objects, 211–212, 445, **1425**
    Organization Unit (OU) container objects, 212–213, 445, **1425–1426**
    [Root] object and, 208–209, *209*
contexts, **131**, **238–243**, **1403**, **1419–1420**
    bindery context, **244**
    changing with CX command, 241, **994–996**
    distinguished names, 240–241
    examples, **253**, **257**
    For your information screen, 140–141, *141*
    how to use to your advantage, **242–243**
    importance of, **239–241**, *239*
    logging in and, 242–243
    naming the Organization and Organizational Units, 139–140, *139*, 148–150, *149*, *150*
    relative distinguished names, 240
    selecting ADMIN name and password, 140, 147, *148*
    setting up user's "home" context, 243
    settings for additional servers, **147–150**
    settings for first NetWare server, **138–141**, *139*
    typeless versus typeful name formats, 238, **1444**
deleting, **184–187**

examples, **194**, **197**
    from multiple-server networks, 187, *188*
    from one-server networks, 185–187, *186*, *187*
    warnings, 185, *186*, *187*
deleting NetWare (NCP) Server objects, **790–792**, *791*
directory services SET commands, **844**, **1370–1372**
DSMERGE program, **873–882**. *See also* server management
    Check Servers In This Tree option, 876, *877*
    Check Time Synchronization option, 877–878, *878*
    examples, **930**
    exiting and cleaning up, 881–882
    Merge Two Trees option, 879–880, *879*
    Rename This Tree option, 880–881, *881*
DSREPAIR program, **779–780**, **853–873**, **1408**. *See also* server management
    Advanced Options menu and submenus, 855, **857–869**
    Create a Database Dump File option, 869, *870*
    Global Schema Options screen, 867–868, *868*
    Local ID to Remote ID List screen, 862, *863*
    Log File/Login Configuration Options screen, 858–859, *859*
    Repair Local Database Options screen, 859–860, *860*
    repairing NDS corruption, **779–780**
    Replica and Partitions Operations options, 863–866, *863*
    Replica Ring Options submenu, 865–866
    Security Equivalence Synchronization option, 866–867, *867*
    Servers found in this Directory Services Database screen, 861–862, *861*
    Servers That Have Replicas of This Partition screen, 865
    Unattended Full Repair option, 854, **856–857**, *857*
    View Repair Log File option, 855, 868–869, *869*
DSTRACE program and, **851–853**, *852*, **926**, **929**
importing employee database records with UIMPORT, **803–805**, **1338–1339**, **1444**
installing for first NetWare server, **130–141**, **151–157**, **192–197**
    context settings, **138–141**, *139*
    copying files to new servers, 154–155, *155*

editing AUTOEXEC.NCF file, **153–154**, *154*
editing STARTUP.NCF file, **151–153**, *152*
For your information screen, 140–141, *141*
installation completion, 157, *157*
MegaCorp example, **195–197**
MiniCo example, **192–194**
naming NDS tree, 133–134, *135*
naming the Organization and Organizational Units, 139–140, *139*
NetWare 4.11 new products and installations, 188–190, *189*, *190*
selecting ADMIN name and password, 140
selecting your time zone, 136, *136*
terms defined, **131**
time setting adjustments, 137–138, *137*
time setting considerations, 135
installing servers into existing 4.1 networks, **141–150**
context settings, **147–150**
examples, **193**, **195–196**
naming the Organization and Organizational Units, 148–150, *149*, *150*
selecting ADMIN name and password, 147, *148*
selecting NDS trees, 142–144, *143*
time zone and time synchronization settings, 144–147, *145*
using single versus multiple NDS trees, 142, *143*
leaf objects, **131**, *133*, **205**, **214–222**, **1415**. *See also* Group objects; objects; Print Queue objects; Print Server objects; Printer objects; User objects
AFP (AppleTalk Filing Protocol) Server objects, 220, **1398**
Alias objects, 210, 219–220, **1399**
bindery and, 214–215
Bindery and Bindery Queue objects, 221–222, **1400**
Computer objects, 219
creating in NETADMIN, **911–912**
creating in NetWare Administrator, 767–769, *768*, *769*
Directory Map objects, 218, 959–960, *960*, **1406**
Distribution List objects, 221
External Entity objects, 221
Message Routing Group objects, 220
Messaging (MHS) Server objects, 220
moving, 770–771, *771*, 913, *914*
naming, 215
in NETADMIN, **911–916**
in NetWare Administrator, **767–776**
NetWare (NCP) Server objects, **217**, 790–792, *791*, **1421**
NetWare Volume objects, 217
Organizational Role objects, 218, 446, **1425**
Profile objects, 219
renaming, 772–773, *773*, 913–915
[Root] object and, 215, *215*
searching for, 773–776, *775*, 915–916, *916*
Unknown objects, 222, **1445**
MacNDS, 1358
MegaCorp example, **255–258**
MiniCo example, **252–254**
NDS trees, **222–238**, **1406**. *See also* DSMERGE; leaf objects; [Root] object
attribute information and, 206
Bindery Services and, 246, 247–249, *248*, *249*
creating pilot systems, 224–225
departmental, workgroup, user-location, or bottom-up design, **230–232**, *233*, *234*
designing versus implementing, 227
designing for users, 226
Directory schema and, **206**
distributed organization chart with a WAN or mixed design, **236–238**, *237*
examples, **253**, **256–257**
goals for NDS tree design, 223–224
inheritance information and, 206
merging, 879–880, *879*
naming for first NetWare server, 133–134, *135*
naming standards, 227–230
organizational, user function, or top-down design, **233–236**, *235*, *236*
physical versus logical design phases, **225–226**, 232, *233*, *234*
selecting for additional servers, 142–144, *143*
subordination and, 206
teaching users about, **992–994**, *993*
using resources from another tree, 246
using single versus multiple trees, 142, *143*
NDS.VLM file, 296
NetWare 4.1x enhancements, **1356–1358**
NetWare Administrator NDS administration, **761–776**
creating container objects, 762–765, *763*, *764*

creating leaf objects, 767–769, *768*, *769*
examples, **925**, **928**
moving leaf objects, 770–771, *771*
renaming leaf objects, 772–773, *773*
saving search criteria, 776
searching for objects, 773–776, *775*
setting intruder detection, 765–767, *766*
setting search filters, 774–776
Organization and Organizational Units, **131**, *133*
  naming, 139–140, *139*, 148–150, *149*, *150*
Other Installation Items/Products screen, **156–183**
  Change Server Language option, 176–177, *177*
  Configure Network Protocols option, 171–174, *172*, *174*
  Create DOS/MS Windows/OS2 Client Install Diskettes option, 162–164, *163*
  Create NetWare UPGRADE/MIGRATE Diskettes option, 164
  Create a Registration Diskette option, 159–161, *161*
  examples, **193–194**, **196–197**
  Install an Additional Server Language option, 175–176
  Install NetWare for Macintosh option, 165–167, *166*, *167*, *168*
  Install NetWare MHS Services option, 168–171, *170*
  Install Online Documentation and Viewers option, 158–159, 178–181, *179*, *180*, *181*, *182*
  Install a product not listed option, 182–183, *183*
  Upgrade 3.1x Print Services option, 161–162
repairing. *See* DSREPAIR
[Root] object, **205**, **207–214**, **1434**
  ADMIN user and, 208
  container objects and, 208–209, *209*
  container rules for objects, 213–214, *214*
  Country (C) container objects, 210, 222, **1403**
  default property rights, 691, 694, *694*
  examples, **252–253**, **256**
  explaining, 993–994, *993*
  leaf objects and, 215, *215*
  Organization (O) container objects, 211–212, 445, **1425**
  Organization Unit (OU) container objects, 212–213, **1425–1426**
  trustees of, 208

security features, **683–690**. *See also* ADMIN User object
  Access Control List (ACL) object property, 686–687, 751, **1398**, **1433**
  examples, **732**, **736**
  guidelines for, 688–690
  IRFs (Inherited Rights Filters) and object and property rights, 687–688
  object rights versus property rights, 684–687
  rights inheritance, 687, *688*
  setting up Macintosh clients for, **1118–1120**, *1120*, 1358
  X.500 specification and, 206, 222
NetWare Distributed Print Services (NDPS), **652–653**
NetWare DOS Requester (VLM.EXE), **261–262**, 266, **274–276**, **295–310**, **1420**
  examples, 339, 343
  NET.CFG parameters and settings, **297–310**
  NetWare DOS Requester heading in NET.CFG file, 297
  NetWare DOS Requester parameter in NET.CFG file, 295–297
NetWare Internet Access Server (NIAS). *See* NetWare IPX/IP Gateway
NetWare IPX/IP Gateway, **1170–1183**, **1196**, **1361–1362**. *See also* IntranetWare; IPX/SPX protocol
  advantages of, 1182–1183
  Client32 and, 1175
  configuring, **1173–1175**, *1174*
  controlling client access to, **1178–1183**, *1179*, *1180*, *1181*
  examples, **1196**
  installing, **1171–1173**, 1176
  security, **1176–1177**, 1183
  setting up clients for, **1175–1176**, *1176*
  TCP/IP protocol and, 1170–1171, 1175, 1176
  Winsock program and, 1170, 1175
NetWare Link Services Protocol (NLSP), **1276–1279**, **1423**
NetWare Loadable Modules (NLMs), **1415**, **1420**. *See also* VLMs
  DOMAIN.NLM, 1270–1271
  INSTALL.NLM program, **88–89**, *88*, *90*
  installing TCPIP.NLM (NetWare TCP/IP support), **1146–1151**
  listing all loaded NLMs, 885, *885*
  memory management and, 1355

1490 NetWare Loadable Modules (NLMs)—network interface cards (NICs)

for NetWare for Macintosh server software, 1096–1100, *1097*
NetWare NFS Services, **1164–1169, 1421**
 file transfer services, 1168–1169, *1169*
 managing name services, 1165–1166, *1165*
 managing NFS Services, 1164–1165, *1165*
 setting up file sharing, 1166–1168, *1167*
 setting up printing, 1168, *1168*
NWPA.NLM driver, 99, 1263
PUPGRADE.NLM, 1339–1340
SNMP.NLM, 1280–1281
versus Unix daemons and background processes, **1130–1131**
viewing information about, 833–834, *833*
NetWare Message Handling Service. *See* Message Handling Service
NetWare Navigator, **935**
NetWare (NCP) Server objects, **217, 1421**
 deleting from NDS, 790–792, *791*
NetWare NFS Services, **1164–1169, 1421**. *See also* NetWare Loadable Modules; TCP/IP protocol; Unix
 file transfer services, 1168–1169, *1169*
 managing name services, 1165–1166, *1165*
 managing NFS Services, 1164–1165, *1165*
 setting up file sharing, 1166–1168, *1167*
 setting up printing, 1168, *1168*
NetWare Peripheral Architecture (NPA)
 monolithic (.DSK) versus NPA drivers, 98–100, 1360
NETWARE PROTOCOL parameter in NET.CFG, 303
NetWare Requester for OS/2, **1421**
NetWare Settings dialog box
 enabling or disabling F6 hotkey, 1000–1001, *1001*
 sound in, 964
NetWare Settings for LPT dialog box, 1009–1012, *1010*
NetWare Storage Management Services (SMS)
 for PC clients, **285**, *285*
NetWare Tools for OS/2, **1212–1215**, *1212, 1213, 1215*
NetWare User Tools (NWUSER), **997–1025, 1421**. *See also* NETUSER program; user utilities
 adding user-defined hotkeys, 1022, *1023*
 changing contexts with, 241
 changing hotkeys and other NetWare settings, 1019–1021, *1020*
 changing LPT printer settings, 1009–1012, *1010*
 configuring Windows 3.1x for fast network printing, 1012–1014, *1013*
 connecting to NetWare servers, 1014–1017, *1016*
 connecting to network printers, 1006–1008, *1007*
 connecting to network printers permanently, 1008–1009, *1009*
 enabling or disabling F6 hotkey, 1000–1001, *1001*
 examples, **1076–1077, 1080–1081**
 Help system, 1023–1025, *1024*
 keyboard shortcuts, 999–1000
 logging into NetWare 4.10 from, 997–998, *999*
 mapping drives, 1002–1005, *1003, 1004*
 mapping drives permanently, 1005–1006, *1006*
 NetWare 4.11 and, **997–998**
 sending and receiving messages, 1017–1019, *1018*
 sound effects, 1000
 viewing rights, 1004–1005, *1004*
NetWare Volume objects, 217
NetWare Web Server, **1183–1192, 1195–1196, 1361, 1448**. *See also* IntranetWare
 configuring and managing, 1187–1192, *1188, 1190, 1191*
 examples, **1195–1196**
 installing, 1185–1187, *1186*
 NetWare 4.11 and, 1185
NetWare/IP protocol, **1153–1164, 1362, 1420**. *See also* IntranetWare; protocols; TCP/IP protocol
 on Client32 clients, 1159–1160
 installing on servers, 1160–1164, *1163*
 on non-Client32 clients, 1156–1159, *1157, 1158*
NetWire Forum on CompuServe, 1057, **1422**
network accounting. *See* accounting
network address restrictions
 in NETADMIN, 427–428, *429*
 in NetWare Administrator, 389–390, *390*
network administrators. *See* administrators
Network General software, 1305
Network Information screen, SERVMAN program, 850, *851*
Network Information System (NIS), 1139, *1139*
network interface cards (NICs), **1422**
 binding AppleTalk to, 1105–1106, *1105*
 binding IPX protocol to, 102–103
 configuring for Macintosh servers, 1102
 installation and setup for PC clients, **262–266**
  base I/O addresses, 265
  DMA channels, 266

drivers, 262
examples, **339–340, 343–344**
IRQ settings, 264
memory addresses, 265
LAN driver installation, **100–101**, *101*
NetWare requirements, **66–68**, *67*
ODI (Open Data-link Interface) and, 38–39
Network Neighborhood. *See* Microsoft Windows 95
network operating systems. *See also* DOS; Macintosh computers; Microsoft Windows; OS/2; Unix
NetWare 4.1x versus other systems, **1346–1348**, *1348*
troubleshooting operating system problems, 1318–1319, 1322–1323
The Network Press Encyclopedia of Networking (Feibel), 664–665, 1395
NETWORK PRINTERS parameter in NET.CFG, 304
network printing. *See* printing
network training. *See* users
network-aware, network-enabled, and network-integrated applications, 933–934, 981, 984
networks, 4–20. *See also* administrators; cabling
100BaseVG networks, 13–14
AnyLAN networks, 13–14
ARCnet networks, 18–20, *19*, 1326
ATM25 networks, 18
ATM (Asynchronous Transfer Mode) networks, 17
Ethernet networks, **4–7, 10–11**, 1409
CSMA/CD (carrier sense multiple access/collision detect) access method and, **5–6**, 13
Fast Ethernet networks (100BaseT), **13**
MAC (Media Access Control) specifications, 13
MiniCo example, **49**
network interface card (NIC) addresses, 6
switched Ethernet networks, **7**, *8*
versus Token Ring networks, **5**, 10–11, *11*
troubleshooting, **1325–1326**
FDDI (Fiber Distributed Data Interface) networks, 16
hardware scale and costs, **1320–1322**, *1320*
on Macintosh computers, **1089–1094**
AppleTalk Filing Protocol (AFP), 42–43, 44, 1092
AppleTalk protocol, 1089–1092
EtherTalk protocol, 42, 1090
IPX/SPX protocol and, 42–43
LocalTalk protocol, 42
network addresses and zones, 1092–1094, **1449**

TokenTalk protocol, 42
MegaCorp planning example, **52–54**
MiniCo planning example, **49–51**
network monitoring software, **1305–1308**, *1306*, *1307*
peer-to-peer networks, 1321
planning, **741–750**
examples, **924, 927**
planning for the future, 743–744
selling the plan to users, 749–750
selling the plan to your boss, 746–749
recommended reading, **1393–1395**
Token Ring networks, **7–11**
versus Ethernet networks, 5, 10–11, *11*
Unix and, 4
user attitudes toward, **992**
wide area networks (WANs), **1448**
distributed organization chart with a WAN NDS tree design, **236–238**, *237*
wireless networks, 14–16, *15*
NETX.COM program, 261
NETX.VLM file, 296
newsgroups, Novell, 1058
NFS services. *See* NetWare NFS Services
NIAS (NetWare Internet Access Server). *See* NetWare IPX/IP Gateway
NICs. *See* network interface cards
NIS (Network Information System), 1139, *1139*
NLMs. *See* NetWare Loadable Modules
NLSP (NetWare Link Services Protocol), 1276–1279, 1423
NMENU.BAT program, 511–513
NMR.VLM file, 296
NODE ADDRESS Link Driver parameter in NET.CFG file, 314
non-Client32 clients, 276–291, 805–807. *See also* PC clients
attaching to networks for the first time, 290–291
completing the installation, 289–290, *289*, *290*
configuring non-Client32 clients with NCUPDATE, **805–807**, 1358
editing INSTALL.CFG file, 277–278
examples, **340, 344–345**
installing from CD-ROMs, 279–280, 281–282
installing from floppy disks, 280–282
installing from servers, 278–279, 281
loading ODI LAN drivers, 286–288, *286*, *287*, *288*, *289*
MAKEDISK.BAT program and, 280–281

running INSTALL.EXE program, **282–290**, *283*
Target Service Agent (TSA) configuration for Storage Management Services (SMS), 285, *285*
Windows 3.1x configuration, 284–285, *284*
workstation language setting, 276–277
Noorda, Ray, 1347–1348
Normal (N) directory attribute, 679, **1423**
Normal (N) file attribute, 681, 955, **1423**
Norton, Peter, 1130
"not enough memory" errors on workstations, 1314–1315
Novell
    GMHS (Global Message Handling Service), 368
    GroupWise guidelines, **966–968**, *967*, *968*
    Internet resources, **1057–1058**
    LANalyzer software, 1305
    NetWire Forum, 1057, **1422**
    Ray Noorda and, 1347–1348
    Web site, 1057
NPA (NetWare Peripheral Architecture)
    monolithic (.DSK) versus NPA drivers, 98–100, 1360
NPATCH parameter in NET.CFG file, 322
NPRINT command
    examples, **1077**, **1081**
    print job configuration, 370, 371, 645, 648
    printing files from command line, 1035, **1040–1042**
    printing system and, 534
NPRINTER program, 535, 536, **1042–1044**, 1077–1078, 1082
NPTWIN95 program, 650–652, *651*, 658, 662, 1078, 1082
NT7A parameter in NET.CFG file, 317
number sign (#)
    # login script command, 492
    in AUTOEXEC.NCF file, 1301
NVER command, 263–264, 334
NWP.VLM file, 296
NWPA.NLM driver, 99, 1263
NWUSER. *See* NetWare User Tools

O

O (Organization) objects, 211–212, 445
Object menu, in NetWare Administrator, 757–758
object rights, 1424, 1433. *See also* rights; security; trustees
    Group object rights
        in NETADMIN, **475–477**, *476*, *477*

    in NetWare Administrator, **460–463**, *462*
    IRFs (Inherited Rights Filters) and, 687–688
    managing with NETADMIN, **713–714**, *715*
    managing with NetWare Administrator, **702–708**
    versus property rights, **684–686**
    [Public] object rights, 690–691
    [Root] object default property rights, 691, 694, *694*
    supervisory functions and, 750
objects, 131, 204–222, **1424**. *See also* Group objects; NetWare Directory Services; User objects
    ADMIN User object, **131**, **1398**
        creating User objects, 351–352
        naming, 140, 147, *148*
        versus NetWare 3.x SUPERVISOR, 669, 730–731, 735
        NetWare Administrator security management and, 690
        NetWare Directory Services (NDS) security and, 683
        print queue operator assignment, 556–557, *557*
        [Root] object and, 208
        selecting password for, 140, 147, *148*
        and User object management, 444–445
        workgroup administrators and, **752–753**
    Application objects in NetWare Application Launcher, **972–977**, *973*
    classes of, 205, *206*
    container objects, 131, 205, **1403**
        container rules for objects, **213–214**, *214*
        Country (C) container objects, 210, 222, **1403**
        Organization (O) container objects, 211–212, 445, **1425**
        Organization Unit (OU) container objects, 212–213, 445, **1425–1426**
        [Root] object and, 208–209, *209*
    container rules for, **213–214**, *214*
    examples, 252, 256
    leaf objects, **131**, 214–222, **1415**. *See also* Group objects; User objects
        AFP (AppleTalk File Protocol) Server objects, 220, **1398**
        Alias objects, 210, 219–220, **1399**
        bindery and, 214–215
        Bindery and Bindery Queue objects, 221–222, **1400**
        Computer objects, 219
        creating in NETADMIN, **911–912**

creating in NetWare Administrator, **767–769**, *768*, *769*
Directory Map objects, 218, *959–960*, *960*, **1406**
Distribution List objects, 221
External Entity objects, 221
Message Routing Group objects, 221
Messaging (MHS) Server objects, 220
moving, 770–771, *771*, 913, *914*
naming, 215
in NETADMIN, **911–916**
in NetWare Administrator, **767–776**
NetWare (NCP) Server objects, **217**, 790–792, *791*, **1421**
NetWare Volume objects, 217
Organizational Role objects, 218, 445–446, **1425**
Print objects, 217–218
Profile objects, 219
renaming, 772–773, *773*, 913–915
[Root] object and, 215, *215*
searching for, 773–776, *775*, 915–916, *916*
Unknown objects, 222, **1445**
naming, **204**
in NETADMIN program, **911–916**
creating leaf objects, 911–912
moving, 913, *914*
renaming, 913–915
searching for, 915–916, *916*
parent objects, 214
properties, **204**, *205*, *206*, **1430**
Access Control List (ACL) object property, 686–687, 751, **1398**, **1433**
Feature property for Printer objects, *576*, *577*
of User objects, 351–352
[Root] object, **205**, **207–214**, **1434**
ADMIN user and, 208
container objects and, 208–209, *209*
container rules for objects, 213–214, *214*
Country (C) container objects, 210, 222, **1403**
default property rights, 691, 694, *694*
examples, **252–253**, **256**
explaining, 993–994, *993*
leaf objects and, 215, *215*
Organization (O) container objects, 211–212, 445, **1425**
Organization Unit (OU) container objects, 212–213, **1425–1426**
trustees of, 208

searching for in NetWare Administrator, **773–776**, *775*
values of, **204**, *205*, *206*
ODI (Open Data-link Interface), 38–39, **1424–1425**
loading ODI LAN drivers for PC clients, 286–288, *286*, *287*, *288*, *289*
required files for non-Client32 PC clients and, 267, *267*
online documentation. *See* DynaText online documentation; Help
OPEN Link Driver parameter in NET.CFG file, 314
open systems, 1124–1125, **1425**
Open Systems Interconnection (OSI) model, 40, *42*
opening Browser windows in NetWare Administrator, 695, 756–757, *757*
operating systems. *See also* DOS; Macintosh computers; Microsoft Windows; OS/2; Unix
NetWare 4.1x versus other systems, **1346–1348**, *1348*
troubleshooting operating system problems, 1318–1319, 1322–1323
operators
print queue operators, **1428**
ADMIN User object and, 556–557, *557*
managing in NetWare Administrator, 552–557, *553*, *557*
managing in PCONSOLE, 627–628
print server operators, **1429**
managing in NetWare Administrator, 585–586, *586*
managing in PCONSOLE, 615–616
optional installation items. *See* Other Installation Items/Products screen
Options menu, in NetWare Administrator, 759
order of execution for login scripts, 487
ordinary files, in Unix, 1130
Organization (O) objects, 211–212, 445, **1425**. *See also* container objects
Organization Unit (OU) objects, 212–213, 445, **1425–1426**
organizational NDS tree design, 233–236, *235*, *236*
Organizational Role objects, 218, 445–446, **1425**
Organizations and Organizational Units, 131, *133*
naming, 139–140, *139*, 148–150, *149*, *150*
%OS login script identifier variable, 497
OS/2. *See also* DOS; IBM; Macintosh computers; Microsoft Windows; NetWare Administrator; Unix
creating client install disks for, 162–164, *163*

future of, 1199, 1217–1218
NetWare Requester for OS/2, **1421**
NetWare User Tools for OS/2, **1212–1215**, *1212*, *1213*, *1215*
recommended reading, **1394**
running NetWare Administrator from OS/2 workstations, **1215–1217**, *1217*
OS/2 clients, **1198–1218, 1426**. *See also* Macintosh computers; PC clients; troubleshooting, workstation problems
    configuring, **1207–1208**, *1207*
    connecting to servers, **1208–1211**, *1210*, *1211*
    installing OS/2 client software, **1199–1206**
        from CD-ROM, 1205–1206, *1206*
        creating OS/2 client disks from NetWare 4.10 CD-ROM, 162–164, *163*, 1201–1202
        from floppy disks, 1202–1205, *1204*
        workstation requirements, 1200
    NetWare User Tools for OS/2, **1212–1215**, *1212*, *1213*, *1215*
    OS/2 client login screen, 1209–1211, *1210*, *1211*
    running NetWare Administrator from OS/2 workstations, **1215–1217**, *1217*
OS/2 servers, **1220–1239**. *See also* servers
    NetWare 4.1x Server for OS/2, **1220–1232**, 1358
        advantages of, 1221, 1358
        installation steps, 1228–1230
        installing from another network server, 1225–1226
        installing from CD-ROM, 1224–1225
        operation of, **1230–1232**, *1231*, *1232*
        selecting an installation method, 1226–1230, *1227*
        server requirements, 1222–1223
        Simplified Installation method, 1227–1228
    Performance Monitor (PMMon), **1233–1238**
        managing memory allocation, 1235–1236, *1235*
        performance optimization, 1236–1237, *1236*
        setting NET.CFG parameters, 1237–1238
OSI (Open Systems Interconnection) model, 40, *42*
%OS_VERSION login script identifier variable, 497
Other Installation Items/Products screen, NetWare Directory Services, **156–183**
    Change Server Language option, 176–177, *177*
    Configure Network Protocols option, 171–174, *172*, *174*
    Create DOS/MS Windows/OS2 Client Install Diskettes option, 162–164, *163*
    Create NetWare UPGRADE/MIGRATE Diskettes option, 164
    Create a Registration Diskette option, 159–161, *161*
    examples, **193–194, 196–197**
    Install an Additional Server Language option, 175–176
    Install NetWare for Macintosh option, 165–167, *166*, *167*, *168*
    Install NetWare MHS Services option, 168–171, *170*
    Install Online Documentation and Viewers option, 158–159, 178–181, *179*, *180*, *181*, *182*
    Install a product not listed option, 182–183, *183*
    Upgrade 3.1x Print Services option, 161–162
OU (**Organization Unit**) **objects,** 212–213, 445, **1425–1426**
ownership, changing directory and file ownership, 951–953, *953*

P

P (**Purge**) directory attribute, 679, **1430**
P (**Purge**) file attribute, 681, **1430**
Packet Exchange Protocol (PEP), 36
packets, 35, 37, **1426**
parallel printer settings
    in NetWare Administrator, 571–572, *572*
    in PCONSOLE, 632–633, *633*
parent objects, 214, **1426**
parent partitions, 777
Partition Manager. *See* PARTMGR program
partitions, 1407, 1421, **1427**. *See also* hard disk drives; replicas; volumes
    copying server files to DOS partition, 93–94, *94*
    creating
        during NetWare installation, **103–104**, *104*, *105*
        with NDS Manager, 781–783, *782*
        with PARTMGR, 916–917, *917*
    DSREPAIR options for, 863–866, *863*
    management guidelines, 778
    merging, 784–785, *785*
    moving with their containers, 792, *793*
    parent and child partitions, 777
    and recovery from NDS database corruption, 779–780
    viewing server partitions, 789–790, *790*
    versus volumes, **103**

PARTMGR program, 777–778, 916–919. *See also* NDS Manager; NetWare Administrator
creating partitions, 916–917, *917*
examples, **926**, **930**
viewing or modifying replicas, 918–919, *918*
passwords, 1427. *See also* rights; security; trustees
in AUDITCON, 722–723
changing with NETUSER, 1032, *1033*
migrating, **1337–1338**
restricting in NETADMIN, 423–425, *424*
restricting in NetWare Administrator, 381–384, *382*
security guidelines, **715–716**
selecting ADMIN password, 140, 147, *148*
PAUSE login script command, 494
PB BUFFERS parameter in NET.CFG, 304
PBURST READ WINDOWS SIZE parameter in NET.CFG, 304
PBURST WRITE WINDOWS SIZE parameter in NET.CFG, 304
PC clients, 260–346. *See also* Macintosh computers; OS/2 clients; workstations
Client32 clients, **326–338, 1402**. *See also* non-Client32 clients
connecting DOS and Windows 3.1x clients to networks, 331–334
examples, **341–342, 345–346**
installing for DOS and Windows 3.1x systems, 327–331, *328*, *329*
installing for Windows 95 systems, 326–327, 334–338, *336*, *337*
NetWare IPX/IP Gateway and, **1175**
NetWare/IP protocol on, **1159–1160**
upgrading clients to, **1341–1343**
client side of NetWare Application Launcher, **978–979**, *979*
controlling client access to NetWare IPX/IP Gateway, **1178–1183**, *1179*, *1180*, *1181*
MegaCorp example, 343–346
MiniCo example, 339–342
NET.CFG DOS and Windows 3.1x client configuration, **291–325**
core NetWare 4.1x VLMs, **295–296**
examples, **340**, **345**
INSTALL.CFG file and, 277
Link Driver options, 310–315
Link Support options, 315–316
Named Pipes parameters, 322–323
NetBIOS parameters, 319–322
NetWare DOS Requester option, 295–297
NetWare DOS Requester parameters and settings, 297–310
non-core NetWare 4.1x VLMs, **296–297**
Protocol IPX option, 316–318
Protocol ODINSUP option, 323–324
standard options for typical clients, **291–294**
TBMI2 options, 324–325
NetWare DOS Requester and
examples, 339, 343
NetWare DOS Requester option in NET.CFG file, 295–297
NetWare DOS Requester parameter in NET.CFG file, 295–297
parameters and settings in NET.CFG file, 297–310
NetWare/IP protocol on Client32 clients, 1159–1160
NetWare/IP protocol on non-Client32 clients, 1156–1159
network interface card installation and setup, **262–266**
base I/O addresses, 265
DMA channels, 266
drivers, 262
examples, 339–340, 343–344
IRQ settings, 264
memory addresses, 265
non-Client32 clients, **276–291, 805–807**. *See also* Client32 clients
attaching to networks for the first time, 290–291
completing the installation, 289–290, *289*, *290*
configuring non-Client32 clients with NCUPDATE, **805–807, 1358**
editing INSTALL.CFG file, 277–278
examples, **340, 344–345**
installing from CD-ROMs, 279–280, 281–282
installing from floppy disks, 280–282
installing from servers, 278–279, 281
loading ODI LAN drivers, 286–288, *286*, *287*, *288*, *289*
MAKEDISK.BAT program and, 280–281
running INSTALL.EXE program, **282–290**, *283*
Target Service Agent (TSA) configuration for Storage Management Services (SMS), *285*, *285*

Windows 3.1x configuration, 284–285, *284*
workstation language setting, 276–277
required files for non-Client32 clients, **266–276**
  child and multiplexor VLMs, 275–276
  examples, **340**, **344**
  IPXODI.COM program, 266–267, 273–274
  LAN drivers, 266–267, 268–273
  LSL.COM (Link Support Layer) program, 266–267, 268, **1425**
  NetWare DOS Requester (VLM.EXE), 266, 274–276
  ODI (Open Data-link Interface) and, 267, *267*
setting up for NetWare IPX/IP Gateway, 1175–1176, *1176*
Windows 95 clients, **1067–1074**, **1303–1305**, **1315–1317**, **1341–1343**
  examples, **1079**, **1083**
  installing Client32 clients, **334–338**, *336*, *337*
  logging in from Network Neighborhood, 1071–1072, *1072*
  mapping drives from Windows 95, 1072–1074, *1073*
  printing and, 1068, 1074
  protecting against problems, **1303–1305**
  sending messages within Network Neighborhood, 1070–1071, *1070*
  troubleshooting, **1315–1317**
  upgrading to, **1341–1343**
  viewing connection information, 1068–1069, *1069*
PCI (Peripheral Component Interconnect) bus, 1355
PCOMP Link Driver parameter in NET.CFG file, 314
PCONSOLE program, **1427**. *See also* printing
  printing management, *606*, **605–637**, **656–657**, **660–661**
    AppleTalk printer configuration, 633, 635
    Bindery mode, 607
    examples, **656–657**, **660–661**
    parallel printer configuration, 632–633, *633*
    print job management, 620–623, *620*, *621*
    Print Queue object configuration, **619–629**
    Print Queue object creation, **607–608**
    print queue operator management, 627–628
    print queue status management, 624–625, *624*
    print queue user management, 626–627, *627*
    print server audit log viewing or configuration, 618, *619*
    Print Server configuration, **610–618**, *610*, *611*
    print server management for print queues, 628–629
    Print Server object creation, **609–610**, *610*
    Print Server object description changes, 616, *617*
    Print Server object password setup, 616–617
    print server operator management, 615–616
    print server status viewing or change, 613–614, *613*
    print server user and group management, 614, *615*
    Printer object addition, deletion, or renaming, 611–612, *612*
    Printer object configuration, **629–637**, *630*
    Printer object creation, **608–609**
    printer problem notification setup, 637
    printer status configuration, 630–632, *631*
    printer type detail settings, 632–635, *633*
    Quick Setup feature, 606
    serial printer configuration, 632–634
    Unix printer configuration, 633, 634
    viewing print queue system information, 626
    viewing print servers attached to print queues, 625
  Quick Setup feature, **538–542**, 606, **655–656**, **660–661**
    defining print objects, **539–540**, *540*
    examples, **655–656**, **660–661**
    printing management, 606
    saving the setup, 541–542, *542*
    viewing default settings, 540–541
peer-to-peer networks, 1321
Pentium processors, 1355
PEP (Packet Exchange Protocol), 36
percent sign (%), in login script identifier variables, 496–497
PerfectOffice guidelines, **968–971**, *969*
Performance Monitor (PMMon), **1233–1238**. *See also* NetWare 4.1x Server for OS/2
  managing memory allocation, 1235–1236, *1235*
  performance optimization, 1236–1237, *1236*
  setting NET.CFG parameters, 1237–1238
performing audits with AUDITCON, 723–725, *724*
Peripheral Component Interconnect (PCI) bus, 1355
Peter Norton's Guide to Unix (Norton and Hahn), 1130
physical design phase for NDS trees, 225–226, 232, *233*, *234*

physical security for servers. *See also* security
    examples, 50, 53
pilot systems, for NetWare Directory Services, 224–225
planning. *See also* designing NDS trees
    networks, **741–750**
        examples, **924**, **927**
        planning for the future, 743–744
        selling the plan to users, 749–750
        selling the plan to your boss, 746–749
    performance and, **1327–1328**
    security, **665–668**, **730**, **734**
PMMon. *See* Performance Monitor
PNW.VLM file, 296
PORT Link Driver parameter in NET.CFG file, 314
ports, **1427**
    Drives/Ports page in NetWare Application Launcher, 975–976, *975*
    I/O port addresses for network interface cards, 71, 265
postal address information
    in NETADMIN, 411–412, *412*
    in NetWare Administrator, 373, *374*
pound sign (#)
    # login script command, 492
    in AUTOEXEC.NCF file, 1301
power conditioning and protection, 27–28, *28*, **1427**
PREFERRED SERVER parameter in NET.CFG, 304
PREFERRED TREE parameter in NET.CFG, 304
PREFERRED WORKGROUP parameter in NET.CFG, 305
preventing login script changes by users, 692–693, *693*
Primary time servers, **145**, **146–147**, **1428**
PRINT BUFFER SIZE parameter in NET.CFG, 305
print devices, **1428**. *See also* Printer objects
    dot-matrix printers, 531–532, *531*
    laser printers, 532
    in NetWare Administrator
        exporting, 598–599, *599*
        importing or deleting, 596–597, *598*
    in PRINTDEF, **638–645**, **657**, **661**
        creating and changing, 639
        editing, 639–640, *640*
        examples, **657**, **661**
        exporting, 642–643, *643*
        importing, 641–642, *642*
        print mode definition, 640–641, *641*

PRINT HEADER parameter in NET.CFG, 305
print job configuration, **1428**. *See also* Print Queue objects
    in NetWare Administrator, 351, 352, 370–373, *371*, 602–605, *603*
    in PCONSOLE, 620–623, *620*, *621*
    in PRINTCON, **645–648**, **657**, **661**
        creating or editing, 645–648, *646*
        examples, **657**, **661**
        selecting default configuration, 648
print mode definition, in NetWare Administrator, 600–601, *601*
Print Queue objects, **218**. *See also* printing
    in NetWare Administrator, **545–548**, **552–564**
        adding or deleting operators, 554–557, *557*
        adding or deleting users, 558–560, *559*
        assigning print queues, 554–555, *555*
        configuring, 552–564
        creating, **545–548**, *546*, *547*
        identification and operator attributes, 552–554, *553*
        tying printers to print queues, 567, *568*
        viewing or changing print queue job lists, 560–564, *561*, *562*
    in PCONSOLE, **607–608**, **619–629**
        adding or deleting print queue operators, 627–628
        adding or deleting print queue users, 626–627, *627*
        configuring, **619–629**
        creating, **607–608**
        creating in Quick Setup feature, 539–540, *540*
        print job viewing and changes, 620–623, *620*, *621*
        viewing and changing print queue status, 624–625, *624*
        viewing print queue system information, 626
        viewing print servers attached to print queues, 625
    print queue operators, **1428**
        ADMIN User object and, 556–557, *557*
        managing in NetWare Administrator, 552–557, *553*, *557*
        managing in PCONSOLE, 627–628
Print Server objects, **217**, **1429**. *See also* printing
    in NetWare Administrator, **550–552**, **578–589**
        adding or deleting print server operators, 585–586, *586*

adding or deleting users and groups, 583–585, *584*
audit log management, 586–589, *588*
changing assignments, 581–583, *582*
configuring, **578–589**
creating, **550–552**, *551*
identification information, 579–581, *580*
in PCONSOLE, **609–618**
  adding or deleting print server operators, 615–616
  adding or deleting print server users and groups, 614, *615*
  adding or deleting print servers for print queues, 628–629
  changing Print Server object description, 616, *617*
  configuring, **610–618**, *610*, *611*
  creating, **609–610**, *610*
  creating or changing passwords, 616–617
  creating in Quick Setup feature, 539–540, *540*
  viewing or changing print server status, 613–614, *613*
  viewing or configuring audit logs, 618, *619*
  viewing print servers attached to print queues, 625
print server operators, **1429**
  managing in NetWare Administrator, 585–586, *586*
  managing in PCONSOLE, 615–616
  viewing printer status at print server console with RCONSOLE, 649–650, *649*
PRINT TAIL parameter in NET.CFG, 305
PRINT.VLM file, 296
PRINTCON program, 645–648, 657, 661. *See also* printing
  creating and editing print job configurations, 645–648, *646*
  examples, **657**, **661**
  selecting default print job configuration, 648
PRINTDEF program, 638–645, 657, 661. *See also* printing
  creating and modifying print devices, 639
  creating and modifying printer forms, 644–645, *644*
  editing print devices, 639–640, *640*
  examples, **657**, **661**
  exporting print devices, 642–643, *643*
  importing print devices, 641–642, *642*

print mode definition, 640–641, *641*
printer forms, 1429
  in NetWare Administrator, 594–596, *595*
  in PRINTDEF, 644–645, *644*
Printer objects, 217, 1429. *See also* print devices; printing
  in NetWare Administrator, **548–549**, **564–578**
    AIO printer settings, 570, 573–574
    AppleTalk printer settings, 570, 573
    changing configurations, 568–574, *569*, *572*
    configuring, **564–578**
    creating, **548–549**, *550*
    Feature property descriptions, 576, *577*
    identification information, 565–566, *566*
    parallel printer settings, 571–572, *572*
    printer problem notification setup, 574–576, *575*
    See Also page, 577–578, *578*
    serial printer settings, 570, *573*
    tying to print queues, 567, *568*
    Unix printer settings, 570, 573
    viewing and changing printer status, 591–594, *592*
  in NetWare User Tools
    changing LPT printer settings, **1009–1012**, *1010*
    connecting to network printers, **1006–1008**, *1009*
  NPTWIN95 program, **650–652**, *651*, 658, 662, 1078, 1082
  in PCONSOLE, **608–609**, **629–637**
    adding, deleting, or renaming, 611–612, *612*
    AIO printer settings, 633, 635
    AppleTalk printer settings, 633, 635
    configuring, **629–637**, *630*
    creating, **608–609**
    creating in Quick Setup feature, 539–540, *540*
    parallel printer settings, 632–633, *633*
    printer problem notification setup, 637
    printer status configuration, 630–632, *631*
    printer type detail settings, 632–635, *633*
    serial printer settings, 632–634
    Unix printer settings, 633, 634
  remote printer setup with NPRINTER program, 535, 536, **1042–1044**, 1077–1078, 1082
printers. *See* print devices; Printer objects

printing, 530–662. *See also* PCONSOLE program; PRINTCON program; PRINTDEF program
   decentralizing management of, **548**
   Macintosh printing
      AppleTalk printer settings in NetWare Administrator, 570, 573
      AppleTalk printer settings in PCONSOLE, 633, 635
      configuring printing services, 1109–1113, *1110*
      history of, 1111
   MegaCorp example, **659–662**
   migrating print services, **1339–1340**
   MiniCo example, **655–658**
   NDPS (NetWare Distributed Print Services), **652–653**
   NETUSER controls, **1026–1027**, *1027*
   NetWare Administrator printing management, **542–605, 656, 660**
      AIO printer settings, 570, 573–574
      AppleTalk printer settings, 570, 573
      examples, **656, 660**
      parallel printer settings, 571–572, *572*
      print device exporting, 598–599, *599*
      print device importing or deleting, 596–597, *598*
      print job configuration management, 602–605, *603*
      print mode definition, 600–601, *601*
      print queue assignments, 554–555, *555*
      print queue job list management, 560–564, *561*, *562*
      Print Queue object configuration, **552–564**
      Print Queue object creation, **545–548**, *546*, *547*
      Print Queue object identification and operator attributes, 552–554, *553*
      print queue operator management, 554–557, *557*
      print queue user list management, 558–560, *559*
      Print Server audit log management, 586–589, *588*
      Print Server object assignment changes, 581–583, *582*
      Print Server object configuration, **578–589**
      Print Server object creation, **550–552**, *551*
      Print Server object identification information, 579–581, *580*
      Print Server object user and group management, 583–585, *584*
      print server operator management, 585–586, *586*
      printer Feature property descriptions, 576, *577*
      printer forms management, 594–596, *595*
      Printer object configuration, **564–578**
      Printer object configuration modification, 568–574, *569*, *572*
      Printer object creation, **548–549**, *550*
      Printer object identification information, 565–566, *566*
      Printer object See Also page, 577–578, *578*
      Printer object tie-in with print queues, 567, *568*
      printer problem notification setup, 574–576, *575*
      printer status viewing and modification, 591–594, *592*
      printing system layout diagram, 589–591, *590*
      Quick Setup feature, 543–544, *544*
      serial printer settings, 570, 573
      Unix printer settings, 570, 573
   in NetWare NFS Services, **1168**, *1168*
   in NetWare versus Unix, **1131–1132**
   NetWare User Tools printing management
      changing LPT printer settings, 1009–1012, *1010*
      configuring Windows 3.1x for fast network printing, 1012–1014, *1013*
      connecting to network printers, 1006–1008, *1007*
      connecting to network printers permanently, 1008–1009, *1009*
   NPRINTER program, 535, 536, **1042–1044**, 1077–1078, 1082
   NPTWIN95 program, **650–652**, *651*, 658, 662, 1078, 1082
   printing system relationships, **537–538**, 655, 659
   RCONSOLE print server management, 69–70, **649–650**, *649*, 657–658, 662
   troubleshooting workstation problems, **1317–1318**
   upgrading NetWare 3.1x Print Services, **161–162**
   Windows 95 clients and, 1068, 1074
privileges. *See* rights; security; trustees
Processor Utilization screen, MONITOR program, 819–821, *820*
processors
   NetWare requirements, 60–61
   Pentium 4 MB page feature, 1355

Profile login scripts, 486–487, 488–489, 498, 1429.
    See also login scripts
    creating or editing with NETADMIN, 509, *510*
    creating or editing with NetWare Administrator, 506–507
    editing in NETADMIN, 421
    example, 502–503, *502*
Profile objects, 219. *See also* objects
    and managing users and resources, 445–446
PROFS (Professional Office System) e-mail system, 368, 459, 473
programs. *See* applications
properties, 204, *205*, 206, **1430.** *See also* objects
    Access Control List (ACL) object property, 686–687, 751, **1398, 1433**
    Feature property for Printer objects, 576, *577*
    of User objects, 351–352
property rights, 1430, 1433. *See also* rights; security; trustees
    All Property Rights trustee assignment, 751
    IRFs (Inherited Rights Filters) and, 687–688
    managing with NETADMIN, **713–714,** *715*
    managing with NetWare Administrator, **702–708**
    versus object rights, 684–686
    revoking, 692–693, *693*
    [Root] object default property rights, 691, 694, *694*
    supervisory functions and, 751
    User object trustee default property rights, 691, 694, *694*
protecting
    applications and data files, **948–957, 1404**
    changing directory and file ownership, 951–953, *953*
    examples, **982, 985–986**
    setting file attributes with FLAG command, 679–683, *682*, 949–951, *951*, 952, **1046–1047,** *1046*, 1078, 1082, **1410**
    viewing and changing file rights with RIGHTS command, **953–957,** *955*, *956*, **1045,** *1046*, 1078, 1082
    workstations against Windows problems, 1303–1305
Protocol IPX options in NET.CFG file, 316–318
PROTOCOL Link Driver parameter in NET.CFG file, 314
Protocol ODINSUP option, in NET.CFG file, 323–324

protocols, 34–44. *See also* INETCFG program; TCP/IP protocol
    adding during installation, **102–103,** *102*
    AppleTalk protocols, 42–43, 44, **1089–1092, 1399**
        AppleTalk Filing Protocol (AFP), 42–43, 44, 1092
        binding AppleTalk to network interface cards, 1105–1106, *1105*
        configuring AppleTalk protocol stack, 1100–1106
        EtherTalk protocol, 42, 1090
        IPX/SPX protocol and, 42–43
        LocalTalk protocol, 42, 1091
        TokenTalk protocol, 42, 1091
    Clearinghouse protocol, 36
    configuring with INETCFG, **171–174,** *172*, *174*
    FTP (File Transfer Protocol), **1410**
        FTP sites for NetWare Help, 1058
        in NetWare NFS Services, 1168–1169
    IDP (Internet Datagram Protocol), 35
    IPX/SPX. *See also* NetWare IPX/IP Gateway; NetWare/IP protocol
        binding IPX protocol to network interface cards, 102–103
        IPTUNNEL program and, 1152–1153, *1153*
        IPX configuration with INETCFG program, 890–893, *891*
        IPX defined, **1413**
        IPX network numbering, 93, **1414, 1422**
        Macintosh computers and, 42–43
        NetWare Core Protocol (NCP) and, 36–39, *38*
        SPX defined, **1436**
        viewing IPX statistics with IPXCON, 896–897, *897*
    MegaCorp example, **54**
    MiniCo example, **51**
    NCP (NetWare Core Protocol), **1419**
        IPX/SPX protocol and, 36–39, *38*
        NCP SET commands, 844, **1383–1385**
        NetWare (NCP) Server objects, **217,** 790–792, *791*, **1421**
    NDPS (NetWare Distributed Print Services), 652–653
    NetWare/IP protocol, **1153–1164, 1362, 1420**
        on Client32 clients, 1159–1160
        installing on servers, 1160–1164, *1163*
        on non-Client32 clients, 1156–1159, *1157*, *1158*

NLSP (NetWare Link Services Protocol), **1276–1279**, 1423
OSI (Open Systems Interconnection) model and, 40, *42*
PEP (Packet Exchange Protocol), 36
RIP (Routing Information Protocol), **36, 1434**
   RIP tracking, 886–887, *886*
RPC (Remote Procedure Call), 36
SAP (Service Advertising Protocol), **1437**
   SAP tracking, 886–887, *886*
SMTP (Simple Mail Transfer Protocol), 368, 459, 473
SNMP (Simple Network Management Protocol), **1279–1283**
   history of, 1280
   NET.CFG options for NetWare clients, 1281–1283
SPP (Sequenced Packet Protocol), 36
TFTP (Trivial File Transfer Protocol), 1169, 1442
XNS (Xerox Network Services), 35–36
PUBLIC directory, 24–25
[Public] object rights, 690–691
[Public] trustees, 671, 751, **1430**
PUPGRADE.NLM, 1339–1340
Purge (P) directory attribute, 679, **1430**
Purge (P) file attribute, 681, **1430**
purging deleted files, 1056, 1325

Q

question mark (?)
   in Group object names, 450, 468
   in User object login names, 358, 400
Quick Setup feature
   in NetWare Administrator, 543–544
   in PCONSOLE, **538–542**, 606, 655–656, 660–661
      defining print objects, 539–540, *540*
      examples, 655–656, 660–661
      printing management, 606
      saving the setup, 541–542, *542*
      viewing default settings, 540–541
quitting
   DSMERGE, 881–882
   NETADMIN, 396

R

R (Read) directory right, 671, **1431**
R (Read) file right, 674, 955, **1431**
R (Read) property right, 686, **1431**
R (Rename) object right, 685, **1432**

RAID disk systems, 65–66, *1320*, 1321
RAM, **1430**. *See also* memory
   NetWare requirements, 62–63
R-CGI (Remote Common Gateway Interface), 1184
RCONSOLE program, 649–650, 807–813, **1431**. *See also* server management
   Available Options menu, 811–813, *811*
   configuring from client, 809–811, *810*
   configuring with INETCFG, 893–894, *894*
   configuring REMOTE at server, 808–809
   examples, **926, 929**
   viewing printer status at print server console, 649–650, *649*, 657–658, 662
READ ONLY COMPATIBILITY parameter in NET.CFG, 306
Read Only (Ro) file attribute, 681, **1431**
Read (R) directory right, 671, **1431**
Read (R) file right, 674, 955, **1431**
Read (R) property right, 686, **1431**
Read Write (Rw) file attribute, 681
Read/Write replicas, 777, **1432**
reading DynaText online documentation from CD-ROM drives, 1062–1063, *1062*
read-only memory (ROM) addresses, 71–72
Read-Only replicas, 777, **1432**
receiving messages
   with NETUSER, 1028–1030, *1029*
   with NetWare User Tools, 1019
recommended reading, **1392–1396**
   administrator's guides, 1392–1393
   general, 1392
   Internet information, 1395–1396
   internetworking guides, 1393–1394
   networking reference books, 1395
   OS/2 information, 1394
   Windows 95 information, 1394
recovering deleted files with FILER, 1054–1055, *1056*, **1434**
REDIR.VLM file, 296
Reference time servers, 146, **1431**
registration disk, creating, 159–161, *161*
related information tracking
   for Group objects
      in NETADMIN, 474
      in NetWare Administrator, 465–466, *465*
   for User objects
      in NETADMIN, 413, *414*
      in NetWare Administrator, 376, *377*

relative distinguished names, 240
REM file right, 955
Remote Common Gateway Interface (R-CGI), 1184
remote printer setup with NPRINTER program, 535, 536, **1042–1044**, *1077–1078*, *1082*
Remote Procedure Call (RPC) protocol, 36
remote server access. *See* INETCFG program
removing. *See* deleting
Rename Inhibit (Ri) directory attribute, 679, **1432**
Rename Inhibit (Ri) file attribute, 681, **1432**
Rename (R) object right, 685, **1432**
renaming. *See also* naming
    leaf objects in NetWare Administrator, 772–773, 773
    NDS trees with DSMERGE, 880–881, *881*
    objects in NETADMIN, 913–915
Repair Local Database Options screen, DSREPAIR program, 859–860, *860*
repairing NetWare Directory Services. *See* DSREPAIR
Replica Ring Options submenu, DSREPAIR program, 865–866
replicas, 777, **1432**. *See also* partitions; volumes
    DSREPAIR options for, 863–866, *863*
    management guidelines, **778**
    and recovery from NDS database corruption, 779–780
    replica servers in TCP/IP protocol, 1139
    replica synchronization, **1440**
    types of, 777
    viewing or modifying
        in NDS Manager, 786–789, *787*, *788*
        with PARTMGR, **918–919**, *918*
Report Synchronization Status option, DSREPAIR program, 855
Resource Utilization option, MONITOR program, 822–825, *824*
RESPONDER parameter in NET.CFG, 306
revoking property rights, 692–693, *693*
RFC 1244, 666–668
Ri (Rename Inhibit) directory attribute, 679, **1432**
Ri (Rename Inhibit) file attribute, 681, **1432**
rights, **1433**. *See also* file system security; security; trustees
    for application directories, **945–947**
        examples, **982**, 985
        managing rights in application and data directories, 946
        setting, 946–947, *948*

directory rights, **1405**, **1433**
    changing directory ownership, 951–953, *953*
    for Group objects in NETADMIN, 475–477, *476*, *477*
    for Group objects in NetWare Administrator, 460–463, *462*
    managing directory trustees with FILER, 709–711, *711*
    managing with NetWare Administrator, 693–702, *694*
    supervisory functions and, 750
    for User Objects in NETADMIN, 434–437, *436*
    for User Objects in NetWare Administrator, 391–395, *393*, *394*
effective rights, **1408–1409**
    in NetWare Administrator, 672
file rights, **1405**, **1410**, **1433**
    changing file ownership, 951–953, *953*
    for Group objects in NETADMIN, 475–477, *476*, *477*
    for Group objects in NetWare Administrator, 460–463, *462*
    managing with NetWare Administrator, 693–702, *694*
    supervisory functions and, 750
    for User Objects in NETADMIN, 434–437, *436*
    for User Objects in NetWare Administrator, 391–395, *393*, *394*
    viewing and changing with RIGHTS command, 953–957, *955*, *956*, **1045**, *1046*, *1078*, *1082*
Inherited Rights Filters (IRFs), 671, 673, **674–677**, *675*, *676*, **1413**
    managing with FILER, 712–713, *713*
    object and property rights and, 687–688
migrating trustee rights, 1339
object rights, **1424**, **1433**
    Group object rights in NETADMIN, **475–477**, *476*, *477*
    Group object rights in NetWare Administrator, **460–463**, *462*
    IRFs (Inherited Rights Filters) and, 687–688
    managing with NETADMIN, **713–714**, *715*
    managing with NetWare Administrator, **702–708**
    versus property rights, **684–686**
    [Public] object rights, 690–691
    [Root] object default property rights, 691, **694**, *694*
    supervisory functions and, 750

property rights, **1430**, **1433**
All Property Rights trustee assignment, 751
IRFs (Inherited Rights Filters) and, 687–688
managing with NETADMIN, **713–714**, *715*
managing with NetWare Administrator, **702–708**
versus object rights, **684–686**
revoking, 692–693, *693*
[Root] object default property rights, 691, 694, *694*
supervisory functions and, 751
User object trustee default property rights, 691, 694, *694*
stacking and subtracting rights, **676**, *676*
supervisory functions and, **750–753**
examples, **924**, **927–928**
workgroup managers and, 752–753
viewing with NETUSER, 1032
viewing with NetWare User Tools, 1004–1005, *1004*
RIGHTS command
changing file rights, 953–957, *955*, *956*
viewing rights, **1045**, *1046*, 1078, 1082
Ring In (RI) and Ring Out (RO) connections, 9, *9*
RIP (Routing Information Protocol), 36, **1434**
RIP tracking, 886–887, *886*
Ritchie, Dennis, 1125
Ro (Read Only) file attribute, 681, **1431**
ROM (read-only memory) addresses, 71–72
root domains, in TCP/IP protocol, 1137–1138
[Root] object, 205, 207–214, **1434**. *See also* NetWare Directory Services; objects
ADMIN user and, 208
container objects and, 208–209, *209*
container rules for objects, 213–214, *214*
Country (C) container objects, 210, 222, **1403**
default property rights, 691, 694, *694*
examples, **252–253**, **256**
explaining, 993–994, *993*
leaf objects and, 215, *215*
Organization (O) container objects, 211–212, 445, **1425**
Organization Unit (OU) container objects, 212–213, 445, **1425–1426**
trustees of, 208
ROOTs, mapping fake, **959**, **1409**
routers, 35, **1434**
Routing Information Protocol (RIP), 36, **1434**
RIP tracking, 886–887, *886*

RPC (Remote Procedure Call) protocol, 36
RSA.VLM file, 296
running
FirstMail program, 1268, *1269*
INSTALL.EXE program for PC clients, 282–290, *283*
menu scripts, 511–512
NetWare Administrator from OS/2 workstations, **1215–1217**, *1217*
Rw (Read Write) file attribute, 681

S

S (Shareable) file attribute, 681, **1437**
S (Supervisor) directory right, 671, **1440**
S (Supervisor) file right, 674, *955*, **1440**
S (Supervisor) object right, 685, **1440**
S (Supervisor) property right, 686, **1440**
SALVAGE program, 1054
salvaging deleted files with FILER, 1054–1055, *1056*, **1434**
SAP (Service Advertising Protocol), **1437**
SAP tracking, 886–887, *886*
SAPS Link Driver parameter in NET.CFG file, 315
saving
PCONSOLE Quick Setup, 541–542, *542*
volume changes during installation, 115
SBACKUP program, 1272, 1273–1274, **1435**
scheduling groups with GroupWise software, 966–968, *967*, *968*
Scheduling Information screen, MONITOR program, 837–839, *838*
scripts. *See* login scripts; menu scripts
Scripts page, in NetWare Application Launcher, 976–977
SCSI interfaces, **1435**
disk interfaces and drives, 64–65
troubleshooting SCSI conflicts, 68–69, 97–98
SEARCH MODE parameter in NET.CFG, 306, 308–309
searching. *See* finding
searching
DynaText online documentation, 1062–1064, *1064*
for files and directories with FILER, 1052–1053
for objects with NETADMIN, 915–916, *916*
for objects with NetWare Administrator, 773–776, *775*

Secondary time servers, 145, 147, 1435
security, 376–395, 413–437, 664–738, 1435. *See also* rights; trustees
    ADMIN User object, **131**
        and assistant network administrators, 456–457
        creating User objects, 351–352
        versus NetWare 3.x SUPERVISOR, 669, 730–731, 735
        NetWare Administrator security management and, 690
        NetWare Directory Services (NDS) security and, 683
        print queue operator assignment, 556–557, *557*
        [Root] object and, 208
        selecting name and password for, 140
        and User object management, 444–445
        workgroup administrators and, **752–753**
    AUDITCON program, **719–726, 1399–1400**
        examples, **733**, **738**
        performing audits, 723–725, *724*
        setting auditor passwords, 722–723
        starting, 720–721, *722*
        viewing audit reports, 725–726, *726*
    C2 level security rating, **1360**
    CRCs (cyclical redundancy checks), 718
    DOS security utilities, **709–714**
        examples, **732**, **737**
        managing directory or file trustees with FILER, 709–711, *711*
        managing IRFs (Inherited Rights Filters) with FILER, 712–713, *713*
        managing property and object rights with NETADMIN, 713–714, *715*
    file attributes and, **677–683, 1399**
        directory attributes, 678–679
        examples, **731**, **736**
        file attributes, 679–683
        migrating, **1338**
        NDS trees and, 206
        setting with FLAG command, 679–683, *682*, 949–951, *951*, *952*, **1046–1047**, *1046*, 1078, 1082, **1410**
    file system security, **670–677**. *See also* rights
        directory rights for users and groups, 671–673, *673*
        examples, **731**, **735**
        file rights for users and groups, 674
        guidelines for, 677
        hidden protection, 670
        inheritance, 670–671, 687, *688*
        IRFs (Inherited Rights Filters) and, 671, 673, 674–677, *675*, *676*, **1413**
        [Public] trustees, 671
        stacking and subtracting rights, 676, *676*
        trustee assignments, 670
    login security guidelines, **692–693**, *693*, **716**
    management and, **728–729**
    MegaCorp example, **734–738**
    MiniCo example, **730–733**
    NetWare 4.11 security improvements, **726–727**
    NetWare Administrator security management, **690–708**
        ADMIN User object and, 690
        Effective Rights listings, 671
        examples, **732**, **736–737**
        granting trustee rights between multiple objects, 705–708, *706*, *707*, *708*
        granting trustee rights between objects with drag-and-drop, 702–705, *704*
        granting trustee rights to groups or users, 699–702, *700*, *701*
        granting trustee rights to volumes or directories, 696–699, *697*, *698*
        managing directory and file rights, **693–702**, *694*
        managing object or property rights, **702–708**
        opening Browser windows, 695, 756–757, *757*
        preventing login script changes by users, 692–693, *693*
        [Public] object rights, 690–691
        revoking property rights, 692–693, *693*
        [Root] object default property rights, 691, 694, *694*
        User object trustee default property rights, 691, 694, *694*
    NetWare Directory Services (NDS) security, **683–690**. *See also* ADMIN User object
        Access Control List (ACL) object property, 686–687, 751, **1398, 1433**
        examples, **732**, **736**
        guidelines for, 688–690
        IRFs (Inherited Rights Filters) and object and property rights, 687–688
        object rights versus property rights, 684–686
        rights inheritance, 687, *688*
    NetWare IPX/IP Gateway and, **1176–1177**, 1183

security—server management

passwords, **1427**
    in AUDITCON, 722–723
    changing with NETUSER, 1032, *1033*
    migrating, **1337–1338**
    restricting in NETADMIN, 423–425, *424*
    restricting in NetWare Administrator, 381–384, *382*
    security guidelines, **715–716**
    selecting ADMIN password, 140, 147, *148*
physical security for servers, **26–27**, 50, 53
planning, **665–668**, 730, 734
security equivalence, **1436**
    Security Equivalence Synchronization option in DSREPAIR program, 866–867, *867*
    setting up in NETADMIN program, 351, 352, 419–421, *420*
    setting up in NetWare Administrator, 351, 352, 386, *387*
Site Security Handbook, 666–668
for User Objects in NETADMIN, **413–437**
    account balance tracking, 431, *432*
    group membership setup, 351, 352, 418, *419*
    intruder lockout setup, 429–430, *430*
    login restriction setup, 421–423, *422*
    login scripts, 351, 352, 415–416, *417*
    login time restriction setup, 426–427, *427*
    network address restrictions, 427–428, *429*
    password restrictions, 423–425, *424*
    Profile script editing, 421
    rights to files and directories setup, 434–437, *436*
    security equivalence setup, 351, 352, 419–421, *420*
    volume space restriction setup, 432–433, *434*
for User Objects in NetWare Administrator, **376–395**
    account balance tracking, 374–376, *375*
    group membership setup, 351, 352, 384–385, *385*
    intruder lockout setup, 391, *393*
    login restriction setup, 379–381, *380*
    login scripts, 377–379, *378*
    login time restriction setup, 387–389, *388*
    network address restrictions, 389–390, *390*
    password restrictions, 381–384, *382*
    rights to files and directories setup, 391–395, *393, 394*
    security equivalence setup, 351, 352, 386, *387*
virus protection, 678, **717–719**, 733, 737

SECURITY.VLM file, 296
See Also page
    for Group objects
        in NETADMIN, 474
        in NetWare Administrator, 465–466, *465*
    for User objects
        in NETADMIN, 413, *414*
        in NetWare Administrator, 376, *377*
selecting
    ADMIN name and password, 140, 147, *148*
    current directory in FILER, 1053
    NDS trees when installing servers into existing networks, 142–144, *143*
    optional files to install, 118–119, *119, 120*
    time zone setting, 136, *136*
sending messages
    with NETUSER, 1028–1030, *1029*
    with NetWare User Tools, 1017–1019, *1018*
    in Windows 95 clients, 1070–1071, *1070*
separating applications from data files, 936–939, *937, 939*
Sequenced Packet Protocol (SPP), 36
serial printer settings
    in NetWare Administrator, 570, *573*
    in PCONSOLE, 632–634
server management, **807–905**
    console commands, 883–888
        DISPLAY NETWORKS, 883–884, *883*
        DISPLAY SERVERS, 884, *884*
        DOWN, 884
        EXIT, 884–885
        MODULES, 885, *885*
        TRACK ON, 886–887, *886*
        VERSION, 887, *887*
        VOLUMES, 887–888, *888*
    DSMERGE program, **873–882**
        Check Servers In This Tree option, 876, *877*
        Check Time Synchronization option, 877–878, *878*
        exiting and cleaning up, 881–882
        Merge Two Trees option, 879–880, *879*
        Rename This Tree option, 880–881, *881*
    DSREPAIR program, **779–780, 853–873**, 1408
        Advanced Options menu and submenus, 855, 857–869
        Create a Database Dump File option, 869, *870*
        Global Schema Options screen, 867–868, *868*
        Local ID to Remote ID List screen, 862, *863*

Log File/Login Configuration Options screen, 858–859, *859*
in NDS Manager, 870–873, *871*, *872*
Repair Local Database Options screen, 859–860, *860*
repairing NDS corruption, **779–780**
Replica and Partitions Operations options, 863–866, *863*
Replica Ring Options submenu, 865–866
Security Equivalence Synchronization option, 866–867, *867*
Servers found in this Directory Services Database screen, 861–862, *861*
Servers That Have Replicas of This Partition screen, 865
Unattended Full Repair option, 854, 856–857, *857*
View Repair Log File option, 855, 867–868, *869*
DSTRACE program, **851–853**, *852*, 926, 929
examples, **926**, **929–930**
installing additional server licenses, **882–883**
MONITOR program, **813–839**, **1417**
  Active Connections screen, 825–828, *826*
  Allocated Memory for All Modules screen, 821–822, *821*
  Available LAN Drivers screen, 831–832, *832*
  Cache Utilization Statistics screen, 817–819, *817*
  Connection Information screen, 825–828, *826*, *827*
  Disk Information screen, 828–831, *829*
  File Open/Lock Activity option, 835–836, *837*
  General Information screen, 814–816, *814*
  LAN/WAN Information option, 831–832, *832*
  Lock File Server Console option, 834–835, *835*
  Memory Utilization option, 821–822, *821*
  Processor Utilization screen, 819–821, *820*
  Resource Utilization option, 822–825, *824*
  Scheduling Information screen, 837–839, *838*
  Server Memory Statistics screen, 822–825, *824*
  server self-tuning and, 1271, 1356
  System Module Information screen, 833–834, *833*
  tracking server performance, **1295–1297**
  troubleshooting and, *1296*
NetSync program, **897–905**, 1357, **1419**
  installing on NetWare 3.1x servers, 902–904, *903*
  installing on NetWare 4.1x servers, 899–902, *900*
  maintaining NetSync objects, 905, *906*
RCONSOLE program, 69–70, **649–650**, **807–813**, **1431**
  Available Options menu, 811–813, *811*
  configuring from client, 809–811, *810*
  configuring with INETCFG, 893–894, *894*
  configuring REMOTE at server, 808–809
  viewing printer status at print server console, **649–650**, *649*, 657–658, 662
SERVMAN program, **844–850**, **939–943**, **1437**
  copying server parameters, **1300–1301**, *1301*
  Directory Caching Parameters screen, 940–943, *941*
  improving disk-read performance, 942–943
  improving disk-write performance, 939–941
  installing Bindery Services, 246–247, *247*
  Network Information screen, 850, *851*
  opening screen, 844–846, *845*
  Server Parameters screen, 846–848, *848*
  SET commands and, 95, 839–841, 1356
  Storage Objects information screen, 848–849, *849*
  Volume Information screen, 849–850, *850*
SET commands, **839–844**, **1366–1389**
  in AUTOEXEC.NCF file, 95, 153, 154, *154*, 1356
  communication parameters, 841, 1366–1368
  directory caching parameters, 842, 940–943, *941*, 1368–1369, 1402
  directory services parameters, 844, 1370–1372
  disk parameters, 843, 1372–1373
  error handling parameters, 844, 1373–1374
  file caching parameters, 841, 1374–1375, 1402
  file system parameters, 842, 1375–1378
  lock parameters, 842–843, 1379
  memory parameters, 841, 1379–1380
  miscellaneous parameters, 844, 1381–1383
  NCP (NetWare Core Protocol) parameters, 844, 1383–1385
  options during NetWare installation, 95
  SERVMAN and, 95, 839–841, 1356
  SET BINDERY CONTEXT= statement, 246
  SET NWLANGUAGE= statement, 177, 276–277

server management—servers

in STARTUP.NCF, 95
in STARTUP.NCF file, 151–152
time parameters, 843, 1385–1388
transaction tracking parameters, 843, 1388–1389
Server Memory Statistics screen, MONITOR program, 822–825, *824*
Server Parameters screen, SERVMAN program, 846–848, *848*
servers, 26–31, 1332–1344, 1410, 1421, 1436–1437.
See also NetWare 4.1x for Macintosh; NetWare 4.1x Server for OS/2; NetWare 4.1x SFT III
application server guidelines, **936–944**
    consolidating application licenses, 943–944, *945*
    examples, **981–982, 985**
    improving disk-read performance with SERVMAN, 942–943
    improving disk-write performance with SERVMAN, 939–941
    separating applications from data files, 936–939, *937, 939*
booting
    creating server installation boot disk, 72–75
    from floppy disks, 79–81
    from hard disk drives, 76–78, *76, 77*
connecting OS/2 clients to, **1208–1211**, *1210, 1211*
connecting to with NetWare User Tools, **1014–1017**, *1016*
deleting from NDS, **790–792**, *791*
installing additional server licenses, **882–883**
installing NetWare 4.1x Server for OS/2 from, **1225–1226**
installing NetWare from
    from NetWare volumes, 84–87
    from remote CD-ROM drives, 87–88
    from remote server's network installation area, 81, 84–87
installing NetWare/IP protocol on, **1160–1164**, *1163*
installing non-Client32 client software from, **278–279**, 281
language settings, **175–177**
    changing default server language, 176–177, *177*
    console versus default server language settings, 177
    installing additional server languages, 175–176

memory management techniques, **1270–1271, 1355–1356**
    DOMAIN.NLM utility, 1270–1271
    managing memory allocation with Performance Monitor, 1235–1236, *1235*
    MONITOR Allocated Memory for All Modules screen, 821–822, *821*
    in NetWare 4.1x versus NetWare 3.x, **1355**
    server self-tuning, 1271, 1356
mirrored servers, 1245–1246, *1246*
naming, **92–93**
NetWare 4.1x performance versus NetWare 3.x, 1355
NetWare 4.1x requirements, **58–72**
    CD-ROM drives, 68–69
    CPUs, 60–61
    examples, **123–124, 126–127**
    floppy disk drives, 69
    hard disk drives, 63–66
    IDE disk controllers and drives, 64
    IRQ, DMA, I/O port settings and ROM addresses, 70–72
    monitors, 69–70
    network interface cards (NICs), 66–68, *67*
    RAID disk systems, 65–66
    RAM, 62–63
    SCSI disk interfaces and drives, 64–65
NetWare 4.1x Server for OS/2 requirements, **1222–1223**
NetWare 4.1x SFT III requirements, **1250**
NetWare (NCP) Server objects, **217**, 790–792, *791*, **1421**
physical security, **26–27**, 50, 53
power conditioning and protection, 27–28, *28*, **1427**
server log files, 1249, 1297–1300, *1298, 1299, 1300*
starting automatically at PC startup, **95–96**
superservers, *1320*, 1322
tape backup systems, **28–31**, *30*, **1441**
    login time restrictions and, 387–388
    network address restrictions and, 389–390, 427–428
    time restrictions and, 426
time servers, **144–147**, *145*, **1428, 1431, 1435, 1437**
troubleshooting, **1295–1301, 1318–1325**

and copying server configuration files, 1300–1301, *1301*
disk errors, 1324–1325, *1325*
freeing server memory temporarily, 1323
hardware scale and costs, 1320–1322, *1320*
operating system and RAM problems, 1318–1319, 1322–1323
server availability and, 1319–1320
server log files and, 1297–1300, *1298, 1299, 1300*
and tracking normal server performance, **1295–1301**
workstation cannot connect to server, 1310–1312
upgrading to NetWare 4.1x, **1332–1344**
  migrating data, 1336–1337
  migrating file attributes, 1338
  migrating passwords, 1337–1338
  migrating print services, 1339–1340
  upgrade method options, 1332–1334
  upgrading Bindery information, 1338–1339
  versus upgrading server hardware, **1334–1336**, 1340
viewing server information with NETUSER, **1032**, *1033*
viewing server partitions with NetWare Administrator, **789–790**, *790*
Web servers, **1437**
Servers Known To This Database option, DSREPAIR program, 861–862, *861*
Servers That Have Replicas of This Partition screen, DSREPAIR program, 865
Service Advertising Protocol (SAP), 1437
  SAP tracking, 886–887, *886*
SERVMAN program, 844–850, 939–943, 1437. *See also* server management
  copying server parameters, **1300–1301**, *1301*
  Directory Caching Parameters screen, 940–943, *941*
  improving disk-read performance, 942–943
  improving disk-write performance, 939–941
  installing Bindery Services, 246–247, *247*
  Network Information screen, 850, *851*
  opening screen, 844–846, *845*
  Server Parameters screen, 846–848, *848*
  SET commands and, 95, 839–841, 1356
  Storage Objects information screen, 848–849, *849*
  Volume Information screen, 849–850, *850*

SESSION program. *See* NETUSER program
SET commands, 839–844, 1366–1389. *See also* server management
  in AUTOEXEC.NCF file, 95, 153, 154, *154*, 1356
  communication parameters, 841, 1366–1368
  copying parameters to files, **846–847**
  directory caching parameters, 842, 940–943, *941*, 1368–1369, 1402
  directory services parameters, 844, 1370–1372
  disk parameters, 843, 1372–1373
  error handling parameters, 844, 1373–1374
  file caching parameters, 841, 1374–1375, 1402
  file system parameters, 842, 1375–1378
  lock parameters, 842–843, 1379
  memory parameters, 841, 1379–1380
  miscellaneous parameters, 844, 1381–1383
  NCP (NetWare Core Protocol) parameters, 844, 1383–1385
  options during NetWare installation, 95
  SERVMAN and, 95, 839–841, 1356
  SET BINDERY CONTEXT= statement, 246
  SET NWLANGUAGE= statement, 177, 276–277
  in STARTUP.NCF, 95
  in STARTUP.NCF file, 151–152
  time parameters, 843, 1385–1388
  transaction tracking parameters, 843, 1388–1389
SET login script command, 494
SET STATION TIME parameter in NET.CFG, 306
setting up
  clients for NetWare IPX/IP Gateway, 1175–1176, *1176*
  Macintosh clients for NDS, 1118–1120, *1120*, 1358
SFT (System Fault Tolerance), 1440. *See also* NetWare 4.1x SFT III
Shareable (S) file attribute, 681, 1437
sharing files in NetWare NFS Services, 1166–1168, *1167*
shielded twisted-pair (STP) cabling, 12, 16. *See also* cabling
SHORT MACHINE TYPE parameter in NET.CFG, 307, **1437**
shortcut keys. *See also* hotkeys
  in FILER program, 1048–1049
  in NETADMIN, 396
  in NetWare User Tools, 999–1000
SHOW DOTS parameter in NET.CFG, 306
SHOW menu script command, 516

showing. *See* viewing
SIDF (System Independent Data Format), 1272, 1359
SIGNATURE LEVEL parameter in NET.CFG, 307
signatures of viruses, 718
Simple Installation method. *See also* NetWare 4.1x installation
    Bindery Services and, 247–249, *248*, *249*
    disk driver installation, 96–100
    and hard disk configuration, 103
    LAN driver installation, 100–101, *101*
    naming the server, 92–93
    for NetWare 4.1x Server for OS/2, **1227–1228**
    protocol installation and, 102–103
    troubleshooting SCSI conflict problems, 97–98
    Unix utilities and, 91
Simple Mail Transfer Protocol (SMTP), 368, 459, 473
Single Reference time servers, 145, 146, 1437–1438
Site Security Handbook, 666–668
slash (/)
    in Group object names, 450, 468
    in User object login names, 358, 400
slaves, in TCP/IP protocol, 1139
SLOT Link Driver parameter in NET.CFG file, 315
SMS (Storage Management Services), 1271–1273, 1438–1439
    for PC clients, 285, *285*
SMTP (Simple Mail Transfer Protocol), 368, 459, 473
SNA (Systems Network Architecture)
    SNADS (SNA Distributed Services) e-mail system, 368, 459, 473
    TCP/IP protocol and, 41
Sniffer software, 1305
SNMP (Simple Network Management Protocol), 1279–1283. *See also* TCP/IP protocol
    history of, 1280
    NET.CFG options for NetWare clients, 1281–1283
sound
    in NetWare Settings dialog box, 964
    in NetWare User Tools, 1000
spaces in names. *See* underscore (_)
spanned volumes, 107–108
special files, in Unix, **1130**
SPP (Sequenced Packet Protocol), 36
SPX protocol. *See* IPX/SPX protocol
.SRC extension, 512
SSPHWG (Site Security Policy Handbook Working Group), 666–668
ST506 disk controllers and drives, 63

stacking rights, 676, *676*
starting
    AUDITCON, 720–721, *722*
    NETADMIN, 907, *907*
startup files, for NetWare 4.1x SFT III, 1248
STARTUP.NCF file, 1438
    copying, 1301
    editing during NDS installation, **151–153**, *152*
    on NetWare boot disks, 80
    SET command options during installation, 95
%STATION login script identifier variable, 497
Steinke, Steve, 1308–1309, 1392
Storage Management Services (SMS), 1271–1273, 1438–1439
    for PC clients, 285, *285*
Storage Objects information screen, SERVMAN program, 848–849, *849*
STP (shielded twisted-pair) cabling, 12, 16. *See also* cabling
suballocation of disk blocks, 114, **1264**, 1354, **1401**
subdirectories, 1439. *See also* directories
    deleting with FILER, 1051–1052, *1052*
subnetwork masks, in TCP/IP protocol, 1141
Subordinate Reference replicas, 777
subordination, NDS trees and, 206
subtracting rights, 676, *676*
Sun Microsystems, 1127
superservers, *1320*, 1322
SUPERVISOR, versus ADMIN User object, 669, 730–731, 735
Supervisor (S) directory right, 671, **1440**
Supervisor (S) file right, 674, *955*, **1440**
Supervisor (S) object right, 685, **1440**
Supervisor (S) property right, 686, **1440**
switched Ethernet networks, 7, *8*
synchronization, 1440, 1442
    Check Time Synchronization option in DSMERGE program, 877–878, *879*
    replica synchronization, **1440**
    Report Synchronization Status option in DSREPAIR program, 855
    Security Equivalence Synchronization option in DSREPAIR program, 866–867, *867*
    Time Synchronization option in DSREPAIR program, 855
    time synchronization settings, 144–147
    time zone and time synchronization settings, *145*
SYS$LOG.ERR file, 1249, 1297–1298, *1298*

SYS: volumes, 106–107, 109, *109*, 112
SYSCON. *See* NETADMIN; NetWare Administrator
system directories, 24–25
System Fault Tolerance, 1440. *See also* NetWare 4.1x SFT III
System File (Sy) file attribute, 681
System Independent Data Format (SIDF), 1272, 1359
System login scripts, 1440
　migrating, 1339
System Module Information screen, MONITOR program, 833–834, *833*
system requirements. *See* servers, NetWare 4.1x requirements
System (Sy) directory attribute, 679, **1440**
Systems Network Architecture. *See* SNA

T

T (Transactional) file attribute, 681, **1443**
tape backup systems, 28–31, *30*, **1441**. *See also* backing up
　login time restrictions and, 387–388
　network address restrictions and, 389–390, 427–428
　time restrictions and, 426
Target Service Agent (TSA), **1441**
　for PC clients, 285, *285*
TBMI2 options in NET.CFG file, 324–325. *See also* NET.CFG; PC clients
　DATA ECB COUNT, 324
　ECB COUNT, 325
　INT7A, 325
　INT64, 325
　USEMAX PACKETS, 325
　USING WINDOWS 3.0, 325
TCP/IP protocol, 1134–1164, **1441**. *See also* IntranetWare; protocols; Unix
　adding during installation, 102–103
　DNS (Domain Name System), 1137–1138
　forwarders, 1138
　how TCP/IP works, **1136–1137**
　IP addresses, 1140, 1413
　master name servers, 1138
　name servers, 1137–1138
　NetWare IPX/IP Gateway and, 1170–1171, 1175, 1176
　NetWare NFS Services, **1164–1169**, **1421**
　　file transfer services, 1168–1169, *1169*
　　managing name services, 1165–1166, *1165*
　　managing NFS Services, 1164–1165, *1165*
　　setting up file sharing, 1166–1168, *1167*
　　setting up printing, 1168, *1168*
　NetWare TCP/IP support, **1134–1135**, **1143–1153**
　　components of, 1143–1146, *1146*
　　installing TCPIP.NLM, 1146–1151
　　IPTUNNEL program, 1152–1153, *1153*
　　XCONSOLE program, 1151
　NetWare/IP protocol, **1153–1164**, **1362**, **1420**
　　on Client32 clients, 1159–1160
　　installing on servers, 1160–1164, *1163*
　　on non-Client32 clients, 1156–1159, *1157*, *1158*
　NIS (Network Information System), 1139, *1139*
　replica servers, 1139
　root domains, 1137–1138
　SNMP (Simple Network Management Protocol), **1279–1283**
　　history of, 1280
　　NET.CFG options for NetWare clients, 1281–1283
　subnetwork masks, 1141–1143
TCPIPCOMP Link Driver parameter in NET.CFG file, 315
Telnet, **1441**
text files, importing user databases into NDS as, 803–805
TFTP (Trivial File Transfer Protocol), 1169, **1442**
third-party products, installing, 182–183, *183*
Thompson, Ken, 1125
time formats, 175
time restriction setup
　in NETADMIN, 426–427, *427*
　in NetWare Administrator, 387–389, *388*
time servers, 144–147, *145*, **1428**, **1431**, **1435**, **1437**
time SET commands, 843, 1385–1388
time settings, 135–138. *See also* installing NetWare Directory Services
　adjusting, 137–138, *137*
　time zone setting, 136, *136*
　time zone and time synchronization settings, 144–147, *145*
time synchronization, **1440**, **1442**. *See also* synchronization
　Check Time Synchronization Information screen in DSMERGE program, 877–878, *879*

Report Synchronization Status option in
DSREPAIR program, 855
Time Synchronization option in DSREPAIR
program, 855
time zone setting, 136, *136*
time zone and time synchronization settings,
144–147, *145*
Token Ring networks, 7–11, 9. *See also* networks
versus Ethernet networks, 5, 10–11, *11*
TokenTalk protocol, 42, 1091
TokenVision software, 1305
tools. *See* DOS utilities; NETADMIN; NetWare
Administrator; user utilities
Tools menu, in NetWare Administrator, 760,
780–781
top-down NDS tree design, 233–236, *235*, *236*
Topology Specific Module (TSM), 269, **1425**
TRACK ON console command, 886–887, *886*
tracking
normal operations, **1293–1308.** *See also*
troubleshooting
copying server configuration files, 1300–1301,
1301
MONITOR program and, 1295–1297, *1296*
protecting workstations against Windows
program problems, 1303–1305
server log files, 1297–1300, *1298*, *1299*, *1300*
server performance, **1295–1301**
tracking details, **1293–1301**
workstation performance, **1302–1305**, *1302*
related group information
in NETADMIN, 474
in NetWare Administrator, 465–466, *465*
related user information
in NETADMIN, 413, *414*
in NetWare Administrator, 376, *377*
RIP and SAP tracking, 886–887, *886*
transaction tracking SET commands, 843,
1388–1389
user account balances
in NETADMIN, 431, *432*
in NetWare Administrator, 374–376, *375*
training users, 990–992, 1074–1075. *See also* user
utilities
examples, **1076, 1080**
NDS trees and, **992–994**, *993*
TRAN.VLM file, 296
transaction tracking SET commands, 843, 1388–1389

Transactional (T) file attribute, 681, 1443
trees, **131,** 132, *133*, 222–238, **1406.** *See also*
DSMERGE; leaf objects; NetWare Directory Services (NDS); [Root] object
attribute information and, 206
Bindery Services and, 246, 247–249, *248*, *249*
creating pilot systems, 224–225
departmental, workgroup, user-location, or
bottom-up design, **230–232**, *233*, *234*
designing versus implementing, 227
designing for users, 226
Directory schema and, **206**
distributed organization chart with a WAN or
mixed design, **236–238**, *237*
examples, **253, 256–257**
goals for NDS tree design, 223–224
inheritance information and, 206
merging, 879–880, *879*
naming for first NetWare server, 133–134, *135*
naming standards, 227–230
organizational, user function, or top-down design,
233–236, *235*, *236*
physical versus logical design phases, **225–226**,
232, *233*, *234*
selecting for additional servers, 142–144, *143*
subordination and, 206
teaching users about, **992–994**, *993*
using resources from another tree, 246
using single versus multiple trees, 142, *143*
Triticom software, 1305–1308, *1306*, *1307*
Trivial File Transfer Protocol (TFTP), 1169, 1442
troubleshooting, 1286–1328
cabling problems, **1325–1327**
component failure problems, **1308–1309**
general tips, **1287–1293**
prevention tips, 1288–1290
for solving problems, 1291–1293
SCSI conflicts, 68–69, 97–98
server problems, **1295–1301, 1308–1309,
1318–1325**
component failure problems, **1308–1309**
and copying server configuration files,
1300–1301, *1301*
disk errors, 1324–1325, *1325*
freeing server memory temporarily, 1323
hardware scale and costs, 1320–1322, *1320*
operating system and RAM problems,
1318–1319, 1322–1323

server availability and, 1319–1320
server log files and, 1297–1300, *1298*, *1299*, *1300*
and tracking normal server performance, **1295–1301**
tracking normal operations, **1293–1308**
  copying server configuration files, 1300–1301, *1301*
  MONITOR program and, 1295–1297, *1296*
  NET.CFG file and, 1303
  network monitoring software, 1305–1308, *1306*, *1307*
  protecting workstations against Windows program problems, 1303–1305
  server log files, 1297–1300, *1298*, *1299*, *1300*
  server performance, **1295–1301**
  tracking details, **1293–1301**
  workstation performance, 1302–1305, *1302*
workstation problems, **1302–1305, 1308–1318**
  cannot connect to server, 1310–1312
  cannot use an application, 1312–1314
  component failure problems, **1308–1309**
  "not enough memory" errors, 1314–1315
  printing problems, 1317–1318
  and tracking normal operations, **1302–1305**, *1302*
  Windows problems, 1303–1305, 1315–1317
TRUE COMMIT parameter in NET.CFG, 307
trustees, 1433, 1443. *See also* rights; security
  All Property Rights trustee assignment, 751
  granting trustee rights
    to groups or users, 699–702, *700*, *701*
    between multiple objects, 705–708, *706*, *707*, *708*
    between objects with drag-and-drop, 702–705, *704*
    to volumes or directories, 696–699, *697*, *698*
  for Group objects, **464**
    modifying in NETADMIN, 477–478, *478*
    modifying in NetWare Administrator, 463–464, *464*
  managing directory or file trustees with FILER, 709–711, *711*
  migrating trustee rights, 1339
  [Public] trustees, 671, 751, **1430**
  for [Root] object, **208**
  supervisory functions and, **751**
  trustee assignments, **670**
  User object trustee default property rights, **691**, **694**, *694*

TSA (Target Service Agent), 1441
  for PC clients, 285, *285*
TSM (Topology Specific Module), 269, **1425**
TTS$LOG.ERR file, 1297, 1299
typeless versus typeful context name formats, 238, 1443–1444

U

UIMPORT program, 803–805, 1338–1339, **1444**
Unattended Full Repair option, DSREPAIR program, 854, 856–857, *857*
underscore (_)
  in Group object names, 450, 468
  in organization names, 140
  in server names, 134
  in User object login names, 358, 400
Understanding Unix (Kelly-Bootle), 1131
uninterruptible power supplies (UPSs), 27–28, *28*, **1444**, *1444*
Universal Time Coordinated (UTC) adjustments, 137–138, *137*
Unix, 1124–1134, 1194–1195. *See also* DOS; IntranetWare; Macintosh computers; Microsoft Windows; PC clients; TCP/IP protocol
  history of, 1125–1127
  versus NetWare, **1124–1134**
    C2 level security rating, 1360
    case-sensitivity, 1130
    daemons, background processes, and NLMs, 1130–1131
    directories and files in Unix, 1130
    NetWare and Unix kernels, 1131
    networking, print, file, and user services differences, 1131–1134
    philosophical differences, 1132–1133
  NetWare NFS Services, **1164–1169, 1421**
    file transfer services, 1168–1169, *1169*
    managing name services, 1165–1166, *1165*
    managing NFS Services, 1164–1165, *1165*
    setting up file sharing, 1166–1168, *1167*
    setting up printing, 1168, *1168*
  network protocol configuration and, 174
  network types and, 4
  open systems and, **1124–1125, 1425**
  printer settings
    in NetWare Administrator, 570, 573
    in PCONSOLE, 633, 634

Simple Installation method and Unix utilities, 91
TCP/IP protocol for, 40
Unix clients defined, **1445**
UnixWare, 1199, 1217
Unknown objects, 222, **1445**
unshielded twisted-pair (UTP) cabling, 12, **1447.** *See also* cabling
Fast Ethernet networks and, 13
FDDI networks and, 16
installing, 31–32
Token Ring versus Ethernet networks and, 10–11
updating NET.CFG
after DSMERGE changes, 882
with NCUPDATE, 805–807, 1358
UPGRADE/MIGRATE disks, 164
upgrading. *See also* migrating
clients to Windows 95 and Client32, **1341–1343**, **1445**
NetWare 3.1x Print Services, 161–162
NetWare 3.11 SFT III systems, 1252–1253
to NetWare 4.1x, **1332–1344**
migrating data, 1336–1337
migrating file attributes, 1338
migrating passwords, 1337–1338
migrating print services, 1339–1340
migrating trustee rights and login scripts, 1339
upgrade method options, 1332–1334
upgrading Bindery information, 1338–1339
versus upgrading server hardware, **1334–1336**, 1340
uppercase
in Group object names, 450, 468
in login scripts, 496–497
in User object names, 357, 400
UPSs (uninterruptible power supplies), 27–28, *28*, **1444**, 1444
USE DEFAULTS parameter in NET.CFG, 307, 309–310
USEMAX PACKETS parameter in NET.CFG file, 325
Usenet newsgroups, Novell, 1058
User login scripts, 486–487, 489, 498, **1446.** *See also* login scripts
creating or editing with NETADMIN, 509–510, *510*
creating or editing with NetWare Administrator, 507
example, 504–505, *504*
migrating, 1339

User objects, 216, 350–442, 445–446, 1446. *See also* Group objects; login scripts; objects; users
adding to Group objects, 454–457, *455*, 471, *472*
ADMIN User object, **131**
creating User objects, 351–352
naming, 140, 147, *148*
versus NetWare 3.x SUPERVISOR, 669, 730–731, 735
NetWare Administrator security management and, 690
NetWare Directory Services (NDS) security and, 683
print queue operator assignment, 556–557, *557*
[Root] object and, 208
selecting password for, 140, 147, *148*
and User object management, 444–445
workgroup administrators and, **752–753**
creating with NETADMIN, 395–437
account balance tracking, 431, *432*
basic User object creation, **397–400**, *398*, *399*
detail settings, **405–413**
e-mailbox setup, 408–409, *409*
environment information, 407–408, *407*
examples, **440**, **442**
foreign e-mail addresses and aliases, 410–411
group membership setup, 351, 352, 418, *419*
home directory setup, 351, 352, 401–404, *402*, *403*, *404*
identification information, 405–406, *406*
intruder lockout setup, 429–430, *430*
login names, 400
login restriction setup, 421–423, *422*
login scripts, 351, 352, 415–416, *417*
login time restriction setup, 426–427, *427*
naming, 400
network address restrictions, 427–428, *429*
overview of NETADMIN, **395–396**, *395*
password restrictions, 423–425, *424*
postal address information, 411–412, *412*
Profile script editing, 421
related information tracking, 413, *414*
rights to files and directories setup, 434–437, *436*
security configuration, **413–437**
security equivalence setup, 351, 352, 419–421, *420*
user reference information, 413, *414*
volume space restriction setup, 432–433, *434*

creating with NetWare Administrator, **352–395**
    account balance tracking, 374–376, *375*
    basic User object creation, **354–358**, *356*, *357*
    detail settings, **358–376**
    e-mailbox setup, 366–367, *367*
    environment information, 364–366, *365*
    examples, **439**, **441–442**
    foreign e-mail addresses and aliases, 368–369, *369*
    group membership setup, 351, 352, 384–385, *385*
    home directory setup, 351, 352, 359–361, *360*
    identification information, 362–364, *362*
    installing client software and NetWare Administrator, **353–354**
    intruder lockout setup, 391, *393*
    login names, 357–358
    login restriction setup, 379–381, *380*
    login scripts, 351, 352, 377–379, *378*
    login time restriction setup, 387–389, *388*
    naming, 357–358
    network address restrictions, 389–390, *390*
    overview of, 352–353
    password restrictions, 381–384, *382*
    postal address information, 373, *374*
    print job configuration, 352, 370–373, *371*
    related information tracking, 376, *377*
    rights to files and directories setup, 391–395, *393*, *394*
    security configuration, **376–395**
    security equivalence setup, 351, 352, 386, *387*
  deleting from Group objects, **454–457**, *455*, **471**, *472*
  home directories for, **23–24**
  MegaCorp examples, **441–442**
  MiniCo examples, **439–440**
  properties of, **351–352**
  tape backup systems
    and login time restrictions, 387–388
    and network address restrictions, 389–390, 427–428
    and time restrictions, 426
  tools for managing, **445–446**, **522–523**, **525–526**
  trustee default property rights, **691**, **694**, *694*
User Templates, 479–485, 1446
  creating with NETADMIN, **483–484**
  creating with NetWare Administrator, 480–483, *481*, *482*

and managing users and resources, 446
MegaCorp example, **526–527**
MiniCo example, **523**
modifying in NETADMIN, 484, *485*
user utilities, 990–1083. *See also* training users
  CAPTURE command
    examples, **1077**, **1081**
    print job configuration, 370, 371, 645, 648
    printing configuration, 1006, **1035–1040**, *1037*
    printing system and, 533–534
  command-line Help, **1058–1059**, *1058*
  CX command, 241, **994–996**
  DynaText online documentation, **1059–1067**
    AppleTalk documentation, 1093
    installing, 158–159, 178–181, *179*, *180*, *181*, *182*, 1060
    installing and configuring viewer for Windows 3.1x, 1060–1061
    installing and configuring for Windows 95, 1065–1067, *1066*
    navigating and searching, 1062–1064, *1064*
    print migration documentation, 1340
    reading from CD-ROM drives, 1062–1063, *1062*
    SETUPDOC program, 1065–1067, *1066*
    in Windows 95, 1064–1065, *1065*
  FILER program, **709–713**, **1048–1057**, **1410**
    deleting subdirectories, 1051–1052, *1052*
    examples, **1078**, **1082**
    keyboard shortcuts, 1048–1049
    managing directory or file trustees, 709–711, *711*
    managing files and directories, 1049–1052, *1050*
    managing IRFs (Inherited Rights Filters), 712–713, *713*
    purging deleted files, 1056, 1325
    recovering deleted files, 1054–1055, *1056*, **1434**
    searching for files and directories, 1052–1053
    selecting current directory, 1053
    setting default options, 1056–1057
    viewing volume information, 1053–1054, *1054*
  FLAG command, 679–683, **682**, 949–951, **951**, **952**, **1046–1047**, *1046*, **1078**, **1082**, **1410**
  MegaCorp example, **1080–1083**
  MiniCo example, **1076–1079**
  NDIR command, **1047**, **1078**, **1082**, **1324**, *1325*

NETUSER program, 201, **1025–1034**
    changing contexts, 241, 1033–1034, *1034*
    changing login scripts and passwords, 1032, *1033*
    examples, **1077, 1081**
    mapping drives, 1030–1032, *1031*
    printing controls, 1026–1027, *1027*
    sending and receiving messages, 1028–1030, *1029*
    viewing rights, 1032
    viewing server information, 1032, *1033*
NetWare User Tools (NWUSER), **997–1025, 1421**
    adding user-defined hotkeys, 1022, *1023*
    changing hotkeys and other NetWare settings, 1019–1021, *1020*
    changing LPT printer settings, 1009–1012, *1010*
    configuring Windows 3.1x for fast network printing, 1012–1014, *1013*
    connecting to NetWare servers, 1014–1017, *1016*
    connecting to network printers, 1006–1008, *1007*
    connecting to network printers permanently, 1008–1009, *1009*
    enabling or disabling F6 hotkey, 1000–1001, *1001*
    examples, **1076–1077, 1080–1081**
    Help system, 1023–1025, *1024*
    keyboard shortcuts, 999–1000
    logging into NetWare 4.10 from, 997–998
    logging into NetWare from, *999*
    mapping drives, 1002–1005, *1003, 1004*
    mapping drives permanently, 1005–1006, *1006*
    sending and receiving messages, 1017–1019, *1018*
    sound effects, 1000
    viewing rights, 1004–1005, *1004*
NPRINT command
    examples, **1077, 1081**
    print job configuration, 370, 371, 645, 648
    printing files from command line, 1035, **1040–1042**
    printing system and, *534*
NPRINTER program, *535, 536*, **1042–1044**, 1077–1078, 1082
RIGHTS command
    changing file rights, **953–957**, *955, 956*
    viewing rights, **1045**, *1046*, 1078, 1082
user-centric file systems, 22–24, *23*

user-function NDS tree design, 233–236, *235, 236*
user-location NDS tree design, 230–232, *233, 234*
users. *See also* User objects
    attitudes toward networks, 992
    managing with NetWare Administrator, **793–807**
        accounting overview, 793–794, 799
        activating server accounting, *795*
        examples, **926, 929**
        moving employee database records into NDS with UIMPORT, 803–805, 1338–1339, **1444**
        setting charge rates for resources, 795–797, *797*, 799
        setting user account balances and low balance limits, 799–801, *800*
        setting user volume space restriction, 801–803, *802*
        updating NET.CFG with NCUPDATE, 805–807, *1358*
        viewing accounting reports with ATOTAL, 797–798
    overview of tools for managing, **445–446**, 522–523, 525–526
    selling network plans to, 749–750
    training, 990–992, 1074–1075
        examples, **1076, 1080**
        NDS trees and, **992–994**, *993*
user services in NetWare versus Unix, **1131–1133**
Windows 95 user support, **326–327, 1067–1074, 1303–1305, 1315–1317, 1341–1343**
    examples, **1079, 1083**
    installing Client32 clients, **334–338**, *336, 337*
    logging in from Network Neighborhood, 1071–1072, *1072*
    mapping drives from Windows 95, 1072–1074, *1073*
    printing and, 1068, 1074
    protecting against problems, **1303–1305**
    sending messages within Network Neighborhood, 1070–1071, *1070*
    troubleshooting Windows clients, **1315–1317**
    upgrading clients to Window 95, **1341–1343**
    viewing connection information, 1068–1069, *1069*
USING WINDOWS 3.0 parameter in NET.CFG file, 325
UTC (Universal Time Coordinated) adjustments, 137–138, *137*

utilities, 1446–1447. *See also* DOS utilities; NETADMIN; NetWare Administrator; server management; user utilities
Web Manager, 1187–1192, *1188, 1190, 1191*
UTP (unshielded twisted-pair) cabling, 12, **1447.** *See also* cabling
   Fast Ethernet networks and, 13
   FDDI networks and, 16
   installing, 31–32
   Token Ring versus Ethernet networks and, 10–11

V

values of objects, 204, *205,* 206
variables in login scripts, 496–497, **1412**
VERSION console command, 887, *887*
video monitors, NetWare requirements, 69–70
View menu, in NetWare Administrator, 758–759
View Remote Server ID List option, DSREPAIR program, 862, *863*
View Repair Log File option, DSREPAIR program, 855, 868–869, *869*
viewers for DynaText online documentation, 158–159, 178–181, *179, 180, 181, 182,* 1060–1061
viewing
   accounting reports with ATOTAL, 797–798
   AUDITCON reports, 725–726, *726*
   connection information in Windows 95 clients, 1068–1069, *1069*
   directory and file information with NDIR command, **1047,** *1047,* 1078, 1082, **1324,** *1325*
   file compression statistics, 1261–1262, *1261*
   IPX statistics with IPXCON, 896–897, *897*
   NLM information, 833–834, *833*
   PCONSOLE Quick Setup default settings, 540–541
   print jobs in PCONSOLE, 620–623, *620, 621*
   print queue job list in NetWare Administrator, 560–564, *561, 562*
   print queue status in PCONSOLE, 624–625, *624*
   printer status in NetWare Administrator, 591–594, *592*
   printing system layout in NetWare Administrator, 589–591, *590*
   replicas
      in NDS Manager, 786–789, *787, 788*
      with PARTMGR, 918–919, *918*
   rights
      with NETUSER, 1032

   with NetWare User Tools, 1004–1005, *1004*
   server information with NETUSER program, 1032, *1033*
   server partitions with NetWare Administrator, 789–790, *790*
   volume information in FILER, 1053–1054, *1054*
virus protection, 678, **717–719,** 733, 737
VLM parameter in NET.CFG, 308
VLMs (Virtual Loadable Modules), 295–297, **1447.** *See also* NetWare DOS Requester; NetWare Loadable Modules
   child and multiplexor VLMs, 275–276
   core NetWare 4.1x VLMs in NET.CFG file, 295–296
   non-core NetWare 4.1x VLMs in NET.CFG file, 296–297
VOL$LOG.ERR file, 1297, 1298–1299, *1299*
VOLINFO command, 1324
Volume Information screen, SERVMAN program, 849–850, *850*
volumes, 106–115, **1447.** *See also* directories; file systems; partitions; replicas
   adding Macintosh name space support to, 1117–1118
   adding Macintosh name space to, 1117–1118
   block size options, 112–113
   block suballocation, 114, **1264,** 1354, **1401**
   changing segment size, 108–111, *109, 110, 111*
   enabling data migration, 114–115
   file compression settings, 113–114
   getting information with NDIR command, **1047,** *1047,* 1078, 1082, **1324,** *1325*
   installing NetWare from, 84–88
   listing volume information, 887–888, *888*
   naming, 112
   versus partitions, **103**
   saving changes during installation, 114–115
   spanned volumes, **107–108**
   SYS: volumes, 106–107, 109, *109,* 112
   and upgrading to NetWare 4.1x, 1339
   viewing volume information in FILER, 1053–1054, *1054*
   volume space restriction in NETADMIN, **432–433,** *434*
   volume space restriction in NetWare Administrator, **801–803,** *802*
VOLUMES console command, 887–888, *888*
VREPAIR program, 1324

W

Web Manager utility, 1187–1192, *1188, 1190, 1191*
Web Server, 1183–1192, 1195–1196, 1361, 1448. *See also* IntranetWare
    configuring and managing, 1187–1192, *1188, 1190, 1191*
    examples, **1195–1196**
    installing, 1185–1187, *1186*
    NetWare 4.11 and, 1185
Web servers, 1437
wide area networks (WANs), 1448. *See also* networks
    distributed organization chart with a WAN NDS tree design, **236–238,** *237*
Window menu, in NetWare Administrator, 760–761
Windows. *See* Microsoft Windows
Winsock program, 1449
    NetWare IPX/IP Gateway and, 1170, 1175
wireless networks, 14–16, *15*
wiring closets and wiring plans, 33–34, *33*
WordPerfect
    file compatibility, 1089
    guidelines for, 968–971, *969*
workgroup managers, 752–753
workgroup NDS tree design, 230–232, *233, 234*
WORKGROUP NET parameter in NET.CFG, 308
workstations, 1449. *See also* Macintosh computers; OS/2; PC clients; users
    troubleshooting, **1302–1305, 1308–1318**
    cannot connect to server, 1310–1312
    cannot use an application, 1312–1314
    "not enough memory" errors, 1314–1315
    printing problems, 1317–1318
    and tracking normal operations, **1302–1305,** *1302*
    Windows problems, 1303–1305, 1315–1317
World Wide Web. *See also* IntranetWare; Web Server
    Novell Web site, 1057
WRITE login script command, 494, 496–497
Write (W) directory right, 671, **1449**
Write (W) file right, 674, 955, **1449**
Write (W) property right, 686, **1449**
WSANSI.VLM file, 297
WSREG.VLM file, 297
WSSNMP.VLM file, 297
WSTRAP.VLM file, 297

X

X (Execute Only) file attribute, 681, 1409
X.400 e-mail system, 368, 459, 473
X.500 specification, 206, 222
XCONSOLE program, 1151
XENIX software, 1127
XNS (Xerox Network Services) protocol, 35–36

Z

zones, in Macintosh networking, 1092–1094, **1449**

SYBEX BOOKS ON THE WEB!

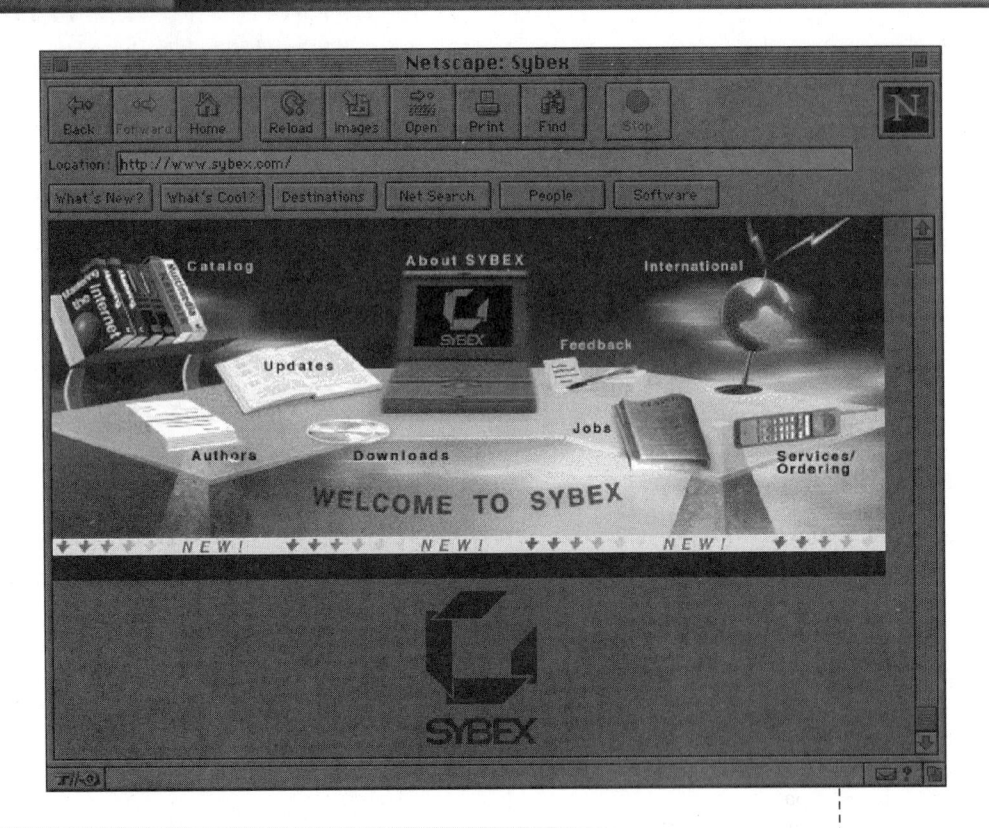

P resenting a truly dynamic environment that is both fun and informative.

- download useful code
- e-mail your favorite Sybex author
- preview a book you might want to own
- find a job
- order books
- learn about Sybex
- discover what's new in the computer industry

http://www.sybex.com

SYBEX Inc. • 1151 Marina Village Parkway • Alameda, CA 94501 • 510-523-8233

A Small Company's NetWare 4.1x Network

This is a high-level overview of the MiniCo network. MiniCo is a book distributor and publisher of a few humorous gimmick books, including *How Gumby Got His Cadillac* and *Mammoths Galore*.

MiniCo has three departments: Accounting, Sales, and Support. As you can see in the diagram, the company has divided its network into three sections, or Organizational Units: Sales, Support, and Management (including the Accounting department). The Organizational Units include:

- **Sales:** Twenty users, one server (486/50, 32 MB RAM, 1.5 GB total disk space, two volumes), and four laser printers.

- **Support:** Thirty-five users, one server (66 MHz Pentium, 64 MB RAM, 2.5 GB total disk space, two volumes), and six laser printers.

- **Management:** Ten users, one server (486/33, 16 MB RAM, 500 MB total disk space, one volume), and one printer.

```
View: MiniCo
ROOT
└─ MiniCo
   ├─ SALES
   │  ├─ SALES_1
   │  ├─ DEALS
   │  └─ SALES_1_SYS
   ├─ SUPPORT
   │  ├─ SUPPORT_1
   │  ├─ SUPPORT_1_SYS
   │  └─ VOL1
   └─ MGMT
      ├─ ACCT
      └─ ACCT_SYS
```

MiniCo's NetWare 4.1x experience? Excellent, finally. The early installation and configuration were delayed by poor planning and lukewarm commitment from the owners. Networks are too important these days to wing them "by the seat of your pants," as MiniCo found out. After some adjustments, MiniCo's network succeeded beyond everyone's expectations.

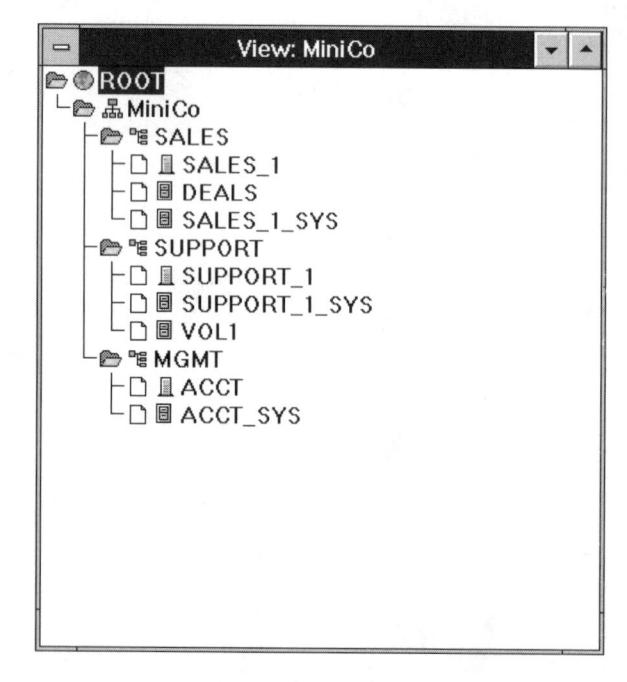

Read the details of MiniCo's (sometimes indirect) route to a successful NetWare 4.1x network starting in Chapter 1, running through Chapter 12, plus a final visit to see how they're doing with IntranetWare in Chapter 14.